Queuing Models

(λ = arrival rate, μ = service rate)

M/M/1 Queue

Service Facility 1

Arrivals

Expected number in system: $L = \dfrac{\lambda}{\mu - \lambda}$

Expected number in queue: $L_q = \dfrac{\lambda^2}{\mu(\mu - \lambda)}$

Expected waiting time (includes service time): $W = \dfrac{1}{\mu - \lambda}$

Expected time in queue: $W_q = \dfrac{\lambda}{\mu(\mu - \lambda)}$

Probability that the system is empty: $P_o = 1 - \dfrac{\lambda}{\mu}$

M/G/1 Queue

Service Facility 1

Arrivals

Expected number in system: $L = L_q + \dfrac{\lambda}{\mu}$

Expected number in queue: $L_q = \dfrac{\lambda^2\sigma^2 + (\lambda/\mu)^2}{2(1 - \lambda/\mu)}$

Expected waiting time (includes service time): $W = W_q + \dfrac{1}{\mu}$

Expected time in queue: $W_q = \dfrac{L_q}{\lambda}$

Probability that the system is empty: $P_o = 1 - \dfrac{\lambda}{\mu}$

M/M/s Queue

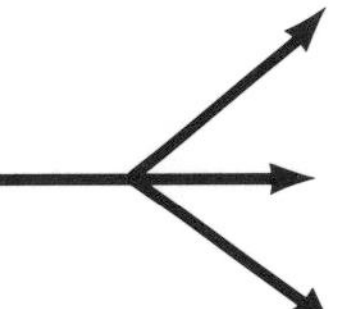

Service Facility 1

Service Facility 2

Service Facility 3

Arrivals

Expected number in system: $L = L_q + \dfrac{\lambda}{\mu}$

Expected number in queue: $L_q = P_o\left[\dfrac{(\lambda/\mu)^{s+1}}{(s-1)!(s - \lambda/\mu)^2}\right]$

Expected waiting time (includes service time): $W = W_q + \dfrac{1}{\mu}$

Expected time in queue: $W_q = \dfrac{L_q}{\lambda}$

Probability that the system is empty: $P_o = \dfrac{1}{\displaystyle\sum_{n=0}^{s-1} \frac{(\lambda/\mu)^n}{n!} + \frac{(\lambda/\mu)^s}{s!}\left(\frac{1}{1 - (\lambda/s\mu)}\right)}$

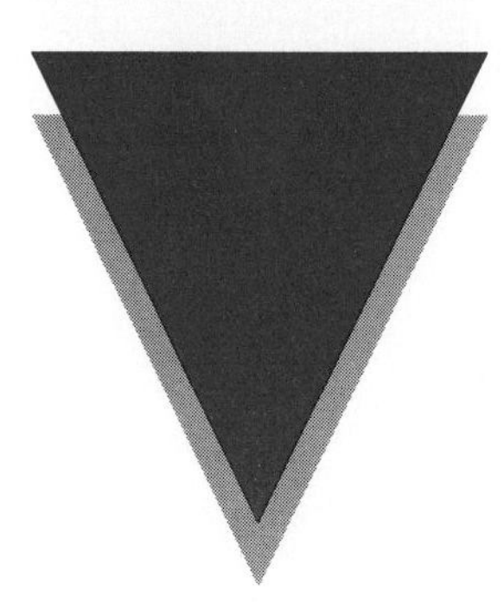

Introductory Management Science

Fourth Edition

ANNOTATED INSTRUCTOR'S EDITION

F.J. GOULD
University of Chicago

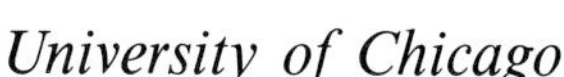
G.D. EPPEN
University of Chicago

C.P. SCHMIDT
University of Alabama

Annotations by

RICK HESSE
Mercer University

PRENTICE HALL, Englewood Cliffs, New Jersey 07632

Acquisition Editor: Valerie Ashton
Editor-in-Chief: Joseph Heider
Development Editor: Daniel Schiller
Production Editor: Carol Burgett
Interior and Cover Designer: Thomas Nery
Copy Editor: Margo Quinto
Prepress Buyer: Trudy Pisciotti
Manufacturing Buyer: Patrice Fraccio
Marketing Manager: Frank Lyman
Supplements Editor: Lisamarie Brassini
Editorial Assistants: Annmarie Dunn, Renee Pelletier

A Simon & Schuster Company
Englewood Cliffs, New Jersey 07632

Printed in the United States of America

10 9 8 7 6 5 4 3 2 1

ISBN 0-13-486481-6

Prentice-Hall International (UK) Limited, *London*
Prentice-Hall of Australia Pty. Limited, *Sydney*
Prentice-Hall Canada Inc., *Toronto*
Prentice-Hall Hispanoamericana, S.A., *Mexico*
Prentice-Hall of India Private Limited, *New Delhi*
Prentice-Hall of Japan, Inc., *Tokyo*
Simon & Schuster Asia Pte. Ltd., *Singapore*
Editora Prentice-Hall do Brasil, Ltda., *Rio de Janeiro*

Take The Uncertainty Out Of Your Textbook Decision

INTRODUCTORY MANAGEMENT SCIENCE FOURTH EDITION

Table of Contents Highlighting New Video Cases and Application Capsules (75% new in the 4/E)

APPLICATIONS

Eppen, Gould and Schmidt emphasize the role of management science techniques as applied to the larger context of business decision-making.

- NEW! Relevant **Application Capsules** now open *every* chapter, and many additional ones are included throughout the text.

—These absorbing accounts show students how the techniques discussed in each chapter have actually been applied by corporations, government agencies, and other organizations (both within the United States and abroad) to solve a great variety of problems.

—Examples include such diverse subjects as building housing in Shanghai, buying aircraft for the Pentagon, choosing tenants for a shopping mall, and scheduling umpires for major-league baseball.

- **Diagnostic Assignments** allow students to analyze a realistic situation and critically evaluate proposed solutions.
- **End-of-Chapter Cases** provide detailed examples of how management science techniques are utilized in practice.

APPLICATION CAPSULE

When Is the Synchronized Swimming, por favor? Management Science Goes to the Barcelona Olympics*

As host for the 1992 summer Olympic games, the city of Barcelona was faced with an extremely complex logistical problem: scheduling more than 2000 events in a 15-day period. The problem was not only very large but included a great many different types of constraints, some of them not ordinarily encountered in the scheduling of more familiar projects.

First were the precedence relationships—for example, qualifying rounds obviously had to take place before quarterfinals, semifinals, and finals. Then, there was the need to spread out the events, in both time and space. One concern was to avoid traffic jams that might result if two or more popular events were scheduled in nearby facilities at the same time. But even when different venues were involved, it was desirable to schedule the most attractive events at different times, to allow the largest possible audience for the greatest number of events. The requirements of live TV coverage of different events for different time zones also had to be considered. For instance, interest in soccer matches would be high in Europe, Africa, and South America, but not in North America. Finally, there were constraints on the available equipment (such as TV cameras) and personnel (for example, security).

This complex problem provided an interesting challenge for two professors at the Universitat Politecnica de Catalunya in Barcelona. It soon became evident that no single existing program was adequate for the task. They therefore developed a collection of interactive algorithms to supplement the more conventional project management software, along with a set of graphical aids to help compare different schedule characteristics.

It was found useful first to create a calendar (assigning competitions to days), and then to refine the precise timetable of events on each day. This approach allowed rough schedules to be generated quickly. It also proved useful to work with time divisions both larger and smaller than an "event."

▶ The modelers discovered that each sport had its own rhythm and that it helped to think in terms of blocks of days that fit that rhythm. A particular sport, for example, might be best served by scheduling three consecutive days of preliminary competition, a day off, and then the finals.

▶ Equally helpful was the concept of a "unit"— a part of an event having intrinsic interest as a spectacle. Thus the end of the marathon, for example, was treated as a unit.

The objective function for the scheduling process incorporated several criteria, each of which was evaluated on a numerical scale. Among these were continuity (the number of days between the first and last activity for a particular event) and temporal profile (a measure of how well the schedule distributed the activities throughout the two-week period, compared to an ideal distribution).

VIDEO CASES

Video Case

Simulation and Time-based Competition at Nissan

Manufacturing competition has passed through many different phases since people first began to produce goods. The dominant form of competition during most of the twentieth century has been based on economies of scale. The essence of this strategy is producing and selling a large number of essentially identical items. With this approach, it pays to make large capital investments in production equipment, since with a large volume of sales the fixed cost that must be absorbed by each unit of output is quite small.

The last ten years or so have brought a major change in the form of competition. The current emphasis is on *time-based competition*. This is a pervasive philosophy that appears throughout the manufacturing process. It is perhaps best known for its impact on production practices and inventory management. Just-in-time inventory control (see Chapter 10) and stockless production systems, pioneered in Japan, are now an integral part of production throughout the world.

However, time-based competition is not restricted to the production floor—it plays a crucial role in product design and new product development. Firms that can reduce the time spent on these processes can move more quickly to satisfy the ever-changing desires of the consumer, putting their less quick-footed competitors at a disadvantage.

A number of techniques and approaches are used to shorten the design cycle. These include synchronous design, the use of design teams, and the use of improved technologies such as CAD (computer-aided design) and CAM (computer-aided manufacturing).

Simulation can and does play an important role in time reduction. The video on designing Nissan automobiles gives some indication of its power.

Questions

1. List several ways in which simulation is used during the design process at Nissan.
2. How do these various simulations influence the time-based strategy of Nissan?

ABC News/Prentice Hall Video Library

Prentice Hall and ABC have worked together to provide you with a Video Library, integrated throughout ***Introductory Management Science, 4/E*** with special **end-of-chapter video cases** that illustrate ways in which management science problem-solving techniques are utilized in real-world situations. These video cases are based on clips from award-winning ABC News shows as well as material provided by the Consortium for Mathematics and its Applications (COMAP) and by individual corporations.

Following is a sampling of some of the video cases:

- Management Science: A Contradiction in Terms? — COMAP
- VRROOM! The Harley Davidson Story — ABC News
- You Are What Your Dinner Eats — Continental Grain

COMPUTER APPLICATIONS

Computer Applications involving popular software packages such as Lotus 1-2-3, @RISK, LINDO, and QSB+ are utilized extensively. New computer examples and problems for spreadsheets and @RISK have been added to most of the chapters in Part II of the book.

MANAGER: First of all, what is the solution to our problem?

MODELER: I have run the problem on the computer, and here's the output [see Figure 5.14]. By "solution" I take it you mean the optimal values of the decision variables. These are printed in the section of output that I've labeled VARIABLE. The optimal values of the variables appear under the second column, headed VALUE. You can see that the rounded optimal values are

$$T1=0.26 \quad T2=0.70 \quad T3=0.04 \quad T4=0.00$$

MANAGER: How much does a ton of this blend cost?

MODELER: The OV, which is the optimal value of the objective function, is also identified. You can see that the minimum cost is $511.11.

MANAGER: I'd like to keep my costs under $500 per ton. Isn't there any way I can do this?

MODELER: It is impossible to find a lower-cost mixture that satisfies the contraints you have imposed.

MANAGER: You mean the requirements on essential elements?

MODELER: Exactly.

MANAGER: Well, maybe I can modify those requirements. I really do want to keep my costs under $500 per ton.

MODELER: Then you certainly will have to loosen your requirements. We can discuss how to do that.

MANAGER: All right. But first, I recall that the requirements were expressed as minimum threshold levels. Is there any way I can tell exactly how much of each essential element gets into the optimal mix?

MODELER: That information is obtained from the second section of the output, which I've identified as CONSTRAINTS. The computer labels the four constraints of the

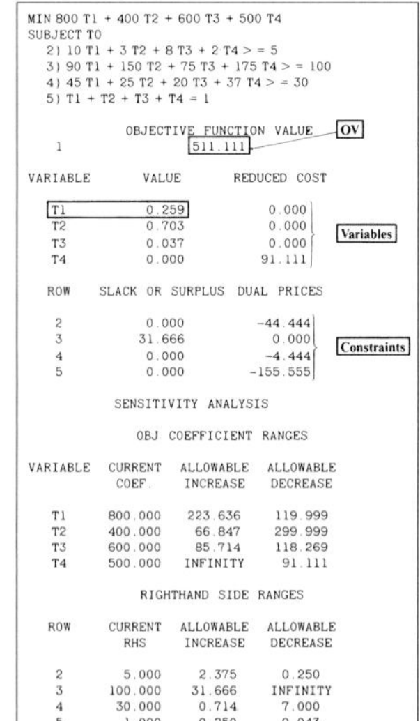

```
MIN 800 T1 + 400 T2 + 600 T3 + 500 T4
SUBJECT TO
   2) 10 T1 + 3 T2 + 8 T3 + 2 T4 >= 5
   3) 90 T1 + 150 T2 + 75 T3 + 175 T4 >= 100
   4) 45 T1 + 25 T2 + 20 T3 + 37 T4 >= 30
   5) T1 + T2 + T3 + T4 = 1

          OBJECTIVE FUNCTION VALUE
   1               511.111

VARIABLE        VALUE        REDUCED COST

   T1           0.259            0.000
   T2           0.703            0.000
   T3           0.037            0.000
   T4           0.000           91.111

  ROW    SLACK OR SURPLUS  DUAL PRICES

   2            0.000          -44.444
   3           31.666            0.000
   4            0.000           -4.444
   5            0.000         -155.555

           SENSITIVITY ANALYSIS

             OBJ COEFFICIENT RANGES

VARIABLE  CURRENT   ALLOWABLE  ALLOWABLE
           COEF.    INCREASE   DECREASE

   T1     800.000   223.636    119.999
   T2     400.000    66.847    299.999
   T3     600.000    85.714    118.269
   T4     500.000   INFINITY    91.111

             RIGHTHAND SIDE RANGES

  ROW     CURRENT   ALLOWABLE  ALLOWABLE
            RHS     INCREASE   DECREASE

   2        5.000     2.375      0.250
   3      100.000    31.666    INFINITY
   4       30.000     0.714      7.000
   5        1.000     0.250      0.043
```


FIGURE 5.14
Output for Crawler Tread

Free LINDO Student Edition software is included for convenience with each student copy of Eppen, Gould and Schmidt's Fourth Edition.

Many new spreadsheet examples are incorporated in the Fourth Edition and add to the text's real-world flavor.

	A	B	C	D	E	F
1	Test	0.853			Utility Lookup Table	
2		E	0.868		-8.5	0.300
3			A	0.711	-8	0.320
4			B	0.868	4.5	0.695
5			C	0.777	5	0.709
6		D	0.042		6.5	0.740
7			A	0.511	7	0.760
8			B	0.809	14.5	0.910
9			C	0.842	15	0.914
10	No Test	0.842			19.5	0.941
11		A	0.609		20	0.943
12		B	0.842		29.5	0.962
13		C	0.822		30	0.963
14						
15	Maximum Utility =		0.853			
16	Optimal Decision: Test					

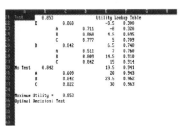

▲ FIGURE 14.40
Spreadsheet Representation of Test/No Test Decision Tree

Sensitivity of the Optimal Decision to Prior Probabilities

Whether cash returns or utilities are used in the decision tree, it is important to see how sensitive the optimal decision is to various parameter values. For example, how sensitive is the optimal decision to the initial estimate of a strong market, the prior probability $P(S)$? Spreadsheets are not particularly suited to solving decision trees, but they are certainly adequate for small problems and do permit easy sensitivity analysis through what-if analysis and Data Table commands. The spreadsheet shown in Figure 14.40 reproduces the graphical analysis shown in Figure 14.39. The main advantage of the spreadsheet formulation is the ease with which various parameters can be changed and the tree recalculated. (The utilities are included in the form of a look-up table to facilitate sensitivity analysis on the utility function.)

The graph of Figure 14.41 was generated by varying the value of $P(S)$ between 0 and 1 in increments of .05. The graph plotted with the square markers is the expected utility of the Test decision, while the pluses plot the expected utility of the No-Test decision. Whenever the two curves cross, the optimal decision changes. Since the curves cross four times (although it is hard to see the last time because the curves are so close together), the optimal decision changes four times: No-Test, Test, No-Test, Test, No-Test. Test is the optimal decision for values of $P(S)$ between (approximately) 0.29 and 0.50 and between 0.94 and 0.96. No-Test is optimal for the values of $P(S)$ between 0 and 0.29 and 0.5 and 0.94, and between 0.96 and 1.

▼ FIGURE 14.41
Expected Utilility of Test and No- Test

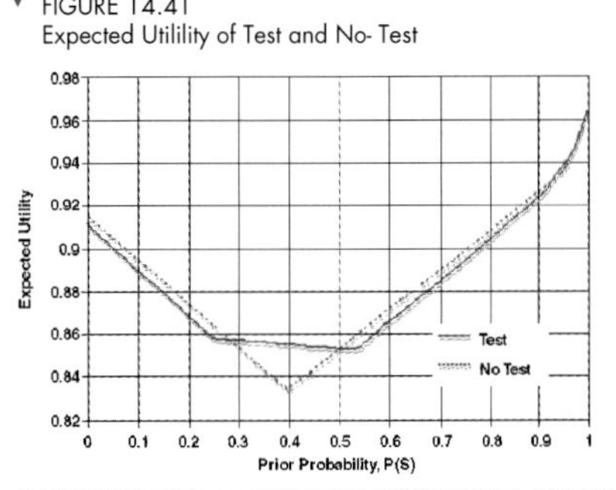

NEW LOGICAL TWO-PART STRUCTURE

By dividing the text into two distinct parts, dealing with deterministic models and probabilistic (stochastic) models, the authors have provided a logical framework for the material while allowing for greater emphasis on, and enhanced coverage of, "hot" areas such as simulation and use of computers in stochastic models.

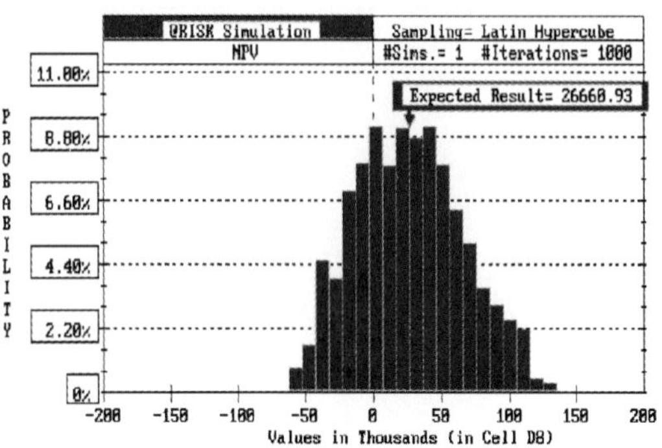

▲ FIGURE 13.8
Histogram of Net Present Value

Fortunately, June has available the spreadsheet add-in called @RISK. @RISK adds a number of @functions to the spreadsheet, corresponding to different probability distributions. To sample from a Poisson distribution with a mean of 10, June has only to enter the formula @POISSON (10). To sample from a continuous uniform distribution between 6 and 14, she enters the formula @UNIFORM (6, 14). The only changes June has to make in her spreadsheet are the following: in cell G6 she enters the formula @POISSON($G$6). While it is possible to generate Poisson random variables without using @RISK (by setting up an appropriate look-up table), it is much easier to use @RISK if it is available. As we will see, @RISK also greatly facilitates the capture and display of the output of the simulation.

@RISK automatically stores the results of these 1000 trials without having to use 1000 rows of the spreadsheet, saving space and time.

June decides to sample 1000 times from the distribution of the NPV and base her estimates on the 1000 values she obtains. She simply tells @RISK to perform 1000 iterations and capture the NPV in cell D8 for each of the iterations. After the 1000 iterations are completed, June can view a histogram of the results. The histogram in Figure 13.8 reveals that the average NPV over the 1000 iterations is $26,660.93, but that there is a definite probability of a negative NPV.

Once the basic relationships have been entered, however, it is very easy to alter the activity times and see what effect this has on the minimum project length and the activities on the critical path. By making the activity times random and recalculating the spreadsheet, one can get a feel for the variability of both the project length and the critical path. Figure 15.20 shows one example. Note that all activity times are between their pessimistic (a) and optimistic (b) times, but that the critical path is different, in this case B-C-F-G-J. This result demonstrates that the path with the longest expected length (B-C-D-E) may not turn out to be the critical path. This fact implies that the expected project length may be greater than the value calculated by the PERT analysis.

To estimate the true expected project length, we should recalculate the spreadsheet many times and average the minimum project lengths obtained on each recalculation. The @RISK add-in makes this easy to do. Since @RISK adds the beta distribution to the spreadsheet as an @function, and the PERT analysis of activity times was based on

672

Chapters 13 & 14 on **Simulation** and **Decision Theory** have been extensively revised and expanded.

Activity	Activity Time	Earliest Start	Earliest Finish	Latest Start	Latest Finish	Slack
A	2	0	2	6	8	6
B	4	0	4	0	4	0
C	3	4	7	4	7	0
D	3	7	10	8	11	1
E	5	10	15	11	16	1
F	2	7	9	7	9	0
G	4	9	13	9	13	0
H	2	9	11	14	16	5
I	5	4	9	11	16	7
J	3	13	16	13	16	0
K	2	9	11	11	13	2

Minimum Project Length 16.0

FIGURE 15.20
Simulated Activity Times for Global Oil

the beta distribution, we set the formulas in column B to sample from the appropriate beta distributions. Figure 15.21 shows the distribution of minimum project length calculated by @RISK based on a sample of 400 simulations. The estimated average project length is in fact larger than what was calculated by the PERT analysis, but only slightly so (20.09917 versus 20.0, about 1/2%). @RISK also makes it easy to calculate the probability that the project length is less than or equal to any given target value of 22 weeks, that probability is 78.49%, slightly lower than the 80% calculated by the PERT analysis. In this case, at least, it seems that PERT's simplifying assumptions are justified.

FIGURE 15.21
Distribution of Project Length

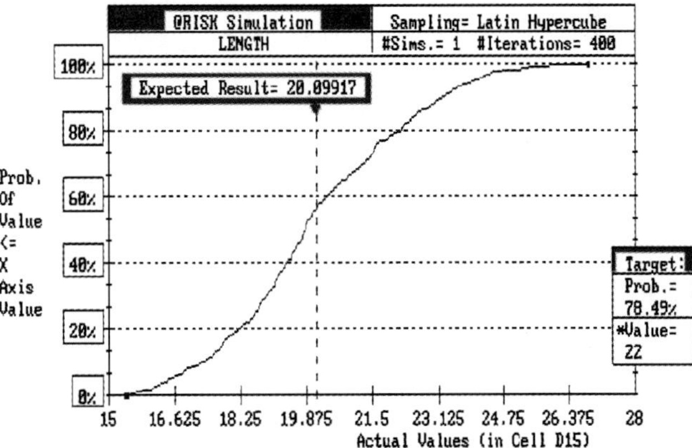

Chapters 15, 16, & 17 on **Project Management, Probabilistic Inventory**, and **Queueing** have been augmented to include additional computer applications.

ANNOTATED INSTRUCTOR'S EDITION

The **Annotated Instructor's Edition**, so well received in the text's third edition, now includes *marginal answers* to all end-of-chapter problems along with marginal notes. Valuable annotations include historical information, teaching tips, points to stress, real-world applications, and references to the *Applications Pack*.

Identical problems are faced by fast-food franchise managers: how many people to put on a shift to keep the average customer wait below a certain value. McDonald's reportedly figures they will lose a customer if the total wait is more than 5 minutes. Burger King has special kitchens set up to time and videotape every aspect of a model franchise. They then try different configurations of the kitchen to get the best possible work flow.

Recall that as we started this chapter, our stated goal was to attack three particular problems at St. Luke's with queueing models. In the preceding sections we have laid the groundwork for this process. We have introduced, defined, and illustrated the characteristics of the systems that we will consider (e.g., expected number in queue, expected waiting time, etc.) We have also made some general results such as Little's flow equation available for use in future analysis. We are now in a position to turn our attention to Monte Jackson's problems.

The system described in Problem 1 of Section 17.1, the blood-testing problem, is illustrated in Figure 17.7. Note that each patient joins a common queue and, on arriving at the head of the line, enters the first examining room that becomes available. This type of system must not be confused with a system in which a queue forms in front of each server, as in the typical grocery store.

Real World Applications

Not only is the choice of distribution important, but the student needs to be reminded that the actual event will happen only once, and that the distribution covers only the *range* of what might happen. Even if Peggy were to choose the correct distibution, she still has to "play the odds." This type of problem could also be set up as a decision tree problem (see Chapter 14).

Importance of the Choice of Distribution. Let us now suppose that Peggy changes her distribution. Instead of using the normal, suppose that she were to assume a *uniform* distribution on the interval from 700 to 1300. In this case,

$$Prob\{\text{demand} \leq x\} = \frac{x - 700}{600} \qquad \text{for } x = 701, 702, ..., 1300$$

and solving (16.4) for Q^* gives

$$Prob\{\text{demand} \leq Q^*\} = \frac{Q^* - 700}{600} \geq 0.588$$

$$Q^* \geq 600(0.588) + 700 = 1052.8$$

and hence $Q^* = 1053$. With the normal assumption she orders 1022. Had she used the uniform distribution, she would order 1053. You can see the assumption about the dist-

Teaching Tip

Marginal solutions make it easier for the instructor to prepare lessons and use the text in the classroom.

(a) Since no queue forms, number in systems is never >3 regardless of arrival rate
(b) 0.182302
(c) 0.427270
(d) 2.147736

17-26. A market research group has three interviewers located in adjacent booths in a suburban shopping mall. A contact person meets people walking in the mall and asks them if they are willing to be interviewed. They estimate that customers willing to agree to the interview arrive at the rate of 15 per hour, and the interarrival time has an exponential distribution. On the average the interview takes 15 minutes. If all booths are occupied, a person who has agreed to be interviewed will not wait and simply goes about his or her business.

(a) Comment on the following statement: Since $\lambda > \mu s$, this system will grow bound.

(b) Calculate the probability that exactly one interviewer is occupied.

(c) Find the probability that all three interviewers are occupied.

(d) Find the average number of busy interviewers.

APPLICATIONS PACK/VIDEO GUIDE

The **Applications Pack and Video Guide** provides instructors with a set of supporting materials for each chapter in the text. It includes chapter outlines, transparency masters, class discussion questions, and articles utilizing material from *Interfaces*. In addition, it offers helpful suggestions for using the Fourth Edition's new video cases in the classroom.

Logo refers instructors to the **Transparency Master** of this figure in the *Applications Pack and Video Guide*.

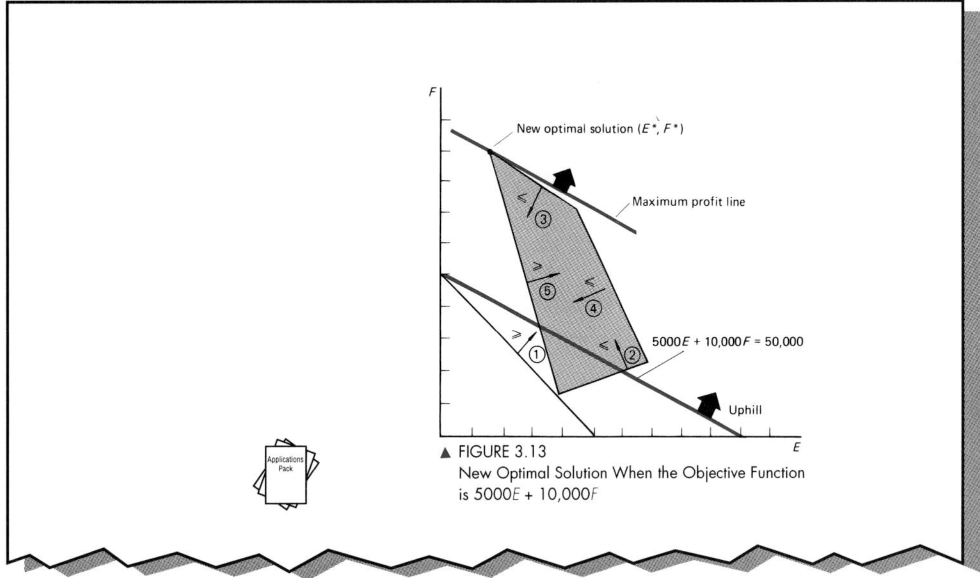

▲ FIGURE 3.13
New Optimal Solution When the Objective Function is 5000E + 10,000F

A special Video Guide included in the *Applications Pack* contains suggestions for classroom discussion topics as well as answers to the questions in the text's Video Cases.

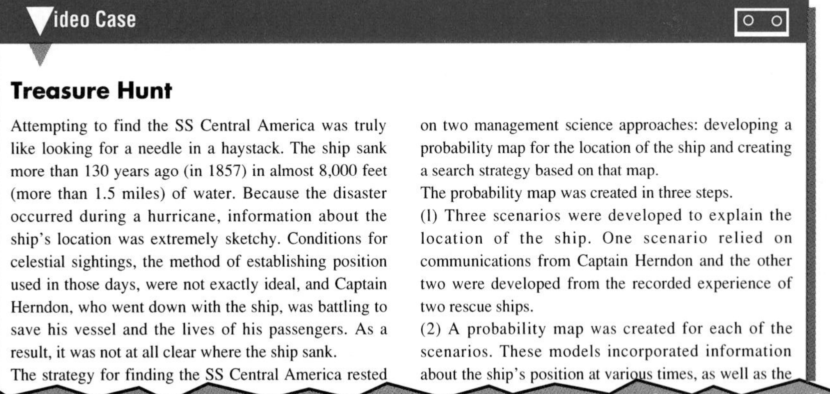

Video Case

Treasure Hunt

Attempting to find the SS Central America was truly like looking for a needle in a haystack. The ship sank more than 130 years ago (in 1857) in almost 8,000 feet (more than 1.5 miles) of water. Because the disaster occurred during a hurricane, information about the ship's location was extremely sketchy. Conditions for celestial sightings, the method of establishing position used in those days, were not exactly ideal, and Captain Herndon, who went down with the ship, was battling to save his vessel and the lives of his passengers. As a result, it was not at all clear where the ship sank.

The strategy for finding the SS Central America rested on two management science approaches: developing a probability map for the location of the ship and creating a search strategy based on that map.

The probability map was created in three steps.

(1) Three scenarios were developed to explain the location of the ship. One scenario relied on communications from Captain Herndon and the other two were developed from the recorded experience of two rescue ships.

(2) A probability map was created for each of the scenarios. These models incorporated information about the ship's position at various times, as well as the

THE DECIDING FACTOR.

INTRODUCTORY MANAGEMENT SCIENCE FOURTH EDITION

Eppen/Gould/Schmidt

SUPPLEMENTS

For You:

- Annotated Instructor's Edition (48648-0)
- Applications Pack and Video Guide (48650-6)
- Prentice Hall/ABC News Video Library (48573-0)
- Instructor's Solutions Manual (48646-4)
- Test Item File (48645-6)
- 5.25″ IBM Test Manager (48652-2)
- 3.5″ IBM Test Manager (48651-4)

For Your Students:

- Study Guide and Solutions Manual (48647-2)
- Prentice Hall/*New York Times* Contemporary View Program newspaper
- QSB+ Version 3.0 (©1993, both 3.5″ & 5.25″) by Yih-Long Chang (04587-2); discounted shrinkwrap package available upon text adoption
- STORM Version 3.0, ©1992 STORM Inc. 5.25″ (84744-3); 3.5″ (84745-0); discounted shrinkwrap package available upon text adoption

CP-012-M1S VA/lmdC/EAS/TN lithoUSA Fall '92

PRENTICE HALL

Simon & Schuster A Paramount Communications Company

Preface

To the Instructor:

These days, most of us are working harder at teaching. A number of factors probably underlie this development. For one thing, student ratings of teachers are now common; the ratings are typically published, and no one enjoys public humiliation. In many business schools, moreover, quantitative courses are under pressure. Courses that were once required are now electives, and good old Quantitative Methods 101 must now compete for students with marketing and finance. In general, students expect more from their courses, and there is institutional pressure to see that these expectations are realized. It follows that most of us are looking for ways to make our courses better.

It is our experience that a good text can play an important role in delivering a good course—that is, a course with lasting value that also catches the current interest of the students. Such a text must be engaging, relevant, up to date, accurate, careful in its use of notation, and clearly written. We have worked hard to make the fourth edition of Introductory Management Science that kind of book.

In this edition we have greatly expanded and strengthened the treatment of probabilistic models. The text has been reorganized to bring the probabilistic chapters together in Part II, creating a logically coherent structure that should help the student to grasp the common features of decision models incorporating uncertainty and the techniques by which such models are solved. We have rewritten Chapters 13 (Simulation) and 14 (Decision Theory), giving greater emphasis to the use of spreadsheets and the spreadsheet add-in @RISK; and we have added sections involving computer simulation to Chapters 15 (Project Management), 16 (Inventory with Probabilistic Demand), and 17 (Queuing) as well. There is also a new appendix on probability, designed to provide students with a concise review of the concepts that underlie the chapters of Part II.

Computing continues to play an increasingly important role in teaching management science, and that trend is also reflected in this revision. All copies of the text now include a student version of LINDO, and LINDO output of both formulations and solutions appears throughout the text. The ability of each student to formulate, solve, and perform sensitivity analysis on small but interesting problems is an important part of the learning process. The fact that the program they are using is exactly the same as the one featured in the text eliminates much unnecessary confusion. We have also increased the use of spreadsheets in the chapters of Part II, and introduced @RISK applications into most of them. Students can be confident that the computing they see in this text is at the level of common computer literacy. The software used is readily available and widely employed by businesses, government agencies, and universities. Indeed, many students will already own and be comfortable with some of these packages.

One of our goals for this edition was the inclusion of even more material to narrow the gap between the classroom and the real world. There are now a total of 37 Application Capsules in the text (compared to 11 in the last edition). These concise accounts of actual problems and their solutions provide a sense of realism that is not obtainable from classroom exercises. Several of the most interesting of these vignettes deal with the experience of managers and modelers in other countries: Canada, Spain, Turkey, Israel, Shanghai. Their inclusion gives the text an international flavor appropriate to today's continuously shrinking world.

Video cases are a new feature of the text. There is a case for each chapter. Some directly supplement the text in that they provide visual support for (or an alternative explanation of) material discussed in the preceding chapter. More often, the cases are used to encourage students to think broadly about the material they have just encountered in the text. The questions associated with such cases are intended to stimulate discussion about key concepts of the chapter. A Video Guide incorporated into the Applications Pack includes suggestions on how to use the videos effectively in the classroom, along with additional discussion questions for classroom use and answers to those in the text.

Other materials that have proved highly effective in the previous edition are still present. These include the copious marginal notes included in the Annotated Instructor's Edition (teaching tips, real-world examples, historical sidelights, useful analogies, etc.), as well as the Diagnostic Assignments and Cases. It is our experience that these last are extremely useful as a basis for class discussion. Problems remain an essential part of the text, and more than half of the even-numbered problems (those whose answers do not appear in the back of the book) are new to this edition. In addition, marginal answers to all the problems are now included in the Annotated Instructor's Edition.

We hope you find that this text and its supporting materials enhance your teaching efforts. We always like to hear from you—especially when it's to pass along your ideas for how the text can be improved—so please feel free to send along your reactions.

In closing, we want to acknowledge the contributions of a number of people who played important roles in creating this edition. Rick Hesse wrote all the marginal annotations, procured many of the videos, and helped in numerous other ways. (He is also the author of the Applications Pack.) Mohan Bala assisted in the preparation of the new problems. We are deeply grateful to the reviewers, listed below, who helped us to make the new edition a better text. We wish also to express our indebtedness to the team from Prentice Hall, including Valerie Ashton, acquisitions editor; Dan Schiller, development editor; Carol Burgett, production editor; Tom Nery, designer; and Debbie Toymil, layout artist. Thanks to all of you. It is literally true that we couldn't and surely wouldn't have done it without you.

Gary D. Eppen
F.J. Gould
Charles P. Schmidt

Reviewers for the Fourth Edition

Prof. Suzanna Cahn	Pace University
Dr. David Carhart	Bentley College
Prof. Robert B. Curry, Jr.	DeVry Institute, Kansas City
Prof. Zvi Goldstein	California State University-Fullerton
Prof. Jamshid Hosseini	Marquette University
Prof. Ron Klimberg	Boston University
Prof. Darlene Lanier	Louisiana State University
Prof. Roger Myerson	Northwestern University
Prof. Jeffrey L. Rummel	Duke University
Prof. Bill Schultz	Buffalo State College
Prof. Gang Yu	University of Texas at Austin

INTRODUCTORY MANAGEMENT SCIENCE

Fourth Edition

F.J. GOULD
University of Chicago

G.D. EPPEN
University of Chicago

C.P. SCHMIDT
University of Alabama

PRENTICE HALL, Englewood Cliffs, New Jersey 07632

Library of Congress Cataloging-in-Publication Data

Gould, F. J. (Floyd Jerome),
Introductory management science / F.J. Gould, G.D. Eppen, C.P. Schmidt.—4th ed.
p. cm.
Includes index.
ISBN 0-13-486440-9 (hard cover)
1. Management—Mathematical models. 2. Management science.
I. Eppen, Gary D. II. Schmidt, C. P. III. Title.
HD30.25.G68 1993
658.4'033—dc20 92-27752
CIP

To our parents and children

Acquisition Editor: Valerie Ashton
Editor-in-Chief: Joseph Heider
Development Editor: Daniel Schiller
Production Editor: Carol Burgett
Interior and Cover Designer: Thomas Nery
Copy Editor: Margo Quinto
Prepress Buyer: Trudy Pisciotti
Manufacturing Buyer: Patrice Fraccio
Marketing Manager: Frank Lyman
Supplements Editor: Lisamarie Brassini
Editorial Assistants: Annmarie Dunn, Renee Pelletier

Printed in the United States of America

10 9 8 7 6 5 4 3 2 1

ISBN 0-13-486440-9

Prentice-Hall International (UK) Limited, *London*
Prentice-Hall of Australia Pty. Limited, *Sydney*
Prentice-Hall Canada Inc., *Toronto*
Prentice-Hall Hispanoamericana, S.A., *Mexico*
Prentice-Hall of India Private Limited, *New Delhi*
Prentice-Hall of Japan, Inc., *Tokyo*
Simon & Schuster Asia Pte. Ltd., *Singapore*
Editora Prentice-Hall do Brasil, Ltda., *Rio de Janeiro*

Brief Table of Contents

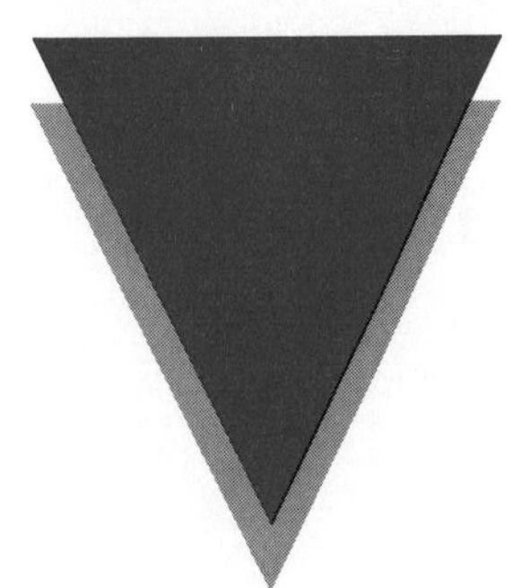

Table of Contents

Index of Applications

Video Cases

Cases and Diagnostic Assignments

Application Capsules

Preface

To the Student:

It's sad, but true: Outside of the engineering school, quantitative courses are not usually very popular. So here you are with another quantitative course to take, and you probably are not filled with enthusiasm. Well, cheer up. Experience has taught us that management science, at least as taught from this text, can be a positive experience. The basic reason is that many students find the problems and approaches of this text intrinsically interesting; and once something becomes interesting, it also becomes "easy."

And why, we hear you asking, will I find this material interesting? The standard answer to this question is that mathematical models are becoming ever more important to today's managers, and therefore students who are concerned with modern management will find them interesting. This argument is usually supplemented with a long list of applications in which such models have made an important contribution. While we certainly do not disagree with this point of view, we feel that it requires some clarification.

Quantitative models are indeed increasingly important, and the list of successful applications is impressive. The fact is, however, that not everyone who takes this course either expects or needs to become expert in mathematical modeling. Most models, such as airline scheduling programs, are produced by specialists—people who make their living by creating and implementing models. Most managers, by contrast, are not model makers—they work with models created by someone else. Their main concern is with seeing that the model gets the appropriate input and with trying to implement the recommendations of the model in the real world.

An approach to management science geared to the needs of the specialist (or prospective specialist) necessarily concentrates on the various solution techniques, or algorithms. These algorithms can be thought of as the "mathematical technology" that takes an input (a specific model) and creates an output (usually a computer printout). An approach geared to the manager (or student of management) differs somewhat in its emphasis. It is based on a view that, in the use of quantitative models, the crucial role of managers occurs during the formulation and implementation phases. It relegates to the computer the mathematical operations needed to solve models, and focuses on helping the manager to understand (1) what sorts of problems are amenable to modeling, (2) what the prospects are for obtaining a computer solution (within an affordable amount of time), and (3) what one can do to get the greatest possible value out of the model and the computer output.

Our goal has been to achieve an effective balance between these approaches. We believe that students will find a course in management science interesting (to say nothing of useful) to the extent that it emphasizes *real-world problems* and the role of models in solving such problems. We have tried, in other words, to keep the focus on *the relationship between problem and model.*

Part of the responsibility for maintaining this focus, however, rests with you. As you work your way through this text, you will find that it is full of specific problems and techniques for solving them. It is easy to become so immersed in these problems and techniques that you lose track of the general skills that you must develop to be either a good manager or a good modeler. Here are four ideas that are fundamental to effective decision making. It is useful to keep them in mind and to see how the specific problems you are working on contribute to your understanding of them.

Problem Framing. To solve a problem, you first have to "frame" it. That is, you must develop an organized way of thinking about the problem. Remember, most problems come to us in the form of symptoms, not as clear problem statements. Your sales representative in Spokane tells you that your chief competitor is beating your pants off by offering 24-hour delivery. In the everyday sense of the word, that's a problem. In our language, that's a symptom. A problem involves possible decisions and a method for measuring their effectiveness. The art of moving from a symptom to a problem statement is called problem framing. It is an essential skill of effective management.

Constrained optimization and *decisions under risk* are two important and useful frames for a wide variety of problems. In textbooks they are presented as mathematical models with the procedures (algorithms) to solve them. What the prospective manager needs is the framing skill, not the mathematics. Unfortunately, it does not seem possible merely to describe the frames and assume that people can then use them correctly. You have to understand how the models are created and the relationships between decisions and results before you can advance to using the frames in an intuitive way. You have to learn about the models and how they are used in various situations before you can make the ideas your own. It takes practice. Thus the book is full of examples and problems.

Optimality and Sensitivity. In this text you will encounter many mathematical models for business problems, and you will see that these models produce "optimal" solutions. That sounds great—what could be better than an "optimal" solution? But language can be deceptive if you do not have a thorough understanding of the concepts behind it. In this context, an *optimal solution* is one that gives the best answer to the mathematical problem formulated in the model—for example, an answer that maximizes profits. But is it the best answer to the real-world problem that prompted us to make the model in the first place? This is what a manager must decide—preferably, *before* implementing the recommendations of the model. Whether or not to implement a particular recommendation is always a judgment call, but the quality of this judgment will depend heavily on how well the manager understands the relationship between the model and the real problem it is designed to mirror.

It is also important to assess the *sensitivity* of the answer—that is, how much the answer given by a model depends on the particular numerical values used for the model's parameters. Managers are usually most comfortable with decisions that hold for a wide range of parameter values, so that a good decision cannot suddenly be transformed into a bad one by a small change in one parameter. Sensitivity analysis is thus an important topic throughout this text.

Cost Concepts. This text deals with individual business decisions, such as how many items to order or where to build a new factory. The basic building blocks for the models you will construct are revenues and costs. You will have the opportunity to work with the concepts of fixed, marginal, and opportunity costs. Determining the proper cost relationships is crucial to arriving at good decisions. It is a skill that will stand you in good stead in any career.

Healthy Skepticism. It is important to be skeptical. Learn to beware of experts, of solutions provided by models, and certainly of your own intuition. Our most valuable associates are those who say, "You can't be right! If you were right, then we would know that the following condition must be true, and it obviously isn't and thus you are wrong." Working with optimization models enhances your ability to analyze and dissect the route from assumptions to conclusions. The Diagnostic Assignments (a unique feature of this text) are specifically designed to illustrate this concept. Asking the right question is the first step in finding a good solution. You have the opportunity to work on developing this skill.

We would like to close with a brief comment about learning and education. We, our editors, and the authors of the various supplements have gone to great effort to make the material correct, easily accessible, and interesting. There are Application Capsules, Cases, Diagnostic Assignments, Video Cases, lists of key terms, problems with solutions, major concept quizzes, etc., etc. The key ingredient, however, is you. It is clearly possible to do the work in this text, get a good grade in the course, and still have the material make no impact on you or your career. To avoid this result, you have to *own* these ideas, which means you must make them a part of your intuition. The text can help, your professor can help, but ultimately you have to do it on the basis of your own participation. Learning something is, after all, a personal experience, and you can achieve it only with personal effort.

Gary D. Eppen
F.J. Gould
Charles P. Schmidt

CHAPTER 1

Introduction: Models and Modeling

APPLICATION CAPSULE

Turnaround at CITGO: Refining Refinery Operations to Make Losses into Profits*

Southland Corporation, the 7-Eleven convenience store giant, acquired Citgo Petroleum partly as a source for the two billion gallons of gasoline per year that it retails through its stores. However, Southland was also determined to make Citgo as successful in the refining and marketing of petroleum products as Southland was in the convenience-store industry.

Citgo had been losing money for some time; in the year immediately prior to the acquisition it had posted a pretax loss of over $50 million. The two previous owners of Citgo had employed a strategy of refining as much crude oil as possible while attempting to minimize incremental costs. Southland management, by contrast, began with the objective of maximizing profit, even if this meant reducing production or incurring higher costs in the short run.

Realizing this objective required the collection of more (and more accurate) data and the use of better management science tools. *The key step taken by Southland was to completely rework the LP models for the refinery.* The importance of having a good model cannot be underestimated. For example, a good model will improve product yields, and an overall increase in product yield of just one-tenth of 1% (0.001) can result in a $3 million per year improvement in earnings.

The new LP system also made possible many insights into refinery operations from a global perspective that helped management increase profits. For instance, the results indicated that separate LP models for individual refinery units were justified. The information provided by these models proved valuable in determining economically efficient run levels for each refinery and helped facility managers fine-tune their operations.

The results of these improvements were dramatic: In the year following the acquisition by Southland, Citgo achieved a pretax profit of over $70 million.

*Klingman, Phillips, Steiger, and Young, "The Successful Deployment of Management Science Throughout Citgo Petroleum Corporation," *Interfaces*, Vol. 17, No. 1 (Jan.–Feb. 1987).

1.1 A Hierarchy of Models

This book is about the use of quantitative models in solving management problems. This chapter is about models—what they are, how they are constructed, how they are used, and what they can tell us.

In our world, many kinds of models are associated with many kinds of activities. Engineers build model airplanes, urban planners build model cities, physicists construct models of the universe, and economists build models of the economy. Business managers and corporate planners work with models of their own particular environments. Such an environment may be a complex multinational corporation or it may simply be a one-room shop where three products are assembled on four machines.

Despite the diversity of these models, they have one aspect in common. They are all idealized and simplified representations of reality. Another way of saying the same thing is that

A model is a selective abstraction of reality.

Quantitative Models

A *quantitative model* uses mathematics to represent the relationship between data of interest. A quantitative model requires these data to be *quantifiable*—that is, expressible in numerical form. We all use such models as part of our everyday lives. Consider the following commonplace examples. A model to evaluate the alternatives of buying a house versus renting an apartment considers the down payments required, mortgage rates, cash flow, appreciation—in brief, numerical data. A model to help you decide whether to work for an MBA degree would consider length of time required, the tuition and other expenses, salary potential—numerical data. In short, numerical data are the guts of quantitative models.

Let us examine more closely a very simple example of such a model. If you are currently in Chicago and plan to be in Cleveland for dinner, you might want to estimate the time it will take you to drive from Chicago to Cleveland. To do so you might look up the mileage in an atlas and divide it by your typical average speed. Your model is therefore

$$T = \frac{D}{S}$$

where T = time, D = distance, and S = speed.

This model is certainly useful. Note, however, that it is *simplification* of reality, for you have intentionally ignored many factors that could influence your travel time. You have made no effort to include considerations such as construction delays, weather conditions, stops to buy gas or to visit the restroom, and so on. Nevertheless, if you are planning to leave at 9 A.M. and $T = 6$ hours, then the model is clearly good enough for your purposes—that is, you can be pretty confident that you will arrive in Cleveland in time for dinner.

Suppose, however, that you cannot leave until noon and have a reservation to meet a very important person at a very fancy restaurant at 6:30. You might then feel that the model is *too* simple for comfort, and you might want to refine it—to incorporate more detail so as to bring it closer to reality. You could, for example, add an expression to represent your stops along the way. The model would then be

$$T = \frac{D}{S} + (R \times N)$$

where R is the average time spent at a rest stop, and N is the number of times you expect to stop.

Clearly, you could go on improving your model by incorporating more factors. Some of those factors might have to be estimates or approximations. The two points that need to be kept in mind are these:

A model usually simplifies reality.

and

You incorporate enough detail into your model so that

1. **the result meets your needs, and**
2. **you can solve it in the time you have to devote to the process.**

Decision Models

In this book we will emphasize *decision models:* models in which some of the variables represent decisions that must be (or at least could be) made. In the example given previously, you obviously cannot change the distance between Chicago and Cleveland. You can, however, choose your speed, the number of times you stop, and the time you take at each stop. These are therefore *decision variables.* (There may be some limits on these variables—you obviously cannot drive at 300 mph, your gas tank can hold only a certain amount of gas, the tank takes a certain amount of time to fill, and so on. We will discuss such limits shortly, because they are central to the construction of realistic models.)

In this book, we will encounter models in which the decision variables are the quantities of a particular tractor to produce, the number of phone lines to install, the amount of money to invest in a certain stock, or the number of green spring suits to order.

Objectives. In addition to decision variables, decision models typically include an *objective.* In the real world, decisions are usually made to achieve a particular objective, and the role of the model is to specify the way in which the decision variables will affect the objective. Consider the following examples:

1. ***Salesforce allocation model:*** The decisions (i.e., decision variables) might be how many salespeople to assign to each territory. A typical objective might be to maximize sales revenues.
2. ***Job-shop scheduling model:*** The decisions (decision variables) might be how many hours to schedule given parts on given machines, and in what sequence. Possible objectives might be to minimize costs, to minimize the total completion time for all parts, or to minimize tardiness on deliveries.
3. ***Cash-management model:*** The decision variables might be the amount of funds to be held in each of several categories (cash, Treasury bills, bonds, stocks) each month. A typical objective might be to minimize the opportunity cost of holding more liquid assets.

To summarize:

1. **Decision models selectively describe the environment.**
2. **Decision models designate decision variables.**
3. **Decision models designate objectives.**

To get a better idea of what a quantitative decision model is like, let us look at an example.

An Example: The Oak Products Spreadsheet

Production at Oak Products, Inc.

Oak Products, Inc. (OP) produces a line of high-quality solid oak chairs. There are six chairs in the product line: Captain, Mate, American High, American Low, Spanish King, and Spanish Queen. These chairs have been designed to use a number of interchangeable component parts—long and short dowels, heavy and light seats, and heavy and light rungs. In addition, each type of chair has a distinguishing rail that caps the back. The interchangeable parts help protect OP against sudden shifts in demand. It is November 15, and Tom Burr, the plant manager, is set to meet James White from production control to finalize the production plan for the next 2 weeks. At OP, the finishing activity (i.e., sanding, spraying, and drying of the component parts) requires 2 weeks. For this reason, only components that are already on hand and finished can be used in chairs that will be produced in the next 2 weeks.

Using Lotus 1-2-3

Production planning at OP is done with a computerized spreadsheet model. Spreadsheet software packages, especially Lotus 1-2-3®[1], have made quantitative models and decision models an everyday part of an enormous number of management activities. These models give managers a "user-friendly" technique for answering a wide range of so-called what if questions. A "what if" question is exactly what the name suggests. The manager wants to know what happens to some quantity of interest if some characteristic of his operating environment changes in a specified way. Obviously, such questions are fundamental to any management task.

"What if" questions

Jim White has run the Lotus 1-2-3 program on his PC. The result is the spreadsheet shown in Figure 1.1.

A spreadsheet is a way of changing data into useful information, something more than a bunch of numbers. Numbers can be arranged so that they make sense in a model form called a "spreadsheet." The spreadsheet is popular because it looks exactly like the sheet of paper on which work is done.

A *spreadsheet* is a kind of representation of the problem. Jim has placed this representation of his problem on a grid with rows labeled 1 through 25 and columns labeled A through K. As you can see, Jim has placed text in many of the rows and columns. This text allows one to readily interpret the numbers in the spreadsheet. For example, the 4 in column C, row 15, is a piece of data indicating that 4 short dowels are used in producing one Captain chair. Also, Jim has placed his suggested production plan in row 8, columns C through H. Thus, Jim's proposal is to produce 40 chairs of each type. Row 3 shows that the total profit will be $8760. The entries in row 15, columns I, J, and K indicate that

1. Jim's production plan will use a total of 1600 short dowels;
2. the starting inventory of short dowels is 1900; and
3. Jim's plan will leave a final inventory of 300 short dowels.

The production planning session proceeds as follows:

JIM: I've used the usual procedure to determine production—that is, to make the same quantity of each product and maximize the total amount produced. This time we run out of long dowels first, but we do pretty well. We produce 40 of each chair and make $8760.

TOM: I know that we've always produced equal quantities of each chair, but this time things are different. The president tells me that solid wood products are a hot item now, and we will sell out no matter what we produce. He says to make as much profit as possible. What should we do?

JIM: I don't know the complete answer, but I do have an idea. American Highs are

[1]Lotus 1-2-3 is a trademark of Lotus Development Corporation.

```
        A     B    C     D     E       F       G       H     I     J     K
1   *****************
2   TOTAL PROFIT:
3       8760
4   *****************
5     Product    Capt  Mate  AmerHi  AmerLo  SpainK  SpainQ
6   Profit\Unit   36    40     45      38      35      25
7
8   Quantity      40    40     40      40      40      40
9   Produced
10  ------------------------------------------------------------------------
11               Product Resource Requirement                Total  Start  End
12                                                           Usage  Inv.  Inv.
13  ------------------------------------------------------------------------
14  Long Do        8     0     12       0       8       4   1280   1280    0
15  Short Do       4    12      0      12       4       8   1600   1900  300
16  Legs           4     4      4       4       4       4    960   1090  130
17  Heavy Se       1     0      0       0       1       1    120    190   70
18  Light Se       0     1      1       1       0       0    120    170   50
19  Heavy Ru       6     0      4       0       5       0    600   1000  400
20  Light Ru       0     4      0       5       0       6    600   1000  400
21  Capt Rail      1     0      0       0       0       0     40    110   70
22  Mate Rail      0     1      0       0       0       0     40     72   32
23  Amer Rail      0     0      1       1       0       0     80     93   13
24  Span Rail      0     0      0       0       1       1     80     85    5
25  ------------------------------------------------------------------------
```

▲ FIGURE 1.1
The First OP Spreadsheet

clearly our most profitable item, but notice that they also use the most long dowels and we're short of long dowels. If I give up 2 American Highs, I lose $90 of profit, but I gain 24 long dowels. I can use those dowels to make 3 Captains, in which case, I'll gain $108. So *what if* we make 100 Captains and no American Highs?

(Jim enters this new proposal into row 8, columns C through H. The Lotus 1-2-3 program automatically fills in new values for those grid cells that depend upon the production plan. The result is shown in Figure 1.2.)

TOM: Jim, that's great! You've increased profits by $360. I wonder if we can do better? I'm sure we can. In fact, I think we can use your idea again. Spanish Kings require 8 long dowels, while Spanish Queens require only 4. I should be able to give up a King and lose $35, but make 2 Queens and gain $50. So, *what if* we make no Kings and a total of 120 Queens?

(The result is shown in Figure 1.3.)

JIM: There's some good news and some bad news. The good news is that your economics was right. Profits increased by $600. The bad news is that we don't have the inventory to support this plan. The spreadsheet shows negative ending inventory for short dowels and a bunch of other things. This means that we have to use more short dowels than we have. It's just not possible.

TOM: I see what you mean. Clearly I overshot the mark. I understand that we could decrease the production of Spanish Kings and increase the production of Spanish Queens somewhat and increase profits. With enough effort, I guess we could figure out how much we can push this trade-off before running out of inventory. But even so, how do we know it's a good solution? I really wonder *what's best.*

	A	B	C	D	E	F	G	H	I	J	K
1	******************										
2	TOTAL PROFIT:										
3	9120										
4	******************										
5	Product		Capt	Mate	AmerHi	AmerLo	SpainK	SpainQ			
6	Profit\Unit		36	40	45	38	35	25			
7											
8	Quantity		100	40	0	40	40	40			
9	Produced										
10	------------										
11			Product Resource Requirement						Total	Start	End
12									Usage	Inv.	Inv.
13	------------										
14	Long Do		8	0	12	0	8	4	1280	1280	0
15	Short Do		4	12	0	12	4	8	1840	1900	60
16	Legs		4	4	4	4	4	4	1040	1090	50
17	Heavy Se		1	0	0	0	1	1	180	190	10
18	Light Se		0	1	1	1	0	0	80	170	90
19	Heavy Ru		6	0	4	0	5	0	800	1000	200
20	Light Ru		0	4	0	5	0	6	600	1000	400
21	Capt Rail		1	0	0	0	0	0	100	110	10
22	Mate Rail		0	1	0	0	0	0	40	72	32
23	Amer Rail		0	0	1	1	0	0	40	93	53
24	Span Rail		0	0	0	0	1	1	80	85	5
25	------------										

▲ FIGURE 1.2
Jim's Revised Spreadsheet

▼ FIGURE 1.3
Tom's Revised Spreadsheet

	A	B	C	D	E	F	G	H	I	J	K
1	******************										
2	TOTAL PROFIT:										
3	9720										
4	******************										
5	Product		Capt	Mate	AmerHi	AmerLo	SpainK	SpainQ			
6	Profit\Unit		36	40	45	38	35	25			
7											
8	Quantity		100	40	0	40	0	120			
9	Produced										
10	------------										
11			Product Resource Requirement						Total	Start	End
12									Usage	Inv.	Inv.
13	------------										
14	Long Do		8	0	12	0	8	4	1280	1280	0
15	Short Do		4	12	0	12	4	8	2320	1900	−420
16	Legs		4	4	4	4	4	4	1200	1090	−110
17	Heavy Se		1	0	0	0	1	1	220	190	−30
18	Light Se		0	1	1	1	0	0	80	170	90
19	Heavy Ru		6	0	4	0	5	0	600	1000	400
20	Light Ru		0	4	0	5	0	6	1080	1000	−80
21	Capt Rail		1	0	0	0	0	0	100	110	10
22	Mate Rail		0	1	0	0	0	0	40	72	32
23	Amer Rail		0	0	1	1	0	0	40	93	53
24	Span Rail		0	0	0	0	1	1	120	85	−35
25	------------										

Optimization Models

The Oak Products model is certainly a quantitative decision model. It specifies the relationship between the decision variables (the quantity of each chair to produce) and various measures of interest (the number of parts used and the total profit). It does not, however, tell us how many chairs to produce. When you think about it, that is a funny question. How many chairs to produce to do what? We might want to know how many chairs to produce to use up as much of our parts inventory as possible. Or how many chairs to produce to satisfy normal customer demand for each model. It is more likely that we would want to know how many chairs to produce in order to maximize our profit. The point is that before we can decide what we want to do, we have to know what we want to accomplish; that is, we have to specify our objective.

Much of this book is devoted to *optimization models:* models in which the goal is to make some function of the decision variables as large or perhaps as small as possible. You might, for example, want to make sales or profits large in one problem and costs or delivery times small in another.

The student does not need to become *computer literate* but rather *computer aware.* It is not necessary to take a course in automotive mechanics (how a car works) to master the fundamentals of driver education (learning to drive an automobile safely and effectively).

If Tom and Jim decide that they want to make their profit as large as possible then the Oak Products problem becomes an optimization problem. Indeed, it is a standard type of managerial planning problem, called a *linear programming (LP)* problem, and the best, or *optimal* solution is easily obtained. There are several PC codes that take a linear programming problem, set up in a Lotus 1-2-3 spreadsheet format as above, and then optimize. Two such codes are VINO™[2] and What's *Best!*™.[3] In both of these programs, only a few additional strokes at the keyboard are required to obtain the optimal plan. The result is shown in Figure 1.4 on page 8. It is interesting to note that profit has increased by $1174 over Jim's revised plan and that no Spanish style chairs are part of the optimal solution.

The above discussion illustrates only what a spreadsheet representation of a problem may look like and what it can do. We've told you nothing about how to actually create a spreadsheet representation. You will see some of that in the discussion of model formulation in Chapter 2, where you'll also see several other specific spreadsheet examples and more of the power that spreadsheets provide.

Constraints and Constrained Optimization. The Oak Products problem is an example of the kind of problem to which most of this text is devoted. It is a *constrained optimization problem:* a problem in which we wish to maximize (or minimize) some function of the decision variables *subject to a set of constraints.* In the language of management science, a *constraint* is a limitation on the range of allowable decisions. In this particular case the constraints are the quantities of various parts available to produce chairs, but there are many different types of constraints. Indeed, most people make most of their personal and professional decisions in situations where the allowable decisions have been restricted in some way. In our private lives we are nearly always dealing with limitations of some sort—of time, of money, of space, of energy. In business, the kinds of constraints encountered are even more numerous. A manager must often take into account capital requirements, personnel availability, delivery schedules, import quotas, union work rules, factory capacities, environmental regulations, inventory costs, and a host of other factors. It is perhaps not surprising, therefore, that constrained optimization—*achieving the best possible result given the restrictions that apply*—is the most active area of management science research. Indeed, one of the most commonly employed management science tools, linear programming, is a special model for carrying out constrained optimization.

Constraints can be thought of in terms of the objective function: *"What keeps me from making an infinite profit?" "What makes me spend money so that my cost isn't $0?"* Asking these questions in English before trying to write equations might help construct the model.

[2]VINO is a trademark of LINDO Systems, Inc.

[3]What's*Best!* is a trademark of General Optimization, Inc.

```
         A    B   C    D      E      F      G      H      I     J     K
1  *******************
2  TOTAL PROFIT:
3      10294
4  *******************
5     Product    Capt  Mate  AmerHi  AmerLo  SpainK  SpainQ
6  Profit\Unit    36    40      45      38      35      25
7
8  Quantity      100    72      40      53       0       0
9  Produced
10 ------------------------------------------------------------------------
11               Product Resource Requirement              Total  Start  End
12                                                         Usage   Inv.  Inv.
13 ------------------------------------------------------------------------
14 Long Do         8     0      12       0       8       4  1280   1280    0
15 Short Do        4    12       0      12       4       8  1900   1900    0
16 Legs            4     4       4       4       4       4  1060   1090   30
17 Heavy Se        1     0       0       0       1       1   100    190   90
18 Light Se        0     1       1       1       0       0   165    170    5
19 Heavy Ru        6     0       4       0       5       0   760   1000  240
20 Light Ru        0     4       0       5       0       6   553   1000  447
21 Capt Rail       1     0       0       0       0       0   100    110   10
22 Mate Rail       0     1       0       0       0       0    72     72    0
23 Amer Rail       0     0       1       1       0       0    93     93    0
24 Span Rail       0     0       0       0       1       1     0     85   85
25 ------------------------------------------------------------------------
```

▲ FIGURE 1.4
The Optimal Solution

Applications of Constrained Optimization Models. Constrained optimization models were first used in decision making in the 1940s. Among the major applications were logistic problems in World War II. The fields of operations research and management science arose from the early defense applications.

Now, applications of constrained optimization models range across all sorts of planning activities in both the public and private sectors. Applications in government are frequent. They have included modeling efforts in the areas of defense, health planning, transportation, energy planning, and resource allocation, to name only a few. In the private sector, applications vary from long-term planning to daily, or even hourly, scheduling of activities. Specific applications in long-term planning include capital budgeting, plant location, long-range marketing strategy, and long-range investment strategy. Shorter-term applications include production and workforce scheduling, inventory management, machine scheduling, aircraft routing, chemical blending, product design, media selection, statistical estimation, feed-mix blending, tanker scheduling, waste disposal, site selection, and project scheduling in the construction of nuclear submarines and major shopping centers. The list could go on and on.

In all these applications, decisions must be made in order to carry out an activity or collection of activities "optimally" according to some criterion (such as minimizing cost, time, waste, or delay, or maximizing profit or total amount shipped). Also, in all these applications, limitations are imposed either by scarce resources that must be allocated or by certain requirements that must be satisfied, or by both. These limitations or requirements place constraints on the decisions that can be made. Other constraints may exist in the form of logical relations or physical laws that must be satisfied by the decision variables. Thus, decisions must be found that optimize the objective subject to all the constraints.

Deterministic and Probabilistic Models

We know that this book is devoted to quantitative decision models. There is, however, a large and diverse body of knowledge that falls under this general heading. It is thus useful to have a taxonomy, or way of organizing the material, so that you can see the forest before getting enmeshed in the trees.

There are several principles used to organize the material in this text. The most obvious one is that there are two main sections. The first part of the text is devoted to deterministic models, and the second part considers probabilistic models.

Deterministic Models. *Deterministic models* are those models in which *all of the relevant data are assumed to be known with certainty.* Oak Products is a deterministic model. We assume that the exact profit per chair and all other data are known. Much of this first part is devoted to *mathematical programming,* or *constrained optimization models.* In this part you will be introduced to linear programming (LP), which is the workhorse of quantitative decision models. There are four reasons why LP is important:

1. An absolutely amazing variety of important management problems can be formulated as LPs.
2. Once they are formulated, we have the technology to solve big problems quickly.
3. The solution technique produces as a by-product a great deal of information that is useful to management.
4. Constrained optimization is an extremely useful way to think about problems even when you are not going to build a model and solve it. Practice with LP problems helps to develop the ability to use the concepts of constrained optimization in an intuitive manner.

The most important mathematical skill is the ability to do the simple mechanics of algebra well, not fancy calculus poorly. Most students have problems adding, subtracting, multiplying, and dividing with numbers and symbols. Usually they grasp the *concepts* of calculus and statistics, but the *mechanics* do them in.

You will learn to formulate LP problems, solve them on the computer, and interpret the solution. You will also have the opportunity to learn the procedures (algorithms) that are used to solve LPs.

A variety of other models also appear in the first part of this text. They include integer and quadratic programming, which are first cousins of LP. There are also chapters on heuristics, network models, and inventory control. Most of the mathematics in this part will be familiar to you. For these topics you should have a good command of high school algebra. An exposure to calculus can be an advantage in that it helps develop mathematical maturity. However, the mathematics of calculus is not required.

Probabilistic Models. *Probabilistic,* or *stochastic,* models are characterized by the fact that some element of the problem is not known with certainty. More specifically some element of the problem is a *random variable,* and the *distribution* of that random variable is known. To get a better idea of what is meant by these terms, consider the following problem from Chapter 14.

> Walter's Dog and Pony Show is scheduled to appear in Cedar Rapids on July 14. The profits obtained are heavily dependent on the weather. In particular, if the weather is rainy, the show loses \$15,000, and if sunny the show makes a profit of \$10,000. (We assume that all days are either rainy or sunny.) Walter can decide to cancel the show, but if he does he forfeits a \$1000 deposit he put down when he accepted the date. The historical record shows that on July 14 it has rained one-fourth of the time in the last 100 years. What decision should Walter make to maximize his expected net dollar return?

Note that in this problem the state of the weather in Cedar Rapids is uncertain. However, a probability distribution is specified—the weather is sunny with probability ¾ and rainy with probability ¼. It is in situations such as this that a probabilistic model would be used. Note that with such models it is not obvious how you know whether you made a good decision or were just lucky (or unlucky). On July 14 Walter will know if it is raining or not and if he made a good decision or not. The problem is to develop a method so that you can decide *in advance* when a decision is good.

In this part of the book you will learn what kinds of criteria you can use when there is uncertainty concerning part of the problem and how to find an optimal decision in view of those criteria. You see that here again we have quantitative decision problems in which we are trying to optimize some function of the decision variables. Topics in this part of the book include decision trees, project management, inventory control when demand is characterized by a random variable, queuing problems, and forecasting. There is also a chapter on simulation, which is an alternative approach to finding good answers to probabilistic models.

This part of the text requires some knowledge of probability and statistics. Appendix A to this text provides a brief overview of the subject. Although it certainly will not make you an expert, it does provide an introduction to (or a review of) the key concepts required for an understanding of these chapters.

1.2 Models and Modeling: A Perspective

By modeling various alternatives for future system design, Federal Express has, in effect, made its mistakes on paper. Computer modeling works; it allows us to examine many different alternatives and it forces the examination of the entire problem.[4]

FREDERICK W. SMITH
Chairman and CEO of Federal Express Corporation

Generally speaking, the material in nearly every chapter of this text can be broken down into five categories:

1. ***Modeling,*** or ***formulation,*** the process of taking real-world problems and describing them in mathematical terms;
2. ***Solution techniques,*** or ***algorithms,*** the mathematical methods used to find answers from the models created in 1;
3. ***Computer solutions,*** the use of standard computer programs to solve the models in 1;
4. ***Interpretation,*** making sure that all available information is obtained from the computer solution in 3;
5. ***Implementation,*** putting the knowledge gained from the solution to work, and
6. ***Philosophy,*** a view of the relationships among the real-world problems, models, managers, and solutions.

[4]Peter Horner, "Eyes on the Prize," *OR/MS Today,* August 1991, pp. 34–35.

Different classes may choose to emphasize different parts of this material, depending on the perspective of the instructor and the needs of the students. A "technical" approach places the emphasis on the mathematics and the algorithms. A "managerial" approach is more concerned with identifying problems, formulating models, interpreting their output, and implementing the solution. We have tried to design this text in such a way that users with either orientation can benefit from all the material. This, we feel, is possible because there is a common central thrust for both types of users: *an interest in real-world problem solving.* Without that, the management scientist would be a pure mathematician, and the manager would be without a job.

Building Models

Although model building is an *art*, the fundamentals can be taught. Thus, even oil painting or playing the guitar can be "taught." The dedicated student spends a lot of time practicing techniques and finally develops a personal style. Here students will be exposed to several different models so that by practicing they will also learn the "art" of modeling.

Whether simple or complex, a model must be constructed by individuals. Unfortunately, the present technology is such that there are no easy rules or automatic methods for model building. The PC revolution and accompanying software developments may someday lead to user-friendly general model-building packages. Currently, however, model building involves a great deal of art and imagination as well as technical know-how.

In a business environment, quantitative modeling involves specifying the interactions among many variables. In order to accomplish this "quantification," the problem must be stated in the language of mathematics. We shall see many examples of model building in the chapters to follow. Do not be misled by the specific examples in the text, for *in the complexity of real-world problems there is usually no single "correct way" to build a model. Different models may address the same situation in much the same way that paintings by Picasso and Van Gogh would make the same view look different.*

As an overall guide, we can break down the process of building a quantitative decision model into three steps:

1. The environment is studied.
2. A selective representation of the problem is formulated.
3. A symbolic (i.e., mathematical) expression of the formulation is constructed.

Studying the Environment. The first of the three model-building steps, a study of the environment, is easily undervalued by those new to modeling. The stated problem is often not the real problem. A variety of factors, including organizational conflicts, differences between personal and organizational goals, and simply the overall complexity of the situation, may stand between the modeler and a clear understanding of the problem. Experience is probably the most essential ingredient for success—both experience in building models and working experience in the environment to be studied.

Students need to ask basic, simple questions at this stage. Many times it is assumed that the facts are known, when they really aren't. This is especially true when someone has been at a company for a long time. (To illustrate this "familiarity block," ask someone to write down the numbers and letters of a telephone dial without looking.)

Formulation. The second step, formulation, involves basic conceptual analysis, in which assumptions and simplifications usually have to be made. The process of formulation requires the model builder to *select* or *isolate* from the total environment those aspects of reality relevant to the problem scenario. Because the problems we are concerned with involve decisions and objectives, these must be explicitly identified and defined. There may be various ways to define the decision variables, and the most appropriate definition may not be apparent initially. The objectives, too, may be unclear. Even the most capable managers may not know precisely what results they want to achieve. Equally problematic, there may be too many objectives to be satisfied, and it may be necessary to choose one out of many. (It will become evident that it is often impossible to optimize two different objectives at the same time. Thus, generally speaking, it is nonsensical to seek to obtain "the most return for the least investment.")

Symbolic Construction. Once a logical formulation is accomplished (and this may be a verbal process), a symbolic form of the model must be constructed. All models are constructed of some medium. A dress designer constructs models out of fabric. The model city is made of clay. The models we are concerned with in this text are constructed in the language of mathematics.

The interactions between formulation and symbolic construction are usually critical. For example, a formulation of a corporate-planning model may involve a decision as to whether to look 3, 5, or 10 years into the future. It may involve judgments as to which divisions and subsidiaries to include. It may then turn out that the model as formulated is far too complex to be constructed in a way that can be useful. Perhaps the required data simply do not exist. Or perhaps the data can be found, but with existing techniques it would take three days to run the model on the computer. This embarrassment can make the cost of using the model outweigh any potential gain. Unemployed management scientists can testify to the fact that, all too often, models are formulated that simply cannot be built.

Does this process of model building sound like too much for one person to accomplish? Often, it is. When operations research (for all practical purposes, today, the terms *operations research* and *management science* are synonymous) began, during World War II, logistic models were built by teams of mathematicians, statisticians, economists, physicists, engineers, and generalists. Today, the picture is not much different, except that econometricians, computer scientists, and management scientists have been added. Usually, management scientists train in the theory and development of models. They are also concerned with the development of algorithms, which are techniques for solving models. Thus, models are frequently built by heterogeneous and interdisciplinary teams of experts from various fields. A management scientist working alone has a very limited repertoire and limited capabilities.

It may be more difficult than you think to work with other people formulating and constructing models. Students grew up being told to sit in straight rows, not look to the right or left, and do their own work. Remember that U.S. culture glorifies the Lone Ranger, Wonder Woman, and Superman (all individual heroes).

Using Models

In the use of quantitative models, the crucial role of managers occurs during the formulation and implementation phases. A manager can often relegate to the computer the mathematical operations needed to solve models, but it is essential that he or she understand

1. What sorts of problems are amenable to modeling,
2. What the prospects are for obtaining a computer solution (within an affordable amount of time), and
3. What one can do to get the greatest possible value out of the model and the computer output.

Models in the Firm. Models often play different roles at different levels of the firm. At the top levels, models more typically provide data and information, not decisions. They are useful as strategic planning tools: to help forecast the future, explore alternatives, develop multiple-contingency plans, increase flexibility, and decrease reaction time. At lower levels, models are actually used to provide decisions. In many plants, for example, assembly-line operations are completely computerized. Decisions are produced by a model of the operation.

Models have different uses at different levels of the firm for a number of reasons. At progressively lower levels of an organization, alternatives and objectives are apt to become clearer. Interactions are easier to specify quantitatively. Data are often more available and the future environment more certain. For example, at the bottom of the hierarchy a decision may concern the scheduling of a particular

An oil company hired a consulting firm to model the acquisition of a plastics and sunglasses company. In the two weeks of questioning required to come up with even a simple flow diagram of merging the two companies, the oil company learned enough to see that this would not be a wise acquisition.

machine. We know the products that will be run on it and the costs of changing the machine from the production of one product to any other product. The goal of the model may be to find a schedule that produces the necessary amounts by the due dates and minimizes changeover and storage costs.

Contrast the clarity and explicitness of that problem with a multibillion-dollar top-management decision between "invest and grow" and "produce and generate current earnings." Models can certainly be applied to such broad and fuzzy problems, but the models themselves are loaded with assumptions and uncertainties. In such cases, the validity of the model may be as difficult to determine as the appropriate decision.

Models and Managers. Models are used in as many ways as there are people who build them. They can be used to sell an idea or a design, to order optimal quantities of nylon hosiery, or to better organize a giant multinational corporation.

In spite of these differences, a few generalities apply to all quantitative decision models. All such models provide a framework for logical and consistent analysis. More specifically, quantitative models are widely used for at least four reasons:

1. Models force managers to be explicit about objectives.
2. Models force managers to identify and record the types of decisions (decision variables) that influence objectives.
3. Models force managers to identify and record pertinent interactions and trade-offs between decision variables.
4. Models force managers to record constraints (limitations) on the values that the variables may assume.

The mathematician Knuth once said, *"The purpose of computing is insight, not numbers."* The same can be said of modeling. What insights are gained into the business or process? How sensitive (or insensitive) is the model to certain data values?

It follows from these features that a model can be used as a consistent tool for evaluating different policies. That is, each policy or set of decisions is evaluated by the same objective according to the same formulas for describing interactions and constraints. Moreover, models can be explicitly adjusted and improved with historical experience.

A final point: Models provide the opportunity for a systematic use of powerful mathematical methods. They can handle a large number of variables and interactions. The mind is capable of storing only so much information.

Models allow us to use the power of mathematics hand in hand with the storage and speed of computers.

A Final Word on Philosophy

"Philosophy" represents our effort to bridge the gap between the classroom experience with models and the experience that awaits you in the real world. In the classroom all the problems are clearly stated (at least we intend them to be so), all the data are given, and the solution may be a single number in the back of the book. None of this is true in the real world. It thus pays to take a moment to think about the role of models in the real world.

Realism. We start with a theme sounded in Section 1.1. No model captures all of reality. Each model is an abstraction—that is, it includes only some of the possible interactions, and only approximately represents the relationship among them.

Consider the Oak Products model. Jim White set the profit for captain's chairs equal to $36.00 per chair in his spreadsheet planning model. That seems reasonable, since it is the average profit per unit over the last six months and no price increases are planned. However, this is indeed an average of a number of sales contracts.

These chairs sell through a variety of marketing channels, and profit per chair can vary with the channel and the number of chairs sold in a particular channel. In particular, direct sales to a major retailing chain can produce a slightly higher profit, since wholesaling costs are saved and Oak Products and the retailer split the savings.

Jim could try to work a forecast of sales by channel into his production planning model. He believes, however, that the extra level of "realism" is not worth the effort. This simple model allows him to plan production quickly and easily. Profitability has increased dramatically since Oak Products moved to the spreadsheet model. Moreover, accurately forecasting short-run sales by channel has generally been very difficult for Oak Products, so Jim cannot be confident of having reliable data for a more elaborate model. In sum, Jim is quite happy with the current model.

This example provides us with a very simple and pragmatic explanation of why—and when—models are used:

A model is valuable if you make better decisions when you use it than when you don't.

There is no guarantee that using a good model will always give a good outcome; but without a perfect crystal ball, it is the most rational approach that can be taken.

The approach is much like that of engineering. The mathematical models may not *exactly* describe the lift on an airplane wing, but we design better planes with the calculations than without them. The same concept holds for business decision models.

Intuition and Quantitative Models. Some students (and non-students as well) think that quantitative models and intuition stand in opposition to each other. Nothing could be further from the truth. The effective use of models depends crucially on good management judgment and intuition.

Emphasize that there is a difference between a *"good decision"* and a *"good outcome."* Using MS models may lead to a good decision, but the outcome may not turn out as desired. However, if enough decisions are made using good logic, mathematics, and common sense, the outcomes should be much more favorable than if we relied on "gut feel."

Intuition plays a major role in problem recognition and formulation. You have to "see" the potential for using a quantitative model to get the process started; that is, you must have an intuitive feeling that a model will capture the essence of a problem and yield a useful result before you are willing to invest in model formulation.

Intuition is also crucial during implementation. Although many of the models in this text are optimization models, it is important to understand that the solution to these models is the optimal solution to a *mathematical* problem. It may or may not be a good solution to the *real* problem.

The term *optimality* is a theoretical (i.e., mathematical) rather than a real-world concept.

Hesse and Woolsey define management science as "the use of mathematics, logic, and computers to solve real-world problems in such a way that it doesn't interfere with common sense."

Only rarely is it meaningful to talk about "optimal solutions" for the real-life problems of business (much less of government). That is why it is crucial that each manager make sure that the actions suggested by a model make sense—that is, satisfy his or her intuition. If the recommendations do not appeal to the manager's intuition, then it is necessary to decide whether the model is wrong. Indeed, a crucial aspect of the manager's role is to evaluate the model itself and to determine just how much weight should be accorded to its recommendations. The model, or even the formulation of the problem, may need to be rethought. The point is that modeling does not provide an opportunity for a manager to put intuition on hold. In fact, one of the worst mistakes a manager can make is to blindly allow a model to make his or her decisions. The environment might change, and a model that was producing perfectly good results could start producing bad advice. (Storming enemy positions with foot soldiers was a plausible, if bloody, tactic until World War I, when the machine gun made it obsolete.) Management must always be alert to the fact that something has changed and that the old answers just won't work anymore.

In business, problems are really circular, not linear. This means that they keep coming up and have to be revised and reworked. Knowing this can relieve a lot of frustration on the job when the same problem keeps cropping up.

Indeed, this fact provides one of the major motivations for studying quantitative models. Your chances for anticipating when a model will and will not yield good real-world results are dramatically improved by understanding the concepts that are used in the model.

With this introduction we think that you are ready to turn to Chapter 2, which begins the examination of linear programming models.

1.3 Summary

This chapter has provided an overview of the use of quantitative decision-making models, with special emphasis on their role as tools for the manager. The interaction between manager and model has been stressed, with attention given to the manager's role as ultimate decision maker and as a user and "evaluator" of models. We have emphasized that the notion of "optimal" is a mathematical, as opposed to real-world, concept. Models are a limited representation of reality, and for this reason a solution to a model is not necessarily the solution for the real problem. If a model is properly formulated and its output carefully interpreted, however, it can provide a wealth of valuable information to a decision maker.

We have introduced the concepts of decision variables, constraints, and objectives, all of which are important components of constrained optimization models. We have also looked at "what-if" models and illustrated the role of spreadsheets in modeling. We have discussed the process by which models are created and the role played by different kinds of models in business organizations. Finally, we have explored the relationship between modeling and managerial intuition in the decision-making process.

Major Concepts Quiz

True-False

1. **T F** The more complicated the model, the more useful it generally is.
2. **T F** Models usually ignore much of the world.
3. **T F** Decision models produce numerical values for decision variables.
4. **T F** A decision model often captures interactions and trade-offs between certain variables or quantities of interest.
5. **T F** There is usually no single correct way to build a model of a realistic problem.
6. **T F** One advantage of the modeling approach is that it often eliminates the need to be very familiar with the environment being studied.
7. **T F** In practice, models are often built by teams of individuals drawn from different disciplines.
8. **T F** Optimization models always provide the best decision for the real problem.
9. **T F** A model is a good substitute for executive judgment and experience.
10. **T F** An important role of management can be the evaluation of a model (determining whether a model should be used and its results implemented).
11. **T F** Although spreadsheets make calculations easy, they have no real impact on decision making.
12. **T F** "What if" models are only useful for examining changes in the values of decision variables.
13. **T F** Lotus 1-2-3 can solve all mathematical programming problems.
14. **T F** You must understand the theory of linear programming to use VINO or What's*Best!*

Multiple Choice

15. A model is
- **a.** a selective representation of reality
- **b.** an abstraction
- **c.** an approximation
- **d.** an idealization
- **e.** all of the above

16. Decisions are often based on
- **a.** an evaluation of numerical data
- **b.** numbers produced by formal models
- **c.** the use of intuitive models that are never written down
- **d.** all of the above

17. Optimization models contain
- **a.** decision variables
- **b.** an objective function
- **c.** both of the above

18. An optimization model
- **a.** provides the best decision in a mathematical sense
- **b.** provides the best decision within the limited context of the model
- **c.** can provide a consistent tool for evaluating different policies
- **d.** all of the above

19. A model
- **a.** cannot be useful unless it mirrors a real situation in great detail
- **b.** is a tool for the decision maker
- **c.** is rarely revised once it has been constructed
- **d.** all of the above

20. A model
- **a.** forces a manager to be explicit about objectives
- **b.** forces a manager to identify explicitly the types of decisions that influence objectives
- **c.** forces a manager to record explicitly constraints placed on the values that variables can assume
- **d.** all of the above

21. Models
- **a.** play different roles at different levels of the firm
- **b.** are rarely used in the strategic-planning process
- **c.** are a costly way of making routine daily decisions
- **d.** all of the above

22. Constrained optimization means
- **a.** that the underlying model is a very precise representation of reality
- **b.** achieving the best possible (mathematical) result considering the restrictions
- **c.** both of the above

23. A constraint
- **a.** is a purely mathematical concept with little relationship to a real situation
- **b.** cannot usually be given a mathematical formulation
- **c.** limits the range of possible decisions
- **d.** all of the above

24. Constraints are generally imposed
- **a.** because it is the only correct way to formulate the problem
- **b.** because of practical considerations
- **c.** to enable us to use the power of constrained optimization
- **d.** all of the above

25. Consider a prospective manager with interests and abilities that lie far from the quantitative techniques field. The point of studying a quantitative modeling course might be
   a. to be able to knowledgeably accept or reject the use of quantitative tools
   b. to acquire new ways of looking at the environment
   c. to become more familiar with the kind of assistance a computer might provide
   d. all of the above

26. With a "What if" analysis, we are sure to find
   a. an optimal solution
   b. a good solution
   c. a feasible solution (if one exists)
   d. none of the above

27. An optimal decision in the Oak Products problem is one that
   a. uses all available component parts
   b. uses as many as possible of the least expensive parts
   c. maximizes contribution margin (revenue minus costs)
   d. maximizes total profit
   e. maximizes the total number of chairs produced

28. In a probabilistic model, some element of the problem
   a. is a random variable with known distribution
   b. is a random variable about which nothing is known
   c. takes on various values that must be precisely calculated before the model can be solved
   d. will not be known until the model has been clearly formulated

29. A manager who wishes to maximize profit and minimize cost
   a. needs two objectives in her model
   b. can get the desired result by maximizing (profit minus cost)
   c. has an impossible goal and must choose one objective
   d. must make use of a probabilistic model

30. Linear programming models in general
   a. can be solved even if they are large
   b. are more useful for analyzing problems than for solving them
   c. are probabilistic in nature
   d. are rarely solved by computer

31. Every quantitative model
   a. represents data of interest in numerical form
   b. requires the use of a computer for a full solution
   c. must be deterministic
   d. all of the above

32. The use of decision models
   a. is possible only when all variables are known with certainty
   b. reduces the role of judgment and intuition in managerial decision-making
   c. requires managers to have a high degree of proficiency with computers
   d. none of the above

Answers

1. F	**9.** F	**17.** c	**25.** d
2. T	**10.** T	**18.** d	**26.** d
3. T	**11.** F	**19.** b	**27.** d
4. T	**12.** F	**20.** d	**28.** a
5. T	**13.** F	**21.** a	**29.** c
6. F	**14.** F	**22.** b	**30.** a
7. T	**15.** e	**23.** c	**31.** a
8. F	**16.** d	**24.** b	**32.** d

Questions for Discussion

1-1. "The hard problems are those for which models do not exist." Interpret this statement. Give some examples.

1-2. Suppose that you want to become a managerial decision maker but your special abilities and interests are far from the quantitative field. What is the point to your studying an introductory quantitative-modeling text?

1-3. What reasons can you think of to explain the fact that many models are built and never implemented? Does the absence of implementation mean that the entire model-development activity was a waste?

1-4. What is your interpretation of the phrase "a successful application of a model"?

1-5. Profit maximization is commonly taken as the objective function for the firm. Is this necessarily the case? Can you think of other objectives that might be appropriate? Do not worry about whether they are readily quantifiable.

1-6. It is often said that there are no optimal decisions for the complex problems of business. Yet optimization models produce "optimal decisions." In what sense, then, are such decisions optimal?

1-7. Consider the following statement: "Our production policy should be to achieve maximum output at minimum cost." Comment on this misunderstanding.

1-8. "An optimization problem has been solved but some of the constraints are violated." Discuss this assertion.

1-9. What is the meaning of a mathematical constraint when the data (parameter values) are not known with precision? What kinds of assumptions would tend to justify the use of models in such situations?

1-10. "Quantifying the elements of a decision problem is the easy part; the hard part is solving the model." Do you agree? Why or why not?

Video Case

Management Science: A Contradiction in Terms?

Webster's New World Dictionary defines *oxymoron* as "a figure of speech in which opposite or contradictory ideas or terms are combined." Common examples include sweet sorrow, thunderous silence, jumbo shrimp, bureaucratic efficiency . . . you can probably think of many more. Perhaps you already have your own favorites.

And management science?

The same dictionary says that *management* is "the act, art, or manner of managing, or handling, controlling, directing, etc." If management is an art, is management science then an oxymoron—a contradiction in terms?

Not to us!

Science is the process of using observation and testing to establish principles and then using these principles to answer questions. Much of business is based on the same approach. Actuaries use statistical models to set insurance rates. Manufacturers use discounted cash flow models to make decisions on capital expenditures. Sales executives use models based on demand elasticity to determine prices, and pension fund managers use investment models to control their investment portfolios. These models are all discussed in other courses you are likely to take or have already taken.

This book and the class in which it is used are devoted to models that may appear in many different situations. Indeed, linear programming, queuing models, decision trees, and forecasting models are *generic* models. Just as the model for discounting cash flows can be used for problems with different time periods, different interest rates, and different cash flows, so can the models studied in this text be used with widely different input parameters. Some of the models, especially linear programming, are even more general in the sense that they apply to situations that seem to have nothing in common. For example, linear programming is used to determine the most profitable way to blend gasolines and the least costly way to route delivery vans.

The video segment you have seen reinforces the generality and widespread usefulness of management science, but it does not deal with what we imagine must be the major question on your mind. You are probably thinking something like this: "Look, I am in business school because I want to be a manager. Indeed, vice president of marketing sounds pretty good to me. If I am a business person, I know that I will have to look at profit-and-loss statements, so I am taking accounting (whether I like it or not). I agree that you can do some nice tricks with mathematics, like blending gasolines. But why do I have to know the math? If I need some math done I will hire a mathematician to do it."

If this is indeed what is on your mind, we offer you three questions to ponder:

1. How will you know when to ask for help from a model if you don't know what models can do?
2. How will you be able to evaluate recommendations from others in your organization or from consultants if you don't understand what they are talking about?
3. How will you do a good job as sales manager or brand manager or any of the other middle-level jobs that require a quantitative analysis of business problems if you haven't practiced working with quantitative models?

Questions

1. What common characteristics do you observe in success stories about management science?
2. What kinds of problems do you think are most amenable to the use of mathematics? What kinds are least suited to this approach?

PART I

Deterministic Models

The next eleven chapters of this book are devoted to deterministic decision models. So it makes sense to ask, "What do we mean by *deterministic*?"

Deterministic Models. The word *deterministic* means that all aspects of the model are *known with certainty*. For example, in a production planning model we will assume that we know *exactly* how long it takes to produce a particular part—say, 20 minutes. We thus know that in 8 hours of work we can produce $(8 \times 60)/20 = 24$ parts. Similarly, we can calculate exactly how many parts can be produced in any given interval of time, or just how long it will take to produce a particular number of parts.

All of us have used deterministic models. From the first time we deduced that five nickel-pieces of candy cost a quarter through the dreaded word problems in college algebra, we always knew the exact value of all the factors in our math problems. Indeed, until we are forced to think about the question in a statistics or probability course, we naturally tend to assume that the world is deterministic. On reflection, however, we realize that it is not. In the example given above, we know that in the real world some of those production times are going to be 19 minutes and others 23. Perhaps it will take only 7 hours and 47 minutes to produce our 24 parts. Or it may turn out that the 24th part will still be in the milling machine at the end of the eighth hour.

Why, then, do we use deterministic models when we know that they do not perfectly describe reality? The answer is simple—the models are useful. Deterministic models may not be perfect, but they are often a reasonably good approximation of reality, almost always better than no model at all. The results they yield make it well worth the time and effort required to construct and solve such models. For this reason, deterministic models are the workhorses in the field of management science.

Decisions and Solutions. This entire book is devoted to problems in which there are decisions to be made. The focus is on management, and the thrust is on using mathematics to help managers make better decisions—that is, to choose the best among a set of possible alternatives. Most often, that means choosing the alternative that yields the largest profit.

In principle this is simple, for with a deterministic model we can calculate exactly what profit we obtain by choosing any alternative. Often, however, there are too many alternatives—it simply is not practical to list all of them and pick the best one, even with a very fast computer to do the evaluations. Indeed, most of the problems in this part of the book are of this type: too many alternatives to consider. To solve such a problem, you must be able to structure (formulate) it in a way that allows the use of an efficient method for finding the best decision. Mathematical programming gives us a way to do just that.

An Overview. Even in the brief summary that follows, you will recognize most of the major themes of this book listed in Chapter 1: modeling or formulation, solution techniques or algorithms, computer solutions, and interpretation of these solutions. The last two topics are so important that we have included a student version of LINDO with the text. We suggest that you start using LINDO right from the beginning. It is our experience that attempting to solve your models with LINDO will help you learn to formulate them clearly. Further, the process of working your way through a problem from the initial statement to the solution and then to its interpretation transforms mathematical programming from a subject you talk about to something you can actually do. It helps you to make your knowledge personal and useful.

CHAPTER 2 **Linear Programming: Formal and Spreadsheet Models**

This chapter deals with the formulation process, largely by developing examples. First the formal and spreadsheet versions of a simple linear programming problem are created. The remainder of the chapter is devoted to illustrations of many important classes of problems that can be modeled using LP. A key element of this chapter is the set of more than 30 end-of-chapter problems, graded by level of difficulty. Formulating LP problems is an art, and you can improve your ability by practice.

CHAPTER 3 **Linear Programming: Geometric Representations and Graphical Solutions**

The structure of LP problems can be illustrated by problems with two decision variables. We can graph such problems in two dimensions and use these graphs to illustrate the fundamental concepts and results in linear programming. This chapter provides a foundation for what is to follow.

CHAPTER 4 **Analysis of LP Models: The Graphical Approach**

Here we use the geometric approach developed in Chapter 3 to develop an understanding of sensitivity analysis—what we have called "interpreting the solution." In particular, we see how it is possible to determine the effect of changing some of the parameter values in a model. Even major structural changes in a problem, such as adding or deleting constraints, can be explored in this way and their consequences evaluated.

CHAPTER 5 **Linear Programs: Computer Analysis, Interpreting Sensitivity Output, and the Dual Problem**

The computer's solution to an LP problem is the centerpiece of this chapter. We see how LINDO produces the solution: the optimal value for the decision variables and the objective function. We also find that a great deal of additional information is available with the solution. For example, we can see at a glance the marginal value of extra capacity in a production planning problem, or determine the impact on the optimal solution of a price change by a specific carrier in a transportation problem. Our ability to understand and use this information is enhanced through the geometric approach developed in Chapter 4.

CHAPTER 6 **Linear Programming: The Simplex Method**

The simplex algorithm is the method used to solve linear programming problems. Here the algorithm is explained and a problem that we have encountered in earlier chapters is solved. (This chapter can be omitted with no effect on the flow of material.)

CHAPTER 7 **Linear Programming: Special Applications**

The transportation and assignment problems are interesting problems in their own right. Each is also an LP problem with a special structure. Algorithms have been developed that exploit these special structures to produce solutions much more rapidly than the simplex algorithm can. Here we consider these problems and algorithms. (This chapter too can be omitted with no effect on the flow of material.)

CHAPTER 8 **Integer and Quadratic Programming**

An Integer Linear Program (ILP) is an LP in which some or all of the decision variables are required to take on integer values. In some important problems this integer condition is crucial. For example, in developing an expansion plan for a banking system, deciding whether to put a branch in a specific location requires an integer-valued decision variable. This chapter considers the formulation and solution of ILPs, which merit special attention for two reasons. First, they are much more difficult to solve than LPs. Second, the logic required to correctly construct ILP models is not as familiar as the logic for LP models; thus some additional practice is useful. The chapter also considers quadratic programming, a class of models that are identical to LP modes with the exception that the objective function is a quadratic function. The Markowitz portfolio problem, a fundamental model in finance, is used to motivate and explain the discussion.

▶ CHAPTER 9

Network Models

We are all familiar with the concept of a network of phone lines or interstate highways. The fundamental components of such systems are nodes (e.g., switching stations or intersections) and arcs or branches (e.g., phone lines or roads). A number of interesting problems, such as finding the shortest or least expensive route between two locations, or determining the best delivery plan with limited resources, involve network structures. Such problems can be formulated as special types of linear programming models called network models. It turns out that a host of other problems having nothing to do with transportation or telephones can be modeled in the same way. This chapter examines such problems and their solution.

▶ CHAPTER 10

Inventory Control with Known Demand

A fundamental question in inventory management is how much to add to inventory at any given time. For a manufacturing firm the question takes the form of how much to produce in a production run. For a distribution company the question is how much to order from a supplier. Increasing the production or order quantity increases the amount of inventory that must be carried but reduces the number of times that the item must be produced or ordered. This chapter considers this trade-off in the context of a classical deterministic model.

▶ CHAPTER 11

Heuristics, Multiple Objectives, and Goal Programming

A number of interesting problems are almost like mathematical programming models in that they have objective functions and constraints. However, they are not LPs, and if they are ILPs they cannot be solved with the techniques developed in Chapter 8 in a reasonable amount of time. The scheduling of jobs through a facility such as a central computer or production job shop exemplifies a rich class of problems of this type. This chapter introduces heuristics—"rules of thumb"—and adaptations of the simplex algorithm that can be used to help solve such problems.

▶ CHAPTER 12

Calculus-Based Optimization and an Introduction to Nonlinear Programming

Linear programming relies on linear functions to represent the objective function and all of the constraints. This approach works well in an amazing variety of circumstances. However, some aspects of our world are simply too nonlinear for such approximations to be reasonable. For example, oil companies must store crude oil from many sources in common storage tanks. The question of which oils to pool in this way and how best to blend the pooled oils to create various products gives rise to a nonlinear programming problem that has a serious impact on the bottom line. To solve such problems, one must turn to nonlinear optimization techniques, based on concepts from differential calculus, including partial derivatives and first- and second-order conditions. This chapter provides an introduction to the concepts and some of the tools in this area.

CHAPTER

2

Linear Programming: Formal and Spreadsheet Models

APPLICATION CAPSULE

A Gallon Saved Is a Bundle Earned: Conserving Airline Fuel with LP*

In recent years, the cost of fuel has become the largest single item in the operating expenses of airlines. The problem of controlling expenditures for fuel is complex. For one thing, the amount of fuel consumed on a particular flight is a function of many variables, including the type of aircraft used, the weight it is carrying (including the weight of fuel on board, which changes continuously during the flight), the flight altitude, the plane's speed, and the weather during the trip. Moreover, both the price and the availability of fuel vary from location to location. As an example of the complicated way in which these factors can interact, it may not pay for a plane to take on extra fuel early in a flight, even at a location where the price is very low, because the additional weight can increase fuel consumption enough to produce a larger total cost.

One major domestic airline constructed and implemented a linear programming model to attack this problem. The model took into account

1. The flight schedule.
2. The price and availability of fuel at each station.
3. The reserve requirement for each plane.
4. The upper bound on weight for each plane.
5. The distance for each segment of a flight.
6. The fuel remaining when a plane arrives at a station.
7. Fuel consumption for each plane as a function of weight, flight altitude, weather, and speed.

The model included 800 constraints and 2400 variables for a flight schedule of 350 flight segments, 50 station/vendor combinations, and multiple aircraft types. In the first month it was used, the average cost that the airline paid for a gallon of fuel dropped nearly 12 percent—at a time when most other airlines experienced a rise in their average per-gallon fuel expenses. The airline's total savings over a two-year period amounted to many millions of dollars. In addition, the sensitivity analysis available with the linear programming solution was most helpful in informing management as to when a change in policy might be required.

*Wayne D. Darnell and Carolyn Laflin, "National Airlines Fuel Management and Allocation Model." *Interfaces*, Vol. 7, No. 2. (February 1977), pp. 1–16.

2.1 Introduction

As we have seen in Chapter 1, a model is an abstract representation of, or a surrogate for, reality. In a decision-making environment, models are important because they capture the essence of many important problems. In a sense, the very notion of being able to *solve* a real-world business problem means that it is possible to formulate successfully the problem as a model. Thus, being able to formulate models—that is, to make the transition between real-world problem and quantitative model (the mathematical problem)—is an important first step in the use of modeling as a management tool.

Constraints

For our purposes, a first step in model formulation will be the recognition of **constraints.** In Chapter 1 we saw numerous "generic" causes for the appearance of constraints. Constraints can be thought of as *restrictions* on the set of allowable decisions. Specific illustrations of such restrictions are particularly evident when dealing with the problems of management. For example

1. A portfolio manager has a certain amount of capital at his or her discretion. Investment decisions are restricted by the amount of that capital and the regulations of the SEC.
2. The decisions of a plant manager are restricted by the capacity of the plant and the availability of resources.
3. The staffing and flight plans of an airline are restricted by the maintenance needs of the planes and the number of employees on hand.
4. An oil company's decision to use a certain type of crude oil in producing gasoline is restricted by the characteristics of the gasoline (e.g., the octane rating and the antiknock capabilities).

In the context of mathematical modeling, a restriction, or constraint, on the allowable decisions is a concept of special importance. Constraints are often in one of two forms: *limitations* or *requirements.* In the examples listed above

1. The portfolio manager is constrained by *limitations* of capital and the *requirements* of the SEC.
2. Production decisions are constrained by *limitations* on capacity and resources.
3. The airlines are constrained by the *requirement* that a crew must spend at least 24 hours on the ground between flights.
4. The oil company is constrained by the *limitation* of the types of crude oil that are available and the *requirement* that the gasoline have at least a specified octane rating.

The Objective Function

All linear programming models have two important features in common. The first feature, illustrated in the examples above, is the existence of constraints. The second feature is that in every linear programming model there is some quantity to be maximized or minimized.

To show this, let us consider again the same four examples. The portfolio manager may want to maximize the return on the portfolio, and the production manager may want to satisfy the demand at minimum production cost. Similarly, the airline wants to meet a given schedule at the minimum cost, and the oil company wants to use the available crude oil in such a way as to maximize profit.

Many students make the Freudian slip of calling the objective function the *objection function!*

Thus, you can see that in each of these examples there is some quantity that the decision maker desires either to maximize (typically profit, return, or effectiveness) or to minimize (typically cost or time). In the language of modeling, this quantity is called the **objective function.**

Every linear programming problem has two important features: an *objective function* to be maximized or minimized, and *constraints.*

Linear programming provides an example of what is called a *constrained decision-making model,* also called a **constrained optimization model.** One common way of describing such a model is as follows:

A constrained optimization model represents the problem of allocating scarce resources in such a way as to optimize an objective of interest.

In this description, the phrase "scarce resources" means resources that are subject to constraints.

Although different and more general types of constrained decision-making models exist, it is nevertheless true that in applications linear programming is the most useful. It has been successfully applied to literally thousands of different types of managerial decision-making problems, and it is for this reason that we give considerable attention to the topic. We shall begin by presenting several specific numerical examples of linear programming formulations. Some of these examples will be illustrated in a spreadsheet format. Then, in the following chapters, it will be shown how linear programming can be used to solve these constrained decisionmaking problems.

2.2 PROTRAC, Inc.

PROTRAC, Inc. produces two lines of heavy equipment. One of these product lines, termed earthmoving equipment, is essentially for construction applications. The other line, termed forestry equipment, is destined for the lumber industry. The largest member of the earthmoving equipment line (the E-9) and the largest member of the forestry equipment line (the F-9) are produced in the same departments and with the same equipment. Using economic forecasts for next month, PROTRAC's marketing manager has judged that during that period it will be possible to sell as many E-9s or F-9s as the firm can produce. Management must now recommend a production target for next month. That is, how many E-9s and F-9s should be produced?

PROTRAC Data

Making this decision requires that the following major factors be considered:

1. PROTRAC will make a profit of $5000 on each E-9 that is sold and $4000 on each F-9.

2. Each product is put through *machining operations* in both department A and department B.

3. For next month's production, these two departments have 150 and 160 hours of available time, respectively. Each E-9 uses 10 hours of machining in department A and 20 hours of machining in department B, whereas each F-9 uses 15 hours in department A and 10 hours in department B. These data are summarized in Figure 2.1.

DEPARTMENT	HOURS		
	per E-9	per F-9	Total Available
A	10	15	150
B	20	10	160

▲ FIGURE 2.1
Protrac Machining Data

4. In order for management to honor an agreement with the union, the total labor hours used in next month's *testing of finished products* cannot fall more than 10% below an arbitrated goal of 150 hours. This testing is performed in a third department and has nothing to do with the activities in departments A and B. Each E-9 is given 30 hours of testing and each F-9 is given 10. Since 10% of 150 is 15, the total labor hours devoted to testing cannot fall below 135. These data are summarized in Figure 2.2.

▼ FIGURE 2.2
Protrac Testing Data

	1 E-9	1 F-9	REQUIREMENT ON TOTAL HOURS
Hours for Testing	30	10	135

5. In order to maintain the current market position, top management has decreed the operating policy that it is necessary to build at least one F-9 for every three E-9s produced.

6. A major customer has ordered a total of at least five E-9s and F-9s (in any combination whatever) for next month, and so at least that many must be produced.

Given these considerations, management's problem is to decide how many E-9s and how many F-9s to produce next month. In technical terms, management seeks to determine the **optimal product mix,** also called the **optimal production plan.** Let us now show how this problem can be expressed as a mathematical model, in particular as a linear program. To do so, we must identify the constraints and the objective function.

The Constraints

We have stated that in each department there is a limitation on the amount of time available for the machining operations in producing E-9s and F-9s. For example, from Figure 2.1 it is seen that for the time period under consideration no more than 150 hours is available in department A. This limited availability of hours is a constraint. To formulate the constraint concisely, let us begin by determining the number of hours that will be used in department A. Recall that both E-9s and F-9s must be machined in department A. From Figure 2.1 we know that each E-9 produced will use 10 hours of machining in department A. Each F-9 produced will use 15 hours in department A. Hence, for any particular production plan

Dept. A constraint

$$\text{total hours used in dept. A} = 10(\text{no. E-9s produced}) + 15(\text{no. F-9s produced})$$

This can be expressed more easily if we introduce some simple notation. Let

$$E = \text{number of E-9s to be produced}$$
$$F = \text{number of F-9s to be produced}$$

Then the expression for the total hours used in department A becomes

$$\text{total hours used in dept. A} = 10E + 15F$$

But, as already stated, we also know from Figure 2.1 that at most 150 hours is available in department A. It follows that the unknowns E and F must satisfy the condition (i.e., the restriction)

$$10E + 15F \leq 150 \qquad \textbf{(2.1)}$$

This is the constraint on hours used in department A. The symbol $\leq$ means *less than or equal to* and condition (2.1) is called an **inequality constraint.** The number 150 is called the **right-hand side** of the inequality. The left-hand side of the inequality clearly depends on the unknowns E and F, and is called a **constraint function.** The mathematical inequality (2.1) is a concise symbolic way of stating the constraint that the total number of hours used in department A to produce E units of E-9 and F units of F-9 must not exceed the 150 hours available.

Dept. B constraint

From Figure 2.1 we also see that each E-9 produced will use 20 hours of machining in department B and each F-9 produced will use 10 hours of machining in department B. Since there are at most 160 hours available in department B, it follows that the values of E and F must also satisfy

$$20E + 10F \leq 160 \qquad \textbf{(2.2)}$$

Inequalities (2.1) and (2.2) represent two of the constraints in the current problem. Are there any others?

The foregoing discussion of major considerations indicates that there is also a union agreement to be honored (i.e., major consideration 4). Figure 2.2 indicates that each E-9 produced will use 30 hours of testing, and each F-9 produced will use 10 hours of testing. Thus

$$\text{total hours used for testing} = 30E + 10F$$

Also from Figure 2.2 we see that the total labor hours used in testing cannot fall below 135 hours. Hence, we obtain the constraint

Testing constraint

$$30E + 10F \geq 135 \tag{2.3}$$

The symbol $\geq$ means *greater than or equal to,* and condition (2.3) is also called an inequality constraint. Note that condition (2.3) is a mathematical inequality of the $\geq$ type (a requirement), as opposed to conditions (2.1) and (2.2), which are mathematical inequalities of the $\leq$ type (limitations).

Another constraint is that at least one F-9 must be produced for every three E-9s produced. This is stated in symbols as

$$E/3 \leq F$$

Product mix constraint

Students often will write the coefficients incorrectly—for example,

$$3E \leq F$$

Encourage them first to write anything, and then check that the constraint does in algebra what it says in English.

Since both sides of an inequality can be multiplied by the same positive number without changing the direction of the inequality, we can multiply both sides of this latter constraint by 3 to obtain

$$E \leq 3F$$

Later it will be seen that it is often convenient to express such an inequality with all of the unknowns on the left side (thereby forming the constraint function). Thus, in this case we subtract $3F$ from both sides to obtain the convenient expression

$$E - 3F \leq 0 \tag{2.4}$$

The sixth major consideration states that at least five units must be produced next month, in any combination whatever. This constraint is simply stated as

Total units constraint

$$E + F \geq 5 \tag{2.5}$$

We have now specified in concise mathematical form five inequality constraints associated with **PROTRAC**'s production problem. Since it does not make physical sense to produce a negative number of E-9s or F-9s, we must include the two additional conditions

Nonnegativity

$$E \geq 0, F \geq 0 \tag{2.6}$$

Conditions such as (2.6), which require E and F to be nonnegative, are called **nonnegativity conditions.** It is important to bear in mind that the term *nonnegative* is not the same as the term *positive.* The difference is that "nonnegative" allows for the possibility of the value zero, whereas the term "positive" forbids this value.

In summary, here are the constraints and the nonnegativity conditions for the **PROTRAC**, Inc. model:

All constraints

$$10E + 15F \leq 150 \tag{2.1}$$
$$20E + 10F \leq 160 \tag{2.2}$$
$$30E + 10F \geq 135 \tag{2.3}$$
$$E - 3F \leq 0 \tag{2.4}$$
$$E + F \geq 5 \tag{2.5}$$
$$E \geq 0, \quad F \geq 0 \tag{2.6}$$

Evaluating Various Decisions

It may help to first define, *in English*:
1. Variables (alternatives, decisions)
2. Constraints (requirement/limitation/both)
   a. **Inputs** (Are there constraints on raw materials?)
   b. **Outputs** (What sales or production constraints are there?)
   c. **Capacity** (What constraints are there on time, labor, machines?)
   d. **Ratio** or **Material Balance** (What ratios must be kept?)
3. Objective function (Maximize profit or revenue, minimize cost.)

Then change the above short statements into algebra. Thus, for this problem:
(a) **Input**—No constraints
(b) **Output**—A production total of at least five vehicles
(c) **Capacity**
   (i) A maximum number of 150 hours in Dept A available
   (ii) A maximum number of 160 hours in Dept B available
   (iii) A minimum number of 135 hours for testing
(d) **Ratio or Material Balance**
   (i) At least one F-9 produced for every three E-9s

In the model above, the choice of values for the pair of variables (E,F) is called a decision; E and F are thus called **decision variables** (i.e., the quantities that management controls). Clearly, in this problem a decision is a production mix. For example, $E = 6$, $F = 5$ is a decision to make six E-9s and five F-9s. Some nonnegative decisions will satisfy all of the constraints (2.1) through (2.5) of our model and some will not. For example, the decision $E = 6$, $F = 5$ can be seen to satisfy constraints (2.1), (2.3), (2.4), and (2.5) and to violate constraint (2.2). To see this, we substitute $E = 6$, $F = 5$ into constraints (2.1) through (2.5) and evaluate the results. Doing this, we obtain

Constraint 1.

$$\begin{aligned} 10E + 15F &\le 150 \\ 10(6) + 15(5) &\le 150 \\ 60 + 75 &\le 150 \\ 135 &\le 150 \text{ true} \end{aligned}$$

Hence, this constraint is satisfied when $E = 6$, $F = 5$.

Constraint 2.

$$\begin{aligned} 20E + 10F &\le 160 \\ 20(6) + 10(5) &\le 160 \\ 120 + 50 &\le 160 \\ 170 &\le 160 \text{ false} \end{aligned}$$

Hence, this constraint is violated when $E = 6$, $F = 5$.

In the same fashion, try to show for yourself that the decision $E = 6$, $F = 5$ satisfies constraints (2.3), (2.4), and (2.5).

Similarly, you can verify for yourself that the production mix $E = 5$, $F = 4$ does indeed satisfy all the constraints.

Allowable = feasible

The mix, or decision, $E = 6$, $F = 5$ is not allowable because, as we have just seen, there are not enough hours available in department B (constraint 2.2) to support this decision. Another way of saying the same thing is that this decision is not allowable because it has violated one of the constraints. Of the infinitely many nonnegative pairs of numbers (E, F), some pairs, or decisions, will violate at least one of the constraints, and some will satisfy all the constraints. In our model, only nonnegative decisions that satisfy *all* the constraints are allowable. Such decisions are called **feasible decisions.**

Reinforce that the objective function cannot be formulated until the variables (decisions, alternatives) are known. Determining these is usually the most difficult part of modeling.

The Objective Function. Of all the allowable, or feasible, decisions, which one should be made? As we have noted earlier, every linear programming problem has a specific objective as well as constraints. The management of PROTRAC, Inc. would like to maximize profit, so this is the objective. PROTRAC's profit clearly comes from two sources.

1. There is profit from the sale of E-9s.
2. There is profit from the sale of F-9s.

In our earlier discussion of major factors to be considered it was stated that the profit is \$5000 for each E-9 and \$4000 for each F-9. Since PROTRAC makes \$5000

When only revenue data are given (or available) the only thing that can be done is to maximize revenue subject to the constraints. If only cost data are available, then all that can be done is to minimize the cost of having to produce a certain product mix. However, if cost *and* revenue data are available, it is usually more advantageous to maximize profit rather than revenue.

for each E-9 produced, and since E denotes the number of E-9s to be produced, we see that

$$5000E = \text{profit from producing } E \text{ units of E-9}$$

Similarly

$$4000F = \text{profit from producing } F \text{ units of F-9}$$

Thus, the decision to produce E units of E-9s and F units of F-9s results in a total profit given by

$$\text{total profit} = 5000E + 4000F \tag{2.7}$$

An Optimal Solution. Of all the infinitely many decisions that satisfy all the constraints (i.e., of all feasible decisions), one that gives the largest total profit will be a *solution* to PROTRAC's problem, or, as often referred to, an **optimal solution.** Thus, we seek a decision that will *maximize* total profit relative to the set of all possible feasible decisions. Such a decision is called an **optimal decision.** Since total profit is a *function* of the variables E, F, we refer to the expression $5000E + 4000F$ as the *objective function,* and we want to find feasible values of E and F that **optimize** (which in this case means maximize) the objective function. Our objective, then, in mathematical terms, is stated concisely as

$$\text{maximize } 5000E + 4000F$$

or, even more simply, this is usually written as

$$\text{Max } 5000E + 4000F \tag{2.8}$$

The objective function is to be maximized *only* over the set of feasible decisions.

For instance, it was seen earlier that the decision $E = 5$, $F = 4$ is feasible because it satisfies all the constraints. Corresponding to this decision, the *objective value* would be

$$\begin{aligned}\text{total profit} &= 5000E + 4000F \\ &= 5000(5) + 4000(4) = 41{,}000\end{aligned}$$

Associated with the decision $E = 6$, $F = 5$ the objective value would be

$$\begin{aligned}\text{total profit} &= 5000E + 4000F \\ &= 5000(6) + 4000(5) = 50{,}000\end{aligned}$$

Improving the Objective Value. Although this objective value is larger than the previous one, and thereby more attractive, we recall that $E = 6$, $F = 5$ is not a feasible decision because it violates one of the constraints. Hence, **PROTRAC** is not able to consider this decision. It must be discarded. Can you find a *feasible* decision for which the objective value exceeds 41,000? Try, for example, the decision $E = 6$, $F = 3.5$. Verify that it satisfies all the constraints and that it yields an objective value of 44,000, which is clearly an improvement over 41,000. Do you believe that this production plan ($E = 6$, $F = 3.5$) is an optimal decision (i.e., a solution to our problem) or that, to the contrary, it is possible to do even better? Remember that only feasible decisions can be considered—that is, the production alternatives that satisfy *all* the constraints.

Observations on the PROTRAC Model

In the following chapters we shall see how to rigorously (i.e., without guesswork) solve this problem and many others like it. Also, we shall see how the computer is used to do much of the work for us. In the remainder of this chapter the goal is to give you more experience in the formulation of linear programming models, for model formulation is one of the early important steps in problem analysis. We shall also show how spreadsheet representations of an LP can be created and used. Let us first, however, take a moment to review the complete mathematical formulation of the PROTRAC, Inc. problem and to make several observations on the form of this model.

The complete formulation of the PROTRAC, Inc. problem

At this point, it might benefit students to get them in the habit of naming their constraints and objective function (maybe even limiting these to eight characters) so they will be ready to put this model into computer form using any of the various PC programs. You might suggest that they use names for the variables instead of X_1, X_2, etc.

In the preceding discussion we translated a verbal description of a real-world problem into a complete mathematical model with an objective function and constraints. This model, which we call the **formal LP model,** is

$$\begin{aligned}
&\text{Max } 5000E + 4000F \quad \text{(objective function)}\\
&\text{subject to (s.t.)}\\
&\quad 10E + 15F \le 150 \text{ (hours in department A)}\\
&\quad 20E + 10F \le 160 \text{ (hours in department B)}\\
&\quad 30E + 10F \ge 135 \text{ (testing hours)}\\
&\quad E - 3F \le 0 \text{ (mix constraint)}\\
&\quad E + F \ge 5 \text{ (total units requirement)}\\
&\quad E, F \ge 0 \text{ (nonnegativity conditions)}
\end{aligned}$$

Linear Functions. Notice that in the formal LP model above, all the constraint functions (recall that the constraint functions are the left-hand sides of the inequality constraints) and the objective function are **linear functions** of the decision variables. As you may recall, the graph of a linear function of two variables is a straight line. In general, a linear function is one where each variable appears in a separate term together with its coefficient (i.e., there are no products or quotients of variables, no exponents other than 1, no logarithmic, exponential, or trigonometric terms). As you can see, this is true of each function in the model above. By contrast, $14E + 12EF$ is a nonlinear function because of the term $12EF$ involving a product of the variables. Also, $9E^2 + 8F$ is nonlinear because the variable E is raised to the power 2. Other examples of nonlinear functions are $6\sqrt{E} + F$ and $19 \log E + 12E^2F$.

As you might imagine, from the mathematical point of view, nonlinear functions are more difficult to deal with. The power of linear programming, in applications, stems from the power of linear mathematics and from the fact that linear models can be readily used in real applications by managers and analysts with little or even no training in the underlying mathematics. For our purposes at this time the important facts to be remembered are

1. A linear program always has an objective function (to be either maximized or minimized) and constraints.
2. All functions in the problem (objective and constraints) are *linear functions.*

Integrality Considerations. In making a final observation, let us take another look at the complete formulation of the PROTRAC, Inc. model. It should be

Note that this means E and/or F can take on values such as 1.26, 0.034, and so on. That is, the values are continuous, not restricted to integers. Fractional parts could be thought of as work in process. For example, 3.12 E-9s could mean that three are made during this production period and part of the fourth is started, with completion planned for the next production period.

pointed out that unless we put in specific additional constraints, which force the decision variables to be integers, we must be prepared to accept fractional answers. In many LP models, such as in the **PROTRAC**, Inc. model, it will be true that fractional values for the decision variables do not have meaningful physical interpretations. For example, a solution that says "produce 3.12 E-9s and 6.88 F-9s" may not be implementable. On the other hand, there are many problems for which fractions obviously have meaning (e.g., "produce 98.65 gallons of crude oil"). In those cases where fractional answers are not meaningful, there are two possible recourses:

1. Add a so-called **integrality condition,** which forces one or more decision variables to take on only integer values. This changes the problem to what is called an **integer program.** Integer programming models involve many additional considerations beyond the usual linear program. Integer programs are discussed at length in Chapter 8.
2. Solve the problem as an ordinary linear program and then round (e.g., to the nearest integer) any decision variable for which a fractional answer cannot be implemented. The advantages and disadvantages of this approach are also discussed in Chapter 8.

When rounding, consider: a) Feasibility: Make sure that the integer answer satisfies the constraints (or "close enough" if these are "fuzzy" constraints), and b) Optimality (discussed in Chapter 8).

In practice, both of these approaches are adopted. For the present, it will suffice to assume that either fractional solutions are meaningful or else (for the purpose of implementation) they will be rounded to integers.

2.3 A Spreadsheet Representation of PROTRAC E and F

Before going on to a new formulation, let us show how the above formal LP model can be put on a spreadsheet. In the process we will be able to provide a balanced view of how the spreadsheet approach fits into the overall modeling context.

Creating a Spreadsheet

In the process of creating a spreadsheet representation the following facts are used:

Various types of cells

1. A **spreadsheet** is a grid, or matrix, with cells, which are the intersections of columns and rows. Letters are used to denote the columns, and numbers designate the rows. For example, *C6* denotes the entry in column C and row 6. Each possible entry in the grid, such as *C6*, is called a cell. In referring to various cells it is customary to designate the column first (C) and then the row (6). In a typical spreadsheet many of the cells will be blank (i.e., unused), while other cells in the spreadsheet will contain various types of information.

Labels

2. In particular, some cells contain user-supplied *labels.* The labels are used in the same way that you would use labels to help read a table of data. Their purpose is to clarify the meaning of other entries in the spreadsheet.

Parameters and decision variables

3. Other cells contain user-supplied *numbers.* Generally these numbers will represent
   a. The numeric value of **parameters,** which are the *data* for the given problem
   b. Numeric values for *decision variables.* These numeric values are called **decision values.**

Formulas **4.** Still other cells contain user-supplied *formulas.* For example, in the spreadsheet representation of an LP model, formulas are required to represent the objective function and the constraint functions. In some instances, there may be underlying formulas that determine the numeric value of various parameters in the model. Thus, for some parameters, as in 3(a) above, numeric values will be entered directly. Other parameters will be computed from formulas that the user has entered.

The above facts are used to create the spreadsheet shown in Figure 2.3. This spreadsheet is called the **symbolic spreadsheet** for the **PROTRAC** E and F problem. A symbolic spreadsheet explicitly shows each formula.

Labels, Data, and Formulas in the E & F Symbolic Spreadsheet

Let us summarize the way in which this spreadsheet has been created (and there are various ways to do this, according to the user's own taste). The first row consists of labels. The first row says that column C will refer to product *E* and column D to product *F.* Row 3 indicates that cell *C*3 will contain the quantity of *E* produced and *D*3 will contain the quantity of *F* produced. The empty blue boxes appearing in *C*3 and *D*3 are simply our convention for drawing special attention to these cells. They are cells that, in a "what if" analysis, the user must manipulate by supplying specific numeric entries (in this case, specific decision values for the variables *E* and *F*). Alternatively, in a What's*Best!* analysis, the computer will determine, and enter in *C*3 and *D*3, the optimal values for *E* and *F.*

In cells *C*4 and *D*4 parameter values have been entered. These are per unit profitabilities for *E* and *F,* respectively, as explained by the label in *A*4. In *A*8 we see a formula. This formula

$$+\ C4 * C3 + D4 * D3$$

represents the objective function for the **PROTRAC** E and F model. The formula

▼ FIGURE 2.3
The Symbolic Spreadsheet for E & F

	A	B	C	D	E	F	G	H	I
1	Product		E	F					
2									
3	Quantity		[ ]	[ ]	Value for F to be Supplied by User				
4	Profit/Unit		5000.00	4000.00					
5									
6	*************								
7	PROFIT								
8	+ C4*C3 + D4*D3				Value for E to be Supplied by User				
9	*************								
10	--								
11			Resource Usage			Constraint	RHS		Slack
12			E	F		Function			
13	--								
14	Dept A		10.00	15.00		(C14*C3) + (D14*D3)	150		+ G14 − F14
15	Dept B		20.00	10.00		(C15*C3) + (D15*D3)	160		+ G15 − F15
16	Test Hrs		30.00	10.00		(C16*C3) + (D16*D3)	135		− G16 + F16
17	Mix		1.00	3.00		− (C17*C3) + (D17*D3)†	0		− G17 + F17
18	Tot Units		1.00	1.00		(C18*C3) + (D18*D3)	5		− G18 + F18
19									
20									

Using a plus to begin a formula

indicates that profit will be computed by multiplying the contents of $C3$ by the contents of $C4$ (the $*$ means multiplication) and adding to it the contents of $D3$ multiplied by the contents of $D4$. The + in front of $C4$ in the formula tells the spreadsheet program that it is indeed looking at a formula and not the text for a label.

With the exception of column I, the other entries in the spreadsheet should be self-explanatory. You can see that the data in columns C and D, rows 14 through 18, come directly from the formal LP model for **PROTRAC** E and F. Although these data have been labeled as "resource usage," the only "resources" in this problem are labor hours in departments A and B, respectively, and hence, strictly speaking, the label is appropriate only for rows 14 and 15. There is, however, no need to be pedantic. In creating a spreadsheet, the user can choose any labeling scheme (or even none) that suits the purpose. Our purpose here is simply to illustrate the process.

In column I, instead of using the mathematical term "slack," you might want to substitute the term "*over/under*," i.e., the amount of resource used *over* a requirement or the amount *under* a limitation.

Computing Slack. It remains to explain the entries, termed *slack,* that appear in column I, rows 14 through 18. This term will be discussed at length in later portions of the text. For present purposes the following is sufficient:

In the symbolic spreadsheet, *slack* is the difference between the constraint function and the right-hand side, computed so that it is nonnegative.

For example, look at the slack formula in cell I14. This slack value corresponds to the department A capacity constraint, which is $10E + 15F \leq 150$. The spreadsheet shows the formula $G14 - F14$ for the slack value. If we substitute the contents of $G14$ and $F14$, we see that $G14 - F14$ is

$$150 - [(C14 * C3) + (D14 * D3)]$$

which is the "right-hand side of the first constraint minus the left-hand side." Thus, the slack value for this constraint is unused capacity. Now consider the mix constraint, which we have rewritten as $-E + 3F \geq 0$. The entry in cell I17 of the spreadsheet shows that the slack formula for the mix constraint is the "left-hand side minus the right-hand side," which is the order of subtraction required to make this slack value nonnegative. What we have just illustrated is the following rule:

**For a ≤ constraint, slack is the right-hand side minus the left-hand side.
For a ≥ constraint, slack is the left-hand side minus the right-hand side.**

This completes our discussion of the symbolic spreadsheet for **PROTRAC** E and F. But this is only the beginning of the story. A typical spreadsheet program allows you to look at two different spreadsheet representations of your model. The first, which we've just created, is the symbolic spreadsheet. The second, which we now discuss, is called the **value spreadsheet.**

The Value Spreadsheet

A value spreadsheet is like a symbolic spreadsheet, except all the formulas have been computed and the numeric values put in the cells. To create the value spreadsheet, let us refer once again to Figure 2.3. We see that in this symbolic spreadsheet there are two distinguished cells that are waiting for specific numeric values to be entered

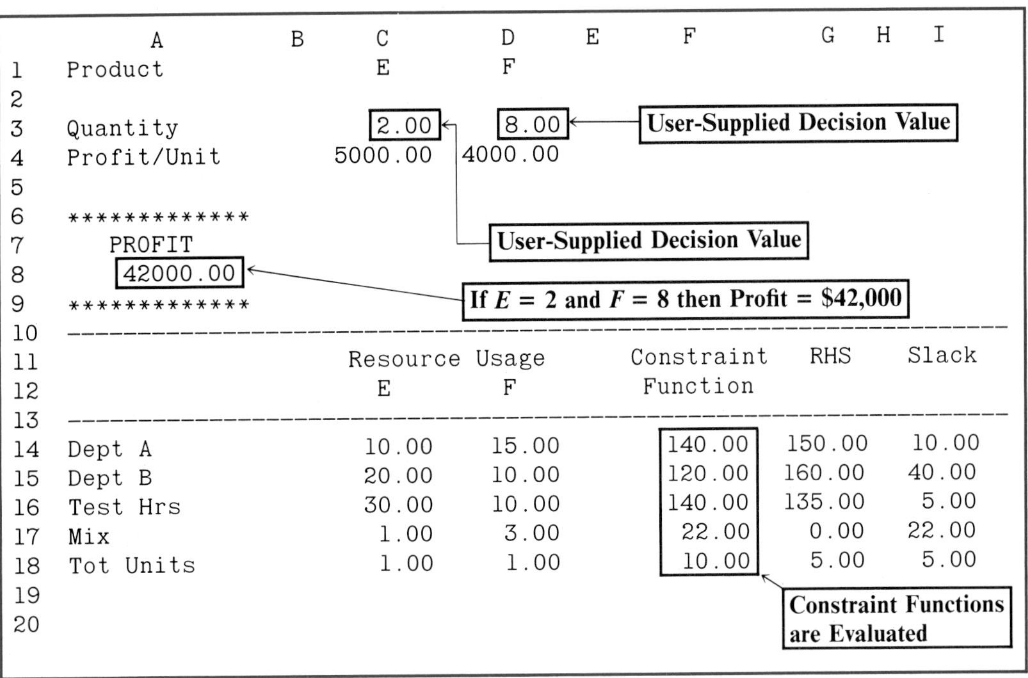

	A	B	C	D	E	F	G	H	I
1	Product		E	F					
2									
3	Quantity		2.00	8.00					
4	Profit/Unit		5000.00	4000.00					
5									
6	*************								
7	PROFIT								
8	42000.00								
9	*************								
10	----------								
11			Resource	Usage		Constraint	RHS		Slack
12			E	F		Function			
13	----------								
14	Dept A		10.00	15.00		140.00	150.00		10.00
15	Dept B		20.00	10.00		120.00	160.00		40.00
16	Test Hrs		30.00	10.00		140.00	135.00		5.00
17	Mix		1.00	3.00		22.00	0.00		22.00
18	Tot Units		1.00	1.00		10.00	5.00		5.00
19									
20									

▲ FIGURE 2.4
The Value Spreadsheet for $E = 2$, $F = 8$

by the user. These are cells *C*3 and *D*3. If, for example, we enter the value 2 into *C*3 and 8 into *D*3 (meaning $E = 2$ and $F = 8$) then the spreadsheet program can (and will) compute ("evaluate") all of the formulas that have been entered in various cells, and these formulas will be replaced with their specific numeric values. The resulting value spreadsheet appears in Figure 2.4.

Computing Value. Note that each cell that previously contained a formula now contains a number. For example, cell *F*14 now contains the number 140, which is the number of labor hours in department A when **PROTRAC** produces the mix ($E = 2$, $F = 8$). Corresponding to this constraint we see, from cell *I*14, that the slack value is 10, which is $150 - 140$. Hence there are 10 hours of unused labor in department A. If you were to enter different values for *E* and *F* the spreadsheet would recompute the values for cells such as *F*14 and *I*14 and the new results would appear. That is how the spreadsheet implements the "what if" analytic process that we described in Chapter 1.

Optimizing the Spreadsheet. If one is interested in the creation and use of spreadsheets for "what if" analyses only, then the above description covers the essentials of the process. However, when considering the spreadsheet representation of an LP, there is generally at least one more step of interest, which is the creation of the optimized spreadsheet. With either of the PC programs VINO or What's*Best!* the user can transform any value spreadsheet to an optimized spreadsheet with one additional stroke at the keyboard (and various graphics of interest can also be produced). Figure 2.5 shows the optimized spreadsheet for **PROTRAC** E and F. This **optimized spreadsheet** is a particular value spreadsheet, one in which the model has computed optimal values for the decision variables *E* and *F*. Thus, we see in Figure 2.5, reading cells *C*3 and *D*3, that the optimal decision values, which we denote as E^*, F^*, are ($E^* = 4.5$, $F^* = 7.0$). The spreadsheet also shows optimal numeric values in the "constraint function" and "slack" columns.

For power spreadsheet users, this model sheet could also represent calculations from several linked spreadsheets. Thus, if needed, the raw data to be examined could appear on several different spreadsheets.

```
         A             B      C          D       E       F             G    H     I
1   Product                   E          F
2
3   Quantity               [4.50]     [7.00] <--- Optimized Decision Value
4   Profit/Unit           5000.00    4000.00
5
6   *************
7      PROFIT                         Optimized Decision Value
8    [50500.00] <------------- Optimized Profit
9   *************
10  ----------------------------------------------------------------------------
11                          Resource Usage       Constraint    RHS      Slack
12                            E          F        Function
13  ----------------------------------------------------------------------------
14  Dept A                  10.00      15.00       150.00     150.00     0.00
15  Dept B                  20.00      10.00       160.00     160.00     0.00
16  Test Hrs                30.00      10.00       205.00     135.00    70.00
17  Mix                      1.00       3.00        16.50       0.00    16.50
18  Tot Units                1.00       1.00        11.50       5.00     6.50
19
20
```

▲ FIGURE 2.5
The Optimized Spreadsheet for E & F

▶ 2.4 The Spreadsheet Versus the Formal LP Model

You have now seen how to capture the **PROTRAC** E and F linear programming problem in two forms:

1. The formal LP model
2. The spreadsheet representation

You may well be wondering, "What should I do? Do I need to do both? What are the relevant considerations?" The purpose of this section is to address such questions.

Advantages of the Spreadsheet

Let us begin with the advantages of a spreadsheet representation. The first advantage has already been discussed:

Reinforce the point that each cell on a spreadsheet is really a calculator, so any type of mathematical calculation can be performed in any cell.

> **The spreadsheet format is a convenient way to perform numerous "what if" analyses.**

"But," we hear you say, "if our ultimate goal is to find *what's best,* do we really need to bother with the spreadsheet? Can't we just put the formal LP model on the PC and then optimize it? Wouldn't that be more efficient, since in any case it looks as if we more or less have to construct the formal LP model before creating the spreadsheet? Otherwise we wouldn't know the formulas for the objective function or the constraint functions, . . ."

Another Level of "What If." As far as it goes, the above point of view is basically correct. But there is another level of "what if" potential associated with the spreadsheet concept that we have not yet discussed. Let us illustrate this with an example.

Suppose that in fact the total hours available in department A depend on the number of workers scheduled to be on duty in the next two weeks. Suppose the dependency is expressed by the following formula:

$$\text{Total hours in dept. A} = 200(1 - e^{-(.05)MA}) \tag{2.9}$$

Converting workers to total hours

where MA denotes the number of people scheduled to work in A. For example, if $MA = 28$ then there are 150.68 hours available. Let us assume that it is the numeric value for MA that the manager really has his hands on. We call this value *raw data,* which means data that are readily available. Expression (2.9) transforms such raw data into the specific data required to formulate the model. Note that in the formal LP model we could not replace the right-hand side of the department A constraint with the right-hand side of expression (2.9) without destroying the linearity of the problem (i.e., treating MA as a variable would make the problem nonlinear). It is precisely the nonlinearity of the formula that prevents us from using it directly in the problem formulated (see Question 28 on p. 67 at the end of this chapter).

Figure 2.6 shows a symbolic spreadsheet for the modified model. In cell *A*2 the label Num Workers has been entered (for number of workers). In cell *C*2 we see that the number of workers in department A must be entered by the user. Thus, in this spreadsheet the user must provide specific values for the two decision variables (*E* and *F*) *and* for one parameter (*MA*). The formula entered in *G*16 represents the right-hand side of equation (2.9).

A value spreadsheet is obtained by entering specific numeric values for *MA* (cell *C*2), *E* (cell *C*5), and *F* (cell *D*5). The value spreadsheet Figure 2.7 was obtained by setting $MA = 28$, $E = 2$, $F = 8$. Note the similarity between Figure 2.4 and Figure 2.7.

A Parametric Analysis. In a typical real-world scenario the manager may, of course, wish to view the optimized spreadsheet for a problem. Actually, for a problem such as E and F, the manager may be thinking, "Well, it is true that I would like to see the optimized spreadsheet corresponding to my assignment of 28 workers to *MA*. But **what if** I decide to put 26 workers in department A? How would the optimized spreadsheet differ from the previous $MA = 28$ case? **What if** I then repeat this with 30 workers, 32 workers, and so on? In fact, my latest accounting run shows that the marginal cost of assigning one additional worker to department A is $400. The same set of data shows that this cost of $400 for each additional worker is the same no matter how many workers have been assigned to department A. I guess I should continue to assign workers to department A as long as the marginal return (i.e., the added return per worker) exceeds $400."

The spreadsheet optimizer is a tool that allows the manager to easily complete such a *parametric analysis.* The manager successively enters values for *MA* (cell *C*2) and obtains the optimal profit (cell *A*10) for each assignment. The result of this procedure, for values of *MA* ranging from 20 to 33, is the curve shown in Figure 2.8. (The data used to generate this curve show *diminishing returns to scale.*)

Graphs such as Figure 2.8 can be generated by the typical spreadsheet program. In our example, the analysis is completed by finding the leftmost point where adding an additional worker produces less than $400 of additional profit. To the left of this point, the marginal return exceeds the marginal cost (of $400 per worker) and to the right the marginal return is less than marginal cost. You can see that this occurs when *MA* is approximately 26. When *MA* is less than 26, the firm will make more money by assigning another worker to department A. If *MA* is greater than 26, the firm will make money by removing a worker from department A. The profit will be maximized when $MA = 26$.

	A	B	C	D	E	F	G	H	I
1			DptA						
2	Num Workers		[ ]						
3	Product		E	F					
4									
5	Quantity		[ ]	[ ]					
6	Profit/Unit		5000	4000					
7									
8	*************								
9	PROFIT								
10	+ C6 * C5 + D6 * D5								
11	*************								
12	------------------------								
13			Resource Usage			Constraint Function	RHS		Slack
14			E	F					
15	------------------------								
16	Dept A		10	15		(C16 * C5) + (D16 * D5)	200 * (1 − @EXP(− 0.05 * C2)		+ G16 − F16
17	Dept B		20	10		(C17 * C5) + (D17 * D5)		160	+ G17 − F17
18	Test Hrs		30	10		(C18 * C5) + (D18 * D5)		135	− G18 + F18
19	Mix		1	3	−	(C19 * C5) + (D19 * D5)		0	− G19 + F19
20	Tot Units		1	1		(C20 * C5) + (D20 * D5)		5	− G20 + F20

Raw Data to be Supplied by User

Decision Values to be Supplied by User

▲ FIGURE 2.6
The Symbolic Spreadsheet with a Formula for Hours Available in Dept. A

	A	B	C	D	E	F	G	H	I
1			DptA						
2	Num Workers		28.00						
3	Product		E	F					
4									
5	Quantity		2.00	8.00		User-Supplied			
6	Profit/Unit		5000.00	4000.00		Entries			
7									
8	*************								
9	PROFIT								
10	42000.00								
11	*************								
12	-----------------								
13			Resource Usage			Constraint	RHS		Slack
14			E	F		Function			
15	-----------------								
16	Dept A		10.00	15.00		140.00	150.68		10.68
17	Dept B		20.00	10.00		120.00	160.00		40.00
18	Test Hrs		30.00	10.00		140.00	135.00		5.00
19	Mix		1.00	3.00		22.00	0.00		22.00
20	Tot Units		1.00	1.00		10.00	5.00		5.00

▲ FIGURE 2.7
The Value Spreadsheet for $E = 2$, $F = 8$, $MA = 28$

Matrix Generators. In typical real-world LP models, there may be many different parameters whose values, like the right-hand side of the department A constraint, are computed from rather complicated *nonlinear* formulas (e.g., expression [2.9] shows that the parameter "total hours in department A" is a nonlinear function of *MA*).

Customarily, computer science practitioners deal with this problem by writing a special "front end" program, called a **matrix generator.** The job of such a program is to take raw data, such as a value for the term *MA,* and, using the appropriate formulas, transform these data into the inputs required by the LP model (the hours

▼ FIGURE 2.8
Optimal Profit vs. Workers in Dept. A

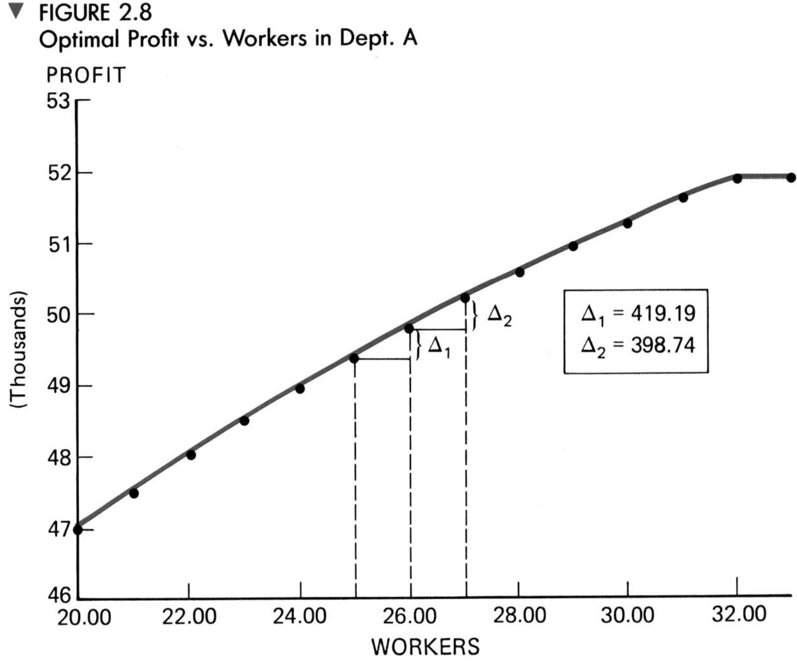

of capacity in department A). The matrix generator allows a user to solve many different LPs without needing to calculate transformed data by hand. The spreadsheet does the same job, but in a more "user-friendly" environment.

A powerful reason for using the spreadsheet approach is that it provides a convenient user-oriented way to generate the data required to formulate the LP. In many real-world applications, such data are generated by directly inputting readily available raw data. The spreadsheet then automatically computes the values for the transformed data.

Reasons for the Formal LP Model

Why then do we bother at all to write out the formal LP model? There are two reasons. As already mentioned, it is almost a prerequisite that in order to create the spreadsheet you must first formulate the problem as a formal LP model. The second reason is that in practice, regardless of which formulation we consider (i.e., spreadsheet or formal model), almost no one formulates a problem correctly on the first try. In other words, formulations often need to be debugged. We have two choices:

Debugging the formal LP model

1. Write out the model as a formal LP and then try to solve it with one of many available interactive computer codes (in this text we use the LINDO code to solve an LP problem). If the model has been incorrectly formulated your first attempt to solve it will generally produce either a diagnostic indication or a nonsensical result. Proceed to debug, which means you examine your formulation and look for errors either in the logic of the formulation or in the way you typed the formulation into the computer.

Debugging the spreadsheet representation of the LP

2. Use the formal LP model as a guide in creating a symbolic spreadsheet representation. Try to optimize. An incorrectly formulated model will, as above, generally trigger some kind of fault indicator. Again, as above, you must now debug your work.

Although either of the above choices can lead to a correct formulation, experience suggests that the first route is easier. For a rather complicated model it is often easier to examine and analyze the formal LP model. Looking at all of the many formulas in the cells of the symbolic spreadsheet can be, to say the least, confusing. The whole purpose of the spreadsheet approach is to get to the value spreadsheet, which the representation managers find easy to work with. But this can be created in a correct manner only after the formulation *has been debugged.*

A two-stage process

Writing the problem as a formal LP model, and then debugging the formulation, seems to be the easiest way to arrive at a correct model. After that, you may choose to create a spreadsheet representation for further manipulation and analysis in a convenient format.

The table shown in Figure 2.9 summarizes some of the important differences between using the formal model in conjunction with an interactive code such as LINDO and using a spreadsheet optimizer.

For all of these reasons, the spreadsheet cannot be viewed as a replacement of the formal LP model, and programs which optimize spreadsheets cannot yet provide satisfactory replacements of interactive computer codes such as LINDO. More appropriately, we shall view the spreadsheet representation of an LP as another tool for the manager's use. It is a tool that in some ways enhances the

APPLICATION CAPSULE

Lotus Blooms in Pennsylvania: Bethlehem Steel Shifts Its Production Planning to a PC Spreadsheet*

Bethlehem Steel had been running a complex production-planning and cost-analysis model on a mainframe computer. The model was slow and not user-friendly; moreover, it had relatively low priority on the mainframe, and users often had to wait to see results. Consequently, the company has switched to a simpler spreadsheet model, developed by University of Pittsburgh MBAs, that uses Lotus 1-2-3 and runs on a PC.

The new system is faster and easier to use. A production-planning module allows managers to determine, for a given product demand, the level of production that will maximize yield, subject to production time constraints. A cost module then uses this information, together with additional cost and price data supplied by the user, to determine the contribution margin (the revenues minus variable costs) for each product. Various what-if calculations, to determine the effects of changes in production or cost parameters, can be performed quickly and easily. It is possible, for example, to pose such questions as, "How would net profit be affected if this year's demand for hot-rolled steel decreased to 250,000 tons?" or "How would the final costs of production change if the price of natural gas increased 10%?"

The model is flexible; a version designed for one plant can be adapted to another with a minimum of effort. Currently, the accounting department uses the model to investigate alternatives at five steel-producing plants for four subsequent quarters. Beyond that time, a yearly analysis is made with the model.

---

*Baker, Clark, Frund, and Wendell, "Production Planning and Cost Analysis on a Microcomputer," *Interfaces*, Vol. 17, No. 4 (July-Aug. 1987).

A spreadsheet is a good way to develop a smaller prototype model before going to a larger, more formal model. In this manner a manager can see the effect of interactions and determine which constraints and variables are important.

manager's ability to have "hands-on-contact" with the problem to be analyzed. The manager who wishes to use the tool effectively will want to understand a good deal about the structure of the underlying formal LP model. Why? Because it is that model and its properties that we are really making use of, regardless of whether it is being represented on a spreadsheet. Elucidating the structure of the underlying LP model will occupy much of our attention for the next few chapters. Before that, however, we shall want to study several other examples, to gain experience both with model formulation and with creating spreadsheet representations.

▼ FIGURE 2.9
A Comparison of Spreadsheet and Formal Models

	FORMAL LP MODEL	SPREADSHEET REPRESENTATION
Matrix Generator:	Would be a separate computer program "not seen" by the manager.	The formulas for generating data are in the spreadsheet cells and can be viewed or modified by the manager.
"What If" Analyses:	Constraints and objective function values computed by hand.	All computations performed automatically on the spreadsheet.
Debugging the Problem Formulation:	Facilitated by looking at a listing of the formal model.	Not easily done with only the spreadsheet representation.

▶ 2.5 Crawler Tread: A Blending Example

Although the PROTRAC, Inc. problem turned out to be a maximization model, many real-world problems occur in a minimization context. When profit is the objective, then clearly maximization is called for; but if, for example, cost is the objective, then minimization is called for. As an example of a minimization model, we consider the following Crawler Tread problem:

The Problem Statement

If students need to have some feel for the contents of each ore, let
A = **A**luminum
B = **B**oron
C = **C**arbon

Iron ore from four different mines will be blended to make treads for a new product at PROTRAC, a medium-size crawler tractor, the E-6, designed especially to compete in the European market. Analysis has shown that in order to produce a blend with suitable tensile qualities, minimum requirements must be met on three basic elements, denoted for simplicity as A, B, and C. In particular, each ton of ore must contain at least 5 pounds of basic element A, at least 100 pounds of basic element B, and at least 30 pounds of basic element C. These data are summarized in Figure 2.10. The ore from each of the four different mines possesses each of the three basic elements, but in different amounts. These compositions, in pounds per ton, are given in Figure 2.11.

Notice that a ton of ore from the first mine contains 10 pounds of basic element A and hence satisfies the minimum requirement on this element of 5 pounds per ton. Similarly, this same ton of ore contains 90 pounds of basic element B and 45 pounds of basic element C, hence satisfying the requirement on basic element C but not on basic element B. Similarly, you can verify that a single ton of ore from the second mine will not satisfy the requirement on A or C. A single ton of ore from mine 3 will not satisfy requirements on B and C, and a single ton from

▼ FIGURE 2.10
Requirements of Basic Elements

BASIC ELEMENT	MINIMUM REQUIREMENT PER TON OF BLEND (LB)
A	5
B	100
C	30

▼ FIGURE 2.11
Compositions from Each Mine (pounds per ton)

BASIC ELEMENT	MINE			
	1	2	3	4
A	10	3	8	2
B	90	150	75	175
C	45	25	20	37

mine 4 will not satisfy the requirement on A. However, many different blends can easily be found that will indeed satisfy the minimal requirements on all three basic elements. An example of such a blend would be a mixture composed of one-half ton from mine 1 and one-half ton from mine 4. The amount of basic element A in this blended ton is computed as follows:

$$\text{pounds of A} = (\text{pounds of A in 1 ton from 1})(1/2) + (\text{pounds of A in ton from 4})(1/2)$$

Hence

$$\text{pounds of A} = 10(1/2) + 2(1/2) = 5 + 1 = 6$$

Since $6 \geq 5$, the minimal requirement on basic element A is satisfied by this blend. Similarly, for the same blended ton, we can compute

$$\text{pounds of B} = (\text{pounds of B in 1 ton from 1})(1/2) + (\text{pounds of B in 1 ton from 4})(1/2)$$

Hence

$$\text{pounds of B} = 90(1/2) + 175(1/2) = 132.5$$

In a similar fashion

$$\text{pounds of C} = 45(1/2) + 37(1/2) = 41$$

Feasibility

Comparing 132.5 with the requirement of 100, and 41 with the requirement of 30, it is seen that this blend of one-half ton from mine 1 and one-half ton from mine 4 easily satisfies all the minimal requirements, and hence this is said to be a *feasible blend.* There are many other possible blends of 1 ton that satisfy all the minimal requirements and hence which are also feasible. See if you can discover one or two. (Of course, a spreadsheet representation would automatically do the calculations for you.) However, since the ore from each mine has a different cost, different blends will also have different costs. The cost data are given in Figure 2.12. For example,

MINE	DOLLAR COST PER TON OF ORE
1	800
2	400
3	600
4	500

▲ FIGURE 2.12
Dollar Cost per Ton from Each Mine

from Figure 2.12 you can see that the cost of the feasible blend one-half ton from mine 1 and one-half ton from mine 4 is (cost per ton from mine 1)(1/2) + (cost per ton from mine 4)(1/2) = 800(1/2) + 500(1/2) = $650. Compare this cost with the cost of some of the other feasible blends that you may have discovered. The objective of management in the Crawler Tread problem is to discover a *least-cost feasible blend.* Let us see how this problem can be formulated as a linear programming model.

Creating the Formal LP Model

Since we are interested in finding an *optimal* 1-ton blend, we set up the *decision variables* as follows:

$$T_1 = \text{fraction of a ton to be chosen from mine 1}$$
$$T_2 = \text{fraction of a ton to be chosen from mine 2}$$
$$T_3 = \text{fraction of a ton to be chosen from mine 3}$$
$$T_4 = \text{fraction of a ton to be chosen from mine 4}$$

Then, using the numerical values given in Figure 2.11, the amounts of the basic elements in 1 ton of blend are calculated as follows:

pounds of basic element A in 1 ton of blend
$$= 10T_1 + 3T_2 + 8T_3 + 2T_4 \quad \textbf{(2.10)}$$
pounds of basic element B in 1 ton of blend
$$= 90T_1 + 150T_2 + 75T_3 + 175T_4 \quad \textbf{(2.11)}$$
pounds of basic element C in 1 ton of blend
$$= 45T_1 + 25T_2 + 20T_3 + 37T_4 \quad \textbf{(2.12)}$$

We can now combine expressions (2.10), (2.11), and (2.12) with the minimal requirements designated in Figure 2.10 to obtain the three (requirement) constraints:

$$10T_1 + 3T_2 + 8T_3 + 2T_4 \geq 5 \quad \textbf{(2.13)}$$
$$90T_1 + 150T_2 + 75T_3 + 175T_4 \geq 100 \quad \textbf{(2.14)}$$
$$45T_1 + 25T_2 + 20T_3 + 37T_4 \geq 30 \quad \textbf{(2.15)}$$

Are there any other constraints in this model? Of course, we must include the usual nonnegativity conditions T_1, T_2, T_3, $T_4 \geq 0$, but there is still another important constraint that must be included. Since there are no other contributions to the 1 ton aside from the four mines, the fractional contributions from each mine must add up to 1. That is, we must include the constraint

This constraint allows T_i to be a percentage of the mix. If 100 pounds of mix are required, 100 T_i pounds would come from mine *i*.

$$T_1 + T_2 + T_3 + T_4 = 1 \quad \textbf{(2.16)}$$

The latter constraint, sometimes called a *balance condition,* is an **equality constraint,** and it restricts the values of the decision variables in such a way that the left-hand side *exactly* equals the right-hand side. This illustrates an important principle:

The constraints in a linear programming model can be equalities as well as inequalities.

Using the data in Figure 2.12, it is easy to see that the cost of any blend is given as follows:

$$\text{cost of 1 ton of blend} = 800T_1 + 400T_2 + 600T_3 + 500T_4$$

Noting that the objective is to minimize cost, we can now write the complete mathematical model for the Crawler Tread problem:

The Formal Crawler Tread Model

$$
\begin{aligned}
\text{Min } & 800T_1 + 400T_2 + 600T_3 + 500T_4 \\
\text{s.t. } & 10T_1 + 3T_2 + 8T_3 + 2T_4 \geq 5 \\
& 90T_1 + 150T_2 + 75T_3 + 175T_4 \geq 100 \\
& 45T_1 + 25T_2 + 20T_3 + 37T_4 \geq 30 \\
& T_1 + T_2 + T_3 + T_4 = 1 \\
& T_1, T_2, T_3, T_4 \geq 0
\end{aligned}
$$

You should verify that all functions in this model are linear and consequently it is a linear programming problem.

Now that you have seen two very detailed examples of model formulation, along with a discussion of spreadsheet representations, we present a number of additional examples for you to work on. These examples will allow you to sharpen your formulation skills. You will also have more opportunities to create spreadsheet representations. Before presenting the examples, let us take a moment to give some loose guidelines on how to translate a word problem into a mathematical model.

2.6 Guidelines and Comments on Model Formulation

In translating a word problem into a formal model, you may find it helpful first to create a verbal model corresponding to the given problem. That is, you might proceed as follows:

1. Express each constraint in words; in doing this, pay careful attention to whether the constraint is a *requirement* of the form $\geq$ (at least as large as), a *limitation* of the form $\leq$ (no larger than), or $=$ (exactly equal to).
2. Then express the objective in words.

Steps 1 and 2 should then allow you to

3. Verbally identify the decision variables.

Variables (decisions, alternatives): *the most important things to determine.* Ask, "What decisions can be made?" "What makes one decision distinct from another?" It is important to distinguish between independent decisions. Thus, using some T_1 and T_2 and no T_3 or T_4 is not a decision. The decision we need to make is, "How much of each individual amount?"

Often a careful reading of the problem statement will reveal that the decision variables and the objective are given to you (in the problem statement) in the exact form that you need. It is usually of great importance that your decision variables be correctly defined. Sometimes you may feel that there are several possible choices. For example, should they represent pounds of finished product or pounds of raw material? One guideline that is often useful is to ask yourself the question, *What decisions must be made in order to optimize the objective function?* The answer to this question will help lead you to identify the decision variables correctly.

Having accomplished steps 1 through 3, invent symbolic notation for the decision variables. Then

4. Express each constraint in symbols (i.e., in terms of the decision variables).
5. Express the objective function in symbols (in terms of the decision variables).

At this stage it is advisable to check your work for consistency of units. For example, if the coefficients in the objective function are in dollars per *pound,* the decision variables that appear in the objective function should be in pounds, not tons or ounces. Similarly, check that for each constraint the units on the right-hand side and the units on the left-hand side are the same. For example, if one of the constraints is a limitation of ≤ form on labor hours, the right-hand side will be labor hours. Then if, as above, the decision variables are pounds, the data for this constraint function (i.e., the numerical coefficients for each decision variable on the left-hand side of the constraint) should be in labor hours per pound. To put it quite simply, you do not want to end up with hours on one side and minutes or seconds or pounds or tons on the other.

At this point it would be a good idea to comment on one other aspect of model formulation. We have seen that inequality constraints may be of the form ≥ or ≤. Students often ask whether a linear programming problem can have a *strict inequality* constraint, such as < or >. The answer is a resounding *no.* The reason for this is mathematical in nature. It is to assure that a well-formulated problem will have a solution. The mathematical details required to justify this assertion lie outside our scope of interest. This is not a costly prohibition, for in just about any real-world situation you can imagine involving inequality constraints, it is true that the ≤ or ≥ representation entirely captures the real-world meaning.

Let us now discuss one final aspect of model formulation. This deals with the nature of the cost data to be employed.

2.7 Sunk Versus Variable Cost

In many real-world problems there are often two types of costs: **sunk costs,** also referred to as **fixed costs,** and **variable costs.** Contrary to the first impressions that students sometimes have, sunk costs play no part in optimization.

Only variable costs are relevant in optimization models.

The sunk cost can be ignored

The sunk, or fixed, costs have already been paid, which means that no future decisions can affect these expenditures. For example, suppose that 800 pounds and 500 pounds of two grades of aluminum (grade 1 and grade 2) have been purchased for future delivery, at specified prices, \$5 and \$10 per pound, respectively, and that the contract has been signed. Management's problem is, in part, to determine the optimal use of these 1300 pounds of aluminum so as, perhaps, to maximize profit obtained from producing aluminum knuckles and conduits. Associated with these two products there will be revenues and variable costs incurred in their production (costs of machining, stamping, and so on). In formulations of this type of model, the sunk costs of \$9000 associated with the contracted purchase are irrelevant. This amount has already been spent and hence the *quantities to be purchased* are no longer variables. The variables will be how much product should be produced, and the relevant cost in this determination is only the variable cost. More specifically, the formulation corresponding to the description above might be as follows. Let

K = number of knuckles to be produced (decision variable)

C = number of conduits to be produced (decision variable)

10 = revenue per knuckle

30 = revenue per conduit

4 = cost of producing a knuckle (variable cost)

12 = cost of producing a conduit (variable cost)

For each product we must calculate what accountants call the *unit contribution margin,* that is, the difference between per unit revenue and per unit variable cost. The unit contribution margins are

$$\text{for knuckles: } 10 - 4 = 6$$

$$\text{for conduits: } 30 - 12 = 18$$

Suppose that each knuckle uses 1 unit of grade 1 aluminum and 2 units of grade 2 aluminum. Each conduit uses 3 units of grade 1 and 5 units of grade 2. Then we obtain the following formal linear programming model:

$$\begin{aligned} &\text{Max } 6K + 18C \\ &\text{s.t. } K + 3C \le 800 \text{ (grade 1 limitation)} \\ &\quad 2K + 5C \le 500 \text{ (grade 2 limitation)} \\ &\quad K \ge 0, \quad C \ge 0 \end{aligned}$$

One way to see the irrelevance of the sunk cost is to note that the objective function in the formulation is the total contribution margin. The net income, or profit, would be

$$\begin{aligned} \text{net profit} &= \text{contribution margin} - \text{sunk cost} \\ &= 6K + 18C - 9000 \end{aligned}$$

However, finding feasible values of K and C that maximize $6K + 18C - 9000$ is the same as finding feasible values that maximize $6K + 18C$. The constant term of 9000 can therefore be ignored. The bottom line here is that maximizing a function plus a constant, or even a positive constant times a function, gives in either case the same result, in terms of optimal values of decision variables, that you would obtain without the constant. However, adding (or subtracting) the same constant to (or from) each coefficient in the objective function may change the result. This is all nicely illustrated in the Red Brand Canners case at the end of this chapter. This case is a good illustration of how both sunk and variable costs arise in real-world problems.

Learning to Formulate Models

The remainder of this chapter contains examples of formulations that you can use to cement your ability to make the transition between the real-world problem and the mathematical model. This transition—the way in which the model has been set up, the way the constraints and the objectives have been formulated—is of prime importance.

Try to work the following problems on your own. Set them up as quickly as possible and *do not read more into a problem than precisely what is given.* Do not introduce additional constraints or logical nuances or flights of imagination of your own that might in your opinion make the model more realistic. Do not, for example, worry about "what happens next week" if the problem never refers to "next week." The problems that we pose are chosen to help you develop a facility for formulation. In order to do this, and so that you may check your work and gauge your progress, it must be true that within the described context the correct formulation should be unambiguous. In other words, there is a "right answer." Later, when you have more experience, the latitude for shades of interpretation and real-world subtleties will be broader. Because the topic of formulation is so important, and because practice is the only way to master this topic, an especially long list of problems appears at the end of this chapter.

One final word of advice: Do not simply read the problem and then immediately read the solution. That would be the best way to deceive yourself about what you understand. Do not read the solution until either (1) you are certain you have correctly solved the problem on your own or (2) you are absolutely convinced that you have hit an impasse.

2.8 Example 1: Astro and Cosmo (A Product Mix Problem)

A TV company produces two types of TV sets, the Astro and the Cosmo. There are two production lines, one for each set, and there are two departments, both of which are used in the production of each set. The capacity of the Astro production line is 70 sets per day. The capacity of the Cosmo line is 50 sets per day. In department A picture tubes are produced. In this department the Astro set requires 1 labor hour and the Cosmo set requires 2 labor hours. Presently in department A a maximum of 120 labor hours per day can be assigned to production of the two types of sets. In department B the chassis is constructed. In this department the Astro set requires 1 labor hour and the Cosmo also requires 1 labor hour. Presently, in department B a maximum of 90 labor hours per day can be assigned to production of the two types of sets. The profit contributions are 20 and 10 dollars, respectively, for each Astro and Cosmo set. These data are summarized in Figure 2.13.

If the company can sell as many Astro and Cosmo sets as it produces, what should be the daily production plan (i.e., the daily production) for each set? Review the **PROTRAC**, Inc. E and F model and then try to formulate Astro and Cosmo as a linear program.

▼ FIGURE 2.13
Astro and Cosmo Data

		LABOR UTILIZATION PER SET (HRS)		
	DAILY CAPACITY	Dept. A	Dept. B	PROFIT PER SET ($)
Astro	70	1	1	20
Cosmo	50	2	1	10
Total Availability		120	90	

Solution to Example 1.

A = daily production of Astros (sets/day)

C = daily production of Cosmos (sets/day)

The formal LP model for Astro and Cosmo

$$\begin{aligned} &\text{Max } 20A + 10C \\ \text{s.t.} \quad & A \le 70 \\ & C \le 50 \\ & A + 2C \le 120 \\ & A + C \le 90 \\ & A, C \ge 0 \end{aligned}$$

Note that in this model not all the decision variables appear in all the constraints. For example, the variable C does not appear in the constraint $A \leq 70$. In general, not all the decision variables have to appear explictly in every constraint.[1] Also, they need not all appear in the objective function.

2.9 Example 2: Blending Gruel (A Blending Problem)

A 16-ounce can of dog food must contain protein, carbohydrate, and fat in at least the following amounts: protein, 3 ounces; carbohydrate, 5 ounces; fat, 4 ounces. Four types of gruel are to be blended together in various proportions to produce a least-cost can of dog food satisfying these requirements. The contents and prices for 16 ounces of each gruel are given in Figure 2.14.

Review the Crawler Tread blending model and then formulate this gruel blending problem as a linear program. HINT: Let x_i denote the proportion of gruel i in a 16-ounce can of dog food, $i = 1, 2, 3, 4$.

This type of model requires a good cost-accounting system and a good information system to easily store, update, and retrieve data. For example, Ralston Purina took just a few months to put together its LP system for blending different "chows" for animals, but required 18 months to get the management information system to supply the needed data.

▼ FIGURE 2.14
Gruel Blending Data

	CONTENTS AND PRICE PER 16 OZ OF GRUEL			
GRUEL	**Protein Content (oz)**	**Carbohydrate Content (oz)**	**Fat Content (oz)**	**Price ($)**
1	3	7	5	4
2	5	4	6	6
3	2	2	6	3
4	3	8	2	2

Solution to Example 2.

The formal LP model for blending gruel

$$
\begin{aligned}
\text{Min } & 4x_1 + 6x_2 + 3x_3 + 2x_4 \\
\text{s.t. } & 3x_1 + 5x_2 + 2x_3 + 3x_4 \geq 3 \\
& 7x_1 + 4x_2 + 2x_3 + 8x_4 \geq 5 \\
& 5x_1 + 6x_2 + 6x_3 + 2x_4 \geq 4 \\
& x_1 + x_2 + x_3 + x_4 = 1 \\
& x_1, x_2, x_3, x_4 \geq 0
\end{aligned}
$$

Note that in Example 1, from the point of view of implementation, fractional values for the decision variables would probably be unacceptable. In Example 2, however, fractional values would be expected and acceptable. Example 3 illustrates another setting where integer values would be needed.

[1]You may think of all decision variables being included, but with zero coefficients in places. Thus, the constraint $A \leq 70$ is the same as $A + 0(C) \leq 70$.

2.10 Example 3: Security Force Scheduling (A Scheduling Problem)

A personnel manager must schedule the security force in such a way as to satisfy the staffing requirements shown in Figure 2.15.

TIME	MINIMUM NUMBER OF OFFICERS REQUIRED
Midnight–4 A.M.	5
4 A.M.–8A.M.	7
8 A.M.–Noon	15
Noon–4 P.M.	7
4 P.M.–8 P.M.	12
8 P.M.–Midnight	9

▲ FIGURE 2.15
Security Staffing Requirements

SHIFT	STARTING TIME	ENDING TIME
1	Midnight	8:00 A.M.
2	4:00 A.M.	Noon
3	8:00 A.M.	4:00 P.M.
4	Noon	8:00 P.M.
5	4:00 P.M.	Midnight
6	8:00 P.M.	4:00 A.M.

▲ FIGURE 2.16
Shift Schedule

Officers work 8-hour shifts. There are 6 such shifts each day. The starting and ending times for each shift are given in Figure 2.16. The personnel manager wants to determine how many officers should work each shift in order to minimize the total number of officers employed, while still satisfying the staffing requirements. We can define the decision variables as follows:

x_1 = number of officers working shift 1

x_2 = number of officers working shift 2

$\vdots$

x_6 = number of officers working shift 6

In formulating the objective function, note that the total number of officers is the sum of the number of officers assigned to each shift. Now write out the objective function, noting that the personnel manager wants to minimize this sum. The objective function is

$$x_1 + x_2 + x_3 + x_4 + x_5 + x_6$$

In formulating the constraints, you want to be sure that a particular set of values for $x_1, \ldots, x_6$ satisfies the staffing requirements. Some device is needed to see what officers are on duty during each of the 4-hour intervals prescribed in Figure 2.15. A tabular arrangement such as the one shown in Figure 2.17 is helpful in making this determination.

SHIFT	TIME INTERVAL					
	Midnight to 4:00 A.M.	4:00 A.M. to 8:00 A.M.	8:00 A.M. to Noon	Noon to 4:00 P.M.	4:00 P.M. to 8:00 P.M.	8:00 P.M. to Midnight
1	x_1	x_1				
2		x_2	x_2			
3			x_3	x_3		
4				x_4	x_4	
5					x_5	x_5
6	x_6					x_6
Requirements	5	7	15	7	12	9

▲ FIGURE 2.17
Officers on Duty in Each Interval

Here we see that the officers who work shift 1 are on duty during each of the first two time intervals, and so on. Figure 2.17 also shows (adding down columns) how many officers work in each time interval (e.g., in the first time interval $x_1 + x_6$ officers are on duty; thus we write the first constraint $x_1 + x_6 \geq 5$). Now try to write out the remaining constraints for this model. The complete solution is given below.

Solution to Example 3.

The formal security force scheduling model

$$
\begin{aligned}
&\text{Min } x_1 + x_2 + x_3 + x_4 + x_5 + x_6 \\
&\text{s.t. } \quad x_6 + x_1 \geq 5 \\
&\qquad x_1 + x_2 \geq 7 \\
&\qquad x_2 + x_3 \geq 15 \\
&\qquad x_3 + x_4 \geq 7 \\
&\qquad x_4 + x_5 \geq 12 \\
&\qquad x_5 + x_6 \geq 9 \\
&\qquad x_i \geq 0, \quad i = 1, 2, \ldots, 6
\end{aligned}
$$

This type of problem has been used to schedule operators for several telephone companies, as well as for companies that have "800" numbers. Typically, each hour is broken into 15-minute segments; thus each 24-hour day has 96 constraints. The number of variables is determined by the different possible shifts allowed.

If you have access to a PC and **Lotus 1-2-3** you can create a spreadsheet representation of this model. One possible symbolic spreadsheet is shown in Figure 2.18. Entering any set of decision values (i.e., numerical values for $x_1, \ldots, x_6$) produces a value spreadsheet. If you have access to a spreadsheet optimizer such as **VINO** or **What's*Best!*,** you can then proceed to optimize the value spreadsheet. This will produce Figure 2.19. This latter figure shows optimal values for the decisions x_1 through x_6.

The examples thus far have shown a product mix model (Astro/Cosmo), a blending model (gruel), and a scheduling model (security force). These are all illustrations of *types* of LPs that you encounter in real-world problem solving. Here is another important type of LP, called a *transportation model.*

	A	B	C	D	E	F	G	H
1								
2	SECURITY STAFFING SPREADSHEET							
3								
4			Num	Num	Num	Xtra		
5		Start	Workers	Workers	Workers	Workers		*******************************
6	Shift	Time	Start	Work	Req'd			Tot Workers
7	-----	-----	-----	-----	-----	-----		Employed
8	1	Mdngt	☐	+ C8 + C13	5	+ D8 − E8		+ C8 + C9 + C10 + C11 + C12 + C13
9	2	4.am	☐	+ C8 + C9	7	+ D9 − E9		*******************************
10	3	8.am	☐	+ C9 + C10	15	+ D10 − E10		
11	4	Noon	☐	+ C10 + C11	7	+ D11 − E11		
12	5	4.pm	☐	+ C11 + C12	12	+ D12 − E12		
13	6	8.pm	☐	+ C12 + C13	9	+ D13 − E13		
14	-----	-----	-----	-----	-----	-----		
15								
16								

Entries in this Column are User-Supplied Decision Values

▲ FIGURE 2.18
Symbolic Spreadsheet for Security Force Scheduling

	A	B	C	D	E	F	G	H	I	J
1										
2	SECURITY STAFFING SPREADSHEET									
3										
4			Num	Num	Num	Xtra				
5		Start	Workers	Workers	Workers	Workers		********		
6	Shift	Time	Start	Work	Req'd			Tot Workers		
7	-----	-----	-----	-----	-----	-----		Employed		
8	1	Mdngt	0	5	5	0		32		**Optimized Objective Value**
9	2	4.am	8	8	7	1		********		
10	3	8.am	7	15	15	0				
11	4	Noon	0	7	7	0				
12	5	4.pm	12	12	12	0				
13	6	8.pm	5	17	9	8				
14	-----	-----	-----	-----	-----	-----				
15										
16										

Optimized Decision Values

▲ FIGURE 2.19
Optimized Spreadsheet for Security Force Scheduling

2.11 Example 4: Transportation Model

A company has two plants and three warehouses. The first plant can supply at most 100 units and the second at most 200 units of the same product. The sales potential at the first warehouse is 150, at the second warehouse 200, and at the third 350. The sales revenues per unit at the three warehouses are $12 at the first, $14 at the second, and $15 at the third. The cost of manufacturing one unit at plant *i* and shipping it to warehouse *j* is given in Figure 2.20. The company wishes to determine how many units should be shipped from each plant to each warehouse so as to maximize profit.

FROM PLANT	TO WAREHOUSE ($) 1	2	3
1	8	10	12
2	7	9	11

▲ FIGURE 2.20
Shipping Costs

Solution to Example 4. Note that the proper choice of the decision variables is given to you in the problem statement itself. Models of this sort are often formulated with decision variables having two rather than a single subscript. Using this device, the decision variables are:

$$x_{ij} = \text{units sent from plant } i \text{ to warehouse } j$$

For each variable, the corresponding profit is the revenue per unit sold at warehouse j minus the cost of shipping a unit from plant i to warehouse j. Thus for items shipped from plant 1 to warehouse 1, for example, the profit is \$12/unit sales − \$8/unit shipping = \$4/unit. Similar calculations for each plant-warehouse combination provide the coefficients for the terms of the objective function. The model is therefore

The formal LP transportation model

$$\begin{aligned}
\text{Max } & 4x_{11} + 5x_{21} + 4x_{12} + 5x_{22} + 3x_{13} + 4x_{23} \\
\text{s.t. } & x_{11} + x_{12} + x_{13} \le 100 \\
& x_{21} + x_{22} + x_{23} \le 200 \\
& x_{11} + x_{21} \le 150 \\
& x_{12} + x_{22} \le 200 \\
& x_{13} + x_{23} \le 350 \\
& x_{ij} \ge 0, \quad \text{all } i,j
\end{aligned}$$

From the formulation above you can see that a transportation model has a very special form. For example, all the nonzero coefficients in the constraints are 1. In fact, a transportation model is an example of an entire class of linear programs called *network problems.* Other examples of transportation models will appear in Chapter 7, and Chapter 9 is devoted to network models.

▶ 2.12 Example 5: Winston-Salem Development Corporation (Financial Planning)

Here is an interesting application of LP to financial planning. Winston-Salem Development Corporation (WSDC) is trying to complete its investment plans for the next two years. Currently, WSDC has \$2,000,000 on hand and available for investment. In 6 months, 12 months, and 18 months, WSDC expects to receive an income stream from previous investments. The data are presented in Figure 2.21. There are two development projects in which WSDC is considering participation.

	6 MONTHS	12 MONTHS	18 MONTHS
Income	$500,000	$400,000	$380,000

▲ FIGURE 2.21
Income from Previous Investments

1. The Foster City Development would, if WSDC participated at a 100% level, have the projected cash flow shown in Figure 2.22 (negative numbers are investment, positive numbers are income). Thus, in order to participate in Foster City at the 100% level, WSDC would immediately have to lay out $1,000,000. In 6 months there would be another outlay of $700,000, and so on.

	INITIAL	6 MONTHS	12 MONTHS	18 MONTHS	24 MONTHS
Income	$−1,000,000	$−700,000	$1,800,000	$400,000	$600,000

▲ FIGURE 2.22
Foster City Cash Flow

2. A second project involves taking over the operation of some old Middle-Incoming Housing on the condition that certain initial repairs be made. The cash flow stream for this project, at a 100% level of participation, would be as shown in Figure 2.23.

	INITIAL	6 MONTHS	12 MONTHS	18 MONTHS	24 MONTHS
Income	$−800,000	$500,000	$−200,000	$−700,000	$2,000,000

▲ FIGURE 2.23
Middle-Income Housing Cash Flow

Because of company policy, WSDC is not permitted to borrow money. However, at the beginning of each 6-month period all surplus funds (those not allocated to either Foster City or Middle-Income Housing) are invested for a return of 7% for that 6-month period. WSDC can participate in any project at a level less than 100%, in which case all of the cash flows of that project are reduced proportionately. For example, if WSDC were to opt for participation in Foster City at the 30% level, the cash flows associated with this decision would be 0.3 times the data in Figure 2.22. The problem currently facing WSDC is to decide how much of the $2,000,000 on hand should be invested in each of the projects and how much should simply be invested for the 7% semiannual return. Management's goal is to *maximize the cash on hand at the end of 24 months.* Formulate this problem as an LP model.

Solution to Example 5. The constraints in this model must say that at the beginning of each of the four 6-month periods

$$\text{money invested} = \text{money on hand}$$

Define the decision variables

F = fractional participation in the Foster City project

M = fractional participation in the Middle-Income Housing project

S_1 = surplus initial funds (not invested in F or M initially) to be invested at 7%

S_2 = surplus funds after 6 months to be invested at 7%

S_3 = surplus funds after 12 months to be invested at 7%

S_4 = surplus funds after 18 months to be invested at 7%

Then the first constraint must say

$$\text{initial investment} = \text{initial funds on hand}$$

or

$$1{,}000{,}000F + 800{,}000M + S_1 = 2{,}000{,}000$$

The equality constraints can be thought of as examples of balance conditions (p. 000) and will occur in many types of linear programming models, especially multiperiod models. They balance the flows from one period or place to another.

Because of the interest paid, S_1 becomes $1.07S_1$ after 6 months, and similarly for S_2, S_3, and S_4, the remaining three constraints are

$$\begin{aligned} 700{,}000F + S_2 &= 500{,}000M + 1.07S_1 + 500{,}000 \\ 200{,}000M + S_3 &= 1{,}800{,}000F + 1.07S_2 + 400{,}000 \\ 700{,}000M + S_4 &= 400{,}000F + 1.07S_3 + 380{,}000 \end{aligned}$$

and the objective function is to maximize the cash on hand at the end of 24 months, which is

$$600{,}000F + 2{,}000{,}000M + 1.07S_4$$

The formal WSDC model

We have thus derived the following model:

$$\begin{aligned} \text{Max } & 600{,}000F + 2{,}000{,}000M + 1.07S_4 \\ \text{s.t. } & 1{,}000{,}000F + 800{,}000M + S_1 = 2{,}000{,}000 \\ & 700{,}000F - 500{,}000M - 1.07S_1 + S_2 = 500{,}000 \\ & -1{,}800{,}000F + 200{,}000M - 1.07S_2 + S_3 = 400{,}000 \\ & -400{,}000F + 700{,}000M - 1.07S_3 + S_4 = 380{,}000 \\ & F \le 1 \\ & M \le 1 \\ & F \ge 0, \quad M \ge 0, \quad S_i \ge 0, \quad i = 1,2,3,4 \end{aligned}$$

2.13 Example 6: Longer Boats Yacht Company—A Vignette in Constrained Break-Even Analysis

The Longer Boats Yacht Company produces three high-performance racing sloops. These three boats are called the Sting, the Ray, and the Breaker. Figure 2.24 gives pertinent revenue and cost data for the next planning period.

SLOOP	SELLING PRICE PER UNIT ($)	VARIABLE COST PER UNIT ($)	FIXED COST ($)
Sting	10,000	5,000	5,000,000
Ray	7,500	3,600	3,000,000
Breaker	15,000	8,000	10,000,000

▲ FIGURE 2.24
Longer Boats' Data

As you can see from these data, the *fixed cost* of each of these activities is considerable. As explained in Section 2.7, fixed cost is a lump cost that is paid regardless of the quantity to be produced. Thus, the same fixed cost of $3,000,000 for Rays will occur whether the production run consists of 0 boats, 1 boat, or 40 boats. The high fixed costs include the costs of design modification, mold reconstruction, and yacht basin testing.

Figure 2.25 shows a break-even analysis of the production of Stings. We see that if Longer Boats were to produce only Stings, it would have to produce at least 1000 boats to break even.

Longer Boats' problem is more complicated, however. First, for the next planning period management has already contracted to produce 700 Stings. Another customer has requested 400 Breakers, a request that management would like to honor. Longer Boats' marketing surveys have convinced management that at most 300 Rays should be produced. Management is still interested in how much it must sell to break even, but now there are three products as well as previous commitments or restrictions to take into consideration. Starting from basic principles, management notes that at break-even

$$\text{total revenue} = \text{total cost}$$

To obtain an expression of this fact in terms of the production quantities, the following decision variables are defined:

$$S = \text{number of Stings to produce}$$

$$R = \text{number of Rays to produce}$$

$$B = \text{number of Breakers to produce}$$

The break-even constraint, then, is

$$10{,}000S + 7500R + 15{,}000B = 5000S + 3600R + 8000B + 18{,}000{,}000$$

or

$$5000S + 3900R + 7000B = 18{,}000{,}000$$

We note that there is an infinite number of sets of values for *S, R,* and *B* that satisfy this constraint. Thus, in the multiproduct case, there are many break-even points, whereas in the single-product case (see Figure 2.25), there is only one. In the multiproduct case, then, management must specify an additional restriction in order to identify a particular break-even point of interest. Since Longer Boats is a relatively new company and is experiencing the cash flow problems associated with rapid growth, management would like to minimize the capital outflow. The fixed costs are of necessity incurred in their totality, and thus the goal becomes one of minimizing total variable costs. The total variable cost (the objective function) is

$$5000S + 3600R + 8000B$$

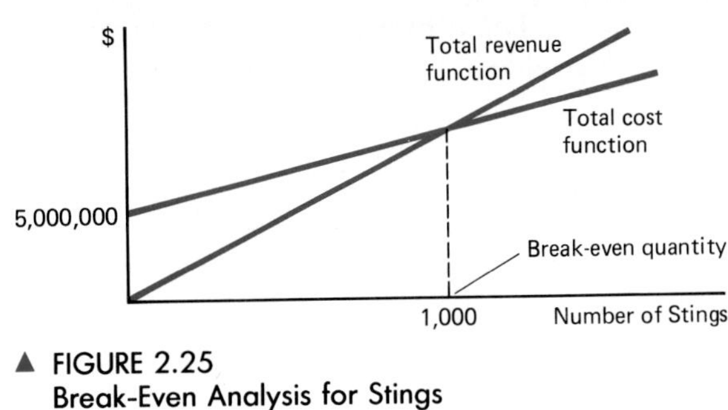

▲ FIGURE 2.25
Break-Even Analysis for Stings

The complete model reflecting the break-even constraint, as well as the preestablished requirements and limits on demand, is as follows:

The formal longer boats LP model

$$
\begin{aligned}
\text{Min } & 5000S + 3600R + 8000B \\
\text{s.t. } & 5000S + 3900R + 7000B = 18{,}000{,}000 \\
& S \geq 700 \\
& B \geq 400 \\
& R \leq 300 \\
& S \geq 0, \quad R \geq 0, \quad B \geq 0
\end{aligned}
$$

2.14 Example 7: Multiperiod Inventory Models

Multiperiod inventory models constitute an important class of models that applies to inventories of materials, cash, and employees carried from one period to the next. Multiperiod models are sometimes referred to as *dynamic problems.* They reflect the fact that the decisions made in this period affect not only this period's returns (or costs) but the allowable decisions and returns in future periods as well. For this reason, multiperiod problems cannot be treated as if they were merely a collection of single-period problems. The topic of inventory management is considered in some detail in later chapters.

This example is a classical, so-called deterministic, single-product inventory problem. It is called *deterministic* because we assume that the demand (i.e., number of orders to be satisfied) in each future period is known at the beginning of period 1. For example, a producer of polyurethane has a stock of orders for the next 6 weeks. Let d_i be a parameter that denotes this known demand (say, in terms of number of gallons that must be delivered to customers during week i), and assume that $d_i > 0$ for all i. Let C_i denote the cost of producing a gallon during week i, and let K_i denote the maximum amount that can be produced (because of capacity limitations) in week i. Finally, let h_i denote the per unit cost of inventory in stock at the end of week i. (Thus, the inventory is measured as the number of gallons carried from week i into week $i + 1$.) Suppose that the initial inventory (at the beginning of period 1 and for which no carrying charge is assessed) is known to be I_0 gallons. Find a production and inventory-holding plan that satisfies the known delivery schedule over the next 6 weeks at minimum total cost.

Before we formulate the constrained optimization model, it will be useful to develop an expression for the inventory on hand at the end of each period. Since there is an inventory carrying charge, this quantity will clearly play a role in the objective function.

Let I_i be the inventory on hand at the end of week i. Define the decision variable x_i to be the gallons of polyurethane produced in week i. We note that

$$I_1 = I_0 + x_1 - d_1$$

That is, the inventory on hand at the end of week 1 is equal to the inventory on hand at the end of week 0 (the beginning of week 1) plus the production in week 1 minus the deliveries in week 1. (We are assuming that all demand must be satisfied. Hence, the known demand in week i, d_i, is by definition the amount delivered in week i.)

Similarly

In English this production model indicates **Production + Old Inventory = Demand + New Inventory.**

$$I_2 = I_1 + x_2 - d_2$$

and, in general, the same reasoning yields, for any period t

$$I_t = I_{t-1} + x_t - d_t$$

This important inventory equation says that

inventory at end of t = inventory at beginning of t
+ production in t − demand in t

If we substitute the known expression for I_1 into the equation for I_2, we obtain

$$I_2 = \underbrace{I_0 + x_1 - d_1}_{I_1} + x_2 - d_2 = I_0 + \sum_{i=1}^{2} x_i - \sum_{i=1}^{2} d_i$$

We could then substitute the foregoing expression for I_2 into the equation for I_3 to obtain

$$I_3 = I_0 + \sum_{i=1}^{3} x_i - \sum_{i=1}^{3} d_i$$

Repeating this procedure leads to an equivalent inventory equation

$$I_t = I_0 + \sum_{i=1}^{t} (x_i - d_i)$$

for any period t.

Note that this last expression relates the inventory at the end of period t to all previous production (the x values). The equation simply says that the inventory at the end of period t is equal to the initial inventory, plus the total production through period t, minus the total deliveries through period t. The variable I_t is sometimes referred to as a *definitional variable* because it is defined in terms of other decision variables (the x_i values) in the problem. The use of definitional variables sometimes makes it easier to see the proper formulation. Before writing the verbal model for this problem, we must figure out a way of saying that production in each period must be *at least* great enough so that demand (i.e., the delivery schedule) can be satisfied. In period 1 this means that $I_0 + x_1 \geq d_1$, or $I_0 + x_1 - d_1 \geq 0$. Since $I_0 + x_1 - d_1$ is the same as I_1, this is the same as saying that the inventory at the end of period 1 is nonnegative. Satisfying period 2 demand means that inventory at the beginning of period 2 (the end of period 1) plus period 2 production $\geq d_2$. That is

$$I_1 + x_2 \geq d_2 \text{ or } I_1 + x_2 - d_2 \geq 0$$

which is the same as saying that the inventory at the end of period 2 is nonnegative. It should now be possible to see the pattern.

The condition that demand in period t must be satisfied is equivalent to the condition that inventory I_t at the end of period t must be nonnegative.

Solution to Example 7. *Diagram*

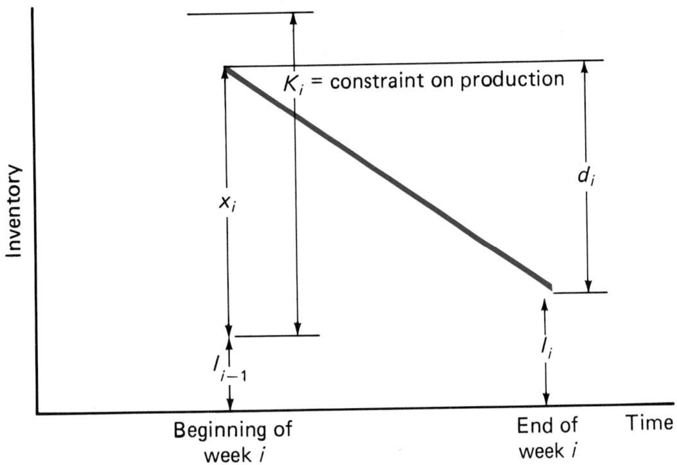

▲ FIGURE 2.26

Verbal Model

Minimize production cost + inventory cost

subject to

inventory at the end of week t	≥ 0	$t = 1,2,\ldots,6$
production in week t	$\leq K_t$	$t = 1,2,\ldots,6$

Decision Variables

$$x_t = \text{production in week } t$$

The Model

$$\begin{aligned} \text{Min } & \sum_{t=1}^{6} C_t x_t + \sum_{t=1}^{6} h_t I_t \\ \text{s.t. } & \left. \begin{aligned} & I_t = I_{t-1} + x_t - d_t \\ & x_t \leq K_t \\ & x_t \geq 0, \quad I_t \geq 0 \end{aligned} \right\} \quad t = 1,2,\ldots,6 \end{aligned}$$

In general, the structure of such models is fairly complex. That is, interactions are occurring between large numbers of variables. For example, inventory at the end of a given period t is determined by all production decisions in periods 1 through t. This is seen from the inventory equation.

$$I_t = I_0 + \sum_{i=1}^{t} (x_i - d_i)$$

Therefore, the cost in period t is also determined by all production decisions in periods 1 through t. Finally, it is noted that the formulation above can be written in an equivalent form without the I_t variables appearing. Try to do this on your own.

2.15 Example 8: The Bumles, Inc. Minicase (Production and Inventory Control)

Bumles, Inc. uses part of its capacity to make hand-painted teapots. One teapot takes 0.5 hours of a painter's time. Bumles has 30 painters available. The plant is used for the teapots on Thursday, Friday, and Saturday each week. During the remainder of the week the productive capacity is devoted to another product line. Not all of the 30 painters will necessarily be engaged, but each painter who is engaged is available to work any part of an 8-hour day, 2 days a week. A painter can be assigned to any 2-day schedule and is paid for 16 hours of regular-time work, no matter what part of that time he actually spends producing teapots. If there is not enough production to keep all the workers assigned to a particular day busy for the entire day, the slack time is spent on cleaning the plant and similar activities.

If labor costs are not taken into account, the revenue from selling a teapot is \$15. Demand must be satisfied on the day on which it occurs or it is lost. Production on a given day can be used to satisfy demand that day or demand later in the week (i.e., teapots produced on Thursday can be used to satisfy demand on Friday or Saturday). However, because of the change of operations to hand-painted statues on Monday, Tuesday, and Wednesday, all teapots produced in a week must be shipped that week (i.e., there is never inventory on Thursday morning). Because of increased handling costs, it costs \$0.50 to carry a teapot in inventory from one day to the next. A unit of lost demand results in an all-inclusive penalty cost of \$1 for a unit on Thursday, \$3 on Friday, and \$5 on Saturday. Painters are paid \$8 per hour. Weekly demand for the teapots is 100 on Thursday, 300 on Friday, and 600 on Saturday.

Ignoring integrality conditions (i.e., allowing the possibility of fractional values of all decision variables), create an LP model that will schedule painters and production in such a way as to maximize revenue minus cost, where cost equals labor plus penalty and inventory-carrying costs. The model should be correct for any set of demands. In your formulation the first three constraints should be

$$DT = 100$$
$$DF = 300$$
$$DS = 600$$

where DT is the demand on Thursday, Friday, and Saturday, respectively. In your formulation of the model, you must pay attention to relationships between production, sales, lost sales, demand, and inventory on any particular day. For example

$$\text{demand on day } x = \text{sales on day } x + \text{lost sales on day } x$$

Solution to Example 8. In addition to the above relation between demand, sales, and lost sales, we also need the following relationship between production, inventory, and sales:

$$\text{production on day } x = \text{sales on day } x + \text{inventory at end of day } x$$
$$- \text{ inventory at end of day } (x-1)$$

Let us define the variables:

S_x = sales on day x

D_x = demand on day x

L_x = lost sales on day x

P_x = production on day x

I_x = inventory at end of day x

where x can be T (Thursday), F (Friday), or S (Saturday).

TF, TS, FS = number of painters assigned to Thursday–Friday, Thursday–Saturday, and Friday–Saturday, respectively.

Then the *formal LP model* is

```
MAX 15 ST + 15 SF + 15 SS − 128 TF − 128 TS − 128 FS − 0.5 IT
    − 0.5 IF − LT − 3 LF−5 LS
SUBJECT TO
  DT = 100 ⎫
  DF = 300 ⎬ ←——————————————————— demand constraints
  DS = 600 ⎭
  − 8 TF − 8 TS + 0.5 PT ≤ 0 ⎫
  − 8 TF − 8 FS + 0.5 PF ≤ 0 ⎬ ←———— production constraints
  − 8 TS − 8 FS + 0.5 PS ≤ 0 ⎭
  ST + IT − PT = 0           ⎫         inventory balance
  SF + IT + IF − PF = 0      ⎬ ←—————— (defines inventory variables in
  SS − IF + PS + IS = 0      ⎭         terms of production and sales)
  IS = 0
  ST + LT − DT =  0 ⎫                  demand sales relationship
  SF + LF − DF =  0 ⎬ ←——————————————— (defines lost sales in terms of
  SS + LS − DS =  0 ⎭                  demand and sales)
  TF + TS + FS ≤ 30 ←————————————————— workforce constraint
```

Figures 2.27 and 2.28 show symbolic and optimized spreadsheets for the Bumles problem. In the spreadsheet representation we let the decision variables be sales on each day, production on each day, and number of painters on each schedule. Then the lost sales on each day and ending inventory on each day are interpreted as definitional variables. Another way of saying this is that the inventory and lost sales are interpreted as dependent variables. The production and sales (as well as workers on each schedule) are interpreted as independent variables.

2.16 Summary

Constraints were defined to be mathematical conditions that rule out certain combinations of values for the decision variables, and feasible or allowable decisions were defined to be values of the variables that satisfy *all* the constraints. Linear programming was seen to involve a search for a feasible decision that optimizes an objective function. More specifically, linear programming was defined to be a mathematical model with the following properties:

1. There is a linear objective function that is to be maximized or minimized.
2. There are linear constraints, each a mathematical inequality (either $\leq$ or $\geq$) or an equality.
3. There are nonnegative decision variables.

	A	B	C	D	E	F	G	H	I
1	BUMLES SPREADSHEET								
2									
3	Days		Thurs	Fri	Sat				
4	Demand		100	300	600				
5	Production						**Decision**		
6	Sales						**Variables**		
7	Lost Sales		+ C4 − C6	+ D4 − D6	+ E4 − E6				
8	End Inventory		+ C5 − C6	+ C8 + D5 − D6	+ D8 + E5 − E6				
9			TF	TS	FS				
10	Painters								
11	REVENUE–COST								
12	15*(C6 + D)*								
13	------------								
14		TF	TS	FS			Used	Avail	Slack
15			Hrs/day		Hrs/Teapot				
16	------------								
17	Prod–T	8	8		0.5		+ C5	(1/E17) ∗ (B17 ∗ C10 + C17 ∗ D10)	+ H17 − G17
18	Prod–F	8		8	0.5		+ D5	(1/E18) ∗ (B18 ∗ C10 + D18 ∗ E10)	+ H18 − G18
19	Prod–S		8	8	0.5		+ E5	(1/E19) ∗ (C19 ∗ D10 + D19 ∗ E10)	+ H19 − G19
20	Workforce						+ C10 + D10 + E10	30	+ H20 − G20

*A12: 15 ∗ (C6 + D6 + E6) − 128 ∗ (C10 + D10 + E10) − 0.5 ∗ (C8 + D8) − C7 − (3 ∗ D7) − (5 ∗ E7)

▲ FIGURE 2.27
Symbolic Bumles Spreadsheet

	A	B	C	D	E	F	G	H	I
1	BUMLES SPREADSHEET								
2									
3	Days		Thurs	Fri	Sat				
4	Demand		100.00	300.00	600.00				
5	Production		60.00	420.00	480.00				
6	Sales		60.00	300.00	600.00				
7	Lost Sales		40.00	0.00	0.00		Optimal Decision Values		
8	End Inventory		0.00	120.00	0.00				
9			TF	TS	FS				
10	Painters		0.00	3.75	26.25				
11	REVENUE-COST								
12	10460.00								
13	---								
14		TF	TS	FS			Used	Avail	Slack
15			Hrs/day		Hrs/Teapot				
16	---								
17	Prod-T	8.00	8.00		0.50		60.00	60.00	0.00
18	Prod-F	8.00		8.00	0.50		420.00	420.00	0.00
19	Prod-S		8.00	8.00	0.50		480.00	480.00	0.00
20	Workforce						30.00	30.00	0.00

▲ FIGURE 2.28
Optimized Bumles Spreadsheet

Examples were given to show how a real-world "word problem" can be translated into a formal LP model. The examples illustrated that a profit objective leads to a Max model, whereas a cost objective gives a Min model. We also saw that a constraint of the "limitation" type is usually translated into a mathematical inequality of the $\leq$ form, and a constraint of the "requirement" type is usually translated into a $\geq$ inequality. In some situations, such as in blending problems, logical considerations will require the presence of equality constraints. Guidelines were also given on how to proceed with model formulation. *Spreadsheet representations* of an LP problem were shown, via specific examples, to have useful properties when the user is interested in manipulating the data in the model. Spreadsheet representations were compared with the *formal LP model,* and advantages of each were discussed.

▶ Key Terms

Constraint. A mathematical inequality (an inequality constraint) or equality (an equality constraint) that must be satisfied by the variables in the model. (*p. 24*)

Objective Function. Every linear program has a linear objective function that represents the goal to be either maximized or minimized. (*p. 25*)

Constrained Optimization Model. A model whose objective is to find values of decision variables that optimize an objective function subject to constraints. (*p. 25*)

Optimal Product Mix. Alternative term for optimal production plan. (*p. 26*)

Optimal Production Plan. The optimal decision for a production model, that is, the optimal quantities of each product to be produced. (*p. 26*)

Inequality Constraint. A constraint requiring some function of the decision variables in a model to be $\geq$ (greater than or equal to) or $\leq$ (less than or equal to) a constant. (*p. 27*)

Right-Hand Side. The number on the right-hand side of a constraint. Abbreviated RHS. (*p. 27*)

Constraint Function. The left-hand side of a constraint. It depends on the unknowns. (*p. 27*)

Nonnegativity Conditions. Conditions in

a model that stipulate that the decision variables can have only nonnegative (*positive* or *zero*) values. (*p. 28*)

Decision Variables. The variables under the decision maker's control. These are the variables that appear in the mathematical models that we have formulated in this chapter. (*p. 29*)

Feasible Decision. A decision that satisfies *all* the constraints of a model, including the nonnegativity conditions. Feasible means allowable. (*p. 29*)

Optimal Decision. A feasible decision that optimizes the objective function. (*p. 30*)

Optimal Solution. Alternative term for optimal decision. (*p. 30*)

Optimize. To maximize or minimize. (*p. 30*)

Formal LP Model. The mathematical representation of an LP problem. (*p. 31*)

Linear Function. A function in which each variable appears in a separate term. There are no powers other than 1, and there are no logarithmic, exponential, or trigonometric terms. (*p. 31*)

Integrality Condition. A requirement that one or more variables in a model have only integer values. (*p. 32*)

Integer Program. A model in which one or more variables can have only integer values. (*p. 32*)

Spreadsheet. A grid whose cells contain labels, parameters, numbers, or formulas. (*p. 32*)

Parameter. A number or symbol in a model that must have a numerical value supplied by the user. (*p. 32*)

Decision Values. A set of numerical values for the decision variables. (*p. 32*)

Symbolic Spreadsheet. A spreadsheet representation with each formula explicitly shown. (*p. 32*)

Value Spreadsheet. A spreadsheet representation with all formulas numerically evaluated. (*p. 34*)

Optimized Spreadsheet. A value spreadsheet that is optimal. (*p. 34*)

Matrix Generator. A computer program that transforms raw data into numbers to be directly employed in a model. (*p. 39*)

Equality Constraint. A constraint requiring some function of the decision variables in a model to be exactly equal to a constant. (*p. 44*)

Sunk Costs. Costs whose values have already been determined, and therefore cannot be affected by subsequent decisions. (*p. 46*)

Fixed Costs. Alternative term for sunk costs. (*p. 46*)

Variable Costs. Costs whose values will be determined by decision yet to be made, and which can therefore serve as variables in an optimization model. (*p. 46*)

Lotus 1-2-3. A spreadsheet program for the PC. (*p. 51*)

VINO. A spreadsheet program that can also optimize the spreadsheet representation of an LP. (*p. 51*)

What's*Best!* A spreadsheet program that can also optimize the spreadsheet representation of an LP. (*p. 51*)

Major Concepts Quiz

True-False

1. T F In the context of modeling, restrictions on the allowable decisions are called constraints.

2. T F Not every LP has to have constraints.

3. T F Any model with an objective function, constraints, and decision variables is an LP.

4. T F A limitation is expressed as a $\geq$ constraint.

5. T F The nonnegativity conditions mean that all decision variables must be positive.

6. T F Since fractional values for decision variables may not be physically meaningful, in practice (for the purpose of implementation) we often round the optimal LP solution to integer values.

7. T F All the constraints in an LP are inequalities.

8. T F Properly defining the decision variables is an important step in model formulation.

9. T F The objective function of a cost-minimization model need only consider variable, as opposed to sunk, costs.

10. T F The way in which a problem has been formulated as a model is of considerable interest to the manager, who may one day have to pass judgment on the validity of the model.

Multiple Choice

11. A constraint limits the values
a. that the objective function can assume
b. that the decision variables can assume
c. neither of the above
d. both a and b

12. Constraints may represent
a. limitations
b. requirements
c. balance conditions
d. all of the above

13. Linear programming is
a. a constrained optimization model
b. a constrained decision-making model
c. a mathematical programming model
d. all of the above

14. In an LP Max model
a. the objective function is maximized
b. the objective function is maximized and then it is determined whether this occurs at an allowable decision
c. the objective function is maximized over the allowable set of decisions
d. all of the above

15. The *distinguishing* feature of an LP (as opposed to more general mathematical programming models) is
a. the problem has an objective function and constraints
b. all functions in the problem are linear
c. optimal values for the decision variables are produced

16. In translating a word problem into a formal model, it is often helpful to
a. express each constraint in words
b. express the objective in words
c. verbally identify the decision variables
d. all of the above

17. Model formulation is important because
a. it enables us to use algebraic techniques
b. in a business context, most managers prefer to work with formal models
c. it forces management to address a clearly defined problem
d. it allows the manager to better communicate with the management scientist and therefore to be more discriminating in hiring policies

18. The nonnegativity requirement is included in an LP because
a. it makes the model easier to solve
b. it makes the model correspond more closely to the real-world problem
c. neither of the above
d. both a and b

Questions 19 through 26 refer to the following problem:

Three itinerant industrialists, Lotta Joy, Claire Sailing, and Fickle Pickle, are en route to Hollywood to seek their fortune. The flight time is 40 hours at a fuel cost of $100 per gallon. In a Hollywood deli they strike up a quick friendship with the notorious Peter Putter. Peter's total income per year is $40,000—his alimony payments are $60,000. Knowing almost everyone in town, Peter is able to spin out a stairway to the stars for our three fortune seekers. They are now inspecting capsule medicine products by passing the capsules over a special lighting table where they visually check for cracked, partially filled, or improperly tainted capsules. Currently, any of our three moguls can be assigned to the visual inspection task. These women, however, differ in height, accuracy, and speed abilities. Consequently, their employer (Flora Fortune) pays them at slightly different wage rates. The significant differences are summed up in Figure 2.29.

INSPECTOR	SPEED (units/hr)	ACCURACY (%)	HOURLY WAGE ($)	HEIGHT
Lotta	300	98	2.95	7 ft 2 in.
Claire	200	99	2.60	4 ft 3 in.
Fickle	350	96	2.75	5 ft 2 in.

▲ FIGURE 2.29

Operating on a full 8-hour shift, Flora needs to have at least 2000 capsules inspected with no more than 2% of these capsules having inspection errors. In addition, because of the devastating carpal tunnel syndrome, no one woman can be assigned this task for more than 4 hours per day. Let

$$X_1 = \text{number of hours worked by Lotta}$$
$$X_2 = \text{number of hours worked by Claire}$$
$$X_3 = \text{number of hours worked by Fickle}$$

The objective is to minimize the cost of 8 hours of inspection. Assume that the inspection process must be in operation for all 8 hours. In other words, continuous production must occur during the 8-hour period. In addition, Lotta, Claire, and Fickle are the only inspectors, no more than one inspector can work at a time, and the plumber works at most 4 hours per day.

19. A correct accuracy constraint is
a. $(0.98)(300)X_1 + (0.99)(200)X_2 + (0.96)(350)X_3 \geq 2000$
b. $(0.02)(300)X_1 + (0.01)(200)X_2 + (0.04)(350)X_3 \leq (0.02)(2000)$
c. $-2X_2 + 7X_3 \leq 0$
d. none of the above

20. The production requirement constraint is correctly written as $300X_1 + 200X_2 + 350X_3 = 2000$.
a. T
b. F

21. Excluding the nonnegativity constraints, a proper formulation for this problem will contain six constraints.
a. T
b. F

22. It is possible that the correct formulation for this problem will have no feasible decisions. (Answer this question for the given data.)
a. T
b. F

23. If it were not for the accuracy requirement and the 4-hour limitation, the optimal solution would have only Fickle working.
   a. T
   b. F

24. The optimal solution will require that at least two of the three employees inspect.
   a. T
   b. F

25. A feasible policy is provided by
   a. 4 hours Claire, 4 hours Fickle
   b. 4 hours Lotta, 4 hours Claire
   c. both a and b

26. Let policy A be $X_1 = 4$, $X_2 = 4$, $X_3 = 0$. Let policy B be $X_1 = 3$, $X_2 = 4$, $X_3 = 1$. Note that each policy is feasible. Since A produces 2000 capsules and B produces 2050, A is preferred.
   a. T
   b. F

Questions 27 through 39 deal with spreadsheet concepts.

27. A parameter in a model can be a number or a symbol.
   a. T
   b. F

28. Consider the constraint $10E + 15F \leq R$, where R is a parameter denoting hours in department A. Now suppose values of R are given by $(1 - e^{-(.05)MA})$. If we substitute this into the original constraint it becomes $10E + 15F \leq 200\,(1 - e^{-(.05)MA})$. This new constraint is linear in E, F, and the new parameter MA.
   a. T
   b. F

29. The symbolic spreadsheet is derived from a value spreadsheet.
   a. T
   b. F

30. One advantage of the spreadsheet representation is that it provides a convenient way to do parametric analysis.
   a. T
   b. F

31. In the symbolic spreadsheet representation of an LP, a constraint function is represented as a formula in a cell.
   a. T
   b. F

32. A spreadsheet representation can sometimes eliminate the need for a matrix generator and thereby enable the manager to directly manipulate raw data.
   a. T
   b. F

33. For feasible decisions, the slack cells in the value spreadsheet will contain nonnegative numbers.
   a. T
   b. F

34. Lotus 1-2-3 can be used to create a spreadsheet representation of an LP but it will *not* optimize the spreadsheet.
   a. T
   b. F

35. A parameter
   a. is a number in a model, or symbol which is exogenous to the model (i.e., a symbol whose numerical value must be supplied to the model)

b. may be represented by a symbol (such as *R*) whose value must be determined by the model
c. both of the above

36. A suggested way to create a spreadsheet representation of an LP is to first write out the formal LP model and then use this as a guideline to create a symbolic spreadsheet.
a. T
b. F

37. A spreadsheet representation of an LP can be useful because
a. parameters representing raw data may enter into the model nonlinearly
b. it makes the model easy to debug
c. both of the above

38. A matrix generator
a. transforms raw data into numbers which are needed in the LP
b. is often employed in real-world problem solving
c. is often fit in as a "front end" for traditional LP codes
d. all of the above

39. A spreadsheet is a grid whose cells may contain
a. labels
b. numbers
c. parameters
d. formulas
e. all of the above

Answers

1. T	**11.** d	**21.** a	**31.** T
2. F	**12.** d	**22.** b	**32.** T
3. F	**13.** d	**23.** b	**33.** T
4. F	**14.** c	**24.** a	**34.** T
5. F	**15.** b	**25.** b	**35.** a
6. T	**16.** d	**26.** b	**36.** T
7. F	**17.** c	**27.** T	**37.** a
8. T	**18.** b	**28.** F	**38.** d
9. T	**19.** c	**29.** F	**39.** e
10. T	**20.** b	**30.** T	

▶ Problems

All end-of-chapter Problems in this text have been graded by level of difficulty: ▲ = simple, ▲▲ = intermediate, ▲▲▲ = challenging. Computer-related problems have been identified by a marginal icon.

a-8, b-2, c-3, d-4, e-1, f-6, g-7, h-5.

2-1. ▲ Match each of the following terms with the most appropriate description below.

(a) Linear program.	**1.** The unknowns in an LP that represent decisions to be made.
(b) Requirement.	**2.** Usually, a constraint of ≥ form.
(c) Variable cost.	**3.** A concept that is proper to include in the model.
(d) Sunk cost.	**4.** Usually, not relevant to the model (break-even analysis would be an exception).
(e) Decision variables.	**5.** Usually, a constraint of ≤ form.
(f) Constraint function.	**6.** The left-hand side of the constraint.

(g) Restriction. — 7. Synonymous with constraint.

(h) Limitation. — 8. A special type of constrained optimization model.

Expressions a, c, and g could be found in an LP; but b, d, e, f, and h contain non-linear terms (see IM).

2-2. ▲ Which of the following mathematical relationships could be found in a linear programming model? For those relationships that could not be found in an LP, state the reasons.

(a) $3x_1 + x_2 \leq \sqrt{5}$

(b) $\sqrt{x_1} + x_2 \leq 10$

(c) $\sqrt{2}x_1 - \pi x_3 \leq e$

(d) $x_1^2 + 2x_2 = 0$

(e) $x_1 + x_1x_2 + x_3 = 5$

(f) $x_1 + \log(x_2) = 5$

(g) $\log(10)x_1 + e^2x_2 = 6$

(h) $e^{x_1} + x_2 = 23$

Let A_1 = number of product 1 produced
A_2 = number of product 2 produced
The model is:
Max $12A_1 + 4A_2$
s.t.
$A_1 + 2A_2 \leq 800$
$A_1 + 3A_2 \leq 600$
$2A_1 + 3A_2 \leq 2000$
$A_1, A_2 \geq 0$

2-3. ▲ *A Production Problem (see Example 1).* The Swelte Glove Company manufacturers and sells two products. The company makes a profit of $12 for each unit of product 1 sold and a profit of $4 for each unit of product 2. The labor-hour requirements for the products in each of the three production departments are summarized in Figure 2.30. The supervisors of these departments have estimated that the following numbers of labor hours will be available during the next month: 800 hours in department 1, 600 hours in department 2, and 2000 hours in department 3. Assuming that the company is interested in maximizing profits, show the linear programming model of this problem.

	LABOR-HOUR REQUIREMENT	
DEPARTMENT	**Product 1**	**Product 2**
1	1	2
2	1	3
3	2	3

▲ FIGURE 2.30
Swelte Glove Company Production Data

The model is:
Max 25A + 20B + 50C + 30UC
s.t.
$3A + B + 4C + 4UC \leq 150$
$4A + 2B + 5C + 5UC \leq 200$
$5A + 5B + 4C \leq 300$
$A, B, C, UC \geq 0$

2-4. ▲ *A Production Problem (see Example 1).* Wood Walker owns a small furniture shop. He makes three different styles of tables: A, B, C. Each model of table requires a certain amount of time for cutting component parts, for assembling, and for painting. Wood can sell all the units he makes. Furthermore, model C may be sold without painting. Wood employs several individuals who work on a part-time basis, so the time available for each of these activities varies from month to month. Use the data in Figure 2.31 to formulate an LP model that will help Wood determine the product mix that will maximize his profit next month.

▼ FIGURE 2.31
Wood Walker Data

MODEL	CUTTING (hrs)	ASSEMBLING (hrs)	PAINTING (hrs)	PROFIT PER TABLE ($)
A	3	4	5	25
B	1	2	5	20
C	4	5	4	50
Unpainted C	4	5	0	30
Capacity	150	200	300	

Let G = number of Gofer stocks
C = number of Can Oil stocks
S = number of Sloth Petroleum stocks

The model is:
Max 7G + 3C + 3S
s.t.
60G + 25C + 20S $\leq$ 100,000
60G $\leq$ 60,000
25C $\leq$ 25,000
20S $\leq$ 30,000
G, C, S $\geq$ 0

2-5. ▲ *Financial Planning.* Willie Maykit is president of a one-person investment firm that manages stock portfolios for a number of clients. A new client has just requested the firm to handle a $100,000 portfolio. The client would like to restrict the portfolio to a mix of the three stocks shown in Figure 2.32. Formulate an LP to show how many shares of each stock Willie should purchase to maximize the estimated total annual return.

STOCK	PRICE PER SHARE $	ESTIMATED ANNUAL RETURN PER SHARE $	MAXIMUM POSSIBLE INVESTMENT $
Gofer Crude	60	7	60,000
Can Oil	25	3	25,000
Sloth Petroleum	20	3	30,000

▲ FIGURE 2.32
Portfolio Mix

Min 45A + 38B + 27C
s.t.
.62A + .55B + .36C $\geq$ 8/16
.05A + .10B + .20C $\geq$ 1/16
.03A + .02B + .01C $\leq$ .5/16
A, B, C, $\geq$ 0

2-6. ▲ *A Blending Problem (see Example 2).* Doug E. Starr, the manager of Heavenly Hound Kennels, Inc., provides lodging for pets. The kennels' dog food is made by mixing three grain products to obtain a well-balanced dog diet. The data for the three products are shown in Figure 2.33. If Doug wants to make sure that each of his dogs consumes at least 8 ounces of protein, 1 ounce of carbohydrate, and no more then 0.5 ounces of fat each day, how much of each grain product should each dog be fed in order to minimize Doug's cost? (Note: 16 ounces = 1 pound.)

GRAIN PRODUCT	COST PER POUND $	PROTEIN (%)	CARBOHYDRATE (%)	FAT (%)
A	0.45	62	5	3
B	0.38	55	10	2
C	0.27	36	20	1

▲ FIGURE 2.33
Well-Balanced Dog Diet

See IM.

2-7. ▲ *A Blending Problem.* McNaughton, Inc. produces two steak sauces, Spicy Diablo and mild Red Baron. These sauces are both made by blending two ingredients, A and B. A certain level of flexibility is permitted in the formulas for these products. The allowable percentages, along with revenue and cost data, are given in Figure 2.34. Up to 40 quarts of A and 30 quarts of B could be purchased. McNaughton can sell as much of these sauces as it produces. Formulate an LP whose objective is to maximize the net revenue from the sale of the sauces.

▼ FIGURE 2.34
Allowable Percentages for McNaughton, Inc.

SAUCE	INGREDIENT A	INGREDIENT B	SALES PRICE PER QUART ($)
Spicy Diablo	at least 25%	at least 50%	3.35
Red Baron	at most 75%	*	2.85
Cost per Quart	$1.60	$2.59	

*No explicit maximum or minimum percentage.

Let T = bottles of turmeric; P = bottles of paprika; HBO1, HBO2, HBO3 = ounces of these ingredients sold.

The model is:

Max 3.25T + 2.75P + .60HBO1 + .70HBO2 + .55HBO3

s.t.

4T + 3P + HBO1 ≤ 8000

2T + 2P + HBO2 ≤ 9000

T + 3P + HBO3 ≤ 7000

T ≤ 1700

P ≥ 600

T, P, HBO1, HBO2, HBO3 ≥ 0

2-8. ▲ *A Blending Problem (see Example 1).* Corey Ander's Spice Company has a limited amount of three ingredients that are used in the production of seasonings. Corey uses the three ingredients—HBO1, HBO2, and HBO3—to produce either turmeric or paprika. The marketing department reports that the firm can sell as much paprika as it can produce, but it can sell up to a maximum of 1700 bottles of turmeric. Unused ingredients can be sold on the open market. Prices are quoted in \$/ounce. The current prices are: HBO1-\$0.60, HBO2-\$0.70, HBO3-\$0.55. In addition, Corey has signed a contract to supply 600 bottles of paprika to Wal-Mart. Additional data are shown in Figure 2.35. Formulate Corey's problem as a revenue-maximizing LP.

	INGREDIENTS (oz/bottle)				
	HB01	**HB02**	**HB03**	**DEMAND (bottles)**	**SALES PRICE PER BOTTLE (\$)**
Turmeric	4	2	1	1700	3.25
Paprika	3	2	3	Unlimited	2.75
Availability (ounces)	8,000	9,000	7,000		

▲ FIGURE 2.35
Corey Ander's Spice Company

Let A_1 = thousand lbs of fertilizer I

A_2 = thousand lbs of fertilizer II

A_3 = thousand lbs of fertilizer III

The model is:

Min $10A_1 + 8A_2 + 7A_3$

s.t.

$25A_1 + 10A_2 + 5A_3 \geq 10$

$10A_1 + 5A_2 + 10A_3 \geq 7$

$5A_1 + 10A_2 + 5A_3 \geq 5$

$A_1, A_2, A_3 \geq 0$

2-9. ▲▲ *A Blending Problem.* Guy Wires, superintendent of buildings and grounds at Gotham University, is planning to put fertilizer on the grass in the quadrangle area early in the spring. The grass needs nitrogen, phosphorus, and potash in at least the amounts given in Figure 2.36. Three kinds of commercial fertilizer are available; analysis and prices are given in Figure 2.37. Guy can buy as much of each of these fertilizers as he wishes and mix them together before applying them to the grass. Formulate an LP model to determine how much of each fertilizer he should buy to satisfy the requirements at minimum cost.

MINERAL	MINIMUM WEIGHT (lb)
Nitrogen	10
Phosphorus	7
Potash	5

▲ FIGURE 2.36
Total Grass Requirements

▼ FIGURE 2.37
Fertilizer Characteristics (per 1000 lb)

FERTILIZER	NITROGEN CONTENT (lb)	PHOSPHORUS CONTENT (lb)	POTASH CONTENT (lb)	PRICE (\$)
I	25	10	5	10
II	10	5	10	8
III	5	10	5	7

Let x_{ij} be the number of cans shipped from warehouse *i* to retail outlet *j*.

The model is:

Min $5x_{11} + 7x_{12} + 6x_{13} + 8x_{21} + 9x_{22} + 10x_{23} + 4x_{31} + 3x_{32} + 11x_{33}$

2-10. ▲▲ Slick Oil Company has three warehouses from which it can ship products to any of three retail outlets. The demand in cans for the product Gunkout is 100 at retail outlet 1; 250 at outlet 2; and 150 at outlet 3. The inventory of Gunkout at warehouse 1 is 50; at warehouse 2 is 275; and at warehouse 3 is 175. The cost of transporting one unit of Gunkout from each warehouse to each retail outlet is given in Figure 2.38.

s.t.
$x_{11} + x_{12} + x_{13} \leq 50$
$x_{21} + x_{22} + x_{23} \leq 275$
$x_{31} + x_{32} + x_{33} \leq 175$
$x_{11} + x_{21} + x_{31} \geq 100$
$x_{12} + x_{22} + x_{32} \geq 250$
$x_{13} + x_{23} + x_{33} \geq 150$
$x_{ij} \geq 0;\ i, j = 1, 2, 3.$

	RETAILER		
WAREHOUSE	**1**	**2**	**3**
1	5	7	6
2	8	9	10
3	4	3	11

▲ FIGURE 2.38
Shipping Costs

Formulate an LP to determine how many units should be shipped from each warehouse to each retailer so the demand at each retailer is met at minimum cost.

Let X = pounds of product 1
Y = pounds of product 2
The model is:
Max 4X + 3Y
s.t.
3X + 2Y ≤ 10
1X + 4Y ≤ 16
5X + 3Y ≤ 12
X, Y, ≥ 0

2-11. ▲▲ Two products are manufactured on each of three machines. A pound of each product requires a specified number of hours on each machine, as presented in Figure 2.39. Total hours available on machines 1, 2, and 3 are 10, 16, and 12, respectively. The profit contributions per pound of products 1 and 2 are $4 and $3, respectively. Define the decision variables and formulate this problem as a profit-maximizing linear program.

	MACHINE-HOUR REQUIREMENT	
MACHINE	**Product 1**	**Product 2**
1	3	2
2	1	4
3	5	3

▲ FIGURE 2.39
Machine-Time Data (hr)

Let S = sedans produced,
W = wagons produced,
C = coupes produced
The model is:
Min 12S + 15W + 24C
s.t.
6000S + 8000W + 11000C ≥ 12,000,000
S ≥ 100
W ≥ 200
C ≥ 300
S, W, C ≥ 0

2-12. ▲▲ Sally's Solar Car Co. has a plant that can manufacture family sedans, station wagons, and sports coupes. The selling price, variable cost, and fixed cost for manufacturing these cars are given in Figure 2.40.

MODEL	PROFIT CONTRIBUTION ($)	VARIABLE PRODUCTION TIME (hours)	FIXED COST ($)
Sedan	6,000	12	2,000,000
Station Wagon	8,000	15	3,000,000
Coupe	11,000	24	7,000,000

▲ FIGURE 2.40
Solar Car Data

Sally currently has orders for 100 sedans, 200 station wagons, and 300 coupes. She must satisfy these orders. She wants to plan production so she will break even as quickly as possible—that is, she wants to make sure that the total contribution margin will equal total fixed costs and that total variable production cost is minimized. Formulate this problem as an LP.

Let U = units of Umidaire
D = units of Depollinator
The model is:
Min 240U + 360D
s.t.
210U + 340D = 390,000
U ≥ 500
U, D ≥ 0

2-13. ▲▲ *Break-Even Analysis (see Example 6).* Reese Eichler, a manufacturer of superfluous air filtration equipment, produces two units, the Umidaire and the Depollinator. Data pertaining to sales price and costs are shown in Figure 2.41. Reese's firm has already contracted to provide 500 Umidaires and would like to calculate the break-even quantities for both types of units. Formulate the cost-minimizing LP model.

PRODUCT	SELLING PRICE PER UNIT ($)	VARIABLE COST PER UNIT ($)	FIXED COST ($)
Umidaire	450	240	150,000
Depollinator	700	360	240,000

▲ FIGURE 2.41
Sales Price and Cost

See IM.

2-14. ▲▲ Wonka Widget, Inc. faces the following three-period inventory problem. The manufacturing cost per widget varies from period to period. These costs are \$2, \$4, and \$3 for periods 1, 2, and 3 respectively. A cost of \$1 is incurred for each unit of inventory that is carried from one period to the next. Demand is 10,000, 20,000, and 30,000 units in periods 1, 2, and 3 respectively. Formulate an LP to determine how much the manufacturer should produce during each period to satisfy demand at minimum cost.

Let TB = millions of \$ in Treasury Bonds
CS = millions of \$ in Common Stock
MM = millions of \$ in Money Markets
MB = millions of \$ in Municipal Bonds
The model is:
Max $.08TB + .06CS + .12MM + .09MB$
s.t.
$TB \le 5$
$CS \le 7$
$MM \le 2$
$MB \le 4$
$TB + CS \ge 3$
$MM + MB \le 4$
$TB + CS + MM + MB = 10$
$TB, CS, MM, MB \ge 0$

2-15. ▲▲ *Portfolio Planning.* An investment company currently has \$10 million to invest. The goal is to maximize expected return earned over the next year. Their four investment possibilities are summarized in Figure 2.42. In addition, the company has specified that at least 30% of the funds must be placed in common stock and treasury bonds, and no more than 40% in money market funds and municipal bonds. All of the \$10 million currently on hand will be invested. Formulate an LP model that tells how much money to invest in each instrument.

INVESTMENT POSSIBILITY	EXPECTED EARNED RETURN (%)	MAXIMUM ALLOWABLE INVESTMENT (MILLIONS \$)
Treasury Bonds	8	5
Common Stock	6	7
Money Market	12	2
Municipal Bonds	9	4

▲ FIGURE 2.42
Summary of Investment Possibilities

See IM.

2-16. ▲▲ A manufacturer faces a three-period inventory problem for an item sale priced at \$4. The manufacturing cost is \$4 during the first period and \$3 during the other two periods. The demand and inventory costs are the same as in Problem 2-14. The manufacturer does not have to meet the demand. However, each unit of lost sales costs them \$1.50. The production is restricted to 40,000 units during the first period and to 10,000 units during the other two periods. Formulate an LP to determine the production schedule that maximizes their profit.

Let A_i = number of packages shipped to wholesaler i from packing location 1
B_i = number of packages shipped to wholesaler i from packing location 2
The model is:
Min $5.31A_1 + 5.29A_2 + 5.37A_3 + 5.34A_4 + 5.30A_5 + 5.85B_1 + 5.79B_2 + 5.75B_3 + 5.78B_4 + 5.78B_5$
s.t.
$A_1 + B_1 = 4000$
$A_2 + B_2 = 6000$

2-17. ▲▲ *Transportation Model (see Example 4).* Bob Frapples packages holiday gift-wrapped exotic fruits. His packages are wrapped at two locations from which they are sent to five wholesalers. The costs of packaging at locations 1 and 2 are \$5.25 and \$5.70, respectively. Bob's forecasts indicate demand for shipments as in Figure 2.43. Wrapping capacity at location 1 is 20,000 packages and at location 2 is 12,000 packages. The distribution costs from the two locations to the five wholesalers are given in Figure 2.44. Formulate an LP model to determine how many packages Bob should send from each location to each wholesaler.

▼ FIGURE 2.43
Wholesaler Demand

WHOLESALER	1	2	3	4	5
Shipment Required	4000	6000	2000	10,000	8000

$A_3 + B_3 = 2000$
$A_4 + B_4 = 10000$
$A_5 + B_5 = 8000$
$A_1 + A_2 + A_3 + A_4 + A_5 \leq 20000$
$B_1 + B_2 + B_3 + B_4 + B_5 \leq 12000$
$A_i, B_i \geq 0$

FROM LOCATION	TO WHOLESALER ($)				
	1	2	3	4	5
1	0.06	0.04	0.12	0.09	0.05
2	0.15	0.09	0.05	0.08	0.08

▲ FIGURE 2.44
Distribution Costs

More-challenging problems ▲▲▲

2-18. *A Scheduling Problem.* In a calculated financial maneuver, **PROTRAC** has acquired a new blast furnace facility for producing foundry iron. The company's management science group has been assigned the task of providing support for the quantitative planning of foundry activities. The first directive is to provide an answer to the following question: How many new slag-pit personnel should be hired and trained over the next six months? The requirements for trained employees in the pits and monthly wage rates for the next six months are given in Figure 2.45.

See IM.

	MONTH					
	Jan.	**Feb.**	**Mar.**	**Apr.**	**May**	**June**
Labor Requirements (hr)	7800	7500	7500	9200	10000	9000
Monthly Wage Rates ($)	1200	1200	1300	1300	1400	1400

▲ FIGURE 2.45
Labor Requirements and Wage Rates

Trainees are hired at the beginning of each month. One consideration to take into account is the union rule that workers must have one month of classroom instruction before they can work in the pits. Therefore, a trainee must be hired at least a month before a worker is actually needed. Each classroom student uses 80 hours of a trained slag-pit employee's time, so the employee has 80 less hours for work in the pit. Also, by contractual agreement, each trained employee can work up to 165 hours a month (total time, instructing plus in the pit). If the maximum total time available from trained employees exceeds a month's requirements, management may lay off at most 15% of the trained employees at the beginning of the month. All employees are paid a full month's salary even if they are laid off. A trainee costs $600 a month in salary and other benefits. There are 40 trained employees available at the beginning of January. Formulate the hiring-and-training problem as a linear programming model. HINT: Let x_t denote the number of trained employees on hand at the beginning month t before any layoffs, let y_t denote the number of trainees hired in month t, and let z_t denote the number of trained employees laid off at the beginning of month t.

See IM.

2-19. ▲▲▲ *Farm Management.* A firm operates four farms of comparable productivity. Each farm has a certain amount of usable acreage and a supply of labor hours to plant and tend the crops. The data for the upcoming season are shown in Figure 2.46. The organization is considering three crops for planting. These crops differ primarily in their expected profit per acre and in the amount of labor they require, as shown in Figure 2.47. Furthermore, the total acreage that can be devoted to any particular crop is limited by the associated requirements for harvesting equipment. In order to maintain a roughly uniform work load among the farms, management's policy is that the percentage of usable acreage planted must be the same at each farm. However, any combination of the crops may be grown at any of the farms as long as all constraints are satisfied (including the uniform-work-load requirement). Management wishes to know how many acres of each crop should be planted at the respective farms in order to maximize expected profit. Formulate this as a linear programming model.

FARM	USABLE ACREAGE	LABOR HOURS AVAILABLE PER MONTH
1	500	1700
2	900	3000
3	300	900
4	700	2200

▲ FIGURE 2.46
Acreage and Labor Data by Farm

CROP	MAXIMUM ACREAGE	MONTHLY LABOR HOURS REQUIRED PER ACRE	EXPECTED PROFIT PER ACRE ($)
A	700	2	500
B	800	4	200
C	300	3	300

▲ FIGURE 2.47
Acreage, Labor, and Profit Data by Crop

Let X_{ij} = gallons of vintage i in Blend j (i = 1,2,3,4; j = A,B,C)
The model is:
Max $80X_{1A} + 80X_{2A} + 80X_{3A} + 80X_{4A} + 50X_{1B} + 50X_{2B} + 50X_{3B} + 50X_{4B} + 35X_{1C} + 35X_{2C} + 35X_{3C} + 35X_{4C}$
s.t.
$X_{1A} + X_{1B} + X_{1C} \leq 130$
$X_{2A} + X_{2B} + X_{2C} \leq 200$
$X_{3A} + X_{3B} + X_{3C} \leq 150$
$X_{4A} + X_{4B} + X_{4C} \leq 350$
$X_{2A} + X_{3A} \geq .75X_{1A} + .75X_{2A} + .75X_{3A} + .75X_{4A}$
$X_{4A} \geq .08X_{1A} + .08X_{2A} + .08X_{3A} + .08X_{4A}$
$X_{2B} \geq .10X_{1B} + .10X_{2B} + .10X_{3B} + .10X_{4B}$
$X_{4B} \leq .35X_{1B} + .35X_{2B} + .35X_{3B} + .35X_{4B}$
$X_{2C} + X_{3C} \geq .35X_{1C} + .35X_{2C} + .35X_{3C} + .35X_{4C}$
$X_{ij} \geq 0$, (i = 1,2,3,4; j = A, B, C)

2-20. ▲▲▲ *A Blending Problem.* A vineyard wishes to blend four different vintages to make three types of blended wine. The supply of the vintages and the sales prices of the blended wines are shown in Figure 2.48, together with certain restrictions on the percentage composition of the three blends. In particular, vintages 2 and 3 together must make up at least 75% of Blend A and at least 35% of Blend C. In addition, Blend A must contain at least 8% of vintage 4, while Blend B must contain at least 10% of vintage 2 and at most 35% of vintage 4. Any amounts of Blends A, B, and C can be sold. Formulate an LP model that will make the best use of the vintages on hand.

BLEND	VINTAGE 1	VINTAGE 2	VINTAGE 3	VINTAGE 4	SALES PRICE PER GALLON
A	*	at least 75% 2 & 3 in any proportion		at least 8%	80
B	*	at least 10%	*	at most 35%	50
C	*	at least 35% 2 & 3 in any proportion		*	35
SUPPLY (gallons)	130	200	150	350	

*indicates no restriction

▲ FIGURE 2.48
Composition of Blends

Let W_i = number of waiters who start their workweek on day i (Monday = 1)
The model is:
Min $W_1 + W_2 + W_3 + W_4 + W_5 + W_6 + W_7$
s.t.
$6(W_1 + W_4 + W_5 + W_6 + W_7) \geq 150$

2-21. ▲▲▲ *A Scheduling Problem (see Example 3).* A certain restaurant operates 7 days a week. Waiters are hired to work 6 hours per day. The union contract specifies that each must work 5 consecutive days and then have 2 consecutive days off. All waiters receive the same weekly salary. Staffing requirements are shown in Figure 2.49. Assume that this cycle of requirements repeats indefinitely, and ignore the fact that the number of waiters hired must be an integer. The manager wishes to find an employment schedule that satisfies these requirements at a minimum cost. Formulate this problem as a linear program.

$6(W_1 + W_2 + W_5 + W_6 + W_7) \geq 200$
$6(W_1 + W_2 + W_3 + W_6 + W_7) \geq 400$
$6(W_1 + W_2 + W_3 + W_4 + W_7) \geq 300$
$6(W_1 + W_2 + W_3 + W_4 + W_5) \geq 700$
$6(W_2 + W_3 + W_4 + W_5 + W_6) \geq 800$
$6(W_3 + W_4 + W_5 + W_6 + W_7) \geq 300$
$W_i \geq 0$

DAY	MINIMUM NUMBER OF WAITER HOURS REQUIRED
Monday	150
Tuesday	200
Wednesday	400
Thursday	300
Friday	700
Saturday	800
Sunday	300

▲ FIGURE 2.49
Staffing Requirements

Let A,B,C,D be the pounds of each of these products produced and sold
M_i = time in minutes used on machine i (i = 1,2,3,4)
The model is:
Max $5A + 6B + 5C + 4D - (2/60)M_1 - (2/60)M_2 - (3/60)M_3 - (3/60)M_4$
s.t.
$5A + 3B + 4C + 4D = M_1$
$10A + 6B + 5C + 2D = M_2$
$6A + 4B + 3C + D = M_3$
$3A + 8B + 3C + 2D = M_4$
$M_1 \leq 3600$
$M_2 \leq 3600$
$M_3 \leq 3600$
$M_4 \leq 3600$
$A \leq 400$
$B \leq 100$
$C \leq 150$
$D \leq 500$
All variables ≥ 0

2-22. ▲▲▲ *A Production Problem.* A plant can manufacture four different products (A, B, C, D) in any combination. Each product requires time on each of four machines as shown in Figure 2.50. Each machine is available 60 hours per week. Products A, B, C, and D may be sold at prices of \$9, \$7, \$6, \$5 per pound, respectively. Variable labor costs are \$2 per hour for machines 1 and 2 and \$3 per hour for machines 3 and 4. Material cost for each pound of product A is \$4. The material cost is \$1 for each pound of products B, C, and D. Formulate a profit-maximizing LP model for this problem.

PRODUCT	MACHINE 1	2	3	4	MAXIMUM DEMAND
A	5	10	6	3	400
B	3	6	4	8	100
C	4	5	3	3	150
D	4	2	1	2	500

▲ FIGURE 2.50
Machine Time (Minutes per Pound of Product)

See IM.

2-23. ▲▲▲ A manufacturer has four jobs, A, B, C, and D, that must be produced this month. Each job may be handled in any of three shops. The time required for each job in each shop, the cost per hour in each shop, and the number of hours available this month in each shop are given in Figure 2.51. It is also possible to split each job among the shops in any proportion. For example, one-fourth of job A can be done in 8 hours in shop 1, and one-third of job C can be done in 19 hours in shop 3. The manufacturer wishes to determine how many hours of each job should be handled by each shop in order to minimize the total cost of completing all four jobs. Identify the decision variables and formulate an LP model for this problem.

SHOP	TIME REQUIRED (hr) A	B	C	D	COST PER HOUR OF SHOP TIME (\$)	SHOP TIME AVAILABLE (hr)
1	32	151	72	118	89	160
2	39	147	61	126	81	160
3	46	155	57	121	84	160

▲ FIGURE 2.51
Job-Shop Data

See IM.

2-24. ▲▲▲ *Financial Planning.* An investor has two money-making activities, coded Alpha and Beta, available at the beginning of each of the next four years. Each dollar invested in

Alpha at the beginning of a year yields a return two years later (in time for immediate reinvestment). Each dollar invested in Beta at the beginning of a year yields a return three years later. A third investment possibility, construction projects, will become available at the beginning of the second year. Each dollar invested in construction yields a return one year later. (This option will be available at the beginning of the third and fourth years also.) The investor starts with \$50,000 at the beginning of the first year and wants to maximize the total amount of money available at the end of the fourth year. The returns on investments are given in Figure 2.52.

(a) Identify the decision variables and formulate an LP model. HINT: Let M_i be the money available at the beginning of year i and maximize M_5 subject to the appropriate constraints.

(b) Can you determine the solution by direct analysis?

ACTIVITY	RETURN PER DOLLAR INVESTED (\$)
Alpha	1.50
Beta	1.80
Construction	1.20

▲ FIGURE 2.52
Return on Investment

Let X_1 = hours of process 1 used
X_2 = hours of process 2 used
The model is:
Max $p_1X_1 + p_2X_2$
s.t.
$3X_1 + 12X_2 \leq 300$
$9X_1 + 6X_2 \leq 450$
$15X_1 + 9X_2 \geq 600$
$6X_1 + 24X_2 \geq 225$
$X_1, X_2 \geq 0$

2-25. ▲▲▲ *A Process Mix Problem.* A small firm has two processes for blending each of two products, charcoal starter fluid and lighter fluid for cigarette lighters. The firm is attempting to decide how many hours to run each process. The inputs and outputs for running the processes for one hour are given in Figure 2.53. Let x_1 and x_2 be the number of hours the company decides to use process 1 and process 2, respectively. Because of a federal allocation program, the maximum amounts of kerosene and benzene available are 300 units and 450 units, respectively. Sales commitments require that at least 600 units of starter fluid and 225 units of lighter fluid be produced. The per hour profits that accrue from process 1 and process 2 are p_1 and p_2 respectively. Formulate this as a profit-maximizing linear programming model.

	INPUTS		OUTPUTS	
PROCESS	Kerosene	Benzene	Starter Fluid	Lighter Fluid
1	3	9	15	6
2	12	6	9	24

▲ FIGURE 2.53
Units of Input and Output per Hour

See IM.

2-26. ▲▲▲ *A Scheduling Problem.* While it is operating out of Stockholm, the aircraft carrier *Mighty* is on maneuvers from Monday through Friday and in port over the weekend. Next week the captain would like to give shore leave for Monday through Friday to as many of the 2500-sailor crew as possible. However, he must carry out the maneuvers for the week and satisfy navy regulations. The regulations are

(a) Sailors work either the A.M. shift (midnight to noon) or the P.M. shift (noon to midnight) any day they work, and during a week they must remain on the same shift every day they work.

(b) Each sailor who works must be on duty exactly four days, even if there is not enough "real work" on some days.

The number of sailors required each shift of each day is shown in Figure 2.54. Formulate this problem as a linear programming problem. Define your variables in such a way that it is obvious how to implement the solution if one were to solve the LP you suggest (i.e., so that one would know how many sailors work on each day).

	M	TU	W	TH	F
A.M.	900	1000	450	800	700
P.M.	800	500	1000	300	750

▲ FIGURE 2.54
Sailors per Shift Day

See IM.

2-27. ▲▲▲ In the human diet, 16 essential nutrients have been identified. Suppose that there are 116 foods. A pound of food j contains a_{ij} pounds of nutrient i. Suppose that a human being must have N_i pounds of each nutrient i in the daily diet and that a pound of food j costs c_j cents. What is the least-cost daily diet satisfying all nutritional requirements? Use summation notation in the formulation of this problem. Aside from the question of palatability, can you think of an important constraint that this problem omits?

See IM.

2-28. ▲▲▲ *An Arbitrage Problem.* A speculator operates a silo with a capacity of 6000 bushels for storing corn. At the beginning of month 1, the silo contains 5000 bushels. Estimates of the selling and purchase prices of corn during the next four months are given in Figure 2.55. Corn sold during any given month is removed from the silo at the beginning of that month. Thus 5000 bushels are available for sale in month 1. Corn bought during any given month is put into the silo during the middle of that month, but it cannot be sold until the following month. Assume that the cost of storing the corn is based on average inventory and that it costs \$0.01 to store one bushel for one month. The storage cost for a month must be paid at the end of the month. All purchases must be paid for with cash by the delivery time. The speculator has \$100 to invest and has no intention of borrowing to buy corn or pay storage costs. Therefore, if he has no cash at the beginning of a month, he must sell some of his stock to pay the storage charge at the end of the month and to pay for the corn if he purchases any. Given the sales and purchase prices and the storage cost, the speculator wishes to know how much corn to buy and sell each month so as to maximize total profits shortly after the beginning of the fourth month (which means after any sale that may occur in that month). Formulate an LP model for this problem. HINT: Let A_t denote bushels in the silo immediately after delivering the quantity sold in month t (x_t), and B_t bushels in the silo immediately after receiving the quantity purchased in month t (y_t), and P_t the cash position at the end of month t.

MONTH	PURCHASE PRICE PER 1000 BUSHELS (\$)	SELLING PRICE PER 1000 BUSHELS (\$)
1	45	40
2	50	45
3	60	56
4	70	65

▲ FIGURE 2.55
Selling and Purchase Price Data

The model is:
Min $20P_1 + 20P_2 + \ldots + 22P_9 + .2(I_1 + I_2 + \ldots + I_9)$
s.t.
$I_1 = P_1 - 1000$
$I_2 = I_1 + P_2 - 900$
⋮
$I_9 = I_8 + P_9 - 500$
$I_t, P_t \geq 0 \; t = 1, \ldots 9$

2-29. ▲▲▲ *Purchasing.* Jack Bienstaulk is responsible for purchasing canned goods for GAGA food service at a large university. He knows what the demand will be over the course of the school year, and he has estimated purchase prices as well. These data are shown in Figure 2.56. He may purchase ahead of demand to avoid price increases, but there is a cost of carrying inventory of \$0.20 per case per month applied to inventory on hand at the end of a month. Formulate a cost-minimizing LP that will help Jack determine the timing of his purchases. HINT: Let P_t be the number of cases purchased in month t and I_t be the number of cases in inventory at the end of month t.

Problems 2-30 to 2-34 require the use of LOTUS 1-2-3 to formulate and VINO or What'sBest! to optimize.

	SEP.	OCT.	NOV.	DEC.	JAN.	FEB.	MAR.	APR.	MAY
Demand (cases)	1000	900	850	500	600	1000	1000	1000	500
Cost per Case $	20	20	20	21	21	21	22	22	22

▲ FIGURE 2.56
Demand and Cost Data

Spreadsheet-related problems

See IM.

2-30. *Portfolio Planning with the CAPM Model.* (*Note:* This problem will be especially interesting to students with a background in investments. Others should be cautioned that it includes terms not defined in this text.) An investment company currently has \$10 million to invest. Its goal is to maximize expected return over the next year. The company wants to use the capital asset pricing model (CAPM) to determine each investment's expected return. The CAPM formula is:

$$ER = Rf + b\,(Rm - Rf)$$

where

ER = expected return

Rf = risk-free rate

b = investment beta (market risk)

Rm = market return

The market return and risk-free rate fluctuate, and the company wants to be able to reevaluate its decision on a weekly basis. Its four investment possibilities are summarized in Figure 2.57. In addition, the company has specified that at least 30% of the funds must be placed in treasury bonds and money markets, and no more than 40% in common stock and municipal bonds. All of the \$10 million currently on hand will be invested.

(a) Formulate this problem as an LP model using LOTUS 1-2-3 and VINO or What's*Best*! The spreadsheet should be constructed in such a way that the market return and the risk-free are entered directly and the appropriate LP model is generated.

(b) Optimize the model if the market return is 12% and the risk-free rate is 6%.

INVESTMENT POSSIBILITY	BETA	MAXIMUM ALLOWABLE INVESTMENT (MILLIONS $)
Treasury Bonds	0	7
Common Stock	1	2
Money market	$\frac{1}{3}$	5
Municipal Bonds	$\frac{1}{2}$	4

▲ FIGURE 2.57

See IM.

2.31. *Work Force and Production Planning.* Review the **PROTRAC** E and F model discussed in Section 2.2. (see Figures 2.3 through 2.7). Now assume that the available production hours in departments A and B depend on the number of workers assigned to each department. Management decides that it is reasonable to approximate the capacity in these departments with the functions shown below:

$$\text{Capacity Dept. A} = 200(1 - e^{-0.05(MA)})$$
$$\text{Capacity Dept. B} = 250(1 - e^{-0.08(MB)})$$

where MA and MB are the number of people assigned to departments A and B respectively. In the original version of this problem, it was assumed that 28 people were assigned to department A (i.e., $MA = 28$) and 13 were assigned to department B (i.e., $MB = 13$). Thus

$$\text{Capacity Dept. A} = 200(1 - e^{-1.4}) = 150.68$$
$$\text{Capacity Dept. B} = 250(1 - e^{-1.04}) = 161.64$$

The capacities were rounded to 150 and 160 respectively for that particular problem.

(a) Create a spreadsheet in which the number of people in departments A and B and the number of units of E and F can be entered directly. The resulting spreadsheet should include all of the information presented in the spreadsheet in Figure 2.6.

(b) Assume that 36 people are assigned to department A and 17 people are assigned to department B. Use your spreadsheet to determine if the plan $E = 6$ and $F = 9$ is feasible and what profit it would yield. Find the best solution you can in three attempts.

(c) Use VINO or What's*Best*! to find the optimal production policy when $MA = 36$ and $MB = 17$.

(d) Assume $MA = 28$. Plot the optimal profit as a function of MB for MB ranging from 10 to 30 in intervals of 2. To do this, your optimizer will have to be run 11 times and you then plot the data. Alternatively, after the 11 runs of data have been obtained, you may wish to use the graphics capabilities of LOTUS 1–2–3 to plot the data. What phenomenon does the graph of this optimal profit function illustrate?

More-difficult spreadsheet exercises

The following three problems are for those who wish to have more practice and depth in spreadsheet usage. The problems illustrate LOTUS 1–2–3 capabilities for "table lookups," use of a SUM function, and use of the IF function. These features are explained in the LOTUS 1–2–3 manual. In the answers to these problems you will see a "$" symbol in some of the formulas. This symbol can be ignored in reading these formulas. The "$" symbol is yet another useful feature of LOTUS 1–2–3, one that makes it easier to construct and copy expressions. Your LOTUS 1–2–3 manual will explain this usage.

See IM.

2-32. *Waitress Scheduling. Using Table Lookup* (*see Example 3 and Problem 2-21*). In order to create the spreadsheet for this problem, you will need to use a "Table Lookup" command. This shows another versatile feature of spreadsheet usage. A certain restaurant operates 7 days a week. Waitresses are hired to work 6 effective hours per day. The restaurant attracts individuals and small groups, which we will call regular demand. In addition, the restaurant attracts a number of larger groups (Rotary, Lions, Quarterback Club, etc.) that schedule weekly meetings. The union contract specifies that each waitress must work 5 consecutive days and then have 2 consecutive days off. All waitresses receive the same weekly salary. The minimum required waitress hours is a function of the regular daily demand plus the waitress hours needed to staff the scheduled group meetings for the day. The regular daily demands (in waitress hours) and the number of group meetings currently scheduled each day are given in Figure 2.58. The manager uses the table in Figure 2.59 to determine the waitress hours required for the larger group meetings. The manager would like to find an employment schedule that satisfies required waitress hours at a minimum cost. Assume that this

▼ FIGURE 2.58

	REGULAR DAILY DEMAND (WAITRESS HOURS)	SCHEDULED LARGER GROUP MEETINGS
Monday	125	1
Tuesday	200	0
Wednesday	350	1
Thursday	300	0
Friday	650	3
Saturday	725	4
Sunday	250	2

cycle repeats indefinitely, and ignore the fact that the number of waitresses hired must be an integer.

(a) Create a spreadsheet representation of this LP using LOTUS 1–2–3. Because demand may change from time to time, the spreadsheet should be constructed in such a way that the "Scheduled Larger Group Meetings" data and the "Regular Daily Demand" data are entered directly into their own cells. Note that the table shown in Figure 2.59 must also be entered. The spreadsheet should represent the appropriate LP for any set of these data.

(b) Using VINO or What's*Best*!, optimize the spreadsheet for the data presented in Figures 2.58 and 2.59.

NO. OF GROUP MEETINGS/DAY	WAITRESS HOURS NEEDED
0	0
1	24
2	36
3	52
4	64
5	80

▲ FIGURE 2.59

See IM.

2-33. ▲▲▲ *Farm Management with the "SUM" Function* (*see Problem 2-19*). A firm operates four farms of comparable productivity. Each farm has a certain amount of usable acreage and a supply of labor hours to plant and tend the crops. The data for the upcoming season are shown in Figure 2.60. The organization is considering three crops for planting. These crops differ in their expected profit per acre and in the amount of labor required, as shown in Figure 2.61. Also shown is the fact that each crop requires a different type of harvester, with a different cost. The total acreage that can be devoted to any particular crop is limited by the firm's decision as to how many hours of harvesting equipment to rent. The firm has made a fixed investment of $19,000 in a harvesting equipment cooperative. For this investment, it can use any of the three types of harvesters at the costs given in Figure 2.61, up to the fixed $19,000. A harvester typically works at a slower rate when it is first put into operation on a farm. Each season, as the crew once again becomes familiar with the machine and any small problems are worked out the rate of production increases. This phenomenon is generally referred to as learning. In this case, the harvesting rate after t hours is given by

FARM	USABLE ACREAGE	LABOR HOURS AVAILABLE PER MONTH
1	500	1700
2	900	3000
3	300	900
4	700	2200

▲ FIGURE 2.60

CROP	MONTHLY LABOR HOURS REQUIRED PER ACRE	EXPECTED PROFIT PER ACRE ($)	λ	n	HARV. MACHINE COST/hr ($)
A	2	500	.02	2	15
B	4	200	.02	3	20
C	3	300	.03	1	20

▲ FIGURE 2.61

the equation

$$\text{rate} = n\,(1-e^{-\lambda t}) \text{ acres per hour}$$

where

n = long-run rate of harvesting, in acres per hour
λ = short-run adjustment factor

The total acreage harvestable in a certain time period, say T hours, can then be found by integrating the rate with respect to time:

$$\text{total acreage harvestable in } T \text{ hours} = \int_0^T n(1-e^{-\lambda t})dt$$
$$= n[T-(1/\lambda)(1-e^{-\lambda T})]$$

The long-run rates and short-run adjustment factors for each type of equipment can be found in Figure 2.61. Management has decided to use 400, 315, and 335 harvesting machine hours for crops A, B, and C, respectively. In order to maintain a roughly uniform work load among the farms, management's policy is that the percentage of usable acreage planted must be the same at all farms. However, any combination of the crops may be grown at any of the farms as long as all constraints are satisfied (including the uniform-work-load requirements). Managements wishes to know how many acres of each crop should be planted at the respective farms in order to maximize expected profit.

(a) Use LOTUS 1–2–3 and the "SUM function" in creating a spreadsheet representation of this LP. The spreadsheet should be constructed in such a way that the rental hours for each of the harvesting machines are entered directly. A cell should show the cost of the total hours requested. There should also be constraints that say, "the total acreage of each crop (across farms) cannot exceed total harvestble acreage for that crop."

(b) Optimize this model.

(c) Suggest another choice of harvesting machine hours that the farm could select. Does your choice yield a higher profit? Can you find a choice that does?

See IM.

2-34. ▲▲▲ *Producing Forestry and Earthmoving Equipment, Using the "If Function."* Suppose that forestry equipment produces a net revenue of \$802 per unit and requires 700 pounds of iron, 50 hours of labor, 30 hours of heat treatment, and 1 transmission per unit. Earthmoving equipment yields a net revenue of \$660 per unit and requires 4200 pounds of iron, 110 hours of labor, 12 hours of heat treatment, and 1 transmission per unit. The company's capacity during this period is 680,000 pounds of iron, 21,000 hours of labor, and 6000 hours of heat treatment. Transmissions are supplied by a wholly owned subsidiary that produces transmissions for the entire product line. The capacity for transmissions for forestry and earthmoving equipment is then determined by the number of production hours dedicated to their production at the subsidiary plant. Production of transmissions involves three phases: setup, startup, and regular production. The duration and production rates for these phases are given in Figure 2.62.

PHASES	DURATION (hrs)	TRANSMISSION (units/hr)
Setup	8	0
Startup	120	.5
Regular Production	—	1

▲ FIGURE 2.62

(a) For example, if 10 hours are available at the subsidiary, 8 of these are required for setup, during which there is no production, and 2 are in the startup phase, during which 2(.5) = 1 transmission would be produced. If $H \geq 128$ hours are used, 120 of the hours will produce .5 transmission/hr, while $H - 128$ hours will produce one transmission/hr. Hence, the total transmissions produced would be $60 + H - 128$

= H − 68. Show the equations that determine the limit on transmissions capacity if T hours are available at the subsidiary for T = 6, T = 108, T = 308.

(b) Evaluate the equations you created in (a). Your answers should be 0, 50, 240.

(c) Define the decision variables and formulate this as a revenue-maximizing linear program using LOTUS 1-2-3 and VINO or What's*Best*! The spreadsheet should be constructed in such a way that the number of labor hours in the subsidiary plant can be entered directly, and the appropriate constraint will be created in the LP. HINT: In your spreadsheet manual, read how to use the built-in @If function. In this problem, you can nest the @If to determine which phase the scheduled hours will reach.

(d) Find the optimal solution if 358 hours of production time are available at the subsidiary plant.

Case

Red Brand Canners*

Here is a simple but interesting case that captures several points that are important in real-world problem formulation. In any real problem it is important for the manager to distinguish between those facts and data that are relevant and those that are not. Distinguishing the two may be especially difficult because on occasion confused or incorrect concepts will be strongly held by members of the management team. This case is designed to reproduce such a situation. The present task will simply involve model formulation. You will deal with this case again, however, in Appendix 5.2, where you will be asked to produce solutions, analyses, critiques, and interpretations.

On Monday, September 13, 1965, Mitchell Gordon, vice-president of operations, asked the controller, the sales manager, and the production manager to meet with him to discuss the amount of tomato products to pack that season. The tomato crop, which had been purchased at planting, was beginning to arrive at the cannery, and packing operations would have to be started by the following Monday. Red Brand Canners was a medium-sized company that canned and distributed a variety of fruit and vegetable products under private brands in the western states.

William Cooper, the controller, and Charles Myers, the sales manager, were the first to arrive in Gordon's office. Dan Tucker, the production manager, came in a few minutes later and said that he had picked up Produce Inspection's latest estimate of the quality of the incoming tomatoes. According to their report, about 20 percent of the crop was grade "A" quality and the remaining portion of the 3,000,000-pound crop was grade "B."

Gordon asked Myers about the demand for tomato products for the coming year. Myers replied that for all practical purposes they could sell all the whole canned tomatoes they could produce. The expected demand for tomato juice and tomato paste, on the other hand, was limited. The sales manager then passed around the latest demand forecast, which is shown in Exhibit 1. He

EXHIBIT 1
Demand Forecasts

PRODUCT	SELLING PRICE PER CASE ($)	DEMAND FORECAST (CASES)
24-2½ Whole Tomatoes	4.00	800,000
24-2½ Choice Peach Halves	5.40	10,000
24-2½ Peach Nectar	4.60	5,000
24-2½ Tomato Juice	4.50	50,000
24-2½ Cooking Apples	4.90	15,000
24-2½ Tomato Paste	3.80	80,000

▼ EXHIBIT 2
Product Item Profitability

COSTS	24–2½ Whole Tomatoes	24–2½ Choice Peach Halves	24–2½ Peach Nectar	24–2½ Tomato Juice	24–2½ Cooking Apples	24–2½ Tomato Paste
Selling Price (per case)	$4.00	$5.40	$4.60	$4.50	$4.90	$3.80
Variable Costs						
Direct Labor	1.18	1.40	1.27	1.32	0.70	0.54
Variable Overhead	0.24	0.32	0.23	0.36	0.22	0.26
Variable Selling	0.40	0.30	0.40	0.85	0.28	0.38
Packaging Material	0.70	0.56	0.60	0.65	0.70	0.77
Fruit[a] (cost per case)	1.08	1.80	1.70	1.20	0.90	1.50
Total Variable Costs	3.60	4.38	4.20	4.38	2.80	3.45
Net Profit (per case)	0.40	1.02	.040	0.12	2.10	0.35

[a]Product usage is as given below.

PRODUCT	POUNDS PER CASE
Whole Tomatoes	18
Peach Halves	18
Peach Nectar	17
Tomato Juice	20
Cooking Apples	27
Tomato Paste	25

reminded the group that the selling prices had been set in light of the long-term marketing strategy of the company, and potential sales had been forecast at those prices.

Bill Cooper, after looking at Myers's estimates of demand, said that it looked as if the company "should use the entire crop for whole tomatoes and should do quite well (on the tomato crop) this year." With the new accounting system that had been set up, he had been able to compute the contribution for each product, and according to his analysis the incremental profit on the whole tomatoes was greater than for any other tomato product. In May, after Red Brand had signed contracts agreeing to purchase the growers' production at an average delivered price of 6 cents per pound, Cooper had computed the tomato products' contributions (see Exhibit 2).

Dan Tucker brought to Cooper's attention that, although there was ample production capacity, it was impossible to produce all whole tomatoes, because too small a portion of the tomato crop was "A" quality. Red Brand used a numerical scale to record the quality of both raw produce and prepared products. This scale ran from zero to ten, the higher number representing better quality. Rating tomatoes according to this scale, "A" tomatoes averaged nine points per pound and "B" tomatoes averaged five points per pound. Tucker noted that the minimum average input quality for canned whole tomatoes was 8 points per pound, and for juice it was 6. Paste could be made entirely from "B" grade tomatoes. Thus whole tomato production was limited to 800,000 pounds.

Gordon stated that this was not a real limitation. He had recently been solicited to purchase any amount up to 80,000 pounds of grade "A" tomatoes at 8½ cents per pound and at that time had turned down the offer. He felt, however, that the tomatoes were still available.

Myers, who had been doing some calculations, said that although he agreed that the company "should do quite well this year," it would not be by canning whole tomatoes. It seemed to him that the tomato cost should be allocated on the basis of quality and quantity rather than by quantity only, as Cooper had done. Therefore, he had recomputed the marginal profit on this basis (see Exhibit 3), and from his results, Red Brand should use 2 million pounds of the "B" tomatoes for paste, and the remaining 400,000 pounds of "B" tomatoes and all the "A" tomatoes for juice.

▼ EXHIBIT 3
Marginal Analysis of Tomato Products

Z = cost per pound of "A" tomatoes in cents
Y = cost per pound of "B" tomatoes in cents
(1) (600,000 lb × Z) + (2,400,000 lb × Y) = (3,000,000 lb × 6)

(2) $\frac{Z}{9} = \frac{Y}{5}$

Z = 9.32 cents per pound
Y = 5.18 cents per pound

PRODUCT	CANNED WHOLE TOMATOES	TOMATO JUICE	TOMATO PASTE
Selling Price	$4.00	$4.50	$3.80
Variable Cost (excluding Tomato Cost)	2.52	3.18	1.95
	$1.48	$1.32	$1.85
Tomato Cost	1.49	1.24	1.30
Marginal Profit	($0.01)	$0.08	$0.55

If the demand expectations were realized, a contribution of $48,000 would be made of this year's tomato crop.

Questions

1. Why does Tucker state that the whole tomato production is limited to 800,000 pounds (i.e., where does the number 800,000 come from)?
2. What is wrong with Cooper's suggestion to use the entire crop for whole tomatoes?
3. How does Myers compute his tomato costs in Exhibit 3? How does he reach his conclusion that the company should use 2,000,000 pounds "B" tomatoes for paste, the remaining 400,000 pounds of "B" tomatoes, and all of the "A" in juice? What is wrong with Myers's reasoning?
4. Without including the possibility of the additional purchases suggested by Gordon, formulate as an LP the problem of determining the optimal canning policy for this season's crop. Define your decision variables in terms of pounds of tomatoes. Express the objective function coefficients in cents per pound.
5. How should your model be modified to include the possibility of the additional purchases suggested by Gordon?

Alternate Questions for Red Brand Canners

Suppose Produce Inspection could use three grades to estimate the quality of the tomato crop. "A" tomatoes average nine points per pound, "B" tomatoes average six points per pound, and "C" tomatoes average three points per pound. Using this system their report would indicate that 600,000 pounds are grade "A" quality, 1,600,000 pounds are grade "B," and the remaining 800,000 pounds are grade "C." Paste has no minimum average quality requirement.

6. What is the maximum production in pounds of canned whole tomatoes? Can Cooper's suggestion be implemented?

Myers extends his analysis to three grades in Exhibit 4. On the basis of Exhibit 4, Myers recommends using all grade "C" tomatoes and 1,200,000 pounds of grade "B" tomatoes for paste, and all grade "A" tomatoes and all remaining grade "B" tomatoes for juice.

7. How does Myers compute his tomato costs in Exhibit 4? How does he reach his conclusion to use 800,000 pounds of grade "C" and 1,200,000 pounds of grade "B" for paste, and the rest of the tomatoes for juice? What is wrong with Myers's reasoning?
8. Without including the possibility of the additional purchases suggested by Gordon, formulate as an LP the problem of determining the optimal canning policy for this season's crop. Define your decision variables in terms of pounds of tomatoes. Express the objective function in cents.
9. How should your model be modified to include the possibility of the additional purchases suggested by Gordon?

EXHIBIT 4
Myers's Marginal Analysis

X = cost per pound of "C" tomatoes in cents

(1) (600,000 lb × Z) + (1,600,000 lb × Y) + (800,000 lb × X) = (3,000,000 lb × 6)

(2) $\frac{Z}{9} = \frac{Y}{6}$

(3) $\frac{Y}{6} = \frac{C}{3}$

Z = 9.31 cents per pound
Y = 6.21 cents per pound
X = 3.10 cents per pound

PRODUCT	CANNED WHOLE TOMATOES	TOMATO JUICE	TOMATO PASTE
Selling Price	$4.00	$4.50	$3.80
Variable Cost (excluding Tomato Cost)	2.52	3.18	1.95
	$1.48	$1.32	$1.85
Tomato Cost	1.49	1.24	.78
Marginal Profit	($0.01)	$0.08	$1.07

Case

An Application of Spreadsheet Analysis to Foreign Exchange Markets

The following case shows a more realistic and, as you might expect, more difficult, illustration of spreadsheet usage. The major purposes of this case are to show what the spreadsheet can do and to gain a more complete understanding of the logic captured by the spreadsheet through the formal LP model for this problem.

PROTRAC has manufacturing and sales operations in five major trading countries: United States, United Kingdom, France, Germany, and Japan. Due to the different cash needs in the various countries at various times, it is often necessary to move available funds from one country and denomination to another. In general, there will be numerous ways to rearrange funds to satisfy cash requirements out of availabilities. On this particular morning the divisions in France and Japan are short of cash. Specifically, the requirements are, respectively, 8 million francs and 1280 million yen. The divisions in the United States, Britain, and Germany are long on cash. They have surpluses of 2 million dollars, 5 million pounds, and 3 million marks. Since there are many possible ways of redistributing the cash to satisfy the shortages out of the surpluses, the issue to be addressed is how one compares the possible conversion strategies. Because of high short-term U.S. interest rates, the firm has decided to evaluate its final cash position by this measure: the equivalent total dollar value of its final cash holdings.

On this morning, as usual, at 7:00 A.M. Jack Walker, the corporate treasurer, and Ezra Brooks, V.P. for overseas operations, meet at corporate headquarters to determine what funds, if any, should be moved. Refer to Exhibits 1 and 2 on pp. 89–91 as you go through the dialogue. The conversation proceeds as follows:

EZRA: Good morning, Jack. I have something to show you. I've asked Fred to set this exchange problem up on a 1–2–3 spreadsheet. I think it will make our lives considerably easier.

JACK: I like the idea, but you'll have to tell me how to use it.

EZRA: Sure, Jack. It contains all the usual information, but let's go through it step by step. The figures in the rectangle defined by Columns B through F and Rows 5 through 9 are the exchange rates. If we let a_{ij} be the rate in row i and column j, then one unit of currency i will exchange for a_{ij} units of currency j. In fact, these data reflect the bid-ask prices. For example, if we sell one pound we get \$1.425. That is, 1.425 is the bid price, in dollars, for a pound. On the other hand, if we sell one dollar we will receive 0.6998 pounds. This means we can buy a pound for 1/0.6998 = \$1.429 (the asking price, in dollars, for a pound is 1.429). Hence the bid-ask spread is 1.425, 1.429. You can see that if we start with \$1 and buy as many pounds as possible and then use those pounds to buy dollars we end up with 0.6998 × 1.425 = \$0.9972 dollars—we lose money.

JACK: That's the transaction cost. So obviously we want to minimize these transaction costs by not moving more money around than we have to. But where does this spreadsheet say something about our cash needs today?

EZRA: Our current cash holdings are shown in column B Rows 32 to 36. All figures are in millions; we have 2 million dollars, 5 million pounds and 3 million marks. Our requirements appear in column F in the same rows. You can see that we need 8 million French francs and 1280 million yen. As you know, our policy is to satisfy requirements in such a way that the dollar value of final holdings is maximized.

JACK: Great! So let's figure out what to do.

EZRA: That's the good part. We simply put our decisions in the appropriate cells in the section labeled "Currency Transactions" and the program does all the calculations. I've already entered what I think would be our typical decisions in this set of circumstances. Cells *B*19 through *B*25 show that I've sold 2.64 million marks and 4.00 million pounds in return for 6.70135 million dollars. I've then taken a million of those dollars and purchased 8.078 million francs, and with the remaining 5.70 million dollars I bought 1280.79 million yen. All of these numbers appear in cells *D*19, *F*19, *D*25, and *F*25 of the Currency Transactions section. For example you see in *D*19 that we used 1 million dollars to buy francs, and *D*25 shows that this purchase yielded 8.078 million francs. You can see by comparing *C*32 through *C*36 with *F*32 through *F*36 that we have satisfied our goals. Indeed, *G*32 through *G*36 show how much additional cash we have in each denomination. As you can see, the policy I've entered gives final holdings worth 10.24922 million dollars.

JACK: I see that we've met our cash requirements, and 1–2–3 certainly makes the calculations easier, but you know how I am, Ez. I'd feel that I understood better if I could see all of the formulas used to do the calculations.

EZRA: That's easy. I'll simply print out the symbolic spreadsheet and you can look through it at your leisure!

JACK *(Some time later that morning.):* All of this seems clear, Ez, but why did we follow such a complicated strategy?

EZRA: As you know, we have always run our exchange operation through Country Bank in New York, and this is their recommended strategy.

JACK: I guess that seeing the problem in the spreadsheet representation makes it easier to think about the trading strategy. I sure would like to know if this really is a good approach.

EZRA: I worried about that for a while, too, but the foreign exchange market is very efficient for these major currencies, so it probably doesn't make much difference what strategy we follow.

JACK: I can't say that banal invocations of efficiency make me any more confident. As you know, I've made millions exploiting inefficiencies. Anyway, I don't have more time this morning to look for a better approach. Let's go with what we have.

As you are already aware, the foreign exchange problem presented in Exhibits 1 and 2 (pp. 89-91) is an LP problem, and the optimal solution can be easily found with VINO or What's *Best!* The spreadsheet for the optimal solution is shown in Exhibit 3 on p. 92. The optimal dollar value of the final cash positions is 10.26839, as compared with the 10.2492 that was obtained with Ezra's solution. We note that in some sense Ezra is right. The difference is less than .2%: (10,268,390 − 10,249,220)/10,268,390 = .001867. On the other hand, when large sums are being transferred, even a small percentage can be a lot of money. In this example, the difference is \$19,170, a handsome quantity that can be captured with almost no effort.

Questions

1. Write out the formal LP model for the foreign exchange problem. In your model use the following notation for the data given in the problem description:

a_{ij} = exchange rate from currency i into

currency j (i.e., 1 unit of currency i will exchange for a_{ij} units of currency j)

c_i = ½(a_{i1} + 1/a_{1i}) = "average dollar value" of currency i

b_i = initial holding in currency i

L_i = minimum amount of currency i required as final holding

Denote the decision variables, as follows:

X_{ij} = amount of currency i changed into currency j, $j \neq i$

Y_i = final holding in currency i

2. In the dialogue, Jack says, "We want to minimize these transaction costs by not moving more money around than we have to." Suppose we define

OV_1 = maximum "average dollar value" that can be generated from initial holdings

Note that finding the value of OV_I requires more than simply evaluating each initial position in terms of average dollar value. For example, converting 1 pound to average dollar value gives \$1.42699; converting 1 pound to 11.55 francs to average dollar value gives (11.55)(.12360) = \$1.42758. Thus it is preferable to convert initial holdings of pounds into francs rather than to leave the pound position intact. In fact, in order to find OV_1 one must solve a linear program. The solution is shown in Exhibit 4 (p. 93), which was created by setting the final cash requirement to zero and then optimizing the value of final holdings. We see that OV_1 = 10.27773. Now let OV_2 = maximum "average dollar value" of final holdings subject to the cash requirements constraints. That is, OV_2 is the optimized objective value shown in Exhibit 3 (OV_2 = 10.26839).

In a case like this, as you will learn in Section 4.7, a more highly constrained LP cannot have a better OV than a less highly constrained LP, so it must always be true that $OV_2 \leq OV_1$. Let us define, for the problem,

$$\text{Transactions Costs} = OV_1 - OV_2$$

Using this definition, is the statement by Jack correct? That is, does the optimized solution in Exhibit 3 minimize transaction costs?

3. Recall the Conversion Strategies Spreadsheet presented in Exhibit 1. Use this spreadsheet and VINO or What's*BEST!* on your personal computer as required to answer the following questions:

(a) Suppose that the exchange rates for two currencies (say the franc and the mark) are such that if we start with 1 franc and execute the trade 1 franc → marks → francs we end up with more than 1 franc. What would the optimal value of the objective function be under these circumstances? What economic term is used to describe this condition?

(b) Comment on the following statement: If PROTRAC has no specific cash requirements, the optimal solution would be to stand pat (i.e., in order to maximize "average dollar value" of final holdings, one should do no trading).

(c) Comment on the following statement: Because the foreign exchange market is efficient, we have seen that the best solution isn't much better (in percentage terms) than Ezra's solution. It is also true, for the same reason, that the worst solution isn't much worse (again in percentage terms) than Ezra's. HINT: Find the solution that *minimizes* "average dollar value" of final holdings.

(d) Comment on the following statement: Consider a general problem like the PROTRAC problem. Such a problem might include hundreds of currencies. However, those currencies for which PROTRAC has no initial holding or no required cash position can be dropped from the formulation without affecting the optimal value of the objective function.

EXHIBIT 1
A Value Spreadsheet for Currency Trading

	A	B	C	D	E	F	G	H
1	CONVERSION STRATEGIES SPREADSHEET							
2	**Can Sell a Pound for $1.425 = Bid Price**			**Can Buy a Pound for $1.429 = Ask Price**				
3							''Dollar	**(1.425 + 1.429)/2**
4		Dollar	Pound	Franc	Mark	Yen	Value''	
5	Dollar	1.00000	0.69980	8.07800	2.62700	224.70	1.00000	
6	Pound	1.42500	1.00000	11.55000	3.75400	320.70	1.42699	
7	Franc	0.12340	0.08647	1.00000	0.32500	27.76000	0.12360	**This Row is Exchange Rates For 1 Franc**
8	Mark	0.37930	0.26620	3.07300	1.00000	85.51000	0.37998	
9	Yen	0.00443	0.00310	0.03586	0.01163	1.00000	0.00444	

10	--	
11		
12		******************************
13		Dollar Value of Final Holding
14		10.24922
15		******************************

	A	B	C	D	E	F	G
16				**Dollars Sold**			Total
17	Currency Transactions						Currency
18		Dollar	Pound	Franc	Mark	Yen	Sold
19	Dollar	0.00	0.00	1.00	0.00	5.70	6.70000
20	Pound	4.00	0.00	0.00	0.00	0.00	4.00000
21	Franc **Sold**	0.00	0.00	0.00	0.00	0.00	0.00000
22	Mark	2.64	0.00	0.00	0.00	0.00	2.64000
23	Yen	0.00	0.00	0.00	0.00	0.00	0.00000
24	Currency						
25	Purchased	6.70135	0.00000	8.07800	0.00000	1280.79	
26	--						
27	Balance Equations		**Dollars Bought**		**Francs Bought**	**Yen Bought**	
28	--						

	A	B	C	D	E	F	G
29		Initial	Final	Amt	Amt	Cash	Excess
30		Holding	Holding	Sold	Purch	Req'd	Held
31							
32	Dollar	2.00000	2.00135	6.70000	6.70135	0.00000	2.00135
33	Pound	5.00000	1.00000	4.00000	0.00000	0.00000	1.00000
34	Franc	0.00000	8.07800	0.00000	8.07800	8.00000	0.07800
35	Mark	3.00000	0.36000	2.64000	0.00000	0.00000	0.36000
36	Yen	0.00000	1280.79	0.00000	1280.79	1280.00	0.79
37							
		Cash Available		**Final Requirements are Satisfied**			**Cash Required**

▼ **EXHIBIT 2**
Symbolic Spreadsheet for Currency Trading

	A	B	C	D
1	CONVERSION STRATEGIES: SYMBOLIC SPREADSHEET			
2				
3				
4		Dollar	Pound	Franc
5	Dollar	1	0.6998	8.078
6	Pound	1.425	1	11.55
7	Franc	0.1234	0.08647	1
8	Mark	0.3793	0.2662	3.073
9	Yen	0.004428	0.003103	0.03586
10	------------------------------			
11				
12	***			
13	Dollar Value of Final Holding			
14	+ G5*C32 + G6*C33 + G7*C34 + G8*C35 + G9*C36			
15	***			
16				
17	Currency Transactions	**User-Entered Decision Values**		
18		Dollar	Pound	Franc
19	Dollar			
20	Pound			
21	Franc			
22	Mark			
23	Yen			
24	Currency			
25	Purchased	+ B6*B20 + B7*B21 + B8*B22 + B9*B23	+ C5*C19 + C7*C21 + D5*D19	
26	------------------------------			
27	Balance Equations			
28	------------------------------			
29		Initial	Final	Amt
30		Holding	Holding	Sold
31				
32	Dollar	2	+ B32 − D32 + E32	+ G19
33	Pound	5	+ B33 − D33 + E33	+ G20
34	Franc	0	+ B34 − D34 + E34	+ G21
35	Mark	3	+ B35 − D35 + E35	+ G22
36	Yen	0	+ B36 − D36 + E36	+ G23

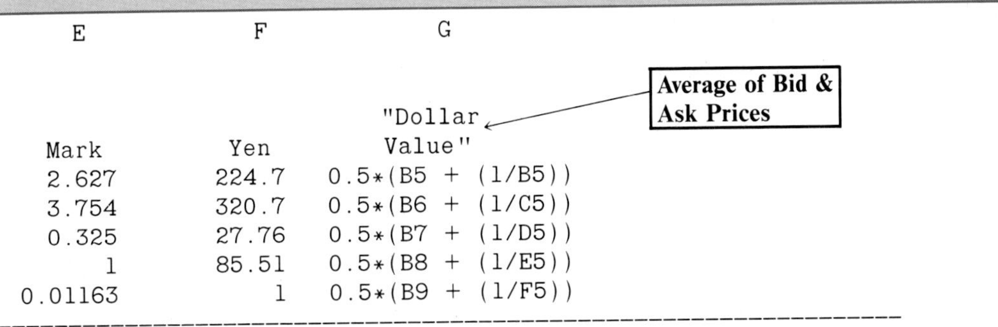

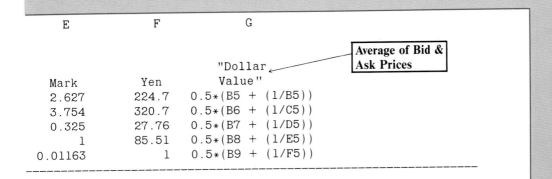

E
F
G
"Dollar
Value"
Mark
Yen
2.627
224.7
0.5*(B5 + (1/B5))
3.754
320.7
0.5*(B6 + (1/C5))
0.325
27.76
0.5*(B7 + (1/D5))
1
85.51
0.5*(B8 + (1/E5))
0.01163
1
0.5*(B9 + (1/F5))
Average of Bid & Ask Prices

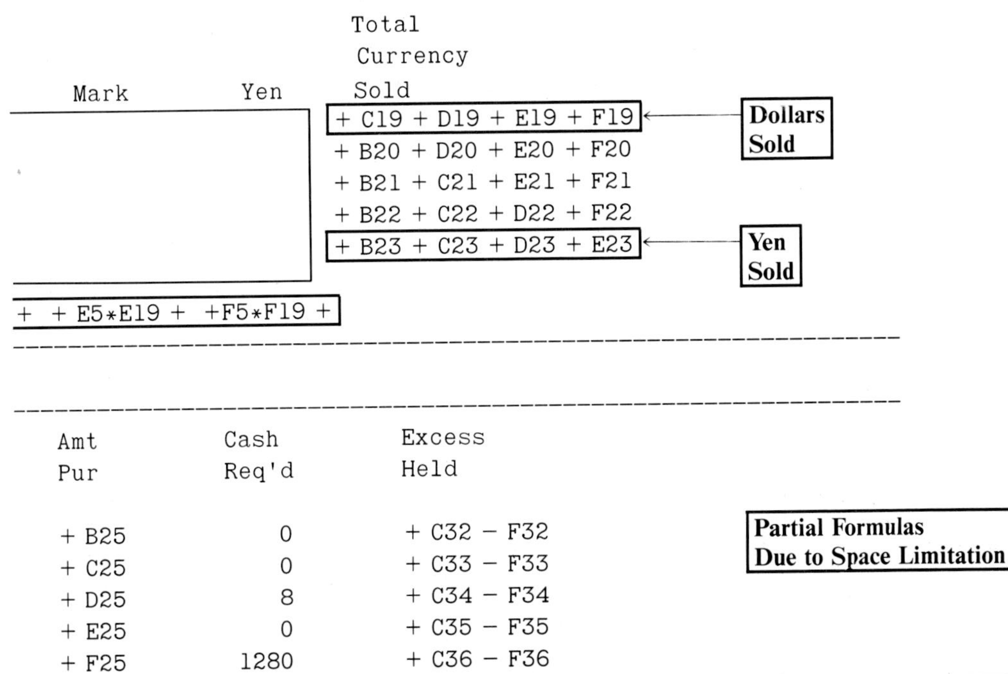

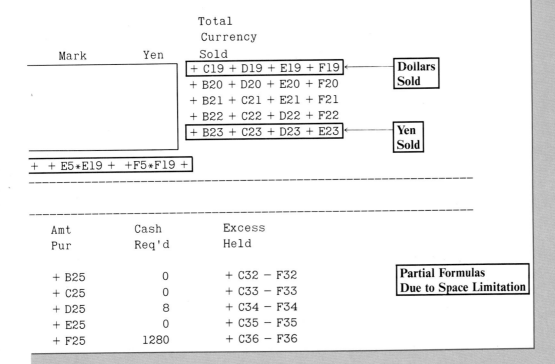

Total
Currency
Sold
Mark
Yen
+ C19 + D19 + E19 + F19
+ B20 + D20 + E20 + F20
+ B21 + C21 + E21 + F21
+ B22 + C22 + D22 + F22
+ B23 + C23 + D23 + E23
Dollars Sold
Yen Sold
+ + E5*E19 + +F5*F19 +
Amt
Pur
Cash
Req'd
Excess
Held
+ B25
0
+ C32 − F32
+ C25
0
+ C33 − F33
+ D25
8
+ C34 − F34
+ E25
0
+ C35 − F35
+ F25
1280
+ C36 − F36
Partial Formulas Due to Space Limitation

▼ **EXHIBIT 3**
Optimized Spreadsheet for Currency Trading

	A	B	C	D	E	F	G	H
1	CONVERSION STRATEGIES: OPTIMIZED SPREADSHEET							
2								
3							''Dollar	
4		Dollar	Pound	Franc	Mark	Yen	Value''	
5	Dollar	1.00000	0.69980	8.07800	2.62700	224.70	1.00000	
6	Pound	1.42500	1.00000	11.55000	3.75400	320.70	1.42699	
7	Franc	0.12340	0.08647	1.00000	0.32500	27.76000	0.12360	
8	Mark	0.37930	0.26620	3.07300	1.00000	85.51000	0.37998	
9	Yen	0.00443	0.00310	0.03586	0.01163	1.00000	0.00444	
10	------------							
11								
12		****************************						
13		Dollar Value of Final Holding						
14		10.26839						
15		****************************						
16							Total	
17	Currency Transactions						Currency	
18		Dollar	Pound	Franc	Mark	Yen	Sold	
19	Dollar	0.00	0.00	0.00	0.00	0.00	0.00000	
20	Pound	0.00	0.00	1.81	3.19	0.00	5.00000	
21	Franc	0.00	0.00	0.00	0.00	0.00	0.00000	
22	Mark	0.00	0.00	0.00	0.00	14.97	14.97000	
23	Yen	0.00	0.00	0.00	0.00	0.00	0.00000	
24	Currency							
25	Purchased	0.00000	0.00000	20.92168	11.97000	1280.08		
26	------------							
27	Balance Equations							
28	------------							
29		Initial	Final	Amt	Amt	Cash	Excess	
30		Holding	Holding	Sold	Purch	Req'd	Held	
31								
32	Dollar	2.00000	2.00000	0.00000	0.00000	0.00000	2.00000	
33	Pound	5.00000	.00000	5.00000	0.00000	0.00000	.00000	
34	Franc	0.00000	20.92168	0.00000	20.92168	8.00000	12.92168	
35	Mark	3.00000	.00000	14.97000	11.97000	0.00000	.00000	
36	Yen	0.00000	1280.08	0.00000	1280.08	1280.00	0.08	

▼ EXHIBIT 4
Optimized Spreadsheet with Final Cash Requirements Equal Zero

```
A1: 'CONVERSION STRATEGIES
        A           B           C           D           E          F          G
1   CONVERSION STRATEGIES
2
3                                                                           Dollar
4                 Dollar        Pound       Franc        Mark      Yen      Value
5   Dollar              1      0.6998       8.078       2.627    224.7          1
6   Pound           1.425           1       11.55       3.754    320.7   1.426989
7   Franc          0.1234     0.08647           1       0.325    27.76   0.123596
8   Mark           0.3793      0.2662       3.073           1    85.51   0.379981
9   Yen          0.004428    0.003103     0.03586     0.01163        1   0.004439
10  ------------------------------------------------------------------------------
11
12               **********************************
13               Dollar Value Of Final Holding
14               10.27773
15               **********************************
16                                                                        Total
17  Currency Transactions                                                 Currency
18                Dollar        Pound       Franc        Mark      Yen    Sold
19  Dollar              0           0           0           0        0          0
20  Pound               0           0    5.798600           0        0   5.798600
21  Franc               0           0           0           0        0          0
22  Mark                0           3           0           0        0          3
23  Yen                 0           0           0           0        0          0
24  Currency
25  Purchased           0      0.7986    66.97383           0        0
26  ------------------------------------------------------------------------------
27  Balance Equations
28  ------------------------------------------------------------------------------
29                Initial      Final       Amt          Amt       Cash     Excess
30                Holding      Holding     Sold         Pur       Req'd    Held
31
32  Dollar              2           2           0           0        0          2
33  Pound               5   - 0.00000    5.798600      0.7986        0   -0.00000
34  Franc               0    66.97383           0    66.97383        0   66.97383
35  Mark                3           0           3           0        0          0
36  Yen                 0           0           0           0        0          0
```

Video Case

Shopping in the USSR

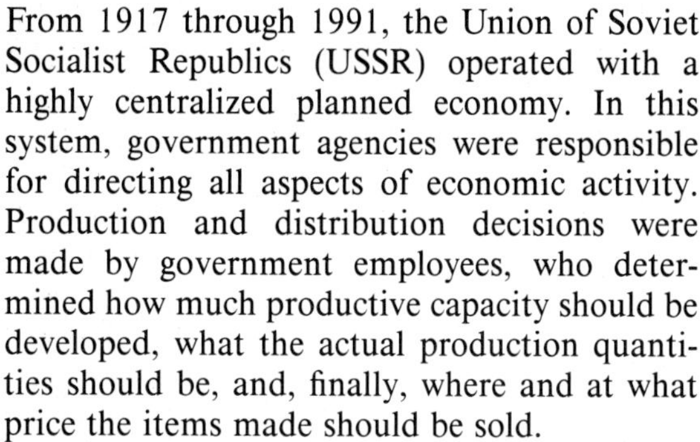

From 1917 through 1991, the Union of Soviet Socialist Republics (USSR) operated with a highly centralized planned economy. In this system, government agencies were responsible for directing all aspects of economic activity. Production and distribution decisions were made by government employees, who determined how much productive capacity should be developed, what the actual production quantities should be, and, finally, where and at what price the items made should be sold.

This system produced a massive military establishment, a number of impressive scientific and technological achievements, and many world-class athletes. However, its performance in the consumer economy was dismal. Many of the products that are taken for granted in the West, such as meat, toilet paper, razor blades, fashionable clothing, and gasoline, were in constant short supply. Prices were often quite reasonable, but the items simply were not available. Effective rationing of these items was accomplished through waiting. In the 1970s and 1980s in Saint Petersburg (then called Leningrad), it was common to see Soviet citizens standing in long lines to buy vegetables that would have been thrown away by a Western supermarket. The average Soviet citizen spent an estimated two hours per day just trying to buy consumer goods. Delays for apartments, autos, and even telephones were enormous.

Although this system had obvious problems, it did have some virtues. Almost no one went hungry in the USSR. The government made sure that the price of bread was very low and that there was always an adequate supply. (Perhaps they really had learned something from French history.) There were other advantages, at least in the eyes of those sympathetic to central planning. Such observers were quick to point out that no time or money was wasted on the bourgeois activities of advertising and marketing. Certainly people waited, but was that any more wasteful than the billions of dollars spent on advertising, which creates no useful product?

Even in this "workers paradise" not everyone waited equally. Special shops were available to leaders of the Communist party and to high-ranking military officials. Moreover, goods were in plentiful supply (though much more expensive) in hard-currency stores that accepted dollars and other Western currencies rather than rubles. These stores existed because the Soviet currency, the ruble, was not traded internationally. The official exchange rates were set by the government and so had to be respected inside the USSR.

Unfortunately, the rates chosen by the government were much higher than the rates that would have prevailed if the ruble had traded. Thus suppliers of foreign goods were reluctant to be paid in rubles, since the artificially high official exchange rates in favor of the ruble meant that any earnings taken out of the USSR were worth only a fraction of their nominal value in the USSR.

In late 1991, the USSR ceased to exist. The various states that had made up the union became independent and formed a federation. In an amazingly short period of time, a superpower that, with the United States, had dominated the world scene for more than 70 years disappeared. By 1992 it was clear that the economic status of the various states was desperate. The Western democracies (including Japan) were planning a bailout of hundreds of millions of dollars. Analysis of the reasons for the demise of "the world's last great empire" started with the first signs of weakness and will undoubtedly provide grist for the mills of historians for many years. However, from early on, it is clear that the inability of the Soviet economy to provide a first class lifestyle for its citizens played a crucial role in this fall.

Questions

It is interesting to use the framework of mathematical programming to consider the economy of the USSR.

1. Think of the short-run problems in such an economy. For example, assume that the planners are attempting to use present capacity to plan production for this year. What crucial assumptions are they implicitly making if they try to use a PROTRAC-like model?
2. Now take a longer perspective—say, that of a 10-year plan. What important element is missing from a PROTRAC-like model?

CHAPTER

Linear Programming: Geometric Representations and Graphical Solutions

APPLICATION CAPSULE

More Bang for the Buck: LP Helps the USAF Stock Its Arsenal*

The United States Air Force has a distinguished record of winning important battles. Americans recall with pride the success of our pilots in the skies over Germany during World War II, and more recently in the Persian Gulf. This success results in part from a relentless search for new tactics and technology. Thus it is no surprise that in recent years the Air Force has turned to a modern approach—using linear programming—in the evaluation and procurement of weapon systems and in the annual battle of the budget.

Each year the Air Force must present a weapons development plan to Congress. To prepare this plan, it is necessary to decide (1) what new projects to start, (2) what current projects to continue, and (3) what projects to discontinue. The final recommendation is highly dependent on the level of funding available.

A key consideration is the effectiveness of each weapon system and its possible contribution, in a mix of weapons, to achieving a desired increase in target value destroyed. Effectiveness estimates must be made for a great many combinations of aircraft, munitions, and targets (tanks, command and communication facilities, bridges, and the like). These factors interact in complex ways. Different munitions require aircraft to fly at different altitudes for different durations, and their vulnerability to enemy antiaircraft fire will vary accordingly. Even a small change in the rate at which aircraft are lost can have a major effect on the cost-effectiveness of a system, to say nothing of the loss of human life.

The Air Force must also assess annually the consequences of a possible increase or decrease in the budget—that is, how sensitive a given proposal might be to a change in the level of funding. Budget changes can affect the mix of weapon systems purchased as well as the number of any particular weapon acquired. The number of items purchased, in turn, can drastically affect the purchase price per unit.

For analyses of this kind, the Air Force has developed a linear program that can evaluate tradeoffs among both aircraft types and munitions. It can not only specify the optimal mix of weapons needed to destroy a particular target set, but also display graphically such relationships as

- the ratio of funds expended on aircraft versus munitions
- target value destroyed as a function of expenditure on individual weapons, or on a mixture of weapons
- target value destroyed versus expenditure as a function of conflict duration.

This information is plotted out in the form of two-dimensional graphs, with axes properly scaled, so that managers and analysts can study possible tradeoffs and perform "what-if" analyses.

*Might, "Decision Support for Aircraft and Munitions Procurement," *Interfaces*, Vol. 17, No. 5 (Sept.–Oct. 1987).

3.1 Introduction

Graphs of a two-dimensional model help us to "see" linear programming models and connect the brain (logic) and intuition (gut feel) of what LP is all about. Above two dimensions a stretch of imagination is needed to visualize what an LP model with several variables "looks" like.

Two-dimensional geometry can be used as a "picture" to illustrate many of the important elements of linear programming models. Although two-dimensional geometry is a very special case, it is easy to work with, and many general concepts that apply to higher-dimensional models can be communicated with two-dimensional pictures. In particular, two-dimensional geometry is useful in providing the basis for the graphical solution approach. This is a simple way to solve a linear programming problem having only two decision variables. Although most real-world problems have more than two decision variables, and hence the graphical solution method will not be applicable, it nevertheless provides a good intuitive basis for much that follows. In other words, the purpose of this chapter is to provide graphical insights into the general LP model. This will provide a good foundation for the use of LP in a variety of real-world applications. Moreover, in our later discussions of computer printouts, the simplex method, and sensitivity analysis, we shall make frequent use of geometric illustrations.

At the outset we briefly recall the technique for plotting inequalities, for this technique provides the basis for the graphical analysis that follows.

3.2 Plotting Inequalities and Contours

Let us begin by plotting the set of points (x_1, x_2) that satisfies the *inequality*

$$2x_2 - x_1 \leq -2 \tag{3.1}$$

Plotting Inequalities

To accomplish this we will use the following general procedure for plotting inequalities:

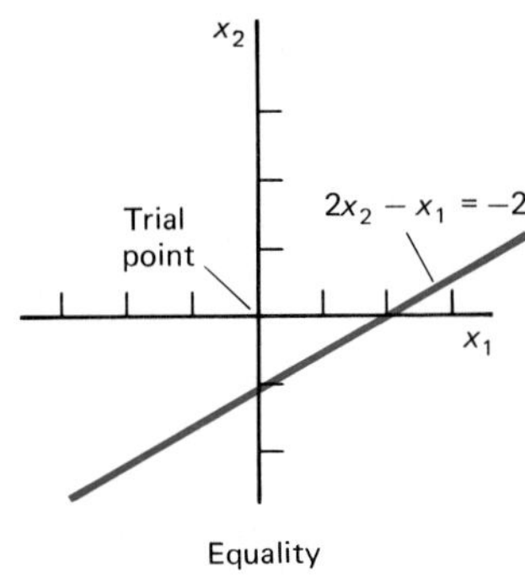

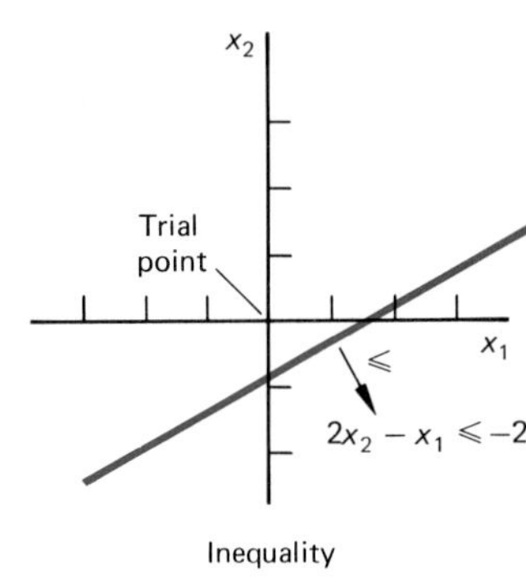

▲ FIGURE 3.1
Plotting $2x_2 - x_1 \leq -2$

Some students have difficulty even plotting a straight line; it may seem ridiculous, but doing this example might help.
(a) Set $x_1 = 0$ and solve for x_2. $x_2 = -2/2 = -1$ and find that point on the x_2 axis.
(b) Set $x_2 = 0$ and solve for x_1. $-x_1 = -2$; $x_1 = 2$ and find that point on the x_1 axis.
(c) Connect the two points.

- ***Step 1: Plot equality.*** Convert the inequality to an equality and plot the straight line that represents this equation. In our example the equality is $2x_2 - x_1 = -2$. The plot of this equation is shown in Figure 3.1.
- ***Step 2: Choose trial point.*** Choose any trial point that is not on the line. If the point $x_1 = 0, x_2 = 0$ is not on the straight line, then it is a convenient point. In our example, we select $x_1 = 0, x_2 = 0$ as the trial point. See Figure 3.1.
- ***Step 3: Evaluate left-hand side expression.*** Substitute the trial point into the expression on the left-hand side of the inequality. In the example, the expression is $2x_2 - x_1$. Substituting in the values $x_1 = 0, x_2 = 0$ yields a numerical value of 0.
- ***Step 4: Determine if the trial point satisfies the inequality.***
  a. If the trial point *satisfies* the original inequality, then the straight line plotted in step 1, and all points on the *same* side of the line as the trial point, satisfy the inequality.
  b. If the trial point *does not satisfy* the original inequality, then the straight line, and all points *not* on the same side as the trial point, satisfy the inequality.

In our example, since 0 *is not* ≤ -2, the trial point does *not* satisfy the inequality. Condition b above holds, and the straight line and all points on the opposite side of the line from (0, 0) satisfy the inequality. This set is shown in Figure 3.1. Note the convention of denoting the relevant side of the equality line with an arrow and ≤ or ≥, as appropriate.

An incorrect method

Students often acquire the incorrect impression that the < side of an inequality plot is always below the equality line. Hence, to plot the points satisfying a ≤ relation, they change the ≤ to =, graph the equality, and then hastily include all points that lie below the equality line. This may be incorrect, since the < side can be above and not below. For example, let us graph the inequality $2x_1 - x_2 \leq 2$. Following the procedure outlined above, we first plot the equation $2x_1 - x_2 = 2$ as shown in Figure 3.2. Now consider the trial point ($x_1 = 0, x_2 = 0$), which is *above* the

▼ FIGURE 3.2
Plotting $2x_1 - x_2 \leq 2$

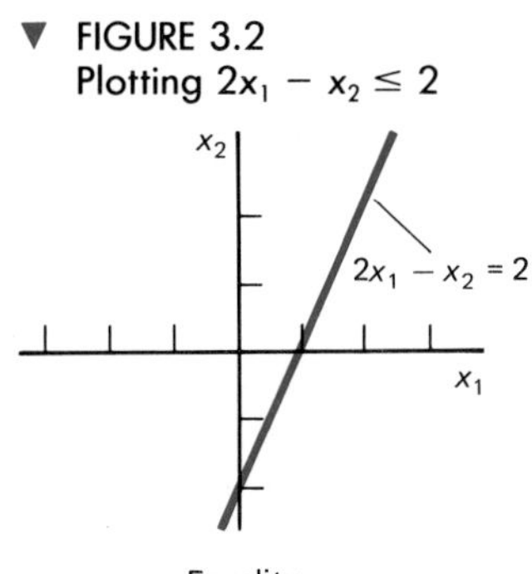

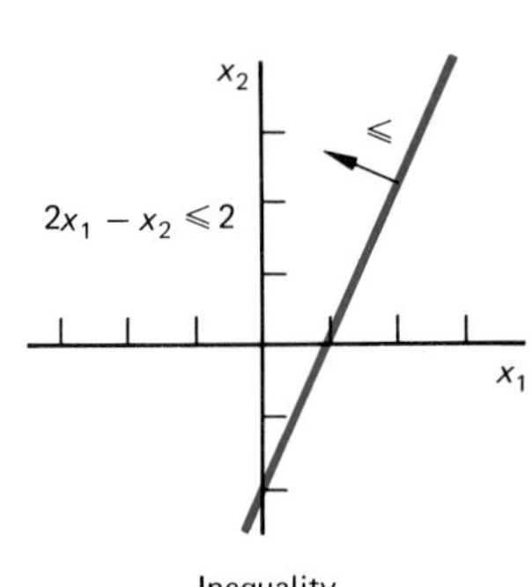

line. At this point $2x_1 - x_2 = 2(0) - 0 = 0$ and, since 0 is less than 2, we have identified the $<$ side of the line in Figure 3.2. Hence, in this case, the points satisfying the $\leq$ inequality are the points on the line along with all the points on the same side as ($x_1 = 0, x_2 = 0$), that is, points *on* and *above* the line. This is also shown in Figure 3.2. A comparison of Figures 3.1 and 3.2 should convince you that there is no general relationship between the sense of the inequality (i.e., $\leq$ or $\geq$) and the *above* or the *below* side of the equality plot. The appropriate side can always be found using a trial point, as we have demonstrated.

The technique described above provides the basic tool for plotting the constraints in an LP, for such constraints are always mathematical equalities or inequalities. In summary, to plot an inequality constraint of either the $\leq$ or the $\geq$ type:

1. Change the inequality to an equality, to obtain an equation, and then plot the straight line that represents this equation.
2. Choose any trial point that is not on this line. (If the point $x_1 = 0, x_2 = 0$ is not on the straight line, it is the easiest trial point.)
3. Substitute this trial point into the left side of the inequality constraint. Since the trial point is not on the line, the result is either less than the right-hand side or greater than the right-hand side. If the result is less than the right-hand side, the line and all points on the side containing the trial point satisfy the $\leq$ inequality, and the line and all points on the other side satisfy the $\geq$ inequality. If the result is greater than the right-hand side, the conclusion is reversed.

Contour Lines

Contours, also called **isoquants,** play an important role in the geometric representation of LP models. A *contour* of a function f of two variables is the set of all pairs (x_1, x_2) for which $f(x_1, x_2)$ takes on some specified *constant value.* When f is a profit function, the contours are often referred to as **isoprofit lines,** and when f is a cost function the contours represent **isocost lines.**

As an example of a contour, suppose that we are selling two products. The profit per unit of product 1 is \$2, and the profit per unit of product 2 is \$4. Then the total profit obtained from selling x_1 units of product 1 and x_2 units of product 2 is given by a function f of two variables defined by

$$\text{profit} = f(x_1, x_2) = 2x_1 + 4x_2$$

Let us now plot all possible sales combinations of x_1 and x_2 for which we obtain \$4 of profit. To do this we plot the equation

$$2x_1 + 4x_2 = 4 \tag{3.2}$$

The plot is shown by the lowest of the three lines in Figure 3.3. This line is called the 4-contour of the function f. In reality, since negative sales do not make sense, we would be interested in only that part of the 4-contour in Figure 3.3 that lies between the two distinguished points on the axes. Do not worry about this now. It will be dealt with in the next section.

Clearly, we can replace the value 4 in the right-hand side of expression (3.2) with any other constant and then plot the result to obtain a different contour of f. Figure 3.3 also shows two other contours of f, those corresponding to right-hand sides, in expression (3.2), with values 6 and 8. You can readily see that these contours are parallel lines, and you can deduce that in fact there are infinitely many such contours, one for each possible numerical value of the right-hand side in (3.2).

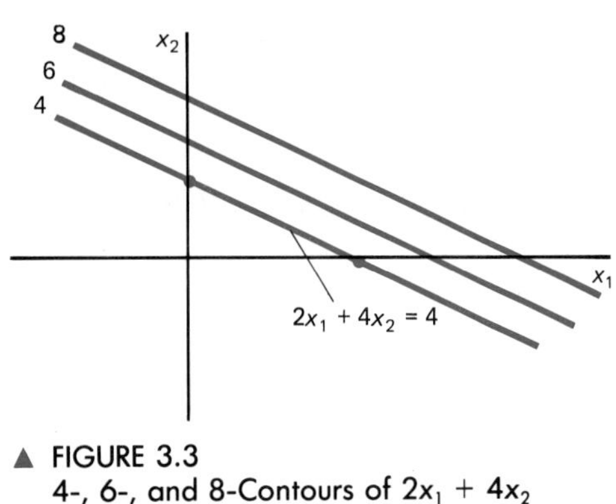

▲ FIGURE 3.3
4-, 6-, and 8-Contours of $2x_1 + 4x_2$

Plotting contours and inequalities

The two concepts reviewed in this section, plotting equalities and plotting contours, will be employed to obtain graphical solutions of linear programming problems with two decision variables.

In summary:

Plotting contours reduces to plotting equalities. The contours of a linear function are a family of parallel lines. Plotting inequalities also reduces to plotting equalities, or contours, and then identifying the correct side.

3.3 The Graphical Solution Method Applied to PROTRAC, Inc.

The **graphical solution method** provides an easy way of solving linear programming problems with two decision variables. Since the **PROTRAC**, Inc. model from Chapter 2 has only two decision variables, *E* and *F*, we can employ that problem to illustrate the graphical approach. The complete model for this problem is

PROTRAC, Inc. Model

$\text{Max } 5000E + 4000F$	(max profit)	(3.3)
$\text{s.t.} \quad E + F \geq 5$	(minimal production requirement)	(3.4)
$E - 3F \leq 0$	(market position balance)	(3.5)
$10E + 15F \leq 150$	(capacity in department A)	(3.6)
$20E + 10F \leq 160$	(capacity in department B)	(3.7)
$30E + 10F \geq 135$	(hours used in testing)	(3.8)
$E, F \geq 0$	(nonnegativity conditions)	(3.9)

where we recall that the decision variables are defined as

$$E = \text{number of E-9s to be produced}$$
$$F = \text{number of F-9s to be produced}$$

The labels (3.3) through (3.9) are used in the following discussion to distinguish the objective function and the constraints.

Plotting the Constraints

Our first goal is to show how all the feasible decisions for this problem can be graphically portrayed. Let us first construct a coordinate system with values of E on the horizontal axis and values of F on the vertical. Thus, every point in the two-dimensional space is associated with a specific production alternative. For example, the point in Figure 3.4 is identified with the production alternative $E = 3$, $F = 4$. We now wish to see which of the possible combinations of (E, F) are feasible, that is, satisfy the restrictions (3.4) through (3.9).

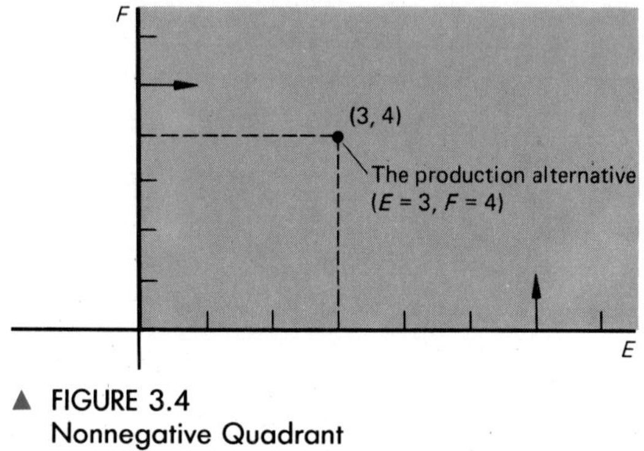

▲ FIGURE 3.4
Nonnegative Quadrant

Since the nonnegativity conditions (3.9) require $E \geq 0$ and $F \geq 0$, we need only consider the so-called **nonnegative quadrant** in looking for feasible production combinations, that is, feasible combinations of the decision variable (E, F). This is indicated in Figure 3.4. In this figure the arrows point in the direction of nonnegative values of E and F, and the nonnegative quadrant is shaded.

Clearly, not every point in the nonnegative quadrant is feasible. For example, consider the first constraint, (3.4):

$$E + F \geq 5 \tag{3.4}$$

Clearly, the combination $(E = 1, F = 1)$, although corresponding to a point in the nonnegative quadrant, violates this constraint. Obviously, we must further limit our graphic representation of the candidates for feasibility.

In order to depict accurately the feasible combinations, we must proceed by taking one constraint at a time. We begin with the first constraint,

$$E + F \geq 5 \tag{3.4}$$

To simplify the process of determining the optimal solution, we will begin to eliminate possible areas of the graph. With each added constraint, the feasible area will get smaller.

The discussion in Section 3.2 indicated that to plot this constraint you should first plot the line $E + F = 5$ and then find the $>$ side, which in this case is seen to be all points above the diagonal line. Following this procedure you should verify that all points in the nonnegative quadrant that satisfy the first constraint are precisely those shown in the shaded region in Figure 3.5. This region represents nonnegative production plans that satisfy the one single constraint, (3.4), but not necessarily the others. For example, you can quickly verify that the plan $(E = 10, F = 10)$ violates constraint (3.6). Clearly, we must restrict the candidate decisions still further by reapplying the prescription just followed.

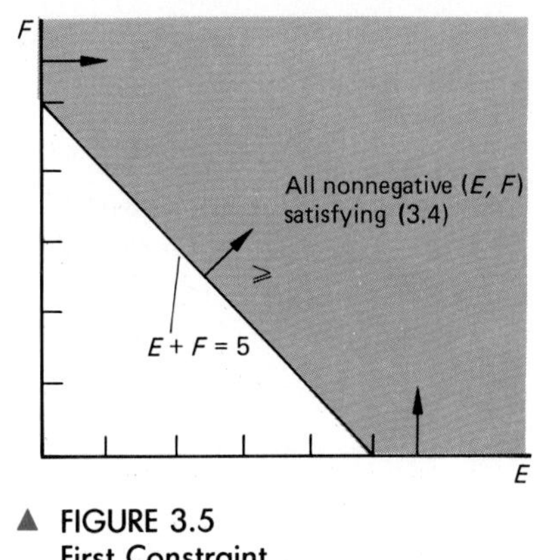

▲ FIGURE 3.5
First Constraint

Thus, we now consider the second constraint,

$$E - 3F \leq 0 \tag{3.5}$$

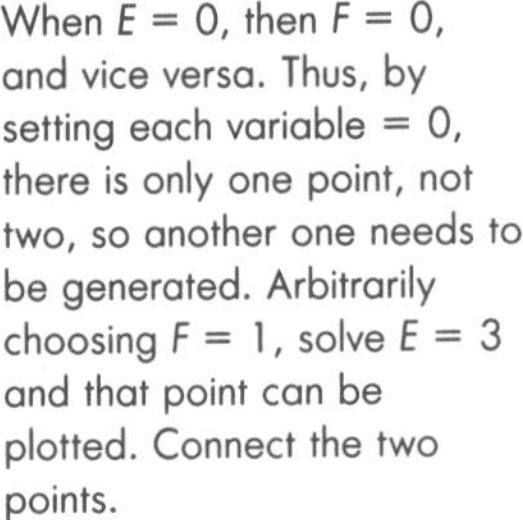

When $E = 0$, then $F = 0$, and vice versa. Thus, by setting each variable = 0, there is only one point, not two, so another one needs to be generated. Arbitrarily choosing $F = 1$, solve $E = 3$ and that point can be plotted. Connect the two points.

In Figure 3.6 the plot of this condition appears together with condition (3.4). The production alternatives in the shaded region of Figure 3.6 satisfy

$$E + F \geq 5 \tag{3.4}$$

$$E - 3F \leq 0 \tag{3.5}$$

$$E \geq 0, \qquad F \geq 0 \tag{3.9}$$

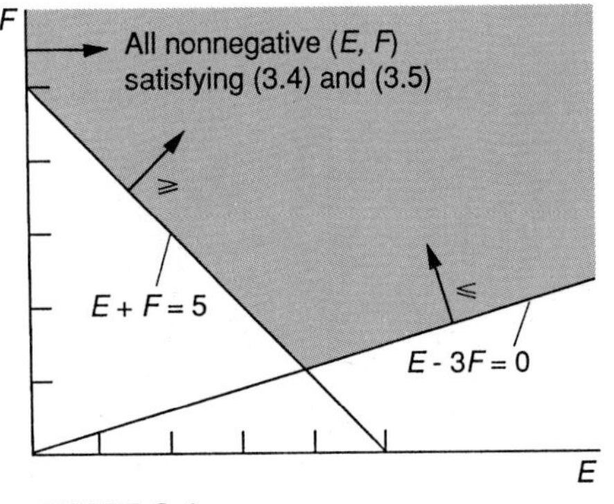

▲ FIGURE 3.6
First Two Constraints, (3.4) and (3.5)

Effect of Adding Constraints

However, this shaded region will still contain some points that will violate some of the remaining constraints (3.6), (3.7), and (3.8). Thus, we must continue to superimpose one by one the remaining constraints. First, however, let us note that superimposing the second constraint (3.5) on the picture in Figure 3.5 has further restricted the decision variables and, graphically, has "trimmed down" the set of candidates for feasible decisions. As we continue to superimpose "tighter and tighter" conditions (i.e., more and more restrictions) on the decision variables, it should be clear that from the geometric point of view these restrictions will tend to trim down the constraint set even further. This phenomenon, the successive trimming down of the constraint set, illustrates the following important general principle. (*General* in this context means "also valid for problems with more than two decision variables.")

Adding more constraints will always either trim down the set of allowable decisions or leave the set unaffected. Adding additional constraints can never enlarge the set of allowable decisions.

The Feasible Region

The culmination of superimposing constraints (3.6), (3.7), and (3.8) on Figure 3.6 yields Figure 3.7, which is a graphic portrayal of all feasible values of the decision variables. This figure, with all five constraints plotted in the nonnegative quadrant, shows the set of production plans that *simultaneously* satisfies *all five* of the constraints, as well as the nonnegativity conditions. In linear programming terminology, this set is called the **constraint set,** *feasible set,* or **feasible region.** That is, the shaded area in Figure 3.7 is the feasible region for the **PROTRAC**, Inc. model.

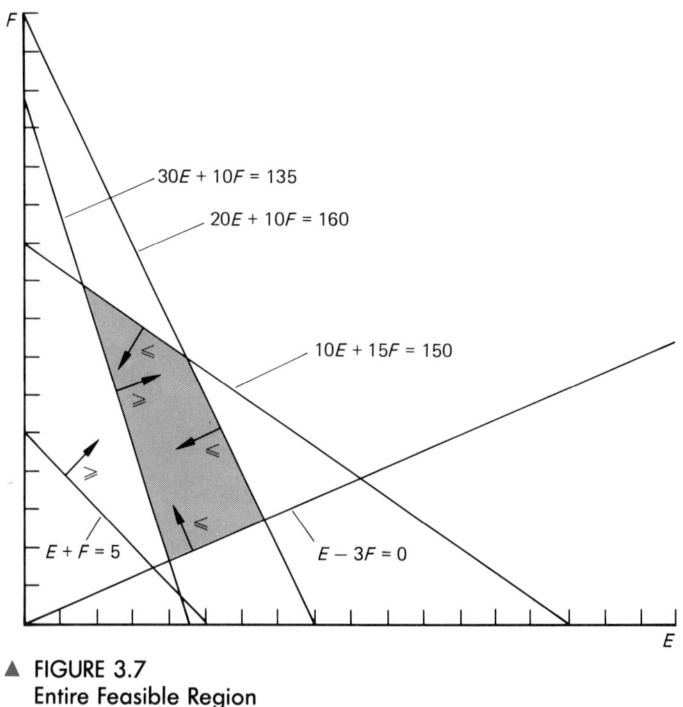

▲ FIGURE 3.7
Entire Feasible Region

The set of all nonnegative values of the decision variables that satisfies all the constraints simultaneously is called the constraint set, or the feasible region.

Can a number be feasible?

In keeping with our definition of feasible region, any production plan [i.e., any pair of values for (E, F)] that satisfies all the constraints, including the nonnegativity conditions, is known as a **feasible solution** or *feasible decision.* These feasible plans, or decisions, are the allowable production alternatives according to our model. Note that it is *incorrect* to speak of a feasible value of E separately, or a feasible value of F separately. Think carefully about this statement, for it is important to understand

Emphasize that a "solution" is more than just two values. It is a point on the graph. If there were three variables, it would be a point in three-dimensional space, and for four variables, it couldn't be "pictured."

that *the term "feasible," in this two-dimensional illustration, always applies to a pair of numbers, not to a single number.*

To illustrate these feasible pairs geometrically, we have seen that you merely plot the constraint set. We used several pictures to lead up to our graph of the entire constraint set simply for illustrative purposes. In practice you would plot everything on the same coordinate systems, superimposing one constraint at a time. To accomplish this, for each constraint

1. Change the inequality to an equality.
2. Plot the equality.
3. Identify the correct side for the original inequality.

Having performed steps 1, 2, and 3 for each constraint, the feasible set is the region that, simultaneously, is on the correct side of all the lines.

Plotting the Objective Function

Obtaining a graphical portrayal of the constraint set is the first step in the graphical solution procedure. Now we want to use the graphical portrayal to find the *optimal* solution to the problem. Since we are dealing with a profit-maximization model, we must find a feasible production alternative that gives the highest possible value to the objective function

$$\text{profit} = 5000E + 4000F \tag{3.10}$$

If we begin to arbitrarily select feasible plans from Figure 3.7 and evaluate the objective function at each such point, trying to find the largest possible profit, we would soon realize that this process could be endless. There are infinitely many feasible pairs (E, F). How would this trial-and-error process ever terminate? We must find, systematically and quickly, a way to discover a profit-maximizing feasible plan.

In order to present a more robust approach, let us first redraw just the shaded feasible region on a new uncluttered graph, as shown in Figure 3.8. Now recall that, since in this case the objective function is a profit function, the contours of the objective function are called isoprofit lines, or, more simply, *profit lines.* Our next task is to superimpose on Figure 3.8 several arbitrary profit lines. For example, let

▼ FIGURE 3.8
Constraint Set for PROTRAC, Inc.

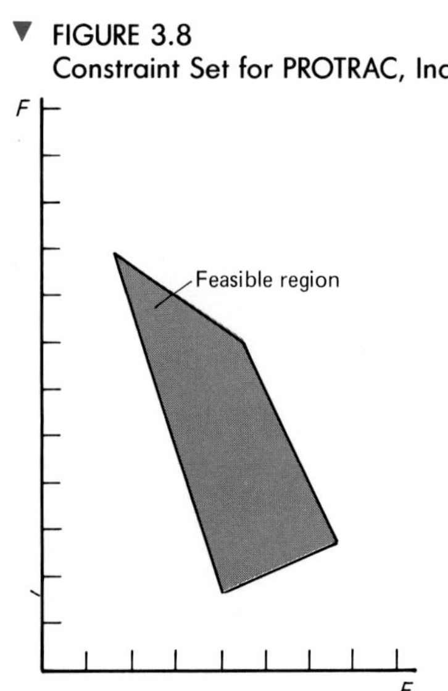

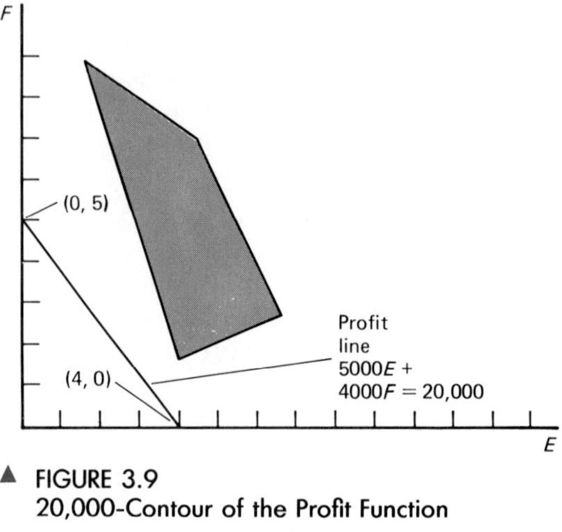

▲ FIGURE 3.9
20,000-Contour of the Profit Function

us begin by setting expression (3.10) equal to 20,000 and superimposing on Figure 3.8 the corresponding profit line, as shown in Figure 3.9. We have restricted this line to the nonnegative quadrant because we are interested only in nonnegative values for E and F. Thus, any point on the line in Figure 3.9 corresponds to a production plan that will yield a profit of $20,000. You can see from this figure that there are an infinite number of nonnegative production plans that will yield a profit of $20,000. However, the fact that the profit line in Figure 3.9 does not intersect the shaded feasible region means that none of the production plans on this line are feasible.

Let us therefore experiment by selecting a different profit line to superimpose on Figure 3.9. For example, let us set expression (3.10) equal to 32,000 and plot the profit line

$$\text{profit} = 5000E + 4000F = 32{,}000$$

This is shown in Figure 3.10. You can see from Figure 3.10 that the 32,000-contour intersects the feasible region. Every production plan that lies on the intersection of this line with the feasible region is feasible, and yields a profit of $32,000. There are, as you can see, infinitely many such plans.

Our objective is to find a point in the feasible region that yields the highest profit. Are there any feasible plans that yield a higher profit than $32,000? Look at Figure 3.10 and see if you can answer this question.

▼ FIGURE 3.10
Two Profit Lines

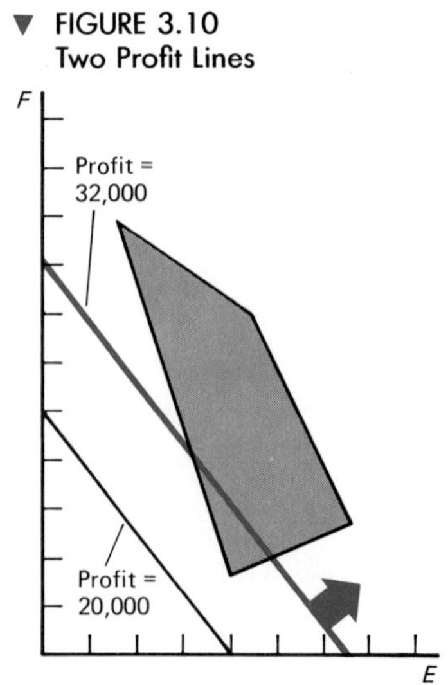

The "uphill" direction

The key to correct identification of feasible plans with a profit greater than \$32,000 lies in noting that the 32,000 profit line is parallel to the 20,000 profit line and lies above it (i.e., to the northeast). In general, as we increase profit, we increase the value of C in the profit equation

$$\text{profit} = 5000E + 4000F = C$$

and the profit line moves parallel to the 20,000 and the 32,000 profit lines. The direction of the motion is northeasterly because this is, in this particular example, the direction in which profit increases. The direction of increasing contour values is called the **optimizing direction.** In this case we will call it the **uphill direction,** identified with an arrow in Figure 3.10.

Finding the Optimal Solution

Now that we have seen how to plot the feasible region and the objective function contours, we are armed with enough information to find the solution to the PROTRAC, Inc. model. As, in our mind's eye, we move, or "slide," the profit lines out to the northeast, without changing the tilt, we can identify feasible plans that yield higher and higher values for the objective function. At some point we will discover that any further movement in this direction will take the profit line beyond the feasible region, at which point all production plans on the line will be unacceptable. Can you now identify the position of the highest-valued contour that touches the feasible region in at least one point? Any feasible plan on this line will be an **optimal solution** to the PROTRAC, Inc. model.

Using either your imagination or a straight edge, and making a parallel outward displacement of the profit line in Figure 3.10, you will see that the highest-valued contour is the one shown in Figure 3.11. This is called the maximum profit line.

In this model only one point in the feasible region lies on the maximum profit line, so this point is called a **unique optimal solution** to our problem. Although we have located our solution graphically, the accuracy with which we can determine the *optimal values* of the decision variables E and F would seem to depend on the accuracy of our graph. We shall see that this impression is incorrect. Also, we have not yet established the value of the **maximum profit line** (i.e., the maximum

▼ FIGURE 3.11
Optimality in the PROTRAC, Inc. Model

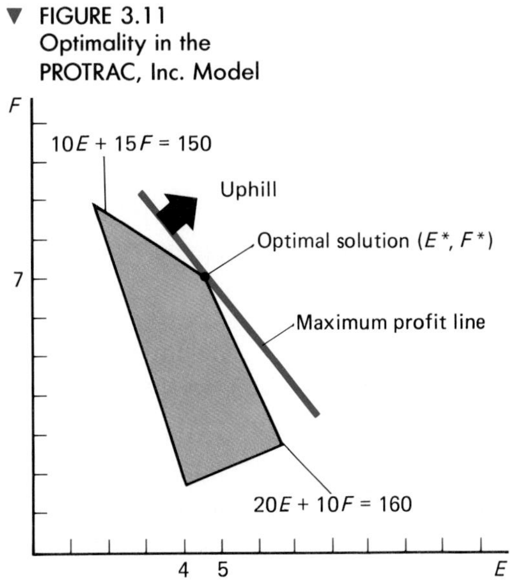

attainable profit). These two points are readily resolved by resorting to some easy algebra, as follows.

Figure 3.11 indicates that the optimal value of E is somewhere between 4 and 5, and the optimal value of F is approximately 7. Let us suppose that greater accuracy is desired. You can see in Figure 3.11 that the optimal solution occurs at *the intersection* of the two constraint lines.

$$10E + 15F = 150 \tag{3.11}$$

$$20E + 10F = 160 \tag{3.12}$$

Knowing alternative ways of solving two equations in two unknowns allows students to experience a little less anxiety on tests.

We thus have two linear equations, which can be solved for the two unknowns, E and F. This can be done either by elimination or by substitution. To illustrate the former method, we can multiply Equation 3.11 by 2 to obtain the new system:

$$2 \times (\text{Eq. } 3.11)\text{:} \quad 20E + 30F = 300 \tag{3.13}$$

$$20E + 10F = 160 \tag{3.12}$$

Then, subtracting (3.12) from (3.13), we find that

$$\begin{aligned} 20F &= 140 \\ F &= \frac{140}{20} = 7 \end{aligned} \tag{3.14}$$

Substituting the value of F from (3.14) back into either (3.11) or (3.12), say (3.12), we obtain

$$\begin{aligned} 20E + 10(7) &= 160 \\ E &= \frac{90}{20} = 4.5 \end{aligned} \tag{3.15}$$

It is important to stress that regardless of how the values of E and F are obtained, they should be inserted back into the original equations to see if indeed these values do solve the equations. Students good at math do this automatically; those poor at math will avoid "extra" work at all costs.

Alternatively, we can rearrange one of the equations to give an expression for either of the variables in terms of the other, and then substitute this expression into the second equation. For example, equation 3.12 can be rearranged to give

$$10F = 160 - 20E'$$

or

$$F = 16 - 2E$$

Substituting this expression into Equation 3.11 gives $E = 4.5$. This value for E can in turn be inserted into either of the original equations, yielding $F = 7$.

Distinguishing the optimal solution

Let us use the notation E^* and F^* to distinguish the optimal values of the decision variables, E and F, respectively. From (3.14) and (3.15) we have found the optimal production plan $E^* = 4.5$ and $F^* = 7$. This is the *optimal solution,* or, more simply, *the solution* to the **PROTRAC**, Inc. model. Using these optimal values ($E^* = 4.5$, $F^* = 7$) we can now compute the value of the maximum profit as follows:

$$\begin{aligned} \text{maximum profit} &= 5000E^* + 4000F^* \\ &= 5000(4.5) + 4000(7) \\ &= 22{,}500 + 28{,}000 = 50{,}500 \end{aligned}$$

Optimal solution and optimal value are different

This is the value of the maximum profit contour in Figure 3.11 and is called the **optimal objective value,** or, sometimes, merely the **optimal value.** The term *solution,* or *optimal solution,* always refers to the optimal values of the decision variables.

The term *optimal value* (singular), which we often call the OV, refers to the objective function evaluated at the solution. In the **PROTRAC**, Inc. model, the optimal production plan ($E^* = 4.5$, $F^* = 7$) is the solution; the optimal profit of $50,500 is the OV.

3.4 Active and Inactive Constraints

In addition to the optimal production plan and the optimal profit, the management of **PROTRAC**, Inc. may want additional information about the solution. For example, management may ask

1. How many labor hours will the optimal solution use in department A?
2. How many labor hours will the optimal solution use in department B?
3. How many hours will the optimal solution use in testing?

Recall that the labor hours used in department A are given by the left-hand side of the inequality (3.6). That is, referring back to the model, we see that

$$\text{hours used in department A} = 10E + 15F \tag{3.16}$$

Since we are going to assign the optimal values $E = E^* = 4.5$, and $F = F^* = 7$, the expression (3.16) is evaluated as follows:

$$\begin{aligned}\text{hours used (at optimality) in department A} &= 10E^* + 15F^* \\ &= 10(4.5) + 15(7) = 150\end{aligned}$$

This means that the answer to question 1 is 150, and we say that "at optimality, 150 hours are used in department A." In order to answer question 2 we recall that the labor hours in department B are given by the left-hand side of inequality (3.7). Hence, at optimality

$$\begin{aligned}\text{hours used in department B} &= 20E^* + 10F^* \\ &= 20(4.5) + 10(7) = 160\end{aligned}$$

Finally, to answer question 3 we employ the left-hand side of inequality (3.8) to discover that, at optimality

$$\begin{aligned}\text{hours used in testing} &= 30E^* + 10F^* \\ &= 30(4.5) + 10(7) = 205\end{aligned}$$

Let us now pursue these elaborations a bit further to introduce some important new terminology. We have just seen that the optimal production plan will consume 150 hours in department A. But we also recall from the model that 150 hours is the total amount of labor *available* in department A. Hence, for the optimal policy we see that

$$\text{hours of labor used} = \text{hours of labor available}$$

and the constraint is satisfied with *equality*. But how can that be, for the constraint on labor hours in department A is an *inequality* constraint, not an equality constraint? The answer is simple if you interpret the $\leq$ symbol correctly. Our $\leq$

constraint on labor in department A allows the use of labor to be either < the amount *or* = the amount available. Hence, equality is permissible. What is *not* permissible is for the labor usage to *exceed* the availability.

If it was known ahead of time which r variables would be > 0 and which r constraints would be active, it would be simple to solve r equations in r unknowns for the optimal solution.

For this constraint, since there is no labor left unused, the constraint is said to be **active,** or equivalently, **binding.** Note that from management's point of view an active constraint plays a role of considerable importance. For example, if there were any further production of E-9s or F-9s, this active constraint would be violated. In this sense the active constraint prevents the earning of additional profits.

By applying analogous reasoning to the constraint on labor hours in department B you can easily verify that this constraint is also active.

Active constraint

In Chapter 2 we saw that the constraints in a linear programming model are always of the form =, ≤, or ≥. *An equality constraint is always active. An inequality constraint, of either the ≤ or ≥ type, is active only if, when evaluated at optimality, equality holds between the left-hand side and the right-hand side.*

Inactive constraint

Let us now consider the constraint on testing. Recall that this constraint requires, by a union agreement, that *at least* 135 hours (the right-hand side of the constraint) be used, whereas the answer to question 3 has shown that 205 hours (the left-hand side) will actually be used. Since we are using 70 hours in *excess* of what is required, there is said to be, at optimality, a *surplus* of 70 hours in this constraint. Here we have an example of an inequality constraint that is *not* active at optimality. As you might guess, such a constraint is said to be **inactive.**

The terms *active* and *inactive* are applicable to each constraint in the model. For example, if we evaluate, at optimality, the left-hand side of the constraint labeled (3.5), we see that

$$E - 3F = 4.5 - 3(7) = 4.5 - 21 = -16.5$$

Since constraint (3.5) stipulates that

$$E - 3F \leq 0$$

and since the actual value of the left-hand side is −16.5, we see that the left-hand side falls 16.5 units *below* the right-hand side. This constraint is said to have a *slack* of 16.5 units, and is also *inactive.*

Summarizing this terminology, we see that

1. If, at optimality (i.e., when evaluated at the optimal solution), the left-hand side of a constraint equals the right-hand side, that constraint is said to be *active,* or *binding.* Thus, an *equality* constraint is always active. An inequality constraint may or may not be active.

Slack and surplus

2. If a constraint is not active, it is said to be *inactive.* For a constraint of the ≥ type, the difference between the left-hand side and the right-hand side (the excess) is called **surplus.** For a constraint of the ≤ type, the difference between the right-hand side and the left-hand side (the amount unused) is called **slack.**
3. At optimality, each *inequality* constraint in a model has a slack or surplus value, and for feasible decisions this value is always nonnegative. For a given constraint the slack or surplus value is zero if and only if that constraint is active.

Graphical Interpretations of Active and Inactive

We have seen how to identify algebraically those constraints that are active and those that are inactive, and hence have positive surplus or slack. We obtained this information by "plugging" the optimal values of the decision variables into the constraints. It will be useful to understand how the active and inactive constraints can also be easily identified from the graphical solution. To see this, let us recall the statement of the model:

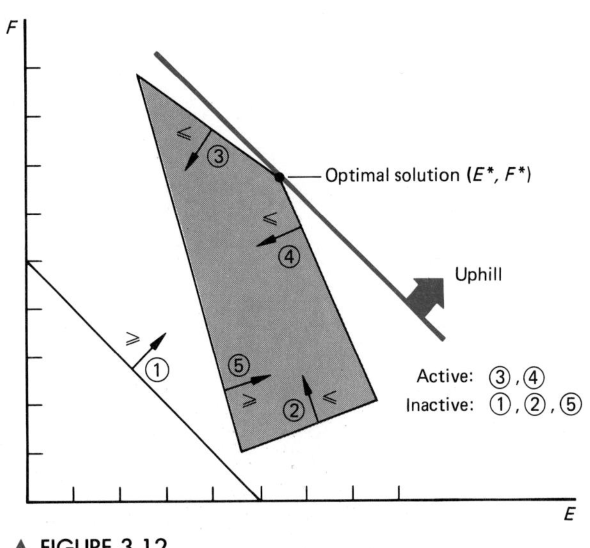

▲ FIGURE 3.12
Active and Inactive Constraints

$$
\begin{array}{lrl}
\text{Max} & 5000E + 4000F & \\
\text{s.t.} & E + F \geq 5 & ① \\
& E - 3F \leq 0 & ② \\
& 10E + 15F \leq 150 & ③ \\
& 20E + 10F \leq 160 & ④ \\
& 30E + 10F \geq 135 & ⑤ \\
& E, F \geq 0 & ⑥
\end{array}
$$

In truth, equation ⑥ is really two equations, ⑥ & ⑦, which are the two axes pictured in Figure 3.12.

and let us again graph the constraints, but this time with each constraint line labeled. This is shown in Figure 3.12. The label ① is on the first line that we plotted, $E + F = 5$. The label ② is on the second line that we plotted, $E - 3F = 0$, and so on. That is, the line labeled ① is the first constraint in the model above, the line labeled ② is the second constraint, and so on. We have just seen that the third and fourth constraints, which represent labor capacity in departments A and B, are active in this model. From Figure 3.12 you can see that these constraints "pass through" the optimal solution. In other words, the optimal solution "lies on" these constraints. Although we did not use the term *active,* we indeed solved for the values of E^* and F^* by implicitly recognizing that constraints ③ and ④ are active.

Identifying an active constraint

Geometrically, an active constraint is one that passes through the optimal solution.

We have seen that constraints ② and ⑤ are inactive. A quick check also shows that constraint ① is inactive. That is,

$$E^* + F^* = 4.5 + 7 = 11.5 > 5$$

Thus, we can see that

Identifying an inactive constraint

Geometrically, an inactive constraint is one that does not pass through the optimal solution.

APPLICATION CAPSULE

Shanghai Story: LP Lays the Foundations for a More Efficient Building Program*

A consistent theme of this book is that models are important because they can help to formulate or clarify concepts. The perspectives provided by a model often have as much impact on managerial decision making as the actual numerical solution. Here is an example of how a model affected a capacity-planning decision.

The Shanghai Urban Construction Bureau (UCB) is responsible for all residential construction in Shanghai. It controls the factories that produce building materials as well as the construction brigades that put up the buildings. Under great pressure to expand and update the city's housing stock, the UCB decided to add two new factories to make wall materials from fly ash (the residue from burning coal), thus putting an environmentally hazardous waste product to constructive use.

The question facing the UCB was what mix of materials—bricks, blocks, and panels—should be produced. Bricks were the cheapest to make and required the least investment; panels were the most expensive and required the most investment. At prevailing costs and prices, the most profitable output would have been a mix of bricks and blocks. However, in construction, bricks were the most labor-intensive and thus entailed the highest construction costs. Both blocks and panels required less labor, and so were much preferred by the construction brigades.

The research arm of the UCB turned the problem over to a student, who formulated an LP model similar to that developed for the PROTRAC example discussed in the text. The objective was to minimize the total cost of both manufacturing wall materials *and* constructing houses.

The model had three types of bricks, six types of block, and four types of panels as decision variables. Constraints were developed to ensure that all of the fly ash was used and that the expected needs for building materials were met. Other constraints limited the factory's usage of coal, electricity, and labor, and set a limit on the allowable capital investment level. Finally, there were constraints that limited the usage of cement, steel, and labor by the construction brigades and limited the total building weight.

The basic solution to this model called for a product mix of bricks, 17%; blocks, 47%; and panels, 36%. Binding constraints were those for the usage of fly ash, coal, construction labor, and steel, as well as building weight. This result suggested that if two factories were to be constructed, one should manufacture blocks and the second a mix of bricks and panels. Perhaps even more important, the model allowed decision makers to explore the results of changes in various parameters. For example, the model revealed that if more construction labor were available, usage of bricks and blocks could be increased, with total savings outweighing the cost of the additional laborers. Thus, it might make good sense for the planners of the UCB to consider expanding the construction brigades. In this way, the LP model dramatized to decision makers the value of viewing the production of building materials and the construction of buildings as a single integrated system.

*Graves, "Reflections on Operations Management in Shanghai," *Interfaces*, Vol. 15, No. 2 (March–April 1986).

The active and inactive constraints are easy to spot in the process of applying the graphical solution method. Indeed, that is the very goal of the graphical method, for once the active constraints are identified, as you have seen, we then solve simultaneous equations to obtain the optimal solution. Each inactive constraint will have surplus or slack, depending upon whether the corresponding inequality is ≥ or ≤. However, the numerical value of the surplus or slack cannot be read from the picture. It must be determined algebraically, as in the foregoing illustrations.

3.5 Extreme Points and Optimal Solutions

As you have seen, the solution to the **PROTRAC**, Inc. problem occurs at a corner of the feasible region—namely, at the corner where (what we have called) the third and fourth constraints intersect. In linear programming jargon the corners of the feasible region are called **extreme points.** The two terms, *extreme points* and *corners,* will be used interchangeably in our discussion.

A New Objective Function

To understand the importance of the extreme points, let us take a different linear objective function, with the same constraint set, and solve the problem again. For example, suppose that we change the price of F-9s in such a way that the profitability is raised from \$4000 to \$10,000 per unit. Let us see how this change in the objective function affects the solution to the problem. First, since we have changed only the objective function, leaving the constraints as they were, the feasible region remains unchanged. All that is new is that the contours of the objective function will assume a new tilt. A profit line of this new objective function (the 50,000-contour) is shown in Figure 3.13. Sliding the new profit line uphill, the new optimal solution is found, as shown in Figure 3.13.

▼ FIGURE 3.13
New Optimal Solution when the Objective Function Is $5000E + 10{,}000F$

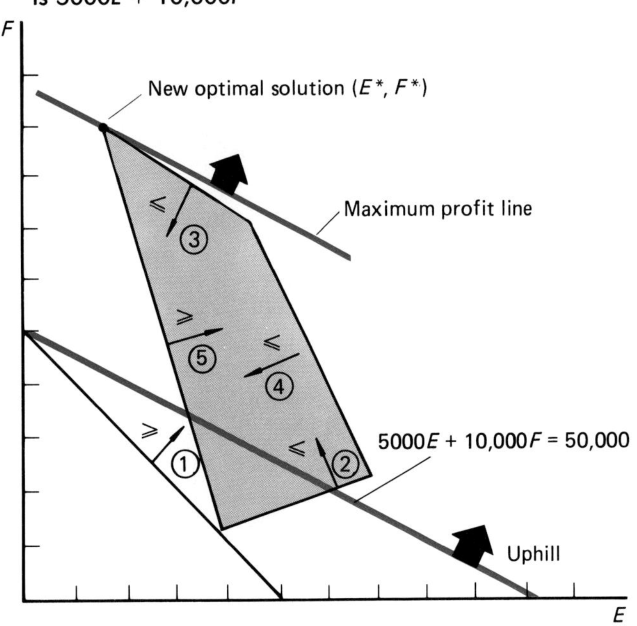

It may be easier to label the extreme points (A, B, C, D, etc.), usually starting in the bottom left-hand corner with A and then moving clockwise. Solving for the values of E-9s and F-9s and the ensuing profit:
A: (4.05, 1.35) profit = \$33,750
B: (1.50, 9.00) profit = \$97,500
C: (4.50, 7.00) profit = \$92,500
D: (6.86, 2.28) profit = \$57,100

Note from Figure 3.13 that at the new optimal point the *active* constraints have changed. Now the third and fifth constraints are active, whereas previously the third and fourth were active. Thus, you can see that the change in the slope of the objective function has moved the optimal solution away from the previous corner, but it has moved to another *corner,* or extreme point. As previously, we can obtain the exact value of the new optimal policy by simultaneously solving the third and fifth constraint equations. Thus we have

$$10E^* + 15F^* = 150 \qquad \text{(third constraint)}$$

$$30E^* + 10F^* = 135 \qquad \text{(fifth constraint)}$$

A New Optimal Corner

Solving these equation yields $E^* = 1.5$ and $F^* = 9$. This is the new optimal policy. As you might have predicted, the new price structure, which has increased the relative profitability of F-9s, leads to an optimal production plan that specifies a cutback in E-9s and an increase in F-9s. You can also note from Figure 3.13 that at the new optimal solution there is now positive slack in labor in department B (constraint ④).

What we have seen is that with each of two different objective functions for **PROTRAC**'s problem we obtained an optimal corner solution. In fact, you can experiment for yourself to see that no matter how much you change the objective function, as long as it remains linear, there will always be an optimal corner solution. You can even change the constraint set and there will still always be an optimal corner solution, as long as everything is kept linear.

In Figure 3.14 you see an arbitrary six-sided constraint set and contours of three *different* objective functions, denoted *f, g,* and *h.* For each objective function the arrow indicates the direction in which we want to slide the plotted contour to optimize the objective function. Note that in each case there is an optimal solution at a corner. The objective function *g* in Figure 3.14 illustrates the interesting case in which *the optimal objective contour coincides with one of the constraint lines on the boundary of the feasible region. In this case there will be many optimal solutions, namely the corners B and C and all the boundary points in between.* This is called a case of **multiple optima,** or **alternative optima.** However, even in this case, when there is not a *unique* optimal solution, it is still true that there is a corner solution that is optimal (in fact, there are two). Thus, the geometry illustrates an important fact about any LP problem with any number of decision variables:

In an LP problem, if there is an optimal solution, there is always at least one optimal corner solution.

▼ FIGURE 3.14
You Always Get a Corner Solution

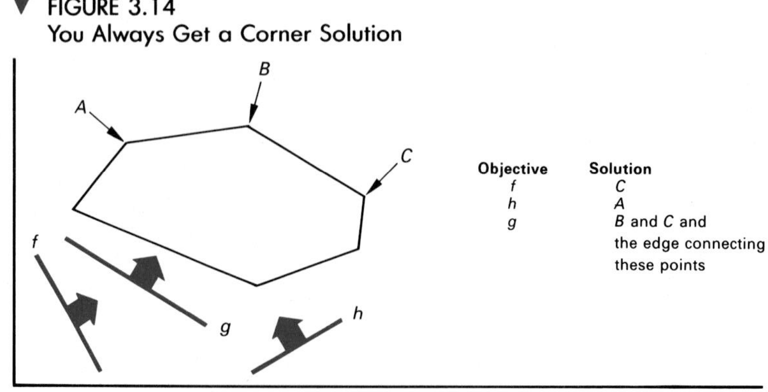

This result has a powerful implication in terms of using the graphical method for solving an LP. It means that you need not be overly meticulous in your plotting. Your diagram need only be sufficiently accurate to identify an optimal corner (i.e., the active constraints) of the feasible region. You then solve two equations in two unknowns to determine the exact optimal values of the decision variables.

In future chapters we will see other important implications of the fact that if there is an optimal solution, there will always be at least one at a corner.

3.6 Summary of the Graphical Solution Method for a Max Model

Our discussion thus far has presented the following procedure for solving a linear programming problem in two decision variables:

1. Superimpose the graph of each constraint on the same nonnegative quadrant. The nonnegative values of the decision variables that simultaneously satisfy (lie on the correct side of) *all* the constraints form the *feasible region,* also called the *constraint set.*
2. Draw an arbitrary *profit line,* also called a *contour,* of the objective function to obtain the slopes of the objective function *contours.*
3. Determine the uphill direction by, for example, evaluating the objective function at any trial point that is not on the profit line you have just constructed.
4. Now, given the slope of the profit line from step 2, and the uphill direction from step 3, determine visually the corner of the constraint set that lies on the highest possible profit line that still intersects this set.
5. The values of the decision variables at this corner (i.e., the coordinates of the corner) give the solution to the problem. These values are found by identifying the active constraints and then simultaneously solving two linear equations in two unknowns. Thus, in order to implement the graphical method, your drawing need only be accurate enough to identify the active constraints.
6. The optimal value of the objective function (i.e., the maximum profit) is obtained by "plugging in" the optimal values for the decision variables and evaluating the objective function.
7. You have already identified the active constraints. The inactive constraints can also be read from your graph. They are those that do not pass through the solution.

3.7 The Graphical Method Applied to a Min Model

The "Downhill" Direction

As we noted in Section 2.5, many real-world problems occur in a minimization context, and this was illustrated with the Crawler Tread problem. Thus far we have dealt only with the graphical representation of a Max model. The method applied to a Min model is quite similar, the only difference being that *the optimizing direction of the objective function* is now **"downhill"** rather than "uphill." Recall that in a Max model the objective function contours are often isoprofit lines or, more simply, profit lines. In a Min model, the objective function contours are often isocost lines or, more simply, cost lines. Our goal, in a Min model, is to determine a corner of the feasible region that lies on the *lowest-valued* objective function contour that still intersects the feasible region. As an example, let us apply the graphical method to the following simple minimization model in two decision variables, which we denote as x_1 and x_2.

$$\begin{aligned} &\text{Min } x_1 + 2x_2 \\ &\text{s.t.} \quad -3x_1 + 2x_2 \le 6 \qquad (1) \\ &\qquad\quad x_1 + x_2 \le 10.5 \qquad (2) \\ &\qquad\quad -x_1 + 3x_2 \ge 6 \qquad (3) \\ &\qquad\quad x_1, x_2 \ge 0 \end{aligned}$$

The feasible region for this problem is shown in Figure 3.15.

It might help again to label the extreme points, starting at the bottom left with *A*, *B*, *C*, and *D*, moving clockwise. By solving the two equations in two unknowns:

	Point	Cost
A:	(0.000, 2.000)	4.000
B:	(0.000, 3.000)	6.000
C:	(3.000, 7.500)	18.000
D:	(6.375, 4.125)	14.625

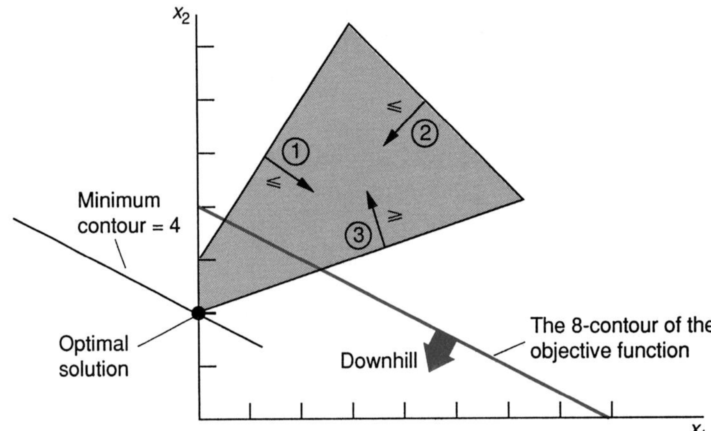

▲ FIGURE 3.15
Feasible Region for the Min Model

Finding the Optimal Solution

In order to find an optimal corner solution, we must

1. Plot a typical objective function contour to obtain the slope of such contours.
2. Determine the optimizing direction, which, since we are dealing with a Min model, is in this case the downhill direction.
3. With a parallel displacement of the objective function contour (from step 1), in the downhill direction (from step 2), determine which corner of the feasible region is optimal.
4. Solve the appropriate equations to obtain the exact optimal values of the decision variables. Then obtain the OV.

An example

Let us now carry out these steps.

1. In Figure 3.15 we superimpose the contour, objective value $= x_1 + 2x_2 = 8$.
2. To determine the downhill direction, we evaluate the objective function at the trial point ($x_1 = 0, x_2 = 0$). We obtain $x_1 + 2x_2 = 0 + 2(0) = 0$. Since 0 is less than 8, we see that the southwest side of our contour in Figure 3.15 is downhill.

3. By imagining a parallel displacement to the southwest, we obtain the optimal solution shown in Figure 3.15.
4. Note that the optimal solution lies on the intersection of the third constraint and the x_2 axis. The equation of the x_2 axis is $x_1 = 0$. Hence, the optimal solution is given by the two equations $x_1^* = 0$ and $-x_1^* + 3x_2^* = 6$. Thus, $x_1^* = 0$, and $x_2^* = 2$. The OV (optimal objective value) is obtained by evaluating the objective function at the optimal values for the decision variables.

$$\begin{aligned} \text{OV} = \text{optimal objective value} &= x_1^* + 2x_2^* \\ &= 0 + 2(2) = 4 \end{aligned}$$

The example above shows that the graphical analysis for a Min problem is exactly the same as that for a Max problem, as long as the objective contours are always moved in the *optimizing direction.* We shall always represent this direction with an arrow: The direction of the arrow is always uphill in a Max model, downhill in a Min model.

A faulty approach

One caveat here always deserves emphasis. Students on occasion fall into the trap of thinking that in a Max model the solution will always be the corner "farthest away" from the origin. And for a Min model, they instinctively feel that if the origin is feasible, it must be optimal, and if the origin is not feasible, then the corner "closest to" the origin will be optimal. *Such reasoning may be false.* The incorrect logic has to do with the false impression that the uphill direction is always outward from the origin (the northeast), and the downhill direction is always inward toward the origin. In fact, there is no general relationship between uphill or downhill and the origin, just as there is no general relationship between the sense of an inequality ($\leq$ or $\geq$) and the above or below side of the equality plot in our graphical representation (see Section 3.2).

3.8 Unbounded and Infeasible Problems

Thus far we have developed a geometric portrayal of LP problems in two decision variables. This portrayal has provided the basis for solving such problems and has also illustrated the important conclusion that "*if* there is an optimal solution, there will always be at least one at a corner." But how can an LP fail to have an optimal solution? In this section we use the geometric representation to see how that can occur.

Unbounded Problems

When running a larger LP model on the computer (can't be graphed), getting a message such as "Unbounded Solution" means that the model should be checked for either:
1. Data input error
   a. Check sign of constraints.
   b. Check values of coefficients.
2. Model formulation error
At least one constraint is missing.

Recall the graphical display of the **PROTRAC**, Inc. model as shown in Figure 3.12, but let us now change the model by supposing that the constraints labeled ③ and ④ have been inadvertently omitted. Thus, we obtain the model

$$\begin{aligned} &\text{Max } 5000E + 4000F \\ &\text{s.t.} \quad E + F \geq 5 \qquad (1) \\ &\qquad E - 3F \leq 0 \qquad (2) \\ &\qquad 30E + 10F \geq 135 \qquad (5) \\ &\qquad E, F \geq 0 \end{aligned}$$

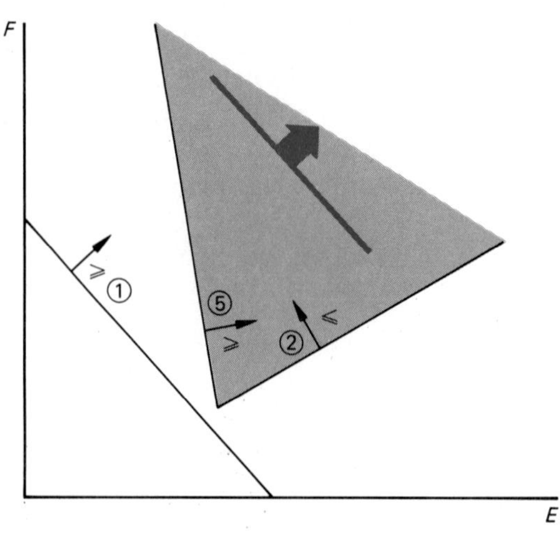

▲ FIGURE 3.16
Unbounded Problem

A chemical company designed a plant to produce ammonia (NH_3) using a five-year LP model with 8000 variables and 200 constraints, which gave an unbounded solution the first time it was run. The model included input restrictions on scarce nitrogen but not on hydrogen. Because any extra hydrogen could be sold internally at a profit of \$0.01/ft^3, the LP model was essentially pumping as much hydrogen as it could straight through the plant. Once an extra set of constraints was put in limiting hydrogen availability, the model started producing ammonia and had a finite, bounded solution.

The graphical analysis for this new problem is shown in Figure 3.16. You can see that the constraint set now extends indefinitely to the northeast, and it is possible to slide the profit line arbitrarily far in this direction. Since for this particular problem the northeast is the optimizing direction, we can find allowable decisions that give arbitrarily large values to the objective function. In other words, we can obtain profits approaching infinity. Such a problem has no solution, because the objective function is **unbounded.** That is, for any set of allowable values for the decision variables we can always find other allowable values that improve the objective value. Problems of this type are termed **unbounded problems.** Unbounded problems are "pathological." They can arise, as in Figure 3.16, when one or more important constraints have been left out of the model, or possibly because of typing errors when entering a problem into the computer for solution. In real life no one has yet discovered how to obtain an infinite profit, and you can be assured that when a model is correctly formulated and correctly entered into the computer it will not be unbounded.

Unbounded constraint set

Students sometimes confuse the term *unbounded problem* with the concept of an **unbounded constraint set.** The latter terminology refers to a feasible region in which at least one decision variable can be made arbitrarily large in value. If an LP is unbounded, the constraint set must also be unbounded, as illustrated by Figure 3.16. However, it is possible to have an unbounded constraint set without having an unbounded problem. This is illustrated graphically in Figure 3.17, which shows a

▼ FIGURE 3.17
Unbounded Constraint Set but a Solution

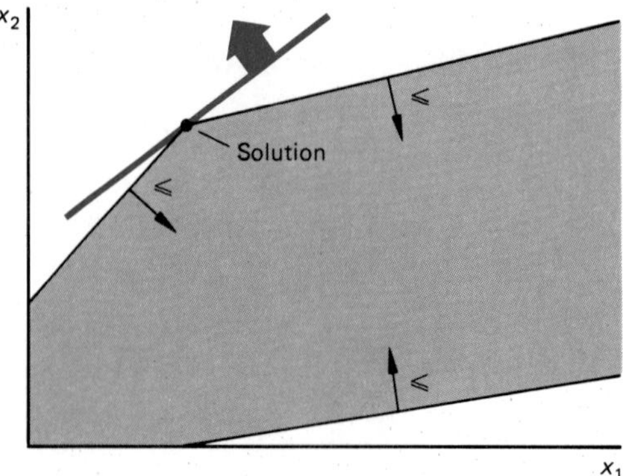

hypothetical LP model in two decision variables, x_1 and x_2. The model has three constraints and an unbounded constraint set, but there is an optimal solution.

Infeasible Problems

An infeasible LP

The most dreaded message for computer LP output is "Infeasible Solution." In this case, at least one of the constraints is too "tight." There are two things that can be done here:

1. Check input data for errors.
2. Check model formulation.
   a. Using a spreadsheet, input some possible solution numbers and see which constraints are violated.
   b. Then, if possible, "loosen" those constraints for the LP computer model and run the model again.

There is another type of pathology to be aware of in linear programming. It is called **infeasibility** or, alternatively, **inconsistency.** This term refers to a problem with an empty constraint set; that is, there is no combination of values for the decision variables that simultaneously satisfies all the constraints. A graphical illustration of an **infeasible problem** is obtained by changing the first constraint in the **PROTRAC,** Inc. model to $E + F \leq 5$ instead of $E + F \geq 5$. This gives us the new model

$$\begin{aligned}
&\text{Max } 5000E + 4000F \\
\text{s.t. } \quad & E + F \leq 5 \\
& E - 3E \leq 0 \\
& 10E + 15F \leq 150 \\
& 20E + 10F \leq 160 \\
& 30E + 10F \geq 135 \\
& E, F \geq 0
\end{aligned}$$

The constraint set for this LP is graphically represented in Figure 3.18. You can see that there is no pair of values (E, F) that satisfies *all* the constraints.

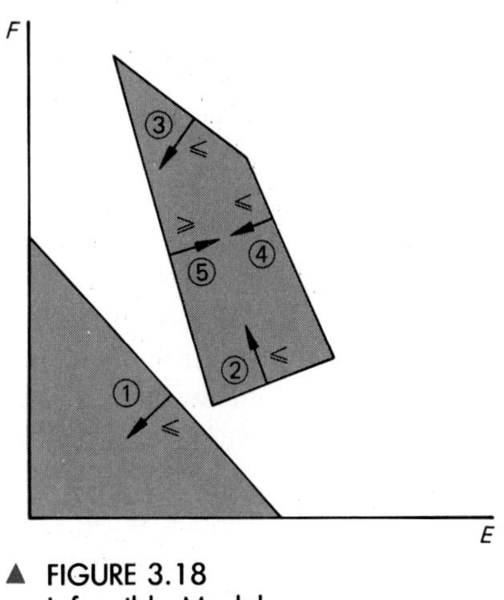

▲ FIGURE 3.18
Infeasible Model

As Figure 3.18 illustrates, *infeasibility depends solely on the constraints and has nothing to do with the objective function.* Obviously, an infeasible LP has no solution, but this pathology will not appear if the problem has been formulated correctly. In other words, in well-posed real problems, infeasibility always means that the model has been incorrectly specified, either because of logical errors or because of typing errors when entering the problem into the computer. Logical errors may mean that either too many constraints, or the wrong constraints, have been included.

In summary:

Every linear program will fall into one of the following three nonoverlapping categories:

1. **The problem has an optimal solution.**
2. **There is no optimal solution, because the problem is unbounded.**
3. **There is no optimal solution, because the problem is infeasible.**

In practice, a correctly formulated real-world LP will always have a solution. States 2 and 3 can arise only from (1) errors in model formulation, (2) errors in entering the problem into the computer.

3.9 Summary

The powerful role of two-dimensional geometry in illustrating certain important concepts has been explained in this chapter. In particular, we used the geometric approach to solve linear programming problems in two decision variables, to illustrate the meaning of active and inactive constraints, to show the important connection between optimal solutions and corners to the feasible region, and finally, to illustrate pathological properties.

We saw that the graphical solution method involves two main steps: determining the set of feasible decisions and then selecting the best of these decisions. The underlying prerequisite for these steps is the ability to plot linear equalities and linear inequalities. The techniques needed were briefly reviewed in Section 3.2.

The task of determining the set of feasible decisions typically reduces to portraying the values of the decision variables that satisfy a collection of linear inequalities. (There could also be equalities in the system, but this merely means that the feasible decisions must also lie on each equality line.) In Section 3.3 we saw that this set is determined by successively superimposing the plots of the constraints and then identifying the points that lie on the correct side of *all* the inequalities.

To find the best feasible decision, you plot a single objective function contour, identifying the optimizing direction (uphill for a Max model, downhill for a Min model), and then, with an imaginary parallel displacement of the contour in the optimizing direction, identify a corner solution. We saw in Section 3.5 that if an LP has an optimal solution, there will always be at least one optimal corner solution, also called an extreme point solution.

The graphical procedure is not limited by the necessity of creating a highly accurate picture, for it is only necessary to be able to identify the active constraints. Then, the optimal values of the decision variables are obtained by simultaneously solving these equations. From the geometric point of view, active constraints were defined as those that pass through the optimal corner of the feasible region. Algebraically, an active constraint is one for which the left-hand side, when evaluated at optimality, is equal to the right-hand side. *Surplus* and *slack* are terms used to denote the nonnegative difference between the two sides of an inequality constraint. The term *surplus* is used for a $\geq$ constraint, *slack* for a $\leq$ constraint.

Section 3.6 is devoted to a summary of the graphical solution method for a Max problem, and in Section 3.7 we saw that the technique was easily extended to Min problems. The only necessary modification for a Min problem is to make sure that the contours of the objective contour are displaced in a downhill direction in the process of finding the best feasible decision.

Finally, Section 3.8 considered two pathological cases in which an LP model does not have an optimal solution. In an unbounded Max problem the objective function can assume arbitrarily large values (arbitrarily negative values in an unbounded Min problem). This typically implies that one or more important constraints have been omitted in formulating the model. An infeasible problem is one in which there are no feasible solutions; that is, the set of decision variable values that satisfy all the constraints is empty. Such a result may occur because of incorrect formulation, such as insisting that two or more contradictory conditions must hold. Unbounded and infeasible problems can also occur as a result of transcription errors made when entering the model in the computer.

Key Terms

Contour. A contour of the function $f(x_1, x_2)$ is the set of all combinations of values for the variables (x_1, x_2) such that the function f takes on a specified constant value. (p. 98)

Isoquant. A synonym for contour. (p. 98)

Isoprofit Line. A contour of a profit function. (p. 98)

Isocost Line. A contour of a cost function. (p. 98)

Graphical Solution Method. A two-dimensional geometric analysis of LP problems with two decision variables. (p. 99)

Nonnegative Quadrant. The northeast sector of the two-dimensional coordinate system in which both variables have nonnegative values. (p. 100)

Feasible Region. The set of combinations of values for the decision variables that satisfies the nonnegativity conditions and *all* the constraints simultaneously, that is, the allowable decisions. (p. 102)

Constraint Set. A synonym for feasible region. (p. 102)

Feasible Solution. One that satisfies the nonnegativity conditions and all the constraints. Graphically, the feasible solutions are in one-to-one correspondence with the points in the feasible region. (p. 102)

Optimizing Direction. The direction in which decisions with better objective function values lie. (p. 105)

Uphill Direction. The optimizing direction for a Max model. (p. 105)

Optimal Solution. A point in the feasible region that maximizes the objective function. (p. 105)

Unique Optimal Solution. Refers to the case in which an LP has one and only one optimal solution. (p. 105)

Maximum Profit Line. The optimal contour of the objective function in a two-dimensional graphical analysis. (p. 105)

Optimal Objective Value (Optimal Value). The optimal value of the objective function; that is, the value of the objective function when evaluated at the optimal solution. Abbreviated as OV. (p. 106)

Active Constraint. A constraint for which, when evaluated at optimality, the left-hand side equals the right-hand side. Geometrically, this corresponds to a constraint line on which the optimal solution lies. (p. 108)

Binding Constraint. A synonym for active constraint. (p. 108)

Inactive Constraint. One that is not active. Consequently, an inactive constraint always has positive slack or surplus. (p. 108)

Surplus. The amount by which the left-hand side of a $\geq$ constraint, when evaluated at optimality, exceeds the right-hand side. Surplus is always nonnegative. (p. 108)

Slack. The amount by which the left-hand side of a $\leq$ constraint, when evaluated at optimality, is less than the right-hand side. Slack is always nonnegative. (p. 108)

Extreme Point. Corner of the feasible region. If an LP has a solution, there is always at least one extreme point solution. (p. 111)

Alternative Optima. Refers to the case in which an LP has more than one optimal solution. (p. 112)

Multiple Optima. A synonym for alternative optima. (p. 112)

Downhill Direction. The optimizing direction for a Min model. (p. 114)

Unbounded Objective Function. An objective function that, over the feasible region, can be made arbitrarily large (positive) for a Max model, arbitrarily negative for a Min model. (p. 116)

Unbounded Problem. An LP problem for which the optimal value can be increased without limit. Such a problem has no solution. (p. 116)

Unbounded Constraint Set. Constraint set in which at least one decision variable can be made arbitrarily large in value. (p. 116)

Infeasibility. A term referring to an infeasible problem. (p. 117)

Inconsistency. A synonym for infeasibility. (p. 117)

Infeasible Problem. An LP problem with an empty feasible region. Such a problem has no solution. (p. 117)

Major Concepts Quiz

True-False

1. T F The feasible region is the set of all points that satisfy at least one constraint.

2. T F In two-dimensional problems, the intersection of any two constraints gives an extreme point of the feasible region.

3. T F An optimal solution uses up all of the limited resources available.

4. T F A well-formulated model will be neither unbounded nor infeasible.

5. T F Infeasibility, as opposed to unboundedness, has nothing to do with the objective function.

6. T F If an LP is not infeasible, it will have an optimal solution.

7. T F Consider any point on the boundary of the feasible region. Such a point satisfies all the constraints.

8. T F An active inequality constraint has zero slack or surplus, which means that the optimal solution satisfies the constraint with equality.

Multiple Choice

9. The graphical method is useful because
- **a.** it provides a general way to solve LP problems
- **b.** it gives geometric insight into the model and the meaning of optimality
- **c.** both a and b

10. The phrase *unbounded LP* means that
- **a.** all decision variables can be made arbitrarily large without leaving the feasible region
- **b.** the objective contours can be moved as far as desired in the optimizing direction and still touch at least one point in the constraint set
- **c.** not all of the constraints can be satisfied

11. Consider an optimal solution to an LP. Which of the following must be true?
- **a.** At least one constraint (not including nonnegativity conditions) is active at the point.
- **b.** Exactly one constraint (not including nonnegativity conditions) is active at the point.
- **c.** Neither of the above.

12. Active constraints
- **a.** are those on which the optimal solution lies
- **b.** are those which, at optimality, do not use up all the available resources
- **c.** both a and b

13. An isoprofit contour represents
- **a.** an infinite number of feasible points, all of which yield the same profit
- **b.** an infinite number of optimal solutions
- **c.** an infinite number of decisions, all of which yield the same profit

14. Which of the following assertions is true of an optimal solution to an LP?
- **a.** Every LP has an optimal solution.
- **b.** The optimal solution always occurs at an extreme point.
- **c.** The optimal solution uses up all resources.
- **d.** If an optimal solution exists, there will always be at least one at a corner.
- **e.** All of the above.

15. Every corner of the feasible region is defined by
- **a.** the intersection of two constraint lines
- **b.** some subset of constraint lines and nonnegativity conditions
- **c.** neither of the above

16. An unbounded feasible region
  a. arises from an incorrect formulation
  b. means the objective function is unbounded
  c. neither of the above
  d. a and b

Answers

1. F	5. T	9. b	13. c
2. F	6. F	10. b	14. d
3. F	7. T	11. c	15. b
4. T	8. T	12. a	16. c

▶ Problems

See IM.

3-1. ▲ Plot the set of points (x_1, x_2) that satisfy each of the following conditions:
(a) $2x_1 + 6x_2 = 12$
(b) $2x_1 + 6x_2 > 12$
(c) $2x_1 + 6x_2 \geq 12$
(d) $2x_1 + 6x_2 < 12$
(e) $2x_1 + 6x_2 \leq 12$

See IM.

3-2. ▲ Plot the set of points (x_1, x_2) that satisfy each of the following conditions:
(a) $4x_1 + 3x_2 = 12$
(b) $4x_1 + 3x_2 > 12$
(c) $4x_1 + 3x_2 \geq 12$
(d) $4x_1 + 3x_2 < 12$
(e) $4x_1 + 3x_2 \leq 12$

(a) See IM
(b) Below
(c) Same as 3-1(d)

3-3. ▲ (a) Plot the set of points that satisfy $-\ 2x_1 - 6x_2 > -\ 12$.
(b) Is this plot above or below the line $-\ 2x_1 - 6x_2 = -\ 12$?
(c) This plot is the same as which of the sets plotted in Problem 3-1?

(a) See IM
(b) Above (does not include line)
(c) Same as 3-2(b)

3-4. ▲ (a) Plot the set of points that satisfy $-4x_1 - 3x_2 < -12$.
(b) Is this plot above or below the line $-4x_1 - 3x_2 = -12$?
(c) This plot is the same as which of the sets plotted in Problem 3-2?

See IM.

3-5. ▲ Claire Voyant, a colorful dealer in stereo equipment, puts together amps and preamps. An amp takes 12 hours to assemble and 4 hours for a high-performance check. A preamp takes 4 hours to assemble and 8 hours for a high-performance check. In the next month Claire will have 60 hours of assembly time available and 40 hours of high-performance check time available. Plot the combinations of amps and preamps that will satisfy
(a) The constraint on assembly time.
(b) The constraint on performance check time.
(c) Both constraints simultaneously.

See IM.

3-6. ▲ One can of grade A dog food contains 12mg of protein and 4mg of fat, while one can of grade B dog food contains 3mg of protein and 8mg of fat. Del Mation manages a small kennel that boards dogs. To feed his boarders tomorrow he would like to obtain a blend of dog foods that contains at least 30 mg of protein and 24 mg of fat. Plot the combination of cans of grade A and grade B that Del can buy to satisfy

(a) The constraint on the amount of protein.
(b) The constraint on the amount of fat.
(c) Both constraints simultaneously.

See IM.

3-7. ▲ In Problem 3-5, suppose that Claire makes a profit of \$10 on each amp and \$5 on each preamp. Plot the \$10, \$20, and \$60 profit contours.

See IM.

3-8. ▲ In Problem 3-6, assume that one can of grade A food costs \$0.80 and one can of grade B food costs \$0.60. Plot the combinations of the two grades that Del can buy for
(a) \$4.80
(b) \$2.40

Problems 3-9 through 3-22 can be solved graphically with the use of the QSB+ software. If the display of the graph is too small on your monitor, you may enlarge it by entering scale factors for the *X* and *Y* axes.

(a) $A^* = 4$, $P^* = 3$
(b) OV $= 10A^* + 5P^* = \$55$
(c) Active constraints are assembly and high-performance testing.
(d) Inactive are $A \leq 6$, slack $= 2$; $P \leq 4$, slack $= 1$.

3-9. ▲ Consider Claire's activity as described in Problems 3-5 and 3-7. Suppose that because of limitations on transistor availability she has determined that there are two additional constraints in her model. Namely, she can produce a maximum of 4 preamps and 6 amps in the next month. Taking all constraints into account,
(a) Find Claire's optimal (profit-maximizing) production plan, using graphical analysis.
(b) What is the OV?
(c) Which constraints are active?
(d) Which constraints are inactive, and what are their slack values?

2 cans A, 2 cans B; cost = \$2.80

3-10. ▲ Assuming the costs presented in Problem 3-8, find how many cans of each grade of dog food Del should buy to satisfy the requirements from Problem 3-6 at minimum total cost.

No.

3-11. ▲▲ Could the omission of any two constraints make Claire Voyant's problem unbounded?

1 can A, 6 cans B; cost = \$4.40

3-12. ▲ Suppose that when Del arrives at the store there is only one can of grade A dog food available and that he cannot buy the dog food anywhere else. Does this change the minimum cost solution you found in Problem 3-10? If so, how?

Makes it infeasible

3-13. ▲ Suppose that Claire's constraint on amps, $A \leq 6$, is replaced by $A \geq 6$. How does this affect the problem?

1.75 cans A, 3 cans B; cost = \$3.20

3-14. ▲ If Del must buy at least three cans of grade B dog food, does this affect the minimum cost solution you found in Problem 3-10? If so, how? (Note: For the purposes of this problem it is assumed that Del can buy fractional cans of dog food.)

(a) $x_1^* = 3$, $x_2^* = 1.5$, OV = 4.5
(b) $x_1^* = 0$, $x_2^* = 3$
(c) Four extreme points: (0,0), (4,0), (3,1.5), (0,3)

3-15. ▲ Consider the following LP:

$$\begin{aligned} \text{Max } & x_1 + x_2 \\ \text{s.t. } & x_1 + 2x_2 \leq 6 \\ & 3x_1 + 2x_2 \leq 12 \\ & x_1, x_2 \geq 0 \end{aligned}$$

(a) Use the graphical method to find the optimal solution and the OV.
(b) Change the objective function to $2x_1 + 6x_2$ and find the optimal solution.
(c) How many extreme points does the feasible region have? Find the values of (x_1, x_2) at each extreme point.

3-16. ▲ Consider the following LP:

(a) $x_1 = 1, x_2 = 3$; OV = 11
(b) $x_1 = 3.5, x_2 = 0.5$
(c) Three: $x_1 = 1.75, x_2 = 0.75$
$x_1 = 1, x_2 = 3$
$x_1 = 3.5, x_2 = 0.5$

$$
\begin{aligned}
\text{Max } & 2x_1 + 3x_2 \\
\text{s.t. } & 3x_1 + x_2 \geq 6 \\
& x_1 + 7x_2 \geq 7 \\
& x_1 + x_2 \leq 4 \\
& x_1, x_2 \geq 0
\end{aligned}
$$

(a) Use the graphical method to find the optimal solution and the OV.
(b) Change the objective function to $3x_1 + 2x_2$ and find the optimal solution.
(c) How many extreme points does the feasible region have? Find (x_1, x_2) at each extreme point.

(a) $x_1^* = 6\frac{2}{3}, x_2^* = 2\frac{2}{3}$, OV = $30\frac{2}{3}$
(b) First constraint: slack = $18\frac{2}{3}$
Second constraint: 0 slack
Third constraint: 0 surplus

3-17. ▲ Consider the following LP:

$$
\begin{aligned}
\text{Max } & 3x_1 + 4x_2 \\
\text{s.t.} & -2x_1 + 4x_2 \leq 16 \\
& 2x_1 + 4x_2 \leq 24 \\
& -6x_1 - 3x_2 \geq -48 \\
& x_1, x_2 \geq 0
\end{aligned}
$$

(a) Use the graphical method to find the optimal solution and the OV.
(b) Find the slack and surplus values for each constraint.

(a) $x_1 = 10, x_2 = 0$; OV = 60
(b) 1: Slack = 0
2: Surplus = 15
3: Surplus = 7

3-18. ▲ Consider the following LP:

$$
\begin{aligned}
\text{Max } & 6x_1 + 2x_2 \\
\text{s.t. } & 2x_1 + 4x_2 \leq 20 \\
& 3x_1 + 5x_2 \geq 15 \\
& x_1 \geq 3 \\
& x_2 \geq 0
\end{aligned}
$$

(a) Use the graphical method to find the optimal solution and the OV.
(b) Find the slack and surplus values for each constraint.

(a) $x_1^* = 1\frac{1}{11}$, $x_2^* = 3\frac{7}{11}$, OV = $12\frac{8}{11}$
(b) Active constraints are second and third; inactive constraints are first and fourth.
(c) Zero associated with second and third
First constraint: surplus is $7\frac{1}{11}$
Fourth constraint: slack is $12\frac{6}{11}$
(d) 4
(e) $x_1^* = 1\frac{1}{11}, x_2^* = 3\frac{7}{11}$; $x_1^* = 2\frac{2}{3}, x_2^* = 1\frac{2}{3}$

3-19. ▲▲ Consider the following LP:

$$
\begin{aligned}
\text{Min } & 5x_1 + 2x_2 \\
\text{s.t. } & 3x_1 + 6x_2 \geq 18 \\
& 5x_1 + 4x_2 \geq 20 \\
& 8x_1 + 2x_2 \geq 16 \\
& 7x_1 + 6x_2 \leq 42 \\
& x_1, x_2 \geq 0
\end{aligned}
$$

(a) Use the graphical method to find the optimal solution and the OV.
(b) Which constraints are active? Which are inactive?
(c) What are the slack and surplus values associated with each constraint?
(d) The feasible region has how many extreme points?
(e) Change the objective function to $15x_1 + 12x_2$. What are the alternative optimal corner solutions?

(a) $x_1 = 3$, $x_2 = 3.5$; OV = 13.5
(b) 1: Slack = 0
2: Surplus = 11.5
3: Surplus = 0

3-20. In Problem 3-18 change the objective function to $x_1 + 3x_2$. Answer parts (a) and (b) for the new problem.

3-21. Consider the following LP:

$$\begin{aligned} \text{Max} \quad & 600E + 1000F \\ \text{s.t.} \quad & 100E + 60F \le 21{,}000 \\ & 4000E + 800F \le 680{,}000 \\ & E + F \le 290 \\ & 12E + 30F \le 6000 \\ & E, F \ge 0 \end{aligned}$$

(a) $E^* = 118.4$, $F^* = 152.6$, OV = 223,684
(b) $E + F \le 290$
(c) −18.496
(d) 0.1599
(e) 1667

(a) Let E be the horizontal axis and F the vertical axis, and use graphical means to find the optimal solution to this problem and the OV. Label the corners of the constraint set as I, II, III, IV, and V, where I is on the vertical axis above the origin and you continue clockwise, ending with V at the origin.

(b) One of the constraints is redundant in the sense that it plays no role in determining the constraint set. Which one is it?

(c) What is the minimum change in the RHS of this constraint that would cause the constraint to become active?

(d) The coefficient of E in the third constraint is currently 1. What is the minimum increase in this coefficient that would cause the constraint to become active?

(e) Suppose that the coefficient of E, say C_E, in the objective function is increased, whereas the coefficient of F, say C_F, remains fixed. At what value for the coefficient of E would alternative optima first become encountered?

(a) $x_1 = 5$, $x_2 = 0$; OV = 15 (See IM)
(b) B = 2; $x_1 = x_2 = 1.33$; OV = 4
(c) $\frac{5}{6}A \le B \le \frac{7}{6}A$ (See IM)

3-22. Consider the following problem:

$$\begin{aligned} \text{Max} \quad & 3x_1 + x_2 \\ \text{s.t.} \quad & 6x_1 + 3x_2 \ge 12 \\ & 4x_1 + 8x_2 \ge 16 \\ & 6x_1 + 5x_2 \le 30 \\ & 6x_1 + 7x_2 \le 36 \\ & x_1, x_2 \ge 0 \end{aligned}$$

(a) Use graphical means to find the optimal solution and the OV.

(b) Consider a Min problem with the constraint set above. Assume that the objective function is $x_1 + Bx_2$. What is the largest value of B so that the optimal solution lies at the intersection of the lines $6x_1 + 3x_2 = 12$ and $4x_1 + 8x_2 = 16$? Find the optimal solution and the OV.

(c) In a Max problem, assume that the objective function is $Ax_1 + Bx_2$. Determine the set of values for A and B for which the optimal solution lies at the intersection of $6x_1 + 5x_2 = 30$ and $6x_1 + 7x_2 = 36$. Use a graph to show the set of values.

Video Case

The Art and Science of Model Formulation

The Juicy Juice problem provides a clear and graphic representation of the process by which models are formed: (1) an economic problem is identified; (2) variables are defined, corresponding to decisions that are under the control of management; and (3) a linear program is created. This example was selected to be absolutely clear and easy to follow, and it succeeds admirably. However, some aspects of the true art (and science) of modeling are downplayed in the effort to achieve that clarity. Here are a few points that may contribute to a more realistic picture.

- The real problem is often not obvious. In most real-world situations management sees a *symptom* of a problem, not the problem itself. For example, management may feel that work-in-process inventory is too large. But what decisions can management make that will improve this situation? That is a much harder question to answer.
- Even when the problem is clear, the decision variables may not be. The security force scheduling problem (Section 2.10, Example 3) provides a good example. You have seen how this model was formulated in the text. If you hadn't, however, it might not be at all obvious to you at first glance that the number of persons assigned to each possible schedule is a good definition for the decision variables (i.e, that this definition yields a model that can be quickly and easily solved.).
- The relationships between the decision variables and characteristics of interest are not always as obvious as they are in the Juicy Juice problem. In that problem it is clear that when you add one quart of apple and one quart of cranberry juice you get two quarts of mixed juice, and the cost of the mixture is also clear. Suppose, however, that you are considering an advertising campaign and deciding how many ads to put in each of several possible publications, such as the *Wall Street Journal* and the *Chicago Tribune.* You have a budget constraint that restricts the amount you can spend on these ads. Now you face a host of additional questions:

1. What is the objective? Should we maximize the *total* number of readers who might see the ad? Or should we try to maximize the number from some particular segment of the population (lawyers, perhaps, or heads of households with incomes over $50,000)?
2. Are the results additive—that is, are two exposures to one person as effective as one exposure each to two different people?
3. Is the response linear or are there diminishing returns—that is, is the second or third exposure to a person as important as the first?

A modeler clearly faces considerable difficulties in trying to describe this problem with mathematics. The task does not become any easier when the model of choice is an LP, in which additivity and linearity of response must hold.

These issues do not go away if the manager chooses not to model the problem and to rely on "seat-of-the-pants" methods instead. Indeed, part of the value of the modeling process is that it brings questions into bold relief. You have to specify the relationship between decisions and outcomes with great exactness if you are going to express them in mathematical terms. Other languages, such as English, contain much more ambiguity.

Questions

The problems in this text are intended to be clear and unambiguous. They thus avoid many of the issues discussed above. However, the real problems that these simplified versions represent can be used to illustrate some of the potential complications.

1. Consider Problem 2.6. What factors have been ignored? What assumptions have been made?

2. Consider Problem 2.15. What factors have been ignored? Why might the upper bounds on the amount to be invested in each instrument have been added to the problem?

CHAPTER

4

Analysis of LP Models: The Graphical Approach

APPLICATION CAPSULE

Bye-Bye Backlogs: LP Workforce Scheduling Breaks Up a Costly Canadian Logjam*

Tax systems have a strong influence on human behavior. Consider, for example, the strain on the U.S. Postal Service (not to mention on taxpayers' nerves) just before midnight on April 15 each year. This is now an international phenomenon—tax authorities in Canada have created a similar problem. Fortunately, one firm was able to achieve some measure of control over a costly and chaotic situation by the use of linear programming.

Canada's income-tax laws allow tax-deductible contributions to a retirement fund, the RRSP, that is much like our IRA. Contributions for a given tax year are permitted not only during the year itself but also in January and February of the following year. It is generally during this two-month "grace period" that most contributions are made. The companies that handle these accounts thus face a tremendous surge in transactions for a few weeks of the year.

One such company, the Financial Services Group (FSG) of the Canada Systems Group (CSG) of Toronto, found its resources severely strained by the annual flood of transactions, which created serious overload and staffing problems. By the mid-1980s the company was incurring extra costs of $500,000 per year. To deal with this problem, FSG made a strategic decision: It would hire temporary staff for specific, single tasks. This approach minimized training time and provided a quick boost in productivity. It also created a new problem, since now schedules had to be devised for a large number of temporary workers.

This problem was solved with an LP model that took into account the different jobs for which personnel were needed, the availability of personnel from different sources, and the various possible work shifts during the six-week period for which the temps were to be employed. This model, consisting ultimately of 202 constraints (including 95 upper bounds) and 226 variables, yielded a solution that could be implemented immediately, producing a huge gain in efficiency.

As we have often emphasized, the solution to a real problem typically requires more than just the "right answer." This is a case in point. One of the most interesting benefits of the model was in the area of morale (and thus, indirectly, of productivity). The LP solution involved a necessary but rather intimidating buildup of work in the data-preparation department toward the end of February. Rather than allowing employees to become aware of the seemingly overwhelming backlog, and perhaps become discouraged or demoralized, managers made sure that at the beginning of each shift each employee received only as much work as he or she could effectively do. Thus employees developed a sense of pride in finishing their assigned quotas and started thinking of themselves as "backlog busters."

All in all, the LP model made possible a saving of more than \$300,000 in its first year of use. In addition, FSG's reputation as a reliable processor of financial transactions was greatly enhanced, helping it to secure new business.

*Von Lanzenauer, Harbauer, Johnston, and Shuttleworth, "RRSP Flood: LP to the Rescue," *Interfaces*, Vol. 17, No. 4 (July–Aug. 1987).

4.1 Introduction to Sensitivity Analysis (PROTRAC, Inc. Revisited)

The LP solution is not just a graphical point but a set of ranges for which that solution is valid. As will be seen, the solution of a model will provide a lot of information about the situation being modeled.

The **PROTRAC**, Inc. model was formulated in Chapter 2 and solved in Chapter 3. You may well feel that if this were a real problem, management would now have a good solution to its problem and would thus be free to turn attention to other matters. In many, if not most, cases this simply is not true. Often the solution to a model is only a starting point and is, in itself, the least interesting part of the analysis of the real problem. Remember that the model is an abstraction of the real problem. Typically a manager would need to ask numerous additional questions before she would be confident enough about the results to apply them to her real problem. For example, there may be rather significant considerations that because of their complexity have not been built into the model. To the extent that a model is a simplification of reality there will always be factors that are left out. These factors may, for example, be of a political or ethical nature. Such considerations are usually difficult to quantify. Having solved her simplified model, the manager may now wish to know how well the optimal solution "fits in" with other considerations, which may not have been included. There may, as another example, be inexactitudes and uncertainty in some of the data that were used in the model. In real-world problem solving this is the norm rather than the exception. The motto is: "Do the best with what you have."

Omitted factors

Inexact data

Other factors that can affect the objective function coefficients are variations in the time it takes to make products and increases or decreases in the cost of raw materials. In such cases, if the solution stays the same within the ranges of those costs, there is no need to determine the costs more precisely.

In such cases, the manager will want to know: How *sensitive* is the optimal solution to the inexact data? We may have an estimate of the absentee rate for next month's labor force, and the model has been run using this estimate. What happens to the optimal solution if we change the estimate by 5%, 10%, or even 15%? Will the OV (i.e., the optimal objective value) vary wildly, or will it remain more or less unchanged? Obviously, the answer to such questions will help to determine the credibility of the model's recommendations. For example, if the OV changes very little with large changes in the value of a particular parameter, we will not be concerned about uncertainty in that value. If on the other hand the OV varies wildly with small changes in that parameter, we cannot tolerate much uncertainty in its value. In this case either the model might be rejected or more resources might be committed to establishing a more precise value for the parameter in question.

Although some of the foregoing considerations can be dealt with only informally, we fortunately do have some rigorous and precise tools at our disposal. These tools are in the realm of **parametric analysis,** or **sensitivity analysis,** or **postoptimality analysis.** All of these terms mean essentially the same thing, and the topic is of such significance that an entire chapter (Chapter 5) is devoted to understanding the sensitivity information contained in the computer solution to an LP problem. Making good use of computer analysis is, of course, a problem faced by managers in the real world. In this chapter we lay some of the groundwork for being able to understand clearly the meaning of the computer results. The graphical approach that we worked with in Chapter 3 will make it relatively easy to do this. The ability to *see,* geometrically, how changes in the model affect the solution in the special two-decision-variable case makes it much easier to understand the changes that will occur in larger realistic models.

Technically, the terminology is *postoptimal analysis.* If only one value is being changed at a time, it is usually called *sensitivity analysis,* but if more than one value is being changed, it is called *parametric analysis.* However, over the years these terms have become intertwined and have lost some of their original meaning.

In order to introduce the topic in a very specific way, let us again refer to our illustrative **PROTRAC**, Inc. model:

$$
\begin{array}{llr}
\text{Max } 5000E + 4000F & & \text{(max profit)} \\
\text{s.t.} \quad E + \quad F \geq 5 & & \text{(minimal production requirement)} \\
E - 3F \leq 0 & & \text{(market position balance)} \\
10E + 15F \leq 150 & & \text{(capacity in department A)} \\
20E + 10F \leq 160 & & \text{(capacity in department B)} \\
30E + 10F \geq 135 & & \text{(contractual labor agreement)} \\
E, F \geq 0 & & \text{(nonnegativity conditions)}
\end{array}
$$

Recall that the purpose of this model, as discussed in Chapter 2, is to recommend a production target *for next month.* Therefore, all the numerical data in the model are supposed to be pertinent to this period of interest, namely one month in the future.

A major application of linear programming involves planning models such as this, where future plans and policies are to be determined, and in such models future data are naturally required. Obviously in many real-world situations such data may not be known with complete certainty. Suppose, for example, that the stated profitabilities of $5000 per E-9 and $4000 per F-9 are only estimates based on revenues and projected costs for next month and that some of the costs of raw materials to be purchased next month are subject to change. Unfortunately, in order to achieve the lead time required in the planning process, the model must be run now, before the exact data are known. Thus, we must use the numbers above, which are our best current estimates, knowing full well that the actual profitabilities next month could differ. We might have some fairly solid ideas about the possible ranges in which the true values will lie, and the profitabilities of $5000 and $4000 might be our best estimates with such ranges. But how do we deal with the fact that the data are not known with complete certainty? That is one important topic covered in sensitivity analysis.

Uncertain revenues and costs

Uncertain RHS data

Another possible concern may involve uncertainty in some of the constraint data. In linear programming, this type of uncertainty usually focuses on the righthand sides of the constraints. For example, consider the number 135, which is the right-hand side of the contractual labor agreement constraint. It represents the minimal number of hours that must be spent on product testing next month. In a real-life application it is possible that such a number could also be uncertain. The actual minimal requirement that will be in force next month could be arrived at in a rather complicated way depending, for example, on the results of quality tests of this month's production, results that can be *estimated* only at the time the planning process occurs. Thus, the value of 135 is only a "best estimate." Again, management must cope with the uncertainty in such data.

These two examples reflect the major focus of sensitivity analysis and the topics discussed in the following two sections. The first example, in which profitabilities are uncertain, illustrates what we call *changes in the objective function coefficients.* The second example illustrates *changes in the right-hand side.* In an LP model, the objective function coefficients and the right-hand sides are often called **parameters,** and for this reason the term *parametric analysis* is sometimes used for the investigation of the effects of changing the values of these parameters. Let us see how graphical analysis can provide insight into the effects of such changes.

4.2 Changes in the Objective Function Coefficients

Suppose that the constraint data remain unchanged and only the objective coefficients are changed. Then the only effect on the model, from the geometric viewpoint, is that the slope of the profit lines is changed. We have, in fact, already seen an illustration of this phenomenon in Section 3.5. In Figure 3.13 all data in the **PROTRAC,** Inc. model remained unchanged except for the fact that the profitability of F-9s was raised from \$4000 to \$10,000 per unit. We saw that the effect of this change was to change the tilt of the profit lines to such an extent that a new corner solution was obtained.

A large overhead transparency of this figure might effectively show how changing one coefficient tilts the objective function toward a neighboring extreme point.

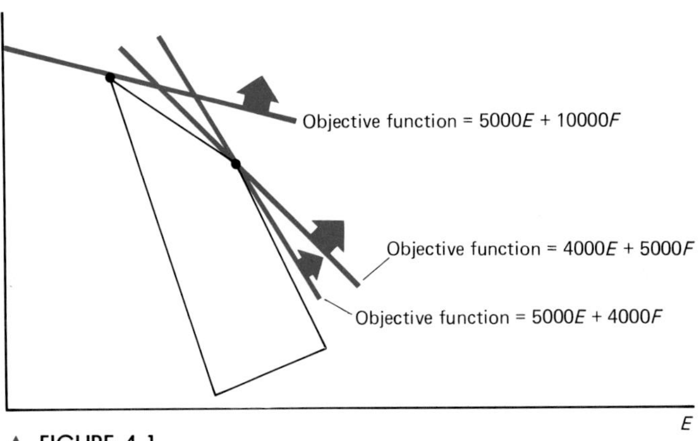

▲ FIGURE 4.1
PROTRAC, Inc. Model with Contours of Three Different Profit Functions and the Corresponding Solutions

You can also quickly see that some changes in the objective function coefficients will *not* change the optimal solution, even though the profit lines will have a different slope. For example, let us replace the old objective function $5000E + 4000F$ with a new objective function $4000E + 5000F$. As we saw in Figure 3.11, the solution with the old objective function is $E^* = 4.5$, $F^* = 7.0$. The new objective function $4000E + 5000F$ assigns a lower profitability to E-9s and a higher profitability to F-9s. You might therefore expect to obtain an optimal solution calling for production of fewer than 4.5 E-9s and more than 7.0 of the more profitable F-9s. However, Figure 4.1 presents a graphical analysis that shows that this is not the case. In this figure there are three different objective functions:

$$5000E + 4000F$$
$$4000E + 5000F$$
$$5000E + 10{,}000F$$

It is evident that the negative slopes of the contours associated with each of the three functions become progressively less steep (i.e., the contours become flatter) as the profitability of F-9s increases relative to E-9s (i.e., as the ratio [coefficient of F/coefficient of E] increases). However, although the objectives $5000E + 4000F$ and $4000E + 5000F$ have contours with different slopes, *the slopes are not sufficiently different to give us a new corner solution.* For each of these two objectives the optimal solution is the same, namely $E^* = 4.5$ and $F^* = 7.0$.

Same solution

On the other hand, it is important to note that in this case the optimal profits (i.e., the optimal objective values) will differ. In the former case we have

Different OVs

$$\text{optimal profit} = 5000E^* + 4000F^*$$
$$= 5000(4.5) + 4000(7) = 50{,}500$$

whereas in the latter case

$$\text{optimal profit} = 4000E^* + 5000F^*$$
$$= 4000(4.5) + 5000(7) = 51{,}200$$

In conclusion, what we have just seen can be summarized thus:

Changing the objective function coefficients changes the slopes of the objective function contours. This may or may not affect the optimal solution and the optimal value of the objective function.

For an LP problem with three variables, the objective function and constraints are planes in three dimensions. A change in any coefficient in the objective function then "tilts" the plane. With four or more variables (dimensions), one cannot "see" the results, but if one understands what happens in two dimensions, one should be able to extrapolate what happens in "*n*" dimensions.

This geometric analysis, although conducted on a two-dimensional problem, gives you good insight into more general problems, for even in models with more than two decision variables the summary statement above is correct. In the next chapter we will see how the computer can be used to provide for higher-dimensional models a wealth of sensitivity information on the effects of changes in the objective function coefficients. We shall also see how such information can be used to management's advantage.

4.3 Changes in the Right-Hand Sides

Let us now ignore the objective function and focus on the right-hand sides of the constraint functions. Again, graphical analysis will nicely explain the effects of changes in these parameters. As a specific example, let us suppose that the fifth constraint of the **PROTRAC**, Inc. model

$$30E + 10F \geq 135 \qquad \text{(contractual labor)} \tag{4.1}$$

is changed to

$$30E + 10F \geq 210 \tag{4.2}$$

Again, taking the original graph and using a large overhead transparency might be an effective way to show how increasing (or decreasing) the right-hand side of the labor constraint changes the feasible area. (Compare with Figure 4.3.)

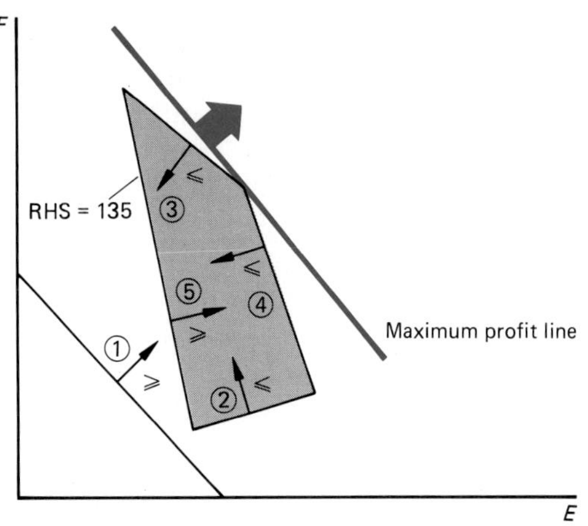

▲ FIGURE 4.2
Graphical Analysis of the Original Model

and suppose that all other constraint data remain as they are given. Since 135 is a smaller number than 210, expression (4.1) is easier to satisfy than (4.2). For example, the pair (E = 3, F = 5) satisfies (4.1) for

$$30E + 10F = 30(3) + 10(5) = 90 + 50 = 140$$

Since 140 is ≥ 135, (4.1) is satisfied. But 140 is less than 210 and hence the pair (E = 3, F = 5) does *not* satisfy condition (4.2). Another way of saying this is that *fewer combinations of values for E and F will satisfy (4.2).*

Because of this fact, it would be reasonable to expect that the change from (4.1) to (4.2) might, in some sense, "shrink" the feasible region. From the geometric point of view, you can see that changing the right-hand side of a constraint creates a parallel shift in the constraint line. In this case, then, the reasoning above suggests that, in changing the RHS from 135 to 210, the fifth constraint line (corresponding to [4.1]) will shift in such a way as to eliminate some of the feasible region. Figure 4.2 shows the original constraint set with the constraints labeled ① through ⑤. Figure 4.3 shows the new constraint set with the fifth constraint (4.1) replaced by (4.2).

Parallel shift in the constraint line

Although, geometrically speaking, the constraint set in Figure 4.3 looks quite different from the one in Figure 4.2, all that has been done is to slide the constraint labeled ⑤ farther outward from the origin to its new position. You should

▼ FIGURE 4.3
Graphical Analysis of the Model with New RHS for the Fifth Constraint

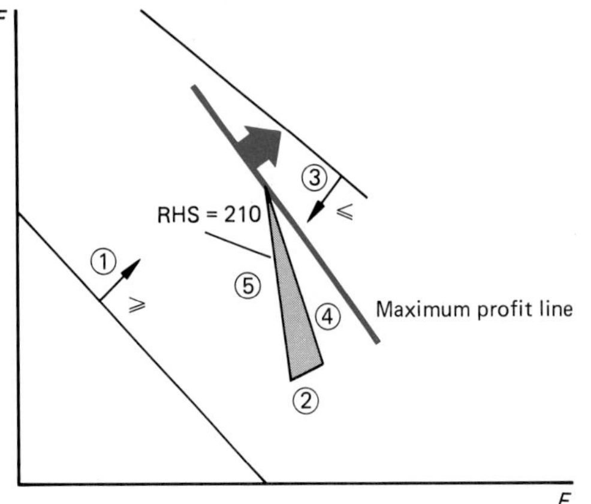

experiment by assigning different values to this right-hand side, and to the other right-hand sides, to see the variety of different-looking feasible regions that can arise from such simple perturbations. One particularly interesting case arises if you further increase the right-hand side of the fifth constraint to 270, leaving all the other constraint data unchanged. You are asked in Problem 4-5 to show that in this case you will have created an inconsistent set of constraints. That is, the problem becomes infeasible.

Return now to Figure 4.3. The optimal solution is shown for the objective function $5000E + 4000F$. Comparing this with the graphical analysis for the original problem, Figure 4.2, you can see that the solution to the new problem is entirely different from the old. We have

Old problem:

Active constraints: ③ and ④
Inactive constraints: ①, ②, and ⑤
Solution (by solving active constraints): $E^* = 4.5$, $F^* = 7$
Optimal profit = OV = 50,500

New problem:

Active constraints: ④ and ⑤
Inactive constraints: ①, ②, and ③
Solution is computed as follows:

$$
\begin{array}{lrcl}
\text{Constraint ④:} & 20E + 10F & = & 160 \\
\text{Constraint ⑤:} & \underline{30E + 10F} & \underline{=} & \underline{210} \\
\text{Subtracting:} & -10E & = & -50 \\
 & E & = & 5 \\
\text{Substituting:} & 20(5) + 10F & = & 160 \\
 & F & = & 6
\end{array}
$$

Hence, $E^* = 5$, $F^* = 6$, and

The new solution

$$
\begin{aligned}
\text{optimal profit} = \text{OV} &= 5000E^* + 4000F^* \\
&= 5000(5) + 4000(6) = 49{,}000
\end{aligned}
$$

It should be clear from this analysis that changing even one right-hand-side value can have a profound effect on the solution. In Chapter 5 we shall develop additional tools for precisely determining the impact of certain RHS changes. Again, it will be shown that the computer can be used to provide sensitivity information on the effects of such changes. For now, we summarize what we have graphically seen in this section for two-dimensional models. These results, as with the previous results for changing an objective function coefficient, are also valid for problems with more than two decision variables.

Changing a right-hand-side value results in a parallel shift of the changed constraints. This *may* affect both the optimal solution and the OV (the optimal objective value). The effect will depend on exactly which right-hand-side values are changed, and by how much.

4.4 Tightening and Loosening an Inequality Constraint

We conclude this discussion on parametric changes by making some general observations on the effects of right-hand-side changes for *inequality constraints.* This will lead us to several useful new terms.

In the discussion above we compared the two constraints

$$30E + 10F \geq 135 \tag{4.1}$$

and

$$30E + 10F \geq 210 \tag{4.2}$$

and noted that since each constraint is of the ≥ form, and since the right-hand side of (4.2) is larger than the right-hand side of (4.1), the constraint (4.2) is more difficult to satisfy. This process of increasing the RHS of a ≥ constraint is called **tightening the constraints.** The constraint (4.2) is *tighter* than (4.1). Similarly, if the RHS of a ≤ constraint is decreased, the constraint becomes more difficult to satisfy and hence is tighter.

Tightening

Tightening an inequality constraint means making it more difficult to satisfy. For a ≥ constraint this means increasing the RHS. For a ≤ constraint this means decreasing the RHS.

Suppose that instead of increasing the RHS of (4.1) we decrease it so that, for example, the constraint becomes

$$30E + 10F \geq 100 \tag{4.3}$$

You should be able to see that since the right-hand side has become smaller, and since (4.3) is a ≥ constraint, there are now *more* combinations of values for E and F that will satisfy the constraint. Thus, the constraint has become easier to satisfy. This process of decreasing the RHS of a ≥ constraint is called **loosening the constraint.** The constraint (4.3) is *looser* than (4.1). Similarly, if the RHS of a ≤ constraint is increased, the constraint becomes easier to satisfy and hence is looser.

Loosening

Loosening an inequality constraint means making it easier to satisfy. For a ≥ constraint this means decreasing the RHS. For a ≤ constraint this means increasing the RHS.

The geometric effects of tightening and loosening are easily illustrated. We see that in moving from Figure 4.2 to Figure 4.3, constraint ⑤ has been tightened and the feasible region contracted. Moving from Figure 4.3 to Figure 4.2 loosens constraint ⑤ and the feasible region expands. These geometric results, that tightening contracts and loosening expands, are what you probably would have predicted, but another possibility must be considered.

Consider constraint ①, $E + F \geq 5$. Note in Figure 4.2 that it currently plays no role in determining the shape of the feasible set. Also, with a suitably small change in the right-hand side, say from 5 to 5.1 or 4.9, the line will incur a small parallel displacement and still not intersect the original feasible set. Thus, in this case we see that a suitably small amount of tightening or loosening of constraint ① has no effect on the feasible set. We now summarize our observation on the geometric effects of tightening and loosening inequality constraints.

Effect on constraint set

For three variables, the feasible region is a solid, the constraints are planes forming the sides, the edges are intersections of two constraints, and the tips or points of the figure are the feasible extreme points. An interesting visual model could be made using a block of styrofoam for a simple 3-variable LP model. Using a knife, one could cut each plane to show the feasible region.

Tightening an inequality constraint either contracts the constraint set or leaves it unaffected. Loosening an inequality constraint either expands the constraint set or leaves it unaffected.

These results are generally true for inequality constraints and do not depend on the dimension of the model (the number of decision variables) or on whether the constraint is of $\leq$ or $\geq$ form. It should be emphasized that in this analysis we have assumed that one constraint is manipulated while all the others remain fixed. The effects of tightening (loosening) several at a time are also to contract (expand) or, possibly, to leave the feasible region unchanged. However, if some constraints are tightened and others simultaneously loosened, there is little that can be categorically stated about the result. We conclude this section with the observation that tightening a constraint too much can produce infeasibility, as occurred when the RHS of constraint ⑤ was increased to 270.

4.5 Redundant Constraints

A constraint such as constraint ① in Figure 4.2 is termed **redundant.** Although five constraints are plotted in this figure, only four of them are required to define the feasible region. This is because, as the figure clearly indicates, any combination of E and F values that satisfies the constraints labeled ②, ③, ④, and ⑤ will automatically satisfy the constraint labeled ① as well. In this sense the first constraint is superfluous. Here is a precise definition.

A redundant constraint is one whose removal does not change the feasible region.

Since a redundant constraint could, by definition, be discarded without changing the feasible region, its elimination will also have no effect on the optimal solution to the problem. Why bother, then, to include such a constraint in the model? There are two important reasons:

Keep redundant constraints

1. Redundant constraints are not generally very easy to recognize. Even in the simple case of problems with two decision variables, if you are looking only at the algebraic form of the mathematical model, the redundant constraints are not immediately spotted. For example, it is not obvious from the mathematical formulation that the constraint $E + F \geq 5$ is redundant in the **PROTRAC**, Inc. model. The graphical representation, of course, makes it clear for this two-dimensional problem. However, since graphical analysis is limited to two-dimensional problems, it is not useful for detecting redundancy in general real-world applications.

2. A constraint that is redundant today may not be redundant tomorrow. For example, suppose that the management of **PROTRAC**, Inc. decides to explore the effects of a new policy decision to produce at least seven, rather than five, units of E and F in total. Then the RHS of the first constraint changes to 7 instead of 5. The

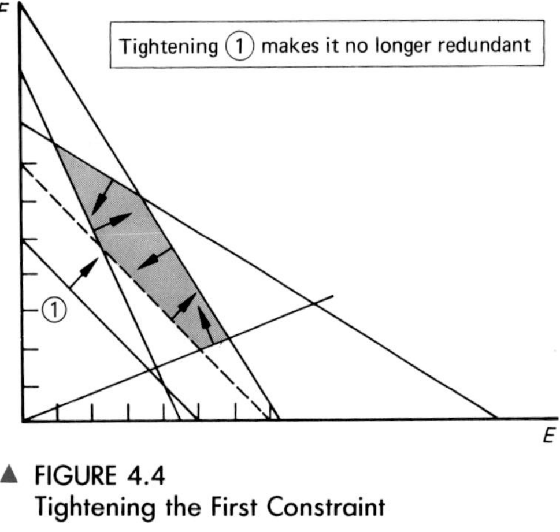

▲ FIGURE 4.4
Tightening the First Constraint

modified first constraint is plotted as a dashed line in Figure 4.4, and it is seen that the new constraint is no longer redundant. In other words, *tightening* the requirement from 5 to 7 forces us to cut off some previously allowable decisions.

It is quite possible that a constraint that is redundant for a given set of data may no longer be redundant when some of the data are changed.

It is often for this reason that a redundant constraint is in a model. It is common practice to solve planning models many times with different sets of data in order to gain insight into possible future scenarios. The model builder may intuitively know that there are conditions of interest (values of the data) for which this constraint may become *important,* and that is why she included this constraint in her model.

4.6 What Is an Important Constraint?

As suggested previously, there may be a distinction between "important" and "unimportant" constraints. Indeed, we have seen that, in general, an LP model may have numerous constraints. It would be of interest to know whether some of the many constraints may have special importance in the model. The management of **PROTRAC**, Inc. certainly has an interest in knowing which constraints are most restrictive in the sense of limiting the possibilities for greater profit.

Redundant Constraints

Redundant constraints are least important

The discussion in the section above suggests that, *for a given set of data, the redundant constraints (if there are any) are the least important.* That is, we have already observed that constraint ① is redundant, which means that it can be ignored without changing the constraint set and hence without changing the optimal solution. Since it does not affect the solution, it is, *for the given set of data,* of little importance. But can we say more? Just in terms of what we have so far learned, can you identify other constraints in the model that seem to be "more important" than the others?

Active and Inactive Constraints

Indeed, if it was known ahead of time that the optimal solution would have $E>0$ and $F>0$ and constraints ③ & ④ would be binding, one could solve for these two equations in two unknowns. In higher dimensions a problem might have 50 variables and 10 inequalities but in the optimal solution have only 3 variables > 0 and 3 inequalities active (binding). By simply solving 3 equations in 3 unknowns, the optimal solution could be found.

In Figure 4.5 the graphical analysis of the **PROTRAC**, Inc. model is reproduced. This figure shows that there are indeed other constraints in the model that can be ignored without affecting the solution, namely, constraints ② and ⑤. The graphical

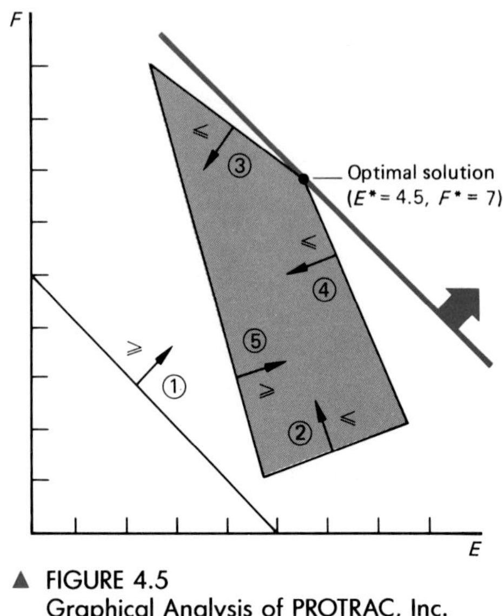

▲ FIGURE 4.5
Graphical Analysis of PROTRAC, Inc.

analysis of the model with constraints ①, ②, and ⑤ deleted is given in Figure 4.6. Although the feasible region has become greatly enlarged, the optimal solution remains unchanged. Recall that in this problem constraints ①, ②, and ⑤ are the **inactive constraints.**

Inactive constraints

The phenomenon we have just observed is generally true, even in higher-dimensional problems.

In any LP model, *for a fixed set of data,* the inactive constraints can be removed without affecting the optimal solution. The optimal solution is determined entirely by the active constraints.

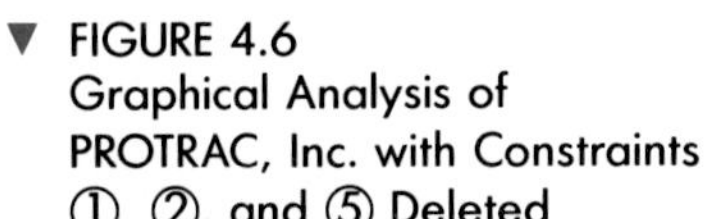

▼ FIGURE 4.6
Graphical Analysis of PROTRAC, Inc. with Constraints ①, ②, and ⑤ Deleted

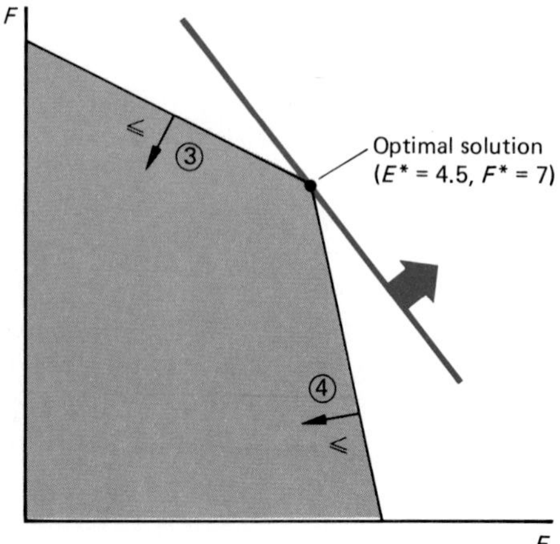

Active constraints are most important

Thus, for a given set of data the **active constraints** are the important ones, in the sense that they completely determine the solution. If we could only know in advance which constraints are active, the task of solving an LP would reduce to the relatively easy problem of solving a system of simultaneous linear equations, such as the equations for the lines labeled ③ and ④ in Figure 4.6. Thus, although we may agree that the active constraints are most important, this information becomes available only *after* the problem is solved, for unfortunately the modeler has no way of knowing, in advance, which of the inequality constraints will be active.[1] Consequently, a more complicated algorithm is needed to solve the general LP. This algorithm, called the simplex method, will be studied in Chapter 6.

In concluding this section, we wish to emphasize that when the data in a model change, the set of active and inactive inequality constraints can also change. *In other words, the unimportant (inactive) constraints for one set of data may become important (active) when the model is re-solved with different data.* You can think of a model as being "a logical framework or structure" that underlies the assigned numerical values of the parameters. This logical framework captures interactions among variables as well as requirements and limitations. The logical framework in a sense is independent of the actual values assigned to the parameters (i.e., the data). Different data values will give different realizations to the model. In this larger context it is not really meaningful to label some constraints as being more important than others. *The importance of the constraints is a relative question whose answer will depend on the values assigned to the data.*

4.7 Adding or Deleting Constraints

Effect on feasible region

The graphical analysis immediately demonstrates one final general observation concerning the effects of adding or deleting constraints. Comparing Figures 4.5 and 4.6 shows immediately what can happen when constraints are deleted. Deleting the constraint labeled ① (the redundant constraint) had no effect on the model. Deleting ② allowed the feasible region to enlarge. Deleting ⑤ allowed it to further enlarge, as represented in Figure 4.6. Thus for any LP problem we can make this general statement:

Deleting constraints leaves the feasible region either unchanged or larger.

We previously observed the impact of adding constraints to a model. This impact was demonstrated during the course of plotting the constraint set for the **PROTRAC**, Inc. model. You will recall that superimposing successive constraints had the effect of "trimming down" the constraint set. This too is true in general.

Adding constraints leaves the feasible region either unchanged or smaller.

Since adding constraints may have the effect of trimming down the feasible region, adding a new constraint to a model may happen to "trim off" a piece of the constraint set that contains the previous optimal solution. If this happens, the result may be a reduced OV (optimal objective value) for the new problem. This effect is

[1] Recall that an equality constraint, by definition, is always active.

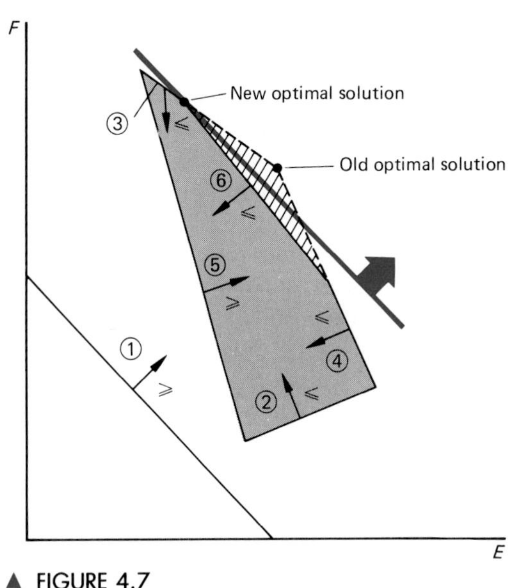

▲ FIGURE 4.7
Addition of a Sixth Constraint

shown in Figure 4.7, where a sixth inequality constraint has been added to the **PROTRAC**, Inc. model. The crosshatched region in Figure 4.7 portrays the part of the constraint set that is eliminated by the addition of the constraint labeled ⑥. The uphill direction in this diagram is to the northeast, and the new maximum profit line is not as far uphill as the former maximum profit line. Hence, the imposition of a new constraint has led to a reduction in the optimal profit. This is why management often prefers to operate with as few constraints as possible. *The larger the number of constraints, the greater the chance that the optimal objective value is less desirable.* The general result can be formulated thus:

Effect on OV

Adding constraints to a model will either impair the OV or leave it unchanged. Deleting constraints will either improve the OV or leave it unchanged.

Conversely, *adding variables* will either improve the OV or leave it unchanged, while *deleting variables* will either impair the OV or leave it unchanged.

The results of adding and deleting constraints are analogous to the results of tightening and loosening inequality constraints, both in terms of effects on the feasible region and on the optimal objective value. Thus, in the above displayed result, the phrase "tightening inequality constraints" could be substituted for "adding constraints to a model." The phrase "loosening inequality constraints" could be substituted for "deleting constraints." The effects on the optimal objective value of tightening and loosening inequality constraints are explored in more detail in Chapter 5.

4.8 Summary

The point of showing the graphical analysis is to give the student a comfortable feeling of knowing that there is a logical, orderly process behind the solution of LP models, but it is impossible to

This chapter used graphical analysis on problems with two decision variables to introduce the topic of parametric analysis, which is also called sensitivity analysis or postoptimality analysis. The general approach in sensitivity analysis is to assume that an LP model has been solved and then to investigate the effect of making various changes in the model. Typically, one is interested in the effect of the changes on the optimal solution and on the optimal value of the objective function.

"see" models with more than three variables. Thus Chapters 3 and 4 should build up a trust that the solutions derived by mathematics and computers do have some sense and order to them.

In Section 4.2 we saw that changing the objective function coefficients changes the slope of the objective function contours. This may or may not affect the optimal solution and the optimal value of the objective function.

Sections 4.3 and 4.4 dealt with changes in the right-hand side of the constraints. We first observed that changing a right-hand-side value results in a parallel shift of the changed constraint. This may affect both the optimal solution and the optimal objective value. The effect will depend on exactly which right-hand-side values are changed. Changes in the right-hand side of an inequality constraint can be thought of as tightening or loosening the constraint. Tightening a constraint means making it more difficult to satisfy. For a ≥ constraint this means increasing the RHS. For a ≤ constraint this means decreasing the RHS. Similarly, loosening a constraint means making it easier to satisfy. For a ≥ constraint this means decreasing the RHS. For a ≤ constraint this means increasing the RHS. From a geometric point of view, tightening an inequality constraint either contracts the constraint set or leaves it unaffected. Loosening an inequality constraint either expands the constraint set or leaves it unaffected. From a practical point of view, these operations can further limit, further augment, or leave unchanged the options available to the decision maker.

Another way in which a model could be modified after its original formulation and solution is by adding or deleting constraints. The effect of these changes was investigated in Section 4.7. En route to this analysis it was noted that a redundant constraint is one whose removal does not change the feasible region. Also, as discussed in Section 4.6, an inactive constraint can be removed from the model without changing the optimal solution. One might therefore be tempted to remove redundant or inactive constraints from a model before solving it, if it were possible to identify such constraints. In fact, however, redundant constraints are usually not recognizable, and the inactive constraints are revealed only after the problem has been solved. Moreover, the concepts of redundant and inactive are data-dependent. If you change the data, the redundant constraints and the inactive constraints may change. It is productive to think of the model as being the "logical framework or structure" that describes the operation of the system under consideration, independently of the numerical values assigned to the parameters. Since constraints that are redundant or inactive for one set of parameter values may not remain in that status when the parameter values are changed, the notion of searching for redundant or inactive constraints seems as inappropriate as it is difficult. Deleting constraints leaves the feasible region either unchanged or enlarged, whereas adding constraints leaves the feasible region either unchanged or smaller, and hence the effects of deleting and adding are analogous to the effects of loosening and tightening.

Key Terms

Sensitivity Analysis. A California approach to management based on group phenomena and of particular interest to aspiring young actors. In LP this has a more restricted meaning: Analyzing the effect on the problem, in particular the effect on the optimal solution and the optimal value of the objective function, of changes in various parameters. (*p. 128*)

Parametric Analysis. A synonym for sensitivity analysis. (*p. 128*)

Postoptimality Analysis. Another synonym for sensitivity analysis. (*p. 128*)

Parameters. Refers to the numerical data in an LP model. The values of parameters may change, and the problem may be resolved with these changed values. (*p. 129*)

Tightening a Constraint. Refers to changes in the RHS of an inequality constraint that make the constraint more difficult to satisfy. This is accomplished by increasing the RHS of a ≥ constraint and decreasing the RHS of a ≤ constraint. (*p. 133*)

Loosening a Constraint. Refers to changes in the RHS of an inequality constraint that make the constraint easier to satisfy. This is accomplished by decreasing the RHS of a ≥ constraint and increasing the RHS of a ≤ constraint. *(p. 133)*

Redundant Constraint. A constraint whose removal does not change the feasible region. *(p. 134)*

Inactive Constraint. An inequality constraint that does not pass through the optimal solution. Hence, for a given set of data, the removal of an inactive constraint will not change the optimal solution. *(p. 136)*

Active Constraint. A constraint that passes through the optimal solution. An equality constraint is always active. An inequality constraint is either active or inactive. *(p. 137)*

Major Concepts Quiz

True-False

1. **T F** Sensitivity analysis greatly increases the possibility that a model can be useful to management.
2. **T F** Consider a model in which, for some of the data, we know there is error. For example, some of the data represent estimates of future values for certain parameters. Suppose sensitivity analysis reveals that the OV is highly sensitive to these parameters. Such information provides more confidence in the recommendations of the model.
3. **T F** Sensitivity analysis is a precise tool.
4. **T F** Changing the RHS of a constraint changes its slope.
5. **T F** Changing an RHS cannot affect the set of inactive constraints.
6. **T F** Loosening an inequality constraint means changing the RHS to make it easier to satisfy.
7. **T F** A ≥ constraint is tightened by increasing the RHS.
8. **T F** Tightening a redundant inequality constraint cannot affect the feasible region.
9. **T F** For a given set of data, the inactive constraints are less important than the active ones.
10. **T F** Adding constraints to a model may help (i.e., improve) the OV.

Multiple Choice

11. Sensitivity analysis
    - **a.** allows us to more meaningfully interpret the computer solution
    - **b.** is done after the optimal solution is obtained, and is therefore called postoptimality analysis
    - **c.** is sometimes called parametric analysis
    - **d.** all of the above

12. Sensitivity analysis
    - **a.** can be done graphically in two dimensions
    - **b.** can increase our confidence in a model
    - **c.** can weaken our confidence in the recommendations of a model
    - **d.** all of the above
    - **e.** a and b

13. The value of the geometric approach, in two dimensions, is
    - **a.** to solve the problem quickly
    - **b.** to understand what is happening in higher dimensions
    - **c.** to better understand two-dimensional algebra

14. In LP, sensitivity analysis
    a. can deal with changes in the objective function coefficients
    b. can deal with changes in RHS
    c. both of the above

15. Changing an objective function coefficient
    a. produces a new optimal solution
    b. changes the tilt of the objective function contours
    c. gives a new OV
    d. all of the above

16. Tightening an inequality constraint
    a. improves the OV
    b. cannot improve the OV
    c. hurts the OV

17. A redundant constraint
    a. may not be easy to recognize
    b. should always be dropped from the model
    c. may not be redundant if the data are changed
    d. all of the above
    e. a and c
    f. a and b
    g. b and c

Answers

1. T	**7.** T	
2. F	**8.** F	**13.** b
3. T	**9.** T	**14.** c
4. F	**10.** F	**15.** b
5. F	**11.** d	**16.** b
6. T	**12.** d	**17.** e

▶ Problems

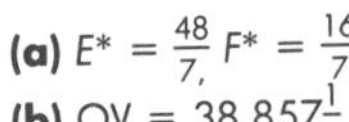
(a) $E^* = \frac{48}{7}, F^* = \frac{16}{7}$
(b) OV = $38{,}857\frac{1}{7}$

4-1. ▲ In the **PROTRAC**, Inc. model, suppose that the objective function is changed to $5000E + 2000F$.

(a) Use graphical analysis (e.g., Figure 4.1) to determine the effect on the optimal solution.

(b) What is the effect on the OV?

(a) $E_1^* = 1.5, F_2^* = 9$
(b) OV = 48,750

4-2. ▲ In the **PROTRAC**, Inc. model, suppose that the objective function is changed to $2500E + 5000F$.

(a) Use graphical analysis (e.g., Figure 4.1) to determine the effect on the optimal solution.

(b) What is the effect on the OV?

See IM.

4-3. ▲ Notice in Figure 4.1 the two objective functions

$$5000E + 4000F$$

$$5000E + 10{,}000F$$

The figure indicates that when the per unit profitability of F is increased from 4000 to 10,000, without changing the per unit profitability of E, the optimal value of E decreases. Why should the optimal value of E depend on the coefficient of F? Try to answer this question in words.

(**a**) Yes, there will be alternative optima.
(**b**) OV = 15,000

4-4. ▲ In the **PROTRAC**, Inc. model, suppose that the objective function is changed to $1000E + 1500F$.

(a) Use graphical analysis to decide whether there will be a new optimal solution.

(b) What is the effect on the OV?

Becomes infeasible

4-5. ▲ In the **PROTRAC**, Inc. model, replace the RHS of the fifth constraint (contractual labor agreement), which is currently 135, with the value 270. State the effect on the constraint set.

(**a**) RHS can increase to 8
(**b**) RHS can decrease to −25.5

4-6. ▲▲ In the **PROTRAC**, Inc. model, how much can you increase the RHS of constraint 2 before it becomes redundant? How small can the RHS be made without destroying feasibility?

(**a**) $x_1^* = 2$, $x_2^* = 0$
(**b**) Increase coefficient of x_2 to 15
(**c**) 2; ($x_1^* = 2$, $x_2^* = 0$) and ($x_1^* = 1$, $x_2^* = 2$)
(**d**) Can be infinitely increased. Can be decreased by 2 units.
(**e**) A change in either direction will change the optimal solution.
(**f**) The first constraint is active. The second is inactive.
(**g**) The optimal solution changes to ($x_1^* = \frac{1}{3}$, $x_2^* = 2\frac{2}{3}$) and the OV changes accordingly.
(**h**) No effect
(**i**) Satisfies, satisfy

4-7. ▲▲ Consider the LP

$$\begin{aligned} \text{Max } & 30x_1 + 10x_2 \\ \text{s.t. } & 2x_1 + x_2 \le 4 \\ & 2x_1 + 2x_2 \le 6 \\ & x_1, x_2 \ge 0 \end{aligned}$$

(a) Solve graphically and state the optimal solution.

(b) Keeping all other data as is, what per unit profitability should the product, whose current optimal value is zero, have in order that this product enter the optimal solution at a positive level?

(c) How many optimal corner solutions exist after making the change described in part (b)? What are they?

(d) In the original problem, how much can the RHS of the second constraint be increased (decreased) before the optimal solution is changed?

(e) Answer part (d) for the RHS of the first constraint.

(f) How do you explain the difference between parts (d) and (e)?

(g) What will be the impact of adding the constraint $4x_1 + x_2 = 4$ to the original model?

(h) What is the impact (on the optimal solution) of adding the constraint $3x_1 + 3x_2 \le 15$ to the original model?

(i) Fill in the blanks: The difference between parts (g) and (h) is that the original optimal solution already ______ the constraint in (h) but does not ______ the constraint in (g).

(**a**) $x_1 = 4$, $x_2 = 0$
(**b**) 2
(**c**) Two: $x_1 = 4$, $x_2 = 0$ and $x_1 = 3$, $x_2 = 1$
(**d**) RHS can decrease to 4, increase without limit.
(**e**) RHS cannot increase or decrease without changing the optimal solution.
(**f**) The first constraint is active.
(**g**) Optimal solution at $x_1 = \frac{6}{11}$, $x_2 = \frac{20}{11}$
(**h**) Optimal solution at $x_1 = 1$, $x_2 = 0$

4-8. ▲▲ Consider the LP

$$\begin{aligned} \text{Max } & 2x_1 + x_2 \\ \text{s.t. } & 3x_1 + 3x_2 \le 12 \\ & x_1 + 3x_2 \le 6 \\ & x_1, x_2 \ge 0 \end{aligned}$$

In terms of this model, answer (a-g) in Problem 4-7.

(h) What will be the impact of adding the constraint $x_1 + x_2 \le 1$ to the original model?

First is tighter; both; second only

4-9. ▲ Of the two constraints

$$\begin{aligned} -3x_1 + 2x_2 &\ge -6 \\ -3x_1 + 2x_2 &\ge -10 \end{aligned}$$

which is tighter? Which of the constraints, if either, does the point ($x_1 = 2, x_2 = 1$) satisfy? What about the point ($x_1 = 3, x_2 = 0$)?

(a) The second
(b) Both
(c) The first

4-10. ▲ Of the constraints

$$4x_1 - 3x_2 \leq 12$$
$$4x_1 - 3x_2 \leq -12$$

(a) which is tighter?
(b) Which of the constraints, if either, does the point ($x_1 = -2, x_2 = 3$) satisfy?
(c) What about the point ($x_1 = 2, x_2 = 3$)?

The second

4-11. ▲ Which of the two constraints in Problem 4-9 is looser?

The first

4-12. ▲ Which of the two constraints in Problem 4-10 is looser?

more, loosening

4-13. ▲ Fill in the blanks: Increasing the RHS of a ≤ constraint means that there will be ______ combinations of decision-variable values that satisfy the constraint. This means that one is ______ the constraint.

fewer, tightening

4-14. ▲ Fill in the blanks: Increasing the RHS of a ≥ constraint means that there will be ______ combinations of decision-variable values which satisfy the constraint. This means that one is ______ the constraint.

enlarge, smaller, unchanged

4-15. ▲ Using the words *enlarge, diminish, smaller, larger, unchanged,* fill in the blanks: Tightening a constraint cannot ______ the constraint set and may leave it ______ or ______.

diminish, larger, unchanged

4-16. ▲ Using the words supplied in Problem 4-15, fill in the blanks: Loosening a constraint cannot ______ the constraint set and may leave it ______ or ______.

The first; no

4-17. ▲▲ In the **PROTRAC**, Inc. model, which constraint is redundant? Will this constraint remain redundant if its RHS value is increased by 10%, all other data held fixed?

RHS < 50

4-18. ▲▲ In the **PROTRAC**, Inc. model, for what values of the RHS will constraint 5 become redundant, assuming all other data are held fixed?

No; it may not be redundant for other values of parameters used in the model.

4-19. ▲▲ Suppose that you have created a model and that by some means you are able to identify a redundant constraint. Would you say it is generally true that such a constraint should be dropped from the model? Why (or why not)?

Constraint should be dropped.

4-20. ▲▲ How would your answer to Problem 4-19 differ if the model is to be run one and only one time?

No.

4-21. ▲▲▲ Suppose you know that in a given run of a model a particular constraint will be redundant. Does it follow that this constraint will also be inactive?

See IM.

4-22. ▲ Discuss briefly the notion of "important" versus "unimportant" constraints.

(a) 2, 5
(b) 1, 4
(c) 3
(d) 2, 5
(e) 1, 4

4-23. ▲ Match up the phrases in the two columns. (Note: Some phrases may have more than one match.)

(a) Adding constraints	**1.** May enlarge the feasible region
(b) Deleting constraints	**2.** May make the feasible region smaller
(c) Important constraints	**3.** Depend on the data set
(d) Tightening constraints	**4.** May improve the OV
(e) Loosening constraints	**5.** May hurt the OV

Video Case

Vrroom! The Harley-Davidson Story

The Harley-Davidson story read like a novel, but it is just one of many interesting episodes in the revolution taking place in American manufacturing. Perhaps the Harley-Davidson case is a bit more fascinating because of its rich historical background and the extent to which a Harley is a quintessential American product.

Harley-Davidson was founded in 1903 and by 1970 had survived four crises brought on by external events. The company produced 29,000 motorcycles in 1920. However, output quickly dropped to 10,000 vehicles as the economy softened and Americans turned to the auto for basic transportation. About the time demand had rebounded to previous levels, the Great Depression struck, and production sunk to 3700 units. World War II brought renewed demand—which ended with the war. Finally, postwar sales surged to record levels on the strength of the purchasing power of returning veterans, only to slack off once again.

The 1970's, however, were another story. This time Harley-Davidson was facing a challenge from a group of strong Japanese competitors: Honda, Yamaha, Kawasaki, Suzuki. These companies were producing motorcycles that were less expensive, more powerful, and of higher quality—that is, more reliable—than those made by Harley-Davidson. Once the company had ruled the super-weight class, but by the early 1980s that was no longer true. In 1973, Harley-Davidson held a 77.5% share of the domestic market for motorcycles with a capacity of at least 851 cc. By 1983, that share had tumbled to less than 24%.

Harley-Davidson's turnaround is quite remarkable. In 1983 Honda was the leader in the super-weight class with a market share of 44.3%. Just five years later Harley and Honda had reversed roles: Harley had 46.5% of the market to Honda's 24.1%. Harley-Davidson achieved these results by implementing a three-pronged strategy: (1) a new production approach based on employee involvement, just-in-time manufacturing, and statistical operator control; (2) a "close-to-the-customer" marketing strategy; and (3) an emphasis on cash management.

Harley's management was faced with many tough decisions during its rise from the ashes. One such event occurred during the Honda-Yamaha motorcycle war. In January 1982, Yamaha president Hisao Koike told his shareholders, "In one year we will be the domestic leader. And in two years, we will be number one in the world." When he heard of this statement, Kiyoshi Kawashima, Honda's president, replied, "Yamaha wo tsubusu"—freely translated, "No way, Jose." In the ensuing war, Honda used every weapon at its disposal: deep price cuts, intense promotion, and a wave of new products. Yamaha responded in kind. Harley-Davidson was caught in the middle. Just when it was starting to get its new strategy off the ground, "all hell broke loose."

Harley responded by appealing to the International Trade Commission for protection under the 1974 Trade Act on the grounds that its Japanese competitors were "dumping" motorcycles on the American market. The result was that on April 1, 1983, President Reagan agreed to a plan recommended by the ITC. This plan added a 45% tariff to the existing level of 4.4% for one year for motorcycles with engines of 700 cc or larger. The add-on decreased to 35%, then 20%, then 15%, and finally to 10% until it expired in 1988. Although the Japanese firms found an effective way to mitigate the effect of the tariff by building cycles with 699-cc engines, the tariff gave Harley-Davidson some breathing room.

Questions

Think of the problem faced by Harley's management after the start of the Honda-Yamaha war as a constrained optimization problem.

1. In broad strategic terms, what do you think Harley's objective would be?
2. Strategically, what constraints do you see?
3. In the context of Question 2, how would you describe Harley's decision to seek tariff protection?
4. Use this characterization to explain what effect you would expect the tariff to have.

CHAPTER

Linear Programs: Computer Analysis, Interpreting Sensitivity Output, and the Dual Problem

APPLICATION CAPSULE

Keep on Truckin': An LP Model Slashes Inventory Costs*

The Fleet Administration Division of North American Van Lines, Inc., has primary responsibility for planning and controlling the company's fleet of truck tractors. The task is complicated because drivers in the North American system are independent contractors. That is, they own and are responsible for the maintenance of their tractor equipment, whose service is in turn leased to North American. In particular, Fleet Administration (1) recruits and trains owner-drivers; (2) buys new tractors from manufacturers and sells used tractors; (3) sells new tractors to drivers and buys used tractors from them; and (4) provides warranty, insurance, and financing arrangements to contract truckers.

Historically, Fleet Administration used a manual system to discharge its responsibilities. This system started with a forecast of demand for shipments that was translated into a forecast for the number of new contract owners required during each remaining week of the fiscal year. This forecast, in turn, led to recruiting and training plans as well as plans for tractor purchases and sales. Some 120 labor hours of computational effort was needed for each pass through the planning process. The manual system thus entailed both high costs and a lack of ability to evaluate alternative purchase and sales plans. In other words, the process simply evaluated the plan selected. It gave no information on what decisions could be made to improve it.

In the face of this situation North American created and implemented a decision support system with two main functions:

1. It used a large-scale LP model to determine a new/used, purchase/sales plan for tractors.
2. It used the LP results to generate a series of reports that illustrate the financial impact of the suggested plan.

The model has had an important effect on three areas within the firm. First, the average inventory has been reduced by 100 tractors, or approximately $3,000,000. This yields an approximate annual savings in inventory carrying costs of $600,000. Second, the ability to run up to three scenarios per day makes it possible for management to react quickly to changes in demand forecasts. Finally, the personnel used in the old manual system can be productively reassigned.

*Dan Avramovich, Thomas M. Cook, Gary O. Langston, and Frank Sutherland, "A Decision Support System for Fleet Management: A Linear Programming Approach," *Interfaces*, vol. 12, no. 3 (June 1982), pp. 1–9.

5.1 Introduction

Remember that an LP solution is not just a "point" but a range of values—not just a number but information that will lead to decisions for the analyst. These ranges are printed out by the computerized LP programs and show how sensitive each resource or price is.
There are really no mathematics for solving simultaneous linear inequalities. Mathematics can only solve *n* equations in *n* unknowns. Thus, the computer algorithm must solve a series of these by first changing inequalities into equalities, and then deciding which *n* variables and which *n* equations to solve.

In Chapter 4 we stated that the manager is typically interested in much more than simply the solution to an LP model. The analysis of a real-world problem often begins with the solution. We stated that the process of analyzing a model after the solution has been derived is termed *sensitivity analysis,* and we then dealt with some of the geometry that underlies sensitivity analysis. In this chapter we look in detail at how the manager might, in practice, use the wealth of information contained in the computer analysis of an LP. This can be an important, even daily, problem faced by managers in the real world—the problem of making good use of computer analysis. This discussion culminates in Section 5.4, in a realistic scenario involving the manager and the management scientist.

To begin the development of this chapter, it is important to understand the form of the LP model that the computer actually solves. This is called the **standard equality constraint form.** After illustrating some relevant properties of this form, we proceed to study the computer output for two problems already seen: **PROTRAC,** Inc. and Crawler Tread.

In concluding this chapter, we introduce a new topic, called *duality,* which is closely connected to sensitivity considerations, and which provides a more profound knowledge of the LP model. We discuss several aspects of the dual problem, highlighting its theoretical, computational, and economic significance.

5.2 The Problem the Computer Solves

Constraints come in two "flavors": limitations (≤) and requirements (≥), so, an equality constraint (=) is really *both* a limitation and a requirement simultaneously.

We shall show that any linear program, regardless of the sense of the constraints (i.e., whether they are ≥, =, or ≤), can be transformed into an equivalent problem all of whose constraints are equalities. This step is accomplished with the use of **slack** and **surplus variables.**

Slack and Surplus Variables

Let us begin by considering a single constraint, say

$$x_1 + x_2 \leq 5 \tag{5.1}$$

This constraint is plotted in Figure 5.1, illustrating the constraint line, the ≤ side, and the ≥ side. The mechanics of plotting such a constraint were presented in

All variables in LP are assumed nonnegative (≥ 0). If they are allowed to have negative values, the computer program will make the necessary changes. Graphically, these are the implied "constraints" $x_1 \geq 0$ (the x_2 axis) and $x_2 \geq 0$ (the x_1 axis). This assures that all variables are nonnegative.

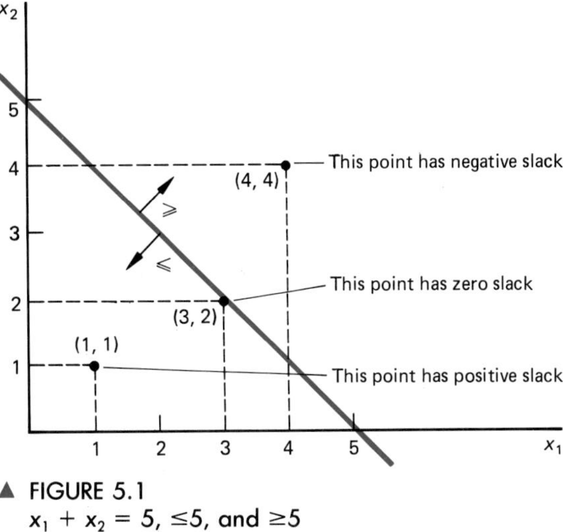

▲ FIGURE 5.1
$x_1 + x_2 = 5, \leq 5$, and ≥ 5

Chapter 3. Recall that each point on the constraint line satisfies $x_1 + x_2 = 5$. All the points on one side of the line (in this case below the line) satisfy $x_1 + x_2 < 5$, and all the points on the other side satisfy the reverse inequality. We now point out that the inequality (5.1) can be transformed to an equality constraint as follows. First, we add a new variable, say s, called a *slack variable,* and rewrite (5.1) as

Adding slack

$$x_1 + x_2 + s = 5 \tag{5.2}$$

Now, note that a point will satisfy (5.1) if and only if it satisfies (5.2) with s nonnegative. Consider, for example, the point ($x_1 = 1, x_2 = 1$). This point satisfies (5.1). It also satisfies (5.2) with $s = 3$. By trying several pairs of values, such as (3, 2) and (4, 4) as illustrated in Figure 5.1, we are led to the following observations:

1. If a point (x_1, x_2) satisfies (5.1), it will, in Figure 5.1, lie on or below the plotted line, and *the value of the slack variable in* (5.2) *will be nonnegative.* Thus, (5.1) is equivalent to the following *two conditions:*

$$\begin{aligned} x_1 + x_2 + s &= 5 \\ s &\geq 0 \end{aligned} \tag{5.3}$$

   The nonnegativity of s ensures that the point (x_1, x_2) lies on the $\leq$ side of the line.

2. If a point (x_1, x_2) satisfies (5.1) with equality, the value of the slack variable in (5.2) will be zero.
3. If the point (x_1, x_2) does not satisfy (5.1), it will lie strictly above the plotted line in Figure 5.1 (e.g., the point [$x_1 = 4, x_2 = 4$]). In this case the value of the slack variable in (5.2) will be negative, thereby violating (5.3).

Slack can be thought of as the slack in a rope or line that can be taken up if need be. When the rope is taut (active constraint), there is no "slack."

We thus see that the slack variable s is the "slack," or extra amount that must be added to the left-hand side to turn the $\leq$ into $=$.

Now that we have used the notion of a slack variable to convert a single $\leq$ inequality constraint to an equality constraint, let us see what must be done to handle a *collection* of $\leq$ inequality constraints. Consider, for example, the three constraints

$$\begin{aligned} 4x_1 - x_2 &\leq 12 \\ 2x_1 + 6x_2 &\leq 21 \\ -3x_1 + 2x_2 &\leq 6.5 \end{aligned}$$

To continue the analogy of the rope, there is different slack for each of three ropes (constraints), not the same amount of slack.

In this case, converting to inequalities requires the introduction of *three* new nonnegative slack variables, say x_3, x_4, x_5 (the three slacks could just as well be labeled s_1, s_2, and s_3). We then obtain the following equivalent system of inequalities:

$$\begin{aligned} 4x_1 - x_2 + x_3 \qquad\qquad &= 12 \\ 2x_1 + 6x_2 \qquad + x_4 \qquad &= 21 \\ -3x_1 + 2x_2 \qquad\qquad + x_5 &= 6.5 \\ x_3, x_4, x_5 &\geq 0 \end{aligned}$$

Note that there is a *different* slack variable associated with each constraint.

We have now to consider the problem of converting a $\geq$ constraint into an equivalent equality. Let us take as an example

$$2x_1 + 4x_2 \geq 13$$

Subtracting surplus

To convert this $\geq$ constraint to an equality, we *subtract* a nonnegative variable from the left-hand side and change the inequality to equality. This produces the two conditions

$$\begin{aligned} 2x_1 + 4x_2 - s &= 13 \\ s &\geq 0 \end{aligned} \tag{5.4}$$

"Surplus" means how much more the constraint has than its minimum (=) value.

When a nonnegative variable is subtracted from a $\geq$ constraint, it is often termed a *surplus variable* (as opposed to a slack variable, which is added to a $\leq$ constraint). A surplus variable is the "surplus" that must be deducted from the left-hand side to turn the $\geq$ into =.

The foregoing discussion demonstrates two important points:

- **Any $\leq$ constraint can be converted to an equality by adding a new nonnegative slack variable to the left-hand side.**
- **Any $\geq$ constraint can be converted to an equality by subtracting a new nonnegative surplus variable from the left-hand side.**

Standard Equality Constraint Form

In solving linear programs, the computer uses an algorithm called the simplex method, which is designed to attack problems with only equality constraints. Given any LP, the discussion above shows how to convert it easily to the required form. As an illustration, recall the **PROTRAC**, Inc. model

$$\begin{aligned} \text{Max } & 5000E + 4000F \\ \text{s.t. } & E + F \geq 5 \\ & E - 3F \leq 0 \\ & 10E + 15F \leq 150 \\ & 20E + 10F \leq 160 \\ & 30E + 10F \geq 135 \\ & E, F \geq 0 \end{aligned} \tag{5.5}$$

This LP problem has two variables and five constraints, two of them $\geq$ and three of them ≤. To convert this problem into an equivalent problem in *standard equality constraint form,* we must add slack variables to the second, third, and fourth constraints (the ≤ constraints) and subtract surplus variables from the first and fifth constraints (the ≥ constraints). Letting s_1, s_2, s_3, s_4, and s_5 denote the five new variables, we obtain

$$\begin{aligned} &\text{Max } 5000E + 4000F \\ &\text{s.t.} \quad E + F - s_1 = 5 \\ &\quad E - 3F + s_2 = 0 \\ &\quad 10E + 15F + s_3 = 150 \\ &\quad 20E + 10F + s_4 = 160 \\ &\quad 30E + 10F - s_5 = 135 \\ &\quad E, F, s_1, s_2, s_3, s_4, s_5 \geq 0 \end{aligned} \tag{5.6}$$

The LP problem changes from 5 inequalities in 2 unknowns to 5 equalities in 7 unknowns.

This is the standard equality constraint form of the **PROTRAC**, Inc. model. This form of the problem still has five constraints, but the addition of slack and surplus has increased the number of variables to seven instead of two. Notice that slack and surplus variables do not explicity appear in the objective function. However, since

$$5000E + 4000F = 5000E + 4000F + 0s_1 + 0s_2 + 0s_3 + 0s_4 + 0s_5$$

it is acceptable to think of the surplus and slack variables as being included in the objective function, but with zero coefficients.

Optimal Values of Slack and Surplus Variables. In Chapter 3 we used the graphical solution method to show that $E^* = 4.5$ and $F^* = 7$ is the solution to the **PROTRAC**, Inc. inequality model (5.5). This means that the optimal values of the other variables (the slacks and surpluses) in the equality constraint model (5.6) are given by

$$\begin{aligned} s_1^* &= E^* + F^* - 5 = 11.5 - 5 = 6.5 \\ s_2^* &= 0 - (E^* - 3F^*) = -(4.5 - 21) = 16.5 \\ s_3^* &= 150 - (10E^* + 15F^*) = 150 - (45 + 105) = 0 \\ s_4^* &= 160 - (20E^* + 10F^*) = 160 - (90 + 70) = 0 \\ s_5^* &= (30E^* + 10F^*) - 135 = (135 + 70) - 135 = 70 \end{aligned}$$

Since there are 2 more unknowns than equalities, 2 variables should be set = 0 (s_3 and s_4) and 5 equations in 5 unknowns solved.

Again, if it were known that the final solution was to make both Es and Fs and that department A and B constraints would be binding, then 2 equations in 2 unknowns could be solved, rather than 5 equations in 5 unknowns. Using that solution, the slacks and surpluses for the other constraints could be determined.

It would be useful at this point for you to review the material on active and inactive constraints in Section 3.4. We recall from that material: An *active* or *binding* constraint is one for which, *at optimality,* the left-hand side equals the right-hand side. From the geometric point of view, an active constraint is one on which the optimal solution lies. We saw that in the **PROTRAC**, Inc. model the active constraints are the third and fourth. The calculation above shows that their slack variables (s_3^* and s_4^*) are zero. On the other hand, the first, second, and fifth constraints are inactive, and their slack/surplus variables are positive. Thus, we can make these generalizations:

- **Active constraints are those for which the optimal values of the slack or surplus variables are zero.**
- **Inactive constraints are those for which the optimal values of the slack or surplus variables are positive.**

It is not difficult to see that all of the discussion in Section 3.4 could be phrased in terms of these new entities, the slack and surplus variables. In particular, when at optimality a constraint has a zero value for the slack or surplus variable,[1] it means, geometrically speaking, that the solution to the problem lies on that constraint.

In order to check your understanding of the standard equality constraint form, try to convert the following model to one with only equality constraints.

$$
\begin{aligned}
\text{Max } & x_1 + 3x_4 \\
\text{s.t. } & 2x_1 + 3x_3 + x_4 \le 12 \\
& x_1 + 13x_2 + 6x_3 + 0.5x_4 \le 41 \\
& 0.4x_2 + 2x_3 \ge 22 \\
& -3x_1 + 12x_4 = 15 \\
& x_1, x_2, x_3, x_4 \ge 0
\end{aligned}
$$

In this example there are four constraints and four decision variables.[2] Since only three of the constraints are inequalities we need to introduce only three new variables, in this case one surplus (for the third constraint) and two slacks (for the first and second constraints). The fourth constraint is already an equality, and hence *we do not introduce a slack or surplus variable for this equality constraint.* Thus, the standard equality constraint form for the model above is

$$
\begin{aligned}
\text{Max } & x_1 + 3x_4 \\
\text{s.t. } & 2x_1 + 3x_3 + x_4 + s_1 = 12 \\
& x_1 + 13x_2 + 6x_3 + 0.5x_4 + s_2 = 41 \\
& 0.4x_2 + 2x_3 - s_3 = 22 \\
& -3x_1 + 12x_4 = 15 \\
& x_1, x_2, x_3, x_4, s_1, s_2, s_3 \ge 0
\end{aligned}
$$

To summarize the discussion above, we have shown how slack and surplus variables are used to convert any LP problem into standard equality constraint form.

Geometry of the Standard Equality Constraint Problem

A brief look at the geometry of our new model will reveal a property that is important both in understanding the mechanics of the simplex algorithm (developed in Chapter 6) and in appreciating and correctly interpreting the information contained in the computer printout. This property has to do with the number of positive variables at any corner (and in particular at an optimal corner) of the constraint set.

In the preceding section we have seen that all variables (decision variables, slack and surplus variables) in the standard equality constraint problem (e.g., [5.6])

[1] In the language of Chapter 3 we simply said that such a constraint has zero slack or surplus, without introducing the concept of a slack or surplus variable.

[2] Students are sometimes confused by a model such as this in which not all decision variables appear in the objective function and all the constraints, but this form is perfectly valid. Think of the variables as being everywhere included but with zero coefficients in places.

are required to be nonnegative (positive or zero). In this section we illustrate that at any corner of the constraint set (and in particular at an optimal corner), the maximum number of positive (*greater than zero*) variables, counting decision variables, slacks, and surpluses, is at most equal to the number of constraints in the model (not counting the "nonnegativity conditions").

To illustrate this "count property," consider the model shown in (5.7).

$$\begin{aligned}
&\text{Max } x_1 + x_2 \\
&\text{s.t.} \quad 8x_1 + 7x_2 \le 56 \quad ① \\
&\quad -6x_1 - 10x_2 \ge -60 \quad ② \\
&\quad x_1 \le 6 \quad ③ \\
&\quad -x_1 + x_2 \le 6 \quad ④ \\
&\quad x_1 \ge 0, \quad x_2 \ge 0
\end{aligned} \tag{5.7}$$

The constraint set for this model is plotted in Figure 5.2, where the appropriate constraints are labeled ① through ④. Now consider the standard equality constraint form of the same model. It is

$$\begin{aligned}
&\text{Max } x_1 + x_2 \\
&\text{s.t.} \quad 8x_1 + 7x_2 + s_1 = 56 \quad ① \\
&\quad -6x_1 - 10x_2 - s_2 = -60 \quad ② \\
&\quad x_1 + s_3 = 6 \quad ③ \\
&\quad -x_1 + x_2 + s_4 = 6 \quad ④ \\
&\quad x_1, x_2, s_1, s_2, s_3, s_4 \text{ all nonnegative}
\end{aligned} \tag{5.8}$$

The original model had four constraints and two variables. The standard equality constraint form has the same number of constraints, but six variables. It is important to note that, when referring to the number of variables in the standard equality constraint model, *we count slack and surplus as well as decision variables.* Since (5.8) has two decision variables and four slack/surplus variables, there are six variables in this form of the model. Also, in referring to the number of constraints, *we do not count the nonnegativity conditions.*

Our geometric representation of (5.8) is nearly the same as that of (5.7), the only difference being that each constraint will be labeled with its slack or surplus

▼ FIGURE 5.2
Constraint Set for the Inequality Constrained Model (5.7)

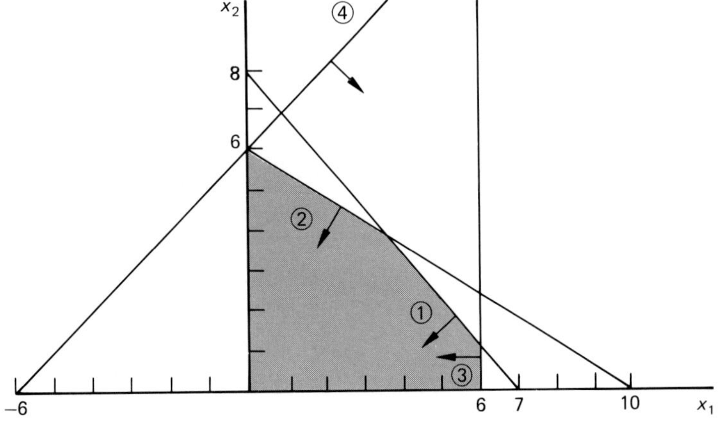

Figure 5.3 is an attempt to show a graph in six variables using only two dimensions. If one could graph six axes and view it, mathematicians would call it a *simplex*, a term from which the name for solving LP models comes.

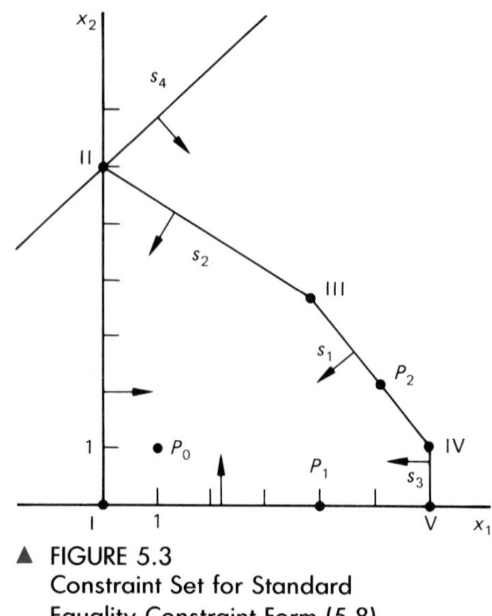

▲ FIGURE 5.3
Constraint Set for Standard Equality Constraint Form (5.8)

variable. This is shown in Figure 5.3, where for convenience we have labeled the five corners (with Roman numerals) and also identified several points that will be of interest. Labeling the constraints with the slack and surplus variables allows you to make the following "visual" observations:

1. At any point interior to the feasible region, all variables are positive. This is illustrated by point P_0 in Figure 5.3. At this point you can directly read $x_1 = 1$ and $x_2 = 1$. Using the values and the constraints in (5.8) you could explicitly calculate the values for s_1, s_2, s_3, and s_4 at P_0, and you would see that these values are also positive. However, you need not perform this algebra, for the figure immediately shows us that all slacks and surpluses are positive at P_0.

2. At any point on the boundary, at least one variable will be zero. This is illustrated at points P_1 and P_2. At P_1, you can see that $x_2 = 0$; all other variables are positive. Similarly, at P_2, which lies on the first constraint line, only s_1 is zero. Special boundary points of interest are the corners of the feasible region. For example, since the corner labeled III lies on the first and second constraint lines, the two variables s_1 and s_2 are zero at this corner, with all other variables positive. These examples show that the zero variables on the boundary could be decision variables as well as slack or surplus variables. Corner V, for example, shows that a decision variable (x_2) and a slack variable (s_3) can both be zero on the boundary.

Mathematical theory shows that the optimal solution *has* to occur on at least one corner point.

Positive Variables and Corner Solutions. On the basis of such observations, we can now illustrate the main result of this section by counting the positive variables at each of the five corners of the constraint set. The result is shown in Figure 5.4.

What this table shows, quite simply, is *which* variables are positive at each

▼ FIGURE 5.4
Counting Positive Variables at Corners

CORNER	ZERO VARIABLES	POSITIVE VARIABLES	POSITIVE COUNT
I	x_1, x_2	s_1, s_2, s_3, s_4	4
II	x_1, s_2, s_4	x_2, s_1, s_3	3
III	s_1, s_2	x_1, x_2, s_3, s_4	4
IV	s_1, s_3	x_1, x_2, s_2, s_4	4
V	x_2, s_3	x_1, s_1, s_2, s_4	4

corner, and, in addition, *how many* variables are positive at each corner. Remember that there are four constraints in the model (5.8). Figure 5.4 thus illustrates an important general fact:

For any LP problem in standard equality constraint form, the number of positive variables at any corner is less than or equal to the number of constraints.

In practice, the number of positive *decision* variables is a small percentage of the number of constraints. For a problem for the U.S.D.A. with 8000 inequality constraints and 50,000 decision variables, only about 250 decision variables were positive, about 0.5%.

This result has an important implication for the computer solution of an LP. You may recall from Section 3.5 that in an LP problem, if there is an optimal solution, there is always an optimal corner solution (there may be noncorner optima as well). As you will see in Chapter 6, the simplex method, which is the main algorithm used by computers to solve LP problems, always produces an optimal corner (assuming, of course, that the problem is neither infeasible nor unbounded). Moreover, the simplex algorithm (as well as the computer) solves a problem in standard equality constraint form and, for such a problem, in accord with the conclusion displayed above: The number of positive variables at *any* corner (hence at an optimal corner) is less than or equal to the number of constraints. Thus, we can now see one reason why the above "count property" is of interest:

The computer solution to an LP problem always has at most *m* positive variables, where *m* is the number of constraints.

We have a practical need for this last conclusion for the following reason:

When the computer solution has less than *m* positive variables, the solution is called degenerate, and in this case special care must be taken in interpreting some of the computer output.

In two dimensions, the intersection of two lines determines a point; in three dimensions the intersection of three planes determines a point. In this case, four planes determine a point, so one is not needed to determine the point. By removing any one of the planes, CDE for instance, the feasible region would open indefinitely to the right. Thus, if the removal of an "extra" constraint would change the feasible area, that "extra" constraint is not truly redundant.

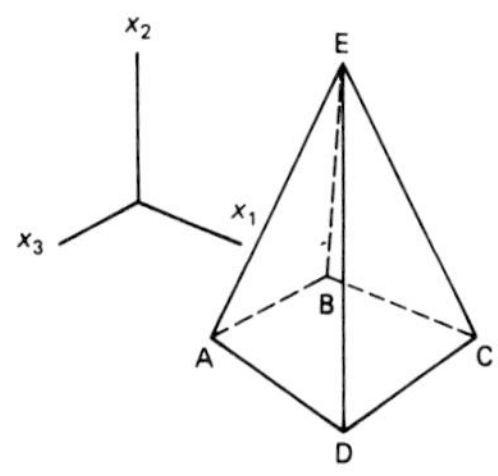

Degeneracy and Nondegeneracy. Since the ramifications of degeneracy are noteworthy, let us briefly pause to define the concept formally. We will then advance to the topic of computer analysis. A corner such as II in Figure 5.3, where the number of positive variables is *less than* the number of constraints, is termed a *degenerate corner.*[3] The remaining corners, I, III, IV, and V, where the number of positive variables is exactly equal to the number of constraints, are termed *nondegenerate corners.* If the optimal computer solution to an LP has less than *m* positive variables, it is termed a **degenerate solution** since it occurs at a degenerate corner. Analogously, a solution with exactly *m* positive variables is called a **nondegenerate solution.**

[3]Here is a subtle point for those who wish to descend slightly deeper into the pits of degeneracy. Figure 5.3 shows that the degenerate corner II has a redundant constraint passing through it (namely, the fourth constraint). Although this is true of any degenerate corner in two dimensions, do not conclude that this must always be the case. As a counterexample, visualize a three-dimensional constraint set that has the shape of a great pyramid standing inside the nonnegative orthant. This figure has four triangular sides and a base, corresponding to five inequality constraints. Thus, the original model has five inequality constraints in three variables, and the corresponding standard equality constraint model will have five constraints and eight variables. At each of the four base corners, A, B, C, and D, three slack variables are zero and hence five variables are positive. Hence, since there are five constraints and at each of these corners five positive variables, these are nondegenerate corners. However, at corner E, four slacks are zero and hence only four variables are positive. Thus, corner E is degenerate but there are no redundant constraints. What this illustrates is the fact that in three or more dimensions, contrary to the two-dimensional case, a degenerate corner need not have a redundant constraint passing through it.

APPLICATION CAPSULE

Milking Profits: Planning with LP Keeps Production Inefficiencies from Skimming the Cream off Earnings*

We have already encountered several examples of blending problems, such as Crawler Tread (Section 2.3). These are essentially assembly problems, in which a finished product is created by the combination of various components. There is another interesting class of problems that you might think of as disassembly (fractionating) problems, in which a single product becomes the source of several new products. Oil refining is a good example, and so is milk processing in a dairy. LP can help with these problems also.

The Dairyman's Cooperative Creamery Association (DCCA) is the largest single milk-processing facility at one location in the United States. This cooperative receives about 5,000,000 pounds of raw milk per day and makes some 50 different products. Their goals are quite clear. First, they must be sure to satisfy consumer demand for this assortment of products. But if they are to remain profitable, they must also efficiently turn any excess product into butter, cheese, or powdered milk, to be sold to the government.

Although the goals are simple, achieving them is not. Production planning and inventory forecasting for plants such as DCCA are very complicated, and traditionally have had to rely heavily on past experience and intuition. The reason is that, while all dairy products are derived from raw milk, some are byproducts of others, and many compete for the same processing equipment. For example, when raw milk is pumped to the cheese plant for processing, not only will cheese be produced but also whey, salty whey, fines, and scrap cheese. Some of these will in turn become the raw materials for other processes, such as the production of buttermilk, in a highly complex web of interactions. Many of the products DCCA makes require processing by the plant's evaporators and dryers, which have a limited capacity and thus tend to create a scheduling bottleneck.

Until recently, supervisors at DCCA had tried to calculate the maze of relationships among the products and processes by hand. All that was changed by the milk-flow analysis program (MFAP), an interactive, user-friendly software package that runs on a PC. This program has two modules: (1) a preprocessor program that prompts the operator to provide information and estimates needed to plan operations, and (2) an LP that uses these data to determine daily production and inventory levels so as to maximize plant throughput. (Maximizing throughput may seem like a strange objective; but when the government will buy all product not sold to consumers, it makes sense.)

Now, at 4:00 A.M. every day, current inventory levels, estimates of milk to be received, and estimates of the product demand for that day are put into the preprocessor. The model has only 36 constraints, and the entire planning process that once occupied several hours every day now takes less than 30 minutes. The output is extremely simple: the quantity of each product to be made that day. Supervisors can also rerun the system several times with modified data and pose "what-if" questions.

MFAP has increased plant throughput by an estimated 150,000 pounds per day while making it possible to avoid a host of production and quality problems. In addition, more management time is now available to deal with the problems of running the company. Overall, the contribution to annual profits is estimated at $100,000. By contrast, the total development cost of the system, including hardware procurement and system design, was less than $15,000.

*Sullivan and Secrest, "A Simple Optimization DDS for Production Planning at Dairyman's Cooperative Creamery Association," *Interfaces*, Vol. 15, No. 5 (Sept.–Oct. 1985).

We have now become acquainted with the problem that the computer solves, namely the standard equality constraint model. We have seen an important property of this model, namely that any optimal solution produced by the computer will have at most m positive variables (exactly m meaning nondegenerate), where m is the number of constraints in the model; and we have learned that the correct interpretation of the printout will require the awareness of whether or not the optimal solution is nondegenerate. Let us now, in the following two sections, look at some actual computer output.

5.3 The Computer Analysis of PROTRAC, Inc.

In this section we use the computer to analyze the **PROTRAC**, Inc. problem that we have already studied from the geometric point of view in Chapter 3. Your understanding of what you are reading on the computer printout will be deepened by relating, wherever possible, the concepts being presented to the geometric notions already developed.

For ease of reference let us reproduce the model here together with the graphical analysis displayed in Figure 3.11.

$$\begin{array}{llll}
\text{Max } 5000E + 4000F & & & \\
\text{s.t.} \quad E + F \ge 5 & \text{(total units requirement)} & ① & \\
E - 3F \le 0 & \text{(market balance)} & ② & \\
10E + 15F \le 150 & \text{(department A)} & ③ & \quad (5.5) \\
20E + 10F \le 160 & \text{(department B)} & ④ & \\
30E + 10F \ge 135 & \text{(contractual labor)} & ⑤ & \\
 & E,\ F \ge 0 & &
\end{array}$$

As we have already observed, the graphical analysis produces the optimal solution $E^* = 4.5$, $F^* = 7.0$. In Chapter 3 we used the term OV to denote the optimal value of the objective function. For the model (5.5) we have

$$\begin{aligned}
\text{OV} = \text{maximum profit} &= 5000E^* + 4000F^* \\
&= 5000(4.5) + 4000(7) = 50{,}500
\end{aligned}$$

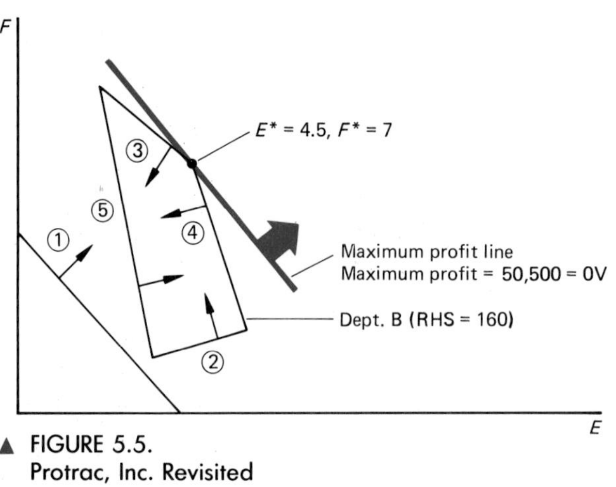

▲ FIGURE 5.5.
Protrac, Inc. Revisited

Also note that the number of positive decision variables will always be less than or equal to the number of binding or active constraints. If it is less than, there is a degenerate solution.

as shown in Figure 5.5. We have also seen (see Section 3.4) that the two constraints on labor hours available in departments A and B are active at optimality. The three remaining constraints are inactive.

Setting Up the Problem for the Computer

As we have already mentioned, the computer processes the standard equality constraint form of the model. However, as we have seen, the process of converting a problem to standard equality constraint form is quite mechanical. For this reason, most LP computer codes will accept, as input, your original model, which may have some inequality constraints, and then the computer will automatically change the model to standard equality constraint form before it solves the problem. Thus, we can input directly the original model, (5.5). There are, however, two important formalities to be observed when setting up a problem for the computer. First, *the simplex algorithm for solving linear programs requires that all variables be nonnegative.* Therefore, this must be true of the model that you input directly to the computer. However, since the computer always assumes that this is true, you do not need to write these nonnegativity conditions explicitly. In Appendix 5.1 we discuss the modifications you must perform on a problem in which not all of your decision variables are nonnegative. The second point is that *all variables in the constraints must appear on the left, with the constant terms on the right.* Of course, the model is the same whether or not all variables are on the left and all constants on the right, and in simply writing out the formulation of a model this formality need not be observed. But to satisfy the computer, the problem must be submitted in this form, and that is our present goal—to solve the problem on the computer. Let us now proceed to the task.

Computer programs still have a long way to go to allow "human input" and give readable output, but they have improved over the years. Remember that most of these programs were written by mathematicians and computer experts, not managers.

The Solution

We have solved the original **PROTRAC**, Inc. model (Figure 5.5) on our computer. The output appears in Figure 5.6.

We make the following observations:

1. This formulation of the model that was input appears at the top of the output. This is immediately followed by the OV of 50,500.
2. The optimal values of the decision variables are then shown in the "VALUE" column. There you see that $E^* = 4.5$, $F^* = 7.0$. In this column you find the optimal values of all variables that explicitly appear in the model that you input (we did not input slack or surplus variables, and hence they do not appear in this column).

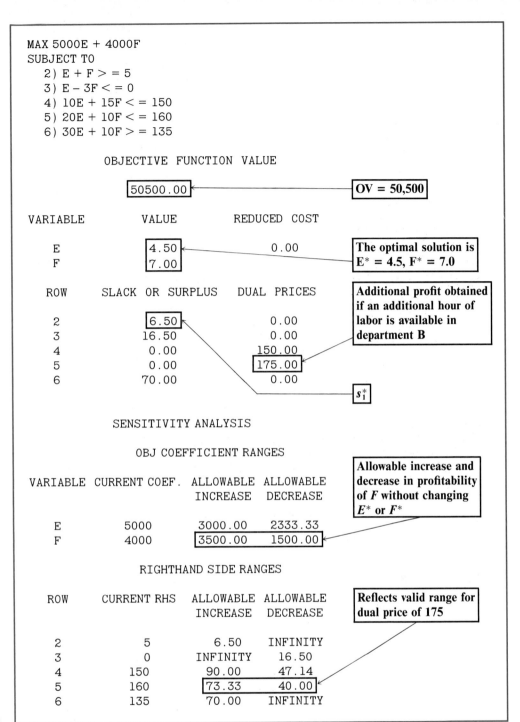

```
MAX 5000E + 4000F
SUBJECT TO
   2) E + F > = 5
   3) E - 3F < = 0
   4) 10E + 15F < = 150
   5) 20E + 10F < = 160
   6) 30E + 10F > = 135

             OBJECTIVE FUNCTION VALUE

             50500.00                        OV = 50,500

VARIABLE          VALUE          REDUCED COST

   E               4.50              0.00        The optimal solution is
   F               7.00                          E* = 4.5, F* = 7.0

   ROW       SLACK OR SURPLUS    DUAL PRICES     Additional profit obtained
                                                 if an additional hour of
   2               6.50              0.00        labor is available in
   3              16.50              0.00        department B
   4               0.00            150.00
   5               0.00            175.00
   6              70.00              0.00        s1*

             SENSITIVITY ANALYSIS

             OBJ COEFFICIENT RANGES
                                                 Allowable increase and
VARIABLE  CURRENT COEF.  ALLOWABLE  ALLOWABLE    decrease in profitability
                         INCREASE   DECREASE     of F without changing
                                                 E* or F*
   E          5000        3000.00    2333.33
   F          4000        3500.00    1500.00

             RIGHTHAND SIDE RANGES

   ROW    CURRENT RHS  ALLOWABLE  ALLOWABLE      Reflects valid range for
                       INCREASE   DECREASE       dual price of 175

   2           5         6.50     INFINITY
   3           0       INFINITY     16.50
   4         150        90.00       47.14
   5         160        73.33       40.00
   6         135        70.00     INFINITY
```

▲ FIGURE 5.6
Computer Output for PROTRAC, Inc.

3. The computer labels *rows* rather than constraints. It considers the objective function to be row 1, the first constraint to be row 2, and so on.
4. The "SLACK OR SURPLUS" column of the output gives the values of the slack and/or surplus variables. In the geometric analysis (Figure 5.5) we saw that the constraints on departments A and B are active. All others are inactive. In the output, you can see that this shows up as zero slack values on rows 4 and 5 and positive slack or surplus on the remaining three rows.
5. The solution is nondegenerate. In Figure 5.5 only two lines intersect at the optimal corner. That is the geometric interpretation. In the output, nondegen-

eracy is revealed by the fact that there are five positive variables (E^*, F^*, and the slacks on rows 2, 3, and 6), which equals the number of constraints in the formulation at the top of the printout.

In mathematical terms, sensitivity analysis is the concept of the partial derivative, where all variables are held constant except for one. This is also known in economics as *marginal value* or *shadow price*.

Let us now move on to the portion of the output that deals with sensitivity analysis. It is important to note that *sensitivity analysis is based on the proposition that all data except for one number in the problem are held fixed,* and we ask for information about the effect of changing the one piece of data that is allowed to vary. The information we might be interested in could include (1) the effect on the OV (i.e., the maximum possible profit) and (2) the effect on the optimal policy E^*, F^*. In Section 5.4 you will see a realistic scenario in which sensitivity analysis is employed.

RHS Sensitivity and the Dual Price

First consider a situation in which we hold all numbers fixed except for the availability of labor hours in department B. What if, instead of having 160 hours available, we were to have 161 hours available? What would be the effect on the OV? Since this constraint on labor-hour availability is the $\leq$ form, we can say, using the language of Section 4.4, that increasing the RHS amounts to "loosening" the constraint, which means making it easier to satisfy. Hence, you would certainly expect that the change from 160 to 161 will not decrease the OV. Will it, though, improve the OV; and if so, by how much?

It is tremendously helpful for students to keep comparing the graphical picture and the computer output. If they can trust a two-dimensional problem which they can see, they will begin to trust computer outputs of problems that couldn't possibly be drawn.

First, let us use the tools we have already acquired, namely geometric analysis, to answer our questions. Then we shall relate this analysis to the computer output. Let the symbol b denote the value of the RHS on the department B constraint. Thus, in Figure 5.5, $b = 160$. In Figure 5.7 we superimpose the department B constraint for the values $b = 161$, $b = 233\frac{1}{3}$, and $b = 250$. We know from the discussion in Section 4.3 that these three new values for b correspond, geometrically, to parallel displacements (away from the origin) of the constraint line. Also since an increase in b means that we are loosening this constraint, the geometric interpretation is that the constraint set, if it changes at all, will expand. The new constraint sets, together with the optimal solutions corresponding to the labor availabilities 161, $233\frac{1}{3}$, and 250, are shown in Figures 5.8, 5.9, and 5.10, respectively.

These figures reveal some interesting facts:

1. $b = 161$. When $b = 161$ (Figure 5.8) the constraints on departments A and B continue to be active. This means that the new solution is given by the two equations

$$10E + 15F = 150$$

$$20E + 10F = 161$$

Solving, we obtain $E^* = 4.575$, $F^* = 6.95$.[4] The new maximum profit becomes

$$\begin{aligned} \text{OV} &= 5000E^* + 4000F^* \\ &= 5000(4.575) + 4000(6.95) = 50{,}675 \end{aligned}$$

Notice that

$$\begin{aligned} \Delta\text{OV} = \text{increase in profit} &= (\text{profit when } b = 161) - (\text{profit when } b = 160) \\ &= 50{,}675 - 50{,}500 = 175 \end{aligned}$$

[4]Here is an interesting point. You might have intuitively supposed that adding another hour of labor to department B should lead to producing a little more E and a little more F in some appropriate mix, but we see that this is not what happens. Our new solution shows that the optimal policy gives 0.075 more E but 0.05 *less* F. The geometry (Figure 5.7) shows you why this happens.

Note that the optimal point moves at a different angle from the "fat" arrow (along Dept. A constraint).
Also reinforce the fact that the hours for department A still haven't been increased, even though the model has exhausted them. Thus, the increased profit is due to trading off—making more Es and fewer Fs (a different product mix) while still using the same number of hours for department A.

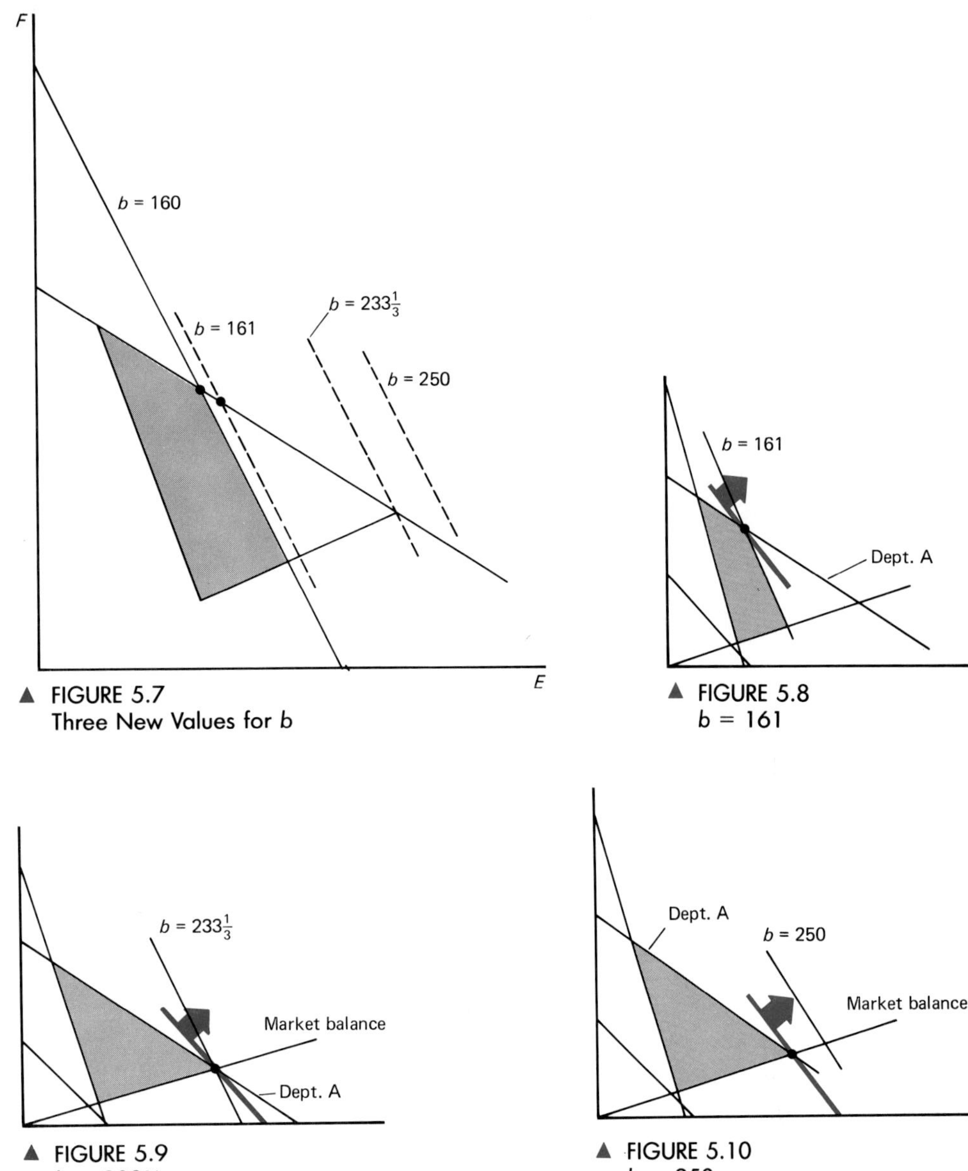

▲ FIGURE 5.7
Three New Values for b

▲ FIGURE 5.8
b = 161

▲ FIGURE 5.9
b = 233⅓

▲ FIGURE 5.10
b = 250

and 175 is also, in the computer output shown in Figure 5.6, the dual price corresponding to row 5, the constraint on department B.

> **In general, the *dual price* on a given constraint can be interpreted as the rate of improvement in OV as the RHS of that constraint increases with all other data held fixed.**

The dual price

What we have just illustrated is that on the computer printout, the dual price for the department B constraint shows the amount of improvement in the optimal objective value as the RHS of that constraint is increased a unit, with all other data held fixed.

2. ***b = 233⅓.*** Figure 5.9 shows that when $b = 233\frac{1}{3}$ the three constraints, department A, department B, and market balance are all active. The computer output for this problem is shown in Figure 5.11. Figure 5.11 shows zero slack values on the three active constraints. There are only four positive variables. Since this problem has five constraints and since the optimal solution has only four positive

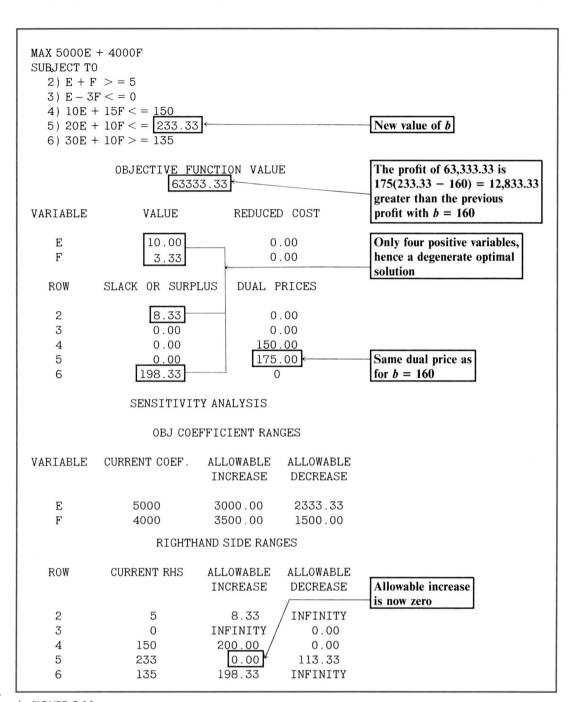

```
MAX 5000E + 4000F
SUBJECT TO
   2) E + F  >= 5
   3) E - 3F <= 0
   4) 10E + 15F <= 150
   5) 20E + 10F <= 233.33      <-- New value of b
   6) 30E + 10F >= 135

              OBJECTIVE FUNCTION VALUE
                   63333.33              <-- The profit of 63,333.33 is
                                             175(233.33 - 160) = 12,833.33
                                             greater than the previous
VARIABLE         VALUE          REDUCED COST profit with b = 160

   E             10.00              0.00     Only four positive variables,
   F              3.33              0.00     hence a degenerate optimal
                                             solution
  ROW      SLACK OR SURPLUS     DUAL PRICES

   2              8.33              0.00
   3              0.00              0.00
   4              0.00            150.00
   5              0.00            175.00     <-- Same dual price as
   6            198.33              0            for b = 160

                SENSITIVITY ANALYSIS

                 OBJ COEFFICIENT RANGES

VARIABLE   CURRENT COEF.   ALLOWABLE   ALLOWABLE
                           INCREASE    DECREASE

   E           5000         3000.00     2333.33
   F           4000         3500.00     1500.00

                 RIGHTHAND SIDE RANGES

  ROW      CURRENT RHS     ALLOWABLE   ALLOWABLE
                           INCREASE    DECREASE     Allowable increase
                                                    is now zero
   2             5            8.33      INFINITY
   3             0         INFINITY       0.00
   4           150          200.00        0.00
   5           233            0.00      113.33
   6           135          198.33      INFINITY
```

▲ FIGURE 5.11
Computer Output for b = 233.33

variables, the solution is, according to the definition given in the preceding section, *degenerate.* Note on the output that the current solution is $E^* = 10$, $F^* = 3\frac{1}{3}$. Also,

$$\begin{aligned} \text{OV} &= 5000E^* + 4000F^* \\ &= 5000(10) + 4000(3\tfrac{1}{3}) = 63{,}333\tfrac{1}{3} \end{aligned}$$

When $b = 233\frac{1}{3}$, the RHS on department B's labor constraint has been increased $73\frac{1}{3}$ units beyond the original value of 160. Consistent with the interpretation above of the dual price, which was 175, we see that the OV has increased by

$$\Delta\text{OV} = 63{,}333\tfrac{1}{3} - 50{,}500 = 12{,}833\tfrac{1}{3} = (175)(73\tfrac{1}{3})$$

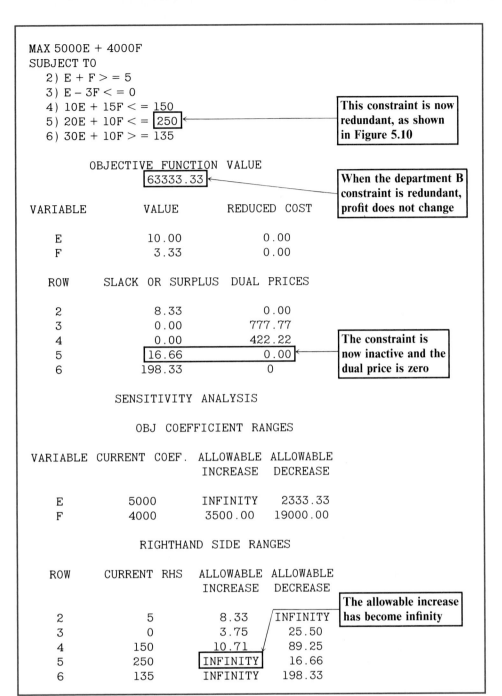

```
MAX 5000E + 4000F
SUBJECT TO
   2) E + F > = 5
   3) E - 3F < = 0
   4) 10E + 15F < = 150
   5) 20E + 10F < = 250
   6) 30E + 10F > = 135

          OBJECTIVE FUNCTION VALUE
                  63333.33

VARIABLE          VALUE          REDUCED COST

   E              10.00               0.00
   F               3.33               0.00

  ROW      SLACK OR SURPLUS    DUAL PRICES

   2               8.33               0.00
   3               0.00             777.77
   4               0.00             422.22
   5              16.66               0.00
   6             198.33               0

             SENSITIVITY ANALYSIS

              OBJ COEFFICIENT RANGES

VARIABLE  CURRENT COEF.  ALLOWABLE  ALLOWABLE
                          INCREASE   DECREASE

   E          5000        INFINITY    2333.33
   F          4000         3500.00   19000.00

              RIGHTHAND SIDE RANGES

  ROW      CURRENT RHS   ALLOWABLE  ALLOWABLE
                          INCREASE   DECREASE

   2            5           8.33     INFINITY
   3            0           3.75       25.50
   4          150          10.71       89.25
   5          250        INFINITY      16.66
   6          135        INFINITY     198.33
```

This constraint is now redundant, as shown in Figure 5.10

When the department B constraint is redundant, profit does not change

The constraint is now inactive and the dual price is zero

The allowable increase has become infinity

▲ FIGURE 5.12
Computer Output for b = 250

3. $b > 233\frac{1}{3}$**.** When b increases up to and beyond the value $233\frac{1}{3}$, Figures 5.9 and 5.10 show that the labor constraint on department B becomes redundant. The values of E^* and F^* and the OV remain as in Figures 5.9 and 5.11. For example, the computer output corresponding to $b = 250$ appears in Figure 5.12. Note that the solution is once again nondegenerate, with the active constraints (0 slack) now being those on department A and market balance (compare with Figure 5.10). Also note that the dual price on the department B constraint has dropped from 175 to zero. This change in the dual price shows that the interpretation of its meaning given above must be restricted to a specific range in RHS values. The range of RHS values for which the dual price remains constant is the **allowable RHS range.** The appropriate range appears on the computer output in the "RIGHTHAND SIDE

RANGES" section under the "ALLOWABLE INCREASE" and "ALLOWABLE DECREASE" columns. Thus, Figures 5.6, 5.11, and 5.12 tell us that

a. When $b = 160$ (Figure 5.6) the dual price of 175 is valid for an allowable increase (in b) of 73⅓ hours and an allowable decrease of 40 hours. Since $160 - 40 = 120$, and $160 + 73⅓ = 233⅓$, we see that *for b values between 120 and 233⅓ hours, the improvement in the OV for each unit of RHS increase, with all other data held fixed, is 175.*

b. When $b = 233⅓$ (Figure 5.11) the dual price remains at 175, but the allowable increase is 0, which means that the value 175 does not apply to RHS values any larger than 233⅓. Indeed, the geometric analysis shows that the constraint becomes inactive and redundant when $b > 233⅓$. *Small changes in the RHS of an inactive constraint cannot affect the OV, and hence for an inactive constraint the dual price will always be zero.*

c. When $b = 250$ (Figure 5.12) we see that now, with the relevant constraint inactive, the dual price is indeed zero and the allowable increase is infinite. That is, for any further increase in b the constraint will remain inactive and the dual price will remain at the value 0. In Figure 5.12 the allowable decrease of 16.66 will take the RHS back to 233⅓. For values of b less than 233⅓ we have seen in Figure 5.11 that the dual price is 175, not zero.

In summary,

Dual price and the valid range

An inactive constraint means that the constraint has slack or surplus (i.e., not binding). Thus, the price for buying more (considering there already is more) is zero!

1. The dual price on a given constraint can be interpreted as the rate of improvement in OV as the RHS of that constraint increases (i.e., the improvement per unit increase in RHS) with all other data held fixed.[5] "Rate of improvement" means "rate of increase" for a Max model and "rate of decrease" for a Min model. If the RHS is decreased, the dual price is the rate at which the OV is *impaired.* This distinction is treated in more detail in Section 5.4. The interpretation of the dual price is valid only within a range for the given RHS. This range is specified by the "ALLOWABLE INCREASE" and "ALLOWABLE DECREASE" columns in the "RIGHTHAND SIDE RANGES" section of the computer printout. It is a range in which the dual price is constant. Outside this allowable range the dual price may change to a different value.

Dual price and inactive constraints

2. According to the interpretation above, the dual price of an inactive constraint will always be zero.

Effect on optimal policy

3. Note that the RHS sensitivity information that the computer provides does not tell us how the optimal policy E^*, F^* changes. It merely explains the way in which the OV will change as the RHS changes.

Effect of degeneracy

This is an area in which the computer fails and human analysis is needed.

4. When we have a degenerate solution some of the dual prices will have either a zero allowable increase or zero allowable decrease. In this case we obtain in the printout only a limited amount of information. Namely, we know only about the effect on the OV of one-sided changes in the RHS.

Objective Function Coefficient Sensitivity and Alternative Optima

Consider increasing the coefficient of F in the objective function, that is, increasing its per unit profitability, while holding the coefficient of E fixed. We have seen (in Figure 4.1) that the contours of the objective function become flatter (have a less negative slope) as this coefficient increases. Figure 5.5 shows that the optimal solution remains at the corner $E^* = 4.5$, $F^* = 7.0$ until the coefficient of F increases

[5]The sensitivity output will not apply when more than one parameter is being changed.

Using a transparency of the graph, it may help to "rock" the objective function at the optimal point to show that the slope could change within certain limits and point III remain the optimum. Then, when the slope is parallel to constraint 3, there are alternate optima; likewise, when the slope is parallel to constraint 4, there are alternate optima.

enough that contours of the objective function are parallel to constraint ③. When the contours of the objective function are parallel to constraint ③, there are *two* optimal solutions: the current corner ($E^* = 4.5$, $F^* = 7.0$), and the corner determined by the intersection of constraints ③ and ⑤. In general, the term **alternative optimal solutions** is used for situations such as this one, in which there is more than one set of decision variables that yield the same optimal value of the objective function.

If the coefficient of F continues to increase, the current solution ($E^* = 4.5$, $F^* = 7.0$) will no longer be optimal, and the point determined by the intersection of constraints ③ and ⑤ will be the unique optimum. The allowable increase for the coefficient of F is thus determined by the increase in the coefficient that makes the contours of the objective function parallel to constraint ③. When, we may ask, does this occur?

The contours of the objective function are parallel to constraint ③ when the two lines have the same slope, which means that the coefficients satisfy the equality:

$$\frac{\text{coefficient of } E \text{ in ③}}{\text{coefficient of } F \text{ in ③}} = \frac{\text{coefficient of } E \text{ in objective}}{\text{coefficient of } F \text{ in objective}}$$

Thus

$$\frac{10}{15} = \frac{5000}{\text{coefficient of } F \text{ in objective}}$$

and

$$\text{coefficient of } F \text{ in objective} = (5000)(^{15}/_{10}) = 7500$$

The current coefficient of F in the objective function is 4000. It becomes parallel to ③, that is, alternative optima occur, if this value increases to 7500. Thus, the current optimal solution remains valid as long as the increase in F is ≤ 3500. *This is termed the allowable increase in the coefficient of F.* It is the value shown in Figure 5.6 under "ALLOWABLE INCREASE" for F. This combination of algebra and geometry explains both the meaning and the value of this entry on the printout.

In general, the **objective coefficient ranges** give the ranges of objective function coefficients over which no change in the optimal solution will occur. Further, by observing how the change in coefficients affects the slope of the objective function, we can make the following important generalizations:

Effect on objective function contours

Changing the objective function coefficients changes the slope of the objective function contours. This change in slope may or not affect the optimal solution and the optimal value of the objective function.

Now recall that as the coefficient of F increased (holding the coefficient of E fixed) we eventually obtained a new solution in which the optimal value of F increased. This result agrees with your intuition since increasing the profitability of F would not cause you to produce F at a lower level! This case illustrates a general concept:

Effect on activity in a Max model

In a Max model, increasing the profitability of an activity and keeping all other data unchanged cannot reduce the optimal level of that activity.

The situation for a cost-minimization model is just reversed. Since we want to minimize total cost, we certainly would not expect that increasing the cost of an activity, while keeping all other data unchanged, could lead to a higher optimal level of that activity. This case illustrates another general concept:

Effect on activity in a Min model

In a Min model, increasing the cost of an activity and keeping all other data unchanged cannot increase the optimal level of that activity.

Meaning of "OBJ COEFFICIENT RANGES." We can now summarize the significant points concerning the "OBJ COEFFICIENT RANGES" of the printout. In interpreting this portion of the output you must be careful to distinguish between the cases of a degenerate and a nondegenerate solution.

For a nondegenerate solution

For a nondegenerate solution

1. The columns "ALLOWABLE INCREASE" and "ALLOWABLE DECREASE," under the "OBJ COEFFICIENT RANGES" heading, tell you how much the coefficient of a given variable in the objective function may be increased or decreased without changing the optimal solution, where all other data are assumed to be fixed. Of course, as the profitability varies in this range the OV values are given by

$$\text{OV} = 5000E^* + [(\text{profitability of } F) \cdot F^*]$$

As an illustration, imagine that the coefficient of F is assigned the value 6000, which is within the allowable range shown in Figure 5.6. Then the solution remains at ($E^* = 4.5$, $F^* = 7$) and

$$\begin{aligned}\text{OV} &= 5000E^* + 6000F^* \\ &= 5000(4.5) + 6000(7) = 64{,}500\end{aligned}$$

Reinforce the fact that changing two or more objective function coefficients simultaneously means that the model will have to be rerun to find out what will happen. These ranges are good for changes in only one coefficient; all the others coefficients stay the same.

2. When a coefficient is changed by less than the allowable amounts, the current optimal solution remains the unique optimal solution to the model.
3. When a particular coefficient is increased by its allowable amount, there will be an alternative optimal solution with, for a Max model, a larger optimal value for the distinguished variable. (For a Min model, increasing a coefficient the allowable amount will produce an alternative optimum with a lower optimal value for the distinguished variable.)
4. When a variable's coefficient is decreased by its allowable amount, there will be another alternative optimal solution with the distinguished variable having a lower (higher) optimal value for a Max (Min) model.

Signal for alternative optima

One other fact of interest applies to a *nondegenerate* solution. *When you see, for some variable in the "OBJ COEFFICIENT RANGES" section of the output, a zero entry under either of the columns "ALLOWABLE INCREASE" or "ALLOWABLE DECREASE," you know that there is at least one alternative optimal solution to the problem at hand.* Moreover, whenever there are alternative optima such a signal will appear. This principle is illustrated in Figure 5.13, a hypothetical maximization LP in two decision variables and three inequality constraints. The objective function contour is parallel to the second constraint (labeled ②), and in employing the graphical solution technique you can see that the corners labeled I and II are alternative optima for this problem. The computer, because of the algorithm it employs to solve the problem, will find only one of these corners as an optimal solution and the computer output applies only to that corner. Let us suppose that corner I is the solution found by the computer. The geometry in Figure 5.13 shows that any increase in the coefficient of x_1 will change the objective function contour to a tilt like that of the dashed line, and corner II becomes the unique optimal solution. The computer output for the solution at corner I would have, as a signal for this phenomenon, a zero value next to x_1 under the "ALLOWABLE INCREASE" column.

Technically, there is an alternative solution (another way of finding the solution values), but in a degenerate case it is the same point superimposed on the first solution. The computer output will give some different information on the "half-ranges" and dual prices for the constraints.

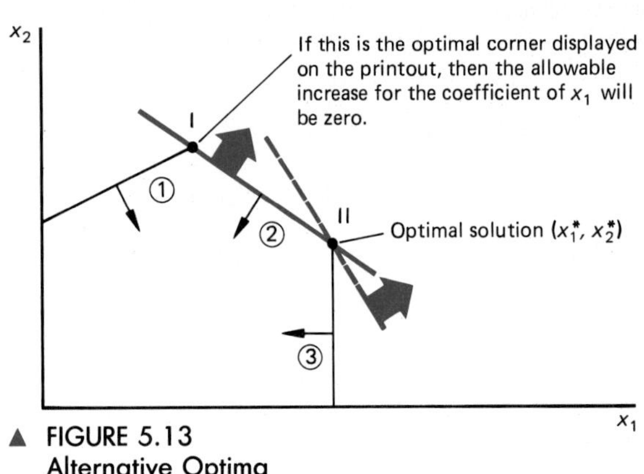

▲ FIGURE 5.13
Alternative Optima

Caveats for degenerate solutions

Let us now consider the case of a printout showing a *degenerate optimal solution.* In this case two caveats must be observed.

For a degenerate solution

1. The signals described above for alternative optima should be ignored.
2. As long as an objective function coefficient is varied in the indicated range the optimal solution will not change. This fact was also true in the nondegenerate case. In the latter case, however, alternative optima were obtained when the coefficient was changed to the limit of its range, and then, as this direction of change continued, the original optimal solution dropped out. In the degenerate case this result can no longer be guaranteed. All we can say is that any objective function coefficient must be changed by *at least, and possibly more than,* the indicated allowable amounts in order to produce a new optimal solution.

Reduced Cost

We have explained everything in our computer output except for the entries under the column "REDUCED COST." The following facts pertain to these entries. This is another instance where, in order to give a correct interpretation, you must first observe whether the optimal solution is nondegenerate.

Nondegenerate case

The sign of the reduced cost is important. Thus, for a Max problem, it can be called *increased profit* (revenue). See the output for Buster Sod on page 195, for example.

1. In a *nondegenerate* optimal solution, the reduced cost of any particular decision variable is defined to be *the amount the coefficient of that variable in the objective function would have to change in order to have a positive optimal value for that variable.* Thus, if a variable is already positive at optimality, its reduced cost is zero (as is the case for both decision variables in Figures 5.6, 5.11, and 5.12). If the optimal value of a variable is zero, then from the definition of reduced cost you can see that the reduced cost is either the "ALLOWABLE INCREASE" or "ALLOWABLE DECREASE" that corresponds to the given variable (one of these values will be infinite; the other will be the reduced cost). For example, suppose that we change the data in the **PROTRAC** E and F model in such a way that the optimal value $E^* = 0$. Then the reduced cost of E is the amount its profitability (the coefficient of E in the objective function) would have to be *increased* in order to have an optimal solution with $E^* > 0$. This is precisely the entry that you would find corresponding to E in the "ALLOWABLE INCREASE" column. In this case, for any decrease in the coefficient of E (making E less profitable) the value E^* will remain at zero. Hence, the corresponding "ALLOWABLE DECREASE" would be infinite.

2. Another equivalent interpretation of reduced cost, for a nondegenerate solution, can be given. In a nondegenerate solution, the reduced cost of a decision variable (whose optimal value is currently zero) is the rate (per unit amount) at which the objective value is hurt as that variable is "forced into" (i.e., is forced to assume positive values in) an optimal solution. In the example above, with $E^* = 0$, the OV would decrease if we forced ourselves to find an optimal solution with the *additional* constraint that $E = 1$. (To see that the OV would *decrease* you need merely recognize that in the current model the optimal value of E is zero. Forcing E to be 1, then, can only yield us less return.) This *rate of decrease* as E^* is initially forced to be positive would be given by the reduced cost of E. Additional examples of the two interpretations above will appear in Section 5.4.

Degenerate case

3. Now consider a *degenerate solution* with a decision variable whose optimal value is zero. The coefficient of that variable in the objective function must be changed by *at least, and possibly more than,* the reduced cost in order for there to be an optimal solution with that variable appearing at a positive level.

This completes our exploration of the meaning of each entry in the computer output. Although our discussion has been introductory, if you have mastered the material presented from Chapter 2 up to this point, you are now able to use LP in practical situations; to formulate problems, solve them on a computer, and correctly interpret the output. The final sections of this chapter go in two different directions. Section 5.4 is intended to increase your familiarity with output interpretation by showing you how the printout might be employed in a realistic scenario. The orientation is managerial, with an emphasis on the sensitivity information and its use. In Section 5.5, we give a synopsis of how to interpret the sensitivity information on the printout. Then, in Section 5.6, the direction changes and the dual problem is discussed. It is a topic that is fundamental to a thorough knowledge of LP and takes you deeper into several aspects of the subject.

Most real-world LP modeling involves taking the computer output and either writing a report in common English or using a "report writer" language that will do it automatically, using both common English and the terms of the industry or business involved.

5.4 The Crawler Tread Output: A Dialogue with Management (Sensitivity Analysis in Action)

This problem was introduced in Section 2.3. Recall that the ore from four different locations is blended to make crawler tractor treads. Each ore contains three essential elements, denoted for simplicity as A, B, and C, that must appear in the final blend at minimum threshold levels. **PROTRAC** pays a different price per ton for the ore from each location. The cost-minimizing blend is obtained by solving the following LP model, where T_i = the fraction of a ton of ore from location i in one ton of the blend.

$$
\begin{array}{llr}
\text{Min } 800T_1 + 400T_2 + 600T_3 + 500T_4 & & \text{(total cost)} \\
\text{s.t. } 10T_1 + 3T_2 + 8T_3 + 2T_4 \geq 5 & & \text{(requirement on A)} \\
90T_1 + 150T_2 + 75T_3 + 175T_4 \geq 100 & & \text{(requirement on B)} \\
45T_1 + 25T_2 + 20T_3 + 37T_4 \geq 30 & & \text{(requirement on C)} \\
T_1 + T_2 + T_3 + T_4 = 1 & & \text{(blend condition)} \\
T_1 \geq 0, \quad i = 1, 2, 3, 4 & &
\end{array}
$$

One can again show from the output that if it had been known that T_1, T_2, and T_3 would be positive and that constraints for A, C, and blend would be binding, one could solve those 3 equations in 3 unknowns to get the values of variables and slacks and surpluses.

APPLICATION CAPSULE

Against the Grain: LP Modeling Helps a Cabinet Company Save on Its Raw Materials*

Wellborn Cabinet, Inc. owns a cabinet manufacturing facility in Alabama. The operation consists of a sawmill, four dry kilns, and a wood cabinet assembly plant with a rough mill for making blanks (cabinet components). Wellborn obtains the lumber used for manufacturing the cabinets in two ways: (1) buying logs that are processed by its sawmill to make lumber, which is then used in the assembly plant; (2) buying lumber that has been sawed elsewhere. Currently, about 73% of the input comes from the company's own sawmill.

Both logs and lumber are graded #1 or #2; #1 is of better quality and more expensive. About two-thirds of the total volume of logs that Wellborn had been buying were #1. Purchased lumber, accounting for about 27% of the lumber used, was of two types: green (18%), which had to be dried in the company's kilns, and dry (9%). Nearly all of the dry lumber was also grade #1.

The cost of wood makes up about 45% of the total material cost of making cabinets. Management thus wanted to know if its approach to buying wood for the cabinet assembly plant was the most economical. To help answer this question, Auburn University's Technical Assistance Center, in cooperation with the School of Forestry, analyzed the company's operation. An LP model of blank production was created, with constraints that included the capacities of the sawmill and kilns, the required output of blanks, and the available supply of raw materials.

Running the model on a mainframe computer revealed that the company could minimize the cost of producing blanks by purchasing only two kinds of wood: #2 grade logs with small-end diameters of 9 to 15 inches (88% by volume) and #2 common green lumber (12%). This purchasing policy would reduce Wellborn's raw materials costs by nearly one-third, an annual saving of about $412,000.

The model provided managers with much additional useful information:

- Shadow prices associated with the purchase of logs of various sizes enabled management to make the most cost-effective selection from among the logs available at any given time.
- Sensitivity analysis revealed the price ranges for which the solution prescribed by the model would remain optimal. In particular, it indicated that reductions of up to 20% in the price of dry lumber or #1 grade logs would not affect the optimal purchase policy.
- A slack value of zero for the operation of the dry kilns indicated that this operation represented a bottleneck—kiln capacity was the only factor limiting increased production. A 22% increase in kiln capacity would permit an increase of 29% in blank output without any additional changes.

---

*Carino and LeNoir, "Optimizing Wood Procurement in Cabinet Manufacturing," *Interfaces*, Vol. 18, No. 2 (March–April, 1988).

A good analyst should be able to raise more questions about the situation being modeled than simply coming up with a "number" as the solution to the problem.

Let us now discuss and analyze the computer output for the solution to this problem. Place yourself in the position of the manager who is responsible for planning future production. A number of questions are on the manager's mind. The modeler responds.

MANAGER: First of all, what is the solution to our problem?

MODELER: I have run the problem on the computer, and here's the output [see Figure 5.14]. By "solution" I take it you mean the optimal values of the decision variables. These are printed in the section of output that I've labeled VARIABLE. The optimal values of the variables appear under the second column, headed VALUE. You can see that the rounded optimal values are

▼ FIGURE 5.14
Output for Crawler Tread

```
MIN 800 T1 + 400 T2 + 600 T3 + 500 T4
SUBJECT TO
   2) 10 T1 + 3 T2 + 8 T3 + 2 T4 >= 5
   3) 90 T1 + 150 T2 + 75 T3 + 175 T4 >= 100
   4) 45 T1 + 25 T2 + 20 T3 + 37 T4 >= 30
   5) T1 + T2 + T3 + T4 = 1

                OBJECTIVE FUNCTION VALUE        [OV]
     1                     511.111

VARIABLE          VALUE          REDUCED COST

   T1              0.259             0.000  \
   T2              0.703             0.000   |
   T3              0.037             0.000   |  [Variables]
   T4              0.000            91.111  /

   ROW     SLACK OR SURPLUS   DUAL PRICES

    2              0.000          -44.444  \
    3             31.666            0.000   |  [Constraints]
    4              0.000           -4.444   |
    5              0.000         -155.555  /

                SENSITIVITY ANALYSIS

                  OBJ COEFFICIENT RANGES

VARIABLE    CURRENT    ALLOWABLE    ALLOWABLE
             COEF.     INCREASE     DECREASE

   T1       800.000     223.636      119.999
   T2       400.000      66.847      299.999
   T3       600.000      85.714      118.269
   T4       500.000    INFINITY       91.111

                  RIGHTHAND SIDE RANGES

   ROW      CURRENT    ALLOWABLE    ALLOWABLE
              RHS      INCREASE     DECREASE

    2         5.000      2.375        0.250
    3       100.000     31.666      INFINITY
    4        30.000      0.714        7.000
    5         1.000      0.250        0.043
```

$$T1 = 0.26$$

$$T2 = 0.70$$

$$T3 = 0.04$$

$$T4 = 0.00$$

MANAGER: How much does a ton of this blend cost?

MODELER: The OV, which is the optimal value of the objective function, is also identified. You can see that the minimum cost is $511.11.

MANAGER: I'd like to keep my costs under $500 per ton. Isn't there any way I can do this?

MODELER: It is impossible to find a lower-cost mixture that satisfies the constraints you have imposed.

MANAGER: You mean the requirements on essential elements?

MODELER: Exactly.

MANAGER: Well, maybe I can modify those requirements. I really do want to keep my costs under $500 per ton.

MODELER: Then you certainly will have to loosen your requirements. We can discuss how to do that.

MANAGER: All right. But first, I recall that the requirements were expressed as minimum threshold levels. Is there any way I can tell exactly how much of each essential element gets into the optimal mix?

MODELER: That information is obtained from the second section of the output, which I've identified as CONSTRAINTS. The computer labels the four constraints of the problem as rows 2 to 5, respectively, since it regards the objective function as row 1. The first three constraints of the problem are the requirements on essential elements. This corresponds to the output labeled as rows 2, 3, and 4.

MANAGER: I see a column labeled SLACK OR SURPLUS and one labeled DUAL PRICES, but where are the amounts of the essential elements in the optimal blend?

MODELER: Those have to be deduced. Remember that before the inequality problem was solved, the computer had to transform it to standard equality constraint form. For this model, the column labeled SLACK OR SURPLUS is the optimal value of the surplus variable associated with each constraint in the transformed problem.

MANAGER: I think I see what you're getting at. The surplus in row 2 is zero. The first constraint is the requirement on A, which was 5 pounds. Since the original constraint is $\geq$, after conversion to equality form it must look like

$$10T1 + 3T2 + 8T3 + 2T4 - S1 = 5$$

MODELER: Exactly.

MANAGER: Okay, and I understand what happens for rows 3 and 4. But the last constraint in the original model was an equality constraint. That means that it has neither a slack nor a surplus variable in standard form. Right?

MODELER: Correct.

MANAGER: Then why is there a slack or surplus value of zero printed on the output for row 5? Doesn't that suggest there is a slack or surplus variable in that row?

MODELER: You may be right, but the suggestion is unintended. For a constraint that was originally an equality the entry in this column is always zero. As you have correctly observed, the actual surplus variables in this problem are associated only with the first three constraints of the original model: That is, rows 2, 3, and 4.

MANAGER: Fine. Now let's return to the surplus variable on row 2. I see that its optimal value is zero. What does that have to do with the amount of essential element A in the final mix? I thought I saw the answer before, but now I'm confused.

MODELER: It's easy. Since the optimal surplus value is zero, and since we know the other optimal values, it must be true that if we substitute the optimal values of all the variables into the equality form of the constraint we will obtain the following result:

$$10(0.25926) + 3(0.70370) + 8(0.03704) + 2(0.0000) - 0 = 5$$

In other words, since the optimal surplus value is zero, the optimal mix contains exactly 5 pounds of A.

MANAGER: I see. And since the surplus in row 4 is zero, the optimal mix must contain exactly 30 pounds of C. Is that right?

Another way of looking at this solution: If you had to provide extra elements *A*, *B*, and/or *C*, extra *B* would be better than the others (more cost-effective).

MODELER: Precisely, and you can also figure out how much B there is.

MANAGER: Okay. For B, I have to look at row 3. Since the surplus is 31.6666 it must be true that

$$90(0.25926) + 150(0.70370) + 75(0.03704) + 175(0.0000) - 31.6666 = 100$$

But where do I go from here?

MODELER: Well, your equation means that in the optimal mix the minimum requirement of 100 pounds is actually exceeded by 31.6666. That is, there are 131.6666 pounds of B actually included.

MANAGER: Isn't that odd? You'd think I could make a cheaper blend by using less B. Why should I use more than 100 pounds if I need only 100?

MODELER: That is a very good question. You see, the combination of ores that satisfies the requirements on A and C at a minimum cost just happens to contain more than 100 pounds of B. Any combination of ores that includes less B will either not have enough of A and/or C, or, if it does have enough, it will cost more than $511.11 per ton. In other words, forcing yourself to include less of the excess amount of B while still satisfying the requirements on A and C will end up costing you more. You may have to think about that assertion, but it is exactly what the solution to the model is telling us.

MANAGER: Okay. I guess I can see your point. So how can I get my total cost down to $500 or less?

MODELER: You will have to loosen your constraints. This means loosening the requirements on A or C.

MANAGER: Why not on B?

MODELER: Because, in order to satisfy the requirements on A and C at minimum cost, you're already including over 100 pounds of B, which is more than your minimal threshold. In other words, the requirement on B is not active. You could loosen this requirement to a smaller number, such as 98, and the optimal mix would still contain the same composition and cost. Thus, loosening the requirement on B to a smaller number won't get us anywhere. You have to loosen one of the active requirements.

MANAGER: You mean one where there's zero surplus.

MODELER: Precisely.

MANAGER: Okay. So I have to relax the requirement on A or C. But which one? And how much?

MODELER: We can use the information under the DUAL PRICES heading to analyze these questions.

MANAGER: I was wondering what that column meant.

MODELER: It means rate of improvement in the OV as we increase the right-hand side. Since we are interested in loosening a $\geq$ constraint, we will be decreasing the right-hand side. Now let's look at the dual price on row 2. It is −44.44. The negative sign means that as the right-hand side is *increased* the OV is "negatively improved," or hurt. Thus, as the right-hand side is loosened, or *decreased,* the OV is improved. What all of this boils down to is the common-sense idea that, as your requirement for A is loosened, your minimum cost will go down. The dual price tells us it goes down at the rate of $44.44 per pound.

MANAGER: Loosening the requirement for A must mean reducing it from 5 pounds to something less. Right?

MODELER: Right.

Again, also note that the number of *positive decision variables* will always be equal to the number of binding or active constraints for a nondegenerate solution.

MANAGER: And the dual price of −44.44 says that for each pound of reduction that cost goes down $44.44?

MODELER: Right.

MANAGER: Great. This means if I require only 4 pounds per ton of A, instead of 5, the cost goes down to about $466.67 and I'm under $500. Right?

MODELER: Well, not quite. But you're right in spirit. You have the correct rate of change, but this rate applies only to some *interval* of values around the original value of 5. The appropriate interval may not allow you to analyze the decrease of a whole unit—maybe only half a unit, for example.

MANAGER: Even so, if I cut the requirement to 4.5 pounds, I'd save (½)(44.44), which is over $22. My final cost would still be under $500!

MODELER: True enough, but the allowable interval may not even include 4.5.

MANAGER: Obviously, we need to know that interval.

MODELER: Right. And it appears on the bottom of the output under the section labeled RIGHTHAND SIDE RANGES.

MANAGER: I see. In the ALLOWABLE DECREASE column for row 2 we have 0.250. That must mean I can analyze a change from 5 down to 4.75. Right?

MODELER: Right.

MANAGER: So my saving would be 0.25(44.44), which is $11.11, and this gets me down exactly to $500. But what if I relaxed the requirement a little more, like to 4.50. Wouldn't that reduce the cost further?

MODELER: Probably, but I can't tell you exactly how much because the rate of change may be different after a decrease of 0.25.

MANAGER: In technical language, that must mean the dual price may change.

MODELER: Exactly.

MANAGER: Okay. Now just to see if I have it all straight, let me analyze the potential savings if I relax the requirement on C.

MODELER: Go ahead.

MANAGER: The requirement on C is identified as row 4. The original right-hand side is 30. The output shows an allowable decrease of 7, so I can go down to 23. The dual price on row 4 is −4.44. This is my rate of savings as I decrease the right-hand side from 30. Hence, if I decrease the requirement to 23, I save

$$7(4.44) = \$31.08$$

This also gets me well under $500. In fact, if I cut down the requirement only 2.5 pounds, I can apply the same rate of change, and consequently I should save

$$(2.5)(4.44) = \$11.10$$

and this just about gets me down to a cost of $500. How am I doing?

MODELER: Very well.

MANAGER: Okay. I see that I can get the cost per ton down to $500 if I relax the requirement on A to 4.75 pounds per ton *or* the requirement on C to 27.5 pounds per ton. But what if I relax both requirements on A and C, perhaps a little less but both at the same time? Then what?

MODELER: Sorry, but again we don't have precise information on the output to that. The only way to tackle that question would be to rerun the model numerous times with different right-hand sides for A and C.

MANAGER: So when I use the dual price on one of the right-hand-side values, it's important to keep the others unchanged.

MODELER: Correct.

MANAGER: So let me review this. I know that I can get my cost per ton down to \$500 if I relax the requirement on A to 4.75 pounds per ton *or* the requirement on C to 27.5 pounds per ton. Which should I do?

MODELER: The computer cannot give you a guideline on that. You might note that the required relaxation on A would be 0.25/5, or 5%, and on C it would be $2.5/30 = 8\frac{1}{3}\%$. But I don't know whether that is helpful. The point is that you, as the manager, have to decide on which change would do more harm to the properties of the blend. I think it probably boils down to an engineering question.

MANAGER: Yes, I think you are right, and I know who to talk with about that.

MODELER: Good.

MANAGER: By the way, I've also been noticing the column of your printout that says ALLOWABLE INCREASE. I would guess that pertains to increases in the right-hand side.

MODELER: Right again.

MANAGER: Would you just run through the analysis on the increase side to make sure that I'm with you?

MODELER: Let's take row 2, the requirement on A. Suppose that you want to tighten this requirement.

MANAGER: Since we are dealing with a ≥ constraint, tightening would mean an increase in the right-hand side, which is the required amount of A.

MODELER: Correct. Tightening a requirement can never help the OV and may hurt. In this case the dual price of −44.44 tells us that increasing the right-hand side will hurt. This means that the cost will go up. The allowable increase of 2.375 tells us that if we increase the original amount, 5, by any amount up to 2.375, the increase in cost is given by 44.44 times that amount.

MANAGER: In other words, the same dual price pertains to both increases and decreases in the right-hand side. The allowable increase and decrease are provided by the computer, and the dual price is the rate of improvement in the objective value as the right-hand side increases over that entire allowable range. If this rate is negative, it hurts the OV.

MODELER: Right. And loosening a constraint will always mean that the OV cannot be hurt and may be improved. Tightening means that the OV cannot be improved and may be hurt.

MANAGER: I even notice that the dual price on B is zero, which means that the changes in the value of 100 don't have any effect. I guess that means we don't even need a constraint on B. Why is that?

MODELER: Because, as I mentioned earlier, if you satisfy the requirements for A and C at a minimum cost, the requirement for B will be satisfied automatically.

MANAGER: So am I correct? Could the constraint on B be discarded?

MODELER: I would think not. If you would ever want to change some of the data and then rerun the model, the constraint on B could become important. In particular, we can see from the ALLOWABLE INCREASE of 31.666 under RIGHTHAND SIDE RANGES that if the RHS were to exceed 131.666, this constraint would become binding. So I don't really want to say that it can be removed from the model.

MANAGER: Could you be a little more explicit, without getting into a lot of terminology?

MODELER: All right. Just as an example, last week I heard from Mr. Shmootz that the cost of ore from location 2 might increase.

MANAGER: Mr. Shmootz?

MODELER: Yes.

MANAGER: Well, I must admit that such a possibility is something I'm concerned about. But I don't see how we can take that kind of uncertainty into account.

MODELER: This relates to your question. The cost of ore from location 2 is the coefficient of T2 in the objective function, namely 400. If this cost is increased, we would expect our OV to increase. If the cost of ore from location 2 goes up enough, we might even expect that less of it, or maybe even none of it, would be used in the optimal blend. This means more of the others must be used because the total amount used has to sum up to 1. This means that the relative importance of the constraints could change. Previous constraints that had been tight might not be, and vice versa. A lot of things can happen when you start playing with the data.

MANAGER: Tell me again what you mean by a tight constraint.

MODELER: It means a constraint with an optimal slack or surplus value of zero. Such a constraint is also called *active,* or *binding,* or *effective.*

MANAGER: I'm glad you told me that. What about an equality constraint? Is it considered active or binding or whatever?

MODELER: Yes. Always. In this terminology, although the constraint on B is currently inactive, it could become active if the data in the model are changed.

MANAGER: Fine. But I'm still confused. What does all this have to do with the cost of ore from location 2? Or is the whole thing just too complicated to explain?

MODELER: Not at all. Let's look at the cost of ore from location 2. We can actually determine the range over which this cost can vary without influencing the optimal blend. In particular, look at the portion of output headed OBJ COEFFICIENT RANGES. In the row corresponding to T2 there are items called ALLOWABLE INCREASE and ALLOWABLE DECREASE. This gives the range in which the cost of T2 can vary.

MANAGER: You mean without changing the optimal mix?

MODELER: Yes.

MANAGER: Okay. In other words, the cost of T2 is now \$400 in our model. You mean that the output says it could be anywhere between \$100 and \$466.84 and the optimal mix stays the same?

MODELER: Exactly.

MANAGER: I don't see how we can know that.

MODELER: It's all in the mathematics.

MANAGER: I'll take your word for that. So if the cost increases from \$400 to \$450, we have nothing to worry about.

MODELER: Well, I don't know about that. We know that the optimal mix will stay the same. This means that the optimal values of all the variables, including the slacks, stay the same. But our total cost will increase by 50 times the amount of T2 being used in the current solution.

MANAGER: I see. The OV will go from the old value, \$511.11, to the new value

$$511.11 + 50(0.70370) = \$546.30$$

Yes, I see what you mean. Everything stays the same except the total cost. Did you say that even the surplus values stay the same?

MODELER: Yes. If all the decision variables stay the same, you can see from the algebra that the surplus variables would have to also.

MANAGER: That must mean the constraints that are active also stay the same.

MODELER: Good for you.

MANAGER: I see. By the way, what happens if the cost of T2 increases by more than the allowable amount?

MODELER: Well, since we have a Min model I know that increasing the cost of an input cannot increase its use. Therefore, as the cost of T2 increases I know that the optimal value of T2 can never increase. In fact, since the current solution is nondegenerate I know that when the cost of T2 increases by more than the allowable amount, the optimal value of T2 will in fact surely decrease.

MANAGER: Wait a minute. Slow down. You said nondegenerate?

MODELER: Yes. This simply means that in the computer output the number of variables with a positive optimal value, including both decision and slack or surplus variables, is equal to the number of constraints. Figure 5.14 shows that at optimality three decision variables and one surplus variable are positive. Thus there are four positive variables and four constraints, which means that we have a nondegenerate solution. This is a technicality but it is important in interpreting some of the output.

MANAGER: All right. Fine. So if the per unit cost of ore from mine 2 increases by more than its allowable amount, we will get an optimal solution with a smaller value of T2.

MODELER: Yes. And not only that. The optimal values of some of the other variables may also change, but it isn't possible to say exactly which ones or how much. This means that a surplus that was positive could become zero, and hence a constraint that was inactive could become active, if you know what I mean.

MANAGER: Yes, I think I'm with you.

MODELER: Good. And it could also mean that a constraint that previously had zero surplus could now become inactive in the sense that its surplus becomes positive. In other words, once the cost change exceeds the limit of the indicated range, all sorts of things can happen.

MANAGER: You're talking about a cost change that *exceeds* the allowable limit. What if it actually hits the limit?

MODELER: Then, again since the current solution is nondegenerate, we know that there will be alternative optimal solutions, the current solution together with a new one that has less T2 in it.

MANAGER: Well, it seems to me that we have considerable information about the influence of uncertainty. That strikes me as remarkable.

MODELER: I agree.

MANAGER: Okay. Thank you very much. I think I can do pretty well now on my own with the output analysis. We should really call it model analysis, shouldn't we?

MODELER: I guess so.

MANAGER: Okay. Thanks again. I'm amazed at how much we can learn about the actual problem, above and beyond the solution.

MODELER: Right. That is because of the relative simplicity of linear mathematics. By the way, do you mind if I ask you just one question to more or less check you out?

MANAGER: Okay. Shoot.

MODELER: You have already noticed on the output that the optimal value of T4 is zero.

MANAGER: True.

MODELER: I happen to know that ore from location 4 has some desirable tensile properties that haven't really been built into the model.

MANAGER: That is true.

MODELER: Also, I understand from Mr. Shmootz that it isn't unreasonable to renegotiate the cost of T4 periodically.

MANAGER: Are you referring to the fact that PROTRAC has some family connections in the location 4 enterprise?

MODELER: Something like that. But my point is this. How much would the cost of T4 have to decrease before you're willing to buy some?

MANAGER: Let's see. The current cost of T4 is $500 per ton. I think what you're trying to ask me is this: How much must this cost decrease before we obtain an optimal policy that uses T4? Is that your question?

MODELER: Yes.

MANAGER: Okay. To find the answer I look at the SENSITIVITY ANALYSIS, where I see that if the cost of T4 decreases by less than $91.11 per ton, then, according to what you just said, the optimal value of this variable remains unchanged. That means it remains at zero. Consequently, taking into account what you just said about nondegeneracy, I know that if its cost is negotiated down to 408.89 or less, there will be an optimal solution with T4 positive. Right?

MODELER: Correct. Now can you tell me what happens to the optimal objective value?

MANAGER: I guess I can figure that out. If the cost decreases by no more than $91.11, no change occurs in the optimal values of any of the variables. In the objective function only the cost of T4 is changing. But since the value of T4 stays at zero, the OV won't change either. I guess it stays at $511.11 as long as the reduction in cost is less than $91.11.

MODELER: Correct.

MANAGER: But what happens if the reduction exactly equals 91.11? You've told me that in this case the optimal value of T4 will become positive. Is that right?

MODELER: Not quite. There will be two optimal solutions: the current one, and another one that has a positive optimal value of T4 and some new values for some of the other variables. But I don't know exactly how the others will change.

MANAGER: Okay, but does this mean that when the cost of T4 is reduced by exactly $91.11, the total cost suddenly drops down from $511.11?

MODELER: No, since these are alternative optima the OV equals 511.11 at each.

MANAGER: Can we tell how much of T4 will be used in the alternative optimum?

MODELER: I'm afraid not. All we know is that there will be some positive value for this variable.

MANAGER: And how do you know all that?

MODELER: From the mathematics. And remember that these statements about alternative optimal solutions depend on the nondegeneracy of the current solution on the printout.

MANAGER: Okay. Great. And I suppose that if the decrease in the cost of T4 exceeds the allowable amount, the OV will then begin to decrease.

MODELER: Again, this is true because of the nondegeneracy.

MANAGER: What if the nondegeneracy weren't satisfied?

MODELER: Then we would have what is termed a degenerate solution. All we could say then is that the optimal solution will not change if the cost of T4 stays within the allowable range. Conceivably, the cost would decrease by *more than* 91.11 and we would still not get a new optimal solution. Thus you can see that in the degenerate case the output gives us somewhat less information.

MANAGER: Well, by now I think I know all that I need to about what's going on. Do you agree?

MODELER: Yes. Shall we stop?

MANAGER: Really, since I'm doing so well, I have to ask one final question. What about that column in the first section of the output under the heading REDUCED COST?

MODELER: It is really meaningful only for a decision variable whose optimal value is zero. It tells how much the per unit cost of that variable can be reduced before the optimal value of the variable will become positive.

MANAGER: We just answered that question about T4.

MODELER: I know.

MANAGER: But we didn't use this column. We used the sensitivity analysis part of the output. In fact, I see that exactly the same value, 91.11, appears in both places.

MODELER: Right.

MANAGER: So why bother with this reduced-cost column if the same value appears under the sensitivity analysis column?

MODELER: Simply for convenience. The reduced cost pertains to variables whose optimal value is zero. You can easily spot these variables in the top section of the output. In the next column you can immediately read the reduced cost, which is a little easier than going down into the sensitivity section. That's all there is to it.

MANAGER: Thank you. It's been very instructive!

MODELER: My pleasure.

5.5 A Synopsis of the Solution Output

When a linear program is solved, the computer output contains the following information:

Optimal values

1. Optimal values are given for the decision variables, the slack and surplus variables, and the objective function. From the optimal value of the slack and surplus variables you can quickly deduce the value of the constraint functions (the amount of resources used, the levels of requirements satisfied, and so on) at an optimal solution. The constraints with zero slack or surplus are called *active, effective, or binding.* Those with positive slack or surplus are called *inactive,* or *nonbinding.*

Dual price and RHS ranges

2. The dual price tells you the rate of improvement in the OV (optimal value of the objective function) as the right-hand side of a constraint increases. "Improvement" means increase in a Max model and decrease in a Min model. RIGHTHAND SIDE RANGES gives you an allowable range in right-hand-side (RHS) changes over which the dual price is valid.

Objective coefficient ranges

3. OBJ COEFFICIENT RANGES tell you the allowable changes that can be made in the objective function coefficients without changing the optimal solution (the optimal values of the variables). Under normal conditions (termed *nondegenerate*), if an objective function coefficient is changed by an amount that *equals* an allowable change, there will be an alternative optimal solution with new values for the variables. If the coefficient is changed by an amount that *exceeds* the allowable change, there will be a new (assuming nondegeneracy) optimal solution.

Reduced cost

4. "Reduced cost output" applies to decision variables whose optimal value is zero. It provides the same information as the OBJ COEFFICIENT RANGES for these variables.

In concluding, it should be noted that the format used for the solution of LP problems differs in minor details from one software package to another. However, a solid understanding of one system prepares you to deal with any system with a minimum of effort.

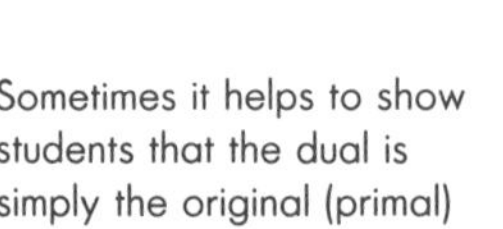

5.6 The Dual Problem

Sometimes it helps to show students that the dual is simply the original (primal) problem "turned on its side." Rows become columns and columns become rows.

Given any set of data for an LP model, we can use the same data to form a *different* LP model. The resulting problem is called the **dual** of the original, or **primal,** problem and the decision variables in this problem are called **dual variables.** The dual has theoretical, economic, and computational importance, which we shall discuss. First, let us see exactly how the dual problem is formed.

Transformation Rules

In order to discuss duality theory in a satisfactory way we must drop the restriction that all variables in an LP model are nonnegative. For example, let us consider the following problem:

Problem (E1)

Given a model with actual names for the constraints, it becomes very instructive to use the constraint names as the names of the dual variables. Thus, it is easier to show that the dual variables are the marginal values of each constraint (resource).

$$\begin{array}{rlr} \text{Max } 3x_1 + 4x_2 - 2x_3 & & \textit{dual variables} \\ \text{s.t. } 4x_1 - 12x_2 + 3x_3 \le 12 & & y_1 \\ -2x_1 + 3x_2 + x_3 \le 6 & & y_2 \\ -5x_1 + x_2 - 6x_3 \ge -40 & & y_3 \\ 3x_1 + 4x_2 - 2x_3 = 10 & & y_4 \\ x_1 \ge 0, \quad x_2 \le 0, \quad x_3 \text{ unconstrained in sign} & & \end{array} \qquad \textbf{(E1)}$$

In this problem we see the appearance of each type of constraint ($\le$, $\ge$, and $=$). Moreover, we have dropped the requirement that all variables must be nonnegative. In this example we have required that only the variable x_1 be nonnegative. The variable x_2 is required to be nonpositive, and x_3 is unconstrained in sign. (That is, the optimal value of x_3 can be positive, negative, or zero.) The dual of this problem (E1) is created by applying the following rules:

- ▶ ***Rule 1:*** The number of variables in the dual problem is equal to the number of constraints in the original problem. The number of constraints in the dual problem is equal to the number of variables in the original problem.

Since (E1) has four constraints and three variables, the dual to (E1) will have three constraints and four variables. We shall see that each of the four variables in the dual to (E1) will correspond to one of the constraints in (E1). For this reason we show the column of dual variables y_1, y_2, y_3, y_4 to the right of (E1).

- ▶ ***Rule 2:*** Coefficients of the objective function in the dual problem come from the right-hand side of the original problem.

Thus, according to rule 2, the objective function for the dual problem is

$$12y_1 + 6y_2 - 40y_3 + 10y_4$$

- ▶ ***Rule 3:*** If the original problem is a Max model, the dual is a Min model. If the original problem is a Min model, the dual is a Max model.

Thus, since (E1) is a Max model the complete objective function for the dual problem is

$$\text{Min } 12y_1 + 6y_2 - 40y_3 + 10y_4$$

- ▶ ***Rule 4:*** The coefficients for the first constraint function for the dual problem are the coefficients of the first variable in the constraints for the original problem, and similarly for the other constraints.

Thus, the first constraint function for the dual is

$$4y_1 - 2y_2 - 5y_3 + 3y_4$$

The second constraint function is

$$-12y_1 + 3y_2 + y_3 + 4y_4$$

Note that these constraints are obtained by reading "down" the rows of (E1). Using the same pattern, try to write out the third constraint function. (By rule 1, there are only three constraints in the dual.) You should get

$$3y_1 + y_2 - 6y_3 - 2y_4$$

► ***Rule 5:*** The right-hand sides of the dual constraints come from the objective function coefficients in the original problem.

Thus, by applying rules 4 and 5 we have obtained the following constraint functions and respective right-hand sides for the dual

constraint function	*RHS*
$4y_1 - 2y_2 - 5y_3 + 3y_4$	3
$-12y_1 + 3y_2 + y_3 + 4y_4$	4
$3y_1 + y_2 - 6y_3 - 2y_4$	-2

► ***Rule 6:*** The sense of the *i*th dual constraint is = if and only if the *i*th variable in the original problem is unconstrained in sign.

Thus, since the third variable in the original problem (E1) is unconstrained in sign, the third dual constraint is an equality:

$$3y_1 + y_2 - 6y_3 - 2y_4 = -2$$

► ***Rule 7:*** If the original problem is a Max (Min) model, then after applying rule 6, assign to the remaining dual constraints a sense the same as (opposite to) the corresponding variable in the original problem.

To apply rule 7, note that the first variable in the original (Max) model is ≥ 0 and the second is ≤ 0. This means that the first dual constraint is $\geq$ and the second dual constraint is $\leq$:

$$4y_1 - 2y_2 - 5y_3 + 3y_4 \geq 3$$
$$-12y_1 + 3y_2 + y_3 + 4y_4 \leq 4$$

Also, rule 7 means that if (E1) had been written as a Min model the inequalities above would be written as ≤ 3 and ≥ 4, respectively.

► ***Rule 8:*** The *i*th variable in the dual problem is unconstrained in sign if and only if the *i*th constraint in the original problem is an equality.

Since the fourth constraint in the original problem is =, rule 8 dictates that the fourth dual variable, y_4, must be unconstrained in sign.

► ***Rule 9:*** If the original problem is a Max (Min) model, then after applying rule

8, assign to the remaining dual variables a sense opposite to (the same as) the corresponding constraint in the original problem.

Since the first and second constraints in the original Max problem are $\leq$, rule 9 dictates that $y_1 \geq 0$, $y_2 \geq 0$. Since the third constraint in the original problem is $\geq$, we must have $y_3 \leq 0$.

Dual of problem (E1)

Application to (E1) of the nine rules above has created the following dual problem:

$$\begin{aligned} \text{Min } & 12y_1 + 6y_2 - 40y_3 + 10y_4 \\ \text{s.t. } & 4y_1 - 2y_2 - 5y_3 + 3y_4 \geq 3 \\ & -12y_1 + 3y_2 + y_3 + 4y_4 \leq 4 \\ & 3y_1 + y_2 - 6y_3 - 2y_4 = -2 \\ & y_1 \geq 0, \quad y_2 \geq 0, \quad y_3 \leq 0, \quad y_4 \text{ unconstrained in sign} \end{aligned} \tag{E2}$$

You could now imagine that (E2) is the original problem. Let x_1, x_2, and x_3 be the variables in the problem that is dual to (E2), and you can verify that an application of the foregoing rules to (E2) will return us to (E1). This means that *taking the dual of the dual gives back the original problem.* We have called (E2) the dual of (E1), but it would be equally correct to call (E1) the dual of (E2). It just depends on which problem is considered the original one.

The rules above may at first seem like a lot to remember. However, compare rules 6 and 8 and note that they are symmetric, merely stipulating that in either problem a variable that is unconstrained in sign corresponds to an equality constraint in the other problem. Similarly, rules 7 and 9 are nearly symmetric. In schematic representation they say:

Max model	*Min model*
$x_i \geq 0$	$\Leftrightarrow$ ith constraint is $\geq$
$x_i \leq 0$	$\Leftrightarrow$ ith constraint is $\leq$
ith constraint is $\leq$ $\Leftrightarrow$	$y_i \geq 0$
ith constraint is $\geq$ $\Leftrightarrow$	$y_i \leq 0$

Here, now, are several examples of these rules.

Examples of Dual Problems

It is very instructive to show computer outputs for both the primal and dual problems. This can really help students understand the relationship between the two problems, especially if both of them can be put on an overhead transparency and shown to the class.

Example 1.

	dual variables
Max $3x_1 + 4x_2$	
s.t. $-2x_1 + 3x_2 \leq 6$	y_1
$5x_1 - x_2 \leq 40$	y_2
$x_1 + x_2 \leq 7$	y_3
$x_1 \geq 0, \quad x_2 \geq 0$	

The dual is

$$\begin{aligned} \text{Min } & 6y_1 + 40y_2 + 7y_3 \\ \text{s.t. } & -2y_1 + 5y_2 + y_3 \geq 3 \\ & 3y_1 - y_2 + y_3 \geq 4 \\ & y_1 \geq 0, \quad y_2 \geq 0, \quad y_3 \geq 0 \end{aligned}$$

Notice how the dual constraint functions are formed by reading "down" the data in the original constraints. Incidentally, when, as in this example, the Max model has all constraints $\leq$ with all variables nonnegative (and hence the Min model has all constraints $\geq$ with all variables nonnegative) the pair of problems carries the label *symmetric dual problems.*

Example 2.

$$\begin{aligned} \text{Max } & 19x_1 - 22x_2 & \textit{dual variables} \\ \text{s.t. } & 4x_1 + 5x_2 = 12 & y_1 \\ & x_1 \geq 0, \quad x_2 \geq 0 & \end{aligned}$$

The dual is

$$\begin{aligned} \text{Min } & 12y_1 \\ \text{s.t. } & 4y_1 \geq 19 \\ & 5y_1 \geq -22 \\ & y_1 \text{ unconstrained in sign} \end{aligned}$$

Example 3.

$$\begin{aligned} \text{Min } & x_1 + 12x_2 - 2x_3 & \textit{dual variables} \\ \text{s.t. } & 4x_1 + 2x_2 + 12x_3 \leq 10 & y_1 \\ & 2x_1 - x_2 + 11x_3 \geq -2 & y_2 \\ & x_1 \leq 0, \quad x_2 \text{ unconstrained in sign}, \quad x_3 \geq 0 & \end{aligned}$$

The dual is

$$\begin{aligned} \text{Max } & 10y_1 - 2y_2 \\ \text{s.t. } & 4y_1 + 2y_2 \geq 1 \\ & 2y_1 - y_2 = 12 \\ & 12y_1 + 11y_2 \leq -2 \\ & y_1 \leq 0, \quad y_2 \geq 0 \end{aligned}$$

Relations between Primal and Dual

In referring to a pair of dual problems it is often said that one of them (usually the original model) is the *primal* problem and the other is the *dual* problem. From a historical point of view, the term *primal* was invented by the mathematician Tobias Dantzig to denote the problem whose dual is a particular problem. The point to stress, however, is that duality is what is called a *symmetric* and *reflexive* relationship. This means that either problem may be considered to be the dual of the other.

Using the analogy from Star Trek about "another universe," one in which everything is the opposite of this universe, might help here. In this Star Trek episode a Dual Starship Enterprise faced a "bad" Captain Kirk, Spock, etc. The "good" Kirk was trying to minimize evil in the dual universe while trying to maximize good in the original universe.

Whichever of the problems is designated as the primal, the dual of the dual problem is again the primal problem.

For convenience, in this section let us adopt the convention that the Max model with, in general, m constraints and n variables, is the *primal,* and the Min model, with n constraints and m variables, is the *dual.*

The theoretic relationships between the primal and the dual are very simply stated, yet these relations have considerable importance in the theory of linear problems.

Let us say that a set of decision variable values is *feasible* for a given model if the set of values satisfies the constraints and sign requirements that are specified by the model. Moreover, we shall say that a specific set of decision variable values $(x_1, \ldots, x_n)$ is *primal feasible* if these values are feasible in the Max model, and similarly that a specific set of values $(y_1, \ldots, y_m)$ is *dual feasible* if these values are feasible in the Min model. The following result is important:

If $(x_1, \ldots, x_n)$ is any set of primal feasible values and $(y_1, \ldots, y_m)$ is any set of dual feasible values, the primal objective function (i.e., the function to be maximized) for the x values cannot exceed the dual objective function (i.e., the function to be minimized) for the y values.

Objective Function Values

Another good pictorial example is that of a horse saddle. The "saddle point" in the middle of the saddle can be either a local minimum, coming down from the horn of the saddle, or a local maximum, coming up from the side of the saddle. Optimum is the point at which the rider meets the horse. Any farther up and it's only the rider; farther down and it's only the horse.

As an example of this fact, let us refer to Example 1. The max model is the primal and the Min model is the dual. Verify that the values (3,2) are primal feasible (i.e., $x_1 = 3$, $x_2 = 2$) since they satisfy all the primal constraints and nonnegativity conditions. The associated primal objective value is

$$3x_1 + 4x_2 = 3(3) + 4(2) = 17$$

The values (0, 1, 6) are dual feasible (i.e., $y_1 = 0, y_2 = 1, y_3 = 6$) since they satisfy all the constraints and nonnegativity conditions of the dual problem. The associated objective value is

$$6y_1 + 40y_2 + 7y_3 = 6(0) + 40(1) + 7(6) = 82$$

and since $82 > 17$, the dual objective value exceeds the primal value. You may wish to select other sets of primal feasible values and other dual feasible values. No matter what values are selected, as long as they are primal and dual feasible, the primal objective value will not exceed the dual value.

Now suppose that primal and dual feasible values are found that produce equal objective function values. If there were a different primal feasible value that produced a larger value for the primal objective function, it would also be larger than the dual objective value and this would contradict the foregoing result. Hence, there can be no primal feasible values for the decision variables that produce a larger value of the primal objective function. This means that the originally found primal feasible values are optimal. Similar reasoning applies to the dual. In other words, if primal and dual feasible values are found that produce equal objective function values, those decision variable values are optimal in their respective problems. In fact, an even stronger result links the primal and dual problems:

- ▶ **Either of the two problems has a solution if and only if the other does.**
- ▶ **When there is a solution, the optimal value of the objective function in the primal is the same as the optimal value of the objective function in the dual.**

This elegant result says that solving either problem yields the same optimal objective value. It does *not* say that the *optimal solution* to each problem (i.e., the optimal values of the decision variables) is the same. Such a result would not be reasonable since the two problems are in spaces of different dimension. That is, there are n of the x variables (the primal variables) and m of the y variables (the dual variables). As an illustration of this, refer to Example 1. There the primal variables are in two-dimensional space and the dual variables in three-dimensional space.

To explain the relations between the primal and dual problems more fully, it is necessary to recall from Section 3.8 the technical terms *infeasible* (or *inconsistent*) and *unbounded.* An LP problem is said to be *infeasible,* or *inconsistent,* if the constraints (including the nonnegativity conditions) cannot all be simultaneously satisfied. This means that the set of points described by the constraints is an empty set. An LP problem is said to be *unbounded* if the objective contour can be slid arbitrarily far in the desired direction without leaving the constraint set behind. This means that in a Max problem there are allowable decision variable values that make the value of the objective function arbitrarily large. The reverse interpretation holds for a Min problem.

It turns out that any linear program falls into one of the following three categories:

1. The problem has an optimal solution. (This implies a finite optimal objective value.)
2. The problem is unbounded. (This implies consistent constraints but, if you like, an infinite—or negatively infinite, for a Min model—optimal objective value.)
3. The problem is infeasible. (This implies that there is no allowable choice for the decision variables.)

The most dreaded message from LP computer output is **"Infeasible solution."** One should *first* check the input data for errors; if that is not the problem, *then* begin to "loosen" constraints to get some solution and analyze from there.

Note that the third category describes two possibilities: the primal is unbounded and the dual inconsistent, or vice versa. Although perfectly respectable as mathematical possibilities, the second and third phenomena are, in terms of applied problems, abnormal. Infinite profits do not exist, and a real-world problem, correctly formulated, cannot lead to an inconsistent model.

Dual Theorem of LP

Using the foregoing terminology, we can now more completely characterize the relations between any pair of dual linear programs. These relations are known as the **dual theorem of linear programming.** This is the most important theoretic result in the study of LP problems. The dual theorem says that of the nine possible states for a pair of dual problems (e.g., one optimal, the other optimal; one optimal, the other unbounded; one optimal, the other infeasible; and so on), only four possibilities can actually occur.

1. In any pair of dual linear programs, both may have optimal solutions, in which case the optimal objective values will be the same.
2. In any pair of dual linear programs, both may be inconsistent.
3. In any pair of dual linear programs, one may be unbounded and the other inconsistent.

The dual theorem states that these combinations are mutually exclusive and exhaustive. For example, the possibility that both the primal and the dual are unbounded is ruled out. The possibility is also ruled out that one problem can be unbounded while the other has an optimal solution. Thus, the dual theorem implies that if it is known that either problem is unbounded, the other *must* be inconsistent.

There is a final theoretic relationship between the primal and dual problems of considerable importance in applications. This is called the **principle of complementary slackness:**

Consider an inequality constraint in any LP problem. If that constraint is inactive for any optimal solution to the problem, the corresponding dual variable will be zero in any optimal solution to the dual of that problem.

We have now presented essentially all the important theoretic relationships between pairs of dual linear programs. This theory is of considerable mathematical interest in its own right. In addition, the theory of duality has economic and computational significance. This will become apparent in the following sections.

Dual Prices and Dual Variables

From the point of view of applied analysis, the most important aspect of the dual problem is probably the associated economic interpretation. The fact is firmly established by the following relationships:

In a Max problem:

$$\textbf{dual price on printout} = \textbf{dual variable}$$

In a Min problem:

$$\textbf{dual price on printout} = -\textbf{dual variable}$$

Thus, all of the economic analysis in this chapter concerning changes in the RHS could have been presented in terms of *dual variables* rather than the *dual prices* in the printout. Indeed, the theory on which this analysis is based was originally developed in the context of the dual problem.

Rather than dwelling on how the change in the sign convention requires a somewhat different interpretation, we shall simply state that

1. The optimal value of the *i*th dual variable is the rate at which the primal optimal objective value will increase as b_i increases, assuming that all other data are unchanged; that is,
2. If an increase in the RHS increases (decreases) the optimal value, the dual variable is positive (negative), regardless of whether the primal is a Max or a Min problem.

Note that in discussing dual prices we used the term *rate of improvement.* In talking about dual variables we use the term *rate of increase.* The two rates have the same sign for a Max model, opposite signs for a Min model.

Evaluating a Resource. To illustrate the interpretation of the dual variables, let us imagine ourselves in a profit-maximization production context with constraints on the input resources. Suppose that aluminum is one of our resources and that the first constraint of our model is of ≤ form and represents a limitation on the availability of aluminum. Imagine that 8000 pounds of aluminum are currently in our stockpile, so we solve the model using the value 8000 for the first RHS, b_1. Let us suppose that in reading the computer output we find that the dual price for the first constraint is \$16.50, which is the optimal value of y_1 in the dual problem. This means that the *marginal* contribution of aluminum (the value of the last, or the next, unit consumed) to the total profit is \$16.50. Suppose the sensitivity information shows that this value of \$16.50 holds for b_1 values between 7500 and 9000, and suppose the market price of aluminum is \$20.00 per pound. Using the lower limit of 7500, and the fact that we have 8000 pounds in the stockpile, we can infer that each pound of our last 500 pounds of aluminum yields us less than the market value (the OV increases only \$16.50 per unit, the market value is \$20.00 per unit). In theory, then, we might sell 500 pounds on the market for a return of (20)(500) = \$10,000, whereas the cost, in terms of the output profit, would be (16.50)(500) = \$8250. The transaction would net us an additional \$1750 above current profits.[6]

On the other hand, suppose that the market value of aluminum is only \$14.00 per pound. In this case, the dual price of \$16.50 indicates that we may want to consider purchasing an additional 1000 pounds of aluminum, for this would net us 16.50 − 14.00 = \$2.50 per pound, or \$2500 above and beyond the current profit.

The discussion above assumes the existence of a market for resources and illustrates how the dual variables enable the planner to compare the market values with the value obtained from the consumption of those resources in this own operations. Although this discussion illustrates one possible economic interpretation of dual variables, one caveat should be issued. When a model includes constraints on resources, it generally implies that these resources are genuinely scarce over the planning period under consideration. This could occur, for example, because of bottlenecks, lead times to delivery, and so on. In such a situation, there is, in essence, no market for the scarce resource.

Economic Significance of the Dual Problem

Let us now focus on the interpretation of the dual problem as a whole. Often, for example, the primal problem has the interpretation of finding profit-maximizing levels of production subject to constraints on scarce resources. How might we interpret the dual to this problem? Since the dual will be a Min model, we could say that it is a cost-minimization model. But it minimizes the cost of doing what? The following scenario will provide an answer to this question:

Suppose that a firm owns two factories in two different marketing districts. For simplicity, assume that the two factories use the same three scarce raw materials. Factory 1 makes two products, lawn mowers and sprinklers, in quantities x_1 and x_2. Factory 2 makes three different products, doorknobs, refrigerator handles, and cowbells, in quantities z_1, z_2, and z_3. Let us imagine that the factory 1 data are as given in Figure 5.15.

▼ FIGURE 5.15
Factory 1 Data

RAW MATERIAL	INPUT PER LAWN MOWER	INPUT PER SPRINKLER	TOTAL AVAILABILITY
1	6	4	38
2	1	3	34
3	10	7	44
Per Unit Profitability (\$)	4	3	

[6]In a realistic situation the manager may not wish to exercise this option because he "may not be in the business of selling aluminum."

Then we obtain

Factory 1 Production Model.

$$
\begin{aligned}
\text{Max } & 4x_1 + 3x_2 \\
\text{s.t. } & 6x_1 + 4x_2 \le 38 \\
& x_1 + 3x_2 \le 34 \\
& 10x_1 + 7x_2 \le 44 \\
& x_1 \ge 0, \quad x_2 \ge 0
\end{aligned}
\tag{F1}
$$

The data for factory 2 appear in Figure 5.16.

RAW MATERIAL	INPUT PER DOORKNOB	INPUT PER REFRIGERATOR HANDLE	INPUT PER COWBELL	TOTAL AVAILABILITY
1	4	2	7	54
2	3	9	8	126
3	6	5	2	33
Per Unit Profitability ($)	6	2	1	

▲ FIGURE 5.16
Factory 2 Data

From that figure we obtain

Factory 2 Production Model.

$$
\begin{aligned}
\text{Max } & 6z_1 + 2z_2 + z_3 \\
\text{s.t. } & 4z_1 + 2z_2 + 7z_3 \le 54 \\
& 3z_1 + 9z_2 + 8z_3 \le 126 \\
& 6z_1 + 5z_2 + 2z_3 \le 33 \\
& z_1 \ge 0, \quad z_2 \ge 0, \quad z_3 \ge 0
\end{aligned}
\tag{F2}
$$

What Is a Fair Price? Now recall our assumption that the same firm owns both of these factories and that the factories are located in different marketing districts. We also assume that the three raw materials are scarce in the sense of long lead times to delivery. Now we suppose that management obtains information indicating that for various economic reasons the prices (i.e., the profitabilities) in the factory 2 marketing district are going to increase drastically. It is not known exactly how much the prices will increase, but management is confident that the increase will be so large that it will be desirable for factory 2 to take over all production. Thus, all of the factory 1 stockpile of raw materials should be transferred to factory 2. However, management decides that factory 2 should pay factory 1 a "fair price" for the transfer of these raw materials. What is such a fair price? It seems intuitively clear that, at least from factory 1's point of view, a fair price would be one that is equal to the maximum possible profit factory 1 would make if it retained use of its resources that may now be shifted to factory 2. This is the factory 1 OV, and it would be a fair overall "lump-sum payment" for the three raw materials. The firm, however, needs to know more than the lump-sum payment. It must have per unit prices for each material. These prices are required for financial reporting (i.e., tax) purposes. All accounting for individual products is carried out on a per item basis. The firm thus must find fair unit prices that can stand the scrutiny of a careful review. In order to obtain fair per unit prices, we make the following observations. If factory 2 pays per unit prices of y_1, y_2, and y_3, for the three raw materials, then since factory 1 possesses 38, 34, and 44 units, respectively, of each raw material

$$\text{amount factory 2 pays} = 38y_1 + 34y_2 + 44y_3$$

Factory 2 wants to look as profitable as possible; thus, its goal is to

$$\text{Min } 38y_1 + 34y_2 + 44y_3$$

Factory 1, however, wants to make sure that it makes as much profit as it would if it remained in business for itself. From Figure 5.15 we see that if factory 1 had 6 units of raw material 1, 1 unit of raw material 2, and 10 units of raw material 3, it could produce one lawn mower for a profit of \$4. Recall that y_i is the sales price of raw material i. Thus, factory 1 will insist that

$$6y_1 + y_2 + 10y_3 \geq 4$$

If this condition does not hold, factory 1 will choose not to sell its raw materials to factory 2. Making use of the raw materials to produce lawn mowers will be more profitable.

Similarly, factory 1 will insist that

$$4y_1 + 3y_2 + 7y_3 \geq 3$$

Otherwise, it is more profitable to make sprinklers than to sell the raw materials to factory 2.

The factory 1 liquidation model

In summary, then, the problem of determining fair prices is

$$\begin{aligned} \text{Min } & 38y_1 + 34y_2 + 44y_3 \\ \text{s.t. } & 6y_1 + y_2 + 10y_3 \geq 4 \\ & 4y_1 + 3y_2 + 7y_3 \geq 3 \\ & y_1, y_2, y_3 \geq 0 \end{aligned}$$

and this problem is the dual of (F1). Thus we have shown that the dual to the production problem has the following interpretation:

It provides "fair prices" in the sense of prices that yield the minimum acceptable liquidation payment.

Computational Significance of the Dual

When the simplex algorithm is used to solve an LP problem, optimal solutions to both the original problem (which may be either a Max or Min model) and its dual are obtained. We have already seen this fact on the printout (subject to a possible sign change), and it will be demonstrated mathematically in Chapter 6.[7] Thus, if you want to solve a particular problem, you can, of course, go about it by solving the problem directly. Alternatively, you can take the dual of the original problem and then solve the dual problem on the computer. This method will also provide a solution to the dual of the dual, which is the original problem. Since both of these possible routes lead to the same result, it is of interest, from the computational point of view, to inquire which procedure is more efficient.

To shed light on this question, we take note of the empirical fact that the amount of time required to solve a linear program depends more critically on the number of constraints than on the number of variables. If the original problem has m constraints and n variables, the dual problem has n constraints and m variables. It is then apparent that, *all other things being equal,* you should choose to solve the problem with fewer constraints.

Although the foregoing rule of thumb is a reasonably good general prescription, when you get into fairly large and structured models it may well break down, for in such cases, all other things may not be equal. Possible reasons for departure from this rule of thumb tend to become quite technical in nature. In some cases, irrespective of the number of constraints, one of the two problems, because of its form, may be solvable with a special code, such as what we call a *network code,* as opposed to a general-purpose LP code. The other problem, however, may not have the required special structure and hence may have to be solved with the general purpose code. Since special structure codes tend to be computationally more efficient than general-purpose codes, this is an important consideration.

Other technical considerations have to do with the fact that even with a general LP code it may be easier to "get started" with one problem than with the other. We will explain this startup procedure, sometimes called *phase I of the simplex method,* briefly in Chapter 6.

The choice between solving the original problem or its dual does not have much computational significance for small problems, say when either model has no more than several hundred constraints, since such problems can be handled with great speed on modern computing equipment. As the problems grow larger, into the ballpark of several thousand constraints, the choice between the original problem and its dual can become very important. On such occasions, technical consultation with a professional linear programmer may well be worthwhile.

5.7 Notes on Implementation

Batch processing mode versus conversational mode

In practice, linear programming has been and continues to be a very important tool. There are essentially two different ways that users work with the computer in solving LP problems: (1) the batch processing mode and (2) the conversational mode (often called the interactive mode). In batch processing the user submits previously prepared data, such as a deck of data cards or a magnetic tape of data, to a central computer center and then waits, perhaps for several hours or several days, to receive the output from the run. In the conversational mode, the user sits at a console, types in data, then runs the model and, typically, within seconds the output is printed on the console. The user may then modify the problem and rerun it. The advantages of the conversational mode are quick access to results and the ability to manipulate the model (change data, change constraints, and so on), rerun it, access

[7] It can also be shown that the same sensitivity information is produced on the output, whether one solves the primal or the dual.

the output, and then, if desired, change and rerun again. The disadvantage is the work required to type in the data at the console. For such a reason, the conversational mode is not typically used for solving large-scale problems. For such problems the batch processing mode is considered more suitable. The relative disadvantage of the latter mode is longer turnaround time and the inability to manipulate the model "on line." That is, the benefits of direct interaction with the computer are lost.

Although LP is certainly the most widely used tool of management science, and although it has been applied to a very broad spectrum of problems, most of the real-world applications are probably clustered in the areas of distribution, transportation, and logistics planning. It has historically been true, and probably still is, that the biggest commercial users of LP are oil firms. In the petroleum industry LP is used in refinery processing and distribution planning.

Most of the latest-generation computers have their own LP batch software, and the associated output will usually be more complicated than that associated with the (conversational mode) printouts seen in this chapter. Given your familiarity with the material in this chapter, not more than an hour or two of additional study would be required to digest the formats of other LP systems such as MPSX (associated with IBM) or FMPS (associated with Univac).

Topics of importance in commercial applications of LP are matrix generation and report writing, both of which are too specialized to present in any detail in this text. Matrix generation involves writing subroutines that transform raw data into a format that is acceptable to a particular software system such as MPSX. Report generation is a way to specify formats for output in ways that will be of specific interest to the user.

Where is LP used in the firm? It used to be the case that the management science group or the operations research department would be the only place in which terms such as *linear programming* or *optimization* would even be understood. All of that has changed. Recent surveys have shown that management science capabilities tend to be much more spread out within the firm. Today you might well find LP studies in the corporate planning department, in marketing, in operations, or in distribution.

One firm that produces feed mix spent only three weeks finalizing its standard-mix LP model (daily running from 30 to 50 models), but took nine months to develop the real-time data base for the costs of all the ingredients.

As a final point, one great difference between textbook problems and real-world applications must be emphasized. In the textbook the data you need in order to solve a problem are always available. In real-world implementation, problems such as the reliability of one's data, even the existence of the needed data, are often a nightmare. Collecting needed data and forming and maintaining data banks can well determine the success or failure of an intended LP analysis.

5.8 Summary

The emphasis in this chapter was on the interpretation of the computer output for an LP, as presented in Sections 5.3, 5.4, and 5.5. We stressed the wealth of information available through sensitivity analysis on the right-hand sides and on the objective function coefficients. The role of degeneracy and signals for alternative optima were also discussed.

In the first part of this chapter (Section 5.2) we explored the role of slack and surplus variables and studied the construction and the geometry of the standard equality constraint form of an LP. Since the simplex algorithm and thus computers solve this form of an LP problem, this material provides a necessary introduction to the material that follows.

In concluding this chapter (Section 5.6) the role of the dual problem was presented in terms of its economic and computational importance.

Key Terms

Standard Equality Constraint Form. The form of the LP model that is solved by the computer. (*p. 146*)

Slack or Surplus Variable. Used to convert an inequality constraint to an equality constraint. (*p. 146*)

Degenerate Solution. A solution for which the number of variables in the standard equality form (counting decision variables, surpluses, and slacks) with positive optimal value is less than the number of constraints. (*p. 153*)

Nondegenerate Solution. A solution for which the number of variables in the standard quality form (counting decision variables, surpluses, and slacks) with positive optimal value is equal to the number of constraints. (*p. 153*)

Dual Price. The *i*th dual price on the computer printout is the rate of improvement in OV as the *i*th RHS is increased. (*p. 159*)

Allowable RHS Range. Range of RHS values for which the dual price (or dual variable) remains constant. (*p. 161*)

Alternative Optimal Solutions. The existence of more than one optimal solution. (*p. 163*)

Objective Coefficient Ranges. Gives ranges of objective function coefficients over which no change in the optimal solution will occur. (*p. 163*)

Dual Problem. A new LP, derived from the original problem according to a set of transformation rules. (*p. 177*)

Primal Problem. The original LP. (*p. 177*)

Dual Variables. The variables in the dual problem. The optimal value of the *i*th dual variable is the rate of increase in the OV as the *i*th RHS is increased in the original problem. (*p. 177*)

Dual Theorem of Linear Programming. States a theoretic relationship between the primal and dual problems. (*p. 182*)

Principle of Complementary Slackness. If an inequality constraint in an LP problem is inactive for any solution the corresponding dual variable will be zero in any optimal solution to the dual of that problem. (*p. 183*)

Major Concepts Quiz

True-False

1. T F Any inequality constraint can be converted to an equivalent equality constraint by properly introducing slack or surplus variables that are unconstrained in sign.

2. T F Suppose that a $\leq$ constraint is converted to an equality. If a point does not satisfy the $\leq$ constraint, the associated slack value is negative.

3. T F In the standard equality form, inactive constraints, at optimality, have an optimal value of zero for the associated slack or surplus variables.

4. T F Degeneracy is important because we must give more restrictive interpretations to the computer output when the optimal solution is degenerate.

5. T F Dual price, for a given constraint, is the rate of change in OV as the RHS increases.

6. T F The dual price on the *i*th constraint is a nonconstant linear function of b_i over the range given by allowable decrease and allowable increase.

7. T F Assuming an optimal solution exists, the simplex method for a Max model produces optimal values for the variables in both the primal and the dual problem.

8. T F In most cases it is more efficient to solve the primal as opposed to the dual.

9. T F The optimal value of the *i*th dual variable is the rate of increase of OV as the RHS b_i increases.

10. T F Positive slack variables at optimality indicate redundant constraints.

11. T F A $\leq$ constraint with positive optimal slack will always have an infinite allowable increase for the RHS.

The following questions refer to the computer output shown in Figure 5.14:

12. T F If the requirements on A and C are each increased by 0.5 pound, sensitivity analysis tells us that the optimal cost will increase by \$24.44.

13. T F The fact that the dual prices are all ≤ 0 is exclusively explained by the fact that we are dealing with a Min model.

Multiple Choice

14. Conversion to the standard equality constraint form
- **a.** is entirely automatic and hence can be done by the computer
- **b.** must be performed before the problem can be solved because this is the form of the problem solved by the simplex algorithm
- **c.** leads to an important observation about the number of positive variables in the computer solution
- **d.** all of the above

15. A degenerate optimal solution
- **a.** has fewer than m positive variables (where m is the number of constraints)
- **b.** provides no information on alternative optima
- **c.** may not provide information on the full range of allowable increase and allowable decrease in objective coefficients
- **d.** all of the above

16. "Improvement" means
- **a.** the OV is increased for a Max model
- **b.** the OV is decreased for a Min model
- **c.** both a and b

17. For a nondegenerate optimal solution to a Max model, if the objective function coefficient c_1 increases by (exactly) the allowable increase
- **a.** the OV may change
- **b.** the previous optimal solution remains optimal.
- **c.** there will be a new optimal solution with a larger optimal value of x_1
- **d.** all of the above

18. We have just solved a cost Min model and $x_1^* = 0$. Management wants to know: "How much does the cost of x_1 have to be reduced before we will begin to use it at a positive level in an optimal solution?" The answer appears in which portion of the printout?
- **a.** values of variables
- **b.** allowable changes in RHS of first constraint
- **c.** allowable increase in the coefficient of x_1
- **d.** reduced cost

19. The primal is a Max model in m equality constraints and n nonnegative variables. The dual
- **a.** has n constraints and m nonnegative variables
- **b.** is a Min model
- **c.** both a and b

20. Consider any primal problem (P) and its dual (D).
- **a.** The OVs in (P) and (D) will be the same.
- **b.** (P) will have an optimal solution if and only if (D) does also.
- **c.** Both (P) and (D) cannot be infeasible.
- **d.** All of the above.

21. Let x be a nonoptimal feasible point in a maximization primal model. Let y be a dual feasible point. Then
- **a.** the primal objective value, at x, is greater than the dual objective value at y
- **b.** the primal objective value, at x, is less than the OV for the dual
- **c.** the primal objective value, at x, could be greater than the dual objective value at y

22. Consider the standard equality constraint form. Suppose that the first constraint, evaluated at a given point P_0, has a zero value for the slack variable. Then

a. P_0 lies on the boundary of the feasible region
b. P_0 lies on the first constraint line
c. both a and b

23. A correct relationship is
a. a constraint with zero dual price must be inactive
b. a constraint with positive dual price must be active
c. both a and b

The following questions refer to the computer output shown in Figure 5.14:

24. If the requirement on A is changed from 5 to 6.5
a. the OV will decrease by $66.66
b. the OV will improve by $66.66
c. the OV will increase by $66.66
d. the OV will not change

25. If the requirement on C is reduced from 30 to 20
a. the OV will decrease by $44.44
b. the OV will increase by $44.44
c. the OV will improve by at least $31.00

26. If the cost of ore from location 2 is decreased to $300 per ton
a. the OV will not change
b. the optimal solution will not change
c. neither a nor b
d. both a and b

27. If the cost of ore from location 1 is reduced to $680 per ton
a. there will be a new optimal solution with T1* > 0.25926
b. there will be alternative optima
c. the optimal solution above remains optimal
d. all of the above

Answers

1. F	**8.** F	**15.** d	**22.** b
2. T	**9.** T	**16.** c	**23.** b
3. F	**10.** F	**17.** d	**24.** c
4. T	**11.** T	**18.** d	**25.** c
5. F	**12.** F	**19.** b	**26.** b
6. F	**13.** F	**20.** b	**27.** d
7. T	**14.** d	**21.** b	

Problems

Max $3x_1 - 4x_2$
s.t. $8x_1 + 12x_2 + s_1 = 49$
$14x_1 - 6x_2 + s_2 = 29$
$3x_1 + 14x_2 - s_3 = 12$
$x_1 + x_2 = 2$
$x_1, x_2, s_1, s_2, s_3 \geq 0$

5-1. ▲ Use slack and surplus variables as required to convert the following problem to standard equality constraint form:

$$\begin{aligned} \text{Max } & 3x_1 - 4x_2 \\ \text{s.t. } & 8x_1 + 12x_2 \leq 49 \\ & 14x_1 - 6x_2 \leq 29 \\ & 3x_1 + 14x_2 \geq 12 \\ & x_1 + x_2 = 2 \\ & x_1 \geq 0, \quad x_2 \geq 0 \end{aligned}$$

(a) Max $x_1 + x_2$
s.t. $x_1 + x_2 - s_1 = 3$
$2x_1 + x_2 + s_2 = 12$
$x_1 + 2x_2 + s_3 = 12$
$x_1, x_2, x_3, s_1, s_2, s_3 \geq 0$
(b) See IM; no degenerate corners
(c) Yes: $x_1 = 4$, $x_2 = 4$

5-2. ▲ **(a)** Use slack and surplus variables as required to convert the following problem to standard equality constraint form:

$$
\begin{aligned}
\text{Max } & x_1 + x_2 \\
\text{s.t. } & x_1 + x_2 \geq 3 \\
& 2x_1 + x_2 \leq 12 \\
& x_1 + 2x_2 \leq 12 \\
& x_1 \geq 0, \quad x_2 \geq 0
\end{aligned}
$$

(b) Give a geometric representation of the problem in which each constraint is labeled with its slack or surplus variable. Provide all the corner solutions. Are there any degenerate corners?

(c) Add the constraint $x_1 + x_2 \leq 8$. Now are there any degenerate corners?

5-3. ▲ Consider the constraint

$$3x_1 - x_2 + s = 12$$

where s is a slack variable. What is the slack value associated with the points

(a) $x_1 = 4$, $x_2 = 0$?
(b) $x_1 = 1$, $x_2 = 3$?
(c) $x_1 = 5$, $x_2 = 2$?

(a) 0
(b) 6
(c) −5

5-4. ▲ Consider the constraint

$$3x_1 - 2x_2 - s = 6$$

where s is a surplus variable.

(a) What is the surplus value associated with the points
- **(i)** $x_1 = 0$, $x_2 = 0$?
- **(ii)** $x_1 = 4$, $x_2 = 3$?
- **(iii)** $x_1 = 5$, $x_2 = 4$?

(b) Determine feasibility of the points in part (a).

(a) (i) $s = -6$
(ii) $s = 0$
(iii) $s = 1$
(b) **(i)** infeasible
(ii) & (iii) feasible

QSB+, LINDO, or some other LP software can be used to verify your answers to the problems marked with the computer symbol.

14

5-5. ▲ Consider an LP in 3 variables and 14 constraints. An optimal computer solution will have at most how many positive variables?

(a) 30
(b) Fewer than 30

5-6. ▲ Consider an LP in 80 variables and 30 constraints.

(a) An optimal nondegenerate computer solution will have how many positive variables?

(b) An optimal degenerate computer solution will have how many positive variables?

(a) Increases by 750
(b) Decreases by 3000
(c) Between $-\infty$ and 11.50

5-7. ▲ Refer to the computer printout shown in Figure 5.6.

(a) Suppose that 5 more hours of labor are made available in department A (row 4). What will be the change in the OV?

(b) Suppose that 20 fewer hours of labor are available in department A. What will be the change in the OV?

(c) The dual price on row 2 is valid for what range of values of the RHS?

See IM.

5-8. ▲ The dual price on an inactive constraint always has what value? What can you say about the dual price on an active constraint?

Zero

5-9. ▲ Consider a constraint with a positive optimal slack value. What must the dual price be?

(a) No effect
(b) 6.5
(c) Increases by 50 × 175 = 8750

5-10. ▲ Refer to the computer printout shown in Figure 5.6.

(a) Suppose that the right-hand side of the second constraint is changed to 6. What is the effect on the OV?

(b) By how much can the total unit requirements constraint be tightened before the dual price could possibly change?

(c) Suppose that 50 more hours of labor are available in department B. By how much will the OV change?

Current solution is degenerate

5-11. ▲▲ Note that in Figure 5.11 there is an allowable increase of zero on row 5. What anomaly is responsible for this?

Degenerate (see IM)

5-12. ▲ Refer to Figure 5.11. Is the exhibited solution degenerate or nondegenerate? Support your answer.

(a) Same as before ($E^* = 4.5$, $F^* = 7.0$)
(b) OV decreases by 4500

5-13. ▲ Refer to Figure 5.6. Suppose that the profitability of E is reduced to 4000 per unit.

(a) What is the resulting optimal solution?

(b) What is the *change* in the OV?

(a) $E^* = 4.5$, $F^* = 7.0$ (unchanged)
(b) Increases by 1000 × 7 = 7000

5-14. ▲ Refer to Figure 5.6. Suppose that the profitability of F is increased to 5000 per unit.

(a) What is the resulting optimal solution?

(b) What is the *change* in the OV?

(a) $91.11
(b) Optimal solution unchanged, OV decreases by 20.8
(c) No; cost increases by $25.96

5-15. ▲ Refer to Figure 5.14.

(a) How much would the price per ton of ore from location 4 have to decrease in order for it to become attractive to purchase it?

(b) Suppose that the price of ore from location 1 decreases by $80 per ton. Is there any change in the optimal solution or in the OV?

(c) Suppose that the price of ore from location 1 increases by $100 per ton. Is there any change in the optimal solution? What, if any, is the associated change in the cost of an optimally blended ton?

(a) No change in solution; OV increases by 50 × 0.037 = 1.85.
(b) Solution still optimal, but there are alternative optima.
(c) 511.111 − (118.269 × 0.037) = 506.735

5-16. ▲ Refer to Figure 5.14.

(a) Suppose that the price of ore from location 3 increases by $50 per ton. Is there any change in the optimal solution? What, if any, is the associated change in the OV?

(b) Analyze the effect on the optimal solution of decreasing the cost of ore from location 3 by exactly $118.269 per ton. (For example, does the present solution remain optimal? Is there an additional optimal solution, and if so how can it be characterized?)

(c) For the change described above in part (b), what is the new OV?

There are alternative optima.

5-17. ▲ You have just solved an LP model. You observe that you have a nondegenerate solution and for some objective function coefficient you see a zero entry under the "ALLOWABLE INCREASE" column. What does this tell you?

Max $5x_1 + 15x_2 + 9x_3$
s.t. $x_1 + 3x_3 \le 2$
$5x_2 + 4x_3 \ge -3$
$2x_1 + 7x_2 + x_3 = 6$
$x_1 \ge 0$, $x_2 \le 0$, x_3 unconstrained

5-18. ▲ What LP problem will have the following dual?

$$\begin{aligned} \text{Min } & 2y_1 - 3y_2 + 6y_3 \\ \text{s.t. } & y_1 + 2y_3 \ge 5 \\ & 5y_2 + 7y_3 \le 15 \\ & 3y_1 + 4y_2 + y_3 = 9 \\ & y_1 \ge 0,\ y_2 \le 0,\ y_3 \text{ unconstrained in sign} \end{aligned}$$

Max $3x_1 + 17x_2$
s.t. $18x_1 + 6x_2 \le 4$
$12x_1 + 2x_2 \le 13$
$x_1 \le 0$, x_2 unconstrained in sign

5-19. ▲ Find the dual to the following LP:

$$\begin{aligned} \text{Min } & 4y_1 + 13y_2 \\ \text{s.t. } & 18y_1 + 12y_2 \le 3 \\ & 6y_1 + 2y_2 = 17 \\ & y_1 \ge 0, \quad y_2 \ge 0 \end{aligned}$$

See IM.

5-20. ▲ Explain how to use the reduced costs to know if there are alternative optimal solutions.

(a) 1500
(b) 120
(c) The dual

5-21. ▲ Suppose that the primal problem has 120 variables and 1500 constraints.

(a) How many variables are in the dual problem?

(b) How many constraints are in the dual problem?

(c) All other things being equal, which problem should you prefer to solve (the primal or the dual)?

(a) 120
(b) 1500
(c) The primal

5-22. ▲ Change the data in Problem 5-21 to a primal problem with 1500 variables and 120 constraints and answer the same three questions.

Special structure

5-23. ▲▲ Regarding Problem 5-21(c), give a reason why all other things may *not* be "equal."

True

5-24. ▲ "Except for a possible sign difference, the dual prices on the computer output are the same as the optimal values of the variables in the dual of the problem being solved." Answer True or False.

(a) Rate of improvement in OV as RHS increases
(b) Rate of change in OV as RHS increases

5-25. ▲ Employing the terms *rate* and *OV*, give the correct interpretation of

(a) Dual price on computer output.

(b) Optimal dual variable.

(a) L
(b) K
(c) See IM

5-26. ▲ Let $c_1x_1 + c_2x_2 + \cdots + c_Kx_K$ denote the primal objective function (a Max model) and $b_1y_1 + b_2y_2 + \cdots + b_Ly_L$ the dual objective function.

(a) How many constraints are in the primal problem?

(b) How many constraints are in the dual problem?

(c) If $(u_1, \ldots, u_K)$ is primal feasible and $(v_1, \ldots, v_L)$ is dual feasible, what can you say about the two objective values?

Let $z_1 = x_1$; $z_2 = y_1$; $z_3 = y_2$; $z_4 = x_3$ to obtain
Max $4z_1 + z_2 - z_3$
s.t. $3z_1 + 2z_2 - 2z_3 - z_4 + z_5 = 0$
$z_1 - 3z_2 + 3z_3 - z_6 = 14$
$z_i \ge 0$, $i = 1, 2, 3, 4, 5, 6$

5-27. ▲ Consider the following problem:

$$\begin{aligned} \text{Max } & 4x_1 + x_2 \\ \text{s.t. } & 3x_1 + 2x_2 - x_3 \le 0 \\ & x_1 - 3x_2 \ge 14 \\ & x_1, x_3 \ge 0 \end{aligned}$$

Thus, the variable x_2 is unconstrained in sign. As discussed in Appendix 5.1, replace x_2 with $y_1 - y_2$, $y_1 \ge 0$, and $y_2 \ge 0$ to convert this problem to an equivalent form in which all variables are nonnegative. Then convert the latter model to a problem in standard equality constraint form, with all variables denoted by the symbol z_j (replace x's, y's, and so on, with z's).

5-28. ▲▲ Consider the Buster Sod problem: Buster Sod operates an 800-acre irrigated farm in the Red River Valley of Arizona. Sod's principal activities are raising wheat, alfalfa, and beef. The Red River Valley Water Authority has just given its water allotments for next year (Sod was allotted 1000 acre-feet), and Sod is busy preparing his production plan for next year. He figures that beef prices will hold at around \$500 per ton and that wheat will sell at \$2 per bushel. Best guesses are that he will be able to sell alfalfa at \$22 per ton, but if he needs more alfalfa to feed his beef than he can raise, he will have to pay \$28 per ton to get the alfalfa to his feedlot.

Some technological features of Sod's operation are wheat yield, 70 bushels per acre; alfalfa yield, 4 tons per acre. Other features are given in Figure 5.17. Define the variables:

W = wheat raised and sold (acres)
AR = alfalfa raised (tons)
B = beef raised and sold (tons)
AB = alfalfa bought (tons)
AS = alfalfa sold (tons)

An LP formulation and solution to Buster Sod's problem are shown in Figure 5.18.

ACTIVITY	LABOR, MACHINERY, AND OTHER COSTS ($)	WATER REQUIREMENTS (ACRE-FT)	LAND REQUIREMENTS (ACRES)	ALFALFA REQUIREMENTS (TONS)
1 acre of wheat	20	2	1	
1 acre of alfalfa	28	3	1	
1 ton of beef	50	0.05	0.1	5

▲ FIGURE 5.17
Data for Buster Sod Problem

▼ FIGURE 5.18
LP Formulation for Buster Sod Problem

```
MAX 120W - 7 AR + 450 B - 28 AB + 22 AS
SUBJECT TO
   2) W + 0.25 AR + 0.1 B < = 800
   3) 2W + 0.75 AR + 0.05 B < = 1000
   4) -AR + 5 B - AB + AS = 0

          OBJECTIVE FUNCTION VALUE
                 2480000.00

VARIABLE        VALUE          REDUCED COST

   W             0.00            2980.00
   AR            0.00             754.00
   B          8000.00               0.00
   AB        40000.00               0.00
   AS            0.00               6.00

   ROW     SLACK OR SURPLUS    DUAL PRICES

   2)            0.00            3100.00
   3)          600.00               0.00
   4)            0.00              28.00

           SENSITIVITY ANALYSIS

             OBJ COEFFICIENT RANGES

VARIABLE   CURRENT   ALLOWABLE   ALLOWABLE
            COEF.    INCREASE    DECREASE

   W       120.00     2980.00    INFINITY
   AR       -7.00      754.00    INFINITY
   B       450.00    INFINITY      298.00
   AB      -28.00        6.00       55.85
   AS       22.00        6.00    INFINITY

              RIGHTHAND SIDE RANGES

   ROW     CURRENT   ALLOWABLE   ALLOWABLE
           RHS       INCREASE    DECREASE

   2        800.00    1200.00      200.00
   3       1000.00   INFINITY      600.00
   4          0.00   40000.00    INFINITY
```

(a) See IM
(b) 400 acre-ft
(c) 8000 tons
(d) Buys 40,000 tons
(e) Nothing
(f) See IM
(g) Both unchanged
(h) $2,480,00
(i) OV decreases by $40,000
(j) $6/ton

(a) Show calculations that explain the values of the coefficient of W in the objective function and the coefficients of AR in the first and second constraints.

(b) How much water is being used?

(c) How much beef is being produced?

(d) Does Sod buy or sell alfalfa?

(e) How much should Sod pay to acquire another acre-ft of water?

(f) Interpret the dual price on row 2.

(g) What happens to the optimal planting policy if the price of wheat triples? What happens to the OV?

(h) How much profit will Sod receive from the optimal operation of his farm?

(i) What happens to the optimal value of the objective function if the cost of alfalfa purchased increases from $28 to $29?
NOTE: The coefficient of AB is currently −$28 and it will become −$29. Thus the coefficient will *decrease* by $1.

(j) How much can the cost of buying alfalfa decrease before the current optimal planting policy will change?

(a) 128 hours on 1 & 2, 76.8 hours on 3
(b) $/minute
(c) $0.60
(d) $1.38/lb

5-29. ▲ A plant can manufacture five different products in any combination. Each product requires time on each of three machines, as shown in Figure 5.19. All figures are in minutes per pound of product. Each machine is available 128 hours per week. Products A, B, C, D, and E are purely competitive, and any amounts made may be sold at per pound prices of $5, $4, $5, $4, and $4, respectively. Variable labor costs are $4 per hour for machines 1 and 2, and $3 per hour for machine 3. Material costs are $2 for each pound of products A and C, and $1 for each pound of products B, D, and E. You wish to maximize profit to the firm. The LP formulation and solution are shown in Figure 5.20.

(a) How many hours are spent on each of the three machines?

(b) What are the units of the dual prices on the constraints that control machine capacity?

(c) How much should the firm be willing to spend to obtain another hour of time on machine 2?

(d) How much can the sales price of product A increase before the optimal production plan changes? State your answer in the proper units.

▼ FIGURE 5.19
Machine-Time Data

PRODUCT	MACHINE-TIME (min/lb) 1	2	3
A	12	8	5
B	7	9	10
C	8	4	7
D	10	0	3
E	7	11	2

More-challenging problems

5-30. ▲▲ *A Product Mix/Process Selection Problem.* Two products, A and B, are processed on three machines. Both products have two possible routings. Routing 1 processes the product on machines 1 and 2 while routing 2 processes the product on machines 1 and 3. Processing times in hours per unit are given in Figure 5.21.
The costs per hour on machines 1, 2, and 3 are $20, $30, and $18, respectively. Each machine is available for 40 hours per week. Any amount of products A and B may be

```
MAX 1.416 A + 1.433 B + 1.85 C + 2.183 D + 1.7 E
SUBJECT TO
  2) 12 A + 7 B + 8 C + 10 D + 7 E <= 7680
  3) 8 A + 9 B + 4 C + 11 E <= 7680
  4) 5 A + 10 B + 7 C + 3 D + 2 E <= 7680

          OBJECTIVE FUNCTION VALUE
                  1817.59

VARIABLE         VALUE          REDUCED COST

   A              0.00             1.38
   B              0.00             0.24
   C            512.00             0.00
   D              0.00             0.75
   E            512.00             0.00

   ROW     SLACK OR SURPLUS   DUAL PRICES

   2              0.00             0.22
   3              0.00             0.01
   4           3072.00             0.00

            SENSITIVITY ANALYSIS

              OBJ COEFFICIENT RANGES

VARIABLE   CURRENT   ALLOWABLE   ALLOWABLE
            COEF.    INCREASE    DECREASE

   A        1.41       1.38      INFINITY
   B        1.43       0.24      INFINITY
   C        1.85       0.09        0.04
   D        2.18       0.07      INFINITY
   E        1.70       0.11        0.08

               RIGHTHAND SIDE RANGES

   ROW     CURRENT   ALLOWABLE   ALLOWABLE
             RHS     INCREASE    DECREASE

   2       7680.00    2671.30     2792.72
   3       7680.00    4388.57     3840.00
   4       7680.00    INFINITY    3072.00
```

▲ FIGURE 5.20
Solution for Five-Product, Three-Machine Problem

▼ FIGURE 5.21
Processing-Time Data

PRODUCT	ROUTING	MACHINE-TIME (hr/unit) 1	2	3
A	1	2	1	
A	2	2		1.5
B	1	1	2	
B	2	1		3

sold at $110 and $150 per unit, respectively. The LP formulation and solution are shown in Figure 5.22 where

A_i = units of A produced by routing i (i = 1,2)

B_i = units of B produced by routing i (i = 1,2)

▼ FIGURE 5.22
LP Formulation for Problem 5-30

```
MAX 40 A1 + 43 A2 + 70 B1 + 76 B2
SUBJECT TO
  2) 2 A1 + 2 A2 + B1 + B2 ≤ 40
  3) A1 + 2 B1 ≤ 40
  4) 1.5 A2 + 3 B2 ≤ 40
END

LP OPTIMUM FOUND AT STEP   3

  OBJECTIVE FUNCTION VALUE

  1) 2435.5560

VARIABLE          VALUE          REDUCED COST

   A1            4.444445           .000000
   A2             .000000           .000000
   B1           17.777780           .000000
   B2           13.333330           .000000

   ROW     SLACK OR SURPLUS    DUAL PRICES

   2)             .000000          3.333333
   3)             .000000         33.333330
   4)             .000000         24.222220

RANGES IN WHICH THE BASIS IS UNCHANGED:

                  OBJ COEFFICIENT RANGES

VARIABLE    CURRENT    ALLOWABLE   ALLOWABLE
             COEF.     INCREASE    DECREASE

   A1      40.000000   99.999990     .000000
   A2      43.000000     .000000   INFINITY
   B1      70.000000     .000000   50.000000
   B2      76.000000   INFINITY      .000000

                  RIGHTHAND SIDE RANGES

   ROW      CURRENT    ALLOWABLE   ALLOWABLE
              RHS      INCREASE    DECREASE

   2       40.000000   53.333340    6.666667
   3       40.000000   13.333330   26.666670
   4       40.000000   20.000000   40.000000
```

(a) See IM
(b) 31.11 units/week; 17.78 units/week
(c) 40 hours/week on each machine
(d) $/hour
(e) Yes

(a) Show calculations that explain the values of the coefficients in the objective function.

(b) How much product B is being produced? How much by the first routing? (Interpret the numbers as production rates. Thus 4.44 would represent 4.44 units per week. This could be accomplished by producing 4 units the first week and starting the 5th, finishing the 5th through the 8th units the second week and starting the 9th, etc.)

(c) How many hours are used on each of the three machines?

(d) What are the units of the dual prices on the machine capacity constraints?

(e) Suppose that there is an opportunity to work up to 8 hours of overtime on machine 2 at a cost of $45 per hour (50% more than the regular time cost of $30 per hour). Should machine 2 be scheduled for 8 hours of overtime?

5-31. ▲▲ *A Blending Problem.* This problem is similar to Problem 2-20. A vineyard wishes to blend four different vintages to make three types of blended wine. Restrictions are placed on the percentage composition of the blends (see Figure 5.23). The LP formulation and solution are shown in Figure 5.24 where

$$X_{ij} = \text{gallons of vintage } j \text{ used in blend } i$$

$$\text{TOTAL } i = \text{total blend } i \text{ produced}$$

BLEND	VINTAGE 1	2	3	4	SALES PRICE PER GALLON ($)
A	at least 75% 1 & 2		*	at most 5%	70
B	*	at least 35% 2 & 3		*	40
C	at least 50% 1 & 3, no restriction on 2			at most 40%	30
Supply (gallons)	180	250	200	400	

*Indicates no restriction

▲ FIGURE 5.23
Data for Problem 5-31

(a), (b), (c) See IM
(d) $54,675
(e) See IM
(f) Degenerate; 12 constraints, only 9 positive variables
(g) Increase by at least $22.50
(h) 1, 2, 3: $72.50/gallon 4: $22.50/gallon
(i) Optimal solution would change; OV would decrease by $7,250

(a) What is the purpose of rows 2 through 4?

(b) What is the purpose of rows 5 through 8?

(c) What restriction does row 9 represent? Explain why the coefficients and RHS of this constraint have the values they do.

(d) What is the maximum revenue that can be achieved by blending the four vintages?

(e) How much of each blend should be produced? What is the composition of each blend?

(f) Is the current solution degenerate or nondegenerate? How can you tell?

(g) What is the minimum amount by which the selling price of blend C would have to change, and in what direction, before it would become optimal to produce blend C?

(h) What are the dual prices of the four vintages? What are the units of these dual prices?

(i) Suppose an earthquake destroys half of the available vintage 3. What can you say about the impact on the optimal solution and the optimal revenue?

5-32. ▲▲ The Party Nut Company has on hand 550 pounds of peanuts, 150 pounds of cashews, 90 pounds of brazil nuts, and 70 pounds of hazelnuts. It packages and sells four varieties of mixed nuts in standard 8-ounce (half-pound) cans. The mix requirements and net wholesale prices are shown in Figure 5.25. The firm can sell all that it can produce at these prices. What mixes of products should it produce?

▼ FIGURE 5.24
LP Solution for Problem 5-31

```
MAX 70 TOTALA + 40 TOTALB + 30 TOTALC
SUBJECT TO
   2) TOTALA − XA1 − XA2 − XA3 − XA4 = 0
   3) TOTALB − XB1 − XB2 − XB3 − XB4 = 0
   4) TOTALC − XC1 − XC2 − XC3 − XC4 = 0
   5) XA1 + XB1 + XC1 ≤ 180
   6) XA2 + XB2 + XC2 ≤ 250
   7) XA3 + XB3 + XC3 ≤ 200
   8) XA4 + XB4 + XC4 ≤ 400
   9) −0.75 TOTALA + XA1 + XA2 ≥ 0
  10) −0.05 TOTALA + XA4 ≤ 0
  11) −0.35 TOTALB + XB2 + XB3 ≥ 0
  12) −0.5 TOTALC + XC1 + XC3 ≥ 0
  13) −0.4 TOTALC + XC4 ≤ 0
END

LP OPTIMUM FOUND AT STEP   7

        OBJECTIVE FUNCTION VALUE

  1) 54675.000

VARIABLE        VALUE         REDUCED COST

 TOTALA      449.166700          .000000
 TOTALB      580.833300          .000000
 TOTALC         .000000          .000000
    XA1      180.000000          .000000
    XA2      246.708300          .000000
    XA3         .000000          .000000
    XA4       22.458330          .000000
    XB1         .000000        50.000000
    XB2        3.291661          .000000
    XB3      200.000000          .000000
    XB4      377.541700          .000000
    XC1         .000000        37.500000
    XC2         .000000        37.500000
    XC3         .000000        37.500000
    XC4         .000000          .000000

ROW    SLACK OR SURPLUS    DUAL PRICES

 2)         .000000          72.500000
 3)         .000000          22.500000
 4)         .000000          35.000000
 5)         .000000          72.500000
 6)         .000000          72.500000
 7)         .000000          72.500000
 8)         .000000          22.500000
 9)       89.833340            .000000
10)         .000000          50.000000
11)         .000000         −50.000000
12)         .000000            .000000
13)         .000000          12.500000
```

```
NO. ITERATIONS=     7

RANGES IN WHICH THE BASIS IS UNCHANGED:

                 OBJ COEFFICIENT RANGES

VARIABLE     CURRENT      ALLOWABLE    ALLOWABLE
              COEF.       INCREASE     DECREASE

 TOTALA    70.000000     38.571430   12.857140
 TOTALB    40.000000      4.736842   14.210530
 TOTALC    30.000000     22.500000    7.500000
    XA1      .000000      INFINITY   37.500000
    XA2      .000000     40.601500     .000000
    XA3      .000000       .000000    INFINITY
    XA4      .000000    771.428600   46.153840
    XB1      .000000     50.000000    INFINITY
    XB2      .000000       .000000   40.601500
    XB3      .000000      INFINITY     .000000
    XB4      .000000      7.287449   21.862350
    XC1      .000000     37.500000    INFINITY
    XC2      .000000     37.500000    INFINITY
    XC3      .000000     37.500000    INFINITY
    XC4      .000000     56.250000    7.500000

             RIGHTHAND SIDE RANGES

ROW     CURRENT       ALLOWABLE    ALLOWABLE
          RHS         INCREASE     DECREASE

 2        .000000    112.856900   414.615400
 3        .000000    445.188000     5.939839
 4        .000000       .000000      .000000
 5     180.000000    112.856900   180.000000
 6     250.000000    112.856900   239.716600
 7     200.000000      3.198375   200.000000
 8     400.000000    445.188000     5.939839
 9        .000000     89.833340     INFINITY
10        .000000      5.642848    20.730770
11        .000000    155.815800     2.078944
12        .000000       .000000     INFINITY
13        .000000       .000000      .000000
```

▲ FIGURE 5.24 (Continued)

▼ FIGURE 5.25 Nut Mix Data

MIX	CONTENTS	PRICE PER CAN
1 (peanuts)	Peanuts only	$0.26
2 (party mix)	No more than 50% peanuts; at least 15% cashews; at least 10% brazil nuts	0.40
3 (cashews)	Cashews only	0.51
4 (luxury mix)	At least 30% cashews; at least 20% brazil nuts; at least 30% hazelnuts	0.52

▼ FIGURE 5.26
Solution for the Party Nut Problem

```
MAX    52 P1 + 80 P2 + 80 C2 + 80 B2 + 80 H2 + 102 C3 + 104 P4
     + 104 C4 + 104 B4 + 104 H4
SUBJECT TO
        2)      P1 + P2 + P4 ≤ 550
        3)      C2 + C3 + C4 ≤ 150
        4)      B2 + B4 ≤ 90
        5)      H2 + H4 ≤ 70
        6)      0.5 P2 − 0.5 C2 − 0.5 B2 − 0.5 H2 ≤ 0
        7)     −0.15 P2 + 0.85 C2 − 0.15 B2 − 0.15 H2 ≥ 0
        8)     −0.1 P2 − 0.1 C2 + 0.9 B2 − 0.1 H2 ≥ 0
        9)     −0.3 P4 + 0.7 C4 − 0.3 B4 − 0.3 H4 ≥ 0
       10)     −0.2 P4 − 0.2 C4 + 0.8 B4 − 0.2 H4 ≥ 0
       11)     −0.3 P4 − 0.3 C4 − 0.3 B4 + 0.7 H4 ≥ 0

                   OBJECTIVE FUNCTION VALUE
        1)              63760.0000

VARIABLE              VALUE           REDUCED COST
       P1            380.000             0.000
       P2            123.333             0.000
       C2             80.000             0.000
       B2             43.333             0.000
       H2              0.000            24.000
       C3              0.000             6.000
       P4             46.667             0.000
       C4             70.000             0.000
       B4             46.667             0.000
       H4             70.000             0.000

  ROW             SLACK OR SURPLUS     DUAL PRICES
        2)            0.000
        3)            0.000
        4)            0.000             108.000
        5)            0.000             132.000
        6)            0.000              56.000
        7)           43.000               0.000
        8)           18.667
        9)            0.000             −56.000
       10)            0.000             −56.000
       11)            0.000             −80.000

                   SENSITIVITY ANALYSIS

                       OBJ COEFFICIENT RANGES

                 CURRENT        ALLOWABLE          ALLOWABLE
VARIABLE          COEF          INCREASE           DECREASE
       P1        52.000           6.000             12.000
       P2        80.000           9.000              6.000
       C2        80.000          24.000              6.000
       B2        80.000          36.000             56.000
       H2        80.000          24.000           INFINITY
       C3       102.000           6.000           INFINITY
       P4       104.000         INFINITY            36.000
       C4       104.000          56.000             24.000
       B4       104.000          56.000             36.000
       H4       104.000         INFINITY            24.000
```

RIGHTHAND SIDE RANGES

ROW	CURRENT RHS	ALLOWABLE INCREASE	ALLOWABLE DECREASE
2	550.000	INFINITY	380.000
3	150.000	93.333	61.429
4	90.000	143.333	23.333
5	70.000	56.000	70.000
6	0.000	93.333	61.667
7	0.000	43.000	INFINITY
8	0.000	18.667	INFINITY
9	0.000	46.667	70.000
10	0.000	23.333	46.667
11	0.000	28.000	56.000

▲ FIGURE 5.26 (Continued)

The problem can be formulated as the linear program shown in Figure 5.26, where

Pi = pounds of peanuts used in mix i

Ci = pounds of cashews used in mix i

Bi = pounds of brazil nuts used in mix i

Hi = pounds of hazelnuts used in mix i

Note that in the model given in Figure 5.26

(1) The coefficient of $P1$ in the objective function is 52 rather than 26 because there are two 8-ounce cans for each pound of peanuts sold as peanuts only.

(2) Row 6 is a rewritten version of the constraint $P2/(P2 + C2 + B2 + H2) \leq 0.5$. A similar comment applies to each of the rows 7 through 11.

In the output in Figure 5.26 we have purposely deleted several of the dual prices. Use this output to answer the questions. If it is impossible to answer the question, state why.

(a) See IM
(b) 493.33
(c) ≥ (See IM)
(d) 0 (See IM)
(e) See IM
(f) See IM
(g) 52 (See IM)
(h) See IM
(i) See IM

(a) Explain the calculation that justifies 102 as the coefficient of $C3$ in the objective function.

(b) How many cans of mix 2 are produced in the optimal solution?

(c) Is the dual price on row 3 (the second constraint) ≥ 0 or ≤ 0? Explain why.

(d) What is the value of the dual price on row 8? How do you know?

(e) What is the meaning of the fact that the surplus variable on row 7 is positive? Explain (not using LP jargon).

(f) What is the effect on the optimal solution and the OV if the sales price of mix 1 (peanuts only) increases to \$0.27 per can?

(g) What is the numerical value of the dual price on row 2? (Hint: What would you do with another pound of peanuts if you had them?)

(h) Why is the allowable increase for the RHS of row 2 INFINITY? (Hint: The answer to part (g) provides the basis for the rationale.)

(i) Provide an explanation as to why it is possible to have an optimal solution even though there is a positive surplus on row 7.

See IM.

5-33. ▲▲ Consider the problem (P)

$$\begin{aligned} \text{Max } & 2x_1 + x_2 \\ \text{s.t. } & 4x_1 + 12x_2 \leq 100 \\ & 19x_1 - 3x_2 \geq 6 \\ & x_1 \geq 10, \quad x_2 \geq 10 \end{aligned}$$

Let D_1 be its dual. Now put (P) into standard equality constraint form and let D_2 be its dual. Show that D_1 and D_2 are equivalent.

See IM.

5-34. ▲▲ Note that the RHS of row 3, which is the market balance constraint, has an allowable increase of ∞ in Figure 5.11 and 3.75 in Figure 5.12. Yet, as you can see by comparing Figures 5.9 and 5.10, the optimal corner is the same in both cases. Use the geometry to explain this difference in the values of allowable increase.

See IM.

5-35. ▲▲ Why is the allowable decrease on the coefficient of *F* equal to 1500 in Figure 5.11 and 19,000 in Figure 5.12?

See IM.

5-36. ▲▲ Suppose that you solve (P) on the computer and then solve (D). Can you explain why all sensitivity information for both problems appears on both printouts?

▶ Appendix 5.1 Solving an LP When Not All Variables Are Required to Be Nonnegative

Suppose that, for logical reasons, some of the variables in your LP model are *not* required to be nonnegative. For example, suppose that in the particular LP model you have formulated there is a variable z such that when z is positive it denotes the quantity of an item sold, and when z is negative it represents the quantity bought. Thus, z may be positive, negative, or zero. In order to solve this LP on the computer it must be transformed into the standard form, in which *all* variables must be nonnegative.

To do this, introduce *two* new *nonnegative* variables, say z_1 and z_2, and let $z = z_1 - z_2$. Everywhere a z appears in your original model, simply replace it by $z_1 - z_2$ and rewrite the model.

For example, suppose that the original model is

$$\text{Max } 2x + 3z$$
$$\text{s.t.} \quad 4x + 5z \leq 30$$
$$x \geq 0, \qquad z \text{ not constrained in sign}$$

The equivalent LP problem with all variables nonnegative is

$$\text{Max } 2x + 3z_1 - 3z_2$$
$$\text{s.t.} \quad 4x + 5z_1 - 5z_2 \leq 30$$
$$x, z_1, z_2 \geq 0$$

We then solve this new problem on the computer to obtain optimal values x^*, and z_1^*, and z_2^*. The optimal value of z in the original model is given by

$$z^* = z_1^* - z_2^*$$

It can be shown that the solution to the second model, which the simplex method obtains, will have the property that at most one of the pair z_1^*, z_2^* is positive. That is, at least one and possibly both have the value zero.

Appendix 5.2 Questions Based on the Red Brand Canners Case

We first saw the Red Brand Canners case in Chapter 2, where the model was formulated and assumptions were discussed. In the following questions, the analysis continues. You are asked to solve several formulations on the computer and then analyze the outputs.

1. Run on your own computer your LP formulation of the Red Brand Canners production problem. Do not include the option of purchasing up to 80,000 additional pounds of grade A tomatoes.

2. What is the net profit obtained after netting out the cost of the crop?

3. Myers has proposed that the net profit obtained from his policy would be \$48,000. Is this true? If not, what is his net profit (taking into account, as in Question 2, the cost of the crop).

4. Suppose Cooper suggests that, in keeping with his accounting scheme as advanced in Exhibit 2 on page 84, the crop cost of 6 cents per pound should be subtracted from each coefficient in the objective function. Change your formulation accordingly, and again solve the problem. You should obtain an optimal objective value that is greater than that obtained in Question 2. Explain this apparent discrepancy (assume that unused tomatoes will spoil).

5. Suppose that unused tomatoes could be resold at 6 cents per pound. Which solution would be preferred under these conditions? How much can the resale price be lowered without affecting this preference?

6. Use the sensitivity output from Question 1 to determine whether the additional purchase of up to 80,000 pounds of grade A tomatoes should be undertaken. Can you tell how much should be purchased?

7. Use a reformulated model to obtain an optimal product mix using the additional purchase option. The solution to your reformulated model should explicitly show how the additional purchase should be used.

8. Suppose that in Question 1 the Market Research Department feels it could increase the demand for juice by 25,000 cases by means of an advertising campaign. How much should Red Brand be willing to pay for such a campaign?

9. Suppose in Question 1 that the price of juice increased 10 cents per case. Does your computer output tell you whether the optimal production plan will change?

10. Suppose that RBC is forced to reduce the size of the product line in tomato-based products to 2. Would additional computer runs be required to tell which product should be dropped from the line?

11. Suppose that in Question 1 an additional lot of grade B tomatoes is available. The lot is 50,000 pounds. How much should RBC be willing to pay for this lot of grade B tomatoes?

Alternate Questions on Red Brand Canners

For the following questions assume 3 grades of tomatoes, as in the alternate questions in Chapter 2.

12. Run on your own computer your LP formulation of Question 8 of the Alternate Questions for Red Brand Canners from Chapter 2.

13. What is the net profit obtained after netting out the cost of the crop?

14. Myers claims the net profit from his policy of producing 2,000,000 lb paste and 1,000,000 lb juice is $89,600. Is this correct? If not, what is his net profit (taking into account, as in Question 13, the cost of the crop)?

15. Suppose Cooper suggests that, in keeping with his accounting scheme as advanced in Exhibit 2 on page 84, the crop cost per pound should be subtracted from each coefficient in the objective function. Change your formulation accordingly, and again solve the problem, assuming a crop cost of 7 cents per pound. You should obtain a solution that is different from that obtained in Question 12. Which solution has a higher net profit (assume unused tomatoes will spoil)? Is it correct to include tomato costs in the objective function?

16. If in Question 15 unused tomatoes could be resold for 7 cents a pound, which solution would be preferred? How much can the resale price be lowered without affecting this preference?

17. Use the sensitivity output from Question 12 to determine whether the additional purchase of up to 80,000 pounds of grade A tomatoes should be undertaken. Can you tell how much should be purchased?

18. Use a reformulated model to obtain an optimal product mix using the additional purchase option. The solution to your reformulated model should explicitly show how the additional purchase should be used.

19. Suppose that in Question 12 the Market Research Department feels they could increase the demand for paste by 3000 cases by means of an advertising campaign. How much should Red Brand be willing to pay for such a campaign?

20. Suppose in Question 12 that the price of canned whole tomatoes decreased by 16 cents per case. Does your computer output tell you whether the optimal production plan will change?

21. Suppose that the Market Research Department suggests that if the average quality of paste is below 4 the product will not be acceptable to customers. Would an additional computer run be necessary to determine the optimal production plan if this constraint were added to the model?

22. Suppose that in Question 12 an additional lot of grade C tomatoes is available. The lot is 200,000 lb. How much would RBC be willing to pay for this lot of grade C tomatoes?

▶ Diagnostic Assignment

Crawler Tread and a New Angle

In important respects, part of a manager's task invokes analysis and evaluation of the work of others as opposed to producing "from rock bottom" his or her own formulation and analysis. In this diagnostic role the manager will judge someone else's model. Have the correct questions been asked? Has a correct analysis been performed? The following vignette captures the spirit of such a situation. You are asked to comment on the analysis of a new opportunity.

Ralph Hanson has been the chief metallurgist at PROTRAC's cast iron foundry for the last five years. He brings several important qualities to this position. First, he has an excellent technical background. He graduated from Case Western with an MMS (master of material science) and had five years' experience with U.S. Steel before joining PROTRAC. He has used this training and experience to implement several changes that have contributed to product quality and process efficiency. In addition, he has become an effective manager. Through a combination of formal course work and self-education, he has become familiar with many modern management techniques and approaches and has worked to see that these new methods are exploited whenever it is appropriate. Indeed, Ralph is responsible for introducing the use of LP models into the ore-blending and scrap-recycling activities at **PROTRAC**.

Ralph was the chief metallurgist when Crawler Tread, the first ore-blending application, was completed. By now both Ralph and Sam Togas, the plant manager, are comfortable with the use of LP models in the ore-blending area. Ralph typically formulates, solves, and interprets the output himself. Currently, he is facing a new problem. The recession has seriously affected the demand for heavy equipment, and **PROTRAC** has excess capacity in most departments, including the foundry. However, the defense industries are booming. A manufacturer of tanks requires a high-grade ore for producing tank treads. Indeed, the requirements are exactly the same as **PROTRAC** used in the Crawler Tread problem (see Section 5.4). The tank manufacturer is willing to pay **PROTRAC** $850 per ton of ore for up to 150,000 tons to be delivered within the next month. Ralph learns that he can have up to 98,000 tons of ore available. This is made up of 21,000 tons from mine 1; 40,000 from mine 2; 15,000 from mine 3; and 22,000 from mine 4.

On the basis of these data, Ralph formulates a new LP model. In this model, T_i is the number of tons of ore from mine i (for i = 1, 2, 3, 4) that are used in the blend, and B is the number of tons of blended ore. He carefully annotates the formulation so that he can easily explain his analysis to Sam, the plant manager. The formulation and solution that Ralph used in his presentation are shown in Figure 5.27.

Sam was delighted with the project. It yielded a contribution margin of $30,500,000 and occupied resources (labor and machinery) that otherwise would have been idle. He immediately had the legal department draw up a contract for the sale of 98,000 tons of ore.

When Ralph arrived the next morning, Sam was waiting for him. The following discussion took place:

SAM: The contract is ready and I was about to call and confirm the arrangement, but there is a new development. We've just received a telex from mine 1. Due to the cancellation of another order, we can have up to another 3000 tons of ore at the standard price of $800 per ton if we want it. What should we do? Why don't you go back and re-solve your problem including the possibility of the additional 3000 tons from mine 1 and draw up a new contract if the new solution is better. Obviously, we can't do worse than we are doing now, and that's not bad.

RALPH: Actually, we don't have to do that. One of the great things about LP is that we can answer many questions involving changes from the original problem. In particular, the dual price on the amount of T_1 available (row 8) provides an upper bound on how much more we should pay to have the opportunity of buying an additional ton of ore from mine 1. If the dual price is positive, say $10, we should be willing to pay up to $10 more for the opportunity to buy another ton of ore (i.e., up to $810 for a ton of ore from mine 1). If it is zero, increasing the amount of ore that is available from mine 1 will not enable us to increase our profit.

A quick inspection of the solution reveals that the dual price on row 8 is zero.

RALPH: Since we can't increase our contribution margin, let's just leave the contract as it is and get back to work.

SAM: Damn it, Ralph, I don't understand this. We can buy the ore for $800 a ton and sell it for $850 a ton and you tell me we shouldn't do it.

RALPH: I know it's hard to see, but I know that if the right-hand side of row 8 is increased, the optimal value of the objective function will remain the same. This implies that additional tons of ore from mine 1 won't help us. I suppose it's because we can't add this additional ore to our blend and still satisfy the minimum elements requirements. Remember that the ore from mine 1 has only 90 pounds of element B per ton, and the blend must have at least 100.

SAM: Look, Ralph, I have to meet with the grievance committee now. I just can't spend any more time on this project. I can't say I understand your answer, but you're the expert. Let's go with the current contract.

Questions

1. Is Ralph's interpretation of the numbers on the printout correct?
2. Is Ralph's response to the additional purchase opportunity correct? If you believe he has erred, where is the flaw?
3. Suppose row 2 were dropped from the model. What would be the dual price on row 8? on row 9?

4. Can you figure out what will happen to the OV if the RHS of row 9 is changed to 39,999?

5. Suppose the RHS of row 9 is increased to 40,001. What are the new optimal values of T_1, T_2, T_3, and T_4?

6. Figure out why the Allowable Increase on row 9 is 571.42.

7. Can you tell which constraint causes the degeneracy in Ralph's model?

▼ FIGURE 5.27
Ralph's Formulation

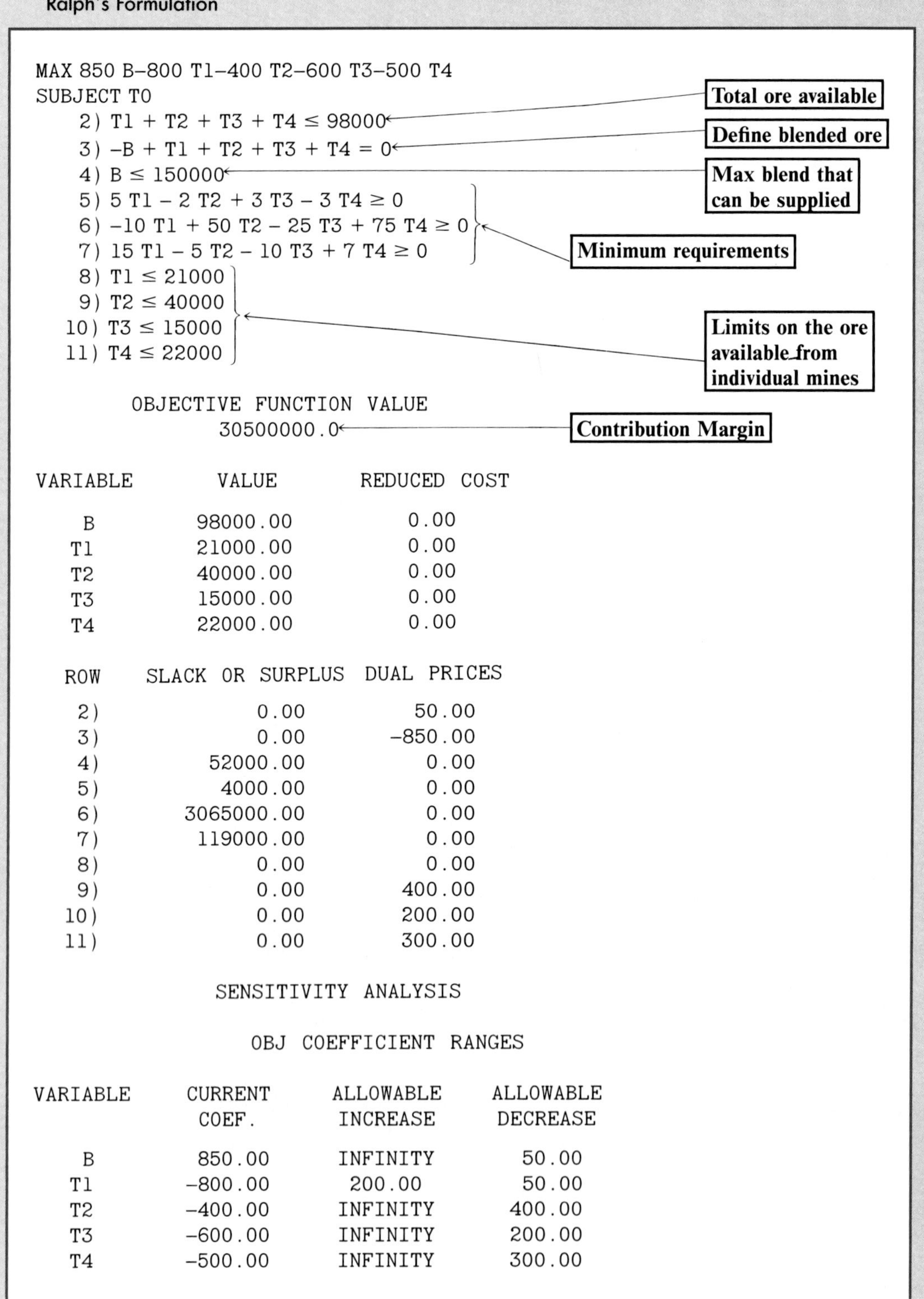

MAX 850 B–800 T1–400 T2–600 T3–500 T4
SUBJECT TO
2) T1 + T2 + T3 + T4 ≤ 98000
3) –B + T1 + T2 + T3 + T4 = 0
4) B ≤ 150000
5) 5 T1 – 2 T2 + 3 T3 – 3 T4 ≥ 0
6) –10 T1 + 50 T2 – 25 T3 + 75 T4 ≥ 0
7) 15 T1 – 5 T2 – 10 T3 + 7 T4 ≥ 0
8) T1 ≤ 21000
9) T2 ≤ 40000
10) T3 ≤ 15000
11) T4 ≤ 22000

OBJECTIVE FUNCTION VALUE
30500000.0

VARIABLE	VALUE	REDUCED COST
B	98000.00	0.00
T1	21000.00	0.00
T2	40000.00	0.00
T3	15000.00	0.00
T4	22000.00	0.00

ROW	SLACK OR SURPLUS	DUAL PRICES
2)	0.00	50.00
3)	0.00	-850.00
4)	52000.00	0.00
5)	4000.00	0.00
6)	3065000.00	0.00
7)	119000.00	0.00
8)	0.00	0.00
9)	0.00	400.00
10)	0.00	200.00
11)	0.00	300.00

SENSITIVITY ANALYSIS

OBJ COEFFICIENT RANGES

VARIABLE	CURRENT COEF.	ALLOWABLE INCREASE	ALLOWABLE DECREASE
B	850.00	INFINITY	50.00
T1	-800.00	200.00	50.00
T2	-400.00	INFINITY	400.00
T3	-600.00	INFINITY	200.00
T4	-500.00	INFINITY	300.00

RIGHTHAND SIDE RANGES

ROW	CURRENT RHS	ALLOWABLE INCREASE	ALLOWABLE DECREASE
2	98000.00	0.00	800.00
3	0.00	98000.00	52000.00
4	150000.00	INFINITY	52000.00
5	0.00	4000.00	INFINITY
6	0.00	3065000.00	INFINITY
7	0.00	119000.00	INFINITY
8	21000.00	INFINITY	0.00
9	40000.00	571.42	0.00
10	15000.00	2000.00	0.00
11	22000.00	500.00	0.00

Case

Saw Mill River Feed and Grain Company

The purpose of this case is to exercise both judgmental and technical skills. You will have to decide, on the basis of Mr. Overton's objectives, just what information you should provide him. You will then have to formulate an LP model (or models), run it (or them) on the computer, and present, in a summary report, the relevant results.

On Monday, August 28, 1986, Mr. Overton called in his sales manager and purchasing manager to discuss the company's policy for the coming month. Saw Mill had accepted orders from Turnbull Co. and McClean Bros. and had the option of accepting an order from Blue River, Inc. It also had the option of buying some additional grain from Cochrane Farm. Mr. Overton, managing director of Saw Mill, had to decide by the end of the week what action to take.

Usually, all purchases of grain are completed by the end of August. However, Saw Mill still has the possibility of an extra purchase of grain from Cochrane Farm. This commitment has to be made by September 1. The grain would be delivered to the Midwest Grain Elevator by the 15th of the month. This elevator acts simply as a storage facility for Saw Mill.

It is immutable company policy to charge a markup of 15% on the cost of the grain supplied to customers. Payments to the Midwest Grain Elevator are treated as an overhead, and this policy is not to be challenged. Turnbull, McClean, and Blue River have agreed to pay, for their current orders, whatever price Saw Mill charges. However, Saw Mill realizes that if its price becomes too high, future business will be lost.

The details of the Turnbull, McClean, and Blue River orders are presented in Exhibit 1. The quantity, as well as the maximum moisture content, minimum weight per bushel, maximum percentage damaged, and maximum percentage foreign material are presented.

The company has the option to supply any amount of grain that it wishes, within the specified range. It must, of course, satisfy the requirements. By September 4, Saw Mill must inform Turnbull and McClean how much grain they will receive. By the same date it must inform Blue River if it will accept its order and how much grain will be delivered if it accepts.

Saw Mill blends the grains that it owns to satisfy customer orders. On August 28 the company had 326,000 bushels of corn stored in the elevator. Obviously, it would be impossible to identify the exact composition of each kernel of corn that the Saw Mill River Feed and Grain Company delivered to the elevator. Hence, Exhibit 2 represents aggregated amounts and characteristics of different types of corn credited to Saw Mill River's account with the elevator. The

ORDERING COMPANY	QUANTITY (BUSHELS)	MAXIMUM PERCENT MOISTURE (per lb)	MINIMUM WEIGHT PER BUSHEL (lb)	MAXIMUM PERCENT DAMAGE (per lb)	MAXIMUM PERCENT FOREIGN MATERIAL (per lb)	DELIVERY DATE
Turnbull	40,000–45,000	13	56	2	2	9/20
McClean	32,000–36,000	15.5	54	5	3	9/22
Blue River	50,000–54,000	15	56	2	4	9/26

▲ EXHIBIT 1
Data on Grain Orders

TYPE OF CORN	QUANTITY (BUSHELS)	COST PER BUSHEL ($)	PERCENT MOISTURE CONTENT	WEIGHT PER BUSHEL (lb)	PERCENT TOTAL DAMAGE (per lb)	PERCENT FOREIGN MATERIAL (per lb)
1	30,000	1.45	12	57	2	1.5
2	45,000	1.44	15	57	2	1
3	25,000	1.45	12	58	3	3
4	40,000	1.42	13	56	4	2
5	20,000	1.38	15	54	4	2
6	30,000	1.37	15	55	5	3
7	75,000	1.37	18	57	5	1
8	15,000	1.39	14	58	2	4
9	16,000	1.27	17	53	7	5
10	20,000	1.28	15	55	8	3
11	10,000	1.17	22	56	9	5

▲ EXHIBIT 2
Characteristics of Corn Types

326,000 bushels are segregated into 11 types of corn, which differ according to (1) quantity available, (2) cost per bushel, (3) percentage moisture content, (4) weight per bushel, (5) percentage damaged, and (6) percentage foreign material.

The grain on offer from Cochrane Farm is one load of up to 50,000 bushels, with an average of 15% moisture, 3% damage, and 2% foreign material. The load has a density of 57 pounds per bushel, and Straddle (the purchasing manager) is convinced that the order can be obtained at a cost of $1.41 per bushel.

Use linear programming to help analyze Mr. Overton's problem. (Use notation T_i = bushels of corn type i to be sent to Turnbull. Similarly for M_i and B_i. Also let corn type 12 denote the corn from Cochrane Farm.) In no more than one page, labeled "Executive Summary," provide as concisely as possible information that will help Overton answer his questions. His main objectives are to maximize profit and to keep prices to the customers sufficiently low to attract future business. He can be expected to use his judgment to make the eventual decision; your job is to provide information that will enable him to look at the important trade-offs. You should also make your own recommendations.

Your presentation will be judged on the economy of your formulation (i.e., formulate your model, or models, *for the given set of data* as efficiently as possible) as well as on your recommendations concerning

(a) to buy or not to buy from Cochrane;

(b) to accept or not to accept the Blue River option;

(c) how much corn to supply to Blue River, Turnbull, and McClean.

From an idea by Jonathan Kornbluth, based on data originally published in *Introduction to Linear Programming: Methods & Cases* by Thomas H. Naylor, Eugene T. Byrne, and John M. Vernon. © 1971, Wadsworth Publishing Co., Inc.

Case

Kiwi Computer

Kiwi Computer of Australia manufactures two types of personal computers: a portable model and a desktop model. Kiwi assembles the cases and printed circuit boards at its only plant, which also manufactures the cases and stuffs the circuit boards with components. Monthly production is limited by the following capacities:

Monthly Capacity

OPERATION	PORTABLE	DESKTOP
Case Production	4000	2000
Board Stuffing	2500	3000
Portable Assembly	2000	—
Desktop Assembly	—	1800

For example, 4000 portable cases can be produced in a month and no desktop cases, or no portable cases and 2000 desktop cases, or if equal time is devoted to both, 2000 portable and 1000 desktop cases can be produced. In order to be feasible, production of portable and desktop computers for a month must satisfy all the constraints simultaneously. The set of feasible production plans is the shaded area in Exhibit 1.

The prices to retail computer stores are $1500 for the desktop and $1400 for the portable. In order to be competitive, Kiwi has to price its computers several hundred dollars below those of a very large and well-known computer manufacturer.

The entry of this manufacturer has caused a boom in the industry as the market has shifted from one aimed primarily at computer "hackers" to business professionals. Currently, Kiwi sells as many computers of either model as it produces. During the first quarter of the year Kiwi produced 2000 portables a month and 600 desktops. Both board stuffing and portable assembly were operating at capacity, but there was slack in case production and desktop assembly. Cost accountants determined standard costs and fixed overhead as shown in Exhibits 2 and 3. The fixed overhead data in Exhibit 2 are derived from the fixed overhead totals in Exhibit 3.

At a quarterly meeting of the company's executives, the sales manager pointed out that the desktop computer was not yielding a profit. He suggested that it be dropped from the company's product line.

The controller objected, saying, "If we produce more desktop computers, we can lower the

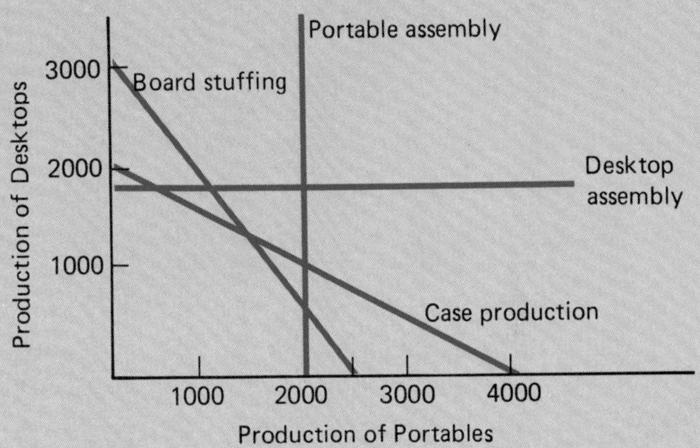

▲ EXHIBIT 1

▼ EXHIBIT 2

	DESKTOPS		PORTABLES	
Direct Materials		$ 800		$ 690
Direct Labor				
Case Production	$ 20		$15	
Board Stuffing	100		90	
Final Assembly	5	125	10	115
Fixed Overhead				
Case Production	$ 95		$ 95	
Board Stuffing	205		205	
Final Assembly	415	715	115	415
Total		$1640		$1220

▼ EXHIBIT 3

	TOTAL FIXED OVERHEAD ($000)*	FIXED OVERHEAD PER UNIT ($)
Case Production	247	95
Board Stuffing	533	205
Desktop Assembly	249	415
Portable Assembly	230	115
Total	1259	

*Based on production of 600 desktop and 2000 portable computers per month.

fixed final assembly cost of $415. It's high now because we are producing so few units."

The production manager responded, "We can increase production if we subcontract out board stuffing. We could supply the boards and components and reimburse the subcontractor for its overhead and labor costs."

The president concluded the meeting by asking the sales manager, the controller, and the production manager to get together and come up with a recommendation concerning the company's product mix and subcontracting. He told them to assume that demand would remain high and current capacity would remain fixed.

Questions

Part A. Subcontracting not allowed.

1. In Exhibit 2 the standard overhead cost assigned to desktop computers for final assembly is $415. Clearly indicate how this figure was derived.
2. **(a)** Do the desktop units make a contribution to profit? In other words, given that the overhead costs are fixed in the short run, is the company's profit higher than it would be if no desktop units were produced?

   (b) A correct computation of per unit profitabilities will show that the portable is more profitable than the desktop. Does this mean that more (or only) portables should be produced? Why?
3. In answering this question assume that boards cannot be stuffed by a subcontractor. Formulate a linear program for determining the optimal product mix.
4. Run your model using LINDO or whatever linear programming package is available and indicate the optimal mix of desktop and portable computers. Noninteger answers are acceptable for this problem.
5. Find the best feasible integer answer that can be achieved by rounding to adjacent integers your answers from Question 4.
6. **(a)** Go back and recalculate the company's "standard costs" using your integer answers from Question 5 and compare with those in Exhibit 2.

   (b) How much larger is the profit using the new mix (using the integer answers from Question 5) than the old (i.e., 600 desktops, 2000 portables)?

Part B. Subcontracting allowed.

We now allow some boards to be stuffed by subcontractors. Assume that production of a computer with a board stuffed by the subcontractor requires the same amount of time in case production and final assembly as production of a computer with a board stuffed at the factory.

7. Assume that the subcontractor is going to charge $110 for each desktop board stuffed and $100 for each portable board stuffed. Kiwi provides the subcontractor with the necessary materials. Should Kiwi employ the subcontractor to stuff boards? Argue why or why not without formulating and solving a new linear program.
8. Now formulate a linear program that includes subcontracting. In your formulation, distinguish between computers produced with internally and externally stuffed boards. Solve using LINDO or some other LP package.
9. Assume that in addition to the per board charge the subcontractor is now going to include a fixed charge for stuffing a batch of boards (same charge regardless of the number of boards or their type). For what fixed charge will Kiwi be indifferent between subcontracting and stuffing all boards internally?

Part C. Sensitivity analysis.

10. Refer to the linear programming formulation in Question 8. Is the optimal solution degenerate? Explain.
11. Refer to the linear programming formulation in Question 8. Do alternative optima exist? Explain.
12. Refer to the linear programming formulation in Question 8. The subcontractor currently charges $110 for each desktop board stuffed. By how much would this charge have to decrease so that it would be optimal for Kiwi to have the subcontractor stuff desktop boards? Why?
13. Refer to the linear programming formulation in Question 3. Assume Kiwi can increase the board-stuffing capacity so that either 600 additional desktop boards or 500 additional portable boards or any equivalent combination can be stuffed. Should Kiwi increase the capacity if the cost would be $175,000 per month? Answer *without* resolving the linear program.

14. Refer to the linear programming formulation in Question 3. Suppose a redesign of the desktop unit to use fewer chips reduces the cost of direct materials by $200. Does your computer output tell you whether the optimal production plan will change? Explain.

Alternative Questions on Kiwi Computer

Kiwi is considering consolidating desktop assembly and portable assembly into one department. The new department would be capable of assembling 3000 portables in a month and no desktops, or no portables and 2200 desktops, or if equal time were devoted to both, 1500 portables and 1100 desktops could be assembled. They estimate that the monthly fixed overhead for this department would be less than $479,000, the current combined overhead for the desktop and portable assembly departments. In answering the following questions assume the departments will be combined.

Part A. Subcontracting not allowed.

1. Let *D,P* equal the monthly production rate of desktops and portables, respectively, and *F* the fixed overhead of the new unified assembly department. Express total profit as a function of *D,P,* and *F.*
2. Must the value of *F* be known in order to determine the optimal product mix? Assume that fixed overhead is not affected by the values of *D* and *P.*
3. In answering this question assume that boards cannot be stuffed by a subcontractor. Formulate a linear program for determining the optimal product mix.
4. Run your model using LINDO or whatever linear programming package is available, and indicate the optimal mix of desktop and portable computers. Noninteger answers are acceptable for this problem.
5. Find the best feasible integer answer that can be achieved by rounding to adjacent integers your answers from Question 4.
6. Suppose that the optimal profit (revenue minus *all* costs) is $330,286 if the two assembly departments are not combined. What is the largest that the fixed overhead of a combined assembly department could be and Kiwi still prefer to combine the departments?

Part B. Subcontracting allowed.

7. Assume that the subcontractor is going to charge $150 for each desktop board stuffed and $135 for each portable board stuffed. Kiwi provides the subcontractor with the necessary materials. Should Kiwi employ the subcontractor to stuff boards? Argue why or why not without formulating and solving a new linear program.
8. Now formulate a linear program that includes subcontracting. In your formulation, distinguish between computers produced with internally and externally stuffed boards. Solve using LINDO or some other LP package.
9. Assume that in addition to the per board charge the subcontractor is now going to include a fixed charge for stuffing a batch of boards (same charge regardless of the number of boards or their type). For what fixed charge will Kiwi be indifferent between subcontracting and stuffing all boards internally?

Part C. Sensitivity analysis.

10. Refer to the linear programming formulation in Question 8. Is the optimal solution degenerate? Explain.
11. Refer to the linear programming formulation in Question 8. Do alternative optima exist? Explain.
12. Refer to the linear programming formulation in Question 8. The subcontractor currently charges $150 for each desktop board stuffed. Could the subcontractor lower his price enough so that it would be optimal for Kiwi to have him stuff desktop boards? Explain.
13. Refer to the linear programming formulation in Question 3. Assume Kiwi can increase the board stuffing capacity so that either 600 additional desktop boards or 500 portable boards or any equivalent combination can be stuffed. Should Kiwi increase the capacity if the cost would be $175,000 per month? Answer *without* resolving the linear program.
14. Refer to the linear programming formulation in Question 3. Suppose a redesign of the desktop unit to use fewer chips reduces the cost of direct materials by $200. Does your computer output tell you whether the optimal production plan will change? Explain.

▶ Case

Production Planning at Bumles

(The Bumles problem was first discussed and solved in Chapter 2. Before attacking this case you will want to review the solution in Chapter 2, for the correct formulation of this problem will be similar.) Bumles, Inc. uses part of its capacity to make two types of hand-painted statues. The finished products can reasonably be grouped into two categories, A and B. A requires 0.5 hours of a painter's time and B requires 0.75 hours. Bumles has 45 painters available, but not all of these painters need to be used. The plant is used for hand-painted statues on Monday, Tuesday, and Wednesday each week. During the remainder of the week the productive capacity is devoted to another product line. Each painter who is engaged is available to work painting statues any part of an eight-hour day, two days a week. A painter can be assigned to any two-day schedule and is paid for 16 hours of regular-time work, no matter what part of that time he actually spends producing statues. If there is not enough production to keep all the workers assigned to a particular day busy for the entire day, the slack time is spent on cleaning the plant and similar activities. In addition, on any day, Bumles can request each working painter to work up to 4 hours of overtime (i.e., if Ed Jones normally works on Tuesday, Bumles can have him work 2, 3, or any other number between 0 and 4, hours of overtime on that day).

Revenue from selling an A is $21 and a B is $30. Demand must either be satisfied on the day on which it occurs or it is lost. Production on a given day can be used to satisfy demand that day or demand later in the week, i.e., statues produced on Monday can be used to satisfy demand on Monday, Tuesday, or Wednesday, and statues produced on Tuesday can be used to satisfy demand on Tuesday or Wednesday. However, because of the change of operations in production, all statues produced in a week must be shipped that week, i.e., there is never inventory on hand Monday morning. Because of increased handling costs, it costs $0.25 to carry an A and $0.30 to carry a B in inventory from one day to the next. A unit of lost demand results in an all-inclusive penalty cost of $2 for a unit of A on Monday, $4 on Tuesday, and $5 on Wednesday. The per unit penalty costs for B are $5 on Monday, $10 on Tuesday, and $11 on Wednesday. Painters are paid $10 per hour of regular time and $15 per hour of overtime.

Demand varies significantly at Bumles. Management is considering two generic demand patterns.

Pre-Christmas Rush

	M	T	W
A	1500	1000	150
B	240	90	1100

After-Christmas Slump

	M	T	W
A	240	48	64
B	160	32	64

Bill Bumle, the Executive V.P., notes that A's yield a contribution of 21/0.5 = $42 per labor hour, whereas B's yield a contribution of 30/0.75 = $40 per labor hour. He also notes that the penalty for lost sales increases as the week goes on. He concludes that Bumles should first satisfy all demand for A's starting with Wednesday, then Tuesday, then Monday, and then use any leftover capacity to produce B's.

Specific Questions

1. Comment on the approach suggested by Bill Bumle.
2. Ignoring integrality conditions (i.e., allowing the possibility of fractional values of all decision variables), create an LP model that will schedule painters and production in such a way as to maximize revenue minus cost, where cost equals labor plus penalty and inventory-carrying costs. The model should be correct for any set of demands. In your formulation the first six constraints should be:

(i) $DAM =$
(ii) $DAT =$
⋮
(vi) $DBW =$

where *DAM* is the demand for A's on Monday, etc.

Thus, to solve the model for any set of demands one must provide only the RHSs for these constraints. In your formulation of the model, pay attention to relationships between production, sales, lost sales, demand, and inventory on any particular day. For example,

demand on day t = sales on t + lost sales on t

3. What are the decision variables? Define them carefully.

4. Show the formulation and briefly describe the purpose of each constraint.

For the above two specific demand patterns, solve the model. Then, in terms that would be understood by a general manager, state

5. How many items of what to produce each day.

6. How to schedule as many of the painters as you use, e.g., schedule 14.3 painters to work a Monday/Tuesday schedule, etc.

7. How many hours of overtime to use each day.

8. How much inventory of each product to carry each day.

9. How many units of lost sales to have each day.

10. Use your solution to answer the following question: Assume that a year consists of 32 weeks of pre-Christmas rush demand and 18 weeks of after-Christmas slump demand. If Bumles wants each of the 45 painters to work an equal number of weeks, how many weeks will each painter work?

Additional Considerations

[The questions in this section should be answered by using the model created in Question 2, with new parameters and performing additional analysis as needed.]

The painters' union has suggested a contract with a guaranteed annual wage (GAW) provision. In particular, this agreement specifies that a painter must be paid at least $11,500 per year for work on hand-painted statues. If, at the end of the year, the amount earned is less than $11,500, the firm simply gives the painter a check to make up the difference. Bumles plans to use all 45 painters even if the GAW provision is not accepted, but if it is all 45 painters will earn at least $11,500 per year.

To estimate the effect of this proposal on the Bumles operation, Bill assumes that 30 weeks of the 50-week year will have pre-Christmas rush demands, and the other 20 weeks will have the demand schedule shown below.

	M	T	W
A	240	48	300
B	160	32	200

He also assumes that a detailed schedule can be worked out so that each painter earns the same pay during a year. Based on your LP model and Bill's assumptions

11. What is Bumles' total annual profit without the GAW provision?

12. Does your solution to Question 11 satisfy the GAW provision? What effect will accepting the GAW provision have on Bumles' profitability (increase, decrease, or no effect)? Show the calculations to support your answers. There is no need to solve another LP at this point.

13. How much would average wages have to be in the low-demand weeks for the annual wage to be $11,500? For the low-demand weeks, formulate an LP that Bumles could use to find a production plan that would meet the GAW provision. Present a justification for your model and solve it.

14. Suppose the GAW provision is accepted. How much would Bumles save per year by using the plan found in Question 13 compared with the plan of Question 11 where additional payments would have to be made to the painters at the end of the year?

Sensitivity Questions

[These questions refer to the models you created to answer Questions 1–10.]

15. In the current solution to the pre-Christmas

problem, if we combine regular and overtime pay then each painter is paid $280/week. If another painter should become available, what is the maximum weekly amount that Bumles should pay him or her?

16. Suppose that, in the pre-Christmas problem, the demand for A on Monday increases by 10 units. What happens to the OV?

17. Answer Question 16 for the post-Christmas problem.

18. What is responsible for the major difference in the answers to Questions 16 and 17?

19. Suppose that, in the pre-Christmas problem, management's recent experience calls for an adjustment in the penalty cost for unsatisfied demand for A on Monday. The new value is set at $3. What happens to the optimal solution and the OV?

20. In Question 19, suppose the new value is reset to $4. What is the effect on the optimal solution and the OV? (Give the best answer you can based on the computer output.)

21. Suppose that, in the pre-Christmas problem, the selling price of A is reduced to $15 and B is reduced to $20. Can you give a bound on the new OV?

Video Case

You Are What Your Dinner Eats

Agriculture, certainly the most important of all industries, is probably the oldest as well. Perhaps for this reason, growing the food we eat has long been thought of as a highly conservative activity, little changed from the practices of past centuries. Today, however, as fast-increasing populations put ever-greater pressure on our food supply, this "traditional" industry has become more and more dependent on the contributions of modern science. Geneticists develop hardy, high-yielding strains of crops and breeds of animals; chemists produce fertilizers to promote the growth of crops and pesticides to preserve them from parasites; agronomists study farming methods that conserve precious water and topsoil. One way to measure the importance of these efforts is to note that in 1820 one farmer raised enough food to feed four people. Today, one farmer raises enough to feed 31 people.

Among the areas of agriculture that have benefited from scientific study is animal nutrition. Proper nutrition is crucial to animal productivity: It influences birth rates, growth rates, fat levels, longevity, and the ability to produce healthy offspring. Appropriate nutrition depends on the ingredients in a wide variety of possible feeds. Are you surprised to learn that the products currently used as animal feed include dry distillers grain, palm oil pellets, citrus pulp pellets, and marigold petals? All of these commodities except the marigold petals, which are used as a colorant in chicken feed, are byproducts of other manufacturing processes. (Distillers grain, for example, comes from the producers of ethyl alcohol and various alcoholic beverages.) These commodities are an inexpensive source of animal nutrition. Currently, approximately 80% of cow fodder in one European country is derived from materials other than whole grain.

Questions

The video deals with an experimental approach to finding good diets for pigs. In Chapter 2 of this text, Example 2 (Section 2.9) also considers a diet problem. The following questions explore the compatibility of these two approaches and the ways in which both might be used by someone who raises pigs for market.

1. Consider the relationship between the experimental results and the LP model discussed in Chapter 2. What information is generated by the experiments? How well can this information be used in the LP model? What additional work might be required to apply the model to the experimental results?
2. Discuss the challenges of implementing the research results on an individual farm.

CHAPTER

6

Linear Programming: The Simplex Method

APPLICATION CAPSULE

Nipped in the Bud: The Simplex Algorithm Helps the Maine Forest Service Fight a Parasite

The spruce budworm is the most destructive pest of the spruce-fir forests of North America. Since 1972, the Maine Forest Service has been conducting an aerial spraying campaign over 5,000,000 acres of severely infested forests. Finding the most economical way of performing the spraying is a complex problem. The infected area is first divided into 250 to 300 blocks. Different sprays may be used on different areas. Moreover, several kinds of planes are available, each with its own characteristics of range and spraying ability. These planes can be based at up to eight airfields scattered throughout the region. Finally, the window of time in which the spraying must be done is rather restrictive, owing to the life cycle of the budworm and the times of day when spraying can be effectively accomplished.

This problem would seem to be a natural candidate for integer programming (discussed in Chapter 8), in that the decision variables of which airports to use and which aircraft to assign to each are clearly integers (whole numbers). However, an attempt to create an IP for this problem produced a model that was too large and complex to be practical. An alternative approach was developed in which the problem was split into two parts. First, the planners selected various combination of airfields and aircraft that seemed plausible on the basis of experience and common sense. (For the choice of airfields, political and logistic considerations also entered into the decision.) Then, each set of airfield/aircraft assignments, or *scenario,* was evaluated with an LP model to determine how the flying time of each aircraft (a continuous variable) should be allocated to the various blocks so as to minimize total cost. The LP model thus made it possible to compare the costs of alternative scenarios quickly and in a consistent manner.

The model itself included two types of constraints. One set dealt with the amount of time needed for spraying each block. The second set dealt with the available flying time for each plane. The model, consisting of about 750 variables and 300 constraints, was solved using a revised simplex algorithm written in FORTRAN.

The results of the model had several important implications. Obviously, they yielded a detailed operating plan for the scenario selected. Moreover, the project staff relied heavily on the results in preparing bid specifications for contracting aircraft and crews, which together accounted for one-third of the total cost of the program. With the help of the model they were able to produce a more efficient spraying plan, which led to a lower bid cost. (Previous projects, it turned out, had recommended 20% more aircraft than were necessary.)

The model also allowed planners to examine a number of interesting "what-if" scenarios. For example, they were able to analyze the effect of closing a particular airfield and constructing a new airfield in a more advantageous location. The model suggested that the savings in operating costs might well justify this action.

*Rumpf, Melachrinoudis, and Rumpf, "Improving Efficiency in a Forest Pest Control Spray Program," *Interfaces*, Vol. 15, No. 5 (Sept.–Oct. 1985).

6.1 Introduction

Many students think that because the word "simple" is in "simplex" that this method should be simple. WRONG! However, it doesn't have to be made excessively difficult either.

In Chapter 3 we studied the graphical method for solving an LP in two decision variables. The geometric presentation was useful in exploring important general properties of the LP model. However, since most real-world problems contain more than two decision variables, the graphical method is not generally applicable. Such problems are usually solved by using the *simplex method,* or *simplex algorithm*[1] (or some variation thereof). This method, which is described in this chapter, was created by George Dantzig in the late 1940s. Since then Dantzig and others have advanced its development, especially for special applications, some of which will be studied in later chapters.

Overview of the simplex method

There are many variations of the simplex algorithm. Some try to find a feasible and an optimal solution simultaneously while others "crash" an initial feasible solution and then are concerned only with optimality. Each code has its advantages and disadvantages, depending on the structure of the LP model.

The **simplex method** can be summarized briefly as follows: It is a systematic algebraic way of examining the corners (also called **vertices,** or **extreme points**) of an LP constraint set in search of an optimal solution. In particular, the algorithm first seeks an initial corner. This step is called **phase I.** If the problem is *inconsistent,* phase I will discover this fact. Otherwise, the algebraic representation of an initial corner is found, and phase I is complete. Then the algorithm proceeds to move along the constraint set from corner to *adjacent* corner. As we shall see, each corner of the LP constraint set can be represented algebraically as a particular kind of solution to a set of linear equations. Different solutions are generated in such a way as to produce a sequence of adjacent corners. Each move in the sequence (from corner to adjacent corner) is called an **iteration,** or **pivot,** and the move involves a manipulation on a linear system. The simplex algorithm is designed in such a way that the objective function will not decrease (increase) for a Max (Min) model and will generally increase (decrease) at each successive corner in the sequence. If the problem is unbounded, the algorithm will discover this during its execution. The mathematics of the uphill (or downhill for a Min model) move from one corner to an adjacent corner will be expressed in terms of a *pivoting operation* on a tableau of data. When an optimal corner has been reached, the algorithm recognizes this fact

[1]An *algorithm* is a repetitive mathematical procedure designed to solve a particular problem, such as the algorithm for long division, or for taking square roots. In later chapters a variety of other algorithms are given for solving various models.

and terminates. Optimal solutions to both the primal and dual problems are provided.

From the description above, you can see that linear equations, and solutions to linear equations, play an important role. To understand the algorithm clearly, it is necessary to study this topic. It will occupy our attention in Sections 6.3 through 6.6. In previous chapters you learned a great deal about the geometric representation of LP models. In order to deepen your understanding of the current material, we will relate, whenever possible, the algebraic approach of this chapter to the geometry with which you are already familiar.

At the heart of the simplex algorithm is the algebraic representation of corners of the feasible region. We shall develop this representation in the context of a problem already encountered in Chapter 2.

6.2 The Astro/Cosmo Problem Revisited

The Astro/Cosmo model was presented as Example 1 in Section 2.8. The annotated model is

Max $20A + 10C$	(profit)
s.t. $A + 2C \le 120$	(labor constraint, department A)
$A + C \le 90$	(labor constraint, department B)
$A \le 70$	(Astro production line capacity)
$C \le 50$	(Cosmo production line capacity)
$A \ge 0, \quad C \ge 0$	
where A = units of Astro to be produced	
C = units of Cosmo to be produced	

We do not have the mathematics to solve m inequalities in n variables. Thus, we must change inequalities into equalities and set n-m variables to zero in order to solve m equalities in m unknowns.

The graphical representation of this problem is shown in Figure 6.1. Our first goal is to obtain an algebraic representation of the corners of the feasible region. To do this, the problem must first be converted to the equivalent standard equality constraint form. This is accomplished by adding a nonnegative slack variable to each $\le$ constraint and converting the $\le$ to =. In this way we obtain the problem

Max $20A + 10C$

s.t. $A + 2C + s_1 = 120$		(department A)	**(6.1)**
$A + C + s_2 = 90$		(department B)	**(6.2)**
$A + s_3 = 70$		(Astro capacity)	**(6.3)**
$C + s_4 = 50$		(Cosmo capacity)	**(6.4)**

Note that this problem has four equality constraints in the six variables A, C, s_1, s_2, s_3, and s_4. At the onset of our discussion we want to focus on the equations in the standard equality constraint form of the LP model. For convenience these are referred to as the **original equations.** We know from Chapter 5 that every nonnega-

The "original equations

Note that the two nonnegativity constraints are also represented as equalities (the two axes). Thus, the optimal solution will be one of the feasible intersections (labeled I–VI). On the graph we are solving two equations in two variables, but in algebra (equations 6.1–6.4) we need to solve 4 equations in 4 unknowns (2 variables must = 0).

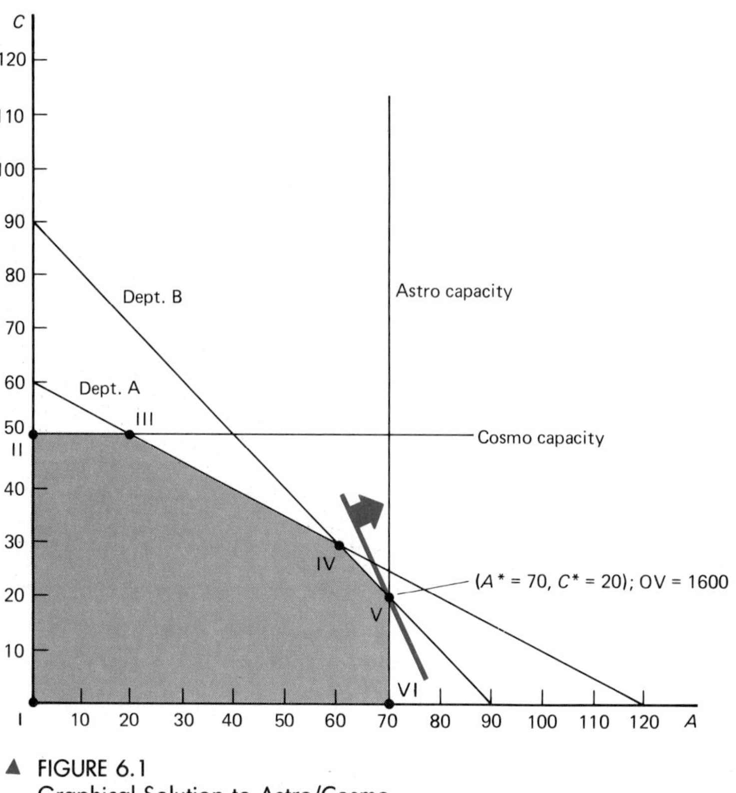

▲ FIGURE 6.1
Graphical Solution to Astro/Cosmo

tive solution to these equations corresponds to a point in the feasible region, and vice versa. In particular, we need to identify the nonnegative solutions that correspond to the constraint set corners.

6.3 Types of Solutions to the Original Equations

Previously, the term *solution* has been used on occasion to denote a solution to the LP. From this point on we must be more precise with this term. By *solution,* we shall mean *a solution to the original equations.* The LP solution is often referred to in the literature as an **optimal solution.** Henceforth we shall conform to this usage. Thus, a solution to the LP problem will be termed an *optimal solution;* the unqualified term *solution* will refer to any set of values for the variables that satisfy the original equations.

For our purposes, four types of solutions (in addition to optimal solutions) must be distinguished. These are *solutions, feasible solutions, basic solutions,* and *basic feasible solutions.*

Solutions

The term **solution** simply refers to *any* set of values for the six variables (A, C, s_1, s_2, s_3, s_4) that satisfy equations (6.1) through (6.4), *ignoring the nonnegativity conditions.* In this problem there are an *infinite* number of solutions. One can see this in a variety of ways. For example, by a simple rearrangement of (6.1)–(6.4) we can solve for A, C, s_1, and s_2 in terms of s_3 and s_4 as follows:

$$
\begin{aligned}
A + 2C + s_1 \quad\quad &= 120 && (6.5)\\
A + \ \ C \quad\quad + s_2 &= \ \ 90 && (6.6)\\
A \quad\quad\quad\quad\quad &= \ \ 70 - s_3 && (6.7)\\
C \quad\quad\quad &= \ \ 50 - s_4 && (6.8)
\end{aligned}
$$

We usually assume nonnegativity conditions in any LP model and especially in any LP computer code. However, some codes will allow you to specify certain variables as "free" (allowed to be negative). In this Astro/Cosmo example, negative values for variables would not make sense.

Equations (6.5)–(6.8), which are equivalent to (6.1)–(6.4), show that we can find a solution to the original system by arbitrarily setting s_3 and s_4 equal to any values, then solving for A, C, s_1, and s_2. For example, if $s_3 = s_4 = 0$, we see that ($A = 70$, $C = 50$, $s_1 = -50$, $s_2 = -30$, $s_3 = 0$, $s_4 = 0$) is a solution to the original equations. In a similar way it is clear that s_3 and s_4 could be arbitrarily set in an infinite number of ways, and (6.5)–(6.8) would determine a solution to the original equations.

How many solutions are there?

In the general LP in standard equality constraint form there will be m equality constraints in n variables, with $m < n$. In this setting, (1) either there will be no solution (in which case the LP is infeasible), or (2) there will be an infinite number of solutions. This is illustrated by considering two linear equations in three unknowns. From a geometric point of view, the two equations represent two planes in three-dimensional space. If the planes do not intersect (which implies that they are parallel) the equations have no solution. Otherwise, the planes must intersect, which means that either they coincide or they determine a line. In either case there are infinitely many points in the intersection, which means that the two equations have an infinite number of solutions.

Feasible Solutions

The term **feasible solutions** refers to solutions that are *nonnegative,* which means that the values of all the variables (decision variables, slacks, and surpluses) must be nonnegative. In other words, a feasible solution satisfies *all the constraints and the nonnegativity conditions of the model.* From the geometric point of view, a feasible solution to Astro/Cosmo is one that corresponds to a point in the shaded region of Figure 6.1.

Basic Solutions

The third type of solution is called a **basic solution.** We first define this concept in the Astro/Cosmo context. There are four equations and six variables in this problem. We used (6.5)–(6.8) to show that this set of equations will have an infinite number of solutions. We shall now focus on a particular kind of solution, obtained by setting $s_3 = s_4 = 0$ in (6.5)–(6.8). Note that when we do this we are left with four equations in four unknowns, and the solution to this square system, namely ($A = 70$, $C = 50$, $s_1 = -50$, $s_2 = -30$) is *unique* (meaning that with $s_3 = s_4 = 0$, there is *one and only one* set of values for the remaining variables that will satisfy the equations).

Here are four equations in six variables. To find a solution, we can set two of the variables to zero, allowing us to solve four equations in four unknowns.

In general, in (6.1)–(6.4), if any two variables are set equal to zero, they are, in principle, eliminated from the equations, leaving us with four rather than six variables. We shall see that *when certain pairs of variables are set equal to zero, the resulting system of equations (four equations in four unknowns) will have a unique solution.* Indeed, we have just shown that (s_3, s_4) is such a pair. This property cannot be guaranteed for all pairs, for the resulting 4×4 system may have no solutions or infinitely many solutions. However, when there *is* in fact a unique solution, the solution obtained thereby is called a basic solution. The two variables that were set equal to zero are called **nonbasic variables,** or sometimes, a **nonbasic set** (of variables). The remaining variables that can be solved for uniquely are called the **basic variables,** or sometimes, a **basic set** (of variables). Also, the set of basic variables is often referred to as a **basis.** Thus, we have shown that A, C, s_1, and s_2 are a basic set of variables, and that s_3 and s_4 constitute a nonbasic set.

As another example, let us set the pair of variables (s_1, s_3) equal to zero (i.e., let $s_1 = 0$, and $s_3 = 0$). Doing this, the original equations (6.1)–(6.4) reduce to the following 4×4 system:

$$\begin{aligned} A + 2C \quad\quad\quad &= 120 \\ A + \quad C + s_2 \quad &= \ \ 90 \\ A \quad\quad\quad\quad\quad &= \ \ 70 \\ C \quad\quad + s_4 &= \ \ 50 \end{aligned}$$

There is a *unique* (one and only one) solution to these equations, namely

$$A = 70, \qquad C = 25, \qquad s_2 = -5, \qquad s_4 = 25$$

Consequently, since this solution to the 4×4 system is unique, we say that

$$A = 70, \qquad C = 25, \qquad s_2 = -5, \qquad s_4 = 25, \qquad s_1 = 0, \qquad s_3 = 0$$

is a basic solution. The nonbasic variables are those that were set equal to zero, namely s_1 and s_3. The basic variables are A, C, s_2, and s_4, and these variables are said to form a basis. Note that *in the basic solution the values of both the basic and the nonbasic variables appear.*

How many basic solutions are there?

We have just seen two examples of basic solutions to the Astro/Cosmo equations (remember, we are for the time being ignoring the nonnegativity conditions and considering only the original equations). Since there are six variables in the original Astro/Cosmo equations,

$$\binom{6}{2} = \frac{6!}{4!\,2!} = \frac{6 \cdot 5}{2} = 15$$

possible pairs of variables can be formed.[2] Conceivably, then, there could be 15 basic solutions. However, only 13 basic solutions exist; these are represented in Figure 6.2 by heavy dots. To see why this occurs, note in Figure 6.2 that the pair $(s_3 = 0, A = 0)$ is *not* part of a basic solution. From the geometric point of view, this is because the lines in Figure 6.2 determined by $s_3 = 0$ and $A = 0$ are parallel. Hence, they do not intersect, which means that the original equations have *no solution* when $s_3 = 0$ and $A = 0$. This is also easily seen algebraically. If we set $A = 0$ and $s_3 = 0$, the original equations (6.1) through (6.4) reduce to four equations in four unknowns. One of the equations, namely (6.3), becomes

$$0 = 70$$

which shows that the resulting system is inconsistent.

Similar comments apply when we consider the pair $(s_4 = 0, C = 0)$. Thus two of the 15 possible pairs are eliminated, and we are left with 13 basic solutions.

For 100 variables and 20 constraints, there are $\binom{100}{20} \approx 10^{20}$ possible basic solutions. If a computer could solve a million of these 20 equations in 20 variables each second, it would take several million years to find the optimal solution by investigating each possibility. Thus, there must be some way to look at only a few of these if we hope to find the optimal solution within a lifetime!

[2]The symbol $\binom{6}{2}$ denotes the number of distinct pairs that can be taken out of six items. The factorial symbol ! is defined by $n! = n(n-1)(n-2)\cdots 1$. It is a convention that $0! = 1$. In general,

$$\binom{r}{s} = \frac{r!}{(r-s)!\,(s!)}$$

Also, it is true that

$$\binom{r}{s} = \binom{r}{r-s}$$

If there is no feasible area, then there will be no basic feasible solution. The best of the basic feasible solutions (b.f.s.) is the optimal solution.

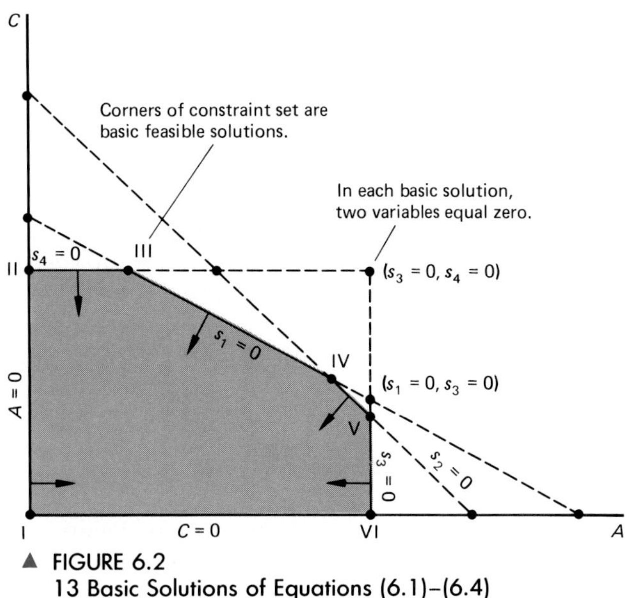

▲ FIGURE 6.2
13 Basic Solutions of Equations (6.1)–(6.4)

What we have just illustrated with Astro/Cosmo is the following general result:

A general result concerning basic solutions

Consider m simultaneous linear equations in n unknowns, with $m < n$. Either there is no solution or there are infinitely many solutions. In the latter case, *certain sets* (possibly all $\binom{n}{n-m}$, which equals $\binom{n}{m}$ sets) of $n - m$ of the unknowns can be set equal to zero, and the resulting square system of m equations in m unknowns will have a unique solution.[3] Any set for which this is true provides what is termed a *basic solution.* The $n - m$ variables that were set to zero are called *nonbasic variables.* The remaining m variables are called *basic variables.* These m variables are said to form a *basis.* The term *basic solution* encompasses the values of *all* the variables, the nonbasic variables (which are all zero), and the basic variables (each of which may be positive, negative, or zero).

Basic Feasible Solutions

The fourth, and for our purposes most important, type of solution is called a **basic feasible solution.** Recall from above that a feasible solution is a solution that satisfies all nonnegativity conditions of the model. Hence, *a basic feasible solution is, simply, a basic solution that is also feasible,* that is, *all* of whose variables are nonnegative. In a basic solution, by definition, the nonbasic variables are always at the value zero. Hence, *a basic solution is a basic feasible solution if and only if all the basic variables have nonnegative values* (which means, as a special case, that some of them could be zero). If we look once more at Figure 6.2, we see that of the 13 basic solutions, only 6 are basic feasible, namely those labeled I through VI. We also see the striking fact that these are the corners of the Astro/Cosmo constraint set. In other words, we have found the algebraic representation of corners, which is what we had set out to do. This equivalence of basic feasible solutions and corners is the topic to be discussed next.

[3]To give a complete theoretic characterization of these sets requires the notion of linear independence, which takes us too far astray for our purposes.

6.4 Basic Feasible Solutions and Extreme Points

In this section we wish to examine further the relationship between the corners of the feasible set (a geometric concept) and basic feasible solutions (an algebraic concept). In general, for an LP in standard equality constraint form with m constraints (equations) and n unknowns, we learned in Chapter 5 that the number of positive variables (including slack and surplus) at any corner is *equal to or less than m.* Let us consider these two possibilities in turn.

Nondegenerate Corner

In the first case, the number of positive variables is exactly m. This is, by the definition given in Chapter 5, a nondegenerate corner. We can illustrate the important features of this case by referring to Figure 6.2, where the corners are labeled I through VI. First note that all of those corners are nondegenerate. Now consider any one of the corners—IV, for example. Since this point lies on constraints (6.1) and (6.2), we know that s_1 and $s_2 = 0$ at point IV. This fact uniquely determines the values of the other variables (i.e., $A = 60$, $C = 30$, $s_3 = 10$, $s_4 = 20$).

Since this corner corresponds to a solution with two variables at the value zero, and the others uniquely determined, it is a basic feasible solution to the original equations. Since the corner is nondegenerate, the basic feasible solution is termed **nondegenerate.** At any nondegenerate corner, such as IV, there is only one set of nonbasic variables (e.g., s_1 and s_2) and one set of basic variables (e.g., A, C, s_3, and s_4).

Degenerate Corner

In the second case, the number of positive variables is less than m. This is, by definition, a degenerate corner. In this case the corner also corresponds to a basic feasible solution, but there will be more than one set of nonbasic (and hence basic) variables at such a corner.[4]

An Example of Degeneracy. Since the corner is degenerate, the corresponding basic feasible solution is also termed **degenerate.** This is illustrated by the feasible region for the inequalities:

$$\begin{aligned} x + y &\le 10 \\ x \quad\; &\le 5 \\ y &\le 5 \\ x, y &\ge 0 \end{aligned}$$

[4]For this reason, some expositions state that "more than one basic feasible solution is associated with a degenerate corner." We find this potentially confusing, since any corner, degenerate or nondegenerate corresponds to a *unique solution* to the original equations. In the nondegenerate case there is a single basic set associated with this solution. In the degenerate case, there are multiple basic sets, all associated with the same solution.

Converting to equalities, we obtain

$$\begin{aligned} x + y + s_1 \quad\quad\quad\quad &= 10 \\ x \quad\quad + s_2 \quad\quad &= 5 \\ y \quad\quad + s_3 &= 5 \\ x, y, s_1, s_2, s_3 &\geq 0 \end{aligned}$$

The geometric representation of the feasible set is shown in Figure 6.3. We note that, since corner A lies on the first, second, and third constraints, we have at that corner $s_1 = 0$, $s_2 = 0$, and $s_3 = 0$. Plugging these values into the equations implies that $x = 5$ and $y = 5$. Thus, corner A corresponds to the solution ($x = 5, y = 5, s_1 = 0, s_2 = 0, s_3 = 0$). Since there are only two positive variables and three constraints, corner A is degenerate. It is also a basic feasible solution since when, for example, s_1 and s_2 are set to zero, the values of the remaining variables are uniquely determined. Figure 6.4 shows the basic and nonbasic sets associated with the corners in Figure 6.3.

Note that there are

$$\binom{5}{2} = \frac{5 \cdot 4}{2 \cdot 1} = 10$$

basic solutions on this graph. Two are impossible due to the parallel lines, and corner A is really three (3) points given by the three sets of 2 equations in 2 unknowns:

1. ($x = 5, x + y = 10$)
2. ($x = 5, y = 5$)
3. ($x + y = 10, y = 5$)

These points lie on each other and are unseen by the nonmathematical eye (see *Flatland*, Edwin A. Abbot, Dover Publications, Inc. New York, 1952, for further explanation).

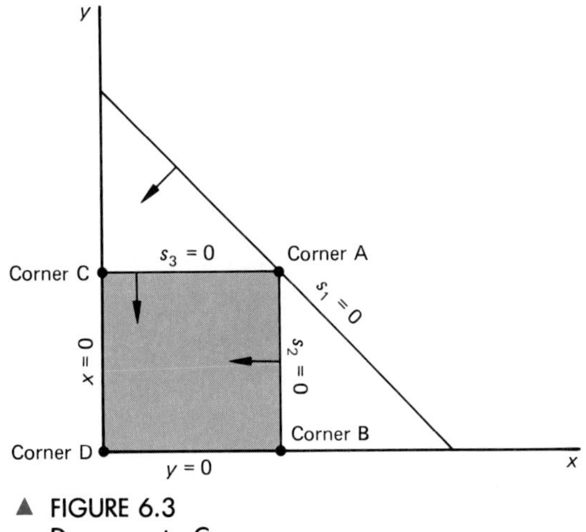

▲ FIGURE 6.3
Degenerate Corner

What Figure 6.4 reveals is that at the degenerate corner A there are three different sets of basic variables. Note that in each such set one of the basic variables has a zero value. At each of the other, nondegenerate, corners (B, C, and D) there is a unique set of basic variables. Moreover, the basic variables at corners B, C, and D are all positive. This is an illustration of the fact that, for a general model with m constraints, a degenerate basic feasible solution has $<m$ positive variables. A nondegenerate basic feasible solution has exactly m positive variables.

▼ FIGURE 6.4
Basic and Nonbasic Variables at the Corners of Figure 6.3.

NONBASIC VARIABLES	BASIC VARIABLES AND VALUES	CORNER ON FIGURE 6.3
x, y	$s_1 = 10, s_2 = 5, s_3 = 5$	D
y, s_2	$x = 5, s_1 = 5, s_3 = 5$	B
s_1, s_2	$x = 5, y = 5, s_3 = 0$	A
s_1, s_3	$x = 5, y = 5, s_2 = 0$	A
s_2, s_3	$x = 5, y = 5, s_1 = 0$	A
x, s_3	$y = 5, s_2 = 5, s_1 = 5$	C

The Correspondence Property

It turns out that, in fact, the correspondence between corners and basic feasible solutions is one to one. The general property is summarized as follows:

1. *Associated with every basic feasible solution to the original equations* is a unique corner (extreme point) of the constraint set. If the basic feasible solution is *nondegenerate,* so is the corner, and there is a unique set of basic variables associated with the corner. These are the positive variables at the corner. If the basic feasible solution is *degenerate,* so is the corner, and there is more than one set of basic variables associated with the corner. In each set, some basic variables will have a value of zero.
2. *Associated with every corner of the constraint set* is a unique basic feasible solution. If the corner is degenerate, so is the basic feasible solution, and there will be more than one associated set of basic variables. If the corner is nondegenerate, so is the basic feasible solution, and there will be exactly one associated set of basic variables.

The correspondence noted above is important because it ties together the geometry and the algebra. We know from geometric analysis that if an LP problem has an optimal solution, there is an optimal corner. This observation, plus the fact that every corner corresponds to a basic feasible solution, permits us to state:

If an LP has an optimal solution, there is a basic feasible solution that is optimal.

The simplex algorithm searches among basic feasible solutions to find an optimal solution. In the next sections we see how this is done.

6.5 Transformed Equations

Transformed equations corresponding to a corner

We have learned thus far that every constraint set corner (i.e., the values of the variables at the corner) is a basic feasible solution to the original equations. The simplex method will search corners by moving from one basic feasible solution to another. To accomplish this, the original equations will be recast into different but equivalent representations. In particular, consider the feasible region for any LP model in standard equality constraint form. Corresponding to any corner of this feasible region is at least one (exactly one if the corner is nondegenerate) set of basic and nonbasic variables. Consider any such corner. Select any basic and associated nonbasic set corresponding to this corner. The original equations can be algebraically transformed into the following equivalent form:

Each basic variable appears in one and only one equation and, in that equation, its coefficient is +1 **(6.9)**

Only constant terms are on the right side of the equations, and these constant terms are nonnegative **(6.10)**

Such a representation of the original equations will be denoted as a set of **transformed equations** corresponding to the corner under consideration.

An illustration

Let us illustrate these sets of transformed equations by referring to corners I and II in Figure 6.2. The original equations for Astro/Cosmo are

These equations can be rewritten in terms of A and C (which are initially set to zero):

$S_1 = 120 - A - 2C$
$S_2 = 90 - A - C$
$S_3 = 70 - A$
$S_4 = 50 - C$

This corresponds to corner I, where the nonbasic variables A and $C = 0$.

$$A + 2C + s_1 = 120 \quad (6.1)$$
$$A + C + s_2 = 90 \quad (6.2)$$
$$A + s_3 = 70 \quad (6.3)$$
$$C + s_4 = 50 \quad (6.4)$$

At corner I, the nonbasic variables are A and C (at corner I, $A = C = 0$). Hence, the basic variables are s_1, s_2, s_3, and s_4. Note that in (6.1)–(6.4) each basic variable appears in one and only one equation, and in that equation its coefficient is +1. Hence, (6.9) is satisfied. Similarly, you can see that (6.10) is satisfied. Thus, at corner I, (6.9) and (6.10) are satisfied by the original equations. What about corner II? We note that, at corner II, C, s_1, s_2, and s_3 are basic. We need to transform the original equations so that (6.9) and (6.10) are satisfied in terms of this basic set. We can proceed as follows: From (6.4) we obtain

$$C = 50 - s_4 \quad (6.11)$$

Similarly, (6.3) yields

$$s_3 = 70 - A \quad (6.12)$$

Substituting in (6.1) the expression for C given by (6.11) yields

$$A + 2(50 - s_4) + s_1 = 120$$

or

$$A + s_1 - 2s_4 = 20 \quad (6.13)$$

Using the same approach on (6.2), we see that

$$A + (50 - s_4) + s_2 = 90$$

or

$$A + s_2 - s_4 = 40 \quad (6.14)$$

Transformed equations for corner II

Thus, the transformed equations for the basic set at corner II are

Again these could be rewritten in terms of the basic variables:

$C = 50 - s_4$
$s_1 = 20 - A + 2s_4$
$s_2 = 40 - A + s_4$
$s_3 = 70 - A$

Now the nonbasic variables are A and s_4, and these equations correspond to corner II.

$$C + s_4 = 50 \quad (6.4)$$
$$A + s_3 = 70 \quad (6.3)$$
$$A + s_2 - s_4 = 40 \quad (6.14)$$
$$A + s_1 - 2s_4 = 20 \quad (6.13)$$

Although this set of equations does not "look like" the original set (6.1)–(6.4), they are indeed equivalent in the sense that they have precisely the same solutions. These transformed equations will reappear when we solve Astro/Cosmo with the simplex algorithm.

6.6 The Characterization of Adjacent Extreme Points

As already noted, the corners of the constraint set in Figure 6.2 are known as *extreme points.* There are six extreme points in this figure, which we have labeled as I through VI. Just as in the discussion in Chapter 5 on the geometry of the equality constraint model and as we did in Figure 6.4, we can with the aid of Figure 6.2 explicitly identify the positive variables and the zero variables at each corner (see Figure 6.5). Indeed, it is the corresponding zero variables that distinguish the different corners. For example, corner V is distinguished by the fact that at this point $s_2 = s_3 = 0$. These are the nonbasic variables at corner V. The basic variables at this corner, namely (s_1, s_4, A, C), are all positive. According to a previous definition, since there are four positive variables and four constraints in the model, this corner is nondegenerate.

The table simply summarizes the four basic variables that will be solved for each equation and the two nonbasic variables that will be on the right-hand side.

CORNER	NONBASIC VARIABLES	BASIC VARIABLES	POSITIVE COUNT
I	A, C	s_1, s_2, s_3, s_4	4
II	A, s_4	s_1, s_2, s_3, C	4
III	s_4, s_1	A, s_2, s_3, C	4
IV	s_1, s_2	A, s_4, s_3, C	4
V	s_2, s_3	A, s_4, s_1, C	4
VI	s_3, C	A, s_4, s_1, s_2	4

▲ FIGURE 6.5
Basic and Nonbasic Variables at the Corners

Exchanging a basic variable with a nonbasic variable

As already stated, the simplex algorithm will proceed by moving from corner to adjacent corner of the constraint set. The mathematics of this move, or pivot, is the essence of the algorithm. The mathematical procedure is based on an important fact. In moving, for example, from corner I to the adjacent corner II, you can see by comparing the two top rows of Figure 6.5 that the basic variable s_4 is exchanged with the nonbasic variable C (i.e., at corner II, C has become basic and s_4 has become nonbasic). Three of the four variables that were basic at corner I, namely s_1, s_2, and s_3, remain basic at corner II. One of the two variables that was nonbasic at corner I, namely A, remains nonbasic at corner II. Thus, there is a simple *exchange operation* in moving from corner I to corner II. You can verify that this fact characterizes the move between all adjacent corners in Figure 6.2. For example, in moving from corner III to adjacent corner IV, Figure 6.5 shows that the roles of s_2 and s_4 are exchanged.

We have now acquired all of the understanding necessary to apply the simplex method to Astro/Cosmo.

6.7 The Initial Solution

The first part of the simplex method, as mentioned earlier, is called phase I. Phase I *is designed to find a set of transformed equations corresponding to any initial corner of the constraint set.* In the Astro/Cosmo example, phase I is trivial, for we can arbitrarily select corner I in Figure 6.2 as the initial corner. As we have already noted, the transformed equations corresponding to corner I are precisely the original equations (6.1) through (6.4).

Tableau representation for Astro/Cosmo

A convenient way of representing the transformed equations corresponding to the initial corner is in the form of a *tableau.* For the Astro/Cosmo problem, taking corner I as the initial corner, the transformed equations are

$$A + 2C + s_1 = 120 \quad \textbf{(6.1)}$$

$$A + C + s_2 = 90 \quad \textbf{(6.2)}$$

$$A + s_3 = 70 \quad \textbf{(6.3)}$$

$$C + s_4 = 50 \quad \textbf{(6.4)}$$

The tableau representation of these equations is shown in Figure 6.6. Each row of the tableau represents an equation. The coefficient for each variable in the equation appears under the appropriate column in the tableau. The RHS appears under the VALUE column. Equations (6.1) through (6.4) are thus easily read from the tableau. The column headed BASIC VARIABLE simply identifies the basic set associated with these transformed equations. In particular, we see which variable is basic in each row. Thus, the first row of the tableau is read

$$1A + 2C + 1s_1 + 0s_2 + 0s_3 + 0s_4 = 120$$

BASIC VARIABLE	A	C	s_1	s_2	s_3	s_4	VALUE
s_1	1	2	1	0	0	0	120
s_2	1	1	0	1	0	0	90
s_3	1	0	0	0	1	0	70
s_4	0	1	0	0	0	1	50

▲ FIGURE 6.6
Tableau Representation of Transformed Equations at Corner I

The tableau representation was developed by mathematicians as a shorthand representation of the transformed equations. This format is useless for most human beings and professional computer programs. Most people need the equations in less abstract form, and computers need the information in a more compact manageable form. No one actually uses these tableaux in the real world. They are included to show students how the results could be found.

and this is precisely (6.1). Also, the BASIC VARIABLE column tells us that s_1 is the basic variable in the first equation. Read the remaining three rows of the tableau to verify that they represent (6.2), (6.3), and (6.4).

Given the initial corner of the feasible region and the associated tableau, phase I of the method is complete and phase II begins. In the first step of phase II we wish to move to an *adjacent* (and we emphasize *adjacent*) corner at which the value of the objective function is improved (in this case, since we are dealing with a Max model, we wish to increase the objective value). Note that at corner I the value of the objective function is zero.

From Figure 6.1 it is clear that either of the adjacent corners II or IV will give a higher value to the objective function. Moreover, this figure indicates that the path of adjacent corners, to the optimal solution (corner V), will be either the sequence I–II–III–IV–V or the sequence I–VI–V, depending on whether the first chosen is II or VI.[5] Figure 6.5 shows the sets of basic variables at any of the corners on the path. All of this information is visible from the geometric interpretation. Our goal now is to see how this information can be obtained algebraically, for remember that most

[5]Since by stipulation the values of the objective function must be increasing from corner to adjacent corner, it should be clear that previously visited corners cannot be encountered again.

real-world problems will not be two-dimensional and hence will not have nice geometric representations. Consequently, all aspects of their solution must be obtained by algebraic manipulations.

6.8 Improving the Solution: The Enter Variable

Let us now recall the definitions

$$
\begin{aligned}
A &= \text{units of Astros produced}\\
C &= \text{units of Cosmos produced}\\
s_1 &= \text{labor slack in department A}\\
s_2 &= \text{labor slack in department B}\\
s_3 &= \text{slack in Astro production capacity}\\
s_4 &= \text{slack in Cosmo production capacity}
\end{aligned}
$$

Nonbasic Columns

Our desire to increase the objective function will be well served by giving physical interpretations to the *nonbasic columns* of the tableau. By *nonbasic columns* we mean those columns headed by the nonbasic variables. Since in Figure 6.6 A and C are nonbasic, there are two nonbasic columns, namely

$$A \text{ column} = \begin{pmatrix} 1 \\ 1 \\ 1 \\ 0 \end{pmatrix}$$

$$C \text{ column} = \begin{pmatrix} 2 \\ 1 \\ 0 \\ 1 \end{pmatrix}$$

We shall see that these columns reveal certain specific information about the Astro/Cosmo production technology.

To explain this, let us rewrite the transformation equations from Figure 6.6 in the form

$$s_1 = 120 - A - 2C \tag{6.15}$$

$$s_2 = 90 - A - C \tag{6.16}$$

$$s_3 = 70 - A \tag{6.17}$$

$$s_4 = 50 - C \tag{6.18}$$

At corner I, $A = C = 0$, there is no production of either Astros or Cosmos. The values of the variables s_1, s_2, s_3, and s_4 at corner I are 120, 90, 70, and 50, respectively. Equation (6.15) tells us that if we maintain Cosmo production at the level zero and increase the production of Astros to 1 unit, then in order to satisfy our constraints

Incrementing A by 1

- s_1, labor slack in department A, will *decrease* by a unit to 119. Similarly, from (6.16), (6.17), and (6.18)
- s_2, labor slack in department B, will *decrease* by a unit to 89.
- s_3, slack in Astro production capacity, will *decrease* by a unit to 69.
- s_4, slack in Cosmo production capacity, will be unaffected and hence will remain at 50.

Now note that the data in the tableau (Figure 6.6) under column A are (1, 1, 1, 0). These data show the amount by which the current values of the basic variables must be *reduced* when (1) another unit of A is produced and (2) C is held at zero.

Incrementing C by 1

Let us now consider the changes in the current values of the basic variables that would be incurred if C were incremented a unit while holding A at the value zero. You can see from (6.15)–(6.18) that the respective *reductions* in s_1, s_2, s_3, and s_4 are 2, 1, 0, and 1. Thus, the data in the tableau under column C, namely (2, 1, 0, 1), show the amounts by which the current values of the basic variables must be reduced when (1) another unit of C is produced and (2) A is held at zero. Because of these interpretations, the data in the nonbasic column are often referred to by the term **substitution coefficients.**

Substitution coefficients

Effects on Objective Function

Let us now see how this relates to the objective function. The Astro/Cosmo objective function is

$$\text{profit} = 20A + 10C + 0s_1 + 0s_2 + 0s_3 + 0s_4 \tag{6.19}$$

The basic variables at corner I are (s_1, s_2, s_3, s_4). The coefficients in the objective function that correpond to these basic variables are (0, 0, 0, 0). These are called the **basic coefficients.** Thus, at corner I

Basic coefficients at corner I

$$\text{basic coefficients} = \begin{pmatrix} 0 \\ 0 \\ 0 \\ 0 \end{pmatrix}$$

Analysis of the A Column. Now suppose that C is held at zero and A is incremented a unit. We have seen that this will induce certain changes in the basic variables. That is, the values of the basic variables will be *reduced* by the coefficients in the A column, namely the amounts (1, 1, 1, 0). Ignoring the *direct effect* (on the objective function) of increasing the nonbasic variable A, and taking into account only the *indirect effect* of the induced changes in the basic variables, the objective function will be *reduced* by

$$(\text{basic coefficients}) \cdot (A \text{ column})$$

This is a convenient shorthand notation to denote the operation of "adding the products of the corresponding terms" of the two columns. Thus, we see that when A is incremented by a unit, with C held at zero,

Indirect effect on objective function

$$\begin{aligned} \textit{indirect} \text{ decrease in profit} &= (\text{basic coefficients}) \cdot (A \text{ column}) \\ &= 0(1) + 0(1) + 0(1) + 0(0) = 0 \\ &= \text{contribution due only to basic variable changes} \end{aligned}$$

Thus, in this case, the resultant changes in the basic variables will not change the objective function. Let us now take the change in A (the *direct effect*) into account.

You can see from (6.19) that if A is incremented by a unit, the *marginal contribution* to profit (i.e., not taking the indirect effects into account) will be to increase it by \$20. Thus, we have shown that *having one more unit of A in the solution would net us a gain of \$20.* In the language of economics this means that the **opportunity cost** of *not* having one more unit of A in the solution is

Opportunity cost for A

$$\begin{aligned} \text{opportunity cost} &= \text{potential gain} - \text{potential decrease} \\ &= \text{direct effect} - \text{indirect effect} \\ &= 20 - 0 = 20 \end{aligned}$$

Analysis of the C Column. Let us conduct the same analysis on the other nonbasic column of Figure 6.6, that headed by C. Since the column of substitution coefficients, the C column, is (2, 1, 0, 1), we see that incrementing C by a unit while holding A at zero gives

$$\begin{aligned} \text{indirect decrease in profit} &= (\text{basic coefficients}) \cdot (C \text{ column}) \\ &= 0(2) + 0(1) + 0(0) + 0(1) = 0 \\ &= \text{contribution due only to basic variable changes} \end{aligned}$$

Also, from (6.19) we see that incrementing C by a unit will have a *direct effect.* Namely, this will cause a marginal contribution to the objective value of +10. In this case, then,

Opportunity cost for C

$$\begin{aligned} \text{opportunity cost} &= \text{potential gain} - \text{potential decrease} \\ &= \text{direct effect} - \text{indirect effect} \\ &= 10 - 0 = 10 \end{aligned}$$

Having computed the current opportunity cost *for all the nonbasic variables,* we have completed the algebra required in our search for an adjacent corner at which the objective function will improve. Recall from our discussion of Figure 6.5 that when moving from any corner to an adjacent corner, it must be true that only one of the currently nonbasic variables can be made basic. In other words, at an adjacent corner all of the currently nonbasic variables will remain at zero except for one, which will be incremented. What we have done in the discussion above is compute the *per unit change* in the objective function as each of the nonbasic variables, A and C, is incremented one at a time with the other held at zero. The term *per unit change* means change in profit per unit increase in the nonbasic variable. This is precisely the opportunity cost. *It follows that a desirable adjacent corner can be reached by increasing any current nonbasic variable with a positive opportunity cost.*

The Enter Rule. This gives us the algebraic rule for perceiving adjacent corners at which the objective function will increase. It is called the **enter rule,** and the variable that becomes positive is called the **enter variable,** since it is the variable chosen to become basic (i.e., to enter the basis). For a general LP this rule can be stated:

> *Enter Rule:* **Increasing any nonbasic variable with a positive opportunity cost, keeping all other nonbasic variables at the value zero, will lead to an adjacent corner with a higher objective value. The variable chosen to be increased is called the enter variable. Usually, in order to have a systematic rule, the variable with the most positive opportunity cost is chosen to enter, but *any* variable with a positive opportunity cost will serve the purpose.**

In the Astro/Cosmo model we have thus computed the result that the geometry in Figure 6.1 has already revealed. A move to either corner VI (i.e., increasing A) or corner II (i.e., increasing *C*) will improve the objective function. Before moving on to the next corner, let us take a moment to show how the initial tableau can be slightly expanded so as to facilitate the opportunity cost computations.

6.9 The Simplex Tableau

With each *nonbasic column* of the tableau in Figure 6.6, let us associate a so-called z_j value defined as follows:

z_j the indirect decrease

z_j = *indirect decrease* in the value of the objective function induced by bringing into the solution one unit of the variable above the *j*th nonbasic column of the tableau, keeping all other nonbasic variables at zero

If we let c_j denote the coefficient in the objective function corresponding to the *j*th nonbasic variable in the model, then

$$\begin{aligned} c_j - z_j &= \text{direct effect} - \text{indirect effect} \\ &= \text{opportunity cost} \end{aligned}$$

For example, if we let *A* denote the first variable in the Astro/Cosmo model, then as we have computed in Section 6.8

$$\begin{aligned} z_1 &= \ \ 0 \\ c_1 &= 20 \\ c_1 - z_1 &= 20 = \text{opportunity cost} \end{aligned}$$

Similary, if we let *C* denote the second variable in the model, then

$$\begin{aligned} z_2 &= \ \ 0 \\ c_2 &= 10 \\ c_2 - z_2 &= 10 = \text{opportunity cost} \end{aligned}$$

To represent these quantities in the tableau format, we proceed as follows:

1. Add a new leftmost column to the tableau. This column explicitly shows the coefficients in the objective function associated with each basic variable.
2. Add a new row above the tableau. This row shows the coefficients of *all* the variables in the objective function (including slack and surplus variables with zero coefficients).
3. Append two new rows to the bottom of the tableau. The first is the z_j row. The second is the $c_j - z_j$ row. This is the opportunity cost row.

Filling in the z_j Row

Let us illustrate by completing the tableau shown in Figure 6.6 in the prescribed manner. We show a partially completed tableau in Figure 6.7. To fill in the z_j row we

BASIC COEFFICIENT	BASIC VARIABLE	20 A	10 C	0 s_1	0 s_2	0 s_3	0 s_4	VALUE
0	s_1	1	2	1	0	0	0	120
0	s_2	1	1	0	1	0	0	90
0	s_3	1	0	0	0	1	0	70
0	s_4	0	1	0	0	0	1	50
z_j								
$c_j - z_j$								

▲ FIGURE 6.7
Partially Completed Tableau at Corner I

use the data in Figure 6.7 as follows:

$$z_j = (\text{basic coefficients}) \cdot (j\text{th column of data})$$

Thus,

$$z_1 = 0(1) + 0(1) + 0(1) + 0(0) = 0$$
$$z_2 = 0(2) + 0(1) + 0(0) + 0(1) = 0$$
$$z_3 = 0(1) + 0(0) + 0(0) + 0(0) = 0$$
$$z_4 = 0(0) + 0(1) + 0(0) + 0(0) = 0$$
$$z_5 = 0(0) + 0(0) + 0(1) + 0(0) = 0$$
$$z_6 = 0(0) + 0(0) + 0(0) + 0(1) = 0$$

$z_j = c_j$ for basic variables

Although basic variables are never candidates for entry, notice that we have used the same equations to compute z_j values for the basic as well as the nonbasic columns. For basic variables the z_j value computed by this formula will always equal c_j, and $c_j - z_j$ will be zero. Thus, the calculations are innocuous, and it is merely for convenience of display that these entries are included in the tableau.

Calculating the Current Objective Value

Notice also that the objective value at the current corner is easily calculated from the expanded tableau. The values of the basic variables at the current corner are given by the VALUE column of the tableau. The remaining variables, which are nonbasic at the current corner, have the value zero. Consequently, they make no contribution to the current value of the objective function. This shows that

$$\text{current objective value} = (\text{basic coefficients}) \cdot (\text{values})$$
$$= 0(120) + 0(90) + 0(70) + 0(50) = 0$$

The c_j–z_j row

Finally, the above z_j values are used with the top row of c_j values to give

The c_j–z_j values show what will happen to the objective function for each unit increase in variable j.

$$c_1 - z_1 = 20 - 0 = 20$$
$$c_2 - z_2 = 10 - 0 = 10$$
$$c_3 - z_3 = 0 - 0 = 0$$

$$c_4 - z_4 = 0 - 0 = 0$$

$$c_5 - z_5 = 0 - 0 = 0$$

$$c_6 - z_6 = 0 - 0 = 0$$

The complete tableau at corner I is shown in Figure 6.8. Notice that the current objective function value is placed in the $c_j - z_j$ row under the VALUE column. In general, the term **simplex tableau** is used for such a tabular representation of the transformed equations plus an opportunity cost row. There is a simplex tableau corresponding to each corner of the feasible region.

Beginning at corner I, the simplex method will produce a sequence of tableaux having the form of Figure 6.8. Each such tableau will correspond to a corner of the feasible region, representing the transformed equations at that corner and the appropriate opportunity costs.

We have already discussed the enter rule, which says that, at corner I, either A or C can be chosen to enter. Although A is the variable with the most positive opportunity cost ($c_1 - z_1 = 20$), and hence might be the usual choice for entry, we shall for expository reasons choose to enter C into the basis. Geometrically, this will correspond in Figure 6.1 to a vertical move from corner I to corner II. Let us now examine the algebra associated with this move.

		20	10	0	0	0	0	
BASIC COEFFICIENT	**BASIC VARIABLE**	**A**	**C**	**s_1**	**s_2**	**s_3**	**s_4**	**VALUE**
0	s_1	1	2	1	0	0	0	120
0	s_2	1	1	0	1	0	0	90
0	s_3	1	0	0	0	1	0	70
0	s_4	0	1	0	0	0	1	50
	z_j	0	0	0	0	0	0	
	$c_j - z_j$	20	10	0	0	0	0	0

▲ FIGURE 6.8
Complete Tableau at Corner I

Since this is the first tableau used in the simplex method, it is called the **initial tableau.**

6.10 Keeping the Solution Feasible: The Exit Variable

We know from the corresponding value of $c_2 - z_2$, namely the value 10, that for each unit our enter variable C is incremented (holding the other nonbasic variable, A, at zero), the profit will increase by \$10. We wish to increase C as much as possible, in order to increase the objective function as much as possible, but at the same time we do not want to violate any of the constraints in the model. With this proviso, let us see just how much C can be increased.

What Is the Maximum Increase of *C*?

Recall that the first row of the current tableau (Figure 6.8) corresponds to the first constraint, (6.1), which is

$$A + 2C + s_1 = 120 \qquad \text{(department A)} \qquad \textbf{(6.1)}$$

We see that each Cosmo produced uses 2 hours of labor in department A. Therefore, if we produce zero Astros and C Cosmos we will use $2C$ hours of labor in department A. Since we have only 120 hours available (the RHS of [6.1]), the maximum possible value of C, considering the labor constraint in department A, is calculated by solving the equation

$$2C = 120$$

Thus, there is enough department A labor available to produce only 60 Cosmos.

Now consider the department B labor constraint given by the second row of the current tableau:

$$A + C + s_2 = 90 \qquad \text{(department B)} \qquad \textbf{(6.2)}$$

This shows that every Cosmo produced uses 1 hour of labor in department B. Thus, keeping Astro production at zero, the maximum number of Cosmos that could be produced while still satisfying the department B constraint is

$$C = 90$$

However, we know that it is impossible to produce 90 Cosmos because there is not enough labor available in department A. In fact, we saw that the department A labor constraint will allow a maximum of only 60 Cosmos to be produced. Thus, the value of $C = 60$ is the maximum production of Cosmos that will satisfy (6.1) and (6.2) simultaneously.

Proceeding with the remaining two rows in the body of the current tableau (those corresponding to constraints [6.3] and [6.4]), you should verify that (1) (6.3) places no constraint on the value of C, and (2) (6.4) permits a maximum value of $C = 50$. Thus, the value $C = 50$ is the largest value of C (keeping A at the value zero) that will simultaneously satisfy all four constraints.

Geometric Interpretation

Let us now make the geometric interpretation. It is seen in Figures 6.1 and 6.2 that as C is increased, keeping A at the value zero, we will move upward from corner I, along the C axis, until reaching corner II, at which A and s_4 are nonbasic and at which C will have the value 50. Thus, at corner II the variables C and s_4 have exchanged roles. The variable C was nonbasic at corner I; at corner II it is basic. The variable s_4 was basic at corner I; at corner II it is nonbasic. For this reason s_4 is termed the **exit variable.** The other basic and nonbasic variables at corner II are the same as at corner I (which is not to imply that their *values* are the same, for clearly some of the basic variables at the two corners have different values).

The exit variable

We now show how the exit variable, s_4, and the largest possible value of C, computed as 50 in the discussion above, can be read from the tableau in Figure 6.8. To see this, we again look at (6.15)–(6.18), which express the basic variables at corner I in terms of the nonbasic variables.

$$s_1 = 120 - A - 2C \tag{6.15}$$

$$s_2 = 90 - A - C \tag{6.16}$$

$$s_3 = 70 - A \tag{6.17}$$

$$s_4 = 50 - C \tag{6.18}$$

At corner I we have $A = 0$, and in moving vertically upward to corner II A will remain at the value zero, since for this nonbasic pair only C will be increased. Thus, since throughout this move we have $A = 0$, we can rewrite (6.15)–(6.18) as

$$s_1 = 120 - 2C \tag{6.15}$$

$$s_2 = 90 - C \tag{6.16}$$

$$s_3 = 70 \tag{6.17}$$

$$s_4 = 50 - C \tag{6.18}$$

You can see from these equations that in moving upward to corner II, as C gradually becomes positive the variable s_3 remains unchanged (from its value of 70 at corner I) and the variables s_1, s_2, and s_4 will decrease from their values at corner I (where $s_1 = 120$, $s_2 = 90$, $s_4 = 50$). You can also see that some simple algebra confirms our geometric observation that s_4 will be the first of these variables to hit zero. This is because

$$s_1 = 120 - 2C = 0 \text{ implies } C = \frac{120}{2} = 60 \tag{6.20}$$

$$s_2 = 90 - C = 0 \text{ implies } C = 90 \tag{6.21}$$

$$s_4 = 50 - C = 0 \text{ implies } C = 50 \tag{6.22}$$

Relations (6.20), (6.21), and (6.22) show that as C increases from the value zero the variable s_4 will be the first basic variable to become zero, and this will occur when $C = 50$. Now, we can see from (6.20)–(6.22) how the exit variable and new value of C can be read from Figure 6.8. Notice that at corner II, C must be the minimum of the three ratios

$$\left\{\frac{120}{2}, \frac{90}{1}, \frac{50}{1}\right\}$$

In Figure 6.8, these are the ratios of each number in the VALUE column to the corresponding number in the enter column (the C column) for which the number in the enter column is positive. That is, in (6.20) we compute the ratio of the first number in the VALUE column, namely 120, to the first number in the C column, namely 2; and similarly, for (6.21) and (6.22). For any row in which the enter column has a zero coefficient, such as the third row in the C column, which corresponds to (6.17), you can see that increasing C has no effect on the associated basic variable. That is, as C is increased (6.17) shows that the basic variable s_3 is unaffected. Also, it is not difficult to show that any row that has a negative entry in the enter column would have the property that the associated basic variable would *increase* as the enter variable increases. For example, if the first entry in the C column happened to be -2 instead of $+2$, the analog of (6.15) would be

$$s_1 = 120 - A + 2C$$

In this case it is clear that s_1 increases as C increases. Thus we need not consider either 0 entries or negative entries in the enter column.

The Exit Rule. These observations lead to the following **exit rule.**

> *Exit Rule:* **Consider the ratio of each number in the VALUE column to the corresponding number in the enter column, for which the number in the enter column is positive. The minimum ratio is the value of the enter variable at the next corner. The basic variable corresponding to the row with a minimum ratio is the exit variable.**

6.11 The Simplex Method Step by Step

Now that we have seen how to use the initial tableau, Figure 6.8, to determine algebraically the enter and exit variables, we must update the initial tableau to a new tableau that will correspond to corner II. The body of this tableau will represent the transformed equations corresponding to corner II. We have already seen (at the end of Section 6.5) that these equations are

$$C \qquad\qquad\qquad + s_4 = 50 \qquad (6.4)$$

$$A \qquad\qquad + s_3 \qquad = 70 \qquad (6.3)$$

$$A \qquad + s_2 \qquad - s_4 = 40 \qquad (6.14)$$

$$A + s_1 \qquad\qquad - 2s_4 = 20 \qquad (6.13)$$

Let us see how to operate on the initial tableau, Figure 6.8, to obtain these equations. The sequence of operations that we shall describe is called **Gaussian elimination.** Here are the first three steps:

Gaussian elimination

- ***Step 1:*** The entry in the enter column and the exit row of the current tableau (Figure 6.8) is called the *pivot element.* This is the circled element in Figure 6.8. Divide each entry in the exit row (the fourth row) by this element. In the BASIC VARIABLE column replace the exit variable with the enter variable and update the BASIC COEFFICIENT column as appropriate. This gives the row of the new tableau corresponding to the enter variable. Thus, the basic variable s_4 is replaced with C. Since the pivot element is 1, and since division by 1 produces no change, the entries in the fourth row stay the same (see the fourth row of Figure 6.9).

FIGURE 6.9
Partial Update of Figure 6.8

		20	10	0	0	0	0	
BASIC COEFFICIENT	BASIC VARIABLE	A	C	s_1	s_2	s_3	s_4	VALUE
0	s_1		0	1	0	0		
0	s_2		0	0	1	0		
0	s_3		0	0	0	1		
10	C	0	1	0	0	0	1	50
	z_j							
	$c_j - z_j$							

Transformed exit row and basic columns

- ▶ ***Step 2:*** The columns under each former basic variable other than the exit variable remain the same in all rows but the last two. Hence, the columns under s_1, s_2, and s_3 remain the same in the main body of the tableau (see this in Figure 6.9).
- ▶ ***Step 3:*** By virtue of step 1, the enter column already contains the number 1. Make the remaining entries zero in all rows except the last two.

Following steps 1, 2, and 3 we obtain the partial tableau shown in Figure 6.9. All remaining entries in the main body of the tableau (all rows, including the VALUE column, but the last two) can be obtained by the *pivot rule,* which works as follows: Suppose that we want the new entry in the s_2 row and the A column. You see in Figure 6.8 that the former entry was a 1. This number, together with the pivot element, defines a rectangle whose four corners are distinguished in Figure 6.8. (Note that any missing entry in the main body of Figure 6.9, together with the pivot element, will similarly define a unique rectangle.) The new entry in the s_2 row and the A column is given by a *pivoting operation,* which consists of the following *opposite corner rule:*

Opposite corner pivot rule

$$\text{new entry} = \text{old entry} - \frac{\text{product of opposite corners}}{\text{pivot element}}$$

Applying this rule, we obtain

$$\text{new entry} = 1 - \frac{(0)(1)}{1} = 1$$

On the basis of this pivoting operation, we can now state:

- ▶ ***Step 4:*** Apply the pivot rule to obtain all new entries for the remaining positions in the main body of the new tableau.

We now use step 4 to obtain the appropriate entries. For example, the new entry in the s_1 row and the s_4 column is

$$\text{new entry} = 0 - \frac{(1)(2)}{1} = -2$$

The main body of the tableau, completed by applying step 4, is shown in Figure 6.10. Observe that we have indeed derived the transformed equations correspond-

▼ FIGURE 6.10
Main Body of the Tableau at Corner II

		20	10	0	0	0	0	
BASIC COEFFICIENT	**BASIC VARIABLE**	***A***	***C***	s_1	s_2	s_3	s_4	**VALUE**
0	s_1	1	0	1	0	0	−2	20
0	s_2	1	0	0	1	0	−1	40
0	s_3	1	0	0	0	1	0	70
10	C	0	1	0	0	0	1	50
	z_j							
	$c_j - z_j$							

Updating by pivoting

BASIC COEFFICIENT	BASIC VARIABLE	20 A	10 C	0 s_1	0 s_2	0 s_3	0 s_4	VALUE
0	s_1	1	0	1	0	0	−2	20
0	s_2	1	0	0	1	0	−1	40
0	s_3	1	0	0	0	1	0	70
10	C	0	1	0	0	0	1	50
	z_j	0	10	0	0	0	10	
	$c_j - z_j$	20	0	0	0	0	−10	500

Last two rows are filled in

▲ FIGURE 6.11
Complete Tableau at Corner II

ing to corner II (i.e., [6.4], [6.3], [6.14], and [6.13]). The tableau is completed by calculating the new z_j's, $(c_j - z_j)$'s, and the new objective value. We obtain

$$z_1 = 0(1) + 0(1) + 0(1) + 10(0) = 0; \quad c_1 - z_1 = 20 - 0 = 20$$
$$z_2 = 0(0) + 0(0) + 0(0) + 10(1) = 10; \quad c_2 - z_2 = 10 - 10 = 0$$
$$z_3 = 0(1) + 0(0) + 0(0) + 10(0) = 0; \quad c_3 - z_3 = 0 - 0 = 0$$
$$z_4 = 0(0) + 0(1) + 0(0) + 10(0) = 0; \quad c_4 - z_4 = 0 - 0 = 0$$
$$z_5 = 0(0) + 0(0) + 0(1) + 10(0) = 0; \quad c_5 - z_5 = 0 - 0 = 0$$
$$z_6 = 0(-2) + 0(-1) + 0(0) + 10(1) = 10; \quad c_6 - z_6 = 0 - 10 = -10$$

The new objective value, at corner II, is given by

$$(\text{basic coefficients}) \cdot (\text{values}) = 0(20) + 0(40) + 0(70) + 10(50) = 500$$

Inserting these new entries, the complete tableau for corner II is given in Figure 6.11. We have exercised step 5.

► ***Step 5:*** Compute the values of z_j, $(c_j - z_j)$, and the current value of the objective function, and fill in the last two rows.

► 6.12 Applying the Simplex Method

The complete tableau at corner II, shown in Figure 6.11, shows that the current value of the objective function (meaning its value at corner II) is 500. This number appears in the last row of the VALUE column. We can also see that one of the currently nonbasic variables, namely *A*, has a positive opportunity cost, that is, the value of 20, which appears in the last row of the *A* column. This means that increasing the nonbasic variable *A* while keeping the other nonbasic variable, s_4, fixed at zero will further increase our objective value. Verify that increasing *A* while keeping s_4 at zero initiates in Figure 6.2 a move, or pivot, from corner II to corner III, where the variable s_1 becomes nonbasic. Any additional increase in *A* while keeping s_4 fixed at zero would force s_1 to become negative, which means we would be leaving the feasible region. Hence, we see from the geometry that *A* should enter and s_1 should exit. Let us now apply the enter and exit rule to Figure 6.11 to obtain the same result.

Applying the Exit Rule

We have already noted that since the only positive entry in the last row is the value 20 under the A column, the enter rule says that A must enter the basis. To find the exit variable, we must check the ratios

$$\frac{20}{1}, \frac{40}{1}, \frac{70}{1}$$

The minimum ratio is 20/1. Accordingly, the exit rule says that s_1 leaves the basic set, and 1 is the new pivot element, as indicated in Figure 6.11.

Using the five steps outlined above, we obtain Figure 6.12. Try to derive this tableau on your own. If you have a problem, continue with the exposition. You will get more detail at the next step.

		20	10	0	0	0	0	
BASIC COEFFICIENT	**BASIC VARIABLE**	***A***	***C***	s_1	s_2	s_3	s_4	**VALUE**
20	A	1	0	1	0	0	−2	20
0	s_2	0	0	−1	1	0	(1)	20
0	s_3	0	0	−1	0	1	2	50
10	C	0	1	0	0	0	1	50
	z_j	20	10	20	0	0	−30	
	$c_j - z_j$	0	0	−20	0	0	30	900

s_4 enters
s_2 exits

▲ FIGURE 6.12
Complete Tableau at Corner III

Pivoting from Corner III

The new tableau in Figure 6.12 indicates that s_4 should enter the basis because 30 is the only positive entry in the last row. The ratios

$$\frac{20}{1}, \frac{50}{2}, \frac{50}{1}$$

indicate that s_2 should leave the basic set because 20/1 is the minimum ratio. The pivot element is 1, as indicated in Figure 6.12. This latest tableau shows that the value of the objective function has increased to 900 at corner III. The main body of this tableau is now updated to give Figure 6.13. To fill in the z_j row we use the data in Figure 6.13 as follows:

$$z_j = (\text{basic coefficients}) \cdot (j\text{th column of data})$$

Thus,

$$\begin{aligned}
z_1 &= 20(1) + 0(0) + 0(0) + 10(0) = 20\\
z_2 &= 20(0) + 0(0) + 0(0) + 10(1) = 10\\
z_3 &= 20(-1) + 0(-1) + 0(1) + 10(1) = -10\\
z_4 &= 20(2) + 0(1) + 0(-2) + 10(-1) = 30\\
z_5 &= 20(0) + 0(0) + 0(1) + 10(0) = 0\\
z_6 &= 20(0) + 0(1) + 0(0) + 10(0) = 0
\end{aligned}$$

Updating by pivoting

BASIC COEFFICIENT	BASIC VARIABLE	20	10	0	0	0	0	VALUE
		A	*C*	s_1	s_2	s_3	s_4	
20	*A*	1	0	−1	2	0	0	60
0	s_4	0	0	−1	1	0	1	20
0	s_3	0	0	1	−2	1	0	10
10	*C*	0	1	1	−1	0	0	30
	z_j							
	$c_j - z_j$							

▲ FIGURE 6.13
Partial Update of Figure 6.12

Using these values in conjunction with the top row of c_j values, we compute

$$c_1 - z_1 = 20 - 20 = 0$$
$$c_2 - z_2 = 10 - 10 = 0$$
$$c_3 - z_3 = 0 - (-10) = 10$$
$$c_4 - z_4 = 0 - 30 = -30$$
$$c_5 - z_5 = 0 - 0 = 0$$
$$c_6 - z_6 = 0 - 0 = 0$$

Moreover, the objective function value at corner IV is also easily computed from the data in Figure 6.13.

$$\begin{aligned}\text{objective function value at corner IV} &= \text{(basic coefficients)} \cdot \text{(values)}\\ &= 20(60) + 0(20) + 0(10) + 10(30)\\ &= 1500\end{aligned}$$

Pivoting from Corner IV

The simplex method could also go from corner I to corner VI and then to corner V to find the optimal solution in three iterations.

Thus, the completed tableau at corner IV is shown in Figure 6.14. The tableau shown in Figure 6.14 shows that the value of the objective function has increased to 1500. The enter rule says that the objective function should further increase if s_1, the only nonbasic variable with a positive opportunity cost, now becomes basic.

▼ FIGURE 6.14
Complete Tableau at Corner IV

BASIC COEFFICIENT	BASIC VARIABLE	20	10	0	0	0	0	VALUE
		A	*C*	s_1	s_2	s_3	s_4	
20	*A*	1	0	−1	2	0	0	60
0	s_4	0	0	−1	1	0	1	20
0	s_3	0	0	(1)	−2	1	0	10
10	*C*	0	1	1	−1	0	0	50
	z_j	20	10	−10	30	0	0	
	$c_j - z_j$	0	0	10	−30	0	0	1500

s_1 enters
s_3 exits

BASIC COEFFICIENT	BASIC VARIABLE	20 A	10 C	0 s_1	0 s_2	0 s_3	0 s_4	VALUE
20	A	1	0	0	0	1	0	70
0	s_4	0	0	0	−1	1	1	30
0	s_1	0	0	1	−2	1	0	10
10	C	0	1	0	1	−1	0	20
	z_j	20	10	0	10	10	0	
	$c_j - z_j$	0	0	0	−10	−10	0	1600

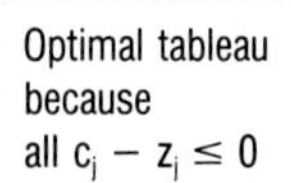

▲ FIGURE 6.15
Tableau at Corner V

The exit rule tells us to consider the ratios

$$\frac{10}{1}, \frac{30}{1}$$

and since 10/1 is the minimum we must choose s_3 to exit. The pivot element is 1, as indicated in Figure 6.14. The complete tableau at corner V is shown in Figure 6.15. We now observe that this tableau is optimal because all the opportunity costs (the $c_j - z_j$ entries) are *negative*. This is a special case of the following *stopping rule,* also called the **optimality criterion:**

Optimality criterion

In a Max problem, when all opportunity costs are nonpositive, an optimal corner solution has been obtained.

The optimal solution is obtained by setting the nonbasic variables, in the optimal tableau, to zero and then reading the values of the basic variables (i.e., the VALUE column). Thus, reading from Figure 6.15, we see that

$$A^* = 70, \quad C^* = 20, \quad s_1^* = 10, \quad s_2^* = 0, \quad s_3^* = 0, \quad s_4^* = 30$$

and the OV is 1600. This coincides with the optimal solution produced by graphical analysis in Figure 6.1.

▶ 6.13 Extensions to More General Problems

The essence of the simplex method, as described above, is:

1. Find any *corner* of the constraint set (which means, find the transformed equations corresponding to some corner). This will be *the initial corner.* Construct the tableau *corresponding to the initial corner.* This is called *phase I* of the method.
2. Beginning at the initial corner, pivot from corner to adjacent corner in such a way that the value of the objective function improves at each iteration and so that, therefore, an optimal solution is obtained.

APPLICATION CAPSULE

An Alternative to Simplex: Karmarkar's Algorithm Helps with the Really Big Problems*

The simplex method, developed in the 1940s, is still widely used to solve linear problems having a huge number of possible solutions. Some problems faced by modern governments and businesses, however, are so big that not even the simplex algorithm is capable of solving them. These LPs may have hundreds of thousands of variables and tens of thousands of constraints.

Narendra Karmarkar, a mathematician at AT&T's Bell Laboratories, devised an algorithm that takes a unique shortcut to rule out whole groups of solutions even more efficiently than does the simplex method. AT&T has marketed this algorithm as the KORBX System. One of its most prominent customers is the Military Air Command (MAC).

MAC, well known for orchestrating the logistics of the Desert Storm airlift operations in the Persian Gulf, is responsible for scheduling more than 900 aircraft worldwide in peacetime and more than 1700 during war operations. The task, involving 5000 pilots flying 700,000 hours annually, has been tackled by LP models run on mainframe computers. Even so, the problem of scheduling the U.S. and Pacific basin traffic is so large that it had to be cut into two models. Four hours of computer time were required just to run scaled-down problems of "only" 36,000 variables and 10,000 constraints. It has been reported, however, that with KORBX system the entire model can be run in one piece in 20 minutes. The even more complicated European routes (150,000 variables and 12,000 constraints) are said to run in one hour with KORBX.

Thanks to KORBX, MAC is now able to investigate problems so large that they could not previously be run even on mainframe computers. One example is the transportation of casualties to hospitals worldwide, which involves more than 500,000 variables and 70,000 constraints.

*"Karmarkar Algorithm Finds a Home at MAC," *OR/MS Today*, June 1989, pp. 22–24.

There are several possibilities that may interfere with the successful execution of these steps. These are *difficulties in phase I, infeasible problems, unbounded problems,* and *degenerate problems.* We shall address these circumstances in order.

Difficulties in Phase I

Let us review some of what we have learned thus far. Phase I, as described above, amounts to finding some corner, indeed, *any* corner, for which we can construct the corresponding tableau. At any corner the main body of the tableau represents a special set of equations that are equivalent to the original equations. This special set of equations is what we have been calling the *transformed equations.* The important fact about these equivalent equations is this: They are in a form such that when the nonbasic variables at the corner being considered are set equal to zero, the values of the *basic variables* are obtained directly. From these data in the main body of the tableau we can easily construct the remainder of the tableau, that is, the rows z_j and $c_j - z_j$ and the current objective value.

The reason that phase I was so easy for Astro/Cosmo is that the original equations (6.1) through (6.4) were already, without any modification, in the required form. That is,

1. At corner I in Figure 6.2 the variables A and C are nonbasic.
2. When A and C are set equal to zero in (6.1)–(6.4), the values of the *basic variables* s_1, s_2, s_3, and s_4 are obtained directly without further manipulation. That is, they are simply read from the RHSs of the original equations. Review (6.1)–(6.4) to verify these statements.

In Astro/Cosmo there is a simple reason for the initial equations already being in the required form. The reason is that each constraint in the original model was of $\leq$ form, and all of the RHS values were nonnegative. This guaranteed that after adding the slack variables the required form was immediately at hand.

Not every set of equations in standard equality constraint form will be as nice as Astro/Cosmo. For example, consider the constraints

$$3x_1 + 4x_2 \geq 6$$
$$2x_1 - 6x_2 \leq 4$$
$$x_1 \geq 0, \qquad x_2 \geq 0$$

The standard equality constraint form contains $m = 2$ equations in $n = 4$ variables. The standard equality constraint form is

$$\begin{aligned} 3x_1 + 4x_2 - s_1 \qquad &= 6 \\ 2x_1 - 6x_2 \qquad + s_2 &= 4 \end{aligned}$$
$$x_1 \geq 0, \qquad x_2 \geq 0, \qquad s_1 \geq 0, \qquad s_2 \geq 0$$

If the variables x_1 and x_2 are set equal to zero, we obtain a *unique* solution for the remaining variables, namely

$$s_1 = -6$$
$$s_2 = 4$$

The fact that $n - m$ of the variables could be set equal to zero to give a unique solution for the remaining m variables means, by definition, that the $n - m$ variables are a nonbasic set. That is, (x_1, x_2) are a set of nonbasic variables and (s_1, s_2) are a set of basic variables. Hence, the solution $(x_1 = 0, x_2 = 0, s_1 = -6, s_2 = 4)$ is a *basic solution.* But it is *not a basic feasible solution,* because s_1 is negative. Consequently, it cannot correspond to a corner. (Remember, corners correspond to basic feasible solutions!) Thus, for the equations above we cannot so easily construct an initial tableau.

When is phase I easy?

In summary, then, the Astro/Cosmo example possesses the following *two key properties,* which guarantee that the initial tableau can be easily constructed.

Property 1. Property 1 is essentially condition (6.9). It says that for a problem in standard equality constraint form, with n variables and m constraints, each constraint must contain a nonnegative variable with the coefficient *plus one,* and that variable must appear only in that constraint. Any nonnegative variable with the property that it has coefficient *plus one* and appears in only one equation will, in our exposition, be referred to as a **distinguished variable.** If there is a distinguished variable in every constraint, property 1 will be satisfied. In (6.1)–(6.4) the variables s_1, s_2, s_3, and s_4 are *distinguished variables.* That is, the *i*th slack variable s_i appears in the *i*th and only in the *i*th equation, and its coefficient in that equation is plus one. Since there is a distinguished variable in every constraint, property 1 is satisfied.

Whenever property 1 is satisfied, you can see that if we set the remaining (i.e., undistinguished) $n - m$ variables equal to zero, we obtain a *unique* solution for the m distinguished variables. By definition, this means that we have a *basic solution.* For example, consider again the foregoing system of constraints in standard equality form

$$\begin{aligned} 3x_1 + 4x_2 - s_1 \quad &= 6 \\ 2x_1 - 6x_2 \quad + s_2 &= 4 \\ x_1 \geq 0, \quad x_2 \geq 0, \quad s_1 \geq 0, \quad & s_2 \geq 0 \end{aligned}$$

A simple, almost trivial, transformation of this system will convert it into an equivalent system with two distinguished variables. See whether you can deduce how to do this. Here is the answer: Multiply the first of the two equations by -1 on both sides of the equality sign. You then obtain the equivalent system

A system with property 1

$$\begin{aligned} -3x_1 - 4x_2 + s_1 \quad &= -6 \\ 2x_1 - 6x_2 \quad + s_2 &= 4 \\ x_1 \geq 0, \quad x_2 \geq 0, \quad s_1 \geq 0, \quad & s_2 \geq 0 \end{aligned}$$

In this system s_1 and s_2 each have a coefficient of *plus one.* Each variable appears in only one equation, and each equation contains one such variable. This means that s_1 and s_2 satisfy the definition of distinguished variables. Property 1 is satisfied. Property 1 now allows us to easily find a basic solution. In this example, set the undistinguished variables x_1 and x_2 equal to zero. Then, as previously observed, we obtain the basic solution ($x_1 = 0$, $x_2 = 0$, $s_1 = -6$, $s_2 = 4$). But this is not a basic *feasible* solution. Because we must have a basic feasible solution we also need

Recall that for a solution to be *feasible*, all values must be nonnegative (≥ 0).

Property 2. Property 2 is (6.10). It says that the values on the right-hand side of the equality constraints are *nonnegative.* If this property holds *simultaneously with property 1,* the values of the basic variables (i.e., the distinguished variables) will be the RHS, and since this is nonnegative we will have a basic feasible solution, and the initial tableau can be constructed.

Modifying Systems, without Both Properties: Artificial Variables

We must now show how a set of original equations that do not satisfy properties 1 and 2, such as the example above, can be modified. To do this, let us look at another, slightly more complicated, illustration. For example, consider the following LP (a completely general system with $\leq$, $\geq$, $=$ constraints, as well as positive and negative RHSs):

The original system

$$\begin{aligned} \text{Max } & 12x_1 + 20x_2 + 8x_3 \\ \text{s.t. } & 3x_1 \qquad\quad - 2x_3 \geq -2 \\ & -4x_1 - x_2 + 12x_3 \geq 4 \\ & -x_1 \qquad\quad + 3x_3 \leq -6 \\ & 3x_1 + 4x_2 - 6x_3 = -12 \\ & \qquad\quad x_2 + 9x_3 = 31 \\ & x_1 \geq 0, \quad x_2 \geq 0, \quad x_3 \geq 0 \end{aligned}$$

When this is converted to standard equality form we obtain

$$
\begin{array}{llr}
\text{Max } 12x_1 + 20x_2 + 8x_3 & & \\
\text{s.t. } 3x_1 \qquad\quad - 2x_3 - s_1 & = -2 & (6.23) \\
-4x_1 - x_2 + 12x_3 \qquad - s_2 & = 4 & (6.24) \\
-x_1 \qquad + 3x_3 \qquad\qquad + s_3 & = -6 & (6.25) \\
3x_1 + 4x_2 - 6x_3 & = -12 & (6.26) \\
x_2 + 9x_3 & = 31 & (6.27)
\end{array}
$$

$$x_1 \ge 0, \quad x_2 \ge 0, \quad x_3 \ge 0, \quad s_1 \ge 0, \quad s_2 \ge 0, \quad s_3 \ge 0$$

This system of original equations does not satisfy either property 1 or property 2—certainly, then, not both properties simultaneously. To deal with such a system, we proceed in the following series of steps.

Step 1: Satisfying Property 2. For each of the equality constraints with a negative RHS, multiply both sides by -1. This will guarantee that property 2 is satisfied. For example, in the system above we must perform this transformation on (6.23), (6.25), and (6.26). We then obtain the *equivalent* problem:

$$
\begin{array}{llr}
\text{Max } 12x_1 + 20x_2 + 8x_3 & & \\
\text{s.t. } -3x_1 \qquad + 2x_3 + s_1 & = 2 & (6.28) \\
-4x_1 - x_2 + 12x_3 \qquad - s_2 & = 4 & (6.24) \\
x_1 \qquad - 3x_3 \qquad\qquad - s_3 & = 6 & (6.29) \\
-3x_1 - 4x_2 + 6x_3 & = 12 & (6.30) \\
x_2 + 9x_3 & = 31 & (6.27)
\end{array}
$$

$$x_1 \ge 0, \quad x_2 \ge 0, \quad x_3 \ge 0, \quad s_1 \ge 0, \quad s_2 \ge 0, \quad s_3 \ge 0$$

The term *artificial* means that there is no physical interpretation of this variable, such as those that exist for the decision, slack, or surplus variables. The variable is used to allow a feasible solution to be gained (when all the artificial variables = 0), and then can be discarded.

Step 2: Satisfying Property 1. Add a nonnegative variable to each constraint that does not now, after multiplication by -1 as required in step 1, contain a distinguished variable. (Note that the order of these steps is important!) Each such variable, called an **artificial variable,** is included in the objective function with a very large negative coefficient, denoted for convenience as $-M$. For example, think of $-M$ as meaning "minus a million." The reason for the large negative coefficient will become clear later. However, before pursuing this point, let us, as an example, refer to the system (6.28), (6.24), (6.29), (6.30), (6.27). Equation (6.28) already contains a distinguished variable, namely s_1. The remaining equations contain no such variable. Why is x_2, which appears in the last equation with coefficient $+1$, not a distinguished variable? Because it appears in other equations as well. Since the last four equations contain no distinguished variables, we must *add an artificial variable* to each one. Doing this, and including the artificial variables, as prescribed, in the objective function, we obtain

The modified system

$$
\begin{array}{llr}
\text{Max } 12x_1 + 20x_2 + 8x_3 - Ma_1 - Ma_2 - Ma_3 - Ma_4 & & \\
\text{s.t. } -3x_1 \qquad + 2x_3 + s_1 & = 2 & (6.28) \\
-4x_1 - x_2 + 12x_3 \qquad - s_2 \qquad + a_1 & = 4 & (6.31) \\
x_1 \qquad - 3x_3 \qquad\qquad - s_3 \qquad + a_2 & = 6 & (6.32) \\
-3x_1 - 4x_2 + 6x_3 \qquad\qquad\qquad + a_3 & = 12 & (6.33) \\
x_2 + 9x_3 \qquad\qquad\qquad\qquad + a_4 & = 31 & (6.34)
\end{array}
$$

$$x_1 \geq 0, \quad x_2 \geq 0, \quad x_3 \geq 0, \quad s_1 \geq 0, \quad s_2 \geq 0, \quad s_3 \geq 0,$$
$$a_1 \geq 0, \quad a_2 \geq 0, \quad a_3 \geq 0, \quad a_4 \geq 0$$

The artificial variables provide the needed distinguished variables for the last four equations. The initial *basic feasible solution* to this new system is

$$x_1 = 0, \quad x_2 = 0, \quad x_3 = 0, \quad s_2 = 0, \quad s_3 = 0,$$
$$s_1 = 2, \quad a_1 = 4, \quad a_2 = 6, \quad a_3 = 12, \quad a_4 = 31$$

The five basic variables are the distinguished variables s_1, a_1, a_2, a_3, a_4, and the nonbasic variables are x_1, x_2, x_3, s_2, s_3. *This new problem is not the same as the original one. It is equivalent to the original problem only when all four artificial variables have the value zero.* If we were actually going to attempt to solve the original problem (with constraints [6.23]–[6.27]), we would first set up the initial tableau for the new problem (constraints [6.28] and [6.31]–[6.34]). We would then pivot on this tableau with the hope that, after a sequence of pivots, all the artificial variables will be *nonbasic* (this is related to the motive for $-M$). Once they are nonbasic, their value is zero, and we will then have a valid initial tableau for the original problem, and phase I will have been successfully completed.

The tableau for the modified system

The initial tableau for the foregoing problem with artificial variables is given in Figure 6.16. Notice how the BASIC COEFFICIENT column now contains a coefficient $-M$ for each artificial variable in the basis. Also notice how the z_j and $c_j - z_j$ rows are computed using the symbols $-M$ just as if they stood for real numbers.

Given this initial tableau, the next step would be to perform a sequence of pivots in the attempt to drive all artificial variables out of the basis (thereby forcing their value to zero as desired). Since the terms $-M$ represent some very negative number such as "minus a million," and since the simplex method will at each iteration improve (in this example, increase) the value of the objective function whenever possible, the very large negative coefficients on the artificial variables in the objective function will guarantee that these will all be made nonbasic *if possible.*

Finding the Enter Variable. In Figure 6.16 note that the only positive opportunity cost is $8 + 24M$, which means that x_3 would be the enter variable. (The number M is assumed to be so large that any $c_j - z_j$ entry containing $+M$ is positive and any $c_j - z_j$ containing $-M$ is negative.) Now, in Figure 6.16 the exit variable would be obtained by finding the minimum of the ratios

$$\frac{2}{2}, \frac{4}{12}, \frac{12}{6}, \frac{31}{9}$$

Since the minimum is 4/12, a_1 would be the exit variable, and, as shown in Figure

▼ FIGURE 6.16
Initial Tableau with Artificial Variables

		12	20	8	0	0	−M	−M	−M	−M	
BASIC COEFFICIENT	**BASIC VARIABLE**	x_1	x_2	x_3	s_1	s_2	a_1	a_2	a_3	a_4	**VALUE**
0	s_1	−3	0	2	1	0	0	0	0	0	2
−M	a_1	−4	−1	(12)	0	−1	1	0	0	0	4
−M	a_2	1	0	−3	0	0	0	1	0	0	6
−M	a_3	−3	−4	6	0	0	0	0	1	0	12
−M	a_4	0	1	9	0	0	0	0	0	1	31
	z_j	$6M$	$4M$	$-24M$	0	M	$-M$	$-M$	$-M$	$-M$	
	$c_j - z_j$	$12 - 6M$	$20 - 4M$	$8 + 24M$	0	$-M$	0	0	0	0	$-53M$

6.16, 12 is the pivot element. From this point on we could follow the usual rules for updating successive tableaux. Now here is an important point:

Removing columns

Each time an artificial variable is removed from the basis, the corresponding column can also be eliminated from the tableau. However, if you also desire to obtain sensitivity analysis (such as dual prices) from the results of your hand calculations, the artificial columns should be retained in each iteration.

The derivation of sensitivity information will be discussed in the appendixes to this chapter, where it will be seen that the artificial columns play an important role, from the sensitivity point of view, in the final tableau. These sensitivity calculations are obviously important, but let us not lose sight of the fact that in real-world problem solving the computer does them for you. Of course, the computer does it all for you, including the addition of artificial variables as needed to perform phase I and then the sequence of pivots to optimality. The point here is that constraints on space do not allow us to give a detailed exposition of all aspects of the process. We have chosen to list the steps carefully from the initial problem to the optimal solution, including phase I as required. The appendixes provide a more terse analysis of the *postoptimality,* or *sensitivity,* calculations. This does not reflect any attempt to give less emphasis to sensitivity *interpretations,* for as we have discussed at length in previous chapters, it is the sensitivity considerations that are often at the heart of managerial decision making. However, the purpose of this chapter is to understand the essentials of the simplex method per se, so it is these calculations that we describe in detail.

Now, proceeding with our main thrust, the goal, after setting up the initial tableau, is to drive all artificial variables out of the basis. When and if this is accomplished, phase I will be complete, and we will have an initial basic feasible solution to our original problem. The pivoting algorithm then continues to proceed as formerly described. Later in this section we will consider the possibility that *not all* of the artificial variables can be driven out of the basis. It will be shown that in this case the original problem is infeasible.

A Complete Example: PROTRAC, Inc. Revisited

Figure 6.16 has now served its purpose, namely to demonstrate the initial tableau for a problem with artificial variables. Rather than continuing to pivot on this tableau, we choose to return to a problem we have already visited—the **PROTRAC,** Inc. model. We shall carry out, by hand, the complete solution to this problem. This will give you the opportunity to check your understanding of how the simplex algorithm is applied to the general LP. Try to verify each step of the algorithm. The problem is

$$\begin{aligned}
\text{Max } & 5000E + 4000F \\
\text{s.t. } & E + F \geq 5 \\
& E - 3F \leq 0 \\
& 10E + 15F \leq 150 \\
& 20E + 10F \leq 160 \\
& 30E + 10F \geq 135 \\
& E, F \geq 0
\end{aligned}$$

We have previously discussed the graphical solution to this problem, shown in Figure 5.5, and the computer output is shown in Figure 5.6. Thus, doing the hand calculations will provide our third solution to this problem.

The first step in applying the simplex method is to convert to standard equality constraint form

$$
\begin{aligned}
&\text{Max } 5000E + 4000F \\
&\text{s.t.} \quad E + F - s_1 = 5 \\
&\quad E - 3F + s_2 = 0 \\
&\quad 10E + 15F + s_3 = 150 \\
&\quad 20E + 10F + s_4 = 160 \\
&\quad 30E + 10F - s_5 = 135 \\
&\quad E, F, s_1, s_2, s_3, s_4, s_5 \geq 0
\end{aligned}
$$

The RHS is nonnegative, and hence property 2 is already satisfied. However, in these original equations only the second, third, and fourth constraints contain distinguished variables. Therefore, to satisfy property 1, we must add artificial variables to the first and last constraints. This gives

Modified form for phase I

$$
\begin{aligned}
&\text{Max } 5000E + 4000F - Ma_1 - Ma_2 \\
&\text{s.t.} \quad E + F - s_1 + a_1 = 5 \\
&\quad E - 3F + s_2 = 0 \\
&\quad 10E + 15F + s_3 = 150 \\
&\quad 20E + 10F + s_4 = 160 \\
&\quad 30E + 10F - s_5 + a_2 = 135 \\
&\quad E, F, s_1, s_2, s_3, s_4, s_5, a_1, a_2 \geq 0
\end{aligned}
$$

Pivoting in Phase I. We now have five distinguished variables, a nonnegative RHS (note that the zero value for the second RHS is permissible), and hence can easily construct the initial tableau as shown in Figure 6.17. The most positive opportunity cost is $5000 + 31M$, so we choose E to enter the basis. The minimum of the ratios

Notice the use of fractions instead of decimal equivalents (from which roundoff errors can produce incorrect answers). This is one of the main numerical analysis difficulties in doing computer algorithms for LP.

$$\frac{5}{1}, \frac{0}{1}, \frac{150}{10}, \frac{160}{20}, \frac{135}{30}$$

is 0/1, which means that s_2 leaves the basis, and hence 1 is the pivot element. The updated tableau is given in Figure 6.18. In Figure 6.18 the only positive opportunity cost is $19{,}000 + 104M$, which means that F enters the basis. The minimum of the ratios

$$\frac{5}{4}, \frac{150}{45}, \frac{160}{70}, \frac{135}{100}$$

is 5/4, which means that a_1 leaves the basis, and hence 4 is the pivot element. The updated tableau is given in Figure 6.19. In this figure we could choose to omit the a_1 column since the artificial variable a_1 has now been driven to zero. However, in order to obtain sensitivity information we shall include the artificial variables in each successive tableau. The only positive opportunity cost is now $4750 + 25M$, which means that s_1 enters the basis. The minimum of the ratios

BASIC COEFFICIENT	BASIC VARIABLE	5000	4000	0	0	0	0	0	$-M$	$-M$	
		E	F	s_1	s_2	s_3	s_4	s_5	a_1	a_2	VALUE
$-M$	a_1	1	1	−1	0	0	0	0	1	0	5
0	s_2	(1)	−3	0	1	0	0	0	0	0	0
0	s_3	10	15	0	0	1	0	0	0	0	150
0	s_4	20	10	0	0	0	1	0	0	0	160
$-M$	a_2	30	10	0	0	0	0	−1	0	1	135
z_j		$-31M$	$-11M$	M	0	0	0	M	$-M$	$-M$	
$c_j - z_j$		5000 $+31M$	4000 $+11M$	$-M$	0	0	0	$-M$	0	0	$-140M$

▲ FIGURE 6.17
Initial Tableau for PROTRAC, Inc.

BASIC COEFFICIENT	BASIC VARIABLE	5000	4000	0	0	0	0	0	$-M$	$-M$	
		E	F	s_1	s_2	s_3	s_4	s_5	a_1	a_2	VALUE
$-M$	a_1	0	(4)	−1	−1	0	0	0	1	0	5
5000	E	1	−3	0	1	0	0	0	0	0	0
0	s_3	0	45	0	−10	1	0	0	0	0	150
0	s_4	0	70	0	−20	0	1	0	0	0	160
$-M$	a_2	0	100	0	−30	0	0	−1	0	1	135
z_j		5000	−15,000 $-104M$	M	5000 $+31M$	0	0	M	$-M$	$-M$	
$c_j - z_j$		0	19,000 $+104M$	$-M$	−5000 $-31M$	0	0	$-M$	0	0	$-140M$

▲ FIGURE 6.18
First Updated Tableau

▼ FIGURE 6.19
Second Updated Tableau

BASIC COEFFICIENT	BASIC VARIABLE	5000	4000	0	0	0	0	0	$-M$	$-M$	
		E	F	s_1	s_2	s_3	s_4	s_5	a_1	a_2	VALUE
4000	F	0	1	−1/4	−1/4	0	0	0	1/4	0	5/4
5000	E	1	0	−3/4	1/4	0	0	0	3/4	0	15/4
0	s_3	0	0	45/4	5/4	1	0	0	−45/4	0	375/4
0	s_4	0	0	70/4	−10/4	0	1	0	−70/4	0	290/4
$-M$	a_2	0	0	(25)	−5	0	0	−1	−25	1	10
z_j		5000	4000	−4750 $-25M$	250 $+5M$	0	0	M	4750 $+25M$	$-M$	
$c_j - z_j$		0	10	4750 $+25M$	−250 $-5M$	0	0	$-M$	−4750 $-26M$	0	95,000/4 $-10M$

$$\left(\frac{375}{4}\right)\Big/\left(\frac{45}{4}\right), \left(\frac{290}{4}\right)\Big/\left(\frac{70}{4}\right), \frac{10}{25}$$

is 10/25, which means that a_2 leaves the basis, and hence 25 is the pivot element. The updated tableau is given in Figure 6.20. At this point both artificial variables have been driven out of the basis, and therefore phase I is complete. Since s_2 and s_5 are the nonbasic variables, this tableau corresponds to the southwest corner of the constraint set in Figure 5.5, at which the market balance (constraint ②), and contractual labor (constraint ⑤) constraints are active.

		5000	4000	0	0	0	0	0	$-M$	$-M$	
BASIC COEFFICIENT	**BASIC VARIABLE**	E	F	s_1	s_2	s_3	s_4	s_5	a_1	a_2	**VALUE**
4000	F	0	1	0	−0.30	0	0	−0.01	0	0.01	1.35
5000	E	1	0	0	0.10	0	0	−0.03	0	0.03	4.05
0	s_3	0	0	0	(3.5)	1	0	0.45	0	−0.45	89.25
0	s_4	0	0	0	1	0	1	0.70	0	−0.70	65.50
0	s_1	0	0	1	−⅕	0	0	−1⁄25	−1	1⁄25	0.40
z_j		5000	4000	0	−700	0	0	−190	0	190	
$c_j - z_j$		0	0	0	700	0	0	190	$-M$	$-M$ −190	25,650

▲ FIGURE 6.20
Phase I Is Complete

Pivoting in Phase II. The most positive opportunity cost is 700, so we choose s_2 to enter the basis. The minimum of the ratios—4.05/0.10, 89.25/3.5, 65.5/1—is 89.25/3.5, which means that s_3 leaves the basis, and hence 3.5 is the pivot element. Thus, the new nonbasic variables are s_3 and s_5. This gives the corner in Figure 5.5 at which the contractual labor (constraint ⑤) and the department A (constraint ③) are active. The tableau is shown in Figure 6.21.

The only positive opportunity cost is 100, which means that s_5 enters the basis. The minimum of the ratios

$$9/(0.2/7),\ 25.5/(0.9/7),\ 40/\left(\frac{4}{7}\right)$$

is 40/(4/7), which means that s_4 leaves the basis, and hence 4/7 is the pivot element.

▼ FIGURE 6.21
Contractual Labor and Department A Are Active

		5000	4000	0	0	0	0	0	$-M$	$-M$	
BASIC COEFFICIENT	**BASIC VARIABLE**	E	F	s_1	s_2	s_3	s_4	s_5	a_1	a_2	**VALUE**
4000	F	0	1	0	0	0.3/3.5	0	0.2/7	0	−0.2/7	9
5000	E	1	0	0	0	−0.1/3.5	0	−0.3/7	0	0.3/7	1.50
0	s_2	0	0	0	1	−1/3.5	0	0.9/7	0	−0.9/7	25.5
0	s_4	0	0	0	0	−1/3.5	1	(4/7)	0	−4/7	40
0	s_1	0	0	1	0	1/17.5	0	−12.5/875	−1	12.5/875	5.50
z_j		5000	4000	0	0	200	0	−100	0	100	
$c_j - z_j$		0	0	0	0	−200	0	+100	−M	−M −100	43,500

BASIC COEFFICIENT	BASIC VARIABLE	5000	4000	0	0	0	0	0	−M	−M	
		E	F	s_1	s_2	s_3	s_4	s_5	a_1	a_2	VALUE
4000	F	0	1	0	0	0.1	−0.05	0	0	0	7
5000	E	1	0	0	0	−0.05	0.075	0	0	0	4.5
0	s_2	0	0	0	1	0.35	−0.225	0	0	0	16.5
0	s_5	0	0	0	0	−0.5	1.75	1	−1	0	70
0	s_1	0	0	1	0	0.05	0.025	0	0	−1	6.5
z_j		5000	4000	0	0	150	175	0	0	0	
$c_j - z_j$		0	0	0	0	−150	−175	0	−M	−M	50,500

▼ FIGURE 6.22
Optimal Tableau

Refinery models for quarterly production typically run to 50,000 to 100,000 variables with thousands of constraints, taking up to 24 hours to solve on mainframe computers. (Usually there is an automatic "save" every hour for these long-running models, so if the computer crashes, you are no more than an hour away from your most recent save.)

Now that s_3 and s_4 are nonbasic, we know from Figure 5.5 that the optimal corner is obtained. The updated tableau is given in Figure 6.22.

The fact that there is no positive opportunity cost tells us that this tableau is optimal. Hence the optimal solution is

$$F^* = 7, \quad E^* = 4.5, \quad s_2^* = 16.5, \quad s_5^* = 70, \quad s_1^* = 6.5, \quad s_3^* = 0, \quad s_4^* = 0$$

and the OV is $50,500. This coincides with the information given on the computer printout shown in Figure 5.6.

The effort required to solve this problem by hand will lead you to appreciate the fact that computers routinely solve problems in thousands of variables and hundreds of constraints in seconds.

Infeasible Problems

A linear program is *infeasible* if there is no solution that simultaneously satisfies all the constraints and nonnegativity conditions. This means that the constraint set is empty. A geometric interpretation of infeasible problems has already been presented in Section 3.8. It would be well to review that discussion at this time.

In terms of the simplex procedure, if phase I can be successfully completed, the original problem cannot be infeasible, for completion of phase I produces an extreme point of the constraint set of the original problem. This implies that that constraint set cannot be empty.

The signal for infeasibility is that we obtain a tableau with the properties that

Signal for infeasibility

1. All opportunity costs are *nonpositive* (i.e., the stopping, or *optimality, criterion,* has been encountered).
2. One or more artificial variables remains in the solution at a *positive level.* That is, one or more artificial variables remains in the basis, and the associated entry in the VALUE column is positive.

It is worth pointing out that if all the constraints in the original problem are inequalities, and if (1) each ≤ constraint has a nonnegative RHS and (2) each ≥ constraint has a nonpositive RHS, the problem cannot be infeasible, for the origin will satisfy all the constraints. For such a problem, after conversion to standard equality constraint form and then changing signs as required in step 1, the slack and surplus variables will all be distinguished variables. Hence, for such a problem (as with Astro/Cosmo) the initial tableau can be directly set up without the inclusion of artificial variables.

Again, infeasibility is the worst message to get! Often in large complicated models it is very difficult to find which constraints are causing the infeasibility. If the data are "correct," then the company may be asking for the impossible.

As a final point, we recall from Section 3.8 that infeasibility is not a real-world phenomenon. That is, no corectly formulated real-world problem can be infeasible. Infeasibility is a mathematical anomaly introduced by the analyst. Either the constraints are too tight, so tight that not all of them can be simultaneously satisfied, or the analyst has made a clerical error in entering the data to the computer.

If you begin with an infeasible problem, then phase I of the simplex method will always detect this, and the computer will tell you that the problem is infeasible.

Unbounded Problems

A linear programming problem is *unbounded* if the objective function can be arbitrarily improved over the feasible region. This implies that the feasible region must also be unbounded.

Unbounded problems were also discussed in Section 3.8. There the geometric analysis was given, and it was also stated that unboundedness is not a real-world phenomenon. No one has yet discovered a way to make infinite profits. Unboundedness is another mathematical anomaly introduced either by incorrect formulation (e.g., not enough constraints) or by errors in data entry.

Signal of unboundedness

The simplex signal for an unbounded problem occurs in phase II (i.e., after all artificial variables have been driven to zero). The signal is (1) a column with a positive opportunity cost and (2) all entries in the main body of the tableau, in that column, being ≤ 0. Suppose, for example, that the column headed by the variable x_j gives such a signal. Then statements (1) and (2) imply that as x_j (currently nonbasic, since all basic variables have zero opportunity cost) is made positive, holding all other nonbasic variables at zero, the objective function will be increased (at a constant rate given by the opportunity cost) while no basic variable will decrease. Thus, this can be done indefinitely without forcing any of the basic variables to zero.

(*Section 6.14*)
Mathematically, there should be no difference between alternative optima, but in a real situation you probably want to investigate them. The Protrac Crawler Tread problem, *Section 2.5*, involved blending ores from four different mines. Changing the cost of the fourth ore (T_4) from \$500/ton to \$408.889/ton, gives us two alternate solutions:

	SOLUTION I	SOLUTION II
OV	511.11	511.11
T_1	25.9%	4.9%
T_2	70.4%	0.0%
T_3	3.7%	43.5%
T_4	0.0%	51.6%
B surplus	31.667	27.364

The blends are different, and each one eliminates one type of ore. Also, solution II has less surplus of basic element B. It may be that PROTRAC prefers one solution over the other due to qualitative or intangible factors of which we are not aware.

Degenerate Problems

We know that a degenerate corner is one at which there are fewer than m positive basic variables, where m is the number of constraints in the model and hence the number of rows in the main body of the tableau. Thus, a degenerate corner will be encountered when the tableau shows a zero in the VALUE column. When this happens in the tableau, it is possible that the variable that we are trying to enter will come into the basis at zero level, and hence in this pivot we remain at the same corner, merely changing the basic set, and the value of the objective function does not change. This is illustrated by the tableaux for the **PROTRAC**, Inc. model shown in Figures 6.17 and 6.18. At the corner corresponding to Figure 6.17 we see a degenerate solution, since at this corner the value of the basic variable s_2 is zero. The nonbasic variable E satisfies the entry criterion, and s_2 with corresponding ratio zero is the exit variable. However, you can see in Figure 6.18 that E has entered at the level zero, and the value of the objective function has not improved on this pivot. It has remained the same. A zero variable has left the basis, a new variable has entered at the level zero, and in short, the values of *all* variables have remained the same (hence, the corner has not changed). This phenomenon can occur for the reason that more than one set of basic variables is associated with a degenerate corner. This was discussed in connection with Figures 6.3 and 6.4.

In the case of the **PROTRAC**, Inc. model, although degeneracy was encountered, it did not cause a problem, and the algorithm proceeded with no special provision for this phenomenon. In theory the algorithm could move back and forth among the several sets of basic variables at a degenerate corner, thus causing what is termed a *cycling phenomenon.* This rarely occurs in practice, although it is possible theoretically.

It has been shown that cycling can be avoided with certainty if the following provision is appended to the exit rule. Recall that the exit variable is identified by starting at the top of the VALUE column and computing prescribed ratios to determine a minimum ratio.

Whenever a tie occurs in the ratios for the exit variable, choose as the pivot row the first (i.e., the uppermost) row that produced the minimum ratio.

With this rule, cycling will always be avoided, and the simplex method becomes a perfect algorithm in the following sense. The simplex algorithm will always terminate in a finite number of steps in one of the following states:

1. You obtain an infeasibility signal.
2. You obtain an unbounded signal.
3. You obtain an optimal solution.

6.14 Alternative Optima

Recall that the optimality signal for the complete tableau is that all entries in the last row (the opportunity costs) are ≤ 0.

When you encounter an optimal tableau with a zero entry in the last row, under a *nonbasic* column, that variable can be brought into the basis without changing the objective value. If the optimal solution is *nondegenerate,* the variable brought into the basis will be positive. This means that a new corner is obtained, and hence an alternative optimal solution exists.

The geometric interpretation of alternative optima was discussed in Section 3.5. This phenomenon occurs when more than one corner of the feasible region lies on the optimal objective function contour. This implies that there is more than one optimal basic feasible solution and infinitely many nonbasic optimal solutions.

6.15 The Simplex Method for a Min Model

All of the development in this chapter has pertained to solving a Max LP model. The modifications required to solve a Min model are very simple. Either of two possible approaches can be taken.

Approach 1 is usually easier for the student than Approach 2, because all the same rules are used in the tableau iterations.

Approach 1. Take the negative of the objective function and solve the problem as though it were a Max model. This trick works because for any function $f(x)$, any point that minimizes $f(x)$ will also maximize $-f(x)$. Thus, by taking the negative of a Min objective function, and then solving as though it were a Max model, we obtain the correct optimal solution for the original Min model. To obtain the correct OV for the original Min model we multiply the OV for the Max model by -1.

Professional computer codes simply have the user indicate "Max" or "Min," and the computer takes care of all the dirty work.

Approach 2. Keep the Min objective as given, but artificial variables must appear in the objective function with coefficient $+M$. Also, reverse the entry rule and the stopping criterion. In other words, for a Min model enter the variable with the *most negative* opportunity cost. An optimal tableau is obtained when all opportunity costs are nonnegative.

APPLICATION CAPSULE

The Human Factor: Why Planners in Turkey Didn't Cotton to an LP Solution*

So far we have spent a good deal of time on the technical side of LP: tableaux, surplus variables, active constraints, and the like. All of these concepts belong to the orderly world of mathematics. In Chapter 1, however, we stressed that the techniques of management science are used by real people to solve real problems in a real and often very disorderly world. And where people are involved, there are usually complications: psychological, political, cultural, and so on. In the real world, therefore, the mere fact that a problem can be formulated as an LP model and solved to produce an attractive result does not mean that the solution will be put to use.

A case in point is the work of the Operations Research division of the Scientific and Technical Research Council of Turkey. This organization created a multiperiod LP for that country's cotton textile industry. The goal was to help prepare the annual budget and production plans for 18 factories manufacturing more than 300 different products. The objective function was to maximize profits (defined as sales revenues minus operating costs, the cost of transferring partly finished products between factories, inventory costs, and penalties for idle capacity). Constraints included:

- The capacity of each machine used and the operating time required for each product
- Balance equations for production quantities, inventories, sales of each product, and so on, for each time period
- Capacity and demand bounds.

When the model was first run, it indicated the possibility of a reduction in annual operating costs of $1,780,000, together with an increase in total production of over 4%. Nevertheless, the production plans produced by the model were never implemented. The reasons have very little to do with LP and a lot to do with people, politics, and bureaucracies:

- During the 14 months of the study there were three different national governments, each bringing in different general managers. Even factory managers were reshuffled.
- Because the OR team consisted of outsiders, middle level management had no sense of ownership of the project and was skeptical of its recommendations.
- Factory managers were resistant to making changes in their production programs.
- There was no authority behind the project recommendations, and no final decision makers were designated to carry out implementation.

You can lead a horse to water. . . .

*Nebol, "Macro Production Planning: An Applied Research Project." *Interfaces*, Vol. 17, No. 4 (July–Aug. 1987).

6.16 Notes on Implementation

The simplex algorithm as presented in this chapter gives, in most respects, the essential ideas originally employed in solving linear programs. However, in current practice, some of the details have been considerably refined in order to produce greater computational efficiency, which generally means greater capabilities for the successful solution of larger and larger models. In particular, most LP software systems for today's modern computers employ what is called the revised simplex method.

Although the details of this are beyond our introductory scope, it can be stated that the main difference between the procedure given in the text and the revised simplex method has to do with the way in which the tableau is represented in computer memory. The major reason for improving this representation is to exploit special structures in the LP data, such as sparsity of the data matrix. As an illustration, suppose that the problem has 500 rows (constraints) and 1000 columns (variables). If the original algorithm as herein presented is used, the tableau would require one coefficient for each variable in each constraint, a total of 500,000 numbers. But most of these coefficients are typically 0. It is not unusual for real problems of this size to have only about four nonzero entries per column, which implies there are only about 4000 pieces of nonzero data. It is this sort of special structure that is exploited in current software to cut down on storage requirements and hence to give greater computing power. As a result, modern batch processing codes can handle problems with thousands of rows and essentially an unlimited number of columns.

Another rule of thumb: When you increase the problem size by p, the running time increases by p^2. Thus, if you double the number of variables, the running time increases by a factor of four. Accordingly, if a 15-variable, 3-constraint problem runs in 1 second, then a 45-variable, 6-constraint problem would run in 36 seconds [(45 × 6)/(15 × 3) = 6 times "bigger" and 36 times slower to run].

As this discussion suggests, the continuing development of sophisticated LP software is a special field in its own right and involves a solid background in both computer science and numerical analysis.

In concluding this section, we should point out that, according to empirical folklore, the number of pivots required to solve an LP problem is roughly from m to $3m$, where m is the number of constraints. The number of pivots, of course, is a measure of how much computer time is involved in solving the problem. This "m to $3m$ rule" explains why, in practical applications, one typically attempts to formulate the LP model with as few constraints as possible, and with less concern given to the number of variables.

6.17 Summary

In this chapter we showed how the simplex method is used to solve an LP problem in standard equality constraint form (all constraints are equalities, all variables, nonnegative). It was seen that the simplex method moves from corner to adjacent corner of the feasible region. Associated with each corner is a basic feasible solution and a simplex tableau that represents this solution, in terms of the transformed equations at the corner. The move from one corner to another is performed algebraically by performing the pivot operation on the tableau of data. In order to begin using the simplex method, it may be necessary to add artificial variables to the problem.

Steps of the Simplex Method

Here is a detailed, step-by-step outline of how to apply the simplex method:

- ***Step 1:*** Cast the original problem into standard equality constraint form by introducing slack and surplus variables as required. If the original model is a Min problem, multiply the objective function by -1 and convert to Max.
- ***Step 2:*** Make all the right-hand sides nonnegative by multiplying both sides of the equalities by -1 wherever required.
- ***Step 3:*** Add artificial variables as necessary to obtain m distinguished variables. Each such variable, by definition, appears in only one constraint and has a coefficient, in that constraint, of $+1$. Each artificial variable is included in the objective function with coefficient $-M$, which stands for a very negative number ("minus a million").
- ***Step 4:*** Set up the main body of the initial tableau. This is simply a tabular representation of the equations coming out of step 3.
- ***Step 5:*** Compute the z_j row and the $c_j - z_j$ row, the latter being the opportunity costs of not having another unit of the variable x_j in the solution. Also compute the current value of the objective function. Now choose the entering nonbasic variable to be the one whose opportunity cost is most positive. (If there is no positive $c_j - z_j$, the current solution is optimal.)
- ***Step 6:*** The pivot column is defined in step 5. Choose the pivot row by finding the Min of the ratios of VALUE entries to positive entries in the pivot column. Then update the main body of the tableau by writing in the new basic variable, filling in the pivot row and the basic columns, and then pivoting on the remaining data.
- ***Step 7:*** Fill in the new z_j row, $c_j - z_j$ row, and the new value of the objective function.
- ***Step 8:*** Test for optimality: If optimal, all entries in the last row are ≤ 0.
- ***Step 9:*** If not optimal, update again. If optimal and at least one artificial variable remains in the basis at a positive level, the original problem is infeasible. If optimal and no artificial variables remain in the basis, you have the optimal solution to the original problem. As soon as all artificial variables have been removed from the basis, phase I is complete.
- ***Step 10:*** As each iteration after phase I is completed, test for an unbounded problem: a positive entry in the last row and all elements ≤ 0 in the corresponding column of the main body of the tableau.

The sequence of operations described above will lead you to the solution of any LP problem. In concluding, however, let us mention the fact that the efficient computational implementation of the simplex method is quite complicated and is a topic worthy of study in its own right. Nevertheless, at the heart of the simplex method is the above-described tabular representation of extreme points and the concept of pivoting in order to update from one basic feasible solution to another.

Key Terms

Simplex Method. An algorithm used to solve linear programming problems. (*p. 218*)

Vertex. Pl. *vertices.* A corner of an LP constraint set. (*p. 218*)

Extreme Point. Synonym for vertex. (*p. 218*)

Phase I. The first part of the simplex method, designed to find the transformed equations corresponding to any initial corner of the constraint set of the given problem. (*p. 218*)

Iteration. In the simplex method, the move from one corner to an adjacent corner. (*p. 218*)

Pivot. Synonym for iteration. (*p. 218*)

Original Equations. The m constraint equations in the standard equality constraint form of the original problem with n variables, including decision variables, surplus variables, and slack variables, and where $m < n$. (*p. 219*)

Solution. Although in many contexts the terms *solution* and *optimal solution* are synonymous, in the study of the simplex method the term *solution* means any solution (i.e., set of values for the n variables), not necessarily optimal, to the original equations.(*p. 220*)

Optimal Solution. A solution that is optimal for the given problem. (*p. 220*)

Feasible Solution. A solution for which all variables are nonnegative. (*p. 221*)

Basic Solution. A solution to m simultaneous linear equations in n unknowns, $m < n$, with the property that $n - m$ of the variables have the value zero, and the values of the remaining m variables are uniquely determined; obtained when a set of nonbasic variables are assigned the value zero. (*p. 221*)

Nonbasic Variables. A set of $n - m$ variables such that, when these variables are set equal to zero, the values of the remaining variables are uniquely determined. (*p. 221*)

Nonbasic Set. A set of nonbasic variables (refers to the set of variables). (*p. 221*)

Basic Variables. Given a set of $n - m$ nonbasic variables, the remaining m variables are termed basic. (*p. 221*)

Basic Set. A set of basic variables (refers to the set of variables, not their values). (*p. 221*)

Basis. The set of basic variables in a corner solution to an LP. (*p. 221*)

Basic Feasible Solution. A basic solution for which the values of all variables are nonnegative; corresponds to a corner of the LP feasible region. (*p. 223*)

Nondegenerate Basic Feasible Solution. A basic feasible solution with exactly m positive variables (hence exactly $n - m$ zero variables). (*p. 224*)

Degenerate Basic Feasible Solution. A basic feasible solution with fewer than m positive variables (hence more than $n - m$ zero variables). (*p. 224*)

Transformed Equations. Corresponding to each corner of the feasible region is a set of transformed equations that represent the basic feasible solution at that corner. These equations are equivalent to the original equations and have the following special form: (1) Each basic variable appears in a different equation only, and in that equation its coefficient is +1, and (2) Only constant terms are on the right-hand side of the equalities, and they are nonnegative. (*p. 227*)

Substitution Coefficients. The data in a nonbasic column that show the reductions that must occur (so that the original equations remain satisfied) in the current values (at a given corner) of the basic variables when the nonbasic variable is incremented a unit and all other nonbasic variables are held fixed at zero. (*p. 231*)

Basic Coefficients. The coefficients in the objective function that correspond to a set of basic variables. (*p. 231*)

Opportunity Cost. A term applying to the nonbasic variables at each corner; it is the cost of *not* incrementing a nonbasic variable by a unit (while keeping all other nonbasic variables at zero and allowing basic variables to adjust appropriately); this is equivalent to the improvement in OV obtained per unit increment in the nonbasic variable. (*p. 232*)

Enter Rule. A procedure for selecting the enter variable in the simplex method. (*p. 232*)

Enter Variable. At the current corner, the nonbasic variable that is chosen to become basic in the move to the next corner. (*p. 232*)

Simplex Tableau. A tabular representation of the transformed equations plus an opportunity cost row; there is a tableau corresponding to each corner of the feasible region. (*p. 235*)

Initial Tableau. The first tableau used in the simplex method. (*p. 235*)

Exit Variable. At the current corner, the basic variable that is chosen to become nonbasic at the next corner. (*p. 236*)

Exit Rule. A procedure for selecting the exit variable on the simplex method. (*p. 238*)

Gaussian Elimination. The sequence of operations that uses the values in a simplex tableau and produces the values in the successor to that tableau. (*p. 238*)

Optimality Criterion. The criterion for recognizing the tableau corresponding to an optimal corner, this is, for a Max problem, all opportunity costs ≤ 0. Also called the stopping rule. (*p. 243*)

Distinguished Variable. A nonnegative variable that appears in only one constraint and has coefficient +1. (*p. 245*)

Artificial Variable. In phase I, a variable added to a constraint lacking a distinguished variable. (*p. 247*)

Major Concepts Quiz

True–False

1. T F Every basic solution to the original equations corresponds to a corner of the constraint set.

2. T F At a nondegenerate corner there will be more than one set of basic variables.

3. T F At a degenerate corner the basic variables are all positive.

4. T F Basic solutions that are not feasible will never be encountered in phase II of the simplex method.

5. T F Each constraint in the standard equality form model (excluding nonnegativity conditions) is represented by a row of the simplex tableau.

6. T F Since the z_j row gives the *loss* of profit (in a Max model) resulting from adding one unit of the column variable to the current solution, we can select the best variable to add to the current solution by choosing any column with a negative z_j value.

7. T F For a Max LP model, it is the enter rule that guarantees a nondecreasing objective function in each move.

8. T F The enter rule can be modified to prevent cycling.

9. T F In solving a Min model, as opposed to a Max model, the enter rule and optimality criterion are the only differences.

10. T F You can solve either the primal or the dual with the simplex method, but not both.

11. T F Degeneracy will result whenever a tie occurs in the minimum ratio for the enter rule.

12. T F An unbounded problem is discovered in phase I.

Multiple Choice

13. Every simplex iteration for a Max problem replaces a variable in the current basis with another variable that has
- **a.** a larger per unit profitability as shown in the c_j (i.e., objective function coefficient) row
- **b.** a positive $c_j - z_j$ value
- **c.** the smallest $c_j - z_j$ value
- **d.** any negative $c_j - z_j$ value

14. Every tableau in the simplex method
- **a.** exhibits a solution to the original equations
- **b.** exhibits a basic feasible solution to the equations in the standard equality form of the model
- **c.** corresponds to an extreme point of the constraint set
- **d.** exhibits a set of transformed equations
- **e.** all of the above

15. Artificial variables
- **a.** are used to aid in finding an initial solution
- **b.** are used in phase I
- **c.** can be used to find optimal dual prices in the final tableau
- **d.** all of the above

16. The signal for optimality in a Max model is
- **a.** $c_j - z_j \leq 0$, for all j
- **b.** $z_j \leq 0$, for all j
- **c.** $c_j - z_j > 0$, for all j

17. Suppose that in a nondegenerate optimal tableau a slack variable s_2 is basic for the second constraint, whose RHS is b_2. This means that
- **a.** the original problem is infeasible
- **b.** all of b_2 is used up in the optimal solution

c. both the dual price and the optimal value of the dual variable, for the second constraint, are zero

d. a better OV could be obtained by increasing b_2

18. Which of the following is not true of the simplex method?
    a. At each iteration, the objective value either stays the same or improves.
    b. It indicates an unbounded or infeasible problem.
    c. It signals optimality.
    d. It converges in at most m steps, where m is the number of constraints.

19. Infeasibility is discovered
    a. in computing the enter variable
    b. in computing the exit variable
    c. in phase I

20. Cycling
    a. can always be prevented
    b. is a real-world concern
    c. will cause more pivots to occur before termination

Answers

1. F	6. F	11. F	16. a
2. F	7. T	12. F	17. c
3. F	8. F	13. b	18. d
4. T	9. T	14. d	19. c
5. T	10. F	15. d	20. a

▶ Problems

(a) iv, (b) vi, (c) i, (d) vii, (e) ix, (f) xi, (g) v, (h) viii, (i) iii, (j) ii, (k) x

6-1. ▲ Consider, as appropriate, (1) a system of m linear equations in n unknowns and (2) an LP. Pertaining to the appropriate system, match each of the following terms with the correct definition below.

(a) Feasible region.

(b) Solution.

(c) Basic variables.

(d) Basis.

(e) Feasible solution.

(f) Nonbasic variables.

(g) Basic feasible solution.

(h) Substitution coefficient.

(i) Basic solution.

(j) Artificial variable.

(k) Opportunity cost.

(i) A set of m variables whose values (in order that the equations be satisfied) are uniquely determined when the values of the remaining variables are set to zero.

(ii) A variable added to a constraint in order to obtain easily an initial tableau.

(iii) The solution (to the equations) obtained when the nonbasic variables are set equal to zero.

(iv) The set of points that satisfies all the constraints and nonnegativity conditions for the original problem.

(v) A basic solution in which no variable has a negative value.

(vi) Any set of values of the n variables such that the equations are satisfied.
(vii) A set of basic variables.
(viii) The trade-off between an entering nonbasic variable and a basic variable.
(ix) Any set of nonnegative values of the n variables such that the equations are satisfied.
(x) Improvement in OV obtained per unit increase in a nonbasic variable.
(xi) $n - m$ variables that, when assigned values of zero, uniquely determine the values of the remaining variables (such that the equations are satisfied).

(a) Max $9x_1 + 21x_2 + 25x_3$
s.t. $3x_1 + x_3 \le 35$
$5x_1 + 5x_2 \le 25$
$-x_2 + 2x_3 \le 15$
$x_1, x_2, x_3 \ge 0$
(b) See IM.
(c) initial set of basic variables s_1, s_2, s_3
(d) x_1, x_2, x_3
(e) $(x_1, x_2, x_3, s_1, s_2, s_3) = (0, 0, 0, 35, 25, 15)$
(f) x_3
(g) s_3
(h) row s_3, column x_3
(i) See IM.

6-2. ▲ Consider the partial initial simplex tableau shown in Figure 6.23 for a Max model.
(a) Write the original LP corresponding to this tableau.
(b) Complete the tableau.

		9	21	25	0	0	0	
BASIC COEFFICIENT	**BASIC VARIABLE**	x_1	x_2	x_3	s_1	s_2	s_3	**VALUE**
		3	0	1	1	0	0	35
		5	5	0	0	1	0	25
		0	−1	2	0	0	1	15
	z_j							
	$c_j - z_j$							

▲ FIGURE 6.23

(c) What is the initial set of basic variables?
(d) What is the initial set of nonbasic variables?
(e) Give the coordinates of the corner of the feasible region that corresponds to the initial basic feasible solution.
(f) What is the enter variable?
(g) What is the exit variable?
(h) What is the pivot element?
(i) Solve the problem using the simplex method.

(a) $3x_1 + x_3 + s_1 - 2s_2 = 100$
$x_1 + x_2 + s_2 = 200$
$-5x_1 - 2s_1 + 4s_2 + s_3 = 400$
$x_i \ge 0, \quad i = 1, 2, 3$
$s_j \ge 0, \quad j = 1, 2, 3$
(b) $\{x_2, x_3, s_3\}$
(c) $\{x_1, s_1, s_2\}$
(d) See IM.
(e) No. s_2 should enter and s_3 should exit.
(f) See IM.

6-3. ▲ Consider the partial simplex tableau shown in Figure 6.24 for a Max model.
(a) Write the transformed equations corresponding to this tableau.
(b) What are the basic variables?

▼ FIGURE 6.24

		20	30	25	0	0	0	
BASIC COEFFICIENT	**BASIC VARIABLE**	x_1	x_2	x_3	s_1	s_2	s_3	**VALUE**
		3	0	1	1	−2	0	100
		1	1	0	0	1	0	200
		−5	0	0	−2	4	1	400
	z_j							
	$c_j - z_j$							

(a) There are 6 basic solutions
(i) ($x_1 = 2, x_2 = 2, s_1 = 0, s_2 = 0$)
(ii) ($x_1 = 3, x_2 = 0, s_1 = 0, s_2 = 3$)
(iii) ($x_1 = 0, x_2 = 3, s_1 = 3, s_2 = 0$)
(iv) ($x_1 = 0, x_2 = 0, s_1 = 6, s_2 = 6$)
(v) ($x_1 = 6, x_2 = 0, s_1 = -6, s_2 = 0$)
(vi) ($x_1 = 0, x_2 = 6, s_1 = 0, s_2 = -6$)

(b) i, ii, iii, iv.

(a) See IM.

(b) $x_1 = 0, x_2 = \frac{4}{3}, s_1 = 0, s_2 = \frac{56}{3}$;
$x_1 = \frac{8}{3}, x_2 = 0, s_1 = 0, s_2 = 8$;
$x_1 = 0, x_2 = 0, s_1 = 8, s_2 = 24$

(a) 10
(b) No.
(c) At least 1, at most 10

(a) 6
(b) No.
(c) At least 1, at most 6

(a) 1, 5
(b) 6
(c) 1, 4
(d) 3
(e) 1
(f) 2

(c) What are the nonbasic variables?

(d) Complete the tableau.

(e) Is the current solution optimal? If not, which variable should enter and which should exit?

(f) Use the simplex method to finish solving the problem.

6-4. ▲ Consider the following LP:

$$\begin{aligned} \text{Max } & 2x_1 + 3x_2 \\ \text{s.t. } & 2x_1 + x_2 \le 6 \\ & x_1 + 2x_2 \le 6 \\ & x_1 \ge 0, \quad x_2 \ge 0 \end{aligned}$$

(a) Either by algebraic or geometric analysis, find all basic solutions.

(b) Which of these correspond to extreme points of the feasible region?

6-5. ▲ Consider the following LP:

$$\begin{aligned} \text{Max } & 5x_1 + 6x_2 \\ \text{s.t. } & 3x_1 + 6x_2 \le 8 \\ & 6x_1 + 4x_2 \le 24 \\ & x_1 \ge 0, \quad x_2 \ge 0 \end{aligned}$$

(a) By either algebraic or geometric analysis, find all basic solutions.

(b) Which of these correspond to extreme points of the feasible region?

6-6. ▲▲ Consider an LP in standard equality constraint form. There are three constraints and five variables, including slack or surplus variables.

(a) What is the maximum number of basic solutions to this problem?

(b) Need it be true that there are, in fact, this number of basic solutions?

(c) Suppose that the problem has an optimal solution. Can you say anything about the number of basic feasible solutions?
HINT: Can you give an upper and a lower bound?

6-7. ▲▲ Answer parts (a), (b), and (c) of Problem 6-6 for an LP in two constraints and four variables.

6-8. ▲▲▲ Each of the following tableaux is associated with a Max model. One or more of the following descriptions applies to each tableau: (1) optimal; (2) shows problem is unbounded; (3) shows problem is infeasible; (4) current corner is degenerate; (5) there are alternative optima; (6) the problem is feasible, and the current corner is not optimal. Label each tableau with the applicable descriptor.

(a)

		9	3	0	0	
BASIC COEFFICIENT	**BASIC VARIABLE**	x_1	x_2	s_1	s_2	**VALUE**
9	x_1	1	⅓	⅓	0	10
0	s_2	0	3	−½	1	12
	z_j	9	3	3	0	
	$c_j - z_j$	0	0	−3	0	90

(b)

BASIC COEFFICIENT	BASIC VARIABLE	4	6	8	0	0	0	VALUE
		x_1	x_2	x_3	s_1	s_2	s_3	
6	x_2	½	1	0	−½	0	⅔	100
8	x_3	0	0	1	½	0	−¼	100
0	s_2	0	0	0	−½	1	−⅓	200
	z_j	3	6	8	1	0	2	
	$c_j - z_j$	1	0	0	−1	0	−2	1400

(c)

BASIC COEFFICIENT	BASIC VARIABLE	1	6	8	0	0	0	VALUE
		x_1	x_2	x_3	s_1	s_2	s_3	
6	x_2	⅓	1	0	−½	0	⅔	100
8	x_3	0	0	1	½	0	−¼	200
0	s_2	0	0	0	−½	1	−⅓	0
	z_j	2	6	8	1	0	2	
	$c_j - z_j$	−1	0	0	−1	0	−2	2200

(d)

BASIC COEFFICIENT	BASIC VARIABLE	4	10	0	$-M$	$-M$	VALUE
		x_1	x_2	s_1	a_2	a_3	
0	s_1	0	12	1	0	−12	10
4	x_1	1	1	0	0	1	4
$-M$	a_2	0	−1	0	1	0	3
	z_j	4	$4+M$	0	$-M$	4	
	$c_j - z_j$	0	$6-M$	0	0	$-4 - M$	$16 - 3M$

(e)

BASIC COEFFICIENT	BASIC VARIABLE	9	−4	0	0	VALUE
		x_1	x_2	s_1	s_2	
9	x_1	1	−⅓	⅓	0	10
0	s_2	0	−3	−½	1	12
	z_j	9	−3	3	0	
	$c_j - z_j$	0	−1	−3	0	90

(f)

BASIC COEFFICIENT	BASIC VARIABLE	9	6	0	0	
		x_1	x_2	s_1	s_2	VALUE
0	s_1	−1	1	1	0	11
0	s_2	−2	3	0	1	15
	z_j	0	0	0	0	
	$c_j - z_j$	9	6	0	0	0

QSB+ may be used to verify your paper-and-pencil calculations of the sequence of tableaux leading to the optimal solution.

See IM.

6-9. Use the simplex method to solve

$$\begin{aligned} &\text{Max } 40x_1 + 60x_2 + 50x_3 \\ &\text{s.t.} \quad 10x_1 + 4x_2 + 2x_3 \leq 950 \\ &\qquad 2x_1 + 2x_2 \leq 410 \\ &\qquad x_1 + 2x_3 \leq 610 \\ &x_1 \geq 0, \quad x_2 \geq 0, \quad x_3 \geq 0 \end{aligned}$$

See IM.

6-10. Use the simplex method to solve

$$\begin{aligned} &\text{Max } x_1 + 2x_2 + 5x_3 \\ &\text{s.t.} \quad 3x_1 + x_2 - x_3 \leq 6 \\ &\qquad 2x_1 - x_2 + 6x_3 \leq 6 \\ &x_1 \geq 0, \quad x_2 \geq 0, \quad x_3 \geq 0 \end{aligned}$$

See IM.

6-11. Use the simplex method to solve

$$\begin{aligned} &\text{Max } 25x_1 + 50x_2 \\ &\text{s.t.} \quad 2x_1 + 2x_2 \leq 1000 \\ &\qquad 3x_1 \leq 600 \\ &\qquad x_1 + 3x_2 \leq 600 \\ &x_1 \geq 0, \quad x_2 \geq 0 \end{aligned}$$

See IM.

6-12. Fill in the missing elements in the following optimal simplex tableau:

BASIC COEFFICIENT	BASIC VARIABLE			0	0	
		x_1	x_2	s_1	s_2	VALUE
		1	0		¼	3
4		0	1	⅜		3/2
	z_j					
	$c_j - z_j$	0	0	−¾	−¼	15

See IM.

6-13. ▲▲ Use the simplex method to solve

$$\begin{aligned} \text{Min } & 6x_1 + 8x_2 + 16x_3 \\ \text{s.t. } & 2x_1 + x_2 \geq 5 \\ & x_2 + 2x_3 \geq 4 \\ & x_1, x_2, x_3 \geq 0 \end{aligned}$$

Final tableaux same as 6-12.

6-14. ▲▲ Use the simplex method to solve

$$\begin{aligned} \text{Max } & 3x_1 + 4x_2 \\ \text{s.t. } & 2x_1 + 4x_2 \leq 12 \\ & 6x_1 + 4x_2 \leq 24 \\ & x_1, x_2 \geq 0 \end{aligned}$$

See IM.

6-15. ▲▲ Use artificial variables and set up the initial tableau for

$$\begin{aligned} \text{Min } & 6x_1 + x_2 + 3x_3 - 2x_4 \\ \text{s.t. } & x_1 + x_2 \leq 42 \\ & 2x_1 + 3x_2 - x_3 - x_4 \geq 10 \\ & x_1 + 2x_3 + x_4 = 30 \\ & x_1, x_2, x_3, x_4 \geq 0 \end{aligned}$$

See IM.

6-16. ▲▲▲ Consider the following problem:

$$\begin{aligned} \text{Min } & 5x_1 + 2x_2 + 3x_3 \\ \text{s.t. } & 2x_1 + 2x_2 + x_3 \geq 7 \\ & -x_1 + 5x_2 + 2x_3 \geq 11 \\ & x_1, x_2 \geq 0 \\ & x_3 \text{ unconstrained} \end{aligned}$$

(a) Write the dual problem.
(b) Set up the initial tableau for the dual problem.

$x_1 = 7.27$, $x_2 = 0$, $x_3 = 6.36$, $x_4 = 0$

6-17. ▲▲▲ Use artificial variables and the simplex method to solve

$$\begin{aligned} \text{Min } & -2x_1 - x_2 - 4x_3 - 5x_4 \\ \text{s.t. } & x_1 + 3x_2 + 2x_3 + 5x_4 \leq 20 \\ & 2x_1 + 16x_2 + x_3 + x_4 \geq 4 \\ & 3x_1 - x_2 - 5x_3 + 10x_4 \leq -10 \\ & x_1, x_2, x_3, x_4 \geq 0 \end{aligned}$$

See IM.

6-18. ▲▲▲ Write the dual to Problem 6-13 and use the optimal tableau from Problem 6-13 to obtain the optimal values of the dual variables.

Variable	AI	AD
x_1	0	∞
x_2	∞	5.0
x_3	5.5	0
x_4	∞	5.0
Constraint		
1	∞	14.3
2	16.9	∞
3	70.0	40.0

6-19. ▲▲▲ Compute all sensitivity information (all allowable increases and decreases) from the optimal tableau to Problem 6-17. (See footnote 8, Appendix 6.3.)

(a) 10
(b) 8; (x, s_2), (y, s_3)
(c) 6
(d) 4

6-20. Refer to Figure 6.3.
▲▲▲ **(a)** What is the theoretic limit on the number of nonbasic sets this model can have?
(b) How many nonbasic sets are there? Which pairs of variables do not form a nonbasic set?
(c) How many distinct basic solutions are there?
(d) How many basic feasible solutions are there?

Appendix 6.1 Sensitivity Analysis: Computing the Optimal Dual Variables

It is important to stress that these values don't appear out of thin air, but can be computed manually. However, it is nice having a computer program that does this automatically! These dual variable values are extremely important, in that they give the marginal value of an extra unit of resource for each constraint (adding 1 to the right-hand side).

In Chapter 5 we discussed the fact that corresponding to any LP there is another LP, called the dual problem. We stated that either of these two problems will have an optimal solution if and only if the other one does also, and in this case the two optimal objective values are equal. As an example, consider the **PROTRAC**, Inc. model solved with the simplex method in Section 6.13 (the computer output for the solution appears in Figure 5.6). The model is

$$
\begin{array}{llll}
\text{Max } 5000E + 4000F & & & \\
\text{s.t.} \quad E + F \geq 5 & \text{(total units requirement)} & ① & \\
E - 3F \leq 0 & \text{(market balance)} & ② & \\
10E + 15F \leq 150 & \text{(department A)} & ③ & \text{(P)} \\
20E + 10F \leq 160 & \text{(department B)} & ④ & \\
30E + 10F \geq 135 & \text{(contractual labor)} & ⑤ & \\
E \geq 0, & F \geq 0 & &
\end{array}
$$

The dual of this problem is[6]

$$
\begin{array}{ll}
\text{Min } 5y_1 + 150y_3 + 160y_4 + 135y_5 & \\
\text{s.t.} \quad y_1 + y_2 + 10y_3 + 20y_4 + 30y_5 \geq 5000 & \\
y_1 - 3y_2 + 15y_3 + 10y_4 + 10y_5 \geq 4000 & \text{(D)} \\
y_1, y_5 \leq 0; \quad y_2, y_3, y_4 \geq 0 &
\end{array}
$$

Recall that for a Max model the dual prices on the computer printout are the same as the optimal values of the variables in the dual problem. For a Min model, dual

[6]If the primal problem (P) is written in standard equality constraint form, the dual problem, let us call it (D′), would have five variables free in sign, seven rather than two constraints, and hence would look different from (D). However, you may wish to verify for yourself, by writing out (D′), that in fact the difference is in appearance only. The extra five constraints in (D′) are the five sign conditions that appear in (D).

prices and optimal dual variables are the same in magnitude (absolute value) but opposite in sign. Since the **PROTRAC**, Inc. problem is a Max model, the dual prices and the optimal solution to the dual problem are the same. Thus, we can read from the DUAL PRICES column of Figure 5.6 to obtain

$$y_1^* = 0, \qquad y_2^* = 0, \qquad y_3^* = 150, \qquad y_4^* = 175, \qquad y_5^* = 0$$

Locating dual variables in the optimal tableau

The following result shows where the optimal values of the dual variables are located in the tableau:

> **For either a Max or a Min model, the optimal value of the kth dual variable can be found in the z_j row of the optimal tableau, in the column headed by the distinguished variable in the kth constraint (the variable in the original standard equality constraint form that appears only in the kth constraint and has coefficient + 1).**

It is beyond the scope and intent of this text to give a formal proof of this result. However, it can be intuitively shown as follows. Consider, for example, the labor constraint in department B (constraint ④). In the standard equality form, the slack variable on this constraint is s_4. Since constraint ④ is a $\leq$ constraint, we also know that s_4 is the distinguished variable associated with this constraint. As seen in Figure 6.22, s_4 is nonbasic (i.e., has the value zero) at the optimal corner. We know, also from Figure 6.22, that the opportunity cost of s_4 is the entry in the s_4 column in the $c_j - z_j$ row, namely -175. This means that if s_4 were increased by a unit, then the value of the objective function would decrease by \$175. But increasing s_4 a unit is tantamount to decreasing by 1 unit the availability of labor in department B. Thus, 1 less hour of labor availability in department B decreases profit by \$175, and we interpret this to mean also that 1 more hour of labor would increase profit by \$175, which is the negative of the entry in the $c_j - z_j$ row, the s_4 column. That is, $175 = z_j - c_j$ and, since c_j is zero because s_4 is a slack variable, we have $175 = z_j$ (i.e., 175 is the entry in the s_4 column in the z_j row). This is y_4^*.

Let us further illustrate the rule above in terms of Figure 6.22. Recall that the variables s_2 and s_3 are the distinguished variables for the second and third constraints, respectively. Therefore, the values of y_2^* and y_3^* noted above are found in the z_j row of Figure 6.22, in the columns headed by s_2 and s_3, respectively. The distinguished variables for the first and fifth constraints are a_1 and a_2 and consequently the y_1^* (y_5^*) noted above is found in the z_j row under the a_1 (a_2) column. Thus, you see that all dual prices can be obtained from the optimal tableau, with the caveat:

> **If you wish to obtain the dual prices from the tableau, you should keep (at each iteration) all columns corresponding to any artificial variables that had to be added to the model.**

Sensitivity analysis is also referred to as *postoptimality analysis* for two reasons. First, the *interpretations* are always with reference to a current optimal solution. Second, most of the *computations* are performed after the optimal tableau is obtained. In the discussion above you saw that the dual prices can in fact be read directly from the optimal tableau. In the following two appendixes you will see that the remainder of the sensitivity analysis is obtained with additional computation based on data in the optimal tableau.

Appendix 6.2 Sensitivity Analysis: Computing Allowable Changes in the RHS[7]

In Appendix 6.1 it was seen that the z_j row of the distinguished variable columns gives the dual prices. Let b_i denote the current (original) value of the ith RHS, and let b_i' denote a different value. Let d_i denote the dual price on the ith constraint. In the discussion of sensitivity analysis in Chapter 5 it was stated that *for some limited range of values b_i'*, the product

$$(b_i' - b_i)d_i$$

gives the improvement in OV as b_i is changed to b_i', with all other data held fixed. Let us see how to compute this range.

At the current optimal corner solution there is a set of current basic and nonbasic variables. Suppose that in the original equations you change b_i to b_i', leaving all other data fixed, and then consider the new basic solution to these equations, in terms of the current set of basic and nonbasic variables. Changing b_i to b_i' will change the values of at least some basic variables. *The allowable values for b_i'* are precisely those values for which the new basic solution remains feasible (i.e., for which the values of the basic variables remain nonnegative). This is because the change from b_i to b_i' has no effect on substitution coefficients, or z_j's, or $(c_j - z_j)$'s, and hence an optimal tableau for the new problem will be precisely the same as the current optimal tableau except for new nonnegative numbers in the VALUE column (i.e., the numbers giving the new values for the basic variables and for the objective function).

Consider, for example, the RHS, b_i, associated with an *inactive constraint.* The optimal value of the corresponding slack or surplus variable, call it s_i^*, is positive, and therefore s_i is basic. Consider the sets of basic and nonbasic variables at an optimal basic feasible solution. As b_i changes, the only basic variable to change value will be s_i. For example, in Figure 5.5 verify that when the RHS of the market balance constraint is changed, then in the current optimal solution only the value of the slack variable, s_2, will change. All other basic variables will retain their current values, and the current nonbasic variables of course remain at zero. The current value of s_2 is 16.5, as shown in the optimal tableau, Figure 6.22. This is the amount the RHS can be decreased without destroying the feasibility of the current optimum. If b_2 is decreased by more than 16.5 units, the slack value s_2, at the current optimum, will be negative. We also observe that the RHS can be arbitrarily increased.

Rule for Inactive Constraints

Thus, *for an inactive constraint the RHS can be tightened by an amount equal to the optimal slack value (found in the optimal tableau) without destroying feasibility. It can be arbitrarily loosened.* This dictates the "allowable increase" and "allowable decrease" values for such right-hand sides (i.e., for inactive constraints). As specific cases, note in Figure 5.6 that on the market balance constraint, a $\leq$ constraint, the allowable increase (loosening) is infinite, and the allowable decrease (tightening) is s_2^*, namely 16.5. Since the first constraint is of $\geq$ form, and since its

[7] The discussion in this section is equally applicable to a Max or a Min model.

optimal surplus value is 6.5., the allowable decrease (loosening) is infinite, while the allowable increase (tightening) is s_1^*, namely 6.5.

Now consider the RHS, b_i, associated with an *active constraint.* As this RHS changes, the values of the basic variables, in the basic solution, will also change. Whenever one of them becomes negative the allowable range will have been exceeded.

To calculate the allowable range we must first identify the distinguished variable associated with the constraint under consideration. Suppose that, in the **PROTRAC**, Inc. model, we are interested in constraint ③ (i.e., in the equality $10E + 15F + s_3 = 150$). We identify s_3 as the distinguished variable and note that since the constraint is active, we have $s_3^* = 0$. Now rewrite the equation as $10E + 15F = 150 - s_3$. We see then that as far as the basic variables E and F are concerned, increasing s_3 is equivalent to decreasing the RHS value 150 by the same amount, and decreasing, s_3 is equivalent to increasing the RHS value 150 by the same amount.

Thus, the following two questions are equivalent:

1. Given the optimal solution, how much can the RHS of constraint ③ be decreased before one of the currently nonnegative basic variables becomes negative?
2. Given the optimal solution, how much can s_3 be increased before one of the currently nonnegative basic variables becomes negative?

We have answered a question just like question 2 each time we have pivoted a nonbasic variable into the basic feasible solution. Thus, we can now use the same process to achieve our goal of finding an answer to question 1. As before, the answer is determined by the following calculation: Let k be the column identified by the distinguished variable, i be an index indicating a row in the optimal tableau, V_i be the entry in the value column of i, and a_{ik} the substitution coefficient in row i, column k.

Allowable decrease for active constraint

Allowable decrease in RHS equals minimum over all i for which $a_{ik} > 0$ of V_i/a_{ik}.

Returning to our example of constraint ③ in the **PROTRAC**, Inc. model, we have already identified the slack variable s_3 as the distinguished variable. According to our prescription the allowable decrease should be equal to the minimum of (7/0.1, 16.5/0.35, 6.5/0.05). The minimum ratio is 16.5/0.35 = 47.14. You can see in the computer output, Figure 5.6, that indeed this is the allowable decrease for the RHS of the third constraint.

Using the same type of reasoning allows us to derive the following rule for determining the allowable increase:

Allowable increase for active constraint

The allowable increase in the RHS equals the minimum over all i for which $a_{ik} < 0$ of $-V_i/a_{ik}$.

Continuing our example of constraint ③, we see that the allowable increase in the RHS of constraint ③ equals the minimum of (−4.05/−0.05, −70/−0.5), which is −4.5/−0.05, or 90. Again the computer output verifies that this is indeed the allowable increase.

Performing the same calculations for constraint ④, we obtain

$$\text{allowable decrease} = \text{Min}(4.5/0.075, 70/1.75, 6.5/0.025)$$
$$= \text{Min}(60, 40, 260) = 40$$
$$\text{allowable increase} = \text{Min}(7/0.05, 16.5/0.225)$$
$$= \text{Min}(140, 73.33) = 73.33$$

Verify that these are the numbers that appear in Figure 5.6.

Appendix 6.3 Sensitivity Analysis: Computing Allowable Changes in the Objective Function Coefficient[8]

In Chapter 5 it was shown how the computer output provides, for each objective function coefficient, a range of values such that the coefficient may be varied within that range without changing the optimal solution. We also used the geometry to interpret these ranges and to show how these values could be determined in a problem with two decision variables. Recall that the *interpretation always assumes that all other data in the model are unchanged.*

In this appendix we show how the objective function coefficient ranges that appear on the computer output can be derived from the optimal tableau. The discussion focuses on a somewhat altered version of the Astro/Cosmo problem. The formulation and computer solution are presented in Figure 6.25. The only change between the original problem and this revised version is that the total capacity in department B is reduced from 90 to 60. In other words, the RHS of the second constraint is now 60. To obtain the standard equality form of this model, we simply add a slack variable to each constraint as follows:

$$
\begin{aligned}
&\text{Max } 20A + 10C \\
&\text{s.t. } A + 2C + s_1 = 120 \\
&\qquad A + C + s_2 = 60 \\
&\qquad A + s_3 = 70 \\
&\qquad C + s_4 = 50 \\
&\qquad A, C \geq 0
\end{aligned}
$$

The simplex algorithm is now applied to this problem. The optimal tableau is shown in Figure 6.26.

[8]The discussion in this section applies to a Max model. If your initial problem is a Min model, you could proceed as follows: (1) multiply the objective function by −1, and compute the simplex solution to the Max problem; (2) use the optimal tableau to compute allowable increases and decreases in objective coefficients, as described in this appendix; and (3) interchange the terms "allowable increase" and "allowable decrease." That is, the allowable increase computed for the Max model turns out to be the allowable decrease for the Min model.

From both Figures 6.25 and 6.26 we see that the optimal solution to the problem is $A^* = 60$, $C^* = 0$, $s_1^* = 60$, $s_2^* = 0$, $s_3^* = 10$, $s_4^* = 50$. Further, we note in Figure 6.26 that s_1, A, s_3, and s_4 are basic variables, whereas C and s_2 are nonbasic. We now turn our attention to determining the allowable increase and allowable decrease for each coefficient in the objective function. There are two different cases to consider: (1) coefficients for nonbasic variables and (2) coefficients for basic variables.

In the following discussion it may be helpful to visualize the geometric analysis of the problem. This is produced in Figure 6.27.

▼ FIGURE 6.25
Printout for Astro/Cosmo, Revised

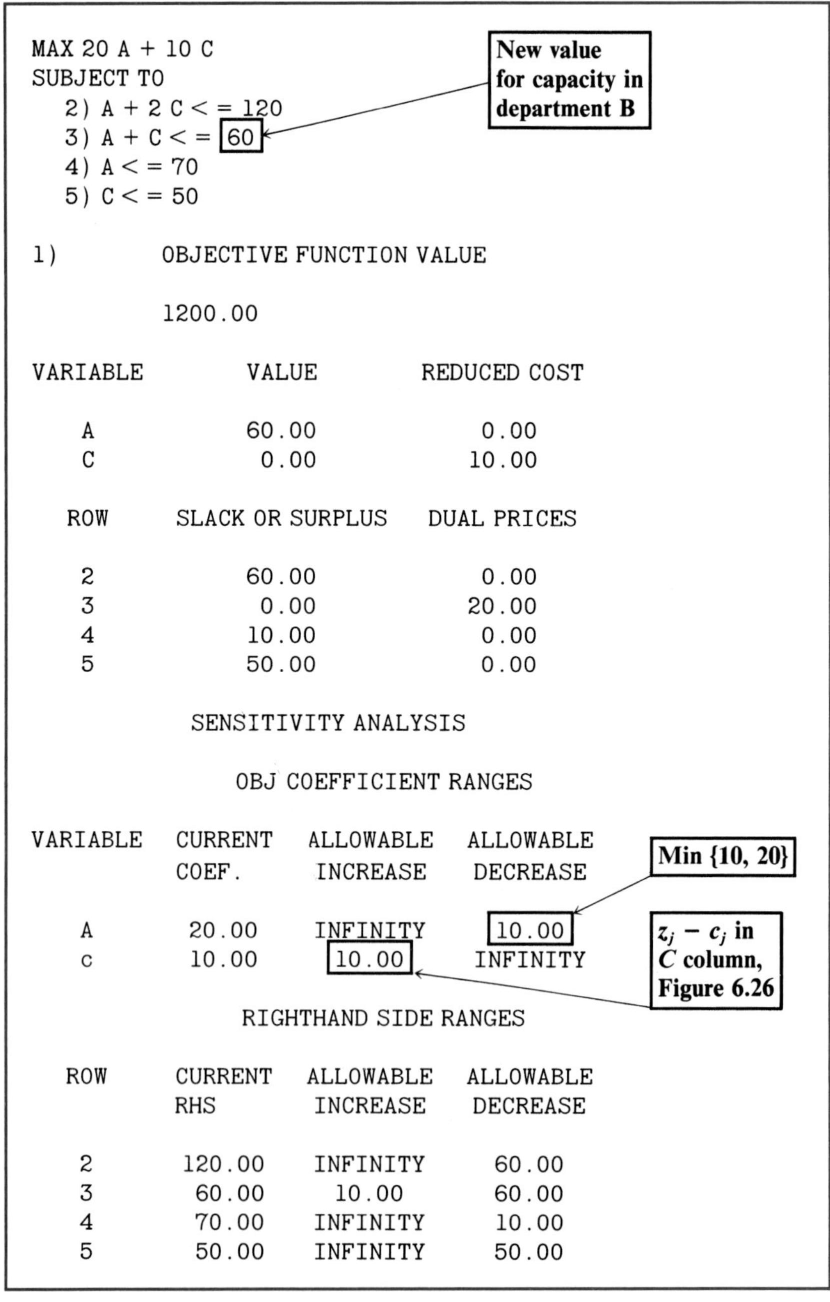

```
MAX 20 A + 10 C
SUBJECT TO
   2) A + 2 C <= 120
   3) A + C <= 60
   4) A <= 70
   5) C <= 50

1)         OBJECTIVE FUNCTION VALUE

           1200.00

VARIABLE        VALUE          REDUCED COST

   A            60.00             0.00
   C             0.00            10.00

  ROW      SLACK OR SURPLUS    DUAL PRICES

   2            60.00             0.00
   3             0.00            20.00
   4            10.00             0.00
   5            50.00             0.00

             SENSITIVITY ANALYSIS

               OBJ COEFFICIENT RANGES

VARIABLE   CURRENT    ALLOWABLE   ALLOWABLE
           COEF.      INCREASE    DECREASE

   A        20.00     INFINITY     10.00
   C        10.00      10.00      INFINITY

               RIGHTHAND SIDE RANGES

  ROW      CURRENT    ALLOWABLE   ALLOWABLE
           RHS        INCREASE    DECREASE

   2       120.00     INFINITY     60.00
   3        60.00      10.00       60.00
   4        70.00     INFINITY     10.00
   5        50.00     INFINITY     50.00
```

BASIC COEFFICIENT	BASIC VARIABLE	20 A	10 C	0 S_1	0 S_2	0 S_3	0 S_4	VALUE
0	S_1	0	1	1	−1	0	0	60
20	A	1	1	0	1	0	0	60
0	S_3	0	−1	0	−1	1	0	10
0	S_4	0	1	0	0	0	1	50
	z_j	20	20	0	20	0	0	
	$c_j - z_j$	0	−10	0	−20	0	0	1200

▲ FIGURE 6.26
Optimal Tableau for Astro/Cosmo, Revised

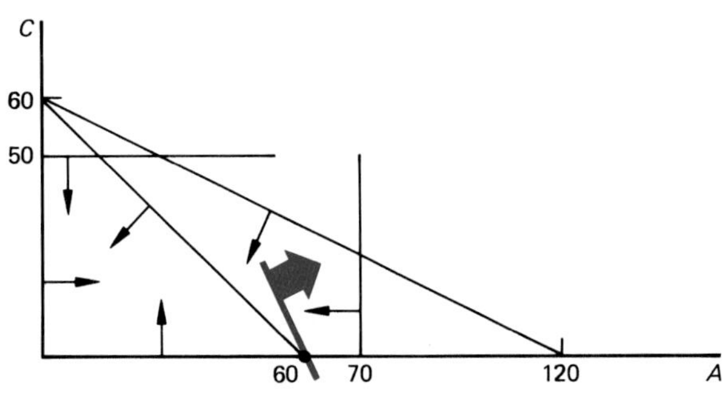

▲ FIGURE 6.27
Geometric Analysis of Astro/Cosmo, Revised

Coefficients of Nonbasic Variables

Consider the variable C. We have already noted that it is nonbasic. That is, $C^* = 0$ in the optimal solution. Decreasing the coefficient of C in the objective function makes it an even less profitable product, and hence, since this is a Max model, it is intuitively clear that decreasing this coefficient could not possibly persuade us to start producing C. This intuitive argument is consistent with the fact that the ALLOWABLE DECREASE for the coefficient of C presented in Figure 6.25 is infinity. The geometric support for this argument is that as the coefficient of C decreases, the objective function contour in Figure 6.27 rotates clockwise, approaching, but never attaining, a horizontal position.

Now consider increasing the coefficient of C in the objective function. Referring to Figure 6.26, we recall that the current solution remains optimal as long as all values of $c_j - z_j$ remain ≤ 0. Suppose that the coefficient of C is increased from 10 to 12. Only two numbers in the optimal tableau change, and both changes occur in the C column. In the top row, the value of the coefficient increases from 10 to 12, and in the last row, the value of $c_j - z_j$ increases from -10 to -8. Thus, an increase of 2 in c_j increased $c_j - z_j$ by 2. We see then that if the coefficient of C increases by more than the current magnitude (absolute value) of $c_j - z_j$ in the C column, the new value of $c_j - z_j$ in the C column will be positive, and the current solution is no longer optimal. This explains the allowable increase of 10 shown for the coefficient of C in Figure 6.25. From the geometric point of view (Figure 6.27) an increase of 10 in the coefficient C will rotate the objective function contour counterclockwise so that it is parallel to the constraint $A + C \leq 60$. At this point there are two optimal corners.

The discussion above illustrates the following general fact:

> For a nonbasic variable in a Max model,
>
> allowable decrease = infinity
>
> allowable increase = value of $z_j - c_j$ in the optimal tableau

Coefficients of Basic Variables

The procedure for basic variables is more complicated, since the coefficient of a basic variable plays a role in determining the value of z_j for all of the *nonbasic* columns in the model. For example, in Figure 6.26 you can see that the coefficient of A influences the value of z_j in the C and s_2 columns. From the geometry (Figure 6.27) you can see that as the coefficient of A is increased, the objective function contour rotates clockwise, approaching, but never reaching a slope of $-\infty$. Thus, the allowable increase should be infinity, as indeed it is in the computer printout (Figure 6.25). Moreover, as the coefficient of A is decreased, the objective contour becomes less steep. As soon as the coefficient has decreased 10 units the objective contour is parallel to the constraint $A + C \leq 60$, at which point there will be two optimal corners. Again, this allowable decrease of 10 agrees with the information provided in the output. Our goal now is to see how these values are obtained algebraically from the optimal tableau (Figure 6.26).

In order to study the effect of changes in the coefficient of A, let us change the current value, 20, to some new value, say $20 + \Delta C_A$. If $\Delta C_A < 0$, the coefficient of A decreases. If $\Delta C_A > 0$, it increases. Let us now see what happens to the optimal tableau (Figure 6.26) when this change is made. The new tableau is given in Figure 6.28. Note that the change ΔC_A has affected the values of $c_j - z_j$ only for the nonbasic variables C and s_2. It has also affected the z_j values in the A, C, *and* s_2 columns, and the objective function value.

▼ FIGURE 6.28
Changing the Coefficient of A

		$20 + \Delta C_A$	10	0	0	0	0	
BASIC COEFFICIENT	**BASIC VARIABLE**	A	C	s_1	s_2	s_3	s_4	**VALUE**
0	s_1	0	1	1	−1	0	0	60
$20 + \Delta C_A$	A	1	1	0	1	0	0	60
0	s_3	0	−1	0	−1	1	0	10
0	s_4	0	1	0	0	0	1	50
z_j		$20 + \Delta C_A$	$20 + \Delta C_A$	0	$20 + \Delta C_A$	0	0	
	$c_j - z_j$	0	$-10 + \Delta C_A$	0	$-20 - \Delta C_A$	0	0	$1200 + 60\Delta C_A$

The optimal solution from Figure 6.26 will remain optimal if all $c_j - z_j \leq 0$ in Figure 6.28. Since the $(c_j - z_j)$'s for basic columns remain unchanged, we need examine only the nonbasic columns. Thus, we see that

$$-10 - \Delta C_A \le 0 \text{ if and only if } -10 \le \Delta C_A$$
$$-20 - \Delta C_A \le 0 \text{ if and only if } -20 \le \Delta C_A$$

This shows that the coefficient of A can be decreased by as much as Min {10, 20} = 10 units without destroying the optimality of the solution in Figure 6.26. It can be arbitrarily increased. This explains how the allowable increase and allowable decrease are determined algebraically from the optimal tableau. The general rule for determining the allowable changes for coefficients of basic variables is derived from reasoning entirely analogous to that presented above. In order to present this rule, let i be the row in the optimal tableau associated with the basic variable of interest; let j be a nonbasic column, and a_{ij} the value of the substitution coefficient in row i, column j of the optimal tableau. Then

$$\text{allowable increase} = \text{Min}\left(\frac{c_j - z_j}{a_{ij}}\right) \text{ for those nonbasic columns}$$

where $a_{ij} < 0$

$$\text{allowable decrease} = \text{Min}\left[\frac{-(c_j - z_j)}{a_{ij}}\right] \text{ for those nonbasic columns}$$

where $a_{ij} > 0$

Returning to Figure 6.26 and the variable A and applying the general rule, we note that there are no negative entries in the A row, and thus there is no limit on the allowable increase in the coefficient of A (i.e., no $a_{Aj} < 0$). Similarly, we see that the allowable decrease must equal the minimum of $-(-10/1)$ and $-(-20/1)$ or 10, which is the value we already computed.

For more practice with this rule, refer to the **PROTRAC**, Inc. problem in Figure 6.22. Concerning the coefficient for F

$$\text{allowable increase} = \text{Min}\left(\frac{-175}{-0.05}\right) = 3500$$

$$\text{allowable decrease} = \text{Min}\left[\frac{-(-150)}{0.1}\right] = 1500$$

Similarly, for the coefficient for E

$$\text{allowable increase} = \text{Min}\left(\frac{-150}{-0.05}\right) = 3000$$

$$\text{allowable decrease} = \text{Min}\left[\frac{-(-175)}{0.075}\right] = 2333.33$$

Verify that these are indeed the values provided in the computer output in Figure 5.6.

Video Case

The Simplex Algorithm

Today we take for granted the ability to solve linear programming problems. Students who are new to management science quickly learn to type an LP into a mathematical programming software package such as LINDO. After a few repetitions to eliminate keyboarding errors, they can solve the problem by simply typing "GO." But it hasn't always been this way.

In 1982 George Stigler won the Nobel Prize in economics for his "seminal studies of industrial structures, functioning of markets, and causes and effects of public regulation." You may be surprised to learn that earlier in his career he was working on what we would now call the diet problem (see Example 2 in Chapter 2). He had set out to find the least expensive diet that would satisfy the nine nutritional requirements determined by the National Research Council in 1943. Stigler had 77 foods, ranging from wheat flour to strawberry jam, to choose from. His formulation of the problem was the same as the one we saw in Chapter 2.

In a 1945 paper reporting his results, titled "The Cost of Subsistence," Stigler wrote that "there does not appear to be any direct method of finding the minimum of a linear function subject to linear conditions." George Dantzig changed all that when he developed the simplex method in the late 1940s. Without the simplex to help him, Stigler "solved" his diet problem by a combination of clever insights and brute force. At the time, he could not prove that he had a good—to say nothing of optimal—solution. Later, when the problem was solved with the simplex, it turned out that his methods had produced a solution that was very close to (though not quite) optimal.

The cost-minimizing diet suggested in Stigler's paper and its annual cost (based on 1939 prices) are shown below. (Obviously, there was not a constraint for taste in this model.)

COMMODITY	QUANTITY	ANNUAL COST ($)
Wheat Flour	370 lbs	13.33
Evaporated Milk	57 cans	3.84
Cabbage	111 lbs	4.11
Spinach	23 lbs	1.85
Dried Navy Beans	285 lbs	16.80
Total Cost		$39.93

It is interesting to think that in less than 50 years the diet problem has gone from a puzzle that challenged one of the finest economic scholars of all time to a simple exercise for beginning students.

Questions

The simplex method is essentially a hill-climbing method. Once it has found a corner solution, it looks at all of its immediate neighboring corners and asks, "If I move to one of these corners, will the value of the objective function be improved?" If the answer is yes, the algorithm moves to one such corner and then again asks whether or not a move to a neighbor will improve things further. If the answer is no, the algorithm proclaims victory and quits.

1. Consider Figure 3.12 and assume that the simplex algorithm started at the corner created by the intersection of constraints 2 and 5. Show how a hill-climbing algorithm is guaranteed to arrive at the optimal solution.
2. Create a diagram like Figure 3.12 with a different feasible region for which a hill-climbing algorithm is *not* guaranteed to yield an optimal or even a good solution. Can a feasible region like the one you have created occur in a linear programming problem?
3. Use a diagram like Figure 3.12 to show a situation in which a hill-climbing algorithm might take many or a few steps in its route to find an optimal solution.
4. Consider a diagram with the value of the decision variable on the x axis and the value of the objective function on the y axis. Use such a diagram to illustrate the fact that in general a hill-climbing algorithm will not lead to an optimal solution.

CHAPTER

7

Linear Programming: Special Applications

APPLICATION CAPSULE

Ici on parle HASTUS: Montréal Streamlines Its Transportation Scheduling with LP*

Controlling the costs of public transportation is a problem that knows no national boundaries. One highly successful approach was developed by the Société de la Communauté urbaine de Montréal (S.T.C.U.M.) in Canada. This organization, with a staff of 8000 and an annual budget of more than $575 million, provides close to 400 million passenger trips per year. To do so, it runs 1700 buses and 750 subway cars, for which it must schedule 3000 drivers and other personnel daily.

Efficient scheduling is extremely important—it improves service and working conditions and can have a dramatic impact on operating costs. Such scheduling is difficult because of the large variation in service levels required during the course of the day. During peak demand hours, nearly 1500 vehicles may be needed, compared to a fifth that number during slack periods. Scheduling must take into account vehicle frequencies on each route during the day, as well as the effect on average vehicle speed of traffic conditions (such as rush-hour congestion) at different times.

Transit-system scheduling is done in two successive operations. Vehicle scheduling is done first. The aim is to provide the number of buses and subway trains required to maintain desired service frequencies on each route. Crew scheduling then assigns drivers to the vehicles. To facilitate these tasks, S.T.C.U.M., in cooperation with the Center for Research on Transportation of the University of Montreal, develped the HASTUS system. The program consists of three main software modules:

- One module is used to provide optimum vehicle scheduling, using network algorithms such as those that will be discussed in Chapter 9.
- A second module uses the LP techniques described in Chapters 2–6 to obtain a "good" initial solution for crew scheduling. Carefully chosen simplifications reduce the enormous number of variables to 3000, so that the model can be solved very rapidly.

- The final module refines the solution to produce detailed driver scheduling assignments, using assignment and shortest-route techniques discussed in this chapter.

The scheduling department has carefully compared the costs of parallel manual and computer-generated solutions. HASTUS was found to reduce manual scheduling errors, saving at least $100,000 per year in unnecessary wages. The system thus paid for itself in less than three months. In addition, HASTUS has been shown to reduce unproductive paid time of drivers and other employees by 20% compared to existing manual solutions. The total annual savings amount to some $4 million: $3 million in manpower scheduling and an additional $1 million in vehicle scheduling.

The system also permits managers to perform sensitivity and "what-if" analysis. Simulations that would have required weeks using manual techniques can now be done in minutes. Such analyses have helped management to tailor the most cost-effective proposals in negotiations with its labor unions.

HASTUS is easy to learn and use, and has proved popular with schedulers because it makes their jobs more interesting and challenging. The success of the program has been so great that today versions of HASTUS in several languages are helping planners in 40 cities around the world.

*Blais, Lamont, and Rousseau, "The HASTUS Vehicle and Manpower Scheduling System at the Société de la Communauté urbaine de Montréal," *Interfaces*, Vol. 20, No. 1 (Jan.–Feb. 1990).

7.1 Introduction

Linear programming is the workhorse of the world of quantitative models. The ability to handle hundreds of constraints, thousands of decision variables, and the incredible number of interactions that these numbers imply makes LP an important tool in a wide variety of problems.

Management scientists, by taking advantage of the special structure of these types of problems, have been able to develop special algorithms that are an order of magnitude (ten times) faster than the standard simplex algorithm. However, each algorithm was developed by using the simplex method in one form or another and then introducing computational shortcuts.

In this chapter we concentrate on some special applications of linear programming. In particular, we consider four specific models. Sections 7.2 through 7.4 are devoted to the *transportation problem.* In this problem, management must determine how to allocate products from its various warehouses to its customers in order to satisfy demand at the lowest possible cost. This model is important because of its successful applications and because it can be solved quickly and efficiently with special algorithms. These algorithms are presented in Section 7.3.

Sections 7.5 through 7.7 are devoted to the *assignment problem.* This model enables management to determine the optimal assignment of salespeople to districts, jobs to machines, or editors to manuscripts. The model itself is a special type of transportation problem. It can be solved with a special algorithm, the Hungarian method, which is presented in Section 7.6.

A financial and production planning model is presented in Section 7.8. Although it is small and relatively simple by the standards of actual applications, it illustrates how more complicated planning models can be constructed and solved. Finally, Section 7.9 considers an important marketing problem. The problem, called the *media selection problem,* is concerned with designing an effective advertising campaign. More precisely, management must decide how many ads to place in each of several possible advertising media. The decision is constrained by an overall budget allocation, the number of openings for ads in the various media, and rules of thumb insisted on by management. The media selection problem is a specific example of an important class of management problems. These are profit-maximization problems in which a decision variable yields declining marginal profits for increased values of the variable.

7.2 The Transportation Problem

PROTRAC's Distribution Problem: Sending Diesels from Harbors to Plants

PROTRAC has four assembly plants in Europe. They are located in Leipzig, Germany (1); Nancy, France (2); Liege, Belgium (3); and Tilburg, the Netherlands (4). The engines used by these plants are produced in the United States, shipped to harbors in Amsterdam (A), Antwerp (B), and Le Havre (C) and are then sent to the plants for assembly.

Production plans for the third quarter, July through September, have been set. The *requirements* (the *demand* at **destinations**) for E-4 diesel engines are as follows:

PLANT	NUMBER OF ENGINES REQUIRED
(1) Leipzig	400
(2) Nancy	900
(3) Liege	200
(4) Tilburg	500
	2000

The *available* number of E-4 engines at harbors (the *supply* at **origins**) in time to be used in the third quarter are shown below.

HARBOR	NUMBER OF ENGINES AVAILABLE
(A) Amsterdam	500
(B) Antwerp	700
(C) Le Havre	800
	2000

Note that this is a balanced problem in the sense that the total supply of engines available equals the total number required. Figure 7.1 illustrates the problem. In this figure the number above the harbors indicates the supply available; and the number above the plants indicates the quantity demanded. The lines indicate the possible delivery routes.

PROTRAC must decide how many engines to send from each harbor to each plant. The engines are transported by common carrier, and charges are on a per engine basis. The relevant costs are given in Figure 7.2. For ease of presentation, we will refer to the harbors with letters and the plants with numbers, as indicated in the supply and demand information above.

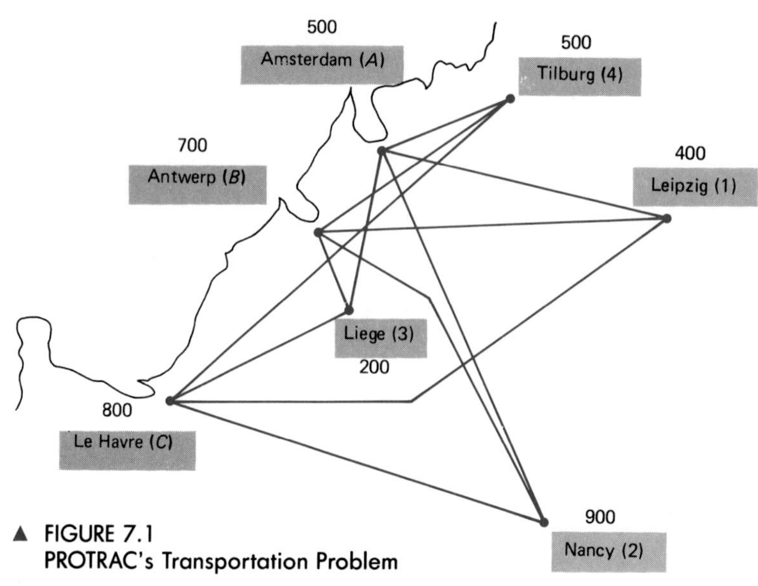

▲ FIGURE 7.1
PROTRAC's Transportation Problem

FROM ORIGIN	TO DESTINATION 1	2	3	4
A	12	13	4	6
B	6	4	10	11
C	10	9	12	4

▲ FIGURE 7.2
Cost to Transport an Engine from an Origin to a Destination ($)

The LP Formulation and Solution

PROTRAC's goal is to minimize the total cost of transporting the E-4 engines from the harbors to the plants. Since the transportation cost for any specific harbor-plant combination (e.g., Antwerp–Nancy) is directly proportional to the number of engines sent from the harbor to the plant ($4 per engine in the Antwerp–Nancy example), we can formulate this problem as an LP model. To do so, we let

The decision variables

$$x_{ij} = \text{number of engines sent from harbor } i \text{ to plant } j$$
$$i = \text{A, B, C}$$
$$j = 1, 2, 3, 4$$

Thus, x_{C4} is the number of engines sent from C, Le Havre, to 4, Tilburg. With this definition, the total transportation cost, which is our objective function, becomes

The objective

$$12x_{A1} + 13x_{A2} + \cdots + 4x_{C4}$$

The constraints

The problem has two general types of constraints:

1. The number of items shipped from a harbor cannot exceed the number that are available. For example,

$$x_{A1} + x_{A2} + x_{A3} + x_{A4}$$

is the total number of engines shipped from A. Since only 500 engines are available at A, the constraint is

$$x_{A1} + x_{A2} + x_{A3} + x_{A4} \le 500$$

A similar constraint is required for each origin.

2. Demand at each plant must be satisfied. For example,

$$x_{A1} + x_{B1} + x_{C1}$$

is the total number of engines sent to plant 1. Since 400 engines are demanded at plant 1, the constraint is

$$x_{A1} + x_{B1} + x_{C1} = 400$$

A similar constraint is required for each plant.

It is also possible to write each demand constraint as ≥ since total supply = total demand. In this case, all the constraints could be written as = constraints. In the case where total supply > total demand, all the supply constraints would be written as ≤ and the demand as =. Where total supply < total demand, supply constraints would be written as = and demand as ≤. In either instance, the simplex method will determine where the extra supply or demand will be left most economically.

The complete formulation and solution to **PROTRAC**'s transportation problem are presented in Figure 7.3. In this figure we see that 6 of the 12 possible routes are used (6 x_{ij}'s are positive), and that the minimum possible transportation cost is $12,000.

▼ FIGURE 7.3
PROTRAC's Transportation Problem

```
MIN 12 XA1 + 13 XA2 + 4 XA3 + 6 XA4 + 6 XB1 + 4 XB2 + 10 XB3
    + 11 XB4 + 10 XC1 + 9 XC2 + 12 XC3 + 4 XC4
SUBJECT TO
   2) XA1 + XA2 + XA3 + XA4 < = 500
   3) XB1 + XB2 + XB3 + XB4 < = 700
   4) XC1 + XC2 + XC3 + XC4 < = 800
   5) XA1 + XB1 + XC1 = 400
   6) XA2 + XB2 + XC2 = 900
   7) XA3 + XB3 + XC3 = 200
   8) XA4 + XB4 + XC4 = 500

          OBJECTIVE FUNCTION VALUE

                       12000.00

VARIABLE              VALUE              REDUCED COST

  XA1                 300.00                 0.00
  XA2                   0.00                 2.00
  XA3                 200.00                 0.00
  XA4                   0.00                 0.00
  XB1                   0.00                 1.00
  XB2                 700.00                 0.00
  XB3                   0.00                13.00
  XB4                   0.00                12.00
  XC1                 100.00                 0.00
  XC2                 200.00                 0.00
  XC3                   0.00                10.00
  XC4                 500.00                 0.00

ROW                   SLACK               DUAL PRICES

   2                   0.00                 0.00
   3                   0.00                 7.00
   4                   0.00                 2.00
   5                   0.00               -12.00
   6                   0.00               -11.00
   7                   0.00                -4.00
   8                   0.00                -6.00
```

7.3 Solving the Transportation Problem

In general, the term **transportation problem** refers to an LP model to find the least expensive way of satisfying demands at n destinations with supplies from m origins.

We have just used a general-purpose linear programming code based on the simplex algorithm to solve a transportation problem. The fact that this works is not surprising, since the simplex algorithm can be used to solve any LP problem and the transportation problem is an LP problem. However, because of the special structure of the transportation problem, we can use other algorithms that are designed to exploit the unique characteristics of this class of problems. In general, these algorithms make it possible to solve very large problems in a fraction of the time that would be required with the simplex algorithm.

The northwest corner rule and Vogel's approximation methods are known as "quick and dirty" techniques, giving a feasible but not necessarily optimal solution. The stepping stone and MODI methods are very visual and easy to do by hand for small problems but inefficient to use for solution by computer. What is important in this section is to show that the basic information needed to model the problem can be set up in a table of rows and columns, that the solution can be found in different ways, and that the optimal solution balances supply and demand by trading off various costs.

In particular, we will discuss four specific algorithms: the *northwest corner rule, Vogel's approximation method,* the *stepping-stone method,* and *MODI* (the *modified distribution method*). These algorithms serve two different purposes. The northwest corner rule and Vogel's approximation method are alternative methods of finding an initial feasible solution. The stepping-stone method and MODI are alternative methods of proceeding from an initial feasible solution to the optimal solution. As this discussion suggests, the first step in solving the transportation problem is to find an *initial feasible solution.* A *feasible solution,* by definition, is any allocation of supplies that satisfies all demand (i.e., a set of x_{ij}'s that satisfies all the constraints).

Once an initial feasible solution has been obtained, the algorithm proceeds in a step-by-step manner. At each step the goal is to find a feasible solution with a "better" (smaller) value for the objective function. When no better feasible solutions are available, the optimal solution has been found. An *optimal solution* is a cost-minimizing feasible solution. We see, then, that the transportation problem algorithm uses the same general approach as the simplex algorithm that was discussed in Chapter 6. In this case, however, the calculations are much simpler.

The Transportation Tableau

It is convenient to illustrate how these algorithms work by employing tableaux. Figure 7.4 shows the appropriate tableau for **PROTRAC**'s transportation problem. This tableau indicates the supply at each origin (e.g., 500 at A) and the demand at each destination (e.g., 200 at 3). We note that total supply equals total demand. Each **cell** represents a route from an origin to a destination, and the number in the upper righthand corner of the cell is the per unit cost of sending an engine along that route (e.g., 4 is the cost to send an engine from B to 2). Our goal is to find a way to use the given supplies to satisfy the demands at the minimum transportation cost.

We will now show two different methods of finding an initial feasible solution, the northwest corner rule and Vogel's approximation method.

The Northwest Corner Rule

The **northwest corner rule** starts in the northwest corner (the upper left-hand cell, route A1), and allocates *as many units as possible* to that route. In our example, 400 units are demanded at 1 and 500 are available at A. The entire demand at 1 is thus allocated from A, and our tableau is modified as shown in Figure 7.5.

Further allocations are then made either by moving to the right or by moving down. Demands are satisfied by moving sequentially from left to right, and supplies

The northwest corner rule is known as a **zero-order** method. That is, the costs are not taken into account. If the worst costs happen to be down the diagonal of the tableau, this would be the worst feasible solution you could find (but it's fast and simple!). **First-order** methods would look at the cheapest cost in each row (or column or whole tableau) and allocate as many units as possible. This can also be a shortsighted method because it is greedy, and so does not recognize that by trading off an allocation in a cell that is one unit more expensive, you might save ten units of expense for an ensuing allocation.

Applications Pack

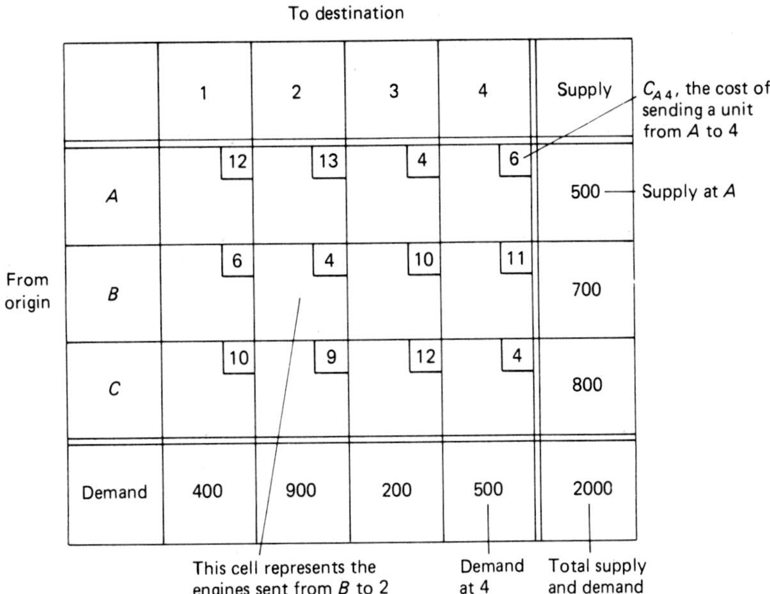

▲ FIGURE 7.4
Transportation Tableau for PROTRAC's Transportation Problem

are allocated by moving from the top to the bottom. In the example, since all the demand at destination 1 was satisfied, and since there is positive supply remaining at origin A, we remain in the same row and move to the right to consider the demand at destination 2, which is 900 engines. To satisfy this we allocate the 100 units still available at A, and then needing more supply, we move down to use the 700 units available at B, and then down once again to use 100 of the 800 units available at C. With these allocations the tableau appears as shown in Figure 7.6. Continuing in this manner, a move to the right to destination 3 leads us to allocate 200 of the 700 units still available at C to 3 and finally the remaining 500 units to 4. The resulting tableau is shown in Figure 7.7. This tableau exhibits an initial feasible solution. We note that all demands are satisfied and that all supplies are exhausted.

▼ FIGURE 7.5
First Allocation

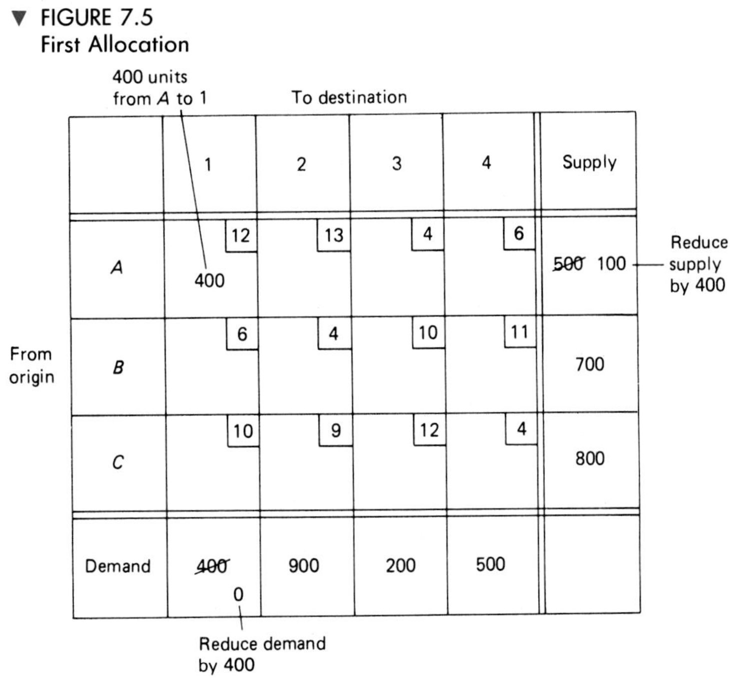

To destination

From origin	1	2	3	4	Supply
A	[12] 400	[13] 100	[4]	[6]	~~500~~ ~~100~~ 0
B	[6]	[4] 700	[10]	[11]	~~700~~ 0
C	[10]	[9] 100	[12]	[4]	~~800~~ 700
Demand	~~400~~ 0	~~900~~ 0	200	500	

▲ FIGURE 7.6
Next Three Allocations

To destination

From origin	1	2	3	4	Supply
A	[12] 400	[13] 100	[4]	[6]	~~500~~ ~~100~~ 0
B	[6]	[4] 700	[10]	[11]	~~700~~ 0
C	[10]	[9] 100	[12] 200	[4] 500	~~800~~ ~~700~~ ~~500~~ 0
Demand	~~400~~ 0	~~900~~ 0	~~200~~ 0	~~500~~ 0	

▲ FIGURE 7.7
Initial Feasible Solution

The value of the objective function for the initial feasible solution produced by the northwest corner rule is shown in Figure 7.8.

The northwest corner rule has the advantages that it is extremely easy to use and yields an initial feasible solution quickly with a minimum of computational effort. On the other hand, there is no reason to believe that it will yield a good feasible solution, that is, one for which the value of the objective function is close to the optimal value. Indeed, we note that the northwest corner rule does not even consider costs in the process of allocating supplies. Thus, this procedure will yield a good feasible solution only by chance.

Vogel's Approximation Method

Vogel's approximation method (VAM) uses cost information by employing the concept of an opportunity cost to determine an initial feasible solution. Consider, for example, origin A. The cheapest route emanating from origin A is the route to

ROUTE	NUMBER OF ENGINES	COST PER ENGINE ($)	COST ($)
A1	400	12	4,800
A2	100	13	1,300
B2	700	4	2,800
C2	100	9	900
C3	200	12	2,400
C4	500	4	2,000
Total Cost			14,200

▲ FIGURE 7.8
Total Cost for the Northwest Corner Rule Solution

destination 3, which has a cost of $4 per engine. The next cheapest route emanating from A is the route to 4, with a cost of $6 per engine. Roughly, then, any engine at A that is not sent to 3 will incur an additional cost of *at least* $2 = $6 − $4. VAM thus assigns a penalty cost (opportunity cost) of $2 to the first row (origin A). We emphasize that this is the penalty based on *not* using the best route in that row. A penalty cost is calculated for each row and each column in a similar fashion. The results of these calculations are shown in Figure 7.9.

VAM is a **second-order** method, in that it looks at the differences between costs instead of being greedy and looking at only the cheapest cost. It might be pointed out that the "penalty" for not using a certain cell is an approximation of the marginal value for that row or column.

VAM proceeds by attempting to avoid large penalties. The first step is to locate the largest of all the row and column penalties, and then make an allocation that avoids that penalty. In this case, we see that the third column (destination 3) has the largest penalty, namely 6. To avoid this penalty we must use the cheapest available route (find the best origin) for that column. We thus allocate as many units as possible to A3, the cheapest route in column 3. Since demand at 3 is 200 and the supply at A is 500, 200 units are allocated to route A3. This allocation is represented in Figure 7.10. The following steps are then employed to update the values for supply, demand, and the penalties, taking into account the allocation we have just made of 200 units to A3:

▼ FIGURE 7.9
Row and Column Penalties

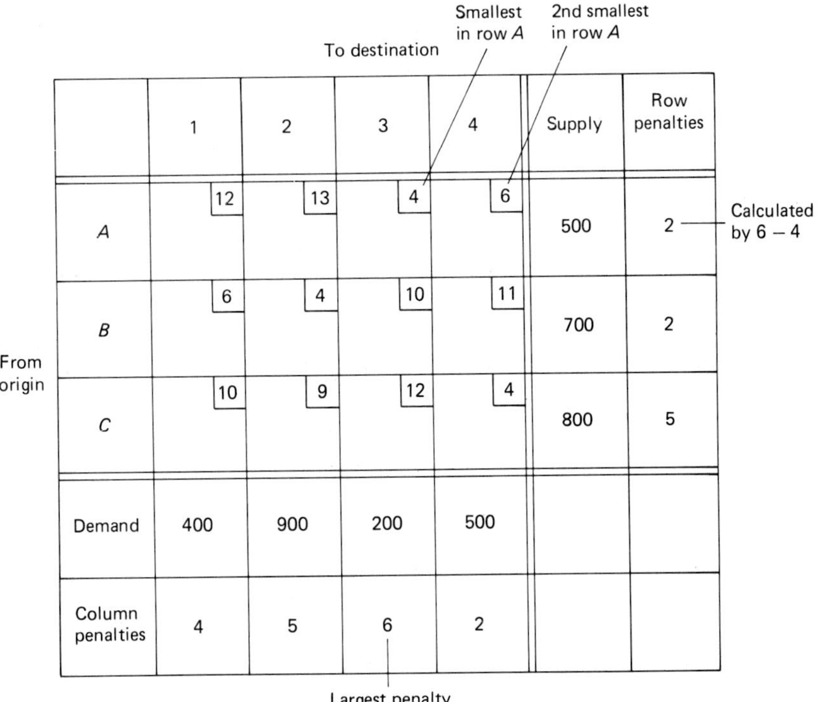

Smallest in row A
2nd smallest in row A
To destination
1
2
3
4
Supply
Row penalties
A
12
13
4
6
500
2
Calculated by 6 − 4
B
6
4
10
11
700
2
From origin
C
10
9
12
4
800
5
Demand
400
900
200
500
Column penalties
4
5
6
2
Largest penalty

	1	2	3	4	Supply	Row penalties
A	12	13	4 200	6	~~500~~ 300	6
B	6	4	10	11	700	2
C	10	9	12	4	800	5
Demand	400	900	~~200~~ 0	500		
Column penalties	4	5	0	2		

To destination; From origin. Assign max possible to minimum cost cell (A3). New row penalty (row A: 6).

▲ FIGURE 7.10
Allocation and New Penalties

Updating the tableau

If costs in column 3 were 5, 11, and 12 for rows A, B, and C, VAM would still compute the penalty for column 3 as 6 (which would be the highest). Thus, the penalty indicates that although a cost of 5 is not the lowest one, it is the most important; units *not* allocated from A to 3 will be forced to incur a cost at least $6 higher per unit. This is the type of tradeoff that LP is able to compute, determining the best allocation that balances these types of tradeoffs.

1. The allocation of 200 to route A3 reduces the supply at A and the demand at 3. The supply becomes 300 and the demand is now 0.

2. Since the demand at 3 is now satisfied, no additional engines will be sent to this destination. Column 3 is shaded out to indicate that the costs in this column should not be used to calculate new penalty costs. Thus, the routes in column 3 are now considered "unavailable."

3. Column and row penalties are calculated for this tableau as before. For example, in the first row, since A4 is the cheapest *available* route, with a cost of 6 and A1 is the next cheapest *available* route, with a cost of 12, the penalty for row A is $12 − $6 = $6. We also note that since a column (column 3) was removed from use in further calculations, the value of the column penalties for the remaining columns did not change from the first to the second tableau.

In summary, then, we see that a four-step process was used to move from the first tableau to the second. In particular, VAM

1. Identifies the row or column with the largest penalty.
2. Makes the largest possible allocation to the unused route with the minimum cost in the row or column selected in step 1. (Ties may be broken arbitrarily.)
3. Adjusts the appropriate supply and demand in view of this allocation.
4. Eliminates any column with 0 remaining demand (or row with 0 remaining supply) from further consideration.
5. Calculates new penalty costs.

Many students forget to update the new penalty costs. It is important to stress that this can significantly change the allocations and resulting cost. If a row is eliminated, then only the column penalties might change and vice versa. If both a row and column are eliminated then any of the penalties might change.

VAM continues to apply this process in a sequential manner until an initial feasible solution is obtained.

Applying the four-step process to the second tableau yields the result shown in Figure 7.11. Note that, in this case, the largest penalty, 6 units, was on the first row of Figure 7.10. Since all of the remaining 300 units of supply were sent to A4, the first row was eliminated. The same four-step procedure is now applied to Figure

To destination

From origin	1	2	3	4	Supply	Row penalties
A	[12]	[13]	[4] 200	[6] 300	~~500~~ ~~300~~ 0	
B	[6]	[4]	[10]	[11]	700	2
C	[10]	[9]	[12]	[4]	800	5
Demand	400	900	~~200~~ 0	~~500~~ 200		
Column penalties	4	5		7		

▲ FIGURE 7.11
Two Allocations

7.11. Since destination 4 now has the largest penalty (7), an allocation of 200 units is made to route C4, the cheapest route in that column. The next tableau is shown in Figure 7.12. Continuing as before yields the tableau shown in Figure 7.13.

At this point there is only one possible way to allocate the 600 units available at C to obtain a feasible solution. We must allocate 400 units to C1 and 200 units to C2. This yields the final tableau shown in Figure 7.14.

The initial feasible solution produced by VAM is presented and evaluated in

▼ FIGURE 7.12
Three Allocations

To destination

From origin	1	2	3	4	Supply	Row penalties
A	[12]	[13]	[4] 200	[6] 300	~~500~~ ~~300~~ 0	
B	[6]	[4]	[10]	[11]	700	2
C	[10]	[9]	[12]	[4] 200	~~800~~ 600	1
Demand	400	900	~~200~~ 0	~~500~~ ~~200~~ 0		
Column penalties	4	5				

To destination

From origin		1	2	3	4	Supply	Row penalties
	A	12	13	4 200	6 300	~~500~~ ~~300~~ 0	
	B	6	4 700	10	11	~~700~~ 0	
	C	10	9	12	4 200	~~800~~ 600	1
	Demand	400	~~900~~ 200	~~200~~ 0	~~500~~ ~~200~~ 0		

▲ FIGURE 7.13
Four Allocations

To destination

From origin		1	2	3	4	Supply
	A	12	13	4 200	6 300	~~500~~ ~~300~~ 0
	B	6	4 700	10	11	~~700~~ 0
	C	10 400	9 200	12	4 200	~~800~~ ~~600~~ 0
	Demand	~~400~~ 0	~~900~~ ~~200~~ 0	~~200~~ 0	~~500~~ ~~200~~ 0	

▲ FIGURE 7.14
Initial Feasible Solution

Figure 7.15. VAM clearly requires more computational work than the northwest corner rule. The hope is that it will yield a better initial feasible solution, that is, one closer to the optimal solution. In this case we see that the value of the objective function is $12,000, compared with a cost of $14,200 that was produced by the northwest corner solution (see Figure 7.8). This is a substantial improvement. Indeed, if we refer to Figure 7.3, we see that the optimal value of the objective function is $12,000. Thus, *in this case* Vogel's approximation method produced an optimal solution. But this will not occur frequently. There are two important points to make at this time:

Will the solution be optimal?

1. In general, neither Vogel's approximation method nor the northwest corner rule is guaranteed to yield *directly* an optimal solution. They simply yield an *initial feasible solution.*
2. Even in cases when these procedures yield an optimal solution, *you will not know that it is optimal.*

Students may jump to conclusions that are generally not true:
Since VAM is more work than the northwest corner rule, it must give a better solution;
Since VAM gave an optimal solution for this example, it always does!
Emphasize again that these two techniques are "quick and dirty," especially when compared with the hand calculations needed for the simplex method!

ROUTE	NUMBER OF ENGINES	COST PER ENGINE ($)	COST ($)
A3	200	4	800
A4	300	6	1,800
B2	700	4	2,800
C1	400	10	4,000
C2	200	9	1,800
C4	200	4	800
Total Cost			12,000

▲ FIGURE 7.15
Total Cost for Vogel's Approximation Method

Thus, we clearly need a procedure whereby we can move from an initial feasible solution to the optimal solution. The stepping-stone method is such a procedure and it is the next topic to consider. Before turning to a new topic, however, let us summarize the material on finding initial feasible solutions.

Summary of Procedures for Finding Initial Feasible Solutions

Northwest Corner Rule.

1. Start in the upper left-hand corner (origin A, destination 1) and allocate as many units as possible to this cell. That is, use as much supply from origin A as possible to satisfy demand at destination 1. This means that the amount allocated is the minimum of supply at A and demand at 1.
2. Reduce the available supply at the current origin and unsatisfied demand at the current destination by the amount of the allocation.
3. Identify the first origin with available supply. This is either the current origin or the one directly below it.
4. Identify the first destination with unsatisfied demand. This is either the current destination or the one immediately to the right of it.
5. Allocate, as in step 1, as many items as possible to the route associated with the origin-destination combination identified in steps 3 and 4.
6. Return to step 2.

Vogel's Approximation Method.

In general, the more time you spend finding an initial solution, the less time you will need to find the optimal one. Thus, the northwest corner rule can get you started very quickly, but it might take six stepping stone tableaux to arrive at the optimal solution. A second-order technique would take longer to find the first solution, but it might be just one or two tableaux from the optimal solution.

1. For each row with an available supply and each column with an unfilled demand, calculate a penalty cost by subtracting the smallest entry from the second smallest entry.
2. Identify the row or column with the largest penalty cost. (Ties may be broken arbitrarily.)
3. Allocate the maximum amount possible to the available route with the lowest cost in the row or column selected in step 2.
4. Reduce the appropriate supply and demand by the amount allocated in step 3.
5. Remove any rows with zero available supply and columns with zero unfilled demand from further consideration.
6. Return to step 1.

The Stepping-Stone Method

Neither of the initial solution methods just discussed requires the problem to be "balanced" (supply = demand). However, the two methods that follow, (stepping-stone and MODI), for checking and reaching optimality, do require that supply = demand.

The **stepping-stone method** is a sequential procedure that starts with an initial feasible solution to a transportation problem (e.g., one produced by the northwest corner rule or Vogel's approximation method) and finds the optimal solution. At each step this procedure attempts to send items along one route *that is unused* in the current feasible solution, while eliminating the use of one of the routes that is currently being used. This changing of routes is done so as to (1) maintain a feasible solution and (2) improve (decrease, in the current context) the value of the objective function. The procedure stops when there is no changing of routes that will improve the value of the objective function. The solution that has this property is the optimal solution.

Let us turn immediately to our example problem. The initial feasible solution produced by the northwest corner rule is reproduced in Figure 7.16. The procedure consists of the following steps.

Step 1: Finding the Marginal Costs. Use the current feasible solution to evaluate the marginal cost of sending material over each of the unused routes, that is, each of the unoccupied cells.

Consider, for example, the currently unused route A3. We wish to determine the marginal cost of using route A3 (i.e., the cost of sending one unit along this route) if we adjust *only* the other currently *used* routes in such a way as to maintain a feasible solution. The adjustment proceeds as follows:

a. Increase the number of units in cell A3 by 1. This is indicated by a + in the A3 cell.

b. An increase in A3 of 1 unit necessitates a decrease in a used cell in the same row (A1 or A2) of 1 unit. Otherwise, we would exceed the supply of 500 items at A. Suppose that we choose A2. This is indicated by a − in the A2 cell.

c. A decrease of 1 unit in A2 necessitates an increase of 1 unit in a used cell of

The "routes" in the tableau are the allocations and can be imagined to look like stepping stones in a pond, hence the name "stepping-stone algorithm." Starting at a cell without allocation, there exists a unique path that continually makes right-angle turns (and may jump over other stones) until it returns to the original cell. Thus, there will always be at least four turns, and always an even number of them.

▼ FIGURE 7.16
Initial Feasible Solution Produced by the Northwest Corner Rule

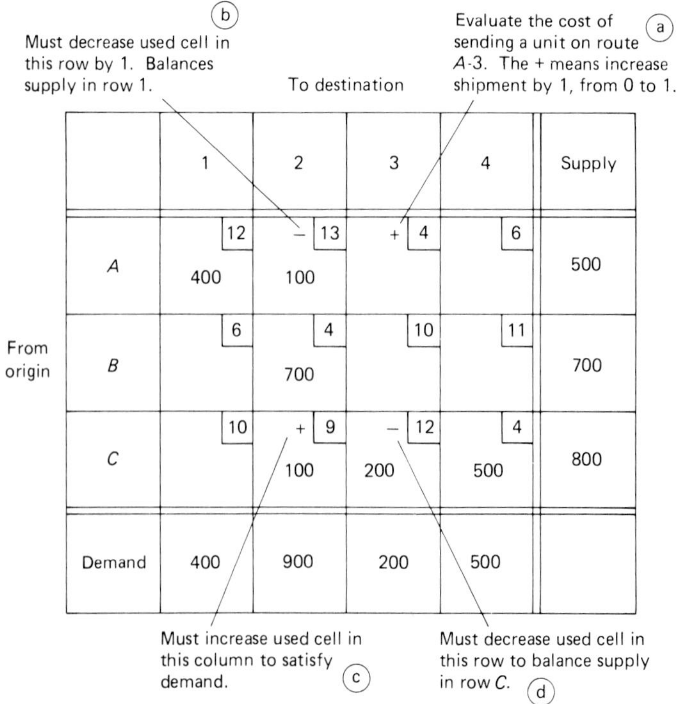

	1	2	3	4	Supply
A	[12] 400	− [13] 100	+ [4]	[6]	500
B	[6]	[4] 700	[10]	[11]	700
C	[10]	+ [9] 100	− [12] 200	[4] 500	800
Demand	400	900	200	500	

column 2 (either B2 or C2). Otherwise, we will not satisfy the demand of 900 at 2. Suppose that we choose C2. This is indicated by a + in the C2 cell.

d. An increase of 1 unit in C2 necessitates a decrease of 1 unit in a used cell in row C (C3 or C4). Otherwise, we would exceed the supply of 800 at C. Suppose that we choose C3. This is indicated by a − in the C3 cell.

e. The decrease of 1 unit in C3 is balanced by the increase (step a) in A3. Thus, no further changes are required.

In steps a–e we have found a way to increase A3 by a unit and to adjust the *currently used routes* to maintain a feasible solution.

The sequence of operations just described is the heart of the stepping-stone process. The example, however, may be misleadingly simple. Complications can occur in attempting to apply it to other problems or even other unused routes in this problem. At this point it is useful to make several comments about the adjustment process in general terms.

Degenerate solutions

1. Suppose that, in the general problem, there are m origins and n destinations. In the present example, $m = 3$ and $n = 4$. If a feasible solution uses fewer than $m + n - 1$ routes ($3 + 4 - 1 = 6$ routes in this example) the problem is termed degenerate. Special adjustments must be made to use the stepping-stone method on a degenerate problem. This topic is discussed in Section 7.4.

"Dead ends"

2. The determination of the appropriate path is more complicated than merely jumping from the cell of interest to *any* used cell in the same row or column. "Dead ends" may be encountered, in which case you must make another try. For example, suppose that we had chosen A1 in step b. Then we would have found no occupied cell in column 1 to balance the decrease in A1. This would also have been true if we had chosen B2 in step c. Similarly, it would not have been possible to choose C4 in step d.

Number of cells in a path

3. The path obtained in steps 1-a through 1-e above contains four cells (including the initial unused cell). The fact that any row or column with a + must also have a − dictates this fact. Although there must always be at least four cells, the path may require more than four.

Let us summarize the adjustment process as we have just set forth:

a. Put a + in the unoccupied cell of interest (A3 in the example).

b. Put a − in a used cell in the same row (A2 in the example).

c. Put a + in a used cell in the column determined in step b (C2 in the example).

Stopping conditions for a stepping-stone path

The process continues by altering +'s and −'s as well as rows and columns until a sequence of cells is established that satisfies two conditions:

- It has a + in the original unused cell of interest.
- Any row (or column) that has a + placed in it also has a −, and vice versa.

The sequence of steps with these properties is called a **stepping-stone path.**

Calculating the marginal costs

We now return to the example problem and calculate the marginal cost of introducing, as above, the use of route A3.

ACTION	ROUTE	EFFECT ON THE OBJECTIVE FUNCTION
Increase 1 Unit	A3	+4
Decrease 1 Unit	A2	−13
Increase 1 Unit	C2	+9
Decrease 1 Unit	C3	−12
Marginal Cost		−12

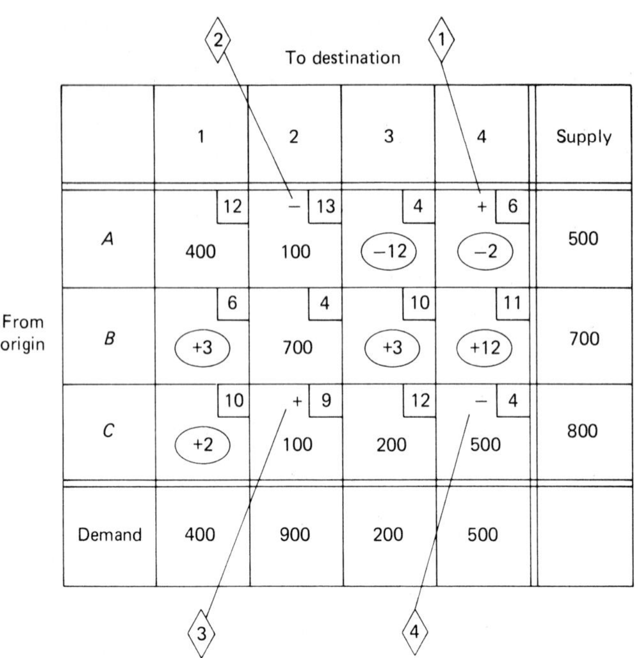

▲ FIGURE 7.17
Marginal Cost of Unused Routes

We see, then, that every time we increase by 1 unit the quantity shipped from A to 3 by making the adjustments indicated in our calculation, the value of the objective function will decrease by 12.

It is now obvious that the initial feasible solution is not optimal and that we will want to find a new solution. To do so, we evaluate, in an analogous way, the marginal cost of using each of the other currently unused routes. Let us look at cell A4. In Figure 7.17, the +'s in cells A4 and C2 and the −'s in cells A2 and C4 are provided to illustrate how the value −2 was calculated. This number results from the following calculation. (The numbers in diamonds below correspond to the numbers in diamonds in Figure 7.17 and indicate the sequence in which the route to evaluate cell A4 was constructed.)

SEQUENCE	ACTION	ROUTE	EFFECT ON THE OBJECTIVE FUNCTION
◇1	Increase 1 Unit	A4	+6
◇2	Decrease 1 Unit	A2	−13
◇3	Increase 1 Unit	C2	+9
◇4	Decrease 1 Unit	C4	−4
	Marginal Cost		−2

It might be faster to simply stop evaluating empty cells once you have found one that is not optimal. There is no guarantee that choosing the cell with the best savings will get you to the optimal solution the fastest.

You should evaluate the other unused cells to check your understanding. The results are indicated by the encircled numbers in Figure 7.17.

Step 2: Choosing an Unused Route. If all the marginal costs are greater than or equal to zero, stop; you have an optimal solution. If not, select that cell with the most negative marginal cost. In the example, cell A3 has the most negative value, −12.

Step 3: Generating the New Tableau. Determine the maximum number of items that can be allocated to the *route* selected in step 2 (cell A3) and adjust the allocations appropriately. The following table can be used to determine the number of units to allocate to cell A3 in the example:

It may happen that two cells have the minimum, and thus both of them would "disappear." In this case, simply set one of the cells to zero ("0") so that you still have the proper number of "stepping-stones."

ACTION	ROUTE	NUMBER AVAILABLE IN DECREASING CELLS
Increase 1 Unit	A3	
Decrease 1 Unit	A2	100
Increase 1 Unit	C2	
Decrease 1 Unit	C3	200

Here we see that the procedure that yields a marginal cost of −12 can be followed only 100 times. After the process has been performed 100 times the solution will have a zero in cell A2 (i.e., no items being shipped from A to 2). In other words, at this point the shipments from A to 2 cannot be further reduced. Thus, in moving from the current solution (the initial feasible solution in this case) to the next solution, we increase the + cells (A3 and C2) by 100 units and decrease the − cells (A2 and C3) by 100 units. This yields the tableau shown in Figure 7.18.

Step 4: Repeat Steps until Optimal. Return to step 1. Thus, we must reevaluate the marginal cost of introducing each of the currently unused routes. For example, the numbers in diamonds in Figure 7.18 show the stepping-stone path required to evaluate cell B1. This path, which contains six cells, illustrates the above-mentioned possibility that more than four cells may be required.

The evaluation of each currently unused route produces the circled numbers in Figure 7.18. These are the marginal costs of using each of these routes.

▼ FIGURE 7.18
Improved Solution

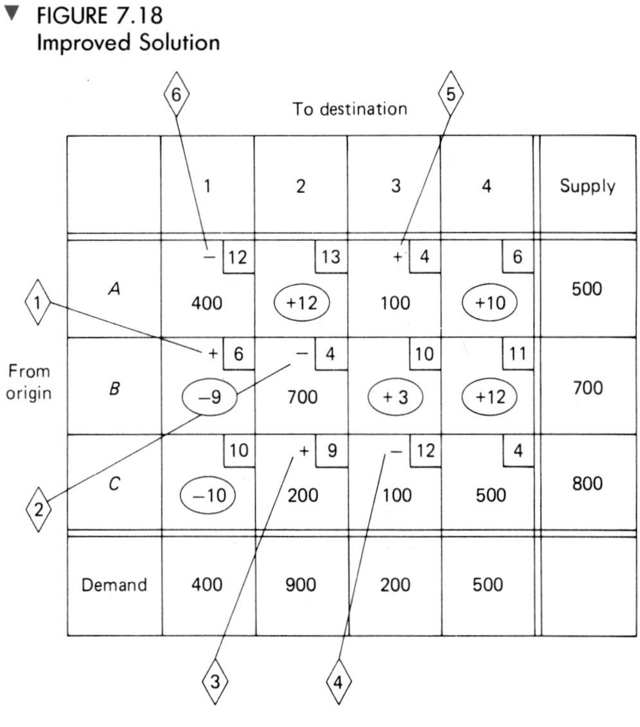

To destination
From origin
1
2
3
4
Supply
A
− 12
13
+ 4
6
400
+12
100
+10
500
B
+ 6
− 4
10
11
−9
700
+ 3
+12
700
C
10
+ 9
− 12
4
−10
200
100
500
800
Demand
400
900
200
500
1
2
3
4
5
6

To destination

From origin	1	2	3	4	Supply
A	cost 12; 300	cost 13; (+2)	cost 4; 200	cost 6; (0)	500
B	cost 6; (+1)	cost 4; 700	cost 10; (+13)	cost 11; (+12)	700
C	cost 10; 100	cost 9; 200	cost 12; (+10)	cost 4; 500	800
Demand	400	900	200	500	

▲ FIGURE 7.19
Optimal Solution

Proceeding to step 2 we see that the greatest improvement will be obtained by using route C1, since its marginal cost is the lowest. In step 3 we determine that at most 100 units can be allocated to this route. (The current value of 100 in cell C3 determines this value.) The adjusted tableau and the marginal costs that result from it are shown in Figure 7.19. Since all of the marginal costs are now greater than or equal to zero, we know that we have found an optimal solution. The optimal value of the objective function can be calculated as shown in Figure 7.20.

Comparison with Computer Solution. Let us now compare the final transportation tableau for this problem with the solution the computer produced with the simplex algorithm in Figure 7.3. We note that both approaches yield the same value for the objective function and the same solution. In addition, we see that what we have called marginal costs for the unused cells (the numbers in circles on the final transportation tableau) have the same values as reduced costs produced by the computer. This is reassuring, since both entities have the same interpretation, that is, the marginal cost of increasing the value of a particular variable.

▼ FIGURE 7.20
Optimal Solution for PROTRAC's Transportation Problem

ROUTE	NUMBER OF ENGINES	COST PER ENGINE ($)	COST ($)
A1	300	12	3,600
A3	200	4	800
B2	700	4	2,800
C1	100	10	1,000
C2	200	9	1,800
C4	500	4	2,000
Total Cost			12,000

Comparison with VAM Solution. We have already seen that the initial feasible solution produced by Vogel's approximation method is also optimal, because the total cost is $12,000. Comparing Figures 7.19 and 7.14, we see that the two solutions are different, even though the objective values are the same. Thus, for this problem, VAM produced an alternative optimal solution to the one we found by using the northwest corner rule and the stepping-stone method. Had we started with VAM, we would have known that we had an optimal solution after the first time we evaluated the marginal costs of the unused routes. When we started with the solution produced by the northwest corner rule, a series of three iterations was required to find an optimal solution.

As a final point, we note that, in using the stepping-stone method, the existence of an alternative optimum can be recognized by the appearance of a zero marginal cost in the optimal tableau. Thus, in Figure 7.19 the zero marginal cost on the unused cell A4 means that this route could be introduced without increasing the cost. You should verify that introducing this route gives the VAM solution of Figure 7.14.

The stepping-stone method is a useful way to present the computation of marginal costs, since there is a physical interpretation that is easy to follow. There is, however, an easier way to compute these values. It is the modified distribution (MODI) method.

The Modified Distribution (MODI) Method

The **MODI method** is a two-step procedure for finding the marginal costs. Again, we will assume that *each feasible solution encountered used* $m + n - 1$ *routes.*

The variables, u_i and v_j, are actually the linear programming dual variables (marginal values of the rows and columns). The derivation of this algorithm, although elegant and clever mathematics, is better left to management science majors.

Step 1. Determine an index for each row (u_i for row i) and an index for each column (v_j for column j) such that $u_i + v_j = c_{ij}$ for every *used* cell where c_{ij} is the cost of sending a unit from origin i to destination j. If we start with the initial feasible solution produced by the northwest corner rule (see Figure 7.16), we must select the u_i's and v_j's to satisfy the following constraints:

ROUTE BEING USED	COST PER ENGINE ($)	EQUATION
A1	12	$u_A + v_1 = 12$
A2	13	$u_A + v_2 = 13$
B2	4	$u_B + v_2 = 4$
C2	9	$u_C + v_2 = 9$
C3	12	$u_C + v_3 = 12$
C4	4	$u_C + v_4 = 4$

Since there are seven variables and only six equations, we can arbitrarily select the value of one of these variables and then use the equations to solve for the other values. For example, if we let $u_A = 0$, we can substitute this value into the first equation and then determine the following index values by working our way down the system of equations. In each case we can substitute a numerical value for one of the variables in an equation.

$$v_1 = 12, \quad v_2 = 13, \quad u_B = -9, \quad u_C = -4, \quad v_3 = 16, \quad v_4 = 8$$

It is particularly easy to make these calculations on a transportation tableau, as shown in Figure 7.21. Setting $u_A = 0$ forces v_1 to be 12 since A1 is occupied and $c_{A1} =$ 12. With the same logic we see that v_2 must equal 13. This, in turn, implies that $u_B =$ -9, and so on. Now, having determined the u_i's and the v_j's for the occupied cells, we are ready for step 2.

It is extremely helpful to show this on a transparency and go through the computations of the u_i's and v_j's using the table rather than just the equations. The beauty of this method is its visual (versus mathematical) impact. Again, as a computer algorithm, although ten times faster than LP, it is ten times slower than using the out-of-kilter algorithm.

$u_A + v_1 = c_{A1}$ ②
$0 + V_1 = 12$

u_i \ v_j		To destination 12	13	16	8	
		1	2	3	4	Supply
Arbitrary start ① 0	A	[12] 400	[13] 100	[4]	[6]	500
From origin −9	B	[6]	[4] 700	[10]	[11]	700
−4	C	[10]	[9] 100	[12] 200	[4] 500	800
	Demand	400	900	200	500	

▲ FIGURE 7.21
Row and Column Indices

Step 2. Calculate the marginal costs for the *unused* cells. If *i, j* is an *unused* cell, the marginal cost of using it (call the marginal cost e_{ij}) is given by the equation

$$e_{ij} = c_{ij} - (u_i + v_j)$$

In our example, cell A3 is unoccupied. We see that $u_A = 0$, $v_3 = 16$, and $c_{A3} = 4$. Thus

$$e_{A3} = 4 - (0 + 16) = -12$$

The same process is used to determine e_{ij} for every unused cell, and the results are shown in Figure 7.22. Comparing this with Figure 7.17 reveals that the e_{ij} values in Figure 7.22 are exactly the same as the marginal cost figures produced by the stepping-stone method. However, they are much easier to find since it is not necessary to find the stepping-stone path for every unused route.

Once the MODI method is used to compute the marginal costs, the system of solving the transportation problem is the same as for the stepping-stone method. In particular, the next step is to select which of the unused routes, if any, to start using. When a cell is selected, it is then necessary to determine how many items to allocate to that cell. To answer that question it is necessary to locate the stepping-stone route for that particular cell. To clarify the similarities and differences between the stepping-stone method and the MODI method of solving a transportation problem, the two approaches are summarized in the following section.

A Summary of the Stepping-Stone and MODI Methods

For each of the two methods we will assume that the procedure starts with an initial feasible solution that has $m + n - 1$ routes (used cells), each used cell representing an x_{ij} variable at a positive level.

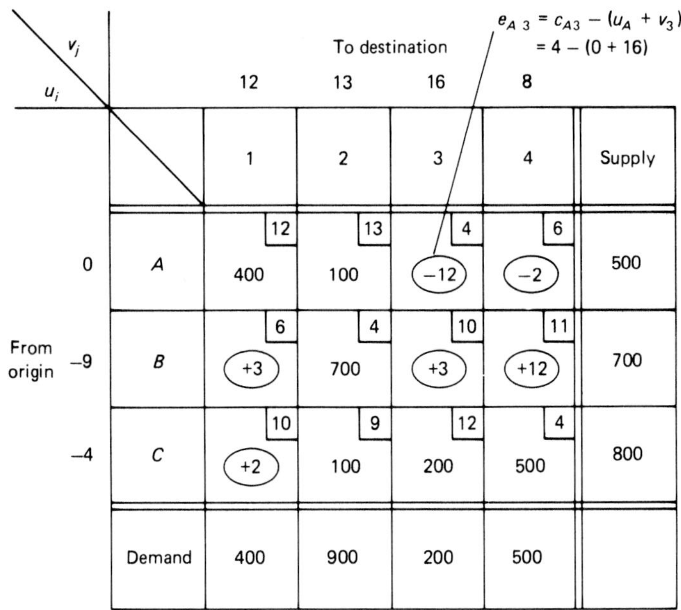

▲ FIGURE 7.22
Marginal Costs of Unused Routes

Stepping-Stone Method.

1. Use the current solution to create a unique stepping-stone path for each unused cell. Use these paths to calculate the marginal cost of introducing each unused route into the solution.
2. If all the marginal costs are greater than or equal to zero, stop; you have the optimal solution. If not, select that cell with the most negative marginal cost. (Ties may be broken arbitrarily.)
3. Using the stepping-stone path, determine the maximum number of items that can be allocated to the route selected in step 2 and adjust the allocation appropriately.
4. Return to step 1.

MODI Method.

1. Use the current solution and operations (a) and (b) below to evaluate the marginal cost of sending material over each of the unused routes.
   a. Set $u_1 = 0$. Find row indices $u_2, \ldots, u_m$ and column indices $v_1, \ldots, v_n$ such that $c_{ij} = u_i + v_j$ for every *used* cell.
   b. Let $e_{ij} = c_{ij} - (u_i + v_j)$ for every *unused* cell; e_{ij} is the marginal cost of introducing cell i, j into the solution.

Steps 2 through 4 are the same as in the stepping-stone method.

▶ 7.4 The Transportation Model: Other Considerations

This section is devoted to extensions of the basic transportation problem introduced in Section 7.2 and to a discussion of special problems that can occur in applying the stepping-stone or MODI solution algorithms. In particular, we will consider

APPLICATION CAPSULE

Meals, Wheels, and Models: A Low-Tech Solution Helps Feed the Needy*

Not all models have to be complex, sophisticated formulations that must be run on a computer. In 1983, John Bartholdi and Loren Platzman studied the problems of Meals on Wheels, a charitable organization that delivers meals daily to elderly and infirm people in their inner-city homes. The organization, which relies heavily on volunteers and near-minimum-wage employees, has limited resources and no access to sophisticated computer technology.

Distribution costs represent a large fraction of direct operating costs for Meals on Wheels. Bartholdi and Platzman ingeniously applied transportation and assignment techniques to devise a scheme for assigning drivers to vehicles and vehicles to routes. The system required only two card files, with no need for a computer. Nevertheless, it provided solutions vastly superior to those obtained by previous methods while cutting the time required for daily planning from 3 hours to a mere 15 minutes. The model is now widely used throughout the United States, not only for delivering meals but also for supplying fresh pastries to restaurants and servicing automated teller machines at banks.

*Richard C. Larson, "OR/MS and the Services Industries," *OR/MS Today*, April 1989, pp. 12–18.

1. Solving max transportation problems.
2. The case when supply exceeds demand.
3. Eliminating unacceptable routes.
4. Degeneracy in transportation problems.
5. Special properties of the transportation model.

Solving Max Transportation Problems

Suppose that in the example problem your goal was to maximize the value of the objective function rather than minimize it. You could use the same solution procedure with one small, but fundamental, change. Think of the marginal values as returns rather than costs. You would thus want to allocate units to the cell with the *largest* marginal value, and the procedure would terminate when all the unused routes had *negative* marginal values.

When Supply Exceeds Demand

When supply exceeds demand, the costs in the extra column represent the costs of storing the excess supply (production). These might be the inventory or carrying costs of keeping the excess supply at each location.

Suppose that in the example problem the supply at A was 600 engines rather than 500. Then, when all demand is satisfied, the sum, over the three origins, of the engines left over will be 100. In the computer solution to the model, as formulated in Figure 7.3, this causes no special problems. The supply that was not allocated at each origin would appear as a slack variable for that origin. In order to solve the problem by hand using the tableau methods discussed in the preceding section, you must add a **dummy destination** to the transportation tableau. The dummy destination is an imaginary destination that is added to a transportation problem so that total supply equals total demand. The modified tableau is shown in Figure 7.23. Note that the cost of supplying the dummy destination, from any origin, is set at

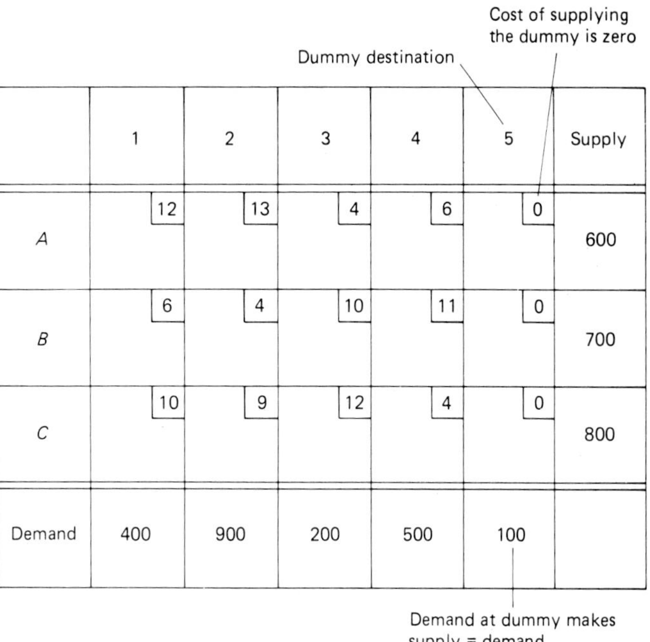

	1	2	3	4	5	Supply
A	12	13	4	6	0	600
B	6	4	10	11	0	700
C	10	9	12	4	0	800
Demand	400	900	200	500	100	

▲ FIGURE 7.23
Adding Dummy Destinations

zero, and the demand at the dummy destination is set equal to the total excess supply (100 units). Hence, in the solution to this problem, a total of 100 items will be sent to the dummy destination. In reality, any items sent to the dummy destination remain at the origin and thus incur a transportation cost of 0.

When demand exceeds supply (as often happens in the real world), the costs for the extra row might be the cost of customer good will or some other penalty for being out of that product.

We note that if demand exceeds supply, the real problem has no feasible solution. Management might, however, be interested in supplying as much demand as possible at minimum cost. To solve this problem we append a **dummy origin** with supply equal to the difference between total actual demand and total actual supply. This dummy origin is an imaginary source that is added to a transportation problem so that total supply equals total demand. The cost of supplying any destination from this origin is zero. Any supply allocated from the dummy origin to a destination is interpreted as unfilled demand.

Eliminating Unacceptable Routes

Assume that certain routes in a transportation problem are unacceptable. Organizational constraints such as regional restrictions or delivery time could indicate that certain origins could not serve certain destinations. (For example, assume that route A3 could not be used.) This fact is handled in formulating transportation problems by assigning an arbitrarily large cost identified as M to that cell. M is so large that M plus or minus a finite number is still larger than any other number in the tableau. This would then automatically eliminate the use of cell A3 since the cost of doing so would be very large.

The same general approach was used in Section 6.13 to eliminate artificial variables from the basis when using the simplex algorithm to solve LP problems.

Degeneracy in Transportation Problems

The initial feasible solution, produced by either the northwest corner rule or VAM, and all subsequent feasible solutions encountered with either the stepping-stone method or MODI, will have *at most* $(m + n - 1)$ positive variables (used cells).

u_i \ v_j		12	13			
		To destination				
		1	2	3	4	Supply
0	A	[12] 400	[13] 100	[4]	[6]	500
−9	B	[6]	[4] 700	[10]	[11]	700
	C	[10]	[9]	[12] 200	[4] 600	800
	Demand	400	800	200	600	

(From origin: A, B, C)

▲ FIGURE 7.24
Degenerate Solution

Degeneracy may occur, as in the example below, when finding an initial solution or while improving a solution. It is possible to spend several iterations "moving zeros" around the tableau (and obviously not improving the objective function). In fact, some computerized MODI codes (usually made up for teaching purposes) can cycle indefinitely!

When there are fewer than $(m + n - 1)$ used cells, that feasible solution is termed **degenerate.** This condition may arise either in the initial feasible solution or at some intermediate feasible solution. Since both the stepping-stone and the MODI methods, as represented above, require $(m + n - 1)$ used cells (we have not carefully explained *why* this is true, but we have stated it as an assumption), we need a procedure to handle the cases when degeneracy occurs. Consider as an example the PROTRAC transportation problem with a small modification. Assume that demand at destination 2 is 800 units and demand at destination 4 is 600 units. The initial feasible solution produced by applying the northwest corner rule is shown in Figure 7.24. Since there are only five used cells, this feasible solution is degenerate. With some reflection, you may see that this situation arose because the allocation to route B2 simultaneously exhausted the supply at origin B and satisfied the remaining demand at destination 2. Whenever such a phenomenon occurs, in the application of the northwest corner rule, you will end up with fewer than $(m + n - 1)$ used routes, and hence degeneracy.

Problems Determining Marginal Costs. Now, beginning with the degenerate initial feasible solution (Figure 7.24), let us attempt to determine the marginal cost for each unused cell. Let us take the MODI approach, which means that we need to find row and column indices such that

$$u_A + v_1 = 12, \quad u_A + v_2 = 13, \quad u_B + v_2 = 4, \quad u_C + v_3 = 12, \quad u_C + v_4 = 4$$

We start by setting $u_A = 0$. This implies that $v_1 = 12$ and $v_2 = 13$. This, in turn, implies that $u_B = -9$. At this point the process breaks down. We have three unknowns in the last two equations. The system, thus, is not entirely determined, as it was in our earlier example. This situation occurs because the feasible solution is degenerate. If you tried to calculate marginal costs by using stepping-stone paths, the method, in this degenerate case, would also fail because there would be cells for which a stepping-stone path did not exist. This is true, for example, of cell B3. Can you find others?

The Remedy. The process of solving a transportation problem in which degeneracy occurs consists of employing one of the unused cells as what might be called *"an*

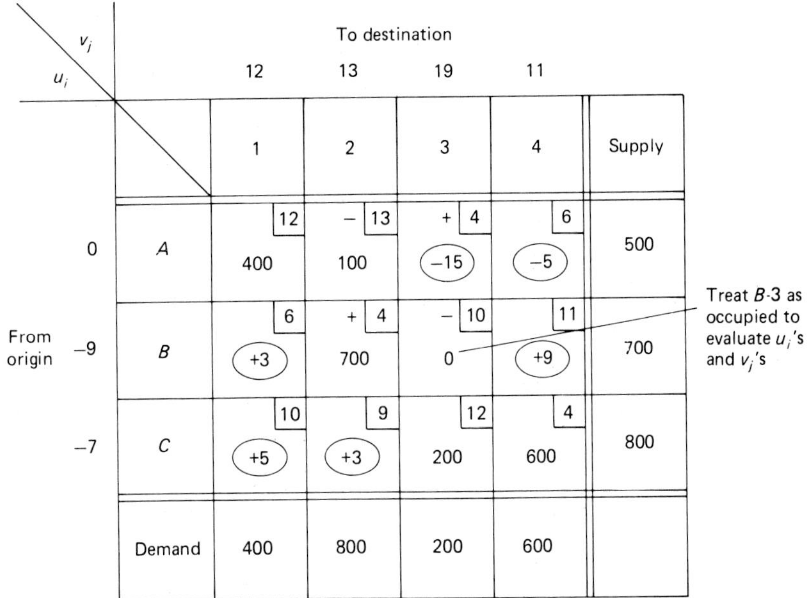

To destination
v_j
u_i
12
13
19
11
1
2
3
4
Supply
0
A
12
− 13
+ 4
6
400
100
−15
−5
500
From origin
−9
B
6
+ 4
− 10
11
+3
700
0
+9
700
Treat B-3 as occupied to evaluate u_i's and v_j's
−7
C
10
9
12
4
+5
+3
200
600
800
Demand
400
800
200
600

▲ FIGURE 7.25
Solving a Degenerate Problem

artificial used cell." We simply select any unused cell that will permit us to find the values for u_i and v_j. In our example problem there are several such cells. In particular, if A3, B3, A4, B4, or C2 were used, values for v_3, v_4, and u_C could be found. We proceed by selecting cell B3. As you see in Figure 7.25, a value of 0 is placed in this cell. That is, it is being used "artificially" at the level zero. The explicit assignment of "zero use" is made simply to remind us to treat cell B3 as *used.* (You can think of the zero as actually representing an infinitesimally small positive quantity whose presence, though, gives us $(m + n - 1)$ used cells.) Let us now follow the MODI method:

- ▶ ***Step 1:*** The values of u_i and v_j are determined as usual. These, in turn, are used to calculate the marginal cost for each unoccupied cell. The marginal costs are circled.
- ▶ ***Step 2:*** We wish to introduce cell A3.
- ▶ ***Step 3:*** To determine how many units can be sent on route A3, we must determine the stepping-stone route. This is indicated by the +'s in cells A3 and B2 as well as the −'s in cells A2 and B3. We then use the following table to determine the number of units to allocate to A3.

ACTION	ROUTE	NUMBER AVAILABLE IN DECREASING CELLS
Increase	A3	
Decrease	A2	100
Increase	B2	
Decrease	B3	0

Since B3 has 0 items available, this is the amount that we can transfer into A3 and B2. The transfer of 0 to A3 allows us now to treat A3 as used (whereas in Figure 7.25 A3 is unused). Thus, we obtain the tableau and the new values for u_i and v_j shown in Figure 7.26.

Since cells C1 and C2 have negative marginal costs, the current solution is not

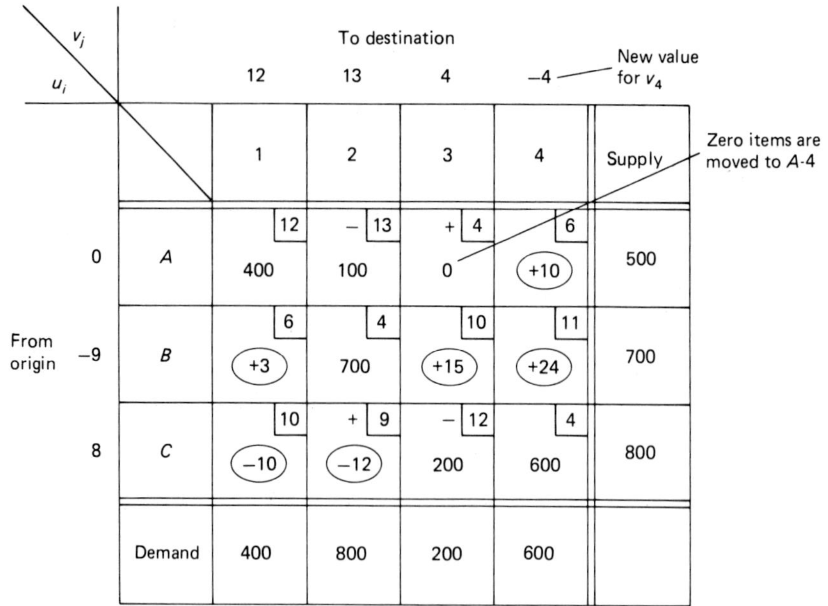

▲ FIGURE 7.26
Zero Transfer

optimal. We choose to use route C2. The stepping-stone path for this cell is indicated by the +'s and −'s on the tableau. The maximum amount that can be reallocated is determined by the 100 unit allocation in cell A2. The new tableau and the values for u_i and v_j are shown in Figure 7.27. Note that the solution is no longer degenerate. The last application of the MODI method moved 100 units into two previous unused cells (A3 and C2) while setting only one cell (A2) to zero. The solution of this problem is achieved in one more application of the MODI method. The final tableau appears in Figure 7.28.

▼ FIGURE 7.27
Transfer into C2

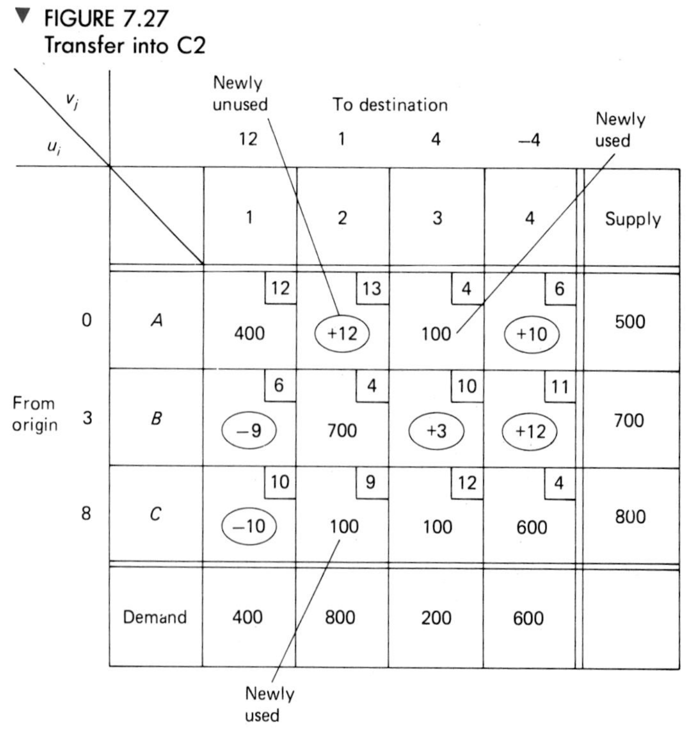

	v_j / u_i	To destination 12	11	4	6	
		1	2	3	4	Supply
0	*A*	[12] 300	[13] (+2)	[4] 200	[6] (+0)	500
From origin −7	*B*	[6] (+1)	[4] 700	[10] (+13)	[11] (+12)	700
−2	*C*	[10] 100	[9] 100	[12] (+10)	[4] 600	800
	Demand	400	800	200	600	

▲ FIGURE 7.28
Optimal Solution

In summary, we see that degeneracy in the initial feasible solution is easily handled. If the number of used cells, say *u*, is less than $(m + n - 1)$, we simply locate $(m + n - 1) - u$ of the unused cells to treat as being "artificially used" for purposes of calculating the values of u_i and v_j.

In a degenerate problem we see that it is possible to pass through an iteration of the MODI method (or the stepping-stone method) without improving the value of the objective function. This occurs when 0 items are reallocated. This phenomenon occurred in passing from the first to the second tableau in the example just completed.

In concluding this discussion, we state that degeneracy may suddenly occur with an intermediate feasible solution. In the adjustment process, when decreasing the − cells on the stepping-stone path, two or more of these could conceivably become zero. When this happens a degenerate feasible solution results. Suppose, for example, that three − cells simultaneously became zero. Then place 0 in *two* of the cells that have just been decreased to zero. That is, two of these cells are treated as being artificially used. We then continue as previously.

Special Properties of the Transportation Model

These specialized algorithms are quick because integer addition and subtraction is ten times faster than decimal multiplication and division on any computer.

Two aspects of the transportation model and the algorithms used to solve it deserve special mention. First, note that, in addition to employing the simplex method, four special algorithms have been presented; the northwest corner rule, Vogel's approximation method, the stepping-stone method, and the MODI method. Addition and subtraction are the only arithmetic operations used in each of these special algorithms. Contrast this with the simplex algorithm, which also requires division in its implementation.

The fact that the solution algorithms require only addition and subtraction is one of the reasons that transportation problems can be solved so rapidly. This characteristic is shared by some other network algorithms. This topic is discussed in Chapter 9. Thus, our first observation is:

It is possible to solve a transportation problem with algorithms that use only addition and subtraction.

The second observation is concerned with the fact that the transportation model has integer solutions under quite general conditions. From earlier chapters we know that, in general, LP models do *not* produce integer solutions. Even general LP models in which all of the parameters are integer (e.g., the **PROTRAC**, Inc. problem) do not necessarily produce integer solutions. The transportation model is an exception.

If all of the supplies and demands in a transportation problem have integer values, the optimal values of the decision variables will also have integer values.

The specialized transportation algorithms, based on networks (out-of-kilter algorithms), allow for upper and lower bounds on supply, on demand, and on any cell or route.

It is not uncommon for large LP models to have, as part of their formulation, a transportation module. In such cases, it might be incorporated in the overall LP formulation or solved separately using faster codes and algorithms.

This result is interesting in its own right, and explains why, at the outset, the simplex method produced integer solutions to **PROTRAC**'s problem in Figure 7.3.

The special algorithms specifically designed for the transportation problem make it possible to solve large transportation models quickly, often more quickly than with a general-purpose LP code based on the traditional simplex algorithm. However, the use of a general-purpose LP routine offers the advantage of flexibility in model formulation. For example, using the general LP approach, upper and lower bounds can be placed on route usage (i.e., on the x_{ij}'s) and/or more general linear constraints can be enforced. In order to handle such generalizations conveniently, and because of the widespread availability of general LP codes, the general simplex approach is not an uncommon way, in practice, of solving transportation-like models.

Let us now turn to an important special case of the transportation model. This is *the assignment problem.*

7.5 The Assignment Problem

Another way to state the assignment problem is to say, "Each person must do one job and each job must be done by one person."

The **assignment problem** occurs in many management contexts. In general, it is the problem of determining the optimal assignment of *n "indivisible"* agents or objects to *n* tasks. For example, management might have to assign salespeople to sales territories or service reps to service calls or editors to manuscripts or commercial artists to advertising copy. The agents or objects to be assigned are indivisible in the sense that no agent can be divided among several tasks. The important constraint, for each agent, is that *he or she be assigned to one and only one task.*

PROTRAC-Europe's Auditing Problem

Let us illustrate the assignment model with a particular problem facing the president of PROTRAC-Europe. PROTRAC's European headquarters is in Brussels. This year, as part of his annual audit, the president has decided to have each of the four corporate vice-presidents visit and audit one of the assembly plants during the first two weeks in June. As you recall, the assembly plants are located in Leipzig, Germany; Nancy, France; Liege, Belgium; and Tilburg, the Netherlands.

There are a number of advantages and disadvantages to various assignments of the vice-presidents to the plants. Among the issues to consider are:

1. Matching the vice-presidents' areas of expertise with the importance of specific problem areas in a plant.
2. The time the audit will require and the other demands on each vice-president during the two-week interval.
3. Matching the language ability of a vice-president with the dominant language used in the plant.

Attempting to keep all these factors in mind and arrive at a good assignment of vice-presidents to plants is a challenging problem. The president decides to start by

V.-P.	PLANT			
	Leipzig (1)	Nancy (2)	Liege (3)	Tilburg (4)
Finance (F)	24	10	21	11
Marketing (M)	14	22	10	15
Operations (O)	15	17	20	19
Personnel (P)	11	19	14	13

▲ FIGURE 7.29
Assignment Costs for Every Vice-President–Plant Combination

estimating the cost to **PROTRAC** of sending each vice-president to each plant. The data are shown in Figure 7.29. With these costs, the president can evaluate any particular assignment of vice-presidents to plants. For example, if he chooses the assignment below he incurs a total cost of 79 units.

ASSIGNMENT		
V.-P.	Plant	COST
F	1	24
M	2	22
O	3	20
P	4	13
Total Cost		79

Solving by Complete Enumeration

For 20 jobs done by 20 people, there are $20! \approx 10^{17}$ possible feasible solutions. If the problem could be solved at a rate of one million solutions per second, it would still take 6 billion years to find the optimal solution! This shows how quickly combinatorial problems can grow. While it is easy to solve smaller problems by inspection, insight, or intuition, when they grow larger, a methodical, sure, and efficient algorithm is needed.

One way to find an optimal solution is to list all possible solutions, calculate the cost of each solution, and pick the best. This process is called *complete enumeration.* Let us see how many solutions there are to this problem. Consider assigning the vice-presidents in the order F, M, O, P. We have the following steps:

1. F can be assigned to any of four plants.
2. Once F is assigned, M can be assigned to any of the three remaining plants.
3. Similiarly, O can be assigned to any of the two remaining plants.
4. P must be assigned to the only available plant.

There are, thus, $4 \times 3 \times 2 \times 1 = 24$ possible solutions. In general, if there were n vice-presidents and n plants, there would be $n(n - 1) \times \cdots \times 2 \times 1$ solutions. This series of multiplications is represented by the symbol $n!$ and called n factorial. As n increases, $n!$ increases even more rapidly. In particular, here is the relation between n and $n!$ for (integral) values of n between 1 and 10:

n	1	2	3	4	5	6	7	8	9	10
$n!$	1	2	6	24	120	720	5040	40,320	362,880	3,628,800

Thus, if the president were currently worrying about which of his 10 salespeople to assign to each of the 10 sales districts, it is clear that complete enumeration would not be a reasonable approach.

Relation to the Transportation Problem

An effective way of representing **PROTRAC**'s assignment problem is with a tableau of the type shown in Figure 7.30. In this figure we note that there is only one of each type of vice-president available (the supply), and one vice-president is required at each plant (the demand). Also, it is a balanced problem in the sense that the total number of vice-presidents available equals the total number required. Each cell represents the assignment of a specific vice-president to a specific plant. The number in the upper right-hand corner is **PROTRAC**'s cost for that assignment.

This hauntingly familiar representation is, of course, reminiscent of the standard transportation problem tableau of the sort introduced in Figure 7.4. There is only one difference. In the assignment problem, we must respect the additional feature that supply cannot be distributed to more than one destination. That is, as previously mentioned, each unit of supply (each vice-president) must go to one and only one destination. An answer that sent three-fourths of a vice-president to Leipzig and the remaining one-fourth to Liege would not be meaningful and is, therefore, prohibited. Let us now recall the discussion under the heading "Special Properties of the Transportation Model" at the end of Section 7.4. There we learned that, if all the supplies and demands are integers, the optimal allocations will also be integers. In the assignment problem, all supplies and demands are one; and hence integer. Thus, we can be assured that we will not obtain fractional allocations. Thus, we can see that:

The *assignment problem* can be solved as a *transportation problem* in which the supply at each origin and the demand at each destination is equal to 1.

▼ FIGURE 7.30
PROTRAC's Assignment Problem

V.P.'s \ Plants j	Leipzig 1	Nancy 2	Liege 3	Tilburg 4	Number of V.P.'s available
Finance (F)	24	10	21	11	1
Marketing (M)	14	22	10	15	1
Operations (O)	15	17	20	19	1
Personnel (P)	11	19	14	13	1
Number of V.P.'s required	1	1	1	1	4

This cell represents assigning P to 2

Total V.P.'s available and required

The LP Formulation and Solution

Since the assignment problem is a special kind of transportation problem, it can be formulated as an LP problem. To create this formulation we use the same definition of variables as we used for the transportation problem. In particular, we let

$$x_{ij} = \text{number of vice-presidents of type } i \text{ assigned to plant } j$$
$$i = \text{F, M, O, P}$$
$$j = 1, 2, 3, 4$$

The formulation and solution are shown in Figure 7.31. In this formulation the first

These inequalities could also be written as equalities. Note that for "n" people and jobs, the LP formulation would have n^2 variables and $2n$ constraints.

▼ FIGURE 7.31
LP Formulation and Solution of PROTRAC's Assignment Problem

```
MIN 24 XF1 + 10 XF2 + 21 XF3 + 11 XF4 + 14 XM1 + 22 XM2
    + 10 XM3 + 15 XM4 + 15 XO1 + 17 XO2 + 20 XO3 + 19 XO4 + 11 XP1
    + 19 XP2 + 14 XP3 + 13 XP4
SUBJECT TO
  2) XF1 + XF2 + XF3 + XF4 <= 1      <-- Number of VP's from F ≤ 1
  3) XM1 + XM2 + XM3 + XM4 <= 1
  4) XO1 + XO2 + XO3 + XO4 <= 1
  5) XP1 + XP2 + XP3 + XP4 <= 1
  6) XF1 + XM1 + XO1 + XP1 = 1       <-- Number of VP's assigned to 1 = 1
  7) XF2 + XM2 + XO2 + XP2 = 1
  8) XF3 + XM3 + XO3 + XP3 = 1
  9) XF4 + XM4 + XO4 + XP4 = 1

      OBJECTIVE FUNCTION VALUE

               48.00

VARIABLE       VALUE        REDUCED COST
  XF1          0.00            15.00
  XF2          1.00             0.00    <-- Assign F to 2
  XF3          0.00            15.00
  XF4          0.00             0.00
  XM1          0.00             1.00
  XM2          0.00             8.00
  XM3          1.00             0.00
  XM4          0.00             0.00
  XO1          1.00             0.00
  XO2          0.00             1.00
  XO3          0.00             8.00
  XO4          0.00             2.00
  XP1          0.00             0.00
  XP2          0.00             7.00
  XP3          0.00             6.00
  XP4          1.00             0.00

ROW            SLACK        DUAL PRICES
  2            0.00             6.00
  3            0.00             2.00
  4            0.00             0.00
  5            0.00             4.00
  6            0.00           -15.00
  7            0.00           -16.00
  8            0.00           -12.00
  9            0.00           -17.00
```

Note: **Optimal Decision Variables all 0 or 1; see discussion under "Special Properties"**

The Reduced Cost of 15 for XF1 has two meanings:
(a) how much the objective coefficient of 24 needs to be reduced (down to 9) before XF1 = 1 and OV = 48, or
(b) the change in the objective function value (+15) if XF1 were forced to be 1 (OV = 63).

constraint (row 2) states that the number of vice-presidents sent from F must be less than or equal to 1. Rows 3 through 5 place similar restrictions on vice-presidents M, O, and P, respectively. Row 6 requires 1 vice-president to be assigned to plant 1. Rows 7 through 9 place a similar requirement on plants 2, 3, and 4, respectively.

In the optimal solution part of Figure 7.31 we see that all decision variables are 0 or 1, and the optimal assignment is

Even for a small problem, such as the example, using a greedy (locally optimal) method will not always yield an optimal solution. In this case, pick the smallest cost in each column. After choosing the smallest in row 1, cross off the corresponding row, and continue. In this instance, a value of 50 is found.

	1	2	3	4
F	24	10	21	11
M	14	22	10	15
O	15	17	20	19
P	11	19	14	13

ASSIGNMENT		
V.-P.	Plant	COST
F	2	10
M	3	10
0	1	15
P	4	13
Total Cost		48

Also, the optimal value of the objective function is 48 units.

7.6 Solving the Assignment Problem: The Hungarian Method

Management science can either:
1. Change the **model** to fit the **method,** or
2. Change the **method** to fit the **model.**
Thus, the assignment problem could be changed into a linear programming model or a transportation model and use methods already developed. In this section the simplex method will be changed to fit the assignment problem using the *Hungarian method.*

Since the assignment problem is an LP problem, it can be solved with the simplex algorithm. That was the approach used to obtain the solution presented in Figure 7.31. Further, since the assignment problem is a special variety of transportation problem, we could use the approach presented in Section 7.3 (e.g., a combination of the VAM and MODI algorithms) to find the optimal assignment.

However, the special structure of the assignment problem has enabled mathematicians to devise a particularly simple algorithm for solving this problem. This algorithm, which is called the **Hungarian method,** will be illustrated in the context of PROTRAC's assignment problem. The general approach of this algorithm is to "reduce" the cost matrix by a series of arithmetic operations. These **matrix reductions** are used to create "reduced" costs of zero in the cost matrix. The optimal assignment is achieved by selecting among the cells with a zero "reduced" cost. Let us start, however, at the beginning. We start with the cost matrix shown in Figure 7.32 and move to the Hungarian method.

▼ FIGURE 7.32
Cost Matrix

	PLANT			
V.-P.	1	2	3	4
F	24	10	21	11
M	14	22	10	15
0	15	17	20	19
P	11	19	14	13

It makes no difference if you start reducing column by column. The answer will be the same, although it is possible that the numbers in the final tableau may be different. The optimal zeros will be in the same place. For row F, it is obvious that person F will have to do one of the four jobs, so that at a minimum it will cost 10 units. Thus, subtracting 10 from each cost gives us a "reduced cost" row of how much **more** it will cost than 10 units for person F.

Step 1: Row Reduction. Create a new cost matrix by selecting the minimum cost in each row and subtracting it from every cost in that row. For example, subtracting 10 from each cell in row F yields the following revised row:

	PLANT			
V.-P.	**1**	**2**	**3**	**4**
F	14	0	11	1

Changing the cost coefficients in this way will have no effect on the optimal solution, for F must still be assigned to one of the four plants, and each such assignment has been reduced by *the same constant.* This means that, were we to use the new costs above, the optimal value of the objective function (i.e., the minumum total cost) would be 10 units less than had we used the original costs. We now apply the same procedure (i.e., subtracting the minimum cost in the row from each element) to the remaining rows. The result is shown in Figure 7.33. As above, this change in costs will not affect the optimal solution to the problem. That is, using the costs from Figure 7.33 produces the same optimal assignment as that obtained by using the original costs (Figure 7.32). However, with the new costs the optimal objective value will be 10 + 10 + 15 + 11 = 46 units less than with the original costs.

	PLANT				
V.-P.	**1**	**2**	**3**	**4**	**ROW REDUCER**
F	14	0	11	1	10←
M	4	12	0	5	10
0	0	2	5	4	15
P	0	8	3	2	11

Subtracted from row F in Figure 7.32

▲ FIGURE 7.33
Row Reductions

One of the most common student mistakes is to miss the zeros (as if they didn't exist) and find the next smallest number in each column. Thus, you might get:

10	0	8	0
0	10	0	4
0	0	2	3
0	6	0	1

Since the minimum in columns 1, 2, and 3 is zero, subtracting zero should not change these columns.

Step 2: Column Reduction Select the minimum-cost entry in each column and subtract it from every entry in that column. This step yields the matrix in Figure 7.34. Again, this will not affect the optimal solution. The new optimal objective value will now be 47 units less than previously.

▼ FIGURE 7.34
Column Reduction

	PLANT			
V.-P.	**1**	**2**	**3**	**4**
F	14	0	11	0
M	4	12	0	4
0	0	2	5	3
P	0	8	3	1
Column Reducer	0	0	0	1

Subtracted from column 4 in Figure 7.33

The minimum number of row and column straight lines necessary to cover all the zeros will be equal to the number of zero assignments that can be made. The lines may not be unique, and there may be several alternate ways to arrive at the same solution.

Step 3: Determine If Matrix Is Reduced. Find the minimum number of row and column straight lines necessary to cover all the zeros in Figure 7.34. If the minimum number equals the number of rows (or columns), the matrix is termed *reduced;* go to step 5. If the number of lines is less than the number of rows (or columns), go to step 4. In our example, only three lines, as shown in Figure 7.35, are required to cover all the zeros. Thus, the matrix is not reduced and we go to step 4.

	PLANTS			
V.-P.	**1**	**2**	**3**	**4**
F	14	0	11	0
M	4	12	0	4
0	0	2	5	3
P	0	8	3	1

Covering zeros in row F

▲ FIGURE 7.35
Covering Zeros

This may look like "magic," but there is some very elegant mathematics behind it all. Since each row and column now has a zero, we are reducing both rows and columns simultaneously. Because of this, we need to add back the value of the minimum uncovered cell at the intersection.

Step 4: Further Reductions. Find the minimum uncovered (unlined) cell. Subtract the value of this cell from every uncovered cell. Add it to the value of the cell at every intersection of the lines drawn in step 3. Leave other cells unchanged. Return to step 3. Thus, since the 1 in cell P4 is the smallest uncovered cost, this operation yields the matrix shown in Figure 7.36.

	PLANT			
V.-P.	**1**	**2**	**3**	**4**
F	15	0	12	0
M	4	11	0	3
0	0	1	5	2
P	0	7	3	0

▲ FIGURE 7.36
Further Reductions

Since we now have four (4) assignments, it will take four lines to cover all the zeros. There are several ways to draw these. One is to cover all rows, another, all columns.

Step 3 (again). It now takes four lines to cover all the zeros. One possible set of covering lines is shown on the matrix in Figure 7.36. Note that there are other such sets of four lines. We now go to step 5.

	PLANT			
V.-P.	**1**	**2**	**3**	**4**
F	15	⊠	12	0
M	4	11	⊠	3
0	⊠	1	5	2
P	0	7	3	⊠

▲ FIGURE 7.37
Optimal Solution

Step 5: Locate the Optimal Solution. It is now possible to find an assignment using only cells with a zero cost. We wish to assign one vice-president to each plant. In terms of the cost matrix, this means that we must choose one and only one cell in each column and in each row. To have an optimal assignment, we must select cells with a zero cost. The solution to PROTRAC's assignment problem is shown in Figure 7.37. The cells with zero cost that are part of the solution are indicated by putting an × across the cell. Note that cell P1 has a cost of 0. It, however, cannot be part of an optimal solution. If P is assigned to plant 1, this eliminates row P and column 1 from further use. (Recall that we can use only one cell in each row and column.) Since column 1 is eliminated, we are unable to assign vice-president O at a zero cost (i.e., the only zero in row O occurs in column 1). The value of the objective function can be found by referring to the original cost matrix:

Point out to students that they must be careful to select single zeros in rows or columns first.

ASSIGNMENT		
V.-P.	**Plant**	**COST**
F	2	10
M	3	10
0	1	15
P	4	13
	Total Cost	48

Cost of assigning F to 2 (see Figure 7.32)

Note that this cost is the sum of all reductions that have been applied. We see, then, that the Hungarian method provides a simple algorithm for solving the assignment problem. Again, we note that addition and subtraction are the only arithmetic operations required by this method.

7.7 The Assignment Problem: Other Considerations

PROTRAC's assignment problem is a minimization problem in which the number of vice-presidents equals the number of plants, and every possible assignment is acceptable. In this section we consider assignment-like problems in which all these conditions do not hold. In particular, we consider problems where

1. There are an unequal number of "persons" to assign and "destinations" needing assignees.
2. There is a maximization problem.
3. There are unacceptable assignments.

Unequal Supply and Demand: The Auditing Problem Reconsidered

We wish to consider two cases. First, assume that supply exceeds demand. In particular, assume that the president himself decides to audit the plant in Tilburg. He must than decide which of the four vice-presidents to assign to each of the three remaining plants. His problem is represented by the matrix in Figure 7.38.

APPLICATION CAPSULE

Play Ball! The American League Uses an LP Assignment Model to Schedule Its Umpiring Crews*

Each year, the American League, after the difficult task of scheduling 162 games for its 14 teams, must assign the umpiring crews that will work each game. Typically, teams play one another in series consisting of 2, 3, or 4 games, with each team playing a total of 52 series in the course of the 26-week season. One of the League's seven umpiring crews must be assigned to each series.

Not surprisingly, with teams in cities across the entire North American continent, from Baltimore to Seattle and from Texas to Toronto, minimizing total travel costs is one of the principal goals of the schedulers. However, it is not the only factor that must be taken into consideration. To guarantee fairness, there are limits to the number of times each crew is exposed to each team, for both its home and its away games. Moreover, every effort is made to avoid a crew being assigned to the same team for more than two consecutive series.

Travel restrictions impose additional constraints on the schedule. Some of the more important examples include:

- A crew cannot work a night game in one city and an afternoon game in another city the next day.
- Because of time changes, a crew cannot travel from a West Coast city to Chicago or any eastern city without a day off between series.
- Because of limited airline flight schedules, a crew traveling into or out of Toronto must have a day off if it is coming from or going to any city other than New York, Boston, Detroit, or Cleveland.

While the total number of possible crew assignments is far too large for each one to be evaluated individually, the scheduling of umpires can be formulated as a relatively simple assignment problem. The League now uses a PC-based decision support system, developed by Dr. Jim Evans of the University of Cincinnati, that produces a better schedule in less than half the time previously required. In its first year of use, the system saved the American League some $30,000 in travel costs.

Taking advantage of a color monitor, the program color-codes each crew in the screen display of schedule assignments. This makes it easy for the user to follow a particular crew and examine the flow of its assignments. In addition to the assignment scheduling algorithm, the system includes a statistical computation and database program that makes it easy to keep track of crew/team combinations. As a result, the balance of crew exposures has improved since the system came into use.

*Evans, "A Microcomputer-Based Decision Support System Scheduling Umpires in the American Baseball League," *Interfaces*, Vol. 18, No. 6 (Nov.–Dec., 1988).

V.-P.	PLANT 1	2	3	NUMBER OF V.-P.s AVAILABLE
F	24	10	21	1
M	14	22	10	1
0	15	17	20	1
P	11	19	14	1
Number of V.-P.s Required	1	1	1	3 \ 4

▲ FIGURE 7.38
Supply Exceeds Demand

To solve this problem with the simplex algorithm we would simply drop the constraint that required a vice-president at plant 4, that is, the last constraint (row 9) in Figure 7.31. The result of this change is that the slack variable in one of the four first constraints would be 1 in the optimal solution to our modified LP problem. In other words, one vice-president would not be assigned to a plant.

Remember, you can either change the problem to fit the algorithm or change the algorithm to fit the problem. In this case, it is easier to change the problem (adding a dummy plant or "warehouse" to make supply = demand).

Supply > Demand: Adding a Dummy Plant. The Hungarian method requires an equal number of vice-presidents and plants. In order to adapt the president's new problem to this requirement, we simply add a "dummy" plant to the problem. The appropriate cost matrix is shown in Figure 7.39. Note that the cost of assigning any vice-president to the dummy plant is zero. In the optimal solution to this problem, one of the vice-presidents will be assigned to the dummy plant. This, of course, implies that in the real problem he is not assigned to a plant.

V.-P.	PLANT 1	2	3	Dummy	NUMBER OF V.-P.s AVAILABLE
F	24	10	21	0	1
M	14	22	10	0	1
0	15	17	20	0	1
P	11	19	14	0	1
Number of V.-P.s required	1	1	1	1	4

There is no cost to satisfy demand at the dummy

Dummy demand; now supply = demand

▲ FIGURE 7.39
Adding a Dummy Plant

We now consider the case where demand exceeds supply. For example, assume that the vice-president of personnel had to visit the International Headquarters in East Moline, Illinois, during the first two weeks in June and is thus unable to participate in the management audit. The president's problem is then represented by the cost matrix in Figure 7.40.

V.-P.	PLANT 1	2	3	4	NUMBER OF V.-P. AVAILABLE
F	24	10	21	11	1
M	14	22	10	15	1
0	15	17	20	19	1
Number of V.-P.s required	1	1	1	1	4 \ 3

▲ FIGURE 7.40
Demand Exceeds Supply

Demand > Supply: Adding a Dummy Vice-President. In this form the problem is infeasible. It is clearly impossible to satisfy the demand for four vice-presidents with a supply of three. If the president wanted to find which three plants to audit in order to minimize his cost, he could add a dummy vice-president as shown to the cost matrix in Figure 7.41.

The problem could now be solved by any of the methods we have discussed. In the solution, the dummy vice-president would be assigned to a plant. In reality, this plant would not be audited. The optimal solution is the solution that minimizes the cost of the audits undertaken by F, M, and O. The president should make sure that this is the problem he wants solved, however. It might make more sense to think that **PROTRAC** would incur some cost if a plant was not audited by a vice-president and that this cost could vary from plant to plant. Under these assumptions the new row of the matrix could be labeled "not audited" and the appropriate cost should be entered in each cell. At any rate, when demand exceeds supply, one or more new rows of supply, with appropriate costs, must be appended to the cost matrix before a feasible solution can be found.

V.-P.	PLANT 1	2	3	4	NUMBER OF V.-P. AVAILABLE
F	24	10	21	11	1
M	14	22	10	15	1
0	15	17	20	19	1
Dummy	0	0	0	0	1
Number of V.-P.s required	1	1	1	1	4

Dummy supply; now supply = demand

Zero cost to assign the dummy

▲ FIGURE 7.41
Adding a Dummy Vice President

Maximization Problems

Consider an assignment problem in which the response from each assignment is a profit rather than a cost. For example, suppose that **PROTRAC** must assign new salespeople to sales territories. Four trainees are ready to be assigned and three territories require a new salesperson. One of the salespeople will have to wait until

SALESPERSON	TERRITORY 1	2	3	NUMBER OF SALESPEOPLE AVAILABLE
A	40	30	20	1
B	18	28	22	1
C	12	16	20	1
D	25	24	27	1
Number of salespeople required	1	1	1	3 \ 4

Profit if A is assigned to 3

▲ FIGURE 7.42
Maximization Assignment Problem

another territory becomes available before he or she can be assigned. The effect of assigning any salesperson to a territory is measured by the anticipated marginal increase in net profit due to the assignment. Naturally, **PROTRAC** is interested in maximizing total net profit. The *profit* matrix for this problem is presented in Figure 7.42. The only new feature of this figure is that the number in each cell represents a profit rather than a cost.

Only one change is required to create the LP formulation of this problem. The word "Max" now precedes the objective function. The formulation is shown in Figure 7.43. We see that this problem can be solved with the simplex algorithm. An optimal solution could also be found by using transportation algorithms presented earlier in the chapter.

Using the Hungarian method to solve the problem is somewhat more complicated, however. First, since we have more salespeople than districts, a dummy district, as in the preceding section (Figure 7.39), must be added to the matrix. This change is shown in the matrix in Figure 7.44.

Since the number of salespeople now equals the number of territories, we have satisfied one of the requirements of the Hungarian method. However, a more fundamental problem remains. The assignment problem is by definition a minimization problem, and the Hungarian method is designed to solve this minimization problem. We now wish to use it to solve our Max problem. Our problem is thus to convert the Max problem into a Min problem in such a way that the optimal solution to the Min problem is also the optimal solution to the original Max problem. There are a variety of ways to accomplish this; we will consider one of them.

Calculating the Equivalent Cost Matrix. This approach involves subtracting each entry in a column from the maximum value in that column. We note that 40 is the largest value in column 1. Subtracting each value from 40 yields the following new column of "costs":

Again, it is easier here to change the problem (from maximization to minimization) than to change the method.

SALESPERSON	TERRITORY 1
A	40 − 40 = 0
B	40 − 18 = 22
C	40 − 12 = 28
D	40 − 25 = 15

```
MAX 40 XA1 + 30 XA2 + 20 XA3 + 18 XB1 + 28 XB2 + 22 XB3
    + 12 XC1 + 16 XC2 + 20 XC3 + 25 XD1 + 24 XD2 + 27 XD3
SUBJECT TO
   2) XA1 + XA2 + XA3 <= 1
   3) XB1 + XB2 + XB3 <= 1
   4) XC1 + XC2 + XC3 <= 1
   5) XD1 + XD2 + XD3 <= 1
   6) XA1 + XB1 + XC1 + XD1 = 1
   7) XA2 + XB2 + XC2 + XD2 = 1
   8) XA3 + XB3 + XC3 + XD3 = 1

        OBJECTIVE FUNCTION VALUE

                   95.00
VARIABLE           VALUE            REDUCED COST

 XA1               1.00                 0.00
 XA2               0.00                 0.00
 XA3               0.00                 4.00
 XB1               0.00                20.00
 XB2               1.00                 0.00
 XB3               0.00                 0.00
 XC1               0.00                24.00
 XC2               0.00                10.00
 XC3               0.00                 0.00
 XD1               0.00                18.00
 XD2               0.00                 9.00
 XD3               1.00                 0.00

ROW                SLACK            DUAL PRICES

  2                0.00                 4.00
  3                0.00                 2.00
  4                1.00                 0.00
  5                0.00                 7.00
  6                0.00                36.00
  7                0.00                26.00
  8                0.00                20.00
```

Profit if A is assigned to 3

This is the Optimal Profit

Assign D to 3

▲ FIGURE 7.43
The LP Formulation of a Max Assignment Problem

Another way to convert the maximization problem is to take the largest value in the table and subtract all other values from it.

▼ FIGURE 7.44
Adding a Dummy Territory to the Max Problem

SALESPERSON	TERRITORY 1	2	3	Dummy	NUMBER OF SALESPEOPLE AVAILABLE
A	40	30	20	0	1
B	18	28	22	0	1
C	12	16	20	0	1
D	25	24	27	0	1
Number of salespeople required	1	1	1	1	4

Column entries = 40 − entry in Figure 7.44

SALESPERSON	TERRITORY 1	2	3	4
A	0	0	7	0
B	22	2	5	0
C	28	14	7	0
D	15	6	0	0

▲ FIGURE 7.45
Equivalent Cost Matrix

Following this procedure for each column yields the cost matrix in Figure 7.45.

To understand the rationale behind this procedure, it is perhaps easiest to think of the cost matrix as representing *opportunity costs.* For example, we know that we must select one cell in column 1. Suppose that no assignments had been made; that is, we could select any row we wanted. If we were maximizing profit, we would, in Figure 7.44, select row 1 since 40 is the largest profit. If we were minimizing opportunity cost we would also select row 1 since 0 is the smallest cost (see Figure 7.45). Now assume that salesperson A had already been assigned, that is, that row 1 was not available. Then if we were maximizing profit, still wishing to assign to column 1, we would select row D because 25 is the largest available profit (see Figure 7.44). If we were minimizing opportunity costs, we would also select row D because 15 is the lowest available cost (see Figure 7.45).

This example illustrates why minimizing opportunity costs yields a solution that maximizes profits.

You can also keep "score" with the Hungarian method. Start with the amount subtracted from each column (40 + 30 + 27 + 0 = 97), and then subtract each amount computed using the Hungarian method. Thus, after Figure 7.45, you could draw lines through row A and down columns 3 and 4, leaving a "2" as the minimum element. The new score becomes 97 − 2 = 95, which is the same total profit as in Figure 7.46.

Optimal solution derived from equivalent cost matrix, Figure 7.45

ASSIGNMENT Salesperson	Territory	PROFIT
A	1	40
B	2	28
C	4	0
D	3	27
Total Profit		95

Profit from original problem, Figure 7.44

▲ FIGURE 7.46
Optimal Solution by the Hungarian Method

At this point the Hungarian method can be applied to this matrix in the usual fashion. Doing so yields the optimal solution shown in Figure 7.46. This solution is the same as the solution presented in Figure 7.43. Here we note that salesman C is assigned to the dummy territory; that is, he is not assigned. In Figure 7.43 this conclusion is shown by the fact that XC1, XC2, and XC3 are all zero.

Note that the optimal solution is found by applying the Hungarian method to the equivalent opportunity cost matrix. Finding the correct value for the optimal value of the objective function requires us to combine the optimal solution produced by the Hungarian method with the profit figures in the original problem formulation.

Problems with Unacceptable Assignments

Note that "0's" in the assignment table allow for certain combinations to take place, while "M's" keep them from happening.

Suppose that you are solving an assignment problem and you know that certain assignments are simply unacceptable. For example, assume that because of a strong personality conflict the president of **PROTRAC**-Europe is sure that he does not want to have the vice-president of operations (O) audit the assembly plant at Nancy (2). To achieve this goal, he simply assigns an arbitrarily *large cost,* represented by the letter M, to the cell in row O column 2. M is such a large number that subtracting any finite number from M still leaves a value of M that is larger than other relevant numbers. Such an assignment will automatically eliminate the assignment of vice-president O to 2.

This is, of course, the same general approach used to ensure that unacceptable routes are not part of the optimal solution in a transportation problem and to eliminate artificial variables from the solution to LP problems.

7.8 Financial and Production Planning

The Production Problem

The **PROTRAC**, Inc. model was introduced in Chapter 2. It is a product-mix problem, that is, a problem in which **PROTRAC** is deciding how many E-9s and F-9s to make in the coming month, in view of a number of constraints. Recall that E is the number of E-9s to produce and F is the number of F-9s. The complete model is

$$
\begin{array}{lll}
\text{Max } 5000E + 4000F & & \\
\text{s.t.} \quad E + F \geq 5 & & \text{(total unit requirements)} \\
\quad E - 3F \leq 0 & & \text{(mix requirements)} \\
\quad 10E + 15F \leq 150 & & \text{(hours in department A)} \\
\quad 20E + 10F \leq 160 & & \text{(hours in department B)} \\
\quad 30E + 10F \geq 135 & & \text{(testing hours)} \\
\quad E, F \geq 0 & &
\end{array}
$$

The production manager is satisfied that from his perspective this model captures the essence of the problem. He sends to the management committee a proposal that the recommendations of the model be considered for implementation.

Financial Considerations

When the management committee reviews the activities that are proposed for the coming month, it soon becomes clear that the **PROTRAC** production model captures only a part of **PROTRAC**'s real situation. In particular, certain important financial considerations have been ignored. Specifically, **PROTRAC** must incur material and direct labor costs in the next month, whereas payments from the eventual customers will not be forthcoming for another three months. The current

PRODUCT	PER UNIT MATERIAL AND LABOR COSTS ($)	PROFIT CONTRIBUTION ($)	SALES PRICE ($)
E	75,000	5,000	80,000
F	20,000	4,000	24,000

▲ FIGURE 7.47
Financial Data

formulation ignores the fact that **PROTRAC** will have to borrow funds to cover at least part of the current expenditures.

The data in Figure 7.47 are relevant to the financial considerations. **PROTRAC** has budgeted \$100,000 of cash on hand to cover the current material and labor costs and plans to borrow any additional funds for these material and labor costs. **PROTRAC** can borrow money at an annual interest rate of 16%, but in order to hedge against downside risks, the bank has limited the total due to the bank (principal plus interest) to be no more than two-thirds of the sum of **PROTRAC**'s cash on hand and accounts receivable. The management committee is concerned that the time value of money has been ignored in calculating the profit contributions. It feels that if present value of net cash flow is maximized fewer E-9s and more F-9s will be produced, because of the relatively high material and labor costs of the E-9s. The committee cannot agree, however, on what the proper discount rate should be. Some members argue for a 12% annual discount rate, others for a 16% rate, and a few for a 20% rate.

The Combined Model

PROTRAC's problem is to formulate a new objective function, determine how much to borrow (if any), and devise a production plan incorporating this new information. To solve this problem, it is convenient to introduce a variable. Let

D = debt (i.e., total dollars borrowed), in thousands of dollars

The net cash flow next month will be $1{,}000D - 75{,}000E - 20{,}000F$, while (since payments will not be forthcoming for another three months) the net cash flow three months later will be $80{,}000E + 24{,}000F - 1{,}040D$. The coefficient 1,040 is derived from the above statement that **PROTRAC** can borrow at 16% per annum, and hence at 4% for three months. Define the discount factor, α, based on the annual discount rate, R, as

$$\alpha = \frac{1}{1 + R/4}$$

The objective is to maximize present value of net cash flow, so the objective function becomes

The new objective function

$$\text{Max } 1{,}000D - 75{,}000E - 20{,}000F + \alpha(80{,}000E + 24{,}000F - 1{,}040D)$$

For example, if $R = 20\%$ and $\alpha = 0.952381$, the objective function becomes

$$\text{Max } 1190.48E + 2857.14F + 9.52381D$$

Note that D actually has a positive coefficient here, because **PROTRAC** is assuming it can earn 20% on its investments, but has to pay back only 16% interest on borrowed funds. If $R = 16\%$ or $R < 16\%$, then the coefficient of D would be zero or negative, respectively.

Additional constraints are also required:

Minimum debt constraint

1. **PROTRAC** must borrow enough so that it is able to cover the material and labor costs associated with production. In general terms, the appropriate inequality is

   debt + cash on hand ≥ material and labor costs

   To expand this expression, we note that **PROTRAC** has \$100,000 of cash on hand. In addition, from Figure 7.47 we see that total material and labor costs are \$75,000 for each E and \$20,000 for each F. Thus, our equation becomes, expressing everything in thousands,

   $$D + 100 \geq 75E + 20F$$

   or in computer-acceptable format

   $$D - 75E - 20F \geq -100$$

2. The bank requires that the total amount due the bank (i.e., debt plus interest) must be no greater than two-thirds of **PROTRAC**'s cash on hand plus the accounts receivable. In other words

Maximum debt constraint

   $$\frac{2}{3}(\text{cash on hand} + \text{accounts receivable}) \geq \text{debt} + \text{interest}$$

   From Figure 7.47 we see that each E sells for \$80,000 and each F sells for \$24,000. Thus, in thousands, the total accounts receivable is

   $$80E + 24F$$

   and the constraint becomes

   $$100 + 80E + 24F \geq 1.5(1.04D)$$

   or in computer-acceptable format

   $$80E + 24F - 1.56D \geq -100$$

   Note that the lower bound on the value of D (implicit in the first of the above constraints) depends upon the cost of labor and materials, whereas the upper limit of D (implicit in the last of the above constraints) is based on the sales prices.

The complete formulation and solution for the case $R = 20\%$ is shown in Figure 7.48. In the solution we see that $D = 279.4872$. Since this variable is in thousands of dollars, we know that **PROTRAC** must borrow \$279,487.20. The surplus variables for rows 7 and 8 indicate that (since row 8 is active) **PROTRAC** will borrow as much as possible, which (since row 7 has positive surplus) is more than is required to finance material and labor costs. This occurs because the model assumes that excess funds can be invested to earn 20% interest, while the cost of those funds is only 16%.

Effect of Financial Considerations

Finally, we note that inserting the financial considerations in the pure production model leads to quite a different plan from the one determined on the basis of only the production constraints. Figure 7.49 summarizes the results for the pure

```
MAX   1190.47998 E + 2857.14014 F + 9.52381 D
SUBJECT TO
   2)   10 E + 15 F <= 150
   3)   20 E + 10 F <= 160
   4)   30 E + 10 F >= 135
   5)      E -  3 F <=   0
   6)      E +    F >=   5
   7) -75 E - 20 F + D >= -100
   8)   80 E + 24 F - 1.56 D >= -100

         OBJECTIVE FUNCTION VALUE

   1)           30161.7700  <-- This compares with 50,500 for the Pure Production Problem

VARIABLE              VALUE            REDUCED COST
   E                 1.500000            .000000
   F                 9.000001            .000000
   D               279.487200            .000000

(E, F: These compare with E = 4.5, F = 7.0 in the Pure Production Problem)

ROW              SLACK OR SURPLUS       DUAL PRICES
   2)                .000000            209.488600
   3)              40.000000              .000000
   4)                .000000            -13.866840
   5)              25.500000              .000000
   6)               5.500000              .000000
   7)              86.987180              .000000
   8)                .000000             -6.105007
```

▲ FIGURE 7.48
E and F Financial and Production Planning Model

	PURE PRODUCTION	PRODUCTION AND FINANCE		
		R = 12%	R = 16%	R = 20%
E	4.5	1.5	1.5	1.5
F	7.0	9.0	9.0	9.0
D	—	192.5	192.5	279.5
OV	50,500	31,844.65	30,576.90	30,161.77

▲ FIGURE 7.49
Results from Models with and without Financial Considerations

production model and the model with financial constraints for three different values of the discount rate, R. The optimal value of the objective function is less in the production and finance models because future cash flows are discounted and interest costs are included. In the production and finance model the optimal production plan does not depend on the value of the discount rate within the observed range of 12% to 20%. The optimal debt does, but in a simple manner. If $R < 16\%$, borrow as little as possible, namely \$192,500. If $R > 16\%$, borrow as much as possible, namely \$279,487.20. If $R = 16\%$ there are alternative optimal solutions where D lies between \$192,500 and \$279,487.20.

7.9 The Media Selection Problem

The Problem in General

This is a good example of a blending or mix problem. In this case, we are looking for the blend or mix of advertising media instead of ingredients for a feed mix or raw materials for an aluminum alloy.

The media selection problem is faced by a firm or advertising agency as they try to develop an effective promotional campaign. Basically, the question is how many "insertions" (ads) the firm should purchase in each of several possible media (e.g., radio, TV, newspapers, and magazines). The goal, in a not very specific sense, is to have the advertising campaign be as effective as possible. As we shall see, the explicit objective we will adopt is subjective. Constraints on the decision maker are typically provided by the total advertising budget and the number of opportunities to place an ad that are available in each of the media. Management may further constrain the decision by insisting on various rules of thumb. For example, it might be insisted that at least a certain dollar amount be spent on a specific medium (e.g., at least $10,000 must be spent on newspaper advertising). Alternatively, it might be stipulated that no more than a certain percentage of the budget (say 50%) be spent on any one medium.

Finally, the decision may be influenced by "the law of diminishing returns"; that is, management may believe that the effectiveness of an ad decreases as the number of exposures in a medium increases during a specified period of time. For example, the tenth exposure of a TV ad in a given week would typically not have the same impact on the audience as the first or second exposure.

We present a media selection problem in detail in the following section. It is at first, however, interesting to point out that the model has an unusual objective function. Clearly, management would like to select its advertising campaign to maximize demand. Conceptually, then, the model should find the advertising campaign that maximizes demand and satisfies the budget and other constraints. Unfortunately, the link between demand and the advertising campaign is sufficiently vague so that it is difficult to construct a useful model based on this approach. The approach used is to measure the response to a particular ad in a particular medium in terms of what are called **exposure units.** This is a subjective measure based on management's assessment of the quality of the particular ad, the desirability of the potential market, and so on. In other words, it is an arbitrary measure of the "goodness" of a particular ad. An exposure unit can be thought of as a kind of utility function. Management's problem then becomes one of maximizing total exposure units, taking into account other properties of the problem (e.g., cost per number of potential customers reached, and so on). A specific example follows.

Promoting PROTRAC's New Product

The small-tractor division at **PROTRAC** has decided to enter the recreational vehicle market with the Rover, a motorcycle-like machine with three oversized tires. Since this is a new product line, a rather extensive advertising campaign is planned during the introductory month, and a budget of $72,000 is set up to fund the campaign.

PROTRAC decides to use daytime radio, evening TV, and daily newspaper ads in its advertising campaign. Data concerning the cost per ad in each of these media and the number of purchasing units reached by each ad are provided by **PROTRAC**'s advertising agency. The data are summarized in Figure 7.50.

We have already mentioned that the effectiveness of an ad is measured in exposures. Management arbitrarily selects a scale from 0 to 100 for each offering of an ad. In particular, it is assumed that each of the first 10 radio ads has a value of 60 exposure units, and each radio ad after the first 10 is rated as having 40 exposures. Figure 7.51 shows a plot of total exposures as a function of the number of daytime radio ads during the month.

ADVERTISING MEDIUM	NUMBER OF PURCHASING UNITS REACHED PER AD	COST PER AD ($)
Daytime Radio	30,000	1700
Evening TV	60,000	2800
Daily Newspaper	45,000	1200

▲ FIGURE 7.50
Media Data

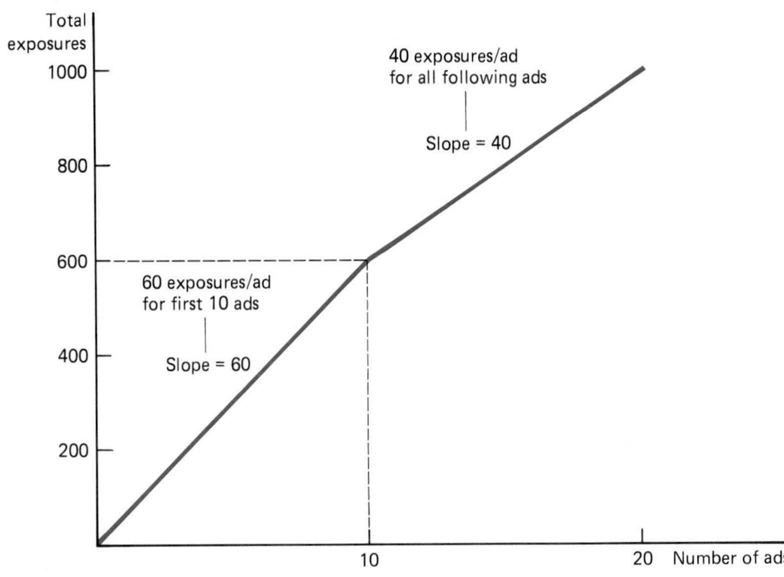

▲ FIGURE 7.51
Total Exposures vs. Number of Radio Ads

Note that in this figure, since each of the first 10 radio ads is rated as having 60 exposures, the slope of the first line segment is 60. After the first 10 ads, since each radio ad is rated as having 40 exposures, the slope of the second line segment is 40. Radio ads, then, suffer from diminishing returns. It is management's subjective evaluation that the first ads are more effective than later ones. This evaluation is based primarily on the assumption that a large proportion of those who see the later ads in a given medium will also have seen the earlier ones.

PROTRAC's analysts feel that the same situation will occur with TV and newspaper ads; that is, they, too, will suffer from diminishing returns. Indeed, they assume that in all three cases the slope (i.e., the exposures per ad) will change at the tenth ad. The exposures per ad (i.e., the slope of the two line segments), however, vary with the particular medium. The data are summarized in Figure 7.52. The total exposures as a function of the number of ads in each medium are plotted in Figure 7.53.

Management wants to ensure that the advertising campaign will satisfy certain criteria that it feels are important. In particular: (1) no more than 25 ads should appear in a single medium, (2) a total number of 1,800,000 purchasing units must be reached across all media, and (3) at least one-fourth of the ads must appear on evening TV. To model **PROTRAC**'s media selection problem as an LP problem, we let

The decision variables

x_1 = number of radio ads up to the first 10

y_1 = number of radio ads after the first 10

ADVERTISING MEDIUM	FIRST 10 ADS	ALL FOLLOWING ADS
Daytime Radio	60	40
Evening TV	80	55
Daily Newspaper	70	35

▲ FIGURE 7.52
Exposures per Ad

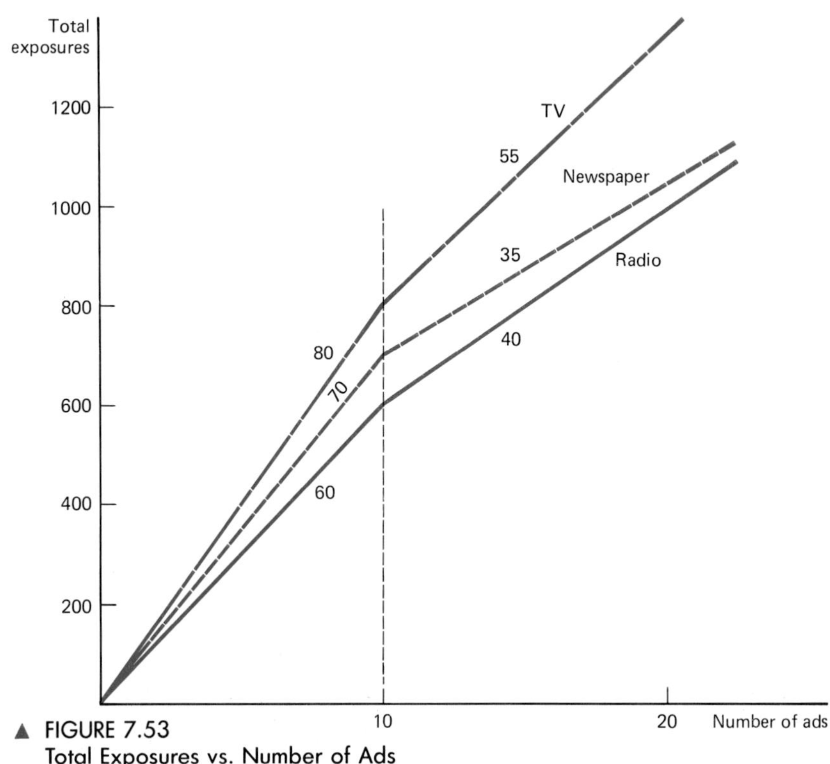

▲ FIGURE 7.53
Total Exposures vs. Number of Ads

x_2 = number of TV ads up to the first 10

y_2 = number of TV ads after the first 10

x_3 = number of newspaper ads up to the first 10

y_3 = number of newspaper ads after the first 10

With this notation we note that $60x_1$ is the total exposures from the number of "first 10" radio ads and $40y_1$ is the total exposures from the remaining radio ads. Thus, the objective function is

The objective function

$$\text{Max } 60x_1 + 40y_1 + 80x_2 + 55y_2 + 70x_3 + 35y_3$$

Turning to the constraints, we note that

$$x_1 + y_1 = \text{total radio ads}$$

$$x_2 + y_2 = \text{total TV ads}$$

$$x_3 + y_3 = \text{total newspaper ads}$$

Referring to Figure 7.50, we see that each radio ad costs \$1700. The expression for the total spent on radio ads is $1700(x_1 + y_1)$. Since TV ads cost \$2800 each and newspaper ads cost \$1200 each, the total advertising expenditure is $1700(x_1 + y_1) + 2800(x_2 + y_2) + 1200(x_3 + y_3)$. **PROTRAC** has allocated \$72,000 for the promotional campaign. This constraint is enforced by the following inequality:

Budget constraint

$$1700x_1 + 1700y_1 + 2800x_2 + 2800y_2 + 1200x_3 + 1200y_3 \le 72{,}000$$

The constraint that no more than 25 ads appear on daytime radio is imposed by the inequality $x_1 + y_1 \le 25$. A similar constraint is required for each medium.

Referring again to Figure 7.50, we see that each radio ad reaches 30,000 purchasing units. Thus, the total number of purchasing units reached by radio ads is $30{,}000(x_1 + y_1)$. The requirement that the entire campaign reach at least 1,800,000 purchasing units is imposed by the inequality

Purchasing unit constraint

$$30{,}000x_1 + 30{,}000y_1 + 60{,}000x_2 + 60{,}000y_2 + 45{,}000x_3 + 45{,}000y_3 \ge 1{,}800{,}000$$

Finally, the constraint that at least one-fourth of the ads must appear on evening TV is guaranteed by the constraint

TV exposure constraint

$$\frac{x_2 + y_2}{x_1 + y_1 + x_2 + y_2 + x_3 + y_3} \ge \frac{1}{4}$$

or

Definitional constraints

$$-x_1 - y_1 + 3x_2 + 3y_2 - x_3 - y_3 \ge 0$$

The complete formulation is presented in Figure 7.54. Note that the last three constraints enforce the definition of the variables x_1, x_2, and x_3. There is, however, one additional point to be noted. According to the definitions x_1 is the number of radio ads up to the first 10 and y_1 is the number of radio ads after the first 10. Let x_1^* and y_1^* be the optimal values of these variables. Clearly it would not make sense to have an optimal solution with $x_1^* < 10$ and $y_1^* > 0$; that is, it does not make sense to

```
MAX 60 X1 + 40 Y1 + 80 X2 + 35 Y2 + 70 X3 + 35 Y3
SUBJECT TO
     2) 1700 X1 + 1700 Y1 + 2800 X2 + 2800 Y2 + 1200 X3 +      [Budget]
        1200 Y3 < = 72000
     3) - X1 - Y1 + 3 X2 + 3 Y2 - X3 - Y3 > = 0                [Proportion for evening TV]
     4) 30000 X1 + 30000 Y1 + 60000 X2 + 60000 Y2 +            [Number of purchasing units]
        45000 X3 + 45000 Y3 > = 1800000
     5) X1 + Y1 < = 25 )
     6) X2 + Y2 < = 25 }  [No more than 25 ads per medium]
     7) X3 + Y3 < = 25 )
     8) X1 < = 10 )
     9) X2 < = 10 }  [Definition]
    10) X3 < = 10 )
```

▲ FIGURE 7.54
Formulation of the Media Selection Problem

have placed ads after the first 10 when not all of the first 10 have been placed. Nothing in the constraints prevents this. However, it will not occur. The reason is that the marginal contribution of x_1, in the objective function, is larger than that of y_1. If $x_1 < 10$ and $y_1 > 0$ is feasible, you can see from the constraints that the values $x_1 + E$ and $y_1 - E$ will also be feasible, where E is a very small positive number.

Moreover, in the objective function, since the coefficient of x_1 is larger than the coefficient of y_1, this substitution will give an improved objective value. In prosaic terms, the maximization will push x_1 to its limit (10 ads) before making y_1 greater than zero. Analogous comments apply to x_2, y_2 and x_3, y_3.

7.10 Summary

This chapter was devoted to special applications of the linear programming model. Four models were presented in some detail.

Sections 7.2 through 7.4 covered the transportation problem. The generic problem is one of determining the least-cost method of satisfying demands at a number of destinations by shipping materials from supplies available at several origins. This problem is motivated by a specific problem faced by **PROTRAC**-Europe. In Section 7.2 this problem was formulated as an LP problem and solved on the computer. Section 7.3 presented two algorithms for finding an initial feasible solution—the northwest corner rule and Vogel's approximation method—as well as two algorithms for moving from an initial feasible solution to the optimal solution—the stepping-stone method and MODI, the modified distribution method. The final section in this group, Section 7.4, covered a pot-pourri of topics related to the transportation problem. The first four subsections discussed the adaptations that are necessary in order to use the algorithms (those given in Section 7.2) for solving the transportation problem when the models differ from the original model. Finally, we saw that the transportation problem has two special properties. First, if all supplies and demands are integer quantities, there is an optimal integer solution. Second, the algorithms for solving the transportation problem use only addition and subtraction. This fact helps explain why the special algorithms are able to obtain optimal solutions so quickly.

Sections 7.5 through 7.7 treated the assignment problem following the pattern of the preceding three sections. The generic assignment problem is one of assigning n persons to n tasks in order to minimize the total cost of the assignments. This problem was again motivated by a specific problem faced by **PROTRAC**-Europe. The problem was formulated as an LP problem and solved on the computer. In this process we noted that the assignment problem is a special type of transportation problem in which all supplies and demands equal 1. Section 7.6 presented the Hungarian method, an efficient algorithm for solving the assignment problem. Finally, Section 7.7 treated a variety of special subjects dealing with the use of the Hungarian algorithm.

Section 7.8 discussed and formulated examples of several other important classes of LP models used for financial and production planning. Media selection in the marketing context was discussed in Section 7.9.

Key Terms

Destination. A location with a demand for material in a transportation problem. (*p. 279*)

Origin. A source of material in a transportation problem. (*p. 279*)

Transportation Problem. An LP model to find the least expensive way of satisfying demands at n destinations with supplies from m origins. (*p. 282*)

Transportation Tableau. A table used to display the parameters for a transportation problem and to provide a convenient way of applying the solution algorithms. (*p. 282*)

Cell. The rectangle in a transportation tableau used to identify the route between an origin and a destination. (*p. 282*)

Northwest Corner Rule. An algorithm

that finds an initial feasible solution to a transportation problem by satisfying demands and exhausting supplies in a prescribed order. (*p. 282*)

Vogel's Approximation Method (VAM). An algorithm that finds an initial feasible solution to a transportation problem by considering the "penalty cost" of not using the cheapest available route. (*p. 284*)

Stepping-Stone Method. A sequential algorithm that starts with a feasible solution and produces an optimal solution to a transportation problem. (*p. 290*)

Stepping-Stone Path. A series of adjustments in a feasible solution to a transportation problem that incorporates a new route and retains a feasible solution. (*p. 291*)

Modified Distribution Method (MODI). A simpler way of calculating the parameters needed in the stepping-stone method. (*p. 295*)

Dummy Destination. An imaginary destination that is added to a transportation problem so that total supply equals total demand. Used in the algorithms specifically designed for the transportation problem. (*p. 298*)

Dummy Origin. An imaginary source that is added to a transportation problem so that total supply equals total demand. Used in the algorithms specifically designed for the transportation problem. (*p. 299*)

Degeneracy. A condition indicated in a transportation problem by the fact that fewer than $(m + n - 1)$ routes are being used. (*p. 300*)

Assignment Problem. The problem of determining the optimal assignment of n "indivisible" agents or objects to n tasks. (*p. 304*)

Hungarian Method. An algorithm specifically designed to solve the assignment problem. (*p. 308*)

Matrix Reduction. The process used in the Hungarian method to convert the original cost matrix to one in which the optimal assignment is selected from assignments with a cost of zero. (*p. 308*)

Exposure Units. An arbitrary measure of the "goodness" of an ad used in solving media selection problems. (*p. 322*)

▶ Major Concepts Quiz

True-False

1. T F The coefficient of x_{ij} in the objective function of a transportation problem is the cost of sending a unit from i to j.

2. T F Vogel's approximation method is based on the concept of a break-even quantity.

3. T F The stepping-stone method requires a feasible solution as a starting point.

4. T F In the MODI method you must determine an index for each row (u_i for row i) and an index number of each column (v_j for column j) such that $u_i + v_j = x_{ij}$ for every used cell.

5. T F To solve a Max transportation problem you stop when all the unused routes have negative marginal values.

6. T F If total supply exceeds total demand in a transportation problem, to find a solution you should add a dummy destination with a transportation cost of zero from every origin.

7. T F A transportation problem cannot have an optimal integer solution unless all of the supplies, demands, and transportation costs are integers.

8. T F One way to transform a Max assignment problem into a problem that can be solved with the Hungarian algorithm is to subtract each entry in a column from the maximum value in that column.

Multiple Choice

9. The northwest corner rule
   a. is used to find an initial feasible solution
   b. is used to find an optimal solution
   c. is based on the concept of minimizing opportunity cost
   d. none of the above

10. In Vogel's approximation method the opportunity cost associated with a row is determined by
   a. the difference between the smallest cost and the next smallest cost in that row
   b. the difference between the smallest unused cost and the next smallest unused cost in that row
   c. the difference between the smallest cost and the next smallest unused cost in the row
   d. none of the above

11. The maximum number of items that can be allocated to an unused route with the stepping-stone algorithm is
   a. the maximum number in any cell
   b. the minimum number in any cell
   c. the minimum number in an increasing cell
   d. the minimum number in a decreasing cell on the stepping-stone path for that route

12. The MODI method uses the stepping-stone path
   a. to calculate the marginal cost of unused cells
   b. to determine how many items to allocate to the selected unused cell
   c. to determine the values of the row and column indexes
   d. not at all

13. Degeneracy occurs in a transportation problem when
   a. demand exceeds supply
   b. exactly one used cell becomes unused while moving items to a currently unused cell
   c. fewer than $(m + n - 1)$ cells are used
   d. none of the above

14. The assignment problem
   a. is a special case of the transportation problem
   b. can be solved with the simplex algorithm
   c. always has an optimal integer solution when treated as an LP
   d. all of the above

Answers

1. T
2. F
3. T
4. F
5. T
6. T
7. F
8. T
9. a
10. b
11. d
12. b
13. c
14. d

Problems

QSB+ has modules for the transportation and assignment problems. You may use these modules to verify your intermediate tableaux and final solutions.

(a) (i) $x_{A1} = 45$, $x_{B1} = 45$, $x_{B2} = 5$, $x_{C2} = 25$, $x_{C3} = 20$, $x_{D3} = 30$; cost = \$1390.
(ii) $x_{A3} = 45$, $x_{B1} = 15$, $x_{B2} = 30$, $x_{B3} = 5$, $x_{C1} = 45$, $x_{D1} = 30$; cost = \$785
(b) As expected, VAM yields a better solution.

7-1. ▲ Consider the transportation tableau in Figure 7.55.
(a) Find an initial feasible solution and evaluate its cost with
   (i) The northwest corner rule.
   (ii) Vogel's approximation method.
(b) Comment on the relative quality of the solutions determined in part (a).

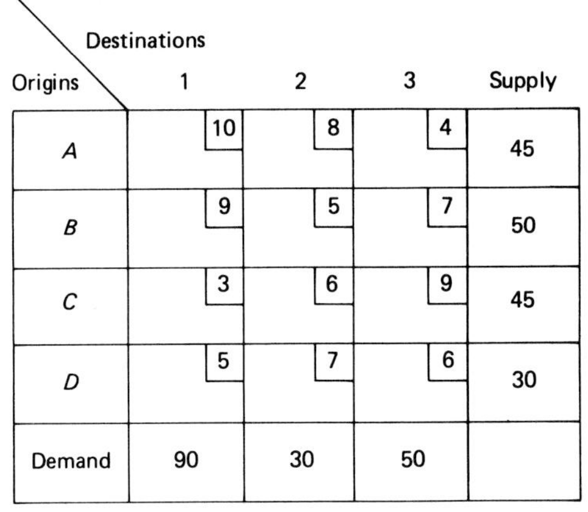

Origins \ Destinations	1	2	3	Supply
A	10	8	4	45
B	9	5	7	50
C	3	6	9	45
D	5	7	6	30
Demand	90	30	50	

▲ FIGURE 7.55

Origin \ Destinations	1	2	3	Supply
A	41	45	40	600
B	31	29	38	300
C	46	36	35	600
Demand	500	800	200	

▲ FIGURE 7.56

(a) **(i)** $x_{A1} = 500$, $x_{A2} = 100$, $x_{B2} = 300$, $x_{C2} = 400$, $x_{C3} = 200$; cost = 55,100
(ii) $x_{A1} = x_{A2} = x_{A3} = 200$, $x_{B1} = 300$, $x_{C2} = 600$; cost = 56,100
(b) Not true—part (a) is a counterexample

7-2. ▲ Consider the transportation tableau in Figure 7.56.

(a) Find an initial feasible solution and evaluate its cost with

(i) The northwest corner rule.

(ii) Vogel's approximation method.

(b) Comment on the following statement: Vogel's approximation method always yields a better initial feasible solution than the northwest corner rule because it considers costs in making its allocation decisions.

(a), (b) $x_{A3} = 45$, $x_{B1} = 15$, $x_{B2} = 30$, $x_{B3} = 5$, $x_{C1} = 45$, $x_{D1} = 30$; OV = 785
(c) Zero
(d) 70

7-3. ▲ Consider the transportation problem presented in Problem 7-1. Find the optimal solution by

(a) Starting with the solution produced by the northwest corner rule and then using the stepping-stone method. Specify the optimal value of the objective function.

(b) Starting with the solution produced by Vogel's approximation method and using the MODI method, specify the optimal value of the objective function.

(c) What is the additional cost if management insists on sending at least 10 units from C to 1?

(d) What is the additional cost if management insists on sending 10 units from C to 2?

(a) $x_{A1} = 500$, $x_{A3} = 100$, $x_{B2} = 300$, $x_{C2} = 500$, $x_{C3} = 100$; cost = 54,700
(b) Same as (a)
(c) 0
(d) 1000

7-4. ▲ Consider the transportation problem presented in Problem 7-2. Find the optimal solution by

(a) Starting with the solution produced by the northwest corner rule and then using the stepping-stone method, find the optimal solution.

(b) Starting with the solution produced by Vogel's approximation method and using the MODI method, find the optimal solution.

(c) What is the additional cost if management insists on sending at least 400 units from A to 1?

(d) What is the additional cost if management insists on sending 100 units from C to 1?

85

7-5. ▲▲▲ What additional cost will management incur in Problem 7-3 if 15 units are sent from D to 3?

1400

7-6. ▲▲ What additional cost will management incur in Problem 7-4 if no item can be sent from B to 2?

$x_{A2} = 150$, $x_{A3} = 250$, $x_{B2} = 300$, $x_{C1} = 150$, $x_{C2} = 50$; OV = 7600

7-7. ▲ Use the northwest corner rule and the stepping-stone method to find the optimal solution to the *maximization* transportation problem shown in Figure 7.57. State the optimal value of the objective function.

$x_{A1} = 150$, $x_{A2} = 250$, $x_{B2} = 300$, $x_{c3} = 200$; OV = 7550

7-8. ▲▲ Use the northwest corner rule and the MODI method to find the optimal solution to the *maximization* problem shown in Figure 7.58. State the optimal value of the objective function.

7-9. ▲▲ Use the northwest corner rule and the stepping-stone method to solve the transporta-

	1	2	3	Supply
A	5	7	10	400
B	4	9	6	300
C	8	3	2	200
Demand	150	500	250	900

▲ FIGURE 7.57

	1	2	3	Supply
A	10	7	5	400
B	6	9	4	300
C	2	3	8	200
Demand	150	550	200	900

▲ FIGURE 7.58

$x_{A2} = 200$, $x_{B1} = 100$, $x_{C1} = 100$, $x_{C2} = 100$, $x_{C3} = 100$; OV = 2500

tion problem shown in Figure 7.59. State the optimal value of the objective function. Note that supply exceeds demand.

7-10. ▲▲▲ Consider Figure 7.60.

(a) Use Vogel's approximation method and the stepping-stone method to find the optimal solution and the OV for this transportation problem. Are there alternative optimal solutions? If so, state one.

(b) If location 3 is eliminated, what is the best way in which the other two locations can be serviced?

(c) If in the original problem supplier C is no longer available, what is the least costly way of meeting as much of the demand as possible?

(a) $x_{A1} = 150$, $x_{A3} = 50$, $x_{B1} = 50$, $x_{B2} = 250$, $x_{C1} = 100$; OV = 1650
Alternative solution: $x_{A1} = 200$, $x_{B1} = 50$, $x_{B2} = 250$, $x_{C1} = x_{C3} = 50$; cost = 1650
(b) Alternate solution from part A is optimal where location 3 is now a dummy with 0 costs.
(c) Original solution still optimal where C is now a dummy with 0 costs.

	1	2	Supply
A	7	5	200
B	4	8	100
C	5	6	300
Demand	200	300	

▲ FIGURE 7.59

	1	2	3	Supply
A	2	6	3	200
B	5	1	9	300
C	7	9	8	100
Demand	300	250	50	

▲ FIGURE 7.60

See IM.

7-11. ▲ Johnson Electric produces small electric motors for four appliance manufacturers in each of its three plants. The unit production costs vary with the locations because of differences in the production equipment and labor productivity. The unit production costs and monthly capacities (supplies) are shown in Figure 7.61. The customer orders that must be produced next month are shown below.

CUSTOMER	DEMAND
1	300
2	500
3	400
4	600

The cost of supplying these customers varies from plant to plant. The unit transportation costs in dollars are given in Figure 7.62. Johnson must decide how many units to produce in each plant and how much of each customer's demand to supply from each plant. It wishes to minimize total production and transportation costs. Formulate Johnson's problem as a transportation problem and show the original tableau.

See IM.

7-12. ▲▲▲ Fernwood Lumber produces plywood. The cost to produce 1000 board feet of plywood

PLANT	UNIT PRODUCTION COST ($)	MONTHLY PRODUCTION CAPACITY
A	17	800
B	20	600
C	24	700

▲ FIGURE 7.61

FROM	TO 1	2	3	4
A	3	2	5	7
B	6	4	8	3
C	9	1	5	4

▲ FIGURE 7.62
Unit Transportation Costs ($)

varies from month to month because of the variation in handling costs, energy consumption, and raw materials costs. The production cost per 1000 board feet in each of the next 6 months is shown below.

MONTH	1	2	3	4	5	6
Production cost ($)	900	950	1250	1050	900	850

Demand for the next 6 months is as follows:

MONTH	1	2	3	4	5	6	Total
DEMAND	60	70	110	80	70	60	450

Fernwood can produce up to 90,000 board feet per month. It also has the option of carrying inventory from one month to the next for a carrying cost of $25 per 1000 board feet per month. For example, 1000 board feet produced in month 1 for demand in month 2 incurs a carrying charge of $25. Furthermore, unsatisfied demand in one month can be filled in later periods at the cost of $40 per 1000 board feet per month-delay. Fernwood would like to know how much to produce each month and how much inventory to carry in order to satisfy demand at minimum cost. Formulate Fernwood's problem as a transportation problem and show the original transportation tableau.

A1, B4, C3, D2; OV = 68

7-13. ▲ A partner at Foot, Thompson and McGrath, an advertising agency, is trying to decide which of four account executives to assign to each of four major clients. The estimated costs of each assignment for each executive are presented in Figure 7.63. Use the Hungarian method to find the optimal solution to this problem. State the optimal value of the objective function.

A2, C1, D3; cost = 99; no alternative optima

7-14. ▲▲ Sam has four repair bays in the maintenance shop and three jobs to assign to them. Because of differences in the equipment available, the people assigned to each bay, and the characteristics of the job, each job requires a different amount of time in each bay. The estimated times for each job in each bay are shown in Figure 7.64. Sam would like

▼ FIGURE 7.63

EXEC.	ACCOUNT 1	2	3	4
A	15	19	20	18
B	14	15	17	14
C	11	15	15	14
D	21	24	26	24

▼ FIGURE 7.64

BAY	JOB 1	2	3
A	27	48	30
B	38	51	28
C	27	55	23
D	35	59	24

to minimize the total time required. Use the Hungarian method to obtain the optimal solution to this problem. State the optimal value of the objective function. Are there alternative optimal solutions?

A4, B3, C1, D2; OV = 320

7-15. ▲▲ PROTRAC is deciding which of four salespeople to assign to each of four midwestern sales districts. Each salesperson is apt to achieve a different sales volume in each district. The estimates are shown in Figure 7.65. **PROTRAC** would like to maximize total sales volume. However, it is impossible to assign salesperson B to district 1 or salesperson A to district 2 since these assignments would violate personnel rotation policies. Use the Hungarian method to solve this problem. State the optimal value of the objective function.

	DISTRICT			
SALESPERSON	**1**	**2**	**3**	**4**
A	65	73	55	58
B	90	67	87	75
C	106	86	96	89
D	84	69	79	77

▲ FIGURE 7.65

	DEVELOPER				
PLOT	**1**	**2**	**3**	**4**	**5**
A	19	19	29	23	24
B	23	21	27	19	25
C	19	19	22	0	20
D	23	0	19	21	18

▲ FIGURE 7.66

A3, B5, C2, D1; OV = 84

7-16. ▲▲ A realtor plans to sell four plots of land and has received individual bids from each of five developers. Because of the amount of capital required, these bids were made with the understanding that no developer would purchase more than one plot. The bids are shown in Figure 7.66. The realtor wants to maximize total income from these bids. Solve this problem using the Hungarian method. State the value of the objective function.

Video Case

Concepts, Analysis, and Technology

You have now seen a brief clip of how the UPS system works at its hub in Louisville, Kentucky. It is hard not to be impressed: hundreds of airplanes, millions of packages, and just hours to clear the system.

UPS uses what is often called a hub-and-spoke system for delivering its domestic packages. At the base of the system is the major hub in Louisville. As we have seen, planes begin arriving at this hub early in the morning, whereupon a truly amazing package sorting and reassignment process takes place. All the packages from the Minneapolis plane are removed and sent to the planes that will take them to their destinations in cities such as Los Angeles, Miami, and New York. Meanwhile, packages from all of these origins are being sorted, and those that are bound for Minneapolis will be placed on the Minneapolis plane. In a time window that is sometimes only three or four hours long, all of the planes are reloaded and are winging their way back to the place where they started.

If you think about it for a minute, you can see that there are many questions that had to be answered in designing this system. Consider a package that originates in Rochester, Minnesota, a city of 58,000 people that is about 90 miles from Minneapolis and has a good airport. Should Rochester's packages go directly to Louisville or should they go to Minneapolis first? If they go to Minneapolis, how early do they have to leave in order to make the flight to Louisville? Then there is Zumbrota, a city of 2200 that is 30 miles from Rochester and 60 miles from Minneapolis, with no airport. Where should *these* packages go, and when? Such problems are related to the transportation and assignment problems discussed in this chapter, as well as to the network problems discussed in Chapter 9.

Questions

1. Compare the problem of designing the hub-and-spoke network to a transportation problem. How are these problems similar? How are they different? In particular, let p_{ij} be the number of packages at origin i that will go to destination j and think about definitions for supply and demand. What do these new definitions mean and how do they compare to the definitions in the transportation problem?
2. It seems fair to say that the hub-and-spoke design of the operating system is a fundamental concept at UPS. The video suggested some other basic UPS concepts. List and describe them.

CHAPTER 8

Integer and Quadratic Programming

APPLICATION CAPSULE

Brushing Up: American Airlines Uses an Integer Program to Tackle a Complex Scheduling Problem*

Each month between 500 and 600 American Airlines crew members from 10 different crew bases are scheduled to receive a short course in the company's recurrent training program, given at the American Airlines Flight Academy at the Dallas/Fort Worth Airport. A variety of rules govern (1) when a crew member is due to receive recurrent training (in order to remain qualified to fly on a particular type of equipment) and (2) the pay a crew member is entitled to receive during the recurrent training period (the pay depends on whether the crew member is trained on free time or is relieved of an assignment). The scheduling must satisfy a variety of constraints. For example, there must be enough people available in reserve to replace those trainees relieved of a flying assignment.

A manual procedure had previously been used for the scheduling. In an attempt to redress numerous problems associated with the manual system, the American Airlines Operations Research group undertook an effort to model the system. A major component of the overall model was an integer linear program involving more than 26,000 variables and 500 constraints. Because of the need for quick turn-around in solving this problem, a three-phase heuristic approach was devised. The system has become an integral component of the crew-scheduling procedure, and by conservative estimates has saved $250,000 per year in crew costs.

*Monroe Shapiro, "Scheduling Crewmen for Recurrent Training," *Interfaces*, vol. 11, no. 3 (June 1981), pp. 1–8.

8.1 Introduction to Integer Programming

The first half of this chapter is devoted to problems that could be formulated and solved as linear programming problems except for the unpleasant complication that some or all of the variables are required to assume integer values. Such problems are called **integer linear programming (ILP)** problems.[1] Integer linear programming has become an important specialized area of management science. In this introductory chapter, it will be possible only to scratch the surface—to illustrate the importance of the topic, as well as one of the most useful solution methods.

Rounded solutions

At the outset, let us recall from previous chapters that in a linear programming problem the variables are permitted to take on fractional values, such as 6.394, and in keeping with the principle that "whatever is allowed will occur," fractional answers must be expected.[2] In spite of this, actual (real-world) decision variables often must be integers. For example, a firm produces bags of cattle feed. A solution that requires them to make 3000.472 bags does not make sense. In such situations a noninteger solution is often adapted to the integer requirement by simply rounding the results to a neighboring integer. This method produces what we call a **rounded solution.** Using such a solution is acceptable to management in situations where, in a significant practical sense, the rounding does not matter. For example, there is no significant difference either in the objective function or in the constraints between producing 19,283.64 and 19,283 bags of Big Bull cattle feed. Indeed, there are probably enough approximations used in assembling the data for the model that management would be content with any production figure near the 19,000-bag level.

Generally, the larger the LP solution values, the more likely that a rounded integer answer will be acceptable *and* not violate the constraints.

When Integer Solutions Matter

There are, however, a number of important problems where this rather cavalier attitude toward the integer requirements of the real problem does not work. This complication can be caused by the scale of the variables under consideration. For example, if the solution to an LP model suggested that Boeing should build 11.6 747s and 6.8 727s, management probably would not be comfortable just going ahead and deciding to build eleven 747s and six 727s, or, for that matter any other rounded combination. The magnitude of the return and the commitment of resources associated with each unit of this problem make it advisable to determine the best possible *integer solution.*

Again, make sure that the rounded answer is substituted back into the constraints and does not cause an infeasibility.

As another example, it will be seen that many models use integer variables to indicate logical decisions. For example, we will see problems where we want X_7 to equal 1 if we should build a warehouse in Kansas City and X_7 to equal 0 if we should not. Suppose that the solution to an LP version of this problem yielded a noninteger value (e.g., $X_7 = 0.38$). We shall see that this value contains no useful information about the solution to the real problem. Clearly, we cannot build 0.38 of a warehouse. We certainly could select warehouses of different sizes, but nevertheless, either we have a warehouse in Kansas City or we do not. You might guess that, in a case such

[1]Not all integer programming problems are necessarily linear, and many of the things we say in this chapter about ILPs apply to integer programs in general. However, since we deal only with linear models in this chapter, we will use the abbreviation ILP throughout to avoid the need for additional terminology and minimize the possibility of confusion.

[2]An exception to this is described in Chapter 7. Transportation models with integral supplies and demands will always produce integer-valued optimal solutions. As will be seen in Chapter 9, this remarkable property is true of a more general class of models called network models. Transportation models are a special type of network models.

as this, rounding to the nearest integer (0 in this case) would be a way to approach this difficulty. Unfortunately, that is not guaranteed to give a good (to say nothing of optimal) solution. Indeed, we shall see that rounding may not even lead to a feasible solution in cases such as these.

There are many important management problems that would be linear programming problems except for the requirement of integer values for some of the decision variables, where you *cannot* find a good solution by using the simplex method and then rounding off the resulting optimal values of the decision variables. These problems must be solved with algorithms designed especially to solve integer programming problems.

Management scientists have been aware of the importance of integer linear programming problems for years, and a great deal of time and effort has been devoted to research on the solution of these problems. These efforts have returned some dividends, and marked progress has been made in this area. The great strides in computer technology have also made a crucial contribution to the increased ability to solve integer linear programming problems.

LP versus ILP

Integer programming problems can take at least ten times longer to solve when using computer codes than when not using integer restrictions.

In spite of the impressive improvement in our ability to solve integer programming problems, the technology is still quite different from what we have available to attack programming problems in which the decision variables need not be integer. Many problems that can be solved easily as LP problems become unsolvable for practical purposes if the decision variables are required to be integers (i.e., the time and cost needed to compute a solution are too large).

The graphical representation again helps the student to visualize the problem and see the difficulties in finding the optimal solution.

In the following sections we first describe two general classes of integer linear programming models and use graphical analysis to illustrate the relationship between linear programming, integer linear programming, and the process of rounding LP solutions to obtain a possible solution to the ILP. This graphical approach will provide an intuitive feeling for the nature of the problem we are confronting. We then turn our attention to a special variety of integer programs in which the integer variables are restricted to the values of 0 or 1. Using such "indicator" or "Boolean" variables allows us to *formulate* a variety of logical conditions that are not otherwise easily captured. A number of important practical problems involve such conditions, and several of these formulations are discussed. We then turn to the topic of *solving* integer linear programs. First we consider the branch-and-bound algorithm that is used to solve these problems. Then our attention turns to the topic of integer linear programming in practice, emphasizing strategic considerations as well as discussing possibilities for sensitivity analysis.

In real applications, integer programs are *never* solved by hand. In order to convey the context of how you would, in practice, deal with such problems we have provided in this chapter, as in others, several computer printouts. Some of these are annotated in order to highlight the interpretation of various numbers. In looking over these printouts, review the problem and the formulation; ask yourself whether the solution is intuitively plausible and, if not, try to explain why. This type of analytic thinking can be developmental; it plays a useful role in management.

8.2 Types of Integer Linear Programming Models

Integer programming is a general term for mathematical programming models with *integrality conditions* (conditions stipulating that some or all of the decision variables must have integer values). We have already pointed out that integer linear programming (ILP) models are linear programming models with the additional characteristic that some or all of the decision variables are required to take on integer values. There are several classifications within this category of models.

All-integer programs

An **all-integer linear program** is, as the name suggests, a problem in which *all* of the decision variables are required to be integers. For example

$$\begin{aligned} \text{Min } & 6x_1 + 5x_2 + 4x_3 \\ \text{s.t. } & 108x_1 + 92x_2 + 58x_3 \geq 576 \\ & 7x_1 + 18x_2 + 22x_3 \geq 83 \\ & x_1, x_2, x_3 \geq 0 \text{ and } \textit{integer} \end{aligned} \tag{8.1}$$

is an all-integer model. Without the additional constraints x_1, x_2, x_3 integer (i.e., the integrality conditions), this problem is an LP problem.

Mixed integer programs

A problem in which *only some* of the variables are restricted to integer values and others can assume any nonnegative number (i.e., *any continuous value*) is referred to as a **mixed integer linear program (MILP).** For example, suppose that in the previous problem only x_1 and x_2 were required to be integer and x_3 was not. This problem then becomes

$$\begin{aligned} \text{Min } & 6x_1 + 5x_2 + 4x_3 \\ \text{s.t. } & 108x_1 + 92x_2 + 58x_3 \geq 576 \\ & 7x_1 + 18x_2 + 22x_3 \geq 83 \\ & x_1, x_2, x_3 \geq 0 \qquad x_1 \text{ and } x_2 \text{ integer} \end{aligned}$$

0–1 integer programs

In some problems the integer variables are restricted to the values 0 or 1. Such problems are called **binary, or 0–1, integer linear programs.** These problems are particularly important because the 0–1 variables may be used to represent dichotomous decisions (yes/no decisions). A variety of scheduling, plant location, production planning, and portfolio construction problems are 0–1 integer linear programming problems. They are discussed in some detail in Section 8.4. As we shall see, 0–1 variables can be found in all-integer models and in MILPs.

In this chapter we often consider the linear programming problem (LP) that results if we start with an ILP and ignore the integer restrictions. This LP problem is referred to as the **LP relaxation** of the ILP. For example, if we remove the phrase "and *integer*" from the ILP presented in model (8.1), the resulting LP is the LP relaxation of the original integer program.

8.3 Graphical Interpretations

In Chapter 4 we saw that it is possible to gain substantial insight into the nature and the solution of LP problems by examining the graphical analysis of a problem with two decision variables. The same approach is useful for an ILP problem, and we now turn our attention to that topic.

Solving the ILP Problem: A Modification of PROTRAC, Inc.

Consider a modified version of the PROTRAC *E* and *F* problem discussed in Chapters 2 through 5. In particular, consider the problem

$$
\begin{array}{llr}
\text{Max } 18E + 6F & & \\
\text{s.t.} \quad E + F \geq 5 & (1) & \\
42.8E + 100F \leq 800 & (2) & \\
20E + 6F \leq 142 & (3) & \qquad \textbf{(8.2)} \\
30E + 10F \geq 135 & (4) & \\
E - 3F \leq 0 & (5) & \\
E, F \geq 0 \text{ and integer} & &
\end{array}
$$

For a detailed description of the original problem, see Section 2.2. In brief, E is the number of E-9s and F is the number of F-9s that **PROTRAC** decides to produce. The objective function is the profit as a function of the production decision. Constraint (1) reflects a need to meet previous commitments. Constraints (2) and (3) are production time restrictions in departments A and B, respectively. Constraint (4) represents part of a union agreement, and constraint (5) is imposed because of management's attitude about the appropriate product mix. The only important change between (8.2) and the LP problem in Section 2.2 is the word *integer.* As we shall see shortly, the impact of this single word is profound.

To solve this problem with a graphical approach, we prescribe three steps:

1. Find the feasible set for the LP relaxation of the ILP problem.
2. Identify the integer points inside the set determined in step 1.
3. Find, among those points determined in step 2, one that optimizes the objective function.

The first two steps have been accomplished in Figure 8.1. The shaded region is the

▼ FIGURE 8.1
Feasible Set for PROTRAC ILP

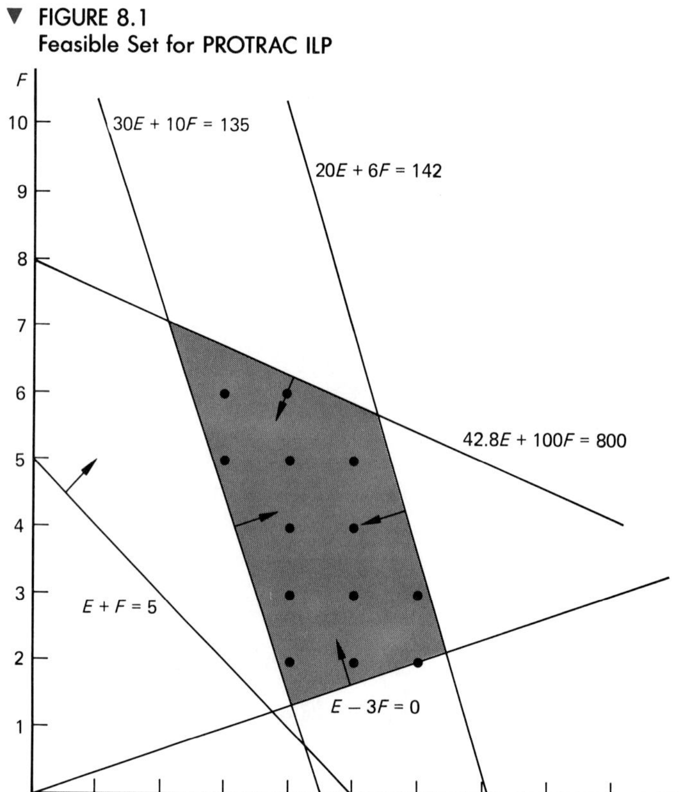

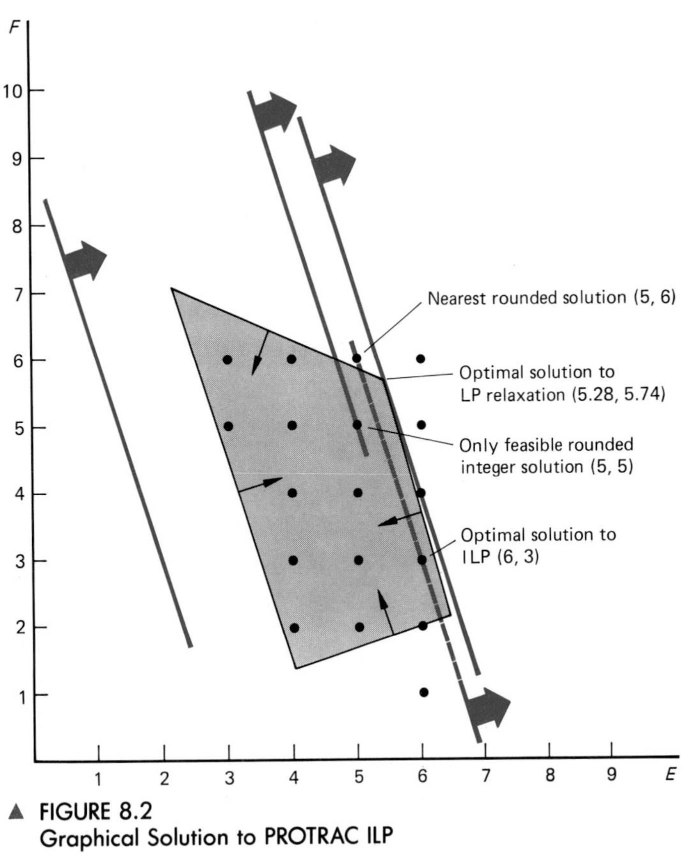

▲ FIGURE 8.2
Graphical Solution to PROTRAC ILP

Using an overhead transparency and a straightedge, you can show that rounded solutions are not optimal. You might also point out how integer solutions lie neatly in rows and columns, and what makes IP difficult to solve mathematically is that LP takes advantage of the fact that the optimal solution cannot be in the interior of the feasible set, and there could be a large number of feasible integer solutions.

feasible set for the LP relaxation, and the dark dots are the integer points contained in this set. This set of integer points is the set of feasible solutions to the ILP. In other words, there are only 13 feasible solutions to the ILP problem. They are the points (3, 6), (4, 6), (3, 5), (4, 5), (5, 5), (4, 4), (5, 4), (4, 3), (5, 3), (6, 3), (4, 2), (5, 2), and (6, 2).

To solve the problem, we must now determine which of the feasible points yields the largest value of the objective function. We proceed as in an LP problem; that is, by moving a contour of the objective function in an *uphill direction* (since we are dealing with a Max model) until it is not possible to move it farther and still intersect a feasible point.

The result of this process is shown in Figure 8.2. We see that the optimal solution to the ILP is the point $E = 6$ and $F = 3$. Since the objective function is $18E + 6F$, this solution yields an optimal value of the objective function of $18(6) + 6(3) = 126$.

The LP Relaxation

We can use Figure 8.2 to illustrate some important facts about the LP relaxation. We first note that the optimal solution to the LP relaxation occurs at the intersection of lines $42.8E + 100F = 800$, $20E + 6F = 142$ in Figure 8.1. This result is obtained by pushing, uphill, the contour of the objective function as far as possible and still have it intersect the feasible set for the LP relaxation. Since the intersection of the two constraints does not occur at an integer point, the optimal solution to the LP relaxation is not feasible for the ILP. To find the optimal solution (i.e., the optimal values of the decision variables) for the LP relaxation, we solve for the intersection of the two binding constraints. Solving these two equations in two unknowns yields

$E^* = 5.28$, $F^* = 5.74$. Thus, the **optimal value** of the objective function, termed the **OV,** for the LP relaxation is $18(5.28) + 6(5.74) = 129.48$.

Comparing these two optimal values (126 for the ILP and 129.48 for the LP relaxation), we see that the OV for the LP relaxation is larger than for the original ILP. This fact is a special case of a phenomenon that we observed in our earlier discussions of linear programming. Think of creating an ILP or an MILP by starting with the LP relaxation and adding the integer restrictions. We know that *in any mathematical programming problem, adding constraints cannot help and may hurt the optimal value of the objective function.* Thus, our optimal value decreases with the addition of the integer constraint. With this observation we are prepared to make the following comments:

1. **In a *Max* problem the OV of the LP relaxation always provides an *upper bound* on the OV of the original ILP. Adding the integer constraints either hurts or leaves unchanged the OV for the LP. In a Max problem, hurting the OV means making it smaller.**
2. **In a *Min* problem the OV of the LP relaxation always provides a *lower bound* on the OV of the original ILP. Again, adding the integer constraints either hurts or leaves unchanged the OV for the LP. In a Min problem, hurting the OV means making it larger.**

Rounded Solutions

We have observed that the optimal solution to the LP relaxation is $E^* = 5.28$, $F^* = 5.74$. Each of these variables could be rounded up or down and hence there are four rounded solutions ([5, 5], [5, 6], [6, 5], [6, 6]) near the optimal solution to the LP relaxation. In general, with two decision variables there are four rounded neighbor solutions; with n decision variables there could be 2^n such points.

Let us now examine in more detail some of the potential problems that can arise when using a rounded solution. Refer to Figure 8.2. If we solve the LP relaxation and round each variable to the nearest integer, we obtain (5, 6), which is infeasible. In this case the point (5, 5) is the *only* feasible point that can be obtained by rounding (5.28, 5.74). The other candidates, (5, 6), (6, 6), and (6, 5), are all infeasible.

This problem illustrates two important facts about rounded solutions:

1. ***A rounded solution need not be optimal.*** In this case the value of the objective function at the only feasible rounded solution is

$$18(5) + 6(5) = 120$$

This compares with a value of 126 for the optimal value of the ILP. We see, then, that a proportional loss of $6/126$, or almost 5%, is incurred by using this rounded solution rather than the optimal solution.

2. ***A rounded solution need not be near the optimal ILP solution.*** Students often have an intuitive idea that even though a rounded solution may not be optimal, it should be "near" the optimal ILP solution. Referring again to Figure 8.2, we see that the rounded solution is not one of the immediate integer neighbors of the optimal ILP solution. Indeed, only four points in the feasible set ([3, 6], [4, 6], [3, 5], and [4, 5]) are farther from the optimal solution than the rounded solution. It seems hard to claim that in this example the rounded solution is near the optimal ILP solution.

In Figure 8.3 we introduce another ILP that illustrates an additional and even more drastic problem associated with rounded solutions. In this figure the shaded

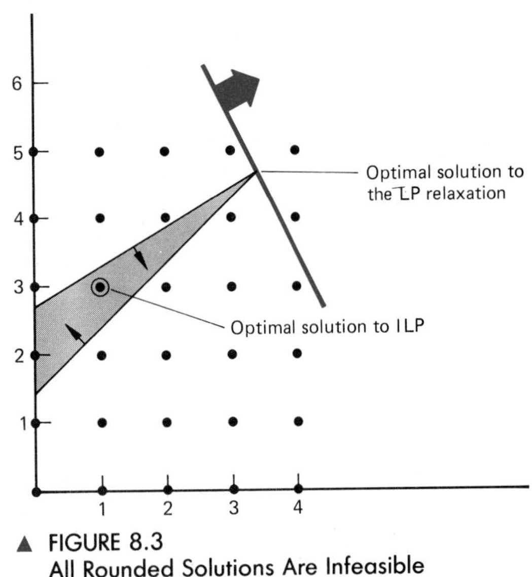

▲ FIGURE 8.3
All Rounded Solutions Are Infeasible

area is the feasible set for the LP relaxation, the dots are integer points, and the circled dot is the only feasible solution to the ILP. The optimal solution to the LP relaxation is indicated at the tip of the wedge-shaped feasible set. Notice that if we start with the optimal solution to the LP (roughly [3.3, 4.7]) and then round this to any of the four neighboring integer points, we obtain an infeasible point. That is, for this example, *no manner of rounding can produce feasibility.*

In summary, we have noted that an intuitively appealing way of attacking an ILP is to solve the LP relaxation of the original problem and then round the solution to a neighboring integer point. We have seen that this approach can have certain problems.

1. **None of the neighboring integer points may be feasible.**
2. **Even if one or more of the neighboring integer points is feasible**
   a. **Such a point need not be optimal for the ILP.**
   b. **Such a point need not even be near the optimal ILP solution.**

Enumeration

The problem with enumeration in several dimensions is that the number of combinations gets large extremely fast. A good visual way to demonstrate this is to challenge the class with this assertion: *"It is impossible to fold a square piece of paper in half more than eight times, regardless of how large or how thin the paper is."* This is an astonishing demonstration of 2^n and how quickly it can grow.

The graphical approach was used to illustrate some important ideas about ILPs. However, since there are only 13 feasible points in Figure 8.1 for the **PROTRAC** ILP, a student may get the mistaken impression that one can reasonably list all the feasible points, evaluate the objective function at each of them, and select the best one; that is, solve the problem by **complete enumeration.** In this case, one could do that. Unfortunately, however, complete enumeration is not a reasonable procedure for most ILPs. Suppose, for example, that we had an ILP with 100 0–1 variables. In this case there could be up to 2^{100}, which is 1.27×10^{30}, feasible points. Even with the fastest computer, it would take more than a lifetime to enumerate all of these points.

It is interesting to compare the enumeration method for ILPs with the simplex algorithm for LPs. As we have seen, the simplex method can be viewed as a way of visiting corners of the constraint set and evaluating the objective function at the corners visited. It is also true that there can be billions of corners on the constraint set of a large LP. The important point, however, is that *not all corners are visited.* Indeed, the simplex algorithm is very efficient. It proceeds in such a way as to improve the value of the objective function at each successive corner. Once no improvement is possible, the procedure stops and indicates that an optimal solution has been reached. At this time there is no comparable algorithm for ILPs. There are methods (to be discussed later) that are better than complete enumeration, but they are not able to eliminate large numbers of alternative solutions as quickly and efficiently as the simplex algorithm does for LPs.

8.4 Applications of 0–1 Variables

Binary, or 0–1, variables play an especially important role in the applications of ILPs. These variables make it possible to incorporate yes-or-no decisions, sometimes called dichotomous decisions, into a mathematical programming format. Two quick examples will illustrate what we mean:

1. In a plant location problem we let $x_j = 1$ if we choose to have a plant at location j and $x_j = 0$ if we do not.
2. In a routing problem we let $x_{ijk} = 1$ if truck k goes from city i to city j and $x_{ijk} = 0$ if it does not.

Thus, you can see from these examples that the use of 0–1 variables provides us with a new formulational tool. In this section we will see some examples of how 0–1 variables are used to make dichotomous decisions in several applications. We will also see how they can be manipulated to enforce various types of logical conditions.

Capital Budgeting: An Expansion Decision

A Canadian firm wished to do a capital budgeting model for 1000 projects over a period of 60 months. For each project and month it was necessary to know the initial investment, salvage value, interest rate, monthly disbursement, and income. The amount of data needed was so large that the company realized the cost of collecting and keeping it would exceed any possible profits resulting from use of the model, and so had to greatly simplify the alternatives and data.

Many firms make decisions on capital investments on an annual basis. In large firms the decisions are often the culmination of a long process that starts with recommendations from individual departments and continues through various firmwide and divisionwide competitions. It is not unusual for the final selection to rest with the board of directors. In smaller firms the process is not so elaborate, but the capital budgeting decision is still a fundamental part of an annual evaluation of the firm's future.

In its simplest form, the capital budgeting decision is a matter of choosing among n alternatives in order to maximize the return subject to constraints on the amount of capital invested over time. As a particular example, suppose that PROTRAC's board of directors faces the problem summarized in Figure 8.4. The dollar amounts in this figure are in thousands. The board must select one or more of the alternatives. If they decide to expand the Belgian plant, the present value of the

▼ FIGURE 8.4
Capital Budgeting Problem

ALTERNATIVE (i)	PRESENT VALUE OF NET RETURN, c_i (\$000)	CAPITAL REQUIRED IN YEAR j BY ALTERNATIVE i				
		1	2	3	4	5
Expand Belgian Plant	40	10	5	20	10	0
Expand Small Machine Capacity in U.S.	70	30	20	10	10	10
Establish New Plant in Chile	80	10	20	27	20	10
Expand Large Machine Capacity in U.S.	100	20	10	40	20	20
Capital Available in Year j (b_j)		50	45	70	40	30

net return to the firm is \$40,000. This project requires \$10,000 of capital in the first year, \$5000 in the second, and so on. The board has previously budgeted up to \$50,000 for all capital investments in year 1, up to \$45,000 in year 2, and so on.

An ILP Model for Capital Budgeting at PROTRAC. This problem can be modeled as an ILP in which all the variables are 0–1 variables. This is called a 0–1 ILP. In particular, let $x_i = 1$ if project i is accepted and $x_i = 0$ if project i is not accepted. The problem then becomes

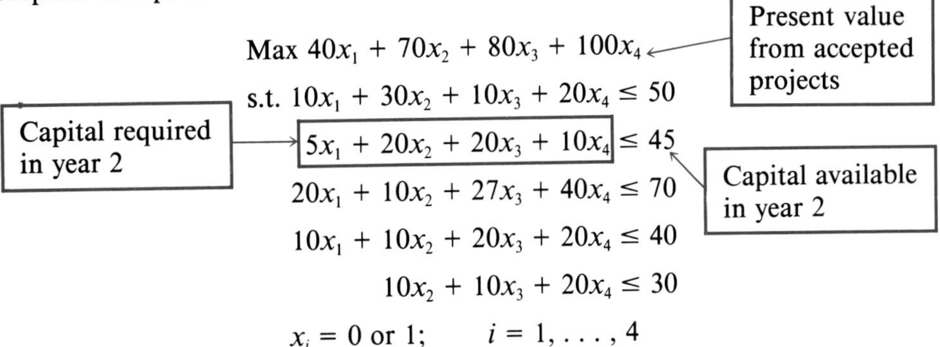

$$\begin{aligned}
\text{Max } & 40x_1 + 70x_2 + 80x_3 + 100x_4 \\
\text{s.t. } & 10x_1 + 30x_2 + 10x_3 + 20x_4 \le 50 \\
& 5x_1 + 20x_2 + 20x_3 + 10x_4 \le 45 \\
& 20x_1 + 10x_2 + 27x_3 + 40x_4 \le 70 \\
& 10x_1 + 10x_2 + 20x_3 + 20x_4 \le 40 \\
& 10x_2 + 10x_3 + 20x_4 \le 30 \\
& x_i = 0 \text{ or } 1; \qquad i = 1, \ldots, 4
\end{aligned}$$

Here the objective function is the total present value of the net returns and each constraint controls the amount of capital used in each of the five periods.

The LP Relaxation. Let us approach this problem by first solving the LP relaxation. The formulation and solution are shown in Figure 8.5. Note that in working with the LP relaxation to a 0–1 ILP, we ignore the constraints $x_i = 0$ or 1. Instead, we add the constraints $x_i \le 1$, $i = 1, 2, 3, 4$ (as shown in Figure 8.5). Of course, in an LP, each x_i is always nonnegative. Thus, in the relaxation, instead of $x_i = 0$ or 1, we have x_i constrained to an interval (i.e., $0 \le x_i \le 1$). It would be nice if in the optimal solution each x_i were, fortuitously, to take one extreme or the other of these allowable values (either 0 or 1), for then the original ILP would be solved. Unfortunately, as Figure 8.5 shows, this happened only with x_4; the values of x_1, x_2,

▼ FIGURE 8.5
LP Relaxation of PROTRAC's Capital Budgeting Problem

```
MAX 40 X1 + 70 X2 + 80 X3 + 100 X4
SUBJECT TO
   2) 10 X1 + 30 X2 + 10 X3 + 20 X4 < = 50
   3) 5 X1 + 20 X2 + 20 X3 + 10 X4 < = 45
   4) 20 X1 + 10 X2 + 27 X3 + 40 X4 < = 70
   5) 10 X1 + 10 X2 + 20 X3 + 20 X4 < = 40
   6) 10 X2 + 10 X3 + 20 X4 < = 30
   7) X1 < = 1 }
   8) X2 < = 1 }  Constraints associated
   9) X3 < = 1 }  with the relaxation
  10) X4 < = 1 }  of 0-1 conditions

          OBJECTIVE FUNCTION VALUE

                   200.00

 VARIABLE     VALUE     REDUCED COST

   X1          0.67         0.00
   X2          0.67         0.00
   X3          0.33         0.00
   X4          1.00         0.00
```

```
MAX 40 X1 + 70 X2 + 80 X3 + 100 X4
SUBJECT TO
  2) 10 X1 + 30 X2 + 10 X3 + 20 X4 < = 50
  3) 5 X1 + 20 X2 + 20 X3 + 10 X4 < = 45
  4) 20 X1 + 10 X2 + 27 X3 + 40 X4 < = 70
  5) 10 X1 + 10 X2 + 20 X3 + 20 X4 < = 40
  6) 10 X2 + 10 X3 + 20 X4 < = 30

INTEGER - VARIABLES = 4

          OBJECTIVE FUNCTION VALUE

                   190.00

VARIABLE           VALUE          REDUCED COST

  X1               1.00             -15.00
  X2               1.00               0.00
  X3               1.00               0.00
  X4               0.00             -50.00
```

▲ FIGURE 8.6
ILP Model of PROTRAC's Capital Budgeting Problem

and x_3 are fractional. Since x_3 should equal 1 if **PROTRAC** establishes a plant in Chile and 0 if it does not, the result $x_3 = 0.33$ is not meaningful. We also note that attempting to find a solution to the ILP problem by solving the LP relaxation and then rounding does not work very well. Standard nearest-integer rounding rules (i.e., round numbers ≤ 0.499 to 0 and numbers ≥ 0.500 to 1) yield the solution $x_1 = 1, x_2 = 1, x_3 = 0, x_4 = 1$. A quick check reveals that this solution is infeasible since it grossly violates the first constraint.

All-integer solution

The Optimal ILP Solution. To obtain the optimal ILP solution for the **PROTRAC** capital budgeting problem, we must turn to *an integer programming code*—in this case, a computer program that employs an algorithm specifically designed to solve the 0–1 ILP. The formulation and solution of the ILP are shown in Figure 8.6.

Note that the four constraints that require the x_i's to be ≤ 1 have been dropped. In this particular program (LINDO), the phrase "integer-variables = 4" indicates that all four of the variables are 0–1 variables.

Note that the optimal ILP solution (1, 1, 1, 0) is not the rounded LP solution (1, 1, 0, 1), which violates the 1st constraint (in Figure 8.5).

The solution shows that management should accept the first three alternatives; x_4 is now zero, whereas in the LP relaxation it was 1. Note also that the objective function is now 190. This is a reduction of 10 (5%) from the optimal value of the objective function for the LP relaxation. In practice, one may well be interested in solving integer programs with hundreds of 0–1 variables. After seeing the analysis of this small example and the problems associated with the relaxation approach, you can well appreciate the even greater importance, in larger and more complex applications, of having special algorithms to solve the ILP problem.

Logical Conditions

An important use of 0–1 variables is to impose constraints that arise from logical conditions. Several examples are cited below.

No More Than k of n Alternatives. Suppose $x_i = 0$ or 1, for $i = 1, \ldots, n$. The constraint

$$x_1 + x_2 + \cdots + x_n \leq k$$

implies that, at most, k alternatives of n possibilities can be selected. That is, since each x_i can be only 0 or 1, the above constraint says that not more than k of them can equal 1. For the data in Figure 8.4, assume that PROTRAC feels that not more than one foreign project can be accepted. For this reason, the board wants to rule out a decision that includes both the Belgian expansion and a new plant in Chile. Adding the constraint

$$x_1 + x_3 \leq 1$$

to the ILP in Figure 8.6 implies that the solution can contain at most one of the overseas alternatives.

Dependent Decisions. You can use 0–1 variables to force a dependent relationship on two or more decisions. Suppose, for example, that management does not want to select alternative k unless it first selects alternative m. The constraint

$$x_k \leq x_m \qquad \textbf{(8.3)}$$

or

$$x_k - x_m \leq 0$$

enforces this condition. Note that if *m is not* selected, then $x_m = 0$. Condition (8.3) then forces x_k to be 0 (i.e., alternative k is not selected). Alternatively, if m is selected, $x_m = 1$; then (8.3) becomes $x_k \leq 1$. This leaves the program free to select $x_k = 1$ or $x_k = 0$.

As an example, again consider Figure 8.4, and suppose that PROTRAC's management feels that, if they are going to expand within the United States, their competitive position implies that they must definitely expand the large machine capacity. Adding the constraint

$$x_2 - x_4 \leq 0$$

to the ILP in Figure 8.6 assures that the model cannot select "expand small machine capacity" unless "expand large machine capacity" is also selected.

Similarly, suppose the board decided, "If we're going to expand our domestic capacity, we're going to expand both lines." Adding the constraint

$$x_4 - x_2 = 0$$

to the ILP in Figure 8.6 would enforce this condition since it implies that x_4 and x_2 must take the same values.

Lot Size Constraints. Consider a portfolio manager with the following constraints: (1) If he purchases security j, he must purchase at least 20 shares; and (2) he may not purchase more than 100 shares of security j. Let x_j be the number of shares of security j purchased. The constraint that *if* j is purchased, then at least 20 shares must be purchased, is called a "minimum lot size" or "batch size" constraint. Note that we cannot create such a constraint in an LP model. The constraints

$$20 \leq x_j \leq 100$$

do not do the job since they insist that x_j always be at least 20. We want the conditions either $x_j = 0$ or $20 \leq x_j \leq 100$. To achieve this we will make use of a 0–1 variable, say y_j, for security j. The variable y_j has the following interpretation:

- If $y_j = 1$, then purchase security j.
- If $y_j = 0$, do not purchase security j.

Now consider the two constraints

$$x_j \leq 100y_j \qquad \textbf{(8.4)}$$

$$x_j \geq 20y_j \qquad \textbf{(8.5)}$$

0–1 variables are a very convenient way to model "either/or" conditions.

We see that if $y_j = 1$, then (8.4) and (8.5) imply that $20 \leq x_j \leq 100$. On the other hand, if $y_j = 0$, then (8.4) implies that $x_j \leq 0$. Similiarly, (8.5) implies that $x_j \geq 0$. These two inequalities together imply that $x_j = 0$. Thus, if $y_j = 1$ when we purchase j, and 0 when we do not, we have the proper conditions on x_j.

How can we be sure that $y_j = 1$ if we purchase security j? The inequality (8.4) ($x_j \leq 100y_j$) guarantees it. We see that in this inequality you cannot have both $x_j > 0$ and $y_j = 0$. Thus, if $x_j > 0$, y_j must equal 1. We see then that inequalities (8.4) and (8.5) together guarantee the "minimum lot size" constraint.

***k* of *m* Constraints.** Mischa Gaas, an exchange student from the Middle East, came to the university for graduate work. He was told by his adviser that anyone intending to earn a Ph.D. degree in history had to satisfy at least two of the following criteria: "You must be single, rich, or crazy." Unfortunately Mischa was destitute and married. In fact, before entering into matrimony, he spent years looking for a bride who was tall, dark, beautiful, and rich. Finally in frustration he said to himself, "Three out of four ain't bad"; and the woman he chose (who chose him) was not rich. These are examples of problems in which k of m constraints must be satisfied. In general notation, let the "superset" of m constraints be

$$g_i(x_1, \ldots, x_n) \leq b_i, \qquad i = 1, \ldots, m$$

Now introduce m new 0–1 variables y_i and let U be chosen so large that, for each i, $g_i(x_i, \ldots, x_n) \leq U$ for every x satisfying any set of k inequalities taken from the above m. Then the following $m + 1$ constraints express the desired condition:

$$\sum_{i=1}^{m} y_i = k$$

$$g_i(x_1, \ldots, x_n) \leq b_i y_i + (1 - y_i)U, \qquad i = 1, \ldots, m$$

Note that $\sum_{i=1}^{m} y_i = k$ forces k of the y_i variables to have the value 1. This means that exactly k of the above inequalities are equivalent to

$$g_i(x_1, \ldots, x_n) \leq b_i$$

The remaining inequalities are equivalent to

$$g_i(x_1, \ldots, x_n) \leq U$$

and by the assumption on the choice of U such a constraint is redundant.

8.5 An ILP Vignette: Steco's Warehouse Location Problem—Formulation and Computer Analysis

In order to conserve capital, Steco, the steel wholesaler, leases its regional warehouses. It currently has a list of three warehouses it can lease. The cost per month to lease warehouse i is F_i. Also, warehouse i can handle a maximum of T_i trucks per month.

There are four sales districts, and the typical monthly demand in district j is d_j truckloads. The average cost of sending a truck from warehouse i to district j is c_{ij}. Steco wants to know which warehouses to lease and how many trucks to send from each warehouse to each district. A schematic representation of the problem is illustrated in Figure 8.7. The data for this problem are presented in Figure 8.8.

▼ FIGURE 8.7
Warehouse Location Problem

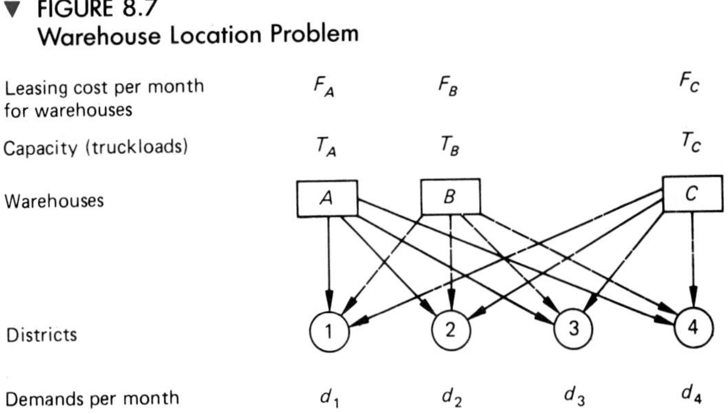

In Figure 8.8 we see, for example, that it costs \$7750 to lease warehouse A for a month and that up to 200 trucks can be dispatched from this warehouse. Also, the monthly demand in sales district 1 is 100 trucks. The numbers in the body of the table are the costs of sending a truck from warehouse i to sales district j (e.g., the cost of sending a truck from B to 3 is \$100).

▼ FIGURE 8.8
Warehouse Location Data

WAREHOUSE	COST PER TRUCK (c_{ij}) SALES DISTRICT (\$)				MONTHLY CAPACITY (NUMBER OF TRUCKS)	MONTHLY LEASING COSTS
	1	2	3	4		
A	170	40	70	160	200	7750
B	150	195	100	10	250	4000
C	100	240	140	60	300	5500
Monthly demand (truck loads)	100	90	110	60		

Modeling Considerations

If you want to attack this problem with a mathematical programming model, you must first decide which variables (if any) you will treat as integers and which (if any) you will treat as continuous variables.

The decision to lease a particular warehouse or not seems to require a 0–1 variable since the cost of leasing warehouse i does not vary with the level of activity (i.e., with the number of trucks sent from it). We will thus let

$$y_i = 1 \text{ if we lease warehouse } i, \qquad y_i = 0 \text{ if we do not}$$

At first glance it also seems appropriate to treat the number of trucks sent from a warehouse to a district as an integer variable. Trucks are, after all, integer entities, and it does not make sense to talk about sending one-third of a truck from here to there. However, several factors could persuade us to treat the number of trucks as a continuous variable.

1. This is a planning model, not a detailed operating system. In actual operation the demands in the districts will vary. Management will have to devise methods of handling this uncertainty. Trucks assigned to a specific warehouse might be allocated among adjacent districts on a daily-as-needed basis, or Steco might use common carriers to satisfy excess demand. At any rate, the number of trucks that the solution to our mathematical programming problem says should go from warehouse i to district j is only an *approximation* of what will actually happen on any given day. Thus, treating these entities as continuous variables and rounding to the nearest integer to determine how many trucks to assign to each warehouse should provide a useful answer and a good approximation of the *average* monthly operating cost.

2. Treating the number of trucks as integer variables may make the problem much more difficult to solve. This is simply a reflection of the general fact that the greater the number of integer variables, the more difficult it is to solve an ILP.

3. It certainly costs much more to lease one of the warehouses than to send a truck from a warehouse to a sales district. The relative magnitude of these costs again implies that it is relatively more important to treat the "lease or not lease" decision as an integer variable, as opposed to the trucks. To illustrate this point, note that it costs \$5500 per month to lease warehouse C and \$60 to send a truck from warehouse C to sales district 4. Suppose that we modeled the problem as an LP. If $y_c = 0.4$ in the optimal solution, rounding to 0 causes a \$2200 change in the OV (optimal value of the objective function), whereas if $x_{C4} = 57.8$, rounding either up or down has less than a \$60 effect.

In summary, there are, in this example, arguments that suggest little advantage to treating the number of trucks as integers. We thus proceed to formulate Steco's warehouse location problem as an MILP, and we will have a pleasant surprise.

The MILP Model

To model Steco's problem as an MILP, we will let

$$y_i = 1 \text{ if lease warehouse } i, \qquad y_i = 0 \text{ if not}; \qquad i = \text{A, B, C}$$

$$x_{ij} = \text{the number of trucks sent from warehouse } i \text{ to district } j;$$

$$i = \text{A, B, C}; \qquad j = 1, \ldots, 4$$

We shall now construct the model by developing each of its component parts.

First consider the objective function. The expression

$$170x_{A1} + 40x_{A2} + 70x_{A3} + \cdots + 60x_{C4}$$

is the total cost associated with the trucks and

$$7750y_A + 4000y_B + 5500y_C$$

is the total leasing cost. Thus, the objective function is

$$\text{Min } 7750y_A + 4000y_B + 5500y_C + 170x_{A1} + \cdots + 60x_{C4}$$

Now consider the constraints. We must consider both demand and capacity. The following constraint guarantees that demand will be satisfied at sales district 1:

$$x_{A1} + x_{B1} + x_{C1} = 100$$

Four constraints like this (one for each district) are required to guarantee that demand is satisfied.

The constraint

$$x_{A1} + x_{A2} + x_{A3} + x_{A4} \leq 200y_A \quad \text{or} \quad x_{A1} + x_{A2} + x_{A3} + x_{A4} - 200y_A \leq 0$$

serves two purposes. It guarantees that capacity at warehouse A is not exceeded, and it forces us to lease warehouse A if we want to send anything out of this warehouse. To see this, recall that y_i, or in this case y_A, must equal 0 or 1. First, assume that $y_A = 1$. The inequality above then becomes

$$x_{A1} + x_{A2} + x_{A3} + x_{A4} \leq 200$$

that is, no more than a total of 200 trucks can be sent out of warehouse A. You have previously seen this type of capacity constraint in transportation models. Now consider the case when y_A is 0. Then the inequality becomes

$$x_{A1} + x_{A2} + x_{A3} + x_{A4} \leq 0$$

Note that the REDUCED COST cannot be interpreted in the same manner as in LP. If YB were forced to be at least 1.0, the cost of the solution would *not* go down by $8500. Thus we lose some of the valuable information given by LP output when we solve IP problems.

that is, no items can be sent out of warehouse A. This constraint then guarantees that nothing can be sent out of warehouse A unless $y_A = 1$. Note that when $y_A = 1$, the term $7750y_A$ in the objective function equals 7750. Thus, we see that nothing is sent out of warehouse A unless we incur the monthly leasing cost for that particular warehouse. Three such constraints, one for each warehouse, are needed in the model.

The complete model and its solution are shown in Figure 8.9.

Output Analysis. A quick glance at the output shows that the optimal values of all truck allocations are integer, even though we decided in the formulation to allow these variables to be continuous. Was this just fortuitous? The answer is no. Here is the reason. We started with a warehouse location problem. Note that once we have decided which warehouse to lease, the problem of finding the optimal allocation of trucks is an LP problem called the transportation problem. In Chapter 7 we saw that if the supply available at each warehouse and the demand at each district are integers, then the optimal solution to the transportation problem will be all integers.

We now have enough information to conclude that the optimal solution to the above warehouse location problem with integer supplies and demands will always include an integer allocation of trucks. The argument involves two steps: (1) the optimal solution must lease some set of warehouses, and (2) every possible set of leased warehouses yields an integer allocation of trucks.

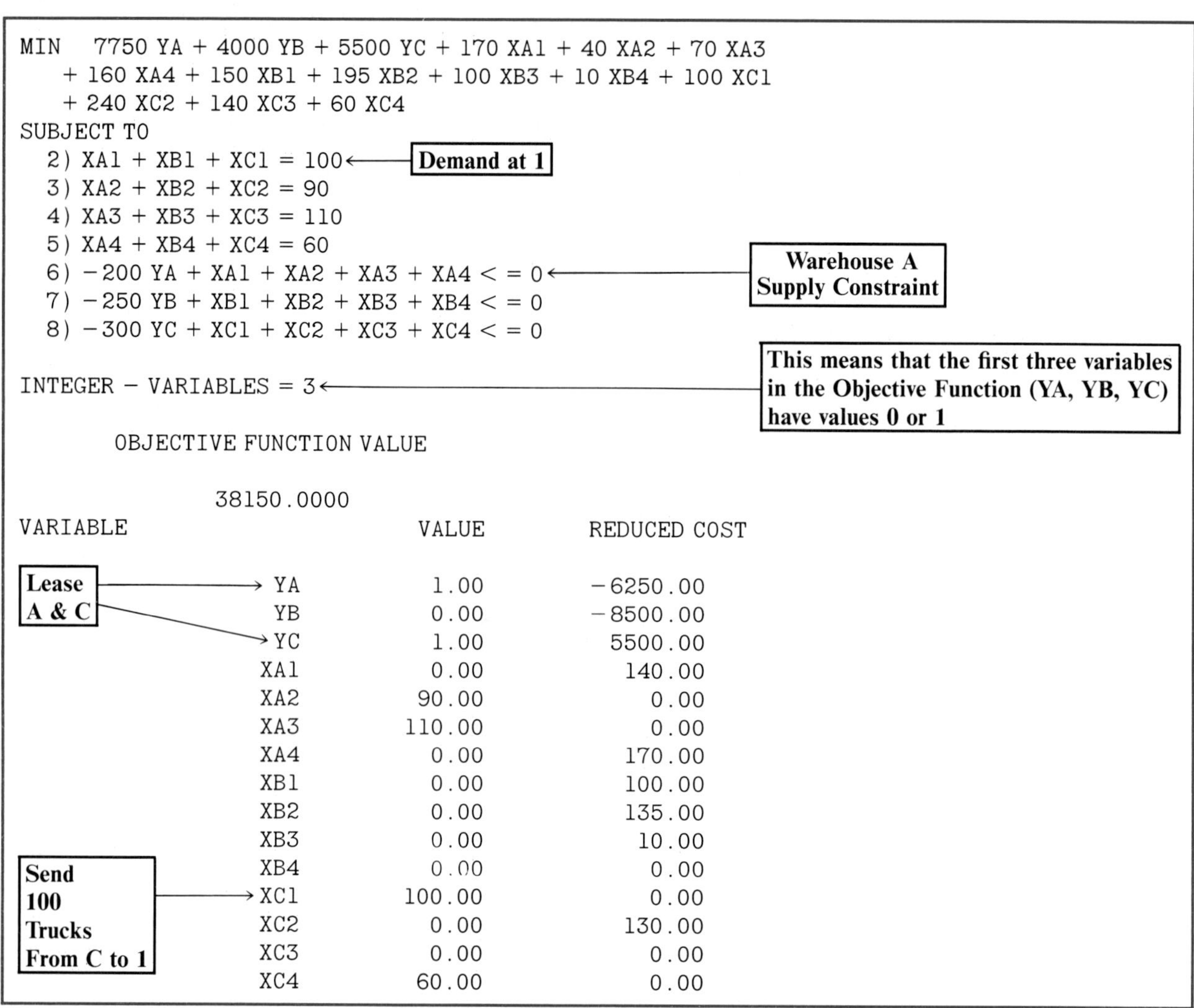

```
MIN   7750 YA + 4000 YB + 5500 YC + 170 XA1 + 40 XA2 + 70 XA3
    + 160 XA4 + 150 XB1 + 195 XB2 + 100 XB3 + 10 XB4 + 100 XC1
    + 240 XC2 + 140 XC3 + 60 XC4
SUBJECT TO
  2) XA1 + XB1 + XC1 = 100
  3) XA2 + XB2 + XC2 = 90
  4) XA3 + XB3 + XC3 = 110
  5) XA4 + XB4 + XC4 = 60
  6) -200 YA + XA1 + XA2 + XA3 + XA4 < = 0
  7) -250 YB + XB1 + XB2 + XB3 + XB4 < = 0
  8) -300 YC + XC1 + XC2 + XC3 + XC4 < = 0

INTEGER - VARIABLES = 3

       OBJECTIVE FUNCTION VALUE

              38150.0000
VARIABLE                     VALUE          REDUCED COST

                   YA         1.00           -6250.00
                   YB         0.00           -8500.00
                   YC         1.00            5500.00
                  XA1         0.00             140.00
                  XA2        90.00               0.00
                  XA3       110.00               0.00
                  XA4         0.00             170.00
                  XB1         0.00             100.00
                  XB2         0.00             135.00
                  XB3         0.00              10.00
                  XB4         0.00               0.00
                  XC1       100.00               0.00
                  XC2         0.00             130.00
                  XC3         0.00               0.00
                  XC4        60.00               0.00
```


▲ FIGURE 8.9
Steco's Warehouse Location Problem

For this problem, then, we now see that it would have been naive and costly to require as additional constraints that the x_{ij}'s be integer. The word is "Never pay for a free good."

8.6 The Assignment Problem and a Social Theorem

The assignment problem was discussed in Sections 7.5, 7.6, and 7.7. Here is an application.

Let there be n men and n women and let c_{ij} be a measure (say on a scale of one to ten) of the mutual pleasure the ith man and the jth woman derive, on the average, per unit of time (e.g., per day) spent together. Let x_{ij} be the fraction of his time that man i spends with woman j. Suppose the men and women do nothing but spend time together. To maximize total happiness, solve

$$\text{Max} \sum_{i=1}^{n} \sum_{j=1}^{n} c_{ij} x_{ij}$$

$$\text{s.t.} \quad \sum_{j=1}^{n} x_{ij} = 1, \qquad i = 1, \ldots, n$$

$$\sum_{i=1}^{n} x_{ij} = 1, \qquad j = 1, \ldots, n$$

$$x_{ij} \geq 0, \qquad i, j = 1, \ldots, n$$

Note the meaning of the constraints:

1. The first n constraints say that each man's time is completely taken up by women.
2. The next n constraints say that each woman's time is completely taken up by men.

Another way of saying this is that the relaxed LP solution will *always* be the optimal IP solution to the assignment problem.

In Chapter 7 it was stated that since the assignment problem is a special case of the transportation model, and since the right-hand side data are integral, there will be an all-integer optimal solution to the assignment problem (as there was for the transportation model in the Steco example). Hence our mating problem has an optimal solution with each $x_{ij} = 0$ or 1, which means that, at optimality, each man is matched with a woman, and vice versa. Thus we have a proof that monogamy is an optimal social arrangement. But be careful. If we replace "Max" with "Min" in the objective function, we obtain an optimal 0–1 solution! (The "integrality property" has nothing to do with whether the objective function is maximized or minimized.) Thus we have also proved that monogamy *minimizes* total happiness!

8.7 The Branch-and-Bound Algorithm

The general approach

To "partially (implicitly) enumerate" means that rather than having to look at every integer possibility, the algorithm is able to eliminate a large number of possibilities that can't be the optimal solution, thus speeding up the search for the optimum.

The **branch-and-bound** approach is currently the most efficient general-purpose method of solving ILPs. Actually, branch and bound is *not* a specific algorithm assigned to solve a specific problem. Rather it is a general approach to problem solving, an approach that must be adapted to a specific setting. The general idea is to partition the set of all feasible solutions to a given problem into smaller and nonoverlapping subsets. Bounds on the value of the best solution in each subset are then computed. Then the branch-and-bound algorithm cleverly allows one to eliminate certain subsets from consideration. In this way one is said to *partially* (as opposed to completely) *enumerate* all of the possible feasible solutions.

An ILP Example

Let us begin with a specific problem, which for convenience we refer to as (P1):

$$\begin{aligned} &\text{Max } x_1 + 5x_2 && \text{(P1)} \\ &\text{s.t.} \quad 11x_1 + 6x_2 \leq 66 \\ &\qquad\quad 5x_1 + 50x_2 \leq 225 \\ &\qquad\quad x_1, x_2 \geq 0 \text{ and integer} \end{aligned}$$

In the following discussion, it will be helpful to use the graphical method discussed in Section 8.3.

Step 1: Solving the LP Relaxation. The first step is to solve the LP relaxation of (P1). If luck is with us, we may have an optimal solution right away, since it is always true that if the solution to the LP relaxation satisfies the integer restriction, it is the optimal solution. We will now use the graphical solution technique to solve the LP relaxation of (P1) and test our luck. Figure 8.10 shows (by shading) the feasible set

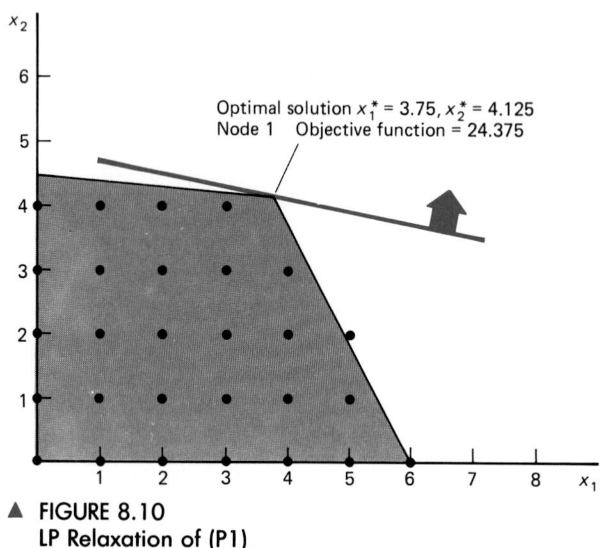

▲ FIGURE 8.10
LP Relaxation of (P1)

for the LP relaxation of (P1). The dots in the shaded region are the feasible points that also satisfy the integrality conditions. Note that there are 27 such points, including the points on the axes such as (0, 4) and (4, 0), which are feasible. Figure 8.10 also shows the optimal corner for the LP. To find the optimal numerical values for the decision variables we solve for the point where the two active constraints intersect; that is, we solve

$$11x_1 + 6x_2 = 66 \qquad \text{and} \qquad 5x_1 + 50x_2 = 225$$

for x_1 and x_2. This yields $x_1^* = 3.75$, $x_2^* = 4.125$. Since these values are not integers, we have *not* solved (P1). We have obtained some information about the problem, however.

1. Recall that OV stands for optimal value of the objective function. When we find the OV for the LP relaxation, we establish an upper bound for the OV of (P1). Let us call this upper bound U. Thus, since the objective function is $x_1 + 5x_2$, we know that

$$\text{OV for (P1)} \leq 3.75 + 5(4.125) = 24.375 = U$$

The true rounded solution (4, 4) is infeasible and violates the first constraint.

2. As you can see in Figure 8.10, if we take the optimal solution to the relaxed problem and round it down to $x_1 = 3$, $x_2 = 4$ (truncate the fractional portion), we obtain a feasible solution to (P1). Now evaluating the objective function at this point (or at any other *feasible* point), we establish a *lower bound* for the OV of (P1). Let us call this value F. Hence,

$$\text{OV for (P1)} \geq 3 + 5(4) = 23 = F$$

The value of F (i.e., 23) may or may not be the OV for (P1). At present, we cannot

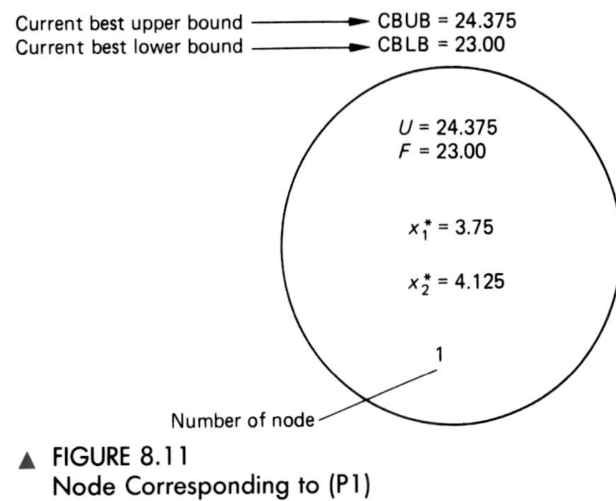

▲ FIGURE 8.11
Node Corresponding to (P1)

tell. All we now know is that $23 \leq \text{OV} \leq 24.375$. We must find out whether a better solution can be found. To do this, we *branch.*

The information about a branch-and-bound solution is typically summarized in a tree-like diagram. The first node in such a diagram is shown in Figure 8.11. This node will look somewhat different from the other nodes in our tree, since we place the values for our *current* best upper bound (CBUB) on the OV and our current best lower bound (CBLB) on the OV above this node.

Stress to students to branch on *either* x_1 or x_2, but not both. Branching on only one variable at any point in the analysis is sufficient. (It may be that because students understand how to add a simple branch constraint, they try to branch on everything in sight!)

Step 2: Branching. We proceed by dividing (P1) into two smaller problems. In this example, we will branch on x_1. This is an arbitrary choice. We could just as well have branched on x_2. The branching process makes use of the fact that in the optimal solution to (P1), either $x_1 \leq 3$ or $x_1 \geq 4$. Why is this true? Because there are no integer values for x_1 in the region eliminated by forcing x_1 to be ≤ 3 or x_1 to be ≥ 4. The values of x_1 that are eliminated are $3 < x_1 < 4$. Since x_1 must be an integer, we have not eliminated any feasible points from the feasible set for (P1). We have, however, eliminated points (i.e., noninteger values) from the feasible set of the LP relaxation of (P1). Indeed, we see that the optimal value of x_1, in the LP relaxation of (P1), is neither ≤ 3 nor ≥ 4, and hence the current optimal point (intentionally) has been eliminated by the branching process. This process creates one of its two new problems by appending the constraint $x_1 \leq 3$ to (P1). The other new problem is created by appending the constraint $x_1 \geq 4$ to (P1). We thus have

$$
\begin{aligned}
&\text{Max } x_1 + 5x_2 && \text{(P2)}\\
&\text{s.t. } 11x_1 + 6x_2 \leq 66\\
&\quad 5x_1 + 50x_2 \leq 225\\
&\quad x_1 \leq 3\\
&\quad x_1, x_2 \geq 0 \text{ and integer}
\end{aligned}
$$

and

$$
\begin{aligned}
&\text{Max } x_1 + 5x_2 && \text{(P3)}\\
&\text{s.t. } 11x_1 + 6x_2 \leq 66\\
&\quad 5x_1 + 50x_2 \leq 225\\
&\quad x_1 \geq 4\\
&\quad x_1, x_2 \geq 0 \text{ and integer}
\end{aligned}
$$

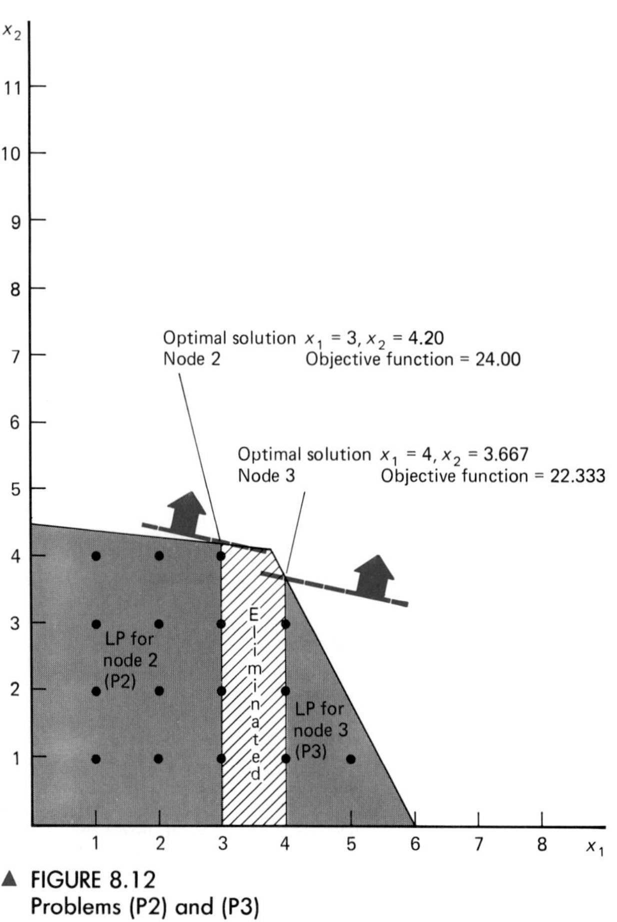

▲ FIGURE 8.12
Problems (P2) and (P3)

These two problems are shown in Figure 8.12.

Figure 8.12 reveals two interesting facts:

1. We have split the (P1) feasible set into two pieces and eliminated from consideration a region containing no integer points. The eliminated region is crosshatched. The boundary lines are *not* in the region eliminated.
2. All of the feasible *integer* solutions to (P1) are now contained in either (P2) or (P3). Since the objective functions for (P1), (P2), and (P3) are identical, it follows that *either the optimal solution to (P2) or the optimal solution to (P3) must be the optimal solution to (P1),* the original ILP. Thus, we may forget (P1) and consider only (P2) and (P3).

Creating a Tree. The branch-and-bound approach proceeds by a process that can be illustrated with a decision tree. The first step in this process is to solve the LP relaxations for problems (P2) and (P3). The optimal solutions are shown in Figure 8.12. In problem (P2) the value of U is provided by the optimal value of the objective function for the LP relaxation (namely 24.00). For (P3), we obtain $U = 22.333$. We have already observed that the optimal solution to (P1) is either in (P2) or (P3); thus the OV for (P1) must be $\leq$ the Max of the values of U provided by these two nodes. Since node 2 yields a U of 24.00 and node 3 yields a U of 22.333, our *current* best upper bound is 24.00. We thus change the value of CBUB above node 1. To change the value of CBLB, we would have to have obtained a point that is feasible in (P1) and yields a value of the objective function > 23.00, our CBLB. Since neither node 2 nor node 3 has an all-integer solution, we have not obtained a new feasible solution. (Although in this problem we could round down at nodes 2 and 3 to obtain new feasible solutions to [P1], in general the search for feasible points may be difficult, and therefore we wish to present a procedure that does not include a new feasible solution at each node.) Thus the value of CBLB remains as it was.

Figure 8.13 incorporates the information from (P2) and (P3) into a decision diagram called a *tree.* To determine what to do next we consider the nodes at the bottom of our tree, nodes 2 and 3 in this case. We note that the upper bound on node 3 is 22.333, and the current value of CBLB is 23.00. We have thus *already found a better solution than we can possibly obtain in the feasible set for (P3).* Therefore, *we can ignore (P3) and concentrate our efforts on (P2).* To indicate that (P3) has now been eliminated from consideration, we place in Figure 8.13 a T below (P3), which means that *that particular branch of the tree is now terminated.* In general, if, after calculating the value of U for a node, we find that $U \leq$ CBLB, then this node can be eliminated from further consideration by writing a T below the node, indicating that this branch of the tree has been terminated.

Let us now continue by considering (P2). We still do not know the optimal solution to (P2), for we still have a noninteger value for x_2^*. Since (P2) is an ILP, we attack it with branch and bound, and to do this we must branch again. The variable x_1 is integer in the optimal solution to (P2). Hence we must branch on x_2, which we do by using the constraints $x_2 \leq 4$ or $x_2 \geq 5$. Doing this, we replace (P2) with the problems

Draw attention to the fact that successive problems contain the new constraint as well as all constraint(s) for "parent" nodes connected above (but not beside) it.

$$\begin{aligned}
&\text{Max } x_1 + 5x_2 && \text{(P4)}\\
&\text{s.t.}\quad 11x_1 + 6x_2 \leq 66\\
&\qquad 5x_1 + 50x_2 \leq 225\\
&\qquad x_1 \leq 3\\
&\qquad x_2 \leq 4\\
&\qquad x_1, x_2 \geq 0 \text{ and integer}
\end{aligned}$$

$$\begin{aligned}
&\text{Max } x_1 + 5x_2 && \text{(P5)}\\
&\text{s.t.}\quad 11x_1 + 6x_2 \leq 66\\
&\qquad 5x_1 + 50x_2 \leq 225\\
&\qquad x_1 \leq 3\\
&\qquad x_2 \geq 5\\
&\qquad x_1, x_2 \geq 0 \text{ and integer}
\end{aligned}$$

Note that the constraints for (P4) are the constraints for (P1); that is,

$$\begin{aligned}
11x_1 + 6x_2 &\leq 66\\
5x_1 + 50x_2 &\leq 225
\end{aligned}$$

plus the constraint that was appended to define (P2) (i.e., $x_1 \leq 3$), plus the new constraint that is appended to define (P4) (i.e., $x_2 \leq 4$). A similar interpretation can be given to (P5). The result of this branch is shown in Figure 8.14, and the new tree is shown in Figure 8.15.

The Final Tree. In comparing Figures 8.14 and 8.12, there are several important features to be noted:

1. Problem (P3) remains unchanged (exactly as it was in Figure 8.12).
2. An additional set of noninteger points, including the optimal solution to the LP

It is important to emphasize that the first integer solution found in this process does not guarantee its being the optimal integer solution.

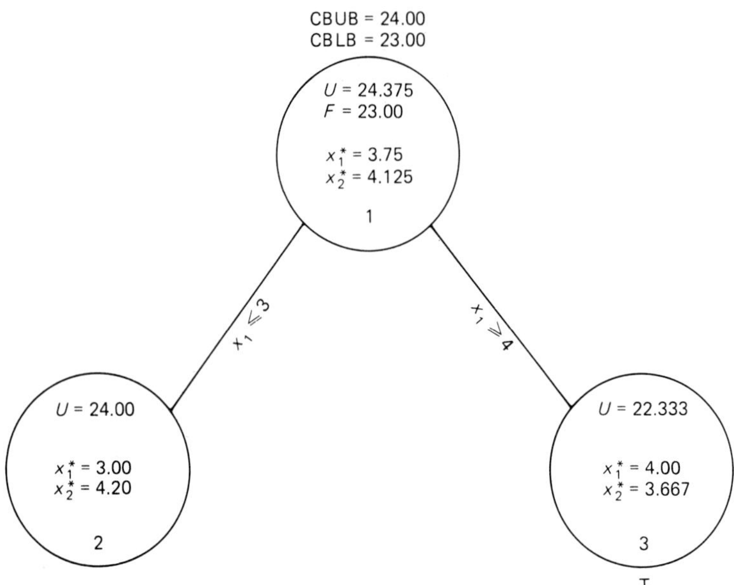

▲ FIGURE 8.13
Tree with Three Nodes Corresponding to (P1), (P2), and (P3)

relaxation of (P2), has been eliminated from consideration. All of the newly eliminated area that was in the feasible set of the LP relaxation of (P1) is double-crosshatched.

3. The constraint set for the LP relaxation of (P5) is empty. There are no points that satisfy the constraints $5x_1 + 50x_2 \le 225$, $x_1 \ge 0$, $x_2 \ge 5$. This also means that (P5) has no feasible solution, which means that we may now forget about (P5). This is indicated by placing, in Figure 8.15, a T below node 5, which terminates another branch of the tree. We now see that there are two causes for termination: Terminate a node when

1. its U is ≤CBLB or
2. it represents an infeasible problem.

▼ FIGURE 8.14
Problems (P3), (P4), and (P5)

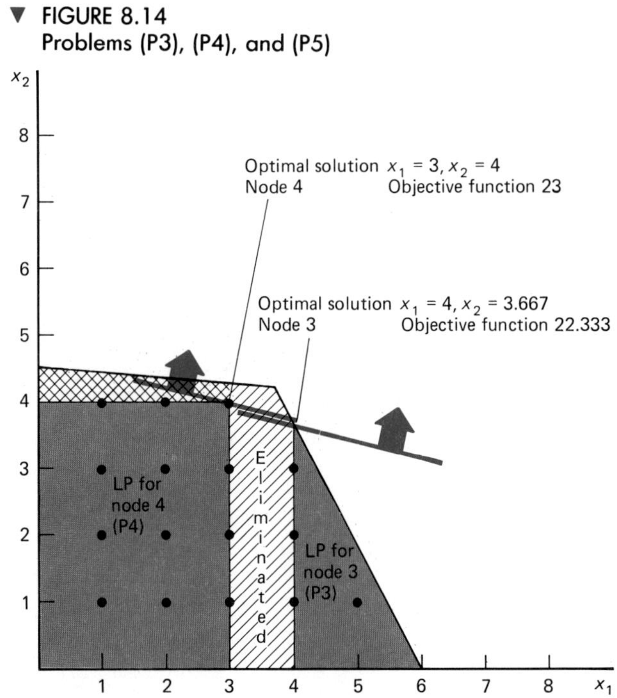

If we had decided to branch on X_2 initially, the tree would have looked different but the result would have been the same:

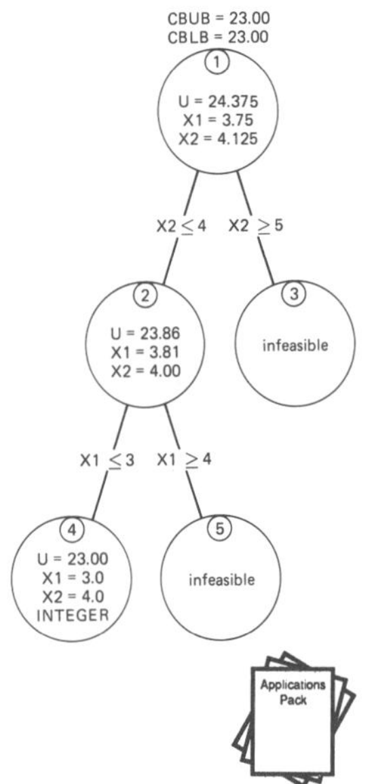

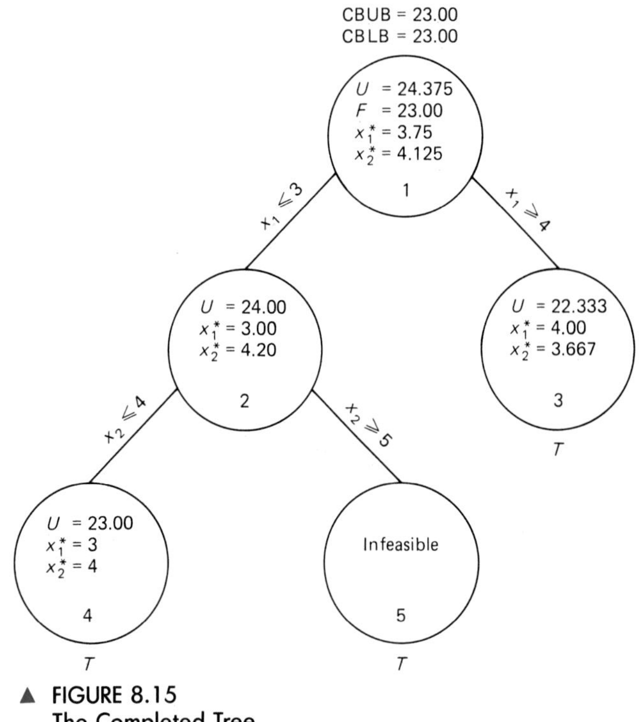

▲ FIGURE 8.15
The Completed Tree

Thus, we need only concentrate on (P4), and solving the LP relaxation of that problem, as shown in Figure 8.14, reveals that the optimal solution to the relaxation of (P4), namely ($x_1^* = 3$, $x_2^* = 4$), is all-integer. This means that ($x_1^* = 3$, $x_2^* = 4$) is the optimal solution to (P4). For this reason, (P4) is another terminal node on our tree and, in Figure 8.15, we have accordingly placed a T under that node. Thus, we have an illustration of the third cause for termination. In summary, terminate a node when

1. its U is ≤CBLB,
2. it represents an infeasible problem, or
3. the LP relaxation provides a solution to the integer problem represented by that node.

Referring again to Figure 8.15, we note that the value of CBUB has changed from the value it held in Figure 8.13. The branch on node 2 yielded an infeasible problem (node 5) and a problem (node 4) with a U of 23.00. Thus the current best upper bound (CBUB) is reduced from 24.00 to 23.00. In node 4, we also have an all-integer solution. This point is thus a feasible solution to (P1). It yields a value of 23.00 for the objective function. Since our current best lower bound is 23.00, we do not change the CBLB.

In general, *when all nodes have been terminated, the branch-and-bound method is complete.* The optimal solution to the original problem (P1) is the solution that established the CBLB. In this case CBLB is 23.00, and thus ($x_1^* = 3$, $x_2^* = 4$) is the optimal solution to (P1). Upon termination, as in Figure 8.15, it will always be the case that CBLB = CBUB.

MILPs

The branch-and-bound procedure described above can be easily modified to work on MILPs. Consider a small modification of the ILP analyzed above. In particular, assume that the problem is

The tree diagram looks as follows:

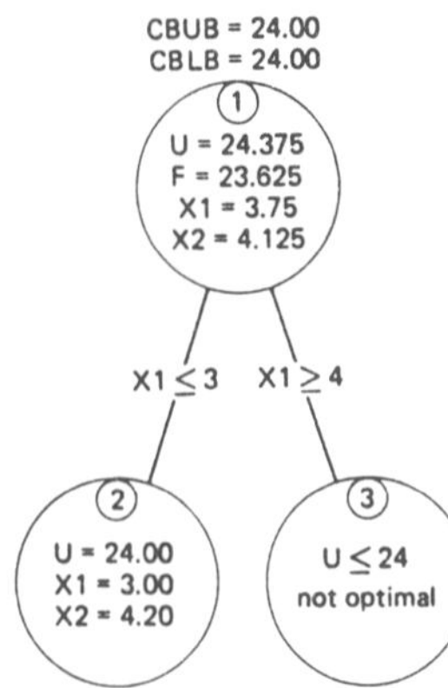

$$\text{Max } x_1 + 5x_2$$

$$\text{s.t.} \quad 11x_1 + 6x_2 \leq 66$$

$$5x_1 + 50x_2 \leq 225$$

$$x_1 \geq 0 \text{ and integer}, \qquad x_2 \geq 0$$

The only change from the previous problem is that x_2 is no longer required to be an integer (i.e., x_2 can be any nonnegative number). To solve this problem, we start as before with the LP relaxation in Figure 8.10. Since x_1^* is not integer (it assumes the value 3.75), we obtain the initial value of F by rounding x_1^* down to 3. The value of x_2 is permitted to remain fractional at 4.125. Thus, we obtain $F = 3 + 5(4.125) = 23.625$. As before, CBUB = 24.375, but now CBLB = 23.625. Now we branch, as previously, on x_1 by introducing the constraints $x_1 \leq 3$ or $x_1 \geq 4$. This yields Figure 8.12. The following information can be read from this figure:

1. Node 2 yields a U of 24.00, and node 3 yields a U of 22.333; thus the CBUB becomes 24.00.
2. The optimal solution to node 2 has an integer value for x_1; thus this is a feasible solution to (P1). It follows that
   a. We achieve a new current best lower bound of 24.00.
   b. Node 2 can be terminated.
3. At node 3 $U \leq$ CBLB; thus node 3 can be terminated.

Since both nodes have been terminated, the optimal solution is the solution that yielded the CBLB. Thus, $x_1^* = 3.00$ and $x_2^* = 4.20$ is the optimal solution.

Summary of Branch and Bound

We summarize the application to ILP. The adaptation for MILP should be obvious. In what follows, the phrase "solve a node" means solve the LP relaxation of the ILP corresponding to the node. A "solved node" is one for which this has been done. Otherwise, the node is "unsolved."

It may not be possible to find an initial feasible IP solution and value of F until an integer solution is reached during the branch and bound process.

1. Draw a node corresponding to the original ILP, and solve the node. The OV for the relaxation is the value of U at the node. If the optimal solution is all-integer, it is optimal for the ILP. Otherwise, use any method to find a feasible point for the ILP, and let F denote the objective value at this point. Set the current best upper bound (CBUB) equal to U and the current best lower bound (CBLB) equal to F.

2. Commence with any solved node that has not been terminated. From this node (the parent) *branch* so as to create two new unsolved nodes (the successors) with the property that the optimal solution to one of the successor ILPs will be the optimal solution to the parent ILP. The branching may be accomplished by taking any fractional component, say x_i^*, of the optimal solution to the parent's relaxation. Let $[x_i^*]$ be the truncation of x_i^* to its integer part. Then $[x_i^*] + 1$ is the next integer larger than x_i^*. One successor will be the parent's problem augmented by the constraint $x_i \leq [x_i^*]$. The other successor is formed by augmenting the parent's problem with $x_i \geq [x_i^*] + 1$. Then either pick another solved node and repeat or go to step 3.

3. Commence with any unsolved node and attempt to *solve*. The OV for the relaxation is the value of U at the node. Write a T under the node, and terminate this branch, if the LP relaxation is infeasible or if $U \leq$ CBLB or if the optimal solution is all-integer. If the optimal solution is all-integer, evaluate the objective function at this point; call the value F. Compare CBLB with F. If $F >$ CBLB, set CBLB $= F$. If the branch is not terminated, either repeat step 3 or go to step 2. If the node is terminated, go to step 4.

4. If all nodes are terminated, the optimal solution to the original ILP is the all-integer solution that produced the value CBLB.

How Can I Help You? AT&T Woos Customers by Saving Them Money with the Aid of a Mixed Integer Program*

AT&T, a major supplier of services to the telemarketing industry, is always looking for ways of helping its customers expand their operations. One of the problems facing companies that do a large volume of telemarketing (using toll-free 800 numbers to take customer orders) is deciding on the number and location of sites for telemarketing offices. It was therefore in AT&T's best interests to develop a set of programs that would aid their customers in this process.

AT&T's researchers soon found that, contrary to the general perception, the location of telemarketing offices was not always dictated primarily by real estate or communications costs. Rather, political or psychological considerations often played a major role. Thus, an office might be located in the same city as the regional headquarters or in a city where upper management wanted to have a presence, even though these might not be cost-efficient choices.

AT&T developed a model that analyzes the costs of plausible candidate sites and allows users to evaluate various site configurations on the basis of both quantitative and qualitative factors. The model, a mixed integer program similar to a facility-location planning model, is solved by means of a branch-and-bound code. It answers four questions:

1. How many telemarketing centers should be opened?
2. Where should centers be located?
3. What geographic regions should be served by each center?
4. How many attendant positions are required at each location?

Originally developed on a mainframe, the model was adapted for use on a PC, with more graphic display and user interaction added. It provides not only an optimal solution that minimizes the three operational cost factors (communications, labor, and real estate) but alternative solutions as well, so that the user can take factors other than costs into account. To this end, an analytical hierarchy process (AHP) has been added to the model, allowing users to include qualitative or subjective factors in the decision process.

The AT&T model has greatly accelerated the siting of telemarketing offices while saving customers many hours of research and consulting costs—savings that some companies estimated at up to \$240,000. Moreover, a number of customers have reported savings averaging \$1 million per year from use of the locations identified by the model rather than ones they had previously considered.

From AT&T's point of view, the model has proven its worth in terms of enhanced customer relations and sales of services. In 1988, 46 AT&T customers made decisions on site locations with the aid of the model, in the process committing themselves to \$375 million per year in network services and \$31 million in new equipment purchases. As a result of business generated by the model, AT&T's share of this market has risen from 30% to 40%.

---

*Spencer, Brigandi, Dargon, and Sheehan, "AT&T's Telemarketing Site Selection System Offers Customer Support," *Interfaces*, Vol. 20, No. 1 (Jan.–Feb. 1990).

It is appropriate, at this point, to make the observation that for very large problems the branch-and-bound method can be stopped before all nodes have been terminated. The node producing the CBLB will provide an *approximate solution* to the original ILP. In this case CBLB will be less than the value CBUB, and the difference CBUB − CBLB indicates the closeness of the approximation.

Finally, let us comment on the application of the branch-and-bound technique to special ILPs with 0–1 variables. In this case, suppose that one is branching on the 0–1 variable y_1. Then one successor will have $y_1 = 0$. The other will have $y_1 = 1$. For the ILP in 0–1 variables another type of branch-and-bound application, sometimes called *partial enumeration,* has enjoyed considerable success. Also, for the general ILP other methods have been applied. These include *cutting-plane methods* and *Lagrangian relaxation.* As stated at the outset of this chapter, our introductory discussion merely touches the surface of this intricate topic.

In practice, the structure of the problem can determine its tractability to being solved by branch and bound or by cutting plane. The experience of working on problems with similar characteristics is the only teacher here.

8.8 ILP in Practice

Strategic Considerations in Solving ILP Problems

As the summary above shows, there is considerable flexibility in the use of branch and bound. For example, after solving the original relaxation and then branching, one could solve the two successors. Alternatively, you might choose to solve just one of the successors and then immediately branch again on that node. Elaborating on this, one possible strategy is a "horizontal attack." One proceeds through the tree according to the sequence of nodes shown in Figure 8.16. To execute this strategy, one solves the original node and then iterates in the following pattern: branch on 1, solve 2, solve 3, branch on 2, solve 4, solve 5, branch on 3, solve 6, solve 7, branch on 4, solve 8, solve 9, and so on. In this way one moves horizontally through the entire tree at each particular level.

Again, stress that although there may be many paths to finding the optimal solution, the process will always yield the same optimal objective function.

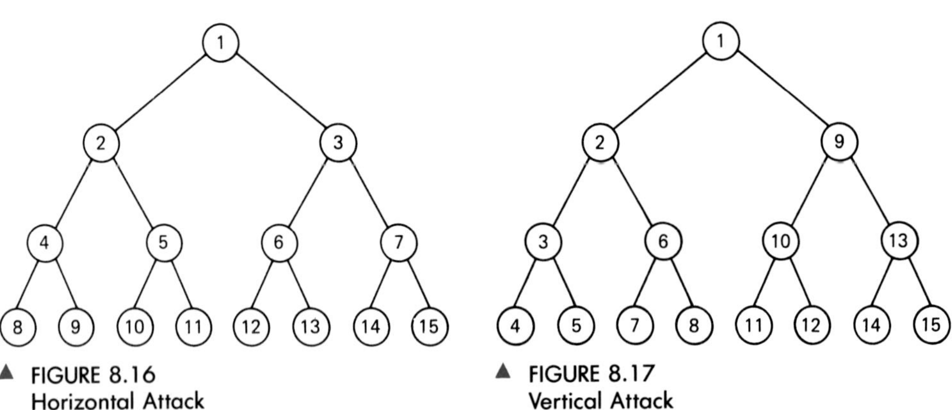

▲ FIGURE 8.16
Horizontal Attack

▲ FIGURE 8.17
Vertical Attack

At the other extreme, Figure 8.17 shows a strategy based on a "vertical attack." These two approaches illustrate just one of the several ways that judgment enters into the solution of ILP problems. Although the details of such strategic considerations become too specialized for this introductory discussion, it is well to understand that in practice there is often considerable room for choice and ingenuity in the application of branch and bound.

Sensitivity

We have seen that the branch-and-bound method uses *numerous* applications of the simplex method to solve an integer program. Thus it is, in general, much more time-consuming to solve ILPs than LPs. Unfortunately, it is also true that the solution to an ILP contains much less information than the solution to an LP. In particular, *the solution to an ILP does not contain sensitivity information.* No information concerning the sensitivity of the OV (i.e., the optimal value of the objective function) to changes in the RHS of a constraint or to a change in the value of an objective function coefficient is produced. In other words, *an ILP solution does not include information that is equivalent to the dual price and cost sensitivity information in an LP.* This does not imply that changes in the RHS or in a cost coefficient do not affect the solution to an ILP. They do. Indeed, the solutions to ILPs can be extremely sensitive to changes in parameter values.

The following somewhat unrealistic, but for the present purpose illustrative, capital budgeting example will illustrate these points:

$$\begin{aligned} &\text{Max } 10x_1 + 100\,x_2 + 1000x_3 \\ &\text{s.t.} \quad 29x_1 + 30x_2 + 31x_3 \le b_1 \\ &\qquad x_1, x_2, x_3 \text{ are 0 or 1} \end{aligned}$$

The problem is easily solved by inspection. The table in Figure 8.18 shows the optimal solution and the optimal value of the objective function (OV) for various values of the parameter b_1. From the data in Figure 8.18 we note that a change in 1 unit in the right-hand side of the constraint (say from 29 to 30) increases the OV by a factor of 10 (from 10 to 100). Clearly, if the manager were aware of such an opportunity, he or she would be anxious to make such a change.

	OPTIMAL SOLUTION			
b_1	x_1	x_2	x_3	OV
29	1	0	0	10
30	0	1	0	100
31	0	0	1	1000

▲ FIGURE 8.18
Sensitivity Data

Unfortunately, no such sensitivity information is produced when you solve an ILP. You can receive only the optimal solution and the OV. Sensitivity information such as that shown in Figure 8.18 can be achieved only by repeatedly solving the model with new parameter values. When the model has a number of constraints, using this approach to generate useful sensitivity data for an ILP can require the analyst to run a large number of alternative programs. This can be an expensive and time-consuming activity.

One final word on sensitivity. Many ILP computer codes are part of LP packages. Thus, they may produce sensitivity data as part of their solution reports, in spite of the fact that these data have no meaning in the ILP context. This is true of LINDO, which is the ILP and LP code used in this text.

Heuristic Algorithms

Because of the importance of the applications, integer programming is currently an active area of research. Much of this research is in the area of heuristic algorithms. These are algorithms designed to efficiently produce "good," although not necessarily optimal, solutions.

From the viewpoint of the manager, a heuristic procedure may certainly be as acceptable as, and possibly even preferable to, a "more exact" algorithm that produces an optimal solution. The dominant considerations should be the amount of insight and guidance the model can provide and the cost of obtaining these.

8.9 Notes on Implementation of Integer Programming

Integer solutions are an important, indeed essential, condition for the application of mathematical programming models to many important real-world problems. Recent advances in research and computer technology have made it possible to make real progress on problems that involve variables that must be treated as integers. An example appeared in the Application Capsule at the beginning of this chapter. Other examples follow.

Kelly-Springfield

Technically, a setup cost is independent of the product previously made. Changeover costs include both teardown and setup costs. In the chemical industry it might make quite a difference which chemical was produced in the vat (or carried in a tank car) before the current one.

The Kelly-Springfield Tire Company has a model-based system to coordinate sales forecasting, inventory control, production planning, and distribution decisions. One crucial link in this system is the production planning model. Central to this problem is the effect of setup time. In the manufacture of each particular line of tires a machine is set up by installing a piece of equipment (called a die) particular to that line. It takes a fixed amount of time (and thus a fixed cost) to remove one die from a machine and insert another. In other words, there is a fixed changeover or setup cost of moving from the production of one line of tires to another, no matter how many tires you decide to produce after the machine is set up. The decision to set up (i.e., to produce a particular line in a given production period) or not, is treated as a 0–1 variable in the MILP used to attack this problem. The total integrated system (including the production planning system) is credited with impressive results. The system implemented in 1970 is estimated to have yielded savings of $500,000 a year. Since an improved system was installed in 1976, average unit inventory decreased by 19%, customer service improved, productivity increased, and additional savings totaling $7.9 million annually resulted. For more details, see "Coordinated Decisions for Increased Profits," *Interfaces* 10, December 1980.

Flying Tiger Line

Another interesting application concerns the use of integer programming by the Flying Tiger Line (an all-cargo airline) in approaching two strategic questions: the design of their service network and the selection and deployment of their aircraft fleet. The size of the MILP used to attack this problem and the cost of solving it are

The Flying Tiger Line was acquired by Federal Express. It would be interesting to see what model they now use or what modifications they have made to the original model.

staggering when your primary exposure has been to classroom problems. One model for 33 cities, 8 hubs (locations where cargo can be interchanged), and 10 aircraft types included 843 constraints, 3807 continuous variables, and 156 integer (aircraft selector) variables. No explicit cost savings are included in the presentation of this application. Management's satisfaction with the project, however, is obvious from the ongoing nature of the investigation. For a detailed account, see "A Mixed-Integer Programming Approach to Air Cargo Fleet Planning," *Management Science,* November 1980.

Hunt-Wesson Foods

This is a classic "Lockbox Problem" wherein a company contracts with several banks to establish P.O. boxes in certain cities. The bank will send a courier several times a day to collect bill payments and deposit them in the company account. From there, they go through the Federal Reserve system, and eventually to the company headquarters. The expense of having a P.O. box (lockbox) usually entails a fixed cost (minimum balance) and some variable costs (per check).

A third application is a major distribution-system study for Hunt-Wesson Foods, Inc. The problem is to select sites for regional distribution centers and to determine what customer zones each distribution center should serve, as well as which of several plants should supply the distribution centers. The problem is an MILP with two types of integer variables:

y_k = 1 if site k is used for a distribution center, and $y_k = 0$ if it is not

y_{kl} = 1 if customer district l is served by the warehouse at site k, and $y_{kl} = 0$ if it is not

The quantities of material shipped are continuous variables.

The problem involves 17 commodity classes, 14 plants, 45 possible distribution center sites, and 121 customer zones. The MILP model used to attack it had 11,854 rows, 727 0–1 integer variables, and 23,513 continuous variables. A special algorithm was constructed to solve the problem. In the article describing this problem the authors stated that the realizable annual cost savings produced by the study were estimated to be in the low-seven figures. For more details, see "Multicommodity Distribution System Design by Benders Decomposition," *Management Science,* January 1974.

The three studies cited here have a number of features in common:

1. Each attacked a major problem of strategic importance to a firm.
2. Each made a significant contribution to successfully dealing with the problem.
3. Each included a large-scale MILP.
4. Clever modeling and/or special algorithms were required in each application.
5. Each project required a major commitment of funds and managerial talent.

The examples illustrate that a good model may enable management to achieve a level of analysis and performance that might otherwise be impossible, but such models are costly to develop and often require an ongoing and time-consuming input from management. In all of the examples the authors (of the articles) stressed a close working relationship between the analysts (modelers) and management. In the case of Kelly-Springfield, the current model has evolved over a 15-year horizon with two major efforts. We see, then, that the use of quantitative models to solve important problems may well entail a serious commitment to a long process. Small tactical problems may be successfully subdued with a quick "off the shelf" treatment. Fundamental strategic problems are seldom that obliging.

8.10 Summary of ILP

The introduction pointed out that integer linear programming (ILP) is an important and developing area of constrained optimization. Section 8.2 identified all-integer models and mixed integer models (MILP) as the two main types of integer linear programs. In MILPs only some of the decision variables are restricted to integer values. Further, the importance of problems involving integer variables that are restricted to the values 0 or 1 was discussed. Finally, the LP relaxation was defined. Section 8.3 used a graphical approach to solve an ILP with two decision variables. This approach was then used to investigate the conceptual relationships between an ILP and its LP relaxation. We saw that:

1. In a *Max* problem the OV of the LP relaxation always provides an *upper bound* on the OV of the original ILP.
2. In a *Min* problem the OV of the LP relaxation always provides a *lower bound* on the OV of the original ILP.

In Section 8.3 we also discussed *rounded solutions.* These are any rounding of the optimal solution to the LP relaxation. Thus, there are many rounded solutions. In some applications, as discussed in Section 8.1, any rounded solution may be an acceptable substitute for the true ILP solution. In other cases, no rounded solution will be acceptable. We saw in Section 8.3 that, in general:

For "n" variables that have fractional answers, there are 2^n possible rounded solutions. Thus, for Flying Tigers there could be $2^{156} = 9.1344 \times 10^{46}$ rounded solutions! If *only* 50 of these variables had fractional answers in the relaxed LP, there would be 1,125,900,000,000,000 (over a quadrillion) solutions to investigate just to find the best rounded feasible solution.

3. it may be that no rounded solution is near the ILP optimum, or
4. it may be that no rounded solution is feasible (i.e., satisfies the constraints of the LP relaxation).

Sections 8.4 and 8.5 considered the use of 0–1 variables in a variety of applications. In particular, models for a capital budgeting problem and a warehouse location problem were considered in some detail. Section 8.6 contained an application of the fact that certain LPs always have all-integer solutions. Section 8.7 explained the branch-and-bound approach used to solve ILPs. The graphical approach was used to show that branching is a matter of dividing the feasible set for a problem into disjoint subsets. Bounding uses the optimum value of the LP relaxation to eliminate subproblems from consideration. Section 8.8 dealt with two important topics concerning the real-world use of ILPs. First, we pointed out the importance of tree-pruning strategies in implementing the branch-and-bound approach. Second, we saw that sensitivity data are not produced as a natural by-product of the solution to an ILP. Further, it was illustrated that ILPs may be inconsistent and erratic in their sensitivity to changes in parameter values. These two facts combine to establish the necessity of using multiple computer runs with different parameters to produce sensitivity information in the ILP setting. This process is often an important part of attacking a real problem with an ILP model. In the final section, 8.9, several major applications of integer programming were cited.

8.11 Introduction to Quadratic Programming

Quadratic programming (QP), like linear integer programming, is a first cousin of linear programming. Compare the following:

- ***Linear Programming Problem.*** Maximize or minimize the value of *linear* objective function subject to a set of linear equality and inequality constraints as well as nonnegativity conditions on the values of the decision variables.
- ***Quadratic Programming Problem.*** Maximize or minimize the value of a *quadratic* objective function subject to a set of linear equality and inequality constraints as well as nonnegativity conditions on the values of the decision variables.

Obviously, the only difference in these two problems is in the functional form of the objective function.

Quadratic Functions. We know about linear functions. Here are some examples of quadratic functions:

$$9x_1^2 + 4x_1 + 7$$

$$3x_1^2 - 4x_1x_2 + 15x_2^2 + 20x_1 - 13x_2 - 14$$

These functions are the sum of terms involving the squares of variables (e.g., $3x_1^2$), cross products (e.g., $4x_1x_2$), linear functions (e.g., $20x_1$), and constants (e.g., 14). In general a quadratic function in N variables can be written in the form

A general quadratic in N variables

$$\sum_{i=1}^{N} A_i x_i^2 + \sum_{i=1}^{N-1} \sum_{j=i+1}^{N} B_{ij} x_i x_j + \sum_{i=1}^{N} C_i x_i + D$$

Note that when all of the coefficients A_i and B_{ij} are zero then the function is linear. Hence, a linear function is a special case of a quadratic function.

Changing from a linear to a quadratic objective function requires a new algorithm to solve the problem. This change also implies that many of the facts we have learned about linear programming problems no longer hold. The following example illustrates some of the differences between quadratic programming problems and linear programming problems. The formal QP model is

A numeric example

$$\begin{aligned} \text{Min } & (x_1 - 6)^2 + (x_2 - 8)^2 \\ \text{s.t. } & x_1 \le 7 \\ & x_2 \le 5 \\ & x_1 + 2x_2 \le 12 \\ & x_1 + x_2 \le 9 \\ & x_1, \quad x_2 \ge 0 \end{aligned}$$

Again, the two basic ways to solve this problem are to:
1. Change the model to fit the method (linearize the objective function), or
2. Change the method to fit the model (use gradient methods).

Geometric Representation. A geometric representation of this problem appears in Figure 8.19. The constraint set, of course, is the same as for an LP and thus needs no new explanation. In order to see that the objective function is a special case of our previous quadratic function, it can be rewritten in the form $x_1^2 - 12x_1 + 36 + x_2^2 - 16x_2 + 64$. You may also recognize the expression

$$(x_1 - 6)^2 + (x_2 - 8)^2 = k$$

as the equation of a circle with radius $\sqrt{k}$ and center at the point (6, 8). Thus, as shown in Figure 8.19, the contours of the objective function are concentric circles around the point (6, 8). Since these contours increase in value as the radius k increases, and since the above problem is a minimization problem, the optimal solution in Figure 8.19 occurs at the point (4, 4). This can be roughly described as the point where the contour "first touches" the feasible set. In this example that "touch" is a point of tangency, though in other cases a solution could occur at a corner, just as in LP. The optimal value of the objective function (i.e., its value at the point (4, 4) is $(4 - 6)^2 + (4 - 8)^2 = 20$.

Comparison with LP This example clearly indicates that, in contrast to linear programming:

1. There need not be an optimal corner solution. An algorithm like the simplex, which searches for the best corner, thus cannot be used to solve this problem.

What makes using NLP difficult is that the optimal solution does not necessarily occur at an extreme point of the feasible region. In this example it occurs on the edge of the feasible region, but it is possible for it to occur in the interior. In either case, there are an infinite number of possible solutions (versus IP which has a large finite number).

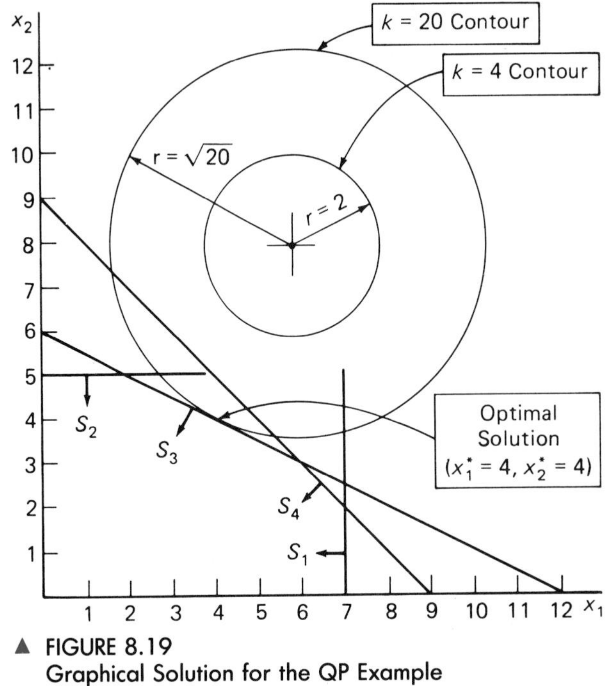

▲ FIGURE 8.19
Graphical Solution for the QP Example

2. As a direct result of 1, there may be more positive variables in the optimal solution than there are constraints. For the example problem there are five positive variables (x_1, x_2, s_1, s_2, s_4) and only four constraints.

8.12 Computer Solution of QP Problems

Real-world QP problems are solved with computers. There are two approaches: One is to use a general nonlinear programming code such as GINO[3] and the other is to use a specially written quadratic programming code. We will restrict our attention to the first approach.

For the example in the previous section, Figure 8.20 shows the input and solution for the GINO code. Except for minor conventions like * for multiplication and for exponentiation, the GINO input reads like the mathematical formulation of the formal QP model.

In the next section the PRICE column of the computer printout is interpreted through a geometric analysis. For the present, concerning the sensitivity output in Figure 8.20, we simply state the following facts:

- Consider the number in the PRICE column corresponding to the *i*th constraint. Just as in LP (e.g., the LINDO output) this represents the rate of improvement in OV as the *i*th RHS is increased, with all other data unchanged.

[3]GINO, which stands for General Interactive Nonlinear Optimizer, much like LINDO, is a user-friendly code for solving NLP problems. There is also a diskette available for personal computer use. For information on either the micro or mainframe versions, interested readers should contact Professor Linus Schrage, Graduate School of Business, University of Chicago, 1101 East 58th Street, Chicago, IL 60637.

```
MODEL:
   1) MIN = (X1 - 6)^2 + (X2 - 8)^2;
   2) X1 < 7;
   3) X2 < 5;
   4) X1 + 2*X2 < 12;
   5) X1 + X2 < 9;
END

SOLUTION STATUS: OPTIMAL TO TOLERANCES. DUAL CONDITIONS: SATISFIED.

            OBJECTIVE FUNCTION VALUE

         1)          20.000000

   VARIABLE           VALUE             REDUCED COST
         X1          4.000000              0.000001
         X2          4.000000              0.000000

        ROW     SLACK OR SURPLUS               PRICE
         2)          3.000000              0.000000
         3)          1.000000              0.000000
         4)          0.000000              3.999999
         5)          1.000000              0.000000
```

▲ FIGURE 8.20
Solving a QP with GINO

- The REDUCED COST applies to a variable whose optimal value is zero. For such a variable, the reduced cost is the rate at which the objective value is "hurt" as that variable is forced to assume positive values in an optimal solution.

8.13 Geometric Interpretation of the Sensitivity Analysis

Let us now consider what happens to the optimal solution and the optimal value of the objective function as the RHS of the third constraint, i.e., the binding constraint, changes. We will refer to the value of the RHS of the third constraint as R. In the current problem $R = 12$. The analysis is geometric and is tied to Figure 8.21. For convenience of exposition let

line 2 be the line $x_2 = 5$

line 3 be the line $x_1 + 2x_2 = 12$

line 4 be the line $x_1 + x_2 = 9$

Each of these lines is identified in Figure 8.21.

Tracing the Optimal Solution

We first note that as R decreases the third constraint will move to the southwest parallel to line 3. Similarly, as R increases the third constraint moves to the northeast parallel to line 3. From geometry we recall the fact that any tangent to a

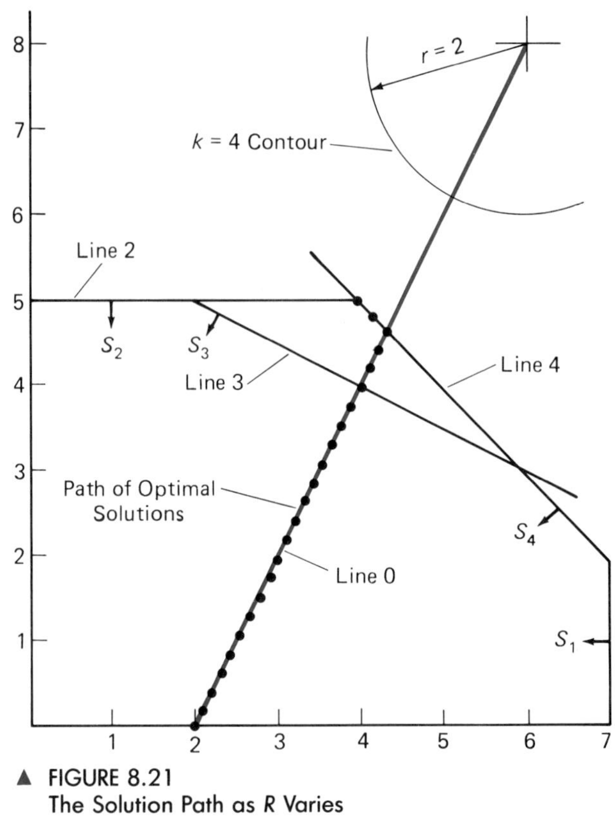

▲ FIGURE 8.21
The Solution Path as R Varies

Changing the RHS

circle is perpendicular to a line connecting the point of tangency and the center. Hence, as R is increased or decreased (within limits), the optimal solution to the problem lies on the line joining the points ($x_1 = 4, x_2 = 4$) and ($x_1 = 6, x_2 = 8$). The equation of this line is $2x_1 - x_2 = 4$, and it is identified as line 0 in Figure 8.21.

From Figure 8.21 we now see that as R decreases the optimal solution moves down line 0 until it reaches the axis (the nonnegativity constraint on x_2). At this point $x_1 = 2$ and $x_2 = 0$ and thus $x_1 + 2x_2 = 2$. Similarly, as R increases the optimal solution moves up along line 0 until R assumes a value such that the third constraint passes through the intersection of line 4 and line 0. This value is determined by solving the equations $x_1 + x_2 = 9$ and $2x_1 - x_2 = 4$ for x_1 and x_2 to obtain the point ($x_1 = 4\frac{1}{3}, x_2 = 4\frac{2}{3}$). Substituting these values in the equation $x_1 + 2x_2 = R$ yields $R = 13\frac{2}{3}$.

As R assumes values greater than $13\frac{2}{3}$, the optimal solution moves along line 4 until R assumes a value such that the third constraint passes through the intersection of line 2 and line 4. This intersection occurs at the point ($x_1 = 4, x_2 = 5$) and since $x_1 + 2x_2 = R$, the third constraint intersects this point when $R = 14$. As R becomes larger than 14, the third constraint becomes redundant and the optimal solution remains at the point ($x_1 = 4, x_2 = 5$). We have now traced the path of the optimal solutions for all possible values of $R \geq 2$. To find the optimal solution for a specific value of R it is only necessary to solve the appropriate two simultaneous linear equations.

A path of solutions

The Optimal Value of the Objective Function (OV)

Once you have the optimal solution, say (x_1^*, x_2^*), the optimal value of the objective function (OV) is obtained by evaluating the expression $(x_1^* - 6)^2 + (x_2^* - 8)^2 = \text{OV}$. We now wish to develop an expression for the OV as a function of R. This function will be identified by the notation OV(R). In particular we will restrict our attention to values of R between 2 and 13⅔, i.e., to those values of R for which the optimal solution lies on line 0.

When the optimal solution lies on line 0, it lies at the intersection of the lines

$$2x_1 - x_2 = 4 \qquad \text{line 0}$$

$$x_1 + 2x_2 = R \qquad \text{third constraint}$$

Solving for x_1 and x_2 in terms of R we obtain

$$x_1 + 2(2x_1 - 4) = R$$

or

$$x_1^* = \frac{R + 8}{5} \qquad \text{and} \qquad x_2^* = 2\left(\frac{R + 8}{5}\right) - 4 = \frac{2R - 4}{5}$$

Note when $R = 12$, $x_1^* = 4$ and $x_2^* = 4$, which is our original result. Since the objective function is $(x_1 - 6)^2 + (x_2 - 8)^2$ its value at x_1^*, x_2^* is

$$\left(\frac{R + 8}{5} - 6\right)^2 + \left(\frac{2R - 4}{5} - 8\right)^2$$

or

$$\text{OV}(R) = \frac{R^2 - 44R + 484}{5}$$

The function OV(R), over the range $2 \leq R \leq 13⅔$, is plotted in Figure 8.22. Note that over this range the OV function is quadratic. Also note that when $R = 12$ the objective function value is 20, the same as the value produced by the computer in Figure 8.20.

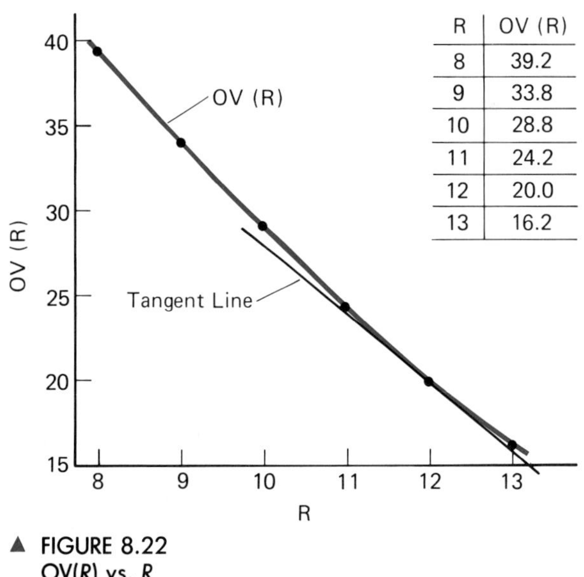

R	OV (R)
8	39.2
9	33.8
10	28.8
11	24.2
12	20.0
13	16.2

▲ FIGURE 8.22
OV(*R*) vs. *R*

Improvement versus Change

Recall that the definition of the dual price on the third constraint is the rate of improvement of the OV as the RHS of the third constraint (i.e., R) is increased. Recall from our discussion of LP that the "rate of improvement" always has the same magnitude (absolute value) as the "rate of change." In a Min problem, however, a negative rate of change (the OV getting smaller) is a positive rate of improvement. Thus in our example problem if we can determine the rate of change we can determine the rate of improvement simply by changing the sign. We observe this somewhat inconvenient distinction because the geometric analysis proceeds naturally in terms of rate of change while both LINDO and GINO produce, in the sensitivity analysis, the rate of improvement.

In geometric terms the rate of change in the function OV(R) at some point, say $R = \hat{R}$, is the slope of the tangent to the graph of the function at the point ($\hat{R}$, OV($\hat{R}$)). In the language of calculus, the rate of change at $\hat{R}$ is the first derivative of OV(R) evaluated at $\hat{R}$. This entity is denoted OV′($\hat{R}$). Figure 8.22 shows the tangent to the graph at the point ($R = 12$, OV $= 20$). To deduce the slope, one can take the first derivative to obtain $\text{OV}'(R) = \frac{2R - 44}{5}$ and thus $\text{OV}'(12) = -4$. We have already noted that since the rate of change is − 4, the rate of improvement (i.e., the dual price) in this Min model must be 4. This result is exactly what we see in the computer output in Figure 8.20.

Rate of change = slope

Note that in Figure 8.22 the slope of the tangent is *different* for every value of R. Thus, comparing QP with LP, we find the following major difference:

No RHS range analysis

- In general for a QP problem there is no allowable increase and decrease in the RHS of a constraint for which the dual price remains the same.

Now let us consider what happens as we change a coefficient of a term in the objective function.

1. If we change the coefficient on some x_j variable we relocate the center of the concentric circles. For example, in the previous objective function let us change the coefficient of x_1 from the value − 12 to − 18, to obtain the new objective

$$x_1^2 - 18x_1 + 36 + x_2^2 - 16x_2 + 64$$

Changing objective function coefficients

This can be rewritten as

$$(x_1 - 9)^2 + (x_2 - 8)^2 - 45$$

which shows that the center of the concentric circles is relocated from the point ($x_1 = 6, x_2 = 8$) to the point ($x_1 = 9, x_2 = 8$). This relocation also produces a new optimal solution.

2. Changing a coefficient on one of the x_j^2 terms in the previous objective function will change the shapes of the contours from circles to ellipses.

Rather than dwelling on this more complicated geometry, it should already be apparent that, in contrast to LP:

No objective function coefficient range analysis

- In general, for a QP problem, for a coefficient in the objective function, it is not possible to give a range of values such that the optimal solution does not change.

This completes the general discussion of quadratic programming. In the next section we turn to a specific application.

8.14 Portfolio Selection

Portfolio selection is a fundamental problem in modern finance. In reality there are enough aspects to portfolio analysis to fill up a book, and indeed volumes have been written on the topic. Our discussion will provide only a brief glimpse into this fascinating practice.

The Problem

The problem of **portfolio analysis** can be stated as follows: An investor has P dollars to invest in a set of n stocks and would like to know how much to invest in each stock. The chosen collection is called the investor's portfolio. The investor has conflicting goals: He or she would like a portfolio with both a large expected return and a small risk. These goals are conflicting because most often, in the real world, portfolios with high expected return also have high risk.

High expected return = high risk

Here is an example of what we mean by the term *return.* Suppose an investment of D_i dollars is put into asset i and suppose that over some specified time period this D_i dollars grows to $1.3D_i$. Then we would say that the *return* over that period is $(1.3D_i - D_i)/D_i = 0.3$. The concept of risk is more subtle and more difficult to elaborate on. For the purpose of this discussion we will assume that *risk is measured by the variance of the return on the portfolio.* Actually, this is consistent with the way that most portfolio analysts would measure risk.

Now, since the portfolio manager seeks low risk and high expected return, one way to frame the problem is to minimize the variance of the return (i.e., minimize risk) subject to a lower bound on expected return. There may also be some constraints on the proportion of the portfolio devoted to particular individual stocks.

Formulating the Portfolio Model

This problem turns out to be a quadratic programming problem. In formulating this model, one can let x_i be the proportion of the portfolio invested in stock i. For example, in a two-stock model if we had P dollars to invest and if the optimal solution were $x_1 = 0.7$ and $x_2 = 0.3$ we would then invest a total of $0.7\,P$ dollars in stock 1, and the remaining $0.3P$ dollars would go to stock 2.

Let us now write out the general model for a two-asset problem. We shall use the following notation:

σ_i^2 = variance of yearly returns from stock, i, $i = 1, 2$

σ_{12} = covariance of yearly returns from stocks 1 and 2

R_i = expected yearly return from stock i, $i = 1, 2$

G = lower bound on expected yearly return from total investment

S_i = upper bound on investment in stock i, $i = 1, 2$

For the present purposes we simply accept the following facts:

1. The ***variance*** *of the yearly returns from stock i* is a number describing the "variability" of these returns from year to year. This will be made more precise in the next section.
2. The ***covariance*** *of the yearly returns from stocks 1 and 2* is a number that describes the extent to which the returns of the two stocks move up or down together. This also will be made more precise in the next section.
3. The *expected return of the portfolio* is defined as the number $x_1R_1 + x_2R_2$.
4. The *variance of the return of the portfolio* is defined as the number $\sigma_1^2 x_1^2 + 2\sigma_{12}x_1x_2 + \sigma_2^2x_2^2$.
5. The ***standard deviation*** of the return of the portfolio is defined as the square root of the variance.

From these definitions it follows that, for the two-stock example, the portfolio problem takes the form

The formal portfolio model—two assets

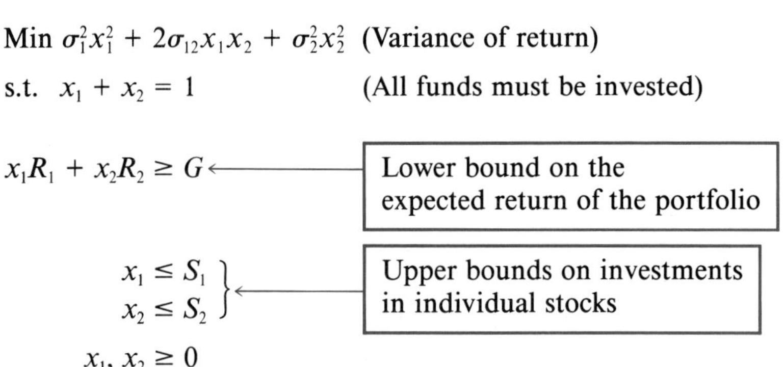

Min $\sigma_1^2 x_1^2 + 2\sigma_{12}x_1x_2 + \sigma_2^2 x_2^2$ (Variance of return)
s.t. $x_1 + x_2 = 1$ (All funds must be invested)
$x_1R_1 + x_2R_2 \geq G$
Lower bound on the expected return of the portfolio
$x_1 \leq S_1$
$x_2 \leq S_2$
Upper bounds on investments in individual stocks
$x_1, x_2 \geq 0$

To create a specific numerical example let

$\sigma_1^2 = 0.09$	$R_1 = 0.06$	$S_1 = 0.75$	$G = 0.03$
$\sigma_2^2 = 0.06$	$R_2 = 0.02$	$S_2 = 0.9$	$\sigma_{12} = 0.02$

The feasible set for this problem is shown in Figure 8.23, where for convenience the objective function and both sides of row 3 have been multiplied by 100. Because of the equality constraint ($x_1 + x_2 = 1$) the feasible set is the heavy line segment connecting the points (0.25, 0.75) and (0.75, 0.25). Each contour of the objective function is an ellipse with its center at the origin and its minor axis lying on a line that forms a 26.55° angle with the x_1 axis. The 2 and 4.54 contours are shown in Figure 8.23.

Note that as the value of the contour increases, the general shape of the ellipse remains the same, but it increases in size. The problem is to select the smallest value for the contour so that the ellipse just touches the feasible set. As indicated in Figure 8.23, the 4.54 contour touches the feasible set at the point ($x_1^* = 0.36$, $x_2^* = 0.64$) which is the optimal solution.

It is not important for you to know how to construct these contours. Real problems are after all solved with the computer, not graphically. The geometric representation, however, is a useful way to understand the model and is helpful in interpreting properties of the solution.

The GINO solution to the above example is shown in Figure 8.24. Note that

▼ FIGURE 8.23
The Portfolio Selection Problem

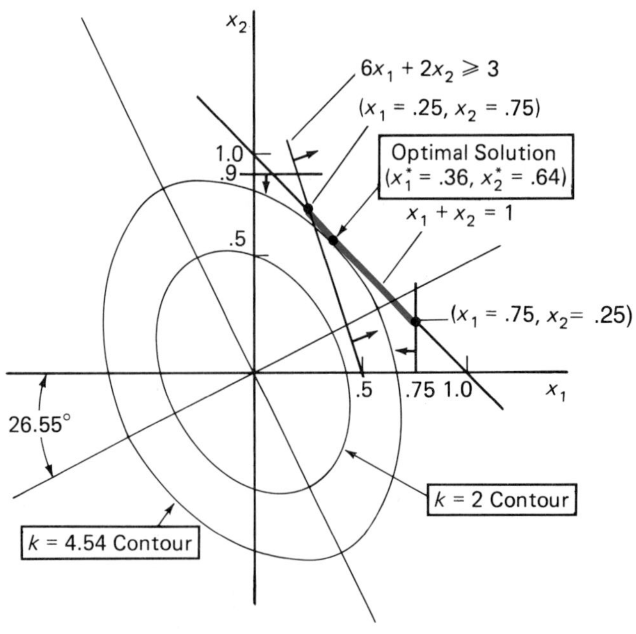

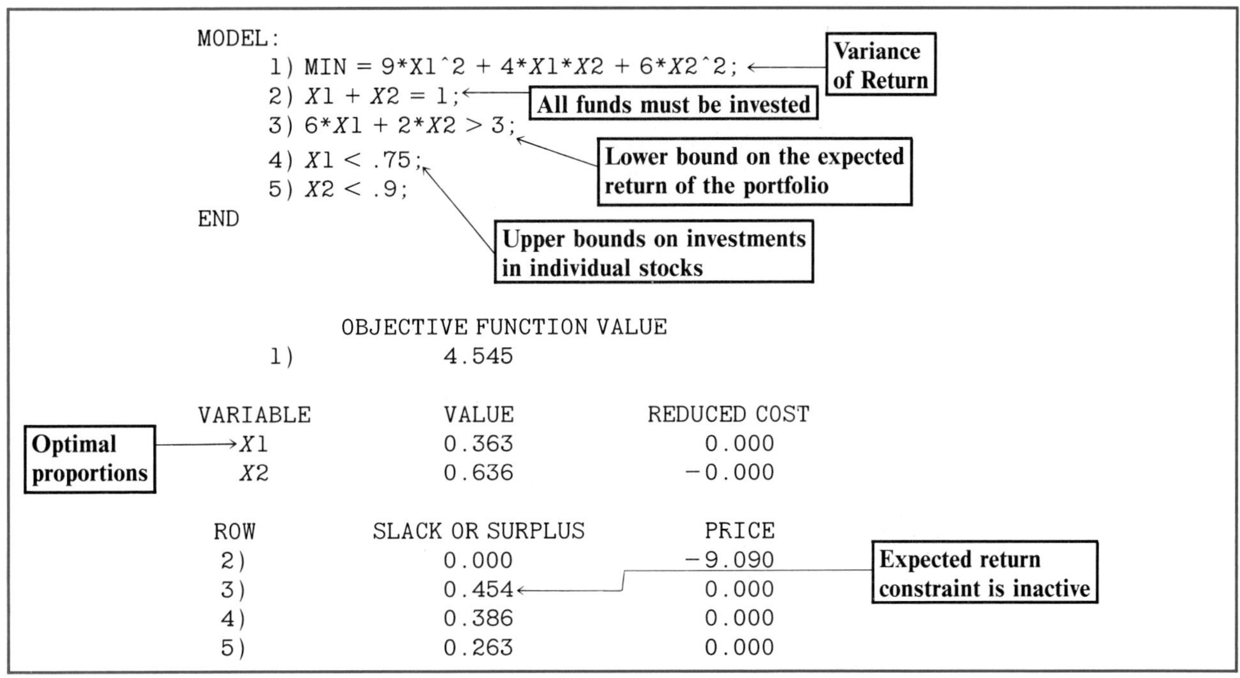

MODEL:
1) MIN = 9*X1^2 + 4*X1*X2 + 6*X2^2;
2) X1 + X2 = 1;
3) 6*X1 + 2*X2 > 3;
4) X1 < .75;
5) X2 < .9;
END
Variance of Return
All funds must be invested
Lower bound on the expected return of the portfolio
Upper bounds on investments in individual stocks
OBJECTIVE FUNCTION VALUE
1) 4.545
VARIABLE VALUE REDUCED COST
X1 0.363 0.000
X2 0.636 -0.000
Optimal proportions
ROW SLACK OR SURPLUS PRICE
2) 0.000 -9.090
3) 0.454 0.000
4) 0.386 0.000
5) 0.263 0.000
Expected return constraint is inactive

▲ FIGURE 8.24
GINO Solution to the Portfolio Selection Problem

only the first constraint (Row 2) is binding. This, of course, was seen in the geometric representation in Figure 8.23. Since the slack in the expected return constraint (Row 3) is 0.454, we know that the expected return from this portfolio is 3.454. Comparing the optimal values of x_1^* and x_2^*, we see that the optimal portfolio contains more of the security with the lower expected yearly return (i.e., security 2). The reason is that the variance of security 2 is lower than that of security 1. The optimal mix is one that minimizes the portfolio variance while guaranteeing an expected portfolio return of at least 3%.

▶ 8.15 A Portfolio Example with Live Data

In this section we turn to a three-asset example. Actual data will be used to estimate the parameters in the model. The problem will then be solved by computer, and we will discuss the solution.

Formulating the Model

In this section the three assets will be designated, at the outset, as *x*, *y*, and *z*. Let

$$X = \text{fraction of asset } x \text{ in the portfolio}$$

$$Y = \text{fraction of asset } y \text{ in the portfolio}$$

$$Z = \text{fraction of asset } z \text{ in the portfolio}$$

The terminology "asset *i*" will be used to refer to asset *x*, or asset *y*, or asset *z*. In the previous sections the portfolio model was presented as if the parameters that describe the distribution of future returns were known, i.e., it was assumed that the expected returns, variances, and covariances were known. In the real world these parameters must be estimated with historical data. In general if n periods (years) of data are available, there will be, for each asset i, an actual historical return R_i^t associated with each period t where t ranges from 1 to n. In other words, each asset will have n historical returns. The expected periodic return from asset i is estimated with $\bar{R}_i = \frac{1}{n}\sum_{t=1}^{n} R_i^t$, which is the average of the asset's historical returns. The periodic historical returns R_i^t, are also used to estimate variances and covariances. The appropriate formulas are

$$\text{estimate of the variance of return for asset } i = \frac{1}{n}\sum_{t=1}^{n}(R_i^t - \bar{R}_i)^2$$

$$\text{estimate of the covariance of returns for assets } i \text{ and } j = \frac{1}{n}\sum_{t=1}^{n}(R_i^t - \bar{R}_i)(R_j^t - \bar{R}_j)$$

As before, we also define

G = lower bound on expected return of the portfolio

S_i = upper bound on the fraction of asset i that can be in the portfolio

In terms of the parameters, the quadratic programming formulation of the three-asset problem is

The formal portfolio model—three assets

$$\text{Min } \sigma_x^2X^2 + \sigma_y^2Y^2 + \sigma_z^2Z^2 + 2\sigma_{xy}XY + 2\sigma_{xz}XZ + 2\sigma_{yz}YZ \qquad \text{quadratic objective}$$

$$\left.\begin{aligned} \text{s.t. } R_xX + R_yY + R_zZ &\geq G \\ X + Y + Z &= 1 \\ X &\leq S_x \\ Y &\leq S_y \\ Z &\leq S_z \end{aligned}\right\} \text{feasible region is same as in LP}$$

$$X, Y, Z \geq 0$$

The objective function is the variance of the portfolio return, which, as stated in Section 8.14, is commonly considered to be the risk of the portfolio. (The rationale for this definition of risk, as well as the derivation of the objective function, is in the domain of statistics and is beyond our scope.) The first constraint expresses the lower bound on the expected return of the portfolio. The second constraint says that the fractions add to one, and the remaining constraints are upper bounds.

When a portfolio is allowed to be constructed from more than three assets the expected return is defined to be $\sum_{i=1}^{n} X_iR_i$. As before, R_i is the expected return from asset i, and X_i is the fraction of asset i in the portfolio. In this general case of N assets, the variance of the return of the portfolio is defined as[4]

$$\sum_{i=1}^{N} X_i^2\sigma_i^2 + 2\sum_{i=1}^{N-1}\sum_{j=i+1}^{N} X_iX_j\sigma_{ij}$$

[4]In matrix notation the variance of the portfolio return is written as X^TYX, where X is the vector $(X_1, \ldots, X_N)$ and Y denotes the symmetric "covariance matrix" whose (i, j)th entry is σ_{ij} (and where $\sigma_{ii} = \sigma_i^2$).

Computer Solution

After numerical estimates are substituted for the parameters, this quadratic programming problem can be solved with GINO. As a specific example let us now consider three stocks and historical returns from 1943 to 1954. The three stocks chosen are AT&T, General Motors, and US Steel. The returns for 1943–1954 are (data from H. M. Markowitz, *Portfolio Selection,* Yale University Press, 1959)

Actual returns

ROW	AT&T	GM	USS
1	0.300	0.225	0.149
2	0.103	0.290	0.260
3	0.216	0.216	0.419
4	−0.046	−0.272	−0.078
5	−0.071	0.144	0.169
6	0.056	0.107	−0.035
7	0.038	0.321	0.133
8	0.089	0.305	0.732
9	0.090	0.195	0.021
10	0.083	0.390	0.131
11	0.035	−0.072	0.006
12	0.176	0.715	0.908

Definition of return

In this table the return in year n is defined by

$$\frac{(\text{closing price, } n) - (\text{closing price, } n-1) + (\text{dividends, } n)}{(\text{closing price, } n-1)}$$

where closing prices and dividends are expressed in dollars per share.[5]

Next, we meet the covariance matrix. Using the above estimation formulas, the result of the calculations is

Estimated variances and covariances

	AT&T	GM	USS
AT&T	0.0108075		
GM	0.0124072	0.0583917	
USS	0.0130751	0.0554264	0.0942268

Finally, we need to calculate the average return for each stock. The result is

Average returns

STOCK	AVERAGE RETURN
AT&T	0.089083
GM	0.213667
USS	0.234583

[5]Note the following unsatisfactory implication of averaging this definition: Suppose there are no dividends, that in year 1 the stock goes from 1.0 to 1.5 (with a return of 0.5) and in year 2 the stock goes from 1.5 to 1 (with a return of −0.33). The average 2-year return is 0.17/2. Would you agree? This shows that estimating expected returns (and covariances) can be a delicate issue. It should be emphasized that this illustration is very introductory in nature.

Now suppose that you wish to minimize the variance of the return of the portfolio, subject to a 15% expected return and a restriction that no more than 75% of the portfolio can be in any individual stock. The quadratic program of interest and GINO solution are given below:

Computer solution to three-asset model

```
MODEL:
   1) MIN = 0.0108075*X^2 + 0.0583917*Y^2 + 0.0942268*Z^2 +
      + 0.0248144*X*Y + 0.0261502*X*Z + 0.1108528*Y*Z;
   2) 0.089*X + 0.21*Y + 0.23*Z > 0.15;
   3) X + Y + Z = 1;
   4) X < 0.75;
   5) Y < 0.75;
   6) Z < 0.75;
END

           OBJECTIVE FUNCTION VALUE

       1)          0.023107

VARIABLE           VALUE           REDUCED COST
       X          0.514878             0.000000
       Y          0.368962             0.000000
       Z          0.116060             0.000000

     ROW     SLACK OR SURPLUS              PRICE
      2)          0.000000            -0.375298
      3)         -0.000100             0.010082
      4)          0.235122             0.000000
      5)          0.381038             0.000000
      6)          0.633940             0.000000
```

Note that the solution to the above problem specifies a portfolio of 51.5% ATT, 36.9% GM, and 11.6% US Steel. Since row 2 is active, the expected yearly return is exactly 15%. The optimal objective value indicates that the variance of yearly return is about 0.023, which means the standard deviation is $\sqrt{0.023} = 15\%$. If in 1955 one had believed in the validity of this model, and if one had further assumed (in addition to the validity of the model) that the portfolio returns are normally distributed with mean 15% and standard deviation of 15%, then according to statistical theory one might reasonably have expected that such a portfolio, in 1955 and ensuing years, would have produced returns roughly between −15% and +45%. In fact, the returns in 1955–57 for the three assets were

	1955	1956	1957
AT&T	.103	.039	.030
GM	.512	−0.50	−.200
USS	.647	.322	−.266

Hence, using the above optimal fractions, the portfolio returns would have been

1955	1956	1957
31.7%	3.9%	−8.9%

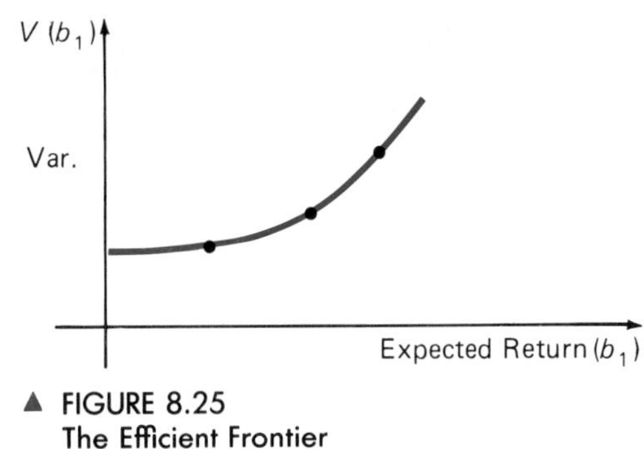

▲ FIGURE 8.25
The Efficient Frontier

In concluding this section, we observe that the dual price on row 2 indicates that a 1% increase in expected return (an increase of 0.01 in the RHS of row 2) would lead to *roughly* an *increase* of 0.00375 in variance (i.e., since increasing the RHS of row 2 will hurt the OV, and since we have a Min model, the OV will increase). Hence the new variance would be about 0.0268, with the standard deviation equal to $\sqrt{0.268} = 16\%$. These numbers are approximate because for a nonlinear program the slopes of $V(b_1)$ are instantaneous (rather than constant in intervals as is the case with LP). This fact was discussed in terms of a general quadratic program in Section 8.13. For the portfolio model, it is reflected by the general shape for $V(b_1)$ as shown in Figure 8.25. (Note that the graph shows that tightening the constraint—i.e., increasing b_1—hurts the OV more and more.)

In the language of finance, this graph is called the **efficient frontier,** and its properties are studied in finance courses. For our purposes we merely observe that it is a piecewise quadratic convex function. To find any point on the graph of this function, one simply selects a value for the RHS of the constraint that sets a lower bound on the expected return (the first constraint), and solves the problem.

Key Terms

Integer Linear Program (ILP). A problem that satisfies all the conditions of a linear program except that some or all of the variables are required to be integers. (*p. 335*)

Rounded Solution. A feasible solution to an ILP found by solving the LP relaxation and rounding each of the integer variables either up or down. (*p. 335*)

All-Integer Linear Program. An integer linear program in which all the decision variables are required to be integers. (*p. 337*)

Mixed Integer Linear Program (MILP). An integer linear program in which only some of the variables are required to be integers. (*p. 337*)

Binary (0–1) Integer Linear Program. An integer linear program in which all the decision variables are required to be either 0 or 1. (*p. 337*)

LP Relaxation. An LP problem that is derived from an ILP by ignoring the integrality constraints. (*p. 337*)

Optimal Value. Short for the optimal value of the objective function. (*p. 340*)

Complete Enumeration. Solving an ILP by listing all the feasible points, evaluating the objective function at each of them, and selecting the best solution. (*p. 341*)

Branch and Bound. A solution technique used on ILPs based on dividing the original problem into mutually exclusive parts and employing the OV from the LP relaxations to obtain bounds. (*p. 351*).

Quadratic Programs. Problems that maximize or minimize the value of a quadratic objective function subject to linear constraints and nonnegativity conditions. (*p. 364*)

Portfolio Analysis. The problem of minimizing the variance of return subject to a requirement on expected return. (*p. 371*)

Variance. A statistical measure of risk. (*p. 371*)

Covariance. A statistical measure of the extent to which random quantities are correlated. (*p. 371*)

Standard Deviation. The square root of variance. (*p. 371*)

Efficient Frontier. The OV function of a portfolio analysis QP. (*p. 377*)

Major Concepts Quiz

Part 1. Integer Programming Questions

True–False

1. T F Rounding LP solutions to meet the real-world requirement for integer decision variables is a common practice.

2. T F In general, it is no more difficult to solve an IP than an LP.

3. T F The binary variable in an IP may be used to represent dichotomous decisions.

4. T F In a *Max* problem, the OV of the LP relaxation always provides a *lower bound* on the OV of the original ILP or MILP.

5. T F The first step in obtaining a rounded solution to an MILP is to solve its LP relaxation.

6. T F Solving an ILP by complete enumeration involves evaluating the objective function at all corners of the feasible set of the LP relaxation.

7. T F In the LP relaxation of the ILP capital budgeting problem there are as many constraints as there are periods.

8. T F In an ILP with n binary decision variables, each of which indicates the selection (or not) of an alternative, the condition that no more than k alternatives be selected can be imposed with the constraint $x_1 + x_2 + \cdots x_n \le k$.

9. T F In Steco's warehouse location problem, the optimal number of trucks to send from each warehouse to each plant was an integer because after the warehouses are selected the problem is a transportation problem with integer supplies and demands.

10. T F Suppose x_1 and x_2 are both binary variables where $x_i = 1$ has the interpretation of building a plant in location i. The condition "a plant can be built in location 2 only if the plant in location 1 is also built" is captured with the constraint $x_1 \le x_2$.

11. T F Consider a transportation model with integer supplies and demands and where, in addition, integrality conditions are imposed on the x_{ij}'s. Since this makes the problem an integer program, it must be solved with special IP codes.

Multiple Choice

12. In an ILP
- **a.** ignoring integrality restrictions, all constraint functions are linear
- **b.** all decision variables must be integers
- **c.** all decision variables must be nonnegative
- **d.** all of the above

13. In an MILP
- **a.** the objective function is linear
- **b.** all decision variables must be integers
- **c.** some coefficients are restricted to be integers, others are not
- **d.** all of the above

14. The LP relaxation of an ILP
- **a.** permits a nonlinear objective function
- **b.** ignores the integrality restrictions on the decision variables
- **c.** relaxes the nonnegativity restrictions on the decision variables
- **d.** all of the above

15. A rounded solution to a Max ILP may not be feasible because
- **a.** it violates the integrality constraints
- **b.** it violates the nonnegativity constraints

c. its OV is smaller than the OV of the LP relaxation
d. none of the above

16. If x_k and x_m are 0–1 variables (the value 1 meaning select) for projects k and m, respectively, the constraint $x_k + x_m \leq 0$ implies that
a. k cannot be selected unless m is selected
b. k must be selected if m is selected
c. m cannot be selected unless k is selected
d. none of the above

17. Suppose a product can be manufactured either not at all or else in lot sizes $\geq L$, and let x be the quantity of the product produced. The following two constraints are appropriate:
a. $x + Uy \leq 0; x - Ly \geq 0$
b. $x - Uy \geq 0; x - Ly \geq 0$
c. $x - Uy \leq 0; x - Ly \geq 0$
d. $x - Uy \leq 0; x - Ly \leq 0$
where U is an arbitrarily large number and y is a 0–1 variable.

18. In solving a Max ILP a lower bound for the OV of the original problem can always be found by
a. solving the LP relaxation of the ILP and using the OV of the LP
b. finding a feasible solution to the ILP by any available means and evaluating the objective function
c. solving the LP relaxation and then rounding fractions <0.5 down, those ≥0.5 up, and evaluating the objective function at this point
d. none of the above

19. In the branch-and-bound approach to a Max ILP, a node is terminated when
a. its $U < CBLB$
b. the LP relaxation is infeasible
c. the LP relaxation provides a solution to the integer problem represented by that node
d. any of the above

20. The computer solution to an MILP
a. contains no sensitivity information
b. contains sensitivity information on only the noninteger variables
c. contains sensitivity information on only right-hand sides
d. contains sensitivity information on only the objective function

More-Challenging Questions. The next 10 questions are based on the following problem:

A firm has 10 outlets that must be supplied with a certain product. The demands (all positive) at the outlets are $d_1, \ldots, d_{10}$, and these demands must be *exactly* satisfied (i.e., d_i units must be distributed to outlet i). The firm may supply these demands by having a supplier deliver directly to each outlet. The supplier charges $50 for each unit delivered, independent of the outlet location. The supplier would charge only $35 per unit for any location if the location would order at least D units. Since each of the $d_i < D$, the firm can make no use of the discount. The firm is considering leasing a centrally located warehouse for $K > 0$ dollars and using this warehouse as an intermediary depot. The depot could order any quantity and could distribute to any number of outlets. It has been agreed that the depot would pay the same as the outlets ($50 per unit if $< D$ units are ordered; $35 per unit if the total order is at least D units).

The cost of sending a unit from the warehouse to outlet i is $C_i > 0$, $i = 1, \ldots, 10$. Assume that $D < \sum_{i=i}^{10} d_i$. Management would like to know

1. Should the warehouse be leased?
2. If so, which outlets should be served by the warehouse and which should be supplied directly by the supplier?

In formulating a model to answer these questions, let

x_i = quantity sent directly from supplier to location i

y_i = quantity sent from warehouse to location i

z = quantity sent from supplier to warehouse

A correct set of constraints for this model is

$$x_i + y_i = d_i, \qquad i = 1, \ldots, 10$$

$$\sum_{i=1}^{10} y_i - z \le 0$$

$$z - tD \ge 0$$

$$z - t\sum_{i=1}^{10} d_i \le 0$$

$$x_i,\ y_i \ge 0 \ (i = 1, \ldots, 10); \qquad z \ge 0; \qquad t = 0 \text{ or } 1$$

21. The correct objective function is

a. Min $\sum_{i=1}^{10} 50x_i + \sum_{i=1}^{10} C_i y_i$

b. Min $\sum_{i=1}^{10} 50x_i + \sum_{i=1}^{10} (C_i + 35)y_i + tK$

c. Min $\sum_{i=1}^{10} 50x_i + 35z + \sum_{i=1}^{10} C_i y_i + tK$

d. Min $\sum_{i=1}^{10} (50x_i + C_i y_i) + 35D$

e. none of the above

22. For the problem as stated, there will never be an optimal solution in which the depot orders a positive amount that is less than D units.

a. T

b. F

23. Management should lease the warehouse if

a. the optimal value of D is positive

b. the optimal value of t is positive

c. the optimal value of z is positive

d. all of the above

e. b and c

24. Consider location k such that $35 + C_k > 50$. Since the marginal cost of shipping directly to k from the supplier is less than the marginal cost of going through the warehouse, there will be no optimal solution in which this outlet (the kth) receives products both from the warehouse and directly from the supplier.

a. T

b. F

25. There always will exist an optimal solution in which no outlet receives deliveries from both the supplier (directly) and the warehouse.

a. T

b. F

26. Suppose $35 + C_i = 50$, $i = 1, \ldots, 10$. Then $t^* = 0$ in any optimal solution.

a. T

b. F

27. This model may have an optimal solution in which the total quantity ordered from the supplier exceeds $\sum_{i=1}^{10} d_i$.
    a. T
    b. F

28. If the optimal value $z^* = \sum_{i=1}^{10} d_i$, then it is certain that the optimal solution will be $x_i^* = 0$, $i = 1, \ldots, 10$, $y_i^* = d_i$, $i = 1, \ldots, 10$, and $t^* = 1$.
    a. T
    b. F

29. This model will allow the possibility of having inventory left at the warehouse after all demands are satisfied.
    a. T
    b. F

30. Suppose each $C_i \geq 15$.
    a. Then the optimal solution to the model is obviously $x_i^* = d_i$, $y_i^* = 0$, $i = 1, \ldots, 10$, $z^* = 0 = t^*$.
    b. For some values of the parameters d_i the solution may differ, and hence it is wisest to run the model.

Part 2. Quadratic Programming Questions

True–False

31. **T F** A quadratic programming program may have quadratic constraint functions.
32. **T F** Maximizing or minimizing any nonlinear objective function subject to a set of linear equality and inequality constraints, as well as nonnegativity conditions on the values of the decision variables, is a quadratic programming problem.
33. **T F** Any LP problem can be solved with a QP code.
34. **T F** It is not possible to characterize extreme points of the feasible region of a QP.
35. **T F** The optimal solution to a QP problem need not be a corner solution.
36. **T F** The optimal solution to a QP problem must include at least as many positive variables as there are constraints.
37. **T F** Loosening a constraint in a QP either will not change or will improve the OV.
38. **T F** In a Max problem the rate of improvement of OV is the negative of the rate of change.
39. **T F** The slope of the tangent to the graph of the function OV(R) at the point ($\hat{R}$, OV ($\hat{R}$)) is the rate of change in the function OV(R) at $R = \hat{R}$.
40. **T F** Changing a coefficient of a term in the objective function of a QP always changes the optimal solution.
41. **T F** The variance of the return from a portfolio is a linear function of the amount invested in each stock in the portfolio.
42. **T F** If there are three stocks in the portfolio, the feasible region will lie on a plane.
43. **T F** The portfolio problem includes a lower bound on the expected return. In general this constraint need not be binding.

Multiple Choice

44. The definition of a QP problem does not include
    a. nonnegativity conditions
    b. quadratic constraint functions
    c. linear equality constraints
    d. nonlinear terms in the objective function

45. In a QP problem in n variables ($x_1, \ldots x_n$), the objective function may not include terms of the form
   a. x_j^2
   b. $x_i x_j$
   c. $x_i^2 \cdot x_j$
   d. $9x_i$

46. An LP is a special case of a QP because
   a. the LP feasible region is a special case of a QP feasible region
   b. the LP constraint functions are a special case of the QP constraint functions
   c. nonnegativity conditions are special to an LP
   d. the LP objective function is a special case of the QP objective function

47. The optimal solution to a QP problem with n constraints may not have
   a. negative values for some decision variables
   b. more than n positive decision variables
   c. fewer than n positive decision variables
   d. zero values for some decision variables

48. The optimal solution to a QP problem
   a. must lie on a corner of the feasible set
   b. cannot be on a corner of the feasible set
   c. is always nondegenerate
   d. none of the above

49. In the optimal solution for a QP problem, slack and surplus variables
   a. have no meaning even though they appear on the computer solution
   b. have the same meaning as in an LP problem
   c. have a different meaning than in an LP problem
   d. are unrestricted in sign

50. GINO can be used to solve
   a. general nonlinear programming problems
   b. QPs
   c. LPs
   d. all of the above

51. Loosening a constraint in a portfolio problem
   a. must increase the dual price on that constraint
   b. must decrease the dual price on that constraint
   c. may change the sign of the dual price on that constraint
   d. cannot increase the objective function

Answers

1. T
2. F
3. T
4. F
5. T
6. F
7. F
8. T
9. T
10. F
11. F
12. d
13. a
14. b
15. d
16. d
17. c
18. b
19. d
20. a
21. c
22. T
23. e
24. F
25. F
26. T
27. T
28. T
29. T
30. a
31. F
32. F
33. T
34. F
35. T
36. F
37. T
38. F
39. T
40. F
41. F
42. T
43. T
44. b
45. c
46. d
47. a
48. d
49. b
50. d
51. d

Problems

Part 1. Integer Programming Problems

(a) See IM
(b) A=1.25, C=5.5, OV=17.75
(c) A=2, C=5, OV=17
(d) A=1, C=5, OV=16; feasible
(e) $1

8-1. ▲ A firm produces two products, A and C. Capacity on the A line is 7 units per day. Each unit of C requires 4 hours of drying time, and a total of 22 drying hours per day is available. Also, each unit of A requires 2 hours of polishing, and each unit of C requires 3 hours of polishing. A total of 19 hours of polishing time is available each day. Each unit of A yields a profit of $1, whereas each unit of C yields a profit of $3. The firm wants to determine a daily production schedule to maximize profits. A and C can be produced only in integer amounts.

(a) Formulate this problem as an ILP.
(b) Use a graphical approach to find the optimal solution to the LP relaxation.
(c) Find the optimal solution to the ILP.
(d) Find an integer solution by rounding each value in the answer to part (b) to its integer part. Is this solution feasible?
(e) How much profit would the firm lose by adopting the latter rounded solution?

(a) x_1=3.5, x_2=4.5, OV=12.5
(b) 29
(c) x_1=2, x_2=5, OV=12
(d) x_1=3, x_2=4, OV=11; No

8-2. ▲ Consider the following ILP:

$$\begin{aligned} \text{Max } & x_1 + 2x_2 \\ \text{s.t. } & 3x_1 + x_2 \le 15 \\ & 3x_1 + 7x_2 \le 42 \\ & x_1, x_2 \ge 0 \text{ and integer} \end{aligned}$$

(a) Use a graphical approach to find the optimal solution to the LP relaxation.
(b) How many feasible points are there?
(c) Using a graphical approach, find the optimal solution to the ILP.
(d) Find an integer feasible solution by rounding the answer to part (a). Is the rounded solution optimal?

Lower bound (See IM)

8-3. ▲ Consider a minimization ILP. Does the optimal value for the LP relaxation provide an upper or a lower bound for the optimal value of the ILP? Explain your answer.

Upper bound (See IM)

8-4. ▲ Consider a minimization ILP. Does the value of the objective function at a feasible rounded solution provide an upper or a lower bound for the optimal value of the ILP? Explain your answer.

Upper bound (See IM)

8-5. ▲ Consider a maximization ILP. Does the optimal value of the LP relaxation of this problem provide an upper or a lower bound for the optimal value of the ILP? Explain your answer.

Lower bound (See IM)

8-6. ▲ Consider a maximization ILP. Does the value of the objective function at a feasible rounded solution provide an upper or a lower bound for the optimal value of the ILP? Explain your answer.

x_i = $ in stock i
y_i = 1 if investing in stock i
(See IM)

8-7. ▲ *Investment Problem* A portfolio manager has just been given $100,000 to invest. She will choose her investments from a list of 20 stocks. She knows that the net return from investing one dollar in stock i is r_i. (Thus, if she invests x_i dollars in stock i she will end up with $[1 + r_i]x_i$ dollars.) In order to maintain a balanced portfolio, she adopts the following two rules of thumb:

1. She will not invest more than $20,000 in a single stock.
2. *If* she invests anything in a stock, she will invest at least $5000 in it.

The manager would like to maximize her return subject to these rules of thumb. Formulate this problem as an MILP. Define your decision variables carefully.

Problems 8-8, 8-9, 8-10, 8-18, 8-20, and 8-21 call for formulation only, but once formulated may be solved with QSB+ or LINDO.

x_{ij} = 1 if flight from i in time j
y_j = number of planes for time j
(See IM)

8-8. ▲▲ *Airline Scheduling* Alpha Airline wishes to schedule no more than one flight out of Chicago to each of the following cities: Columbus, Denver, Los Angeles, and New York. The available departure slots are 8 A.M., 10 A.M., and 12 noon. Alpha leases the airplanes at the cost of $5000 before and including 10 A.M. and $3000 after 10 A.M., and is able to lease at most two per departure slot. Also, if a flight leaves for New York in a time slot, there must be a flight leaving for Los Angeles in the same time slot. The expected profit contribution before rental costs per flight is shown in Figure 8.26. Formulate a model for a profit-maximizing schedule. Define your decision variables carefully.

	TIME SLOT		
	8	**10**	**12**
Columbus	10	6	6
Denver	9	10	9
Los Angeles	14	11	10
New York	18	15	10

▲ FIGURE 8.26
Expected Profit Contribution ($000)

x_{ij} = megawatts produced by generator i in period j
y_i = 1 if generator i is started
(See IM)

8-9. ▲▲ *A Startup Problem* A problem faced by an electrical utility each day is that of deciding which generators to start up. The utility in question has three generators with the characteristics shown in Figure 8.27. There are two periods in a day, and the number of megawatts needed in the first period is 2900. The second period requires 3900 megawatts. A generator started in the first period may be used in the second period without incurring an additional startup cost. All major generators (e.g., A, B, and C) are turned off at the end of each day. Formulate this problem as an MILP. Define your decision variables carefully.

GENERATOR	FIXED STARTUP COST ($)	COST PER PERIOD PER MEGAWATT USED ($)	MAXIMUM CAPACITY IN EACH PERIOD (MW)
A	3000	5	2100
B	2000	4	1800
C	1000	7	3000

▲ FIGURE 8.27

(See IM)

8-10. ▲▲ *Production Planning* A certain production line makes two products. Relevant data are given in Figure 8.28. Total time available (for production and setup) each week is 80 hours. The firm has no inventory of either product at the start of week 1 and no inventory is allowed at the end of week 4. The cost of carrying a unit of inventory from one week to the next is $4 for each product. One unit of unsatisfied demand costs $10 for product A and $15 for product B. Demand data are given in Figure 8.29. The line is shut down and cleaned each weekend. As a result, if a product is produced in a week the appropriate setup time cost is incurred. Only one product can be produced during a week. No production can take place during the time that the line is being set up. Formulate this 4-week planning problem as an MILP. The objective is to maximize the profit over a 4-week period. Define your notation carefully and use summation notation in your formulation.

	PRODUCT	
	A	B
Setup Time	5 hours	10 hours
Per Unit Production Time	0.5 hours	0.75 hour
Setup Cost	\$200	\$400
Per Unit Production Cost	\$10	\$15
Selling Price	\$20	\$30

▲ FIGURE 8.28

	WEEK			
PRODUCT	1	2	3	4
A	80	100	75	80
B	15	20	50	30

▲ FIGURE 8.29

$y_i = 1$ if board accepts investment i
(See IM)

8-11. ▲▲ The board of directors of a large manufacturing firm is considering the set of investments shown in Figure 8.30. Let R_i be the total revenue from investment i and C_i be the cost to make investment i. The board wishes to maximize total revenue and invest no more than a total of M dollars. Formulate this problem as an ILP. Define your decision variables.

INVESTMENT	CONDITION
1	None
2	Only if 1
3	Only if 2
4	Must if 1 *and* 2
5	Not if 1 *or* 2
6	Not if 2 *and* 3
7	Only if 2 *and not* 3

▲ FIGURE 8.30

x_{ij} = amount shipped from warehouse i to retailer j
$y_i = 1$ if warehouse i is used
(See IM)

8-12. ▲▲ A distribution company wants to minimize the cost of transporting goods from its warehouses A, B, and C to the retail outlets 1, 2, and 3. The costs for transporting one unit from warehouse to retailer is given by the following table.

▼ FIGURE 8.31

	RETAILER		
WAREHOUSE	1	2	3
A	15	32	21
B	9	7	6
C	11	18	5
Demand	200	150	175

The fixed cost of operating a warehouse is \$500 for A, \$750 for B, and \$600 for C, and at least two of them have to be open. The warehouses can be assumed to have unlimited storage capacity. Write an ILP to decide which warehouses should be opened and the amount to be shipped from each warehouse to each retailer.

$x_1=0$, $x_2=6$ or $x_1=2$, $x_2=5$; OV=12 (See IM)

8-13. ▲▲ Use a graphical approach and the branch-and-bound algorithm to solve the ILP presented in Problem 8-1. Branch first on A, present each new problem in the process together with its solution, and express the analysis in a decision diagram.

$x_1=4$, $x_2=3$, OV=7 (See IM)

8-14. ▲▲ Use a graphical approach and the branch-and-bound algorithm to solve the ILP presented in Problem 8-2. Branch first on x_1. For each new problem state what constraint you would add to what problem to create the new problem; for example, a phrase like "Add constraint $x_1 \leq 2$ to Problem 1." Express the analysis in a decision diagram like those in the text.

(See IM)

8-15. ▲▲ Consider the following formulation of Problem 8-1:

$$\begin{aligned} \text{Max } & A + 3C \\ \text{s.t. } & A \leq 7 \\ & 4C \leq 22 \\ & 2A + 3C \leq 19 \\ & A \geq 0 \text{ and integer}, \quad C \geq 0 \text{ and integer} \end{aligned}$$

Plot the optimal objective value as a function of the RHS of the second constraint as the value of the RHS ranges between 0 and 24.

HINT: Use the graphical approach and the figure prepared in the solution to Problem 8-1.

(See IM)

8-16. ▲▲ Consider the ILP presented in Problem 8-2. Plot the optimal objective value as a function of the RHS of the constraint

$$3x_1 + x_2 \leq \text{RHS}$$

for $0 \leq \text{RHS} \leq 24$.

(a) $x_1=\frac{8}{3}$, $x_2=\frac{5}{3}$, OV=$\frac{57}{3}$
(b) See IM
(c) $x_1=4$, $x_2=1$, OV=21
(d) $x_1=3$, $x_2=2$, OV=22
(e) No
(f) 1

8-17. ▲ Consider the following ILP:

$$\begin{aligned} \text{Min } & 4x_1 + 5x_2 \\ \text{s.t. } & 3x_1 + 6x_2 \geq 18 \\ & 5x_1 + 4x_2 \geq 20 \\ & 8x_1 + 2x_2 \geq 16 \\ & 7x_1 + 6x_2 \leq 42 \\ & x_1 \geq 0 \text{ and integer}, \quad x_2 \geq 0 \text{ and integer} \end{aligned}$$

(a) Find the optimal solution to the LP relaxation.
(b) List all the feasible points.
(c) Find the optimal solution to the ILP.
(d) Find a feasible rounded solution.
(e) Is (d) optimal?
(f) How large is the cost of using the rounded solution identified above relative to the optimal solution?

$A_i=1$ if operation A done on machine i, etc. (See IM)

8-18. ▲▲ *Line Balancing.* A job requires five operations, A, B, C, D and E, each of which can be done on either machine 1 or machine 2. The time taken for each operation on each of the given machines is given in the following table.

	A	B	C	D	E
Machine 1	5	9	2	3	4
Machine 2	3	4	7	5	4

Formulate an ILP to assign the jobs to the machines so that if T_1 is the total time taken on machine 1 and T_2 the time taken on machine 2, then Max (T_1, T_2) is minimized.

(See IM)

8-19. ▲▲ Consider the printout shown in Figure 8.9. Given the optimal values of YA, YB, and YC, write out the transportation model that the optimal truck allocations solve.

$A=1$ if fire station A open, etc.
(See IM)

8-20. ▲▲ The city council found that to service the city, fire stations have to be opened at either locations A, B, and C or locations A, C, and D or locations B, C, and D. The cost of opening a fire station (in millions of $) at location A is 1.5, at B is 2.3, at C is 1.8, and at D is 2.1. Formulate an ILP which will allow the city council to decide which fire stations should be opened so as to service the city at minimum cost.

(See IM)

8-21. ▲▲ *Capacity Expansion* An electric utility is planning the expansion of its generating capacity for the next five years. Its current capacity is 800 MW, but based on its forecast of demand it will require additional capacity as shown in Figure 8.32. The utility can increase its generating capacity by installing 10-, 50-, or 100-MW generators. The cost

YEAR	MINIMUM CAPACITY (MW)
1	880
2	960
3	1050
4	1160
5	1280

▲ FIGURE 8.32
Capacity Requirements

of installing a generator depends on its size and the year it is brought on line. See Figure 8.33. Once a generator is brought on line its capacity is available to meet demand in succeeding years. Formulate an ILP that minimizes the cost of bringing generators on line while satisfying the minimum capacity requirements. HINT: Let x_t, y_t, and z_t be the number of 10-, 50-, and 100-MW generators brought on line in year t and c_t the total capacity in year t after these generators have been brought on line.

GENERATOR SIZE MW	YEAR 1	2	3	4	5
10	300	250	208	173	145
50	670	558	465	387	322
100	950	791	659	549	458

▲ FIGURE 8.33
Cost of Bringing Generators on Line ($000)

More challenging IP formulations

(a) $B_1 + A_{12} + A_{14} \leq 1$
(b) $B_2 \leq A_{12} + A_{52} + A_{32}$
(c) $A_{21} + A_{41} \leq B_1$
(d) True
(e) True

8-22. ▲▲▲ Norco Home Cosmetics Sales is just moving into a six-county region of southern Utah. The map on page 388 shows the location of the counties and their populations, P_i. Norco plans to assign two salespersons to this region. The company assigns two counties to each salesperson, a base county and an adjacent county. Counties are adjacent if they share a common *side;* a common corner is *not* sufficient.

P_1 1	P_2 2	P_3 3
P_4 4	P_5 5	P_6 6

For example, in the map above, counties 1 and 2 are adjacent, but 1 and 5 are not. Norco's objective is to maximize the total population of the assigned counties. A feasible solution is to make 4 a base with 1 as the assigned adjacent and also make 3 a base with 2 as the assigned adjacent. The value of the objective function for this solution is $P_1 + P_2 + P_3 + P_4$.

Define

$$B_j = \begin{cases} 1 \text{ if county } j \text{ is used as a base} \\ 0 \text{ if not} \end{cases} j = 1, \ldots, 6$$

$$A_{ij} = \begin{cases} 1 \text{ if county } i \text{ is used as a county adjacent to base } j \\ 0 \text{ if not} \end{cases} \begin{matrix} j = 1, \ldots, 6; \\ i \text{ adjacent to } j \end{matrix}$$

Thus the variables are B_1, B_2, B_3, B_4, B_5, B_6, A_{21}, A_{41}, A_{12}, A_{52}, A_{32}, A_{23}, A_{63}, and so on.

(a) In the model for this problem, double counting must not occur (i.e., a county must not be used as both a base and an assigned adjacent). Write a constraint that assures no double counting for county 1.

(b) Write a constraint that says "if any salesperson is assigned to county 2 as a base then a salesperson must also be assigned to an appropriate adjacent county."

(c) Write a constraint that says "if either county adjacent to 1 is scheduled (as an adjacent to 1) then 1 must be used as a base."

(d) This model can be written with 12 inequality constraints and 1 equality constraint. True or False.

(e) This model can be written with 7 equality constraints and 6 inequality constraints. True or False.

See IM.

8-23. ▲▲▲ Refer to the description that precedes exercise 21 in the concepts quiz. Assume in addition to the conditions described there, that there is a fixed cost of $R > 0$ dollars assigned to each shipment that leaves the supplier. This implies, for example, that if the supplier makes direct shipments to locations 3, 5, and 8 and to the warehouse then an additional cost of $4R$ dollars is incurred.

Formulate this problem as an MILP, using the notation introduced earlier and whatever additional notation is required.

Part 2. Quadratic Programming Problems

When proportion constraint not binding

8-24. ▲▲ "If *at least one* of the stocks in the portfolio has an expected return greater-than-or-equal-to the required return on the entire portfolio, then this formulation will never be infeasible." Under what conditions will this statement be true?

No

8-25. ▲▲ Consider the problem solved in Section 8.15. The current solution to this problem is (X = 0.515, Y = 0.369, Z = 0.116). Is this point an extreme point of the feasible region? Why or why not?

Small variance or negative correlation

8-26. ▲▲ Consider the problem solved in Section 8.15. Assume you are considering adding the stock of the IMCRZY corporation to your portfolio selection model. This stock has a *negative* expected return. Under what conditions might the model select stock from IMCRZY to be in the portfolio?

0.381038

8-27. ▲▲ Consider the problem solved in Section 8.15. What is the allowable decrease on the constraint that limits the investment of stock Y to 75% of the portfolio?

No—not linear

8-28. ▲▲ As with pure LP analysis, there is sensitivity analysis output associated with QP. Would you expect this QP sensitivity analysis to include allowable increases and decreases on the RHS? Explain.

Max $= R_xX + R_yY + R_zZ$
$\sigma_x^2X^2 + \sigma_y^2Y^2 + \sigma_z^2Z^2 + 2\sigma_{xy}XY + 2\sigma_{yz}YZ \leq V$, other constraints unchanged

8-29. ▲▲ Consider the problem solved in Section 8.15. Assume your objective is to maximize return subject to the constraint that the variability of the portfolio cannot exceed V. Reformulate the problem with this modification.

15%

8-30. ▲▲ Refer to Problem 8-29. Set $V = 0.023107$. If there are no alternative optima in the original problem, what is the maximum expected return in your reformulated model? Explain.

(a) X=19.48%, Y=35.36%, Z=45.14%
(b) Yes
(c) Predicted=0.01294; actual=0.02327

8-31. ▲▲ Stocks x, y, and z have expected returns of 7%, 6%, and 10%, respectively, and the following covariance matrix:

	x	y	z
x	.01		
y	.001	.04	
z	.001	−.04	.08

(a) Determine the fraction of the portfolio to hold in each stock so as to minimize the variance of the portfolio subject to a minimum expected return on the portfolio of 8%.

(b) Can the variance of the portfolio be smaller than the variance of any individual stock? Explain.

(c) Use the dual price information to estimate what would happen to the variance of the optimal portfolio if the minimum expected return were raised to 9%. Compare your estimate with the actual by resolving the model.

▶ Diagnostic Assignment

Assigning Sales Representatives

One of the main themes in the text is that the manager plays the role of the intermediary between the real problem and the model. The manager must decide if the assumptions are appropriate and if the solution produced by the model makes sense in the context of the real problem.

Sally Erickson is midwest sales director for Lady Lynn Cosmetics. Lady Lynn is a rapidly expanding company that sells cosmetics through representatives. These representatives originally contact most of their customers through house parties. At these parties, the representative demonstrates the products and takes orders. The guests have an opportunity to win some samples of the products and to order products. The hostess receives "gifts" depending on the volume of orders.

Sally is in the process of assigning representatives to the seven eastern Iowa counties shown in Figure 8.34. Actually, she has only two trained representatives to assign at this time. The policy at Lady Lynn is to assign a representative to a base county and one adjacent county. Actual practice is based on a heuristic model that assigns representatives sequentially. The county with the largest population is selected as the base for the first representative, and the adjacent county with the largest population is also assigned to her. The unassigned county with the largest population is assigned as the next base and so on. The populations of the counties are shown below.

1. Buchanan	16,000
2. Delaware	15,000
3. Dubuque	98,000
4. Linn	109,000
5. Jones	4,000
6. Jackson	6,000
7. Clinton	100,000

Using this scheme, the first representative would be assigned to Linn County as a base. As the map

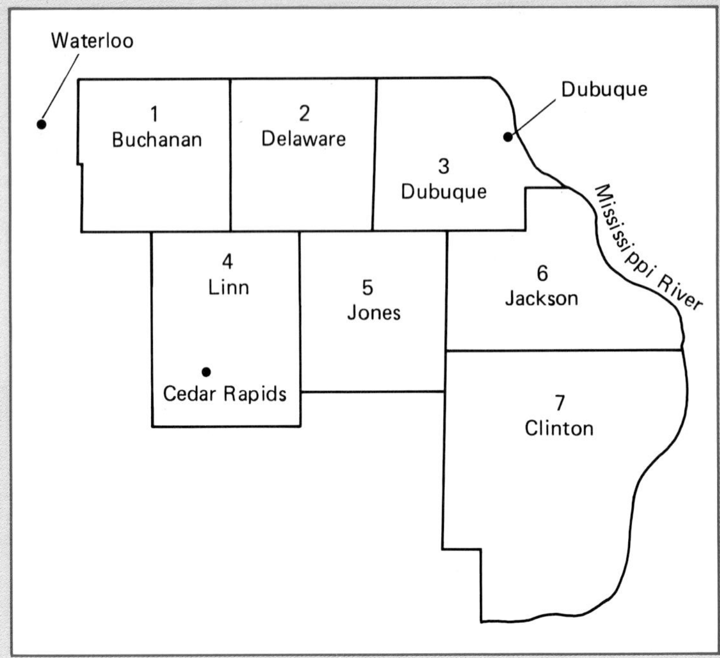

▲ FIGURE 8.34

shows, Buchanan, Delaware, and Jones are the adjacent counties. Since Buchanan has the largest population of these three counties it would be the assigned adjacent county. The second representative would be based in Clinton with Jackson as the assigned adjacent county. Sally realizes that the goal is to maximize the total population assigned to representatives. She is concerned that, since Dubuque County is nearly as large as Clinton, the proposed solution may not be optimal, and after a moment's thought she can see that it clearly is not: The pair Dubuque and Delaware beat Clinton and Jackson. She decides to abandon the traditional heuristic approach and to model the problem as an IP. Although this particular problem is quite simple, she believes that if she can create a successful model it could then be appropriately modified to assign the company's 60 midwest representatives to well over 300 counties. In formulating the problem, she lets

y_i = 1 if county i is a base
= 0 if not

x_{ij} = 1 if adjacent county j is assigned to base i
= 0 if not

The formulation and solution are shown in Figure 8.35. Sally has used an IP code to solve the problem.

The solution shows that y_4 and y_1 = 1; thus, Linn and Buchanan counties are selected as the base counties. It also shows that the optimal value of the objective function is 250, which implies that 250,000 people will be served by the two representatives. Sally thus is pleased to have discovered that the solution suggested by the standard heuristic approach was incorrect before she implemented that solution. She is a bit surprised that the optimal solution does not involve either Dubuque or Clinton county, but she feels sure that the IP code provides the optimal solution to her model and thus she is determined to implement it.

Questions

1. Sally's solution is obviously wrong. Find, by inspection of the data, a correct optimal solution. How many alternative optima are there?
2. What is wrong with Sally's model? Write out seven additional constraints that will give a correct formulation.
3. Solve the reformulated model with LINDO or QSB+.

```
MAX  16 Y1 + 15 Y2 + 98 Y3 + 109 Y4 + 4 Y5 + 6 Y6 + 100 Y7
    + 15 X21 + 109 X41 + 16 X12 + 98 X32 + 109 X42 + 4 X52
    + 15 X23 + 4 X53 + 6 X63 + 16 X14 + 15 X24 + 4 X54 + 15 X25
    + 98 X35 + 109 X45 + 6 X65 + 100 X75 + 4 X56 + 98 X36
    + 100 X76 + 4 X57 + 6 X67
SUBJECT TO
 2) -Y1 + X21 + X41 = 0
 3) -Y2 + X12 + X32 + X42 + X52 = 0
 4) -Y3 + X23 + X53 + X63 = 0
 5) -Y4 + X14 + X24 + X54 = 0
 6) -Y5 + X25 + X35 + X45 + X65 + X75 = 0
 7) -Y6 + X56 + X36 + X76 = 0
 8) -Y7 + X57 + X67 = 0
 9)  Y1 + Y2 + Y3 + Y4 + Y5 + Y6 + Y7 = 2

INTEGER - VARIABLES = 29

        LP OPTIMUM FOUND AT STEP 15

        OBJECTIVE FUNCTION VALUE

           250.000000
```

VARIABLE	VALUE	REDUCED COST
Y1	1.00	0.00
Y2	0.00	0.00
Y3	0.00	0.00
Y4	1.00	0.00
Y5	0.00	0.00
Y6	0.00	0.00
Y7	0.00	0.00
X21	0.00	94.00
X41	1.00	0.00
X12	0.00	94.00
X32	0.00	12.00
X42	0.00	1.00
X52	0.00	106.00
X23	0.00	12.00
X53	0.00	23.00
X63	0.00	21.00
X14	1.00	0.00
X24	0.00	1.00
X54	0.00	12.00
X25	0.00	106.00
X35	0.00	23.00
X45	0.00	12.00
X65	0.00	115.00
X75	0.00	21.00
X56	0.00	115.00
X36	0.00	21.00
X76	0.00	19.00
X57	0.00	21.00
X67	0.00	19.00

▲ FIGURE 8.35

▶ Case

Municipal Bond Underwriting*

The municipal bond market is tough and aggressive, which means that a successful underwriter must be on the cutting edge in terms of competitive bidding. Bond markets often change from hour to hour. An active underwriter may bid on several issues each day with as little as 15 to 20 minutes to prepare a bid. This case has two objectives: (1) The student is familiarized with some of the mechanics of an important financial market; (2) The student will develop an IP model with real-world importance. A variant of this model is actually used by several banks and investment bankers. In practice, bids are routinely prepared in a minute of CPU time on an IBM mainframe for problems involving as many as 100 maturities and 35 coupon rates.

Basic Scenario

Each year billions of dollars of tax-exempt debt securities are offered for sale to the public. This is usually done through an underwriter acting as a broker between the issuer of the security and the public. The issuing of the securities to the underwriter is usually done through a competitive bid process. The issuer will notify prospective underwriters in advance of the proposed sale and invite bids that meet constraints set forth by the issuer. In constructing a proposed sale, the issuer divides the total amount to be raised (say \$10,000) into bonds of various maturities. For example, to raise \$10,000, the issuer might offer a one-year bond with face value of \$2000, a two-year bond with face value of \$3000, and a three-year bond with face value of \$5000. At maturity, the face value of these bonds would be paid to the buyer. Thus in this example, the issuers would pay the buyers \$2000 in principal at the end of year 1, and so on.

A bid by an underwriter (to the issuer) has three components:

1. An agreement to pay the issuer the face value of all the bonds at the issue data (\$10,000 in our example).
2. A premium paid to the issuer at the issue date (more on this later).
3. An annual interest rate for each of the bonds cited in the proposal. These rates are called the coupon rates and determine the amount of interest the issuer must pay the buyers each year. Suppose that the underwriter proposed the following coupon rates for our example.

MATURITY DATE	RATE (%)
1 year	3
2 years	4
3 years	5

The interest to be paid by the issuer would then be calculated as follows:

$$\text{Year 1} = 2000(.03) + 3000(.04) + 5000(.05) = 430$$

$$\text{Year 2} = 3000(.04) + 5000(.05) = 370$$

$$\text{Year 3} = 5000(.05) = 250$$

Historically, the net interest cost (NIC) is the criterion most often employed by the issuer in evaluating bids. The NIC is the sum of interest payments over all years for all maturities minus any premium offered by the underwriter. The winning bid is the one with the minimum NIC. The time value of money is ignored in calculating the NIC. Even though the bid with the lowest NIC may not be best for the issuer when present values are considered, this is immaterial to the underwriter since the bid is evaluated according to the NIC.

The profit of the underwriter is the difference between what the buyer pays him and what he (the underwriter) pays the issuer. That is,

*This modeling approach was derived from the discussion in Robert M. Nauss and B. R. Keeler, *Management Science*, vol. 27, no. 4 (April 1981), pp. 365–376. This case was initially formulated by Professor R. Kipp Martin, Graduate School of Business, University of Chicago.

Profit = (total selling price to public)
− (total face value + premium)

Thus, in preparing a bid the underwriter must

1. determine the coupon (interest) amounts the issuer will pay on each maturity, and
2. for each maturity, estimate the selling price (i.e., the underwriter's selling price to the public) for bonds of each coupon rate. (The selling price for bonds need not be the same as the face value of the bond.)

The underwriter has two conflicting objectives. Higher coupon rates imply the bonds have a higher selling price to the public and hence more money to the underwriter, which can be used both as premium and profit. Thus the coupon rates must be set large enough so that if the bid is accepted the underwriter makes a reasonable profit. But higher coupon rates affect the interest the issuer will have to pay (higher coupon rates imply more interest) as well as the premium that the underwriter can offer the issuer. This tradeoff between premium and interest may imply that lower coupon rates will decrease the cost to the issuer and hence increase the chances of winning the bid.

The approach we take is to incorporate the underwriter's profit as a constraint and then minimize NIC (the cost to the issuer) in order to maximize the chances of winning the bid.

Data for a Specific Scenario

The city of Dogpatch is going to issue municipal bonds in order to raise revenue for civic improvements. Sealed bids will be received until 5:00 P.M. on February 7, 1993 for $5,000,000 in bonds dated March 1, 1993. The bid represents an offer from the underwriter to (1) pay $5,000,000 to Dogpatch, (2) pay an additional (specified) premium to Dogpatch, (3) include an interest schedule that Dogpatch will pay to the bond holders. The interest is payable on March 1, 1994, and annually thereafter. The bonds become due (i.e., Dogpatch must pay off the face value, without option for prior payment) on March 1 in each of the maturity years in Table 1 below and in the amounts indicated. That is, Table 1 indicates Dogpatch's obligation (in terms of principal) to the bondholders.

The bonds will be awarded to the bidder on the basis of the minimum NIC. No bid will be considered with an interest rate greater than 5% or less than 3% per annum. Bidders must specify interest rates in multiples of one-quarter of one percent per annum. Not more than three different interest rates will be considered (a repeated rate will not be considered a different rate). The same rate must apply to all bonds of the same maturity.

Estimating selling prices of various maturities as a function of coupon rates is a complicated process depending upon available markets and various parameters. For the sake of this example, take the data in Table 2 as given. Note that the underwriter may sell bonds to the public at more or less than the face value.

YEAR (MATURITY)	AMOUNT ($000)
1995	250
1996	425
1997	1025
1998	1050
1999	1100
2000	1150

▲ TABLE 1

Face value	250	425	1025	1050	1100	1150
PERCENT	**1995**	**1996**	**1997**	**1998**	**1999**	**2000**
3	245	418	1015	1040	1080	1130
3¼	248	422	1016	1042	1084	1135
3½	250	423	1017	1044	1085	1140
3¾	251	424	1025	1046	1090	1150
4	253	430	1029	1050	1095	1155
4¼	255	435	1035	1055	1096	1160
4½	256	437	1037	1060	1105	1165
4¾	257	440	1038	1062	1110	1170
5	258	441	1040	1065	1115	1175

▲ TABLE 2
Estimating Selling Price ($000)

Example (A Sample Bid)

Assume an underwriter establishes the coupon rates for each maturity as in Table 3.

MATURITY	COUPON RATE (%)	TOTAL INTEREST ($000)
1995	3	15.00
1996	4½	57.375
1997	4¾	194.75
1998	4½	236.25
1999	4½	297.00
2000	4½	362.25

▲ TABLE 3

Given these coupon rates the bonds would be sold to the public (see estimates in Table 2) for \$5,050,000. Assume the underwriter's spread or profit requirement is \$8 per \$1000 of face value of bonds. For a \$5,000,000 issue this will be \$40,000. Thus the premium paid to Dogpatch by the underwriter for this bid is

$$\text{premium} = \$5{,}050{,}000 - \$5{,}000{,}000 - \$40{,}000 = \$10{,}000$$

Questions

1. Calculate Dogpatch's NIC for the example above.
2. Suppose, as in Table 2, the underwriter has a choice between selling a 1995 bond at 4¼% for \$255,000 or a 1995 bond at 4½% for \$256,000. Just in terms of minimizing NIC (ignoring other possible constraints), which would the underwriter prefer to offer? Suppose that the underwriter's profit is the same in both cases.
3. In Table 2, consider the 1995 maturity at 5%. Suppose that you as an investor can with certainty receive 5% interest on money invested on March 1, 1994. What compounded yearly rate of interest would you be receiving if you pay \$258,000 for the 1995 bond and use the above investment opportunity with your first receipt of interest?
4. Formulate a constrained optimization model for solving the underwriter's problem. This formulation should minimize the NIC of the underwriter's bid subject to the underwriter receiving an \$8 margin per \$1000 of face amount and the other constraints given. Be very clear and concise in defining any notation you use, and indicate the purpose of each constraint in your formulation.
5. Solve your constrained optimization model using LINDO.
6. Bid requests often include additional constraints. Assume that one such additional restriction is that coupon rates must be nondecreasing with maturity. Add the necessary constraint(s) to enforce this condition. You do not need to resolve with LINDO.
7. Next assume that the maximum allowed difference between the highest and lowest coupon rates is 1%. Add the necessary constraint(s) to enforce this condition. You do not need to resolve with LINDO.
8. Refer to your formulation in Question 4. If the bonds (regardless of maturity and coupon value) could never be sold in excess of face value will your formulation have a feasible solution? Why or why not?
9. Assume your formulation in Question 4 has a feasible solution. Is it possible that the addition of the constraint(s) from Question 6 or the constraint(s) from Question 7 (or both taken together) make the formulation infeasible?

A Word of Advice One danger of misformulating a rather large integer programming model, and then attempting to run it on a computer, is that you may waste a great deal of computer time (this of course could be true of any large model). Your solution to Question 5 above, using a correctly formulated model, should take no more than one minute of CPU time on any medium-sized mainframe computer. Your model, although rather large, should take no more than an hour to correctly type in at a console.

 Case

Cash Flow Matching

In some applications, a stream of cash flows must be generated over a planning horizon. For example, in a personal injury lawsuit, the plaintiff must be compensated for future medical expenses or lost wages or both. Both parties often agree on an initial lump sum that is "equivalent in value" to the cash flows over time. What is an equivalent lump sum? The plaintiff, who wants to maximize the size of the payment, argues that future interest rates will be low so that a large lump sum is needed. The defendant argues that interest rates will be high and thus a smaller lump sum is required.

One resolution is to purchase a portfolio of bonds so that the return from the bonds satisfies the required cash flow. A bond offers a guaranteed annual payment (determined by the coupon rate) and its face value at maturity. Thus it is clear how much each bond will contribute to meeting the cash flow. The current price of the bonds is also known and thus the "lump payment problem" becomes one of finding the lowest-cost bond portfolio that will satisfy the agreed-upon cash flow.

It is reasonable to think of many pension fund planning problems as cash flow matching problems. In this problem a corporation or a union has an obligation to meet the cash requirements of a pension fund over some planning horizon. The goal is to purchase a minimum-cost, low-risk portfolio that generates an income stream to match the cash-outflow requirements of the pension plan.

Consider the following small but conceptually realistic cash flow problem. The cash requirements (in millions) for the next five years are shown in Table 4.

YEAR	1995	1996	1997	1998	1999
Cash requirement	10	11	12	14	15

▲ TABLE 4

The investment committee is considering five types of low-risk investments: an insured money market fund paying an annual rate of 5% and the four types of AAA bonds described in Table 5.

BOND	CURRENT COST	COUPON (YEARLY)	YEARS TO MATURITY	FACE VALUE
1	.97	.04	1	1.00
2	.947	.05	2	1.00
3	.79	.00	3	1.00
4	.829	.03	4	1.00

▲ TABLE 5
(Values in $000,000)

Assume that all cash transactions associated with investments occur on January 1 of each year. Table 6 shows the cash flows for each bond.

BOND	1995	1996	1997	1998	1999
1	−.970	1.040			
2	−.947	.050	1.050		
3	−.790	.000	.000	1.000	
4	−.829	.030	.030	.030	1.030

▲ TABLE 6
(Values in $000,000)

Note that in the year the bond matures the return is equal to the sum of the coupon plus the face value of the bond. Also note that bond 3 is a zero coupon bond, i.e., it does not pay any interest until maturity.

There is also an opportunity for borrowing in most cash flow matching problems. In this problem assume that the pension fund managers have the opportunity to borrow as much cash as they want at an annual rate of 13%. Loans are made for one year only, i.e., a loan made in 1995 must be paid off in 1996. However, another one-year loan could be taken out immediately.

In the real problem, cash flows (both in and out) occur at various times during the year. In the model it is assumed that:

1. All inflows (returns from the bonds, money

invested in the money market fund as well as interest earned on these funds, funds borrowed during the year under consideration, and the original lump sum) are available on the morning of January 1.

2. All cash outflows (the cash required by the pension fund, payment of debt and interest from the previous year, deposits in the money market account) occur in the afternoon of January 1.

These assumptions make it possible to keep the proper relationship between the various cash flows. For example:

1. In 1995 the cash outflow needed by the pension fund, as well as any purchases of bonds or money to deposit in the money market account, must come from the original lump sum payment or from funds borrowed in 1995.
2. Debt and interest that arise from borrowing in 1995 can be paid for by borrowing funds in 1996.

Questions

1. Plot the yield curve for the four bonds listed in Table 5. To do this you must first determine for each bond the interest rate that makes the present value of the cash flows for that bond equal to zero. This is accomplished with a financial calculator or the Lotus 1-2-3 @IRR function. Otherwise you must use trial and error. Now plot the interest rate as a function of the maturity of the bond for the four bonds.
2. Comment on the general shape of the function you plotted in Question 1. What does this shape suggest about the preferences and expectations of lenders? About borrowers? Does the yield curve have to have this shape? What preferences and expectations of borrowers and lenders might cause it to look otherwise?
3. Assume your goal is to minimize the original lump-sum payment. Formulate an MILP to solve this problem. Assume that only an integral number of bonds may be purchased and that these purchases are made in January 1995. Define the decision variables as follows:

   L = initial lump sum required

   B_i = amount borrowed in year i

   M_i = amount invested in money market fund in year i

   X_i = number of bonds of type i purchased in 1995

   C_i = cash not utilized in year i

   Assume that it is not possible to borrow funds in 1999, the fifth year. In your formulation, there should be a balance constraint in each year that sources of funds must equal uses of funds.
4. In a real problem, the data in Table 4 would in fact be estimates of future requirements since these would not generally be known with certainty. What other significant assumptions were made in creating this model?
5. Will there always be a feasible answer for general models of the type constructed in Question 3? That is, consider the problem in Question 3 with any set of cash demands and rates of return. Will there always be a feasible solution? Explain.
6. Use your computer to solve the problem you formulated in Question 3.
7. Solve the problem using the following heuristic procedure:
   - **(a)** Solve the model from Question 3 as an LP.
   - **(b)** Round the number of bonds to the next largest integer.
   - **(c)** Fix the integer variables at the levels in (b) and resolve the problem as an LP.
8. Calculate the value of the following ratio: OV Question 7(c)/OV Question 6.
   Do you expect this ratio to be greater or less than 1? Why? What does the value of this ratio suggest about solving real (i.e., much bigger) cash flow matching problems?
9. What interpretation do you give to the dual prices produced by the LP solution in Question 7(a)?
10. Comment on the following statement: "The way to minimize the initial lump sum is to limit your purchase of bonds to only the bond with the highest rate of return."
11. Comment on the following statement: "If the rate of return on the money market fund exceeds the rate of return on all the bonds, then there is an optimal solution in which the money market fund is the only investment used."

Video Case

The United States Postal Service

The United States Postal Service (USPS), whether it deserves it or not, has become the butt of jokes about government inefficiency. For example, in stating his opposition to a national health service, Louis Sullivan, Secretary of Health and Human Services, said that the proposed organization would have the compassion of the IRS and the effectiveness of the post office.

The "post office problem" has many facets. It is easy to find individuals ready to point out that the USPS suffers from a bloated bureaucracy, inflexible work rules, union power, and outmoded equipment. Undoubtedly, there is at least some truth in most of these accusations. But even if all of these "problems" were solved, the post office problem would not go away.

It is clear that the USPS has logistical and management problems of truly gigantic proportions. With 760,000 employees, USPS is the nation's largest employer. The USPS system includes 40,000 locations, 300,000 collection points, and 200 facilities for sorting and routing mail. Demands on this system have been growing rapidly. Indeed, mail volume has been doubling every year, reaching 550 million pieces daily in 1991.

In the early 1980s, predictions suggested that the workforce would have to increase to 1 million employees by the year 2000 if current technology were used. Clearly such a system was not viable, and plans had to be made for an alternative approach. It was decided that only a completely automated system could meet the challenge of increased demand and competition from private carriers.

The USPS is a "disassembly" operation. Mail enters the system in a batch that must be sorted into smaller and smaller lots until the individual piece is delivered to the correct address. Sorting is currently performed in one of three ways: (1) manual sorting, in which a person picks up each piece of mail, reads the address, and throws the piece into the proper bin; (2) mechanized sorting, in which a machine presents the piece and distributes it to the proper bin upon receiving a typed command from the operator; and (3) automated sorting, using either bar code readers or optical character readers to sort on the basis of a ZIP code presented in bar code or written form.

It is one thing to decide to completely automate mail sorting and routing, but determining just how to go about this task is another matter. The mail delivery process involves six steps:

1. Sort to destination
2. Transport to destination
3. Sort to 5-digit ZIP code
4. Sort to carrier
5. Sort to sequence
6. Deliver

The major sorting activities, steps 1, 3, and 4, take place in the 250 largest major processing centers, known as general mail facilities or GMFs, using one of the systems described above. The USPS of the future will have to determine the number and location of its GMFs that will best meet the increasing demand for mail service.

Questions

1. In this chapter we have encountered a simple facilities location model. What factors must the USPS model consider that the STECO model ignores?

CHAPTER

9 Network Models

APPLICATION CAPSULE

Farewell to the Magical Mystery Tour: A Little Networking Helps Tulsa Streamline Its School Bus Routes*

A very common type of network problem is the routing of school buses. This task was particularly troublesome for the school system of Tulsa, Oklahoma. Federal guidelines require public school systems to provide transportation for students in special-education programs. Tulsa has about 850 such students, served by 66 different schools. Because both schools and students are dispersed over a wide geographical area, bus routes are longer than for typical students attending neighborhood schools. (The maximum ride time permitted for each student is 3 hours per day, but the school system strives for a limit of no more than 45 minutes each way.) Most bus routes have a number of different destination schools, creating a complex "many-to-several" routing problem.

School officials had previously created these bus routes manually, a process that typically took about two weeks. As an alternative to this difficult and time-consuming method, a consulting team developed a set of heuristic network algorithms to attack the routing problem.

- The first algorithm investigates an existing pair of routes to see if they can be combined into a single route without exceeding the capacity of the bus or the maximum allowable ride time.
- The second algorithm chooses three branches of a route at a time and replaces them with a different pattern of connections to see if the change improves the solution.
- The third algorithm tries to exchange segments *between* different routes. The algorithm stops when no further link exchanges can be found that improve the solution.

Together, these algorithms, which took only minutes to run on the school system's PC, reduced the total route mileage by nearly one-third.

As is often the case, definition of the problem evolved between the start of the analysis and the implementation of a solution. To reduce student ride times and make individual bus routes more compact, management decided to adopt a shuttle system, in which students were first bused to a central location and then transferred to buses bound for their particular schools. These goals were achieved at the cost of "giving back" some of the decrease in total route length.

Implementation of the new system also presented problems. Some drivers resisted the shorter routes, which reduced their driving time and thus their wages. Others found that the new routes interfered with special time arrangements they had made to accommodate parental work schedules. Drivers also complained about computer-generated routes that ignored real-world barriers such as rivers, dead-end streets, one-way streets, and so on. Drivers were therefore allowed to offer their own refinements of the routes. Despite these changes, the total route mileage was reduced by about 11%, producing a potential saving for the Tulsa Public School System of $50,000 to $100,000 per year.

*Russell and Morrel, "Routing Special Education School Buses," *Interfaces*, Vol. 16, No. 5 (Sept.–Oct. 1986).

9.1 Introduction

Throughout this text the introduction to each chapter has been used as a preview of topics covered in the chapter. In the case of networks, we depart from this practice and turn immediately to an example of an important class of management problems. With this example in hand we will be in a position to consider the *network model* and its importance in both theory and practice, as well as several special forms of the model and the algorithms used to solve them. Much of what would normally appear in the introduction is thus contained in Section 9.3.

9.2 An Example: Seymour Miles (A Capacitated Transshipment Model)

Seymour Miles is the distribution manager for Zigwell Inc., **PROTRAC**'s largest midwestern distributor. Zigwell distributes its crawler tractors in five midwestern states. Currently, Seymour has ten E-9s at what we shall designate as site ①. These crawlers must be delivered to two major construction sites denoted as sites ③ and ④. Three E-9s are required at site ③, and seven are required at site ④. Because of prearranged schedules concerning driver availability, these crawlers may be distributed only according to any of the alternative routes shown in Figure 9.1.

Network Terminology

Figure 9.1 is an example of a **network diagram.** Each of the arrows between sites is termed an **arc,** or **branch,** of the network. The arc from ② to ④ is sometimes denoted symbolically by the pair (2, 4). Each site is termed a **node** of the network.

This diagram represents yet another way of modeling a management science problem. It is extremely visual (no equations) and can be very effective when presenting a problem to management (even if it is solved by another algorithm that uses equations).

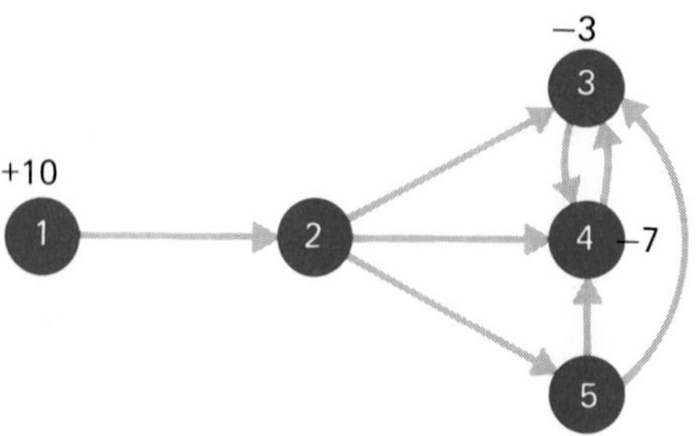

▲ FIGURE 9.1
Network Diagram for Seymour's Problem

The figure shows a +10 identified with site ①. This means that ten E-9s (items of *supply*) are available at this site. The identifiers −3 and −7 attached to sites ③ and ④, respectively, denote the *requirements,* or *demands,* at these two sites. The figure also indicates that E-9s may be delivered to site ③ via any of the alternative routings ①→②→③, ①→②→④→③, ①→②→⑤→④→③, or ①→②→⑤→③.

Which of the allowable routes is ultimately selected will be determined by the associated *costs* of traversing the routes and *capacities* along the routes. These additional data are shown in Figure 9.2. For convenience the costs and capacities are represented in symbolic (i.e., parametric) notation. The costs c_{ij} are *per unit costs.* For example, the cost of traversing arc (5, 3) is c_{53} per crawler. These costs are primarily due to fuel, tolls, and the cost of the driver for the average time it takes to traverse the arc. Because of preestablished agreements with the teamsters, Zigwell must change drivers at each site it encounters on a route. Because of limitations on the current availability of drivers, there is an upper bound on the number of crawlers that may traverse any given arc. Thus, as an example, u_{53} is the upper bound or capacity on arc (5, 3).

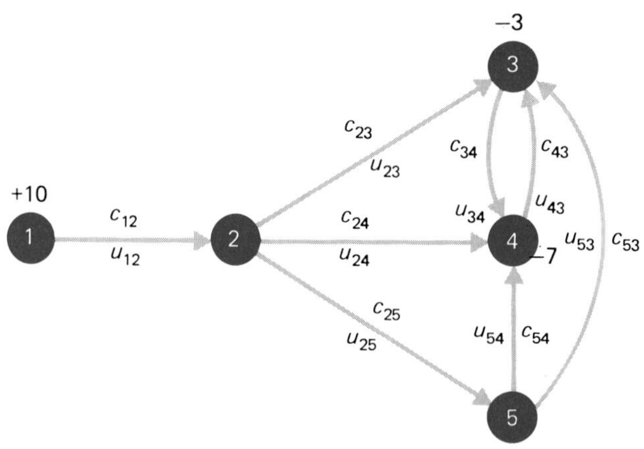

▲ FIGURE 9.2
Capacities and Costs Appended

LP Formulation of the Problem

Seymour's problem is to find a shipment plan that satisfies the demands at minimum cost, subject to the capacity constraints. You can now appreciate the trade-offs facing Seymour. For example, if $(c_{25} + c_{53})$ is less than c_{23}, the route ①→②→⑤→③ will have a total cost that is less than the total cost of route ①→②→③, and hence ①→②→⑤→③ is preferred to ①→②→③. However, the maximum number of E-9s that can be sent across the preferred route is Min $\{u_{12},$

This problem is basically identical to the transportation problem in Chapter 7 except that:

1. Any plant or warehouse can ship to any other plant or warehouse, *and*
2. There can be upper and/or lower bounds (capacities) on each shipment (branch).

Because these *capacities* can be added to the problem, and *shipments* can cross (*trans*) from warehouse to warehouse (or plant to plant), it is called the *capacitated transshipment problem*.

u_{25}, u_{53}}. If this number is less than 3, the number of E-9s required at 3, all of the shipment cannot be accomplished via ①→②→⑤→③. This is a problem in only five nodes and eight arcs, and even in a simplified example such as this the optimal solution may not be obvious. Imagine such a problem with 30 or 40 nodes and many more arcs.

Seymour's problem is called a **capacitated transshipment model.** We now show that this problem can easily be expressed as an LP. First, define the decision variables

$$\begin{aligned} x_{ij} &= \text{total number of E-9s sent on arc } (i, j) \\ &= \text{flow from node (i) to node (j)} \end{aligned}$$

Then the problem is

$$\begin{aligned}
\text{Min } & c_{12}x_{12} + c_{23}x_{23} + c_{24}x_{24} + c_{25}x_{25} + c_{34}x_{34} + c_{43}x_{43} \\
& + c_{53}x_{53} + c_{54}x_{54} \\
\text{s.t. } & + x_{12} = 10 \\
& - x_{12} + x_{23} + x_{24} + x_{25} = 0 \\
& - x_{23} - x_{43} - x_{53} + x_{34} = -3 \\
& - x_{24} + x_{43} - x_{34} - x_{54} = -7 \\
& - x_{25} + x_{53} + x_{54} = 0 \\
& 0 \le x_{ij} \le u_{ij}, \quad \text{all arcs } (i,j) \text{ in the network}
\end{aligned}$$

Properties of the LP

There are now a number of observations to be made about this model.

1. The problem is indeed an LP. There is one variable x_{ij} associated with each arc in the network (Figure 9.2). There are eight arcs in this network and thus eight corresponding variables, x_{12}, x_{23}, x_{24}, x_{25}, x_{43}, x_{53}, x_{34}, and x_{54}. The objective is to minimize total cost.

2. There is one equation associated with each node in the network. The first equation says that the total flow *out of* node ① is ten units. Recall that this is the total supply at node ①. The second equation says that the total flow *out of* node ② (namely, $x_{23} + x_{24} + x_{25}$) minus the total flow *into* node ② (namely, x_{12}) is zero. In other words, the total flow out of node ② must equal the total flow into node ②. The third equation says that the total flow *out of* node ③ (namely x_{34}) must be 3 units less than the total flow *into* node ③ (namely, $x_{23} + x_{43} + x_{53}$). This is the mathematical way of expressing the requirement for a *net delivery* of 3 units to node ③. The equations for nodes ④ and ⑤, respectively, have similar interpretations. Thus, the equation for each node expresses a *flow balance* and takes into account the fact that the node may be either a supply point or a demand point or neither. Intermediate nodes (such as ② and ⑤ in Figure 9.1) that are neither supply points nor demand points are often termed *transshipment nodes.*

3. The positive right-hand sides correspond to nodes that are net suppliers (origins). The negative right-hand sides correspond to nodes that are net destinations. The zero right-hand sides correspond to nodes that have neither supply nor demand. The sum of all right-hand-side terms is zero, which means that the total supply in the network equals the total demand.

NODE	ARC (1, 2)	(2, 3)	(2, 4)	(2, 5)	(4, 3)	(5, 3)	(3, 4)	(5, 4)	RHS
1	+1	0	0	0	0	0	0	0	10
2	−1	+1	+1	+1	0	0	0	0	0
3	0	−1	0	0	−1	−1	+1	0	−3
4	0	0	−1	0	+1	0	−1	−1	−7
5	0	0	0	−1	0	+1	0	+1	0

▲ FIGURE 9.3
Node-Arc Incidence Matrix

Special structure of the LP

4. The *special structure* of this network model is revealed by placing the data of the constraints in the tableau format shown in Figure 9.3, called a **node-arc incidence matrix.** Each row of Figure 9.3 corresponds to a node and contains the data of the corresponding constraint in the LP. Each column of Figure 9.3 corresponds to an arc (or a variable). Since there are eight arcs in the model, there are eight corresponding columns in the tableau. The key to the *special structure* of this network model is the fact that in each column of the node-arc incidence matrix there is a +1 and a −1, and the remaining terms are zero. The +1 is in the row corresponding to the node at which the arc originates. The −1 is in the row corresponding to the node at which the arc terminates. In Figure 9.3, consider the column under arc (2, 5). Since this arc originates at node ②, there is a +1 in row 2. Since the arc terminates at node ⑤, there is a −1 in row 5. All other entries in this column are zero. It should be noted that the node-arc incidence matrix can be created directly from Figure 9.1 without first writing down the LP. Similarly, Figure 9.1 could be constructed from the data in Figure 9.3 (or from the LP). In other words, Figures 9.1 and 9.3 are equivalent ways of communicating the network structure of Seymour's problem.

Notice that all the values of the matrix (not the RHS) are either 0, 1, or −1, and never fractions. When implemented on a computer, a special purpose algorithm is 10 times faster than the simplex because there is no division or multiplication. It is in this manner that management scientists develop faster and better algorithms.

5. Since Seymour's problem is an LP it could be solved with the simplex method like any other LP. In the special case in which the capacity limits u_{ij} are infinitely large, the special network structure can be exploited in the following way: Compute the least cost, say m_{ij}, of distributing a single unit of flow from origin i to destination j. For example, m_{13} denotes the least-cost way of distributing a unit of flow from node ① to node ③. For Seymour's problem the only origin is node ①, and the destinations are ③ and ④. Thus we obtain Figure 9.4.

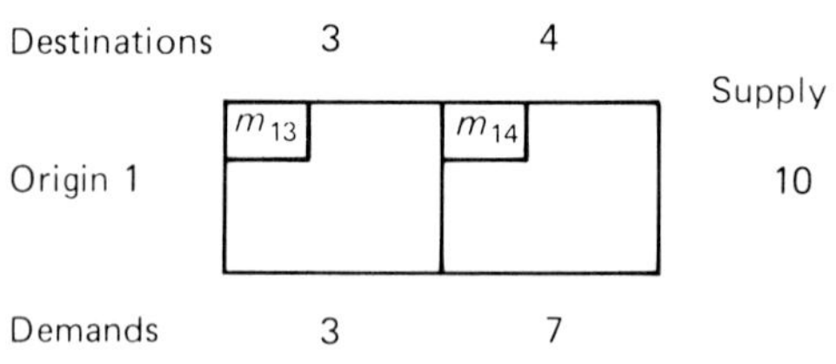

▲ FIGURE 9.4
Transportation Tableau for Seymour's Problem

It is important to understand that a problem can be formulated either as a linear programming model or as a network model. There really are no such things as "linear programming problems," only problems that can be formulated as LP, network, or assignment models. It can be helpful to formulate several alternative models of the same problem. Often, one of these models is far simpler to solve than the others.

In Section 9.4 we present an algorithm for easily computing the values m_{ij}, given the data of the original problem. These computations involve repeated applications of what is termed the *shortest-route algorithm.* For now, the point is that by performing such computations we have been able to reduce the transshipment problem to a standard transportation problem, which can then be solved with the algorithms given in Chapter 7.

9.3 A General Formulation (The Capacitated Transshipment Model)

The Generalized Model

Seymour's problem is a special case of the following general symbolic form of a network model. Again, the decision variables x_{ij} will denote the "flow" from node i to node j across the arc connecting these two nodes, and L_j represents the supply at node j.

$$\text{Min } \sum_{i,j} c_{ij} x_{ij}$$

$$\text{s.t. } \sum_k x_{jk} - \sum_k x_{kj} = L_j, \qquad j = 1, \ldots, n$$

$$0 \le x_{ij} \le u_{ij}, \qquad \text{all } (i,j) \text{ in the network}$$

Let us observe that

1. The sum $\sum_{i,j} c_{ij} x_{ij}$ in the objective function is understood to be over all arcs in the network. Thus, the objective is to minimize the total cost of the flow.
2. Consider the jth constraint, for some fixed value of j. The sum $\sum_k x_{jk}$ is understood to be over all k for which arc (j,k), with j fixed, is in the network. Thus, $\sum_k x_{jk}$ is the total flow *out of* the specified node j. Similarly, $\sum_k x_{kj}$ is over all k for which arc (k, j), with j fixed, is in the network. Thus, $\sum_k x_{kj}$ is the total flow *into* node j. Thus, the jth constraint says

total flow out of node j − total flow into node j = supply at node j

where negative supply (i.e., $L_j < 0$) represents a requirement. Nodes with negative supply are called **destinations,** *sinks,* or *demand points.* Nodes with positive supply (i.e., $L_j > 0$) are called **origins,** *sources,* or *supply points.* Nodes with zero supply are called *transshipment points.*

3. For simplicity it is assumed that $\sum_j L_j = 0$ (i.e., total supply = total demand) and all $c_{ij} \ge 0$.
4. The last set of constraints places *capacities* on the flows x_{ij}. As a special case some of the u_{ij} could be infinitely large, meaning that these are arcs with no capacity constraints. Setting a zero value for a u_{ij} would be equivalent to eliminating arc (i,j) from the network.
5. The given data for the model are the c_{ij}'s, the L_j's, and the u_{ij}'s.

Importance of the network model

The capacitated transshipment model (often called the **network model**) is important because several important management decision problems are special cases. In particular the transportation problem, assignment problem, and shortest-route problem are special cases of the capacitated transshipment model, and the maximal flow problem is closely related.

Integer Optimal Solutions

There are two advantages in being able to identify a problem as a special case of the network (or capacitated transshipment) model. First, theoretical results that are established for the general model apply automatically to the specific cases. The outstanding example of this phenomenon is the integer property of *the* network model. The integer property can be stated thus:

If all terms L_j and u_{ij} are integers in the capacitated transshipment model, there will always be an integer-valued optimal solution to this problem.

From earlier chapters you know that LP models do not in general yield optimal solutions that have integer-valued variables. The network model with integer values for all L_j and u_{ij} does. This has an important implication on the usefulness of the various special versions of the network model.

Efficient Solution Procedures

We can view the assignment problem as a special case of the transportation problem, and the shortest-route problem as a special case of the assignment problem. The transportation problem also can be seen as a huge assignment problem, so that for three plants with a total supply of 50, and five warehouses with a need of 50, we would have a 50 by 50 assignment problem!

The second reason it is useful to identify a problem as a special case of the capacitated transshipment model is that the *special structure* of this model typically makes it possible to find a special algorithm that solves the problem more easily than applying the general simplex algorithm. The transportation and assignment problems discussed in Chapter 7 are two good examples of this phenomenon. The MODI method and the Hungarian algorithm presented there illustrate how management scientists have used the special structure of the network model to create superior ways of attacking the transportation and assignment models, respectively.

The impact of some of the superefficient codes derived from the special structure of the network model is rather amazing. Recently, the Internal Revenue Service constructed a network model with 50,000 constraints and 600 million variables. Only one hour of high-speed computer time was required to solve the problem. It turns out that in such a problem it can require less time to obtain the optimal solution than to read the output.

There is also a general algorithm that will solve *circulation flow networks,* which are more general models than capacitated flows. This is called the out-of-kilter algorithm, and is extremely fast on a computer. However, it is very difficult to solve even a small example by hand. It was formed by looking at the LP structure of the problem and by using both primal and dual simplex to develop it.

The transportation and assignment problems and the special algorithms used to solve them have been discussed at length in Chapter 7. In Problems 9-19 and 9-20 you will be asked to demonstrate that each of these problems is a special case of the capacitated transshipment model.

Sections 9.4, 9.5, and 9.6 are devoted to the shortest-route problem, the minimum spanning tree problem, and the maximal flow problem, respectively. In each case the problem is represented with a network diagram, and a special algorithm for solving the problem is presented. In Problem 9-21 you are asked to demonstrate that the shortest-route problem is another special case of the capacitated transshipment model.

The minimum spanning tree problem is *not* a special case of the capacitated transshipment model. It is an important problem in its own right and illustrates that network diagrams are useful in representing a large variety of problems.

9.4 The Shortest-Route Problem

The **shortest-route problem** refers to a network for which each arc (i,j) has an associated number, c_{ij}, which is interpreted as the distance (or possibly the cost, or time) from node i to node j. A *route,* or a *path,* between two nodes is any sequence of arcs connecting the two nodes. The objective is to find the shortest (or least-cost or least-time) routes from a specific node to each of the other nodes in the network.

An example: Aaron's delivery service

As an illustration, Aaron Drunner makes frequent wine deliveries to seven

APPLICATION CAPSULE

New Merchandise Arriving Daily: Network Models Help a Discount Chain Keep Shipping Costs at Bargain-Basement Levels*

Finding the most economical way of routing merchandise from suppliers to warehouses and from warehouses to retail stores is a complex problem for many retailing chains. The problem is particularly difficult when the company is growing at a rate of 30% per year. This was the case with Marshall's, the off-price clothing retailer. Adding new stores at a rapid rate, Marshall's needed to be able to alter shipping patterns quickly to accommodate its expansion, as well as decide where new distribution centers should be located. To help accomplish these objectives, Marshall's adopted a computerized logistics planning system.

One part of this system, Network Optimization, consists of three software modules designed to minimize shipping costs.

- An "inbound" module deals with the flow of merchandise from suppliers to warehouses and processing centers.
- An "outbound" module deals with shipments from warehouses and processing centers to retail outlets.
- A third module analyzes the placement of new warehouses, a decision which strongly affects the first two modules.

Each module has four components:

1. A network generator, which builds network links and nodes
2. A network editor that allows users to modify the network by directly changing costs demands, and constraints
3. An optimization program
4. A post-processor for downloading the optimization results into readable format for use by management.

Each of the three modules required a separate modeling approach to capture important economic trade-offs of the particular problem and still ensure computational feasibility. Size was a real challange with both the inbound and outbound models, each of which initially required the solution of a network with 350,000 links. Use of a heuristic algorithm (Chapter 11) and other ingenious simplifications reduced that number to around 20,000. Thus streamlined, the models could be run on a PC rather than a mainframe, allowing them to incorporate such user-friendly features as interactive graphics. Now the workhorses of the entire system, they have enabled managers to examine a variety of scenarios, changing such factors as the number of trucks used and their capacities, costs, and warehouse locations, and then quickly reoptimizing. The speed of the process allows interactive feedback for sensitivity analysis.

Use of these models enabled Marshall's to evaluate both costs and service levels of its delivery network, producing estimated savings of $250,000 per year. In addition, the model helped determine the site for a new distribution center, expected to save the company $1.4 million in shipping costs.

*Carlisle, Nickerson, Porbst, Rudolph, Sheffi, and Powell, "A Turnkey Microcomputer-Based Logistics Planning System," *Interfaces*, Vol. 17, No. 4 (July–Aug. 1987).

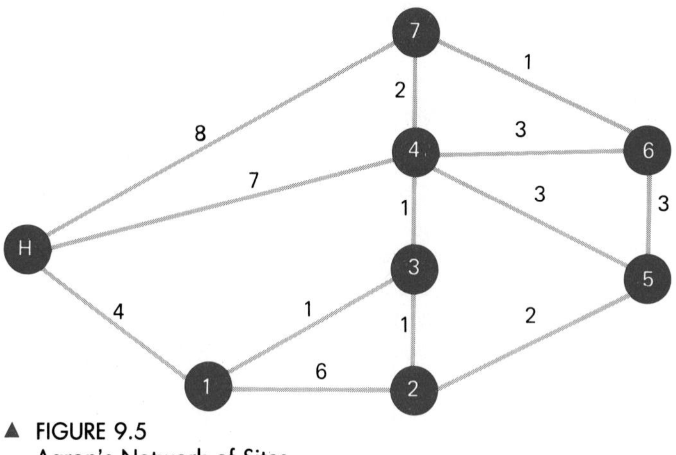

▲ FIGURE 9.5
Aaron's Network of Sites

It is certainly possible to have directed arcs between the nodes, with the cost from node 1 to 2 different than from 2 to 1. This might be the case when there is rush-hour traffic in one direction but not in the other, or to be able to go from 1 to 2 but not from 2 to 1 (one-way street).

different sites. Figure 9.5 shows the seven sites together with the possible travel routes between sites. Note that here, unlike in the transshipment model, the arcs are *nondirected.* That is, on each arc, flow is permitted in either direction. Each arc in Figure 9.5 has been labeled with the distance between the nodes the arc connects. The home base is denoted H. Aaron feels that his overall costs will be minimized by making sure that any future delivery to any given site is made along the shortest route to that site. Thus, his objective is to specify the seven shortest routes from node H to each of the other seven nodes. Note that in this problem, as stated, the task is not to find optimal x_{ij}'s. The task is to find an optimal set of routes.

The Shortest-Route Algorithm

The algorithm for solving this problem will assume that all c_{ij} are nonnegative. The algorithm will find the shortest paths from H to all other nodes in the network. The resulting arcs form what is termed a **shortest-path tree.**[1] The algorithm will take n − 1 steps, where n is the number of nodes in the network. For Aaron's problem there are seven potential delivery sites and a home base. Hence, there are eight nodes in his network, and $n = 8$. The algorithm will take $n - 1 = 7$ steps.

Labels. The algorithm employs what is called a *labeling procedure.* As the algorithm progresses a label for each node will be determined. This label will be a pair of numbers in parentheses. For a particular node, the first number in the label represents a distance from H to that node, along a specific route, and the second number represents the node that precedes the node in question on the specified route. Initially, the labels on nodes other than H are called **temporary labels.** When the shortest distance (i.e., the best route) from H to a given node has been determined, the temporary label on that node becomes a **permanent label.**

Step 1. The algorithm begins by labeling node Ⓗ with the *permanent label* (0, H), where 0 simply means that the shortest route from Ⓗ to itself has length 0, and the H simply identifies this as the starting node.

Next, all nodes that can be reached *directly* (i.e., by traversing a single arc) from node Ⓗ are assigned temporary labels. In Aaron's problem, as shown in Figure 9.5, these are nodes ①, ④, and ⑦. Each node is labeled with the direct distance from node Ⓗ and with the previous node on the route, which is merely Ⓗ.

[1]A **tree** in an n-node network is defined to be n − 1 arcs, with the property that every pair of nodes in the network is connected by some sequence of these arcs.

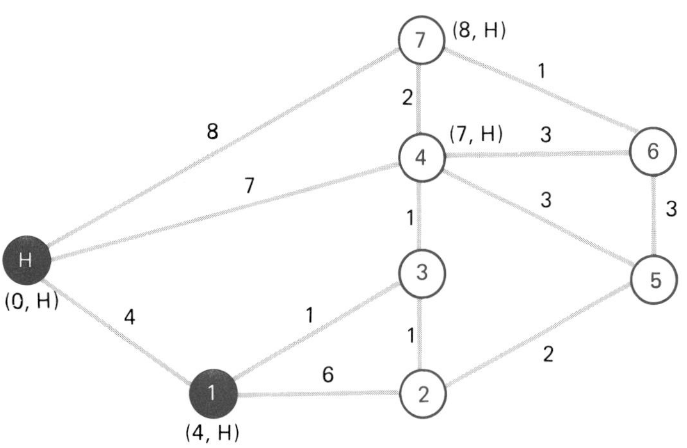

▲ FIGURE 9.6
Initial Assignment of Labels

These labels are shown in Figure 9.6. For example, node ⑦ is a distance of eight units from node Ⓗ. Hence, the label is (8, H). Similarly, the labels on nodes ④ and ① are (7, H) and (4, H), respectively.

Site 1 permanently labeled

Next, of the nodes just labeled, we identify the one with the smallest distance value in its label (ties may be broken arbitrarily). This will identify the node closest to Ⓗ. In Figure 9.6 this is node ①. Since any other route to node ① must pass through nodes ⑦ or ④, the route Ⓗ→① is clearly the shortest route to node ①. For this reason the label (4, H) on node ① becomes a permanent label. The permanently labeled nodes will be shaded in the network diagrams. In Figure 9.6 nodes Ⓗ and ① are shown with their permanent labels. Nodes ④ and ⑦ have temporary labels. This completes step 1, and we now have one of the seven sites with a permanent label.

Step 2. The next step begins by branching outward from the last permanently labeled node. We first assign temporary labels to all nodes that can be reached directly from the last permanently labeled node, which is node ①. Thus, we focus on nodes ② and ③. Since the permanent label on node ① indicates that the shortest distance to node ① is 4, and since the direct distance from node ① to node ② is 6 [i.e., the distance on arc (1, 2) is 6], we deduce that by traveling through the last permanently labeled node the distance to node ② is 4 + 6 = 10 units. For this reason the temporary label on node ② is assigned a distance entry of 10 units. Since this distance is incurred on the route Ⓗ→①→②, node ① is the predecessor of node ②, and the complete temporary label assigned to node ② is therefore (10, 1). Similarly, the temporary label on node ③ is (5, 1). As shown in Figure 9.7, the nodes with labels are now Ⓗ, ①, ②, ③, ④, and ⑦.

Site 3 permanently labeled

We now focus on the nodes with temporary labels, namely ②, ③, ④, and ⑦. First, consider nodes ② and ③. It is clear that since the distance label of 5 on node ③ is less than the distance label of 10 on node ②, the route Ⓗ→①→③ is shorter than any route to ③ commencing with the sequence Ⓗ→①→②. There remain still other possible routes to node ③, but any such route must commence either with the sequence Ⓗ→④ or the sequence Ⓗ→⑦. Since such routes will have distances of at least seven or eight units, respectively (because of the labels on nodes ④ and ⑦), the route Ⓗ→①→③ is the shortest path from Ⓗ to node ③. Consequently, the label on node 3 becomes permanent, as indicated by the shading in Figure 9.7. This completes step 2, and we now have two sites with permanent labels, namely site ①, which is closest to Ⓗ, and site ③, which is the next closest to Ⓗ.

The discussion above indicates that, *upon the completion of each step, the temporary label with the smallest distance component is declared permanent, and this becomes the next closest node to the starting node.*

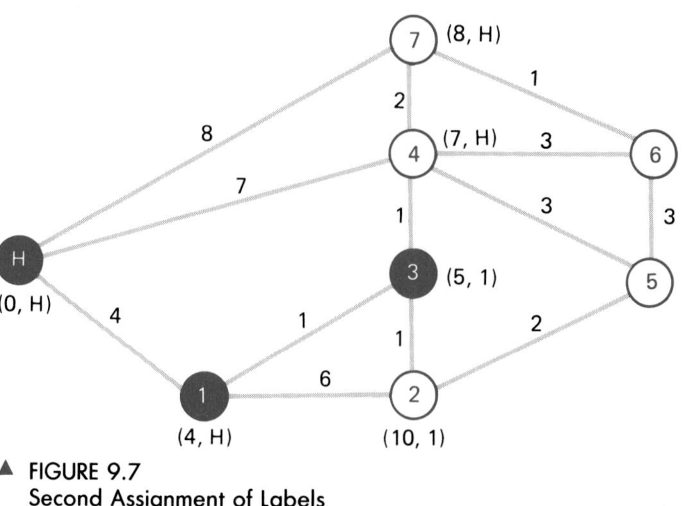

▲ FIGURE 9.7
Second Assignment of Labels

Site 4 permanently labeled

Step 3. Since node ③ was the last permanently labeled node, we next branch outward from this node to consider its "neighbors," nodes ② and ④. Travel to node ② through node ③ can, according to Figure 9.7, be accomplished in six units of distance. Hence, the temporary label on ② is changed from (10, 1) to (6, 3). Similarly, the temporary label on node ④ is revised to (6, 3). The nodes with temporary labels are now ②, ④, and ⑦. As shown in Figure 9.8, nodes ② and ④ are tied for having the smallest distance component in the label. We break the tie by arbitrarily selecting node ④ to be the one declared permanent. The updated assignment at the end of the third step, with permanent labels on sites ①, ③, and ④, is shown in Figure 9.8.

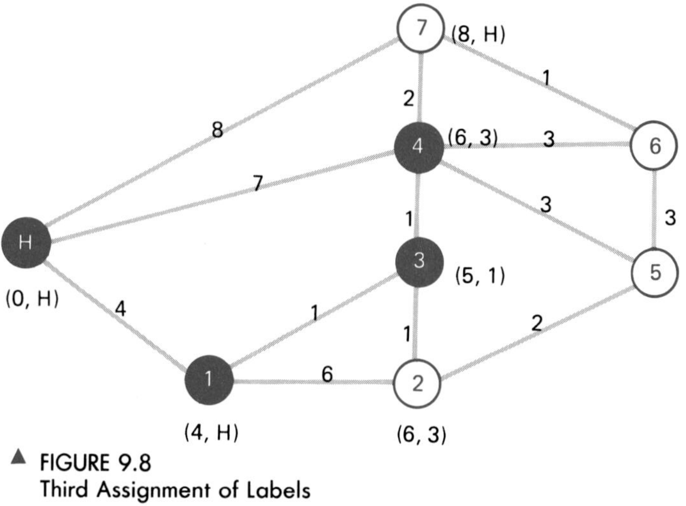

▲ FIGURE 9.8
Third Assignment of Labels

Site 2 permanently labeled

Step 4. The next (fourth) step is to branch out from node ④. Nodes ⑤ and ⑥ are assigned temporary labels, (9, 4) and (9, 4), respectively (see Figure 9.9). Node ⑦ can be reached through 4 in a distance of eight units, which is the same as the distance component on the current label. It is arbitrary whether we leave the label at (8, H) or change it to (8, 4). We choose the former. The nodes with temporary labels are now ②, ⑤, ⑥, and ⑦. Among these, node ② has the smallest distance component. Hence, it is now declared permanent, as shown in Figure 9.9.

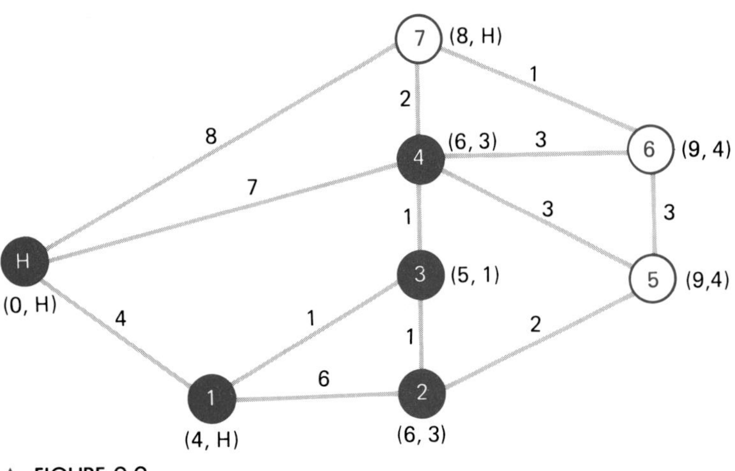

▲ FIGURE 9.9
Fourth Assignment of Labels

Remaining sites permanently labeled

Step 5. The next (fifth) step branches out from ②. Node ⑤ becomes permanently labeled with (8, 2). In the sixth step, the label (8, H) becomes permanent on node ⑦, and in the final (seventh) step the label (9, 4) becomes permanent on node ⑥. The result is shown in Figure 9.10.

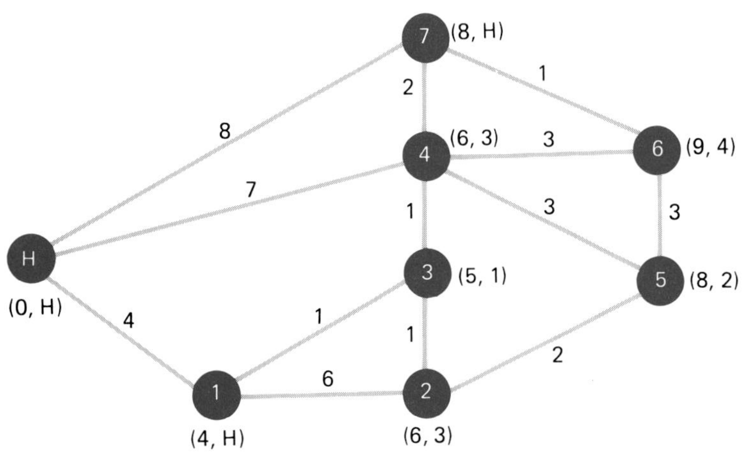

▲ FIGURE 9.10
All Nodes Permanently Labeled

Backtracking. The permanent labels in Figure 9.10 now allow us to find the shortest route from H to any of the sites. For example, consider node ⑥. The permanent label (9, 4) tells us that the shortest route from Ⓗ to ⑥ has a distance of nine units. To find the route that will take us from Ⓗ to ⑥ in nine units, we use the labels to *backtrack* from node ⑥. The label on ⑥ tells us that we reach ⑥ from ④. Moving back to node ④, its label tells us that we reach ④ from ③. Continuing backward, we reach ③ from ①, and ① from Ⓗ. Thus, we see that the shortest route from node Ⓗ to node ⑥ is Ⓗ→①→③→④→⑥. The same approach will produce the shortest routes to all of Aaron's sites. These are identified in Figure 9.11.

The data in Figure 9.11 are used to produce Figure 9.12, in which the shortest route from H to every other node is traced. Any arc that is used in one or more of these routes is indicated by a black line. The set of black lines is the *shortest-path*

NODE	SHORTEST ROUTE FROM NODE H	DISTANCE
1	H-1	4
2	H-1-3-2	6
3	H-1-3	5
4	H-1-3-4	6
5	H-1-3-2-5	8
6	H-1-3-4-6	9
7	H-7	8

▲ FIGURE 9.11
Shortest Routes to All Sites

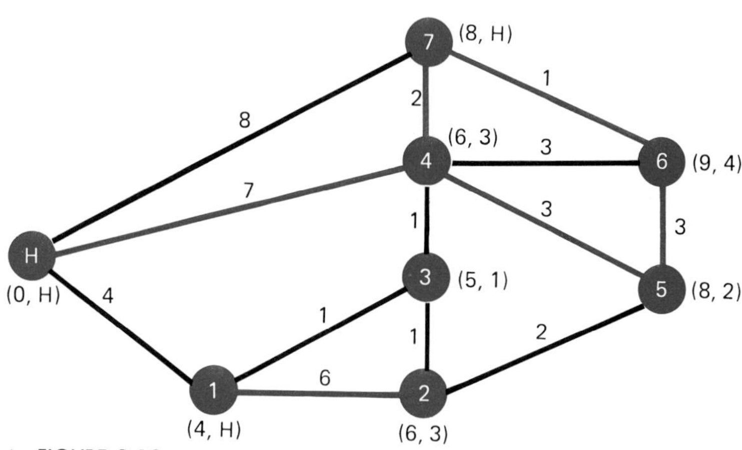

▲ FIGURE 9.12
Shortest-Path Tree for Aaron's Network

tree for Aaron's problem. As defined in footnote 1, a tree in an n-node network consists of a set of $n - 1$ arcs (in this case seven arcs) that connect every pair of nodes. The shortest path from H to any node will traverse only a subset of arcs on the tree.

The algorithm we have presented may seem to require many steps, and indeed for a problem as simple as Aaron's you may well have been able to solve it by inspection. The reason is that with so few nodes there are few alternative routes. However, problems encountered in practice could well involve hundreds or even thousands of nodes. Problems of that size would generally be impossible to solve by inspection. For such problems a systematic method such as the above labeling algorithm is required, and we note that this algorithm is easily implemented on the computer.

Summary of Steps

Let us summarize the method we have presented.

- ***Step 1:*** Consider all nodes that are directly connected (i.e., by a single arc) to the origin. The distance component of the label on each such node is set equal to its distance from the origin. The predecessor component is the origin. These nodes now have temporary labels.
- ***Step 2:*** Of all nodes with temporary labels, choose one whose distance component is minimal, and declare that node to be permanently labeled. Any ties, at any point in the algorithm, may be arbitrarily broken. As soon as all nodes have permanent labels, go to step 4.

- **Step 3:** Each node that currently is not permanently labeled is either unlabeled or has a temporary label. Let Ⓘ denote the last node whose label has been declared permanent. Consider all nodes that are neighbors of Ⓘ (i.e., directly connected to Ⓘ with a single arc). For each such node compute the sum of (its distance to Ⓘ plus (the distance component of the label on Ⓘ)). If the node in question is unlabeled, assign a temporary label consisting of this distance and Ⓘ as predecessor. If the node in question already has a temporary label, give it a new one only if the newly calculated distance is less than its current distance component. If this is the case, the label consists of this distance, with Ⓘ as predecessor. Now return to step 2.
- **Step 4:** The permanent labels indicate the shortest distance from the origin to each node in the network. Permanent labels also indicate the preceding node on the shortest path to each node. To find the shortest path to a given node, start at that node and move backward to its preceding node. Continue with this backward movement until arriving at the origin. The sequence of nodes traced forms the shortest route between the origin and the node in question.

An Application: Equipment Replacement

Lisa Carr is responsible for obtaining reproduction equipment (Xerox-like machines) for **PROTRAC**'s secretarial service. She must choose between leasing newer equipment at high rental cost but low maintenance cost or used equipment with lower rental costs but higher maintenance costs. Lisa has a four-period time horizon to consider. Let c_{ij} denote the cost of *leasing* new equipment at the beginning of period i, $i = 1, 2, 3, 4$, and maintaining it to the beginning of period j, where j can take on the values $2, \ldots, 5$. If the equipment is maintained only to the beginning of period j, for $j < 5$, new equipment must again be leased at the beginning of j. For example, three alternative feasible policies are:

1. Lease new equipment at the beginning of each time period. Presumably, such a policy would involve the highest leasing charges and the minimum maintenance charges. The total (leasing + maintenance) cost of this policy would be $c_{12} + c_{23} + c_{34} + c_{45}$.
2. Lease new equipment only at the beginning of period 1 and maintain it through all successive periods. This would undoubtedly be a policy of minimum rental cost but maximum maintenance. The total (leasing + maintenance) cost of this policy would be c_{15}.
3. Lease new equipment at the beginning of periods 1 and 3. The total cost would be $c_{13} + c_{35}$.

This is another example of changing the model to fit the method. Here, a leasing problem is changed into a shortest-route problem and then solved in a simple fashion.

Of all feasible policies, Lisa desires one with a minimum cost. The solution to this problem is obtained by finding the shortest (i.e., in this case, minimum-cost) route from node 1 to node 5 of the network shown in Figure 9.13. Each node on the shortest route denotes a replacement, that is, a period at which new equipment should be leased.

▼ FIGURE 9.13
Network for Lisa's Decision

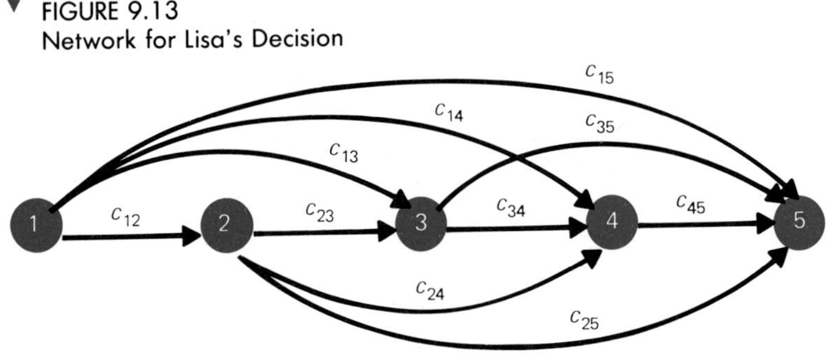

APPLICATION CAPSULE

All Gassed Up: A Network Model Helps Air Products and Chemicals Compress Delivery Costs and Expand Service*

With annual sales exceeding $1.5 billion, Air Products is one of the three largest manufacturers and distributors of industrial gases in North America. In particular, oxygen and nitrogen are manufactured in highly automated plants and transported as liquids at a temperature of −320°F using a fleet of more than 500 tractor-trailer trucks. Storage tanks at customer sites are provided by Air Products under long-term contracts, and inventories are monitored and replenished.

Air Products has made a quantum leap from manual order generation and scheduling to the use of an advanced state-of-the-art on-line constrained optimization model. The computer solves daily a mathematical problem involving 800,000 variables and 200,000 constraints. Input to this model includes a file with distance, travel time, and toll cost between any pair of customers. These data are not immediately available but are derived with a shortest-route algorithm applied to a network representation of the road system of the United States.

This system has since been implemented at 10 depots and continues to be expanded. It has been saving the company between 6% and 10% of operating costs, or more than $2 million annually. Other benefits are its significant impact on the management of the distribution function and the opportunities it has created to piggyback other applications onto the on-line network. It has changed decision making from a reactive to an active mode. The system is being presented to customers as a competitive advantage in providing better service.

* Walter J. Bell et al, "Improving the Distribution of Industrial Gases with an On-line Computerized Routing and Scheduling Optimizer," *Interfaces*, Vol. 13, No. 6 (December 1983), pp 4–23.

9.5 The Minimum Spanning Tree Problem (Communication Links)

A communication link must be installed between twelve cities. The costs of the possible direct links between *permissible* pairs of cities are identified in Figure 9.14. Each unit of cost represents $10,000. The network in Figure 9.14 simply identifies *possible* direct links and their costs. For example, it shows that no direct link is possible between city 1 and city 6. There is a direct link possible between city 1 and city 5, at a cost of 1 unit; and so on. These costs are also reproduced in tabular form in Figure 9.15, where the blank entries correspond to impermissible links. Note that, when there is a possible link between city i and city j, it is true that $c_{ij} = c_{ji}$. This is reflected by the data in Figure 9.15.

The task is to construct a *tree* that connects all nodes of the network at minimum total cost. This is called a **minimum spanning tree.** In Section 9.4 a tree was defined to be $n - 1$ arcs, in an n-node network, which connect every pair of

Consider Figure 9.14 as the layout for a water sprinkler system that must be dug in hard clay. The numbers on the branches represent the hours of digging by hand that must be done. All the nodes (sprinkler heads) must be connected to one another to form a "tree" (not a "loop"), so that the water main can be connected to any of the nodes in order for the system to work.

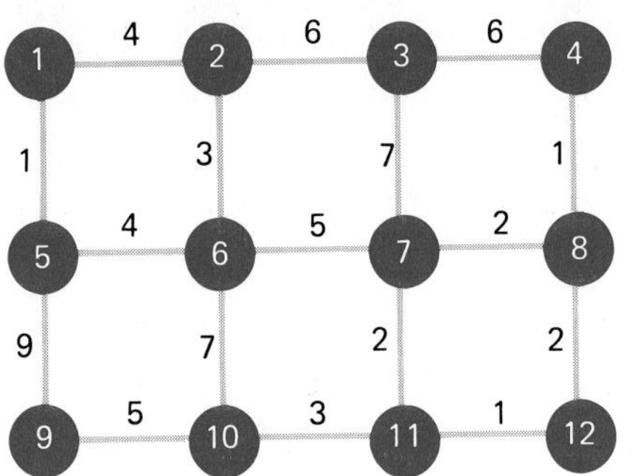

▲ FIGURE 9.14
Costs of Possible Links

FROM CITY	TO CITY 1	2	3	4	5	6	7	8	9	10	11	12
1		4			1							
2	4		6			3						
3		6		6			7					
4			6					1				
5	1					4			9			
6		3			4		5			7		
7			7			5		2			2	
8				1			2					2
9					9					5		
10						7			5		3	
11							2			3		1
12								2			1	

▲ FIGURE 9.15
Cost Table for Communication Links

nodes. Indeed, in that section you saw that the shortest-route algorithm produced a particular tree in the network it addressed. Here we construct another type of tree.

The Greedy Algorithm

The algorithm for solving this problem is extremely simple. We shall give two forms for essentially the same algorithm.

This method is better suited to a visual solution, but is not easily adapted to a computer solution.

The Graphical Method. The first form, the *graphical method,* is particularly easy to implement by hand on a graphical display such as Figure 9.14.

- ***Step 1:*** Arbitrarily begin at any node. Pick the cheapest arc leading out of that node. This is the first link. It forms a *connected* segment of two nodes. The remaining nodes are termed *unconnected.*

▶ ***Step 2:*** Consider all arcs leading from the connected segment to the unconnected nodes. Select the cheapest to be the next link. Break ties arbitrarily. This adds a new node to the connected segment. Repeat this step until all nodes are connected, which requires $n - 1$ steps.

This is called "greedy" because we can be shortsighted and simply find the nearest connection possible (local optimization), and, in this case, greed works.

This is called a *greedy algorithm* because at each step the best possible choice is made. This is one of the few problems in management science where the greedy algorithm is guaranteed to produce an optimal solution. The use of the greedy algorithm as a heuristic approach is discussed in Chapter 12.

Graphical Method Applied. Let us apply the graphical method to the network shown in Figure 9.14. We are allowed to begin at any node. We arbitrarily select node ①. According to Figure 9.14, the cheapest arc emanating from node ① is the arc (1, 5). This is the first link, as shown in Figure 9.16. Nodes ① and ⑤ are now

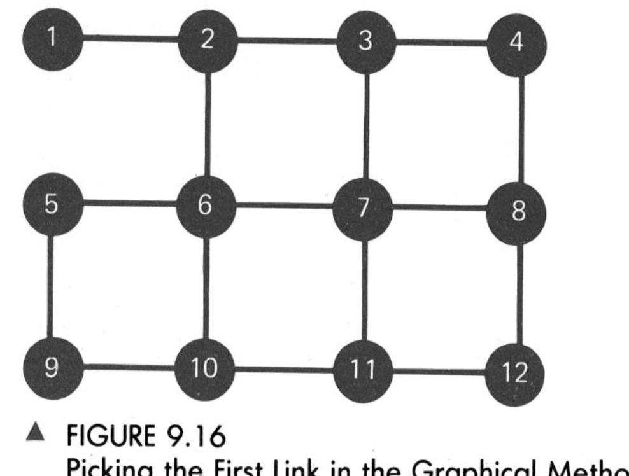

▲ FIGURE 9.16
Picking the First Link in the Graphical Method

connected. The cheapest arc emanating from either of these has a cost of 4. Either of the arcs (1, 2) or (5, 6) can be chosen as the next link. Let us choose (5, 6). Now nodes ①, ⑤, and ⑥ are connected. Next in succession the arcs (6, 2), (6, 7), (7, 8), (8, 4), (7, 11), (11, 12), (11, 10), (10, 9), (4, 3) are selected. The final tree is shown in Figure 9.17. The minimum total cost of connecting all nodes of the network is obtained by adding the costs on the arcs in the minimum spanning tree. In this case the minimum cost is 33 units.

The Tabular Method. The second form of the greedy algorithm for this problem is more suited to be implemented directly on the tabular data in Figure 9.15,

▼ FIGURE 9.17
Minimum-Cost Spanning Tree Produced by the Graphical Method

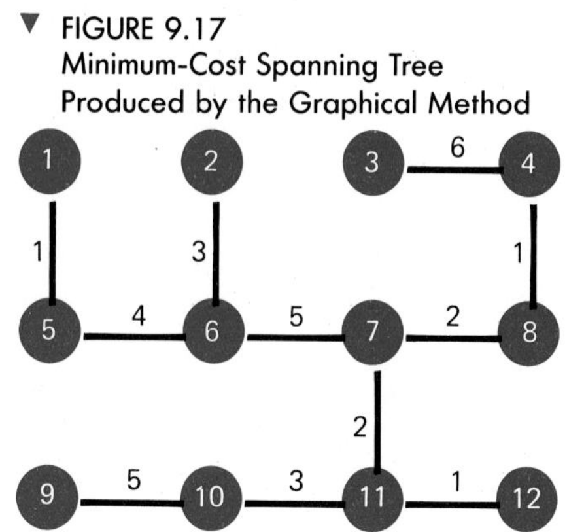

without resorting to the network diagram. This is the form that the computer would employ.

- ▶ ***Step 1:*** Arbitrarily begin with any node. Designate this node as connected and place a √ beside the row corresponding to this node. Cross out the column label corresponding to this node.
- ▶ ***Step 2:*** Considering all rows with a √, find the smallest value in columns with labels not crossed out, and circle this value. Ties are broken arbitrarily. The column containing this circled element designates the new connected node. Cross out this column label, and place a check in the row corresponding to this node. Repeat this step until all nodes are connected.
- ▶ ***Step 3:*** After all nodes are connected, the minimum-cost spanning tree is identified by the circled elements.

Tabular Method Applied. As an illustration, let us apply the algorithm to the data in Figure 9.15. We begin the algorithm arbitrarily with node ①, placing a check next to row 1 and crossing out column 1. Step 2 requires us to identify the smallest value in row 1, which is 1 under column 5. Thus, we circle the value 1, cross out column 5, and put a check next to row 5. At this point nodes ① and ⑤ are connected, and Figure 9.15 has been revised to look like Figure 9.18.

▼ FIGURE 9.18
Nodes 1 and 5 Are Connected

FROM CITY	TO CITY											
	~~1~~	2	3	4	~~5~~	6	7	8	9	10	11	12
√ 1		4			①							
2	4		6			3						
3		6		6			7					
4			6					1				
√ 5	1					4			9			
6		3			4		5			7		
7			7			5		2			2	
8				1			2					2
9					9					5		
10						7			5		3	
11							2			3		1
12								2			1	

Continuing the algorithm, the minimum value in rows 1 and 5, considering the columns not crossed out, is 4 in column 6 (alternatively, the 4 in column 2 could be selected.) Thus, nodes ①, ⑤, and ⑥ are now connected. A check is placed next to row 6, and column 6 is crossed out. Continuing this way, we terminate with Figure 9.19.

FROM CITY	TO CITY											
	~~1~~	~~2~~	~~3~~	~~4~~	~~5~~	~~6~~	~~7~~	~~8~~	~~9~~	~~10~~	~~11~~	~~12~~
√ 1		4			①							
√ 2	4		6			3						
√ 3		6		6			7					
√ 4			⑥					1				
√ 5	1					④			9			
√ 6		③			4		⑤			7		
√ 7			7			5		②			②	
√ 8				①			2					2
√ 9					9					5		
√ 10						7			⑤		3	
√ 11							2			③		①
√ 12								2			1	

▲ FIGURE 9.19
Final Tableau

Reading across the rows of this figure, we see that

- Node ① connects to 5.
- Node ④ connects to 3.
- Node ⑤ connects to 6.
- Node ⑥ connects to 2 and 7.
- Node ⑦ connects to 8 and 11.
- Node ⑧ connects to 4.
- Node ⑩ connects to 9.
- Node ⑪ connects to 10 and 12.

Figure 9.20 shows the graphic realization of these connections. You can see that we have obtained precisely the same tree as we obtained using the graphical method (Figure 9.17). This is because, in each application, ties that occurred were broken in the same fashion. If ties were broken in a different way, an alternative optimal solution would be found.

▼ FIGURE 9.20
Minimum-Cost Spanning Tree
Produced by the Tabular Method

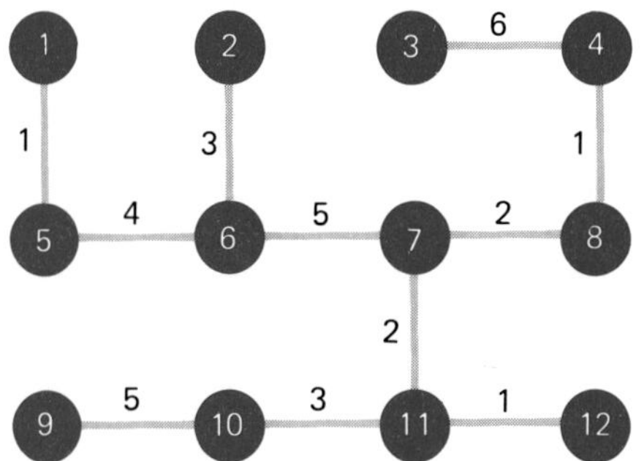

Other Applications of the Minimum Spanning Tree Problem

In the minimum spanning tree problem the c_{ij} terms could represent distances as well as costs, and the applications include the design of transportation systems (the nodes are terminals and the arcs are highways, pipelines, air routes, and so on) as well as communications systems. Nodes could also represent interfacing satellite computer terminals located at various distances from one another. Imagine a system for which communication lines must be installed to connect these terminals. The objective might be to connect all nodes in such a way as to minimize the total length of the communication lines. The solution to this problem would be the minimum spanning tree.

9.6 The Maximal-Flow Problem

In the **maximal-flow problem** there is a single *source* node (the input node) and a single *sink* node (the output node). The problem is to find the maximum amount of total flow (petroleum, cash, messages, traffic) that can be routed through the network (from source to sink) in a unit of time. The amount of flow per unit time on *each arc* is limited by *capacity restrictions.* For example, pipeline diameters limit the flow of crude oil on the links of a distribution system. Flow capacities for nodes are not specified. The only requirement here is that for each node (other than the source or the sink) the balance relation

$$\text{flow out of the node} = \text{flow into the node}$$

must be satisfied.

Formally, letting node ① be the source, and ⓝ be the sink. The problem is

$$\begin{aligned}
&\text{Max } f\\
&\text{s.t.}\quad \textstyle\sum_j x_{ij} - \sum_j x_{ji} = \begin{cases} f, & \text{if } i = 1\\ -f, & \text{if } i = n\\ 0, & \text{otherwise}\end{cases}\\
&0 \le x_{ij} \le u_{ij}, \quad \text{all } (i, j) \text{ in the network}
\end{aligned}$$

We observe that:

1. The variables x_{ij} denote the flow per unit time across the arc (i, j) connecting node ⓘ and node ⓙ.
2. Consider the ith constraint, for some fixed value of i. The sum $\sum_j x_{ij}$ is over all j for which arc (i, j), with i fixed, is in the network. Thus, $\sum_j x_{ij}$ is the total flow *out of* node ⓘ. Similarly, the sum $\sum_j x_{ji}$ is over all j for which there is an arc (j, i) in the network (where i is fixed). Thus, $\sum_j x_{ji}$ is the total flow *into* node ⓘ.
3. The symbol f is a variable denoting the total flow through the network per unit time. By definition this is equal to the flow per unit time leaving the source, node ① (the first constraint). This is also equal to the flow per unit time entering the sink, node ⓝ (the second constraint). The objective is to maximize this quantity.
4. The u_{ij}'s denote the capacities on the flows per unit time across the various arcs.

This problem, together with the shortest-path problem, is of interest in its own right. It also appears as a subproblem in solving other, more complicated, models. For such reasons, as well as because of some of the theoretic underpinnings (which go beyond our present scope of interest), it is sometimes stated that these two problems (shortest path and max flow) are of central importance in network theory.

An Example: The Urban Development Planning Commission

Here is an example of the maximal-flow problem. Gloria Stime is in charge of the UDPC (Urban Development Planning Commission) ad hoc special interest study group. This group's current responsibility is to coordinate the construction of the new subway system with the highway maintenance department. Because the new subway system is being built near the city's beltway, the eastbound traffic on the beltway must be detoured. The planned detour actually involves a network of alternative routes that have been proposed by the highway maintenance department. Different speed limits and traffic patterns produce different flow capacities on the various arcs of the proposed network, as shown in Figure 9.21.

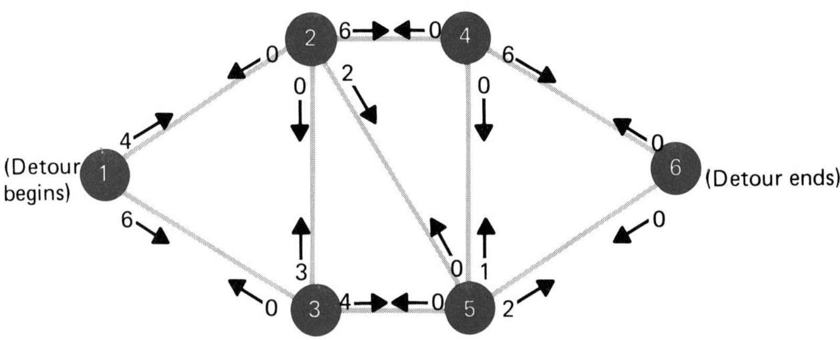

▲ FIGURE 9.21
Proposed Network and Flow Capacities (Thousands of Vehicles per Hour)

Node ① denotes the beginning of the detour, that is, the point at which the eastbound traffic leaves the beltway. Node ⑥ is the point at which the detoured traffic reenters the beltway. Also, in Figure 9.21, the flow capacities depend on the direction of the flow. The symbol 6 on arc (1, 3) denotes a capacity of 6000 vehicles per hour in the 1 → 3 direction. The symbol 0 on the same arc means that a zero capacity exists in the 3 → 1 direction. This is because the indicated arc (1, 3) denotes a one-way street from ① to ③. In this example it is seen that each of the other arcs denotes one-way travel. (The algorithm to be presented will also apply to problems with arcs permitting positive levels of flow in each direction.)

In the following section we present an algorithm for determining the maximum number of vehicles per hour that can flow through the proposed detour network. We also compute, more specifically, how much flow should traverse each link (arc) to achieve the overall maximal flow.

A Maximal-Flow Algorithm

In order to have a better feeling for the algorithm, let us first consider a path of flow from node ① to node ⑥. There are, of course, many such paths. As an example, let us arbitrarily consider ①→②→⑤→⑥. A quantity of flow along such a path is said to be *feasible* if

Feasible flow

1. On no arc of the path does the quantity exceed the arc capacity.
2. With the exception of nodes ① and ⑥, the flow at each node obeys the *conservation condition*

flow entering the node = flow leaving the node

It is important to note the following implication of condition 1:

The maximum amount that can flow from source to sink along a given path is equal to the minimum of the arc capacities on the path.

Flow capacity

Thus for the path ①→②→⑤→⑥ a flow of, for example, 1 unit on each arc is *feasible* since it obeys the conservation condition and does not exceed any arc capacity. Is this the maximum flow along this path? Since the minimum of the arc capacities on the path is 2, we know that another feasible flow is 2 units on each arc, and this is the *flow capacity along this particular path.*

In the maximal-flow algorithm, various trial flows are sequentially considered. The algorithm will revise the trial flows in order to increase the overall flow through the network. In this process it is useful to employ the following procedure. Whenever we assign a flow to a particular arc, we shall adhere to the following rules:

1. *Reduce* the capacity *in the direction of the assigned flow* by the amount of the flow.
2. *Increase* the capacity in the opposite direction by the amount of the flow.

For example, consider arc (1, 2) in Figure 9.21. This arc is

① 4→ ———————— ←0 ②

with a capacity of 4 in one direction and 0 in the other. Suppose, as in the above discussion, that we wish to assign 2 units of flow to this arc. Then, according to rules 1 and 2 of the stated procedure, we will revise the flow capacities as follows:

① 2→ ———————— ←2 ②
(2→)

Undoing trial flows

The (2→) that appears below the arc indicates that 2 units of flow have been assigned in the ①→② direction. We have decreased the capacity in the ①→② direction by 4 − 2 = 2 units. This is the remaining capacity available for flow (considering this arc alone) in the ①→② direction. We have at the same time increased flow in the ②→① direction by 2 units. This provides a "fictitious capacity" in the ②→① direction. It is fictitious because any future flow assigned in the ②→① direction will merely cancel out some of the ①→② flow already assigned. Thus, if at some future point in the course of the algorithm, we should decide to send a single unit of flow in the ②→① direction, it would be necessary (again according to rules 1 and 2) to subtract a unit from the fictitious ②→① capacity and add a unit to the ①→② capacity. Doing this, we would obtain the newly revised capacities.

① 3→ ———————— ←1 ②
(1→)

Thus, rules 1 and 2 provide a device that allows us to "undo" previously assigned trial flows. Since we have "sent back" one of the two initially assigned units, there is now a flow of 1 unit in the ①→② direction, with a remaining capacity of 3 units in this direction. The remaining 1 unit of fictitious capacity in the ②→① direction allows us to undo this single unit of ①→② flow, in which case there is no flow on the arc.

The maximal flow algorithm

We are now in a position to give the steps of the maximal-flow algorithm.

- ***Step 1:*** Find any path from source to sink that has positive flow capacity. That is, considering all arcs on the path, the minimum of the capacities in the direction of flow (source → sink) must be positive. If no such path is available, the optimal solution has been found.
- ***Step 2:*** Let c_{Min} denote the minimum-flow capacity of all arcs on the path selected in step 1. Increase the existing flow through the network by sending an additional flow of c_{Min} over this path.
- ***Step 3:*** For this same path, decrease the capacities in the direction of flow, on each arc, by c_{Min}. Increase the capacities in the opposite direction by c_{Min}, for all arcs in the path. Go back to step 1.

Applying the Algorithm: Solving Gloria's Problem

Let us apply the algorithm to Gloria Stime's problem (Figure 9.21).

Iteration 1. We arbitrarily begin with path ①→③→⑤→⑥. On this path, c_{Min} = 2, the flow capacity in the ⑤→⑥ direction (i.e., the direction of flow from source to sink) on arc (5, 6). Thus, all capacities in the direction of flow are reduced by 2 units. Capacities in the opposite direction are increased by 2 units. Note that (5, 6) will now have a capacity of zero in the ⑤→⑥ direction, which means that the *path* ①→③→⑤→⑥ *now* has zero capacity. The revised network appears in Figure 9.22. In Figure 9.22, the arrow leading into node ① indicates a total flow of 2 units entering the network. This is also, as shown, the amount of flow leaving node ⑥. That is, we now have 2000 vehicles per hour being transported across the network. Is this a maximal flow? The answer is no, because there are remaining paths from source to sink with a positive capacity (e.g., ①→②→④→⑥ in Figure 9.22).

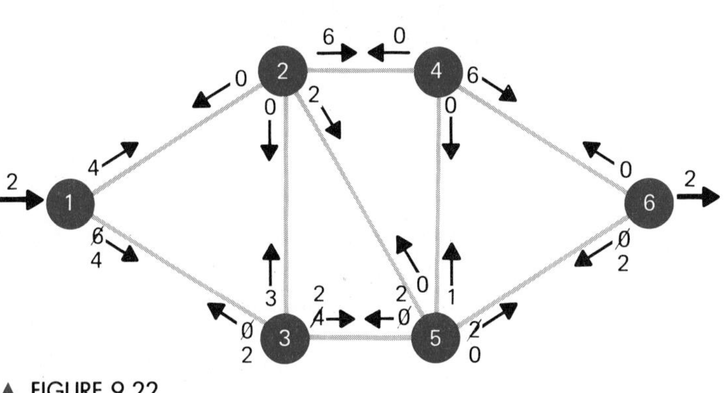

▲ FIGURE 9.22
Gloria's First Update

Iteration 2. Reapplying step 1, we select the path ①→②→④→⑥. The value of c_{Min}, determined by arc ①→②, is 4 units. The revised network appears in Figure 9.23. Note that the total flow through the network is now 6 units, which is the sum of the c_{Min} values from the first two iterations.

Iteration 3. We now select the path ①→③→②→④→⑥. The value of c_{Min} is 2 units, and the revised network appears in Figure 9.24. Note that both arcs leading into node ⑥ now have a capacity of 0 in the direction of node ⑥. Thus, there are no

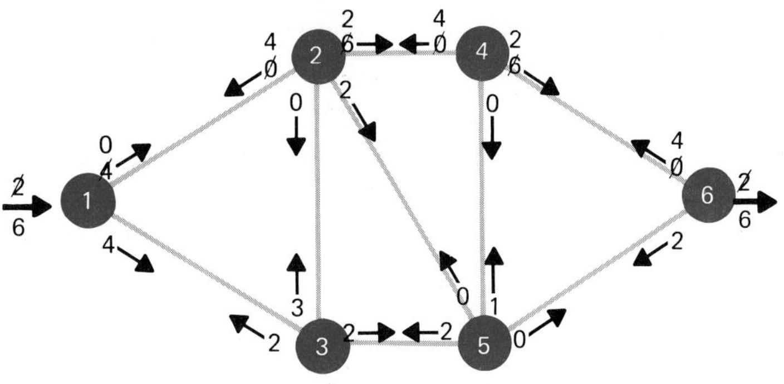

▲ FIGURE 9.23
Gloria's Second Update

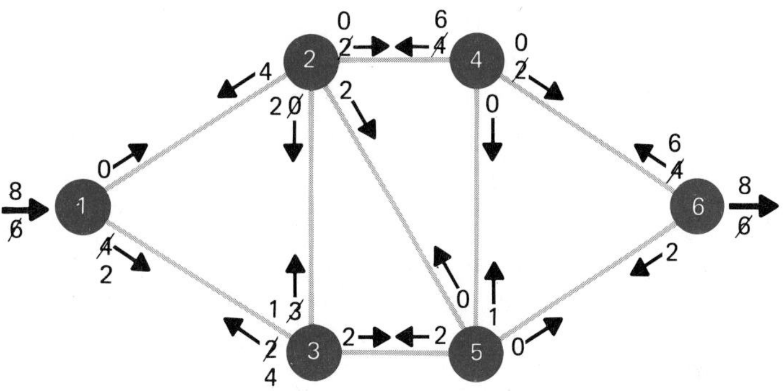

▲ FIGURE 9.24
Gloria's Third Update

remaining paths from node ① to node ⑥ with positive capacity on all arcs of the path. Figure 9.24 shows that the maximal flow for this network is 8000 vehicles per hour. Let us now show how to compute the amount and direction of flow on each arc so that this total flow of 8000 vehicles per hour can be achieved.

Determining the Final Flows. The final flow on each arc is determined by comparing the final arc capacity with the initial arc capacity. The rule for each arc, is:

> **If final capacity is *less than* initial capacity, compute the difference. That difference is the amount of flow traversing the arc.**

For example, Figure 9.21 shows that on arc (3, 5) the initial capacities were

Initial: ③ 4→ ———————————————— ←0 ⑤

The final capacities, shown in Figure 9.24, arc

Final: ③ 2→ ———————————————— ←2 ⑤

Since the final capacity in the ③→⑤ direction is 2 units less than the initial capacity in that direction, the difference $4 - 2 = 2$ is the final *flow* over this arc, and it is in the ③→⑤ direction.

Applying this rule to all arcs in the network produces the maximal-flow pattern shown in Figure 9.25.

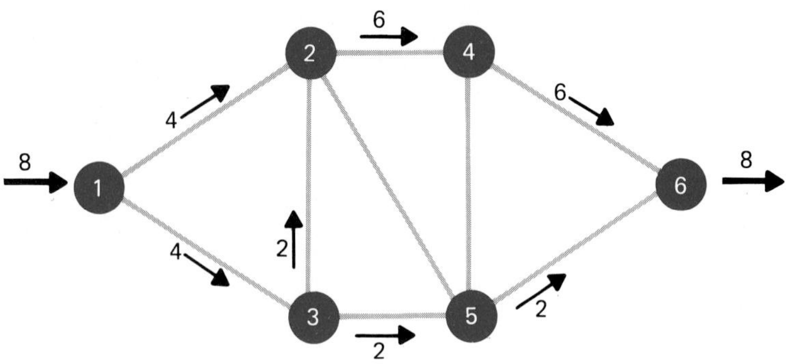

▲ FIGURE 9.25
Maximal-Flow Pattern for Gloria's Problem

The Max Flow/Min Cut Result

One of the key theoretic results in network theory relates to the maximal-flow problem. The result, called the max flow/min cut theorem, is very simple to state. We first define the notion of a **cut** and a **cut capacity.**

- ***Cut:*** A partition of the nodes into two disjoint classes, say C_1 and C_n, where the source is in the C_1 and the sink is in C_n.
- ***Cut Capacity:*** Consider all arcs that directly connect a node in C_1 to a node in C_n. The sum of the capacities on these arcs, in the $C_1 \rightarrow C_n$ direction, is called the cut capacity.

In Gloria's network, Figure 9.21, there are many possible cuts. Several are shown in Figure 9.26.

To calculate the cut capacity of the first cut in Figure 9.26 we must sum up the capacities on each of the arcs connecting a node in C_1 with a node in C_n. In this case we must sum the capacities on arcs (2, 4), (5, 4), and (5, 6). Since these capacities are 6, 1, and 2, respectively, the cut capacity is 9. Other cut capacities are calculated in a similar manner.

You can see in Figure 9.26 that the smallest of the cut capacities is 8, which, as we have seen, is the maximal flow in Gloria's network. The max flow/min cut theorem states that this equality will always be true. Intuitively, it generalizes the concept that the maximal flow on any *path* is equal to the minimal-cut capacities on the path.

Max flow/min cut theorem: **The maximal flow in any network is equal to the minimal-cut capacity.**

▼ FIGURE 9.26
Illustrative Cuts and Cut Capacities

C_1	C_n	CUT CAPACITY
①, ②, ③, ⑤	④, ⑥	9
①, ②, ③	④, ⑤, ⑥	12
①	②, ③, ④, ⑤, ⑥	10
①, ②, ③, ④, ⑤	⑥	8
①, ②	③, ④, ⑤, ⑥	14

9.7 Notes on Implementation

Network models and algorithms are among the most important applications of management science, and specialization in this topic has become a career path in the field. Along this line, in recent years we have seen the appearance of a number of consulting firms that deal exclusively with network applications. The main emphasis of such firms is often on strategic planning problems from the point of view of distribution studies, where the term *distribution* is taken in a quite general sense: flow of physical product, information, vehicles, cash, and so on.

The software libraries for most of the large computer systems include packages for solving various network problems. Some of the state-of-the-art software for very-large-scale applications must be purchased from private vendors.

The application of network models to real problems involves considerable skill and experience in casting problems, which initially may not appear to be network models, into a network representation. For example, an LP model for a problem of interest may not be a network problem, but its dual may in fact have a network structure; or the network structure may emerge in the dual only after some clever manipulation of the original problem. To capitalize on the advantages of the network structure, it is often worth the price of "straining" the initial formulation to cast it (or its dual) into a network representation.

As a final note, as stated in the text, it is worth emphasizing that many real problems contain subproblems that may have a network form.

9.8 Summary

Network problems are important for several reasons. These problems have such a simple special linear form that special superefficient algorithms can be applied to obtain optimal solutions. Also, under mild restrictions on the data it will always be true that integral-valued optimal solutions exist and are provided by the network algorithms. Finally, all of this is of interest because a wide variety of real-world problems can be cast as network problems. The flows may represent physical quantities, paperwork, cash, vehicles, and so on. The type of problem amenable to the network approach is often very large in scale. One can imagine, for example, a network model of an international enterprise involved in paper production. The network might depict the overall multiperiod distribution system from the forest through lumber storage, a variety of paper mills, widely distributed warehouses, and even wholesalers in numerous marketing districts. A model for such a vast operation offers the potential of creating considerable savings in the firm's global operations. The potential size of such models leads one to appreciate the importance of speed in the solution algorithm.

Often the crucial element in network modeling is the analyst's ingenuity in being able to cast the original complex problem into the network format. Usually, this is far from a trivial exercise in model formulation, and considerable on-site experience inside the operation being modeled is often a prerequisite.

Of course, all network models can be solved with an LP algorithm, but in this chapter we have studied special-purpose algorithms for solving three specific network problems of interest: shortest-route, minimum spanning tree, and maximal-flow. These algorithms are of interest in their own right, as well as being useful in solving subproblems of larger or more complex problems.

Key Terms

Network Diagram. A schematic representation consisting of nodes and arcs over which flows may occur. (*p. 399*)

Arc. A connection between two nodes in a network. (*p. 399*)

Branch. A synonym for arc. (*p. 399*)

Node. An element in a network. (*p. 399*)

Capacitated Transshipment Model. A network model with supplies at specified origins, demands at specified destinations, and shipment alternatives through intermediate nodes on capacitated routes from origins to destinations. (*p. 401*)

Node-Arc Incidence Matrix A tableau format for the constraint data in a network model. Corresponding to each arc of the network is a column of the tableau. Corresponding to each node is a row of the tableau. Each column has only two nonzero entries, +1 and −1. The +1 (−1) is in the row corresponding to the node at which the arc originates (terminates). (*p. 402*)

Destination. A node in a network with positive demand. (*p. 403*)

Origin. A node in a network with positive supply. (*p. 403*)

Network Model. Generally refers to the capacitated transshipment model or one of its special forms. (*p. 403*)

Shortest-Route Problem. The problem of finding shortest routes from a specified node (the origin) to each of the other nodes in a network. (*p. 404*)

Shortest-Path Tree. The shortest path from origin to any node will traverse a subset of the arcs on this tree. (*p. 406*)

Tree. $(n - 1)$ arcs, in an n-node network, that connect all pairs of nodes. (*p. 406*)

Temporary Label. Intermediate label on a node in the shortest-route algorithm. (*p. 406*)

Permanent Label. In the shortest-route algorithm, the permanent label on a node shows the shortest distance from origin to the node and shows the predecessor node on the shortest route. (*p. 406*)

Minimum Spanning Tree. A tree that connects all nodes of a network at minimum total cost. (*p. 412*)

Maximal-Flow Problem. The problem of routing the maximal amount of flow through a network. (*p. 417*)

Cut. A partition of the nodes of a network into two disjoint classes, say C_1 and C_n, where the source is in C_1 and the sink is in C_n. (*p. 422*)

Cut Capacity. The sum of the capacities in the $C_1 \rightarrow C_n$ direction over all arcs that directly connect a node in C_1 to a node in C_n. (*p. 422*)

Major Concepts Quiz

True-False

1. **T F** A capacitated transshipment problem has one variable for each node.
2. **T F** A node-arc incidence matrix for the network problem has a +1, a −1, and all other entries 0 in each column.
3. **T F** If the right-hand side of any arc capacity inequality in a capacitated transshipment problem is zero, the problem is infeasible.
4. **T F** In the shortest-route problem a temporary label on a node becomes a permanent label when the node of interest becomes a closest temporary labeled node to the base node.
5. **T F** The minimum spanning tree connects all nodes of a network at minimum total cost.
6. **T F** In the minimum spanning tree problem the greedy algorithm is a useful heuristic but is not guaranteed to find an optimal solution.
7. **T F** The maximal-flow algorithm requires the construction and direct evaluation of every path from the source to the sink.
8. **T F** The maximal flow through any path in a network is equal to the minimum arc capacity on that path.
9. **T F** In the maximal-flow problem a cut is *any* two disjoint sets of nodes.

Multiple Choice

10. A positive right-hand side in a flow balance equation of a capacitated transshipment problem indicates that
    a. the node is an origin
    b. the node is a destination
    c. the node is a transshipment node
    d. none of the above

11. Which of the following is a condition that assures that there is an optimal integer solution to a capacitated transshipment problem?
    a. the right-hand side of all flow equations (the L_j's) be integer
    b. the arc capacities (the u_{ij}'s) be integer
    c. either a or b
    d. both a and b

12. In the shortest-route problem, the first number in a permanent label on the node
    a. is the minimum distance between the base and that node
    b. is the minimum distance between the base and that node on any path that passes through the node indicated by the second number in the label
    c. is the minimum distance between that node and a specified destination
    d. both a and b

13. The shortest-path tree
    a. connects every pair of nodes
    b. is the set of all arcs used in tracing the shortest paths from a base H to every other node
    c. both a and b

14. In the maximal-flow problem the maximized flow is equal to
    a. the flow over an arbitrary cut
    b. the maximal capacity over all cuts
    c. the minimum-cut capacity
    d. none of the above

Questions 15 through 19 refer to the following problem: A company has two plants and three warehouses. The first plant can supply at most 500 pounds of a particular product, and the second plant at most 200 pounds. The demand at the first warehouse is 150, at the second warehouse 200, and at the third warehouse 350. The cost of manufacturing one pound at plant *i* and shipping it to warehouse *j* is given below:

	TO WAREHOUSE		
FROM PLANT	1	2	3
1	8	10.2	12.6
2	7	9	11.8

Suppose the problem is to determine a shipping schedule that satisfies demand at minimum cost.

15. This problem is
    a. a network model
    b. a transportation model
    c. an integer program
    d. all of the above
    e. a and b

16. Let x_{ij} denote the amount sent from plant i to warehouse j. The demand constraint for the first warehouse is properly written as

a. $x_{11} + x_{21} = 150$

b. $x_{11} + x_{21} \geq 150$

c. both a and b are correct (i.e., it does not matter whether = or ≥ is used)

17. Let x_{ij} denote the amount sent from plant i to warehouse j. In symbols, the supply constraints can be written as

a. $\sum_{i=1}^{3} x_{ij} \leq s_j, j = 1, 2$

b. $\sum_{i=1}^{3} x_{ij} = s_j, i = 1, 2$

c. $\sum_{j=1}^{3} x_{ij} = s_j, i = 1, 2$

d. none of the above

e. both a and b are correct (i.e., it does not matter whether = or ≥ is used)

18. The simplex method will always find an integer solution to this problem.

a. T

b. F

19. Since total supply = total demand, all constraints (supply and demand) must be written as equalities.

a. T

b. F

Answers

1. F	**6.** F	**11.** d	**16.** c
2. T	**7.** F	**12.** d	**17.** d
3. F	**8.** T	**13.** c	**18.** a
4. T	**9.** F	**14.** c	**19.** b
5. T	**10.** a	**15.** e	

▶ Problems

See IM.

9-1. ▲ Consider the following linear constraints of a transshipment model. Construct the corresponding incidence matrix and the associated network diagram, labeling each node with its supply or demand.

$$
\begin{aligned}
x_{13} + x_{12} + x_{14} &= 2 \\
-x_{12} + x_{24} &= 1 \\
-x_{13} + x_{35} &= 0 \\
-x_{24} - x_{14} + x_{46} + x_{45} &= 0 \\
-x_{35} + x_{56} - x_{45} &= 0 \\
-x_{46} - x_{56} &= -3 \\
x_{ij} \geq 0, \quad & \text{all } (i, j)
\end{aligned}
$$

See IM.

9-2. ▲ Consider the following constraints:

$$
\begin{aligned}
x_{12} + x_{13} &= 2 \\
- x_{12} + x_{24} + x_{25} &= 0 \\
- x_{13} + x_{34} &= 0 \\
- x_{24} - x_{34} + x_{45} &= -1 \\
- x_{25} - x_{45} &= -1
\end{aligned}
$$

Construct the corresponding incidence matrix and network diagram.

See IM.

9-3. ▲ Write the linear constraints corresponding to the transshipment network of Figure 9.27.

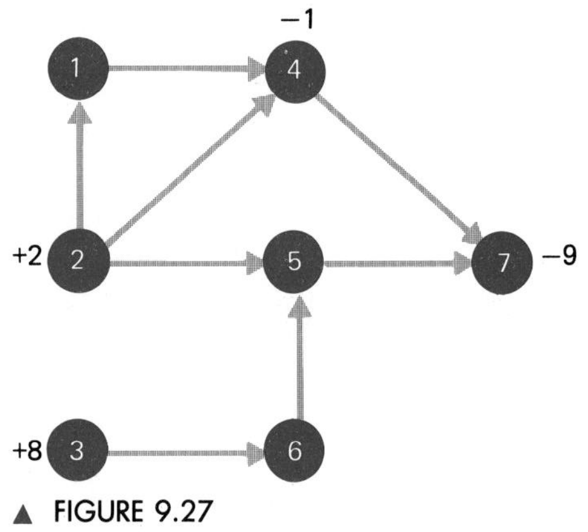

▲ FIGURE 9.27

See IM.

9-4. ▲ Write the linear constraints corresponding to the transshipment network of Figure 9.28.

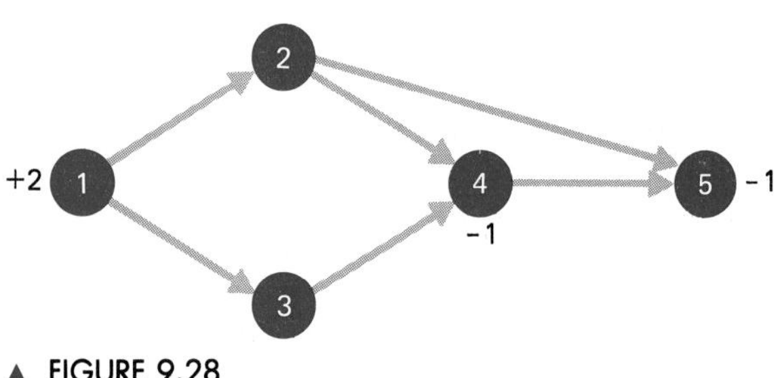

▲ FIGURE 9.28

See IM.

9-5. ▲ Construct the incidence matrix for the network shown in Problem 9-4.

See IM.

9-6. ▲ Consider the distribution network shown in Figure 9.29. Find the shortest route from node ① to all other nodes in the network.

Connect H−1,1−3,2−3,2−5, 3−4,4−7,6−7 (See IM)

9-7. ▲▲ Algorithms were presented in this chapter for determining two types of trees: the shortest-path tree and the minimum spanning tree. Each algorithm can be applied to the same problem, that is, the same network with the same arc parameters. The question arises as to whether the two algorithms produce the same tree. Apply the minimum spanning tree algorithm to Aaron's problem (p. 404) to show that this algorithm can produce the same tree as the shortest-path tree. Construct a simple three-node example to show that in general the two algorithms will produce different trees.

Only 1

9-8. ▲ In Figure 9.29, by how much does the distance on the arc from ④ to ⑦ have to decrease before it can become part of the shortest-path tree from node ①?

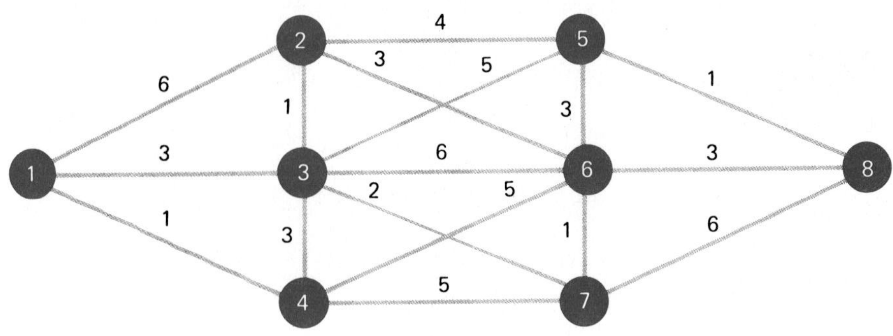

▲ FIGURE 9.29

9-9. ▲ Consider the distribution network shown in Figure 9.30. Find the shortest path from node ① to each of the other nodes.

1–2(8),1–3(17),1–4(10), 1–5(14), 1–6(16), 1–7(20)

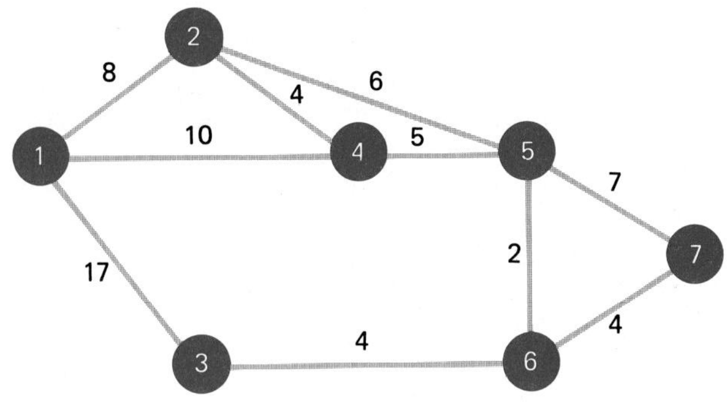

▲ FIGURE 9.30

9-10. ▲ Find the minimum spanning tree for the distribution network in Figure 9.29. Use the graphical method.

Connect 1–4,2–3,3–4, 3–7,5–6,6–7,5–8; min. span = 12

9-11. ▲ Find the minimum spanning tree for the distribution network in Figure 9.30.

See IM.

9-12. ▲▲ Mr. Crimmage is operating the Chicago Health Club with leased equipment and space. Recently, his landlord suggested long-term leasing. Based on the long-term lease plan, Mr. Crimmage obtained Figure 9.31, which displays the expected net cost if he leases from the beginning of year *i* to the beginning of year *j* (in hundreds of dollars). Mr. Crimmage wishes to know when and how long to lease so as to minimize the cost over the next 4 years. Formulate his problem with a network representation and solve it. Find all the solutions.

Lease years 1–2,2–4,4–5 (cost = 43); or lease years 1–2,2–5 (same cost)

	i			
i	**2**	**3**	**4**	**5**
1	13	25	37	45
2		12	21	30
3			10	20
4				9

▲ FIGURE 9.31

9-13. ▲ *Smoke Detector Layout.* Peter Dout is designing the layout of a new coordinated smoke detector system in a warehouse. The required locations as indicated by the insurance company are shown in Figure 9.32. The arcs represent feasible lengths for the electronic connections. The numbers on the arcs represent linear feet. What layout will connect all detectors and use the least total length of electronic connections?

Connect 1–2,2–4,3–4,4–5, 4–6,6–8,7–8,8–9; min. span = 163

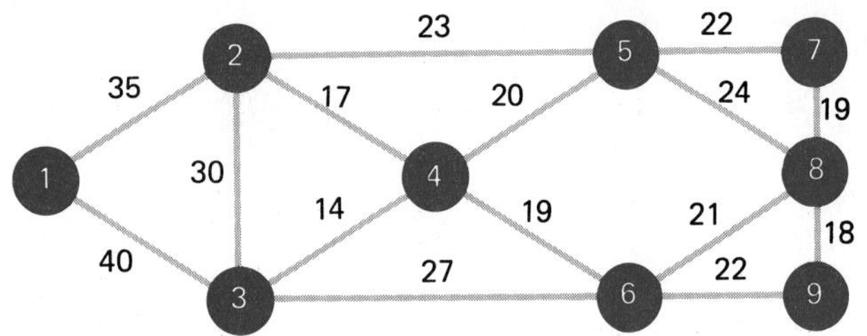

▲ FIGURE 9.32

9-14. ▲ The distances between six different cities are given in Figure 9.33. The cost of building roads is proportional to the distance. How can we build roads at minimum cost so that we can travel from any one city to any other? Use the tabular method.

Connect Aba to Oz, Ur, and Zin; connect Oz to Wu and Wu to Ufa; min. span = 25

FROM CITY	TO CITY					
	Aba	**Oz**	**Ufa**	**Ur**	**Wu**	**Zin**
Aba		6	9	5	8	4
Oz	6		11	10	7	16
Ufa	9	11		14	3	13
Ur	5	10	14		12	17
Wu	8	7	3	12		15
Zin	4	16	13	17	15	

▲ FIGURE 9.33

22 units

9-15. ▲ *Crude Distribution.* Lindsay Doyle is responsible for the transport of crude oil to several storage tanks. A portion of the pipeline network is shown in Figure 9.34. What is the maximal flow from node ① to node ⑦?

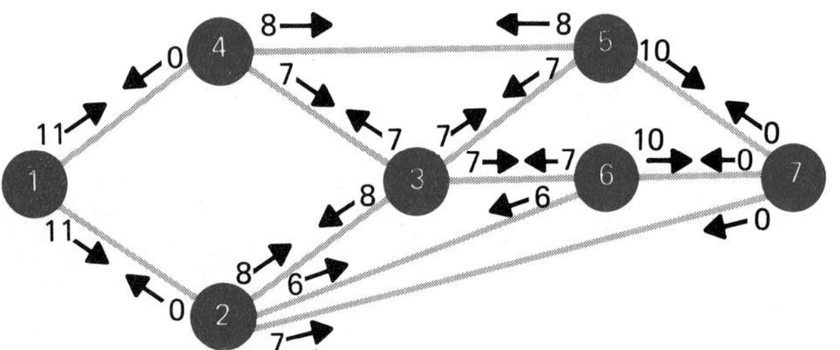

▲ FIGURE 9.34

9-16. ▲▲ Consider the network shown in Figure 9.35. First find the maximal flow, and then find the cut with capacity equal to the maximal flow. Assume ① is the source and ⑦ the sink.

12 units; cuts:3–6,5–6,5–7

18 units

9-17. ▲ Determine the maximal flow from node ① to node ⑥ across the highway network shown in Figure 9.36.

See IM.

9-18. ▲▲ Formulate an LP to solve the maximal flow problem diagrammed in Figure 9.36 (Problem 9-16).

See IM.

9-19. ▲▲▲ Demonstrate that the transportation problem with S origins and D destinations is a special case of the capacitated transshipment model.

See IM.

9-20. ▲▲ Demonstrate that the assignment problem is a special case of the capacitated transshipment model.

9-21. ▲▲▲ Demonstrate that the problem of determining the minimum-cost route from one node to another specific node can be expressed as a special case of the capacitated transshipment model.

Put supply of 1 at origin, demand of 1 at destination; make all other nodes transshipment points.

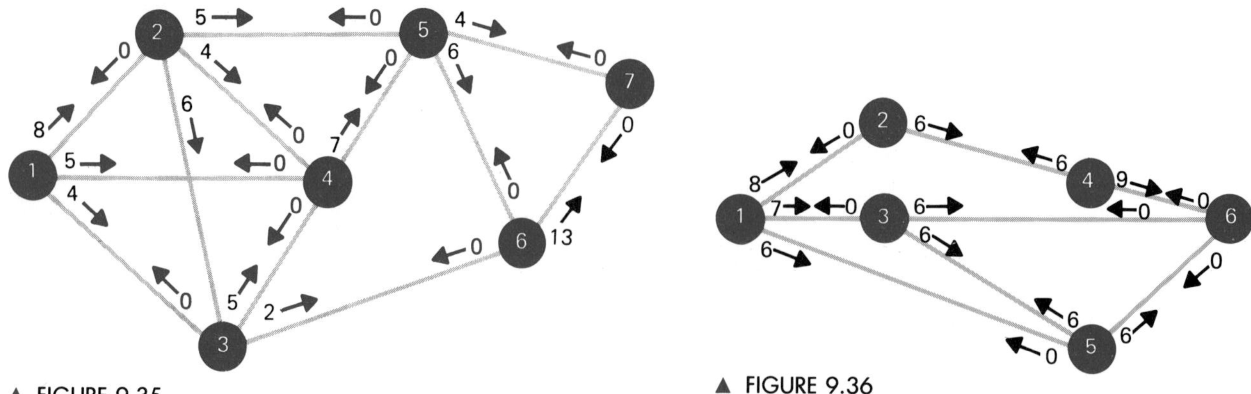

▲ FIGURE 9.35 ▲ FIGURE 9.36

See IM.

9-22. ▲ Consider the transportation tableau shown in Figure 9.37, which represents the cost, c_{ij}, required to move one unit from origin i to destination j.

(a) Draw a network diagram corresponding to the tableau.

(b) Construct the incidence matrix for the network.

To Destination

From Origin	1	2	3	4	Supply
A	18	9	16	∞	100
B	∞	5	3	4	150
C	7	9	∞	8	100
Demand	80	50	100	120	350

▲ FIGURE 9.37

(a) 17
(b) 9
(c) 5, 4, and 10 respectively
(d) 8, 6, and 11 respectively
(e) See IM
(f) 2,000 (See IM)

9-23. ▲▲▲ Consider the transshipment network of Figure 9.38. Nodes 1 and 5 are the plant sites. The plants produce 200 and 150 truckloads, respectively. Nodes 3, 6, and 9 are the outlet sites. The outlets demand 50, 250, and 50 truckloads, respectively. The number on arc (i, j) indicates costs of transporting one truckload from i to j. Assume the cost from i to j is the same as the cost from j to i.

(a) How many variables does the LP formulation of this problem have?

(b) How many constraints does the LP formulation of this problem have?

(c) Find the least costs of moving one truckload from 1 to 3, 6, and 9.

(d) Find the least costs of moving one truckload from 5 to 3, 6, and 9.

(e) Construct the transportation tableau.

(f) Solve the problem with one of the algorithms given in Chapter 7. What is the total cost?

In period 1, produce 2000 units for periods 1 & 2; in period 3 produce 2000 units for periods 3 & 4; cost = $36,000

9-24. ▲▲▲ Moebius Products, Inc. faces the following problem. It has to deliver 1000 Klein bottles per month for the next four months. The production cost per bottle is $5 during month 1, $9 during month 2, $10 during month 3, and $14 during month 4. The inventory carrying cost is $3 per bottle per month. The manager of the company would like to determine the most cost-efficient production schedule—i.e., how many bottles to make at one time, and when. Assume that production is in multiples of 1,000 bottles. That is, production in month i covers demand for months i through j, for some $j \geq i$. Formulate this problem with a network representation and solve it.

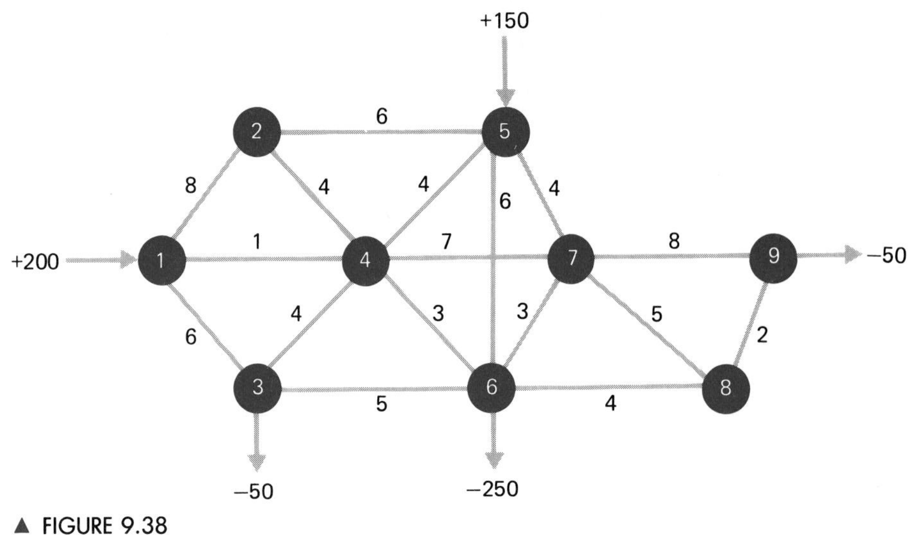

▲ FIGURE 9.38

Appendix 9.1 A PC Approach to Network Problems

This chapter discussed three specific network problems and the algorithms used to solve them. It is not surprising that software has been developed to solve these three classes of problems on the personal computer. This appendix illustrates the use of the QSB system on examples from the text.

The Shortest-Route Problem

A shortest-path tree was shown in Figure 9.12. That figure is reproduced in Figure 9.39 with two modifications: The nodes have been renumbered starting by assigning the number 1 to node H since QSB does not accept 0 as a node number, and for ease

▼ FIGURE 9.39
A Shortest-Path Tree

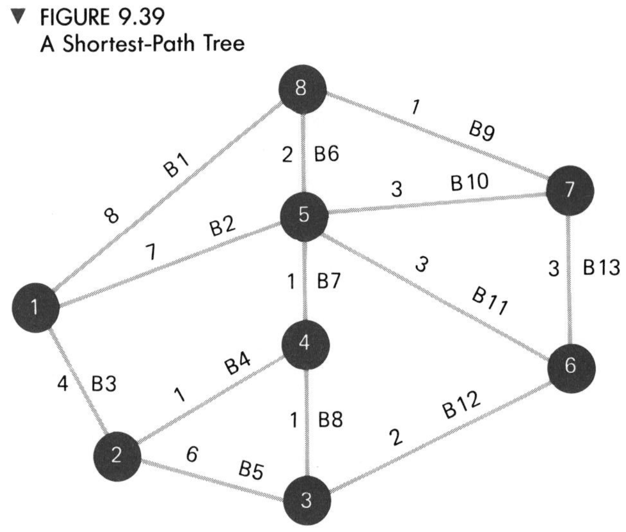

Branch Number	Branch Name	Start Node	End Node	Distance
1	<B1 >	<1 >	<8 >	< 8.0000>
2	<B2 >	<1 >	<5 >	< 7.0000>
3	<B3 >	<1 >	<2 >	< 4.0000>
4	<B4 >	<2 >	<4 >	< 1.0000>
5	<B5 >	<2 >	<3 >	< 6.0000>
6	<B6 >	<5 >	<8 >	< 2.0000>
7	<B7 >	<4 >	<5 >	< 1.0000>
8	<B8 >	<3 >	<4 >	< 1.0000>
9	<B9 >	<8 >	<7 >	< 1.0000>
10	<B10 >	<5 >	<7 >	< 3.0000>
11	<B11 >	<5 >	<6 >	< 3.0000>
12	<B12 >	<3 >	<6 >	< 2.0000>
13	<B13 >	<6 >	<7 >	< 3.0000>

Optimal Solution

Node	Distance	Shortest Route from Node 1
2	4	1- 2 (B3)
3	6	1- 2- 4- 3 (B3–B4–B8)
4	5	1- 2- 4 (B3–B4)
5	6	1- 2- 4- 5 (B3–B4–B7)
6	8	1- 2- 4- 3- 6 (B3–B4–B8–B12)
7	9	1- 2- 4- 5- 7 (B3–B4–B7–B10)
8	8	1- 8 (B1)

▲ FIGURE 9.40
Solving a Shortest-Route Problem with QSB

of translation Figure 9.39 was produced by adding 1 to each node number in Figure 9.12. Also a name, such as "B1," has been appended to each branch. QSB calls for a branch name, and the selected name has been added to the figure for clarity.

The input and solution from the QSB system are presented in Figure 9.40. A quick check reveals that the solution presented here corresponds to the result shown in Figure 9.11.

The Minimum Spanning Tree Problem

Data for a minimum spanning tree problem were originally presented in Figure 9.14. This figure is reproduced in Figure 9.41 where two additional pieces of information are introduced: Each branch is given a name, like "B1," since QSB calls

▼ FIGURE 9.41
A Minimum Spanning Tree Problem

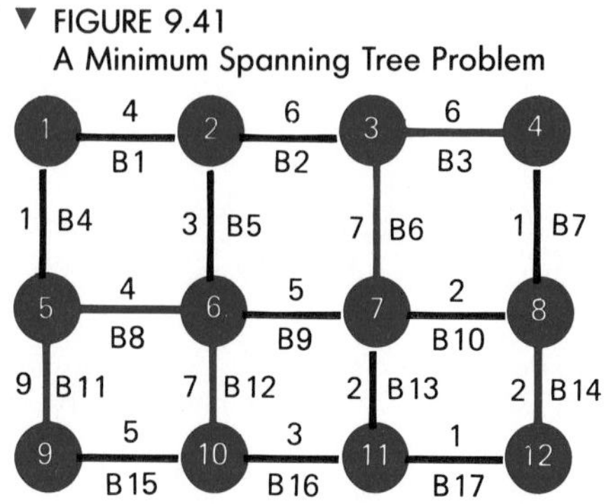

Branch Number	Branch Name	Start Node	End Node	Distance
1	<B1 >	<1 >	<2 >	< 4.0000>
2	<B2 >	<2 >	<3 >	< 6.0000>
3	<B3 >	<3 >	<4 >	< 6.0000>
4	<B4 >	<1 >	<5 >	< 1.0000>
5	<B5 >	<2 >	<6 >	< 3.0000>
6	<B6 >	<3 >	<7 >	< 7.0000>
7	<B7 >	<4 >	<8 >	< 1.0000>
8	<B8 >	<5 >	<6 >	< 4.0000>
9	<B9 >	<6 >	<7 >	< 5.0000>
10	<B10 >	<7 >	<8 >	< 2.0000>
11	<B11 >	<5 >	<9 >	< 9.0000>
12	<B12 >	<6 >	<10 >	< 7.0000>
13	<B13 >	<7 >	<11 >	< 2.0000>
14	<B14 >	<8 >	<12 >	< 2.0000>
15	<B15 >	<9 >	<10 >	< 5.0000>
16	<B16 >	<10 >	<11 >	< 3.0000>
17	<B17 >	<11 >	<12 >	< 1.0000>

Optimal Solution

Branch on the Tree	Distance
1 – 2 (B1)	4
1 – 5 (B4)	1
2 – 3 (B2)	6
2 – 6 (B5)	3
6 – 7 (B9)	5
7 – 8 (B10)	2
7 – 11 (B13)	2
8 – 4 (B7)	1
10 – 9 (B15)	5
11 – 10 (B16)	3
11 – 12 (B17)	1

Total distance = 33

▲ FIGURE 9.42
Solving a Minimum Spanning Tree Problem with QSB

for a branch name, and the arcs in the optimal solution produced by QSB are indicated by black lines.

Figure 9.42 presents the input data and the optimal solution for this problem. Comparing the results with those shown in Figure 9.20 reveals that QSB has produced an alternative optimal solution.

The Maximal-Flow Problem

Data for a maximal-flow problem were presented in Figure 9.21. This figure is reproduced in Figure 9.43, where two additional pieces of information have been appended: Each branch is given a name, like "B1," since QSB calls for branch names, and the optimal solution produced by QSB is indicated by the black arcs, arrowheads, and arc flows.

The input for QSB and the corresponding solution are shown in Figure 9.44.

We observe that QSB produces the same optimal solution that was shown in Figure 9.25.

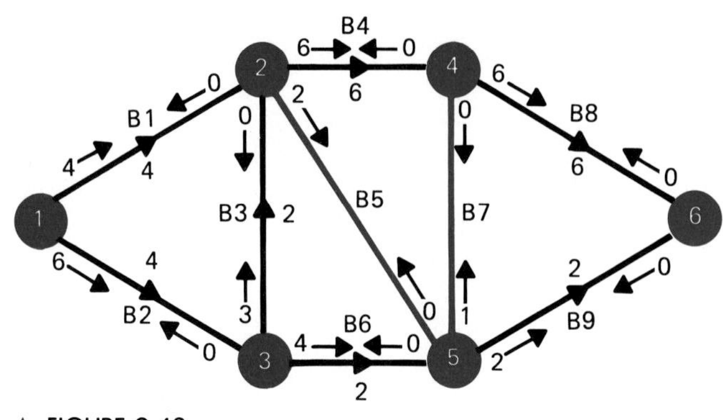

▲ FIGURE 9.43
A Max-Flow Problem

▼ FIGURE 9.44
Solving a Max-Flow Problem

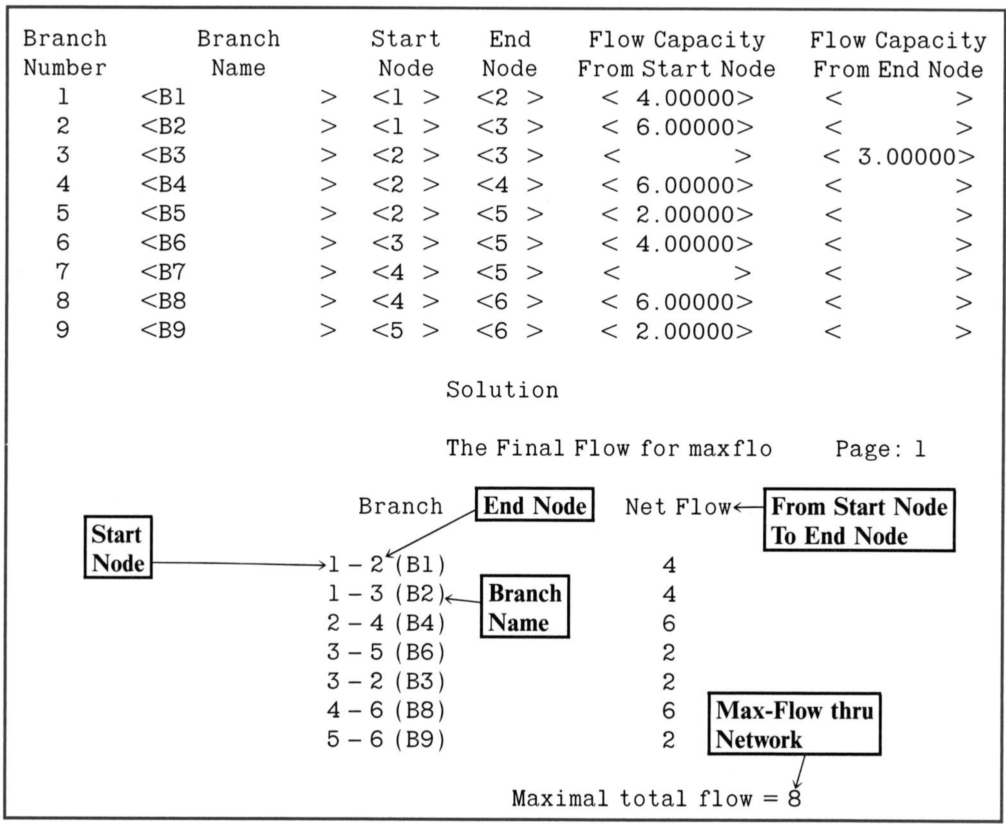

Branch Number	Branch Name	Start Node	End Node	Flow Capacity From Start Node	Flow Capacity From End Node
1	<B1 >	<1 >	<2 >	< 4.00000>	< >
2	<B2 >	<1 >	<3 >	< 6.00000>	< >
3	<B3 >	<2 >	<3 >	< >	< 3.00000>
4	<B4 >	<2 >	<4 >	< 6.00000>	< >
5	<B5 >	<2 >	<5 >	< 2.00000>	< >
6	<B6 >	<3 >	<5 >	< 4.00000>	< >
7	<B7 >	<4 >	<5 >	< >	< >
8	<B8 >	<4 >	<6 >	< 6.00000>	< >
9	<B9 >	<5 >	<6 >	< 2.00000>	< >

Solution

The Final Flow for maxflo Page: 1

Branch	Net Flow
1 – 2 (B1)	4
1 – 3 (B2)	4
2 – 4 (B4)	6
3 – 5 (B6)	2
3 – 2 (B3)	2
4 – 6 (B8)	6
5 – 6 (B9)	2

Maximal total flow = 8

Video Case

Yellow Freight

Anyone who has driven on a U.S. highway knows that trucks are a major component of our transportation system. By any measure, trucking is big business. In 1991 trucks accounted for more than 770 billion ton-miles of transportation. Perhaps 80% of the total amount spent on freight costs is spent on truck transportation. (This figure includes the costs of labor associated with the truck terminals.) It is estimated that there are more than 22 million privately-owned and one million government-owned trucks. The trucking industry has a few major players, but there are literally thousands of small firms. The structure of the industry is determined by the fact that it is not capital intensive—studies show that wages account for nearly 60% of operating revenues. Entry into the trucking industry is relatively easy: Capital costs are low and training requirements are modest. In these circumstances one would expect margins to be thin, and they are.

It is not an easy matter to determine how and when to ship materials by truck. Since trucking is a highly competitive industry, it is crucial to control or minimize operating costs, but there are several factors that make it difficult to determine cost-effective shipping practices.

Load Consolidation. Truck shipping is most economical when full loads are carried. As more organizations turn to just-in-time systems, however, there is increased pressure to ship small loads that must arrive within a small, narrow window. (See the video case in Chapter 10 for a discussion of the just-in-time strategy.) The question of when to send a partial load to meet a JIT requirement and when to consolidate loads, waiting until a full truckload can be arranged, is thus becoming more difficult and more important.

Labor Rules. Work rules, which are greatly influenced by the Teamsters Union, play a major role in determining the cost structure of shipping by truck. For example, in shipping material from Minneapolis to Chicago, it is actually less costlv to use two trucks than to use just one. One truck leaves Minneapolis and the other leaves Chicago; they meet somewhere in Wisconsin and exchange loads. This approach avoids paying a driver for spending a night away from home base.

Government Regulations. All but eight states impose economic regulations on trucking. These controls range from determining what firms can carry what products to setting the price structure. These regulations distort what would appear to be natural economies. For example, Frito-Lay saves $95 per truckload by supplying corn chips needed in its San Antonio plant from Jackson, Mississippi, rather than from Lubbock, Texas, which is 200 miles closer.

Organizational Complexity. A company may organize its shipping through an agent who works with a wide variety of trucking companies to arrange transportation. This means that information must flow across the boundaries of several organizations (shipper to agent to trucker to receiver) as a load travels from origin to destination. Since all companies do not have compatible computers or information-processing approaches, this need greatly complicates matters.

Questions

1. What information does a large shipper need in its effort to manage its truck shipping costs?
2. What advantages do you think a mathematical programming or network approach might have for controlling such costs?
3. What factors make this a hard problem?

CHAPTER 10

Inventory Control with Known Demand

APPLICATION CAPSULE

Sans Blimp: A Tire Company Lowers Costs and Improves Service with the Aid of an Inventory Control Model*

Kelly-Springfield is a major manufacturer of auto and truck tires. This firm operates four factories and produces tires for its own house brands as well as for some 20 private-label customers (department store chains, petroleum companies, auto supply chains, and tire wholesalers). From 1976 to 1979 Kelly expanded its share of the 140-million-unit replacement auto tire industry by nearly 1% and achieved a full 1% increase in the 32-million-unit truck-tire replacement market.

This achievement resulted in no small part from the improved service provided by a management-science–based production and inventory control system. Kelly measures service in terms of the percentage of units shipped within 24 hours of receipt of an order for passenger tires. This percentage steadily increased from 78.5% in 1975 to 85.3% in 1979. This improvement was achieved while average inventory expressed in days' supply decreased from 94.7 days to 78.8 days. During the same period, average inventory for truck tires decreased from 76.0 to 52.2 days. All told, these reductions in inventory generated annual savings of over $2 million.

These remarkable results were achieved with a computer and management-science–based "total system" that includes four major components: sales forecasting, inventory control, production planning, and distribution determination. This complex system has been constructed in two major versions over a 12-year horizon. In the second (current) version, forecasting for each of the 26,000 stocking units for up to 23 months is done in a top-down manner. In other words, Kelly-Springfield sales potential is an assumed share of the projected replacement market. The inventory control section is based on the reorder point, reorder quantity model with a safety stock. The production planning system uses both linear programming and dynamic programming. The distribution system uses a heuristic based on the transportation model of linear programming to determine factory-to-warehouse shipments and transshipments among warehouses to eliminate critical inventory imbalances.

The total benefits from the system come from many sources: reduced inventory investment ($2.2 million), increased productivity ($4.2 million), reduced scrap ($860,000), reduced transfer tonnage ($500,000), and reduced personnel ($175,000). Thus, the total system yields benefits totaling $8.4 million annually, while the improved service due to the system has enabled Kelly-Springfield to expand its market share.

*R. H. King and R. R. Love, Jr., "Coordinating Decisions for Increased Profits," *Interfaces*, vol. 10, no. 6 (December 1980), pp. 4–19.

10.1 Introduction

Steco is the country's second largest steel wholesaler. Its main function is to supply various items to customers. In order to do this the key operations are (1) buying items from the producer; (2) holding these items in inventory; and (3) marketing, selling, and distributing these items in response to demand.

Victor Kowalski is a success at Steco. After 18 years in marketing Victor was recently promoted to vice-president of operations. The purchasing, inventory control, and marketing functions are now his responsibility. He is confident of his ability to handle the marketing aspects of his new position, but he feels less secure in his knowledge of inventory control. Since the holding of inventory is a critical part of Steco's business. Victor's inventory-related decisions will have an important effect on his firm's performance and his own career.

From his favorite management science text, Victor learns

What are inventories?

1. **Inventories** are defined as *idle goods in storage,* waiting to be used.

2. There are many types of inventories; for example, inventories of raw materials, inventories of in-process materials, inventories of finished goods, inventories of cash, and even inventories of individuals.

3. Inventories are held for many reasons. Some distributors hold inventory in order to fill quickly an order placed by a customer. Otherwise, in many cases, the customer would order from a competitor. This, however, is only one reason why inventories are held. They are, in fact, held for any of the following reasons:

a. Inventories smooth out the time gap between supply and demand. For example, the corn crop is harvested in September and October, but user demand for corn (as a raw material for animal feed, corn oil, and so on) is steady throughout the year. Thus, the harvest must be stored in inventory for later use. Users are willing to pay others to worry about storing for the convenience of having the crop available when they need it.

Why are inventories held?

b. The possibility of holding inventory often contributes to lower production costs, for it is more economical to produce some items in large batches even though immediate orders for the items may not exist. One chooses to store the excess in inventory as opposed to producing in a more costly way—that is, a lower but more continuous rate in time.

c. Inventories provide a disguised way of storing labor. For example, in dynamic production problems the availability of labor may be a binding constraint in some later time period but slack in the earlier periods. The possibility of producing excess output in these earlier periods and carrying the product forward in inventory frees labor in the later periods for alternative uses.

d. Finally, as in Steco's case, inventory is a way of providing quick customer service at the time an item is needed, and customers are willing to pay for this convenience.

What are the costs?

4. There are generally three types of costs associated with the inventory activity: *holding costs, ordering costs,* and *stockout costs.*

Students who have had accounting and/or finance will recognize that holding costs are *variable* costs, which vary by the amount of inventory being held. If you want to minimize variable costs, then simply order small quantities.

a. ***Holding costs:*** One of the smaller items stocked by Steco is a piece of 3/10-inch-thick high-carbon steel called an "appliance angle." Victor currently observes that there are 3000 appliance angles in stock. Each angle costs Steco \$8. Thus, Steco currently has

$$(8) \times (3000) = \$24{,}000$$

tied up with the inventory of this item. Suppose that Steco were to reduce this inventory to only 1000 items. Instead of \$24,000, the investment would be reduced to \$8000. It would then be possible to invest some of the \$16,000 that is released—in other words, by holding inventory Steco forgoes the opportunity to make other investments. This so-called **opportunity cost** is perhaps the most important contribution to inventory holding cost. The magnitude of this cost is closely tied to the interest rate. As an indication of its importance, consider that since 1970 the prime interest rate has always been above 5% and that in the early 1980s it hovered near 20%.

There are other holding costs, such as breakage, pilferage, insurance, and special handling requirements. *The larger the inventories, the larger the inventory holding costs.*

These costs are *fixed* costs, and are independent of how much has been ordered. To minimize these costs, order large quantities.

b. ***Ordering costs:*** Each time Steco places an order to replenish its inventories an ordering cost is incurred. *This cost is independent of the quantity ordered.* It is related to the amount of time required for paperwork and accounting when an order is placed and is a direct function of the salaries of involved personnel.

These costs are *variable* costs, and depend on the number of items being backlogged. To minimize this cost, you should never be out of items. Usually, commodity items should never be backlogged; customers can simply go somewhere else and pick them up. However, customized or specialized items can afford to be. The 1989 Mazda Miata had a waiting list for which each customer had to put down a \$500 deposit in October 1989 for delivery in April 1990!

c. ***Stockout costs:*** A **stockout** means that the firm runs out of inventory. In most technical uses, the term *stockout* refers to the more specific phenomenon that orders arrive after inventory has been depleted. There are, at least in the context of a model, two ways to treat such orders. One way is to save up the orders and fill them later after the inventory has been replenished. This is called **backlogging.** (Note that this is really an *assumption* in a model. In the real world, customers usually get to vote on whether they are willing to wait. The extent to which customers are willing to accept backlogging could be a major factor in determining the appropriateness of a model that makes a backlogging assumption.) Another way to deal with stockouts is simply not to accept any orders received when there is no inventory on hand.

The study of inventory includes models that deal with the possibility of stocking out, and in such a case some models assume backlogging; others assume no backlogging. In either case there is a cost of stocking out. This cost could include the lost profit from not making the sale (in the no-backlogging case) or from late delivery (the backlogging case), as well as discounts for a number of more intangible factors, such as the cost of possibly losing the customer, of losing goodwill, and of establishing a poor record of service. In the case of stockouts with no backlogging, we generally use the term **penalty cost,** which means the per unit cost of unsatisfied demand. In the case of stockouts with backlogging we speak of a **backlogging cost,** which means the per unit cost of backlogging demand.

What are the trade-offs?

It is obvious to Victor that, for a company such as Steco, with hundreds of thousands of dollars tied up in inventory, there must be a right way and a wrong way to manage the inventory function. The main trade-offs are clear: On one hand, it is good to have inventory on hand to make sure that customers' orders can be satisfied (i.e., to avoid *stockout costs*). On the other hand, carrying inventory implies a

These trade-offs are found in many noninventory instances. For example, many fast-food franchises opened up for breakfast in the 1980s, realizing that the building was a fixed cost, and that for the small expense of hiring extra employees, they could earn extra money that would defray their larger fixed costs.

holding cost. This cost can be reduced by ordering smaller quantities more often, but that approach involves increased *ordering costs.* These three cost factors must be balanced against each other.

The basic decisions: when and how much

Once the fundamental question of what items to order has been determined, the questions to be answered are the same for all inventory control systems. For every type of item held in inventory, someone must decide (1) *when* a replenishment order should be placed and (2) the **order quantity,** or *how much* should be ordered. Knowing what questions to ask is easy; finding good answers to those questions is not. A multitude of factors combine to make this a difficult problem. Some of the most important considerations are

1. The extent to which future demand is known.
2. The cost of stocking out and management's policy (backlogging or not).
3. The inventory holding and ordering costs.
4. The possibility of long **lead times**—the period of time between when an order is placed and when the material actually arrives.
5. The possibility of quantity discount purchasing plans.

Victor realizes that he has his work cut out for him and decides to give high priority to a review of Steco's inventory system.

10.2 Steco Wholesaling: The Current Policy

In getting started, Victor decides to focus on a small but tractable problem, the current inventory policy for appliance angles. This is what he learns: These angles (used in constructing the frames for many home appliances, such as stoves, refrigerators, and freezers) are a high-volume item for Steco. Figure 10.1 shows the monthly demand for appliance angles during the preceding year.

Demand versus sales

The term **demand** means "orders received." It is not necessarily the same as *sales.* For example, in January of last year 5300 items were demanded. If *at least* 5300 items were in inventory, then sales equaled demand (i.e., sales were 5300). If

▼ FIGURE 10.1
Monthly Appliance Angle Demand

MONTH	DEMAND (UNITS)
January	5,300
February	5,100
March	4,800
April	4,700
May	5,000
June	5,200
July	5,300
August	4,900
September	4,800
October	5,000
November	4,800
December	5,100
Total Annual Demand	60,000
Average Monthly Demand	5,000

fewer than 5300 items were in inventory, say only 5000, then sales were 5000, which is less than the demand of 5300, and consequently a stockout occurred.

As a matter of fact, over a period of several years the demand for appliance angles has remained at a steady rate of about 5000 items per month. Based on this fact, management's policy last year was to add 5000 angle irons to inventory each month. Since demand is expected to hold at about the same level in the future, this is the current policy as well. Victor's question remains: "Is this a good policy?"

One way to attempt to answer this question would be to see how well the policy did last year. This turns out *not* to be an easy task. The answer depends on a considerable amount of information that Victor does not have. Consider:

1. Was there a shortage in January? Demand (5300) is larger than the amount ordered (5000). Thus there might have been. But if Steco had at least 300 angles on hand on January 1, there would not have been. Right? Not necessarily! What if the January replenishment of 5000 angles did not show up until January 10, and there was an order for 300 angles on January 5?

2. Holding costs are equally confusing. Suppose that in March the 5000 angles from the producer arrived on March 1, and an order from one of Steco's customers, for 4800 angles, arrived on March 2. The holding cost was very small. On the other hand, if the customer order for the 4800 angles had occurred on March 31, the holding cost would have been much larger.

Victor quickly gives up the task of calculating last year's actual cost. He simply does not have enough information. Instead, he decides to see what the policy of ordering 5000 angles each month *would* cost in an *abstract, idealized* world. In this world Victor assumes that

Simplifying assumptions

1. Shipments always arrive on the first day of the month.
2. Demand is known and occurs at a constant rate of 5000 units per month.
3. All demand will be satisfied with no backlogging. In other words, stockouts are forbidden.

Victor's incentive for using this *model* is provided by his colleagues. They assure him that *on the average* these assumptions describe rather well the actual circumstances at Steco. He thus decides to use them, realizing that he may have to take the complicating factors of variability and uncertainty into account later. With these assumptions Victor can make a plot of the inventory on hand at any time. Such a plot is shown in Figure 10.2.

Notice how the inventory jumps up by 5000 units at the beginning of each month when a shipment arrives and decreases continuously at a constant rate of 5000 items per month (the constant monthly rate of demand). Also notice that a shipment from the producer arrives at the instant the inventory on hand hits zero. Thus, no stockouts occur. Given assumptions 1, 2, and 3, the cost of operating the system shown in Figure 10.2 depends only on *how much new stock is ordered* and on the *holding and ordering costs.* Since in this ideal world there are no stockouts, Victor need not worry about stockout costs. Let us see how the operating cost arises.

This figure is also called the *Sawtooth Model* because it looks like the teeth of a simple wood saw.

▼ FIGURE 10.2
Inventory on Hand, 5000 Order Quantity

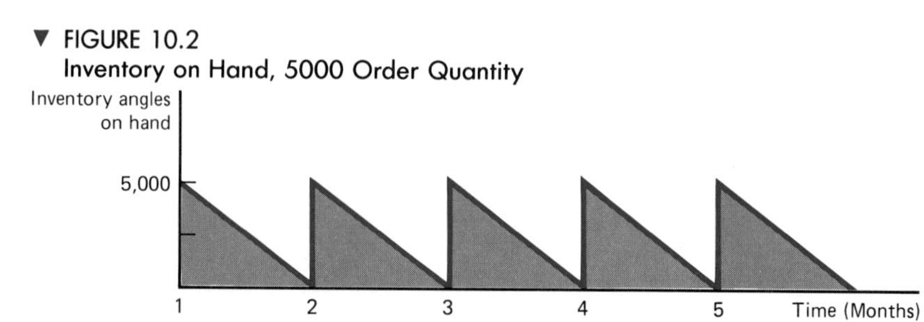

Calculating Annual Ordering and Holding Costs

"In cooperation with his accountants . . ." is a very significant phrase. Management science analysis cannot exist without valid data from the accounting department. It is extremely important to have a good working relationship with accounting.

In cooperation with his accountants Victor learns that (1) it costs \$25.00 to place an order, and (2) it costs \$1.92 to hold an angle in inventory for a year. Given his assumptions, Victor is now in a good position to compute, within his model, the annual cost of *ordering 5000* items per month. Since orders are placed with suppliers once a month

$$\text{annual ordering cost} = 12(25) = \$300$$

To calculate the annual holding cost, Victor uses the following logic:

$$\text{average time each item remains in inventory} = \frac{1}{2} \text{ month}$$

Expressed in terms of years, then, for each batch

$$\text{average time each item remains in inventory} = \frac{1}{24} \text{ year}$$

Since the cost to hold 1 item for 1 year is \$1.92, it must follow that for each batch

$$\text{cost to hold 1 item for } \frac{1}{24} \text{ year} = (1.92)\left(\frac{1}{24}\right)$$

Thus, for each batch of 5000 items

$$\text{holding cost per batch} = 5000(1.92)\left(\frac{1}{24}\right)$$

Since 12 of these batches are ordered each year

$$\begin{aligned} \text{annual holding cost} &= (12)(5000)(1.92)\left(\frac{1}{24}\right) \\ &= (2500)(1.92) \\ &= \$4800 \end{aligned}$$

Victor's simplifying assumptions and calculations in the idealized world have produced an annual holding cost of \$4800. Another derivation may be more intuitive. First note that the average inventory level is one-half of the maximum inventory level when demand is constant (see Figure 10.3). Thus, over the year the average inventory level is 2500 units, and we have

$$\begin{aligned} \text{annual holding cost} &= (\text{average inventory level}) \cdot (\text{holding cost per item per year}) \\ &= (2500) \cdot (1.92) = \$4800 \end{aligned}$$

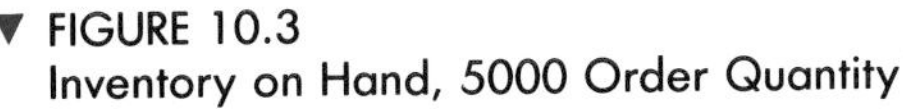

▼ FIGURE 10.3
Inventory on Hand, 5000 Order Quantity

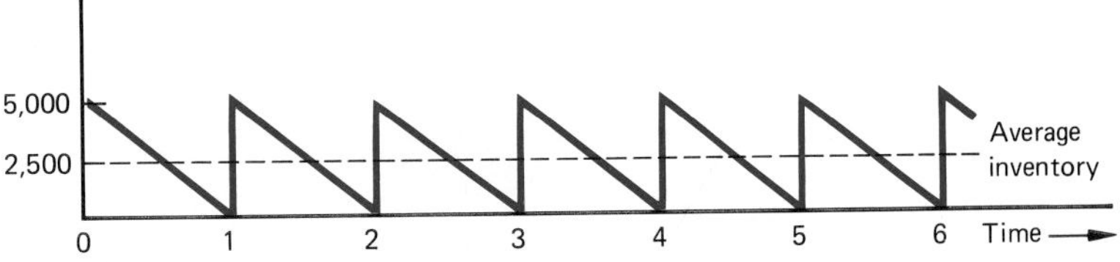

Now combining the yearly holding and ordering costs, Victor computes that, in terms of his model, the annual inventory costs for appliance angles are

Total annual cost

$$\begin{aligned}\text{total annual cost} &= \text{annual holding cost} + \text{annual ordering cost}\\ &= 4800 + 300\\ &= \$5100\end{aligned}$$

As we have pointed out, this figure is based on the policy of ordering 5000 items each month. Suppose that he had placed larger orders, say for 10,000 items each time an order was placed. The effects of this change can be seen by comparing Figures 10.3 and 10.4. Note that an order would now be placed every 2 months (i.e.,

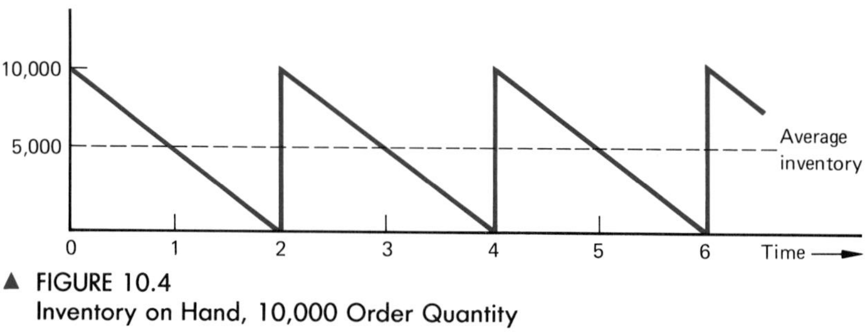

▲ FIGURE 10.4
Inventory on Hand, 10,000 Order Quantity

6 per year) and that the average inventory is 5000 items. The total annual cost would then be computed as follows:

Contrast this with ordering 500 each time, which would give a total annual cost of

(500/2)(1.92) + (60,000/500)(25) = 480 + 3000 = 3480.

$$\begin{aligned}\text{total annual cost} &= \text{annual holding cost} + \text{annual ordering cost}\\ &= (5000)(1.92) + 6(25)\\ &= 9600 + 150\\ &= \$9750\end{aligned}$$

Here, we see that the costs of ordering are now much higher than the holding costs.

Note that *increasing* the order quantity *increased* the annual holding cost and *decreased* the annual ordering cost.

In contrast, suppose that a policy of ordering 2500 items twice a month was followed. Then the average inventory is 1250 items, and 24 orders would be placed each year. In this case

$$\begin{aligned}\text{total annual cost} &= \text{annual holding cost} + \text{annual ordering cost}\\ &= (1250)(1.92) + (24)(25)\\ &= 2400 + 600\\ &= \$3000\end{aligned}$$

Note that *decreasing* the order quantity *decreased* the annual holding cost and *increased* the annual ordering cost.

Seeking the Best Reorder Policy

Victor now clearly understands the general effect of changing the amount that is ordered. What he wonders is whether the policy followed last year by Steco, and currently being followed, is optimal in the *idealized model.* This policy is to order

5000 units per month. It would appear from the last calculation above that a policy of ordering 2500 items twice a month would be better. Is there even a better policy?

In his search for the answer to this question, Victor comes across a computer-based inventory control system called **ICON.**[1] This system is designed to answer two key questions: (1) when to order[2] and (2) how much to order. With reference to the appliance angle policy, this is just what Victor wants to know. When should orders be placed? How much should be ordered?

He decides to explore further this ICON system. He is amazed to discover that this system is based in part on an adaptation of a simple model that he recalls having studied as an undergraduate almost 20 years ago, the **economic order quantity (EOQ) model.** Victor had always thought of it as a textbook model with unrealistic assumptions, a model selected to give a simple and easily taught result. In part, Victor was correct. The EOQ model does ignore a number of important factors. He was, however, wrong in his estimate of its usefulness. This model attempts to balance the cost of placing orders with the cost of holding inventory. In the present appliance angle context, that is just what Victor is looking for. In a larger context, the EOQ model forms the backbone for most of the commercially available computer-based inventory control systems.

As Victor is soon to learn, the ICON system is able to use the EOQ model because it follows a two-step process. First, it uses the EOQ model to answer the "when" and "how much" questions, with or without quantity discounts, and then it modifies these answers to allow for variabilities in demand. The latter topic will be discussed in Chapter 16.

10.3 The Economic Order Quantity Model

Victor decides to see how this system works by first applying the EOQ model to the trial problem posed above. Would any improvements have been obtained?

Developing the EOQ Model

EOQ Assumptions. The EOQ model in its simplest form assumes that

1. No stockouts are allowed. That is, each new order arrives (in totality) as soon as the inventory level hits zero.
2. There is a constant rate of demand.
3. The relevant costs are ordering and holding costs.

Victor notes that these three assumptions are precisely the assumptions he has already made in his calculation (i.e., using his model) that Steco's annual inventory cost is \$5100. Recall that this cost is based on a policy of adding to the stock 5000 angles each month. The EOQ model will give Victor some feeling for the "goodness" of that policy, for it will calculate the **optimal order quantity,** which is defined to be the quantity that under the three assumptions above *minimizes the*

[1]This is a hypothetical system in our scenario that resembles several currently available commercial systems.

[2]We have already seen that, assuming a known rate of demand (5000 items per month), as soon as we choose an order quantity we also implicitly determine how often we order (e.g., once a month, once every 2 months, etc.). The "when to order" question has not yet been addressed. It asks *when* we should order, in terms of the level of the current inventory on hand. This will be seen to depend on lead time to delivery.

total cost per year of ordering appliance angles and holding them in inventory. It is based on

1. ***Ordering cost*** **=** C_0**:** Every time an order is placed, the purchasing department must contact the supplier to determine the current price and delivery time, complete and mail the order form, enter the order into the inventory control system, and initiate the receiving and stock-keeping records. When the order arrives, the receiver must complete the receiving and stock-keeping records and update the order status in ICON. All of this costs money. As we have already seen, Steco estimates the cost of placing an order for appliance angles, *regardless of the number of units ordered,* to be \$25. This includes two thirds of an hour of clerk-category labor at \$18 per hour for wages and fringe benefits, one third of an hour of an assistant purchasing agent's time at \$24 per hour, plus \$5 in material, phone, and mailing costs. Thus,

$$C_0 = \frac{2}{3}(18) + \frac{1}{3}(24) + 5 = \$25$$

2. ***Inventory carrying cost*** **=** C_h**:** Every dollar invested in inventory could be put to use elsewhere by Steco. For example, it could be put in a bank or invested in Treasury bills and earn interest for Steco. When a dollar is tied up in inventory, Steco loses the opportunity to invest it elsewhere. This lost opportunity is called the opportunity cost. Typically, the opportunity cost accounts for a large part of the cost of holding inventory. In addition, there are overhead costs such as rent, light, and insurance that must be allocated to the items in inventory.

Firms sometimes can use their profit margin percentage as their opportunity cost.

The cost of holding inventory is typically expressed as the cost of holding one unit for one year and is calculated as a percentage of the cost of the item. Steco estimates that the cost of holding an appliance angle in inventory for one year is 24% of its purchase price. The 24% figure can be subdivided into an opportunity cost of 20% plus an overhead allocation per item of 4%. Since each angle costs \$8, the cost of holding each item in inventory for one year is

The use of a year as a time frame is important because money earns interest on weekends, holidays, and at night. Keeping it in years avoids having to worry about how many work days there are in a year.

$$C_h = 0.24 \times \$8.00 = \$1.92$$

which is the figure Victor used in his calculations.

The Annual Holding and Ordering Cost. The first step in calculating the optimal (i.e., cost-minimizing) order quantity is to derive an expression for the *annual holding and ordering cost* (AHO) as a function of the order quantity. It consists of two parts, annual ordering cost and annual holding cost.

$$\text{annual ordering cost} = C_0 \times (\text{number of orders per year}) \tag{10.1}$$

Victor notes that if the order quantity is 5000 units, he will place 12 orders a year, since the model assumes a total demand of 60,000, and 60,000/5000 = 12. This leads him to the general formula

$$N = \frac{D}{Q} \tag{10.2}$$

where N = number of orders per year
D = annual demand
Q = order quantity

Students many times forget to make sure that D and C_h are in terms of "per year" and will have demand in months and holding costs in years, etc. In fact, as long as both quantities are in the same time unit, the answer will be correct.

Thus, in general

$$\text{annual ordering cost} = C_0 N = C_0 \left(\frac{D}{Q}\right) \tag{10.3}$$

To compute the annual holding cost Victor makes use of two facts: (1) The annual holding cost is equal to C_h times the average inventory, and (2) the average inventory is equal to one-half of the maximum inventory when demand occurs at a constant rate. Since the order quantity is also the maximum amount of inventory on hand (see Figures 10.3 and 10.4), it follows that

$$\text{annual holding cost} = C_h\left(\frac{Q}{2}\right) \tag{10.4}$$

If we add together expressions (10.3) and (10.4), we see that the assumptions of the EOQ model have enabled Victor to obtain the following expression for the annual holding and ordering cost as a function of the order quantity Q:

AHO

$$\text{AHO}(Q) = C_0\left(\frac{D}{Q}\right) + C_h\left(\frac{Q}{2}\right) \tag{10.5}$$

Since demand occurs at the rate of D units per year, we know that these Q units will be depleted in Q/D years, which is precisely when the inventory level hits the value zero. For example, when $Q = 5000$ and $D = 60{,}000$, the order of 5000 units is depleted in $5000/60{,}000 = 1/12$ year = 1 month, as we have already seen (Figure 10.3). For appliance angles, the relevant values of C_0, D, and C_h can be plugged into expression (10.5) to give:

$$\text{AHO}(Q) = \$25\left(\frac{60{,}000}{Q}\right) + \$1.92\left(\frac{Q}{2}\right) = \left(\frac{1{,}500{,}000}{Q}\right) + 0.96Q \tag{10.6}$$

When $Q = 5000$ it is seen that

$$\text{AHO}(5000) = \$300 + \$4800 = \$5100$$

which is exactly the result Victor obtained in the previous section. Now, however, using expression (10.6), Victor can represent the annual holding and ordering cost for angles as a function of the order quantity Q in graphical form. The result is shown in Figure 10.5.

From this graph it is clear that the optimal order quantity [the one that minimizes AHO(Q)] is somewhat larger than 1000 items. Victor is amazed at how

If the order quantity is 50% higher than optimal (1875), the cost difference (2600.00 – 2400.00) is only about 10% higher. Notice the shallow slope going off to the right (versus the steeper slope on the left for smaller order quantities). This shallow minimum allows for a comfortable margin of error for the order quantity.

▼ FIGURE 10.5
Graph of Annual Holding and Ordering Costs as a Function of Order Quantity

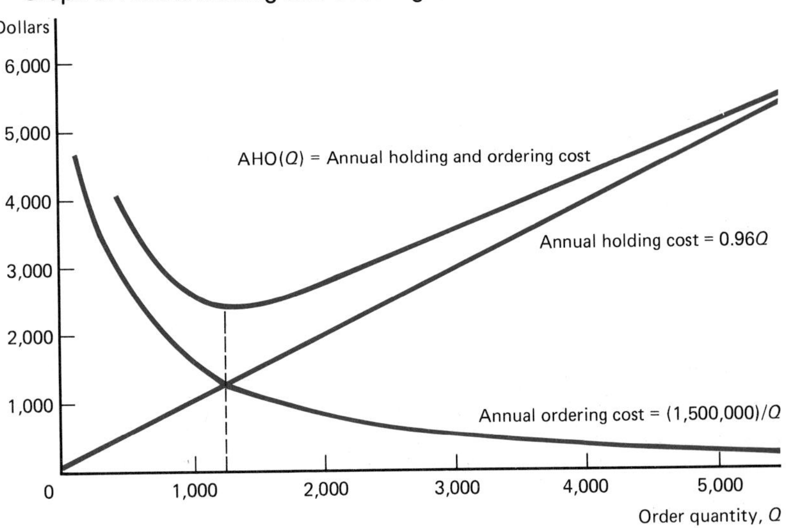

much this differs from the current policy of 5000 items per month. If he felt like it, Victor could find a good value for the order quantity by trial and error, that is, by plugging in for Q in (10.6) various values around 1100 or 1200 until he was satisfied that he was close enough to the optimum.

The EOQ Formula: Q*

It would obviously be useful to have an expression for Q^*, the optimal order quantity. (The asterisk indicates the value of Q that is the optimal solution to the model.) A formula can be derived to calculate its value as a function of the parameters in the problem by using the differential calculus to minimize the function AHO(Q) presented in (10.5) (see Appendix 10.1). A consequence of this approach is that at the optimum, the annual holding cost is equal to the annual ordering cost

$$C_h\left(\frac{Q^*}{2}\right) = C_0\left(\frac{D}{Q^*}\right) \tag{10.7}$$

or

$$(Q^*)^2 = \frac{2C_0D}{C_h} \tag{10.8}$$

or

$$Q^* = \sqrt{\frac{2C_0D}{C_h}} \tag{10.9}$$

It is sometimes convenient to estimate C_h by assuming that it is some percentage (say, i) of the purchase price (P); that is, $C_h = iP$. Equation 10.9 can then be rewritten

Alternative form

$$Q^* = \sqrt{\frac{2C_0D}{iP}} \tag{10.10}$$

In our example, P, the purchase price for angles, is \$8 and i, the fraction of P that is used to calculate C_h, is 0.24.

The quantity Q^* is often termed the **economic order quantity,** and it should be noted that it is expressed in terms of the input parameters C_0, C_h, and D. By substituting the appliance angle values for D, C_0, and C_h into (10.9), Victor can find the optimal order quantity for his problem:

It might be easier for Steco to order weekly (52 times per year), and thus Q would be 60,000/52 = 1153.846 (which may be very awkward to order). The new cost would be \$2407.69 (a very small increase), but it may be that orders must be in the tens, dozens, hundreds, etc., and the analyst must use common sense at this point. Some simple rounding or changing of Q and/or T might make the result more usable in a real situation, without changing the cost much.

$$Q^* = \sqrt{\frac{2 \times 60{,}000 \times 25}{1.92}} = 1250$$

Plugging this value into the expression for the annual holding and ordering cost for angles (equation [10.6]) yields

$$\text{AHO}(Q^*) = \text{AHO}(1250) = \frac{(1{,}500{,}000)}{1250} + (0.96)(1250)$$
$$= \$1200 + \$1200 = \$2400$$

The calculation above illustrates the fact that when Q equals Q^*, the associated annual holding cost ($C_hQ^*/2$) and the annual ordering cost (C_0D/Q^*) are equal. This fact is rigorously proved in Appendix 10.1.

Victor has already observed that the policy of ordering 5000 units at a time produces in the model a total annual cost of \$5100. If the quantity 1250 were to be used instead, the cost in the model would be \$2400, resulting in over a 50% savings. Victor is convinced that the idealized economic order quantity model is a good enough representation of Steco to make these results quite interesting.

Related Expressions: N^* and T^*

Although Victor is happy to learn of the optimal order quantity and the savings that come with it, he is not satisfied. He realizes there are other questions yet to be resolved. For example, he is curious to know the optimum number of times appliance angles should be ordered each year and the **cycle time,** which is defined as the interval between the arrival of two consecutive orders.

He has already used the fact that $N = D/Q$ to calculate the annual ordering cost. Thus, N^*, the optimal number of times to order each year, is given by the expression

$$N^* = \frac{D}{Q^*} \tag{10.11}$$

For angles, this yields a result of $N^* = 60{,}000/1250 = 48$. Recall that with the current policy Steco places only 12 orders per year. The new result is quite different.

Victor has also noted that the cycle time, the time required to use up an order, is Q/D years. Letting T^* denote the optimal cycle time, we see that

$$T^* = \frac{Q^*}{D} = \frac{1250}{60{,}000} = 0.020833 \tag{10.12}$$

which implies that Steco should order angles every 0.25 month since (0.020833)(12) = 0.25. Note that when the cycle time is 0.25 month he must order 4 times per month and thus 48 times per year. This is the same as the value for N^* above. Note that expression (10.5) for AHO(Q) depends on the given parameters C_0, C_h, and D, as well as the variable Q. It is possible to obtain an expression for the *optimal value* of AHO, in terms of only the input parameters C_0, C_h, and D (i.e., eliminating Q) as follows: Substitute the expression for Q^* (expression [10.9]) into (10.5) to obtain

$$\begin{aligned} \text{AHO}^* = \text{AHO}(Q^*) &= C_0\left(\frac{D}{Q^*}\right) + C_h\left(\frac{Q^*}{2}\right) \\ &= C_0\left(D\Big/\sqrt{\frac{2C_0D}{C_h}}\right) + C_h\left(\sqrt{\frac{C_0D}{2C_h}}\right) \\ &= C_0D\sqrt{\frac{C_h}{2C_0D}} + C_h\sqrt{\frac{C_0D}{2C_h}} \\ &= \sqrt{\frac{C_0DC_h}{2}} + \sqrt{\frac{C_0DC_h}{2}} = \sqrt{2C_0DC_h} \end{aligned} \tag{10.13}$$

For angles this becomes $\text{AHO}^* = \sqrt{2 \times \$25 \times 60{,}000 \times \$1.92} = \$2400$, a value that Victor has previously calculated.

Lead Times and When-to-Order

Under the assumptions of the EOQ model, the "how-much-to-order" decision is provided by the derived quantity Q^*. The number of orders per year is given by $N^* = D/Q^*$. The remaining basic question is: "When to order." The answer to this

"When to order" is an important question to those actually implementing an inventory control system (and sometimes a vital missing element). How many times have you asked for something in a store only to be told that someone forgot to order them last week? Lead time can sometimes be shortened by paying extra for special handling.

question is straightforward, but it depends on the *lead time to delivery.* Under the assumptions of the EOQ model, the entire order quantity Q^* arrives in a single batch precisely when the inventory level hits zero. Thus, if it takes ℓ days for an order to arrive, the order should be placed ℓ days before the end of each cycle.

This rule is illustrated for two different values of ℓ in Figure 10.6. Here T^* is the optimal cycle length, i.e., the cycle length that arises from ordering Q^* items,

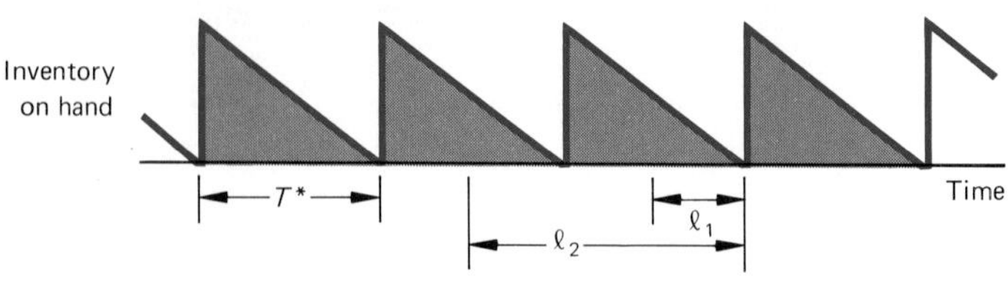

▲ FIGURE 10.6
When-to-Order Decision

and ℓ_1 and ℓ_2 are two examples of lead times. If the order is to arrive at time A and the lead time is ℓ_1, the order should be placed at time $A - \ell_1$. If the order is to arrive at time A and the lead time is ℓ_2, the order should be placed at time $A - \ell_2$. In practice, the actual demand will not strictly obey the constant rate assumption shown in Figure 10.6. For this reason, in reality, point A may not be well defined, and hence "order at time $A - \ell_1$" is not a suitable rule. Rather, in practice, the when-to-order rule is typically stated as follows:

When-to-order rule: **An order should be placed when the *inventory position* equals the demand during the lead time.**

where by definition

Inventory position defined

inventory position = inventory on hand + inventory on order

In the case in which demand is at a constant rate, this rule is equivalent to the more intuitive timing rule; that is, order ℓ days before you want the order to arrive.

We first note that there are 240 working days in a year at Steco. Since yearly demand, *D,* for angles is 60,000 items, assumed to occur at a constant rate, this implies that *d,* the daily demand, is

$$d = \frac{D}{240} = \frac{60{,}000}{240} = 250 \text{ per day}$$

We have seen in (10.12) that the optimal cycle time T^* is 1250/60,000 years. Since there are 240 days per year, this becomes

$$T^* = \frac{1250}{60{,}000} \times 240 = 5 \text{ days}$$

Why the When-to-Order Rule Works. To see why the when-to-order rule works, we first consider a case in which the lead time (ℓ) is less than the optimal cycle time T^*. In particular, let $\ell = 3$. The timing rule says to order 3 days before you want an order to arrive. Thus 2 days after an order of 1250 angles arrives (3 days before the next order) an order for 1250 angles is placed. The situation is illustrated in Figure 10.7. Note that when the order is placed there are no other orders outstanding (no items on order), and since daily demand is 1250/5 = 250, the order is placed when there are 750 items on hand. Since

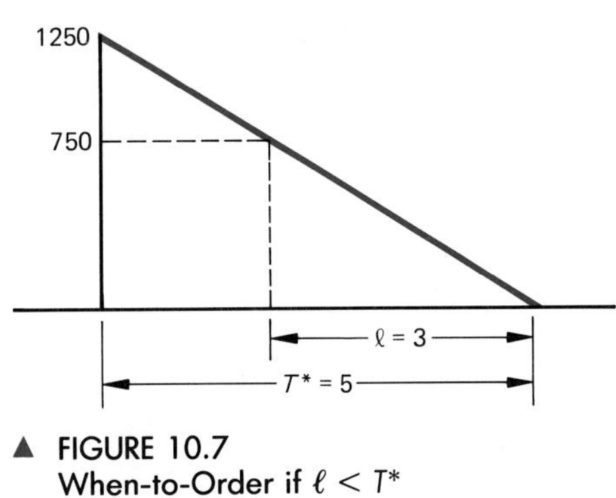

▲ FIGURE 10.7
When-to-Order if $\ell < T^*$

$$\begin{aligned}\text{inventory position} &= \text{inventory on hand} + \text{inventory on order}\\ &= 750 + 0\\ &= 750\end{aligned}$$

and

$$\text{demand over the lead time} = 3 \text{ days} \times 250 \text{ items/day} = 750 \text{ items}$$

we can therefore state that the **reorder point** is when

$$\text{inventory position} = \text{demand over the lead time}$$

Now consider a case where ℓ is greater than T^*. In particular, suppose that $\ell = 8$, $T^* = 5$, and you want the order to arrive on day 30. Then as shown in Figure 10.8,

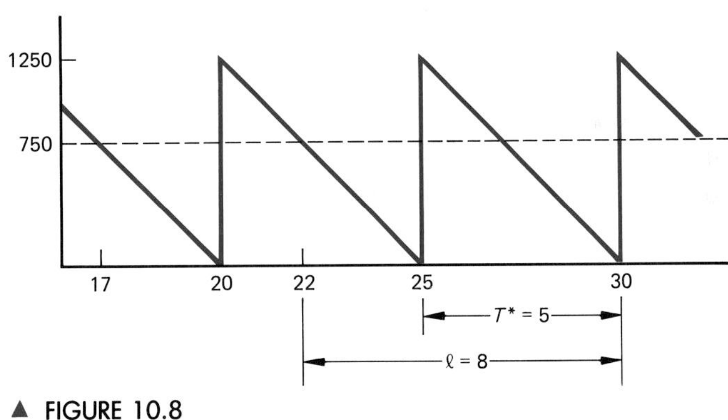

▲ FIGURE 10.8
When-to-Order if $\ell > T^*$

the order must be placed 8 days (on day 22) before you want it to arrive. Note in Figure 10.8 that at time 22

$$\text{inventory on hand} = 750$$

Further, the order that will arrive at time 25 was placed at time 17 because the lead time is 8. This order is still outstanding. It is the only order outstanding. Thus,

$$\text{inventory on order} = 1250$$

Again by definition,

$$\begin{aligned}\text{inventory position} &= \text{inventory on hand} + \text{inventory on order}\\ &= 750 + 1250\\ &= 2000\end{aligned}$$

The demand during the lead time is given by the calculation

$$8 \text{ days} \times 250 \text{ items/day} = 2000$$

Once again we see that the rule *"order when the inventory position equals the demand during the lead time"* yields the same result as the timing rule.

How the Rule Works. The when-to-order rule based on inventory position may seem needlessly complicated. In practice, however, it is easy to implement. The inventory clerk simply keeps a running total of the inventory position for each item. *When an order is placed* (not when an order arrives), *he adds the order quantity to the inventory position.* When an order arrives there is no change in inventory position, for this is merely a transfer of Q^* items from inventory on order to Q^* items on hand. *When an order is sent to a customer, the clerk must subtract the amount from the inventory position.* When the inventory position reaches a specified precomputed number, the demand during the lead time, an order is placed.

In a system where there is uncertainty in demand, we shall see that the concept of safety stock can be easily incorporated within the inventory position rule. This provides a simple and effective inventory control procedure.

Sensitivity

Victor now feels that he understands the application of the EOQ model to angles quite well. But let us at this point very carefully and clearly summarize exactly what he has shown:

1. Using the company's current policy of ordering 5000 items each time an order is placed, the inventory costs in the model are \$5100.
2. If the company would use the optimal EOQ policy of ordering 1250 items each time an order is placed, the inventory costs from the model would be \$2400.

Whether the optimal EOQ policy should be used in the future depends on the realism of the assumptions. After all, the EOQ model, like any other model, is idealized. It is no more than a selective representation of reality: an abstraction and an approximation. In this case, as with all models, the main question is: "How sensitive are the results of the model to the assumptions and the data?"

Victor has already determined that the assumptions (no stockouts are allowed, all goods arrive in a batch, the only relevant costs are ordering and holding costs, demand is on average 5000 items per month) are realistic in terms of Steco's policies and operations. Since the model is fairly realistic, it seems reasonable that the inventory costs obtained within the model are fairly good estimates of the costs that Steco is actually incurring. Therefore, using a policy that is optimal in the model (order quantity of 1250) seems preferable to the traditional policy of ordering 5000. However, Victor must still be concerned about how sensitive the optimal order quantity and, more important, the optimal annual cost are to the data. After all, each of the parameters C_0 and C_h is in itself an estimate. He is worried about how sensitive the EOQ results might be to the estimates for these parameters. If he errs in estimating these parameters, how much effect will that error have on the difference between the calculated Q^* and AHO* and the true Q^* and AHO*? If the results are highly sensitive to the values of the estimates, it is not clear whether the optimal policy for the model should actually be implemented by Steco. Moreover, Victor's

(1) TRUE PARAMETERS		(2)	(3)	(4)	(5)	(6)
C_h	C_0	OPTIMAL Q	MINIMUM COST ($)	VICTOR'S DECISION[a]	VICTOR'S COST ($)	LOSS (%)
(i) 1.72	23	1267	2179	$Q = 1250$	2179	0
(ii) 1.72	27	1372	2361	$Q = 1250$	2371	0.42
(iii) 2.12	23	1141	2419	$Q = 1250$	2429	0.41
(iv) 2.12	27	1236	2621	$Q = 1250$	2621	0

[a]Based on $C_h = \$1.92$, $C_0 = \$25$.

▲ FIGURE 10.9
Sensitivity to C_h and C_0

overall task is to deal with the inventory control on all of Steco's thousands of products. Substantial resources will be needed to estimate the parameters for all the products with great accuracy, if that is required.

Let us therefore consider how the EOQ results might vary with changes in our estimated holding and ordering costs. Recall that Victor assumed that $C_h = \$1.92$ and $C_0 = \$25$. We will consider four cases in which the true parameters are different from the values selected by Victor. These "true values" are shown in the first two columns of Figure 10.9. In case (i) Victor has overestimated both cost parameters by about 10% each. Had he estimated the parameters correctly he would have ordered 1267 items and incurred an annual holding and ordering cost of \$2179. Because of his estimation errors he orders 1250. In order to find out what costs he will actually incur, Victor must evaluate the AHO equation with its true parameter values ($C_h = \$1.72$ and $C_0 = \$23$ in case [i]) and the value of Q determined by his estimates (1250). This calculation follows:

$$\begin{aligned} \text{AHO}(Q) &= C_0\left(\frac{D}{Q}\right) + C_h\left(\frac{Q}{2}\right) \\ &= 23\left(\frac{60{,}000}{1250}\right) + 1.72\left(\frac{1250}{2}\right) \\ &= 23(48) + 1.72(625) \\ &= 1104 + 1075 \\ &= \$2179 \end{aligned}$$

This number is shown as Victor's Cost in column (5). We thus see that if Victor underestimates the two cost parameters as shown, it has no effect on the annual holding and ordering cost (to the nearest dollar). The other three cases show that the effect on the annual holding and ordering cost of any combination of 10% errors in the estimates of C_0 and C_h is negligible.

Precise estimates not required

Our analysis suggests that in Victor's case the EOQ model is insensitive even to approximately 10% variations or errors in the cost estimates. It turns out that this is a property enjoyed by EOQ models in general. Thus, Victor concludes that if he can obtain at least reasonable estimates of ordering and holding costs, the value of Q thereby obtained will yield an AHO very close to the true minimum.

Managerial Considerations

If future demand were known with complete certainty and were truly at a constant monthly rate, then, under the other assumptions (that ordering and holding costs are the only relevant costs and no stockouts are allowed), the values Q^* and

It is important to realize that this analysis gives the manager a good picture of the inventory situation, and that 5000 units each month is way too large an order. If Steco had been ordering 1300 each time, then Victor should be satisfied that everything looks under control.

AHO(Q^*) as produced by the idealized EOQ model would indeed be optimal, not just in the model but in the real problem as well. However, in practice, as we repeatedly emphasize, the real-world problem rarely satisfies the assumptions of the model exactly. For example, in most real-world contexts it would be unlikely that future demand would be known with complete certainty. It is even more unlikely that it would occur at a constant monthly or daily rate. Indeed, in the appliance angle context, as Figure 10.1 shows, last year's demand rate of 5000 items per month is only an average. There was no constant monthly rate. And what about the future? This value of 5000 per month is only an estimate of the rate of demand in the future. In Chapter 15 Victor will enlarge his perspective to see how the ICON system deals with uncertainty in future demand in formal ways.

Protecting against Uncertain Lead Time Demand. As a first step, however, he as the manager might feel that the EOQ assumptions, together with the estimated demand of 5000 items per month, are realistic enough to make the model directly useful as is. On the other hand, he must recognize that using the previously derived reorder point of 750 items (for 3-day lead times) will almost surely lead to some stockouts. A stockout will, in fact, occur whenever the demand during the 3-day lead time (i.e., the 3-day period that commences when the reorder point is achieved) exceeds 750 items. Another possible cause for a stockout could be the occurrence of a longer lead time for unforeseen reasons. The job of the manager is to deal successfully with uncertainty. In the Steco context, if stockouts are truly to be avoided, then Victor as manager may choose to increase the reorder point (leaving the reorder quantity unchanged). He may, for example, choose to reorder when 1000 items are on hand. What would he achieve with such a change?

Since, during the expected 3-day lead time, 750 items are estimated to be demanded (assuming that the constant demand rate holds), we see that 250 items will still remain in inventory when the order arrives. This extra 250 units serves as a precaution against larger-than-expected demand or a delay in the scheduled delivery. It is called a **safety** or **buffer stock.**

Safety stock

A safety stock is the difference between the reorder point and the expected lead-time demand.

In the appliance angle example, carrying a safety stock of 250 items would raise the average inventory level by 250 items. This would affect only the yearly carrying charge, which would increase by

$$C_h(250) = (1.92)(250) = \$480$$

and hence the only effect of the 250-item buffer stock is to raise the annual cost estimate from \$2400 to \$2880, still a considerable savings over the current policy. (This statement ignores any changes in costs due to stockouts.)

Thus, as a first-order consideration, possible uncertainties in demand or in lead time can be treated with a managerial judgment on a suitable safety stock level. This is handled by simple modification of the reorder point rule. Whether a simple modification should be made is in itself a matter of managerial judgment. It is a question of the extent to which stockouts are to be avoided and of whether a deeper treatment should be undertaken. After all, the question of what a suitable safety stock level is remains unanswered. In Chapter 16 this question will be analyzed in greater depth.

Other variations in the basic model might be called for to capitalize on the opportunity to get quantity discounts. This circumstance is treated in the following section.

APPLICATION CAPSULE

A Lot to Learn: Management Scientists Find That the EOQ Model Isn't Always the Last Word on Lot Size*

We have noted that the EOQ model is based on specific (and not always realistic) assumptions. Each manager must decide whether the results are useful for his or her real-world problems.

One environment where the EOQ model may not produce optimal results is the job shop in which many items need to be processed in large batches on several machines. Among the problems that are likely to develop in such operations are high levels of work in progress (WIP), long queues (waiting lines) at some machines, and much lost time as machines stand idle, waiting for the previous step to be completed. In fact, complex, multi-item job shops are estimated to spend only 10–15% of the available time in actual processing.

Studies have shown that the size of the batch (lot size) directly influences waiting times for processing. Management scientists from Eastman Kodak, the University of Rochester, and Carnegie-Mellon University investigated the use of the EOQ model to determine lot sizes for a production cell that contained 10 major work centers with a total of 15 machines. Part flow through the cell was not uniform and varied from part to part, with some parts being worked several times on the same machine.

Simulation (Chapter 13) was used to measure the effect of lot size on WIP and waiting times. Experimentation showed that the lot sizes suggested by the EOQ model were much too large for this situation. A heuristic procedure (Chapter 11) was developed to search for appropriate lot sizes for the 13 parts passing through the manufacturing cell. After a few weeks of experimenting, lead times were reduced by 50% over the initial results.

*Karamarkar, Kekre, Kekre, and Freeman, "Lot-Sizing and Lead-Time Performance in a Manufacturing Cell," *Interfaces*, Vol. 15, No. 2, March–April 1985.

10.4 Quantity Discounts and Steco's Overall Optimum

The EOQ model that Victor has been working with minimizes the annual holding and ordering cost. There was previously no need to take into account the cost of purchasing the product, for the per item cost to Steco was assumed to be a constant independent of Q. Victor now learns that Steco's supplier will offer a **quantity discount** as an incentive for more business. The supplier has agreed to offer a \$0.10 discount on every angle purchased if Steco orders in lots of at least 5000 items. Of course, higher order quantities will also reduce the number of orders placed, and hence the annual ordering cost. However, as already discussed (compare Figures 10.3 and 10.4), a high order quantity leads to a higher average inventory level and hence higher holding costs. Whether the discount will, on balance, be advantageous to Steco is not obvious.

Victor decides to proceed as before, that is, to develop an annual cost curve and then find the order quantity that minimizes it. His annual total cost [ATC(Q)] is the sum of the annual holding and ordering cost [AHO(Q)] and the annual purchase cost (APC), that is,

$$\text{ATC}(Q) = \text{AHO}(Q) + \text{APC}$$

From equation (10.5) and the fact that $C_h = iP$, Victor knows that

$$\text{AHO}(Q) = C_0 \left(\frac{D}{Q}\right) + iP\left(\frac{Q}{2}\right)$$

Note that since C_h depends on the unit price P, the expression for AHO also involves P. The annual purchase cost is simply the unit price times annual demand. Thus,

Annual purchase cost

$$\text{APC} = PD$$

It follows that

Annual total cost

$$\text{ATC}(Q) = C_0 \left(\frac{D}{Q}\right) + iP\left(\frac{Q}{2}\right) + PD$$

Victor wishes to evaluate this function for two different prices, the regular price of \$8.00 per unit and the potential discounted price of \$7.90 per unit. He obtains the following two functions:

Regular price equation:

$$\text{ATC}(Q) = \frac{25 \times 60{,}000}{Q} + (0.24)(8.00)\left(\frac{Q}{2}\right) + (8.00)(60{,}000)$$

Discount price equation:

$$\text{ATC}(Q) = \frac{25 \times 60{,}000}{Q} + (0.24)(7.90)\left(\frac{Q}{2}\right) + (7.90)(60{,}000)$$

The general shape of these curves is shown in Figure 10.10. There are several facts to notice.

1. The discount curve lies below the regular cost curve. This is so because each term in the regular price ATC(Q) is greater than or equal to the corresponding term in the discount price ATC(Q).
2. The value of Q, say Q_D^*, that minimizes the discount price ATC(Q) is larger than the value of Q, say Q_R^*, that minimizes the regular price ATC(Q). This is true because, using (10.10),

$$Q_D^* = \sqrt{\frac{2 \times 25 \times 60{,}000}{(0.24) \times (7.90)}} > \sqrt{\frac{2 \times 25 \times 60{,}000}{(0.24) \times (8.00)}} = Q_R^*$$

▼ FIGURE 10.10
Annual Total Cost for Regular and Discount Prices

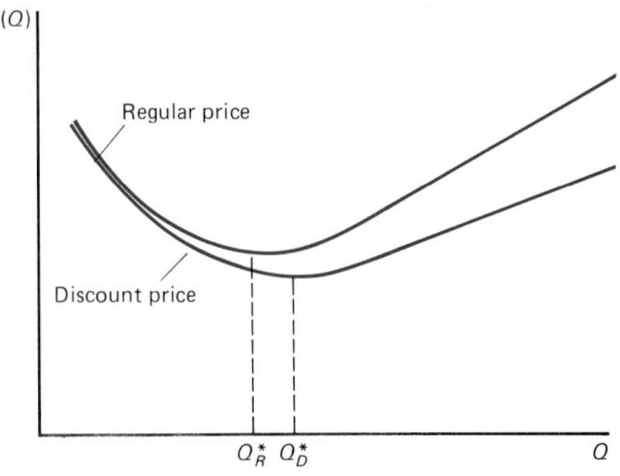

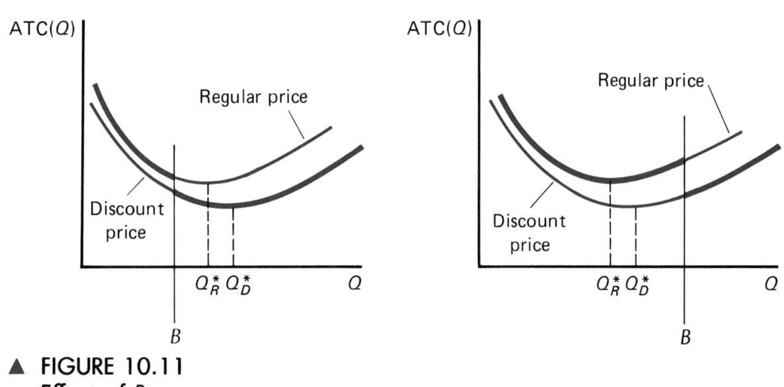

▲ FIGURE 10.11
Effect of *B*

Obviously, Victor would like to minimize his annual total cost, ATC(Q). If he could get the discount price regardless of the order quantity, he would of course order Q_D^*. However, assume that the discount price holds only if he orders at least B items at a time. Two situations could arise. These are illustrated in Figure 10.11.

The shaded curves in these figures indicate the actual cost function that Victor faces. They illustrate that the regular price curve must be used for order quantities of B or less and that the discount price curve can be used for order quantities greater than B.

We see that if $B \leq Q_D^*$, Victor will achieve the minimum cost by ordering Q_D^*. If, however, $B > Q_D^*$, the optimal decision, in general, is not immediately obvious. The best Victor can do on the regular price curve is to order Q_R^*. The best he can do on the discount price curve is to order B. (He cannot order less than B and get the discount price, and ordering more than B increases ATC.) To determine which of these is optimal he must calculate the ATC(Q) at these two points and compare them. The general rule then is

The optimal order quantity

$$\text{If } B \leq Q_D^*, \text{ order } \quad Q_D^*.$$

$$\text{If } B > Q_D^*, \text{ order } \begin{cases} Q_R^* & \text{if regular price ATC}(Q_R^*) \leq \text{discount price ATC}(B) \\ B & \text{if not} \end{cases}$$

To apply this rule, Victor notes that he must order at least 5000 items to get the discount. Thus $B = 5000$. To calculate Q_D^* he uses the EOQ formula as follows:

$$Q_D^* = \sqrt{\frac{2 \times 25 \times 60{,}000}{(0.24)(7.90)}} = 1257.9 \sim 1258 \qquad \textbf{(10.14)}$$

Since $Q_D^* = 1258 < 5000 = B$, he must compare two alternatives to determine the optimal order quantity. From his previous calculations (those following [10.10]) he knows that Q_R^* equals 1250. Thus, the value ATC(Q_R^*) is calculated by the regular price equation above.

$$\text{ATC}(Q_R^*) = \frac{25 \times 60{,}000}{1250} + (0.24)(8.00)\frac{1250}{2} + (8.00)(60{,}000)$$

$$= 1200 + 1200 + 480{,}000 = \$482{,}400$$

Similarly, the value ATC(B) is calculated by the discount price equation, p. 454:

$$\text{ATC}(B) = \frac{25 \times 60{,}000}{5000} + (0.24)(7.90)\frac{5000}{2} + (7.90)(60{,}000)$$

$$= 300 + 4740 + 474{,}000 = \$479{,}040$$

These calculations show that Victor should order 5000 items to take advantage of the quantity discount. This decision saves

$$\$482{,}400 - \$479{,}040 = \$3360$$

per year over the next best decision (ordering Q_R^*). What this discussion suggests is that quantity discounts can play an important role in determining the optimal inventory policy. Indeed, this is so important that Steco's ICON system has been designed to deal with the problem. ICON first solves the basic EOQ model, and then in a second stage, when quantity discounts are available, the system runs through the calculations that Victor has just made.

10.5 The EOQ Model with Backlogging

One of the important functions of inventory is to protect against stockouts. We have already seen earlier in this chapter how a manager will add a safety stock to the reorder point to decrease the likelihood of stockouts with an EOQ model. However, in some cases it may be advantageous to both the buyer and the seller if not all orders are satisfied out of inventory on hand. Indeed, the seller sometimes plans on running out and knows that there will be some demand when there is no inventory on hand. Holding this demand in abeyance and then satisfying it out of later inventory is called *backlogging demand.*

We thus wish to drop the no-stockout assumption in the basic model and examine the implications of doing so. The essence of backlogging in the EOQ context is illustrated in Figure 10.12.

Much of Figure 10.12 is familiar. An order for Q items arrives every T days. The order arrives all at once (in a batch), at which time the inventory on hand jumps up by Q items. Between the arrival of orders inventory depletes at a constant rate, reflecting the fact that demand is occurring at a constant rate. The new wrinkle is the fact that not all demand is satisfied out of inventory on hand. Certain customers are asked to wait, and their demand is satisfied when the next order arrives. In a strict sense those customers whose orders arrive during the first t_1 days of an inventory cycle have their demand satisfied out of inventory on hand. Those whose orders arrive during the rest of the cycle (t_2) wait until the next replenishment to receive their goods. The process of asking customers to wait (or backlogging) is indicated in Figure 10.12 as a negative value of inventory on hand.

▼ FIGURE 10.12
EOQ Model with Planned Backorders

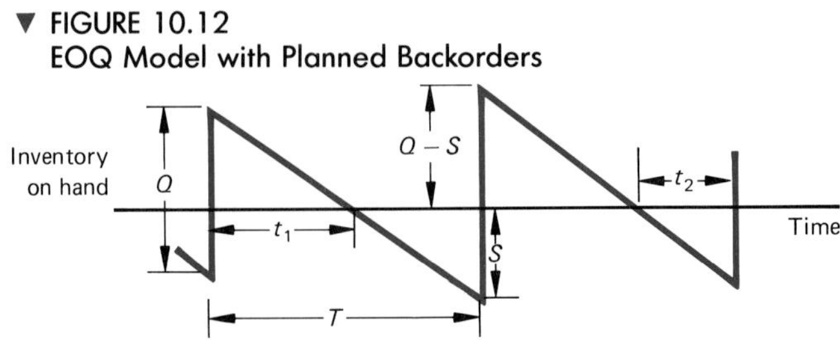

Costs of Backlogging

Typically, the supplier must offer some sort of financial incentive to his customers to accept a waiting period. This incentive might take the form of financial considerations; that is, the supplier might accept payment up to 90 days after delivery at no extra charge, whereas immediate delivery implies immediate payment or the addition of finance charges. Another approach is simply to offer a price reduction for backlogged orders. The point is that the supplier typically incurs a cost for these items, but sometimes it is sensible to incur these costs intentionally.

Returning to Figure 10.12, note that during the cycle time (T) the firm holds inventory during t_1 and accepts backorders (i.e., backlogged demand) during t_2 when the inventory has been depleted. Clearly,

$$t_1 + t_2 = T$$

The symbol S indicates the total number of units backlogged during a cycle, that is, the total number of units of unsatisfied demand accumulated during t_2. We see then that, with an order size of Q, the maximum level of inventory on hand is $Q - S$, since S items from each new order must be used to fill previously backlogged orders, and the remaining $Q - S$ are placed in inventory.

In the basic EOQ model management has to make one decision, the value of Q, since this determines the cycle time and the entire policy. When backorders are permitted, management must select both Q and S. As before, Q, together with the constant rate of demand D, determines T, the cycle length. But S must be specified before it is clear how many units will be backlogged on each cycle and how much inventory will be held. The values of the decision variables Q and S are selected to minimize the sum of the annual ordering, holding, and backlogging costs. Backlogging costs are assessed in exactly the same manner as holding costs; that is, the cost to backlog an item for a year must be specified, and the cost per cycle is built up from this quantity. The cost per cycle is used in turn to calculate the annual cost. A detailed development follows.

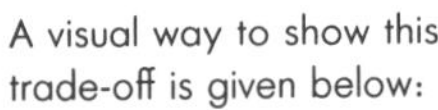
A visual way to show this trade-off is given below:

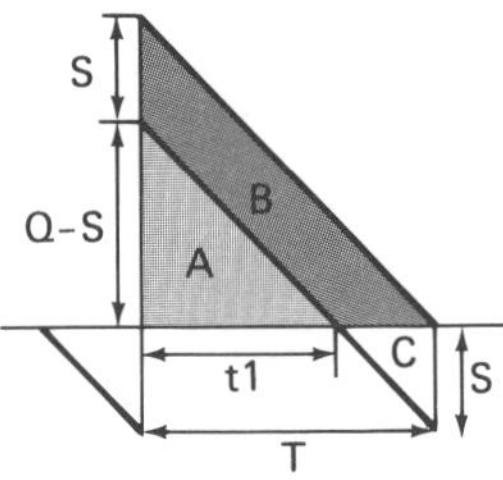

The cost of A and C can be less than the cost of A and B. (Figure reproduced in Application Pack.)

The Annual Cost Expression

Let AHOB(Q, S) be the annual holding, ordering, and backlogging cost as a function of Q and S. Also, let C_b be the cost of backlogging an item for a year. We now proceed to develop the cost of a cycle.

1. ***Ordering cost:*** Since one order is placed each cycle, this is simple. The ordering cost equals C_0.
2. ***Holding cost:*** The maximum inventory level is $Q - S$. Demand occurs at the constant rate of D items per year. It follows that the quantity $(Q - S)$ will last for a time (in years) given by

$$t_1 = \frac{Q - S}{D}$$

if it is consumed at the *rate D*. The average time (in years) that a unit is held in inventory is $t_1/2$, and $(Q - S)$ items are held. Thus, the holding cost per cycle is

$$C_h(Q - S)\left(\frac{t_1}{2}\right) = C_h(Q - S)\left(\frac{1}{2}\right)\left(\frac{Q - S}{D}\right)$$
$$= \frac{C_h}{2}\frac{(Q - S)^2}{D}$$

3. ***Backlogging cost:*** A maximum of S units are backlogged. Since backlogging occurs at the rate of demand D, the time for backlogging must be

$$t_2 = S/D$$

A total of S items are backlogged for an average of $t_2/2$ years; thus, the backlogging cost per cycle is

$$C_b S\left(\frac{t_2}{2}\right) = C_b S\left(\frac{1}{2}\right)\left(\frac{S}{D}\right) = \frac{C_b}{2}\frac{S^2}{D}$$

The annual holding, ordering, and backlogging cost, AHOB(Q, S), can now be obtained by adding the costs from 1, 2, and 3 above to obtain the cost per cycle and then multiplying by the number of cycles per year. As in the basic EOQ model there are D/Q cycles per year (equation [10.2]). Thus,

Annual cost

$$\text{AHOB}(Q, S) = \frac{D}{Q}\left[C_0 + \frac{C_h}{2}\frac{(Q - S)^2}{D} + \frac{C_b}{2}\frac{S^2}{D}\right] \tag{10.15}$$

Management can now use (10.15) to calculate the annual holding, ordering, and backlogging cost for any choice of the decision variables Q and S. With differential calculus one can also use the same equation to derive the expressions for Q^* and S^*, the optimal values of Q and S. The results of this derivation are presented in (10.16) and (10.17).

Optimal values of Q, S

$$Q^* = \sqrt{\frac{2C_0D}{C_h}\left(\frac{C_h + C_b}{C_b}\right)} \tag{10.16}$$

$$S^* = Q^*\left(\frac{C_h}{C_h + C_b}\right) \tag{10.17}$$

Plugging the expressions for Q^* and S^* into (10.15) yields AHOB(Q^*, S^*), the minimum annual holding, ordering, and backlogging cost. The result is shown in (10.18).

$$\text{AHOB}(Q^*, S^*) = \sqrt{2C_0DC_h\left(\frac{C_b}{C_h + C_b}\right)} \tag{10.18}$$

It is interesting to compare these expressions with those for Q^* and AHO(Q^*) in the basic EOQ model. Recall that in the basic model (10.9)

$$Q^* = \sqrt{\frac{2C_0D}{C_h}}$$

and (10.13)

$$\text{AHO}(Q^*) = \sqrt{2C_0DC_h}$$

First compare (10.16) and (10.9). We first note that since $(C_h + C_b)/C_b \geq 1$, the optimal order quantity in the backlogged case is at least as large as the optimal order quantity in the basic model. Similarly, by comparing (10.18) and (10.13) we see that since $C_b/(C_b + C_h) \leq 1$, the annual cost for the backlogged model is at most as large as the annual cost in the basic model.

One way to think about the basic model is to assume that backlogging is allowed, but that since C_b is extremely large (infinite) no orders are ever backlogged. It is reassuring to note that if C_b is set equal to infinity in (10.16), (10.17), and (10.18), then $S^* = 0$, and Q^* and AHOB(Q^*, S^*) reduce to the appropriate expressions for the no-backlog case.

Backlogging as a Profitable Opportunity

The determination of C_b is, typically, not very easy. It may involve a loss of customer goodwill (even if the customer eventually gets the item) and may result in lost sales down the road. Of all the inventory costs, this is the most difficult to quantify exactly. For this reason, doing some sensitivity analysis on this cost can be of utmost importance.

Suppose that the cost of backlogging an item for a year is twice as large as the cost of holding the same item for a year; that is, assume that $C_b = 2C_h$. Does your intuition tell you that you would never choose a backlog in this case? If it does, you have learned again how easily we are misled by our intuition. From (10.17) we see that since $C_h/(C_h + C_b) = 1/3$,

$$S^* = Q^*\left(\frac{1}{3}\right)$$

which implies that one-third of the orders will be backlogged. Now from (10.18) and the facts that

$$\frac{C_b}{C_h + C_b} = \frac{2}{3} \quad \text{and} \quad \sqrt{\frac{C_b}{C_h + C_b}} = 0.816$$

we conclude that the annual cost in the backlogged model is only 0.816 times as much as the annual cost in the basic model. In other words, what to many people seems like an unattractive alternative (backlogging when it is twice as expensive as holding inventory) turns out to play an important role in the optimal inventory policy. One-third of the orders are backlogged. This policy has an important effect on the costs (approximately a 20% reduction).

An Example: Selling Insulating Foam. To illustrate the potential benefits of backlogging, suppose that a supplier of insulating foam is faced with the following situation for his foam panels, which are 2 feet by 8 feet by 2 inches thick:

$$\begin{aligned} D &= 50{,}000 \text{ panels per year} \\ C_h &= \$4 \text{ per year} \\ C_b &= \$8 \text{ per year} \\ C_0 &= \$25 \text{ per order} \end{aligned}$$

From (10.16) we see that

$$Q^* = \sqrt{\frac{2C_0D}{C_h}\left(\frac{C_h + C_b}{C_b}\right)} = \sqrt{\frac{2(25)(50{,}000)}{4}\left(\frac{4 + 8}{8}\right)} = 968 \text{ panels}$$

Equation (10.17) shows that

$$S^* = Q^*\left(\frac{C_h}{C_h + C_b}\right) = 968\left(\frac{4}{4 + 8}\right) = 322 \text{ panels}$$

Finally, (10.18) yields

Cost with backlogging

$$\text{AHOB}(Q^*, S^*) = \sqrt{2C_0DC_h\left(\frac{C_b}{C_b + C_h}\right)}$$

$$= \sqrt{2(25)(50{,}000)(4)\left(\frac{8}{8 + 4}\right)} = \$2580$$

If the firm had not taken advantage of the opportunity to backlog orders, then the optimal order quantity would be calculated as follows:

$$Q^* = \sqrt{\frac{2C_0\,D}{C_h}} = \sqrt{\frac{2(25)(50{,}000)}{4}} = 790 \text{ panels}$$

Similarly, the minimum annual holding and ordering cost would be

Cost without backlogging

$$\text{AHO}(Q^*) = \sqrt{2C_0DC_h}$$
$$= \sqrt{2(25)(50{,}000)(4)} = \$3162$$

These calculations provide a specific example of the general case described above and illustrate again the importance of using the opportunity to backlog orders if the characteristics of the market make that alternative possible. It is important to note that the "when-to-order rule" must be modified when backlogging is permitted. The proper modification is noted in Problem 10.15.

10.6 The Production Lot Size Model: Victor's Heat-Treatment Problem

Although Steco is primarily a steel wholesaler, it does have some productive capacity. In particular, it has an extensive and modern heat-treatment facility that it uses to produce a number of items that it then holds in inventory. The heat-treatment facility has two important characteristics: There is a large setup cost associated with producing each product, and once the setup is complete, production is at a steady and known rate.

Setup cost

The setup cost, which is analogous to the ordering cost in the EOQ model, is incurred because it is necessary to change the chemicals and the operating temperature in the heat-treatment facility to meet the specifications set forth by the metallurgical laboratory. Also, each item must spend a specified time at a specific temperature in each of several chemical baths. Thus, an order quantity of heat-treated steel does not arrive in inventory all at once. Rather, it arrives steadily over a period of several days. This change requires a modification in the EOQ formula, even if the assumptions of a constant rate of demand and the inventory carrying cost being equal to C_h times the average inventory are maintained.

Parameters of the model

It is usually more convenient to work with this model in terms of daily production and demand rates. Thus, consider a product in which

Be sure to emphasize that the time units for d, p, and c_h must be the same. It is disastrous to mix days with years. Note that days are used as time units here because the production rate is easier to work with in days than in fractions of years.

d = number of units demanded each day

p = number of units produced each day during a production run

C_0 = setup cost that is independent of the quantity produced

c_h = cost per *day* of holding inventory
(note the change in notation to emphasize holding cost per day)

It is obvious that p must be greater than d for the problem to be interesting. If $p < d$, demand is greater than Steco's ability to produce, and holding inventory is the least of their problems.

Figure 10.13 presents a plot of what the inventory on hand would look like if Steco decided to produce in lots of Q items each.

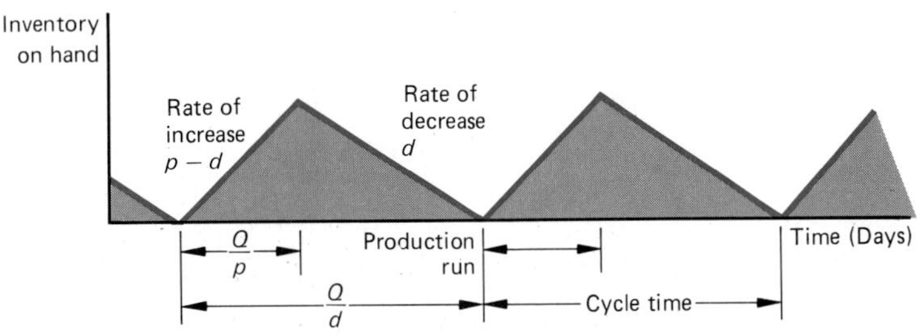

▲ FIGURE 10.13
Inventory on Hand for the Production Lot Size Model

There are several aspects of this graph that must be noted in order to calculate the average holding and setup and cost per day.

1. During a production run items are added to inventory at a rate of p units per day and removed at the rate of d per day. The net effect is an increase at the rate of $p - d$ units per day.
2. At other times, items are removed from inventory at a rate of d items per day.
3. Since Q items are produced in a run, at the rate of p items per day, each production run is Q/p days long.
4. Since Q items are produced in a run, and d is the daily demand rate, each cycle time is Q/d days long.

Facts 1 and 3 can be used to find the maximum amount of inventory on hand (see Figure 10.13).

$$\text{maximum inventory} = (p - d)\frac{Q}{p}$$

Since the average inventory equals one-half of the maximum inventory, it follows that

$$\text{average inventory} = \frac{1}{2}(p - d)\frac{Q}{p}$$

Rearranging the terms in the expression above, we obtain

$$\text{average inventory} = \frac{Q}{2}\left(1 - \frac{d}{p}\right)$$

$$\text{holding cost per day} = c_h\frac{Q}{2}\left(1 - \frac{d}{p}\right)$$

Similarly, since there is one setup every cycle and a cycle lasts Q/d days,

$$\text{setup cost per day} = \frac{C_0}{Q/d} = C_0\frac{d}{Q}$$

Thus, the daily holding and setup cost, denoted DHS(Q), is given by the expression

$$\text{DHS}(Q) = C_0\frac{d}{Q} + c_h\frac{Q}{2}\left(1 - \frac{d}{p}\right)$$

If you think of $c_h(1 - d/p)$ as a constant, this expression takes the same form as given by (10.5), the expression for the annual holding and ordering cost in the EOQ model.

It follows, then, that the value of Q that minimizes DHS(Q) will be given by the EOQ equation (10.9) with c_h appropriately modified. Thus, for the **production lot size model,**

Optimal lot size

$$Q^* = \sqrt{\frac{2C_0 d}{c_h\left(1 - \frac{d}{p}\right)}} \quad \textbf{(10.19)}$$

Students can be shown that if the production rate is infinite, then the term $(1 - d/p) \rightarrow 1$, and thus **Equation 10.19** becomes **Equation 10.9** and DHS(Q) becomes AHO(Q).

The result could also be derived with differential calculus, analogous to the derivation in Appendix 10.1. Substituting Q^* for Q in the expression for DHS(Q) and simplifying gives us an expresssion for the *minimum* daily holding and setup cost:

$$\text{DHS}\ (Q^*) = \sqrt{2C_0 dc_h(1 - \left(1 - \frac{d}{p}\right)}$$

Note that this expression does not depend on Q; it is valid only when the lot size is equal to the value of the expression in Equation (10.9).

Note that the holding cost is per *working day*, and thus the yearly cost is divided by 240 working days rather than 365 calendar days.

To apply this analysis to any particular product, Victor must estimate the various parameters for that product and then evaluate (10.19) to obtain Q^*. Thus, once the parameters are estimated, finding Q^* is reduced to a matter of "plug and chug."

Just to confirm his understanding of the production lot size model, Victor decides to work his way through the calculations for a 3/8-inch hardened reinforcing rod, a product used in reinforced concrete construction.

The demand for this product averages 200 rods per day. It costs \$100 to set up to heat treat the rods, and they can be produced at a rate of 400 rods per day. Victor estimates the holding cost per day as (\$1)(0.24)/240 = \$0.001, where \$1 is the cost of the rod and 0.24 is the annual interest rate used by Steco for all products. The figure 240 is the assumed number of working days per year.

The optimal production lot size for this product, then, is

$$Q^* = \sqrt{\frac{2 \times 200 \times 100}{0.001\left(1 - \frac{200}{400}\right)}} = 8944$$

and the minimum daily holding and setup cost is

$$\sqrt{2 \times 200 \times 100 \times 0.001\left(1 - \frac{200}{400}\right)} = \$4.47$$

A production run of this size yields a supply of rods large enough to satisfy demand for

$$\frac{8944}{200} = 44.72 \text{ days}$$

In practice, Victor might adjust this quantity to take into account the fact that a number of other products also have to make use of the heat-treatment facility. He would perhaps add a safety stock to allow for the possibility that demand might run ahead of production at the beginning of a production run. Quantity discounts would probably not play a role in his decision since the rods that are heat treated are drawn from Steco's general inventory of 3/8-inch high-carbon steel rods. These rods are used for a number of purposes, and their purchase must be determined by total demand.

10.7 Material Requirements Planning: Farmcraft Manufacturing Co.

The directors of Steco have recently approved the purchase of Farmcraft Manufacturing Co., a major producer of planting equipment. As a manufacturer, Farmcraft maintains inventories of intermediate goods that are to be used in producing finished products. During a major restudy of Farmcraft's inventory management, Victor is called in as a consultant. He quickly learns that his experience at Steco has little direct application. Steco maintains finished product inventories to satisfy consumer demand. There is a big difference between this activity and that which occurs at Farmcraft.

In a typical manufacturing process certain parts and subassemblies are used in a number of finished products. For a firm like Farmcraft you would expect to see basic parts like bolts and nuts, custom parts like wheels and treads, and subassemblies like transmissions and engines used in a number of finished products. We shall use the term *intermediate goods* to refer to all parts and subassemblies.

It is, of course, clear that the demand for intermediate goods is generated by the demand for the finished product. The question to be asked is: "What levels of intermediate goods inventories are required to assure that finished product demand will be satisfied?" We shall see that the relationships between intermediate goods and final product, if properly taken into account, can lead to important efficiencies in establishing appropriate inventory levels. **Material requirements planning,** abbreviated **MRP,** is an important technique to deal with dependencies in demand. Let us use a simple example to explain the approach.

Analyzing Requirements

In Figure 10.14 we see a display of some of the requirements for a 12-row beet and bean planter. The flow in this figure illustrates that the gearbox must be available in order to produce the transmission, for indeed the gearbox is part of the transmission. Moreover, the transmission must be available in order to produce the power train, for it is part of the power train, and this power train in turn goes into the final product. Thus, Figure 10.14 gives you an indication of some of the dependencies among intermediate goods. It is this type of dependency that will be used in the MRP analysis of required inventory levels.

Proceeding, suppose that Farmcraft's production schedule calls for 1000 units of finished product (12-row planters) to be assembled by April 1 of next year. In order to meet this schedule the power train, wheel assembly, and earth-turning units

FIGURE 10.14
Material Input List

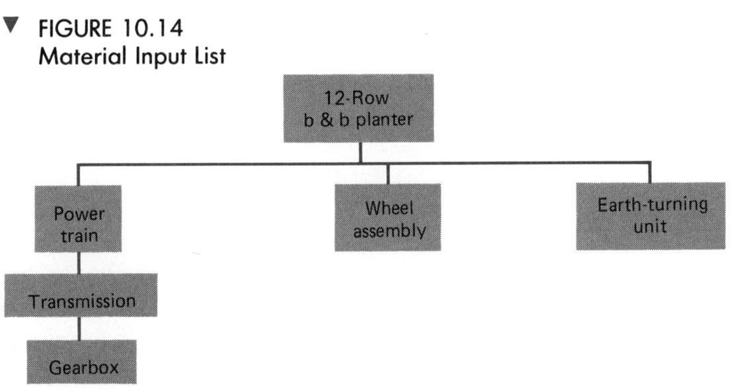

must be completed by March 15, allowing 2 weeks for the final assembly. Let us now focus on the inventory control aspects of the power train. The number of units currently in inventory are shown in Figure 10.15. The first question to be asked is: "How many units of each component will ultimately be required in inventory to fulfill the requirement that 1000 units of finished product be assembled by April 1?"

COMPONENT	UNITS CURRENTLY IN INVENTORY
Power Train	360
Transmission	250
Gearbox	400

▲ FIGURE 10.15
Current Inventory for Farmcraft

COMPONENT	NUMBER REQUIRED TO MEET DEMAND FOR 1000 PLANTERS	NUMBER IN INVENTORY	ADDITIONAL REQUIREMENT
Power Train	1000	360	640
Transmission	1000	250	750
Gearbox	1000	400	600

▲ FIGURE 10.16
Additional Requirements: A Wrong Answer

You may believe that the answer is obvious: namely, 1000 units of each component are required. Therefore, you may say that the *additional requirements,* above and beyond current inventory levels, are obtained by subtracting current levels from 1000, as shown in Figure 10.16. The problem with this answer is that it does not take into account the dependencies revealed in Figure 10.14. It ignores the facts that gearboxes are already installed in the 250 transmissions on hand and that transmissions are already installed in the 360 power trains on hand. Taking these facts into account, the MRP analysis of additional requirements would proceed as follows:

units of finished product to be assembled	1000
total requirement for power trains	1000
power trains in current inventory	360
additional power trains required	640

Now since each additional power train will require a transmission, we have

total requirement for transmissions	640
transmissions in current inventory	250
additional transmissions required	390

Similarly, since each of the additional transmissions will require a gearbox, one obtains

total requirement for gearboxes	390
gearboxes in current inventory	400
additional gearboxes required	0

You can now see how MRP was used to take the dependency of intermediate goods into account and to produce an improved list of additional requirements as given in

COMPONENT	ADDITIONAL REQUIREMENTS WITHOUT DEPENDENCY (FIGURE 10.16)	ADDITIONAL REQUIREMENTS TAKING DEPENDENCY INTO ACCOUNT
Power Train	640	640
Transmission	750	390
Gearbox	600	0

▲ FIGURE 10.17
Comparison of Results

Figure 10.17. The analysis using MRP clearly leads to lower inventory levels and hence lower inventory changes.

Timing of Requirements

Since each component of the power train requires production and assembly time, some planning must be done in order to deliver the 640 additional power trains on schedule. The necessary information is given in Figure 10.18. The lead time in this context is the amount of time it will take to produce the additional requirements, given that all components are available at the start of the process. For example, it requires 20 working days to produce 640 power trains once the 640 transmissions (250 from inventory and 390 newly produced), as well as all of the other materials in the power train, are available.

COMPONENT	ADDITIONAL REQUIREMENTS	LEAD TIME (WORKING DAYS)
Power Train	640	20
Transmission	390	5
Gearbox	0	0

▲ FIGURE 10.18
Additional Requirements and Lead Times for the Power Train Assembly

With the information in Figure 10.18 we can construct the time line shown in Figure 10.19. As previously stated, the 1000 complete planters are due on April 1, the sixtieth working day of the year. This day marks the end of the production and assembly process and the start of our calculation. It was also previously stated that the power trains must be available on March 15, to allow the 10 working days required to assemble final components into the planters. Figure 10.19 was constructed by starting at the desired completion time and working backward. This process is often called **time phasing** or *lead-time offsetting.* We see from this construction that the process of producing the 390 additional transmissions must be

▼ FIGURE 10.19
Time Phasing Planter Production

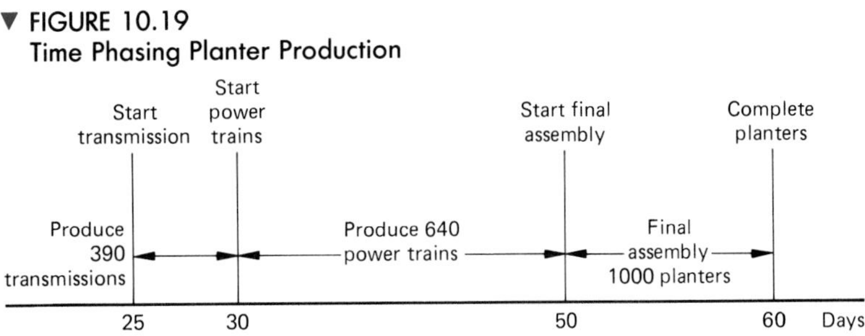

started on the twenty-fifth working day (roughly February 5; the exact date, of course, depends on the year). If Farmcraft did not already have at least 390 gearboxes in inventory, the date at which the entire process of producing power trains started would have been even earlier.

The popularity of MRP in real applications is partly due to its conceptual simplicity.

To apply MRP, start backward from the finished product and successively compute net additional requirements for the dependent intermediate goods.

However, in spite of its simplicity an enormous volume of calculations must be performed to apply MRP in most real manufacturing environments. Consequently, the success of MRP is to a large extent due to the capabilities of large-scale computers.

10.8 Summary

This chapter was devoted primarily to the basic EOQ (economic order quantity) model and its various modifications. The model assumes a constant known rate of demand, with no stockouts, and the relevant costs are those of ordering and holding. A policy with frequent orders gives a high ordering cost and low holding cost. Infrequent orders give a low ordering cost and high holding cost. The EOQ formula determines an order quantity Q^* that balances these two costs, that is, minimizes annual holding and ordering costs. Given Q^*, the number of orders per year is D/Q^*, where D is annual demand, and the amount of time it takes to deplete the quantity Q^*, called the cycle time, is Q^*/D.

After developing the EOQ formula and related expressions (e.g., AHO (Q^*)), our attentions turned to the question of when to order. The concept of a reorder point was introduced, and inventory position, the sum of inventory on hand and inventory on order, was introduced as the appropriate quantity to use in establishing the reorder point. The rule, in the absence of a safety stock is: "Reorder when the inventory position equals lead-time demand." In Section 10.3 we considered the sensitivity of the model to changes in the values of the cost parameters and the use of safety stocks to allow for uncertainty in demand or in lead time. With a safety stock, the reorder point rule is: "Reorder when inventory position equals lead-time demand plus safety stock."

Other sections of this chapter dealt with modifications of the basic model that are important in applications. For example, Section 10.4 showed how the optimal order quantity must be modified in the face of a quantity discount. Section 10.5 investigated the advantages of backlogging demand (delivering orders late) when the market is such that this strategy is feasible. Section 10.6 treated the case in which items are not ordered from an outside source, but are produced internally. In such cases the quantity of material ordered typically does not arrive all at one time in a single batch. Its arrival is spread out over an interval of time. The basic model must be modified to take this fact into account.

The last section in this chapter went deeper into the problem of inventory control in a production facility as compared with a retail or a wholesale firm. The MRP (material requirements planning) technique was introduced. This technique is specifically designed to take into account the interdependencies in the inventories of assembled products. It is also used to plan the time at which various functions must be started in order to satisfy the demand for completed projects (finished product).

Key Terms

Inventory. Units of goods, money, or individuals held in anticipation of future needs. (*p. 437*)

Holding Cost. The cost of holding inventory; it includes opportunity cost plus direct costs such as pilferage, insurance, and obsolescence. (*p. 438*)

Opportunity Cost. If taking one action (say, A) implies that another action (say, B) cannot be taken, the net return associated with action B is an opportunity cost of taking action A. (*p. 438*)

Ordering Cost. One of the cost parameters in the EOQ model. The marginal cost of placing an order. (*p. 438*)

Stockout Cost. Stated in terms of either penalty cost or backlogging cost. (*p. 438*)

Stockout. Not having enough inventory on hand to satisfy demand. (*p. 438*)

Backlogging. The practice of delivering goods to customers some time after the order has been received rather than immediately upon receipt of the order. (*p. 438*)

Penalty Cost. The loss in a no-backlogging model when it is not possible to satisfy demand; usually stated as a per unit cost of unsatisfied demand. (*p. 438*)

Backlogging Cost. One of the cost parameters in the EOQ model expanded to allow for backlogging. The cost of backlogging an item for a specified time. (*p. 438*)

Order Quantity. Part of an inventory control system. The number of items that are ordered when an order is placed. (*p. 439*)

Lead Time. The period of time between when an order is placed and when it actually arrives. (*p. 439*)

Demand. The number of items ordered. Because of stockouts, this may be different from the number of items sold. (*p. 439*)

ICON. A hypothetical inventory control system in this text. Its characteristics are similar to many commercial packages. (*p. 443*)

Economic Order Quantity Model. An inventory control model with constant rate of demand and in which relevant costs are those of ordering and holding, and possibly those of backlogging demand. (*p. 443*)

Optimal Order Quantity. The quantity that minimizes the total annual cost of ordering and holding a particular item. (*p. 443*)

Inventory Carrying Cost. One of the cost parameters in the EOQ model. The cost of holding an item in inventory for a specified time. (*p. 444*)

Economic Order Quantity. The optimal order quantity derived from the EOQ model. (*p. 446*)

Cycle Time. The interval between the arrival of the two consecutive orders. (*p. 447*)

Inventory Position. Inventory on hand plus that on order. (*p. 448*)

Reorder Point. Part of a reorder point-reorder quantity inventory control system. When the inventory position reaches this number, an order should be placed. (*p. 449*)

Safety Stock. Additional items that are added to the reorder point in order to protect against stockouts due to uncertainty in demand over the lead time. (*p. 452*)

Buffer Stock. A synonym for safety stock. (*p. 452*)

Quantity Discount. A purchase plan under which the seller offers a special price to the buyer if he or she purchases a specified quantity or more. (*p. 453*)

Production Lot Size Model. A modification of the EOQ model that allows for a finite rate of receiving materials. (*p. 460*)

Material Requirements Planning (MRP). An inventory control system for manufactured products involving assemblies. (*p. 463*)

Time Phasing. The process of determining when production or purchasing activities should begin in an MRP system. Also called lead-time offsetting. (*p. 465*)

Major Concepts Quiz

True–False

1. T F The opportunity cost segment of the holding cost is determined by factors such as breakage, pilferage, and insurance.

2. T F Demand is always greater than or equal to sales.

3. T F In the EOQ model the annual ordering cost is directly proportional to the order quantity.

4. T F If the lead time is smaller than the cycle time, an order should be placed when the inventory on hand equals the demand during the lead time (assuming zero safety stock).

5. T F In the EOQ model the annual holding and ordering cost is reasonably insensitive to errors in estimating the cost parameters.

6. T F The safety stock is the difference between the reorder point and the actual demand over the lead time.

7. T F For any set of demand and cost parameters, the minimum annual holding and ordering cost (backlogging not permitted) is never smaller than the minimum annual holding, ordering, and backlogging cost (backlogging permitted).

8. T F In the production lot size model, since production is at a steady rate, no setup cost is included in the model.

9. T F Material requirements planning takes the dependency of intermediate goods into account to determine the additional requirements of component parts.

Multiple Choice

10. The following are some of the reasons inventory is held:
 a. protect against uncertainty in demand
 b. lower production costs
 c. store labor
 d. all of the above

11. Important considerations in deciding *when* and *how much* to order include all factors except
 a. the lead time
 b. the proportion of the holding cost that is due to the opportunity cost
 c. the possibility of quantity discounts
 d. the extent to which future demand is known

12. In the EOQ model
 a. shipments arrive in a batch
 b. demand is known and occurs at a constant rate
 c. all demand must be satisfied
 d. all of the above

13. In the EOQ model if the price of the item increases and all other parameters remain the same, the optimal order quantity will typically
 a. increase
 b. decrease
 c. stay the same

14. In the EOQ model the optimal number of orders per year
 a. increases directly with
 b. increases as the square root of
 c. decreases directly with
 d. does not change with
 the annual rate of demand.

15. Consider an EOQ model with a quantity discount where a smaller per unit price applies to all units if B or more units are purchased. If Q_D^* minimizes AHO assuming the smaller price, and Q_R^* minimizes AHO assuming the regular price, and $Q_D^* > B$, the optimal order quantity is always
 a. Q_D^*
 b. either Q_R^* or B, depending on which yields the smaller annual total cost
 c. Q_R^*
 d. B

16. In the EOQ model with backlogging, the optimal number of orders to backlog is
 a. directly proportional to
 b. directly proportional to the square root of

c. not dependent on
d. directly proportional to the reciprocal of
the annual rate of demand.

17. In the production lot size model, increasing the rate of production
 a. increases
 b. does not influence
 c. decreases
 the optimal number of orders to place each year.

Answers

1. F	**6.** F	**11.** b	**16.** b
2. T	**7.** T	**12.** d	
3. F	**8.** F	**13.** b	
4. T	**9.** T	**14.** b	
5. T	**10.** d	**15.** a	

Problems

QSB+ can be used as an aid in solving the following problems. For example, it will calculate AHO(Q) for any Q and even graph the results if your computer has a graphics capability

(a) 7000 lbs
(b) \$420
(c) \$1300
(d) \$1720
(e) \$183,720
(f) Larger lots

10-1. ▲ A local hardware store sells 364,000 pounds of nails a year. It currently orders 14,000 pounds of nails every 2 weeks at a price of \$0.50 per pound. Assume that

1. Demand occurs at a constant rate.
2. The cost of placing an order is \$50 regardless of the size of the order.
3. The annual cost of holding inventory is 12% of the value of the average inventory level.
4. These factors do not change over time.
 (a) What is the average inventory level?
 (b) What is the annual holding cost?
 (c) What is the annual ordering cost?
 (d) What is the annual holding and ordering cost?
 (e) What is the annual total cost?
 (f) Would it be cheaper for the owner to order in lots larger than 14,000 (and less frequently) or smaller lots (and more frequently)?

(a) 90
(b) \$67.50
(c) \$90
(d) See IM
(e) Savings = \$607.50

10-2. ▲▲ The campus ice cream store sells 180 quarts of vanilla ice cream each month. The store currently restocks its inventory at the beginning of each month. The wholesale price of ice cream is \$3 per quart. Assume that

1. Demand occurs at a constant rate.
2. The annual cost of holding inventory is 25% of the value of the average inventory level.
3. Last year the annual total cost was \$7627.50.
4. These factors do not change over time.
 (a) Compute average inventory level.
 (b) Compute annual holding cost.
 (c) Compute the ordering cost.
 (d) Plot a graph of annual holding costs and annual ordering costs as a function of order quantity.
 (e) Graphically show at what point the AHO is minimized. How much can the ice cream store save if it uses the optimal order quantity?

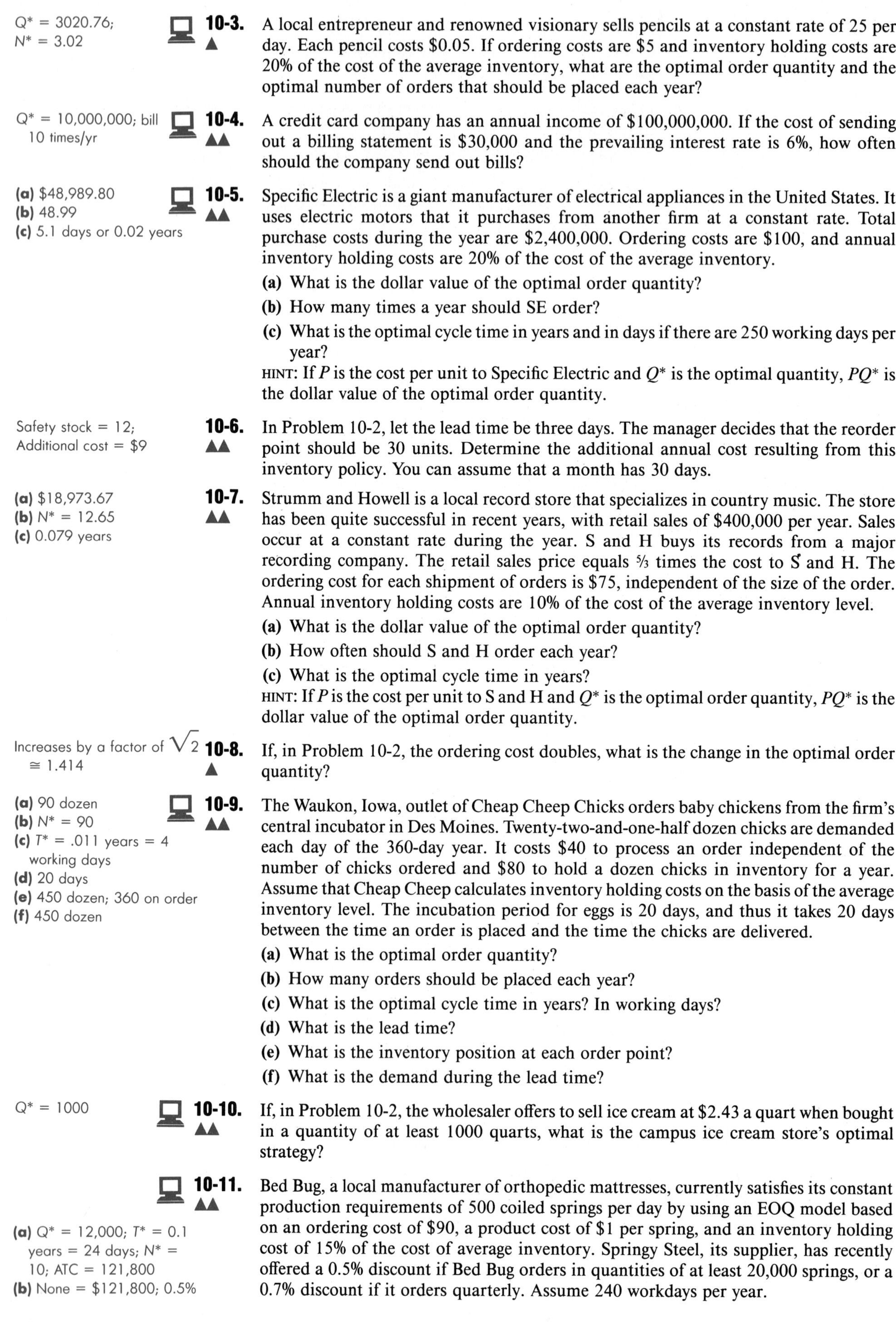

$Q^* = 3020.76$; $N^* = 3.02$

10-3. ▲ A local entrepreneur and renowned visionary sells pencils at a constant rate of 25 per day. Each pencil costs $0.05. If ordering costs are $5 and inventory holding costs are 20% of the cost of the average inventory, what are the optimal order quantity and the optimal number of orders that should be placed each year?

$Q^* = 10{,}000{,}000$; bill 10 times/yr

10-4. ▲▲ A credit card company has an annual income of $100,000,000. If the cost of sending out a billing statement is $30,000 and the prevailing interest rate is 6%, how often should the company send out bills?

(a) $48,989.80
(b) 48.99
(c) 5.1 days or 0.02 years

10-5. ▲▲ Specific Electric is a giant manufacturer of electrical appliances in the United States. It uses electric motors that it purchases from another firm at a constant rate. Total purchase costs during the year are $2,400,000. Ordering costs are $100, and annual inventory holding costs are 20% of the cost of the average inventory.

(a) What is the dollar value of the optimal order quantity?

(b) How many times a year should SE order?

(c) What is the optimal cycle time in years and in days if there are 250 working days per year?

HINT: If P is the cost per unit to Specific Electric and Q^* is the optimal quantity, PQ^* is the dollar value of the optimal order quantity.

Safety stock = 12; Additional cost = $9

10-6. ▲▲ In Problem 10-2, let the lead time be three days. The manager decides that the reorder point should be 30 units. Determine the additional annual cost resulting from this inventory policy. You can assume that a month has 30 days.

(a) $18,973.67
(b) $N^* = 12.65$
(c) 0.079 years

10-7. ▲▲ Strumm and Howell is a local record store that specializes in country music. The store has been quite successful in recent years, with retail sales of $400,000 per year. Sales occur at a constant rate during the year. S and H buys its records from a major recording company. The retail sales price equals 5/3 times the cost to S and H. The ordering cost for each shipment of orders is $75, independent of the size of the order. Annual inventory holding costs are 10% of the cost of the average inventory level.

(a) What is the dollar value of the optimal order quantity?

(b) How often should S and H order each year?

(c) What is the optimal cycle time in years?

HINT: If P is the cost per unit to S and H and Q^* is the optimal order quantity, PQ^* is the dollar value of the optimal order quantity.

Increases by a factor of $\sqrt{2} \cong 1.414$

10-8. ▲ If, in Problem 10-2, the ordering cost doubles, what is the change in the optimal order quantity?

(a) 90 dozen
(b) $N^* = 90$
(c) $T^* = .011$ years = 4 working days
(d) 20 days
(e) 450 dozen; 360 on order
(f) 450 dozen

10-9. ▲▲ The Waukon, Iowa, outlet of Cheap Cheep Chicks orders baby chickens from the firm's central incubator in Des Moines. Twenty-two-and-one-half dozen chicks are demanded each day of the 360-day year. It costs $40 to process an order independent of the number of chicks ordered and $80 to hold a dozen chicks in inventory for a year. Assume that Cheap Cheep calculates inventory holding costs on the basis of the average inventory level. The incubation period for eggs is 20 days, and thus it takes 20 days between the time an order is placed and the time the chicks are delivered.

(a) What is the optimal order quantity?

(b) How many orders should be placed each year?

(c) What is the optimal cycle time in years? In working days?

(d) What is the lead time?

(e) What is the inventory position at each order point?

(f) What is the demand during the lead time?

$Q^* = 1000$

10-10. ▲▲ If, in Problem 10-2, the wholesaler offers to sell ice cream at $2.43 a quart when bought in a quantity of at least 1000 quarts, what is the campus ice cream store's optimal strategy?

(a) $Q^* = 12{,}000$; $T^* = 0.1$ years = 24 days; $N^* = 10$; ATC = 121,800
(b) None = $121,800; 0.5%

10-11. ▲▲ Bed Bug, a local manufacturer of orthopedic mattresses, currently satisfies its constant production requirements of 500 coiled springs per day by using an EOQ model based on an ordering cost of $90, a product cost of $1 per spring, and an inventory holding cost of 15% of the cost of average inventory. Springy Steel, its supplier, has recently offered a 0.5% discount if Bed Bug orders in quantities of at least 20,000 springs, or a 0.7% discount if it orders quarterly. Assume 240 workdays per year.

= $121,432.50; 0.7% = $121,754.25
(c) Order 20,000

(a) Find Q^*, T^*, N^*, and the annual total cost under the current cost assumptions.
(b) Calculate annual total cost for each of the discount alternatives.
(c) What should Bed Bug do?

$Q^* = 1080$

10-12. ▲ If, in Problem 10-2, the ice cream store is allowed to backlog demand at a cost of 20%, what is the optimal order quantity?

(a) $Q^* = 96$ packs; $N^* = 24$; $T^* = 8.33$ days; AHO* = $4800
(b) $40.00
(c) $Q^* = 144$; $S^* = 80$; $N^* = 16$; $T^* = 12.5$ days
(d) Allow backlogs

10-13. ▲▲ The Reefer Tobacco Company, the nation's largest distributor of California-grown smoking products, has a constant demand of 192 packs per month for its most popular product, Wachy Tabachy. Its ordering cost is $100, annual holding costs are 25% of the average inventory (due to the high risk of seizure), and the product costs $200 per pack. Currently, it does not backlog demand and follows the optimal ordering policy. Recently, a local consultant recommended that the company backlog demand. This requires a price discount. Reefer feels that it must offer a discount of $0.20 per day. Allowing for vacations and religious holidays, there are 200 days per year.
(a) Under the current policy (no backlogging), find Q^*, N^*, T^*, and AHO(Q^*).
(b) What is the value for C, the cost of backlogging a unit for a year?
(c) For the suggested backlogging policy, find Q^*, S^*, N^*, T^*, and AHOB(Q^*).
(d) Which policy should Reefer implement?

(a) $Q^* = 600$; $T^* = 8.33$ days; $N^* = 30$; AHO* = 1800
(b) on hand = 504; on order = 0; position = 504
(c) 504

10-14. ▲ The demand for general books at the University Bookstore occurs at a constant rate of 18,000 books per year. The manager satisfies this demand without backlogging. He calculates the optimal order quantity based on ordering costs of $30 and an annual holding cost of $3 per book. Orders are delivered 7 days after they are received by telephone. Assume 250 days per year.
(a) What are the values for Q^*, N^*, T^*, and AHO(Q^*)?
(b) When an order is placed, what is the level of
(i) Inventory on hand?
(ii) Inventory on order?
(iii) Inventory position?
(c) What is the demand during the lead time?

(a) $Q^* = 900$; $T^* = 12.5$ days; $N^* = 20$; AHOB* = 1200
(b) on hand = 4; on order = 0; position = 4
(c) 504
(d) Yes

10-15. ▲▲ Suppose that in Problem 10-14 the bookstore has the option of backlogging orders and that it costs $2.40 to backlog a unit of demand for a year. (When backlogging is permitted inventory position is defined as inventory on hand plus inventory on order minus backorders.)
(a) What are the values for Q^*, N^*, T^*, S^*, and AHOB(Q^*)?
(b) When an order is placed, what is the level of
(i) Inventory on hand?
(ii) Inventory on order?
(iii) Inventory position?
(c) What is the demand during the lead time?
(d) Should the bookstore backlog orders?

(a) $Q^* = 3600$; $T^* = 80$ days; $N^* = 3.75$
(b) Max. inv. = 900; prod. run = 60 days
(c) DHS = $22.50

10-16. ▲ XXX Distillery, a major producer of arthritis and nerve medicine in the Southeast, produces its stock in batches. In order to begin each run, the company owners must select a suitable location and assemble the equipment. The cost of this operation is $900. Production yields 60 gallons of product each day, each of which costs $0.025 per day to hold in inventory. Demand is constant at 1125 gallons per month. Assume 12 months, 300 days per year, and 25 days per month.
(a) Find Q^*, N^*, and T^* for the optimal production lot size.
(b) Find the maximum inventory and the length (in days) of each production run for the optimal production lot size.
(c) Find DHS(Q^*).

(a) $Q = 4500$; $T = 100$ days; prod. run = 75 days; max. inv. = 1125
(b) DHS = $23.06

10-17. ▲ Because of the importance of business confidentiality, XXX Distillery in Problem 10-16 decides to make three production runs per year.
(a) Find the production order quantity, Q, cycle time (in days), length of production run, and maximum inventory level.
(b) Find DHS for the policy in part (a).

10-18. ▲▲▲ Consider Problem 10-16.

(a) $Q^* = 1800$; AHO = \$13,500
(b) DHS is lower; less inventory
(c) See IM
(d) $p = 45$, DTC = \$30; $p = 60$, DTC = \$45

(a) Suppose that XXX Distillery purchased rather than produced its product and that the cost of placing an order is \$900. Find Q^* and AHO(Q^*).

(b) How does AHO(Q^*) in part (a) compare with DHS(Q^*) when there is a production rate of 60 gallons per day? Explain this relationship.

(c) Plot the DHS($Q^*[p]$) as a function of the daily production rate, p.

(d) Due to the economies of scale, unit production costs decrease as p goes up. The exact relationship is $C(p) = 30/p$, where $C(p)$ is the unit production cost when the daily production rate is p. Find the minimum value of the sum of DHS and daily production costs for $p = 45$ and $p = 60$.

0.4% discount

10-19. ▲▲▲ Due to technical obsolescence of its equipment, XXX Distillery (Problem 10-16) stops producing and functions only as a marketing organization. It now purchases its product from another producer. XXX must buy at least 1000 gallons per order to qualify for a quantity discount. What is the smallest discount per gallon that would persuade XXX to order 1000 gallons? Assume that now $P = \$5$, $C_h = \$2.50$, and $C_o = \$200$.

(a) 300 engines; 25 sparks; 250 carbs; 25 throats; 75 butterfly valves
(b) See IM

10-20. ▲ The Clunker Car Company (CCC) produces automobiles based on the latest Model T technology. Some of the materials used in its newest line of import-competing automobiles, the C-Cars, are shown in Figure 10.20. CCC's current inventory levels include 225 throats, 175 butterfly valves, 275 spark plug sets (1 set per engine), 50 carburetors, and 100 engines.

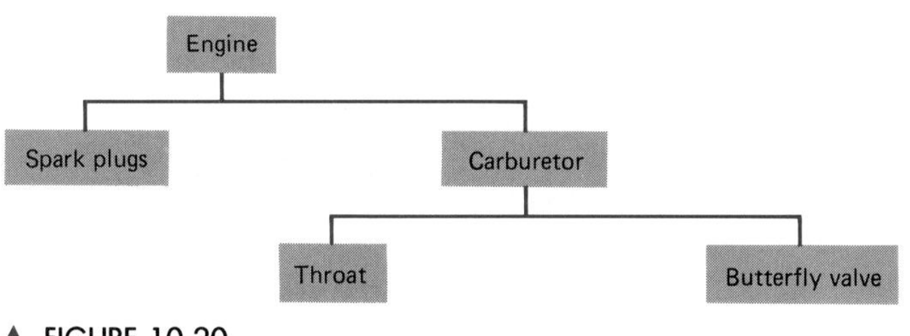

▲ FIGURE 10.20

(a) What additional amounts of each part will be needed to satisfy an order for 400 engines?

(b) Assume that the lead time for assembly is 10 days for engines and 5 days for carburetors. Assume further that the lead time for ordering throats is 3 days, butterfly valves is 2 days, and spark plugs is 6 days. Find the ordering and assembly schedule for an order due in 30 days.

10-21. ▲ Solve Problem 10-20 with the following data:

(a) 270 engines; 145 sparks; 180 carbs; 30 throats; 80 butterfly valves
(b) See IM

Current inventory
- 150 throats
- 100 butterfly valves
- 125 spark plug sets
- 90 carburetors
- 130 engines

Assembly time
- Engines, 8 days
- Carburetors, 6 days

Ordering time
- Throats, 5 days
- Butterfly valves, 3 days
- Spark plugs, 5 days

What is the date that the first action must be taken? Which action is it?

Appendix 10.1 Mathematical Derivation of EOQ Results

The EOQ model

To derive expression (10.9), the optimal value of Q in the EOQ model, you must find the value of Q that minimizes expression (10.5), the annual holding and ordering cost.

$$\text{AHO} = C_0\left(\frac{D}{Q}\right) + C_h\left(\frac{Q}{2}\right)$$

Taking the first derivative with respect to Q yields

$$\frac{d}{dQ}\,\text{AHO} = \frac{-C_0 D}{Q^2} + \frac{C_h}{2}$$

Setting this result equal to 0 and solving for Q gives

$$Q^* = \sqrt{\frac{2C_0 D}{C_h}}$$

which is (10.9).

To demonstrate that Q^* yields a minimum, you take the second derivative of AHO with respect to Q and determine if it is positive:

$$\frac{d^2}{dQ^2}\,\text{AHO} = \frac{2C_0 D}{Q^3}$$

Since the result is positive for all $Q > 0$, you can conclude that Q^* yields a minimum.

Equality of the annual holding and ordering cost

It is useful to show that

$$C_0\left(\frac{D}{Q^*}\right) = C_h\left(\frac{Q^*}{2}\right)$$

that is, that the optimal order quantity yields equal values for the annual holding and annual ordering costs.

The demonstration is achieved by substituting the expression for Q^* into the left-hand side of the inequality and obtaining the right-hand side.

$$C_0\left(\frac{D}{Q^*}\right) = C_0\frac{D}{\sqrt{\frac{2C_0 D}{C_h}}}$$

$$= C_0\left(\frac{2}{2}\right)\left(\frac{D\sqrt{C_h}}{\sqrt{2C_0 D}}\right)\left(\sqrt{\frac{C_h}{C_h}}\right)$$

$$= C_h\frac{1}{2}\sqrt{\frac{2C_0 D}{C_h}}$$

$$= C_h\left(\frac{Q^*}{2}\right)$$

Video Case

Just-in-Time

Just-in-time! Although the just-in-time (JIT) concept is very young, perhaps 10 to 15 years old in this country, it is so widespread in American manufacturing and service that it is almost a cliché. Perhaps this is because the idea is so simple and so appealing. In short, the JIT strategy is to have "the right product at the right place at the right time." It implies that in manufacturing or service, each stage of the process produces exactly the amount that is required for the next step in the process. This notion holds true for all steps within the system. Suppose, for example, that in our plant all products pass through a drilling operation and then a milling operation. With JIT, the drill produces only what the mill will need next. It also holds for the last step—that is, the system produces only what the customer desires.

Implementation of a JIT system typically includes emphasis on the following aspects of the production process:

1. Reduction of setup times and cost. Here the idea is to make it cost-effective to produce in very small lot sizes. The ideal is a lot size of one.
2. Emphasis on preventive maintenance. This is important because the manufacturing process must always be ready to go when you need it if you hope to be just in time.
3. Continuous process improvement to guarantee good quality. If you are going to make just the right number of units, you must be sure that they are of good quality—you cannot select the good items out of a larger lot with this approach. A continuous improvement process is typically based on a high level of employee involvement and empowerment.
4. Reduction of lead times through effective use of information technology and close relationships with vendors.

In many publications, JIT is placed at one end of a continuum with EOQ at the other. The EOQ model is portrayed as being old, out-of-touch, and possibly responsible for many of the problems faced by manufacturing firms in the United States. We would like to suggest an alternative interpretation. Is it possible that the concepts that form the basis for the EOQ model are consistent with the JIT philosophy, and that the problem has been in interpretation and implementation? Let's examine that possibility.

Questions

1. What is the effect of reducing setup cost on lot size in the EOQ model? Is the effect the same in a JIT system?
2. What is the role of quality and preventive maintenance in the EOQ model? Why?
3. Do you sense a difference in philosophy between the EOQ and the JIT approaches? In particular, what aspects of the production problem is it assumed we can influence in the two approaches?
4. Do you think that there are any general lessons to be learned in regard to modeling from the movement from EOQ to JIT?

Heuristics, Multiple Objectives, and Goal Programming

APPLICATION CAPSULE

The Taxman Cometh: Peoria Fine-Tunes Its Tax System with the Help of Goal Programming*

Designing an equitable tax system that provides sufficient revenue to sustain government programs without excessively burdening any single group of taxpayers is an extremely difficult (and unappreciated) task. The loss of revenue sources as residents and businesses flee the city for the suburbs has further complicated the problem for urban tax planners. Historically, property taxes have been the major source of city revenues, as they are for Peoria, Illinois. But reliance on this source has been diminished by a shrinking property base and a simmering taxpayer revolt. Higher property taxes tend to encourage the emigration of more-mobile, high-income households from the city, thus *decreasing* tax revenue in a vicious cycle.

Planners have therefore been forced to place greater reliance on other forms of taxation, including sales taxes. Sales taxes tend to place a proportionally greater burden on lower-income families. However, they also have certain advantages over property taxes:

1. They are less likely to prompt business migration from the city or discourage the start of new ventures.
2. They shift part of the tax burden to non-city residents who benefit from public services.
3. Because sales taxes are paid continually in small amounts, their burden is generally perceived to be less (or at least is felt less acutely) than that of taxes requiring lump-sum payments.

The city manager of Peoria enlisted the help of university consultants to explore ways of improving the city's tax structure. A multiobjective linear programming (MOLP) model was formulated to provide a better understanding of the alternatives available and the tradeoffs involved in various plans. The model had four variables (the tax rates on property, general sales, durable goods, and gas) and several objectives, including

- reducing property taxes
- minimizing the tax burden on low-income households

- minimizing the flight of businesses and shoppers to the suburbs to escape high sales taxes.

It was essential to find ways of achieving these objectives without diminishing tax revenues or increasing the tax burden on the city's middle- and high-income families. Constraints were formulated to embody these requirements and others, such as limiting the general sales tax to between 1% and 3% and eliminating the food and drug tax previously in effect.

The solution produced 12 efficient tax plans for the city to consider. The best of these achieved a substantial decrease in the property tax rate, the lost revenue being made up by a gas tax of $0.033/gallon and an increase in the sales tax from 1% to 2%.

*Chrisman, Fry, Reeves, Lewis, and Weinstein, "A Multiobjective Linear Programming Methodology for Public Sector Tax Planning," *Interfaces*, Vol. 19, No. 5 (Sept–Oct. 1989).

11.1 Introduction

From time to time a manager's problem may be so complex that the mathematical model constructed to attack it cannot be solved with the traditional algorithms available to the analyst. This situation may occur because

1. The model, "correctly formulated," may be too large, too nonlinear, or logically too complex (requiring, for example, the use of many 0–1 variables in the formulation).
2. It is felt that the imposition of simplifying assumptions or approximations, which might make the problem more tractable, would destroy too much of the important real-world structure of the problem (i.e., would carry the model too far from reality to be useful).

Here is a real dilemma. The model at hand is too complex to solve. At the same time we are unwilling to simplify it in any ameliorative way. What does one do in this seemingly hopeless situation?

In part to answer this question, the field of heuristic programming has developed. In the discussion above, when we employed the phrase "the model is too complex to *solve*" we were using the word *solve* in a rigorous mathematical sense. We meant that the mathematical model was so complicated that, although a rigorous solution exists (e.g., an optimal solution in an optimization model), it is too difficult, too time-consuming, perhaps even impossible to discover with existing know-how and technology. In such a case a *heuristic algorithm* might be employed.

An important aspect of a heuristic algorithm is that it never gives a "bad" solution. It is more important always to have a fairly good solution than to have the best solution sometimes and a bad solution once in a while.

A **heuristic algorithm** is one that efficiently provides good approximate solutions to a given problem. Often (but by no means always) in employing such an algorithm one may be able to measure precisely the "goodness" of the approximation. For example, in the optimization context, with some heuristic algorithms one can make a statement like "Upon termination you can be sure of being within _____% of optimality." Or, "Under certain assumptions the heuristic answer will be optimal _____% of the time."

Heuristic programming

The phase I heuristic for LP codes is known as "crashing the basis" (trying to find a quick, initial feasible solution).

The term **heuristic** is also frequently encountered. A **heuristic** is an intuitively appealing rule of thumb for dealing with some aspect of a problem. A collection of heuristics, or heuristic algorithms, is referred to as a **heuristic program.** Some computer codes, for example, employ heuristics in phase 1 of the simplex method to attempt to quickly find an initial corner. Heuristics are employed to get a quick start with the transportation algorithm, and so on.

As you can infer from the definitions above, you no doubt use heuristics frequently in everyday problem solving. You go to the bank, and to minimize your time waiting, you stand in the shortest line. Although this is by no means guaranteed to be optimal, it is a rule of thumb that often works quite well. In checking through customs you may prefer the bench occupied by a smiling officer, although he is certainly not guaranteed to be more lenient than others. The list goes on.

Usefulness of heuristics

In the context of mathematical programming, heuristics are often employed in conjunction with, or as a special case of, more general or more rigorous problem-solving strategies. The important point to remember is that a heuristic procedure or algorithm is intuitively appealing but can guarantee its results, if at all, only statistically or within certain margins of uncertainty. It is employed mainly for *efficiency*—namely, to produce quickly what are hopefully good, if not optimal, results.

Two factors that help this acceptability are that:
1. the user has control over the model, and
2. it is easy to make changes.

Generally speaking, from the viewpoint of a manager, a heuristic procedure may certainly be as acceptable as, and possibly (in terms of cost) even preferable to, a "more exact" algorithm that produces an optimal solution. The dominant considerations should be the amount of insight and guidance that the model can provide and the overall net benefit as measured by the difference "savings due to the model less cost of producing the model and its solution."

Combinatorial optimization

In the first part of this chapter we discuss several examples of heuristic algorithms as applied to large *combinatorial optimization* problems. The term **combinatorial optimization** means there are only a finite number of feasible alternatives, and if all of these are enumerated, the optimal one can be found. The problem is that in practice this finite number often amounts to millions or even billions of possibilities, and hence even on high-speed computers complete enumeration is out of the question. Although such problems can often be formulated as integer programs with 0–1 variables, they are often so large that even the IP formulation is prohibitively expensive to bring to optimality with the usual branch-and-bound or partial enumeration approach.

Goal programming

Following the examples in the first part of the chapter we then look at problems for which the objective is to achieve acceptable levels of certain "goals." For example, consider a problem with multiple but conflicting objectives. The president of a firm wants high profits but also wants to maintain low prices in order to keep from losing clients. An executive with a fixed budget wants to invest in R&D but also wants to purchase raw materials to use in obtaining near-term profits. Such examples of multiple but conflicting objectives are typical in business applications. *Goal programming* deals with such problems. The topic is closely related to heuristic programming, for in a sense goal programming itself could be thought of as a heuristic approach to dealing with multiple objectives.

11.2 Facility Scheduling (Sequencing Computer Jobs)

Sequence-Dependent Setup Time

Consider a single production facility through which numerous jobs must be processed—for example, a computer, a drill press, or an ice cream machine. Typically, the facility may have to shut down after processing one job in order to set

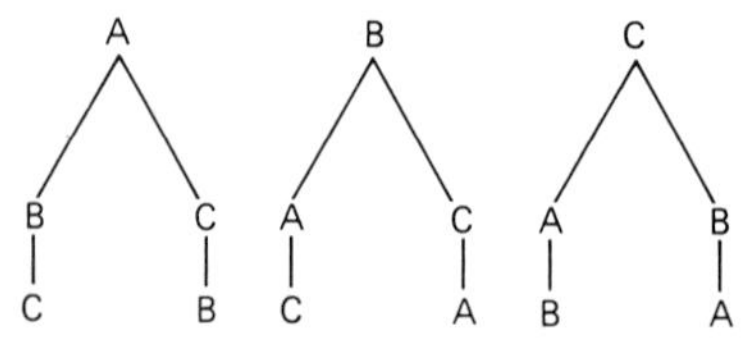

▲ FIGURE 11.1
Tree Showing Six Possible Sequences for Three Jobs A, B, C

This is a typical problem for a company such as Monsanto Chemical, which makes chemicals in common vats or transports them by tank cars. It makes a difference in which order the chemicals are produced or transported, as to the cost of changeover.

up for the next. Such "downtime" is termed **setup,** or *changeover,* time. The length of the setup time may depend on the next job to be processed and the job just completed. A sequence of similar jobs (making French vanilla ice cream after New York vanilla) would be interrupted by less setup time (cleaning out the machine) than a sequence of dissimilar jobs (French vanilla after Dutch chocolate). A typical managerial problem would be to *sequence the jobs in such a way as to minimize total setup time.*

You can easily see that from the combinatorial point of view this can be a very large problem. If there are only three jobs to be processed, say jobs A, B, and C, then any of the three could be taken first, with either of the remaining two second and the third determined (i.e., the single remaining job). The possible sequences can be displayed as a tree with each branch representing one sequence. The six possibilities are shown in Figure 11.1. In general, with n jobs, there are $n! = n(n-1)(n-2)\cdots 1$ possible combinations or sequences.[1] Only 10 jobs produces $10! = 3{,}628{,}800$ different sequences. You can see that this number of possible sequences ($n!$) increases rapidly with the size of n.

If there were 20 jobs, and a computer could calculate 1,000,000 combinations each second, it would take over 75,000 years to determine the optimal answer by listing every possible combination.

Obviously, one way to think about solving the minimization problem above is by complete enumeration. That is, generate each of the $n!$ possible sequences of jobs and compute the total setup time required for each sequence. Then pick the sequence associated with the smallest total time. Although this algorithm would provide a true optimum, it is not practical even for modest values of n because of the large number of sequences that would have to be enumerated.

Heuristic Solutions

Heuristic rules, although they will not guarantee an optimal solution, are often applied to this problem, for they will usually lead quite quickly to a satisfactory solution.

As an example, consider a computer operator who has three rather long jobs to be run on Monday afternoon. The computer is currently idle. For each of these jobs there is a setup time (searching for input tapes, hanging tapes, setting up the disk drive units and other auxiliary equipment) as specified in Figure 11.2. Since there are only

$$3! = 3 \cdot 2 = 6$$

possible sequences, they can all be enumerated. The results appear in Figure 11.3. As you can see, the optimal (minimum total setup time) sequence is $0 \to A \to C \to B$.

A Greedy Heuristic. Let us now see how a heuristic rule might be applied to this problem. The rule we shall illustrate is called the **next best rule,** sometimes called a **greedy algorithm.** The rule goes as follows:

[1] $n!$ stands for the mathematical term "n factorial."

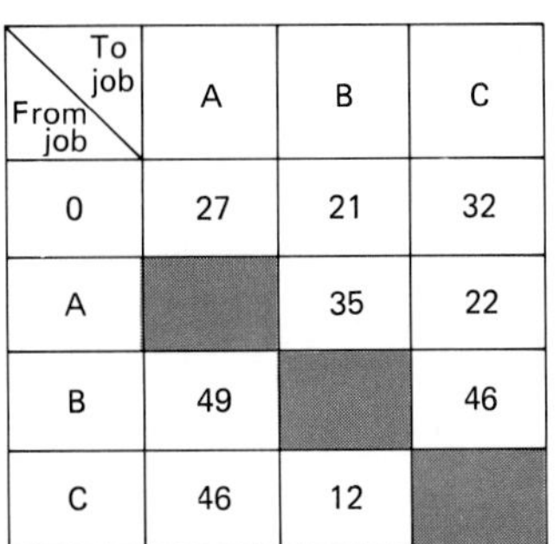

From job \ To job	A	B	C
0	27	21	32
A		35	22
B	49		46
C	46	12	

▲ FIGURE 11.2
Setup Times in Minutes

SEQUENCE	SETUP TIME	TOTAL (MIN)
0 → A → B → C	27 + 35 + 46	108
0 → A → C → B	27 + 22 + 12	61
0 → B → C → A	21 + 46 + 46	113
0 → B → A → C	21 + 49 + 22	92
0 → C → A → B	32 + 46 + 35	113
0 → C → B → A	32 + 12 + 49	93

▲ FIGURE 11.3
Results of Complete Enumeration

1. At step 1 (e.g., in selecting the first job), perform the task with least initial setup time.
2. At each subsequent step, select the task with least setup time, based on the current state.

Let us now apply this rule to the data in Figure 11.2. The task with the least initial setup time is B. Hence, the first step is 0 → B. According to the greedy algorithm, given that we have just completed B, the task to be selected is C, since the setup for B → C is less than for B → A. Thus, we have 0 → B → C, and we can then finish only with A. Thus, we obtain

$$\text{greedy heuristic: } 0 \rightarrow B \rightarrow C \rightarrow A$$

$$\text{total setup time} = 21 + 46 + 46 = 113$$

Notice that this is far from optimal. In fact, in this example, the greedy heuristic, although intuitively appealing, provides the worst possible policy for our problem.[2] However, the rule is extremely easy to apply, and studies on this type of problem have shown that *statistically,* for the above type of sequencing problem, the rule is not bad. For example, one article[3] showed that the heuristic will often produce better results than could be obtained by a purely random selection of tasks.

A Better Heuristic. The same article shows that the following modified heuristic gives even better results:

[2]Although it is true that in general, for sequential decision problems, the greedy algorithm does *not* lead to an optimal solution, there are in fact a few special problems for which it does. See, for example, the problem of finding a minimal spanning tree in Chapter 9.

[3]J. W. Gavett, "Three Heuristic Rules for Sequencing Jobs to a Single Production Facility," *Management Science,* 11 (1965), pp. B166–76.

Students may recognize this as the assignment problem with column 0 missing, which means, in this case, the set of jobs will not repeat itself.

	A	B	C
0	0	9	10
A		23	0
B	22		24
C	19	0	

▲ FIGURE 11.4
Transformed Data

1. Transform the original data in Figure 11.2 by subtracting the minimum setup time in each column from all other entries in that column. This process produces the data in Figure 11.4.
2. Apply the greedy algorithm to this set of transformed data. Doing this, we obtain

Best first step	$0 \rightarrow A$
Best second step	$A \rightarrow C$
Third step	$C \rightarrow B$

and thus the modified heuristic produces the sequence $0 \rightarrow A \rightarrow C \rightarrow B$, which was already shown to be optimal for this problem.

Although this modified heuristic will not always give the optimal solution, it is easy to implement, and in practice, for large problems, it often produces quite good results.

11.3 Scheduling with Limited Resources (Workload Smoothing)

Imagine a sequence of activities to be scheduled in order to complete a project. Basic models such as PERT and CPM, discussed in Chapter 15, will schedule the activities in such a way as to minimize total project completion time subject to the constraint that some activities cannot start until others have been completed. The resources (money, labor, machinery, and so on) needed to complete the individual activities are often considered to be available in any quantities required by any particular schedule. In reality, however, such resources may be limited, in which case resource availability becomes another constraint.

A Simple Example

As a simple example, consider the scheduling problem shown in Figures 11.5 and 11.6. Figure 11.5 shows **precedence relationships** among the various activities. That is, it shows which activities must be completed before others can begin. For example, activity VIII cannot begin until VII is completed, and VII cannot begin until I is completed. Figure 11.6 shows the duration of each activity (in weeks) and the resources required (number of people) to complete each activity.

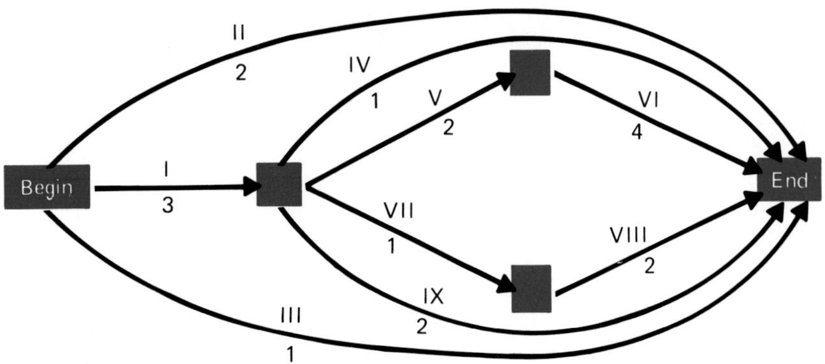

▲ FIGURE 11.5
Precedence Relationships

ACTIVITY	TIME REQUIRED TO COMPLETE (WEEKS)	NO. OF PEOPLE (PER WEEK) REQUIRED TO COMPLETE
I	3	6
II	2	3
III	1	3
IV	1	3
V	2	6
VI	4	5
VII	1	3
VIII	2	4
IX	2	3

▲ FIGURE 11.6
Requirements for Each Activity

This problem is simple, and thus the earliest possible completion time can be easily computed. It is 9 weeks.[4] Figure 11.7 shows a proposed activity schedule that will achieve this overall completion time. Thus, Figure 11.7 respects the precedence relationships of Figure 11.5, and at the same time shows when each activity should start and how long (in weeks) it will take. In this proposed schedule, each activity starts as early as possible. You can see that I, II, and III start immediately (at the beginning of week 1). Activities IV, V, VII, and IX start at the beginning of week 4. Activity VI starts at the beginning of week 6, and activity VIII starts at the beginning of week 5.

▼ FIGURE 11.7
Proposed Schedule of Activities

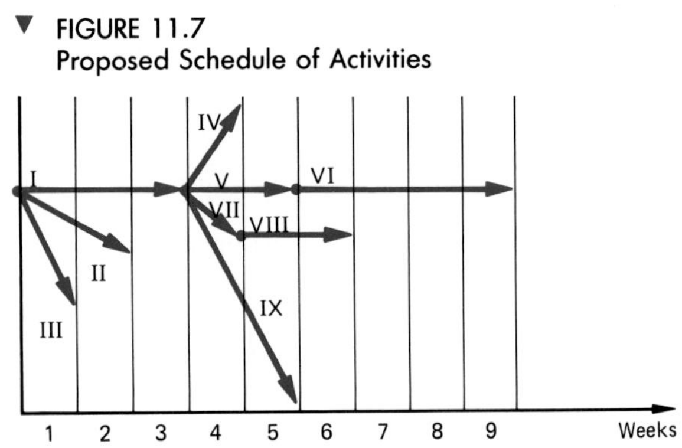

[4]If you have studied PERT, you can see that activities I, V, and VI form the *critical path* (see Section 15.3).

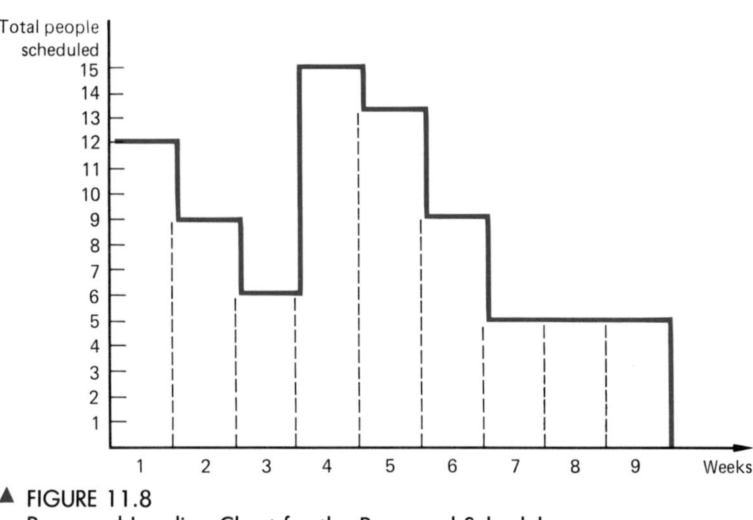

▲ FIGURE 11.8
Personnel Loading Chart for the Proposed Schedule

Personnel loading chart

Now consider the number of people per week required to implement the proposed schedule. The personnel data in Figure 11.6 can be combined with the schedule in Figure 11.7 to produce the **personnel loading chart** shown in Figure 11.8. As you can see, the proposed schedule makes an erratic utilization of personnel, the requirements fluctuating between the extremes of 15 people in week 4 and only 5 in weeks 7, 8, and 9. It may be to management's advantage to have a schedule that employs resources more smoothly. Heuristic programs are often applied to accomplish such an objective.

Workload Smoothing Heuristic

In order to discuss one such heuristic, let us define, for each activity, its **slack.**

Slack is the maximum amount of time an activity can be delayed without delaying overall project completion.

Note in Figure 11.7 that if the completion time of activity V were delayed, then activity VI could not start at the beginning of week 6 and the project could not be completed by the end of the ninth week. Thus activity V has no slack. In contrast, the completion of activity VIII could be delayed by 3 weeks without delaying the completion of the project. Activity VIII thus has a slack of 3 weeks.

Now, using this concept, the following heuristic can be given:

1. Determine the maximum required resources in the proposed schedule, say m.

2. In each week, impose an upper limit of $m - 1$ for resource utilization, and, if possible, revise the proposed schedule to satisfy this constraint. The revision is systematically performed as follows:

  a. Beginning with the earliest week violating the constraint, consider the activities contributing to the overload and move forward the one with *most* slack as little as possible until it contributes to no overloading, but without delaying the completion of the entire project (which means that activities with zero slack may not be moved). If there are ties, move forward the activity that contributes *least* to the overload (i.e., requires the fewest people).

  b. The heuristic terminates when the current overload cannot be decreased.

This table helps to "see" the problem of uneven manpower loading.

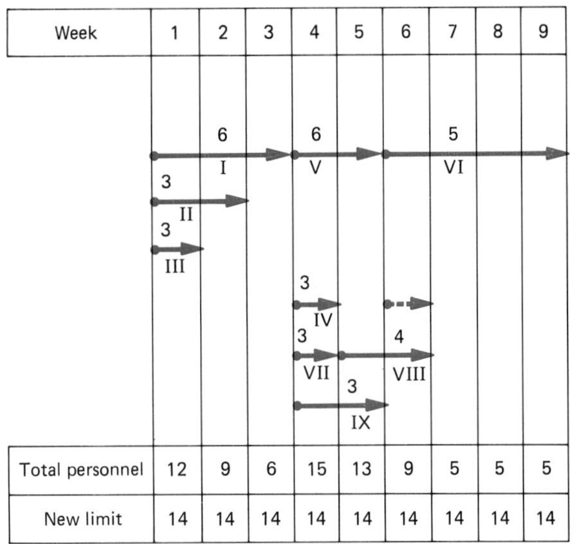

Total personnel	12	9	6	15	13	9	5	5	5
New limit	14	14	14	14	14	14	14	14	14

▲ FIGURE 11.9
First Proposal

To apply this heuristic, let us portray the proposed plan as in Figure 11.9. In this figure, the activity label appears below each arrow. Above each arrow is the number of people required each week. For example, the 6 above activity I implies that 6 people are required for each of the 3 weeks needed to complete activity I. Thus, you can read down the appropriate columns to obtain total personnel utilization in a given week. For example, since week 2 is intersected by activities I and II, the entry in the Total Personnel row, under the week 2 column, is 9. Similarly, the distance from the head of each unfollowed arrow at the end of a *series* of jobs to the end of week 9 indicates the slack for such an arrow. Thus, activity IV has 5 weeks of slack, while activity VIII has 3 weeks of slack, and so on. For activity VII, which is a followed arrow, we compute the slack by noting that VII is followed only by VIII. Since the slack on VIII is 3 weeks, slack on activity VII must also be 3 weeks. Also notice that activities I, V, and VI have zero slack since they cannot be moved forward at all without increasing the overall completion time of 9 weeks. In applying the foregoing heuristic we move forward only activities with positive slack, and hence activities I, V, and VI are not considered.

Applying the Heuristic. Given these observations, we may now employ the heuristic. For the first proposal, the maximum required resource is 15 in period 4. Thus, according to step 2, we impose an upper limit of 14 in each week. This limit is violated only in week 4. The "movable" activities contributing to the overload are IV, VII, and IX (since V need not be considered). Of these, the one with most slack is IV. Moving IV forward 1 period reduces the utilization in week 4 by 3 units to 12 people, but creates a utilization of 3 additional units in week 5, giving a total of 16 in week 5, which overloads week 5 (i.e., violates the imposed upper limit of 14). Hence, it must be moved farther forward. You can see that by moving activity IV forward a total of 2 weeks (into week 6 as illustrated in Figure 11.9) no upper limit will be violated. This gives the second proposal, as shown in Figure 11.10.

In this figure the upper limit of 13 must be reduced to 12. The only overload is caused by VIII and IX in week 5. Activity IX has the most slack, and it must be advanced 3 weeks to begin in week 7, as shown. This gives the third proposal presented in Figure 11.11. Here the upper limit of 12 must be reduced to 11. There are violations in weeks 1 and 6. According to the algorithm, we first move III forward 2 weeks and then IV forward 1 week. Continuing with the heuristic, we obtain the fourth and fifth proposals shown in Figures 11.12 and 11.13.

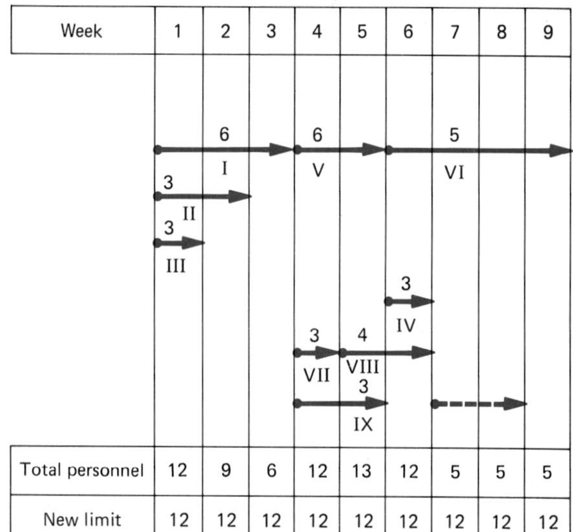

▲ FIGURE 11.10
Second Proposal

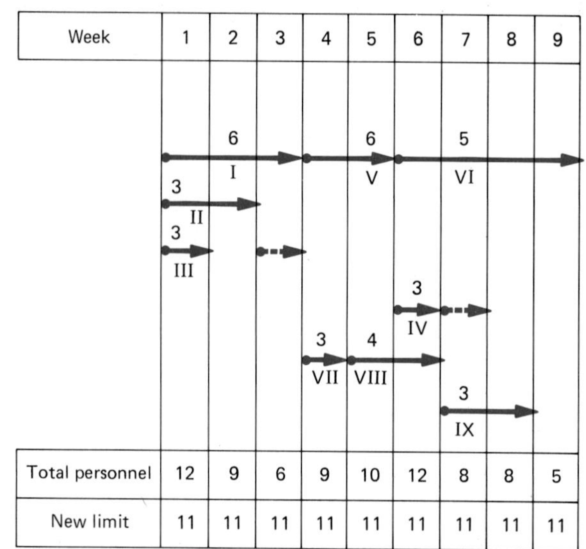

▲ FIGURE 11.11
Third Proposal

Week	1	2	3	4	5	6	7	8	9
Total personnel	9	9	9	9	10	9	11	8	5
New limit	10	10	10	10	10	10	10	10	10

▲ FIGURE 11.12
Fourth Proposal

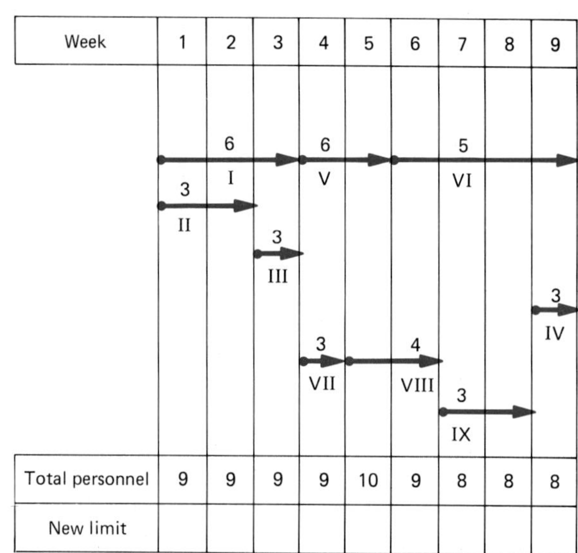

▲ FIGURE 11.13
Fifth Proposal

Heuristic Terminates. The algorithm is unable to improve beyond the fifth proposal. To see this, note that the overload on week 5 can be reduced only by moving forward activity VIII. However, advancing VIII by 1, 2, or 3 weeks would increase the total personnel in weeks 7 and 8, or 8 and 9, to 12. Step 2b of the heuristic *is* thus satisfied, and hence this schedule is the heuristic solution. This final schedule has smoothed the utilization considerably from that shown in Figure 11.8, for the maximum utilization is now 10 (in week 5), and the minimum is 8.

For this problem one might define an optimal solution to be a schedule that *minimizes the maximum utilization* of personnel. An optimal schedule, according to this *minimax* criterion, is shown in Figure 11.14. For this schedule the maximum utilization is 9. Although the heuristic algorithm did not lead to optimality (in this minimax sense—and it must be admitted that the schedule in Figure 11.14 is smoother than that in Figure 11.13), our heuristic approach did quite well. In large

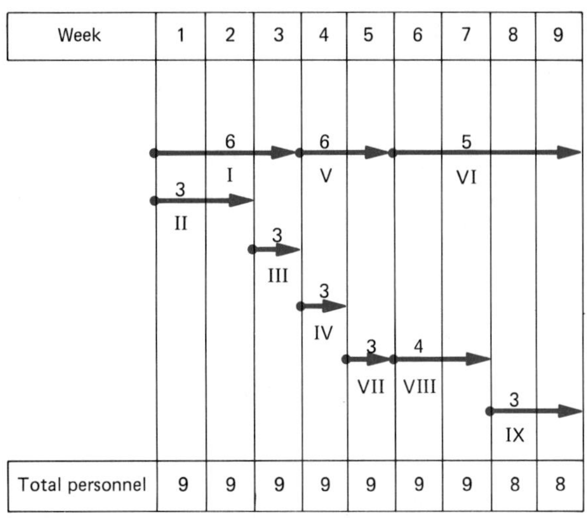

▲ FIGURE 11.14
Optimal Minimax Schedule

problems (i.e., with many activities) it would not be possible to easily generate the optimal minimax schedule. It is for this reason that a heuristic is often employed to smooth requirements.

This section and the preceding one have given only a very brief introduction to the important topic of heuristic algorithms. Another example, assigning facilities to locations, is discussed in Problems 11-2, 11-3, and 11-4 at the end of this chapter.

11.4 Multiple Objectives

The problem of multiple objectives

In many applications, the planner has more than one objective. These different objectives may all be of equal importance or, at the very least, it may be difficult for the planner to compare the importance of one objective with that of another. The presence of multiple objectives is frequently referred to as the problem of "combining apples and oranges." Consider for example the corporate planner whose long-range goals are to (1) maximize discounted profits, (2) maximize market share at the end of the planning period, and (3) maximize existing physical capital at the end of the planning period. These goals are not commensurate, which means that they cannot be *directly* combined or compared. It is also clear that the goals are *conflicting*. That is, there are *trade-offs* in the sense that sacrificing the requirements on any one goal will tend to produce greater returns on the others. For example, spending fewer dollars on marketing is apt to reduce market share and thus prevent the firm from meeting its second goal. However, these dollars can be spent on new machinery in an effort to increase physical capital and satisfy the third goal.

The treatment of multiple objectives is a young but important area in applications. At this time the analytic methods for handling problems with multiple objectives have not been applied as often in practice as some of the other models, such as linear programming, forecasting, and inventory control. However, the concepts involved are important, and some leaders in the management science community feel that they will become more important in the near future. The models have been found to be especially useful on problems in the public sector.

Approaches to the problem

Several approaches to multiple objective problems (also called multicriteria decision making) have been developed. They are: use of multiattribute utility

APPLICATION CAPSULE

Scenes from a Mall: Heuristic Methods Are Employed to Get Useful Results from an "Unsolvable" Model*

The development of a regional shopping center is a complex undertaking with a price tag of about $60 million. Recovery of this investment hinges on the rents paid by the mall's tenants. These rents not only constitute the developer's income while it manages the mall but will also determine the price for which the development can eventually be sold.

Each mall needs two or three "anchor" stores (usually large department stores) to attract customers. Since these tenants are able to negotiate highly favorable occupancy agreements, the developer's profits are derived primarily from rents paid by the numerous smaller stores that occupy the balance of the 1,000,000 square feet of selling space. The leases of these stores are usually for periods of 5–15 years. Thus the initial decision as to how space should be allocated among various potential tenants is crucial to the success of the investment.

The tenant-mix problem is complicated by several factors:

1. Each tenant's annual rent is the maximum of a base (minimum) figure and a specified percentage of the store's sales, or overage. Thus the developer's revenue is the sum of a deterministic amount (base) and a stochastic amount (overage).
2. The worth of a particular store must take into account not only its own profits but also its role in attracting or competing for customers, thereby affecting the profits of other stores in the development. Interactions among stores are of several types:

- In general, each store's sales are increased by the presence of stores of *different* types, since a greater diversity of stores tends to draw more shoppers to the mall.
- A store's sales are also affected by the number of other stores of the *same* type. As the number of (for example) shoe stores increases, customers are attracted and the return for each store initially grows. At some point, however, there is so much competition for the same consumer dollars that profits no longer increase and may in fact be adversely affected. To make the best possible use of this synergy, it is important to include the optimum number of each type of store.

Shopping centers form a major part of the business of the Homart Development Company, a large commercial land developer. In the past, Homart had used rules of thumb, the product of years of experience, to plan its tenant mix. Although this approach had been successful, there was no way of knowing whether the mix could be improved. Homart therefore sought to formulate the problem as an IP model.

The objective function chosen was the worth of the tenant mix over a given time horizon, including both the rental income during the period of Homart's ownership and the eventual sale price of the development. However, the interactions between stores made this function nonlinear. Moreover, the many different store types and sizes produced a model with 180 integer variables and over 100 0–1 variables—too large to solve in any reasonable period of time. Two simplifications were therefore made:

1. The nonlinear objective function was replaced by a linear approximation, with interaction effects approximated by defining new variables.

2. The integrality restrictions were relaxed.

When the resulting LP was then solved, a postprocessor was used to convert the results to an integer solution by various heuristic means. For example, fractions were rounded and fractional parts for the same kind of store combined. Thus, if the model called for half a large store and half a small store, this could be considered the equivalent of one medium-sized store.

Tenant mixes selected by the program have proven to be 10–26% more profitable than those arrived at by conventional methods. In addition, the program can display constraint shadow prices—a benefit of using LP approximation. The value of this feature became apparent in one case when the model suggested including a small drugstore in a particular mall. Because such tenants are hard to procure, management was initially reluctant to pursue this recommendation. The shadow prices, however, indicated that the value of the drugstore would likely outweigh the difficulty of obtaining it. The plan was therefore formulated to include the drugstore, with the shadow price serving as an upper bound on the incentives that should be offered to entice such a tenant.

*Bean, Noon, Ryan, and Salton, "Selecting Tenants in a Shopping Mall," *Interfaces*, Vol. 18, No. 2 (March–April 1988).

theory, search for Pareto optimal solutions via multicriteria linear programming, heuristic search methods, and goal programming. Our discussion is limited to goal programming, a concept introduced by A. Charnes and W. W. Cooper,[5] which in some ways can be thought of as a heuristic approach to the multiple-objectives problem. Goal programming is a powerful approach that builds on the development of linear programming presented in Chapters 2 through 6. It is an area that is now experiencing considerable interest and development and is potentially an important topic for future managers.

Goal Programming

Herbert Simon, Nobel Prize winner in economics, coined the term "satisfice" to describe the desire to maximize several objectives simultaneously to at least satisfactory levels.

Goal programming is generally applied to linear problems; it is an extension of LP that enables the planner to come as close as possible to satisfying various goals and constraints. It allows the decision maker, at least in a heuristic sense, to incorporate his or her preference system in dealing with multiple conflicting goals. It is sometimes considered to be an attempt to put into a mathematical programming context the concept of *satisficing*. This term was coined to communicate the idea that individuals often do not seek optimal solutions, but rather, they seek solutions that are "good enough" or "close enough." We shall illustrate the method of goal programming with several examples.

An example: designing an education program

Suppose that we have an educational program design model with decision variables x_1 and x_2, where x_1 is the hours of classroom work and x_2 is the hours of laboratory work. Assume that we have the following constraint on total program hours:

$$x_1 + x_2 \leq 100 \qquad \text{(total program hours)}$$

[5]*Management Models and Industrial Applications of Linear Programming* (New York: John Wiley & Sons, Inc., 1961).

Two Kinds of Constraints. In the goal programming approach there are two kinds of constraints: (1) *system constraints* (so-called hard constraints) that cannot be violated and (2) *goal constraints* (so-called soft constraints) that may be violated if necessary. The above constraint on total program hours is an example of a system constraint.

Now, in the program we are designing, suppose that each hour of classroom work involves 12 minutes of small-group experience and 19 minutes of individual problem solving, whereas each hour of laboratory work involves 29 minutes of small-group experience and 11 minutes of individual problem solving. Note that the total program time is at most 60(100), or 6000 minutes. The designers have the following two *goals:* Each student should spend as close as possible to one-fourth of the maximum program time working in small groups and one-third of the time on problem solving. These conditions are

$$12x_1 + 29x_2 \cong 1500 \qquad \text{(small-group experience)}$$
$$19x_1 + 11x_2 \cong 2000 \qquad \text{(individual problem solving)}$$

where the symbol $\cong$ means that the left-hand side is desired to be "as close as possible" to the RHS. If it were possible to find a policy that exactly satisfies the small-group and problem-solving goals (that is, exactly achieves both right-hand sides), without violating the system constraint on total program hours, then this policy would solve the problem. A simple geometric analysis will show that no such policy exists. Clearly then, in order to satisfy the system constraint, at least one of the two goals will be violated.

To implement the goal programming approach, the small-group condition is rewritten as the goal constraint

$$12x_1 + 29x_2 + u_1 - v_1 = 1500 \qquad (u_1 \geq 0,\ v_1 \geq 0)$$

where u_1 = the amount by which total small-group experience falls short of 1500
v_1 = the amount by which total small-group experience exceeds 1500

Deviation Variables. The variables u_1 and v_1 are called **deviation variables,** since they measure the amount by which the value produced by the solution deviates from the goal. We note that by definition we want either u_1 or v_1 (or both) to be zero because it is impossible to simultaneously exceed and fall short of 1500. In order to make $12x_1 + 29x_2$ as close as possible to 1500, it suffices to make the sum $u_1 + v_1$ small.

In a similar way, the problem-solving condition is written as the goal constraint

$$19x_1 + 11x_2 + u_2 - v_2 = 2000 \qquad (u_2 \geq 0,\ v_2 \geq 0)$$

and in this case we want the sum of the two deviation variables $u_2 + v_2$ to be small. Our complete (illustrative) model is now written as follows:

The goal programming model

Both u_1 and v_1 can't be > 0.

$$\begin{aligned}
&\text{Min } u_1 + v_1 + u_2 + v_2 \\
&\text{s.t.} \quad x_1 + x_2 \leq 100 \qquad \text{(total program hours)} \\
&\quad 12x_1 + 29x_2 + u_1 - v_1 = 1500 \qquad \text{(small-group experience)} \\
&\quad 19x_1 + 11x_2 + u_2 - v_2 = 2000 \qquad \text{(problem solving)} \\
&\quad x_1, x_2, u_1, v_1, u_2, v_2 \geq 0
\end{aligned}$$

This is an ordinary LP problem and can now be easily solved on the computer. The optimal decision variables will satisfy the system constraint (total program hours). Also, it turns out that the simplex method (for technical reasons that we shall not dwell on) will guarantee that either u_1 or v_1 (or both) will be zero, and thus these variables automatically satisfy this desired condition. The same statement holds for u_2 and v_2 and in general for any pair of deviation variables.

Note that the objective function is the sum of the deviation variables. This choice of an objective function indicates that we have no preference among the various deviations from the stated goals. For example, any of the following three decisions is acceptable: (1) a decision that overachieves the group experience goal by 5 minutes and hits the problem-solving goal exactly, (2) a decision that hits the group experience goal exactly and underachieves the problem-solving goal by 5 minutes, and (3) a decision that underachieves each goal by 2.5 minutes. In other words, we have no preference among the three solutions:

(1)	(2)	(3)
$u_1 = 0$	$u_1 = 0$	$u_1 = 2.5$
$v_1 = 5$	$v_1 = 0$	$v_1 = 0$
$u_2 = 0$	$u_2 = 5$	$u_2 = 2.5$
$v_2 = 0$	$v_2 = 0$	$v_2 = 0$

We must have no preference because each of these three decisions yields the same value (5) for the objective function.

Weighting the Deviation Variables. Such a lack of preference for one solution over another certainly would not hold for all goal programming problems. Differences in units alone could produce a preference among the deviation variables. Suppose, for example, that the individual problem-solving constraint had been written in hours; that is,

$$\frac{19}{60}x_1 + \frac{11}{60}x_2 + u_2 - v_2 = \frac{2000}{60}$$

It is hard to believe that the program designers would not prefer a 1-minute excess of small-group experience ($v_1 = 1$) to a 1-hour shortfall of individual problem solving ($u_2 = 1$).

One way of expressing a preference among the various goals is to assign different coefficients to the deviation variables in the objective function. In the program-planning example one might select

$$\text{Min } 2u_1 + 10v_1 + u_2 + 20v_2$$

as the objective function. Since u_2 (underachievement of problem solving) has the smallest coefficient, the program designers would rather have u_2 positive than any of the other deviation variables (positive u_2 is penalized the least). Indeed, with this objective function it is better to be 9 minutes under the problem-solving goal than to exceed by 1 minute the small-group-experience goal. To see this, note that for any solution in which $v_1 \geq 1$, decreasing v_1 by 1 and increasing u_2 by 9 would yield a smaller value for the objective function.

Goal Interval Constraints. Another type of goal constraint is called a **goal interval constraint.** Such a constraint restricts the goal to a range or *interval* rather than a specific numerical value. Suppose, for example, that in the above illustration the designers were indifferent among programs for which

$$1800 \leq [\text{minutes of individual problem solving}] \leq 2100$$

$$\text{i.e., } 1800 \leq 19x_1 + 11x_2 \leq 2100$$

In this situation the interval goal is captured with two goal constraints:

$$19x_1 + 11x_2 - v_1 \le 2100 \qquad (v_1 \ge 0)$$
$$19x_1 + 11x_2 + u_1 \ge 1800 \qquad (u_1 \ge 0)$$

When the terms u_1 and v_1 are included in the objective function, the LP code will attempt to minimize them. We note that when, at optimality, $u_1^* = 0$ and $v_1^* = 0$ (their minimum possible values), the total minutes of problem solving ($19x_1 + 11x_2$) fall within the desired range (i.e., $1800 \le 19x_1 + 11x_2 \le 2100$). Otherwise it will turn out that, at optimality, 1 of the 2 variables will be positive and the other 0, which means that only one side of the two-sided inequality can be satisfied.

Summary of the Use of Goal Constraints. It may be useful at this point to summarize the various ways in which goal constraints can be formulated and employed. Each goal constraint consists of a left-hand side, say $g_i(x_1, \ldots, x_n)$, and a right-hand side, b_i. Goal constraints are written by using nonnegative deviation variables u_i, v_i. At optimality at least one of the pair u_i, v_i will always be zero. The variable u_i represents *underachievement;* v_i represents *overachievement.* Whenever u_i is used it is *added* to $g_i(x_1, \ldots, x_n)$. Whenever v_i is used it is *subtracted* from $g_i(x_i, \ldots, x_n)$. Only deviation variables (or a subset of deviation variables) appear in the objective function, and the objective is always to minimize. The decision vaiables x_i, $i = 1, \ldots, n$ do not appear in the objective. We have discussed four types of goals:

Following standard LP notation, all the variables (x_i, u_i, v_i) will be on the left-hand side while the constant (b_i) will be on the right-hand side of the constraint.

1. ***Target.*** Make $g_i(x_1, \ldots, x_n)$ as close as possible to b_i. To do this we write the goal constraint as

$$g_i(x_1, \ldots, x_n) + u_i - v_i = b_i \qquad (u_i \ge 0, v_i \ge 0)$$

and in the objective we minimize $u_i + v_i$. At optimality, at least one of the variables u_i, v_i will be zero.

2. ***Minimize Underachievement.*** To do this, we can write

$$g_i(x_1, \ldots, x_n) + u_i - v_i = b_i \qquad (u_i \ge 0, v_i \ge 0)$$

and in the objective we minimize u_i, the underachievement. Since v_i does not appear in the objective function, and it is in only this constraint, it plays the role of a surplus variable, and hence the constraint can be equivalently written as

$$g_i(x_1, \ldots, x_n) + u_i \ge b_i \qquad (u_i \ge 0)$$

If the optimal u_i is positive, this constraint will be active, for otherwise u_i^* could be made smaller. This result is also clear from the equality form of the constraint. That is, if $u_i^* > 0$ then, since v_i^* must equal zero, it must be true that $g_i(x_1, \ldots, x_n) + u_i^* = b_i$.

3. ***Minimize Overachievement.*** To do this, we can write

$$g_i(x_1, \ldots, x_n) + u_i - v_i = b_i \qquad (u_i \ge 0, v_i \ge 0)$$

and in the objective we minimize v_i, the overachievement. Since in this case u_i plays the role of only a slack variable, the constraint can be equivalently written as

$$g_i(x_1, \ldots, x_n) - v_i \le b_i \qquad (v_i \ge 0)$$

If the optimal v_i is positive, this constraint will be active. The argument is analogous to that in item 2 above.

4. ***Goal Interval Constraint.*** In this instance, the goal is to come as close as possible to satisfying

$$a_i \le g_i(x_1, \ldots, x_n) \le b_i$$

In order to write this as a goal, we first "stretch out" the interval by writing

$$a_i - u_i \le g_i(x_1, \ldots, x_n) \le b_i + v_i \qquad (u_i \ge 0, v_i \ge 0)$$

which is equivalent to the two constraints

$$\left.\begin{array}{l} g_i(x_1, \ldots, x_n) + u_i \ge a_i \\ g_i(x_1, \ldots, x_n) - v_i \le b_i \end{array}\right\} \leftrightarrow \left\{\begin{array}{ll} g_i(x_1, \ldots, x_n) + u_i - \hat{v}_i = a_i & (u_i \ge 0, \hat{v}_i \ge 0) \\ g_i(x_1, \ldots, x_n) + \hat{u}_i - v_i = b_i & (\hat{u}_i \ge 0, v_i \ge 0) \end{array}\right.$$

In the case of a goal interval constraint we minimize $u_i + v_i$ in the objective function. The variables $\hat{v}_i$ and $\hat{u}_i$ are merely surplus and slack, respectively (not deviation variables). As usual, at optimality, at least one of the deviation variables u_i, v_i will be 0. In dealing with two constraints representing a goal interval, the constraint with the nonzero deviation variable (if there is one) will be active.

In general, goal constraints are most often expressed in the appropriate equality form using deviation variables, surplus, and slack as required. The equivalent inequality forms that we have displayed will allow us, for problems in two decision variables, to obtain some geometric insight into the solution procedure.

Absolute Priorities

In some cases managers do not wish to express their preferences among various goals in terms of weighted deviation variables, for the process of assigning weights may seem too arbitrary or subjective. In such cases it may be more acceptable to state preferences in terms of **absolute priorities** (as opposed to weights) to a set of goals. This approach, which requires that goals be satisfied in a specific order, is illustrated in the following example.

With weightings, the GP problem is solved just once. With priorities, the GP is solved in stages as a sequence of problems.

Swenson's Media Selection Problem: A Minicase. Tom Swenson, a senior partner at J. R. Swenson, his father's advertising agency, has just completed an agreement with a pharmaceutical manufacturer to mount a radio and television campaign to introduce a new product, Mylonal. The total expenditures for the campaign are not to exceed \$120,000. The client is interested in reaching several audiences with this campaign. To determine how well a particular campaign meets this client's needs, the agency estimates the impact of the advertisements on the audiences of interest. The impact is measured in *rated exposures,* a term that means "people reached per month." Radio and television, the two media the agency is considering using, are not equally effective in reaching all audiences. Data relevant to the Mylonal campaign are shown in Figure 11.15.

▼ FIGURE 11.15
Exposures per \$1000 Expenditure

	TV	RADIO
Total	14,000	6,000
Upper Income	1,200	1,200

After lengthy discussions with the client, Tom accepts the following goals for this campaign. Tom feels that the order in which he has listed his goals reflects the absolute priority among them.

1. He hopes total exposures will be at least 840,000.
2. In order to maintain effective contact with the leading radio station, he hopes to spend no more than $90,000 on TV advertising.
3. He feels that the campaign should achieve at least 168,000 upper-income exposures.
4. Finally, if all other goals are satisfied, he would like to come as close as possible to maximizing the total number of exposures. He notes that if he spends all of the $120,000 on TV advertising he would obtain 120 × 14,000, or 1,680,000 exposures, and this is the maximum obtainable.

This is clearly a problem with a number of constraints. It is not quite a typical mathematical programming problem, however, since Tom has a number of objectives. Nevertheless, he feels that a mathematical programming approach will help him understand and solve the problem. He thus proceeds in the typical manner. To model the problem, he introduces the notation

$$x_1 = \text{dollars spent on TV} \qquad \text{(in thousands)}$$

$$x_2 = \text{dollars spent on radio} \qquad \text{(in thousands)}$$

Since his highest-priority goal is total exposures, he feels that a reasonable way to model the problem is to use total exposures as the objective function and to treat the other goals as constraints.

An Infeasible Problem. The formulation and computer solution of this problem are shown in Figure 11.16. Each constraint and the objective function are labeled to indicate the purpose they serve. We see that the problem is infeasible. Clearly, since

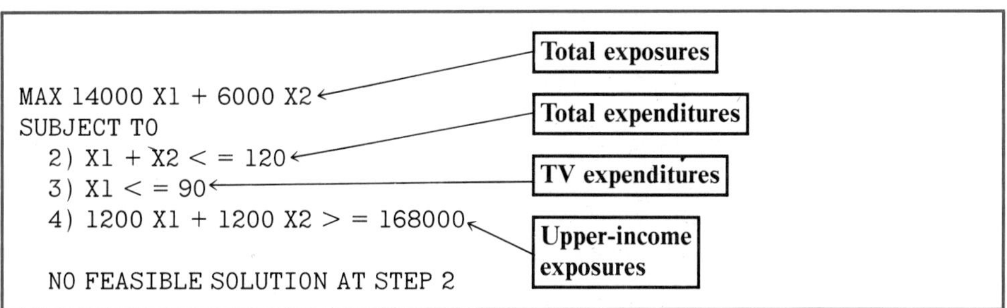

▲ FIGURE 11.16
Maximizing Total Exposures

it is infeasible, there is no way to satisfy simultaneously the three goals (total expenditures, TV expenditure, and upper-income exposures) that Tom has stated as constraints. Since there are only two decision variables in this problem, the graphical approach can be used to investigate Tom's initial formulations. The analysis in Figure 11.17 clearly shows that there are no points that satisfy both the first (total expenditures) and the third (upper-income exposures) constraints. At this point, Tom could attempt to approach the problem somewhat differently. He might change one or more of his goals, or perhaps the objective function, and start again. In general, however, this is not a satisfactory systematic approach. In problems with many decision variables and several conflicting goals, restructuring the problem to

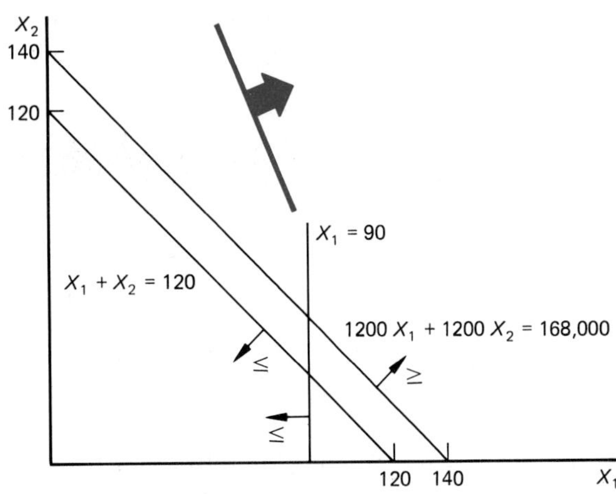

▲ FIGURE 11.17
Maximizing Total Exposures: A Graphical Approach

create a new problem that has a feasible solution could prove to be difficult. More important, in this restructuring process, the essence of the real problem could be lost.

Recall that Tom is not indifferent about the various goals; indeed, he has stated an absolute priority among them. Goal programming with absolute priorities is designed to handle exactly the type of decision process Tom Swenson wants. It is a sequential process in which goals are added one at a time (in the order of decreasing priority) to an LP problem.

Goals as inequalities

Swenson's Goal Programming Model. In order to set up his problem as a goal program, Tom notes that the first goal, if violated, will be underachieved. The second goal, if violated, will be overachieved, and so on. Employing this reasoning, he restates his goals, in descending priority, as

1. Minimize the underachievement of 840,000 total exposures (i.e., Min u_1, subject to the condition $14{,}000x_1 + 6000x_2 + u_1 \geq 840{,}000$, $u_1 \geq 0$).
2. Minimize expenditures in excess of \$90,000 on TV (i.e., Min v_2, subject to the condition $x_1 - v_2 \leq 90$, $v_2 \geq 0$).
3. Minimize underachievement of 168,000 upper-income exposures (i.e., Min u_3, subject to the condition $1200x_1 + 1200x_2 + u_3 \geq 168{,}000$, $u_3 \geq 0$).
4. Minimize underachievement of 1,680,000 total exposures—the maximum possible (i.e., Min u_4, where $14{,}000x_1 + 6000x_2 + u_4 \geq 1{,}680{,}000$, $u_4 \geq 0$).

Note that Tom's priorities are now clearly stated in terms of either minimizing underachievement (i.e., minimizing a u_i) or minimizing overachievement (i.e., minimizing a v_i). His goals, as stated above, have been expressed as inequalities in accord with our previous discussion. This method will facilitate a graphical analysis.

Given that he has correctly formulated his priorities, Tom must distinguish between (1) *system constraints* (all constraints that may not be violated) and (2) *goal constraints*. In his problem, the only system constraint is that total expenditures will be no greater than \$120,000. Thus (since the units of x_1 and x_2 are thousands), we have

$$x_1 + x_2 \leq 120 \qquad \text{(S)}$$

In goal programming notation, Tom's problem can now be expressed as follows:

$$
\begin{array}{lrcr}
\text{Min } P_1u_1 + P_2v_2 + P_3u_3 + P_4u_4 & & & \\
\text{s.t.} \quad x_1 + x_2 & \leq & 120 & \text{(S)} \\
14{,}000x_1 + 6000x_2 + u_1 & \geq & 840{,}000 & (1) \\
x_1 - v_2 & \leq & 90 & (2) \\
1200x_1 + 1200x_2 + u_3 & \geq & 168{,}000 & (3) \\
14{,}000x_1 + 6000x_2 + u_4 & \geq & 1{,}680{,}000 & (4) \\
x_1, x_2, u_1, v_2, u_3, u_4 \geq 0 & & &
\end{array}
$$

Note that the objective function consists only of deviation variables and is of the *Min* form. As already stated, all goal programming formulations are minimization problems, as the objective is to come as close as possible to the goals. The terms serve merely to indicate priorities, with P_1 denoting highest priority, and so on. What the problem statement above means precisely is

Sequential feasible regions

1. Find the set of decision variables that satisfies the system constraint (S) and that also gives the Min possible value to u_1 subject to constraint (1) and $x_1, x_2, u_1 \geq 0$. Call this set of decisions FR I (i.e., "feasible region I"). Considering *only the highest goal,* all of the points in FR I are "optimal" (i.e., the best that Tom can do) and (again considering only the highest goal) he is indifferent as to which of these points he selects.
2. Find the subset of points in FR I that gives the Min possible value to v_2, subject to constraint (2) and $v_2 \geq 0$. Call this subset FR II. Considering only the ordinal ranking of the two highest-priority goals, all of the points in FR II are "optimal," and in terms of these two highest-priority goals Tom is indifferent as to which of these points he selects.
3. Let FR III be the subset of points in FR II that minimize u_3, subject to constraint (3) and $u_3 \geq 3$.
4. FR IV is the subset of points in FR III that minimize u_4, subject to constraint (4) and $u_4 \geq 0$. Any point in FR IV is an optimal solution to Tom's overall problem.

Graphical Analysis and Computer Implementation of the Solution Procedure. Since Tom's marketing problem has only two decision variables, the solution method above can be accomplished with graphical analysis. In all real-world problems, the computer would be used. In the next section we show how this can be done using LP.

1. In Figure 11.18, both the computer output and the geometry reveal that the Min of u_1 s.t. (S), (1), and $x_1, x_2, u_1 \geq 0$ is $u_1^* = 0$. Although the computer prints out optimal values for x_1^* and x_2^*, these values are not of interest. The important information is that $u_1^* = 0$, which tells us that the first goal can be completely attained. Alternative optima for the current problem are provided by all values of (x_1, x_2) that satisfy the conditions

$$
\text{FR I} \begin{cases} x_1 + x_2 \leq 120 \\ 14{,}000x_1 + 6000x_2 \geq 840{,}000 \\ x_1, x_2 \geq 0 \end{cases}
$$

At any such point Tom's first goal is attained ($u_1^* = 0$) so that, in terms of only the first goal, these decisions are equally preferable. Thus FR I is the shaded area ABC.

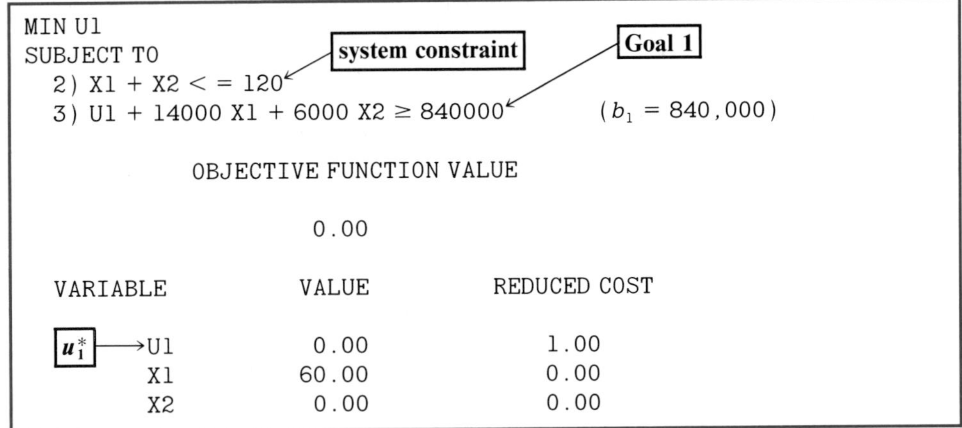

```
MIN U1
SUBJECT TO                          system constraint          Goal 1
  2) X1 + X2 <= 120
  3) U1 + 14000 X1 + 6000 X2 >= 840000                (b1 = 840,000)

              OBJECTIVE FUNCTION VALUE

                       0.00

  VARIABLE             VALUE              REDUCED COST

u1* --> U1              0.00                  1.00
        X1             60.00                  0.00
        X2              0.00                  0.00
```

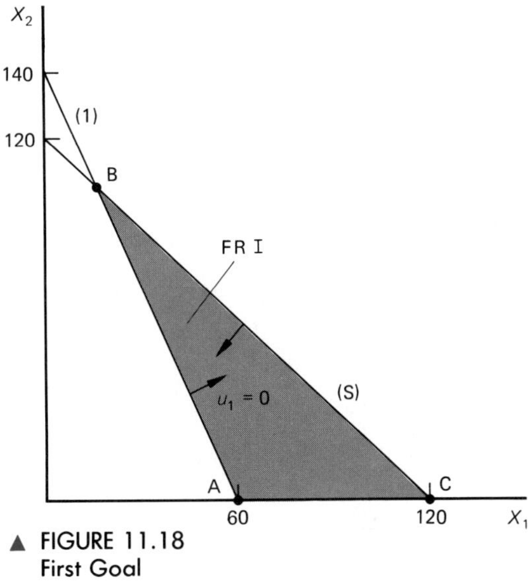

▲ FIGURE 11.18
First Goal

The line labeled (1) represents goal 1. The arrow marked $u_1 = 0$ indicates that at all points to the right of line (1) goal 1 is achieved.

The feasible region becomes smaller

Adding a constraint in linear programming can only keep the feasible area the same or reduce it.

2. In the computer formulation in Figure 11.19, we have entered the constraints defining FR I (rows 2 and 3), together with the new goal constraint (2), and we see that

$$\text{Min } v_2$$
$$\text{s.t. } x \text{ in FR I, goal (2), and } v_2 \geq 0$$

is $v_2^* = 0$. Thus, FR II is defined by

$$\text{FR II} \begin{cases} x_1 + x_2 \leq 120 \\ 14{,}000x_1 + 6000x_2 \geq 840{,}000 \\ x_1 \leq 90 \\ x_1, x_2 \geq 0 \end{cases}$$

which is the shaded area ABDE, clearly a subset of FR I.

```
MIN V2
SUBJECT TO
  2) X1 + X2 < = 120
  3) 14000 X1 + 6000 X2 > = 840000      <- b1 - u1*
  4) X1 - V2 ≤ 90                       <- Goal 2      (b2 = 90)

            OBJECTIVE FUNCTION VALUE

                    0.00

  VARIABLE          VALUE          REDUCED COST

 v2* ->  V2          0.00              1.00
         X1         60.00              0.00
         X2          0.00              0.00
```

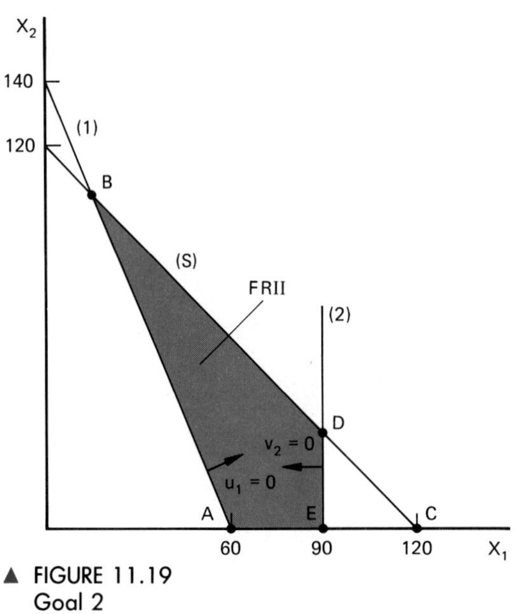

▲ FIGURE 11.19
Goal 2

Goal 3 is not attained

Continuing in this way, Figure 11.20 shows that FR III is the line segment BD. In this case $u_3^* = 24{,}000$. Although the first two goals were completely attained (since $u_1^* = v_2^* = 0$), the third goal cannot be completely attained because $u_3^* > 0$. At this stage, Tom is indifferent about any decision satisfying

$$\text{FR III}\begin{cases} x_1 + x_2 \leq 120 \\ 14{,}000x_1 + 6000x_2 \geq 840{,}000 \\ x_1 \leq 90 \\ 1200x_1 + 1200x_2 \geq 168{,}000 - 24{,}000 = 144{,}000 \end{cases}$$

which defines the line segment BD.

The optimal solution

Finally, Figure 11.21, on page 498, shows the optimal solution at point D. Recall that the fourth goal is to minimize underachievement of the maximum possible number of exposures, which is 1,680,000. Thus, we wish to minimize the underachievement u_4 where

$$14{,}000x_1 + 6000x_2 + u_4 \geq 1{,}680{,}000$$

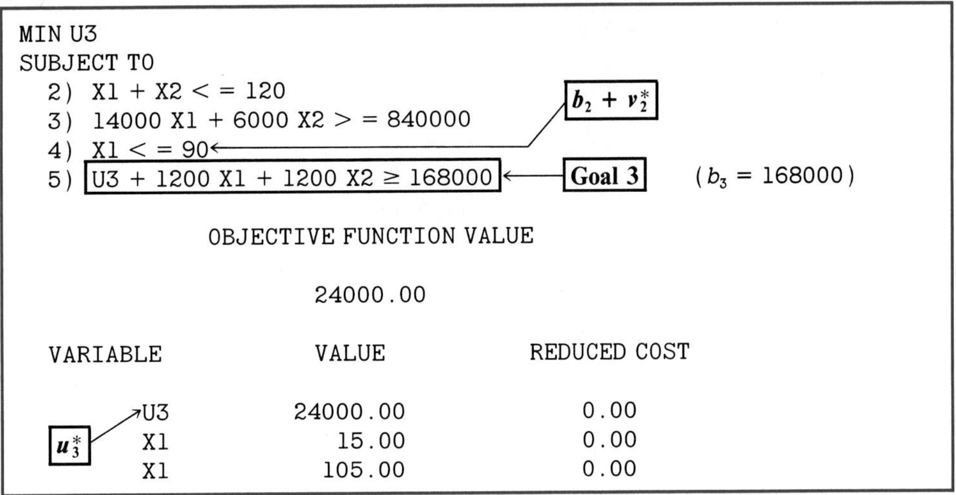

```
MIN U3
SUBJECT TO
  2) X1 + X2 < = 120                                  b2 + v2*
  3) 14000 X1 + 6000 X2 > = 840000
  4) X1 < = 90
  5) U3 + 1200 X1 + 1200 X2 ≥ 168000   <---  Goal 3      (b3 = 168000)

                OBJECTIVE FUNCTION VALUE

                        24000.00

  VARIABLE              VALUE                REDUCED COST

       U3              24000.00                0.00
  u3*  X1                 15.00                0.00
       X1                105.00                0.00
```

The feasible region is now just a line segment.

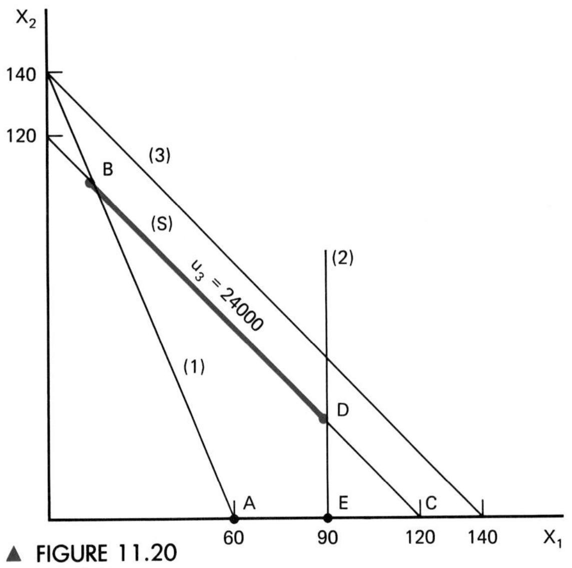

▲ FIGURE 11.20
Goal 3

In Figure 11.21 we find the unique optimum $x_1^* = 90$ and $x_2^* = 30$; that is, Tom should spend $90,000 on TV advertising and $30,000 on radio advertising. This fact is verified in the geometric analysis, where it is clear that point D·($x_1 = 90$, $x_2 = 30$) is closer to the line that describes goal 4 ($14{,}000x_1 + 6000x_2 = 1{,}680{,}000$) than any other point in FR III (i.e., than any other point on the line BD). We also note that $u_4^* = 240{,}000$. Thus, Tom achieves only 1,680,000 − 240,000 = 1,440,000 exposures.

We see, then, that goal programming with absolute priorities allows a manager (like Tom) to solve a problem in which there is no solution that achieves all the goals, but where he is willing to specify an absolute ranking among the goals and successively restrict his attention to those points that come as close as possible to each goal.

Combining Weights and Absolute Priorities

It is possible to combine, to some extent, the concepts of weighted and absolute priority goals. To illustrate this fact, we return to Tom Swenson's advertising problem.

```
MIN U4
SUBJECT TO
  2) X1 + X2 < = 120
  3) 14000 X1 + 6000 X2 > = 84000          b3 − u3*
  4) X1 < = 90
  5) 1200 X1 + 1200 X2 > = 144000
  6) U4 + 14000 X1 + 6000 X2 ≥ 1680000     Goal 4     (b4 = 1,680,000)

              OBJECTIVE FUNCTION VALUE

                   240000.000

  VARIABLE             VALUE            REDUCED COST

x1*    U4           240000.00               0.00
       X1               90.00               0.00
x2* →  X2               30.00               0.00
```

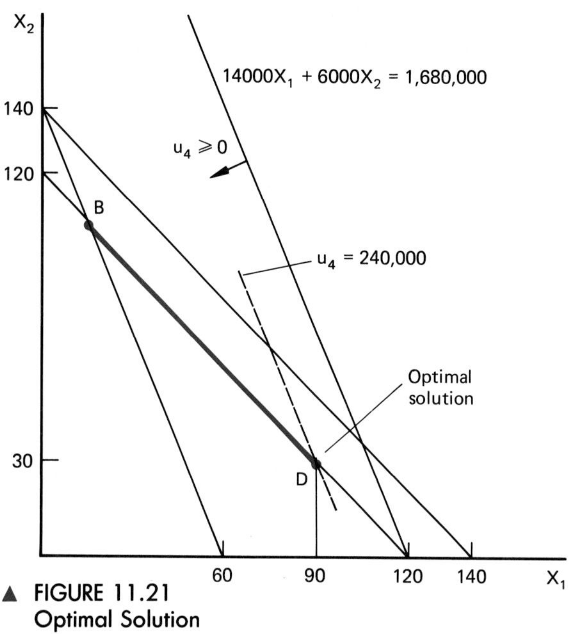

▲ FIGURE 11.21
Optimal Solution

In reviewing the results of the absolute priority study, Tom and his client begin to discuss the importance of the older members of the Mylonal market. In particular, they focus on the number of exposures to individuals 50 years old or older. Again, they see that radio and TV are not equally effective in generating exposures in this segment of the population. The exposures per $1000 of advertising are as follows:

EXPOSURE GROUP	TV	RADIO
50 and over	3000	8000

A new goal

If there were no other considerations, Tom would like as many 50-and-over exposures as possible. Since radio yields such exposures at a higher rate than TV (8000 > 3000), Tom sees that the maximum possible number of 50-and-over

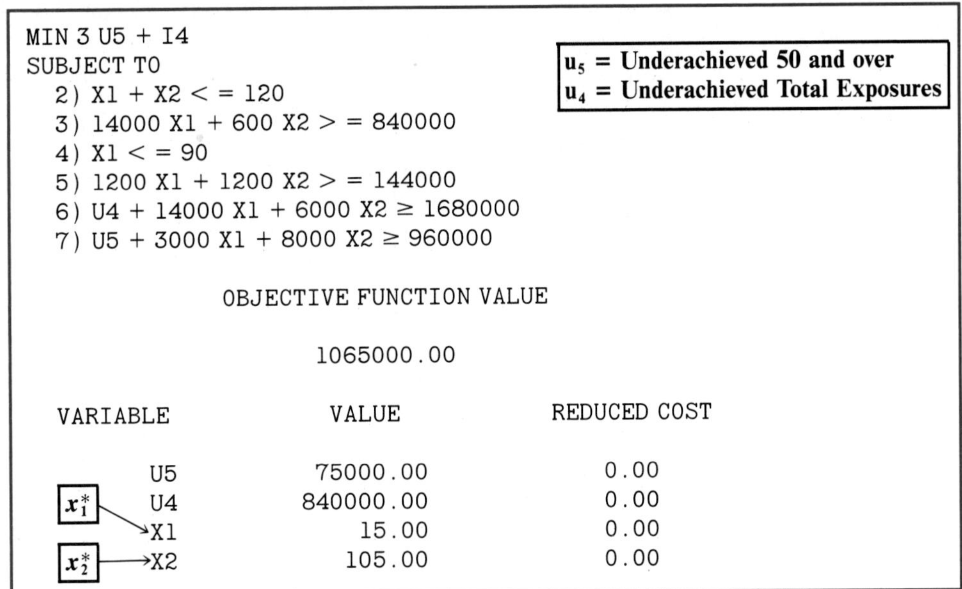

```
MIN 3 U5 + I4
SUBJECT TO
  2) X1 + X2 < = 120
  3) 14000 X1 + 600 X2 > = 840000
  4) X1 < = 90
  5) 1200 X1 + 1200 X2 > = 144000
  6) U4 + 14000 X1 + 6000 X2 ≥ 1680000
  7) U5 + 3000 X1 + 8000 X2 ≥ 960000

              OBJECTIVE FUNCTION VALUE

                   1065000.00

  VARIABLE           VALUE           REDUCED COST

        U5        75000.00              0.00
        U4       840000.00              0.00
        X1           15.00              0.00
        X2          105.00              0.00
```

u_5 = Underachieved 50 and over
u_4 = Underachieved Total Exposures

x_1^* → X1
x_2^* → X2

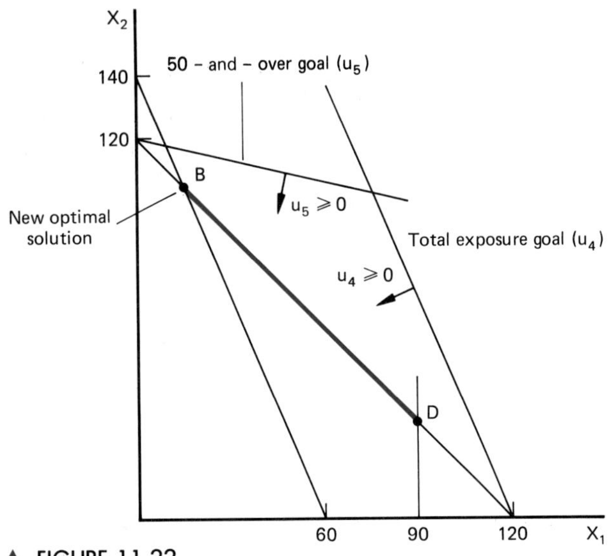

▲ FIGURE 11.22
Weighting the Final Step

exposures would be achieved by allocating all of the \$120,000 available to radio. Thus, the maximum number of 50-and-over exposures is 120 × 8000 = 960,000. Tom and his client would like to come as close as possible to this goal (minimize underachievement) once the first three goals are satisfied. Recall, however, that they also want to come as close as possible to the goal of 1,680,000 total exposures (minimize underachievement) once the first three goals are satisfied. To resolve this conflict of goals, they decide to use a weighted sum of the deviation variables as the objective in the final phase of the absolute priorities approach. It is their judgment that underachievement in the fifth goal (960,000 exposures to the 50-and-over group) is three times as serious as underachievement in the fourth goal (1,680,000 total exposures). The formulation, solution, and graphical analysis are presented in Figure 11.22.

Sensitivity analysis of the weights shows when the solution would change from point B to point D.

From the computer solution we see that the optimal solution to this problem is point B ($x_1^* = 15$, $x_2^* = 105$). Recall that when the objective function was to minimize u_4, the optimal decision was point D ($x_1^* = 90$, $x_2^* = 30$). Thus, in the graphical analysis, we see that the new objective function has moved the optimal solution from one end of FR III to the other. There is no obvious graphical way to find the optimal solution to this problem; that is, there is not an obvious objective function contour to push in a downhill direction that takes us to the point $x_1 = 15$, $x_2 = 105$. It is, however, intuitively appealing to see that the optimal solution is as close as possible to the more heavily weighted goal.

This completes the analysis of Tom Swenson's advertising campaign problem. The general sequential LP procedure described above for goal programming with absolute priorities holds for any problem in which the system constraints and the goal constraints are formulated with linear functions. For each new problem a single constraint is added to the previous model, and the objective function is modified slightly. Generally speaking, a fairly large number of decision variables can be involved. The example with two variables was useful because it made it possible to present, along with the computer output, geometric interpretations, which add insight to the solution technique.

The foregoing problem is useful in indicating how conflicting and noncommensurate goals (i.e., apples and oranges) can be simultaneously considered by means of goal programming. Thus, it gives some insight into why goal programming is a promising and increasingly useful tool in analyzing public policy questions.

11.5 Notes on Implementation

The whole area of expert systems is the natural extension of heuristics and human/machine interaction. It requires an expert who has a "feel" for solving a particular kind of problem, and a way to develop rules of thumb with a human override.

As is true of most types of quantitative models, heuristic approaches are typically implemented with a computer program. One difference, in practice, between using heuristic procedures and using more formal models such as linear or quadratic programming, is that in the latter case the computer software already exists. In the heuristic case, however, the application is often *ad hoc,* which implies that the software must be constructed. A typical application of heuristics is, as stated earlier, the area of large combinatorial problems, for which obtaining a solution either by enumeration or by applying a formal mathematical or integer programming model would be prohibitively expensive. In all applications of heuristics there is an implicit managerial judgment that "acceptability" rather than "optimality" is an appropriate way of thinking. In other words, it is felt that "good solutions" as opposed to "optimal solutions" can be useful and satisfactory. *This philosophy is particularly well suited to problems that are rather vague in their statement, such as high-level problems with surrogate objectives or for which there may be numerous conflicting criteria of interest and for which, consequently, there is not a clear, definitive single-objective function.*

In practice, the use of heuristics is in some cases closely linked to the field of *artificial intelligence,* where the computer is programmed with heuristic techniques to prove theorems, play chess, and even write poems.

Perhaps the most common use of heuristics in management science has been, to date, in problems of assembly-line balancing, job-shop scheduling, and resource allocation in project management. However, recently there has been an increase in the scope of applications to such areas as media selection in marketing, political districting, and scheduling or positioning urban systems.

Interaction between model and decision maker

In the implementation of all heuristic models, managerial interaction and feedback must play perhaps an even greater role than in the case of more formal modeling, for in the heuristic case the manager must assess not only the model but, implicitly, the heuristic algorithm as well. This assessment is necessary because, *for the same model, different heuristics will lead to different "solutions."*

This close interaction between the model and the decision maker is also manifest in goal programming when the decision maker must assign priorities to various goals, such as in the form of ordinal ranking (i.e., *absolute priorities*). Goal programming is an intuitively appealing, and in this sense a "heuristic," approach to problems with multiple objectives. In goal programming with absolute priorities, the manager must consider carefully the relative importance or utility of his or her goals. Depending on model output, the decision maker may wish to change priorities, or even the number of goals, and rerun the model. In other words, just as with LP, sensitivity analysis becomes an important aspect of implementation. Since goal programming is still more or less in its infancy, the field is developing, from a theoretical point of view, at a rapid rate, and it seems clear that this development will prompt greater use of the technique, especially as sensitivity analysis becomes better understood.

In practice, computer codes do exist for solving large-scale goal programs in the batch processing mode, but typically these are not part of the standard program libraries. For problems of modest size, the interactive mode is ideally suited to the sequential technique described in this chapter.

Key Terms

Heuristic Algorithm. An algorithm that efficiently provides good approximate solutions to a given problem, often with estimates as to the goodness of the approximation. (*p. 476*)

Heuristic. An intuitively appealing rule of thumb for dealing with some aspect of a problem. (*p. 476*)

Heuristic Program. A collection of heuristics and/or heuristic algorithms. (*p. 476*)

Combinatorial Optimization. An optimization problem with a finite number of feasible alternatives. (*p. 477*)

Setup Time. Time required before an activity can begin. (*p. 478*)

Greedy Algorithm. An algorithm that says that the maximum improvement should be made at each step of a sequential process. (*p. 478*)

Next Best Rule. Same as the greedy algorithm. (*p. 478*)

Precedence Relationships. Means that certain activities must be completed before others may begin. (*p. 480*)

Personnel Loading Chart. A bar chart showing the total number of people required per week in order to carry out a given schedule of activities. (*p. 482*)

Slack. In the project scheduling context this refers to the maximum amount of time any given activity can be delayed without delaying completion of the overall project. (*p. 482*)

Goal Programming. Seeks allowable decisions that come as close as possible to achieving specified goals. (*p. 487*)

Deviation Variables. Variables used in goal programming to measure the extent to which a specified goal is violated. (*p. 488*)

Goal Interval Constraint. A constraint for which goals are specified by an interval of indifference, rather than by a specific numerical value. (*p. 489*)

Absolute Priority. A form of goal programming in which goals must be satisfied in a specific order. (*p. 491*)

Major Concepts Quiz

True-False

1. T F Heuristic algorithms are guaranteed to be within a specified percentage of optimality at termination.

2. T F The optimal solution to a combinatorial optimization problem can, in principle, be found by complete enumeration.

3. T F An alternative heuristic in the problem of scheduling with limited resources is to move forward that activity that contributes *most* to the overload (i.e., utilizes the largest number of people).

4. T F Goal programming is the only quantitative technique designed for use on problems with multiple objectives.

5. T F Each step in goal programming with absolute priorities introduces a new goal and eliminates from further consideration all current candidates that do not satisfy this new goal as well as possible.

6. T F Consider the goal constraint $12x_1 + 3x_2 + u_1 - v_1 = 100$. Suppose that, because of other constraints in the model, the goal cannot be achieved. If u_1 is positive, the goal is overachieved.

7. T F One way to state priorities among goals is to place weights on deviation variables.

8. T F Consider the goal interval constraint $180 \leq 4x_1 + 12x_1 \leq 250$. A correct goal formulation is

$$4x_1 + 12x_2 - v_1 \leq 250$$

$$4x_1 + 12x_2 - u_1 \geq 180$$

9. T F If a goal interval constraint cannot be achieved (exactly satisfied) then one deviation variable will be positive, and the constraint in which that variable appears will be active.

10. T F In goal programming a system constraint is not permitted to be violated.

11. T F A goal programming problem cannot be infeasible.

Multiple Choice

12. If changeover time of n jobs on a single machine is sequence-dependent, the problem of minimizing total setup time requires the inspection of

a. n sequences

b. 1 sequence

c. $n!$ sequences

d. $\binom{n}{2}$ sequences

13. The intuitively appealing notion that motivates a *greedy* algorithm is

a. get as close as you can to the optimal solution

b. do the best you can at the current step

c. minimize the number of steps required

d. none of the above

14. In the facility scheduling problem, subtracting the minimum setup time in a column from the other entries in that column

a. is a heuristic based on the notion that it is relative costs that matter

b. is guaranteed to yield an optimal solution if the greedy algorithm is applied

c. makes the greedy algorithm not useful

d. all of the above

15. If a goal programming problem includes the constraint $g_1(x_1, \ldots, x_n) + u_1 - v_1 = b_1$ and the term $6u_1 + 2v_1$ in the objective function, the decision maker

a. prefers $g_1(x_1, \ldots, x_n)$ to be greater than, rather than smaller than, b_1

b. prefers $g_1(x_1, \ldots, x_n)$ to be smaller than, rather than larger than, b_1

c. is indifferent as to whether $g_1(x_1, \cdots, x_n)$ is larger than or smaller than b_1

16. Problems with multiple objectives

a. are difficult because it is often true that improving one objective will hurt another

b. are difficult because the objectives may be in noncommensurate units (i.e., the problem of "combining apples and oranges")

c. can sometimes be treated with the goal programming approach

d. all of the above

Questions 17, 18, 19 apply to the following problem:
(1) $g_1(x_1, x_2) \leq b_1$ is a system constraint

(2) minimizing underachievement of $g_2(x_1, x_2) = b_2$ is top priority
(3) minimizing overachievement of $g_3(x_1, x_2) = b_3$ is next in priority

17. The first step of the solution procedure is
a. Min u_2, s.t. $g_1(x_1, x_2) \leq b_1$, $g_2 - u_2 = b_2$, $x_1, x_2, u_2 \geq 0$
b. Min u_2, s.t. $g_1(x_1, x_2) \leq b_1$, $g_2 + u_2 \geq b_2$, $x_1, x_2, u_2 \geq 0$
c. Min u_2, s.t. $g_1(x_1, x_2) \leq b_1$, $g_2 - u_2 \leq b_2$, $x_1, x_2, u_2 \geq 0$

18. Let FR I denote the points (x_1, x_2) obtained in the first step of the solution procedure. The second step is
a. Min $u_3 + v_3$, s.t. (x_1, x_3) in FR I and $g_3(x_1, x_2) + u_3 - v_3 = b_3$
b. Min u_3, s.t. (x_1, x_2) in FR I and $g_3(x_1, x_2) + u_3 \leq b_3$
c. Min v_3, s.t. (x_1, x_2) in FR I and $g_3 - v_3 \leq b_3$

19. In this model
a. at least one goal will be achieved
b. if the first goal is not achieved, the second goal will not be achieved
c. none of the above

20. Consider a goal program with the constraint

$$g_1(x_1, \ldots, x_n) - v_1 \leq b_1, \qquad v_1 \geq 0$$

with v_1 in the objective function. Then
a. the goal is to minimize overachievement
b. if $v_1^* > 0$ then the constraint will be active
c. neither of the above
d. both a and b

Answers

1. F	**6.** F	**11.** F	**16.** d
2. T	**7.** T	**12.** c	**17.** b
3. T	**8.** F	**13.** b	**18.** c
4. F	**9.** T	**14.** a	**19.** c
5. T	**10.** T	**15.** a	**20.** d

▶ Problems

See IM

11-1. ▲ For the minimax scheduling problem, find an alternative optimal solution to the one given in Figure 11.14.

Problems 11-2, 11-3, and 11-4 refer to the following example of the so-called *facilities layout problem:*

Solomon Gemorah, high-priced management consultant, has been hired to redo the layout of a small bank. There are four key departments to be taken into consideration: (1) Trusts, (2) Estates, (3) Accounting, (4) Savings. These four departments must be assigned to four locations. The distances between locations are given in Figure 11.23. Thus the distance from location 2 to location 4 is 1 unit, from 4 to 1 is 1 unit, and so on. A measure of the two-way "daily flows" between the four key departments is shown in Figure 11.24.

The problem is to assign the four departments to the four locations (one department per location) in such a way as to minimize the sum of the distance-weighted

LOCATION	LOCATION 1	2	3	4
1	0	2	3	1
2	2	0	3	1
3	3	3	0	2
4	1	1	2	0

▲ FIGURE 11.23
Distances between Locations

DEPT.	DEPARTMENT 1	2	3	4
1	0	15	20	16
2	15	0	13	9
3	20	13	0	19
4	16	9	19	0

▲ FIGURE 11.24
Flows between Departments

daily flows.[6] For example, if we make the assignment of departments to locations as follows: 1 → 1, 2 → 2, 3 → 3, 4 → 4, then the objective value will be

weighted two-way cost
between facilities 1 and 2 = distance × flow = 2(15) = 30

weighted two-way cost
between facilities 1 and 3 = distance × flow = 3(20) = 60

weighted two-way cost
between facilities 1 and 4 = distance × flow = 1(16) = 16

weighted two-way cost
between facilities 2 and 3 = distance × flow = 3(13) = 39

weighted two-way cost
between facilities 2 and 4 = distance × flow = 1(9) = 9

weighted two-way cost
between facilities 3 and 4 = distance × flow = 2(19) = 38

total cost = 192

(a) Total cost = 170
(b) 24; *n*!

11-2. ▲ **(a)** Suppose Solomon assigned department 1 to location 4, department 2 to location 3, department 3 to location 2, and department 4 to location 1. What would be the distance between departments? What would be the total cost of Solomon's assignments?

(b) What is the total number of possible assignments of facilities to locations that Solomon would consider if he were to attack the problem by complete enumeration? For the general problem of assigning n facilities to n locations, what is the total possible number of assignments?

6 possible assignments
(See IM)

11-3. ▲ Suppose that department 1 is assigned to location 1. Draw a tree, analogous to Figure 11.1, showing the remaining possible assignments of departments 2, 3, and 4 to locations 2, 3, and 4.

[6]This problem can be formally expressed as a 0-1 integer program as follows. Let

$$x_{pq} = \begin{cases} 1 & \text{if facility } p \text{ is to be placed in location } q \\ 0 & \text{if facility } p \text{ is not to be placed in location } q \end{cases}$$

and let c_{ikjl} be the cost of placing facility i in location k and facility j in location l. Then the model is

$$\text{Min } \frac{1}{2}\sum_{i=1}^{n}\sum_{k=1}^{n}\sum_{j=1}^{n}\sum_{l=1}^{n} c_{ikjl}x_{ik}x_{jl}$$

$$\text{s.t.} \quad \sum_{i=1}^{n} x_{ik} = 1, \qquad k = 1,\ldots, n$$

$$\sum_{k=1}^{n} x_{ik} = 1, \qquad i = 1,\ldots, n$$

$$x_{ik} = 0 \text{ or } 1, \qquad \text{all } i, k$$

This problem is called the *quadratic assignment problem.*

(a) 6
(b) See IM

11-4. ▲▲ **(a)** How many different pairs of departments can be selected from four departments?

(b) Start from the answer to part (a) of Problem 11-2 to improve the assignment by employing the following Best Pairwise Exchange Heuristic,[7] as described below:

- ▶ ***Step 1:*** Find the potential improvement in the objective function associated with each pairwise exchange of departments. For example, if departments 1 and 2 are exchanged, the new assignment will be $1 \rightarrow 3$, $2 \rightarrow 4$, $3 \rightarrow 2$, and $4 \rightarrow 1$. That is, the location of departments 1 and 2 are changed, but departments 3 and 4 remain unchanged.
- ▶ ***Step 2:*** Make the pairwise exchange that results in the largest improvement. Then repeat the procedure until no pairwise exchange will improve the value of the objective function.

(a) 4-A, 1-C, 5-B, 3-D, 2-E; Total = 108
(b) 4-A, 1-D, 3-E, 5-C, 2-B; Total = 116

11-5. ▲ Sam Hull is a marketing manager for a pharmaceutical company. He must assign five detail people to five hospitals. The expected sales are shown in Figure 11.25.

(a) Use a greedy heuristic to assign each detail person to each hospital so that total expected sales are maximized.

(b) Use the modified heuristic in Section 11.2: After transforming the data by subtracting the maximum sales in each column from all other entries in that column, use the greedy heuristic.

(a) No setup–J2–J3–J1; Cost = \$100
(b) No setup–J3–J2–J1; Cost = \$105 or no setup–J3–J1–J2; cost = \$104
(c) No

11-6. ▲▲ Three jobs—J1, J2 and, J3—are to be machined on a lathe. The cost of setting up for a job depends on the setup for the previous job. The cost for changeovers is given in Figure 11.26. Currently the lathe is not set up for any job.

(a) Use the greedy heuristic to schedule the jobs. The objective is to minimize the total setup cost.

(b) Use the modified heuristic in Section 11.2.

(c) Does the modified heuristic always produce a better result than the greedy one?

See IM

11-7. ▲▲ Erma McZeal is in charge of quality control for the city of Chicago's water supply. There are currently three test stations located in Lake Michigan. Letting (x_1, x_2) denote coordinates, the three existing locations are placed as follows:

$$\text{station 1: } x_1 = 2, \quad x_2 = 10$$
$$\text{station 2: } x_1 = 6, \quad x_2 = 6$$
$$\text{station 3: } x_1 = 1, \quad x_2 = 3$$

Erma's job is to locate a new station in such a way as to minimize the total distance of the new station from the three existing stations. Assume that, because of existing channel marker locations, distance is measured rectangularly. In other words, if the

▼ FIGURE 11.25

DETAIL PERSON	HOSPITAL A	B	C	D	E
1	25	18	23	22	16
2	20	21	18	15	12
3	23	19	20	21	20
4	30	26	25	22	20
5	28	22	23	20	18

▼ FIGURE 11.26

	J1	J2	J3
No Setup	\$50	\$35	\$39
J1	—	\$30	\$34
J2	\$41	—	\$30
J3	\$35	\$25	—

[7]Many heuristics have been proposed in the literature for attacking the facilities assignment problem. In one study involving 12 facilities (R. Mojena, T. Vollmann, and Y. Okamotot, "On Predicting Computational Time of a Branch-and-Bound Algorithm for the Assignment of Facilities," *Decision Sciences* 7, no. 4 [1976], pp. 856–67), it is reported that achieving a true optimum with a branch-and-bound algorithm required 2 hours on a high-speed computer. In 7 seconds the Best Pairwise Exchange Heuristic produced a proposal that was, in terms of associated objective values, within 3% of the optimum.

new station is located at ($x_1 = 3, x_2 = 4$), then it is a distance of $(3 - 2) + (10 - 4)$, or 7 units, from station 1; and so on. Let (x_1, x_2) denote the coordinates of the new station, and formulate a goal programming model to solve Erma's problem.

Schedule D and H one time-period later.

11-8. ▲▲ Figure 11.27 is the precedence diagram for the activities in a project. The time and the personnel required for each activity are given in Figure 11.28. Use the workload smoothing heuristic to generate a schedule for this project.

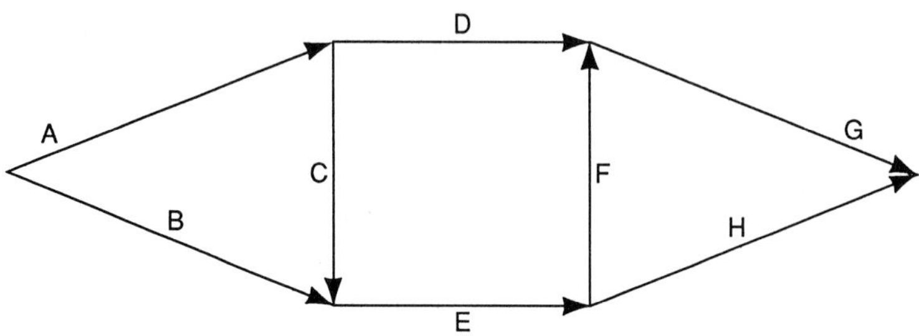

▲ FIGURE 11.27

ACTIVITY	TIME REQUIRED	PERSONNEL
A	1	4
B	2	5
C	1	3
D	2	2
E	2	7
F	1	7
G	1	5
H	1	4

▲ FIGURE 11.28

See IM

11-9. ▲ *Product Mix* A firm produces two products. Each one must be processed through two machines, each of which has available 240 minutes of capacity per day. Each unit of product 1 requires 20 minutes on machine 1 and 12 minutes on machine 2. Each unit of product 2 requires 12 minutes on machine 1 and 20 minutes on machine 2. In determining the daily product mix, management would like to achieve the following goals:

1. Joint total production of 12 units
2. Production of 9 units of product 2
3. Production of 10 units of product 1

Suppose that management wishes to minimize the underachievement of each of these goals and that predetermined priority weights w_1, w_2, and w_3 are to be assigned to the three goals, respectively. Formulate this as a goal programming problem.

(a) $10T + 5C + u_1 - v_1 = 3200$
(b) $T + .5C + u_2 = 300$
(c) $T - v_3 = 200$
(d) $C + u_4 \geq 200$; $C - v_4 \leq 250$

11-10. ▲▲ T & C Furniture Company manufactures tables and chairs. If the variables T and C represent the number of tables and chairs, respectively, produced in a period, write the goal constraints for the following objectives:

(a) A table takes 10 hours to make and a chair 5 hours. The total number of work hours available per period is 3200. Though idle time and overtime are acceptable, T & C Co. would like the total number of work hours to be as close to 3200 as possible.

(b) A table uses one side of wood and a chair half a side; 300 sides of wood are available for a period and no more can be bought. T & C would like to use as much of this wood as possible in one period.

(c) T & C makes tables to order and is committed to providing 200 tables in a period. Extra tables, if produced, have to be held in inventory, and the company would like to minimize the number of tables held in inventory.

(d) The demand for chairs is uncertain, but is estimated to be between 200 and 250. The company would like to produce chairs as close to this range as possible.

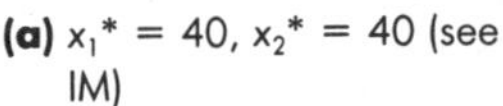

11-11. ▲ Consider the goal programming model

(a) $x_1^* = 40$, $x_2^* = 40$ (see IM)
(b) Min underachievement; no overachievement allowed
(c) Min underachievement; overachievement allowed
(d) $x_1^* = 0$, $x_2^* = 80$

$$\text{Min } P_1v_1 + P_2v_2 + P_3u_3 + P_4(u_4 + v_4)$$

$$\begin{aligned} \text{s.t.} \quad x_2 + u_1 - v_1 &= 100 \\ x_1 + x_2 + u_2 - v_2 &= 80 \\ x_2 + u_3 \quad &= 40 \\ x_1 + 2x_2 + u_4 - v_4 &= 160 \\ x_1, x_2, u_1, u_2, u_3, u_4, v_1, v_2, v_3, v_4 &\geq 0 \end{aligned}$$

(a) Use the graphical method to solve the problem.
(b) Interpret the third goal $x_2 + u_3 = 40$.
(c) Replace $x_2 + u_3 = 40$ with $x_2 + u_3 \geq 40$. What is the new interpretation?
(d) Use the graphical method to solve the problem with the replacement prescribed in (c).

11-12. ▲ Consider the goal programming model

(a) $x_1^* = 40$, $x_2^* = 40$ (See IM)
(b) Min overachievement; no underachievement allowed
(c) Min overachievement; underachievement allowed
(d) $x_1^* = 0$, $x_2^* = 80$

$$\text{Min } P_1v_1 + P_2v_2 + P_3v_3 + P_4(u_4 + v_4)$$

$$\begin{aligned} \text{s.t.} \quad x_2 + u_1 - v_1 &= 100 \\ x_1 + x_2 + u_2 - v_2 &= 80 \\ x_1 - v_3 &= 40 \\ x_1 + 2x_2 + u_4 - v_4 &= 160 \\ x_1, x_2, u_1, u_2, u_3, u_4, v_1, v_2, v_3, v_4 &\geq 0 \end{aligned}$$

(a) Use the graphical method to solve the problem.
(b) Interpret the third goal $x_1 - v_3 = 40$.
(c) Replace $x_1 - v_3 = 40$ with $x_1 - v_3 \leq 40$. What is the new interpretation?
(d) Use the graphical method to solve the problem with the replacement prescribed in (c).

11-13. ▲ Consider the following goal program:

(a) $x_1^* = 100$, $x_2^* = 0$ (See IM)
(b) Yes; overachieved second by 20; underachieved third by 45

$$\text{Min } P_1u_2 + P_2v_1 + P_3u_3$$

$$\begin{aligned} \text{s.t.} \quad x_1 + x_2 + u_1 - v_1 &= 80 \\ x_1 + u_2 - v_2 \quad &= 100 \\ x_2 + u_3 \quad &\geq 45 \\ x_1, x_2, u_1, v_1, u_2, v_2, u_3 &\geq 0 \end{aligned}$$

(a) Solve by the graphical method.
(b) Is the first-priority goal achieved? What about the second and third? In case of underachievement or overachievement state actual numerical amounts of the violations.

Open warehouses 3 & 4; cost = $150

11-14. ▲▲ A1 transportation company operates warehouses and distributes goods to retail outlets. A1 has warehouses at 5 different locations and has four retail customers. The transportation costs per unit, the demands, and the costs of operating the warehouses are given in Figure 11.29. All warehouses have unlimited capacity. A1 would like to decide which warehouses should be operated and which should be closed. The greedy open heuristic for doing this consists of opening the warehouse that saves the most money and continuing to do this as long as money can be saved. Use the greedy open heuristic to solve this problem.

(a) 720
(b) D–C–A–F–E–B; total = 23 (See IM)

11-15. ▲ There are six jobs to be processed on two machines (cutting and grinding). Each job must go through the cutting machine before being processed on the grinding machine. Assume that the sequence in which jobs are processed is the same on both machines.

WAREHOUSE	RETAILER A	B	C	D	FIXED COST OF OPERATING WAREHOUSE
1	5	4	1	6	31
2	9	7	3	5	35
3	8	1	7	4	20
4	4	3	6	2	29
5	6	3	5	2	38
Demand	10	15	6	5	

▲ FIGURE 11.29

Figure 11.30 shows the time (in hours) required to finish a job on each machine. The objective is to schedule the jobs so that the time required to finish all jobs is minimized.

(a) How many alternatives should you compare for complete enumeration?

(b) What is the time required to finish all jobs if the jobs are processed in the ascending order of the total processing time? A figure like Figure 11.9 may be helpful. In this application keep all tasks assigned to machine 1 in one row and those assigned to machine 2 in a second row.

MACHINE	TIME REQUIRED FOR JOB (hours) A	B	C	D	E	F
Cutting	3	4	2	1	5	3
Grinding	2	5	2	1	3	4
Total	5	9	4	2	8	7

▲ FIGURE 11.30

Improves total time to 20

11-16. ▲▲ Given the job-scheduling exercise in Problem 11-15, can you see any improvement when you apply the following heuristic method?

- ▶ ***Step 1:*** List the jobs along with their processing times on the cutting and grinding machines.
- ▶ ***Step 2:*** Find the job with the smallest processing time. If the smallest time is on the cutting machine, schedule the job as early as possible; if it is on the grinding machine, schedule it as late as possible. Break ties arbitrarily.
- ▶ ***Step 3:*** Eliminate the job from the list.
- ▶ ***Step 4:*** Repeat steps 2 and 3 until all jobs have been scheduled.

See IM

11-17. ▲▲ The city of Chicago is considering two projects. Each unit of Project A costs $400, generates 20 jobs, and returns $200 at the end of the year. Each unit of Project B costs $600, generates 40 jobs, and returns $200. The city planner would like to achieve the following goals:

1. Keep total expenditure at or below $2400.
2. Generate at least 120 jobs.
3. Maximize return at end of year.

Suppose that the three goals are in order of descending absolute priority. Use graphical analysis to find the optimal number of units to engage in each project. Are the goals achieved? If not, what are the underachievements? What are the net expenditure and the number of jobs generated?

Close 2, 4, 5 or open 1, 3 for better solution cost of $142

11-18. ▲▲ Another heuristic for solving problem 11-14 is called the greedy close. In this case we start with all warehouses open and close the one which saves the most money. We continue to do this until we cannot close a warehouse without losing money. Solve problem 11-14 using the greedy close heuristic. Is this solution better or worse than that in 11-14?

Video Case

Heuristics

The text says that a heuristic is an intuitively logical "rule of thumb" for dealing with some aspect of a problem. The video shows how a quite-plausible-sounding heuristic for scheduling jobs on machines can produce unexpected results. In the case depicted, increasing the resources available (the number of machines to do the work) while using the same heuristic paradoxically yielded a less desirable solution. This example quite naturally raises the questions, "How do you know a good heuristic when you see one?" and "How do you prove (or demonstrate) that a heuristic is good?"

One approach is to test the heuristic on small (simple) versions of the problem, for which it is possible to find optimal solutions. Suppose, for example, that you are attempting to find a good scheduling rule for a situation in which N jobs must be scheduled on M machines. Each job passes through the M machines in the same order, but each job can take a different amount of time on each machine. There are N! possible ways to schedule these jobs. We have seen that N! gets big rapidly—for instance, 10! = 3,628,800. However, 5! = 120 is quite manageable. We can imagine using a computer to check all 120 schedules to find the best one. Thus we can determine how close the heuristic comes to producing the optimal solution.

Another approach is to use a procedure to find a bound on the optimal value of the objective function. A common example of this approach is to use the LP relaxation to provide an upper (or lower) bound to the OV for a max (or min) IP problem. Heuristics are often used to solve problems that could be formulated as IPs but in practice are not because there is no cost-effective solution procedure. (Examples of this strategy can be found in the Application Capsules on pages 405 and 486–87.) The LP relaxation can be used to find a bound on the OV. This tells us whether the heuristic is "close enough"—that is, whether the current level of achievement is satisfactory or whether it appears worthwhile to look for a better heuristic.

Finally, there is simulation. One can build a simulator that evaluates various heuristics. Conway, Maxwell, and Miller used this approach in the late 1960s to find some good rules for scheduling a job shop. A similar approach is described in the Application Capsule on page 453.

Questions

1. (a) Can you use any of the approaches listed above to *prove* that a heuristic provides an *optimal* solution to a problem? (b) Can you prove that it does *not* provide an optimal solution? (c) Can you prove that it provides a *good* answer?
2. Is the simplex algorithm a greedy algorithm? Explain.
3. Give an example of a heuristic that is discussed in Chapter 7.

CHAPTER 12 Calculus-Based Optimization and an Introduction to Nonlinear Programming

APPLICATION CAPSULE

Water, Water Everywhere? A Nonlinear Program Helps Plan the Expansion of an Irrigation System in Israel*

Short of water and energy, the state of Israel must plan its use of these resources carefully. Among the available sources of both are the Hazbani and Dan rivers, major tributaries of the Jordan River. The Hazbani-Dan System (HDS) supplies water for irrigation, using any surplus to generate energy by means of a hydroelectric power station. Owned by an association of agricultural users, the HDS derives most of its income from selling water and power to users who chose not to share in the original investment and thus are not members. Its main expense is pumping water for irrigation during the summer season.

The HDS has established a set of priorities to govern allocation of its resources:

- Water requirements of members and internal users are met first by gravity-fed irrigation, supplemented by pumping (which is twice as expensive) when necessary.
- External users can utilize only the remaining pumping capacity or must pump themselves.
- Irrigation for both members and nonmembers takes precedence over use of water for energy production.

Considering several proposed expansions, the HDS called on university consultants to evaluate the potential benefits of the options:

- Addition of more internal users (cost, \$25,000–\$75,000)
- Addition of more external users, which would require enlargement of the water distribution network (cost, \$500,000)
- Expanding the system to catch part of the Hazbani River flow (cost, \$750,000).

A program was devised to maximize the expected annual return for the alternative (or combination of alternatives) selected. The solution evaluated the alternatives for 2 types of years (dry and rainy), 7 types of weeks (representing various weather conditions and levels of demand), and 17 time periods each week. The program included four stages:

1. Drawing on historical data, the average inflow and user consumption of water for each time period, the type of week, and the type of year were computed for each of the alternatives.
2. An LP model determined an optimal water-sharing plan for the various users according to the priorities policy specified above.
3. A nonlinear programming model determined the optimal operating plan for the hydroelectric turbine, subject to the water allocations arrived at in stage 2. This model provided for flexibility in water storage, so that more water could be released during periods when the prices for electric power were highest.
4. The average annual returns for the various alternatives were computed by totaling the weekly revenues from water and electricity sales and subtracting pumping costs.

This analysis found that implementing all of the alternatives under consideration would increase the maximum expected annual return from about \$109,000 to \$1 million. Although only the least expensive of the proposed expansions were ultimately carried out, the annual return was expected to total nearly \$423,000.

*Rabinowitz, Mehrez, and Ravivi, "An Economic Evaluation Model of Investment Alternatives in Water Supply Systems," *Interfaces*, Vol. 18, No. 6 (Nov.–Dec. 1988).

12.1 Introduction

This material will appeal especially to students who have specialized in economics, physics, or mathematics. It is the cornerstone of much of the classical optimization that has led to many algorithms in management science. The student needs to be familiar with first and second derivatives for this chapter.

In many business and economics problems the functions or mathematical relationships involved are not all linear. In fact, it is probably true that the real-world problems that fit the strict mold of linearity are the exception rather than the rule. As a simple illustration:

In a linear model, price is usually assumed to be a given constant, say p, and quantity to be sold is a variable x that is assumed to be independent of price. Hence, revenue is given by px, and we say that revenue is proportional to price. In reality, however, price may be a variable, and quantity of sales (demand) might be dependent on price. This dependency is expressed by writing sales = $f(p)$, where f is some specified (nonconstant) function of p. Thus, revenue would be given by

$$\text{revenue} = \text{price} \times \text{sales} = pf \times (p)$$

which is nonlinear in the variable p. In this case a model to find the price level that maximizes revenue would be a nonlinear model.

In general, some of the prominent (and not necessarily distinct) reasons for nonlinearity are (1) nonproportional relationships (in the example above, revenue is not proportional to price, for, depending on the specific form of $f(p)$, price may increase and revenue decrease); (2) nonadditive relationships (e.g., when two chemicals are added together the resulting volume need not be the sum of the two added volumes); and (3) efficiencies or inefficiencies of scale (e.g., when too many workers try to plant beans on the same acre of ground they begin to get into each other's way and the yield per worker will decrease, rather than remain constant.[1] In

[1]Note that this situation leads to a nonproportional relationship between total yield and number of workers.

short, any number of physical, structural, biological, economic, and logical relationships may be responsible for the appearance of nonlinearity in a model.

It must be stated at the outset that, although nonlinear phenomena are common, nonlinear models are considerably more difficult to solve than linear models. Combine this difficulty with the fact that linear models, in many contexts, provide *good approximations* to nonlinear models, and you can understand the popularity of linear models, such as LP.

As we know, a model is not the real world. It is an abstract representation of reality. The important point for the modeler is to know when a linearized version provides an *adequate* representation of the nonlinear world. The answer to such a judgmental question comes with experimentation and much experience, and even then only imperfectly and often without consensus. In this chapter we want to address those situations where nonlinear programming models are deemed to be required. Our objective is to provide some understanding of the tools and concepts necessary to deal with nonlinear programming models.

The chapter is organized as follows. The first two sections review the facts concerning *unconstrained* optimization in several decision variables. Then we give a descriptive and geometric introduction to constrained nonlinear optimization. We then focus on problems with equality constraints, emphasizing the role of Lagrange multipliers and their interpretation in a pricing context. The next section deals with NLP (nonlinear programming) formulation and solution using GINO. (GINO is an interactive computer code used to solve NLP problems.) Following this, we loosely define the concept of concave and convex programs and discuss in a qualitative way the kinds of nonlinear problems that can be routinely solved. The chapter concludes with some notes on implementation of NLP, including a brief discussion of the nature of some of the algorithms used to solve NLP problems.

12.2 Unconstrained Optimization in Two Decision Variables

General Conditions for Optimality

Many engineering design problems are unconstrained optimization problems.

Let us first consider the case of two decision variables, x_1 and x_2. Thus, we consider a function $f(x_1, x_2)$. For the case of two decision variables (that is, two independent variables) we must use partial derivatives to describe local or global optima. We shall use the notation f_{x_i} for first partial derivative, $f_{x_i x_i}$ for second partial derivative, and so on. Any point at which all first partial derivatives vanish is called a **stationary point.** We have the following *necessary condition* for optimality.

At a local max or min both partial derivatives must equal zero (i.e., $f_{x_1} = f_{x_2} = 0$). That is, a local maximizer or a local minimizer is always a stationary point.

However, not all stationary points provide maxima and minima. Thus, we may wish to employ the so-called second-order (meaning that second derivatives are involved) sufficient condition for optimality, which is somewhat more complicated than the necessary condition. The rule for the second-order sufficient condition for optimality is illustrated below.

Suppose that $x^* = (x_1^*, x_2^*)$ is a stationary point of f. Define

$$D = D(x_1^*, x_2^*) = [f_{x_1x_1}(x_1^*, x_2^*)][f_{x_2x_2}(x_1^*, x_2^*)] - [f_{x_1x_2}(x_1^*, x_2^*)]^2$$

Case 1: **If $f_{x_1x_1}(x_1^*, x_2^*) > 0$ and $D > 0$, then (x_1^*, x_2^*) is a local minimizer.**

Case 2: **If $f_{x_1x_1}(x_1^*, x_2^*) < 0$ and $D > 0$, then (x_1^*, x_2^*) is a local maximizer.**

Case 3: **If $D < 0$ then (x_1^*, x_2^*) is a so-called saddle point; that is, it is neither a local minimizer nor a local maximizer. Indeed, at such a point the function will attain a local max with respect to one of the variables and a local min with respect to the other, thereby having a saddle shape at that point.**

Case 4: **If $D = 0$, further analysis (beyond the scope of the present discussion) is required to determine the nature of the stationary point.**

The "saddle point" was named because of the resemblance to a horse's saddle. Looking from the side view, the lowest sitting point on the saddle is both the lowest point looking forward and backward on the horse and the highest point on the saddle looking left or right.

Note, in the above conditions, that if $f_{x_1x_1}(x_1^*, x_2^*) = 0$ then $D \le 0$, and we are in either Case 3 or Case 4.

Evaluating Optimality Conditions: Two Examples

Example 1: Importing Coconut Oil—Profit Maximization. Hoot Spa imports coconut oil from his home town in Jamaica. He uses this oil to produce two kinds of tanning creme: Sear and Char. The price per pound at which he will be able to sell these products depends on how much of each he produces. In particular, if Hoot produces x_1 pounds of Sear and x_2 pounds of Char, he will be able to sell all he produces at the following prices (in dollars):

$$\text{price per pound of Sear} = 80 - 3x_1$$

and

$$\text{price per pound of Char} = 60 - 2x_2$$

The cost of manufacturing x_1 pounds of Sear and x_2 pounds of Char is

$$\text{cost of manufacturing the two cremes} = 12x_1 + 8x_2 + 4x_1x_2$$

Assuming that he can sell all he produces, Hoot wishes to determine how many pounds of each creme he should schedule for production so as to maximize his profit.

We observe that

$$\text{revenue received for Sear} = x_1(80 - 3x_1)$$
$$\text{revenue received for Char} = x_2(60 - 2x_2)$$
$$\text{total revenue received} = x_1(80 - 3x_1) + x_2(60 - 2x_2)$$
$$\text{profit received} = x_1(80 - 3x_1) + x_2(60 - 2x_2) - (12x_1 + 8x_2 + 4x_1x_2)$$

$$= 80x_1 - 3x_1^2 + 60x_2 - 2x_2^2 - 12x_1 - 8x_2 - 4x_1x_2$$
$$= P(x_1, x_2)$$
$$= \text{profit function}$$

To find the optimal production schedule we first locate the stationary points of the profit function. Taking first partial derivatives of $P(x_1, x_2)$ yields

$$P_{x_1} = 80 - 6x_1 - 12 - 4x_2$$
$$P_{x_2} = 60 - 4x_2 - 8 - 4x_1$$

Hence, solving the *necessary* optimality conditions $P_{x_1} = 0$ and $P_{x_2} = 0$ gives

$$6x_1 + 4x_2 = 68$$
$$4x_1 + 4x_2 = 52$$

The solution to these simultaneous equations is

$$x_1^* = 8 \text{ pounds} \qquad \text{and} \qquad x_2^* = 5 \text{ pounds}$$

To see whether this solution actually gives a local maximum, we check the second-order conditions. The second partials of $P(x_1, x_2)$ are

You might recall that $P_{x_1x_2}$ is identical to $P_{x_2x_1} = -4$.

$$P_{x_1x_1} = -6, \qquad P_{x_2x_2} = -4, \qquad P_{x_1x_2} = -4$$

Hence,

$$D = P_{x_1x_1} P_{x_2x_2} - P_{x_1x_2}^2 = (-6)(-4) - (-4)^2 = 8 > 0$$

Since $P_{x_1x_1} = -6 < 0$ and $D > 0$, it follows from Case 2 above that we have a local maximum. In fact (using methods beyond our scope), it can be demonstrated that $P(x_1, x_2)$ is a strictly concave function, and hence the solution ($x_1^* = 8$, $x_2^* = 5$) is in fact a unique global maximizer of the profit. Thus, Hoot should produce 8 pounds of Sear and 5 pounds of Char in order to maximize his profit.

Let us now exercise these tools on a second problem.

Example 2. Define

$$f(x_1, x_2) = 5x_1^2 + 10x_2^2 + 10x_1x_2 - 22x_1 - 32x_2 + 20$$

Let us find all local maximizers and minimizers of this function. To achieve this, we first set both first partials equal to zero and find all solutions. This step gives all stationary points of the function, and among these points will be the points we are seeking. Proceeding, then, we obtain

$$f_{x_1} = 10x_1 + 10x_2 - 22 = 0$$
$$f_{x_2} = 20x_2 + 10x_1 - 32 = 0$$

Solving these two equations in two unknowns yields

$$x_1^* = 1.2, \qquad x_2^* = 1.0$$

Thus, there is only one stationary point. To determine its nature we first compute the second partials at (x_1^*, x_2^*):

$$f_{x_1x_1} = 10, \qquad f_{x_2x_2} = 20, \qquad f_{x_1x_2} = 10$$

Since

$$f_{x_1x_1} = 10 > 0$$

and

$$D = (f_{x_1x_1})(f_{x_2x_2}) - (f_{x_1x_2})^2 = (10)(20) - 10^2 = 100 > 0$$

Case 1 applies, and the point (1.2, 1.0) is a local minimizer of the function.

Thus, we have seen that (just as for functions of a single variable) there is a first-order (first derivative) and second-order (involving second derivatives) test that can be applied to locate unconstrained local optima. These tests are called **first-order optimality conditions** and **second-order optimality conditions.** Note that the first-order conditions are necessary; the second-order conditions are sufficient. Also note that the second-order conditions subsume the first-order ones (that is, the second-order conditions assume that x_1^*, x_2^* is a stationary point).

In the absence of some additional properties of the function, such as convexity or concavity, a local (as opposed to global) optimizer is the most that one can generally hope to find. The first-derivative test (the necessary condition) says that the local optima are contained among the stationary points of the function. The second-derivative test (the sufficient condition) allows us to distinguish between local maximizers and minimizers, and points that are neither.

Let us now move on to the most general case, a function of n variables.

12.3 Unconstrained Optimization in *n* Decision Variables: The Computer Approach

For a differentiable function of n variables, each local optimizer is a stationary point. In order to guarantee that a stationary point is, for example, a local maximizer, second-order sufficiency conditions must be invoked. Although these two types of optimality conditions have theoretic interest they have, for many nonlinear problems in more than two variables, limited *practical relevance.* The reasons are:

1. Setting the first partial derivatives equal to zero gives a system of n equations in n unknowns. Unless this system is linear (i.e., the original function was quadratic) it is not easy to find solutions. It may well be impossible to do by hand.
2. The second-order sufficiency conditions are quite complicated, requiring the evaluation of determinants of certain entries in the matrix of second partial derivatives. Indeed, even in the case of one or two decision variables, if the function f is sufficiently complicated, it may not be possible to hand-solve the optimality conditions, and hence this approach is not generally viable.

A max or min can be identified with a spreadsheet by adding or subtracting .001 from each value of the variables. If all points around this solution give a higher objective function value, a minimum exists. If all points give a lower value, there is a maximum. Otherwise, there is a saddle point.

For these reasons, computer codes have been developed to find local optima of nonlinear functions of n variables (where n is any integer ≥ 1). Often such codes are based on hill-climbing (or hill-descent) behavior. That is, for a maximization problem, an initial point is chosen, and then an uphill direction is determined. Intuitively, the algorithm moves from the initial point, along a straight line in an uphill direction, to the highest point that can be attained on that line. Then a new uphill direction is defined, and the procedure is continued. The algorithm terminates when the first partials are sufficiently close to zero. Such a point, then, will always be a "local peak." Other local maxima are searched for by initiating the computer code at a different point.

An analogy that might help students understand how difficult it is to find a global optimum, is to imagine trying to find the highest peak in a chain of mountains while climbing in a dense fog. Even if you have reached "the top" of something, it isn't guaranteed to be the highest peak. In the same way that you can't "look" to see if you are on the highest mountain, neither can the computer "look" to see if there are any other local or global optima.

The description above reveals the main role of the first-order necessary conditions in applications. They are used indirectly, in the sense that they serve as a *termination criterion* for the "hill-climbing" computer codes that search for local optima. The second-order sufficiency conditions, for the general problem in n variables, are mainly of theoretic interest, and go beyond the introductory nature of this chapter.

In concluding this section we mention one other practical approach that is sometimes taken in maximizing a *concave function.* For a concave function, any stationary point is a global maximizer (for a convex function, any stationary point is a global minimizer). Thus, if we can write out the first derivatives, we can then try to solve the n equations in n unknowns. Special computer codes exist to solve such systems. Whereas in the general case a solution could be a local maximizer or minimizer or neither, in the concave case we are guaranteed that any solution is a global maximizer. This approach is generally limited to the case of a concave or convex function. Moreover, it is limited by the requirement that the first-order partial derivatives can be explicitly written. For some problems this may not be possible.

12.4 Nonlinear Optimization with Constraints: A Descriptive Geometric Introduction

This chapter, up to this point, has focused on *unconstrained* optimization. More typically, in a management-oriented decision-making setting, we are interested in optimizing an objective function subject to constraints. These constraints are in the form of mathematical equalities and/or inequalities, just as in the case of linear programming, except that in this chapter linearity is not assumed. Thus, the *general mathematical programming model,* in symbolic terms, can be written in the form illustrated below.

$$\begin{aligned}
&\text{Max } f(x_1, x_2, \ldots, x_n) \quad \text{(objective)} \qquad (P_0)\\
&\text{s.t. } \left.\begin{aligned} g_1(x_1, \ldots, x_n) &= b_1\\ g_2(x_1, \ldots, x_n) &= b_2\\ &\vdots\\ g_m(x_1, \ldots, x_n) &= b_m \end{aligned}\right\} m \text{ equality constraints}\\
&\qquad \left.\begin{aligned} h_1(x_1, \ldots, x_n) &\le r_1\\ h_2(x_1, \ldots, x_n) &\le r_2\\ &\vdots\\ h_k(x_1, \ldots, x_n) &\le r_k \end{aligned}\right\} k \text{ inequality constraints}
\end{aligned}$$

Graphical Analysis

Just as with LP, we can use two-dimensional geometry to gain insight into this problem. For example, let us use graphical analysis to solve the specific problem

$$\begin{aligned} &\text{Max } x_1 - x_2 \\ \text{s.t.} \quad &-x_1^2 + x_2 \geq 1 \\ &x_1 + x_2 \leq 3 \\ &-x_1 + x_2 \leq 2 \\ x_1 \geq 0, \quad &x_2 \geq 0 \end{aligned}$$

Note that everything in this model is linear except for the first constraint. A model is called nonlinear if at least one of the constraint functions, or the objective function, or both, are nonlinear. Therefore, the model above is properly termed a **nonlinear program (NLP).**

The Feasible Region. In order to use the graphical approach to solve this problem, we proceed just as we did in LP. First we plot the set of points that simultaneously satisfy *all* the constraints. This set of points is called, just as in LP, the *constraint set,* or the *feasible region.* This set represents the allowable decisions. In order to find an allowable decision that maximizes the objective function, we find the "most uphill" (i.e., highest-valued) *contour* of the objective function that still touches the constraint set. The point at which it touches will be an optimal solution (often more simply referred to as a solution) to the problem. Figure 12.1 shows the graphical solution to the problem presented above.

You can see in Figure 12.1 that the nonlinear constraint puts curvature into the boundary of the constraint set. The feasible set is no longer a polyhedron (i.e., a flat-sided figure defined by linear inequalities) as is the case with LP, and the optimal solution does not lie on a corner. Recall that in the LP case the graphical analysis allowed us to identify the active constraints at an optimal corner, and then the *exact solution* was obtained by solving two equations in two unknowns. In general this method does not work in the nonlinear case. As shown in Figure 12.1, there is only one active constraint. In Section 12.5 we will discuss what can be done, in a case like this, to obtain the exact solution algebraically.

Even when there is a series of linear equations, strange things can happen on the computer. Because only a finite number of digits can be stored on a computer, even solving five linear equations in five unknowns can lead to curious results. This area of applied mathematics is known as numerical analysis.

▼ FIGURE 12.1
Graphical Solution to the Nonlinear Model

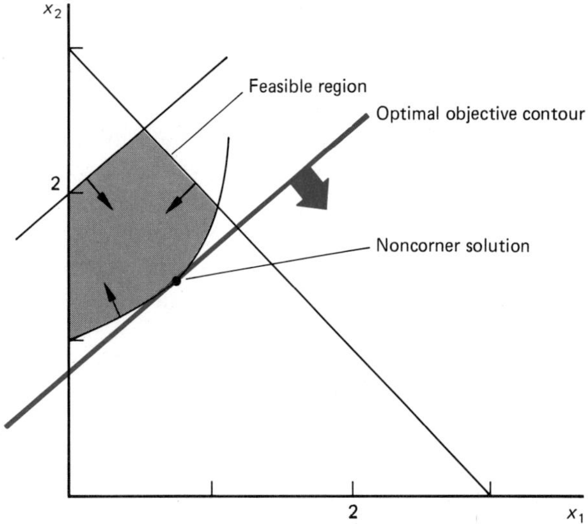

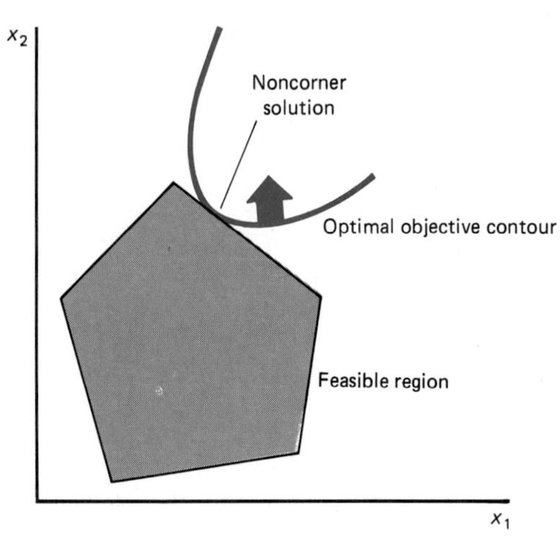

▲ FIGURE 12.2
Noncorner Solution

Noncorner Optima. Another example of an NLP is shown in Figure 12.2, which shows a *hypothetical* nonlinear inequality constrained maximization model. In this figure the constraints are all linear, and hence the constraint set is a polyhedron. The objective function, however, is nonlinear, and again it is seen that the solution does not occur at a corner. In fact, for some nonlinear objective functions the optimal solution may not even lie on the boundary of the feasible region. Of course, a solution *could* appear at a corner, but the important point is that this property is not guaranteed, as it is in the linear model.

The nice thing about "corner-searching" is that there are only a finite number of corner points. Thus, always finding a better corner point guarantees that the optimum will eventually be found.

This fact has significant algorithmic implications. It means that in the nonlinear case, we cannot use a "corner-searching" method such as the simplex algorithm for finding a solution. This restriction enormously complicates the solution procedure. The topic of solution procedures will be taken up in Sections 12.5, 12.6, and 12.7.

Comparisons between LP and NLP

There are several instructive parallels between LP and NLP. For example, the following four statements hold *in either type of model.*

1. Increasing (decreasing) the RHS on a ≤ (≥) constraint loosens the constraint. This cannot contract and may expand the constraint set.
2. Increasing (decreasing) the RHS on a ≥ (≤) constraint tightens the constraint. This cannot expand and may contract the constraint set.
3. Loosening a constraint cannot hurt and may help the optimal objective value.
4. Tightening a constraint cannot help and may hurt the optimal objective value.

Another concept that is common to both LP and NLP is the notion of changes in the OV as a right-hand side changes, with all other data held fixed. In LP we defined (see Chapter 5) the *dual variable* on a specified constraint to be *the rate of change in OV as the RHS of that constraint increases,* with all other data unchanged. In the NLP context this rate of change is often called the **Lagrange multiplier** as opposed to the dual variable, but the meaning is the same.

The Lagrange Multiplier. There is, however, one important property of dual variables associated with LP that Lagrange multipliers in the NLP context will not generally share. Recall that in an LP the dual variable (or dual price) is constant for a range of value for the RHS of interest. It can be easily illustrated that in the NLP context this property does not generally hold true. As an illustration, consider the following simple NLP:

$$\text{Max } x^2$$
$$\text{s.t.} \quad x \leq b$$
$$x \geq 0$$

In order to maximize x^2, we want to make x as large as possible. Thus, the optimal solution is $x^* = b$, and the optimal value of the objective function, which we call the OV, is $(x^*)^2 = b^2$. Thus, you can see that the OV is a function of b. That is,

$$\text{OV}(b) = b^2$$

From basic calculus we know that the rate of change of this function as b increases is the derivative of OV(b), namely $2b$. In other words, the Lagrange multiplier is *not* constant for a range of values of the RHS, b. It varies continuously with b, as might be expected.[2]

Local versus Global Solutions. Another important difference between LP and NLP has to do with *global* versus *local solutions.* In an LP, it is always true that there cannot be a local solution that is not also global. This is not usually true for general nonlinear programming problems. In other words, such problems may have local as well as global solutions. This is illustrated by the hypothetical Max model in Figure 12.3. In this figure, the point identified as "Local max" is termed a *local constrained maximizer* because the value of the objective function at this point is no smaller

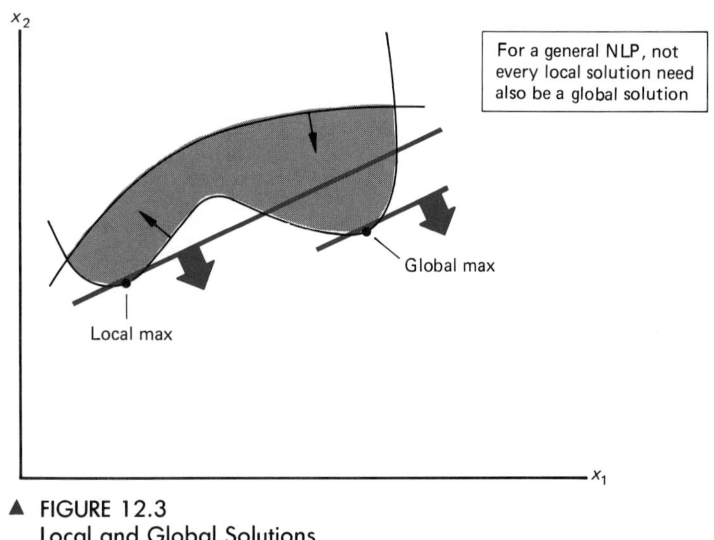

▲ FIGURE 12.3
Local and Global Solutions

than at its *neighboring* feasible points. The point identified as "Global max" is termed a *global constrained maximizer* because the value of the objective function at this point is no smaller than at *all other* feasible points. As was the case with unconstrained optimization, certain convexity and concavity conditions must be satisfied to guarantee that a local constrained optimizer is also global. These properties will be defined in Section 12.7. In the absence of these properties it is generally not possible to know whether a given solution is a local or a global maximizer.

[2]It may be briefly noted that this same example also serves to illustrate that the optimal value for an NLP *max* problem can exhibit increasing marginal returns. This can *never* happen in LP (i.e., the OV for an LP *max* model is *always* concave and hence exhibits nonincreasing marginal returns).

12.5 Equality-Constrained Models and Lagrange Multipliers

Many problems in business and economics are of the following form:

Maximize (or Minimize) $f(x_1, \ldots, x_n)$ **(P$_1$)**

s.t. $g_i(x_1, \ldots, x_n) = b_i, \quad i = 1, \ldots, m \ (m < n)$

That is, the goal is to maximize or minimize an objective function in n variables subject to a set of m $(m < n)$ *equality* constraints. Here are two examples.

Example 3. A manufacturer can make a product on either of two machines. Let x_1 denote the quantity made on machine 1, and x_2 the amount on machine 2. Let

$$a_1x_1 + b_1x_1^2 = \text{cost of producing on machine 1}$$
$$a_2x_2 + b_2x_2^2 = \text{cost of producing on machine 2}$$

Determine the values of x_1 and x_2 that minimize total cost subject to the requirement that total production is some specified value, say R. The formulation of this problem is

$$\begin{aligned} &\text{Min } a_1x_1 + b_1x_1^2 + a_2x_2 + b_2x_2^2 \\ &\text{s.t.} \quad x_1 + x_2 = R \end{aligned}$$

Example 4. Let p_1, p_2, and p_3 denote given prices of three goods, and let B denote the available budget (i.e., B is a specified constant). Let s_1, s_2, and s_3 be given constants, and let $x_1^{s1} + x_2^{s2} + x_3^{s3}$ denote the "utility derived" from consuming x_1 units of good 1, x_2 units of good 2, and x_3 units of good 3. Determine the consumption mix that maximizes utility subject to the budget constraint. The formulation of this problem is

$$\begin{aligned} &\text{Max } x_1^{s1} + x_2^{s2} + x_3^{s3} \\ &\text{s.t.} \quad p_1x_1 + p_2x_2 + p_3x_3 = B \end{aligned}$$

Even inequalities can be rewritten in the form of an equality with the addition or subtraction of a nonnegative variable (such as u^2).

In both of these examples the physical interpretations require the decision variables to be nonnegative. We shall assume that the parameters in the two models (a_i and b_i, $i = 1, 2$ in Example 2; and p_i, s_i, $i = 1, 2, 3$ and B in Example 3) are such that the optimal solutions will turn out to be nonnegative, and hence nonnegativity constraints need not be explicitly included. Such conditions, if appended, would convert the models to more difficult problems with both equality *and* inequality conditions.

The Case with Two Variables

Before analyzing the general problem (P$_1$) above, let us consider the special case of two decision variables and one equality constraint. Thus, we treat the problem as shown below.

$$\text{Max } f(x_1, x_2) \qquad (P_2)$$
$$\text{s.t. } g(x_1, x_2) = b$$

Example 5. As a particular example of (P_2), consider the problem

$$\begin{aligned} \text{Max} \quad & x_1 - x_2 \\ \text{s.t.} \quad & -x_1^2 + x_2 = 1 \end{aligned}$$

The geometric analysis is shown in Figure 12.4. This analysis shows that at the optimal solution the contour of the objective function is tangent to the equality constraint. It also suggests that the optimal solution is approximately $x_1^* = 0.5$ and $x_2^* = 1.25$. We shall now show how to solve this problem analytically. To do this, we make use of the tools of differential calculus.

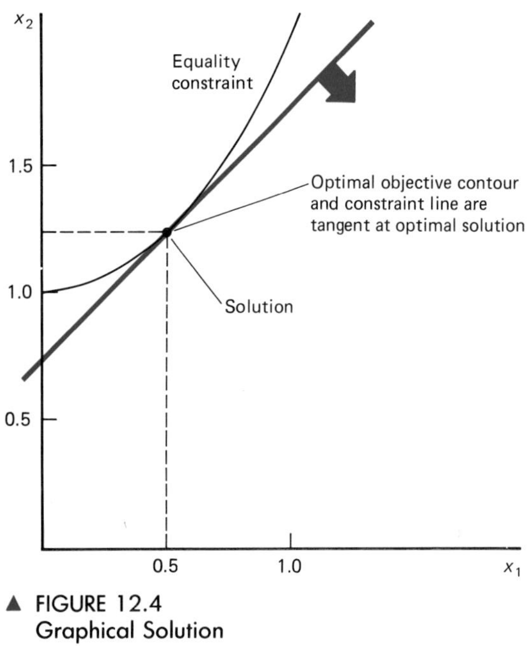

▲ FIGURE 12.4
Graphical Solution

Introducing Lagrange Multipliers. The formal solution procedure is called the *Lagrangian technique* (also called the Lagrange multiplier method). This procedure includes four steps that are specified below for (P_2).

Mathematicians love to designate functions by the Greek equivalent of the first letter in their English name. Thus, instead of using L for "Lagrangian" they use the lower case Greek L, λ.

- ***Step 1: Form Lagrangian:*** Form a *new* function called the *Lagrangian.* This function involves a new variable, which we shall denote as λ, and which is called a *Lagrange multiplier.* The function, *for a maximization model,* is

$$L(x_1, x_2, \lambda) = f(x_1, x_2) + \lambda[b - g(x_1, x_2)]$$

- ***Step 2: Take partial derivatives:*** Compute the partial derivatives of the Lagrangian with respect to x_1, x_2, and λ, and set three partial derivatives equal to zero to obtain

$$L_{x_1} = f_{x_1} - \lambda g_{x_1} = 0 \qquad \textbf{(12.1)}$$
$$L_{x_2} = f_{x_2} - \lambda g_{x_2} = 0 \qquad \textbf{(12.2)}$$
$$L_\lambda = b - g = 0 \qquad \textbf{(12.3)}$$

- **Step 3: Find all solutions:** Find the values x_1^*, x_2^*, λ^* that satisfy the equations derived in step 2. These equations are the first-order necessary optimality conditions for (P_2).
- **Step 4: Check sufficiency conditions:** For each triple (x_1^*, x_2^*, λ^*) determined in step 3, check whether x_1^*, x_2^* yields a constrained maximizer or constrained minimizer of *f.* Often this will be apparent from economic or physical considerations. Mathematically, this check can be performed as follows. Evaluate, at the point (x_1^*, x_2^*), the expression

$$D^* = -(g_{x_2})^2 L_{x_1x_1} - (g_{x_1})^2 L_{x_2x_2} + 2g_{x_1}g_{x_1}L_{x_1x_2} \quad \textbf{(12.4)}$$

If $D^* > 0$, then (x_1^*, x_2^*) is a local constrained maximizer. If $D^* < 0$, then (x_1^*, x_2^*) is a local constrained minimizer. If $D^* = 0$, no conclusion can be drawn.

Let us now apply the steps described above to Example 5, that is, to the problem

$$\text{Max } x_1 - x_2$$
$$\text{s.t.} \quad -x_1^2 + x_2 = 1$$

Implementing the Lagrangian technique

- **Step 1: Form Langrangian:** The problem is already in the form of a *Max model.* Thus, the Lagrangian is

$$L(x_1, x_2, \lambda) = f(x_1, x_2) + \lambda[b - g(x_1, x_2)] = x_1 - x_2 + \lambda(1 + x_1^2 - x_2)$$

- **Step 2: Take partial derivatives:**

$$L_{x_1} = 1 + 2\lambda x_1 = 0$$
$$L_{x_2} = -1 - \lambda = 0$$
$$L_\lambda = 1 + x_1^2 - x_2 = 0$$

- **Step 3: Find all solutions:** The unique solution to the above system of three equations in three unknowns x_1, x_2, λ is obtained by noting, from the second equation, that $\lambda^* = -1$. Substituting into the first equation and solving for x_1 gives $x_1^* = 1/2$. Then the third equation gives $x_2^* = (x_1^*)^2 + 1 = 1\frac{1}{4}$. We have thus obtained

$$\lambda^* = -1, \qquad x_1^* = \frac{1}{2}, \qquad x_2^* = \frac{5}{4}$$

For a quick check on this solution (because this is a small simple problem) we can show that

$x_2 = x_1^2 + 1.$

Substituting into the objective function gives

Maximize $x_1 - x_1^2 - 1.$

Taking the first derivative of $P(x)$ gives

$P'(x) = 1 - 2x_1 = 0.$

Thus $x_1 = 0.5$, which means $x_2 = (0.5)^2 + 1 = 1.25.$

- **Step 4: Check sufficiency conditions:**

$$D^* = [-1(2\lambda^*)] - [4(x_1^*)^2(0)] + [2(-2x_1^*)(1)(0)]$$
$$= 2$$

Since $D^* > 0$, the solution is a constrained maximizer.

Note that the solution in step 3 is consistent with that obtained in the geometric analysis of Figure 12.4.

Example 6. Let us now use the necessary conditions given previously to find the solution to a problem with more than two decision variables. Consider the problem

$$\text{Min } a_1x_1 + a_2x_2 + b_1x_1^2 + b_2x_2^2 + c_1x_1x_2 \quad \textbf{(12.5)}$$

$$\text{s.t.} \quad x_1 + x_2 = R$$

This example will illustrate how the Lagrangian technique can be used to solve a whole class of problems. In other words, we will derive an expression for the optimal values of the decision variables (x_1^*, x_2^*) in terms of the parameters (a_1, a_2, b_1, b_2, c_1, and R). Having done so, we can use these general expressions to find solutions quickly and easily for any problem that is of the general form of problem (12.5). Indeed, our next example will illustrate this fact. We now turn to problem (12.5). Since the problem is in minimization form, we first convert it to Max form as follows.

$$\text{Max} - a_1x_1 - a_2x_2 - b_1x_1^2 - b_2x_2^2 - c_1x_1x_2$$
$$\text{s.t.} \quad x_1 + x_2 = R$$

▶ ***Step 1: Form Lagrangian:*** The Lagrangian for the Max problem is

$$L(x_1, x_2, \lambda) = -a_1x_1 - a_2x_2 - b_1x_1^2 - b_2x_2^2 - c_1x_1x_2 + \lambda(R - x_1 - x_2)$$

▶ ***Step 2: Take partial derivatives:*** Taking first partial derivatives yields

$$L_{x_1} = -a_1 - 2b_1x_1 - c_1x_2 - \lambda = 0$$
$$L_{x_2} = -a_2 - 2b_2x_2 - c_1x_1 - \lambda = 0$$
$$L_\lambda = R - x_1 - x_2 = 0$$

▶ ***Step 3: Find all solutions:*** Solve for x_1^*, x_2^*, and λ^*. From the first two equations

$$a_1 + 2b_1x_1 + c_1x_2 = a_2 + 2b_2x_2 + c_1x_1$$

Thus, assuming that $2b_1 - c_1 \neq 0$,

This assumption needs to be made because ($2b_1 - c_1$) is used to divide to calculate x_1.

$$x_1(2b_1 - c_1) = (a_2 - a_1) + [x_2(2b_2 - c_1)]$$

or

$$x_1 = \frac{(a_2 - a_1) + [x_2(2b_2 - c_1)]}{(2b_1 - c_1)}$$

Substituting this expression into the third equation yields

$$R - \frac{(a_2 - a_1) + [x_2(2b_2 - c_1)]}{(2b_1 - c_1)} - x_2 = 0$$

or

$$[R(2b_1 - c_1)] - (a_2 - a_1) - [x_2(2b_2 - c_1)] - [x_2(2b_1 - c_1)] = 0$$

Thus, assuming that $b_1 + b_2 - c_1 \neq 0$,

The same type of assumption is made because ($b_1 + b_2 - c_1$) is a denominator in (18.6).

$$x_2^* = \frac{(a_1 - a_2) + [R(2b_1 - c_1)]}{2(b_1 + b_2 - c_1)} \qquad \textbf{(12.6)}$$

Once a numerical value of x_2^* is determined, the third equation easily yields

$$x_1^* = R - x_2^* \qquad \textbf{(12.7)}$$

Then the value of λ^* is obtained by substituting x_1^* into the first equation. This yields

$$\lambda^* = -a_1 - (2b_1R) + [x_2^*(2b_1 - c_1)]$$

To determine if x_1^*, x_2^* is a local maximizer, we must check the "sufficiency conditions." The first step is to evaluate the expression for D^* given in (12.4). To perform this task we first note that $g_{x_2} = 1$, $g_{x_1} = 1$, $L_{x_2x_2} = -2b_2$, $L_{x_1x_1} = -2b_1$ and $L_{x_1x_2} = -c_1$. Substituting these values into (12.4) yields

$$\begin{aligned} D^* &= -[(1)^2(-2b_1)] - [(1)^2(-2b_2)] + [2(1)(1)(-c_1)] \\ &= 2(b_1 + b_2 - c_1) \end{aligned}$$

Thus, if $b_1 + b_2 - c_1 > 0$, we know that x_1^*, x_2^* is a local maximizer of the function

$$-a_1x_1 - a_2x_2 - b_1x_1^2 - b_2x_2^2 - c_1x_1x_2$$

which means x_1^*, x_2^* is a local minimizer of

$$a_1x_1 + a\ x_2 + b_1x_1^2 + b_2x_2^2 + c_1x_1x_2$$

We will now apply these general results to a specific problem.

Example 7: Optimal Marketing Expenditures. A restaurant's average daily budget for advertising is \$100, which is to be allocated to newspaper ads and radio commercials. Suppose that we let

x_1 = average number of dollars per day spent on newspaper ads

x_2 = average number of dollars per day spent on radio commercials

In terms of these quantities, the restaurant's total annual cost of running the advertising department has been estimated to be

$$\text{cost} = C(x_1, x_2) = 20{,}000 + 20x_1^2 + x_1x_2 + 12x_2^2 - 440x_1 - 300x_2$$

Find the budget allocation that will minimize this total annual cost.

The model to be solved is

$$\begin{aligned} &\text{Min } 20{,}000 + 20x_1^2 + x_1x_2 + 12x_2^2 - 440x_1 - 300x_2 \\ &\text{s.t.} \quad x_1 + x_2 = 100 \end{aligned}$$

We first note that the first term in the objective function (20,000) is a constant that does not depend on the values of the decision variables. Thus, we can ignore it in determining the optimal value of the decision variables. We thus wish to select x_1^*, x_2^* in order to

$$\begin{aligned} &\text{Min } -440x_1 - 300x_2 + 20x_1^2 + 12x_2^2 + x_1x_2 \\ &\text{s.t.} \quad x_1 + x_2 = 100 \end{aligned}$$

Also note that $(2b_1 - c_1) = 2(20) - 1 = 39 \neq 0$ so that this is a valid solution. $\lambda^* = -1194.85$, which means that for another extra dollar of daily budget, the operating costs of the advertising department would drop by over \$1000. The optimal minimum cost is \$61,987.10.

Observe that this problem is a specific case of the general class of problems given by (12.5). It follows that we can use the general equations (12.6) and (12.7) to determine x_2^* and x_1^*, respectively. To do so we first observe that $a_1 = -440$, $a_2 = -300$, $b_1 = 20$, $b_2 = 12$, $c_1 = 1$, and $R = 100$. Thus, substituting in Equation (12.6),

$$x_2^* = \frac{(a_1 - a_2) + [R(2b_1 - c_1)]}{2(b_1 + b_2 - c_1)}$$

we obtain, after performing the indicated calculations, $x_2^* = 60.645$. Now turning to

(12.7) we obtain $x_1^* = R - x_2^* = 100 - 60.645 = 39.355$. To consider the sufficiency conditions we simply note that $b_1 + b_2 - c_1 = 31 > 0$. Thus, ($x_1^* = 60.645$, $x_2^* = 39.355$) is a local constrained minimizer of the objective function. In Problem 12-11, you are asked to argue that this is indeed a global minimizer.

The General Case

We now turn to the general equality constrained problem (P_1). In this case there are m constraints, and we introduce m new variables, one for each constraint. These m new variables are called Lagrange multipliers. After the problem is put into the maximization form, the Lagrangian function is

$$L(x_1, x_2, \ldots, x_n, \lambda) = f(x_1, \ldots, x_n) + \sum_{i=1}^{m} \lambda_i [b_i - g_i(x_i, \ldots, x_n)]$$

For problem (P_1) we can now state a *necessary condition* for $(x_1^*, \ldots, x_n^*)$ to be optimal. In order to do this, rather technical regularity conditions must be imposed on the constraint functions $g_i(x_1, \ldots, x_n)$ at the point $(x_1^*, \ldots, x_n^*)$.[3] These conditions, called a *constraint qualification,* are usually satisfied and hence are more of theoretical than practical importance. Moreover, a precise discussion of these conditions would lead well beyond the scope of this text. Therefore, as is usually done in practice, *we shall assume that a suitable regularity condition is satisfied* at $(x_1^*, \ldots, x_n^*)$. Under this assumption the following general statement can be made:

A general statement of the first-order conditions

If $(x_1^*, \ldots, x_n^*)$ is a local constrained maximizer in (P_1), then there are m numbers $\lambda_1^*, \ldots, \lambda_m^*$ such that $x_1^*, \ldots, x_n^*, \lambda_1^*, \ldots, \lambda_m^*$ are a solution to the following system of $n + m$ equations in the $n + m$ unknowns $x_1, \ldots, x_n, \lambda_1, \ldots, \lambda_m$.

$$\frac{\partial f}{\partial x_1} - \sum_{i=1}^{m} \lambda_i \frac{\partial g_i}{\partial x_1} = 0 \qquad (L_{x_1} = 0)$$

$$\frac{\partial f}{\partial x_2} - \sum_{i=1}^{m} \lambda_i \frac{\partial g_i}{\partial x_2} = 0 \qquad (L_{x_2} = 0)$$

$$\vdots \qquad\qquad \vdots$$

$$\frac{\partial f}{\partial x_n} - \sum_{i=1}^{m} \lambda_i \frac{\partial g_i}{\partial x_n} = 0 \qquad (L_{x_n} = 0)$$

$$g_1(x_1, \ldots, x_n) = b_1 \qquad (L_{\lambda_1} = 0)$$

$$g_2(x_1, \ldots, x_n) = b_2 \qquad (L_{\lambda_2} = 0)$$

$$\vdots \qquad\qquad \vdots$$

$$g_m(x_1, \ldots, x_n) = b_m \qquad (L_{\lambda_m} = 0)$$

[3]For example, it suffices to assume that the m vectors (each vector n-dimensional) $(\partial g_i/\partial x_1, \ldots, \partial g_i/\partial x_n)$, all evaluated at $(x_1^*, \ldots, x_n^*)$, are linearly independent. Although it was not explicitly mentioned, the optimality conditions for (P_2) also assume that the regularity condition holds.

This necessary condition is a direct generalization of the two-variable case, problem (P_2), discussed above. In other words, each local constrained optimizer (maximizer or minimizer) must be a solution to the system of equations obtained by setting the $n + m$ partial derivatives of the Lagrangian equal to zero.

In theory, a global solution to problem (P_1) could be obtained by finding *all solutions* to the equations above (the necessary conditions) and then finding, among those, one that produces the largest objective value. Alternatively, one could seek a local solution to (P_1) by finding *a solution* to the equations above and then applying a complicated sufficiency test to see whether that solution is a local constrained maximizer. However, it is misleading to suggest that either of these approaches is, in general, a useful practical technique to solving problems of the form (P_1). The situation is analogous to what we encountered in the unconstrained case with n variables. There we saw that, although in special cases the necessary conditions could be explicitly solved, these conditions are more typically employed as a termination criterion in computer codes. In the current context, it is also true that special-purpose computer codes exist for solving the general problem (P_1). The Lagrangian conditions are first-order necessary conditions for a point to be optimal in (P_1). Rather than solving these conditions directly, the codes take other approaches. To describe this in detail would go beyond the scope of this chapter. It suffices to say that the Lagrangian conditions provide *a termination criterion* for such codes. The point to remember is that for all NLP models it is generally true that the necessary conditions are (1) of theoretic interest (i.e., they reveal properties of the real-world model being studied) and (2) used as a termination criterion in computer codes designed to solve the problem.

For (P_1), as for most NLP models, second-order sufficiency conditions also exist. However, these are entirely of theoretic interest and too complicated to discuss in the general case.

Having now discussed the general problem with equality constraints, the next level of difficulty would be to add inequality constraints to the model to obtain the general constrained model (P_0). Necessary optimality conditions for this problem are the so-called Karush-Kuhn-Tucker conditions, of which the Lagrange multiplier conditions in step 2 above are a special case. Again, because of the introductory level of this chapter, a discussion of these conditions cannot be taken further. This is, more appropriately, a topic covered in a course on nonlinear programming.

Economic Interpretation of Lagrange Multipliers

Lagrange multipliers have an interesting and important economic interpretation. Indeed, as stated in Section 12.4, the Lagrange multipliers in NLP have the same interpretation as the dual variables in LP. In other words, the optimal value of the ith Lagrange multiplier λ_i^* is the instantaneous *rate of change* in the OV, the optimal value of the objective function, as the ith RHS, b_i, is increased, with all other data unchanged. Another way of saying this, in economic terminology, is that λ_i^* reflects the marginal value of the ith resource. Thus, the units of λ_i^* are

In fact, if the LP problem is rewritten as a Lagrangian problem then the λ's are the dual variables.

$$\frac{\text{units of objective function}}{\text{units of RHS of constraint } i}$$

Recall Example 3, where a manufacturer wished to minimize total product cost, the objective in dollars, subject to the restriction that the total production, say in tons, of two products had to equal R. The Lagrange multiplier then has units of dollars per ton, and its value is the instantaneous marginal cost of producing the Rth unit.

In order to illustrate specifically the foregoing interpretation of λ^*, for a Max model, consider again the problem posed by Example 5, which was solved with geometric analysis in Figure 12.4. In this case, however, let the parameter b denote the RHS. Thus, the problem is

$$\text{Max } x_1 - x_2$$
$$\text{s.t.} \quad -x_1^2 + x_2 = b$$

The Lagrangian is

$$x_1 - x_2 + \lambda(b + x_1^2 - x_2)$$

and the equations to be solved (for x_1, x_2 and λ) are

$$\begin{aligned} L_{x_1} &= 1 + 2\lambda x_1 &= 0 \\ L_{x_2} &= -1 - \lambda &= 0 \\ L_\lambda &= b + x_1^2 - x_2 &= 0 \end{aligned}$$

The solution is

$$\lambda^* = -1, \qquad x_1^* = \frac{1}{2}, \qquad x_2^* = b + \frac{1}{4}$$

To observe the interpretation of λ^*, we will first find an expression for the optimal value of the objective as a function of b. Let OV (b) be this function. By definition OV(b) $= x_1^* - x_2^*$. Thus, by substitution,

$$\text{OV}(b) = \tfrac{1}{2} - (b + \frac{1}{4}) = \frac{1}{4} - b$$

To determine the rate of change in OV(b) as a function of b we take the first derivative. We see that

$$\frac{d}{db}\text{OV}(b) = -1$$

But $\lambda^* = -1$, and hence, as stated above, λ^* is the rate of change in the OV with respect to b.

In concluding this section, we mention that just as is true with LP, a dual to problem (P_1) can be defined. This dual is a different optimization problem that can be expressed in only the variables $\lambda_1, \ldots, \lambda_m$, and the Lagrange multipliers will be the optimal solution to the dual problem. This topic of *nonlinear duality theory* is studied in more advanced courses in NLP.

12.6 Models with Inequality Constraints and GINO

We have seen from our study of linear programming that it is very natural to construct models with inequality constraints, the simplest of which are the nonnegativity conditions. Since the method of Lagrange multipliers assumes that all constraints are equality constraints, it cannot solve these models. Also, models that contain only equality constraints are in general very difficult to solve manually using this method. For these reasons we now examine a computer program called GINO that allows us to easily enter and solve a model that could contain a nonlinear objective or nonlinear constraint functions or both.

Using GINO

Data entry

GINO is a first cousin of LINDO, and much of what you learned about LINDO will carry over to GINO. There are, however, a number of differences between data entry in GINO and in LINDO. In LINDO "three times X" would be written as "3X," but in GINO the implied multiplication must be explicitly represented as "3*X." GINO allows division and exponentiation as well as addition, subtraction, and parenthesized expressions. For example, the expression

$$\frac{(x^3 - 5x^2 + 3x - 10)(x - 6)}{\sqrt{x^2 + 9}}$$

would be entered as

$$(X\hat{}3 - 5*X\hat{}2 + 3*X - 10)*(X - 6)/(X\hat{}2 + 9)\hat{}0.5$$

Objective function

The objective function in GINO is defined by a constraint of special form. For a maximization problem it is an equation of the form MAX = . . . ; while for a minimization problem it is an equation of the form MIN = ... An objective function is not even necessary; if one is not given, GINO will try to identify a feasible solution. So GINO can be used to test for feasibility of the constraint set or to solve systems of nonlinear equations. It is also not necessary to include any constraints, so that GINO can be used to do unconstrained optimization.

SLBs and SUBs

The end of each constraint is indicated by a semicolon, and variables may appear on both sides of the =, >, or < sign. As in LINDO, > means ≥ and < means ≤. *Nonnegativity of the variables is not assumed.* It can be required by placing a **simple lower bound (SLB)** of zero on each variable that must be nonnegative. It is also possible to put a **simple upper bound (SUB)** on a variable. Both SLBs and SUBs can be indicated without explicitly entering constraints into the model.

Dual prices

The form of the solution output is virtually identical to that of LINDO. Reduced costs and dual prices have a somewhat more restricted meaning, however, and there is no sensitivity analysis section. The dual price of a constraint is found in the column labeled PRICE. The dual price of a constraint is the *initial* (i.e., instantaneous) rate of "improvement" in the optimal value of the objective function as the RHS of the constraint is increased. A negative dual price would indicate that increasing the RHS would initially "hurt" the objective function value. *Improvement* means an increase in the objective in a Max model and a decrease in the objective in a Min model. Similarly, *hurt* means a decrease in the objective in a Max model and an increase in the objective in a Min model. However, in contrast to what we've learned about linear programming, it is not possible to say over what range of increase or decrease of the RHS the stated dual price is valid. In fact, the usual case is for the dual price to change as soon as the RHS changes, so that the allowable increase and decrease are zero. However, this does not prevent us from using the dual price to *estimate* what will happen to the optimal value if the RHS is changed.

Reduced costs

The reduced cost of a variable reported by GINO relates to the optimality of the reported solution. A negative reduced cost for a variable indicates that *increasing* the variable will *improve* the objective function. A positive reduced cost for a variable indicates that *decreasing* the variable will *improve* the objective function. If a variable is at its upper bound, the reduced cost should be nonpositive for the solution to be optimal; otherwise, decreasing the variable would improve the objective function value. If a variable is at its lower bound, the reduced cost should be nonnegative; otherwise, increasing the variable would improve the objective function. If a variable is between its upper and lower bounds, the reduced cost should be zero for the solution to be optimal.

Example 8: Astro/Cosmo Revisited. When the Astro/Cosmo problem was formulated in Chapter 2, it was assumed that the unit profit per set was constant over all feasible product mixes. Suppose that in fact more TV sets can be sold only if the selling price is reduced; that is, the company faces downward sloping demand curves for its products. Suppose further that (for relevant values of A and C) these demand curves are quantified by the following equations:

Demand equations

$$PA = .01A^2 - 1.9A + 314$$

$$PC = -.14C + 243$$

where

$$A = \text{daily production of Astros}$$
$$PA = \text{selling price of Astros}$$
$$C = \text{daily production of Cosmos}$$
$$PC = \text{selling price of Cosmos}$$

In the preceding expression, PA is the price that the company must set for Astros in order to sell all of the Astros it produces. It follows that the profit per unit now depends on the total production. If the unit cost of an Astro is \$210 and the unit cost of a Cosmo is \$230, then the total profit is

Total profit

$$\text{profit} = (PA - 210)A + (PC - 230)C$$

Even if PA were linear, the objective function would be nonlinear.

which gives us a nonlinear objective function. The complete nonlinear program is given below. Note that it contains two equality constraints defining the selling price of each product in terms of its production. One of these constraints is nonlinear. Since PA is a function of A and PC is a function of C, the objective function is also nonlinear.

Reformulated Astro/Cosmo problem

$$\begin{aligned}
&\text{Max } (PA - 210)A + (PC - 230)C \\
&\text{s.t. } PA = .01A^2 - 1.9A + 314 \\
&\qquad PC = -.14C + 243 \\
&A \le 70 && \text{(capacity of Astro line)} \\
&C \le 50 && \text{(capacity of Cosmo line)} \\
&A + 2C \le 120 && \text{(department A labor hours)} \\
&A + C \le 90 && \text{(department B labor hours)} \\
&A, PA, C, PC \ge 0
\end{aligned}$$

The GINO Solution. Figure 12.5 shows how this model would appear in GINO and gives the solution GINO obtained. Note that the slack on row 6 is zero, so that the constraint on labor hours in department A is binding. The dual price on that constraint indicates that initially the OV increases at the rate of about \$0.86 per unit of additional labor hours in department A. If we had 10 more hours available in department A, we might estimate that the objective function would increase by 10 × 0.857663, or 8.57663. However, such an estimate would be quite inaccurate, for actually increasing the RHS by 10 and resolving gives a new objective function

Department A dual price

```
MODEL:
    1) MAX = (PA - 210) * A + (PC - 230) * C;
    2) PA = 0.01 * A ^ 2 - 1.9 * A + 314;
    3) PC = - 0.14 * C + 243;
    4) A < 70;
    5) C < 50;
    6) A + 2 * C < 120;
    7) A + C < 90;
END

SLB    PA    0.000000
SLB     A    0.000000
SLB    PC    0.000000
SLB     C    0.000000

SOLUTION STATUS: OPTIMAL TO TOLERANCES. DUAL CONDITIONS: SATISFIED.

             OBJECTIVE FUNCTION VALUE

       1)        2056.273280

VARIABLE         VALUE            REDUCED COST
      PA       254.668916           0.000000
       A        39.395220           0.000026
      PC       237.357665           0.000000
       C        40.302390           0.000000

   ROW       SLACK OR SURPLUS         PRICE
       2)         0.000000          39.395220
       3)         0.000000          40.302390
       4)        30.604780           0.000000
       5)         9.697610           0.000000
       6)         0.000000           0.857663
       7)        10.302390           0.000000
```

▲ FIGURE 12.5
GINO Solution to Astro/Cosmo Problem

value of 2061.513603, an increase of only 5.240323. This illustrates the previously stated fact that in nonlinear programming dual prices reflect the initial rate of improvement in OV, and this rate may change considerably as the RHS is changed. This is true even when the RHS change is small. The initial, or marginal, information may be useful, but the bottom line is that caution should be used in extrapolating that information.

Corner not optimal

Now there can be an infinite number of possible places for the optimal solution, making finding the optimal solution very difficult.

We have learned that, in linear programming, if an optimal solution exists, some corner of the feasible region must be optimal. Figure 12.6 shows that in the preceding nonlinear model the optimal solution does not occur at a corner of the feasible region, though it is on the boundary. In fact, for different demand curves, the optimal solution may not even be on the boundary of the feasible region.

Optimality in NLPs

In LP models we have become accustomed to looking at the solution produced by LINDO and being confident that we do indeed have the optimal solution. Life is not so simple with NLPs. GINO might stop at a solution that is clearly not optimal, or it might stop at a solution that is a local rather than a global optimum. The manager and analyst must be aware of these possibilities and be prepared to take appropriate action. These ideas are illustrated in the following example.

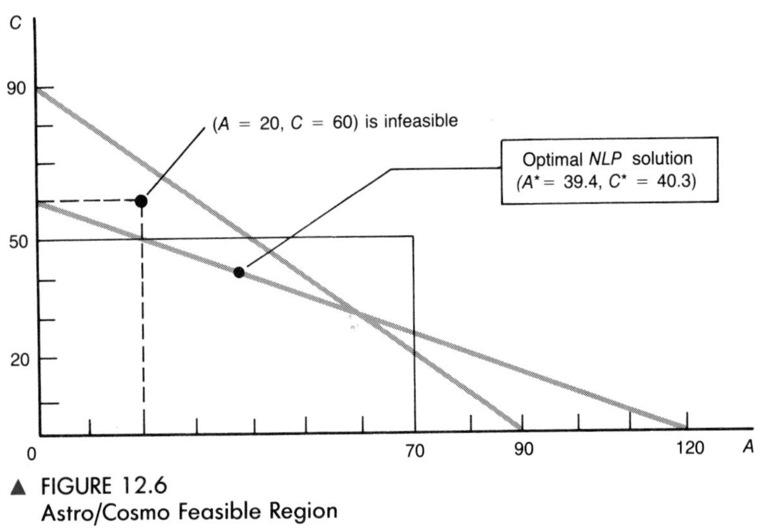

▲ FIGURE 12.6
Astro/Cosmo Feasible Region

Example 9. Example 2 of Chapter 2 is an example of a blending problem that can be formulated as a linear program. Some blending problems, however, require a nonlinear formulation. Consider the case of Gulf Coast Oil that blends gasoline from three components: Domestic Blend, Foreign Blend, and Lead Additive. Foreign Blend is itself a blending of two sources. Foreign Blend is transported monthly to Gulf Coast Oil in one 8000-gallon storage compartment of a large tanker. Because the oil purchased from the two sources loses its separate identities when "pooled" in the storage compartment of the tanker, the problem is a *pooling* problem. As we shall see, this "pooling" process is responsible for introducing nonlinearities into the model. Octane numbers, cost per gallon, and availability information for each component are given in Figure 12.7.

Oil companies have been working with various nonlinearities in gasoline-blending models for over 30 years. The usual approach is making a piece-wise linear approximation to be able to take advantage of the powerful LP algorithm.

COMPONENT	OCTANE NO.	COST PER GALLON	AVAILABILITY (gal/month)
Domestic Blend	85	0.65	10,000
Source 1	93	0.80	†
Source 2	97	0.90	†
Lead Additive	900	1.50	5,000

†Because of the way Gulf Coast Oil obtains Source 1 and Source 2 no more than 8000 gallons of Source 1 *plus* Source 2 may be obtained per month.

▲ FIGURE 12.7
Component Characteristics

The decision variables

The problem Gulf Coast Oil faces is to decide how many gallons of Regular, Unleaded, and Premium Unleaded gasoline to blend each month. Each gasoline is subject to a minimum octane requirement. The octane number of a blend is the weighted average of the octane numbers of its components where the weights are the fraction of each component in the blend. Data on minimum octane numbers and selling prices are given in Figure 12.8.

	MINIMUM OCTANE NO.	SALES PRICE PER GALLON
Regular	89	0.84
Unleaded	87	0.92
Premium Unleaded	93	1.04

▲ FIGURE 12.8
Product Characteristics

The following decision variables are used in the formulation:

R = gallons of regular gas produced

U = gallons of unleaded gas produced

P = gallons of premium gas produced

D = gallons of Domestic Blend purchased

L = gallons of Lead Additive purchased

RD = gallons of Domestic Blend in regular

RF = gallons of Foreign Blend in regular

UD = gallons of Domestic Blend in unleaded

UF = gallons of Foreign Blend in unleaded

PD = gallons of Domestic Blend in premium

PF = gallons of Foreign Blend in premium

Nonlinear pooling constraint

Taking account of the pooling nature of the problem requires three additional decision variables:

$S1$ = gallons purchased from Source 1

$S2$ = gallons purchased from Source 2

OCT = octane number of Foreign Blend

The octane number is determined by the following nonlinear equation:

$$OCT = \frac{93S1 + 97S2}{S1 + S2}$$

The trick of multiplying both sides by the denominator to obtain a linear equation no longer works.

$$OCT(S1 + S2) = 93S1 + 97S2$$

This expression is nonlinear because OCT is now a variable, and hence the left side contains a product of variables.

Nonlinear formulation of Gulf Coast Oil problem

The complete model is given below. Note that the minimum octane constraints are also nonlinear. Also note that the true decision variables are RD, RF, UD, UF, PD, PF, L, $S1$, and $S2$. All other variables can be interpreted as definitional.

$$\text{Max } .84R + .92U + 1.04P - .65D - .8S1 - .9S2 - 1.5L$$

$$
\begin{aligned}
\text{s.t.} \quad R &= RD + RF + L && \text{(composition of regular gas)}\\
U &= UD + UF && \text{(composition of unleaded gas)}\\
P &= PD + PF && \text{(composition of premium gas)}\\
D &= RD + UD + PD && \text{(total Domestic Blend used)}\\
RF + UF + PF &= S1 + S2 && \text{(uses = sources of Foreign Blend)}
\end{aligned}
$$

$$85RD + OCT^*RF + 900L \geq 89R \quad \text{(min octane number for regular)}$$

$$85UD + OCT^*UF \geq 87U \quad \text{(min octane number for unleaded)}$$

$$85PD + OCT^*PF \geq 93P \quad \text{(min octane number for premium)}$$

$$OCT(S1 + S2) = 93S1 + 97S2 \quad \text{(pooling constraint)}$$

$$S1 + S2 \leq 8000 \quad \text{(tank capacity)}$$

$$D \leq 10{,}000 \quad \text{(supply of Domestic Blend)}$$

$$L \leq 5000 \quad \text{(supply of Lead Additive)}$$

These are the nonlinear aspects of the problem

All variables are nonnegative.

The GINO Solution. The GINO formulation is shown in Figure 12.9. The nonnegativity of the variables is handled by the SLB statements. The supply limits on Domestic Blend and Lead Additive are handled by the SUBs on D and L. Since the octane number of Foreign Blend is a weighted average of 93 and 97, we know ahead of time that the octane number cannot be lower than 93 or higher than 97. This information is also passed to GINO with the SLB and SUB statements.

The solution found by GINO is given in Figure 12.10. GINO reports that the

▼ FIGURE 12.9
Product Mix/Blending/Pooling Problem

```
MODEL:
     1)  MAX = 0.84 * R + 0.92 * U + 1.04 * P - 0.65 * D
          - 0.8 * S1 - 0.9 * S2 - 1.5 * L;
     2)  R = RD + RF + L;
     3)  U = UD + UF;
     4)  P = PD + PF;
     5)  D = RD + UD + PD;
     6)  RF + UF + PF = S1 + S2;
     7)  85 * RD + OCT * RF + 900 * L > 89 * R;
     8)  85 * UD + OCT * UF > 87 * U;
     9)  85 * PD + OCT * PF > 93 * P;
    10)  OCT * (S1 + S2) = 93 * S1 + 97 * S2;
    11)  S1 + S2 < 8000;
END

SUB      D      10000.000000
SLB     S1          0.000000
SLB     S2          0.000000
SLB      L          0.000000
SUB      L       5000.000000
SLB     RD          0.000000
SLB     RF          0.000000
SLB     UD          0.000000
SLB     UF          0.000000
SLB     PD          0.000000
SLB     PF          0.000000
SLB    OCT         93.000000
SUB    OCT         97.000000
```

```
SOLUTION STATUS: OPTIMAL TO TOLERANCES. DUAL CONDITIONS: UNSATISFIED

           OBJECTIVE FUNCTION VALUE

      1)          0.019753

VARIABLE        VALUE            REDUCED COST
       R      3.265432               0.000000
       U      2.006173               0.000000
       P      0.685185               0.000000
       D      2.666666               0.000000
      S1      1.981481               0.000000
      S2      0.000000       337769901.448480
       L      1.308642               0.660000
      RD      1.320988              -0.190000
      RF      0.635802               0.200000
      UD      1.345679              -0.270000
      UF      0.660494               0.120000
      PD      0.000000               0.000000
      PF      0.685185               0.000000
     OCT     93.000000     -167321187.115828

ROW     SLACK OR SURPLUS            PRICE
 2)          0.000000               0.840000
 3)          0.000000               0.920000
 4)          0.000000              -3.493750
 5)          0.000000              -0.650000
 6)          0.000000               1.040000
 7)       1058.567781               0.000000
 8)          1.271605               0.000000
 9)          0.000000              -0.048750
10)          0.000000       -84442475.397120
11)       7998.018519               0.000000
```

▲ FIGURE 12.10
Solution with Poor Guess

solution is "optimal to tolerances" but that the dual conditions are "unsatisfied." This is a tipoff that the solution may not be optimal. A profit of less than \$0.02 confirms the suspicion that the reported solution is not optimal, for a feasible solution is to buy 8000 gallons from Source 1 and sell it as regular gas for a net profit of (.84 − .8)(8000) = \$320, and hence the optimal solution must have an OV of at least 320.

Use of an Initial Guess

Guessing all zeros to start an LP model is not great either, but at least the computer code will find the optimum solution, even though it may take much longer. Professional codes will allow the user to specify a starting point other than all zeros.

When GINO solves a problem, it requires an initial guess of the optimal solution (this initial guess is the starting point for the algorithm). If none is specified, GINO guesses the value of 0 for all variables and tries to find a better solution starting at that initial guess. Because of the form of the nonlinear constraints, this particular problem is called a *nonconcave program.* As we will see in the next section, the starting point for the algorithm can be quite important for this class of problem, and several different starting points may be required to find a "good" solution. Guessing all zeros is usually a very poor choice of an initial point—the output in Figure 12.10 resulted from such an initial guess. The solution in Figure 12.11 was found by guessing initial values of $S1$ and $S2$ of 4000. This is done by using the GUES command:

```
SOLUTION STATUS: OPTIMAL TO TOLERANCES. DUAL CONDITIONS: SATISFIED

        OBJECTIVE FUNCTION VALUE

        1)        4220.000188

VARIABLE          VALUE          REDUCED COST
       R         0.000000           0.000000
       U     13333.333333           0.000000
       P      4666.666667           0.000000
       D     10000.000000          -0.230000
      S1      8000.000000           0.000000
      S2         0.000000           0.020000
       L         0.000000           0.000000
      RD         0.000000           0.043255
      RF         0.000000           0.196745
      UD     10000.000000           0.000000
      UF      3333.333333           0.000000
      PD         0.000000           0.000000
      PF      4666.666667           0.000000
     OCT        93.000000           0.000000

 ROW    SLACK OR SURPLUS        PRICE
  2)         0.000000         0.767571
  3)         0.000000        -0.819999
  4)         0.000000        -0.819998
  5)         0.000000        -0.650000
  6)         0.000000         1.040000
  7)         0.000000        -0.000814
  8)         0.000000        -0.020000
  9)         0.000000        -0.020000
 10)         0.000000         0.020000
 11)         0.000000         0.240000
```

▲ FIGURE 12.11
Solution with Improved Guess

```
GUES S1 4000
GUES S2 4000
```

A good initial guess is extremely important in NLP and can be derived from information about the actual situation being modeled.

This solution looks much more reasonable. GINO reports that the dual conditions are now "satisfied," which means that the necessary conditions for a local optimum are satisfied. But it would be prudent to explore different initial guesses, because there may be local optima (discussed in the next section), and the solution GINO has found may not be the global optimum. As we will see, there is a "nice" class of nonlinear programming problems, called *concave* or *convex* programs, where we do not need to worry about a starting point. For this class of problems, the algorithm finds the desired solution, no matter where it starts.

12.7 Different Types of NLP Problems and Solvability

The algorithms for solving general NLP problems are markedly different from the simplex approach. In LP we saw that for a problem that has an optimal solution, we could always be assured that there would in fact be at least one optimal corner solution. This is a critically important characteristic of LP models, for the corners of the feasible region can be defined by linear equations in such a way that a simple algebraic operation allows us to move from one corner to any adjacent corner at which the objective value either improves or remains at the same value. Using this technique, the simplex algorithm provides a fail-safe method for attacking LP problems. None of these comments apply to the general NLP problem (P_0), or even to the special case (P_1) involving only equality constraints.

In contrast to the LP case, there is not a single preferred algorithm for solving nonlinear programs. Without difficulty one can easily find 10 to 15 methods in the literature. However, three classes of algorithms currently seem to be most useful in solving general nonlinear programs: GRG (generalized reduced gradient), SLP (successive linear programming), and SQP (successive quadratic programming). (GINO is an example of a program that uses an algorithm in the GRG class.) But nonlinear programming is a very broad topic, and many interesting special types of problems are identified in the literature. Indeed, many of the solution methods found in the literature are designed to solve special types of NLP problems. For example, some algorithms are designed exclusively for quadratic programming problems, others for problems that are "mostly" linear with the nonlinear terms entering the objective function or constraints in special ways.

Rather than confronting you with a compendium of the numerous types of algorithms for solving NLP problems, we shall give a brief description of a few major classes of nonlinear programs that one might encounter in practical applications. That is, we can "break down" this very general class of problems into more special cases, defined by the nature of the objective function and the constraint functions, and then discuss how easily solvable these special cases are. Indeed, from the managerial perspective these are important issues: to know what type of NLP one may be facing, and the prospects for finding a solution. It will be seen that these prospects are heavily dependent on the type of problem one faces.

We might begin this overview with the observation that nonlinear models are divided into two classes: (1) those that can be solved and (2) those that one can try to solve. The models that can be solved must typically conform to certain qualifications of structure and size. The hierarchy of increasing computational difficulty is shown in Figure 12.12. In this figure, the increasing Roman numerals reflect increasing computational difficulty. Let us now consider these several classes of nonlinear programs in somewhat more detail.

▼ FIGURE 12.12
Increasing Computational Difficulty

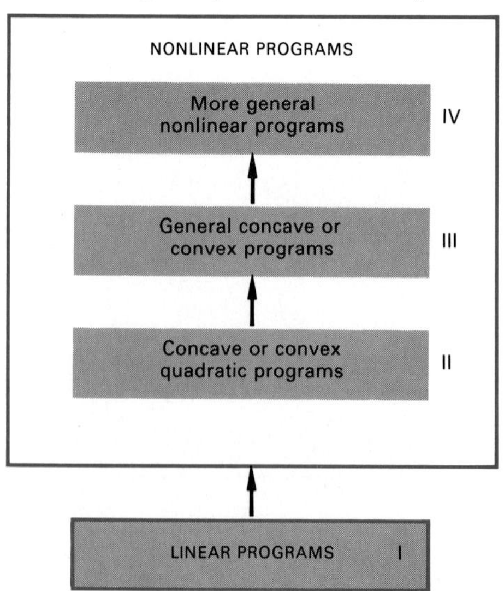

Nonlinear Programs That Can Be Solved: Concave and Convex Programs

To define these problems it is necessary to introduce a new technical term, a **convex set of points.** Loosely speaking, this is a set of points without any "holes" or "indentations." More formally, a convex set is any set that has the following property:

> **Consider all possible pairs of points in the set, and consider the line segment connecting any such pair. All such line segments must lie entirely within the set.**

Figure 12.13 shows two-dimensional sets of points that do not satisfy this property and hence are *not* convex sets, together with sets that are convex. The polygon in the first of these two figures may remind you of the constraint sets that occur in LP problems. This is appropriate since any constraint set for a linear program is a convex set. *The nonlinear programs that we can be reasonably sure of solving must also have convex constraint sets.*

NLP problems may have optimal solutions that are not found at the corner points even of sets that are convex. They may be on a boundary line or at an interior point.

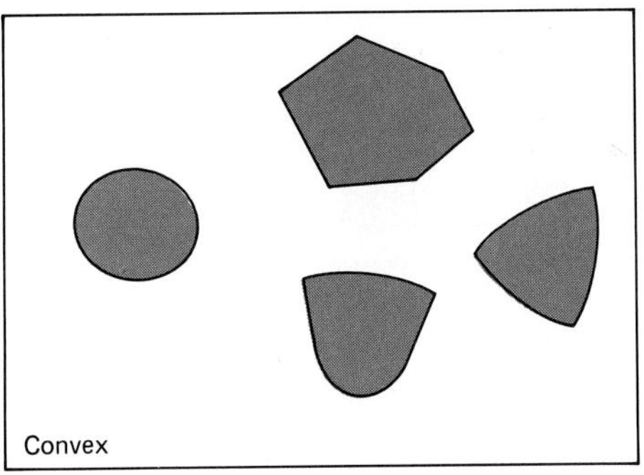

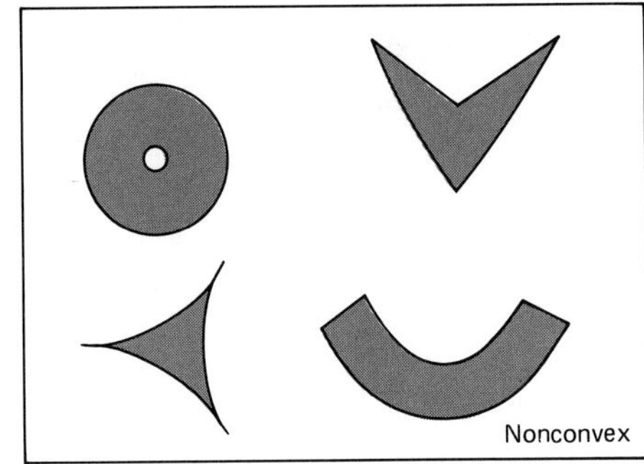

▲ FIGURE 12.13
Convex and Nonconvex Sets of Points

Concave and Convex Functions. The next question to be asked then is: What kinds of nonlinear programs have convex constraint sets? It is useful to be able to use the notion of concave and convex functions in answering this question. If the function has two independent variables, a *concave function* is shaped like an upside-down bowl. In general, a concave function, by definition, has the property that the line segment connecting any two points on the graph of the function never enters the space above the graph (if it always lies strictly under the graph then the function is *strictly concave*). Similarly, if the function has two variables, a *convex function* is shaped like a bowl. In general, a convex function, by definition, has the property that the line segment connecting any two points on the graph of the function never enters the space below the graph (if it always lies strictly above the graph then the function is *strictly convex*). The same ideas hold for functions that have a single variable, or more than two variables. It should also be remarked that a linear function is considered to be both concave and convex (the above mentioned line segments always lie in the graph).

Now suppose that we have a nonlinear program with only inequality constraints.

If the constraint function associated with each ≤ constraint is convex and the constraint function associated with each ≥ constraint is concave, the constraint set will be a convex set.

These facts are illustrated in Figure 12.14, which shows a convex function g of a single variable, given by $g(x) = x^2 + 1$. You can see that the set of x values for which $g(x) \leq 2$ is convex (i.e., this is the set $-1 \leq x \leq 1$), whereas the set of x values for which $g(x) \geq 2$ is not convex (i.e., this is the set $x \leq -1, x \geq 1$). This set is not convex because it is possible to find two points in the set (say, $x = +2$ and $x = -2$) such that the straight line that connects them passes through points (e.g., the point $x = 0$) that are not in the set.

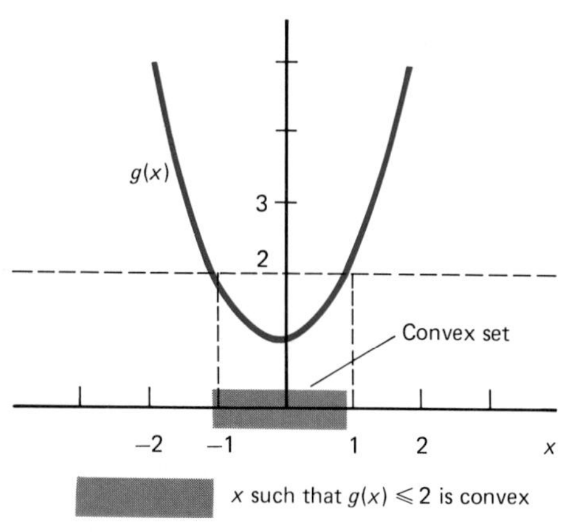

▲ FIGURE 12.14
Constraint Sets $g(x) \leq 2$ and $g(x) \geq 2$

Thus, we see that in this example $g(x)$ is convex and the set defined by the inequality $g(x) \leq 2$ is convex, whereas the set defined by the inequality $g(x) \geq 2$ is not convex. A similar demonstration could be constructed to show that if $g(x)$ is concave, then the set defined by the inequality $g(x) \geq 2$ is convex, whereas the set defined by the inequality $g(x) \leq 2$ is not convex (this is related to the fact that the negative of a concave function is convex and vice-versa). We thus have a test at our disposal that will enable us to verify that certain NLPs have a convex constraint set. This test certainly will not enable us to determine if the constraint set for *any* NLP is convex or not. In particular, in the case of problems involving one or more *nonlinear equality* constraints, there is great difficulty in characterizing whether or not the constraint set is convex. Concerning the discussion in this subsection, it is worth noting that the term *concave* applies only to functions, whereas the term *convex* can apply either to a function or to a set of points, depending on the context.

Now that you understand the meaning of a convex set, it is easy, at least formally, to define a concave or convex program.

- A **concave program** is a Max model with a concave objective function and a convex constraint set.
- A **convex program** is a Min model with a convex objective function and a convex constraint set.

The rationale for this characterization has to do with the fact that in the maximization context, just as in elementary calculus with one variable, concave objective functions are very convenient to work with in terms of the mathematical properties associated with the upside-down bowl shape. Convex objective functions (bowl-shaped) are convenient in the minimization context. Finally, the convexity of the constraint set endows the problem with other attractive mathematical properties that can be exploited both theoretically and computationally. A most important characteristic of concave (or convex) programming problems is that for such problems *any local constrained optimizer is a global constrained optimizer.* This fact has obvious computational implications.

Convexity and global optima

Karmarkar (1987) of AT&T's Bell Labs developed an ingenious way of quickly solving a certain set of LP problems by turning each of them into a convex problem. Then, using gradient search to "cut across" the feasible convex set, the solution arrives close to the optimal corner point (which is found by using LP). This algorithm has proven 10 to 100 times faster on certain kinds of LP problems.

Solution Procedures. Figure 12.12 indicates that the easiest nonlinear programs are concave or convex quadratic programs. These problems, by definition, have linear (equality or inequality) constraints. The objective function must be quadratic and concave if it is a Max model and quadratic and convex if it is a Min model. It turns out that a variation of the simplex method can be used to solve such problems, and in practice this is reasonably efficient. It is not uncommon to solve quadratic programs with hundreds of constraints and several thousand variables. As we have seen in Chapter 8, financial models such as those used in portfolio analysis are often quadratic programs, so this class of models is of some applied importance.

In Figure 12.12 the next level of difficulty involves general (nonquadratic) concave or convex programs. There are numerous mathematical approaches and corresponding algorithms for solving such problems. For example, suppose that the problem to be solved is a Max model. One typical approach proceeds as follows:

1. Find an initial feasible point "inside" the constraint set (not on the boundary).
2. Find an uphill direction and move along this straight line until either reaching a maximum along the line or hitting some boundary of the constraint set.
3. Modify the direction of motion so as to continue uphill while remaining in the feasible region.
4. Terminate the algorithm when a point satisfying the necessary optimality conditions is found.

Termination may also take place when the analyst runs out of time and/or money.

In this type of algorithm, as well as most others that apply to nonlinear programs that are not quadratic, there is considerable use of advanced calculus, and hence it is not possible in this development to go into much detail. Suffice it to say that *for general concave or convex programs, as opposed to linear programs, the number of nonlinear variables (i.e., those that enter into the problem nonlinearly) seems to be more significant than the number of constraints as an indicator of problem difficulty.*

Nonlinear Programs That We Try to Solve

Finally, we consider the highest level of difficulty in Figure 12.12, general nonlinear programs. These problems are often called *highly nonlinear,* which usually means that the convexity and concavity properties discussed above are absent. To attack such problems, it is common practice to use the same algorithm one would use for general concave and convex programs. The results are different, however. Any NLP algorithm will generally terminate at a point at which the necessary (i.e., first-order) optimality conditions are satisfied. For a concave or convex program, such a point is guaranteed to be a global optimizer (indeed, if the objective function is *strictly* concave, or *strictly* convex, we are guaranteed that such a point is a *unique* global optimizer). But for general nonlinear programs this need not be true, as illustrated for a problem in one variable in Figure 12.15. The objective function f, which is to be maximized, is neither concave nor convex. The solution to the problem is given by x^*, but the algorithm may terminate at any of the points x_1, x_2, x_3, or x^* (for they will satisfy the necessary conditions). To date, no one has been smart enough to invent algorithms that guarantee complete immunity from this possibility.

Absence of convexity

In practice, this difficulty is usually overcome by starting the algorithm at several different initial points. For example, if the initial guess is somewhat larger than x_3 in Figure 12.15, any reasonable algorithm would converge to x^*. If x_1 had also been obtained by some other initial guess, it would now be rejected, because

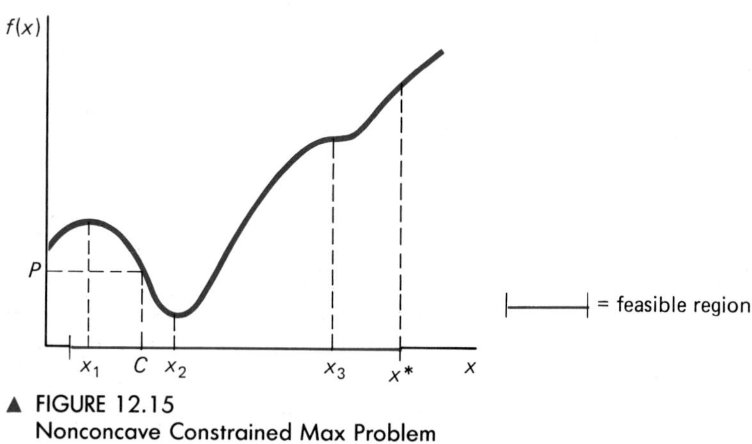

▲ FIGURE 12.15
Nonconcave Constrained Max Problem

although we may not know with certainty that x^* is optimal, we would see that the objective value at x_1 is lower than that at x^*. While the procedure of starting at different points does not guarantee that the global optimum will be found, it has a very practical justification. If the algorithm can produce a *better* solution than is currently being used, then the use of the algorithm might well be justified. This is consistent with the overall theme that in practice there is nothing so pure as a truly optimal solution. *The goal in quantitative modeling is always to assist in the search for better decisions. The general considerations are the cost of improvement (the cost of the modeling effort and obtaining the solution) versus the benefit rendered by the solution.*

In concluding, let us address one additional practical aspect. How can we tell whether a nonlinear program in many variables is concave, convex, or neither? In other words, how do we know whether the objective function and the constraints have the right mathematical form? There are several answers to this question:

1. Sometimes, there are mathematical tests that can be applied to the problem functions to determine whether they are concave, convex, or neither.
2. Sometimes, economic intuition is used to assert that such-and-such a phenomenon reflects diminishing marginal returns or increasing marginal costs, and hence the associated function is concave or convex.
3. In many real problems nothing is done to address the question. One simply attempts to solve the problem and then inquires as to the practical usefulness of the terminal point (the purported "solution" produced by the algorithm). As stated above, for a problem that is thought or known to be nonconvex or nonconcave, one frequently restarts the algorithm from a different initial point, to explore the possibility of producing a better terminal point.

▶ 12.8 Notes on Implementation

The practice of nonlinear programming is in some ways even more of an art than the practice of LP. Concerning LP, almost every computer library will have as part of its standard repertoire an LP software package. Also, all LP codes are, in major respects, the same, since they are variants of the simplex method. Nonlinear programming codes are harder to come by. They are generally not a standard part of computer libraries. Moreover, it would not be difficult to identify as many as 10 or 15 quite different algorithmic procedures for solving NLP problems. To find the best method for a given problem, indeed even to understand the differences between various approaches, the user, at least in this respect, must be more of an expert with mathematics. Another delicate aspect of NLP practice is the existence, from a

Most companies experience "classes" of problems, wherein only a few of the coefficients change. They will use every known algorithm to try to find the optimal solution to one of these, and then settle on two or three algorithms to continually solve the problems on a periodic basis.

mathematical viewpoint, of so many different types of nonlinear problems with different theoretical properties (whereas there is only one type of LP). Associated with this fact is the need to reckon with the issue of local versus global solutions to the model. The user must know enough about the mathematical structure of his or her model to have at least a feeling for the quality of the solution (e.g., local versus global) produced by the code, and often he or she must experiment in order to locate improved solutions.

Although most NLP codes will print out dual prices (i.e., the optimal values of the Lagrange multipliers) along with the solution, additional sensitivity analysis is generally not available. Thus, from the manager's point of view, the NLP output contains less information than an LP output provides.

There are now a number of mainframe codes for medium-sized and large-scale problems, as well as PC codes for medium-sized problems (up to 100 variables). Some mainframe codes are GRG2, SOL/NPSOL for medium-sized problems and MINOS 5.0 for large-scale problems. GAMS/MINOS is a PC program that contains a modeling system (GAMS) as well as a PC implementation of MINOS. Some users of this system have reported solving problems with 200 to 300 constraints.

Although NLP applies to a wide spectrum of problems, the most common applications probably occur in situations where the model has special structure. For example, there may be linear constraints but a nonlinear objective function, and so on. In such cases there is hope of solving reasonably large-scale models—provided that the code makes efficient use of the problem's special structure.

What do we mean by "large-scale" in NLP? Again, this is much less clearly defined than it is for LP. For a concave or convex quadratic program, we can aspire to several thousand constraints and unlimited variables. This power derives from the fact that for such a model a variant of the simplex method is employed. However, for more general nonlinear problems, without special structure that is used to advantage, one would consider a problem with more than 100 variables to be large.

As a final note, NLP applications are probably clustered in such areas as financial analysis and portfolio optimization, engineering design, nonlinear estimation, electrical power transmission, physical applications such as oil drilling, and finally, optimal scheduling and equipment utilization when nonlinear costs are involved.

Key Terms

Stationary Point. A point at which all first partial derivatives vanish. (*p. 512*)

First-Order Optimality Conditions. Necessary conditions for the existence of an optimum; all partial derivatives must equal zero. (*p. 515*)

Second-Order Optimality Conditions. Sufficient conditions for the existence of an optimum. (*p. 515*)

Nonlinear Program. A mathematical programming problem in which at least one of the constraint functions or the objective function or both are nonlinear. (*p. 517*)

Lagrange Multiplier. Associated with a constraint, it is the rate of change in the optimal value of the objective function as the RHS of that constraint increases. Called *dual variable* in LP problems (see Chapter 5). (*p. 518*)

Simple Lower Bound (SLB). A constraint that a decision variable must be greater than or equal to a specified number. (*p. 528*)

Simple Upper Bound (SUB). A constraint that a decision variable must be less than or equal to a specified number. (*p. 528*)

Convex Set of Points. A set of points such that for all possible pairs of points in the set, the lone segment connecting any such pair must lie entirely within the set. (*p. 537*)

Concave Program. A Max model with a concave objective function and a convex constraint set. (*p. 538*)

Convex Program. A Min model with a convex objective function and a convex constraint set. (*p. 538*)

Major Concepts Quiz

True–False

1. T F Economy of scale is a nonlinear relationship.

2. T F An applied problem involving a nonlinear relationship cannot be modeled as an LP.

3. T F If the necessary conditions for a local max occur, a local max occurs.

4. T F If a local min occurs, the necessary conditions for a local min occur.

5. T F If a local min is a global min, it is the only point where the sufficient conditions for a local min hold.

6. T F A straight line is neither a concave nor a convex function.

7. T F In an NLP or an LP, tightening a constraint cannot help and it might hurt.

8. T F For a max model, a Lagrange multiplier has the same interpretation as the dual price that appears on the computer output for LP problems earlier in the text, although in general it is not constant over an RHS interval.

9. T F A quadratic programming problem is always a special type of concave programming problem.

10. T F An NLP is always either a concave or a convex programming problem.

11. T F The constraint set defined by the following inequalities is convex.

$$9x + 4y \le 36$$
$$4x + 12y \le 20$$

12. T F In practice, to find a local max of a function of several variables, one first finds all stationary points. One then applies second-order tests to these points.

13. T F Although nonlinear programs are more difficult than LPs, in terms of finding an optimal solution it is nevertheless true that a corner-searching technique can be applied.

14. T F One problem in NLP is distinguishing between local and global solutions.

Multiple Choice

15. Suppose that f is a function of a single variable. The condition $f''(x^*) > 0$
  a. is a necessary condition for a local min
  b. is a sufficient condition for a local min
  c. is a sufficient condition for a local max
  d. none of the above

16. Suppose that f is a function of a single variable. The condition $f'(x^*) = 0$ is
  a. a necessary condition for x^* to be a local max
  b. a necessary condition for x^* to be a local min
  c. a necessary condition for x^* to be a global min
  d. all of the above

17. In nonlinear models differential calculus is needed
  a. to avoid multiple (local) solutions
  b. to express optimality conditions
  c. both a and b
  d. neither a nor b

18. A point x^* with the property that $f'(x^*) = 0$ and $f''(x^*) > 0$ (where f is a function of a single variable) satisfies the sufficient conditions for x^* to be
  a. a local max
  b. a local min
  c. neither a nor b

19. Which of the following is true of a concave function?
   a. One can attempt to find a global maximizer by using a hill-climbing computer code.
   b. One can attempt to find a global maximizer by setting the first partials to zero and solving the resulting system of equations on the computer.
   c. Any local maximizer is also a global maximizer.
   d. All of the above.

20. Which of the following is true?
   a. For a general NLP, optimality conditions are directly used in solving NLP problems. That is, computer codes exist to directly solve these conditions, and this produces an NLP solution.
   b. For a general NLP, optimality conditions are indirectly used in solving NLP problems. That is, computer codes exist to directly attack the NLP, employing for example a hill-climbing approach. The optimality conditions provide a termination criterion for such algorithms.
   c. Optimality conditions are only of theoretic interest.

21. For concave programming problems
   a. the second-order conditions are more useful
   b. any local optimum is a global optimum as well
   c. both the constraint set and the objective function must be concave

22. Convexity
   a. is a description that applies both to sets of points and to functions
   b. is an important mathematical property used to guarantee that local solutions are also global
   c. is useful in unconstrained as well as constrained optimization
   d. all of the above

23. Which of the following is *not* generally true of a Lagrange multiplier?
   a. It has an economic interpretation similar to that of dual variable.
   b. It is the rate of change of OV as the RHS of a constraint is increased.
   c. It is valid (i.e., constant) over an RHS range.
   d. It enters into the first-order optimality conditions.

24. Which of the following is *not* true?
   a. Even when global solutions cannot be guaranteed, optimization can still be a useful tool in decision making.
   b. In LP, we need never worry about local solutions (i.e., every local solution is also global).
   c. Since we can only guarantee that local solutions are global when the appropriate convexity (or concavity) properties exist, these are the only types of NLP problems that yield useful information.

25. Which is true of corner point solutions in NLP?
   a. It makes no difference what objective function we have the optimal solution will always be at a corner point.
   b. We have to worry about corner points only if the objective function is linear.
   c. In general, the optimum may not be at a corner point.

Answers

1. T	**8.** T	**15.** d	**22.** d
2. F	**9.** F	**16.** d	**23.** c
3. F	**10.** F	**17.** b	**24.** c
4. T	**11.** T	**18.** b	**25.** c
5. F	**12.** F	**19.** d	
6. F	**13.** F	**20.** b	
7. T	**14.** T	**21.** b	

Problems

(a) $x^* = -7/8$
(b) negative: $f''(x^*) = -16$
(c) $x = 1$
(d) Concave, because $f'' < 0$ for all x

12-1. ▲ **(a)** Maximize the function $f(x) = -8x^2 - 14x - 32$.
(b) What is the sign of the second derivative of this function at the maximizing value of x?
(c) Maximize this function over the interval $1 \le x \le 10$.
(d) Can you tell whether this function is concave or convex?

(a) $x^* = 2$
(b) negative: $f''(x^*) = -2$
(c) $x = 3$
(d) Concave, because $f'' < 0$ for all x

12-2. ▲ **(a)** Maximize the function $f(x) = -x^2 + 4x + 6$.
(b) What is the sign of the second derivative of this function at the maximizing value of x?
(c) Maximize this function over the interval $3 \le x \le 12$.
(d) Can you tell whether this function is concave or convex?

$x^* = 25$ pounds

12-3. ▲ Lotta Crumb, manager of Crumb Baking Services, is considering the offer of a distributor who sells an instant croissant mix. The total cost of x pounds of the mix is given by

$$\text{total cost} = x^3 - 50x^2 + 2x$$

What quantity of this mix will minimize *total cost per pound?*

$x = 2, y = 2$ is a local minimizer

12-4. ▲ Find all stationary points of the function

$$f(x, y) = x^2 + 2xy + 2y^2 - 8x - 12y + 6$$

and determine whether they are local minima, local maxima, or neither.

(a) Saddle point
(b) Local maximizer
(c) Local maximizer

12-5. ▲▲ Consider the function

$$f(x_1, x_2) = -2x_1^4 + 12x_1^2 - 2x_1^2x_2 - x_2^2 + 4x_2 - 60$$

Determine whether the points below yield local minima, local maxima, or saddle points.

(a) $(x_1 = 0, x_2 = 2)$ **(b)** $(x_1 = 2, x_2 = -2)$ **(c)** $(x_1 = -2, x_2 = -2)$

$r = 1, h = 2$

12-6. ▲▲ We want to build a solid cylinder of volume 2π. If we would like to minimize the surface area of the cylinder (including both ends), what should be its radius and height? [Hint: volume $= \pi r^2 h$, surface area $= 2\pi rh + 2\pi r^2$]

(a) $a^* = -5.428$, $b^* = 47.714$
(b) $a^* = -2.000$, $b^* = 45.000$

12-7. ▲▲ *Linear Regression Analysis.* In the linear regression model, historical data points (x_i, y_i), $i = 1, \ldots, n$, are given. The linear model is an estimating equation (also called the regression line) $y = ax + b$, where a and b are chosen so as to minimize the sum of squared deviations

$$S(a, b) = \sum_{i=1}^{n} [y_i - (ax_i + b)]^2$$

(a) Use this approach to determine the estimating equation for the following data:

x	8	6	12
y	6	14	−18

(b) Use the same approach to determine the estimating equation for the following data:

x	10	12.6	14.9	17.4	20.1
y	25	20	15	10	5

(a) $x_1^* = 2, x_2^* = 3, \lambda^* = -9$
(b) 9

12-8. ▲▲ (a) Solve the following problem:

$$\text{Min } 2x_1^2 + 3x_2^2 + x_1 - 9x_2 + 16$$
$$\text{s.t. } x_1 + x_2 = 5$$

(b) For this problem, what is the rate of change of OV with respect to the RHS of the constraint?

(a) $x_1^* = 3, x_2^* = 2, \lambda^* = 6$
(b) 6

12-9. ▲▲ Consider the problem:

$$\text{Max } -3x_1^2 + 42x_1 - 3x_2^2 + 48x_2 - 339$$
$$\text{s.t. } 4x_1 + 6x_2 = 24$$

(a) Solve the problem.

(b) Estimate the change in OV if the RHS of the constraint were to increase from 24 to 25.

$x^* = 1000, y^* = 1000$

12-10. ▲▲▲ Ure industries gets a productivity of

$$f(x, y) = 2x^2y + 3xy^2 + 2y^3$$

from x units of labor and y units of capital. If labor costs \$50 per unit and capital costs \$100 per unit, how many units of labor and capital should Ure use, given that their budget is \$150,000?

Unique stationary point means global

12-11. ▲▲ Show that the solution found in the "optimal marketing expenditures" example (Section 12.5) is actually a global (as opposed to local) optimum.

f_x/f_y also $= 1/2$

12-12. ▲▲ Show that the optimum solution to question 12-10 satisfies

$$\frac{\text{Marginal productivity of labor}}{\text{Marginal productivity of capital}} = \frac{\text{Unit price of labor}}{\text{Unit price of capital}}$$

See IM

12-13. ▲▲▲ Solve Example 3 for the optimal x_i^*'s and λ^* with $s_i = \frac{1}{2}$, $i = 1, 2, 3$.

Yes; ≤ constraints convex and ≥ constraints concave

12-14. ▲▲▲ Does the following set of constraints form a convex set? Why?

$$x + y \le 20$$
$$-2x + y \ge 10$$
$$x^2 + 2x + 1 \le 100$$
$$-x^4 - 2x^2 + 60 \ge 36$$

See IM

12-15. ▲▲ Consider the function

$$f(x_1, x_2) = a_1x_1 + a_2x_2 + b_1x_1^2 + b_2x_2^2 + c_1x_1x_2 + d$$

Give a general solution to the problem of minimizing $f(x_1, x_2)$, as follows. Assume that $c_1^2 \neq 4b_1b_2$, and $c_1 \neq 0$. Solve explicitly for the optimizing value of x_2^*. Solve for x_1^* in terms of x_2^*. Express the second-order sufficiency conditions in terms of the data.

Max profit = \$466.67

12-16. ▲▲▲ *A Pooling Problem.* Two chemical products, X and Y, are made by blending three chemical inputs, A, B, and C. The inputs are contaminated by sulfur, and the outputs must meet restrictions on sulfur content. The three inputs are shipped mixed together in two tank cars. A is shipped in car 1, C is shipped in car 2, and B is shipped in car 1 and/or car 2. No more than 100 units of X and 200 units of Y may be sold. Using the data in Figure 12.16, formulate a profit-maximizing nonlinear program and solve using GINO or some other NLP software.

CHEMICAL	COST PER UNIT ($)	SULFUR CONTENT (%)
A	6	3
B	16	1
C	10	2
	SALES PRICE PER UNIT	
X	9	no more than 2.5
Y	15	no more than 1.5

▲ FIGURE 12.16

Max profit = $2864.33
PA = $248.56, A = 70
PC = $238.25, C = 20

12-17. ▲▲ *Economic Substitutes.* Suppose in the Astro/Cosmo problem of Section 12.6 that Astros and Cosmos are economic substitutes. This means that an increase in price of one causes an increase in demand for the other. More specifically, suppose that demand equations are

$$A = 1000 - 4.7PA + PC$$

$$C = 1000 + 2PA - 6.2PC$$

Reformulate the problem, and solve it using GINO or some other NLP software.

Estimated increase = $160.00; actual the same

12-18. ▲▲ Suppose in the Gulf Coast Oil problem of Section 12.6 the octane number from Source 1 varies from month to month. Reformulate the problem by introducing a new variable, $OCTS1$, the octane number of Source 1, and replacing all references to the octane number of Source 1 in the model with this variable. Add a constraint that sets $OCTS1$ equal to 93 and then solve the NLP. Using the output, *estimate* what would happen to the optimal profit if the octane number increased to 94, then actually change the octane number to 94 and resolve, comparing the actual result with your estimate. Note that what we are really doing is a sensitivity analysis on a constraint coefficient.

Video Case

Treasure Hunt

Attempting to find the SS *Central America* was truly like looking for a needle in a haystack. The ship sank more than 130 years ago (in 1857) in almost 8,000 feet (more than 1.5 miles) of water. Because the disaster occurred during a hurricane, information about the ship's location was extremely sketchy. Conditions for celestial sightings, the method of establishing position used in those days, were not exactly ideal, and Captain Herndon, who went down with the ship, was battling to save his vessel and the lives of his passengers. As a result, it was not at all clear where the ship sank.

The strategy for finding the SS *Central America* rested on two management science approaches: developing a probability map for the location of the ship and creating a search strategy based on that map.

The probability map was created in three steps.

1. Three scenarios were developed to explain the location of the ship. One scenario relied on communications from Captain Herndon and the other two were developed from the recorded experience of two rescue ships.
2. A probability map was created for each of the scenarios. These models incorporated information about the ship's position at various times, as well as the effects of current and wind. For each map, the ocean floor in the area under consideration was divided into a grid of two-mile-by-two-mile squares and the probability that the ship lay in each of the grid squares was calculated.
3. The three probability maps were combined by assigning a subjective probability that each of the individual maps was correct and calcutating the combined probabilities.

The search procedure selected was in part dictated by the technology of the sonar used to survey the ocean floor. The sonar could cover only a swath of a certain width, and worked best if the ship using it made as few changes in course as possible. Consequently, the treasure hunters devised a search plan consisting of long, straight lanes chosen to pass through the regions of highest probability. The plan took 40 days and covered approximately 1400 square miles of ocean floor.

The method worked. In the summer of 1989, the search group recovered one ton of gold bars and gold coins from the wreck. Recovery efforts continued in the summers of 1990 and 1991, yielding a number of valuable historical artifacts.

QUESTIONS

Consider the problem of locating the SS *Central America* as a nonlinear programming problem.

1. What function are you trying to maximize?
2. What role does the probability map play?
3. How does this search procedure differ from a typical search for an extreme point?
4. If you were not restricted by the sonar technology, what search procedure might you use?

PART II

Probabilistic Models

We all know the saying: Only two things are sure, death and taxes. Although it can be taken as a complaint about governments, this remark also expresses a rather fundamental view of nature and human enterprise. It suggests that most earthly phenomena include some element of uncertainty and unpredictability. The biblical Book of Ecclesiastes makes the same observation about human endeavors: "Time and chance happeneth to them all."

We respond to this fact of life in various ways. In some situations we choose to ignore the uncertainty, in others we attempt to deal with it explicitly. We have spent the last 11 chapters ignoring uncertainty. In the next six chapters we confront situations in which the level of uncertainty is too great to ignore, and we as managers must take this into account. There are many examples: The entire insurance industry is one. Others include investments in stocks, bonds, and real estate, as well as any business in which a product is created in anticipation of demand.

This part of the book is devoted to clarifying our way of thinking about uncertainty and developing methods for dealing with it in decision models. Our goal is to help you frame problems in which uncertainty plays a major role in a consistent and useful manner and to provide you with some helpful problem-solving techniques. The focus remains the same: We consider situations in which management has the opportunity to choose between several alternatives. But now the problem is complicated by the fact that we are not sure what the payoff will be for each of the alternatives.

Probability is the branch of mathematics that provides the foundation for the analysis in this part of the book. The language of probability is part of our everyday experience: Weather forecasts say that the *chance* of rain is 30%, *odds* on sporting events are quoted in the newspapers, and the government worries about the *probable* effects of the proposed tax law. Closer examination, however, often reveals considerable confusion about what such terms and statements really mean. To understand these chapters you will have to start with (or develop) an understanding of some concepts related to probability. Appendix A in the back of the book contains a brief introduction to the crucial concepts. The material in this appendix should provide an adequate background to enable you to master the material in this part of the text.

Probability is a difficult topic for many students. You may not find it hard to read these chapters and do the assignments; what is hard is making probability a part of your personal approach to problem solving. This will occur only when you come to think naturally about a *distribution* of profits or waiting times or demands and when you have convenient tools to use on real problems. Here again, computing plays an important role—especially in simulation. It is possible to simulate interesting problems using spreadsheets, and especially easy with the spreadsheet add-in @RISK. Both of these tools are discussed in the simulation chapter that opens this Part. We strongly encourage you to use this software and do the simulation exercises, which will greatly enhance the ultimate value of your study.

▶ **CHAPTER 13** **Simulation**

Simulation has been placed at the beginning of this part for two reasons. First, it is widely used to solve a variety of important problems, from scheduling the arrival of supertankers at oil refineries to evaluating risk in capacity-expansion proposals. Second, the chapter provides a detailed illustration of the issues involved in making decisions when the outcomes are uncertain. The availability of simulation routines in convenient software packages makes simulation an easy and accessible tool.

▶ **CHAPTER 14** **Decision Theory and Decision Trees**

A decision tree is a graphical method of attacking problems in which the costs and profits are determined by a sequence of decisions and random events. For example, suppose a manufacturer *decides* to build a prototype in an attempt to become the supplier of a part for a new product. She may or may not actually get the contract—a *random* (uncertain) event. *If* she does, she then must *decide* how to manufacture the part. Her profit will depend both on this decision and on the sales of the product—another *random* event. The technique used to solve a tree is based on the fact that you must know how you will act under all possible sets of future circumstances in order to decide what you will do today. Decision trees provide managers with a valuable framework for thinking intuitively about sequential decisions. They are also a useful tool for dealing with complicated problems in an organization, where the ability both to formulate a problem clearly and to communicate its essential features to other people is crucial.

▶ **CHAPTER 15** **Project Management: PERT and CPM**

A project can be thought of as a sequence of interrelated jobs or activities. PERT and CPM are two closely related techniques used to help managers control complex projects. Today, no major construction proceeds without a PERT analysis, and PERT-like methods are now required by law for those managing many government-funded projects. The fundamental approach of PERT and CPM is deterministic. However, some background in probability is needed to understand the estimation techniques and sensitivity analyses associated with these tools.

▶ **CHAPTER 16** **Inventory Models with Probabilistic Demand**

This chapter shows managers how to include uncertainty in demand in their inventory control policies. It deals with items that are always held in inventory as well as items such as fashion goods that are held for only a specific period of time. In the language of management science, it considers (r, Q) models and the newsboy problem.

▶ **CHAPTER 17** **Queuing Models**

People wait in all societies. Some, like the British, are renowned for forming polite, orderly queues; in other countries, when the bus arrives it's a free-for-all. Here we consider the mathematics of queues, an area rich in insights and potential applications, which range from determining the appropriate number of lines in a telephone receiving system to selecting the ideal number of persons to assign to a machine repair crew.

▶ **CHAPTER 18** **Forecasting**

Forecasting problems are everywhere, and they are important. City and school administrators worry about population trends; investors know that their fortunes depend on anticipating the movement of interest rates; and all businesses must be concerned about future demand for their products. This chapter provides a discussion of the issues in forecasting and an introduction to the basics of "piggyback" and "bootstrap" forecasting.

CHAPTER

13 Simulation

APPLICATION CAPSULE

Robot Riddle: Simulation Helps GM of Canada to Automate Its Auto Assembly*

General Motors of Canada has committed over $2 billion to automating its production facilities. An example of this approach is the GM assembly plant in Oshawa, Ontario. The plant is designed to produce hundreds of cars per shift, using over 600 industrial robots to perform various welding, loading, and assembly tasks. In addition, 1100 automatic guided vehicles (AGVs) will be used to transport cars and parts through various phases of assembly.

AGVs can handle a wide variety of loads, following a path selected by the user. They are controlled by a microprocessor and receive commands through a network of antennae and receivers embedded in the floor. The use of AGVs instead of the familiar conveyer belt has enabled GM to break the assembly line into small work groups, each with the ability to control its own work speed.

The implementation of such an automated, integrated assembly system is very complex. Each component must be tested first in isolation and then as part of an integrated working unit. Any changes in such a unit tend to be costly and time-consuming. It is therefore crucial to have a fast and inexpensive way of evaluating different work configurations. Simulation provides such a tool.

GM performed a simulation study to analyze one important section of the plant—the AGV body-framing system. The basic layout of this section has 100 work stations, each capable of independent operation. Only three of the 28 work stations devoted to actual processing are operated by humans. AGVs are used to deliver heavy parts to machines at each station. The finished product is a fully welded, framed auto body lacking only doors, hood, front fenders, and trunk lid.

The computer simulation investigated such questions as

- What is the system's maximum production rate? Could a reliable throughput of 525 cars/shift be achieved?
- Where could "parking" spots for idle AGVs most effectively be located to avoid bottlenecks?

- What is the sensitivity of the system to increased equipment failure or faster machine cycle time?
- How many AGVs are needed to make production quotas?

This last question was of particular importance—too few carriers starve the system, while too many choke it. Moreover, at $50,000 each, AGVs are a major cost element.

Thirteen configurations of the framing line were modeled, with the number of AGVs ranging from 54 to 79. Each configuration was simulated in 20 separate runs of an 8.5 hour shift (including breaks and lunch). The runs took only 15–20 minutes each on a PC. The study found that the maximum throughput of 630 cars was obtained using 74 AGVs. However, if the aim was simply to achieve the target figure of 525 cars, this could be realized at least 99% of the time using only 42 to 44 AGVs.

The simulation model also investigated the sensitivity of the production system to an increase in the failure rate of the three most important work stations and to changes in the cycle time of the automated processes. Neither factor was found to have a very marked effect on throughput, indicating that the system was both fairly stable and robust.

This study, which required few resources, provided valuable information to help management with an important capital budgeting decision.

*Bookbinder and Kotwa, "Modeling an AGV Automobile Body-Framing System," *Interfaces*, Vol. 17, No. 6 (Nov.–Dec.) 1987.

13.1 Introduction

Many people believe that "experience is the best teacher." Unfortunately, it is often too costly (in time or money) to obtain real experience. This dilemma provides a primary motivation for the use of simulation: to find a quick, inexpensive way to acquire the knowledge that is usually gained through experience.

The basic idea of simulation is to build an experimental device, or *simulator,* that will "act like" (simulate) the system of interest in certain important aspects in a quick, cost-effective manner.

The goal is to create an environment in which information about possible alternative actions can be obtained through experimentation. The use of simulation is fundamental to many applied experiments; for example,

- Testing of medicine on laboratory animals. Here the animal responses *simulate* human responses.
- Driving automobiles on test tracks. Here the test track *simulates* the environment the auto will face.
- Testing wing designs for airplanes in wind tunnels. The wind tunnel *simulates* flight conditions.
- Training airline pilots in actual cabins with *simulated* out-of-the-window displays under *simulated* conditions.

In the context of quantitative analysis, simulation has come to mean experimentation based on a mathematical model. Although simulation and optimization

Simulation versus optimization

(e.g., by means of LP) both use quantitative models, they are based on very different concepts. The fundamental difference lies in the role of decision variables in the two approaches.

- **In an optimization model the values of the decision variables are *outputs.* That is, the model provides a set of values for the decision variables that maximizes (or minimizes) the value of the objective function.**
- **In a *simulation model* the values of the decision variables are *inputs.* The model evaluates the objective function for a particular set of values.**

To see what this means, consider the following example. Suppose that a supermarket wants to decide how to assign checkout personnel (checkers and baggers) during the weekend. The goal is to minimize labor cost, subject to the restrictions imposed by the labor contract and the constraint that customers should not have to wait too long.

If we had an optimization model, we would need to supply the model parameters. Perhaps these would be quantities such as the arrival rate of customers, the distribution of time it takes to check out a customer with and without the use of a bagger, and so on. When the model was solved, the answer would include the best way to assign personnel, the corresponding value of the objective function (the total cost), and an indication as to whether there was slack in any of the constraints. We have seen this approach many times in the mathematical programming sections of this text.

Simulation is usually "trial and error," allowing for a lot of experimentation and interaction with the modeler, but it will not necessarily optimize the goal of interest. The simulator is usually a much cheaper and/or faster way to experiment with many factors of interest.

In a simulation model, the inputs would include the parameters we described above (customer arrival rates and the like), an expression for the objective function (total costs), and *a possible assignment of personnel.* The model would produce a specific set of results showing how well the solution performed by various measures, such as total cost, customer waiting time, staff utilization, and so on. In general, the model measures the *quality* of the suggested solution.

When Should Simulation Be Used?

From this brief description, it seems as if no one would ever want to use a simulation model. Why not use a model that always yields the best answer, that is, an optimization model? Indeed, in the past simulation was often seen as the technique of last resort, to be used only when analytical methods failed. It is true that if an analytical model is available, exact results can be obtained quickly, and often an optimizing procedure can be used to determine the optimal results. However, simulation today is one of the most frequently used tools of quantitative analysis. Why are simulation models so popular?

1. First, analytical models may be difficult or impossible to obtain, depending on complicating factors. What a complicating factor is depends on the specific problem. Complicating factors for queuing models are nonexponential random variables, while complicating factors for inventory models are multiple stocking points or locations.

2. Analytical models typically predict only average or "steady-state" (long-run) behavior. In real-world problems, however, it is often important to understand the possible variability in the performance measures, or how the performance measures vary in the short run.

It is usually *cheaper* to build a mathematical and/or computer model than to change the physical characteristics of a system that has complex interactions. It is also *faster* to make these changes in the model than in physical reality. But it should be kept in mind that:
1. Simulation models are *simplifications* of reality.
2. Even optimal answers to simulation models may not be optimal in the physical reality.

3. Simulation can be performed with a great variety of software, from general computer programming languages (BASIC, FORTRAN) to special purpose simulation languages (GPSS) to spreadsheets (Lotus 1-2-3). As simulation models can now be created and run on a PC or a workstation, the level of computing and mathematical skill required to design and run a useful simulator has been substantially reduced. It is now quite reasonable to build and use a simulator even when it is clear that an analytic (optimization) model could be constructed with more time and effort.

The ability of simulation models to deal with complexity, capture the variability of performance measures, and reproduce short-run behavior make simulation a powerful tool.

Simulation and Random Variables

Simulation models are often used to analyze a *decision under risk*—that is, a problem in which the behavior of one or more factors is not known with certainty. There are many examples: demand for a product during the next month, the return on an investment, the number of trucks that will arrive to be unloaded tomorrow between 8:00 and 9:00 A.M. and so on. In such cases the factor that is not known with certainty is thought of as a **random variable.** The behavior of a random variable is described by a **probability distribution.** (Perhaps at this point we should remind you that we assume some knowledge of probability theory in this section of the book. The basic information you will need, including the definition of a probability distribution and some examples, is contained in Appendix A.) This type of simulation is sometimes called a **Monte Carlo method,** after the roulette wheels in Monte Carlo, which can be seen as devices for generating uncertain or random events. Let us look at several examples of this approach.

If all the numbers corresponded to possible random happenings (all equally likely), then by spinning the wheel you could simulate the occurrence of an event without bias.

Design of Docking Facilities. A typical problem is illustrated in Figure 13.1. Here trucks, perhaps of various sizes carrying different types of loads, arrive at a warehouse to be unloaded. The uncertainties are when a truck will arrive, what kind and size of load it will be carrying, and how long it will take to unload. In modeling these uncertainties, each uncertain quantity would be a random variable characterized by a probability distribution.

▼ FIGURE 13.1
Truck Docking Problem

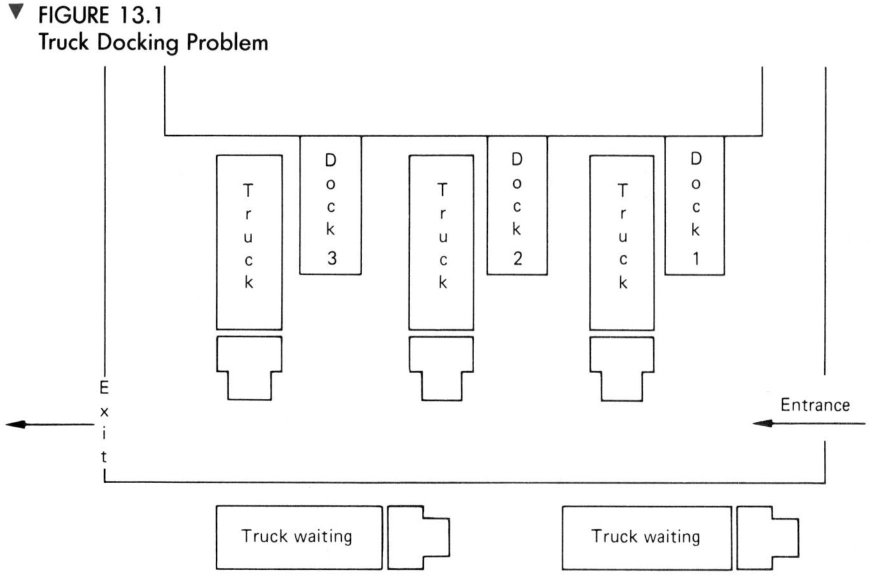

Here planners must address a variety of design questions:

- How many docks should be built?
- What type and quantity of material-handling equipment are required?
- How many workers are required over what periods of time?

The design of the unloading dock will affect its cost of construction and operation. This cost can be reduced by building fewer docks, buying less material-handling equipment, and hiring fewer personnel. However, these options will increase the amount of time it takes to unload the trucks and the amount of time a truck has to wait before unloading begins. Management must balance the cost of acquiring and using the various resources against the cost of having trucks wait to be unloaded.

A similar problem of designing docking facilities for oil tankers is important to the oil companies because of the high cost of having a supertanker full of oil waiting for an open dock. (See the Diagnostic Assignment at the end of this chapter.) Such problems are in the formal domain of "queuing models" (waiting lines), described in Chapter 17. To be solved by the methods of that chapter, however, queuing problems must meet certain strict assumptions. If the arrival and service times can be described by the *exponential distribution,* then the analytical results of Chapter 17 may be used to predict waiting times and other characteristics of the system. (The exponential distribution is discussed later in this chapter, as well as in Appendix A.) If, however, this distribution is not a good fit, or if there are other complexities in the problem that don't fit the standard assumptions, then it may be difficult or impossible to obtain analytic results. Then simulation would have to be used.

The analytical solution of queuing cases becomes extremely difficult as the situations increase in complexity. Often, there is no analytical solution for many queuing situations, and simulation gives you the only chance to find a "good" solution.

Determination of Inventory Control Policies. Simulation can be and is used to study a variety of problems in the general area of inventory control. One such problem is illustrated in Figure 13.2. In this system, the factory produces goods that are sent to the warehouses to satisfy customer demand. Assume that daily demand at each warehouse is a random variable. Shipping times from the factory to a warehouse may also be random. Here some of the operational questions are:

- When should a warehouse reorder from the factory and how much?
- How much stock should the factory maintain to satisfy the orders of the warehouses?

The main costs here are the cost of holding inventory, the cost of shipping goods from the factory to the warehouses, and the cost of not being able to satisfy customer demand at a warehouse. Because the demands at the warehouses are uncertain, unless a warehouse maintains an unreasonably high inventory, there will be times when it will not be able to meet all customer demand. An alternative to high inventories would be to have frequent shipments to the warehouses from the factory. This would keep inventory at the warehouse low, but now the shipping cost would be high. As in the inventory problems with known demand, discussed in Chapter 10, management's objective is to find a stocking and ordering policy that keeps the total of holding plus shipping cost low while meeting a desired fraction of the customers' demands at the warehouses.

Many times simulation is used in this area not to minimize costs but to see what the "worst case" might be and to develop a policy that will cover the company 99% of the time.

This problem is in the domain of inventory theory, discussed in Chapters 10

FIGURE 13.2
Distribution System

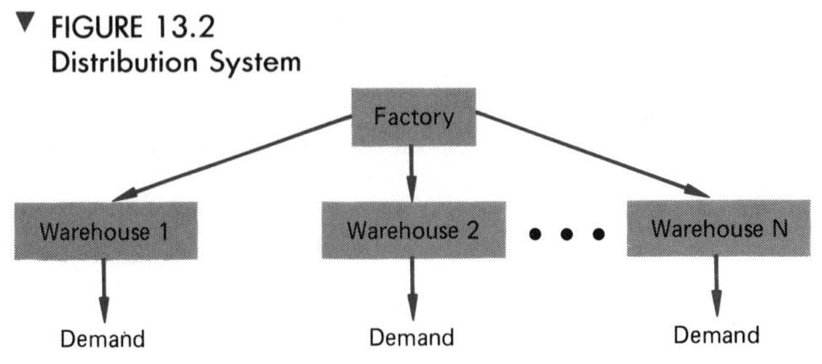

APPLICATION CAPSULE

Getting the Lead Out: Exxon Refines Its Construction Plans with the Aid of Simulation*

In the mid-1970s concern over the use of tetraethyl lead (TEL), as well as the amount of sulfur, in automobile gasoline became a topic of national concern. One result was that the California legislature passed a law requiring a scheduled lead and sulfur phase-down. Under this law the maximum TEL content had to be decreased in phased steps from 1.4 to 0.4 grams per gallon over a 3-year horizon.

This law presented a major challenge to Exxon's Benicia Refinery since it fundamentally changed the way in which gasoline was produced. Gasoline production is performed in two steps: refining, in which crude oil is separated into various components that are stored in large (component) tanks; and blending, in which the components are mixed together to produce finished products that are stored in (finished-product) tanks. TEL was an important part of this process because of the flexibility it provided. If a batch of gasoline did not meet the octane specification, a little more TEL could be added to bring it up to standard.

Reducing the use of TEL had a particularly dramatic influence on the storage of components and finished products. Without the ability to enhance octane ratings with TEL it was necessary to expand the inventory of higher-octane components or blended products or perhaps both to ensure an adequate supply of the full range of finished products. Preliminary calculations indicated at least two new component tanks and one or two new finished-product tanks would be needed. At a cost of over $1 million per tank this was clearly a problem that deserved careful attention.

Exxon constructed a discrete time simulator to analyze this problem. The program simulates the operation of the gasoline production facilities on an hour-to-hour basis. The simulator had several advantages: Gathering of input data was easy and straightforward, management became involved in determining the blending strategy used in the simulation, and results were produced on operations reports very similar to those in actual use. Each of these factors makes the results more "believable" to management and thus made the recommendations more acceptable.

As a result of the analysis, Exxon management decided to change the way in which components and final products were stored and to authorize the construction of one additional component tank and one additional finished-product tank. Thus the company was able to reduce its planned capital expenditure by at least one tank—an estimated savings of at least $1.4 million.

*Lewis Golovin, "Product Blending: A Simulation Case Study in Double-Times," *Interfaces*, vol. 9, no. 5 (November 1979), pp. 64–76.

and 16. Most analytic results in inventory theory are for a single item stocked at a single location. Multi-item, multi-location problems like the one above are much more difficult to analyze, and so are often attacked with simulation.

To gain a fuller understanding of the nature of simulation we will develop a Monte Carlo simulation of a capital budgeting problem. After seeing what is involved in performing a simulation, we will analyze by simulation the Wiles's Housewares problem that is solved by analytic means in Chapter 16 (Section 16.9). This will allow us to compare the simulation approach and the analytic approach.

13.2 Simulating with a Spreadsheet

Most simulations are performed on a computer, because the number of calculations required soon overwhelms human capability. Indeed, there are a number of commercial simulation programs available for both mainframe and personal computers (see Section 13.7 for more details). However, simple simulations can be performed with spreadsheets, and using one of the spreadsheet add-ins such as @RISK makes the job even easier. In this section we present a capital budgeting example to show the use of a spreadsheet for simulation and to establish some important facts about the output from a simulator.

A Capital Budgeting Example: Adding a New Product to PROTRAC's Line

June Wilson is considering the financial implications of a possible addition to PROTRAC's heavy equipment line. Startup costs for the proposed model G-9s (which include purchase of some new equipment, training of personnel, and so on) are estimated at $100,000. The new product would be sold at a price of $25,000 per unit. Fixed costs are estimated to run at $15,000 per year, while variable costs should be about 70% of revenues each year. Tax depreciation on the new equipment would be $10,000 per year over the expected 4-year product life of the G-9. The salvage value of the equipment at the end of the 4 years is uncertain, so June conservatively estimates it to be zero. PROTRAC's cost of capital is 10%, and its tax rate is 40%.

The most uncertain aspect of the proposal is the demand for the new product. If June knew the demand, she could easily calculate the *net present value* (NPV) of the proposal using a spreadsheet program. For example, if June assumes that the demand for G-9s is 10 units for each of the next 4 years, the spreadsheet in Figure 13.3[1] shows that the NPV would be $26,795.

The Model with Random Demand

Modeling demand

However, it is unlikely that the demand will be exactly the same every year. June feels it would be more realistic to model the demand each year not as a common constant value, but as a sequence of *independent and identically distributed (IID)* random variables. This model of demand is appropriate when there is a constant base level of demand that is subject to random fluctuations from year to year. When the base level demand is 10 units, actual demands for the next 4 years might turn out to be 12, 9, 8, and 10, because of the random factors affecting demand.

Sampling Demand with a Random Number Table. June decides to generate random demands for the 4 years to see what effect the variability of the demands has on the NPV. She assumes initially that demand in a year will be either 8, 9, 10, 11, or 12 units with each value being equally likely to occur. This is an example of a **discrete uniform distribution:** discrete, because the random variable can assume only integer values, and uniform, because each value is equally likely. June generates a demand for each year with the aid of a *random number table,* using a procedure

[1]Depreciation is first subtracted to determine before-tax profit and then added back to determine net cash flow.

D8: (C0) @NPV(G3,D19..G19)+C19

	A	B	C	D	E	F	G
1	INPUTS:						
2	Startup Costs		$100,000		Variable Costs		70%
3	Selling Price		$25,000		Cost of Capital		10%
4	Fixed Costs		$15,000		Tax Rate		40%
5	Depreciation		$10,000				
6					Demand Rate		10.0
7	OUTPUT:						
8	Net Present Value			$26,795			
9							
10			Year 0	Year1	Year 2	Year 3	Year 4
11	Demand			10	10	10	10
12	Revenue			250000	250000	250000	250000
13	Fixed Cost			15000	15000	15000	15000
14	Variable Cost			175000	175000	175000	175000
15	Depreciation			10000	10000	10000	10000
16	Before Tax Profit			50000	50000	50000	50000
17	Tax			20000	20000	20000	20000
18	After Tax Profit			30000	30000	30000	30000
19	Net Cash Flows		-100000	40000	40000	40000	40000
20							

▲ FIGURE 13.3
Wilson's Initial Spreadsheet

described more fully in Section 13.4. Since the random number table June uses (Figure 13.14, p. 569) lists the random numbers as pairs of digits, and since each of the 100 possible pairs (00–99) is equally likely, she decides to assign the random numbers to demands according to the table in Figure 13.4.

RANDOM NUMBER RANGE	PROPORTION OF 100 PAIRS ASSIGNED	DEMAND FOR 9-Gs	PROBABILITY OF DEMAND
00–19	0.2	8	0.2
20–39	0.2	9	0.2
40–59	0.2	10	0.2
60–79	0.2	11	0.2
80–99	0.2	12	0.2

▲ FIGURE 13.4
Associating Random Numbers with Demands

For example, suppose June chooses to start in column 8 of Figure 13.14 and read down. The first four random numbers in that column are 13, 22, 63, and 63 which translate into sample demands of 8, 9, 11, and 11.

Figure 13.5 shows that the NPV corresponding to this sequence of demands is $21,348, about 20% less than the NPV if demand were constant at 10 per year. If June were to read the next four random numbers from the table, she would get a different sample of demands, and hence thus possibly a different NPV. Because the demands can vary from sample to sample, the NPV can also vary. Put more technically, the demands are random variables, so the NPV is also a random variable.

G11: 11

	A	B	C	D	E	F	G	H
1	INPUTS:							
2	Startup Costs		$100,000		Variable Costs		70%	
3	Selling Price		$25,000		Cost of Capital		10%	
4	Fixed Costs		$15,000		Tax Rate		40%	
5	Depreciation		$10,000					
6					Demand Rate		10.0	
7	OUTPUT:							
8	Net Present Value			$21,348				
9								
10			Year 0	Year1	Year 2	Year 3	Year 4	
11	Demand			8	9	11	11	
12	Revenue			200000	225000	275000	275000	
13	Fixed Cost			15000	15000	15000	15000	
14	Variable Cost			140000	157500	192500	192500	
15	Depreciation			10000	10000	10000	10000	
16	Before Tax Profit			35000	42500	57500	57500	
17	Tax			14000	17000	23000	23000	
18	After Tax Profit			21000	25500	34500	34500	
19	Net Cash Flows		-100000	31000	35500	44500	44500	
20								

▲ FIGURE 13.5
Wilson's Spreadsheet with Randomly Selected Demands

Sampling Demand with a Spreadsheet. June decides that she needs to perform a number of **trials** (runs of the simulation model) to see just how sensitive the NPV is to variability in demand. She recalls that her spreadsheet has a function, @RAND, that returns a random number between 0 and 1, all values being equally likely. This is an example of a **continuous uniform distribution.** It is continuous because the random number may take on any fractional value. She cleverly devises the formula @INT(8+5*@RAND) to sample from the discrete uniform distribution on the five integers 8, 9, 10, 11, 12. Note that 5*@RAND will result in the creation of a random number between 0 and 5, so that 8+5*@RAND will produce a number between 8 and 13 (i.e., up to 12.99999 . . .). The formula then makes use of the @INT function, which returns the integer part of the number. Figure 13.6 shows what the value of the formula would be for different values of @RAND.

@RAND	@INT(8+5*@RAND)
$0 \le$ @RAND $< 1/5$	8
$1/5 \le$ @RAND $< 2/5$	9
$2/5 \le$ @RAND $< 3/5$	10
$3/5 \le$ @RAND $< 4/5$	11
$4/5 \le$ @RAND < 1	12

▲ FIGURE 13.6
Using @RAND to Generate Discrete Demands

Since the intervals are all of equal length (1/5), @RAND is equally likely to fall into any one of them, and thus the formula is equally likely to yield any one of the five integer values.

Now that June has freed herself from the laborious task of looking up random numbers, converting them to demands, and entering them into her spreadsheet, she decides that she would like to analyze a greater spread of possible demands. The formula she enters into the Demand cells (D11, E11, F11, G11) of her spreadsheet is @INT(5+11*@RAND). This will generate a discrete uniform distribution on the 11 integers 5, 6, . . . , 15. Since the value of @RAND will change every time the spreadsheet is recalculated, June can easily perform **multiple trials**—that is, draw a new sample of demands simply by pressing the calculation key for her spreadsheet. After doing this a few times, she is surprised to find that on some trials she obtains a *negative* NPV.

If demonstrating this in class, press the <F9> key to recalculate and show the new demand and resulting profit.

Evaluating the Proposal

June realizes that she needs to plan a series of experiments to help her answer two questions about the NPV distribution: (1) What is the *mean* or **expected value** of the NPV? and (2) What is the probability that the NPV assumes a negative value? The larger the mean NPV and—perhaps even more important—the less likely it is that the NPV is negative, the more attractive the proposal.

Downside Risk. By using her spreadsheet's data table command, she is able to run the simulation automatically a number of times and capture the resulting NPV. The results of 18 simulations are shown in Figure 13.7. Based on this limited sample, the estimated mean NPV is \$23,671. The probability of a negative NPV can be estimated by calculating the frequency of negative NPVs in the sample, in this case 2/18 or about an 11% chance. Also in this sample, the largest NPV was \$64,120 and the smallest was −\$6898.

▼ FIGURE 13.7
Wilson's Simulation Results

E22: (C0) @AVG(B23..B40)

	A	B	C	D	E	F	G
21	Simulation #	NPV	Max	Min	Avg		
22		(\$22,081)	\$64,120	(\$6,898)	\$23,671		
23	1	\$29,207					
24	2	\$6,626					
25	3	\$38,782					
26	4	\$8,197					
27	5	\$18,299					
28	6	\$51,595					
29	7	\$12,543					
30	8	\$64,120					
31	9	\$37,792					
32	10	\$27,114					
33	11	(\$6,898)					
34	12	(\$477)					
35	13	\$1,309					
36	14	\$40,752					
37	15	\$17,343					
38	16	\$44,843					
39	17	\$14,116					
40	18	\$20,810					

Reinforce how misleading just a few trials can be.

How Reliable Is the Simulation? While it is difficult to answer June's second question by analytical means, in this case there turns out to be an easy answer to her first question. Since the NPV is a linear function of demand, the mean NPV can be calculated by setting demand equal to the mean demand. This is what June did in her initial spreadsheet (Figure 13.3). Thus the mean NPV is $26,795 and her estimate based on a sample of 18 is off by approximately 12%. This suggests that there is also apt to be some error in the estimate of the likelihood of a negative NPV. June thus needs more than 18 trials if she wants more accurate answers to her questions.

Refining the Simulation with @RISK

Simulations with a spreadsheet can be made significantly easier with one of the commercially available add-in simulation packages such as @RISK. In particular, these programs greatly simplify the processes of generating random variables and assembling the results. This fact is illustrated with a refinement of June Wilson's G-9 problem, which also will provide us with some additional insights into the value of simulation output.

June is concerned about the estimates of demand that she used in the previous simulation. In that model she assumed that the mean demand in each period would be 10 units, and then allowed for random variation in demand around that mean. She is quite confident that the mean demand will indeed remain essentially the same in each of the next four years, but she is not at all sure that it will necessarily be 10. If the economy is slow it might be 8; if the federal bridge repair program is approved it might be 13. After some thought, June decides that the mean demand could be anywhere between 6 and 14 units a year, with all values in between being equally likely. To express this uncertainty she decides to model the mean demand as a continuous uniform distribution between 6 and 14.

A more realistic model of demand

She would also like to explore the impact of different demand distributions on the NPV. She has read in an inventory control text that when mean demand is relatively small, a distribution called the **Poisson distribution** is often a good fit. The Poisson is a *one-parameter* distribution, because specifying only one parameter, the mean value of the random variable, completely determines it. The Poisson is also a discrete distribution, since a Poisson random variable can take on only nonnegative integer values. June, however, does not know how to use her spreadsheet program to generate a Poisson random variable.

Fortunately, June has available the spreadsheet add-in called @RISK. @RISK adds a number of @functions to the spreadsheet, corresponding to different probability distributions. To sample from a Poisson distribution with a mean of 10, June has only to enter the formula @POISSON(10). To sample from a continuous uniform distribution between 6 and 14, she enters the formula @UNIFORM(6,14). The only changes June has to make in her spreadsheet are the following: in cell G6 she enters the formula @UNIFORM(6,14) and in cells D11 through G11 she enters the formula @POISSON($G$6). While it is possible to generate Poisson random variables without using @RISK (by setting up an appropriate look-up table), it is much easier to use @RISK if it is available. As we will see, @RISK also greatly facilitates the capture and display of the output of the simulation.

@RISK automatically stores the results of these 1000 trials without having to use 1000 rows of the spreadsheet, saving space and time.

June decides to sample 1000 times from the distribution of the NPV and base her estimates on the 1000 values she obtains. She simply tells @RISK to perform 1000 iterations and capture the NPV in cell D8 for each of the iterations. After the 1000 iterations are completed, June can view a histogram of the results. The histogram in Figure 13.8 reveals that the average NPV over the 1000 iterations is $26,660.93, but that there is a definite probability of a negative NPV.

The graph gives a qualitative impression of the distribution, but more detailed information can be obtained. Some of the simulation statistics June can view (see

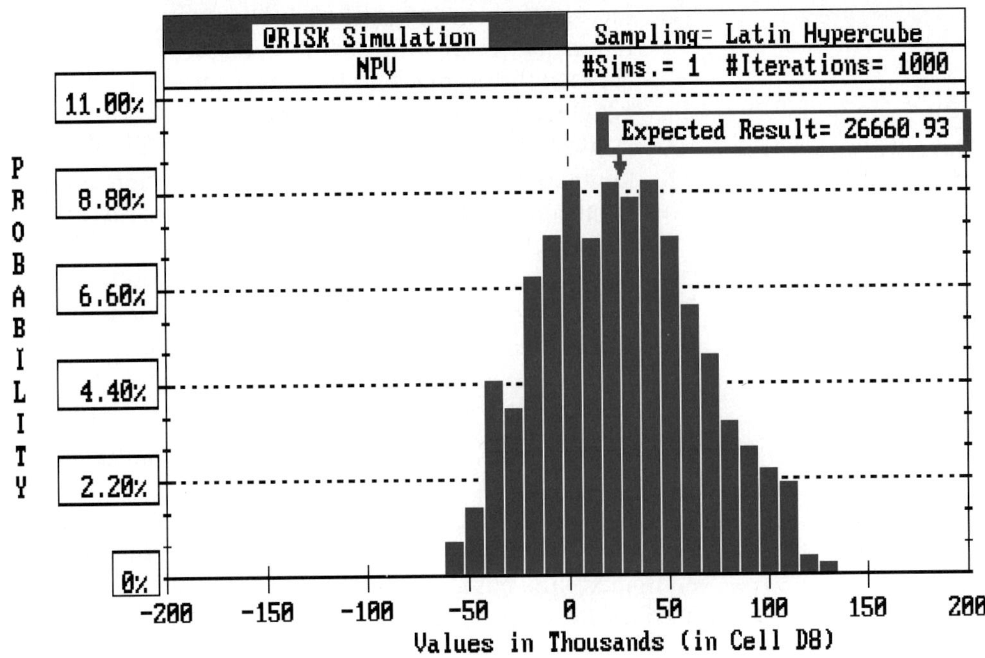

▲ FIGURE 13.8
Histogram of Net Present Value

Figure 13.9) are: the probability of a negative result, 28.3%; the largest value observed, \$135,362; and the smallest value observed, −\$62,237.21.

We have now seen three evaluations of June's G-9 capital budgeting problem: (1) a deterministic model (Figure 13.3), (2) a limited simulation with 18 trials and restricted assumptions about demand (Figure 13.7), and (3) the @RISK simulation with a large number of trials, based on what June feels is a more realistic representation of demand (Figure 13.8). What have we learned?

▼ FIGURE 13.9
NPV Statistics

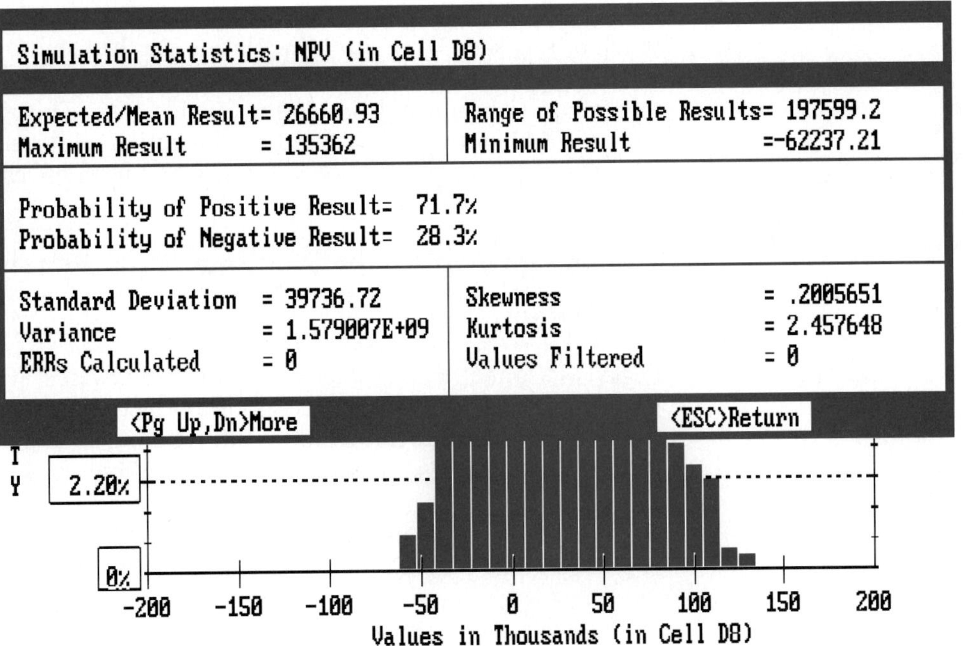

While simulation cannot guarantee an optimum, the more trials that are run, the closer the average gets to the expected values. Unfortunately, it may take a large number of trials (1000 or more) before the results become evident.

1. Increasing the number of trials is apt to give a better estimate of the expected return, but even with a large number of trials there can be some difference between the *average* and the expected return. Note that the expected return is \$26,795; the average return with 18 samples is \$23,671 (a 12% error); and the average return with 1000 observations is \$26,660.93 (a 0.5% error).
2. Simulations can provide useful information on the distribution of results. Even with a small sample of 18 trials there was an indication (a probability of about 0.11) that this project might yield a negative NPV. This, in part, encouraged June to do a "better" simulation.
3. Simulation results are sensitive to assumptions affecting the input parameters. When June changed her assumptions about the distribution of demand, there was a significant impact on the probability of a negative NPV (it increased from about .11 to about .28).

Perhaps the most important impact of the simulation is on the decision-making process.

If June had not performed any simulation analysis, she would have given an enthusiastic recommendation to proceed with the proposed addition to the heavy equipment line based on the mean NPV. However, after performing the analyses, she feels the project is too risky to recommend. While this is a qualitative judgment on her part, she can support it with the quantitative results of the simulation model. As we have noted before, models do not relieve managers from the responsibility of making decisions, but they do supply additional information for making those decisions well informed.

13.3 An Inventory Control Example: Wiles's Housewares

June Wilson's capital budgeting problem provided an example of the use of simulation in a "yes or no" situation: June had to decide whether or not to accept the project. There are other situations, however, in which the question is, "How much of this should we do?" Simulation can be used for problems of this type as well. However, there are some new concerns (or perhaps variations of old concerns) to consider when using simulation in this way. This section uses an inventory control problem to provide another illustration of simulation. It will also serve to motivate a discussion of the proper interpretation of results.

The Omelet Pan Promotion: How Many Pans to Order?

Peggy McConnel is the chief buyer for housewares at Wiles, Chicago's leading retailer. The chief buyer's role is important in a retail organization like Wiles. Peggy is responsible for designing the overall retailing strategy and operating procedures for her area. She also supervises a group of buyers who make specific purchase decisions.

Certain sections of the housewares department have just suffered their second consecutive bad year. Competing shops, such as Box and Barrel, which specialize in imported cooking and dining articles, have made serious inroads into Wiles's once secure position. The gourmet cooking, glassware, stainless flatware, and contemporary dishes sections of Wiles are not generating enough revenue to justify the amount of floor space currently committed to them.

Peggy plans to meet this challenge head-on. She has reorganized the sections that are in trouble to create a store within a store. To achieve the same ambience as her competitors, she has adopted display techniques that feature natural wood and modern lighting. She has essentially created a specialty shop, like her competitors, within the housewares department. With these changes, plus the store's reputation for quality and service, she feels that Wiles can effectively compete.

To introduce the new facility at Wiles, Peggy decides to make the month of October "International Dining Month." This promotion will feature a sale on five special articles, each from a different country. These articles will be especially made for Wiles and include a copper omelet pan from France, a set of 12 long-stem wine glasses from Spain, and so on. Each of the items has been selected by a buyer on Peggy's staff. The design and price are agreed on. The items have to be ordered at least 6 months in advance, and they will not become part of Wiles's regular product line. Any items left at the end of October will be sold to a discount chain at a reduced price. In addition, Wiles has adopted the policy that if it runs out of the special sale items, a more expensive item from its regular line of merchandise will be substituted at the sale price. It is all part of the "once-in-a-lifetime" promotion.

In the case of the omelet pans, Wiles will buy the special pans for \$22 and will sell them for \$35. Any pans left at the end of the sale will be sold to Clampton's Discount Chain for \$15 each. If Wiles runs out of the special pans, it will substitute one of its regular copper omelet pans and sell it for the sale price of \$35. Regular pans, which normally sell for \$65, cost \$32 each.

Peggy's problem is that she must decide how many of the special pans to order without knowing in advance what the demand for them will be. For example, suppose she ordered 1000 pans and the demand turned out to be 1100 pans. Then she would have to buy 100 pans (1100−1000) at \$32 per pan after buying 1000 pans at \$22 per pan and would sell 1100 pans at \$35 per pan. Thus her net profit would be

$$35(1100) - 32(1100 - 1000) - 22(1000) = \$13{,}300$$

In general, let y = number of pans ordered and D = demand. Then for $D < y$,

$$\text{Profit} = 35D - 32(D - y) - 22y = 3D + 10y.$$

If, on the other hand, she ordered 1000 pans and demand turned out only to be 200 pans, then she would sell 200 pans at \$35 and 800 pans (1000−200) at \$15 to Clampton's. Her net profit would be

$$35(200) + 15(1000 - 200) - 22(1000) = -\$3000$$

In general, for $D > y$,

$$\text{Profit} = 35D + 15(y - D) - 22y = 20D - 7y.$$

(You can see that for $D = y$, the two formulas become identical.)

Note that Peggy's calculations assume that using regular pans to satisfy promotional demand will *not* create any unsatisfied regular demand. Because of the location of her regular pan supplier, the supply is large enough that this complication need not be considered.

Profit versus Order Quantity

This will give Peggy an idea of the variation in possible results of her promotion.

Peggy is naturally interested in determining how the number of pans she orders affects her expected profit on the promotion and the likelihood of the promotion losing money. We will see how to attack this question with simulation, beginning with a simple illustrative example. Later, in Section 13.5, we will treat the more realistic assumption of a *normal demand distribution* (μ=1000, σ=100), which is the situation analyzed in Chapter 16. Let us now assume that demand has the following probability distribution.

$$\begin{aligned}
\text{Prob}\{\text{demand} = 8\} &= 0.1 \\
\text{Prob}\{\text{demand} = 9\} &= 0.2 \\
\text{Prob}\{\text{demand} = 10\} &= 0.3 \\
\text{Prob}\{\text{demand} = 11\} &= 0.2 \\
\text{Prob}\{\text{demand} = 12\} &= 0.1 \\
\text{Prob}\{\text{demand} = 13\} &= 0.1
\end{aligned}$$

These demands have been chosen artificially small in order to simplify the example. Let us, for the moment, also assume that we know how to "generate a random demand" from this probability distribution. The technique of doing this will be explicitly treated in the next section.

A simulator for the omelet pan promotion

With this demand information Peggy could construct the simulator shown in Figure 13.10. To see how the simulator works, assume that Peggy decides to order 11 omelet pans. Then $y = 11$. If the random demand turns out to be 9, then $D = 9$, $y > D$, and the simulator takes the "yes" branch in the flowchart. We have seen that when $y > D$, the profit is $20D - 7y$. Thus the profit of this single simulated promotion is $20(9)-7(11) = \$103$.

We are now prepared to use simulation to calculate the average return. To do so, we must make a number of trials, setting $y = 11$ and generating a new demand on each trial. The profit that results on any given trial depends, of course, on the value of demand that was generated on that particular trial. The *average profit* over all trials, then, is an estimate of the expected profit. This process, for 10 trials, is illustrated in Figure 13.11. Since the total profit for the 10 trials is \$1282, the average profit is \$1282/10 = \$128.20. Thus, based on these 10 trials, Peggy's best estimate of the expected profit of ordering 11 pans is \$128.20.

Peggy can use the same approach to calculate the average profit associated with any order quantity. She need only

1. Select an order size (in the example above, the order is 11).
2. Run a number of trials (say, 10).
3. Calculate the average profit.

But note that since the demand is random, the average profit will also be random. This means that if Peggy ran another set of 10 trials with the same order

▼ FIGURE 13.10
Simulating the Cost of Ordering y Pans

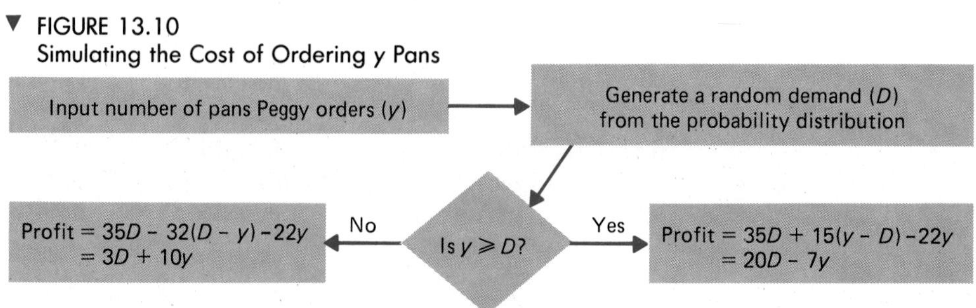

TRIAL NUMBER	QUANTITY ORDERED	RANDOM DEMAND	PROFIT
1	11	9	20(9) − 7(11) = 103
2	11	13	3(13) + 10(11) = 149
3	11	10	20(10) − 7(11) = 123
4	11	10	20(10) − 7(11) = 123
5	11	9	20(9) − 7(11) = 103
6	11	12	3(12) + 10(11) = 146
7	11	11	20(11) − 7(11) = 143
8	11	12	3(12) + 10(11) = 146
9	11	11	20(11) − 7(11) = 143
10	11	9	20(9) − 7(11) = 103
			Total Profit = $1282

▲ FIGURE 13.11
Ten Simulated Trials

size of 11 pans, the simulator could generate a different series of demands and thus would most likely obtain a different average profit.

Expected Value versus Order Quantity. In this simple example Peggy can easily calculate the *expected* profit associated with any order quantity. This can be done by using the simulator shown in Figure 13.10 to calculate the profit resulting from each of the six possible demand levels (8, 9, . . . , 13). Each of these profit values is then multiplied by the probability of that demand occurring (e.g., the profit produced when demand = 10 is multiplied by 0.3, the probability that demand will in fact be 10). Finally, the resulting terms are added. The calculation is shown in Figure 13.12.

(a) ORDER	(b) DEMAND	(c) PROBABILITY OF DEMAND	(d) PROFIT	(e) COLUMN (c) × (d)
11	8	0.1	20(8) − 7(11) = 83	8.3
11	9	0.2	20(9) − 7(11) = 103	20.6
11	10	0.3	20(10) − 7(11) = 123	36.9
11	11	0.2	20(11) − 7(11) = 143	28.6
11	12	0.1	3(12) + 10(11) = 146	14.6
11	13	0.1	3(13) + 10(11) = 149	14.9
			Expected Profit =	**123.9**

▲ FIGURE 13.12
Expected Profit When Ordering 11 Pans

Simulated versus Expected Profits. Assuming that risk is not a factor, Peggy would like to select the order quantity that yields the largest expected profit. To do so, she would calculate the expected profit for the interesting set of order quantities, just as she did for an order quantity of 11, and select the order quantity that yields the largest profit. If she were to use simulation, for each interesting order quantity she would use the same procedure that she used to determine the *average profit* with an order quantity of 11 and then select that order quantity that yielded the largest average profit.

It is no surprise that for any particular order quantity, the average profit generated by one run of the simulator does not equal the expected profit, as we have already seen that different runs will produce different values for the average. The implication of this fact on the process of making a decision is interesting. The computed expected profits and simulated average profits for order sizes of 9, 10, 11, and 12 pans are shown below.

NUMBER ORDERED	EXPECTED PROFIT	SIMULATED AVERAGE PROFIT BASED ON 10 TRIALS
9	119.2	121.8
10	124.1	126.7
11	123.9	128.2
12	120.3	126.3

Stress that *the same random demand is used* while changing only the number ordered each time.

Here we see that if Peggy were to base her decision on the simulated average profit for this particular set of trials, the profit-maximizing decision would be to order 11 pans. To maximize the expected profit, however, she should order 10 pans. This is, of course, a deliberately oversimplified example, but it is an excellent illustration of the fact that *simulation, in general, is not guaranteed to achieve optimality.*

In Peggy's case, the decision to order 11 pans rather than 10 is not critical, for it reduces her expected profit by less than 0.2%. In some instances, however, simulation can lead to results that are far from optimal. Peggy may therefore wonder whether there is anything she can do to improve the accuracy of her simulation. Can she increase the likelihood that a simulation will in fact produce an optimal decision?

More trials = greater reliability

Although the nature of simulation makes it impossible to *guarantee* that an optimal decision will be identified, there is a very simple way to increase the likelihood of this outcome: *increase the number of trials.* The greater the number of trials, the more reliable the results of the simulation tend to be—just as the more often you toss a coin, the more closely the proportion of heads is likely to approach 50%. This fact leads to the following important observation:

Suppose that, in a decision under risk, management would like to make the decision that minimizes expected cost or maximizes expected profit. With simulation, the decision may be wrongly identified if care is not taken to simulate a sufficient number of trials.

We should reemphasize that in a real problem you would not both calculate the expected cost and use simulation to calculate an average cost. Simulation is used when it is computationally impractical or even not possible to calculate the expected cost associated with the alternative decisions, or when it is important to assess the variability of various solutions. This simple example serves to illustrate relationships between simulation and analytic models.

Recapitulation

The next section deals with the technique of generating random variables such as the number of omelet pans demanded. First, let us summarize and comment on several aspects of what we have seen so far:

1. A simulator takes parameters and decisions as inputs and yields a performance measure (or measures) as output.

2. If the simulator uses random variables, each pass through the simulator (for the same parameters and decisions) will generally yield a different value for the performance measure.

3. In Peggy's problem the performance measure for an order of size 11, in each trial, was taken to be profit (each row of Figure 13.11). The 10 trials taken together combine to produce another measure of the goodness of the order size: *average profit.*

Note that even more information is available. Figure 13.11 shows that a shortage occurred in 3 of the 10 trials—demand exceeded the quantity ordered. This is additional data with which to assess the "goodness" of ordering 11 pans, and it shows how, with simulation, numerous "performance measures" can be produced.

Yet another important property of simulation is illustrated by Figure 13.11. The 10 trials have produced a distribution of profit: it varies from 103 to 149, with a mean of 128.2. This provides some indication as to the **variability** associated with the policy being evaluated (ordering 11 pans). Indicators of variability are important products of simulation studies. *Management usually seeks policies for which the potential outcome is highly predictable, which means low variability.*

4. If the simulator contains random events, then increasing the number of passes through the simulator (for the same parameters and decisions) will usually improve the accuracy of the estimate of expected value of the performance measure. In other words, if Peggy had used 100 or 1000 trials in Figure 13.12, the average profit for each order quantity would almost certainly be closer to the corresponding expected profit.

5. In a simulator we can never be sure that we have found the optimal decision. This is because a simulator can provide only an estimate of the expected effectiveness and not the exact value when randomness is present.

6. Management must assess four main factors in a simulation study:

- **a.** Does the model capture the essence of the real problem? (See Section 13.7 for more discussion of this point.)
- **b.** Are the influence of the starting and ending conditions of the simulation properly accounted for? (See Section 13.6 for a specific example.)
- **c.** Have enough trials been performed for each decision so that the average value of the measure (or measures) of performance is a good indication of the expected value?
- **d.** Have enough decisions (and the right decisions) been evaluated so that we can believe that the best answer found is "close enough" to the optimum?

13.4 Generating Random Variables

In our simulation of the capital budgeting problem and the omelet pan problem it was necessary to generate values for random variables. In this section we will explore how to *draw a random sample* from a given probability distribution, which we take to be synonymous with generating a random variable.

If using a computer in class, you may want to go directly to the generalized method and use @RAND on the spreadsheet.

The topic of generating random variables is dealt with at several levels. The first level shows how to use a random number table to generate observations from an arbitrary discrete distribution. This is sufficient to obtain the basic view of how a simulator with random elements operates. The following section on a generalized method shows how to generate random variables from any continuous distribution. It uses the exponential and normal distributions to motivate the presentation.

An analog method for simulating demand

It is easy to think of a physical device that could be used to generate the demand in the omelet pan problem. The game spinner shown in Figure 13.13 is equally likely to point to any point on the circumference of the circle. Therefore, the chance that the spinner lands in a sector that comprises 30% of the circumference (or, equivalently, 30% of the area) is 30%. If the areas of the sectors are made to correspond to the probabilities of different demands, the spinner can be used to simulate demand. For example, if the spinner stops in the sector shown in Figure 13.13, a demand of 9 would be generated. To simulate another trial, we would simply spin again.

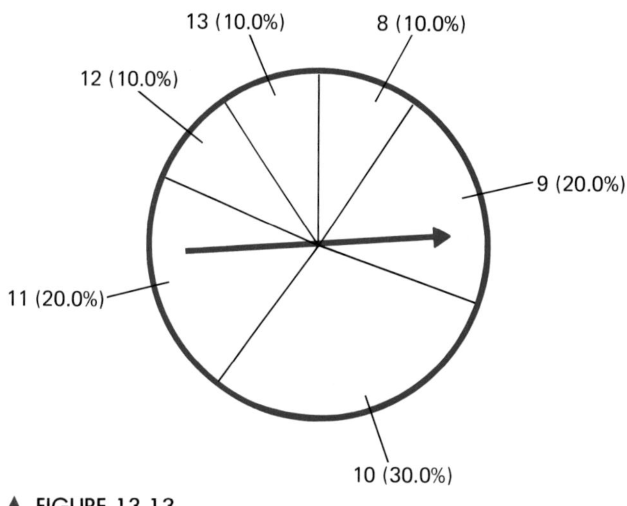

▲ FIGURE 13.13
Game Spinner for Omelet Pan Demand

Using a Random Number Table

While easy to understand, this method has an obvious defect if thousands of trials are necessary or if the process is to be performed on a computer. For this reason *random number generators* have been developed. The output of a random number generator is an integer with the property that each of its digits is a **random digit.** A random digit is a random variable with the following probability distribution:

$$
\begin{aligned}
\text{Prob}\{\text{digit} = 0\} &= 0.1\\
\text{Prob}\{\text{digit} = 1\} &= 0.1\\
\text{Prob}\{\text{digit} = 2\} &= 0.1\\
\text{Prob}\{\text{digit} = 3\} &= 0.1\\
\text{Prob}\{\text{digit} = 4\} &= 0.1\\
\text{Prob}\{\text{digit} = 5\} &= 0.1\\
\text{Prob}\{\text{digit} = 6\} &= 0.1\\
\text{Prob}\{\text{digit} = 7\} &= 0.1\\
\text{Prob}\{\text{digit} = 8\} &= 0.1\\
\text{Prob}\{\text{digit} = 9\} &= 0.1
\end{aligned}
$$

That is, every decimal digit has an equal chance of occurring. A typical output from a random number generator, in the form of a **random number table,** is shown in

	1	2	3	4	5	6	7	8	9	10
1	97	95	12	11	90	49	57	13	86	81
2	02	92	75	91	24	58	39	22	13	02
3	80	67	14	99	16	89	96	63	67	60
4	66	24	72	57	32	15	49	63	00	04
5	96	76	20	28	72	12	77	23	79	46
6	55	64	82	61	73	94	26	18	37	31
7	50	02	74	70	16	85	95	32	85	67
8	29	53	08	33	81	34	30	21	24	25
9	58	16	01	91	70	07	50	13	18	24
10	51	16	69	67	16	53	11	06	36	10
11	04	55	36	97	30	99	80	10	52	40
12	86	54	35	61	59	89	64	97	16	02
13	24	23	52	11	59	10	88	68	17	39
14	39	36	99	50	74	27	69	48	32	68
15	47	44	41	86	83	50	24	51	02	08
16	60	71	41	25	90	93	07	24	29	59
17	65	88	48	06	68	92	70	97	02	66
18	44	74	11	60	14	57	08	54	12	90
19	93	10	95	80	32	50	40	44	08	12
20	20	46	36	19	47	78	16	90	59	64
21	86	54	24	88	94	14	58	49	80	79
22	12	88	12	25	19	70	40	06	40	31
23	42	00	50	24	60	90	69	60	07	86
24	29	98	81	68	61	24	90	92	32	68
25	36	63	02	37	89	40	81	77	74	82
26	01	77	82	78	20	72	35	38	56	89
27	41	69	43	37	41	21	36	39	57	80
28	54	40	76	04	05	01	45	84	55	11
29	68	03	82	32	22	80	92	47	77	62
30	21	31	77	75	43	13	83	43	70	16
31	53	64	54	21	04	23	85	44	81	36
32	91	66	21	47	95	69	58	91	47	59
33	48	72	74	40	97	92	05	01	61	18
34	36	21	47	71	84	46	09	85	32	82
35	55	95	24	85	84	51	61	60	62	13
36	70	27	01	88	84	85	77	94	67	35
37	38	13	66	15	38	54	43	64	25	43
38	36	80	25	24	92	98	35	12	17	62
39	98	10	91	61	04	90	05	22	75	20
40	50	54	29	19	26	26	87	94	27	73

▲ FIGURE 13.14
Table of Random Digits

A digital method for simulating demand

Figure 13.14. What is important for our purposes is how random variables can be generated from random digits. We will give various illustrations of this process.

To generate demand for the omelet pan problem, we first need to assign a range of random numbers to each possible demand. This assignment is arbitrary to a degree. The only requirement for a correct assignment is that the proportion of total numbers assigned to a demand must equal the probability of that demand and that no number is assigned to more than one demand. Since the digits in Figure 13.14 are grouped in pairs, we will assign two-digit random numbers to demands. One possible assignment is shown in Figure 13.15. Note that in this example, 10 (90–99) out of the 100 possible two-digit pairs (00–99) are assigned to a demand of 13. The probability of drawing a random number in the range 90–99 is 10 out of 100 or 0.1, which is exactly the same as the probability that the demand is 13.

The random number table makes a good in-class exercise to reinforce the concept of simulating demand.

Clearly, this is not the only possible correct assignment. We could assign a demand of 13 to *any* 10 numbers—for example, 00, 05, 13, 45, 56, 66, 78, 79, 91, 99—since the probability of drawing one of these 10 values is also 0.1. It is not, however, as convenient because the assignment is not one of contiguous values. This

RANDOM NUMBERS	PROPORTION OF TOTAL NUMBERS ASSIGNED	DEMAND FOR OMELET PANS	PROBABILITY
00–09	0.10	8	0.1
10–29	0.20	9	0.2
30–59	0.30	10	0.3
60–79	0.20	11	0.2
80–89	0.10	12	0.1
90–99	0.10	13	0.1

▲ FIGURE 13.15
Associating Random Numbers with Demands

would make it more difficult to verify that the ranges did not overlap and to identify in what range a particular random number falls.

Note that for this problem we could have assigned only one-digit random numbers: for example, 0 to a demand of 8; 1 and 2 to a demand of 9; 3, 4, and 5 to a demand of 10; 6 and 7 to a demand of 11, and so on. We can get by with single-digit random numbers in this case because the probabilities can be expressed with only one digit to the right of the decimal point. If some probabilities required two digits to the right of the decimal point, we would be forced to use two-digit random numbers. If some of the probabilities required three digits to the right of the decimal point, then we would have to use three-digit random numbers, and so on.

Both the random starting point and the fact that one can read either down rows or across columns contribute to the randomness of the result.

Let us now see how we generated the demand sequence shown in Figure 13.11. We first select an arbitrary place in the table (Figure 13.14) to begin—row 6, column 7. We observe that the random number is 26. Referring to Figure 13.15, we see that a random number of 26 implies a demand of 9. We proceed by reading down the table. The second number is 95, which in Figure 13.15 implies a demand of 13. Another eight observations are produced by continuing to read down the table. The results are the demands shown in Figure 13.11.

A Generalized Method

The method we have just demonstrated is useful for generating discrete random variables. Many problems, however, involve *continuous* random variables, which require a modification of the random number table approach. Fortunately, there is a general method that can be used to generate both discrete and continuous random variables. We will develop this method and illustrate it with several examples.

To generate a discrete random variable with a random number table we need two things: (1) the ability to generate random digits (discrete uniform random variables) and (2) the distribution of the discrete random variable to be generated. Similarly, to generate continuous random variables we need (1) the ability to generate continuous uniform random variables on the interval 0 to 1, and (2) the distribution (in the form of the *cumulative distribution function*) of the random variable to be generated.

Continuous Uniform Random Variables. In what follows, it is important to distinguish between the uniform random variable on the interval 0 to 1, U, and a specific realization of that random variable, u. One way to generate a continuous uniform random variable would be to use a version of the game spinner introduced earlier. Figure 13.16 shows a game spinner that, conceptually at least, can be used to generate values of U. Every point on the circumference of the circle corresponds to a number between 0 and 1. For example, when the pointer is in the 3 o'clock position, it is pointing to the number 0.25.

While this device is useful for gaining an intuitive understanding of the

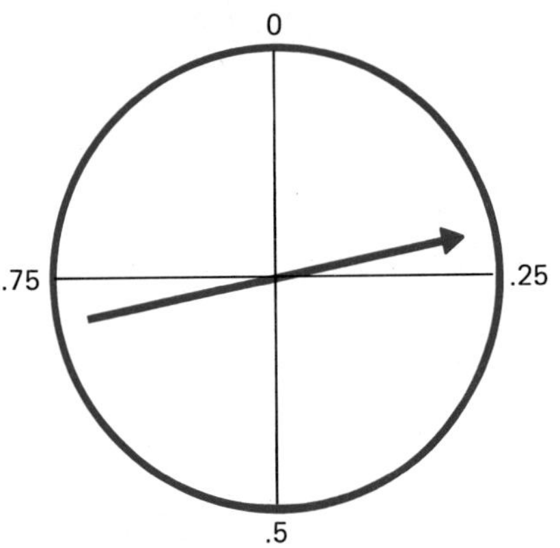

▲ FIGURE 13.16
Game Spinner for Uniform Random Variables

uniform random variable, it is even more limiting in practice than the spinner for the omelet pan problem, in that it requires us to be able to read the exact point at which the pointer is pointing. (For example, imagine trying to discern whether the number indicated is 0.500000 or 0.499999.) We have seen, however, that in practice we do not need to be dependent on such "analog" devices as game spinners. With the use of a random number table, we can approximate *U* to any number of decimal places we choose by sampling as many random digits as we need and placing a decimal point in front of them. In a spreadsheet program, we could accomplish the same thing by using the function @RAND, or, in @RISK, by using @UNIFORM (0,1).

The Cumulative Distribution Function. The second key to generating a random variable is the random variable's **cumulative distribution function** (CDF). Consider a random variable *D*—say, the demand in the omelet pan problem. The CDF for *D*, which we will designate F(x), is then defined as the probability that *D* takes on a value less than or equal to x—that is, F(x) = Prob{$D \geq x$}. Recall that if we know the probability distribution for *D*, as we did in the omelet pan problem, we can easily find the CDF. Indeed, the CDF for key values of *D* is as follows:

x	8	9	10	11	12	13
F(*x*)	0.1	0.3	0.6	0.8	0.9	1

We will show how to use the general approach to generate observations of the random variable *D*. You will see that it is as easy as the approach based on the probability distribution, but certainly no easier. So why adopt this general approach? The answer is a technical one. With a continuous random variable, the probability that any *specific* value occurs is, strictly speaking, 0. Thus you cannot use an approach based on the probability distribution. Indeed, continuous random variables do not have probability distributions; the density function and the CDF are the two functions used to define a continuous random variable.

A graph of the omelet pan CDF is shown in Figure 13.17. To generate a demand using the graph, draw a particular value u of the random variable and locate this value on the vertical axis of the graph. From this value on the vertical axis draw a line horizontally across to the plot of the CDF, and then down vertically to the horizontal axis to obtain the value of the demand, d. For example, when $u = 0.5$, the demand is 10 (see Figure 13.17).

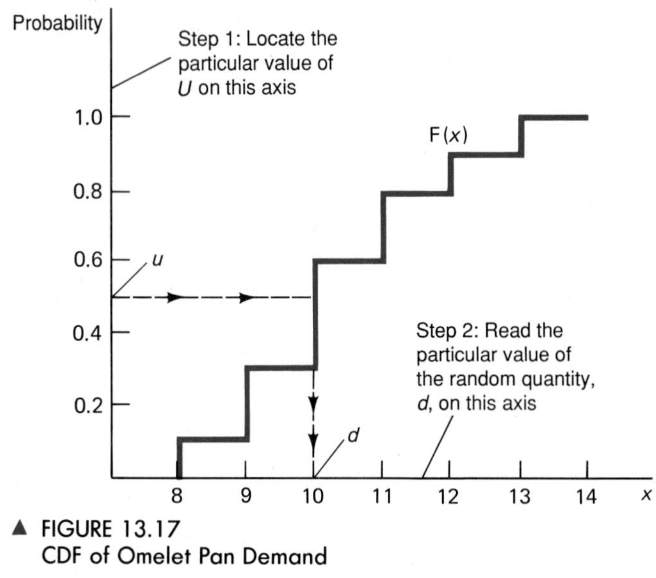

▲ FIGURE 13.17
CDF of Omelet Pan Demand

Why does this procedure work? It works because the probability of generating a particular demand is the probability of that demand occurring. For example, we want the probability of generating a demand of 10 to be 0.3. A demand of 10 will be generated when u lies between 0.3 and 0.6 on the vertical axis of Figure 13.17. But since U is a uniform random variable, this probability is just the length of the interval, $0.6 - 0.3 = 0.3$. Similarly, we want the probability of generating a demand of 11 to be 0.2. A demand of 11 will be generated when the value of u lies between 0.6 and 0.8, which happens with a probability of $0.8 - 0.6 = 0.2$, and so on. (You might wonder what happens if u is exactly 0.6. Should a demand of 10 or 11 be generated? The answer is that it doesn't really matter, as the probability of generating a value of u *exactly* equal to 0.6 is 0. One convention is to take the larger value. This works except when u is 1 when the larger value is not defined. In that case, just take the demand to be 13.)

The technique we have just illustrated with the omelet pan problem can be applied to any discrete distribution. We shall now see how the general method can be used to generate any continuous random variable, with specific illustrations for the exponential and normal distributions.

The General Method Applied to Continuous Distributions

The two-step process for generating a continuous random variable W is illustrated in Figure 13.18. As before, the crucial element in the graph is the cumulative distribution function of W, $F(x) = \text{Prob}\{W \le x\}$. The figure shows a typical function of this type, namely, one that goes from 0 to 1, is nondecreasing, and is *continuous.* (That is, unlike the CDF for a discrete distribution, there are no jumps in the curve.) Exactly as before, the process starts by drawing a particular value u of the random variable U and locating this value on the vertical axis (0.8 in Figure 13.18). You then read horizontally across to the plot of the distribution function and then vertically down to the horizontal axis to obtain the value of the random quantity (approximately 5.1 in Figure 13.18). We should stress that Figure 13.18 motivates the *concept* underlying the technique of generating an arbitrary continuous random variable. In practice, the process is typically performed in the computer with either an analytic or tabular representation of a graph like Figure 13.18. We illustrate both procedures below.

An overhead of Figure 13.18 can be used in class to illustrate generating demand from continuous distributions.

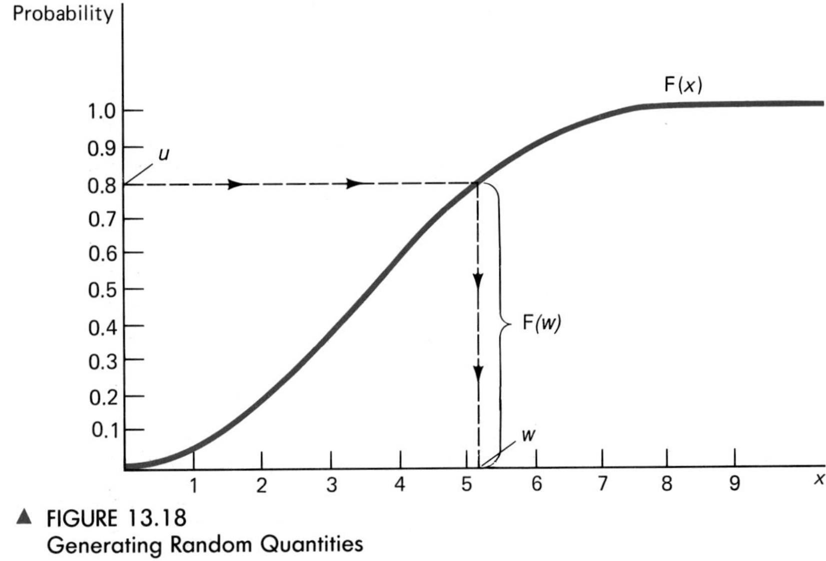

▲ FIGURE 13.18
Generating Random Quantities

The graphical procedure illustrated above is equivalent to an algebraic procedure. That procedure is to solve the equation

$$u = \mathrm{F}(w) = \mathrm{Prob}\{W \leq w\}$$

for w. This can be seen from Figure 13.18 where the vertical distance on the vertical axis is u and is equal to the vertical distance from w on the horizontal axis to the plot of the CDF. When the CDF has a simple enough analytic expression, it is possible to solve for w in terms of u.

Generating from the Exponential Distribution. An important distribution for which this is the case is the **exponential distribution.** As we will see in Section 17.2, the exponential distribution is often used to model the time between arrivals in a queuing model. Its CDF is given by

$$\mathrm{F}(w) = \mathrm{Prob}\{W \leq w\} = 1 - e^{-\lambda w}$$

where $1/\lambda$ equals the mean of the exponential random variable, W. Therefore we want to solve the following equation for w:

$$u = 1 - e^{-\lambda w} \tag{13.1}$$

The solution is

$$w = -\frac{1}{\lambda}\ln(1 - u) \tag{13.2}$$

For example, suppose we want to draw a sample from the exponential distribution with mean equal to 20 using this equation and a random number table. We would

1. Take a number from the random number table and put a decimal point in front of it. For example, suppose that we arbitrarily start in row 2, column 3 of Figure 13.14 and obtain the number 0.75.
2. We then take the natural logarithm of $1 - 0.75 = 0.25$, which is -1.386 and multiply by -20. The observation from the exponential distribution is $(-20)(-1.386) = 27.72$.

Generating from the Normal Distribution. The **normal distribution** plays an important role in many analytic and simulation models. In simulation, we often assume that random quantities are normally distributed. To illustrate, we return to Peggy McConnel and Wiles's omelet pan problem (see Section 13.3). In the next section we will find Peggy making the more realistic assumption that a normal distribution with a mean of 1000 and a standard deviation of 100 described the demand that would occur.

To use simulation to estimate the expected cost of a given order size, Peggy would have to draw on each trial a random demand from a normal distribution with a mean of μ of 1000 and a standard deviation σ of 100. It turns out that if Z is a unit normal random variable (a normal with a mean of 0 and a standard deviation of 1), then $\mu + Z\sigma$ is a normal random variable with mean μ and standard deviation σ. So the problem reduces to drawing from a unit normal distribution. The difficulty here is that the CDF of the unit normal is complicated enough that it is not possible to get an analytical expression for z in terms of u. What we can do instead is to use a tabular representation of the unit normal CDF.

A quick and dirty way used by some to generate a pseudo-normal random number is to take the average of 20 uniform numbers. The central limit theorem states that this average will "tend" to be normal.

This tabular representation is Table A.0, found in Appendix A at the end of the text. The values in the body of the table are, for different z values, the values of the CDF *less* 0.5. For example, $\text{Prob}\{Z \le 0.97\} = 0.3340 + 0.5 = 0.8340$. To solve the equation $\text{Prob}\{Z \le z\} = 0.9345$ we would first subtract 0.5 from 0.9345 to obtain 0.4345. Then we would try to find 0.4345 in the body of the table. In this case no interpolation is required, and $z = 1.51$.

So to generate a normal random variable with mean of 1000 and standard deviation of 100, Peggy follows this three-step process:

1. First she takes a number from the random number table and puts a decimal point in front of it. For example, suppose that we arbitrarily start in row 28, column 3, of Figure 13.15. We would get the number 0.76.
2. Next she finds the number z such that the probability that the unit normal is less than or equal to this value is 0.76. This means she will look for $0.76 - 0.5 = 0.26$ in the body of Table A.0. From this table she sees that z must lie between 0.70 and 0.71. Interpolating between these two values gives 0.706. She now has an observation from the unit normal distribution.
3. Finally, she sets demand equal to $1000 + 0.706(100) = 1070.6$

13.5 A Spreadsheet Simulation of Wiles's Problem

It is important, however, to go through a simulation by hand to see if it is working properly and what results to expect. Then, when the computer simulation is developed, it becomes easier to find any "bugs" in the program.

Simulation by hand is time-consuming and tedious (to put it kindly) even for simple models like the omelet pan problem. For more complicated models, these characteristics are exacerbated and, in addition, it becomes increasingly difficult to avoid making logical or computational errors or both. Fortunately, however, computers are specifically designed to perform a large number of logical and numerical operations rapidly and accurately. In addition, computers can be easily programmed to generate random quantities from any specific distribution. For example, @RISK has a number of different preprogrammed @ functions that will produce random variables, including all the ones we have considered so far (uniform, Poisson, normal, and exponential). For all of these reasons, almost all simulations are performed on computers.

Although we have already analyzed the Wiles's Houseware problem in Section 13.3, by using a spreadsheet program we can do a much more realistic analysis and generate more useful information. Recall that we had assumed a simplified demand distribution in Section 13.3 when a more realistic model of demand is the normal with a mean of 1000 and a standard deviation of 100. Also, we limited our simulation to 10 trials for illustrative purposes. In this section we will use a normal distribution of demand, perform 100 trials, and use a data table to optimize the order quantity.

In the development of this example we will see how to generate a normal random variable with a specific mean and standard deviation. We will also see how variability in a simulation can be reduced, allowing a better estimate of the difference in profit between two decisions. In addition, the example provides an opportunity for examining the distinction between average and expected profit, as well as an illustration of what is meant by the distribution of profits for a specific order quantity.

The Wiles's Spreadsheet: Simulating Demand

Recall from Figure 13.10 that the profit on an order of size y when demand turns out to be D is $20D-7y$ if $y \geq D$ and is $3D+10y$ if $y<D$. This logic is implemented in the spreadsheet shown in Figure 13.19 through the use of an @IF statement. For example, the profit shown in cell C4 is calculated as @IF($B$1>=B4,20*B4−7*$B$1,3*B4+10*$B$1).

```
B4: (F0) [W9] 1000+100*@SQRT(-2*@LN(@RAND))*@SIN(2*@PI*@RAND)
```

	A	B	C	D	E	F	G
1	Order Qty	1000					
2	Avg Profit	$12,435					
3	Trial	Demand	Profit				
4	1	1167	$13,501				
5	2	1051	$13,153				
6	3	1042	$13,127				
7	4	1147	$13,440				
8	5	950	$11,991				
9	6	899	$10,971				
10	7	1084	$13,251				
11	8	904	$11,086				
12	9	997	$12,936				
13	10	878	$10,552				
14	11	1091	$13,273				
15	12	951	$12,024				
16	13	927	$11,536				
17	14	928	$11,553				
18	15	940	$11,801				
19	16	1271	$13,814				
20	17	1136	$13,408				

▲ FIGURE 13.19
Wiles's Spreadsheet

The value in cell B4 is the value of D that is drawn from the normal distribution. There are many ways to generate normal random variables, one of which was discussed in Section 13.4. A convenient method to use to generate normal random variables in a spreadsheet is the Box-Muller transformation. It samples two values, u_1, u_2, from the continuous uniform random variable U. It uses these values and the following formula to generate a specific value, x, of a normal random variable, X, with mean 0 and standard deviation 1:

$$x = \sqrt{-2\ln(u_1)}\,\sin(2\pi u_2)$$

To generate a value from the normal distribution with mean μ and standard deviation σ, simply set $D = \mu + \sigma X$. Thus, the formula in cell B4 is

1000+100*@SQRT(−2*@LN(@RAND))*@SIN(2*@PI*@RAND).

To simulate 100 trials, make 99 copies of cells B4 and C4. The formula in cell B2, @AVG(C4..C103), computes the average profit of the 100 trials. Every time the spreadsheet is recalculated, 100 new trials will be performed and a new average profit calculated. Since we will perform only 100 trials, after the first 100 demands have been created, the formulas can be converted to numbers (using the Range Value command in Lotus 1-2-3) so that the demands will not change every time the spreadsheet is recalculated. It is important that they not change, because we want to compare the average profit for *different* order quantities but the *same* set of demands. Then profit will differ only because of different order quantities and not because a different set of demand values had been sampled. (Also, the spreadsheet will recalculate faster as it does not have to update the values in the demand cells.)

This process of decreasing variability in simulation results is called *variance reduction,* and it is an important technique in reducing the amount of computation necessary to obtain valid simulation results. Indeed, the ability to use the same set of random variables to evaluate competing alternatives is a unique experimental advantage of simulation. All branches of science attempt to reduce exogenous variability in their experiments. For example, agronomists plant different varieties of corn in the same field to insure that weather and soil conditions do not vary. With simulation, using the same sequence of random variables provides us with complete control of random elements.

The Effect of Order Quantity

The Data Table command uses the same set of random numbers (and thus demands) to see the effect of different order quantity policies.

For the 100 sample demands (partially) shown in Figure 13.19, the average profit when the mean demand of 1000 pans is ordered is $12,435. By entering different order quantities in cell B1 and recalculating the spreadsheet, we could get an idea of how the average profit varies with the order quantity. In this example we will use a more efficient procedure than randomly entering values. Using the Data Table command, it is possible to calculate the average profits for a range of order quantities and a *given* set of demands. Figure 13.20 is a graph of average profit as a function of the order quantity for all order quantities between 950 and 1050. It shows that the maximum average profit results for an order quantity between 1020 and 1030 units. The exact quantity found from the table is 1028, with an average profit of $12,460.

While this quantity maximizes the *average* profit *for the given set of 100 demands,* it may not maximize the *expected* profit. In fact, the number of pans that maximizes expected profit, as calculated in Section 16.9, is actually 1022. As we have said before, it is impossible to guarantee that the optimal solution will be found using simulation. But remember, an optimal solution is a theoretical as opposed to a real-world concept. At best, an optimal solution represents a "good decision" for the real-world problem. Given these qualifications on the meaning of an optimal solution, since the solution found using simulation is within 1% of the optimal solution, it is probably good enough.

A "good-enough" solution

The Probability Distribution of Profit. We may, however, want to know more about the solution suggested by simulation (ordering 1028 pans). For example, how much variability can we expect around the average profit of $12,460? Could we make much more or much less than the average? Could this decision *lose* money?

The definitive answer to these questions is given in the form of the probability distribution of profit. This distribution can be approximated by a histogram derived from simulation results. While it is possible to generate such a histogram in a

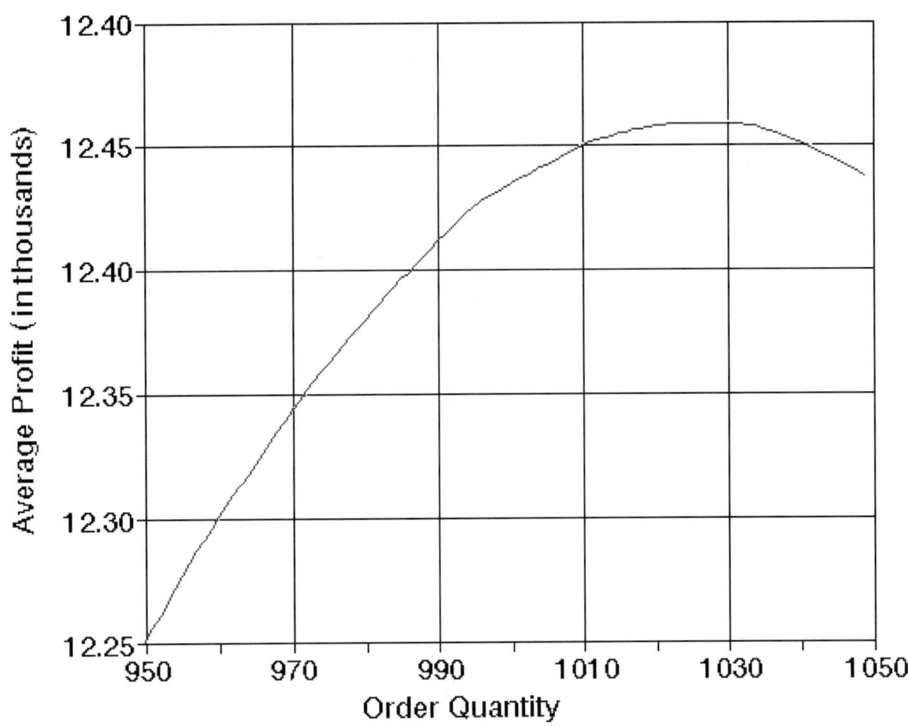

▲ FIGURE 13.20
Simulation of Wiles's Average Profit as a Function of Order Quantity

spreadsheet program (in Lotus 1-2-3 by using the Data Distribution command and then graphing the results), it is much easier to let @RISK do most of the work.

Visualizing the variability

Figure 13.21 shows the @RISK generated distribution of profit for an order quantity of 1028 based on a sample of 1000 trials. The distribution appears to be the combination of two distinct distributions: to the left a flat distribution with long "tails" and to the right a peaked distribution. (It can be shown by analytical means that the distribution is actually what is called a *mixture* of two normal distributions,

This gives a nice visual picture of the range of risk that Wiles will be taking in ordering 1028 pans, and may have more impact than just numbers and averages.

▼ FIGURE 13.21
Profit Histogram (1028 Pans)

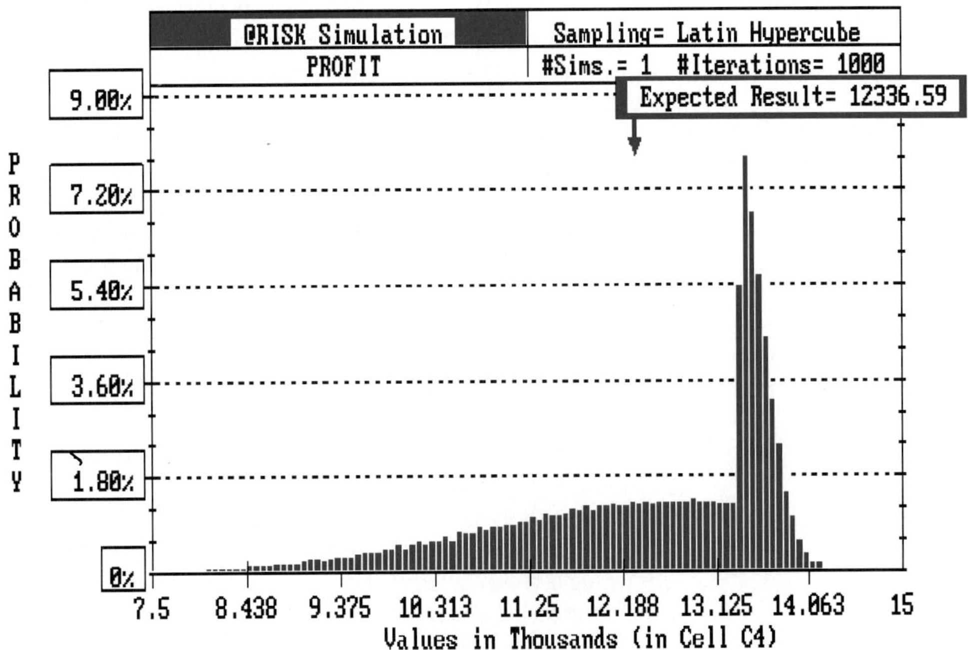

APPLICATION CAPSULE

Checks and Balances: An Ohio Bank Uses Simulation to Streamline Its Operations*

In 1984, BancOhio National Bank had 266 branches statewide. Checks were consolidated at 31 of these branches for encoding and then sent on to Columbus or Cleveland for computer processing, sorting, and preparation for clearance. Realizing that improvements in the efficiency of these activities would reduce costs and improve throughput, management sought to address the following questions:

- How many encoding sites were actually needed to serve the branch network, and at which branches should they be located?
- Which branches should each site serve?
- What resources and costs should be considered in evaluating the alternatives?

To help find answers, BancOhio engaged a consulting company that had developed a simulation package called CHECKSIM. This program generates efficient routes for the messengers who pick up checks at branches and deliver them to the processing centers. The simulation output reports the check volume delivered to the processing center by time of day, thus providing the information needed to make staffing decisions. Since the model can simulate only one processing center at a time, the following procedure was used.

- First, planners would select a particular scenario—that is, a set of branches to function as processing centers.
- Next, a number of plausible schemes for assigning the branches to be served by each center were evaluated with the simulator.
- Finally, once the most economical assignment scheme for each scenario had been determined, the costs of the different scenarios were compared, using the program's interface with Lotus 1-2-3.

In all, management evaluated five different scenarios, involving 31, 22, 16, 11, and 7 processing centers. The two best scenarios were found to be those with 22 and 7 centers. The 22-center scenario had the lower transportation costs. However, the 7-center scenario made more effective use of facilities, resulting in lower encoding costs. Consequently, it was nearly $288,000 per year less expensive.

These results prompted management to consider the possible advantages of consolidating additional functions at the proposed processing centers. Thus the project was expanded to incorporate operations management, returns, customer inquiries, and MICR cash balancing in the same centers. The result was an additional saving in indirect operating costs of $1.38 million per year.

*Davis, Kleindorfer, Kochenberger, Reutzel, and Brown, "Strategic Planning for Bank Operations with Multiple Check-Processing Locations," *Interfaces*, Vol. 16, No. 6 (Nov.–Dec. 1986).

but even if you did not know this fact, it would be strongly suggested by the simulation results.) The peaked distribution to the right of the expected value means that there is a definite probability that the profit will exceed the mean profit. The long tail to the left of the expected profit means that there is some chance of obtaining a result several thousand dollars below the expected profit. There is very little chance, however, of losing money on this promotion: in 1000 trials no profit was less than $7500.

13.6 Simulation and Capacity Balancing

Simulation is a powerful tool for gaining insights into the planning and operation of a manufacturing facility. In this section, we explore the assertion that capacity should be "balanced" throughout a manufacturing plant. We will see that variation in processing times can lead to unexpected results. This example is enlightening in several ways: (1) It shows how to use a spreadsheet to model a multi-period problem in which results from one period are carried into the next. In this problem, as in many real situations, inventory is carried from period to period. (2) It provides a graphic lesson on the risk of drawing conclusions based on relatively short simulation runs. (3) It provides useful intuitive insights into the consequences of balancing production rates in a serial manufactuing operation.

Modeling a Work Cell

John Jones, an industrial engineer at **PROTRAC**, is trying to determine the appropriate capacity to install in the small work cell shown in Figure 13.22. This cell takes a raw material, processes it at the first workstation (WS1), holds it in a temporary storage area if the second workstation (WS2) is busy, and then processes it at WS2. The completed part is used on one of **PROTRAC**'s assembly lines at the rate of 3 per hour.

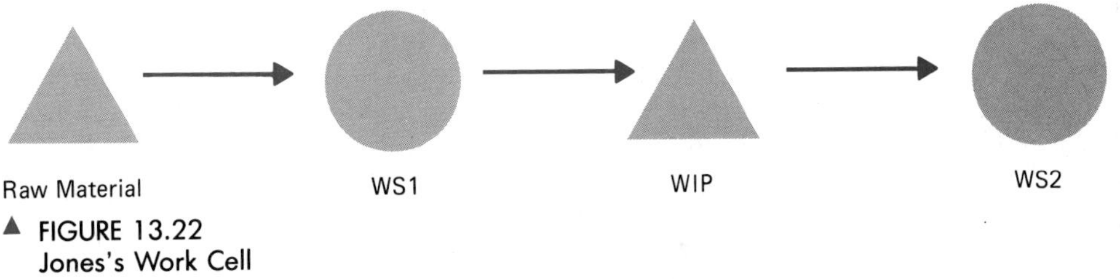

▲ FIGURE 13.22
Jones's Work Cell

Consider how expensive it would be actually to set up a factory to implement and test the work cell for several days, compared to the cost of a spreadsheet simulation!

John has several goals in designing this work cell. He wants to meet the demand for this part on the assembly line, to keep work in process (WIP) between the two workstations down, and (in order to keep costs down) to minimize the capacity of the workstations subject to achieving the first two goals. He decides to do a simulation to help him make his capacity decisions.

Simulating Balanced Capacity

Since the assembly area needs the part at a rate of 3 per hour, John initially decides to set the capacity of both workstations at 3 per hour. That is, the capacities of WS1 and WS2 are *balanced.* However, because of processing time variability, a workstation might be able to process anywhere from 1 to 5 units in an hour. Suppose that during any given hour period, a workstation will have the capability of processing 1, 2, 3, 4, or 5 units with equal probability. Then the *average* output of that workstation will be 3 units per hour *provided it always has something on which to work.* John assumes that sufficient raw material will always be available to WS1 so that it will never be *starved.* However, because the processing times are variable at WS1, there may be times when WS2 is idled for lack of material.

```
E4: @MIN(B4,C4)
```

	A	B	C	D	E	F	H
1			Potential		Actual		
2		Initial	WS2	WS1	WS2	Final	Average
3	Hour	WIP	Output	Output	Output	WIP	WIP
4	1	0	4	4	0	4	4
5	2	4	5	4	4	4	4
6	3	4	1	1	1	4	4
7	4	4	1	4	1	7	5
8	5	7	2	5	2	10	6
9	6	10	1	1	1	10	7
10	7	10	1	1	1	10	7
11	8	10	2	5	2	13	8
12	9	13	3	4	3	14	8
13	10	14	2	1	2	13	9
14	11	13	3	5	3	15	9
15	12	15	4	1	4	12	10
16	13	12	3	5	3	14	10
17	14	14	3	3	3	14	10
18	15	14	5	1	5	10	10
19	16	10	4	5	4	11	10
20							

▲ FIGURE 13.23
Jones's Spreadsheet

It is also possible to vary the initial conditions to determine what effect they have on the model.

The Initial Conditions. Figure 13.23 is the spreadsheet representing the first 16 simulated hours of operation of the work cell. The *initial conditions* at the beginning of the first hour of the simulation are no WIP, and WS1 and WS2 are idle. The columns labeled Potential WS2 Output and WS1 Output contain the formula @INT(1+5*@RAND), which produces values from a discrete uniform distribution with 5 possible values (1, 2, . . . ,5) with equal probability. The column labeled Actual WS2 Output is the row by row minimum of Initial WIP and Potential WS2 Output. For example, the actual output of WS2 during the first hour is 0, because there is nothing for it to work on. The actual output during the second hour is 4, because there were 4 units available to work on and WS2 was able to process up to 5 units during that hour. The actual output during the third hour was 1, because although there were 4 units available for processing, WS2 could process only 1 of them during the hour.

The Final WIP is calculated by adding the Initial WIP to the WS1 Output and subtracting Actual WS2 Output. The Initial WIP is simply Final WIP for the previous hour. Average WIP is defined to be the average of the Final WIP values. For example, the Average WIP for the first 4 hours is $(4+4+4+7)/4 = 4.75$, which displays as 5 since the format has been set to round to the nearest integer. (There is a hidden column [column G] in the spreadsheet that accumulates the Final WIP values so that Average WIP is just the value in the hidden column divided by the number of simulated hours in column A.)

Beyond the Initial Conditions. John realizes that running the simulation for only 16 hours can be very misleading, so he devises a macro[2] that will simulate the next 16 hours starting where the last 16 hours ended. That is, the Initial WIP for the

[2]For those fluent in macroese, it is 1 in cell J2, cell J3 blank, and the following in cells J4 through J12: {PUT A21..A121,0,1,H19}, {LET A4,16+A4}, {LET B4,+F19}, {LET G3,+G19}, {CALC}, {LET J2,1+J2}, {PUT A21..A121,0,J2,H19}, {IF J2-100}{BRANCH J5}, {QUIT}.

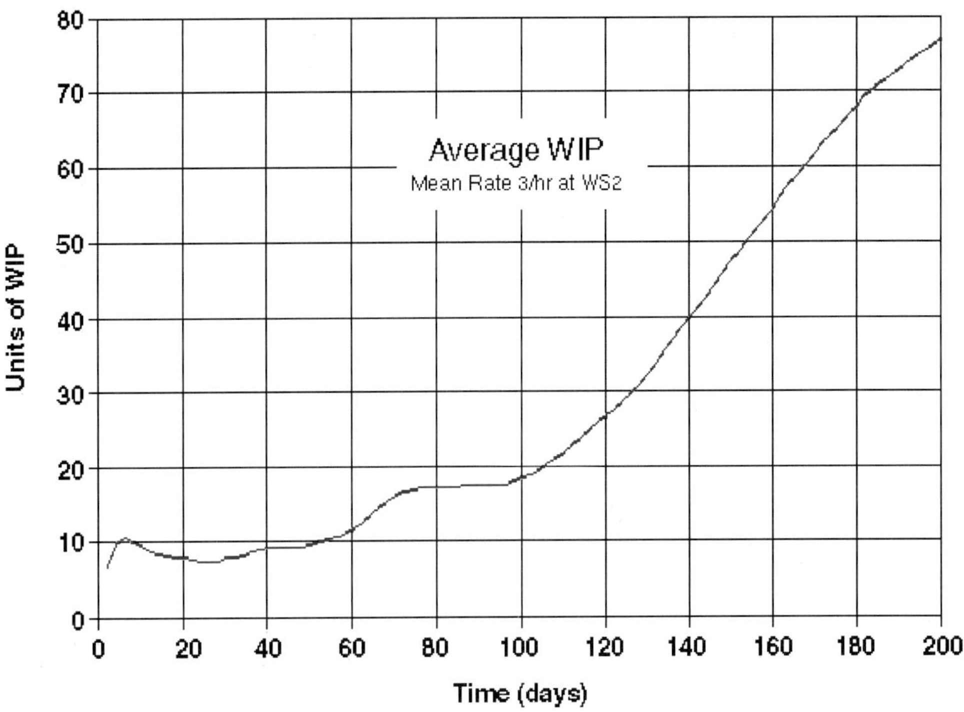

▲ FIGURE 13.24
Average Work in Process, Balanced Capacity

next 16 hours will be the Final WIP for the sixteenth hour of the last simulation. (The macro also updates the Hour column, updates the cumulative WIP in the hidden column, and writes the value of Average WIP for the sixteenth hour to the next cell in a range reserved for capturing these values.)

The steady state

John is quite surprised when he graphs Average WIP versus time for the first 200 days of operation (see Figure 13.24). He knows that the initial condition of 0 WIP should lead to low values of Average WIP initially. He expects to see average WIP grow, but then to level off around some *steady-state* value. What he did not expect was the continued growth of average WIP. It appears that the longer the cell is in operation, the greater the amount of WIP that accumulates. This is somewhat counterintuitive, since it appears that with both workstations operating at an average rate of 3 units per hour there should be no tendency for WIP to grow.

A simple queuing model, however, predicts this unexpected growth. As we shall see in Chapter 17, when the average arrival rate to a queue is equal to the average service rate, the number of customers in the queue will grow without bound. Here "customers" are parts leaving WS1, and the queue is the temporary storage area before WS2. Because raw material is readily available, the output rate of WS1, and hence the average arrival rate to the queue, is 3 units per hour. The average service rate, the rate at which WS2 can process WIP, is also 3 units per hour. Thus, the average arrival rate and average service rate are equal when the capacities of the two workstations are balanced. Hence the continued growth of Average WIP.

Simulating Unbalanced Capacity

On the basis of these considerations, John decides to add capacity to WS2 so that its average production rate is now 3.5 units per hour. He models this in his spreadsheet by changing the formulas in the Potential WS2 Output column to @INT(2+4*@RAND). The graph of average WIP (Figure 13.25) now shows a

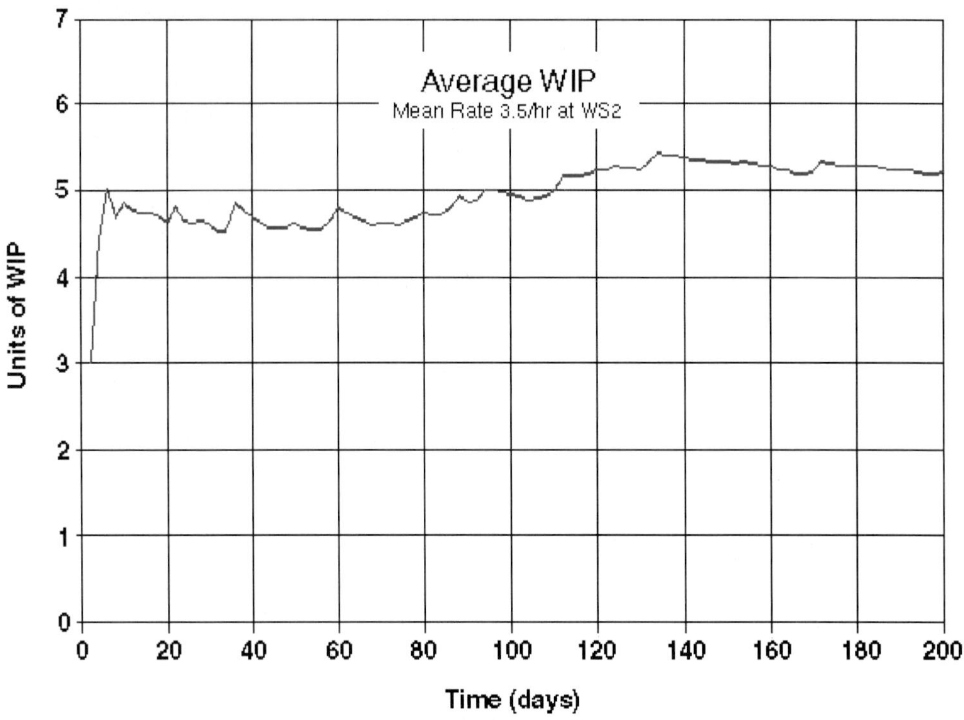

▲ FIGURE 13.25
Average Work in Process, Unbalanced Capacity

much lower average WIP. His results suggest that there is no long-term growth in the Average WIP, with the steady-state value lying somewhere between 5 and 7 units.

John's final conclusion is that the capacity of the two workstations should not be balanced (equal output rates). If WIP is to be kept to reasonable levels, then the downstream workstation (WS2) should have a somewhat greater capacity. If John had simulated fewer than 40 days of operation, he would have been seriously misled about the long term behavior of WIP in the balanced design. By running the simulation for a longer period of time, the effect of the initial conditions was overcome, and the true long-term behavior could be discerned. A general observation about simulation can be drawn from this example:

Simulation results are useful only when care is taken in the experimental design to eliminate extraneous effects such as starting or ending conditions. Simulations that are too short may give very misleading results.

13.7 Notes on Implementation

Simulation is a powerful and flexible analytic tool that can be used to study a wide variety of management problems. It is generally used in cases where a good analytic model either does not exist or is too complicated to solve. Simulation can also demonstrate the effects of variability and initial conditions, as well as the length of time needed to reach steady state. This description encompasses a large segment of real-world problems and, as a result, surveys of the use of management science techniques typically put simulation at or near the top. However, there are a number of important factors for management to consider before making a commitment to a simulation study.

APPLICATION CAPSULE

Cease Fire! Simulation Helps a Shipbuilder Salvage a Sinking Relationship*

Ingalls Shipbuilding, a division of Litton Industries, Inc., is one of the largest shipyards in the world. From 1974 through 1977 the division's sales ranged from $500 million to $800 million with employment of approximately 20,000.

In 1969 and 1970 Ingalls was awarded Total Package Procurement contracts for five amphibious assault ships (LHAs) and 30 DD963 destroyers. These were firm-fixed-price contracts in which Ingalls received performance specifications and assumed sole responsibility for system design, detailed design, material procurement, planning, testing, and construction.

These contracts led to unanticipated cost overruns of $500 million and a claim for this amount against the Navy. The basis for this claim rested on Ingalls' contention that Navy-responsible delays and design changes had created disruptions that had spread difficulties throughout the system and eventually produced the cost overruns. Although detailed data were submitted with the claim the difficulty of estimating the costs of second- and third-order "ripple effects" led to an adversary relationship between Ingalls and the Navy. This relationship endangered not only Ingalls' current profit position but the potential for future business.

To clarify its claim, Litton had a simulation program constructed to correctly quantify Navy-responsible delay and disruption costs and to demonstrate the ripple effects. Simulation was selected because it permitted

1. Direct answering of "what if" questions; in particular, what if the Navy-initiated delays had not occurred?
2. A more complete and realistic representation of the system.
3. Clear and defensible attribution of impacts to specific sources.

The short-run impact of the model was to obtain a $447 million settlement for Ingalls from the Navy. Since the claim was settled out of court both the direct cost of further litigation (perhaps from $170 million to $350 million) and a vast amount of managerial and professional time and talent were saved.

Perhaps the long-run effects are more important. Since its original application eight different shipbuilding programs totaling 55 ships and approximately $7 billion of business have been modeled. In these applications the model is used to estimate the effect of various actions in scheduling or managing resources, as well as the impact of a multitude of external factors.

*Kenneth G. Cooper, "Naval Ship Production: A Claim Settled and a Framework Built," *Interfaces*, vol. 10, no. 6 (December 1980), pp. 20–30.

Simulation versus Analytic Models. As stated above, simulation is frequently used when no convenient analytic model is available. With an analytic model the laws of mathematics can be used, often to obtain optimal decisions and sometimes sensitivity data (provided, of course, that the analysis is not so complex as to be prohibitive). In a simulation with random events, by contrast, optimality is not guaranteed, and it may be difficult to obtain even an approximately optimal solution. Often a number of runs are required just to get a good estimate of the "goodness" of a particular decision. However, simulation models can provide information that analytic models find it difficult or impossible to supply, such as the impact of variability, behavior before steady state is reached, and so on.

Designing a Simulator. The acronym KISS for "Keep It Simple, Stupid" is popular among professionals in the quantitative analysis business. The idea applies with special force to simulation. A common and often fatal error in devising simulation studies is making them too complicated. This may be an overreaction to the freedom gained by moving from analytic models to simulation models. Analytic models are often quite restrictive in their assumptions. Once we depart from linear functions or very simplistic assumptions, the mathematics gets harder by an order of magnitude. The result is that many of the popular analytic models have limited applicability. Simulation can be much more permissive. Since we are typically just generating an observation from a function (rather than solving a set of equations), linear functions do not facilitate the analysis in simulation as much as they do in analytic models.

Whatever the motivation, there is typically a strong urge to include many factors in a simulation model. For example, it may not seem difficult to add a customer return feature to an inventory control model. In essence, all that is required is some additional computer code to generate this feature and incorporate it into the model. "There is no theoretical barrier, so why not do it?" This impression can be seriously wrong.

Large, complicated simulations incorporating a large number of "lifelike" features are at first blush appealing to management. However, they suffer from at least three serious problems:

1. They are often expensive to write and document.
2. They are an expensive experimental device. In the first place, the computer code may become so complex that each run is time-consuming and therefore expensive. Moreover, the more complex the simulation, the more runs one generally wants to make.
3. Complex simulations often produce so much data that the results are difficult to interpret.

Lean, abstract models that capture the essence of the real problem and set encumbering details aside are as important to successful simulation studies as they are to good analytic models. Casual observation suggests that more simulation projects have died from too grand an original conception than from any other disease.

Simulation Packages. The importance and widespread use of simulation has led to the creation of special simulation packages. The first such packages were simulation languages intended to

1. Facilitate model formulation
2. Be easy to learn
3. Provide good debugging and error diagnostics
4. Be flexible enough to use on a wide range of problems

It is now becoming more commonplace for software companies to have student versions of these programs.

Some of the more popular simulation languages are GPSS/H, SIMSCRIPT II.5, and SLAM II. While originally available only for mainframe computers, many of these languages now run on personal computers.

A recent development is the use of animation in conjunction with simulation. For example, if the operation of a factory is being simulated, the user could view on the computer monitor an animation of the movement of material and operation of machines as the simulation is in progress. PROOF (GPSS/H) and SIMGRAPHICS (SIMSCRIPT II.5) are two packages that add animation capabilities to a simulation language. The aim of animation is to make the output of simulation more "user-friendly."

There are now also packages that aim to make the process of building a simulation model more user-friendly. We have seen in this chapter how @RISK can be used by anyone familiar with the spreadsheet paradigm. XCELL+ is a menu-driven, graphically oriented package that also runs on personal computers. It is a special-purpose simulation package in that it aims to enable simulation modeling of manufacturing facilities without requiring the user to do any programming. These are just two of a growing number of such products.

Two guidelines that are useful in all quantitative studies are especially important in simulation studies:

Documentation. Insist on good documentation. A new manager (in contrast to an analyst) should be able to understand the input required, the assumptions of the model, and the meaning of the output with a reasonable amount of effort. This requires clear documentation. Too often the usefulness of a simulation program effectively ends with the tenure of the originator. The only reasonable cure for this problem is good documentation. It is difficult to overemphasize the importance of this guideline.

Group Dynamics. All quantitative modeling efforts require intensive interaction and communication between modeler and user. This is particularly true of simulation projects. The user must understand how to enter decisions and parameters and how to analyze output. The first-hand knowledge of the user is essential in making sure that the simulation captures the essence of the real problem. Also, the fact that the user has an intimate knowledge of the real problem can be an important part of the search for good solutions.

Good documentation and group dynamics are closely interrelated and are an important part of managing any project based on quantitative modeling and analysis.

13.8 Summary

Section 13.1 pointed out that the use of experimentation to evaluate alternatives is an important part of applied science and that computer-based simulation is the most common experimental approach to management problems. It also discussed the use of simulation on decisions under risk, that is, on problems in which the behavior of one or more factors can be represented by a probability distribution.

Sections 13.2 and 13.3 introduced examples dealing with capital budgeting and inventory control, both of which involve an unpredictable element (demand). These problems were used to illustrate how random events are incorporated into a simulation study. The examples showed that experimental results will not necessarily lead to the same decision that would be derived if one could use the analytic criterion of maximizing the expected profit. By its very nature the output from a simulator with random components is random. Generally, using a large number of trials will make the simulated average profit closer to the theoretic expected profit. The examples also demonstrated how multiple measures of effectiveness can be produced and, more important, how simulation with multiple trials provides an indication of the variability with a given policy.

Random numbers are at the basis of the technique of simulating random events. Section 13.4 presented the general technique used to generate random variables from an arbitrary probability distribution. The exponential and normal distributions were presented as special cases.

Section 13.5 returned to the inventory problem discussed in Section 13.3 to show how a spreadsheet program can easily perform much more realistic analysis and generate more valuable information than is possible with calculations by hand.

Section 13.6 turned to an example from manufacturing to explore the question of whether balancing the production capacity of all workstations necessarily leads to an optimal result. The example illustrated the importance of designing a simulation so as to eliminate extraneous effects such as those associated with starting or ending conditions.

The final section was devoted to the topic of implementation. The discussion took a general management point of view and considered such topics as designing a simulator, good documentation, and group dynamics. A brief introduction to commercially available simulation software was also included.

Key Terms

Simulator. An experimental device that in important respects acts like a system of interest. (*p. 551*)

Simulation Model. A series of logical and mathematical operations that provides a measure of effectiveness for a particular set of values of the parameters and decisions. (*p. 552*)

Random Variable. An entity that will take on a numerical value; the likelihood of it assuming any particular value is given by a probability function. (*p. 563*)

Probability Distribution. A means of specifying the likelihood of an uncertain quantity. (*p. 563*)

Monte Carlo Method. A type of simulation that uses probability distributions to determine whether random events occur. (*p. 563*)

Discrete Uniform Distribution. A probability distribution that assigns equal probability to each member of a finite set of consecutive integers. (*p. 556*)

Trial. A single run of a simulation model (i.e., a single pass through the simulator). (*p. 558*)

Continuous Uniform Distribution. A probability distribution that assigns equal likelihood to each member of an interval of real numbers. (See Appendix A for the mathematical form of this function.) (*p. 558*)

Multiple Trials. Multiple passes through the simulator, each pass using the same values for decisions and parameters, but a different series of random numbers and hence possibly different outcomes for random events. (*p. 559*)

Expected Value. A statistical concept referring to the expected value, or mean, of some random quantity with a specified probability distribution. (*p. 559*)

Poisson Distribution. A probability distribution often used to describe the number of arrivals to a queuing system during a specified interval of time. (See Appendix A for the mathematical form of this function.) (*p. 560*)

Variability. In simulation, a reference to the amount of fluctuation in measures of effectiveness as numerous trials are performed. (*p. 567*)

Random Digit. A random variable consisting of a single digit that can take on any value (0–9) with equal probability. (*p. 568*)

Random Number Table. A random sampling of integers in a given range (say, from 0 to 99) where each integer is equally likely to occur. (*p. 568*)

Cumulative Distribution Function. For a specific random variable X, the function giving the probability that $X \leq x$ for all values of x. (*p. 571*)

Exponential Distribution. A probability distribution typically used to describe the time between arrivals at a queuing system. (See Appendix A for the mathematical form of this function.) (*p. 573*)

Normal Distribution. A probability distribution that is a good model for many phenomena that occur in nature and business, such as fluctuating prices and demands; also, the distribution of the sample mean calculated for any random variable. (See Appendix A for details.) (*p. 574*)

Major Concepts Quiz

True-False

1. T F The basic concept of simulation is to build an experimental device that will "act like" the system of interest in important respects.

2. T F A deterministic model (one with no random elements) can be used as a simulation model.

3. T F If a simulator includes random elements, two successive trials with the same parameter values will produce the same value for the measure of effectiveness.

4. T F In a simulation with random elements it is impossible to guarantee that the decision that maximizes expected profit has been selected.

5. T F In real-world problems it is common practice to compare the expected cost associated with a decision with the average cost for that decision produced by a simulator.

6. T F In a simulation with several distinct random outcomes a correct association of random numbers and events implies that each random number must represent one of the outcomes.

7. T F With small sample sizes the results of a simulation can be very sensitive to the initial conditions.

8. T F Simulation is sometimes described as a last-resort technique since it is generally not employed until analytic approaches have been examined and rejected.

9. T F A common error in designing a simulator is to use such restrictive assumptions that the model fails to capture the essence of the problem.

10. T F Additional experimentation with a simulator is sure to increase the simulation cost but may also improve the quality of the solution.

Multiple Choice

11. In a typical simulation model, input provided by the analyst includes
    - **a.** values for the parameters
    - **b.** values for the decision variables
    - **c.** a value for the measure of effectiveness
    - **d.** all of the above
    - **e.** both a and b

12. An advantage of simulation, as opposed to optimization, is that
    - **a.** often multiple measures of goodness can be examined
    - **b.** some appreciation for the variability of outcomes of interest can be obtained
    - **c.** more complex scenarios can be studied
    - **d.** all of the above

13. Consider a simulator with random elements that uses profit as a measure of effectiveness. For a specified assignment of parameter values
    - **a.** the average profit over a number of trials is used as an estimate of the expected profit associated with a decision
    - **b.** the average profit is always closer to the expected profit as the number of trials increases
    - **c.** the average profit over 10 trials is always the same
    - **d.** none of the above

14. A random number refers to
    - **a.** an observation from a set of numbers (say, the integers 0–99) each of which is equally likely
    - **b.** an observation selected at random from a normal distribution
    - **c.** an observation selected at random from any distribution provided by the analyst
    - **d.** none of the above

15. The random number 0.63 has been selected. The corresponding observation, v, from a *normal* distribution is determined by the relationship:
    - **a.** v is "the probability that the normally distributed quantity is ≤ 0.63"
    - **b.** v is the number such that "the probability that the normally distributed quantity is $\leq v$" equals 0.63
    - **c.** v is the number such that "the probability that the normally distributed quantity equals v" is 0.63
    - **d.** none of the above

16. Analytic results are sometimes used before a simulation study
    - **a.** to identify "good values" of the system parameters
    - **b.** to determine the optimal decision

c. to identify "good values" of the decision variables for the specific choices of system parameters
d. all of the above

17. To reduce the effect of initial conditions in a simulation study one can
    a. vary the values of the system parameters
    b. increase the number of alternative decisions studied
    c. increase the sample size and ignore data from a number of the first runs for each set of parameters and decisions
    d. all of the above

18. If both an analytic model and a simulation model could be used to study a problem including random events, the analytic model is often preferred because
    a. the simulator generally requires a number of runs just to get a good estimate of the objective value (such as expected cost) for a particular decision
    b. the analytic model may produce an optimal decision
    c. the simulation study may require evaluating a large number of possible decisions
    d. all of the above

19. Large complicated simulation models suffer from the following problem(s):
    a. average costs are not well defined
    b. it is difficult to create the appropriate random events
    c. they may be expensive to write and to use as an experimental device
    d. all of the above

20. In performing a simulation it is advisable to
    a. use the results of earlier decisions to suggest the next decision to try
    b. use the same number of trials for each decision
    c. simulate all possible decisions
    d. none of the above

Answers

1. T	6. F	11. e	16. c
2. T	7. T	12. d	17. c
3. F	8. T	13. a	18. d
4. T	9. F	14. a	19. c
5. F	10. T	15. b	20. a

▶ Problems

In the following problems you will be asked to perform a number of simulations. In all cases, assign consecutive random numbers to each event and assign smaller values of random numbers to smaller numerical values of the event. For example:

EVENT (DEMAND)	PROBABILITY	PROPER ASSIGNMENT	IMPROPER ASSIGNMENT
3	0.2	00–19	30–49
4	0.7	20–89	00–29 and 60–99
5	0.1	90–99	50–59

In each simulation problem a row and column will be indicated. Select the first random number at this position in Figure 13.14 and read as instructed in the problem statement. Following this procedure will enable you to check your answers with those in the back of the book.

See IM

13-1. ▲ Cite examples of the use of simulation (in the broad sense) by the military.

See IM

13-2. ▲ Cite examples of the use of simulation (in the broad sense) in professional sports.

(a) See IM

(b) BEST = 1700; BEST = 1900

13-3. ▲▲ Consider the Astro/Cosmo production problem that was presented as Example 1 in Section 2.8. The LP formulation of this model is

$$\begin{aligned} &\text{Max } 20A + 30C \\ &\text{s.t.} \quad A \le 70 \\ &\qquad C \le 50 \\ &\qquad A + 2C \le 120 \\ &\qquad A, C \ge 0 \end{aligned}$$

(a) Construct a flowchart showing how to approach this problem as a simulation.

(b) Use the flowchart to evaluate the two potential solutions: ($A = 40$, $C = 30$) and ($A = 50$, $C = 30$).

See IM

13-4. ▲ Given below are 50 weeks of historical car sales at Sally's Solar Car Co.

Number of Sales	Number of Weeks
0	2
1	5
2	12
3	16
4	8
5	7

(a) Assign random numbers to demands so that the probability of a particular demand in the simulation is equal to the relative frequency of that demand over the last 50 weeks.

(b) Starting in row 4 column 5 of Figure 13.14, simulate 13 weeks of demand.

False; simplex is guaranteed to find optimum.

13-5. ▲▲ Comment on the following statement: The simplex algorithm is a type of simulation, since it has to evaluate a number of alternative solutions en route to finding the optimal solution.

Fairly common (See IM)

13-6. ▲▲ Jerry Tate is responsible for the maintenance of a fleet of vehicles used by the power company in constructing and repairing electric transmission lines. Jerry is especially concerned with the cost projections for replacing a large derrick on these vehicles. He would like to simulate the number of derrick failures each year over the next 20 years. Jerry has looked at the last 10 years of data and compiled the following table:

Number of Derrick Failures	Number of Years
0	4
1	3
2	1
3	1
4	1

He decides to simulate the 20-year period by selecting two-digit random numbers from the second column of Figure 13.14 starting in the third row.

Conduct the simulation for Jerry. How common is it for the total number of failures during three consecutive years to exceed 3?

Increase: 00–29; remain the same: 30–79; decrease: 80–99

13-7. ▲ PROTRAC has a cash management problem. In this problem PROTRAC's cash balance is determined each morning. The change in the cash balance from one morning to the next is a random variable. In particular, it increases by \$10,000 with probability 0.3, decreases by \$10,000 with probability 0.2, and remains the same with probability 0.5. Associate random numbers with these events so as to accurately reflect the correct probability in a simulation study.

See IM

13-8. ▲▲ Consider the following brand-switching problem. In this problem probabilities are used to describe the behavior of a customer buying beer. Three particular beers (B, M, and S) are incorporated in the model. Customer behavior is summarized in Figure 13.26. Thus, we see in the first row that a customer who buys beer B in week 1 will buy the same beer in week 2 with probability 0.90, will buy beer M with probability 0.06, and will buy beer S with probability 0.04. A similar interpretation holds for the other rows. Consider a customer who buys beer B in week 1. Assume that you wish to simulate his behavior for the next 10 weeks. We know that in week 2 he would buy beers B, M, and S with probabilities 0.90, 0.06, and 0.04. If in week 2 he bought beer M, he would buy beers B, M, and S with probability 0.12, 0.78, and 0.10, respectively. Define the events you would need and associate random numbers with these events so as to accurately reflect the correct probabilities.

BEER PURCHASED IN WEEK i	PROBABILITY OF PURCHASE IN WEEK $i + 1$		
	B	M	S
B	0.90	0.06	0.04
M	0.12	0.78	0.10
S	0.09	0.07	0.84

▲ FIGURE 13.26

115.55

13-9. ▲ Assume that you want to generate a sample from a normal distribution that has a mean of 100 and a standard deviation of 10. If the number you obtain from the table of random numbers is 94, what is the value of the normal random variable?

16.0

13-10. ▲▲ Assume that you want to generate a sample from the normal distribution that has a mean of 20 and a standard deviation of 15. If the number you obtain from a table of random numbers is 395, what is the value of the normal random variable?

RN = 06, W = 6.0; RN = 60, W = 38.6; RN = 80, W = 44.3

13-11. ▲▲ The probability that $W \leq x$ is plotted in Figure 13.27. Use this function to generate three sequential observations of the random variable W. Start in row 17, column 4 of Figure 13.15 and read down.

RN = 40, x = 1; RN = 60, x = 2; RN = 80, x = 3

13-12. ▲▲ The probability mass function of the Poisson distribution is given by

$$p(x; \lambda) = \frac{\lambda^x}{x!} e^{-\lambda}, \quad x = 0, 1, \ldots$$

Let $\lambda = 2$, and calculate the probability you observe x, $x = 0, 1, \ldots, 5$. What are the observations for the random numbers 40, 60, 80?

(a) 129

(b) 5

13-13. ▲▲ Simulate a sample of 10 periods for the omelet pan problem described in this chapter. Assume that you have 10 pans on hand at the beginning of each period. Use the random numbers starting in row 20, column 8, reading down Figure 13.14. Use the association of random numbers with demand given in Figure 13.15.

(a) Calculate the average profit per period.

(b) Record the number of stockouts (count a stockout as occurring when demand > 10).

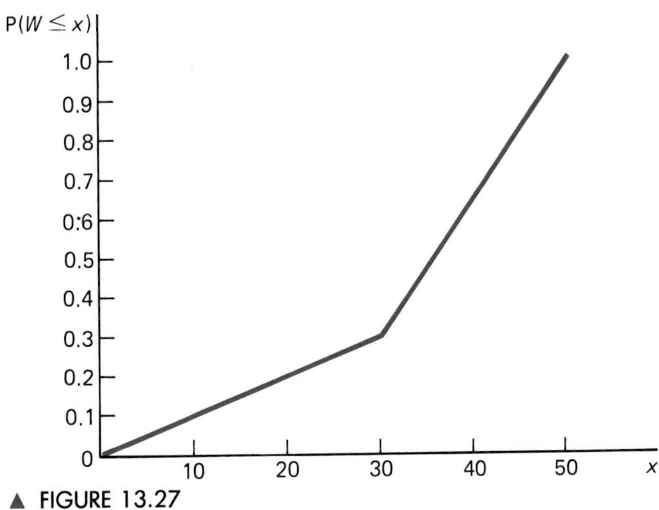

▲ FIGURE 13.27

(b)Average shortage = 1.1; average excess = 0.2

(c)Expected shortage = 0.92; expected excess = 0.36

13-14. ▲▲ The weekly demand for milk for the last 50 weeks at the All-Ways-Open convenient market is shown in Figure 13.28.

(a) Assign random numbers to demands so that the probability of a particular demand in the simulation is equal to the relative frequency of that demand over the last 50 weeks.

(b) The store orders 42 cases every week. What are the average shortage and average excess inventory for 10 weeks? Begin in row 1, column 1 of Figure 13.14 and read down.

(c) What are the expected shortage and the expected excess inventory?

See IM

13-15. ▲▲ The number of disk brake jobs performed by the service department of the Green Cab Company during each of the last 30 weeks is shown in Figure 13.29.

(a) Assign random numbers to the number of brake jobs performed so that the probability of a particular number of jobs in the simulation is equal to the relative frequency of that number of jobs over the last 30 weeks.

(b) Simulate 10 weeks of demand. Begin in row 5, column 3 of Figure 13.14 and read down.

▼ FIGURE 13.28

SALES (CASES)	NUMBER OF WEEKS
40	4
41	10
42	12
43	9
44	8
45	7
Total	50

▼ FIGURE 13.29

NUMBER OF BRAKE JOBS	NUMBER OF WEEKS
5	3
6	8
7	9
8	6
9	4
Total	30

(a)See IM

(b)See IM

(c)Decrease; random effects tend to cancel each other

(d)Yes (See IM)

13-16. ▲▲ Steco currently carries inventory for stainless steel sheets in two nearby cities, L and A. Weekly demands (in trucks) and the probabilities for each city are shown in Figure 13.30. Assume that the demands are independent. L starts each week with 4 trucks of inventory on hand. A starts each week with 6 trucks of inventory on hand.

(a) Simulate 20 weeks of demand at L, and record the number of stockouts. Begin in row 21, column 6 of Figure 13.14 and read down.

(b) Start in row 1, column 7 and read down to simulate 20 weeks of demand at A and record the number of stockouts.

DEMAND	PROBABILITY	
	L	A
1	0.2	
2	0.3	
3	0.3	0.1
4	0.1	0.1
5	0.1	0.3
6		0.3
7		0.2

▲ FIGURE 13.30

Suppose that Steco centralized its stainless steel sheet inventory and satisfied all demand from L and A out of 1 new warehouse (call it LA).

(c) If LA started each week with 10 trucks of inventory on hand, would you expect the number of stockouts to increase, decrease, or remain the same as compared with when L and A operated independently? Why?

(d) Use the same sequence of demands you used in parts (a) and (b) to simulate 20 weeks of operation for the new warehouse, LA. Record the number of stockouts. Does this result agree with your answer to part (c)?

4 customers have to wait (See IM)

13-17. ▲▲ The time between arrivals at the drive-up window of the Slippery Savings and Loan is shown in Figure 13.31. All customers form a single line and are served in the order of arrival. Assume that it takes 8 minutes to serve each customer. Also assume that no one is being served or waiting to be served when the first customer arrives. Simulate the arrival of 16 customers, and record the number of customers who have to wait. Begin in row 1, column 1 of Figure 13.14 and read down.

TIME BETWEEN ARRIVALS (MIN)	PROBABILITY
5	0.25
10	0.50
15	0.25

▲ FIGURE 13.31

(a)$19,418.25 (See IM)

(b) See IM

(c)$42,000 (See IM)

(d)$25,500 (See IM)

13-18. ▲▲ The Homeburg Volunteer Fire Department makes an annual door-to-door solicitation for funds. There are 3000 households to solicit. The department asks households to be supporters (a $10 donation) or patrons (a $25 donation). An analysis of data from previous years indicates that

1. No one is home at 15% of the homes visited. If no one is home, the home is *not* revisited, and thus no donation is obtained. When someone is home, 80% of the time a woman answers the door and 20% of the time a man answers the door.
2. 40% of the women make a contribution; 70% of them are supporters, and 30% are patrons.
3. 70% of the men make a contribution; 25% of them are supporters, and 75% are patrons.

(a) What is the expected value of the return from the solicitation?

(b) Make a flowchart for this process. The output should be the contribution that occurs from calling on a house.

(c) Use the flowchart in part (b) to simulate 5 visits and record the total contribution from these 5 visits. Begin in row 1, column 4 of Figure 13.14 and read down. What is your estimate of the return from the annual solicitation based on this simulation?

(d) Simulate 10 visits to answer the same question as in part (c). Begin in row 1, column 6 of Figure 13.14 and read down.

(a)$14,941

(b)Answers may vary (See IM)

13-19. Not wanting to leave your beloved alma mater, you have come up with a scheme to stay around for 5 more years: You have decided to bid on the fast food concession rights at the football stadium. You feel sure that a bid of $30,000 will win the concession, which gives you the right to sell food at football games for the next 5 years. You estimate that annual operating costs will be 40% of sales and annual sales will average $50,000. Your Uncle Ned has agreed to lend you the $30,000 to make your bid. You will pay him $7700 at the end of each year. Your tax rate is 33%.

(a) Use a spreadsheet program to answer the following question. What is your average annual after-tax profit? Assume that the yearly payments of $7700 are deductible.

(b) You realize that sales will probably vary from year to year. Suppose that sales can vary plus or minus 40% from the average of $50,000. You are concerned about the minimum after-tax profit you can earn in a year. You can survive if it is at least $7000. Model annual sales for the 5 years as 5 continuous uniform random variables. Based on a sample of 400 five-year periods, estimate the probability that over any five-year period the *minimum* after-tax profit for a year will be at least $7000. Will you bid for the concession?

(a)7 TVs. Not necessarily

(b)Answers may vary (See IM).

13-20. You are the manager of Tex Electronics and are planning a promotion on a discontinued model of 27″ color TV. The promotion will last 10 days, at the end of which any sets that you ordered but have not sold will be sold to another retailer for $250 each. You must order the sets from the manufacturer before you know what the demand during the promotion will be. Your cost is $350 per set and you will sell them for $600. You estimate that on 20% of the days you will sell 2 sets, 30% of the days you will sell 1 set, and 50% of the days you will sell no sets.

(a) What is the expected demand during the promotion? Should you necessarily order the expected demand?

(b) Use @RISK to estimate the optimal number of TVs to order. Use the @SIMTABLE function to simulate order quantities of 7, 8, 9, 10, and 11. [Set the cell in the spreadsheet that contains the order quantity to @SIMTABLE(7,8,9,10,11,5) and set the number of Simulations to 5 using the @RISK menu.] In the 10 cells containing the daily demands, put the function @DISCRETE(0,0.5,1,0.3,2,0.2,3). Have one cell that contains the total net profit for the promotion. Based on 400 trials, what order quantity maximizes the average net profit?

Diagnostic Assignment

Scheduling Tanker Arrivals

Simulation is a popular method for studying systems with random components. It follows that managers are often placed in the position of accepting or rejecting recommendations based on simulation studies, or perhaps recommending additional analysis. This vignette illustrates such a situation.

David O'Brien is the manager of Global Oil's St. Croix refinery. This refinery was built in 1954 and is served by a dock facility designed to handle 250,000-barrel tankers. Tankers arrive at the dock and unload into a 700,000-barrel storage tank at the rate of 400,000 barrels per day. The refinery itself accepts oil from the storage tank at the rate of 250,000 barrels per day. This is called the input pipeline capacity. The storage tank thus serves as a buffer storage facility, allowing the tankers to unload more rapidly. If the storage tank is full, however, the rate at which tankers can unload decreases to 250,000 barrels per day.

Global installed the storage tank because the firm must pay a penalty cost, a so-called demurrage fee, if a tanker has to wait too long before it is able to start unloading its oil. In particular, a demurrage fee of $1400 per day is charged if a 250,000-barrel tanker must wait more than 2 days to start unloading. The charge is a pro-rata charge, so if a tanker waits 3.5 days, for example, before the start of unloading, then its total fee is (3.5 − 2.0) × \$1400, or \$2100.

Global is considering servicing the St. Croix refinery with its fleet of new 500,000-barrel supertankers. The harbor is deep and can easily accommodate the new tankers, but because of the limited unloading capacity, demurrage charges are a concern. A 500,000-barrel tanker incurs demurrage fees at the rate of \$3000 per day if it must wait more than 2 days to start unloading.

Currently, one 250,000-barrel tanker arrives every 1.5 days on the average, that is, at a rate of 2/3 tankers per day, or 166,667 barrels of oil per day. Dave has proposed that if Global moves to the 500,000-barrel tankers, demurrage charges should remain about the same as long as the average daily arrival of oil is held constant. He therefore decides that the supertankers should arrive at the rate of 1/3 tanker per day, or 1 every 3 days, since 500,000-barrels/tanker × 1/3 tanker/day equals 166,667 barrels/day.

Dave learns that if the 500,000-barrel tankers are used, Global in fact is willing to incur a small increase in the total annual demurrage charges. This is because 1 supertanker requires fewer crew members than 2 of the current tankers. However, the firm would not like to see a large increase in these charges.

To check his intuitive notion that the effects of doubling the tanker size and cutting the arrival rate in half should cancel each other, Dave decides to use Tanker, Global's on-line simulator, which was written to aid him in operating the dock. This simulator assumes that the arrivals are drawn from an exponential distribution (see Chapter 17) with a user-specified mean. The item of interest is the total annual demurrage charges. The simulation will provide two ways to estimate this quantity:

1. *Average cost per tanker method.* Use the simulated results to compute the average cost per tanker as

$$\frac{\text{total demurrage fees}}{\text{number of tankers}}$$

and multiply this figure by the average number of tankers per year. Since supertankers arrive at the rate of 1 every 3 days, this implies 120 per year (assuming a 360-day year). Thus, for supertankers we obtain the estimate

$$\text{total annual cost} = (\text{average cost per tanker}) \times (120)$$

2. *Average cost per day method.* Use the simulated results to compute the average cost per day as

$$\frac{\text{total demurrage fees}}{\text{number of days}}$$

and multiply this figure by 360, the number of days in a year. Using this method, we obtain the estimate (for either type of tanker)

$$\text{total annual cost} = (\text{average cost per day}) \times (360)$$

▼ FIGURE 13.32
250,000-Barrel Tankers

```
$PARAMS
PIPCAP = 250000.0,        TNKCAP = 700000.0,         UNLOAD = 400000.0,
SHPSIZ = 250000.0         ARRIVAL = 0.6670000,       DEMLMT = 2.000000,
CHARGE = 1400.000,        NUMBAT = 1,                NUMSHP = 44
SEED = 345671
WANT MORE CHANGES? N

END OF SIMULATION AT TIME  50,399

A TOTAL OF           44 TANKERS WERE UNLOADED
AVERAGE TIME IN PORT WAS           1.718
A TOTAL OF           1 TANKERS WERE WAITING AT END
A TOTAL OF           41.142 DAYS WERE SPENT WAITING
A TOTAL OF         7388.640 DOLLARS IN FEES CHARGED
TANK WAS EMPTY           6.774
TANK WAS FULL           18.533
```

```
$PARAMS
PIPCAP = 250000.0,          TNKCAP = 700000.0,          UNLOAD = 400000.0,
SHPSIZE = 500000.0,         ARIVAL = 0.3330000,         DEMLMT = 2.000000,
CHARGE = 3000.000,          NUMBAT = 1,                 NUMSHP = 22,
SEED = 345671
WANT MORE CHANGES? N

END OF SIMULATION AT TIME          52.192

A TOTAL OF          22       TANKERS WERE UNLOADED
AVERAGE TIME IN PORT WAS          1.915
A TOTAL OF          3        TANKERS WERE WAITING AT END
A TOTAL OF          12.364        DAYS WERE SPENT WAITING
A TOTAL OF          3982.445        DOLLARS IN FEES CHARGED
TANK WAS EMPTY           10.992
TANK WAS FULL           6.035
```

▲ FIGURE 13.33
500,000-Barrel Tankers

Actually Dave decides to run two simulations: one with parameters describing the current situation and the other with parameters describing the proposed situation. In each case he decides to sample roughly 2 months of data. He thus plans to simulate the arrival and unloading of 44 of the 250,000-barrel tankers (an expected duration of 44 × 1.5 or 66 days) and 22 of the 500,000-barrel tankers (an expected duration of 22 × 3.0 or 66 days). The simulation with current parameters is used as a test to see if the results are a reasonable approximation of the current situation.

The results of the simulations are shown in Figures 13.32 and 13.33.

The relevant data are summarized in Figure 13.34.

Dave finds the data in Figure 13.34 to be interesting from several points of view. First, concerning the results from the 250,000-barrel tankers (i.e., the current situation), experience has shown that, over the last several years of operation, more than half of the time no demurrage charge has been incurred during a 2-month interval. However, a $7000 charge for a 2-month period in which a charge is incurred is not rare. Dave thus feels that the simulator is by chance giving a conservative estimate (in the sense of an overestimate) of the average demurrage charges,

▼ FIGURE 13.34
Summary Data

TANKER SIZE	250,000	500,000	TANKER SIZE	250,000	500,000
(a) Total demurrage charges	$7388.640	$3982.445	(e) = (a)/(c) Average cost per day	$146.60	$76.304
(b) Numbers of tankers unloaded	44	22	(f) Expected tankers per year	240	120
(c) Number of days	50.399	52.192	(g) = (d) × (f) Tanker-based cost per year	$40,301.52	$21,722.40
(d) = (a)/(b) Average cost per tanker	$167.923	$181.020	(h) = (e) × 360 Day-based cost per year	$52,776.00	$27,469.44

and it should thus be a good test of the proposed system.

Second, he is surprised that 500,000-barrel tankers yield a considerably lower annual cost with both estimation techniques. His intuition had suggested that the costs for the two systems would be about equal. However, he knows that the difference could easily be a random event, because this particular result is, of course, based on a sample. The good news, however, is that there is nothing in the data to suggest that the demurrage charges would be significantly larger with the 500,000-barrel tankers.

The mark of a good manager is to know when to decide as well as what to decide. With the simulation analysis for backup, Dave confidently recommends that Global switch to the 500,000-barrel tankers with a 0.333 rate of arrival.

Questions

1. Explain the cause of the difference Dave encountered with the two methods of estimating total annual demurrage fees in the simulation with 500,000-barrel tankers.
2. Do you believe the results of the study? Comment on Dave's recommendation and study.

Video Case

Simulation and Time-Based Competition at Nissan

Manufacturing competition has passed through many different phases since people first began to produce goods. The dominant form of competition during most of the twentieth century has been based on economies of scale. The essence of this strategy is producing and selling a large number of essentially identical items. With this approach, it pays to make large capital investments in production equipment, since with a large volume of sales the fixed cost that must be absorbed by each unit of output is quite small.

The last ten years or so have brought a major change in the form of competition. The current emphasis is on *time-based competition.* This is a pervasive philosophy that appears throughout the manufacturing process. It is perhaps best known for its impact on production practices and inventory management. Just-in-time inventory control (see Chapter 10) and stockless production systems, pioneered in Japan, are now an integral part of production throughout the world.

However, time-based competition is not restricted to the production floor—it plays a crucial role in product design and new product development. Firms that can reduce the time spent on these processes can move more quickly to satisfy the ever-changing desires of the consumer, putting their less quick-footed competitors at a disadvantage.

A number of techniques and approaches are used to shorten the design cycle. These include synchronous design, the use of design teams, and the use of improved technologies such as CAD (computer aided design) and CAM (computer aided manufacturing).

Simulation can and does play an important role in time reduction. The video on designing Nissan automobiles gives some indication of its power.

Questions

1. List several ways in which simulation is used during the design process at Nissan.
2. How do these various simulations influence the time-based strategy of Nissan?

CHAPTER

14 Decision Theory and Decision Trees

APPLICATION CAPSULE

A Tale of Nine Digits: Decision Trees Help Keep Postal Automation from Becoming a Dead Letter*

In March of 1984, the US Postal Service (USPS) faced a major strategic decision. The USPS had to decide whether to implement phase 2 of their postal automation program as originally planned or to adopt one of a number of possible alternatives.

The automation program included the acquisition of optical character readers (OCRs) and bar code readers (BCRs). Phase 1 was complete: USPS had ordered 252 single-line OCRs and 248 BCRs at a total cost of $234 million. Phase 2, which included plans to order another 403 OCRs and 452 BCRs, would cost an additional $450 million. Potential savings from reduced clerk and carrier costs of as much as $1.5 billion were possible, but highly uncertain. A major reason for the uncertainty was that the savings depended on businesses using the nine-digit ZIP code (ZIP + 4). Since this practice was not mandated, actual use was uncertain. To further complicate matters, a new technology, the multi-line OCR, had become available. The evidence suggested that this device was essentially equivalent to the single-line OCR for reading nine-digit ZIP mail but substantially better for reading five-digit mail.

A decision analysis model (decision tree) was developed to help analyze this problem. Six possible courses of action were considered:

1. *Single-line OCR.* The USPS should proceed with the current plan. No funds would be devoted to multi-line OCR research, development, or testing.
2. *Multi-line with ZIP + 4.* Cancel the current phase 2, purchase multi-line readers, and retain the ZIP + 4 program.
3. *Multi-line without ZIP + 4.* Pursue plan 2, but drop the ZIP + 4 program.
4. *Convert.* Continue phase 2 but initiate testing on single-line to multi-line conversion; then convert all single-line OCRs as soon as possible regardless of the level of ZIP + 4 usage.
5. *Hedge.* Pursue plan 4, with conversion dependent on the level of ZIP + 4 usage.

6. *Abandon ship.* Cancel phase 2, terminate ZIP + 4, and use the current OCRs for five-digit ZIP mail.

Three fundamental types of uncertainty were identified:

1. The level of ZIP + 4 usage.
2. The actual savings rate—that is, how much the USPS would actually save for each piece of mail sorted with these systems.
3. The usage rate—that is, the actual volume of mail.

A decision tree was constructed and the net present values of the different strategies were calculated. All options proved preferable to canceling the program, with the *convert* strategy the best. Subsequently, extensive sensitivity analysis confirmed the advantages of the *convert* strategy and suggested further refinements, in which both single-line and multi-line OCRs were purchased.

The final result of this evaluation was a report prepared for the U.S. Congress by the Office of Technology Assessment. The impact of the report was notable. The Postal Service, which had previously rejected the multi-line OCR technology, accepted it after this analysis, and indeed subsequently purchased multi-line equipment. The resulting savings are estimated at $200 million over the single-line alternative and perhaps as much as $1.5 billion over the alternative of canceling the postal automation program.

*Ulvila, "Postal Automation (ZIP + 4) Technology: A Decision Analysis," *Interfaces,* Vol. 17, No. 2 (March–April 1987); "20/30 Hindsight: The Automatic Zipper," *Interfaces,* Vol. 18, No. 1 (Jan.–Feb. 1988).

14.1 Introduction

The decision criterion is similar to the objective function in linear programming.

Decision theory provides a framework for analyzing a wide variety of management problems. The framework establishes (1) a system of classifying decision problems based on the amount of information about the problem that is available and (2) a decision criterion, that is, a measure of the "goodness" of a decision for each type of problem.

Decisions against nature

In the first part of this chapter we will present the decision theory framework and relate it to models previously discussed. The second half of the chapter is devoted to decision trees. Decision trees apply decision theory concepts to sequential decisions that include uncertain events. They are a pragmatic and practical aid to managerial decision making.

It sometimes "feels" as if nature is perverse and "out to get us" but these states of nature take place regardless of our actions or decisions.

In general terms, decision theory treats decisions against nature. This phrase refers to a situation where the result (return) from a decision depends on the action of another player (nature), over which you have no control. For example, if the decision is whether or not to carry an umbrella, the return (get wet or not) depends on the state of nature that ensues. It is important to note that in this model the returns accrue only to the decision maker. Nature does not care what the outcome is. This condition distinguishes decision theory from game theory. In *game theory* both players have an economic interest in the outcome.

In decision theory problems, the fundamental piece of data is a **payoff table** like Figure 14.1. In this figure the alternative decisions are listed along the side of the table, and the possible states of nature are listed across the top. The entries in the

DECISION	STATE OF NATURE			
	1	2	⋯	m
d_1	r_{11}	r_{12}	⋯	r_{1m}
d_2	r_{21}	r_{22}	⋯	r_{2m}
⋮	⋮	⋮	⋮	⋮
d_n	r_{n1}	r_{n2}	⋯	r_{nm}

▲ FIGURE 14.1
Payoff Table

body of the table are the payoffs for all possible combinations of decisions and states of nature. The decision process proceeds as follows:

1. You, the decision maker, select one of the alternative decisions $d_1, \cdots, d_n$. Suppose that you select d_1.
2. After your decision is made, a state of nature occurs that is beyond your control. Suppose that state 2 occurs.
3. The return you receive can now be determined from the payoff table. Since you made decision d_1 and state of nature 2 occurred, the return is r_{12}.

Emphasize that the decision is made first, then one of the states of nature occurs. Once the decision has been made, it can't be changed after the state of nature occurs.

In general terms the question is, Which of the decisions should we select? We would like as large a return as possible, that is, the largest possible value of r_{ij}, where i represents the decision made and j the state of nature that occurs. It is obvious that the decision we should select will depend on our belief concerning what nature will do, that is, which state of nature will occur. If we believe state 1 will occur, we select the decision associated with the largest number in column 1. If we believe the state of nature is more likely to be state 2, we choose the decision corresponding to the largest payoff in column 2, and so on.

In the following section we will consider different assumptions about nature's behavior. Each assumption leads to a different *criterion* for selecting the "best" decision, and hence to a different procedure.

▶ 14.2 Three Classes of Decision Problems

This section deals with three classes of decision problems against nature. Each class is defined by an assumption about nature's behavior. The three classes are decisions under certainty, decisions under risk, and decisions under uncertainty.

Decisions under Certainty

A **decision under certainty** is one in which you know which state of nature will occur. Alternatively, you can think of it as a case with a single state of nature. Suppose, for example, that in the morning you are deciding whether to take your umbrella to work and you know *for sure* that it will be raining when you leave work in the afternoon. In the payoff table for this problem, Figure 14.2, \$7 is the cost of having your suit cleaned if you get caught in the rain. It enters the table with a minus sign since it is a table of returns and a cost is a negative return. Obviously, the optimal decision is to take the umbrella.

	RAIN
Take Umbrella	0
Do not	−7.00

▲ FIGURE 14.2

All linear programming models, integer programming models, and other deterministic models such as the EOQ model can be thought of as decisions against nature in which there is only one state of nature. This is so because we are sure (within the context of the model) what return we will get for each decision we make. For a concrete example, consider the **PROTRAC** E and F model of Chapter 2:

$$\begin{aligned} \text{Max } & 5000E + 4000F \\ \text{s.t. } & 10E + 15F \leq 150 \\ & 20E + 10F \leq 160 \\ & 30E + 10F \geq 135 \\ & E - 3F \leq 0 \\ & E + F \geq 5 \\ & E, F \geq 0 \end{aligned}$$

Figure 14.3 presents this problem in the form of a payoff table. In this table, a return of $-\infty$ is assigned to any infeasible decision. For example, since $E = 0, F = 0$ violates the third and fifth constraints, the associated return is defined to be $-\infty$. For any feasible pair (E, F) the return is defined to be the objective function value—namely, $5000E + 4000F$. For this model we know exactly what return we get for each decision (each choice of the pair E, F). We can thus list all returns in one column and think of it as representing one state of nature that we are sure will occur.

DECISION	STATE OF NATURE
$E = 0, F = 0$	$-\infty$
$E = 5, F = 4$	41,000
⋮	⋮
$E = 6, F = 3.5$	44,000
⋮	⋮

▲ FIGURE 14.3
Payoff Table for the PROTRAC E and F Problem

Conceptually, it is easy to solve a problem with one state of nature. You simply select the decision that yields the highest return. In practice, as opposed to "in concept," finding such a decision may be another story. Since E and F can take on an infinite number of values, there will be an infinite number of rows for this problem (see Figure 14.3). Even in this simple problem, enumerating the alternatives and selecting the best of them are not possible. Additional mathematical analysis (in this case, the simplex algorithm) is needed to find the optimal decision.

Decisions under Risk

A lack of certainty about future events is a characteristic of many, if not most, management decision problems. Consider how the decisions of the financial vice-president of an insurance company would change if she could know exactly what changes were to occur in the bond market. Imagine the relief of the head buyer for Maxwell House if he could know exactly how large next year's crop of coffee beans would be.

It thus seems clear that numerous decision problems are characterized by a lack of certainty. It is also clear that those who deal effectively with these problems, through either skill or luck, are often handsomely rewarded for their accomplishments. In the first book of the Old Testament, Joseph is promoted from slave to assistant Pharaoh of Egypt by accurately forecasting 7 years of feast and 7 years of famine.[1]

In quantitative modeling, the lack of certainty can be dealt with in various ways. For example, in a linear programming model, some of the data may be an estimate of a future value. In the above **PROTRAC** *E* and *F* model, next month's capacity (availability of hours) in department A (the right-hand side of the first constraint) may depend on factors that will occur next week, but the production plans, let us say, must be spelled out today. As previously described in Chapter 5, management might deal with this lack of certainty by estimating the capacity as 150 and then performing sensitivity analysis.

Definition of Risk. Decision theory provides alternative approaches to problems with less than complete certainty. One such approach is called **decisions under risk.** In this context, the term *risk* has a restrictive and well-defined meaning. When we speak of decisions under risk, we are referring to a class of decision problems for which there is more than one state of nature and for which we make the assumption that *the decision maker can arrive at a probability estimate for the occurrence for each of the various states of nature.* Suppose, for example, that there are $m > 1$ states of nature, and let p_j be the probability estimate that state j will occur. Recall that the expected value of any random variable is the weighted average of all possible values of the random variable, where the weights are the probabilities of the values occurring. Since different returns are associated with different states of nature, the expected return associated with decision i is the sum, over all possible states j, of terms of the form: (return in state j when decision is i) × (the probability of state j), or $r_{ij}\, p_j$. We can then use the following equation to calculate ER_i, the expected return if we make decision i:

$$\mathrm{ER}_i = \sum_{j=1}^{m} r_{ij} \cdot p_j = r_{i1}p_1 + r_{i2}p_2 + \cdots + r_{im}p_m \tag{14.1}$$

For this type of problem, *management should then make the decision that maximizes the expected return.*[2] In other words, i^* is the optimal decision where

$$\mathrm{ER}_{i^*} = \text{maximum over all } i \text{ of } \mathrm{ER}_i$$

[1]As well as being an accurate forecaster, by virtue of his skill in successfully interpreting Pharaoh's dreams, Joseph has been called the first psychoanalyst. Less well known is the fact that Joseph was also the first management scientist. In anticipation of the famine, he advised Pharaoh to build storage facilities to hold inventories of grain. When it was all over and the famine had been survived, Joseph was asked how he had come to acquire such wisdom and knowledge. "Lean-year programming," was his reply.

[2]It will be shown that this is equivalent to another criterion: minimizing *expected regret.*

The Newsboy Problem. An example of such a problem is the following newsboy problem. (Similar problems are treated in Sections 13.3 [simulation] and 16.9 [inventory models], illustrating that there is often more than one method of analyzing a given problem.) A newsboy can buy papers for 10 cents each and sell them for 25 cents. However, he must buy the papers before he knows how many he can actually sell. If he buys more papers than he can sell, he simply disposes of the excess at no additional cost. If he does not buy enough papers, he loses potential sales now and possibly in the future (disgruntled customers may no longer buy their papers from him). Suppose, for the moment, that this loss of *future* sales is captured by a cost of lost goodwill of 12 cents per paper. For illustrative purposes and ease of computation, also suppose that the demand distribution he faces is

$$P_0 = \text{Prob}\{\text{demand} = 0\} = \frac{1}{10}$$

$$P_1 = \text{Prob}\{\text{demand} = 1\} = \frac{3}{10}$$

$$P_2 = \text{Prob}\{\text{demand} = 2\} = \frac{4}{10}$$

$$P_3 = \text{Prob}\{\text{demand} = 3\} = \frac{2}{10}$$

In this problem, each of the four different values for demand is a different state of nature, and the number of papers ordered is the decision. The returns, or payoffs, for this problem are shown in Figure 14.4.

The entries in this figure represent the net cash flow associated with each combination of number ordered and number demanded, less the cost of lost goodwill when the number ordered is not sufficient to meet the number demanded. These entries are calculated with the expression

$$\text{payoff} = 25\ (\text{number of papers sold}) - 10\ (\text{number of papers ordered}) - 12\ (\text{unmet demand})$$

where 25 cents is the selling price per paper, 10 cents is the cost of buying a paper, and 12 cents is the cost of disappointing a customer (cost of lost goodwill). It is important to note that in this model, sales and demand need not be identical. Indeed, sales is the minimum of the two quantities (numbered ordered, number demanded). For example, when no papers are ordered, then clearly none can be sold, no matter how many are demanded, and the unmet demand will equal the demand. Thus, for all entries in the first row, the above expression for the payoff gives $25(0) - 10(0) - 12(\text{demand}) = -12(\text{demand})$. If 1 paper is ordered and none are demanded, then none are sold, the unmet demand is 0, and the payoff is $25(0) - 10(1) - 12(0) = -10$, which is the first entry in row 2. However, if 1 paper is ordered and 1 or more are demanded, then exactly 1 will be sold, the unmet demand will be 1 less than the demand, and the payoff becomes $25(1) - 10(1) - 12(\text{demand} - 1) = 27 - 12(\text{demand})$. Can you verify that the remaining values in the body of Figure 14.4 are correct?

▼ FIGURE 14.4
Payoff Table for the Newsboy Problem

	STATE OF NATURE (DEMAND)			
DECISION	**0**	**1**	**2**	**3**
0	0	−12	−24	−36
1	−10	15	3	−9
2	−20	5	30	18
3	−30	−5	20	45

Once all the data are assembled in Figure 14.4, the process of finding the optimal decision is strictly mechanical. You use equation (14.1) to evaluate the expected return for each decision (ER_i for $i = 0, 1, 2, 3$) and pick the largest. For example, if you order two papers,

$$ER_2 = -20\left(\frac{1}{10}\right) + 5\left(\frac{3}{10}\right) + 30\left(\frac{4}{10}\right) + 18\left(\frac{2}{10}\right) = 15.1$$

The first term is the return if we order 2 papers and 0 are demanded multiplied by the probability that 0 are demanded. The second term is the return if we order 2 papers and 1 is demanded (see Figure 14.4) multiplied by the probability that 1 paper is demanded. The other terms are similarly defined. The expected returns for all of the decisions are calculated as follows:

$$\begin{aligned}
ER_0 &= 0\left(\frac{1}{10}\right) - 12\left(\frac{3}{10}\right) - 24\left(\frac{4}{10}\right) - 36\left(\frac{2}{10}\right) = -20.4 \\
ER_1 &= -10\left(\frac{1}{10}\right) + 15\left(\frac{3}{10}\right) + 3\left(\frac{4}{10}\right) - 9\left(\frac{2}{10}\right) = 2.9 \\
ER_2 &= -20\left(\frac{1}{10}\right) + 5\left(\frac{3}{10}\right) + 30\left(\frac{4}{10}\right) + 18\left(\frac{2}{10}\right) = 15.1 \\
ER_3 &= -30\left(\frac{1}{10}\right) - 5\left(\frac{3}{10}\right) + 20\left(\frac{4}{10}\right) + 45\left(\frac{2}{10}\right) = 12.5
\end{aligned}$$

Since ER_2 is the largest of these four values, the optimal decision is to order 2 papers.

The Cost of Lost Goodwill: A SpreadSheet Sensitivity Analysis. This decision is based on a cost, the cost of lost goodwill, whose value is much less certain than the other two costs, the selling price and the purchase cost. What would happen to the optimal decision if the cost of lost goodwill were different? To answer this question we will perform a sensitivity analysis on the value of the cost of lost goodwill.

Emphasize how much easier it is to let the computer do all of the "what-if" work.

One possible way to do this would be to assume a value for the cost of lost goodwill, recalculate the payoff matrix, recompute the expected returns, and see what happens to the optimal decision. This would be tiresome to do by hand, but is ideally suited to be done in a spreadsheet program. Figure 14.5 shows the spreadsheet for calculating the payoff matrix and expected returns. The formula in cell B7 can be copied to obtain the other formulas in the payoff matrix. The first term calculates the revenue from sales: $C$1, the Selling Price, times @MIN($A7,B$6), the smaller of the number ordered and the number demanded. The second term subtracts the cost of the papers purchased: $C$2, the Purchase Cost, times $A7, the number of papers purchased. The final term subtracts the lost goodwill: $C$3, the Goodwill Cost, times @IF(B$6>$A7,B$6−$A7,0), the unmet demand if the demand exceeds the quantity ordered, 0 otherwise. The expected return column can be generated by copying the formula in cell F7: $B$12*B7+$C$12*C7+$D$12*D7+$E$12*E7, which is just the sum of the products of the probability of receiving a given payoff times the payoff.

Newer versions of spreadsheets now have an @SUMPRODUCT function that simplifies the formula in cell F7: @SUMPRODUCT ($B$12..$E$12,B7..E7).

It is much easier to use the Data Table command than to run this manually on the spreadsheet 31 different times.

Using the Data Table command, a table of expected returns can easily be generated for a range of Goodwill Costs. The table in Figure 14.6 shows the expected returns of different order quantities for values of the Goodwill Cost between 0 and 30 in one-cent increments.

Notice that as the Goodwill Cost increases, the expected returns either decrease or, when 3 papers are purchased, remain constant. For Goodwill Costs less than 25 cents, the optimal decision is to order 2 papers. For a Goodwill Cost of 25 cents, alternative optima exist: order 2 or 3 papers. For a Goodwill Cost greater than 25 cents, the optimal decision is to order 3 papers. Thus, it is not necessary to know the Goodwill Cost precisely, just whether it is greater than or less than 25 cents. These results are reminiscent of the sensitivity analysis of a cost coefficient in a linear programming model where the optimal solution did not change for values of the coefficient in a given range. With this example, we have now illustrated another

Finding the optimal decision may be difficult

Optimality criterion

```
B7: +$C$1*@MIN($A7,B$6)-$C$2*$A7-$C$3*@IF(B$6>$A7,B$6-$A7,0)
```

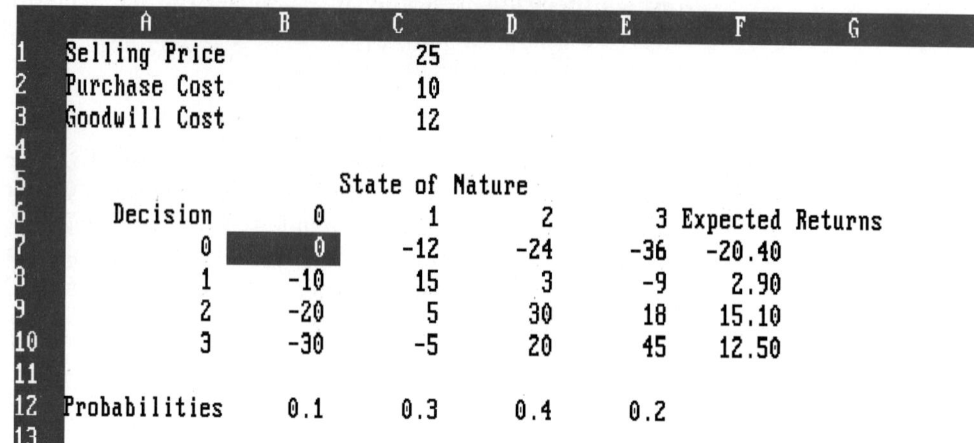

	A	B	C	D	E	F	G
1	Selling Price		25				
2	Purchase Cost		10				
3	Goodwill Cost		12				
4							
5			State of Nature				
6	Decision	0	1	2	3	Expected Returns	
7	0	0	-12	-24	-36	-20.40	
8	1	-10	15	3	-9	2.90	
9	2	-20	5	30	18	15.10	
10	3	-30	-5	20	45	12.50	
11							
12	Probabilities	0.1	0.3	0.4	0.2		
13							

▲ FIGURE 14.5
Newsboy Spreadsheet

▼ FIGURE 14.6 (a)
Expected Returns for Various Goodwill Costs

	Goodwill Cost															
	0	1	2	3	4	5	6	7	8	9	10	11	12	13	14	15
Order 0	0.0	−1.7	−3.4	−5.1	−6.8	−8.5	−10.2	−11.9	−13.6	−15.3	−17.0	−18.7	−20.4	−22.1	−23.8	−25.5
Order 1	12.5	11.7	10.9	10.1	9.3	8.5	7.7	6.9	6.1	5.3	4.5	3.7	2.9	2.1	1.3	0.5
Order 2	17.5	17.3	17.1	16.9	16.7	16.5	16.3	16.1	15.9	15.7	15.5	15.3	15.1	14.9	14.7	14.5
Order 3	12.5	12.5	12.5	12.5	12.5	12.5	12.5	12.5	12.5	12.5	12.5	12.5	12.5	12.5	12.5	12.5

	Goodwill Cost														
	16	17	18	19	20	21	22	23	24	25	26	27	28	29	30
Order 0	−27.2	−28.9	−30.6	−32.3	−34.0	−35.7	−37.4	−39.1	−40.8	−42.5	−44.2	−45.9	−47.6	−49.3	−51.0
Order 1	−0.3	−1.1	−1.9	−2.7	−3.5	−4.3	−5.1	−5.9	−6.7	−7.5	−8.3	−9.1	−9.9	−10.7	−11.5
Order 2	14.3	14.1	13.9	13.7	13.5	13.3	13.1	12.9	12.7	12.5	12.3	12.1	11.9	11.7	11.5
Order 3	12.5	12.5	12.5	12.5	12.5	12.5	12.5	12.5	12.5	12.5	12.5	12.5	12.5	12.5	12.5

▼ FIGURE 14.6 (b)

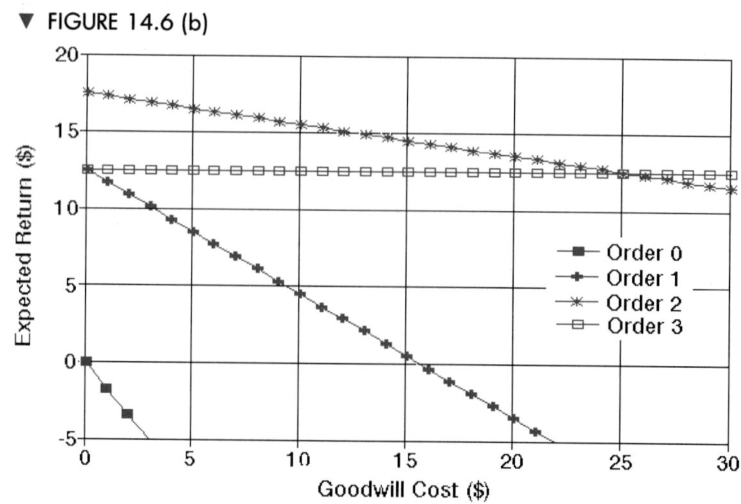

class of decision problems (decisions under risk) and the associated decision criterion (maximize the expected return).

Decisions under Uncertainty

In **decisions under uncertainty** we again have more than one possible state of nature, but now the decision maker is unwilling or unable to specify the probabilities that the various states of nature will occur. There is a long-standing debate as to whether such a situation should exist; that is, should the decision maker always be willing to at least subjectively specify the probabilities even when he or she does not know very much (anything) about what state of nature is apt to occur? Leaving this debate to the philosophers, we turn to the various approaches suggested for this class of problem.

When using the Laplace criterion, since each state has equal probability, all you need do to find the best decision is to add up all the payoffs for each decision.

Decision	0	1	2	3
Payoff	−72	−1	33	30

Decision 3 gives the best payoff and the expected value is 33/4 = 8.25.

Laplace Criterion. The Laplace Criterion approach interprets the condition of "uncertainty" as equivalent to assuming that all states of nature are equally likely. This is the point of view: "If I know nothing, then anything is equally likely." For example, in the newsboy problem, assuming all states are equally likely means that since there are four states, each state occurs with probability 0.25. Using these probabilities converts the problem to a decision under risk, and one could then compute the expected return. You can easily verify that, using these probabilities, expected return would again be maximized by decision 2 (order 2 papers).

Although in some situations this "equally likely" approach may produce acceptable results, in other settings it would be inappropriate. For example, consider your friend from Uzbekistan, about to watch the football game between Notre Dame and USC in a year in which one team is experiencing a bad season and the other is thus heavily favored in the betting. Although your friend knows nothing about football and has no knowledge about the probability of either team winning, these probabilities clearly exist and are *not* equal. In other words, even though one has "no knowledge," there may be underlying probabilities on the various states of nature, and these probabilities may in no way be consistent with the "equal likelihood" assumption. With this realization, there may be contexts in which you would not wish to use the criterion of expected return based on the equal-likelihood assumption (i.e., the Laplace criterion).

Does no knowledge mean equally likely?

For such cases, there are three different criteria that can be used to make decisions under uncertainty: *maximin, maximax,* and *minimax regret.* All of these criteria can be used without specifying probabilities. The discussion will be illustrated with the newsboy problem. Look at the earlier payoff table for a moment and think of what criterion you might use to make a decision. By this we mean, think of a rule that you could describe to a friend. It has to be a general rule so that your friend could apply it to any payoff table and come up with a decision. Remember, you are willing to make no assumptions about the probabilities on states of nature. Now consider the following criteria.

Maximin Criterion. The **maximin criterion** is an extremely conservative, or perhaps pessimistic, approach to making decisions. It evaluates each decision by the worst thing that can happen if you make that decision. In this case, then, it evaluates each decision by the *minimum* possible return associated with the decision. In the newsboy example the minimum possible return if 3 papers are ordered is −30; thus, this value is assigned to the decision "order 3 papers." Similarly, we can associate with each other decision the minimum value in its row. Following this rule enables the decision maker to prepare a table as shown in Figure 14.7.
The decision that yields the maximum value of the minimum return (hence, maximin) is then selected. In this case, the newsboy should order 1 paper.

Maximin is often used in situations where the planner feels he or she cannot afford to be wrong. (Defense planning might be an example, as would investing your

DECISION	MINIMUM RETURN
0	−36
1	−10
2	−20
3	−30

▲ FIGURE 14.7

life savings.) The planner chooses a decision that does as well as possible in the worst possible (most pessimistic) case.

It is, however, easy to create examples in which most people would not accept the decision selected with the maximin criterion. Consider, for example, the payoff table in Figure 14.8. Most people would prefer decision 1. It is much better than decision 2 for all states of nature except state 3, and then it is only slightly worse. Nevertheless, the maximin criterion would select decision 2. If you are among those who strongly prefer decision 1 in this example, you must then ask yourself the following question: "If the maximin criterion provides an answer that I don't like in this simple example, would I be willing to use it on more complicated and important problems?" There is no correct answer to this question. The answer depends on the taste of the decision maker.

	STATE OF NATURE								
DECISION	1	2	3	4	5	6	7	8	9
1	100	100	2	100	100	100	100	100	100
2	3	3	3	3	3	3	3	3	3

▲ FIGURE 14.8
Payoff Table: Maximin Example

Maximax Criterion. The **maximax criterion** is as optimistic as maximin is pessimistic. It evaluates each decision by the best thing that can happen if you make that decision. In this case, then, it evaluates each decision by the maximum possible return associated with that decision. In particular, refer again to the payoff table for the newsboy problem (Figure 14.4). If the newsboy ordered 2 papers, the best possible outcome would be a return of 30. This value is thus assigned to the decision "order 2 papers." In other words, for each decision we identify the maximum value in that row. Using this rule, the decision maker prepares a table as shown in Figure 14.9.

Another way to choose the optimal act using this criterion is to simply find the largest number in the table. However, this doesn't give as much information as Figure 14.9, which shows the second-best decision, and so on.

DECISION	MAXIMUM RETURN
0	0
1	15
2	30
3	45

▲ FIGURE 14.9

The decision that yields the maximum of these maximum returns (hence, maximax) is then selected. In this case, then, the newsboy should order 3 papers.

The maximax criterion is subject to the same type of criticism as maximin;

Students may confuse the decision with the state that produces the optimal payoff. Thus, it is important to stress that the optimal decision under maximax criterion is to order 3 papers. Students might mistakenly say that the optimal decision is to "order 3 papers *and have 3 customers*."

that is, it is easy to create examples where using the maximax criterion leads to a decision that most people find unacceptable. Consider the payoff table presented in Figure 14.10, for example. Most people prefer decision 1 since it is much better than decision 2 for every state of nature except state 3, and then it is only slightly worse. The maximax criterion, however, selects decision 2.

	STATE OF NATURE								
DECISION	**1**	**2**	**3**	**4**	**5**	**6**	**7**	**8**	**9**
1	100	100	100	100	100	100	100	100	100
2	3	3	101	3	3	3	3	3	3

▲ FIGURE 14.10
Payoff Table: Maximax Example

Regret and Minimax Regret. **Regret** introduces a new concept for measuring the desirability of an outcome; that is, it is a new way to create the payoff table. So far, all the decision criteria have been used on a payoff table of dollar returns as measured by net cash flows. In particular, each entry in Figure 14.4 shows the net cash flow for the newsboy for every combination of decision (number of papers ordered) and state of nature (number of papers demanded). Figure 14.11 shows the regret for each combination of decision and state of nature. It is derived from Figure 14.4 by

1. Finding the maximum entry in each column of Figure 14.4 (e.g., 30 is the largest entry in the third column, the column under State of Nature "2").

	STATE OF NATURE			
DECISION	**0**	**1**	**2**	**3**
0	0	27	54	81
1	10	0	27	54
2	20	10	0	27
3	30	20	10	0

Applications Pack

▲ FIGURE 14.11
Regret Table for the Newsboy Problem

2. Calculating the new entry by subtracting the current entry from the maximum in its column. Thus, the new entry in the second row, third column is

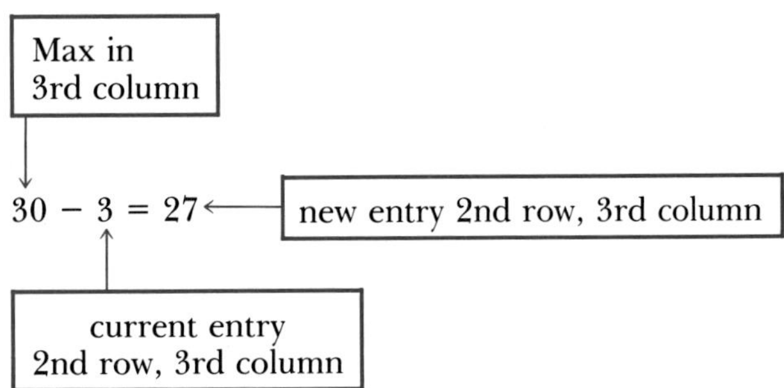

An alternative way of stating the payoff table is to ask for each entry, "How much *more* would I have made if this state occurred and I hadn't made this choice?"

In each column, these new entries, called regret, indicate how much better we can do. In other words, "regret" is synonymous with "opportunity cost" of not making the best decision for a given state of nature. It follows that the decision maker would like to make a decision that minimizes regret, but (same old story) he does not know which state of nature will occur. If he knew a probability distribution on the state of nature, he could minimize the expected regret. (In the next section, we will see that this is equivalent to maximizing expected net cash flow.) If he does not know the probability, the typical suggestion is to use the conservative *minimax criterion,* that is, to select that decision that does the best in the worst case (the decision that has the smallest maximum regret).

For example, consider the regret table for the newsboy problem shown in Figure 14.11. If 1 paper is ordered, the maximum regret of 54 occurs if 3 papers are demanded. The value 54 is thus associated with the decision, "order 1 paper." In other words, the maximum value in each row is associated with the decision in that row. Following this rule produces the table in Figure 14.12.

DECISION	MAXIMUM REGRET
0	81
1	54
2	27
3	30

▲ FIGURE 14.12

Some personnel managers believe that college graduates tend to choose between several first-job choices using minimax regret criterion. They imagine themselves in the various jobs and decide which one would give them the least regret of being there.

The decision maker then selects the decision that minimizes the maximum regret. In this case, the minimax regret criterion implies that the newsboy should order 2 papers. Our newsboy example illustrates that, when making decisions without using probabilities, the three criteria, maximin cash flow, maximax cash flow, and minimax regret, can lead to different "optimal" decisions.

14.3 The Expected Value of Perfect Information: Newsboy Problem Under Risk

Let us return to the newsboy problem under risk (i.e., with the probability distribution on demand shown on p. 602). Recall that, in this case, the optimal policy was to order 2 papers and that the expected return was 15.1. It is useful to think about this problem in a very stylized fashion in order to introduce the concept of the expected value of perfect information. In particular, let us assume that the sequence of events in the newsboy's day (the "current sequence of events") proceeds as follows:

1. A genie, by drawing from the demand distribution for papers, determines the number of papers that will be demanded.
2. The newsboy, not knowing what demand had been drawn, but knowing the distribution of demand, orders his papers.
3. The demand is then revealed to the newsboy and he achieves an *actual* (as opposed to expected) return determined by his order-size decision and the demand.

It is important to stress that the genie can't *make* a certain demand come true; he simply has *perfect knowledge* of what will happen and is willing to sell that knowledge or information.

Now consider a new scenario. The newsboy has an opportunity to make a deal with the genie. Under the new deal the sequence of events proceeds as follows:

1. The newsboy pays the genie a fee.
2. The genie determines the demand as above.
3. The genie tells the newsboy what the demand will be.

4. The newsboy orders his papers.
5. The newsboy achieves the return determined by the demand and the number of papers he ordered.

The question is, What is the largest fee the newsboy should be willing to pay in step 1? This fee is called the **expected value of perfect information.** In general terms,

$$\text{fee} = \begin{pmatrix}\text{expected return}\\ \text{with new deal}\end{pmatrix} - \begin{pmatrix}\text{expected return with current}\\ \text{sequence of events (no deal)}\end{pmatrix}$$

Thus, the probabilities of 0, 1, 2, or 3 papers demanded are still the same but now the newsboy knows exactly how many customers will arrive each day and always has the perfect amount on hand.

With the new deal the newsboy, in step 4, will always order the number of papers that will give him the maximum return for the state of nature that will occur. However, the payment in step 1 must be made *before* he learns what the demand will be. Referring to Figure 14.4 we see that if 0 papers will be demanded, he will order 0 papers and enjoy the maximum return of 0. Since the genie is drawing from the distribution of demand, there is a probability of 1/10 that what the newsboy will learn from the genie is that demand will in fact be 0. Similarly, he will learn with a probability of 3/10 that 1 paper will be demanded. If this occurs, he will order 1 paper and enjoy the maximum return of 15. Following this reasoning, his expected return under the new deal is

$$\text{ER(new)} = 0(\tfrac{1}{10}) + 15(\tfrac{3}{10}) + 30(\tfrac{4}{10}) + 45(\tfrac{2}{10}) = 25.5$$

We have already seen that in the absence of perfect information his optimal decision (order 2 papers) gives an expected return of 15.1. Thus, we can calculate the expected value of perfect information (EVPI) as follows:

EVPI for newsboy

$$\text{EVPI} = 25.5 - 15.1 = 10.4$$

This is the maximum amount our vendor should be willing to pay in step 1 for the deal with the genie. Although the story we have used to develop the concept is far-fetched, the expected value of perfect information (EVPI) has important practical significance. It is an upper bound on the amount that you should be willing to pay to improve your knowledge about what state of nature will occur. Literally millions of dollars are spent on various market research projects and other testing devices (geological tests, quality control experiments, and so on) to determine what state of nature will occur in a wide variety of applications. The expected value of perfect information indicates the expected amount to be gained from any such endeavor and thus places an upper bound on the amount that should be spent in gathering information.

When does EVPI = expected regret?

The expected value of perfect information is always equal to the expected regret of the optimal decision under risk (the decision that maximizes expected return). We will show that this fact holds in the newsboy example.

When the probabilities on the states of nature are specified, it is a straightforward task to compute the expected regret for each decision. Using the previous probability distribution of demand and the regret table (Figure 14.11), we can calculate expected regret if 0 papers are ordered as follows:

$$\text{expected regret (0)} = 0(\tfrac{1}{10}) + 27(\tfrac{3}{10}) + 54(\tfrac{4}{10}) + 81(\tfrac{2}{10}) = 45.9$$

The first term is the regret if 0 papers are demanded times the probability that 0 papers are demanded. The second term is the regret if 1 paper is demanded times the probability that 1 paper is demanded, and so on.

The expected regret for the other possible order quantities is computed in a similar fashion:

$$\text{expected regret (1)} = 10(\tfrac{1}{10}) + \ \ 0(\tfrac{3}{10}) + 27(\tfrac{4}{10}) + 54(\tfrac{2}{10}) = 22.6$$

$$\text{expected regret (2)} = 20(\tfrac{1}{10}) + 10(\tfrac{3}{10}) + \ \ 0(\tfrac{4}{10}) + 27(\tfrac{2}{10}) = 10.4$$

$$\text{expected regret (3)} = 30(\tfrac{1}{10}) + 20(\tfrac{3}{10}) + 10(\tfrac{4}{10}) + \ \ 0(\tfrac{2}{10}) = 13.0$$

We see that ordering 2 papers yields the minimum expected regret.

You might point out that these two problems are the dual of each other and thus their optimums are always equal. Not only are there dual problems in LP (Section 5.6), but every problem has a dual (like the maximum flow, minimal cut network in Section 9.6)

The expected regret of the optimal decision under risk (i.e., the minimum expected regret) equals the expected value of perfect information.

But ordering 2 papers was also the optimal decision when the criterion was to maximize the expected net dollar return.

It is always the case that, in decision making under risk, these two criteria (minimize expected regret, maximize expected net dollar return) will prescribe the same decision as optimal.

14.4 Utilities and Decisions Under Risk

Utility is an alternative way of measuring the attractiveness of the result of a decision. In other words, it is an alternative way of finding the values to fill in a payoff table. Up to now we have used net dollar return (net cash flow) and regret as two measures of the "goodness" of a particular combination of a decision and state of nature.

Utility suggests another type of measure. Our treatment of this topic includes three main sections:

1. A rationale for utility (i.e., why using net cash flow can lead to unacceptable decisions).
2. How to use a utility function.
3. Creating a utility function.

The Rationale for Utility

In the preceding section we saw that the maximin and maximax decision criteria could lead to unacceptable decisions in simple illustrative problems. We now point out that the criterion of maximizing expected net cash flow in a decision under risk can also produce unacceptable results. For example, consider an urn that contains 99 white balls and 1 black ball. You are offered a chance to play a game in which a ball will be drawn from this urn. Each ball is equally likely to be drawn. If a white ball is drawn, you must pay \$10,000. If the black ball is drawn, you receive \$1,000,000. You must decide whether to play. The payoff table based on net cash flow is shown in Figure 14.13.

We now use the information in this table, together with the facts that the probabilities of a white and a black ball are, respectively, 0.99 and 0.01, to calculate the expected return for each decision (play or do not play) in the usual way.

DECISION	STATE OF NATURE	
	White Ball	**Black Ball**
Play	−10,000	1,000,000
Do Not Play	0	0

▲ FIGURE 14.13
Payoff Table (Net Cash Flows)

$$\text{ER(play)} = -10{,}000\left(\frac{99}{100}\right) + 1{,}000{,}000\left(\frac{1}{100}\right)$$
$$= -9900 + 10{,}000 = 100$$
$$\text{ER(do not play)} = 0\left(\frac{99}{100}\right) + 0\left(\frac{1}{100}\right) = 0$$

Since ER(play) > ER(do not play), we should play if we apply the criterion of maximizing the expected net cash flow.

Downside risk

Now step back and ask yourself if you would decide to play this game. Remember that the probability is 0.99 that you will lose $10,000. Many people simply find this large "downside risk" to be unacceptable; that is, they are unwilling to accept the decision based on the criterion of maximizing the expected net cash flow. Thus, once again we see a simple example that shows a need to take care in selecting an appropriate criterion. This is all the more true in dealing with complicated real-world problems.

Note that if the sums involved were 10¢ and $10, many more people would probably be willing to play.

Fortunately, it is not necessary to reject the concept of maximizing expected returns. To adapt the expected return criterion to general decisions under risk it is only necessary to recognize that net dollar returns do not always accurately reflect the "attractiveness" of the possible outcomes of decisions. To show what this means, ask yourself if you would be willing to win or lose 10 cents depending on the flip of a fair coin. (Most people would say yes.) How about winning or losing $10,000, depending on a flip of the same coin? (Here most people would say no.) What is the difference? A 10-cent gain seems to balance a 10-cent loss. Why does a $10,000 gain not balance a $10,000 loss? The answer is that in the latter situation most people are **risk-averse,** which means they would feel that the loss of $10,000 is more painful than the benefit obtained from a $10,000 gain.

Risk-averse

Decision theory deals with this problem by introducing a function that measures the "attractiveness" of money. This function is called a *utility function,* where for the sake of this discussion the word *utility* can be thought of as a measure of "satisfaction." A typical risk-averse function is shown in Figure 14.14. Two characteristics of this function are worth noting:

1. It is nondecreasing, since more money is always at least as attractive as less money.
2. It is concave. An equivalent statement is that the marginal utility of money is nonincreasing. To illustrate this phenomenon, let us examine Figure 14.14.

First suppose that you have $100 and someone gives you an additional $100. Note that your utility increases by

$$U(200) - U(100) \approx 0.680 - 0.524 = 0.156$$

Now suppose that you start with $400, and someone gives you an additional $100. Now your utility increases by

$$U(500) - U(400) \approx 0.910 - 0.850 = 0.060$$

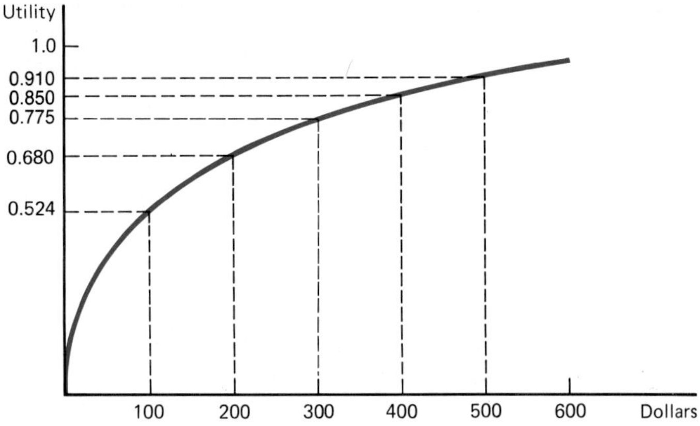

▲ FIGURE 14.14
Typical (Risk-Averse) Utility Function

Students understand that, for most people, receiving \$1,000,000 would be tremendously exciting, but receiving \$2,000,000 would not be twice as exciting. Similarly, finding \$100 would be a nice windfall, but the difference between receiving \$1,000,000 and \$1,000,100 is negligible. Put another way, the same increment has a decreasing utility, or to get the same utility, each increment must be larger.

In other words, 100 additional dollars is less attractive to you if you have \$400 on hand than it is if you start with \$100. Another way of describing this phenomenon is that at any point, the gain of a specified number of dollars increases utility less than the loss of the same number of dollars decreases utility. For example, using the utility function in Figure 14.14, we have already calculated that the gain in utility of going from \$400 to \$500 is 0.060. The loss in utility of going from \$400 to \$300, however, is $U(400) - U(300) = 0.850 - 0.775 = 0.075$, which is greater.

Risk-seeking

Figure 14.15 shows two other general types of utility functions. The first is a **risk-seeking** (convex) function, where a gain of a specified amount of dollars increases the utility more than a loss of the same amount of dollars decreases the utility. For example, if you start with \$200 and increase your holding by \$100 to \$300, your utility increases by

$$U(300) - U(200) \approx 0.590 - 0.260 = 0.330$$

whereas if you start with \$200 and decrease your holding by \$100 to \$100, your utility decreases by

$$U(200) - U(100) \approx 0.260 - 0.075 = 0.185$$

Thus, with a risk-seeking utility function an increase of \$100 increases your utility more than a decrease of \$100 decreases it. As we saw, exactly the opposite statement holds for a risk-averse (concave) function like the one shown in Figure 14.14.

▼ FIGURE 14.15
Some Utility Functions

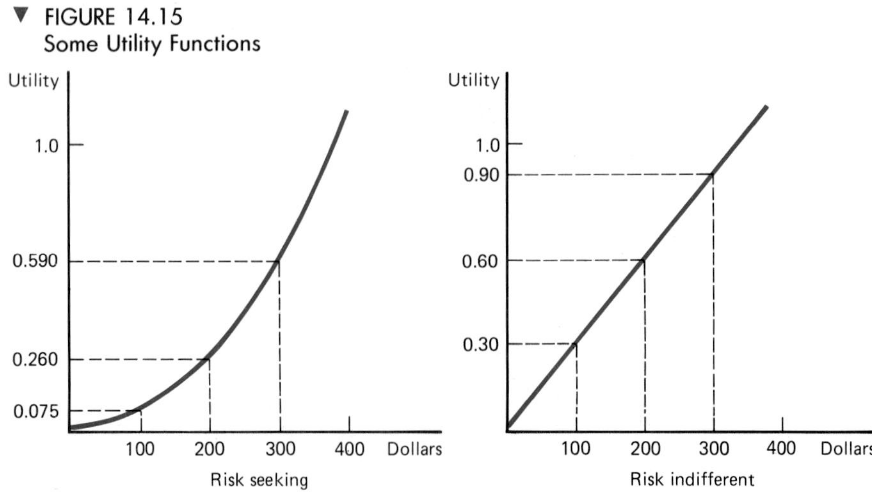

Risk-indifferent For the **risk-indifferent** function shown in Figure 14.15, a gain or a loss of a specified dollar amount produces a change of the same magnitude in your utility.

Using a Utility Function

In the next section we will worry about how you go about creating a utility function. For the meantime, assume that somehow one has been created. Using this function to make decisions when the probabilities of the states of nature are known is a straightforward process. To be specific, you simply redo the payoff table, substituting the utility of the net cash flow for that cash flow, and proceed as before. Consider, for example, the newsboy problem, where we let Figure 14.16 represent

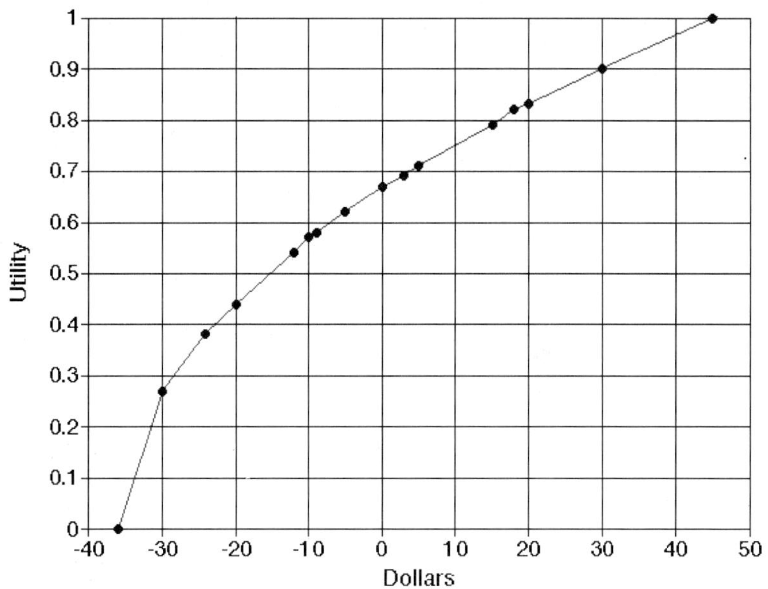

▲ FIGURE 14.16
Newsboy's Utility Function

	STATE OF NATURE			
DECISION	0	1	2	3
0	0.67	0.54	0.38	0.00
1	0.57	0.79	0.69	0.58
2	0.44	0.71	0.90	0.82
3	0.27	0.62	0.83	1.00

▲ FIGURE 14.17
Newsboy Payoff Table (Utilities)

the newsboy's utility for money. The newsboy can use this figure and the payoff table of net cash flows (Figure 14.4) to create a new payoff table where the entries are the utility of the net cash flow associated with each combination of a decision and a state of nature. For example, row 4, column 3 in Figure 14.4 shows a net cash flow of 20. Figure 14.16 translates this into a utility of about 0.83, which becomes the new entry in row 4, column 3. The complete table is presented in Figure 14.17. The newsboy now proceeds as before; that is, he calculates the expected utility for each decision. Using the previously employed probabilities (1/10, 3/10, 4/10, 2/10), and letting EU_i be the expected utility for decision i, the calculations are

You might point out that alternative 1 is now much closer to alternative 2 for expected utilities than with expected monetary values, and is almost tied with alternative 3 for second best choice.

$$EU_0 = 0.67(\frac{1}{10}) + 0.54(\frac{3}{10}) + 0.38(\frac{4}{10}) + 0(\frac{2}{10}) = 0.381$$

$$EU_1 = 0.57(\frac{1}{10}) + 0.79(\frac{3}{10}) + 0.69(\frac{4}{10}) + 0.58(\frac{2}{10}) = 0.686$$

$$EU_2 = 0.44(\frac{1}{10}) + 0.71(\frac{3}{10}) + 0.9(\frac{4}{10}) + 0.82(\frac{2}{10}) = 0.781$$

$$EU_3 = 0.27(\frac{1}{10}) + 0.62(\frac{3}{10}) + 0.83(\frac{4}{10}) + 1(\frac{2}{10}) = 0.745$$

On the basis of a criterion of maximizing the expected utility, the newsboy would order 2 papers. Referring to the discussion of decisions under risk in Section 14.2, we see that if the newsboy based his decision on maximizing the expected net cash flow, he would also order 2 papers. It is not always true, however, that the decision that has the largest expected cash flow will also have the largest expected utility. The fact that this phenomenon occurred in this particular example does not imply that it will occur in general. For example, consider the following gamble. A coin is flipped. If heads turns up you win \$1,000,002, if tails you lose \$1,000,000. Suppose the coin is fair, so that the probability of heads equals the probability of tails. Assign the utility of \$1,000,002 to be 1 and the utility of −\$1,000,000 to be 0, and suppose the utility of \$0 in this case is 0.6. Figure 14.18 shows that maximizing expected utility leads to a different decision than maximizing expected return.

DECISION	EXPECTED RETURN	EXPECTED UTILITY
Play	0.5(1,000,002) + 0.5(−1,000,000) = 1.00	0.5(1) + 0.5(0) = 0.5
Don't Play	0	0.6

▲ FIGURE 14.18
Gambling Example

Creating a Utility Function

One system of creating a utility function like the one shown in Figure 14.16 requires the decision maker, in our case the newsboy, to make a series of choices between a sure return and a lottery. In more formal language, the decision maker is called on to create an **equivalent lottery.** This, however, is the second step. Let us start at the beginning.

The newsboy can arbitrarily select the end points of his utility function. It is a convenient convention to set the utility of the smallest net dollar return equal to 0 and the utility of the largest net return equal to 1. Since in the newsboy example the smallest return is −36, and the largest is +45, he sets $U(-36) = 0$ and $U(45) = 1$. Note that these values are used in Figure 14.16. These two values play a fundamental role in finding the utility of any quantity of money between −36 and 45. It is perhaps easiest to proceed by example.

Assume that the decision maker starts with $U(-36) = 0$ and $U(45) = 1$ and wants to find the utility of 10 [i.e., $U(10)$]. He proceeds by selecting a probability p such that he is indifferent between the following two alternatives:

An equivalent lottery

1. Receive a payment of 10 for sure.
2. Participate in a lottery in which he receives a payment of 45 with probability p or a payment of −36 with probability $1 - p$.

Clearly if $p = 1$, the decision maker prefers alternative 2, since he prefers a

When decision analysts work with corporations to aid in determining utility functions, they have to be very careful that the decision maker uses the corporation's view of money rather than his/her own personal values. Individuals tend either to be afraid to risk a few thousand dollars or to get blasé about millions of dollars. Thus, there is a distinct difference between corporate utility and personal utility.

payment of 45 to a payment of 10. Equally clear, if $p = 0$, he prefers alternative 1, since he prefers a payment of 10 to a loss of 36 (i.e., a payment of -36). It follows that somewhere between 0 and 1 there is a value for p such that the decision maker is indifferent between the two alternatives. This value will vary from person to person depending on how attractive the various alternatives are to them. We call this value of p the utility for 10. For example, suppose that the decision maker chooses p to be 0.6. Then the expected value of the lottery is $0.6(45) + 0.4(-30) = 15$. In other words, he is expressing indifference between a sure payment of 10 and a gamble with a larger expected value, 15. This means he is averse to risk, because he requires an expected value larger than the sure payment to compensate for the riskiness of the lottery. If he had chosen $p = 0.7$, the expected value of the lottery would have been $0.7(45) + 0.3(-30) = 22.5$. In some sense, the larger the value of p he chooses, the more risk-averse he is, because he requires a larger expected value of the lottery to compensate him for its riskiness. Now suppose he had chosen $p = 0.5$. Then the expected value of the lottery is $0.5(45) + 0.5(-30) = 7.5$ which is *smaller* than the sure payment of 10. This means he is seeking risk, because he requires a sure payment larger than the expected return to compensate him for the loss of the possibility of making more than the expected return. By solving the equation

$$p(45) + (1 - p)(-30) = 10$$

$$75p - 30 = 10$$

$$p = \frac{40}{75} = 0.5333$$

we find the value of p for which the expected value of the lottery is equal to the sure payment of 10. If the decision maker chooses a value of p greater than 0.5333 he is averse to risk; equal to 0.5333, indifferent to risk; and less than 0.5333, seeking risk.

We obviously have not *proved* that using the probability p to define an equivalent lottery is a meaningful way to construct a utility function. An understandable discussion of why this approach works would carry us far beyond the scope of this text. We must be content to stop with the how and leave the why to other courses.

14.5 A Mid-Chapter Summary

The preceding three sections provided the theoretical foundation on which the rest of the chapter is based. The ensuing sections are devoted to procedures that play an important role in solving real-world problems. It is useful to summarize what we have achieved before moving ahead.

Section 14.2 provided a general framework for a class of problems identified as decisions against nature. In this framework, the problem can be described by a payoff table in which the returns to the decision maker depend on the decision selected and the state of nature that subsequently occurs. Three specific cases were identified:

1. ***Decisions under certainty:*** The decision maker knows exactly what state of nature will occur. The "only" problem is to select the best decision. Deterministic problems such as linear programming, integer programming, and the EOQ model fall into this category.
2. ***Decisions under risk:*** A probability distribution is specified on the states of nature. The decision maker may use the following criteria to select a "best decision":

a. Maximize expected return as measured by net dollar return
b. Minimize expected regret (opportunity cost)
c. Maximize expected return as measured by utility

We saw that criteria **a** and **b** always lead to the same decision. Many inventory control and queuing problems fall into the category of decisions under risk.

3. ***Decisions under uncertainty:*** Here it is assumed that the decision maker has *no* knowledge about which state of nature will occur. The decision maker might apply the Laplace criterion, that is, assign equal probabilities to the various states of nature and then choose a decision that maximizes expected return. Alternatively, the decision maker may attack the problem without using probabilities. In this case, we discussed three different criteria for making a "best decision":

a. Maximize minimum net dollar return
b. Maximize maximum net dollar return
c. Minimize maximum regret

Each of these criteria will, in general, lead to different decisions.

Section 14.3 was devoted to the concept of the expected value of perfect information (EVPI). This entity plays an important role by establishing an upper bound on the amount you should pay to gain new information about what state of nature will occur. We saw that EVPI is equal to the optimal (Min) value of expected regret.

Finally, in Section 14.4 we discussed utility as an alternative measure of the attractiveness of each combination of a decision and a state of nature. The desire to use a utility function is motivated by the fact that in some cases, for example, because of the magnitudes of the potential losses, the decision that maximizes the expected net dollar return is not the decision that you would want to select.

The remaining sections in this chapter will deal with extensions of the model for decisions under risk. They consider decision trees, a technique of significant practical importance, and introduce two important concepts: the use of new information in decision making and the analysis of sequential decision problems.

14.6 Decision Trees: Marketing Home and Garden Tractors

A simple decision tree can also be represented as a decision table. An advantage of the decision tree is that it can show a series of decisions and states of nature in a chronological pattern.

A **decision tree** is a graphical device for analyzing decisions under risk, that is, problems in which decisions and the probabilities on the states of nature are specified. More precisely, decision trees were created to use on problems in which there is a sequence of decisions, each of which could lead to one of several uncertain outcomes. For example, a concessionaire typically has to decide how much to bid for each of several possible locations at the state fair. The result of this decision is not certain, since it depends on what the competitors decide to bid. Once the location is known, the concessionaire must decide how much food to stock. The result of this decision in terms of profits is also not certain since it depends on customer demand.

Our discussion of decision trees is organized in the following manner: In this section we introduce the basic ideas. Section 14.7 examines the sensitivity of the optimal decision to the assessed values of the probabilities. Section 14.8 shows how Bayes's Theorem is used to incorporate new information into the process, and Section 14.9 considers a sequential decision problem. The entire discussion is motivated by the following production and marketing problem faced by the management of **PROTRAC**.

Alternate Marketing and Production Strategies

The design and product-testing phase has just been completed for **PROTRAC**'s new line of home and garden tractors. Top management is attempting to decide on the appropriate marketing and production strategy to use for this product. Three major alternatives are being considered. Each alternative is identified with a single word.

1. ***Aggressive (A):*** This strategy represents a major commitment of the firm to this product line. A major capital expenditure would be made for a new and efficient production facility. Large inventories would be built up to guarantee prompt delivery of all models. A major marketing campaign involving nation-wide sponsorship of television commercials and dealer discounts would be initiated.
2. ***Basic (B):*** In this plan, production of E-4 (the small crawler tractor) would be moved from Joliet to Moline. This move would phase out the trouble-plagued department for adjustable pelican and excavator production. At the same time, the E-4 line in Joliet would be modified to produce the new home and garden product. Inventories would be held for only the most popular items. Headquarters would make funds available to support local or regional advertising efforts, but no national advertising campaign would be mounted.
3. ***Cautious (C):*** In this plan, excess capacity on several existing E-4 lines would be used to produce the new products. A minimum of new tooling would be developed. Production would be geared to satisfy demand, and advertising would be at the discretion of the local dealer.

Management decides to categorize the condition of the market (i.e., the level of demand) as either strong (S) or weak (W). Figure 14.19 presents the payoff table and management's best estimate of the probability of a strong or a weak market. The payoffs in the body are the net profits measured in millions of dollars. They were generated by carefully calculating the sales, revenues, and costs associated with each decision–state of nature combination. It is interesting to note that a cautious (C) decision yields a higher profit with a weak market than it does with a strong market. If there is a strong market and **PROTRAC** is cautious, not only will the competition capture the small tractor market, but as a result of the carryover effect of these sales, the competition will seriously cut into **PROTRAC**'s current market position for accessories and other home products.

▼ FIGURE 14.19
Payoffs (Millions of Dollars) and Probabilities for the Basic Marketing Problem

	STATE OF NATURE	
	Strong, S	**Weak, W**
	PROBABILITY	
DECISION	**0.45**	**0.55**
Aggressive (A)	30	−8
Basic (B)	20	7
Cautious (C)	5	15

We are dealing here with what we have termed decisions under risk and it is, of course, possible to calculate the expected return for each decision and select the best one, just as we did in Section 14.2. The calculations follow:

$$\text{ER(A)} = 30(0.45) - 8(0.55) = 9.10$$
$$\text{ER(B)} = 20(0.45) + 7(0.55) = 12.85$$
$$\text{ER(C)} = 5(0.45) + 15(0.55) = 10.50$$

The optimal decision is to select (B), the basic production and marketing strategy.

Creating a Decision Tree

This marketing problem can also be represented by a decision tree. The first step in creating it is shown in Figure 14.20. In our exposition of decision trees, a **square node** will represent a point at which a decision must be made, and each line leading from a square will represent a possible decision. The **circular nodes** will represent situations when the outcome is not certain. Each line leading from a circle represents a possible outcome. The term **branches** will be employed for the lines emanating from the nodes, whether square or circular.

For the home and garden tractor problem, the decision tree in Figure 14.20 shows the initial node, labeled I. Since it is square, a decision must be made. Thus, management must choose one of the strategies A, B, or C. Depending on which decision is selected, a new position will be attained on the tree. For example, selecting strategy A leads us from node I to node II. Since II is a circle, the next branch that will occur is not known with certainty. If the market condition turns out to be strong, position V is attained. If, instead, the market proves to be weak, position VI is attained. Since they represent the end of the decision process, positions such as V and VI are referred to as **terminal positions.** Also, since nodes II, III, and IV are not followed by other nodes, they are called **terminal nodes.**

▼ FIGURE 14.20
First Step in Creating a Decision Tree
for the Home and Garden Tractor Problem

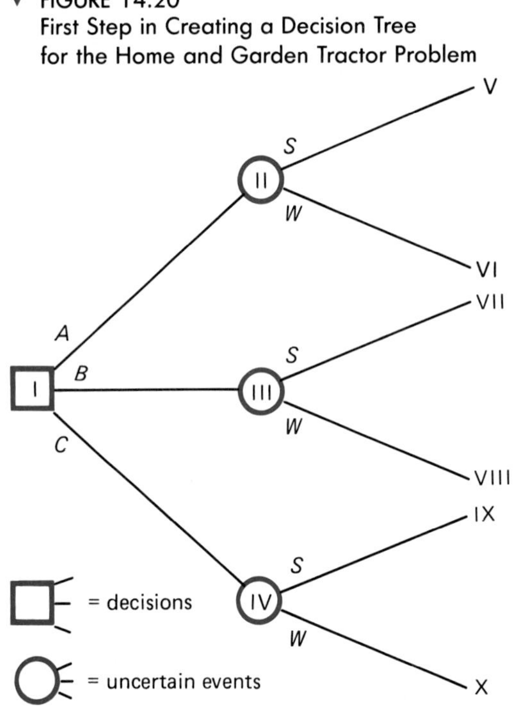

Appending the Probabilities and Terminal Values

The decision tree presented in Figure 14.20 provides an efficient way for management to visualize the interactions between decisions and less-than-certain events. However, if management wishes to use the decision tree to select an optimal decision, some additional information must be appended to the diagram. In particular, one must assign the return associated with each terminal position. This is called the **terminal value.** One must also assign a probability to each branch emanating from each circular node. For the basic model this is a simple task, and performing it yields the decision tree presented in Figure 14.21. You can see that the appended terminal values and branch probabilities are taken directly from Figure 14.19.

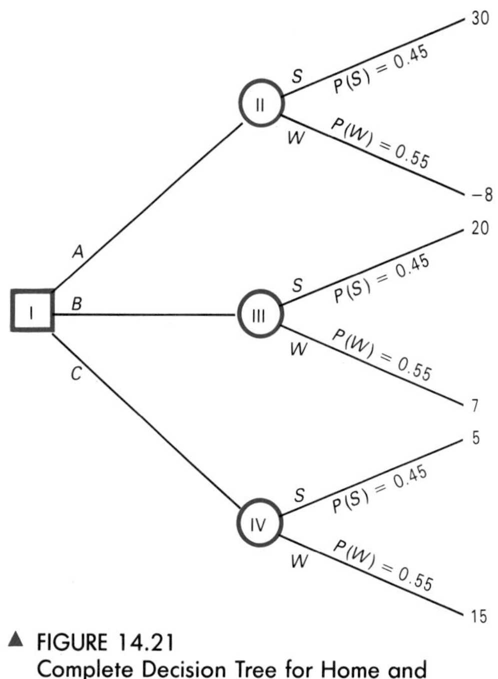

▲ FIGURE 14.21
Complete Decision Tree for Home and Garden Tractor Problem

Folding Back

For decision trees, "forward" is left to right, "backward" is right to left. When a decision tree is folded back, it means that the analysis is done from right to left.

Using a decision tree to find the optimal decision is called solving the tree. To solve a decision tree one works backward or, in the jargon of the trade, by **folding back** the tree. First, the terminal branches are *folded back* by calculating an expected value for each terminal node. For example, consider node II. The calculation to obtain the expected value for this node is

$$\text{expected terminal value} = 30(0.45) + (-8)(0.55) = 9.10$$

In other words, the expected value to be obtained if one arrives at node II is 9.10. Now the branches emanating from the node are folded back (i.e., eliminated) and the expected value of 9.10 is assigned to the node, as shown in Figure 14.22.

The reduced decision tree

Performing the same calculations for nodes III and IV yields what is termed the *reduced decision tree,* shown in Figure 14.23. Note that the expected terminal values on nodes II, III, and IV are identical to the expected returns computed earlier in this section for decisions A, B, and C, respectively. Management now faces the

APPLICATION CAPSULE

Chilled Out: Decision Trees Help Protect a Hot Project (and Its Budget) from Meltdown*

The Palo Verde Nuclear Generating Station near Phoenix, Arizona, is one of the world's largest power facilities. This plant, which is located in the Arizona desert, requires 90 million gallons of cooling water per day. Wastewater from Phoenix is used to meet this need. However, to serve this purpose, the wastewater must be transported some 39 miles to the plant site, treated, stored, used, recycled, and the residue disposed of. Indeed, the water supply system can be thought of as having five major components: conveyance, treatment, cooling, storage, and residue disposal. Each of these components could have been designed in several different ways. For example,

1. The water could have been transported in a single or dual line with one or several pumping stations.
2. The water could have been treated with any of several methods such as bionitrification or reverse osmosis.
3. The water could have been used for one or more cycles in the cooling process. More cycles require less water, but there is an increased probability of fouling the unit because of residue in the water.

The design problem was difficult not only because of the large number of alternatives, but also because of the high level of interdependence. For example,

1. If dual supply lines had been selected, a smaller reservoir could have been chosen since the supply would have been more secure.
2. The quality of material needed in the condenser depended on the quality of water being emitted from the treatment phase.
3. The residue in the water after cooling depends both on the quality of the incoming water and the number of cycles in the cooling process.

Decision trees were particularly useful for analyzing this problem. They allowed engineers and managers to incorporate uncertainty directly in the decision process. Perhaps more important, they provided a valuable device for visualizing and communicating the complex structure of the system.

Decision trees were only one of a spectrum of management science techniques used to develop, evaluate, and select design parameters for the Palo Verde project. The effort was directly responsible for a reduction of $20 million in capital construction costs, or a cash flow savings of $3.5 million per year over the estimated 30-year life of the project.

---

*Carl W. Hamilton and G. William Bingham, "Management Science Applications in the Planning and Design of a Water Supply System for a Nuclear Power Plant," *Interfaces*, vol. 9, no. 5 (November 1979), pp. 50–62.

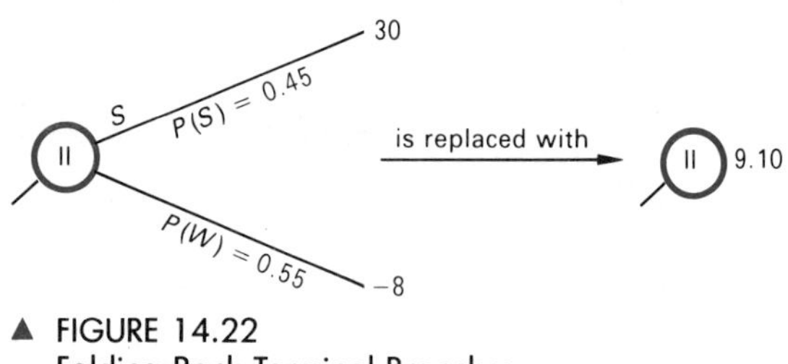

▲ FIGURE 14.22
Folding Back Terminal Branches

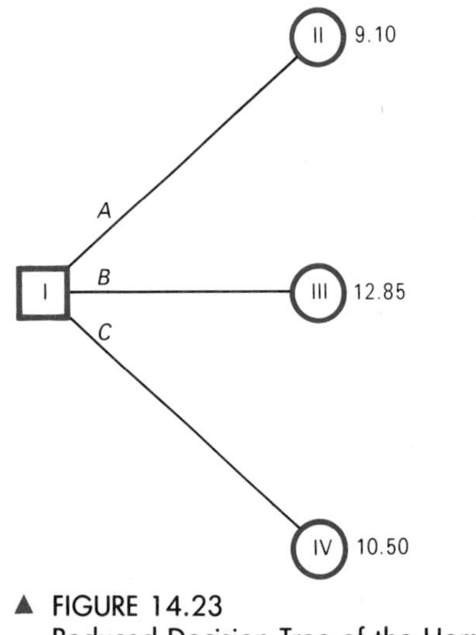

▲ FIGURE 14.23
Reduced Decision Tree of the Home and Garden Tractor Problem

simple problem of choosing the alternative that yields the highest expected terminal value. In this case, as we have seen earlier, the choice is alternative B.

More complex trees can be folded back by following the same procedures. At each circle determine the sum of the expected values of each branch, while at each square choose the "best" branch (maximum or minimum value), going from right to left.

The above discussion provides a simple illustration of how the basic model can be analyzed with a decision tree. In Sections 14.8 and 14.9 you will see the use of decision trees in more structured scenarios. However, this introductory discussion illustrates an important point: *For the basic model a decision tree simply provides another, more graphic, way of viewing the same problem.* Exactly the same information is utilized, and the same calculations are made whether one uses the steps described in Section 14.2 or a decision tree to solve the problem.

14.7 Sensitivity Analysis

Expected Return as a Function of *P*(S)

Before proceeding to the next main topic, a model in which new information becomes available concerning the likelihood of the uncertain events, it will be useful to consider again the expected return associated with each of the decisions in our previous example. We have already noted that to calculate the expected return of strategy A, one uses the relationship

$$ER(A) = (30)P(S) + (-8)P(W)$$

where $P(S)$ is the probability of strong and $P(W)$ is the probability of weak. We also know that

$$P(S) + P(W) = 1, \text{ or } P(W) = 1 - P(S)$$

Thus

$$ER(A) = 30P(S) - 8[1 - P(S)] = -8 + 38P(S)$$

This expected return, then, is a linear function of the probability that the market response is strong.

A similar function can be found for alternatives B and C since

$$ER(B) = 20P(S) + 7[1 - P(S)] = 7 + 13P(S)$$

and

$$ER(C) = 5P(S) + 15[1 - P(S)] = 15 - 10P(S)$$

Plotting expected return

Eventually we are going to plot each of these three functions on the same set of axes. We start in Figure 14.24 with the expected return for decision A, ER(A). The vertical axis is expected return and the horizontal axis is $P(S)$, the probability that the market is strong. Note that when $P(S) = 0$, then $ER(A) = -8$. To see that this makes sense, recall that when $P(S) = 0$, we are sure that the market will be weak; Figure 14.19 shows that if the market is weak and we make decision A the return is -8.

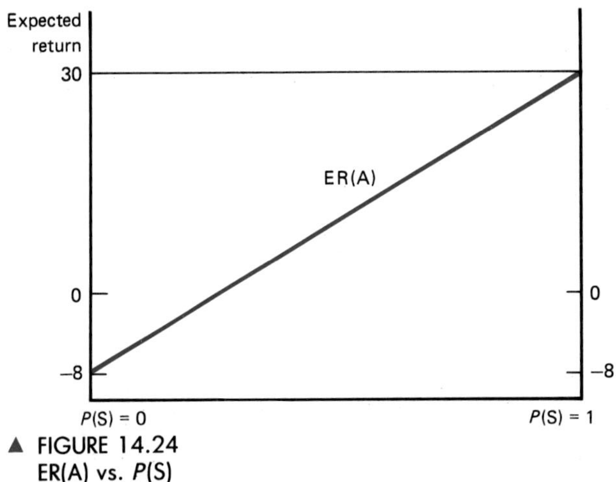

▲ FIGURE 14.24
ER(A) vs. $P(S)$

A similar argument shows that ER(A) should be 30 when $P(S) = 1$ since in this case we are sure that the market is strong. The fact that a straight line connects these two points follows from the fact that

$$ER(A) = -8 + 38P(S)$$

which is a linear function of $P(S)$. In Figure 14.25, ER(A), ER(B), and ER(C) are all plotted on the same set of axes.

Since the criterion for making a decision when you have decisions under risk is

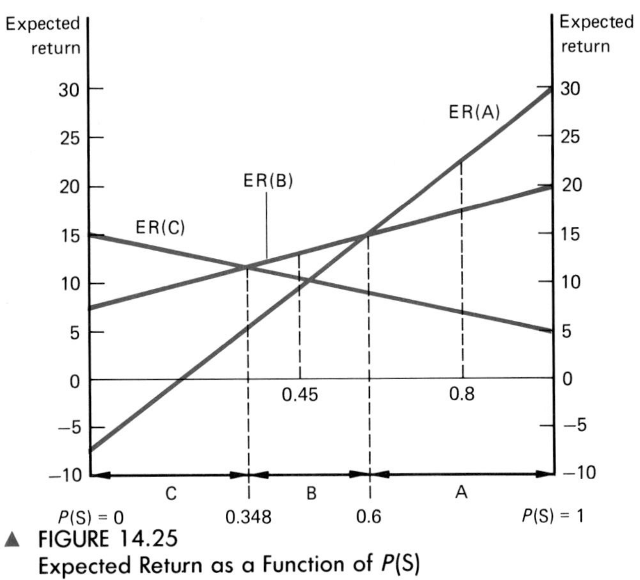

▲ FIGURE 14.25
Expected Return as a Function of P(S)

to select the decision with the highest expected return, Figure 14.25 shows which decision is optimal for any particular value of P(S). For example, if as in Figure 14.19, the value of P(S) is 0.45, then Figure 14.25 shows that ER(B) > ER(C) > ER(A). Hence, as we have already computed, for this value of P(S) the optimal decision is B. On the other hand, if P(S) = 0.8, we see that ER(A) > ER(B) > ER(C) and thus A is the optimal decision.

In more general terms we see that if P(S) is larger than the value of P(S) at which the graphs of ER(A) and ER(B) cross, strategy A should be selected. The P(S) value at which strategy A becomes optimal can be found by setting ER(A) equal to ER(B) and solving for P(S); that is

To show the other point:
$ER(B) = ER(C)$
$7 + 13P(S) = 15 - 10P(S)$
$23P(S) = 8$
$P(S) = 8/23 = 0.348$

$$\begin{aligned} \text{ER(A)} &= \text{ER(B)} \\ -8 + 38P(\text{S}) &= 7 + 13P(\text{S}) \\ 25P(\text{S}) &= 15 \\ P(\text{S}) &= 0.6 \end{aligned}$$

The optimal policy is not very sensitive

In a similar way, it is easily determined that the graphs of ER(C) and ER(B) cross when P(S) = 0.348. (You should try this calculation yourself.) Thus, Figure 14.25 indicates that **PROTRAC** should select the basic production and marketing strategy (i.e., decision B) if P(S) is larger than 0.348 and smaller than 0.6. This is consistent with what we already computed under the assumption that P(S) = 0.45. However, the analysis of Figure 14.25 provides considerably more information than we had previously. It is now clear, for example, that the optimal decision in this case is not very sensitive to the precision of our estimate for P(S). The same strategy, B, remains optimal for an increase or decrease of more than 0.10 in the previously estimated probability of 0.45.

Sensitivity of the Optimal Decision to Returns

It is also important to consider how sensitive the decision is to estimates of the returns. For example, suppose that the return of the aggressive strategy is greater than 30 when the market is strong. Let x represent this return. Then

$$\begin{aligned}
\text{ER(A)} &= (x)P(\text{S})+(-8)P(\text{W}) \\
&= (x)P(\text{S}) + (-8)[1 - P(\text{S})] \\
&= (x + 8)P(\text{S}) - 8
\end{aligned}$$

As x increases beyond 30, the slope of the line in Figure 14.25 labeled ER(A) increases without changing the vertical intercept of the line; that is, the line rotates counterclockwise about the vertical intercept. This means that the lines labeled ER(A) and ER(B) will have a new intersection, which can be found by solving the equation

$$\begin{aligned}
\text{ER(A)} &= \text{ER(B)} \\
(x + 8)P(\text{S}) - 8 &= 7 + 13P(\text{S}) \\
(x - 5)P(\text{S}) &= 15 \\
P(\text{S}) &= \frac{15}{(x - 5)}
\end{aligned}$$

Thus A will be optimal for $P(\text{S}) \geq 15/(x - 5)$, B will be optimal for $0.348 \leq P(\text{S}) \leq 15/(x - 5)$, and C will be optimal for $0 \leq P(\text{S}) \leq 0.348$. Since $15/(x - 5)$ decreases as x increases, the range in which A is optimal will grow, the range in which B is optimal will shrink, and the range in which C is optimal will stay the same. There is, however, an "allowable increase" on x. As x is increased, eventually the three lines labeled ER(A), ER(B), and ER(C) will intersect at a single point (see Figure 14.26). When that happens the optimal decision will be C for $P(\text{S}) \leq 0.348$ and A for $P(\text{S}) \geq 0.348$. The value of x for which this happens can be found by solving

$$\begin{aligned}
P(\text{S}) &= \frac{15}{(x-5)} = 0.348 \\
x - 5 &= \frac{15}{0.348} = 43.1 \\
x &= 48.1
\end{aligned}$$

For values of x greater than 48.1 the range of $P(\text{S})$ values in which C is optimal will start to shrink, and the range in which A is optimal will continue to expand.

▼ FIGURE 14.26
Finding the Allowable Increase

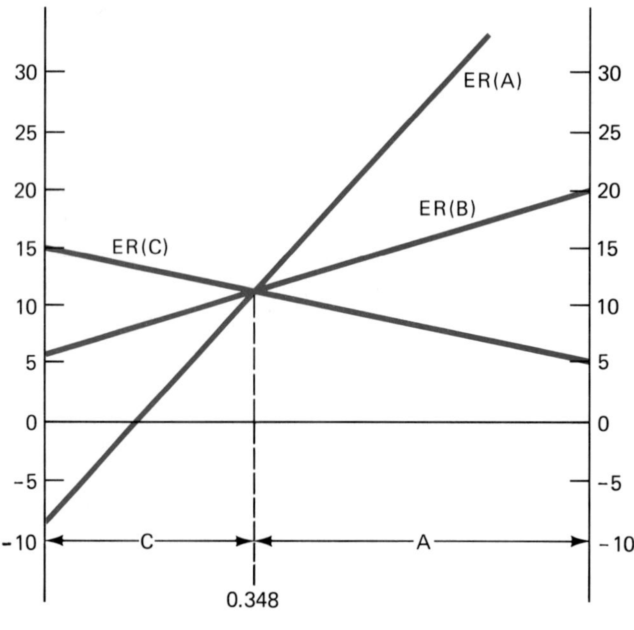

Although a diagram such as Figure 14.25 can be used only when there are two possible states of nature, it provides a useful pedagogical device for illustrating the sensitivity of the optimal solution to the estimates of the probabilities and returns. For higher dimensions, generalizations of this approach exist, but such a discussion would go beyond the introductory level of this chapter.

14.8 Decision Trees: Incorporating New Information

A Market Research Study for Home and Garden Tractors

The management of **PROTRAC**'s domestic tractor division was just on the verge of recommending the basic marketing and production strategy (B) when the board of directors insisted that a market research study had to be performed. Only after such a study would the board be willing to approve the selection of a marketing and production strategy. As a result of the board's decision, management consulted the corporate marketing research group at **PROTRAC** headquarters. It was agreed that this group would perform a market research study and would report within a month on whether the study was encouraging (E) or discouraging (D). Thus, within a month the new-product planners would have this additional information. This new information should obviously be taken into account before making a decision on the marketing and production strategy.

Management could treat the new information informally; that is, once the test results were available, management's estimate of P(S), the probability that the market would be strong, could be updated. If the study turned out to be encouraging (E) presumably management would want to increase the estimate of P(S) from 0.45 to 0.50, 0.60, or maybe more. If the study results were discouraging (D) then P(S) should be decreased. The question is: How should the updating be accomplished? There is a formal way to do this, based on the concept of *conditional probability*. The mathematics of why this approach works is detailed in Appendix 14.2. Here we will take a tabular approach that is suited to implementation in a spreadsheet program.

Obtaining Revised Probabilities Based on New Information

The marketing research group has agreed to report within a month whether according to their study the test is encouraging (E) or discouraging (D). We certainly hope their report will be reliable—that is, if their report is encouraging, then the market is strong and if their report is discouraging, then the market is weak. This would amount to their report revealing the true state of nature. We will see, however, that marketing's report may be useful even if it is not perfectly reliable. This raises the issues of how to quantify "reliability." We will use conditional probabilities.

Conditional Probability. Suppose that A and B are two events. An informal definition of the **conditional probability,** $P(\text{A}|\text{B})$, is the probability that the event A occurs *given* that the event B occurs. For example, P(E|S) would be the conditional probability that marketing gives an encouraging report *given* that the market is in fact strong. If marketing were perfectly reliable, this conditional probability would be 1; that is, they would always give an encouraging report when the market is in fact

REPORT	STATE OF NATURE	
	S	W
E	0.6	0.3
D	0.4	0.7

▲ FIGURE 14.27
Reliability of Marketing Report: Conditional Probabilities

strong. However, marketing's track record is not perfect. In the past when the market has in fact been strong, they have issued an encouraging report only 60% of the time. Thus, $P(\text{E}|\text{S}) = 0.6$. Since marketing always issues an encouraging or discouraging report, the value of $P(\text{D}|\text{S})$ must be $1 - 0.6$, or 0.4; that is, they issue a discouraging report 40% of the time when in fact the market is strong.

What happens when the market is in fact weak? Marketing is somewhat better at predicting weak markets, but is still not perfect: $P(\text{D}|\text{W}) = 0.7$. That is, in the past when the market has in fact been weak, marketing has issued a discouraging report 70% of the time. Of course, $P(\text{E}|\text{W}) = 0.3$. This information about marketing's reliability is summarized in Figure 14.27.

In this figure, the conditional probability, $P(\text{A}|\text{B})$, is found at the intersection of row A and column B. Note that the column sums must be 1, while the row sums may be either greater than, less than, or equal to 1.

Calculating the Posterior Probabilities. Suppose that marketing has come back with an encouraging report. What is the probability that the market is in fact strong? It is the conditional probability $P(\text{S}|\text{E})$. Note that this probability is in general *not* the same as $P(\text{E}|\text{S})$. We will see that it depends on the reliabilities in Figure 14.27 and the initial estimates of the probabilities of a strong or weak market. These initial estimates are called **prior probabilities,** while conditional probabilities such as $P(\text{S}|\text{E})$ are called **posterior probabilities.** The domestic tractor division has already estimated the prior probabilities given in Figure 14.28.

The key to obtaining the posterior probabilities is Bayes's Theorem. We will use a tabular spreadsheet approach that is justified by the argument given in Appendix 14.2. The procedure is as follows:

1. Generate a new table by multiplying each column of the reliability table by the corresponding prior probability. For example, multiply each entry in the S column of Figure 14.27 by $P(\text{S})$. This table is a table of the *joint probabilities.* (See Appendix 14.2.)
2. For each row of this new table, compute the sum of the entries. In the example at hand this gives the *marginal probabilities,* $P(\text{E})$ and $P(\text{D})$.
3. Generate another new table by dividing each row of the joint probability table by its row sum. This final table gives the posterior probabilities.

This process has been carried out in the spreadsheet shown in Figure 14.29.[3]

[3]Note that the posterior probability table in Figure 14.29 is read differently from the reliability table. For example, the probability in row D and column W of the posterior probability table is $P\{\text{W}|\text{D}\}$, whereas the probability in row D and column W of the reliability table is $P\{\text{W}|\text{D}\}$. In general, the probability $P\{A|B\}$ in the posterior probability table is found at the intersection of *column* A and *row* B. This convention is employed to simplify the copying of formulas in the spreadsheet that is used to generate the posterior probability table. If the convention for the reliability table had also to be observed in the posterior probability table, then the first *column* of the table would be the first *row* of the table in step 2 divided by its row sum, the second column of the table would be the second row of the table in step 2 divided by *its* row sum, and so on. These operations would be difficult to perform in one step with most spreadsheet programs.

S	W
0.45	0.55

▲ FIGURE 14.28
Prior Probabilities of Strong or Weak Market

B9: +B2*B$6

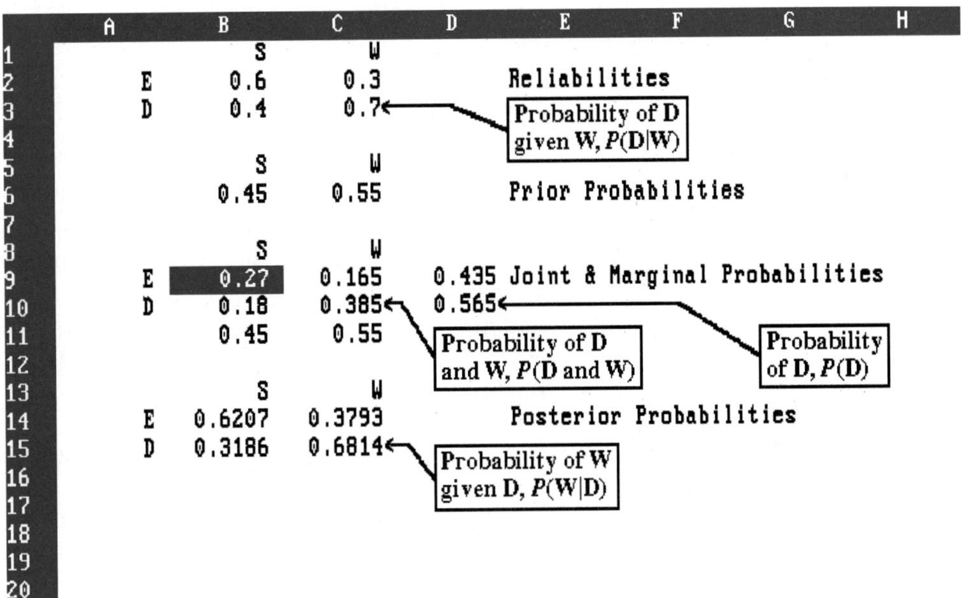

	A	B	C	D	E	F	G	H
1		S	W					
2	E	0.6	0.3		Reliabilities			
3	D	0.4	0.7					
4								
5		S	W					
6		0.45	0.55		Prior Probabilities			
7								
8		S	W					
9	E	0.27	0.165	0.435	Joint & Marginal Probabilities			
10	D	0.18	0.385	0.565				
11		0.45	0.55					
12								
13		S	W					
14	E	0.6207	0.3793		Posterior Probabilities			
15	D	0.3186	0.6814					
16								
17								
18								
19								
20								

▲ FIGURE 14.29
Calculation of Posterior Probabilities

In this spreadsheet the tables labeled Reliabilities and Prior Probabilities are given and the tables labeled Joint & Marginal Probabilities and Posterior Probabilities are calculated according to the three-step procedure above.

The spreadsheet makes it easy to calculate the sensitivity of the posterior probabilities to the reliabilities and the prior probabilities. For example, the Data Table command can be used to generate all posterior probabilities of a strong market for values of $P(\text{S})$ between 0 and 1 in increments of 0.1 [the value of $P(\text{W})$ was set equal to $1 - P(\text{S})$]. The results are shown in Figure 14.30.

Note that as the prior probability of a strong market increases, so does the posterior probability of a strong market given either an encouraging or a discouraging test result. Note too that the posterior probability of a strong market is greater than the prior given an encouraging test result, but the posterior probability is less than the prior given a discouraging test result.

Incorporating Posterior Probabilities in the Decision Tree

We now represent management's problem with the decision tree presented in Figure 14.31. The first node (I) corresponds to performing the marketing research. The node is circular because the outcome is not certain. There are two possible results. The test is either encouraging (E) or discouraging (D); $P(\text{E})$ and $P(\text{D})$ represent the probabilities of those two outcomes.

PRIOR	POSTERIOR	
P(S)	*P*(S|E)	*P*(S|D)
0	0	0
0.1	0.18	0.06
0.2	0.33	0.13
0.3	0.46	0.20
0.4	0.57	0.28
0.5	0.67	0.36
0.6	0.75	0.46
0.7	0.82	0.57
0.8	0.89	0.70
0.9	0.95	0.84
1	1	1

▲ FIGURE 14.30
Sensitivity of Posterior Probabilities to Prior Probabilities

If the test is encouraging, we proceed to node II, which is square because a decision must be made. Management must decide to select A or B or C. Suppose that management selects A. We are then led to node IV, another situation with two possible outcomes, namely whether the market is strong (S) or weak (W). If it turns

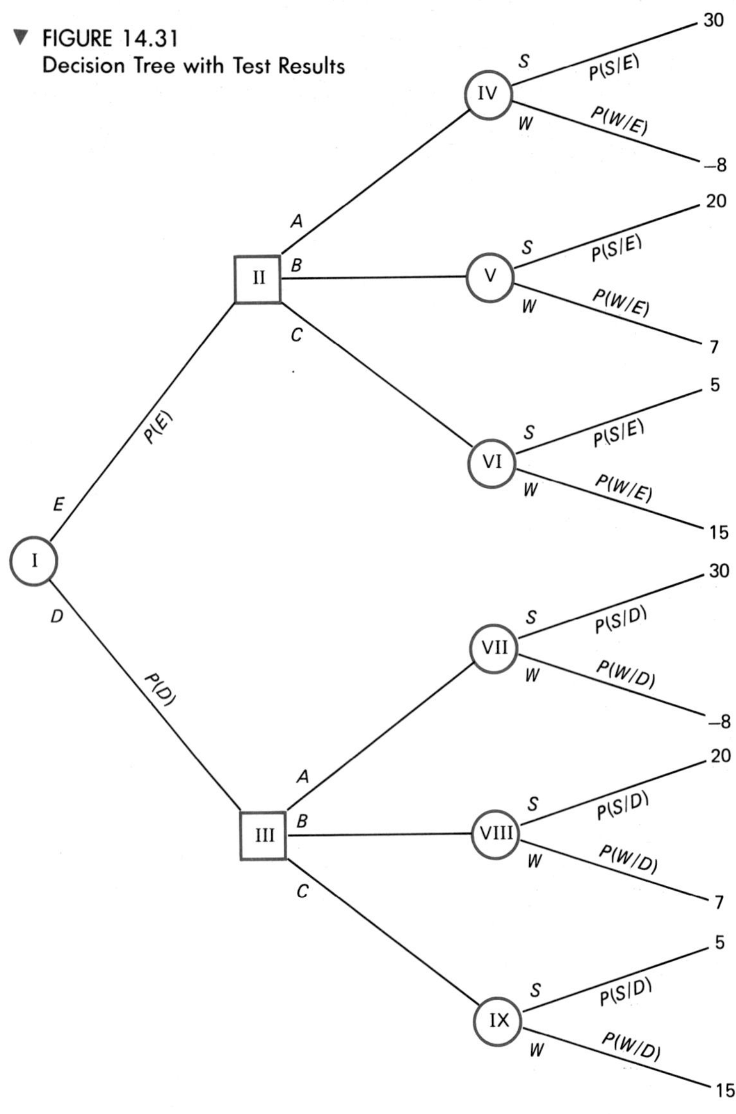

▼ FIGURE 14.31
Decision Tree with Test Results

out to be strong, **PROTRAC** will enjoy a net return of 30, which is the terminal value on the branch.

Importance of chronological order

It is important to note that the tree is created in the chronological order in which information becomes available and decisions are required; that is,

1. Test result.
2. Make decision.
3. Market condition.

In order to solve this tree we must fill in the values for *P*(S|E), *P*(W|E), *P*(S|D), *P*(W|D), *P*(E), and *P*(D). The first four probabilities are found in the table labeled Posterior Probabilities in Figure 14.29. The probability *P*(A|B) is found in *column* A and *row* B of the table (again, note that this is the opposite of the convention used to read the Reliabilities table but is more convenient for the spreadsheet representation). So for example, *P*(W|E) = 0.3793.

Updating *P*(S)

Thus, the event of an encouraging test result, and the use of Bayes's Theorem allow us to update the prior value of *P*(S), namely 0.45, to a higher value, *P*(S|E) = 0.621. Similar calculations yield *P*(W|E) = 0.379, *P*(S|D) = 0.318, and *P*(W|D) = 0.682.

In Figure 14.32 the probabilities are attached to the decision tree. The first step in solving the tree is to fold it back to the terminal nodes.

▼ FIGURE 14.32
Decision Tree with New Information

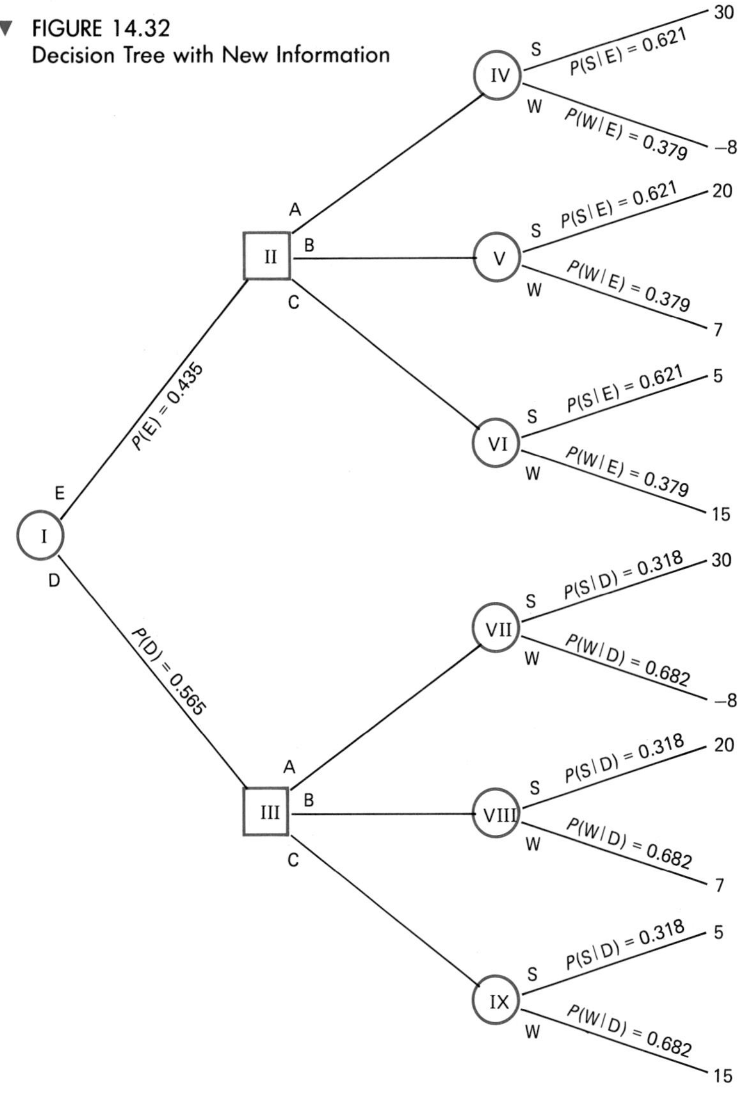

When computing ER, you can use this quick-and-dirty common-sense check. Make sure that the expected value is between the highest and lowest payoffs. If it is not, then a mathematical error has been made.

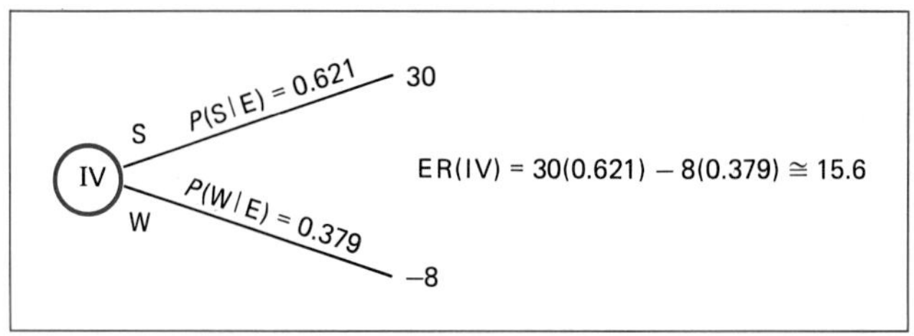

For example, node IV is folded back by calculating its expected return and assigning it to the node. Figure 14.33 shows the tree after the first step. This figure can be used to determine the optimal decisions. We see that if the test is encouraging (E), we arrive at node II. Then to maximize the expected return, we should take action A, that is, follow the aggressive production and marketing strategy. Similarly, if the test result is discouraging, we should take action C. Why? Because 11.81 is the largest possible expected return when the test is discouraging.

▼ FIGURE 14.33
Decision Tree after One Foldback

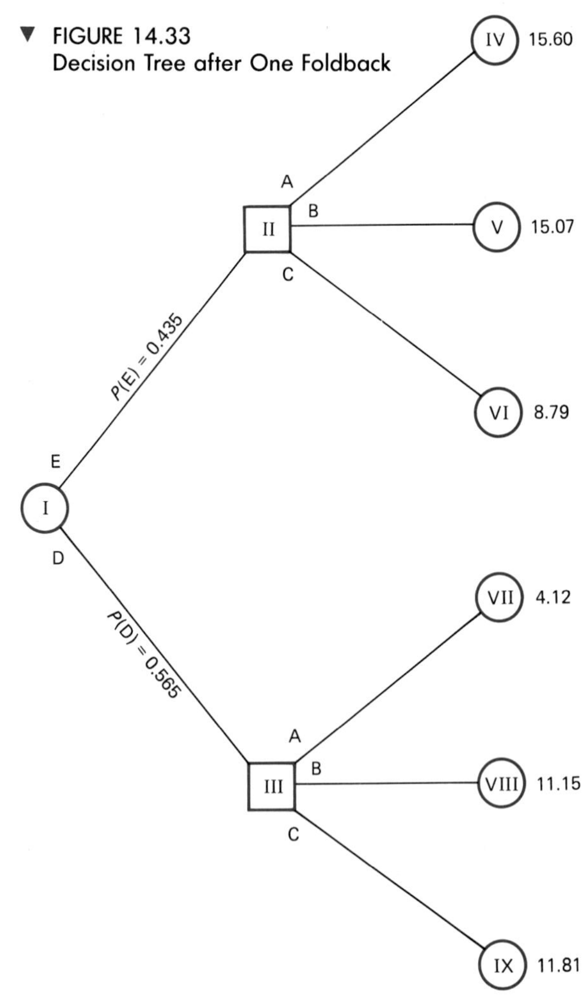

The Expected Value of Sample Information

Suppose that we use the optimal decisions determined above to fold back the decision tree shown in Figure 14.33 one more step. We obtain

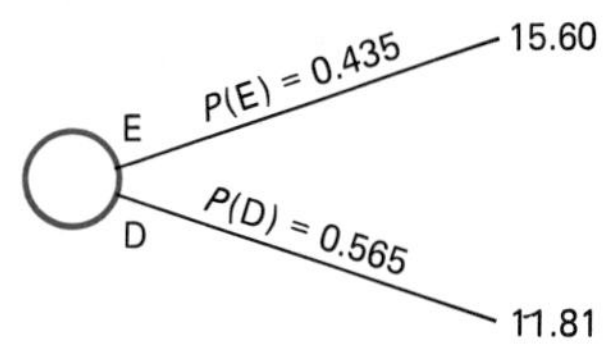

The expected return then is

$$ER = 15.60(0.435) + 11.81(0.565) \approx 13.46$$

This value is the expected return of performing the market test and making optimal decisions.

In Section 14.6 we saw that if the market test is not performed, the optimal decision is to select B, the basic strategy, and that this decision has an expected return of 12.85. Clearly then, performing the market test increases **PROTRAC**'s expected return by 13.46 − 12.85 = 0.61. Even though the market test is not perfectly reliable, it still has some value (0.61, to be precise). Appropriately enough, this quantity is called the **expected value of sample information (EVSI).** In general terms

EVSI

$$\text{EVSI} = \begin{pmatrix}\text{maximum possible}\\ \text{expected return}\\ \text{with sample}\\ \text{information}\end{pmatrix} - \begin{pmatrix}\text{maximum possible}\\ \text{expected return}\\ \text{without sample}\\ \text{information}\end{pmatrix}$$

The EVSI is an upper bound of how much one would be willing to pay for this information.

Let us now calculate the expected value of *perfect* information. Recall from Section 14.3 that this is the amount that management would be willing to pay for perfect information. The payoff table originally presented in Figure 14.19 is reproduced below for your convenience (Figure 14.34).

	STATE OF NATURE	
	S	**W**
	PROBABILITY	
DECISION	**0.45**	**0.55**
A	30	−8
B	20	7
C	5	15

▲ FIGURE 14.34

If it were sure that the market would be strong, management would pick decision A and enjoy a return of 30. Similarly, if it were sure that the market would be weak, management would pick decision C and enjoy a return of 15. How much would management pay for perfect information? Since perfect information will reveal a strong market with probability 0.45, and a weak market with probability 0.55, we see that

$$\text{EVPI} = (30)(0.45) + (15)(0.55) - 12.85 \approx 8.90 \qquad \textbf{(14.2)}$$

EVPI and EVSI compared

Equation (14.2) tells us that perfect information will bring us an expected increase of 8.90 over the previous expected return. This is the maximum possible increase in

As the probabilities of correct sample information increase, EVSI approaches EVPI. In fact, when P(EIS) = 1.00 and P(DIW) = 1.00, then EVSI=EVPI.

the expected return that can be obtained from new information. The expected value of sample information (EVSI) is the increase in the expected return that was obtained with the information produced by the market test. Since EVPI = 8.9 and EVSI = 0.61, we see that the market test is not very effective. If it were, the value for EVSI would be much closer to EVPI.

14.9 Sequential Decisions: To Test or Not to Test

In the preceding section, we assumed that the board of directors had decided to have a market research study done. We then considered the question of how the management of **PROTRAC**'s domestic tractor division should use the information generated by the study to update the decision model. Let us step back for a moment. It seems clear that the decision to have a market study done is in essence no different from the decision to adopt one marketing and production strategy or another. Management must carefully weigh the cost of performing the study against the gain that might result from having the information that the study would produce. It is also clear that the decision on whether to have a market research test is not an isolated decision. If the test is given, management must still select one of the marketing and production strategies. Thus, the value of performing the test depends in part on how **PROTRAC** uses the information generated by the test. In other words, the value of an initial decision depends on a *sequence* of decisions and uncertain events that will follow the initial decision. This is called a **sequential decision problem.**

Sequential decision problems

Analyzing Sequential Decisions

Students may think that a decision is "test and choose option A" rather than first "test," and then, depending upon the state of nature that occurs, choose option A or C.

This is an extremely common type of management problem and is actually the kind of situation that decision trees are designed to handle. It is in situations where there are a number of interrelated decisions and events with more than one possible outcome that the ability to display the problem graphically is especially useful.

Figure 14.35 shows the test or no-test tree. In terms of structure and the probabilities, you see that the upper (test) branch is the tree from Figure 14.32 and the lower (no test) branch is the tree from Figure 14.21.

The terminal values merit some discussion. They are determined in a two-step process:

Determination of terminal values

1. Assign the appropriate cash flow to each decision and uncertain event. In this problem we have assumed that the market test costs $500,000. Since all costs and returns are measured in millions, a figure of −0.5 is placed by the test branch and a figure of 0 is placed by the no-test branch. Similarly, a figure of 30 is placed on the upper branch since this is the profit if **PROTRAC** selects A and the market is strong.

2. Determine a particular terminal value by adding the cash flows on all branches between the first node and the terminal position. For example, the number 29.5 on the uppermost terminal position comes from adding the costs on the path Test-E-A-S (i.e., costs of $-0.5 + 0 + 0 + 30 = 29.5$).

You solve this tree by folding it back. You fold back a circular node by calculating the expected returns. You fold back a square (decision) node by selecting the decision that yields the highest expected return. Three steps are required to solve the test or no-test tree. They are shown in Figure 14.36.

The optimal strategy

The *optimal strategy* is a complete plan for the entire tree. It specifies what

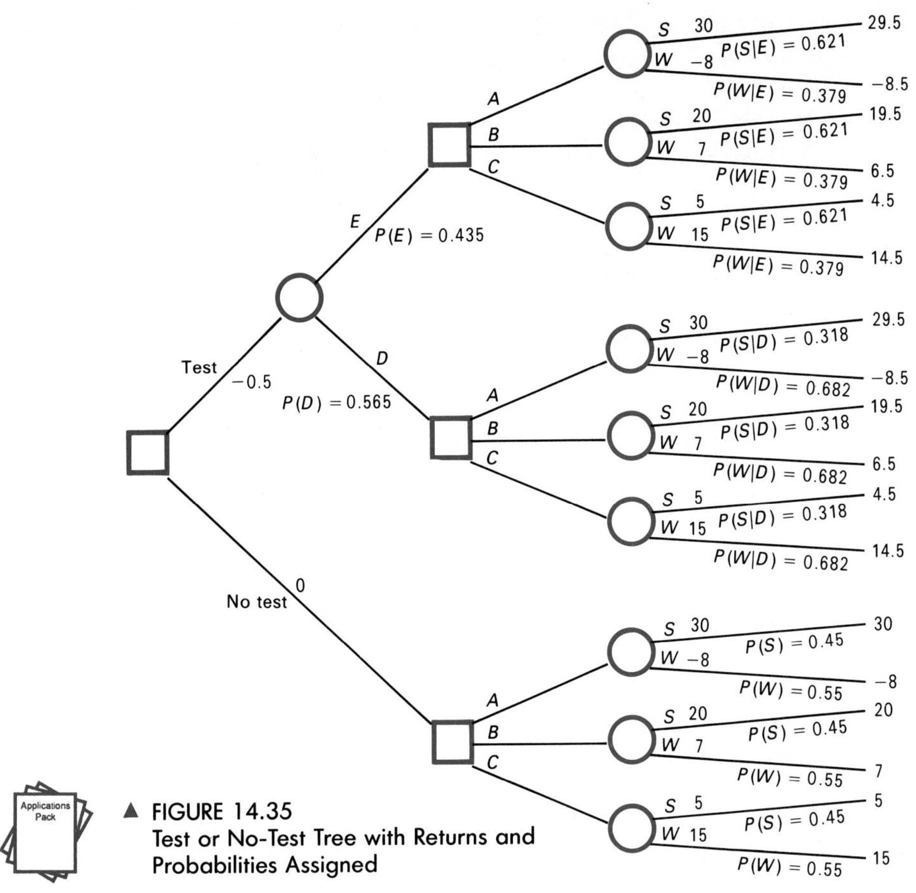

▲ FIGURE 14.35
Test or No-Test Tree with Returns and Probabilities Assigned

▼ FIGURE 14.36
Solving the Test or No-Test Tree

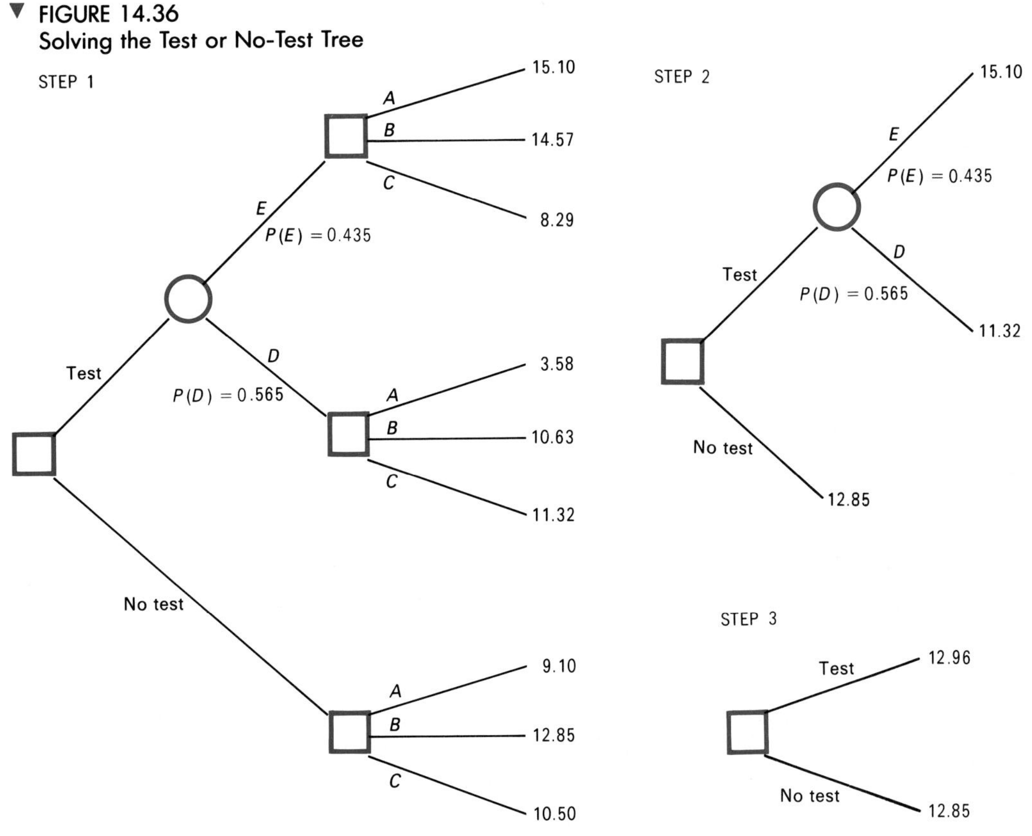

action to take no matter which of the uncertain events occurs. To determine the optimal strategy for the test or no-test tree, we refer to Figure 14.36. From step 3 we see that since 12.96 > 12.85, **PROTRAC** should have the market test. From step 1 we see that if the result of the test is encouraging (E), then A is the best decision since it yields the largest expected return. Similarly, if the result of the test is discouraging (D), then C is the best decision.

The Impact of Utilities

It is simple to incorporate utilities into a decision tree. Suppose that the utilities of all possible payoffs are given in Figure 14.37.

PAYOFF	UTILITY
−8.5	0.300
−8	0.320
4.5	0.695
5	0.709
6.5	0.748
7	0.760
14.5	0.910
15	0.914
19.5	0.941
20	0.943
29.5	0.962
30	0.963

▲ FIGURE 14.37
Utilities of Payoffs

A graph of utility versus payoff would show that **PROTRAC** is risk-averse. For example, the additional utility of increasing the payoff from 20 to 30 is only 0.963 − 0.943 = 0.020, while the additional utility of increasing the payoff from 5 to 15 is 0.914 − 0.709 = 0.205.

To incorporate the utilities into the decision tree, replace the payoffs in Figure 14.35 with their utilities (see Figure 14.38). Now roll back the tree as before. From Figure 14.39, we see that the optimal decision is still to test. However, if the test is encouraging, alternative B is now chosen rather than A. While A's maximum payoff (29.5) is larger than B's (19.5), B's minimum payoff is larger than A's (6.5 versus −8.5). For **PROTRAC**'s utility function and the given posterior probabilities, the expected utility of B is higher than that of A.

Sensitivity of the Optimal Decision to Prior Probabilities

Whether cash returns or utilities are used in the decision tree, it is important to see how sensitive the optimal decision is to various parameter values. For example, how sensitive is the optimal decision to the initial estimate of a strong market, the prior probability *P*(S)? Spreadsheets are not particularly suited to solving decision trees, but they are certainly adequate for small problems and do permit easy sensitivity analysis through what-if analysis and Data Table commands. The spreadsheet shown in Figure 14.40 reproduces the graphical analysis shown in Figure 14.39. The main advantage of the spreadsheet formulation is the ease with which various

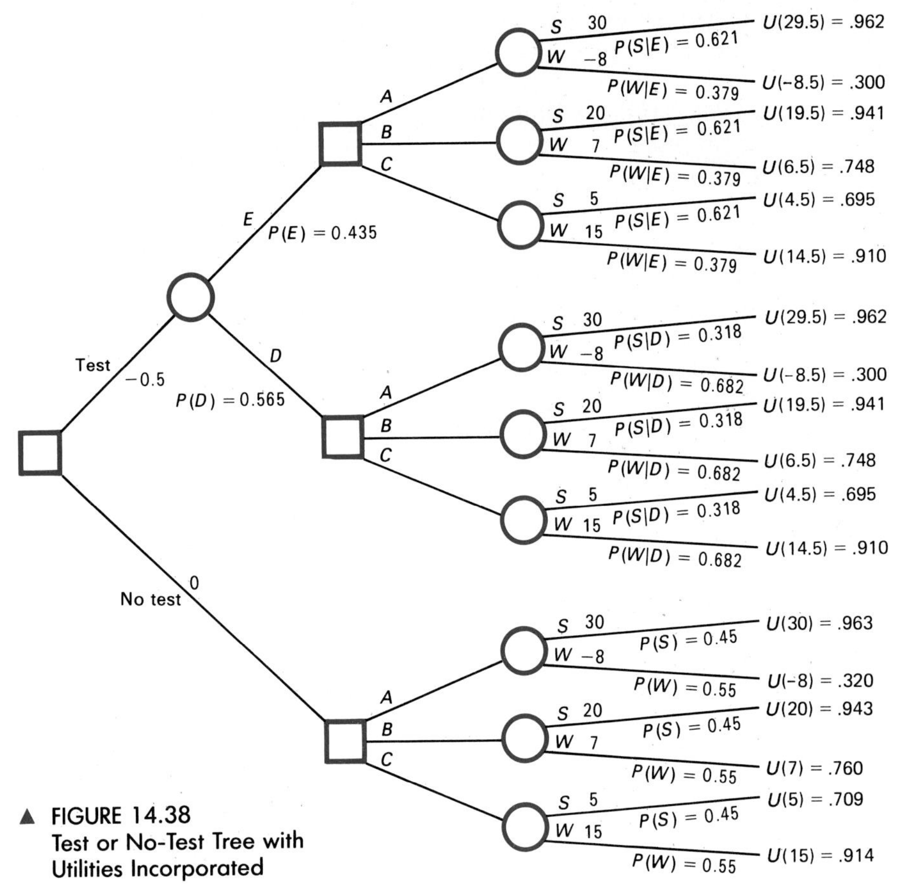

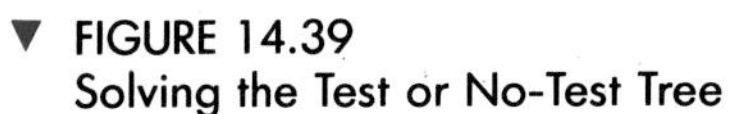
▲ FIGURE 14.38
Test or No-Test Tree with Utilities Incorporated

▼ FIGURE 14.39
Solving the Test or No-Test Tree

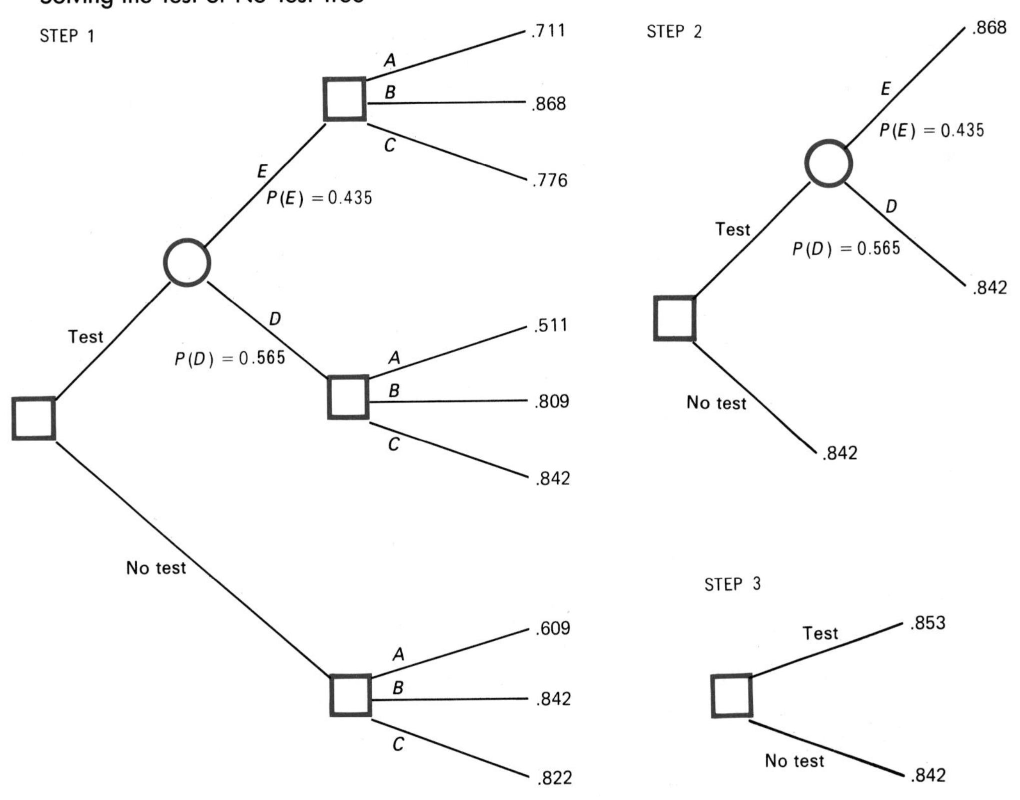

A21: (F3) 'Test

	A	B	C	D	E	F	G	H
21	Test	0.853			Utility Lookup Table			
22		E	0.868		-8.5	0.300		
23			A	0.711	-8	0.320		
24			B	0.868	4.5	0.695		
25			C	0.777	5	0.709		
26		D	0.842		6.5	0.748		
27			A	0.511	7	0.760		
28			B	0.809	14.5	0.910		
29			C	0.842	15	0.914		
30	No Test	0.842			19.5	0.941		
31		A	0.609		20	0.943		
32		B	0.842		29.5	0.962		
33		C	0.822		30	0.963		
34								
35	Maximum Utility =		0.853					
36	Optimal Decision: Test							
37								
38								
39								
40								

▲ FIGURE 14.40
Spreadsheet Representation of Test/No Test Decision Tree

parameters can be changed and the tree recalculated. (The utilities are included in the form of a look-up table to facilitate sensitivity analysis on the utility function.)

The graph of Figure 14.41 was generated by varying the value of $P(\text{S})$ between 0 and 1 in increments of .01. The solid line represents the expected utility of the Test decision, while the dotted line represents the expected utility of the No-Test decision. Whenever the two curves cross, the optimal decision changes. Since the curves cross four times (although it is hard to see the last time because the curves are so close together), the optimal decision changes four times: No-Test, Test, No-Test, Test, No-Test. Test is the optimal decision for values of $P(\text{S})$ between (approximately) 0.29 and 0.50 and between 0.94 and 0.96. No-Test is optimal for the values of $P(\text{S})$ between 0 and 0.29, between 0.5 and 0.94, and between 0.96 and 1.

14.10 Management and Decision Theory

A typical management decision has the following characteristics:

1. It is made once and only once (e.g., should I buy 100 shares of IBM stock today or not?)
2. The return depends on an uncertain event that will occur in the future (e.g., the price of IBM stock will go up or down), and we have no historical information about this event.

We know about related events that may tell us something about the likelihood of the various outcomes (e.g., the behavior of the price of IBM stock last week). But we cannot perform an experiment to provide a good, reliable estimate of the relevant

Another advantage of modeling with a spreadsheet is the ease of storing the sensitivity results from the data table and then graphing them, as shown in Figure 14.41.

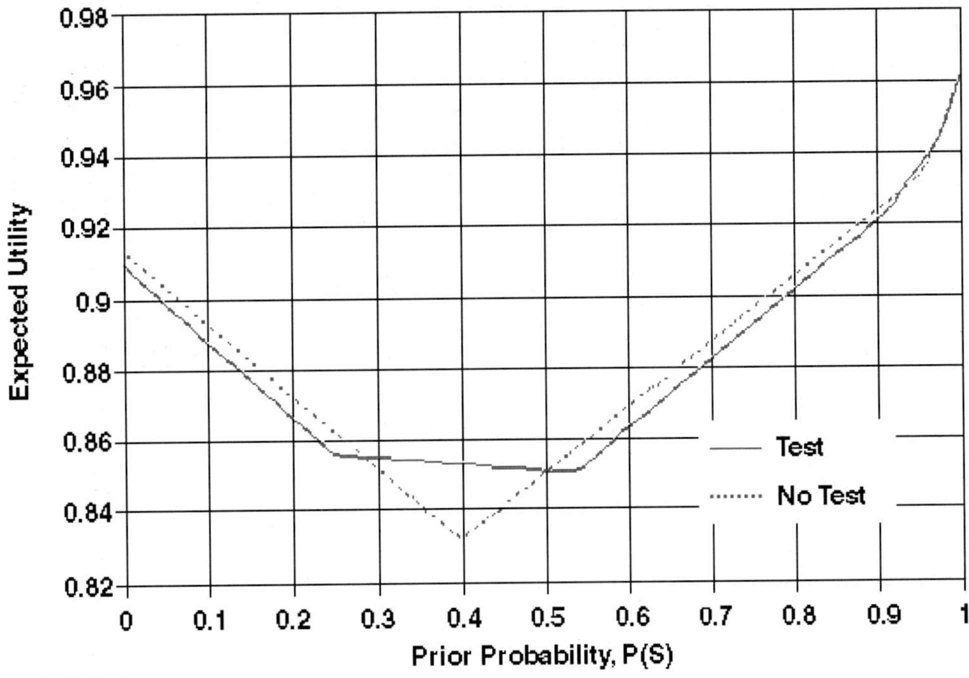

▲ FIGURE 14.41
Expected Utility of Test and No Test

probabilities (e.g., we cannot perform an experiment that tells us about the price of IBM stock next week.)

Reviewing the conceptual framework

What does the material in this chapter contribute to our understanding of how to attack this problem? In brief, this chapter recommends the following conceptual framework:

1. For each decision, determine the utility of each possible outcome.
2. Determine the probability of each possible outcome.
3. Calculate the expected utility of each decision.
4. Select the decision with the largest expected utility.

Once the first two steps have been completed the next two steps are easy, at least conceptually. But how can you *know* the probabilities and the utilities?

Probabilities and utilities are subjective assessments

The answer is that there are no values to *know.* These are not entities, the "true" value of which can be revealed by experimentation or further analysis. Indeed, these two quantities, *probabilities* and *utilities,* are *subjective* and represent the *best judgment and taste of the manager.* Certainly the manager's evaluation of these two quantities can be influenced by study, but there is no opportunity for direct experimentation with the underlying phenomena, as there would be, for example, in physical or biological science.

There is, nevertheless, some structure to cling to in this sea of subjectivity. The structure is provided by a logical device called an *equivalent lottery.* This concept gives one a *consistent framework* for quantifying both probabilities and utilities. We saw in Section 14.4 how a manager can use an equivalent lottery to create a utility function.

Assessing subjective probabilities

The manager can use this approach to assess a subjective probability. Suppose, for example, that on this date you wish to assess the probability that Dan Quayle will be the Republican candidate for President in 1996. The first step is to think of two games. In game 1 you receive \$100 if Quayle is the candidate and \$0 if he is not. In game 2 you receive \$100 with probability p and \$0 with probability $1 - p$. You now adjust the value of p until you are indifferent between the two games. The resulting value of p is *your* subjective probability that Quayle will be the Republican candidate in 1996. It is clear that your assessment may be different from that of George Bush or Dan Quayle.

In corporate settings, a group's utilities will tend to be more conservative than each individual's.

We have argued that the equivalent lottery allows one to quantify both subjective probability and utility. We now stress again that the values obtained through this process are personal and a matter of judgment, and thus by definition they will vary from person to person. Certainly, then, two individuals, each of whom is facing the same decision and using the recommended approach, may arrive at different decisions. And why not? The recommended approach allows the decision maker to incorporate personal knowledge (and experience), and surely there is no reason to believe that everyone will "know" the same things at the moment of decision.

The advantage of the lottery approach

However, a cynic might ask, "Why bother with all this machinery?" If judgment and taste play such an important role in these assessments, isn't it better to use judgment in a holistic approach and simply select the alternative that intuitively seems best? What do we gain from assessing probability and utility separately? The reply is that separating the two assessments makes it possible for a manager to concentrate attention on each of these entities (probability and utility), one at a time. The problem with a simple intuitive approach is that we humans have a hard time thinking about more than one thing at a time. While thinking about payoffs, it is hard to be thinking at the same time about likelihoods and then to combine them in one's head. In other words, the simple, intuitive approach makes it too easy to put heavy emphasis on a particularly awful outcome (or a particularly attractive outcome) and not enough weight on the fact that this outcome may be extremely unlikely. As an example, look at the number of people who won't fly in an airplane, but will drive in a car, even though the probability of being killed in an auto accident is vastly higher than that of dying in a plane crash. (Presumably, they are influenced by the thought that they *might* survive an auto accident, whereas they would be unlikely to live through a plane crash.) *Separating the assessments of probabilities and utilities forces a manager to give appropriate and separate consideration to each before combining the two to determine the final decision.*

The revolution in personal computing and the explosion in software that has accompanied it have had an impact on decision analysis. A few years ago, general-purpose decision analysis programs from commercial software suppliers were not widely available. Some companies created programs for their own purposes, but these were not available to the general public. At this writing at least three microcomputer packages (Arborist, Riskcalc, and Supertree) are similar in the sense that each enables the user to use the power of the personal computer to carry out the various tasks associated with decision trees.

14.11 Notes on Implementation

In practice, the material in this chapter is included under the more general heading of "decision analysis." Ralph Keeney, a leading scholar in the field, defines decision analysis as "a formalization of common sense for decision problems which are too complex for informal use of common sense." Decision analysis, which is based on axioms originally stated by John von Neumann and Oskar Morgenstern, involves assigning probabilities and utilities to possible outcomes and maximizing expected utility. This approach is applied to highly complex problems that are typically sequential in nature. It can be thought of as having four parts: (1) structuring the problem, (2) assessing the probability of the possible outcomes, (3) determining the utility of the possible outcomes, and (4) evaluating alternatives and selecting a strategy.

Much of the material in this chapter concerns item (4), the technical process of evaluating alternatives and selecting a strategy. This is appropriate since this is the conceptual heart of decision analysis. In practice, however, this is the easy part of the problem. A significantly greater proportion of effort is spent on the other three areas. Structuring the problem, which involves generating alternatives and specifying objectives in numerically measurable terms, is a particularly unstructured task. In some of the applications, objectives have been quantified in the areas of environmental impact, public health and safety, and so on.

Role of personal judgment

Indeed, there are many qualitative and nonobjective factors involved in all decision making, but the important role of Decision Analysis is to make it consistent, not just "objective" and devoid of any subjective judgments. There is room for subjectivity, but it should not depend on how you "feel" at the moment.

It is important to understand that decision analysis does *not* provide a completely objective analysis of complicated problems. Many aspects of a decision analysis require personal judgment—whether it be structuring the problem, assessing probabilities, or assigning utilities. In many important complex problems there simply are not enough empirical data to provide a basis for complete analysis. Nevertheless, experience has shown that the framework provided by decision analysis has been useful.

In the early 1960s decision analysis began to be successfully applied to a number of problems in the private sector. These included problems of gas and oil exploration as well as capital investment. Although developments have continued on private-sector problems, two other general problem areas have witnessed a wide variety of applications of decision analysis. In the health-care field, decision analysis has been applied to such diverse problems as the evaluation of new drugs, the analysis of treatment strategies for diseases, and the selection of medical technology for a particular facility. The second problem area concerns applications in the government. In particular, decision analysis has been applied to everything from the seeding of hurricanes, to the negotiation of international oil tanker standards, to the choice between coal and nuclear technology for large-scale power plants. A readable overview of decision analysis with an extensive bibliography is available in "Decision Analysis: An Overview," *Operations Research,* September-October 1982.

14.12 Summary

The first part of this chapter dealt with the fundamentals of decision theory. A summary of that material was provided in Section 14.5.

The following four sections of the chapter expounded on the role of decision trees in facilitating the decision process. A decision tree is a graphical device for attacking problems in which a sequence of decisions must be made, and these decisions are interspersed with events that have several possible outcomes. It is typically true that square nodes are used to represent decisions and circular nodes are used to represent events. The branches emanating from a square node are the possible decisions, and the branches emanating from a circular node are the possible outcomes. When a decision tree has been completed, a path from the start of the tree to a terminal node represents a specific sequence of decisions and uncertain events. The complete tree represents all possible such sequences.

Solving a decision tree is a sequential process that starts at the terminal nodes and proceeds back to the start of the tree in a process that is described as "folding back." The process includes two steps: The branches emanating from a circular node are folded back by assigning to the node the expected value of the chance events; branches emanating from a decision node are folded back by selecting the alternative with the maximum expected return and assigning this value to the decision node. The solution of a decision tree yields an optimal strategy; that is, it specifies what sequence of actions should be taken for any of the possible sequences of chance events.

Bayes's Theorem plays an important role in the construction of decision trees, because this is the device that makes it possible to incorporate new information into the decision process in a formal way. Bayes's Theorem is based on the concept of conditional probability, and thus some time is devoted to that general topic.

The expected value of sample information is a measure of the value of incorporating sample information into a decision under uncertainty. The expected value of perfect information is an upper bound on the expected value of sample information.

Key Terms

Payoff Table. A table showing the returns for each possible state of nature-decision combination in a decision against nature. (*p. 598*)

Decision under Certainty. A decision against nature in which the state of nature is known with certainty. (*p. 599*)

Decision under Risk. A decision against nature in which a probability distribution on the states of nature is known. (*p. 601*)

Decision under Uncertainty. A decision against nature with no knowledge about the likelihood of the various states of nature. (*p. 605*)

Maximin Criterion. A conservative decision criterion of maximizing the minimum return. (*p. 605*)

Maximax Criterion. An optimistic decision criterion of maximizing the maximum return. (*p. 606*)

Regret. A measure of how much better the decision maker could have done had he or she known the state of nature (the opportunity cost of not making the best decision for a given state of nature). (*p. 607*)

Expected Value Of Perfect Information (EVPI). An upper bound on the value of new information. (*p. 609*)

Utility. In this chapter, a measure of the "attractiveness" of an outcome to an individual. (*p. 610*)

Risk-Averse. A preference to avoid downside risks, precisely reflected in a concave utility function. (*p. 611*)

Risk-Seeking. A preference for upside returns, precisely reflected in a convex utility function. (*p. 612*)

Risk-Indifferent. Reflected by a linear utility function. (*p. 613*)

Equivalent Lottery. A device for creating a utility function. (*p. 614*)

Decision Tree. A graphical device for analyzing decisions under risk. (*p. 616*)

Square Node. A point at which a decision must be made. Or a node showing a marked lack of social development and abusively used in certain decision tree diagrams. (*p. 618*)

Circular Node. Indicates a nondeterministic event on a decision tree. (*p. 618*)

Branch. The lines emanating from the nodes in a decision tree. (*p. 618*)

Terminal Position. The end of a branch emanating from a terminal node. (*p. 618*)

Terminal Node. A node in a decision tree that is not succeeded by other nodes. (*p. 618*)

Terminal Value. The net return associated with a terminal position. (*p. 619*)

Folding Back. The process of solving a decision tree by working backward. (*p. 619*)

Conditional Probability. The probability of an event (say, B) given that another event (say, A) occurs; denoted $P(B|A)$ and defined $P(B|A) = P(B \text{ and } A)/P(A)$. (*p. 625*)

Prior Probabilities. The originally assessed values for probabilities. (*p. 626*)

Posterior Probabilities. An updated probability. The updating combines the prior probabilities and new information with Bayes's theorem. (*p. 626*)

Expected Value of Sample Information (EVSI). The difference between the maximum possible expected returns with and without sample information. (*p. 631*)

Sequential Decision Problem. A problem in which the value of an initial decision depends on subsequent decisions and uncertain events. (*p. 632*)

Major Concepts Quiz

True-False

1. **T F** Decision trees involve sequences of decisions and random outcomes.
2. **T F** In decision theory, returns are dependent on the actions of an indifferent adversary termed "nature."
3. **T F** One underlying aspect of decision theory is that, regardless of what we assume about nature, in terms of whether we know probabilities of various states, we are led to the same criterion for selecting a "best decision."
4. **T F** Many deterministic optimization models can be thought of as decision making under certainty, where there is only one state of nature and one selects a decision that maximizes returns.
5. **T F** One way to deal with decision making in the "uncertainty" context is to treat all states of nature as equally likely and maximize expected return.
6. **T F** The computation of the value of perfect information is based on the concept that all randomness has been eliminated.
7. **T F** Maximizing expected net dollar return always yields the same optimal policy as minimizing expected regret.
8. **T F** A risk-averse utility function is convex.
9. **T F** Decision trees are solved by folding forward.
10. **T F** Bayes's Theorem provides a formula for how one can use new information to update a prior probability assessment.

Multiple Choice

11. Decision theory is concerned with
    a. the amount of information that is available
    b. criteria for measuring the "goodness" of a decision
    c. selecting optimal decisions in sequential problems
    d. all of the above

12. Concerning decision making under risk, which of the following is not true?
    a. We assume that the decision maker knows the probability with which each state of nature will occur.
    b. We use the criterion of maximizing return.
    c. We use the criterion of maximizing expected return.
    d. We use the criterion of minimizing expected regret.

13. Which of the following criteria does *not* apply to decision making under uncertainty?
    a. maximin return
    b. maximax return
    c. minimax regret
    d. maximize expected return

14. Maximin return, maximax return, and minimax regret are criteria that
    a. lead to the same optimal decision
    b. can be used without probabilities
    c. both a and b

15. The expected value of perfect information (EVPI)
    a. places two-sided bounds (upper and lower) on how much should be spent in gathering information
    b. can be determined without using probabilities
    c. refers to the utility of additional information
    d. equals the expected regret of the optimal decision under risk

16. The concept of utility is a way to
   a. measure the attractiveness of money
   b. take into account aversion to risk
   c. take into account inclination to take risk
   d. a and b
   e. a, b, and c

17. Which of the following does not apply to a decision tree?
   a. A square node is a point at which a decision must be made.
   b. A circular node represents an encounter with uncertainty.
   c. One chooses a sequence of decisions that has the greatest probability of success.
   d. One attempts to maximize expected return.

18. The expected value of perfect information (EVPI)
   a. shows the cost necessary to produce perfect information about the future
   b. shows the maximum possible increase in expected return with sample information
   c. shows the expected increase in information required to select the optimal decision
   d. all of the above

19. When computing the expected value of perfect information (EVPI) it is important that the payment is made
   a. in advance of receiving the information
   b. after receiving the information
   c. in an irrevocable way
   d. both a and c

20. When decisions are made sequentially in time
   a. decision trees cannot be employed
   b. Bayes's Theorem must be used
   c. the terminal value at the end of each sequence of branches is the net of the cash flows on that sequence
   d. the terminal value at the end of each sequence of branches is an expected net cash flow

Answers

1. T	**6.** F	**11.** d	**16.** e
2. T	**7.** T	**12.** b	**17.** c
3. F	**8.** F	**13.** d	**18.** b
4. T	**9.** F	**14.** b	**19.** d
5. T	**10.** T	**15.** d	**20.** c

▶ Problems

In using QSB+ to solve a problem involving a payoff matrix, if there is no sample information involved enter only one experiment outcome with a conditional probability of 1.0 in any state of nature. Also, the principle of insufficient reason is the same as the Laplace criterion.

(a) 4
(b) 3
(c) 1
(d) See IM
(e) 3

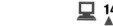

14-1. Consider the payoff table shown in Figure 14.42, in which the entries are net dollar returns. Assume that this is a decision with no knowledge about the states of nature.
   (a) What is the optimal decision if the Laplace criterion is used?
   (b) What is the optimal decision if the maximin criterion is used?
   (c) What is the optimal decision if the maximax criterion is used?
   (d) Create the payoff table in which the entries are regret.
   (e) What is the optimal decision if the criterion of minimax regret is used?

DECISION	STATE OF NATURE 1	2	3	4
1	35	22	25	12
2	27	25	20	18
3	22	25	25	28
4	20	25	28	33

▲ FIGURE 14.42

(a) 1
(b) 2
(c) 3
(d) See IM
(e) 1

14-2. ▲ Consider the payoff table shown in Figure 14.43, in which the entries are net dollar returns. Assume that this is a decision with no knowledge about the states of nature.

(a) What is the optimal decision if the Laplace criterion is used?
(b) What is the optimal decision if the maximin criterion is used?
(c) What is the optimal solution if the maximax criterion is used?
(d) Create the payoff table in which the entries are regret.
(e) What is the optimal decision if the criterion of minimax regret is used?

DECISION	STATE OF NATURE 1	2	3
1	5	7	8
2	6	6	6
3	3	9	1

▲ FIGURE 14.43

(a) 4
(b) 4
(c) Maximizing expected net return and minimizing expected regret always lead to the same optimal decision.

14-3. ▲ Consider the payoff table in Figure 14.42. Assume that the following probabilities are specified for the states of nature:

$$P(1) = 0.1, \qquad P(2) = 0.4, \qquad P(3) = 0.3, \qquad P(4) = 0.2$$

(a) Find the decision that maximizes the expected net dollar return.
(b) Find the decision that minimizes the expected regret.
(c) Comment on the relationship between the answers to parts (a) and (b).

(a) 1
(b) 1
(c) 2 for $0 \le P(2) \le 0.35$, 1 for $0.35 \le P(2) \le 0.625$, 3 for $0.625 \le P(2) \le 1.0$
(d) Same as (c)
(e) They are the same.

14-4. ▲▲ Consider the payoff matrix in Figure 14.43. Assume that the probabilities of the states of nature are as follows:

$$P(1) = 0.3 \qquad P(2) = 0.6 \qquad P(3) = 0.1$$

(a) Find the decision that maximizes the expected net dollar return.
(b) Find the decision that minimizes the expected regret.

Suppose that $P(1)$ and $P(2)$ are not known, but $P(3)$ is estimated to be 0.1

(c) Plot expected net dollar return versus $P(2)$ for the three decisions in the same graph, and find the range for $P(2)$ for which each decision is optimal.
(d) Plot expected regret versus $P(2)$ for the three decisions in the same graph, and find the range for $P(2)$ for which each decision is optimal.
(e) What did you find in the above two answers?

14-5. ▲ Phil Johnson of Johnson's Printing in Chicago must decide either to accept a contract for a government form printing job or fly to L.A. to bid on a brochure. Capacity constraints prohibit him from doing both jobs, and he must decide on the government contract before the bidding process starts. He estimates the payoff table in terms of net dollar return as shown in Figure 14.44.

(a) Accept government contract
(b) Accept government contract
(c) See IM
(d) 0.4
(e) Bid on brochure
(f) Accept government contract
(g) 1000
(h) Expected value of perfect information

(a) What is the optimal decision based on the maximin criterion?

(b) If the probability that he gets the brochure job is ⅓, which decision will maximize his expected net dollar return?

(c) Let $P(\mathrm{J})$ be the probability that he gets the brochure job. Plot the expected return for each decision as a function of $P(\mathrm{J})$ on the same axis.

(d) What is the smallest value of $P(\mathrm{J})$ for which Phil Johnson should decide to go to L.A. if he wishes to maximize his expected net dollar return?

(e) What is the optimal decision if minimax regret is the decision criterion?

(f) What is the optimal decision if minimize expected regret is the decision criterion and $P(\mathrm{J}) = 1/3$?

(g) Assume that the purchasing agent for the brochure job has already decided who will receive the bid but Phil doesn't know the result. If Phil believes that $P(\mathrm{J}) = 1/3$, what is the maximum amount that Phil should pay to have this information?

(h) What would you call the quantity calculated in part (g)?

DECISION	STATE OF NATURE	
	Do Not Get Brochure Job, NJ	Get Brochure Job, J
Accept Government Contract, G	1000	1000
Accept Brochure Job, B	−1000	4000

▲ FIGURE 14.44

(a) Medium or large
(b) Small
(c) Vendor risk-averse

14-6. ▲▲ A souvenir vendor discovers that sales in July depend heavily on the weather. Products must be ordered in January. The wholesaler offers small, medium, and large variety packs at special prices, and the vendor must decide to buy one of them. The payoff table in terms of net dollar return is shown in Figure 14.45.

DECISION	STATE OF NATURE			
	Cold	Cool	Warm	Hot
Small	0	1000	2000	3000
Medium	−1000	0	3000	6000
Large	−3000	−1000	4000	8000

▲ FIGURE 14.45

The utility function for money is presented in Figure 14.46. If the vendor believes that each state of nature is equally likely

(a) Which decision maximizes the expected net dollar return?

(b) Which decision maximizes the expected utility?

(c) Explain the relationship between the answers to parts (a) and (b).

(a) Accept government contract; 1000
(b) No (See IM)
(c) 0.73
(d) ER (bid) = 666.67; U(666.67) = 0.71
(e) EU (bid) = 0.66
(f) No; not in general (See IM)

14-7. ▲▲ Phil Johnson of Johnson's Printing (see Problem 14-5) has decided to use the utility function shown in Figure 14.46 to determine if he should bid on the brochure job.

(a) What is the optimal decision if the decision criterion is to maximize the expected net dollar return and the probability of getting the brochure job is ⅓? What is the expected net dollar return of the optimal decision?

(b) Would you expect the decision to change if the decision criterion is to maximize the expected utility? Discuss.

(c) What is the expected utility of the optimal decision?

(d) What is the utility of the expected dollar return from submitting a bid for the brochure?

(e) What is the expected utility of submitting a bid for the brochure?

(f) Are the answers to parts (d) and (e) the same? Should they be?

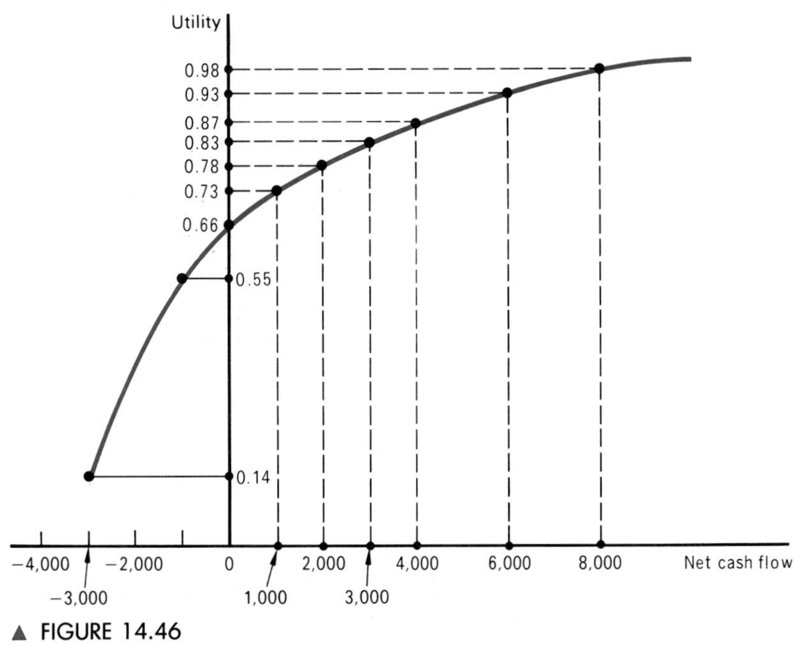

▲ FIGURE 14.46
Utility Function

See IM

14-8. ▲▲ Assign a utility of 0 to a net cash flow of −$20,000 and a utility of 1 to a net cash flow of $50,000. Create your own utility function by the following steps:

(a) Find equivalent lotteries for net cash flows of $0 and $20,000.

(b) Plot the four points on your utility function, and connect them with straight lines.

(c) On the basis of this utility function, are you risk-averse, risk-seeking, risk-indifferent, or none of the above?

(a) $U(30) \geq 0.6$
(b) $U(50) \geq 0.85$
(c) $U(10) \leq 0.55$

14-9. ▲▲▲ Assume you are risk-averse and have assigned the following two end points on your utility function:

$$U(-30) = 0$$
$$U(70) = 1$$

(a) What is a lower bound on $U(30)$?

Suppose that you are indifferent between a sure payment of 30 and a lottery with a probability of 0.7 of winning 70 and a probability of 0.3 of losing 30.

(b) What is a lower bound on your utility for a sure payment of 50?

(c) What is the smallest upper bound of your utility for a sure payment of 10?

HINT: Recall that a utility function is nondecreasing and, if the decision maker is risk-averse, it is concave.

(a) Convex; yes
(b) 0.65; 0.5
(c) 0.25; 0.2125

14-10. ▲▲▲ Assume that you have assigned the following two end points on your utility function:

$$U(-30) = 0$$
$$U(70) = 1$$

Suppose that you are indifferent between a sure payment of 30 and a lottery with a probability of 0.3 of winning 70 and a probability of 0.7 of losing 30. Furthermore, you feel that a sure payment of 10 is equivalent to a gamble with a probability of 0.9 of losing 30 and a probability of 0.1 of winning 30.

(a) How can you describe your utility function? Are you a risk-taker?

(b) What are upper and lower bounds on $U(50)$?

(c) What are upper and lower bounds on $U(25)$?

Ordering error

14-11. ▲▲ The customer service manager for **PROTRAC** is responsible for expediting late orders. To do the job effectively, when an order is late the manager must determine if the lateness is caused by an ordering error or a delivery error. If an order is late, one or the other of these two types of errors must have occurred. Because of the way in which this system is designed, both errors cannot occur on the same order. From experience, the manager knows that an ordering error will cause 8 out of 20 deliveries to be late, whereas a delivery error will cause 8 out of 10 deliveries to be late. Historically, out of 1000 orders, 30 ordering errors and 10 delivery errors have occurred. Assume that an order is late. If the customer service manager wishes to look first for the type of error that has the largest probability of occurring, should it be an ordering error or a delivery error?

(a) 1/2; $425
(b) agents—$214.06, managers—$210.94
(c) agents—7/16, managers—9/16; search the manager file first.

14-12. ▲▲▲ The Scrub Professional Cleaning Service receives preliminary sales contracts from two sources: (1) its own agent and (2) building managers. Historically, ¼ of the contracts have come from Scrub agents and ¾ from building managers. Unfortunately, not all preliminary contracts result in actual sales contracts. Actually, only ⅜ of those preliminary contracts received from building managers result in a sale, whereas ⅞ of those received from Scrub agents result in a sale. The net return to Scrub from a sale is $1000. The cost of processing and following up on a preliminary contract that does not result in a sale is $150.

(a) What is the probability that a preliminary contract leads to a sale? What is the expected return associated with a preliminary sales contract?

(b) Which party, agents or building managers, contributes more to the expected return?

Scrub keeps all of its sales filed by the source of reference; that is, it maintains one file for sales resulting from preliminary contracts submitted by Scrub agents and another for sales resulting from preliminary contracts submitted by building managers. Scrub knows that John Jones holds one of its sales contracts, and it wishes to have more information about him.

(c) Which file should it search first to have the higher probability of finding his name?

(a) $P(1/2) = 0.225$;
(b) $P(A|1/2) = 0.44$;
(c) ER = $188.50

14-13. ▲▲▲ Clyde's Coal Company sells coal by the ½-ton, 1-ton, or 2-ton load. The probability is 0.20 that an order is from town A; 0.30 from town B; and 0.50 from town C. The relative frequency of the number of orders of each size from each town is shown in Figure 14.47.

	LOAD SIZE (TONS)		
TOWN	**½**	**1**	**2**
A	0.50	0.00	0.50
B	0.00	0.50	0.50
C	0.25	0.75	0.00

▲ FIGURE 14.47
Relative Frequencies of Number of Orders for Each Town

(a) What is the probability that an order will be for ½ ton?

(b) If an order is for ½ ton, what is the probability that it came from town A?

Clyde makes a different amount of profit on each type of load of coal in each city. The profit figures are shown in Figure 14.48.

(c) Find the expected profit per load for Clyde.

TOWN	LOAD SIZE (TONS)		
	½	1	2
A	100	190	370
B	90	200	360
C	70	130	270

▲ FIGURE 14.48
Profit in Dollars per Load

(a) Have show
(b) $3500

14-14. ▲ Walter's Dog and Pony Show is scheduled to appear in Cedar Rapids on July 14. The profits obtained are heavily dependent on the weather. In particular, if the weather is rainy, the show loses $15,000, and if sunny the show makes a profit of $10,000. (We assume that all days are either rainy or sunny.) Walter can decide to cancel the show, but if he does he forfeits a $1000 deposit he put down when he accepted the date. The historical record shows that on July 14 it rained ¼ of the time in the last 100 years.

(a) What decision should Walter make to maximize his expected net dollar return?

(b) What is the expected value of perfect information?

(a) If "sun" forecast, go ahead; if "rain" forecast, cancel
(b) $1500

14-15. ▲ Consider the problem faced by Walter in Problem 14-14. Walter has the option to purchase a forecast from Victor's Weather Wonder. Victor's accuracy varies. On those occasions when it has rained, he has been correct (i.e., he predicted rain) 90% of the time. On the other hand, when it has been sunny, he has been right (i.e., he predicted sun) only 80% of the time.

(a) If Walter had the forecast, what strategy should he follow to maximize his expected net dollar return?

(b) How much should Walter be willing to pay for the forecast?

Play first round; if white, quit; otherwise play second round.

14-16. ▲ A gambler has an opportunity to play the following two-stage game. At stage 1 he pays $5 and draws a ball at random from an urn containing 5 white and 5 red balls. The balls are identical except for color. The player may now quit or move on to play stage 2 at the cost of an additional $10. In stage 2, if a white ball was drawn in stage 1, the player draws a ball at random from a white urn that contains 2 blue and 8 green balls. If a red ball was drawn in stage 1, the player draws a ball at random from a red urn that contains 6 blue and 4 green balls. If in stage 2 the player draws a blue ball, the house pays him $35. If he draws a green ball, the house pays him $0. Use a decision tree to determine the optimal strategy for the gambler.

$P(\text{bad risk}|\text{credit}) = 0.024$

14-17. ▲ A certain retail firm places applicants for credit into two categories, bad risks and good risks. Statistics indicate that 10% of the population would be classified as a bad risk by the firm's standards. The firm uses a credit-scoring device to decide whether credit should be granted to an applicant. Experience suggests that if a good risk applies, the person will get credit 90% of the time. If a bad risk applies, credit will be granted 20% of the time. Management believes that it is reasonable to assume that the persons who apply for credit are selected at random from the population. What is the probability that a person granted credit will be a bad risk? (Use Bayes's Theorem.)

(a) 60
(b) 1/2

14-18. ▲ Three workers produce a certain part at the same rate. Larry averages 3 defective parts per hundred while Moe and Curly average 6 and 9 defectives per hundred, respectively.

(a) How many defective parts do you expect out of 1,000 produced?

(b) What is the probability that a defective part selected at random was produced by Curly?

Compete; if order received, use current machines.

14-19. ▲ Johnson's Metal (JM), a small manufacturer of metal parts, is attempting to decide whether to enter the competition to be a supplier of transmission housings for **PROTRAC**. In order to compete, the firm must design a test fixture for the production process and produce 10 housings that **PROTRAC** will test. The cost of development, that is, designing and building the fixture and the test housings, is $50,000. If JM gets the order, an event estimated as occurring with probability 0.4, it will be possible to sell 10,000 items to **PROTRAC** for $50 each. If JM does not get the order, the development cost is essentially lost. In order to produce the housings, JM may either use its current machines or purchase a new forge. Tooling with the current machines will cost $40,000 and the per-unit production cost is $20. However, if JM uses its current machines, it runs the risk of incurring overtime costs. The relationship between overtime costs and the status of JM's other business is presented in Figure 14.49. The new forge costs $260,000, including tooling costs for the transmission housings. However, with the new forge, JM would certainly not incur any overtime costs, and the production cost will be only $10 per unit. Use a decision tree to determine the optimal set of actions for JM.

OTHER BUSINESS	PROBABILITY	OVERTIME COST TO JM
Heavy	0.2	$200,000
Normal	0.7	100,000
Light	0.1	0

▲ FIGURE 14.49
Cost and Probability Data for Johnson's Metal Problem

(a) See IM
(b) Take 1 to court; if win, take 2 to court; if lose, settle 2
(c) $152,500
(d) Both would be settled; savings = $7500

14-20. ▲▲ It is January 1 and Justin Case, chief counsel for Chemgoo, is faced with a difficult problem. It seems that the firm has two related lawsuits for patent infringement. For each suit, the firm has the option of going to trial or settling out of court. The trial date for one of the suits, which we will cleverly identify as suit 1, is scheduled for July 15 and the second (suit 2, of course) is scheduled for January 8, next year. Preparation costs for either trial are estimated at $10,000. However, if the firm prepares for both trials, the preparation costs of the second trial will be only $6000. These costs can be avoided by settling out of court. If the firm wins suit 1, it pays no penalty. If it loses, it pays a $200,000 penalty. Lawyers for the firm assess the probability of winning suit 1 as 0.5. The firm has the option to settle out of court for $100,000. Suit 2 can be settled out of court for a cost of $60,000. Otherwise, a trial will result in one of three possible outcomes: (1) the suit is declared invalid and the firm pays no penalty; (2) the suit is found valid but with no infringement, and the firm pays a penalty of $50,000; or (3) the suit is found valid with infringement, and the firm pays a penalty of $90,000. The likelihood of these outcomes depends in general on the result of suit 1. The judge will certainly view suit 1 as an important precedent. The lawyers' assessment of the probability of the three possible outcomes of suit 2 under three sets of possible conditions (relating to suit 1) are presented in Figure 14.50.

OUTCOMES	NO INFORMATION CONCERNING SUIT 1[a]	FIRM WINS SUIT 1	FIRM LOSES SUIT 1
Invalid	0.3	0.7	0.1
Valid, No infringement	0.3	0.2	0.5
Valid, Infringement	0.4	0.1	0.4

[a]That is, suit 1 is settled out of court.

▲ FIGURE 14.50

(a) Represent the firm's problem with a decision tree.

(b) Solve the decision tree, and find the optimal strategy for the firm.

(c) What is the expected loss that the firm will incur if it follows the optimal strategy?

(d) What decisions would be made if the firm treated each suit independently, ignoring any interactions between the two? What is the expected savings from the decision analysis of this scenario?

HINT: Since all the figures are costs, you may find it easier to work with the cost figures and minimize the expected cost.

To movie company; $210,000

14-21. ▲ Olive Branch is a writer of romance novels. A movie company and a TV network both want exclusive rights to one of her most popular works. If she signs with the network she will receive a single lump sum, but if she signs with the movie company the amount she will receive depends on the market response to the movie. Olive's payoffs are summarized in Figure 14.51.

DECISION	STATE OF NATURE		
	Small Box Office	**Medium Box Office**	**Large Box Office**
Sign with movie company	$200,000	$1,000,000	$3,000,000
Sign with TV network	900,000	900,000	900,000

▲ FIGURE 14.51

If the probability estimates for the states of nature are $P(\text{Small}) = 0.3$, $P(\text{Medium}) = 0.6$, $P(\text{Large}) = 0.1$, to whom should Olive sell the rights? What is the most Olive should be willing to pay to learn what the size of the box office would be before she decides with whom to sign?

(a) Build 50
(b) Build 150
(c) Build 100
(d) Build 100
(e) $170,000

14-22. ▲ Kelly Construction wants to get in on the boom of student condominium construction. The company must decide whether to purchase enough land to build a 100-, 200-, or 300-unit condominium complex. Many other complexes are currently under construction, so Kelly is unsure how strong demand for its complex will be. If the company is conservative and builds only a few units, it loses potential profits if the demand turns out to be high. On the other hand, many unsold units would also be costly to Kelly. Figure 14.52 has been prepared, based on three levels of demand.

DECISION	DEMAND		
	Low	**Medium**	**High**
Build 50	$400,000	$400,000	$400,000
Build 100	100,000	800,000	800,000
Build 150	−200,000	500,000	1,200,000

▲ FIGURE 14.52

(a) What is the optimal decision if the maximin criterion is used?
(b) What is the optimal decision if the maximax criterion is used?
(c) What is the optimal decision if the criterion of minimax regret is used?
(d) If $P(\text{Low}) = 0.3$, $P(\text{Medium}) = 0.5$, and $P(\text{High}) = 0.2$, which decision will maximize the expected net dollar return?
(e) What is the expected value of perfect information?

Make the component.

14-23. ▲ Marple Manufacturing is planning the introduction of a new product. The cost to set up to manufacture one of the product's components is very high, so Marple is considering purchasing that component rather than manufacturing it. Once set up to manufacture the component, however, Marple's variable cost per unit would be low in comparision to the purchase price of the component. Marple's materials manager has calculated the net profit in thousands of dollars for three different levels of demand in Figure 14.53. The states of nature have probabilities $P(\text{Low}) = 0.4$, $P(\text{Medium}) = 0.3$, and $P(\text{High}) = 0.3$. Draw a decision tree and use it to decide whether Marple should make or buy the component.

DECISION	DEMAND		
	Low	Medium	High
Make component	11	32	53
Buy component	15	30	45

▲ FIGURE 14.53

(a) 280–28 minutes, El Camino—35.5 minutes, take 280
(b) See IM

14-24. ▲ Chuck drives to a consulting job in Palo Alto on Wednesdays. He returns to San Jose the same day right at the evening rush hour. If he takes Route 280 home he has observed that his travel time is highly variable from one week to the next, but if he takes El Camino his travel time is relatively constant. On the basis of his experience, Chuck has set up the payoff table shown in Figure 14.54, which gives his travel time in minutes.

(a) Chuck estimates that about 90% of the time the traffic will be light. Which route should he take to minimize his expected travel time?

(b) Chuck's wife Boots gets very worried if he is even a little late in coming home. Which route would you recommend he take now? Explain.

DECISION	STATE OF NATURE	
	Light Traffic	Heavy Traffic
Take 280	25	55
Take El Camino	35	40

▲ FIGURE 14.54

DEMAND	FREQUENCY
0	24 months
1	8
2	4
Total	36 months

▲ FIGURE 14.55

(a) See IM
(b) 2 units

14-25. ▲ A small hospital in rural Greene County buys blood each month from a distant blood bank. A certain rare blood type must be restocked each month because its shelf life is only one month long. If the order is placed one month in advance the cost to the hospital is \$10 per unit. If the demand for the rare blood type during the month exceeds the supply it must be special-ordered at a cost of \$100 per unit. The demand for the past 3 years is shown in Figure 14.55.

(a) Develop a payoff table for the hospital.

(b) How many units should the hospital order each month?

(a) See IM
(b) Vendor A—\$11,020, Vendor B—\$12,300; buy from Vendor A.

14-26. ▲ Martin Gale, head of purchasing at Marple Manufacturing, must decide from which vendor to buy a particular component. Vendor A will supply the components in lots of 1,000 for \$10 a unit while Vendor B will charge only \$9.50 a unit. However, 20% of the time Vendor B's lots will contain 10% defectives and 80% of the time they will contain 1% defectives, while Vendor A's lots will contain 1% defectives 99% of the time and 3% defectives 1% of the time. The cost of a defective to Marple Manufacturing is \$100 due to the high cost of scrapping or reworking the assemblies containing defective components.

(a) Draw a decision tree for this problem.

(b) Using the criterion of expected cost, from which vendor should Martin purchase the component?

(a) See IM
(b) Denver

14-27. ▲ Rick O'Shea is an independent trucker operating out of Tucson. He has the option of either hauling a shipment to Denver or hauling a different shipment to Salt Lake. If he chooses the shipment to Denver, he has a 90% chance of finding there a return shipment to Tucson. If he does not find a return shipment he will return to Tucson empty. If he chooses the shipment to Salt Lake, he has a 50% chance of finding a return shipment to Tucson. His payoffs are shown in Figure 14.56.

	RETURN SHIPMENT	NO RETURN
Salt Lake	$4000	$3500
Denver	3850	3350

▲ FIGURE 14.56

(a) Draw the decision tree for this problem.

(b) Using the criterion of expected net dollar return, to which city should Rick go?

(a) See IM
(b) No; if favorable, sign with movie company; if unfavorable, sign with TV network.
(c) $80,000

14-28 ▲▲ Olive Branch's payoff table (Problem 14-21) is given in Figure 14.57.

DECISION	STATE OF NATURE		
	Small Box Office	Medium Box Office	Large Box Office
Sign with movie company	$200,000	$1,000,000	$3,000,000
Sign with TV network	900,000	900,000	900,000
Probability	0.3	0.6	0.1

▲ FIGURE 14.57

She may hire a market research firm to conduct a survey at a cost of $100,000. The result of the survey would be either a favorable (F) or unfavorable (U) public response to the movie. The firm's ability to assess the market as measured by conditional probabilities is

$$P(F|\text{Small}) = .3 \qquad P(U|\text{Small}) = .7$$
$$P(F|\text{Medium}) = .6 \qquad P(U|\text{Medium}) = .4$$
$$P(F|\text{Large}) = .8 \qquad P(U|\text{Large}) = .2$$

(a) Draw the decision tree for this problem.

(b) Should Olive have the survey conducted? How should she use the results of the survey?

(c) What is the EVSI? What is the most Olive should be willing to pay for the survey?

(a) See IM
(b) If M_1, build 100; if M_2 or M_3, build 200
(c) EVSI = $129,000; EVSI/EVPI = 0.76: The survey is fairly efficient.

14-29. ▲▲▲ Kelly Construction (Problem 14-22) wants to reduce the uncertainty about the number of units it should build. It has decided to conduct a survey which will result in one of three measures of demand: M_1, weak; M_2, moderate; M_3, strong. The payoff table is shown in Figure 14.58.

▼ FIGURE 14.58

DECISION	DEMAND		
	Low, D_1	Medium, D_2	High, D_3
Build 100, B_1	$500,000	$500,000	$500,000
Build 200, B_2	0	1,000,000	1,000,000
Build 300, B_3	−700,000	400,000	1,500,000
Probability	0.3	0.5	0.2

The reliabilities are given in Figure 14.59.

	$P(M_i \mid D_i)$		
	D_1	D_2	D_3
M_1	.7	.3	.1
M_2	.2	.4	.3
M_3	.1	.3	.6

▲ FIGURE 14.59

(a) Draw the decision tree for this problem.
(b) What is Kelly's optimal strategy?
(c) What is the EVSI? Compare it with the EVPI by computing the ratio EVSI/EVPI and noting that the most this ratio could be is 1.

(a) See IM
(b) $12.60
(c) $12.60

14-30. ▲▲▲ The payoff table for the hospital in Greene County (Problem 14-25) is given in Figure 14.60.

ORDER QUANTITY	DEMAND		
	0, D_1	1, D_2	2, D_3
0, Q_1	0	100	200
1, Q_2	10	10	110
2, Q_3	20	20	20
Probability	$\frac{2}{3}$	$\frac{2}{9}$	$\frac{1}{9}$

▲ FIGURE 14.60

	$P(S_i \mid D_i)$		
	D_1	D_2	D_3
S_1	.95	.05	.02
S_2	.04	.8	.08
S_3	.01	.15	.9

▲ FIGURE 14.61

The hospital administrator has decided to check the scheduled surgeries each month to see if there will be any operations requiring the rare blood type. He may find that there are no scheduled surgeries (S_1), one scheduled surgery (S_2), or two scheduled surgeries (S_3), requiring the rare blood type. The conditional probabilities are given in Figure 14.61.

(a) Draw the decision tree for this problem.
(b) What is the EVSI?
(c) How much can the administrator expect to save each month by checking the surgery schedule?

Appendix 14.1 The PC Approach to Decision Trees

The spreadsheets we employed earlier in this chapter are general-purpose tools that can be used for many applications. The price of this versatility is that they are often not as helpful for a given application as a software package designed with that specific application in mind. One such package is Arborist.

Construction and Analysis of a Decision Tree. In Section 14.10 we mentioned that Arborist can be used in the construction and analysis of a decision tree. Here we briefly illustrate some of the features of this approach in the context of the test or no-test tree shown in Figure 14.35. For convenience of reference that figure is reproduced in Figure 14.62.

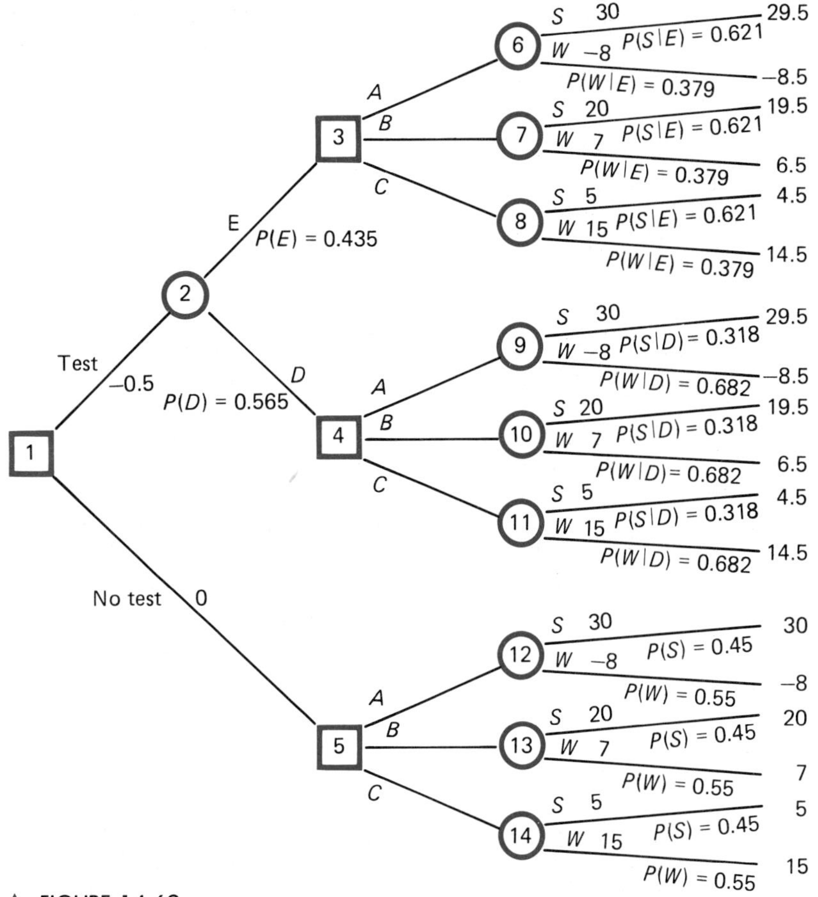

▲ FIGURE 14.62
Test or No-Test Tree with Returns and Probabilities Assigned and Nodes Numbered

The nodes have been numbered to facilitate the discussion. Arborist uses a divided screen to make it possible for you to view simultaneously both the entire tree and a small segment where you are currently working. It also has the ability to copy specific branches of the tree. Note in this example that once the no-test branch is completed, it is a great convenience to produce the branches emanating from nodes 3 and 4 simply by copying the branch emanating from node 5 and changing the probabilities. These features help to simplify the construction process.

The analysis, and particularly the ability to perform sensitivity analysis, is enhanced by the ability to represent each terminal value as a formula. In general the procedure is to assign a variable name to each cash flow as it is entered on a branch. The formula for the terminal value at a particular terminal position is simply the appropriate arithmetic combination of the variables that lie on the path from the root of the tree to that terminal position. For example, suppose that in Figure 14.62 a variable called *Cost,* with a current value of −0.5, is assigned to the test branch emanating from node 1, and a variable called *Return,* with a current value of 30, is assigned to the strong branch emanating from node 6. Then the formula for the uppermost terminal position could be written as

$$\text{Profit} = \text{Return} - \text{Cost}$$

If this approach were used throughout the tree, then to calculate the effect of an increase in the cost of the test you would simply have to enter a new value for "Cost," and Arborist would calculate a complete new set of terminal values. Once the tree is constructed, the optimal policy is determined as the result of a single command.

Risk Analysis. Arborist makes it easy to produce the probability distribution of terminal values (profits in this example). This feature, along with the split-screen capabilities of Arborist, is illustrated in Figure 14.63.

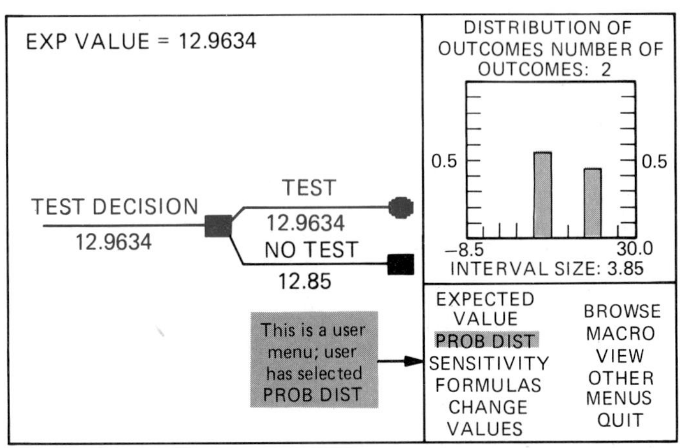

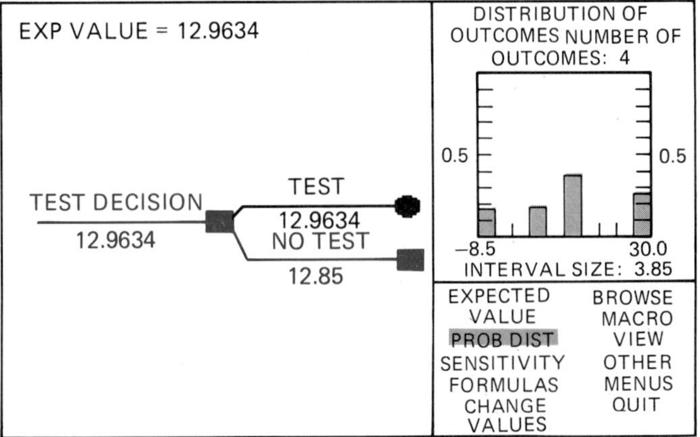

▲ FIGURE 14.63
Arborist Output

Referring back to Figure 14.36, we note that the correct expected returns, and thus the correct decision (i.e., *test*), is also shown in this figure. The upper panel shows a histogram of the probability distribution that results from the *no-test* decision. It shows that values between 6.9 and 10.75 occur with a probability that appears to be equal to about 0.55, and values between 18.45 and 22.30 occur with the remaining probability, a value that appears to be about 0.45. The interval size of 3.85 was automatically selected by Arborist once the number of desired intervals was specified (in this case the user specified 10 intervals). The lower panel presents similar results for the *test* decision.

Consider the importance of this information to a manager. As we know, the *test* decision is optimal if a criterion of expected return is used. In this case, however, the expected return of *test* is only slightly larger ($12.96 - 12.85 = 0.11$) than the *no-test* alternative; and it is much riskier. Selecting the *test* decision and the ensuing optimal decision yields a return between -8.5 and -4.65 with a probability that appears to equal about 0.16. On the other hand, there is a probability that appears to be about 0.26 of realizing a return in the interval between 26.15 and 30.00. It is not hard to imagine that under these circumstances the risk-averse manager would select the no-test branch.

It will not surprise you to learn that it is not necessary to attempt to read the probabilities from these histograms. Printouts with the exact intervals and probabilities are available from Arborist on request. Experience has shown, however, that the graphical display does a better job of capturing the overall sense of the situation for many managers. It is important to recall that subjective probabilities are used to construct most decision trees and therefore it is often not reasonable to assume great precision for these estimates.

Appendix 14.2 Conditional Probability and Bayes's Theorem

While dice and urns filled with balls do not seem to be very relevant to managerial decision making, they do make it easy to assign probabilities, and so we will use them (as statisticians are fond of doing) to explain conditional probability and Bayes's Theorem. Suppose that we draw a ball from an urn according to the following two-stage process:

1. A fair die is thrown.
2. The value of the die is used to determine which of three urns we draw the ball from.

Each urn contains 100 balls, but with a different number of white (W) and black (B) balls. Urn 1, with 28 white and 72 black balls, is chosen if a 1 is thrown. Urn 2, with 40 white and 60 black balls, is chosen if a 2 or 3 is thrown. Urn 3, with 92 white and 8 black balls, is chosen if a 4, 5, or 6 is thrown.

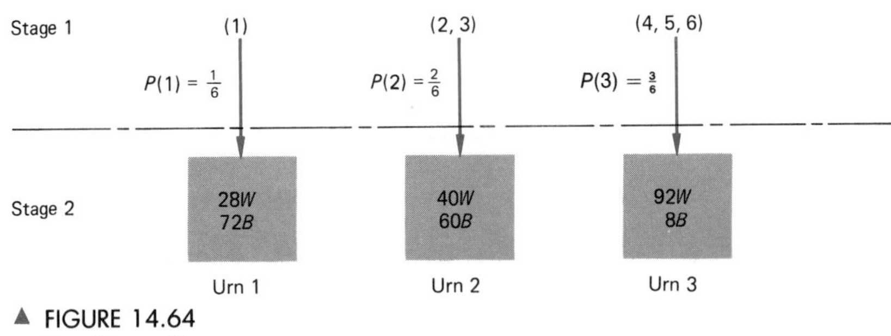

▲ FIGURE 14.64
Two-Stage Process

Since we are throwing a fair die, the probability that Urn 1 is selected is 1/6; that is, $P(1) = 1/6$. Similarly, if we throw a 2 or 3, we will draw a ball from Urn 2. This implies that $P(2) = 2/6$. Finally, if a 4, 5, or 6 is thrown, we will draw a ball from Urn 3, and thus $P(3) = 3/6$ (see Figure 14.64). If this seems unduly abstract, it may be helpful in the following discussion to think of the different urns as representing three different states of nature corresponding to three different levels of market demand, 1 being the smallest level and 3 the largest. Think of the two ball colors as two possible results of a marketing test to assess the true state of nature, W being an encouraging test result and B being a discouraging test result.

Conditional Probabilities. The notation $P(W|1)$ signifies a *conditional probability*. The vertical line is read "given." Thus, $P(W|1)$ is read "the probability of W, given 1." It means the probability of drawing a white ball (W) assuming that the drawing is made from Urn 1 (or the probability of an encouraging test result given that the market strength is 1). Recall that once an urn is selected, a ball is chosen at random, which means that each ball in the urn is equally likely to be drawn. Looking at Figure 14.64, we see that

$$P(W|1) = 0.28 \quad \text{and} \quad P(B|1) = 0.72$$
$$P(W|2) = 0.40 \quad \text{and} \quad P(B|2) = 0.60$$
$$P(W|3) = 0.92 \quad \text{and} \quad P(B|3) = 0.08$$

In the marketing-test example these probabilities are not known precisely. They would have to be estimated from past marketing tests for other products and the assumption would have to be made that the results would be valid for this product. For example, the same values for $P(W|1)$ and $P(B|1)$ would be obtained if in 100 past tests it turned out that the market was weak, in 28 the test was encouraging, and in 72 the test was discouraging.

In the marketing-test example we would also be interested in conditional probabilities such as $P(1|B)$, for this would be the probability that the market strength is 1 given that the market test was discouraging. In the die-and-urn example, this is the probability that the ball was drawn from Urn 1, given that we know it is black. To clarify this, assume that a friend goes through the two-stage process in the next room, after which he comes in and reports that the ball is black. He then asks, "What is the probability that it came from Urn 1?"

Before answering that question, suppose that he had asked, "What is the probability that the ball I drew came from Urn 1?" *without* telling you the color of the ball. In this case all you know is that he would have drawn from Urn 1 if he had thrown a 1 with his fair die. Thus, the *unconditional probability* that the ball came from Urn 1 is $P(1) = 1/6$. In the marketing example, this corresponds to asking what the probability of a strength 1 market is before performing the marketing test.

Now that you know the ball is black and that Urn 1 has the highest percentage of black balls, your intuition probably suggests that the probability of Urn 1 has increased. If so, your intuition is correct. We will now use conditional probabilities to lend some precision to that intuitive feeling.

Joint Probability. In order to calculate $P(1|B)$, we use the following relation, which is developed in courses dealing with probability and statistics. Let X and Y denote *any* two random events. Then

$$P(X \text{ and } Y) = P(X|Y)P(Y) \tag{A.1}$$

$$P(X \text{ and } Y) = P(Y \text{ and } X) \tag{A.2}$$

$$P(Y \text{ and } X) = P(Y|X)P(X) \tag{A.3}$$

$$P(Y|X) = \frac{P(X|Y)P(Y)}{P(X)} \tag{A.4}$$

The first equation says that the *joint probability* of *both* X and Y occurring is equal to the conditional probability of X occurring given that Y occurs times the *marginal probability* that Y occurs. The second equation says that the probability of X and Y occurring is the same as Y and X occurring. The third equation is simply another way of stating the first equation, since X and Y represent any two events. The last equation is implied by the first three and gives a means for finding a given conditional probability if the "reverse" conditional probability is known.

To apply these general results to the case at hand let $Y = 1$ and $X = B$. Then (A.4) allows us to write immediately that

$$P(1|B) = \frac{P(B|1)P(1)}{P(B)} \tag{A.5}$$

We know $P(B|1)$ and $P(1)$ but what is $P(B)$? To find out, we use a common trick in probability theory. The event B occurs (i.e., a black ball is drawn) if and only if a ball is drawn from Urn 1 and it is black or a ball is drawn from Urn 2 and it is black or a ball is drawn from Urn 3 and it is black. Thus

$$\begin{aligned} P(B) &= P(1 \text{ and } B) + P(2 \text{ and } B) + P(3 \text{ and } B) \\ &= P(B \text{ and } 1) + P(B \text{ and } 2) + P(B \text{ and } 3) \\ &= P(B|1)P(1) + P(B|2)P(2) + P(B|3)P(3) \end{aligned} \tag{A.6}$$

Bayes's Theorem and the Calculation of Posterior Probabilities. If we substitute this expression for $P(B)$ in A.5 we get an example of the application of *Bayes's Theorem.*

$$P(1|B) = \frac{P(B|1)P(1)}{P(B|1)P(1) + P(B|2)P(2) + P(B|3)P(3)} \tag{A.7}$$

Since all terms on the right-hand side of A.7 are known, Bayes's Theorem provides a way to compute $P(1|B)$.

$$P(1|B) = \frac{72/100 \times 1/6}{72/100 \times 1/6 + 60/100 \times 2/6 + 8/100 \times 3/6} = \frac{1}{3} \tag{A.8}$$

Recall that the unconditional probability (i.e., with no additional information) that the ball was drawn from Urn 1 is 1/6. Once we are told that the ball is black, the probability that it came from Urn 1 increases. In this particular case it doubles. In terms of the market-test example, based on the information at hand before the test, the probability of a strength 1 market (weakest market) is 1/6. After performing the test and getting a discouraging result (B), the probability increases to 1/3.

We would also like to compute $P(1|W)$ and the other conditional probabilities. We could do it by formulas similar to A.7, but instead we will present a tabular approach that is easy to implement in a spreadsheet program.

	STATE OF NATURE		
TEST RESULT	**1**	**2**	**3**
B	$P(B|1) = .72$	$P(B|2) = .60$	$P(B|3) = .08$
W	$P(W|1) = .28$	$P(W|2) = .40$	$P(W|3) = .92$
Column Sums	1	1	1

▲ FIGURE 14.65
Reliabilities

Figures 14.65 and 14.66 contain the initially known probabilities—what in the marketing-test example might be called *reliabilities,* because they are related to how reliable the test is—and the *prior probabilities* of the states of nature. The joint probabilities in Figure 14.67 are calculated from those tables by multiplying each column of Figure 14.65 by the prior probability found in the corresponding column i of Figure 14.66. The row and column sums of Figure 14.67 give the *marginal probabilities.* The *posterior probabilities* of Figure 14.68 are calculated from Figure 14.67 by dividing the joint probabilities in each row by the row sum.

STATE OF NATURE			ROW SUM
1	2	3	
$P(1) = 1/6$	$P(2) = 2/6$	$P(3) = 3/6$	1

▲ FIGURE 14.66
Prior Probabilities

TEST RESULT	STATE OF NATURE			ROW SUMS
	1	2	3	
B	$P(B \text{ and } 1) = .12$	$P(B \text{ and } 2) = .20$	$P(B \text{ and } 3) = .04$	$P(B) = .36$
W	$P(W \text{ and } 1) = .0467$	$P(W \text{ and } 2) = .1333$	$P(W \text{ and } 3) = .46$	$P(W) = .64$
Column Sums	$P(1) = .1667$	$P(2) = .3333$	$P(3) = .50$	1

▲ FIGURE 14.67
Joint and Marginal Probabilities

TEST RESULT	STATE OF NATURE			ROW SUMS
	1	2	3	
B	$P(1 \mid B) = .333$	$P(2 \mid B) = .556$	$P(3 \mid B) = .111$	1
W	$P(1 \mid W) = .073$	$P(2 \mid W) = .208$	$P(3 \mid W) = .719$	1

▲ FIGURE 14.68
Posterior Probabilities

We conclude with a final point that some find confusing. If in the market-test example the reliabilities are estimated from past data, why can't we use the same data to estimate the posterior probabilities? For example, suppose we have the data shown in Figure 14.69 on 300 past market tests classified according to marketing's test report and the state of nature that actually occurred.

TEST RESULT	STATE OF NATURE			ROW SUMS
	1	2	3	
B	72	60	8	140
W	28	40	92	160
Column Sums	100	100	100	300

▲ FIGURE 14.69
Data on 300 Market Tests

We estimated $P(B \mid 1)$ as 72/100. Why can't we estimate $P(1 \mid B)$ as 72/140?

First note that this does in fact give us a different answer; 72/140 = 0.514 is not the same as 0.333. The reason is that we have implicitly used a different set of prior probabilities. If we set $P(1) = 100/300$, $P(2) = 100/300$, and $P(3) = 100/300$ and apply Bayes's Theorem we will then get $P(1 \mid B) = 0.514$, because we have set the prior probabilities to reflect the historical frequency of states 1, 2, and 3. If we believe the prior probabilities should be different from the historical frequencies, then we will get a different answer. As an extreme example suppose we have information that leads us to believe very strongly that the market demand for the product must be very strong; that is, $P(3) = 1.0$. Then applying Bayes's Theorem gives $P(1|B) = 0$, $P(2|B) = 0$, and $P(3|B) = 1.0$; even a discouraging test report will not alter our prior probabilities. *The point is that the posterior probabilities depend on the prior probabilities, and the prior probabilities may differ from the historical frequencies.*

▶ Diagnostic Assignment

Johnson's Metal

Shirley Johnson, president of Johnson's Metal (JM), is facing the decision presented in Problem 14-19, but a new element has entered the picture. Shirley has the opportunity to hire Compal, a consulting firm that does what it calls "competitive analysis." In particular, in this situation Compal offers to do a detailed study of the other firms that will compete to supply transmission housings to PROTRAC. After the analysis, Compal will report to JM that conditions for JM to get the contract are either encouraging or discouraging.

Compal states that, if conditions are encouraging, then JM will get the PROTRAC contract with probability equal to 0.5. On the other hand, Compal states that if conditions are unfavorable the probability that JM will get the PROTRAC contract is only 0.35. At this time Compal states that the probability of encouraging and discouraging conditions are equally likely. Compal charges $1000 for its services.

Shirley asks Linus Drawer, her assistant, to determine if JM should hire Compal. Indeed she asks Linus to determine the optimal strategy.

Linus prepares the decision tree for the problem and by working back through it, determines that the optimal strategy is

1. Hire Compal
2. If conditions are encouraging
   a. Build the test fixture
   b. If JM gets the order, use current tools
3. If conditions are discouraging
   a. Build the test fixture
   b. If JM gets the order, use current tools

He makes an appointment to discuss the results with Shirley. The meeting proceeds as follows:

SHIRLEY: Linus! I see the decision tree and I'm duly impressed, but the result doesn't make any sense. Why should I pay Compal $1000 if we take the same action no matter what they say?

LINUS: Surely, Shirley, you don't mean that the analysis did not make a difference. I understand that your statement holds now that the analysis is complete, but how would you have known what strategy to follow without the decision tree?

SHIRLEY:Linus! You missed my point! No matter what costs or probabilities are involved, I say that we should build the test fixture, and then use the current tools if we get the order. This simply has to be a better strategy than to hire Compal and then do the same thing no matter what they say.

LINUS: I understand, but I know I've done the decision tree right, so I don't know what to tell you.

SHIRLEY: I don't have the time or interest to check the details of your analysis. All I know is that I want to make a decision about Compal tomorrow morning and I want to have an answer that makes sense. Your job is to provide me with that answer.

Questions

1. Is Shirley right; that is, is it impossible for Linus's strategy to be optimal?
2. Is Linus right; that is, is his analysis correct given the data at his disposal?
3. Assume Linus's role; that is, it is now your job to provide Shirley with an answer that makes sense.

Case

 To Drill or Not to Drill

Terri Underhill has recently been assigned to the economic analysis section of Global Oil. Prescot Oil has just offered to buy the Burns Flat lease from Global for $15,000 and Terri has been assigned the task of preparing Global's response. The Burns Flat lease gives Global the right to explore for oil under 320 acres of land in western Oklahoma. Terri must recommend either to sell the lease or to drill.

If Global drills, the results are uncertain. On the basis of drilling records in western Oklahoma and current market prices, Terri prepares a table showing the possible outcomes, the probability of each outcome, and the net return to Global (Exhibit 1).

▼ EXHIBIT 1

POSSIBLE OUTCOMES	PROBABILITY	NET RETURN
Dry Well	0.2	−100,000
Gas Well	0.4	40,000
Oil and Gas	0.3	90,000
Oil Well	0.1	200,000

Terri, however, knows that she does not have to make the decision simply on the basis of historical records. DRI, Drilling Resource, Inc., which is Etto Oxstein's company, will perform a test for $6000 to determine the underground formation of the Burns Flat terrain. The test will indicate which of three categories (plate, varied, or ridge) best describes the underground structure. The conditional probabilities of the possible outcomes vary with the underground structure. Exhibit 2 shows the results of the last 50 tests.

If the test is taken, the opportunity to sell the lease is forfeited. The market for oil leases understands that a decision to sell after the test has been performed indicates that drilling does not appear to be profitable.

1. On the basis of these data, should Global drill or sell the lease?
2. What is the most that Global should pay in advance to know what the outcome of drilling would be?
3. Use a decision tree to determine the optimal strategy for Global.
4. What is the expected return associated with the optimal policy?
5. What is the maximum *additional* amount that Global should be willing to pay DRI for the test?

▼ EXHIBIT 2

TEST RESULT/OUTCOME	PLATE	VARIED	RIDGE	TOTAL
Dry	8	2	0	10
Gas	2	16	2	20
Gas & Oil	0	14	1	15
Oil	0	0	5	5
	10	32	8	50

Video Case

Decision Trees

It all seems so easy in retrospect. Today, as the video indicates, Maytag Corporation is the parent of four full-line appliance manufacturing companies: Maytag Company, Magic Chef, Admiral, and Norge. It is also the parent of Hoover, the leading maker of floor care products in the United States and a producer of major appliances in Europe and Australia. Maytag enjoys annual sales of nearly $2 billion. It has a secure niche in the upper price range with the widely respected Maytag brand and holds a strong position in the middle range of the appliance market with its Magic Chef, Admiral, and Norge labels. Hoover provides access to overseas markets, which are expecting rapid growth. In summary, Maytag Corporation is in an excellent competitive position.

This didn't just happen. In 1980, Maytag was doing quite well as a small but prestigious manufacturer of top-quality automatic washers, clothes dryers, and dishwashers. Annual sales were $349 million and the company was cash-rich—that is, it was in a mature business generating more cash than it needed for research and development.

Two things occurred that made Maytag decide to take a careful look at itself: (1) The sales of appliances moved from small, privately owned "appliance stores" to large national and regional chains. These chains wanted to limit the number of vendors, to buy in carload lots, and to work with manufacturers who produced a full line of appliances. (2) Mergers and acquisitions were booming, and cash-rich companies were common targets for hostile takeovers. Maytag's comfortable and profitable existence was in jeopardy.

As we know, Maytag reacted to this challenge by moving quickly to make acquisitions of its own, and this strategy has proven to be a good one. Let us, however, try to analyze the question from a 1980 perspective. Suppose you are a member of the 1980 strategic planning group at Maytag and you are using a decision tree to help plan for the future.

Questions

1. What branches (alternatives) will you have emanating from your first decision node? Are some of these branches immediately followed by other decisions?
2. What do you see as the major sources of uncertainty? Where and how might you incorporate them into your decision tree?

CHAPTER 15

Project Management: PERT and CPM

APPLICATION CAPSULE

When Is the Synchronized Swimming, por favor? Management Science Goes to the Barcelona Olympics*

As host for the 1992 summer Olympic games, the city of Barcelona was faced with an extremely complex logistical problem: scheduling more than 2000 events in a 15-day period. The problem was not only very large but included a great many different types of constraints, some of them not ordinarily encountered in the scheduling of more familiar projects.

First were the precedence relationships—for example, qualifying rounds obviously had to take place before quarterfinals, semifinals, and finals. Then, there was the need to spread out the events, in both time and space. One concern was to avoid traffic jams that might result if two or more popular events were scheduled in nearby facilities at the same time. But even when different venues were involved, it was desirable to schedule the most attractive events at different times, to allow the largest possible audience for the greatest number of events. The requirements of live TV coverage of different events for different time zones also had to be considered. For instance, interest in soccer matches would be high in Europe, Africa, and South America, but not in North America. Finally, there were constraints on the available equipment (such as TV cameras) and personnel (for example, security).

This complex problem provided an interesting challenge for two professors at the Universitat Politècnica de Catalunya in Barcelona. It soon became evident that no single existing program was adequate for the task. They therefore developed a collection of interactive algorithms to supplement the more conventional project management software, along with a set of graphical aids to help compare different schedule characteristics.

It was found useful first to create a calendar (assigning competitions to days), and then to refine the precise timetable of events on each day. This approach allowed rough schedules to be generated quickly. It also proved useful to work with time divisions both larger and smaller than an "event."

▶ The modelers discovered that each sport had its own rhythm and that it helped to think in terms of blocks of days that fit that rhythm. A particular sport, for example, might be best served by scheduling three consecutive days of preliminary competition, a day off, and then the finals.

- Equally helpful was the concept of a "unit"—a part of an event having intrinsic interest as a spectacle. Thus the end of the marathon, for example, was treated as a unit.

The objective function for the scheduling process incorporated several criteria, each of which was evaluated on a numerical scale. Among these were continuity (the number of days between the first and last activity for a particular event) and temporal profile (a measure of how well the schedule distributed the activities throughout the two-week period, compared to an ideal distribution).

The TV scheduling problem could be formulated as a binary integer programming model, but solving it would have required an impractical amount of computer time. Instead, a simpler greedy algorithm, designed for the situation, proved useful in developing timetables tailored to the needs of specific audiences.

A key feature of the resulting system, called SUCCESS92, is its speed and flexibility. In the event of weather problems, an alternative schedule can be quickly devised. SUCCESS92 has been received with great enthusiasm by the organizers of the games. Whether it will actually be used in Barcelona, however, is unclear as of this writing.

*Andreu and Corominas, "SUCCESS92: A DSS for Scheduling the Olympic Games," *Interfaces*, Vol. 19, No. 5 (Sept.–Oct. 1989).

15.1 Introduction

Projects ancient and modern

The task of managing major projects is an ancient and honorable art. In about 2600 B.C., the Egyptians built the Great Pyramid for King Khufu. The Greek historian Herodotus claimed that 400,000 men worked for 20 years to build this structure. Although these figures are now in doubt, there is no question about the enormity of the project. The Book of Genesis reports that the Tower of Babel was not completed because God made it impossible for the builders to communicate. This project is especially important, since it establishes a historical precedent for the ever-popular practice of citing divine intervention as a rationale for failure.[1]

Modern projects ranging from building a suburban shopping center to putting a man on the moon are amazingly large, complex, and costly. Completing such projects on time and within the budget is not an easy task. In particular, we shall see that the complicated problems of scheduling such projects are often structured by the interdependence of activities. Typically, certain of the activities may not be initiated before others have been completed. In dealing with projects possibly involving thousands of such dependency relations, it is no wonder that managers seek effective methods of analysis. Some of the key questions to be answered in this chapter are

[1]The *Chicago Tribune* (August 5, 1977) noted the following comment concerning the blackout in New York in July of that year: "Con Ed called the disaster an act of God."

1. What is the expected project completion date?
2. What is the potential "variability" in this date?
3. What are the scheduled start and completion dates for each specific activity?
4. What activities are *critical* in the sense that they must be completed exactly as scheduled in order to meet the target for overall project completion?
5. How long can *noncritical* activities be delayed before a delay in the overall completion date is incurred?
6. How might resources be concentrated most effectively on activities in order to speed up project completion?
7. What controls can be exercised on the flows of expenditures for the various activities throughout the duration of the project in order that the overall budget can be adhered to?

Origins of PERT and CPM

PERT and **CPM,** acronyms for Program Evaluation Review Technique and Critical Path Method, respectively, will provide answers to these questions. Each of these approaches to scheduling represents a project as a network, and hence the material in this chapter can be viewed as an extension of the deterministic networks discussed in Chapter 9. When a project involves uncertain elements, the representation of the project requires a stochastic network, which introduces an additional level of complexity not present in Chapter 9.

The implementation of PERT and CPM had an immediate impact on scheduling projects because it allowed the practice of "management by exception." Although there might be 10,000 activities in the course of a project, perhaps only 150 of them would be "critical" and need to be watched closely.

To put an American on the moon during the days of the Apollo project, North American Aviation used PERT to bring their part of the project in six weeks early. There were over 32,000 events and hundreds of thousands of activities, but only a few hundred needed constant monitoring.

PERT was developed in the late 1950s by the Navy Special Projects Office in cooperation with the management consulting firm of Booz, Allen, and Hamilton. The technique received substantial favorable publicity for its use in the engineering and development program of the Polaris missile, a complicated project that had 250 prime contractors and over 9000 subcontractors. Since that time, it has been widely adopted in other branches of government and in industry and has been applied to such diverse projects as construction of factories, buildings, and highways, research management, product development, the installation of new computer systems, and so on. Today, many firms and government agencies require all contractors to use PERT.

CPM was developed in 1957 by J. E. Kelly of Remington Rand and M. R. Walker of DuPont. It differs from PERT primarily in the details of how time and cost are treated. Indeed, in actual implementation, the distinctions between PERT and CPM have become blurred as firms have integrated the best features of both systems into their own efforts to manage projects effectively.

In keeping with our philosophy throughout the text, we approach the topic of project management on two levels. First, the essential techniques will be developed in an easily grasped illustrative example. Second, the use of the computer will be illustrated to indicate how one would handle the techniques in a large-scale, real-world application.

15.2 A Typical Project: The Global Oil Credit Card Operation

No one would claim that it is like building the Great Pyramid, but the impending move of the credit card operation to Des Moines, Iowa, from the home office in Dallas is an important project for Rebecca Goldstein and Global Oil. The board of directors of Global has set a firm deadline of 22 weeks for the move to be accomplished. Becky is a manager in the Operations Analysis Group. She is in charge of planning the move, seeing that everything comes off according to plan and making sure that the deadline is met.

The move is difficult to coordinate because it involves many different divisions within the company. Real estate must select one of three available office sites.

Personnel has to determine which employees from Dallas will move, how many new employees to hire, and who will train them. The systems group and the treasurer's office must organize and implement the operating procedures and the financial arrangements for the new operation. The architects will have to design the interior space and oversee needed structural improvements. Each of the sites that Global is considering is an existing building with the appropriate amount of open space. However, office partitions, computer facilities, furnishings, and so on, must all be provided.

A second complicating factor is that there is an interdependence of activities. In other words, some parts of the project cannot be started until other parts are completed. Consider two obvious examples: Global cannot construct the interior of an office before it has been designed. Neither can it hire new employees until it has determined its personnel requirements.

The Activity List

This is the *most important* part of any PERT or CPM project and usually is done with several people involved, so that no important activities are missed. This must be a group effort—not done in isolation.

Becky knows that PERT and CPM are specifically designed for projects of this sort, and she wastes no time in getting started. The first step in the process is to define the activities in the project and to establish the proper precedure relationships. This is an important first step since errors or omissions at this stage can lead to a disastrously inaccurate schedule. Figure 15.1 shows the first **activity list** that Becky prepares for the move (the columns labeled "Time" and "Resources" are indications of things to come).

Immediate predecessors of an activity

Conceptually, Figure 15.1 is straightforward. Each activity is placed on a separate line, and its **immediate predecessors** are recorded on the same line. The immediate predecessors of an activity are those activities that must be completed prior to the start of the activity in question. For example, in Figure 15.1 we see that Global cannot start activity C, determine personnel requirements, until activity B, create the organizational and financial plan, is completed. Similarly, activity G, hire new employees, cannot begin until activity F, select the Global personnel that will move from Texas to Iowa, is completed. This activity, F, in turn, cannot start until activity C, determine personnel requirements, is completed.

The activity list with immediate predecessors and the yet-to-be-obtained time estimates will provide the essential ingredients to answer the first five questions at the start of this section. We shall shortly see how PERT and CPM are used to produce these answers. In practice, however, another graphical approach, the Gantt chart, also is used commonly to attack such problems. We thus make a slight detour to consider this precursor of the network approaches (PERT and CPM) before returning to the main thrust of the chapter.

▼ FIGURE 15.1
First Activity List

ACTIVITY	DESCRIPTION	IMMEDIATE PREDECESSORS	TIME	RESOURCES
A	Select Office Site	—		
B	Create Organizational and Financial Plan	—		
C	Determine Personnel Requirements	B		
D	Design Facility	A, C		
E	Construct Interior	D		
F	Select Personnel to Move	C		
G	Hire New Employees	F		
H	Move Records, Key Personnel, etc.	F		
I	Make Financial Arrangements with Institutions in Des Moines	B		
J	Train New Personnel	H, E, G		

The Gantt Chart

Weakness of Gantt charts

Students may be familiar with this chart from the introductory class in production and operations management or lectures on scientific management. It was an early attempt to help others "see" the scheduling problem before them and is another example of a management science model. It had many limitations, which both PERT and CPM were able to overcome.

The Gantt chart was developed by Henry L. Gantt in 1918 and remains a popular tool in production and project scheduling. Its simplicity and clear graphical display have established it as a useful device for simple scheduling problems. The Gantt chart for Becky's problem is shown in Figure 15.2. Each activity is listed on the vertical axis. The horizontal axis is time, and the anticipated as well as actual duration of each activity is represented by a bar of the appropriate length. The chart also indicates *the earliest possible starting* time for each activity. For example, activity C cannot start before time 5 since, according to Figure 15.1, activity B must be completed before activity C can begin. As each activity (or part thereof) is completed the appropriate bar is shaded. At any point in time, then, it is clear which activities are on schedule and which are not. The Gantt chart in Figure 15.2 shows that as of week 13 activities D, E, and H are behind schedule, while G has actually been completed (because it is all shaded) and hence is ahead of schedule.

This simple example shows how the Gantt chart is mainly used as a record-keeping device for following the progression in time of the subtasks of a project. As Figure 15.2 shows, we can see which individual tasks are on or behind schedule. It seems important to note at this point that in the Gantt chart context the phrase "on schedule" means "it has been completed no later than the earliest possible completion time." Thus Figure 15.2 shows that D and H could have been completed, *at the earliest,* by week 12. Since they are not completed by week 13 they are, in this sense, behind schedule. As we shall see, this is too simple a concept for whether an activity is on schedule. The appropriate point of view should be whether *the overall project* is being delayed in terms of a target completion date. The Gantt chart fails to reveal some of the important information needed to attack this question. For example, the Gantt chart fails to reveal which activities are *immediate predecessors* of other activities. In Figure 15.2 it may appear that F and I are immediate predecessors of G since G can start at 10 and F and I can each finish at 10. In fact, however, Figure 15.1 tells us that only F is an immediate predecessor of G. A delay in I would *not* affect the potential starting time of G, or for that matter of any other activity. It is this type of "immediate predecessor" information that must be used to deduce the impact on completion time for the overall project. This latter

A project manager has to know the impact on the whole system of a single activity's being late. In constructing a brick house, having the bricklaying two days late could impact the project much more than if it were just a brick sidewalk for a stucco house. Thus, the analysis of the precedence and dependence of activities is crucial, and Gantt charts are of no help here.

▼ FIGURE 15.2
A Gantt Chart

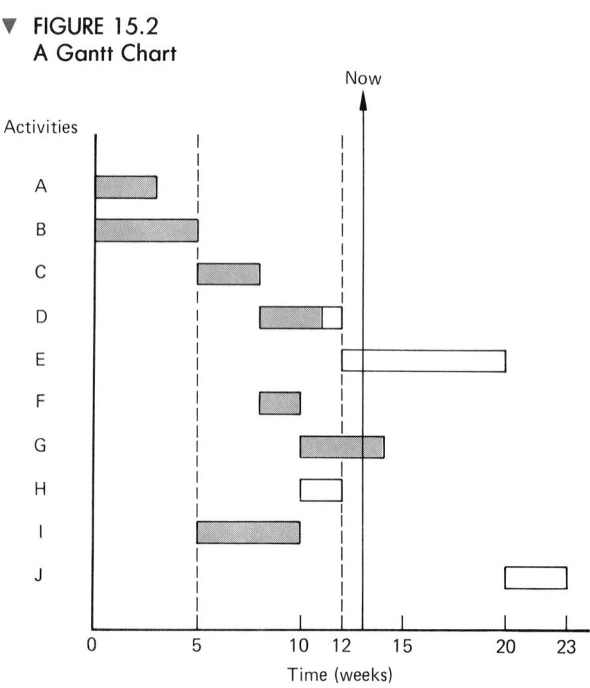

type of information is of obvious importance to the manager. The overall weakness of Gantt charts is reflected by their uselessness in making such inferences. We shall now see that the network representation contains the immediate predecessor information that we need.

The Network Diagram

The activity list is the most important part of the PERT process. Changing the list into a PERT network diagram is the most difficult part for many students.

An event in PERT is like a milestone on the highway. It is an instant in time and represents the beginning and/or end of one or more activities. The numbering of the events (nodes) has no innate significance and can be any set of unique numbers. It is usually simpler to have the nodes in ascending order from left to right.

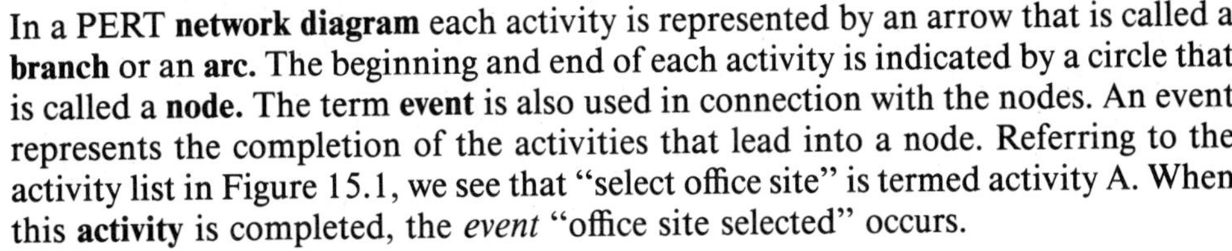

In a PERT **network diagram** each activity is represented by an arrow that is called a **branch** or an **arc.** The beginning and end of each activity is indicated by a circle that is called a **node.** The term **event** is also used in connection with the nodes. An event represents the completion of the activities that lead into a node. Referring to the activity list in Figure 15.1, we see that "select office site" is termed activity A. When this **activity** is completed, the *event* "office site selected" occurs.

Constructing the Network Diagram. Figure 15.3 shows a network diagram for activities A through C. We emphasize at the outset that the numbers assigned to the nodes are arbitrary. They are simply used to identify events and do not imply anything about precedence relationships. Indeed, we shall renumber the node that terminates activity C several times as we develop the network diagram for this project, but *correct precedence relationships will always be preserved.* In the network diagram each activity must start at the node in which its immediate predecessors ended. For example, in Figure 15.3, activity C starts at node ③ because its

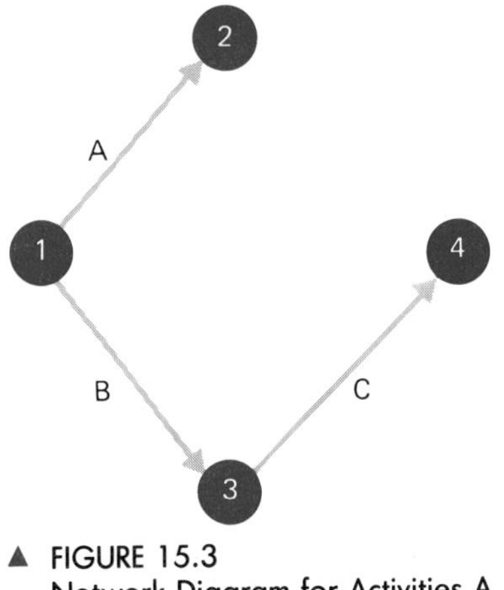

▲ FIGURE 15.3
Network Diagram for Activities A through C

immediate predecessor, activity B, ended there. We see, however, that complications arise as we attempt to add activity D to the network diagram. Both A and C are immediate predecessors to D, and since we want to show any activity such as D only once in our diagram, nodes ② and ④ in Figure 15.3 must be combined, and D should start from this new node. This is shown in Figure 15.4. Node ③ now represents the event that both activities A and C have been completed. Note that activity E, which has only D as an immediate predecessor, can be added with no difficulty. However, as we attempt to add activity F, a new problem arises. Since F has C as an immediate predecessor, it would emanate from node ③ (of Figure 15.4). We see, however, that this would imply that F also has A as an immediate predecessor, which is incorrect.

The Use of Dummy Activities. This diagramming dilemma is solved by introducing a **dummy activity** which is represented by a dashed line in the network diagram in Figure 15.5. This dummy activity is fictitious in the sense that it requires no time or resources. It merely provides a pedagogical device that enables us to draw a network

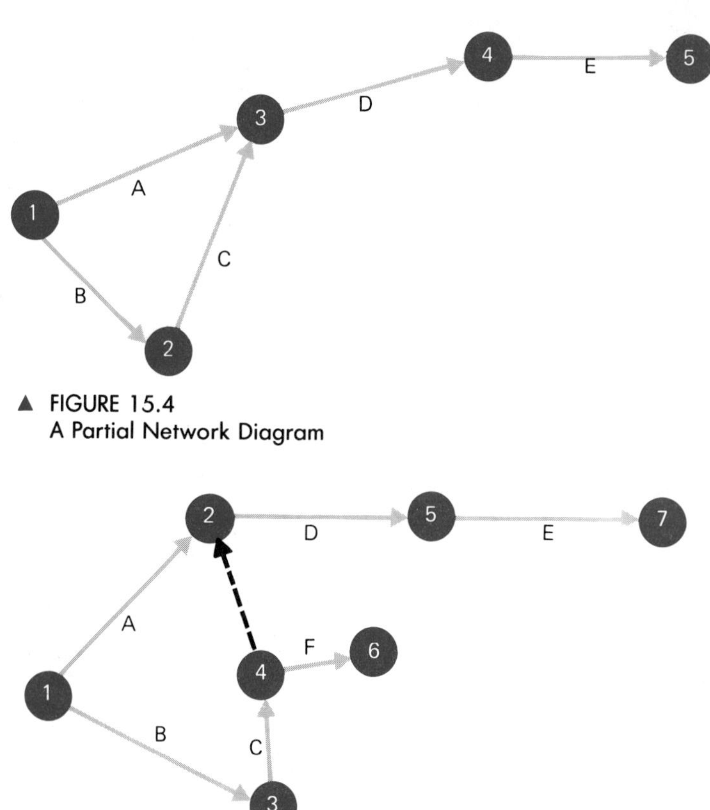

▲ FIGURE 15.4
A Partial Network Diagram

▲ FIGURE 15.5
Introducing a Dummy Activity

This is a very difficult concept for some students to grasp: the necessity of a dummy activity with zero time. While many may be able to understand Figure 15.5 once it has been drawn, being able to draw it from an activities list is another matter.

representation that correctly maintains the appropriate precedence relationships. Thus, Figure 15.5 indicates that activity D can begin only after both activities A and C have been completed. Similarly, activity F can occur only after activity C is completed.

We can generalize the procedure of adding a dummy activity as follows. Suppose that we wish to add an activity A to the network starting at node N, but not all of the activities that enter node N are immediate predecessors of the activity. Create a new node M with a dummy activity running from node M to node N. Take those activities that are currently entering node N and that are immediate predecessors of activity A and reroute them to enter node M. Now make activity A start at node M. (Dummy activities can be avoided altogether if, instead of associating activities with arcs, we associate them with nodes. An example of this approach is presented in the box on p. 669.)

Figure 15.6 shows the network diagram for the first activity list as presented in Figure 15.6. We note that activities G and H both start at node ⑥ and terminate at node ⑦. This does not present a problem in portraying the appropriate precedence relationships, since only activity J starts at node ⑦. This might, however, create a problem for certain computer programs used to solve PERT and CPM problems. In some of these programs, each activity is identified by the number of its *starting and ending* node. If such a program is to be used, the representation of G and H in Figure 15.6 would lead the computer to regard them as the same activity. This would be incorrect, since in fact activities G and H are not the same. A dummy activity can be used to cure this condition. Figure 15.7 illustrates the procedure. Since the dummy activity requires no time, the correct time and precedent relationships are maintained. This new representation has been introduced into Figure 15.9. The computer code that we will employ does not require that these dummy activities be input. Thus, for our purposes, they serve mainly the pedagogical goal of correctly portraying the precedence relations (i.e., as used in Figure 15.5).

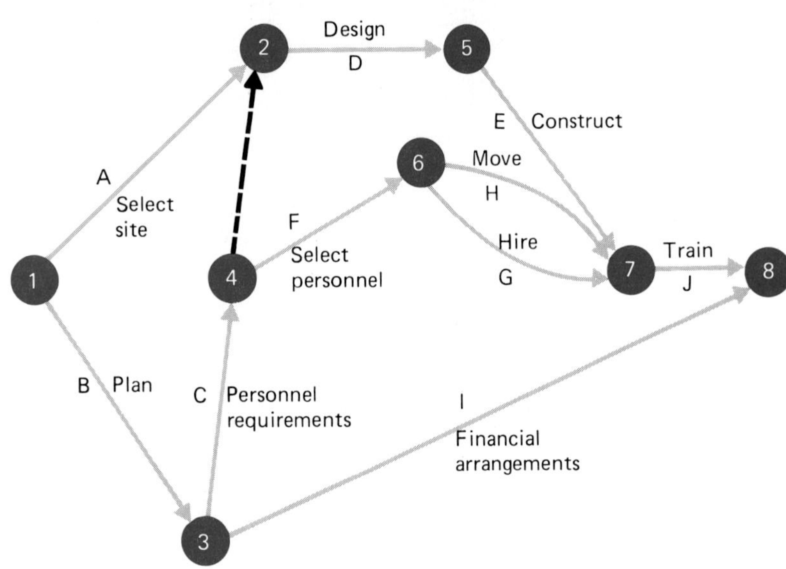

▲ FIGURE 15.6
Network Diagram for the First Activity List for the Move to Des Moines

An alternative way to add a dummy variable is shown below. Either way will accomplish the same end.

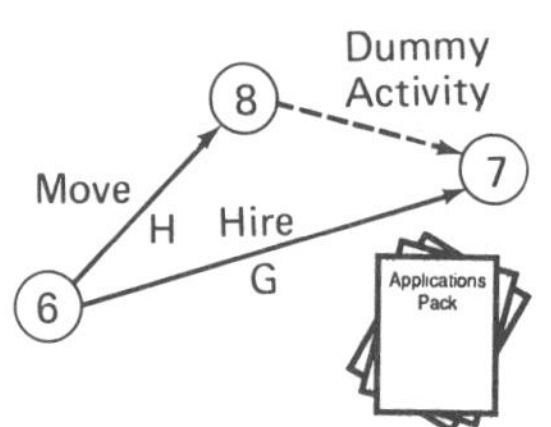

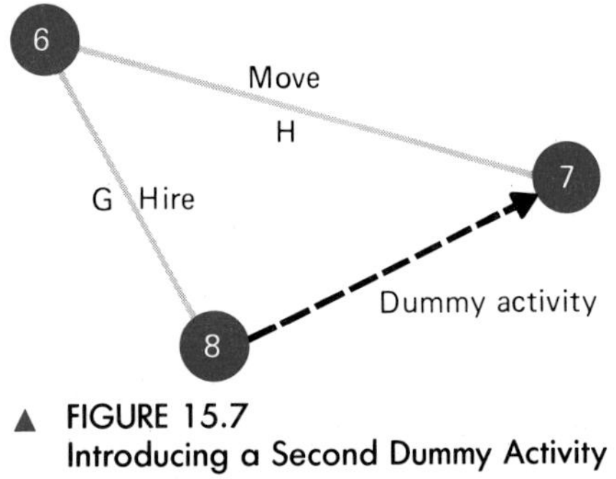

▲ FIGURE 15.7
Introducing a Second Dummy Activity

An Activity-on-Nodes Example

In the activity-on-nodes approach to representing a project as a network, the activities are associated with the nodes of the network while the arcs of the network display the precedence relationships. The Global Oil network in Figure 15.6 would be represented as shown below. For example, activity J has activities E, G, and H as immediate predecessors because there are arcs entering J from the nodes labelled E, G, and H. Note that there is no special difficulty in making A and C immediate predecessors of D, and C but not A an immediate predecessor of F.

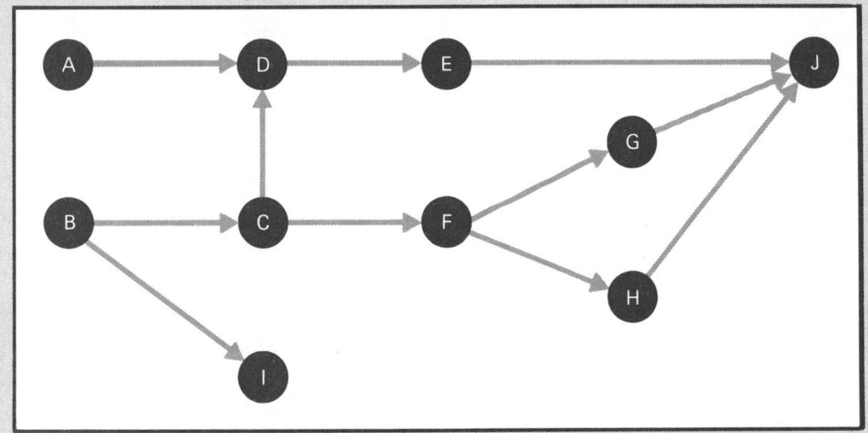

15.3 The Critical Path—Meeting the Board's Deadline

The activity list and an appropriate network diagram are useful devices for representing the precedence relationships among the activities in a project. Recall that the board has set a firm goal of 22 weeks for all the overall project to be completed. Before Becky can tell if she can meet this goal, she will have to incorporate time estimates into the process.

ACTIVITY	DESCRIPTION	IMMEDIATE PREDECESSORS	EXPECTED ACTIVITY TIME (WKS)	RESOURCES
A	Select Office Site	—	3	
B	Create Organizational and Financial Plan	—	5	
C	Determine Personnel Requirements	B	3	
D	Design Facility	A, C	4	
E	Construct Interior	D	8	
F	Select Personnel to Move	C	2	
G	Hire New Employees	F	4	
H	Move Records, Key Personnel, etc.	F	2	
I	Make Financial Arrangements with Institutions in Des Moines	B	5	
J	Train New Personnel	H, E, G	3	

▲ FIGURE 15.8
First Activity List with Expected Activity Times in Weeks

Time assignments

The PERT-CPM procedure requires management to produce an estimate of the expected time it will take to complete each activity on the activity list. Let us assume that Becky has worked with the appropriate departments at Global to arrive at the expected time estimates (in weeks) shown in Figure 15.8. (In Section 15.4 we shall discuss in more detail the way in which these time estimates were produced.) Figure 15.9 shows the network diagram with the expected activity times appended in brackets.

The Critical Path Calculation

This is the opposite problem from the one in Section 9.4 (the shortest-route problem). Here, the longest route from beginning (start) to end (finish) is needed. We can either change this PERT problem to a shortest-route model and use the algorithm in Section 9.4 or change the algorithm to fit the problem. It is easier in this case to change the algorithm.

From Figure 15.8 you can see (by adding up the separate expected activity times) that the total working time required to complete all the individual activities would be 39 weeks. However, the total calendar time required to complete the entire project can clearly be less than 39 weeks, for many activities can be performed simultaneously. For example, Figure 15.9 shows that activities A and B can be initiated at the same time. Activity A takes 3 weeks and B takes 5 weeks. If management arranges to begin both activities at the same time (at calendar time = 0), both will be completed by calendar time = 5. To obtain a prediction of the minimum calendar time required for overall project duration, we must find what is referred to as a *critical path* in the network.

A **path** can be defined as a sequence of connected activities that leads from the starting node ① to the completion node ⑨. For example, the sequence of activities B–I, requiring 10 weeks to complete, is a path. So is the sequence B–C–D–E–J requiring 23 weeks to complete. You can identify several other paths in Figure 15.9. To complete the project, the activities *on all paths* must be completed. In this sense

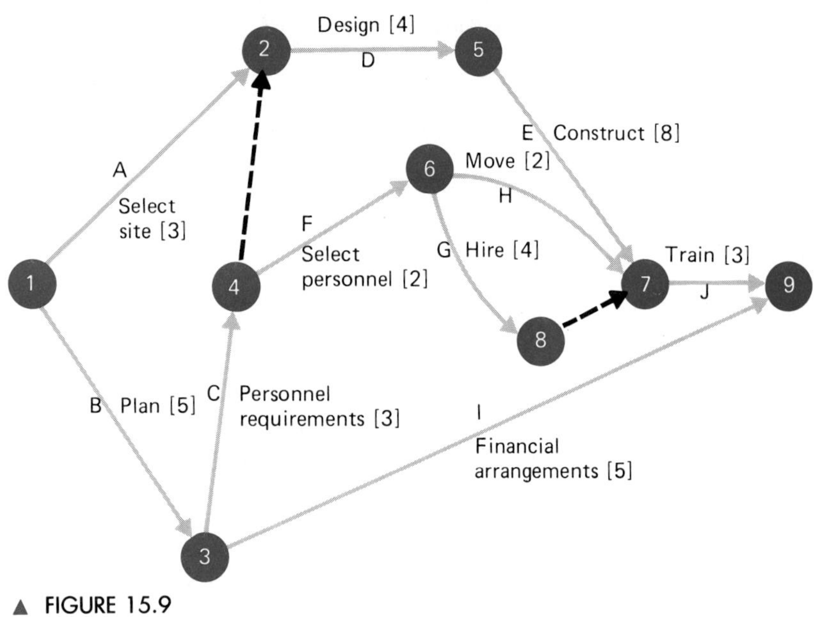

▲ FIGURE 15.9
Network Diagram with Expected Activity Times

we might say that "all paths must be traversed." Thus, we have just seen that our project will take *at least* 23 weeks to complete, for the path B–C–D–E–J must be traversed. However, numerous other paths must also be traversed, and some of these may require even more time. Our task will be to analyze the total amount of calendar time required for all paths to be traversed. Thus, we wish to determine the *longest path* from start to finish. This path, called the **critical path,** will determine the overall project duration, because no other path will be longer. If activities on the longest path are delayed, then, since these activities must be completed, the entire project will be delayed. For this reason the activities on the critical path are called the **critical activities** of the project. It is this subset of activities that must be kept on schedule.

Another difference between the shortest-route problem and this longest route (critical path) is that the interest is not just in the longest path in the network, but in the earliest and latest times each activity can be started and not affect the current solution. Thus, what is needed is *sensitivity analysis* of each activity and, therefore, finding the earliest and latest start times (and finish times) for each activity.

Earliest Start and Earliest Finish Times. We now specify the steps employed in finding a critical path. Fundamental in this process will be the **earliest start time** for each activity. To illustrate this idea, consider activity D, "design facility." Now assume that the project starts at time zero and ask yourself: "What is the earliest time at which activity D can start?" Clearly, it cannot start until activity A is complete. It thus cannot start before time = 3. However, it also cannot start before the dummy activity (that requires 0 time) is complete. Since the dummy cannot start until B and C are complete (a total of 8 weeks), we see that D cannot start until 8 weeks have passed. In this calculation, it is crucial to note that activities A and B both start at time 0. After 3 weeks A is complete, but B still requires another 2 weeks. After a total of 5 weeks, B is complete and C can start. After another 3 weeks, a total of 8 from the start, C is completed. Thus, after 8 weeks, both A and C are complete and D can start. In other words,

$$\text{earliest start time for activity D} = 8 \text{ weeks}$$

Another important concept is **earliest finish time** for each activity. If we let

$$ES = \text{earliest start time for a given activity}$$
$$EF = \text{earliest finish time for a given activity}$$
$$t = \text{expected activity time for a given activity}$$

then, for a given activity, the relation between earliest start time and earliest finish time is

$$EF = ES + t$$

For example, we have just shown that for activity D we have ES = 8. Thus, for activity D,

$$\begin{aligned} EF &= ES + t \\ &= 8 + 4 = 12 \end{aligned}$$

We now recall that each activity begins at a node. We know that a given activity leaving a node cannot be started until *all* activities leading into that node have been finished. This observation leads to the following rule.

LF for arrows going into the node is the smallest number of all the arrows going out of the node.

Earliest Start Time Rule: **The ES time for an activity leaving a particular node is the *largest* of the EF times for all activities entering the node.**

Let us apply this rule to nodes ①, ②, ③, and ④ of Becky's network, Figure 15.9. The result is shown in Figure 15.10. We write in brackets the earliest start and earliest finish times for each activity next to the letter of the activity, as shown in Figure 15.10. Note that the earliest start time rule applied to activity D says that ES for activity D is equal to the largest value of the EF times for the two precedent activities C (via the dummy) and A. Thus, the ES for D is the largest of the two values [8, 3], which is 8.

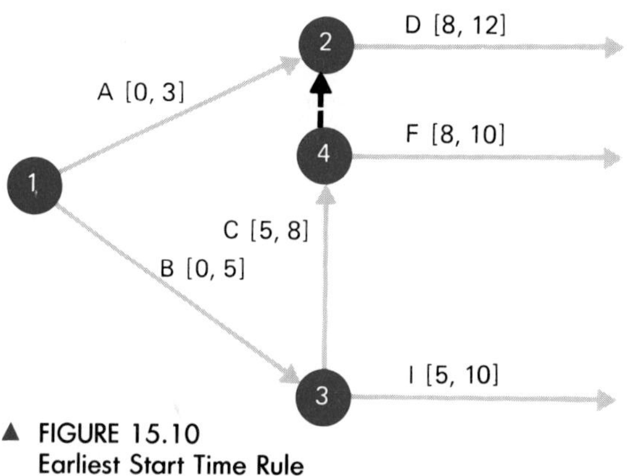

▲ FIGURE 15.10
Earliest Start Time Rule

The forward pass

Continuing to each node in a **forward pass** through the entire network, the values [ES, EF] are then computed for each activity. The result is shown in Figure 15.11. Note that the earliest finish time for J is 23 weeks. This means that the earliest completion time for the entire project is 23 weeks. This answers the first of the questions itemized in Section 15.1: "What is the expected project completion date?"

Latest Start and Latest Finish Times. In order to identify possible start and completion dates, the activities on the critical path, and how long noncritical activities may be delayed without affecting the overall completion date (answering the third, fourth, and fifth questions of Section 15.1), we now proceed with a

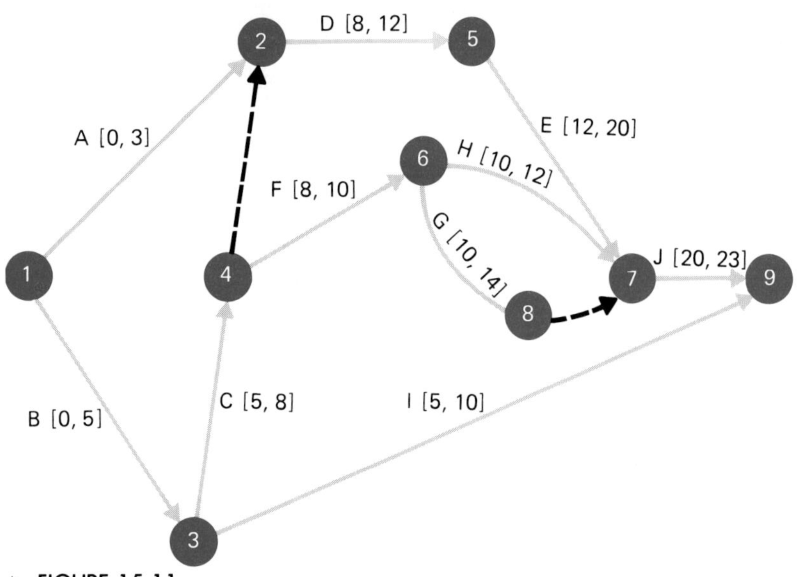

▲ FIGURE 15.11
Global Oil Network with Earliest Start and Earliest Finish Times Shown

The backward pass

backward pass calculation. The idea is that since we now have a target completion date (23 weeks from the start of the project), we can work backward from this date, determining the *latest* date each activity can finish without delaying the entire project. The backward pass begins at the completion node, node ⑨. We then trace back through the network computing what is termed a **latest start time** and **latest finish time** for each activity. In symbols,

LS = latest start time for a particular activity

LF = latest finish time for a particular activity

The relation between these quantities is

$$LS = LF - t$$

For activity J we define the latest finish time to be the same as its earliest finish time, which is 23. Hence, for activity J,

$$LS = LF - t = 23 - 3 = 20$$

Since the latest start time for activity J is 20, the latest activities E, H, and G can finish is 20. Thus, the latest E can start is $20 - 8 = 12$, the latest H can start is $20 - 2 = 18$, and the latest G can start is $20 - 4 = 16$. To determine the latest finish time for activity F is a little more complicated. We apply the following general rule:

ES for the arrows going out of the node is the largest number of all the arrows going into the node.

Latest Finish Time Rule: **The LF time for an activity entering a particular node is the *smallest*** of the LS times for all activities leaving that node.

Thus, for activity F, which enters node ⑥, we apply the rule to see that LF = 16, because the latest start times for the activities leaving node ⑥ (activities H and G) are 18 and 16. The complete network with LS and LF entries is shown in Figure 15.12. These entries appear on the arc for each activity in brackets, directly under the ES and EF times.

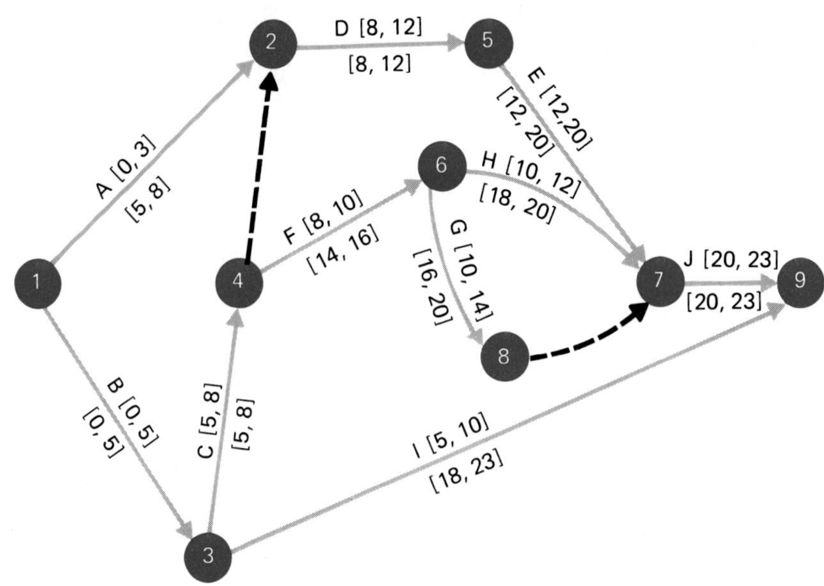

▲ FIGURE 15.12
Global Oil Network with LS and LF Times Shown below Activities

Slack is the same concept covered in LP and is the extra time that could be spent on that path without affecting the length of the critical path. An easy and important mathematical check is that every activity on the critical path should have the same slack, namely 0.

Slack and the Critical Path. Based on Figure 15.12, the next step of the algorithm is to identify another important value, the amount of slack, or free time, associated with each activity. **Slack** is the amount of time an activity can be delayed without affecting the completion date for the overall project. For each activity, the slack value is computed as

$$\text{slack} = \text{LS} - \text{ES} = \text{LF} - \text{EF}$$

For example, the slack for activity G is given by

$$\begin{aligned} \text{slack for G} &= \text{LS for G} - \text{ES for G} \\ &= 16 - 10 \\ &= 6 \end{aligned}$$

and the same value is given by

$$\text{LF for G} - \text{EF for G} = 20 - 14 = 6$$

This means that activity G could be delayed up to 6 weeks beyond its earliest start time without delaying the overall project. On the other hand, the slack associated with activity C is

$$\begin{aligned} \text{slack for C} &= \text{LS for C} - \text{ES for C} \\ &= 5 - 5 \\ &= 0 \end{aligned}$$

Thus, activity C has no slack and must begin as scheduled at week 5. *Since this activity cannot be delayed without affecting the entire project, it is a critical activity and is on the critical path.*

PERT critical paths can also have alternative optimal solutions (again, just as in LP). If activity F took 8 weeks, then the path B-C-F-G-J would also be a critical path.

The critical path activities are those with zero slack.

Activity No.	Activity Name	Activity Exp.Time	Activity Variance	Earliest Start	Latest Start	Earliest Finish	Latest Finish	Slack LS-ES
1	A	+3.00000	0	0	+5.00000	+3.00000	+8.00000	+5.00000
2	B	+5.00000	0	0	0	+5.00000	+5.00000	Critical
3	C	+3.00000	0	+5.00000	+5.00000	+8.00000	+8.00000	Critical
4	D	+4.00000	0	+8.00000	+8.00000	+12.0000	+12.0000	Critical
5	E	+8.00000	0	+12.0000	+12.0000	+20.0000	+20.0000	Critical
6	F	+2.00000	0	+8.00000	+14.0000	+10.0000	+16.0000	+6.00000
7	G	+4.00000	0	+10.0000	+16.0000	+14.0000	+20.0000	+6.00000
8	H	+2.00000	0	+10.0000	+18.0000	+12.0000	+20.0000	+8.00000
9	I	+5.00000	0	+5.00000	+18.0000	+10.0000	+23.0000	+13.0000
10	J	+3.00000	0	+20.0000	+20.0000	+23.0000	+23.0000	Critical
11	DUMMY	0	0	+8.00000	+8.00000	+8.00000	+8.00000	Critical
12	DUMMY	0	0	+14.0000	+20.0000	+14.0000	+20.0000	+6.00000
Expected completion time = 23 Total cost = 0								

▲ FIGURE 15.13
Computer-Generated Scheduling Summary for Global Oil

Computer Output for the Network. The computer solution of this problem, produced by the CPM module of QSB+, is shown in Figure 15.13. This is the type of output you would be likely to see in a real study. Note that the word "Critical" is printed for those activities with zero slack. Thus, we can see from this computer output that the critical path for Becky's project is B-C-D-E-J, where we have excluded any dummy activities that may happen to be critical. The minimum overall completion time is 23 weeks, which is the sum of the times on the critical path, as well as the earliest finish time for the last activity (J). Figure 15.13 also provides the answers to questions 3, 4, and 5 raised in Section 15.1. In other words, we have, up to this point, answered the following questions from that section.

1. What is the expected project completion date?
Answer: 23 weeks.

3. What are the scheduled start and completion dates for each specific activity?
Answer: An activity may be scheduled to start at any date between "earliest start" and "latest start." The scheduled completion date will be "start date + expected activity time." For example, activity G can be scheduled to start anywhere between time = 10 and time = 16. As shown in Figure 15.8, the expected activity time is 4 weeks. Hence, the scheduled completion date will be "start date + 4."

4. What activities are *critical* in the sense that they must be completed exactly as scheduled in order to meet the target for overall project completion?
Answer: The activities on the critical path: namely, B, C, D, E, J.

5. How long can *noncritical* activities be delayed before a delay in overall completion date is incurred?
Answer: Any activity may be started as late as the "latest start" date without delaying the overall project completion.

Three questions, namely 2, 6, and 7, remain to be answered. But first, before proceeding further, let us take an overview of what we have learned. It is clear from the critical path analysis that Becky has a problem. The board of directors wants the credit card operation to start operating in Des Moines in 22 weeks, and with the current plan 23 weeks are required. Obviously, something must change if this goal is to be met.

Ways of Reducing Project Duration

There are two basic approaches to reducing the time required to complete a project:

1. *A strategic analysis:* Here the analyst asks: "Does this project have to be done the way it is currently diagrammed?" In particular, "Do all of the activities on the critical path have to be done in the specified order?" Can we make arrangements to accomplish some of these activities in a different way not on the critical path?
2. *A tactical approach:* In this approach the analyst assumes that the current diagram is appropriate and works at reducing the time of certain activities on the critical path by devoting more resources to them. The current expected times assume a certain allocation of resources. For example, the 8 weeks for construction (activity E) assumes a regular 8-hour workday. The contractor can complete the job more rapidly by working overtime, but at increased costs.

Once the feedback has been received on "solving" the current model, this may lead to questions about the original model and the precedential relationships. This is analogous to solving an LP model and then questioning whether certain constraints are really necessary (or what might be missing).

The tactical approach will get us into consideration of CPM models, to be discussed in Section 15.6. For now, let us deal with the so-called strategic questions.

This is analogous to "what if . . . ?" analysis done on spreadsheets. The analyst's first concern is "can the deadline be met?" (feasibility), and second, "what is the cheapest way of meeting the deadline?" (optimality). There can be many ways of reducing the critical path, and the analyst must use his/her knowledge of the actual project and good common sense in choosing a few alternatives from a possibly large number to find the cheapest cost of meeting the deadline.

A Strategic Analysis. Becky starts with a strategic analysis, since she is anxious to keep the cost of the move as low as possible. After some study she suddenly realizes that the current network assumes that activity J, the training of new employees, must be carried out in the new building (after E is complete), and after records and key personnel have been moved (after H is complete). After reconsidering, she believes that these requirements can be changed. First of all, J can be accomplished independently of H. The previous specification that H should be an immediate predecessor of J was simply incorrect. Moreover, she believes that she can secure an alternative training facility by arranging to use surplus classroom space in Des Moines at a minimal cost. She can then have the new employees trained and ready to start the moment that construction ends. On the other hand, she has to add another activity to the activity list: Secure a training facility (to be denoted as activity K). Although she feels that such a rearrangement may be helpful, it is possible that in this redefined network she may have created a new critical path with a still unsatisfactory minimum time (i.e., one greater than 22 weeks).

Computer Output for the Redefined Network. Figure 15.14 shows the redefined activity list in the form in which it appears on screen as Becky types in the

▼ FIGURE 15.14
Computer Input for Redefined Activity List

```
Activity  Activity  Start   End     Normal     Crash      Normal     Crash
number      name    node    node   duration   duration     cost       cost
   1      <A      > <1    > <2    > <3       > <0       > <0       > <0       >
   2      <B      > <1    > <3    > <5       > <0       > <0       > <0       >
   3      <C      > <3    > <4    > <3       > <0       > <0       > <0       >
   4      <D      > <2    > <5    > <4       > <0       > <0       > <0       >
   5      <E      > <5    > <9    > <8       > <0       > <0       > <0       >
   6      <F      > <4    > <6    > <2       > <0       > <0       > <0       >
   7      <G      > <6    > <7    > <4       > <0       > <0       > <0       >
   8      <H      > <6    > <9    > <2       > <0       > <0       > <0       >
   9      <I      > <3    > <9    > <5       > <0       > <0       > <0       >
  10      <J      > <7    > <9    > <3       > <0       > <0       > <0       >
  11      <K      > <6    > <8    > <3       > <0       > <0       > <0       >
  12      <DUMMY1 > <4    > <2    > <0       > <0       > <0       > <0       >
  13      <DUMMY2 > <8    > <7    > <0       > <0       > <0       > <0       >
```

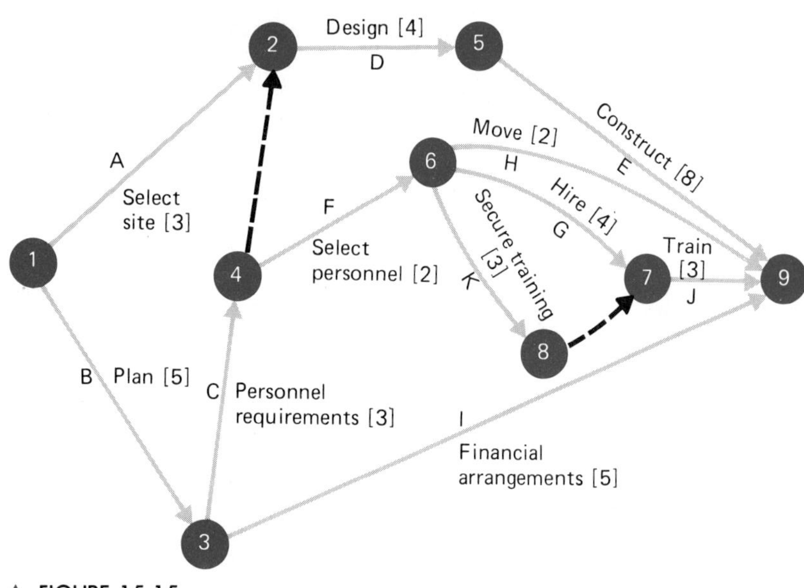

▲ FIGURE 15.15
Network Diagram for the Redefined Project

problem on her personal computer. Note that the dummy activities are given a normal duration (expected activity time) of 0. Some of the entries (Crash duration, Normal cost, and Crash cost) do not have to be specified for this particular analysis. Figure 15.15 shows the network diagram for the redefined project. Becky has to do only a limited amount of typing because she is modifying the input data from her previous definition of the network. Thus, she must add activity K and change the ending node numbers for activities E, G, and H.

Becky then asks the computer to solve the problem, and the report shown in Figure 15.16 is produced. Here we see that the redefined project can be completed in 20 weeks (the sum of the times on the critical path), so the board's deadline can be met. It is also apparent that the activity "train" (J) is no longer on the critical path.

▼ FIGURE 15.16
Computer Solution for the Redefined Project

Activity No.	Activity Name	Activity Exp.Time	Activity Variance	Earliest Start	Latest Start	Earliest Finish	Latest Finish	Slack LS-ES
1	A	+3.00000	0	0	+5.00000	+3.00000	+8.00000	+5.00000
2	B	+5.00000	0	0	0	+5.00000	+5.00000	Critical
3	C	+3.00000	0	+5.00000	+5.00000	+8.00000	+8.00000	Critical
4	D	+4.00000	0	+8.00000	+8.00000	+12.0000	+12.0000	Critical
5	E	+8.00000	0	+12.0000	+12.0000	+20.0000	+20.0000	Critical
6	F	+2.00000	0	+8.00000	+11.0000	+10.0000	+13.0000	+3.00000
7	G	+4.00000	0	+10.0000	+13.0000	+14.0000	+17.0000	+3.00000
8	H	+2.00000	0	+10.0000	+18.0000	+12.0000	+20.0000	+8.00000
9	I	+5.00000	0	+5.00000	+15.0000	+10.0000	+20.0000	+10.0000
10	J	+3.00000	0	+14.0000	+17.0000	+17.0000	+20.0000	+3.00000
11	K	+3.00000	0	+10.0000	+14.0000	+13.0000	+17.0000	+4.00000
12	DUMMY1	0	0	+8.00000	+8.00000	+8.00000	+8.00000	Critical
13	DUMMY2	0	0	+13.0000	+17.0000	+13.0000	+17.0000	+4.00000

Expected completion time = 20 Total cost = 0

In spite of the fact that 3 weeks is needed to secure a training facility, activity J has a slack of 3 weeks. The computer solution shows that the critical path for the redefined project is B-C-D-E. (Recall that "Critical" in the Slack column indicates that an activity is on the critical path and that we ignore dummy activities.)

15.4 Variability in Activity Times

Let us now consider the second question raised in the introduction: "What is the potential variability in the expected project completion date?" So far, we have been acting as though the activity times and the derived values for ES, LS, EF, and LF were all deterministic. This may not be strictly correct, for in reality the activity times are often not known in advance with certainty. In view of this fact, PERT employs a special formula for estimating activity times. We shall now present the details, and in so doing it will be seen that the PERT approach can also be used to calculate the probability that the project will be completed by any particular time.

Estimating the Expected Activity Time

The PERT system of estimating activity times requires someone who understands the activity in question well enough to produce three estimates of the activity time:

The time estimates for optimistic, pessimistic, and most probable may be difficult to obtain because people don't want to make promises they can't keep, and so inflate their estimates.

1. **Optimistic time** (denoted by a): the minimum time. Everything has to go perfectly to achieve this time.
2. **Most probable time** (denoted by m): the most likely time. The time required under normal circumstances.
3. **Pessimistic time** (denoted by b): the maximum time. One version of Murphy's Law is that if something can go wrong, it will. The pessimistic time is the time required when Murphy's Law is in effect.

Consider, for example, activity E, construct the interior. Becky and the general contractor carefully examine each phase of the construction project and arrive at the following estimates:

$$a = 4$$
$$m = 7$$
$$b = 16$$

The relatively large value for b is caused by the possibility of a delay in the delivery of the air-conditioning unit for the computer. If this unit is delayed, the entire activity is delayed. Moreover, in this case, since E is on the critical path, a delay in this activity will delay overall project completion.

In the original development of the PERT approach (during the late 1950s), the procedure for estimating the expected value of the activity times was motivated by the assumption that the activity time was a random variable with a particular probability distribution. This distribution (the **beta distribution**) has a minimum and maximum value, unlike the normal distribution, which has an infinite range of values. It also is capable of assuming a wide variety of shapes, again unlike the normal, which is always symmetrical about its most likely value. A typical beta distribution is shown in Figure 15.17. The expected value of a beta distribution is

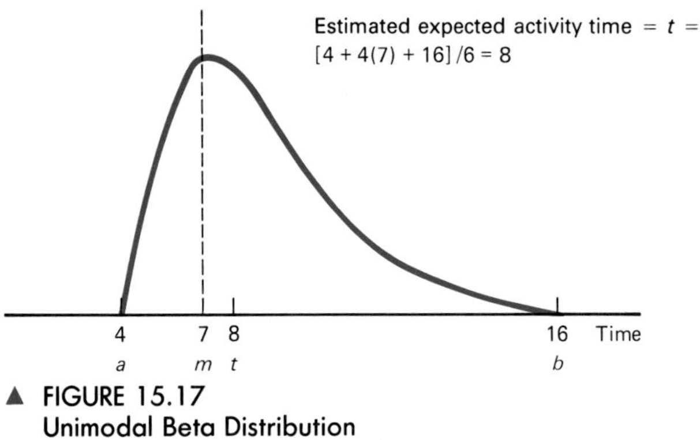

▲ FIGURE 15.17
Unimodal Beta Distribution

approximately $(a+4m+b)/6$; thus the formula used to estimate the expected activity time is

$$\text{estimate of expected activity time} = \frac{a+4m+b}{6} \quad \textbf{(15.1)}$$

Note that the estimate is a weighted average of the values of *a, m,* and *b,* where the weights (1/6, 4/6, 1/6) sum to 1. This means that the estimate will always lie between *a* and *b.* Thus for activity E,

$$\text{estimate of expected activity time} = \frac{4 + 4(7) + 16}{6} = 8$$

By working with the appropriate individuals in Global Oil, Becky used (15.1) to estimate each of the expected activity times that were presented in Figure 15.8 and subsequently used in the critical path analysis.

Estimating the Standard Deviation of an Activity Time. The standard deviation of an activity time is estimated by assuming that there are six standard deviations between the optimistic and pessimistic times:

$$\text{estimate of the standard deviation of activity time} = \frac{b - a}{6} \quad \textbf{(15.2)}$$

Thus, for activity E,

$$\text{estimate of standard deviation} = \frac{16 - 4}{6} = 2$$

Figure 15.18 shows the three estimates (*a, m, b*), the expected activity times, the standard deviation of the activity times, and the *variance* of the activity times for the redefined activity list. The variance is simply the square of the standard deviation. It is useful to record the variance of each activity since these values will be used in making statements about the probability of completing the overall project by a specific date.

In an application, it is of course possible to use any procedure that seems appropriate to estimate the expected value and standard deviation of the activity time. Indeed, in some circumstances data may be available and various statistical procedures can be used to estimate these parameters of the model.

ACTIVITY	a	m	b	$(a + 4m + b)/6$ (EXPECTED VALUE)	$(b - a)/6$ (STD. DEV.)	$[(b - a)/6]^2$ (VARIANCE)
A	1	3	5	3	2/3	4/9
B	3	4.5	9	5	1	1
C	2	3	4	3	1/3	1/9
D	2	4	6	4	2/3	4/9
E	4	7	16	8	2	4
F	1	1.5	5	2	2/3	4/9
G	2.5	3.5	7.5	4	5/6	25/36
H	1	2	3	2	1/3	1/9
I	4	5	6	5	1/3	1/9
J	1.5	3	4.5	3	1/2	1/4
K	1	3	5	3	2/3	4/9

▲ FIGURE 15.18
Time Estimates

Probability of Completing the Project on Time

The fact that activity times are random variables implies that the completion time for the project is also a random variable. That is, there is potential variability in the overall completion time. Even though the redefined project has an *expected* completion time of 20 weeks, there is no guarantee that it will actually be completed within 20 weeks. If *by chance* various activities take longer than their expected time, the project might not be completed within the desired 22-week schedule. In general, it would be useful to know the probability that the project will be completed within a specified time. In particular, Becky would like to know the probability that the move will be completed within 22 weeks.

San Diego State University and Georgia Tech contracted to build parking towers and were given reduced costs if PERT charts were *not* used. The construction firms would not promise when the structures would be done so that if workers were needed on another project (which did have deadlines), they could be taken off the universities' projects for several days or weeks and used elsewhere. In exchange for this uncertainty, the institutions got cheaper construction rates for helping the contractors with their personnel balancing.

The analysis proceeds as follows:

1. Let T equal the total time that will be taken by the activities on the critical path.

2. Find the probability that the value of T will turn out to be less than or equal to any specified value of interest. In particular, for Becky's project we would find Prob$\{T \leq 22\}$. A good approximation for this probability is easily found if two assumptions hold.

a. *The activity times are independent random variables.* This is a valid assumption for most PERT networks and seems reasonable for Becky's problem. There is no reason to believe that the time to construct the interior should depend on the design time, and so on.

b. *The random variable T has an approximately normal distribution.* This assumption relies on the *central limit theorem,* which in broad terms states that the sum of independent random variables is approximately normally distributed.

Now recalling that our goal is to find Prob$\{T \leq 22\}$, where T is the time along the critical path, we will want to convert T to a standard normal random variable and use Table A.0 in Appendix A at the end of the text to find Prob$\{T \leq 22\}$. The first step in this process is to find the standard deviation of T. To do this we need the variance of T. When the activity times are independent, we know that the variance of the total time along the critical path equals the sum of the variances of the activity times on the critical path. Thus, for Becky's problem

$$\text{var } T = \begin{pmatrix}\text{variance for}\\ \text{activity B}\end{pmatrix} + \begin{pmatrix}\text{variance for}\\ \text{activity C}\end{pmatrix} + \begin{pmatrix}\text{variance for}\\ \text{activity D}\end{pmatrix} + \begin{pmatrix}\text{variance for}\\ \text{activity E}\end{pmatrix}$$

Using the numerical values in Figure 15.18 yields

$$\text{var } T = 1 + \frac{1}{9} + \frac{4}{9} + 4 = \frac{50}{9}$$

Finally,

$$\text{std. dev. } T = \sqrt{(\text{var } T)} = \sqrt{\frac{50}{9}} = 2.357$$

We now proceed to convert T to a standard normal random variable, Z, in the usual way: $Z = \frac{T - \mu}{\sigma}$. Recalling that 20 weeks is the mean (i.e., the expected completion time), we have

$$\begin{aligned}\text{Prob}\{T \le 22\} &= \text{Prob}\left\{\frac{T\text{-}20}{2.357} \le \frac{22\text{-}20}{2.357}\right\}\\ &= \text{Prob}\{Z \le 0.8485\}\end{aligned}$$

If we consult Table A.0 at the end of the text for the area under a normal curve from the left-hand tail to a point 0.8485 standard deviations above the mean, we find that the answer is about 0.80. Thus, there is about an 80% chance that the critical path will be completed in less than 22 weeks.

This analysis shows how to shed light on the second of the questions asked in the introduction. In particular, it shows how to find the probability that the *critical path* will be finished by *any* given time. It illustrates the importance of considering the variability in individual activity when considering overall project completion times. The analysis for Becky's problem indicates that, using expected time as our "real-world forecast," the expected project duration will be 20 weeks and, if so, it will be completed 2 weeks ahead of the desired date. The analysis of uncertainty above sheds additional light on this estimate. It shows a significant probability (i.e., $0.2 = 1 - 0.8$) that *the critical path* will not be completed by the desired completion date. The implication is that there is *at least* a probability of 0.2 that the overall project may not be completed by the desired date. The modifier "at least" has been employed because of the following complicating factor: Because of randomness, some other path, estimated as being noncritical, may in reality take longer to complete than the purported critical path.

Testing the Assumptions with Spreadsheet Simulation

For small projects, it is not too cumbersome to use a spreadsheet program to do a critical path analysis. Figure 15.19 shows a spreadsheet for the redefined Global Oil problem. The Earliest Finish column is the Activity Time column plus the Earliest Start column. Similarly, the Latest Start column is the Latest Finish column minus the Activity Time column. The Slack column is either the Latest Start column minus the Earliest Start column or the Latest Finish column minus the Earliest Finish column. The formula for the minimum project length in cell D15 is @MAX(D3..D13), the largest Earliest Finish.

The cumbersome part of creating the spreadsheet is entering the information

D15: (F1) @MAX(D13..D3)

	A	B	C	D	E	F	G	H
1		Activity	Earliest	Earliest	Latest	Latest		
2	Activity	Time	Start	Finish	Start	Finish	Slack	
3	A	3	0	3	5	8	5	
4	B	5	0	5	0	5	0	
5	C	3	5	8	5	8	0	
6	D	4	8	12	8	12	0	
7	E	8	12	20	12	20	0	
8	F	2	8	10	11	13	3	
9	G	4	10	14	13	17	3	
10	H	2	10	12	18	20	8	
11	I	5	5	10	15	20	10	
12	J	3	14	17	17	20	3	
13	K	3	10	13	14	17	4	
14								
15	Minimum Project Length			20.0				
16								
17								
18								
19								
20								

▲ FIGURE 15.19
Spreadsheet for Redefined Global Oil Problem

that is conveyed by the network diagram. For example, since the Latest Finish of activity F is the smallest Latest Start of activities G, H, and K, the formula in cell F8 is @MIN(E9,E10,E13). Since the Earliest Start of activity D is the largest Earliest Finish of activities A and C, the formula in cell C6 is @MAX(D3,D5).

Once the basic relationships have been entered, however, it is very easy to alter the activity times and see what effect this has on the minimum project length and the activities on the critical path. By making the activity times random and recalculating the spreadsheet, one can get a feel for the variability of both the project length and the critical path. Figure 15.20 shows one example. Note that all activity times are between their pessimistic (a) and optimistic (b) times, but that the critical path is different, in this case B–C–F–G–J. This result demonstrates that the path with the longest *expected* length (B–C–D–E) may not turn out to be the critical path. This fact implies that the expected project length may be greater than the value calculated by the PERT analysis.[2]

To estimate the true expected project length, we should recalculate the spreadsheet many times and average the minimum project lengths obtained on each recalculation. The @RISK add-in makes this easy to do. Since @RISK adds the beta distribution to the spreadsheet as an @function, and the PERT analysis of activity times was based on the beta distribution, we set the formulas in column B to sample from the appropriate beta distributions.[3] Figure 15.21 shows the distribution of minimum project length calculated by @RISK based on a sample of 400 simulations. The estimated average project length is in fact larger than what was calculated

[2]The key result needed to show this is that the expected value of the maximum of two random variables is greater than or equal to the maximum of the expected values: $E[\max(X,Y)] \geq \max(E[X],E[Y])$.

[3]Since beta distributions have a range of 0 to 1, what was actually done was to scale a beta random variable to the range a to b and then choose the parameters of the beta to match the expected value and variance calculated by the PERT analysis.

D15: (F1) @MAX(D13..D3)

	A	B	C	D	E	F	G	H
1		Activity	Earliest	Earliest	Latest	Latest		
2	Activity	Time	Start	Finish	Start	Finish	Slack	
3	A	2	0	2	6	8	6	
4	B	4	0	4	0	4	0	
5	C	3	4	7	4	7	0	
6	D	3	7	10	8	11	1	
7	E	5	10	15	11	16	1	
8	F	2	7	9	7	9	0	
9	G	4	9	13	9	13	0	
10	H	2	9	11	14	16	5	
11	I	5	4	9	11	16	7	
12	J	3	13	16	13	16	0	
13	K	2	9	11	11	13	2	
14								
15	Minimum Project Length			16.0				
16								
17								
18								
19								
20								

▲ FIGURE 15.20
Simulated Activity Times for Global Oil

by the PERT analysis, but only slightly so (20.09917 versus 20.0, about ½%). @RISK also makes it easy to calculate the probability that the project length is less than or equal to any given target value. The figure shows that for a target value of 22 weeks, that probability is 78.49%, slightly lower than the 80% calculated by the PERT analysis. In this case, at least, it seems that PERT's simplifying assumptions are justified.

▼ FIGURE 15.21
Distribution of Project Length

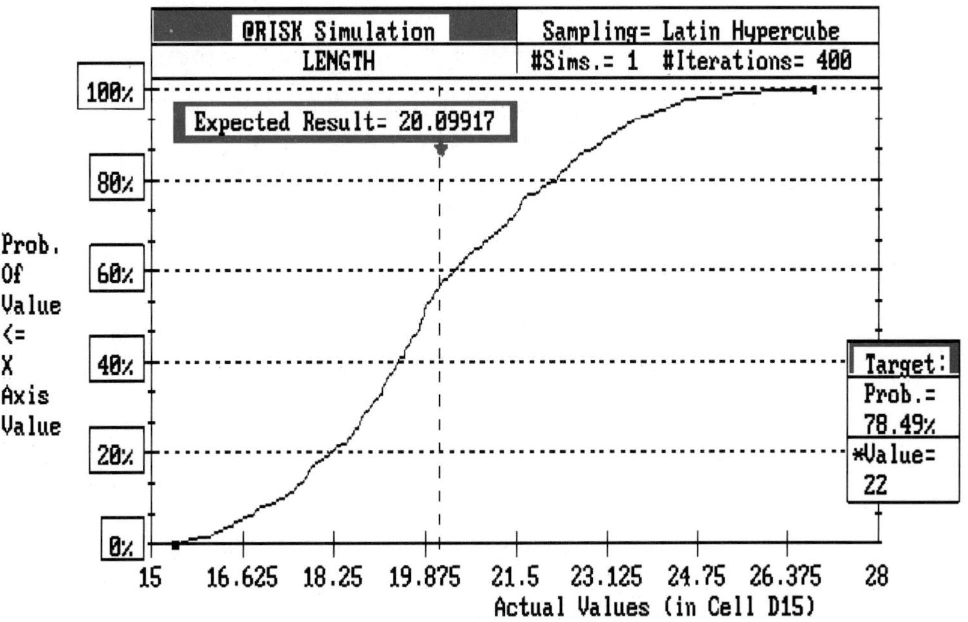

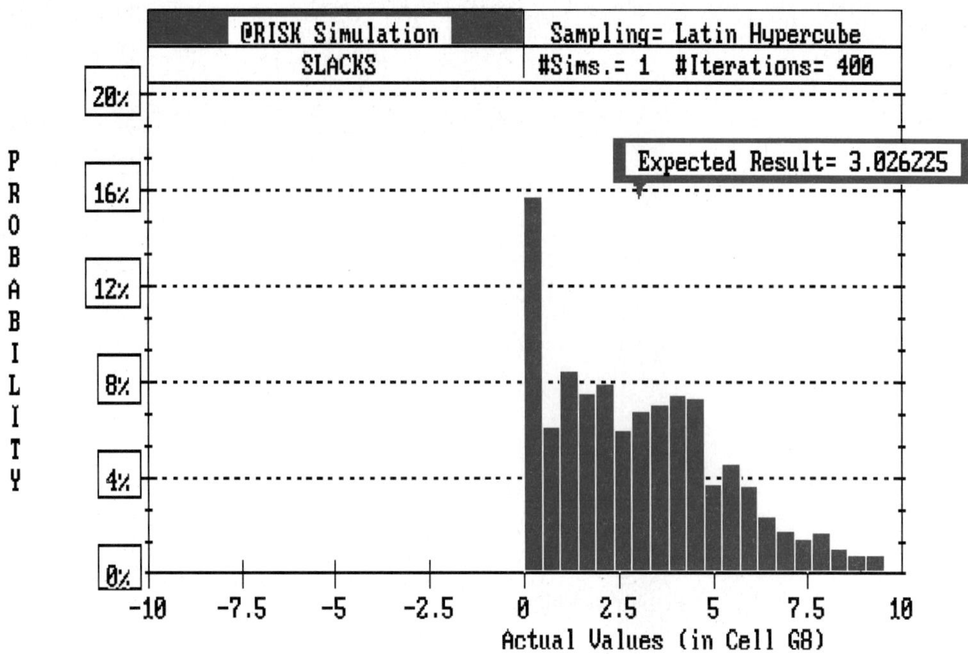

▲ FIGURE 15.22
Distribution of Slack for Activity F

@RISK also makes it easy to generate histograms like the one shown in Figure 15.22. This is a histogram of the slack for activity F. While the *expected* slack is close to the PERT analysis value of 3 weeks, the histogram shows that there is considerable variation around this average value. Note particularly that there is a spike of probability for slacks close to zero. If the slack is zero, then F is on the critical path. If the slack is close to zero, then the schedule for F can slip very little without delaying the entire project. This means that activity F *may* turn out to be a critical activity. This is an insight that the PERT analysis, with its large slack of 3 weeks for activity F, might obscure.

15.5 A Mid-Chapter Summary: PERT

Required PERT inputs

Using the PERT approach the analyst must provide the following inputs:

1. A list of the activities that make up the project.
2. The immediate predecessors for each activity.
3. The expected value for each activity time [using $t = [a + 4m + b)/6]$.
4. The standard deviation for each activity time [using std. dev. $t = (b - a)/6$].

The PERT estimation procedure uses pessimistic, most likely, and optimistic estimates of the activity time to obtain the expected value and the standard deviation for each activity. The standard deviation is required only if the analyst wishes to make probability statements about completing the project by a certain date.

The analysis uses the inputs listed above to

PERT outputs

1. calculate the critical path;
2. calculate the minimum expected time in which the project can be completed;
3. show slack values for each activity, together with the latest expected time that any activity can start (or finish) without delaying the project; and

4. calculate the probability that the current critical path will be completed by a specified date if estimates of the standard deviation are provided.

If the project cannot (or is unlikely to) be completed by a desired date, the project must be redefined either by

PERT and planning

1. strategic analysis, in which the project network is modified by introducing new activities or changing the relationships between existing activities, or
2. tactical analysis, in which activity times are changed by the application of additional resources.

PERT and control

Finally, we can observe that PERT is not only a planning system. You can now see that it can also be used to monitor the progress of a project. Management can compare the actual activity times as they occur with those that were used in the planning process. If, for example, activity B took 6 or 7 weeks, rather than the 5 weeks used in the network diagram, Becky would know that the project is behind schedule. This would give her the opportunity to arrange to assign more resources to some other activity on the critical path in an effort to shorten that activity and meet the desired overall due date.

Identification of the critical path and prompt reporting give management a powerful tool to deal with the difficult problem of bringing a complicated project in on schedule.

15.6 CPM and Time-Cost Trade-Offs

As we have just seen, PERT provides a useful approach to the analysis of scheduling problems in the face of *uncertainty about activity times.* Such uncertainty will often occur in new or unique projects where there is little previous time and cost experience to draw upon. In other types of projects there may be considerable historical data with which one may make good estimates of time and resource requirements. In such cases it may be of interest to deal more explicitly with costs in the sense of analyzing possibilities to shift resources in order to reduce completion time. The concept that there is a trade-off between the time that it takes to complete an activity and the cost of the resources devoted to that activity is the basis of a model that was originally part of the CPM method.

The model assumes that cost is a linear function of time. Consider, for example, Figure 15.23. This figure illustrates that management has the opportunity to aim at an activity time anywhere between a minimum value and a maximum

FIGURE 15.23
Time-Cost Trade-off Function

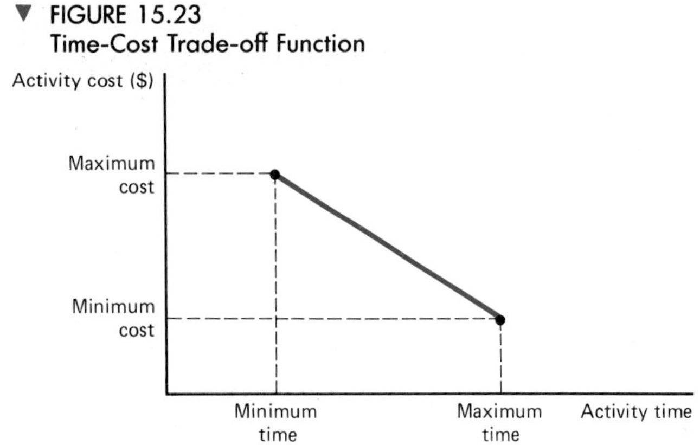

value. The choice of an activity time implies an activity cost as specified by the diagram.

Given the availability of such a time-cost trade-off function for each activity in the project, management has the opportunity to select each activity time (within limits) and incur the associated cost. Clearly, the choice of individual activity times affects the project completion time. The question becomes: "What activity times should be selected to yield the desired project completion time at minimum cost?" The CPM approach to answering this question will be presented in the context of the creation of a financial analysis package by the Operations Analysis Group at Global.

A Financial Analysis Project for Retail Marketing

In addition to the move to Des Moines, Becky is responsible for a new financial analysis package that will be used in the retail marketing section of Global. The program is used in evaluating potential outlets (gas stations) in terms of location and other characteristics. The systems design is complete. The computer programming must still be done, and the package must be introduced to the retail marketing section.

Figure 15.24 shows the activity list and network diagram for this project. The time shown is termed the **normal time.** This corresponds to the maximum time shown in Figure 15.23. Recall that we are here assuming that activity times can be estimated with good accuracy, and hence "normal time" is a known quantity. From Figure 15.24 it is clear that the longest path through the network is DAP–WAP–INT, and hence this is the critical path. The earliest completion time for the project is 194 hours.

ACTIVITY	IMMEDIATE PREDECESSOR	NORMAL TIME (HR)
DIP (Design Information Processor)	—	32
WIP (Write Information Processor)	DIP	40
DAP (Design Analysis Package)	—	50
WAP (Write Analysis Package)	DAP	24
INT (Introduce System)	WIP, WAP	120

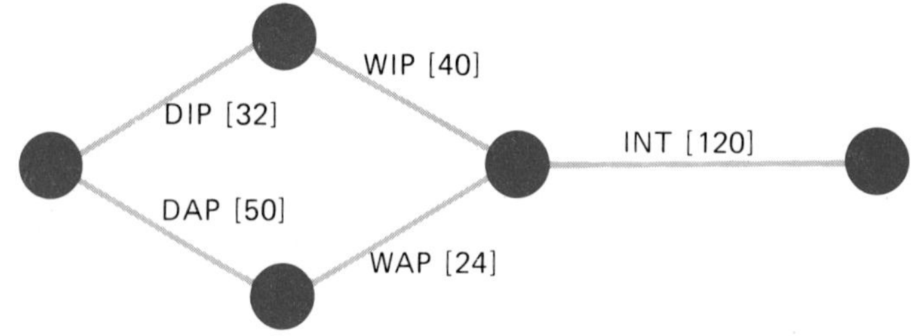

▲ FIGURE 15.24
Activity List and Network Diagram for the Financial Analysis Project

Required Activity Data. The CPM system is based on four pieces of input data for each activity:

1. **Normal time:** the maximum time for the activity.
2. **Normal cost:** the cost required to achieve the normal time.
3. **Crash time:** the minimum time for the activity.
4. **Crash cost:** the cost required to achieve the crash time.

ACTIVITY	(1) NORMAL TIME	(2) NORMAL COST ($)	(3) CRASH TIME	(4) CRASH COST ($)	(5) MAXIMUM CRASH HOURS	(6) COST PER CRASH HOUR ($)
DIP	32	640	20	800	12	13.33
WIP	40	480	30	720	10	24.00
DAP	50	1000	30	1200	20	10.00
WAP	24	288	15	360	9	8.00
INT	120	4800	70	5600	50	16.00
TOTAL		$7208				

▲ FIGURE 15.25
Time–Cost Data for the Financial Analysis Project

These data for the financial analysis project are presented in the first four columns of Figure 15.25. The fifth column shows the maximum crash hours, defined by

$$\text{Max crash hours} = \text{normal time} - \text{crash time}$$

Figure 15.26 shows how these data are used to create the time–cost trade-off function for activity DIP, design the information processor.

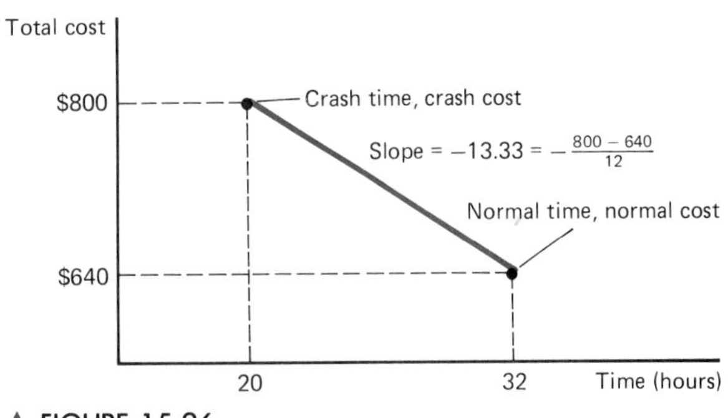

▲ FIGURE 15.26
Time-Cost Trade-off Function for DIP

Note that, according to Figure 15.25, using all normal times leads to a total project cost of $7208. Also note that the last column in Figure 15.25 shows how much it costs per hour (as computed in Figure 15.26) to reduce each activity time to less than its normal time. In CPM jargon, the process of reducing an activity time is called **crashing.** For example, management could choose to have DIP completed in 31 hours, rather than the normal 32 hours, for a marginal cost of $13.33. The normal time of 32 hours costs $640, and a time of 31 hours would therefore cost 640 + 13.33 = $653.33.

Crashing the Project

We have noted that, using only the normal time for each activity, the earliest completion time for this project is 194 hours (along the critical path DAP–WAP–INT). Management is now in a position to determine the minimum-cost method of reducing this time to specified levels. To reduce the project time to 193, Becky would crash an activity on the critical path by 1 hour. Since it costs less per hour to

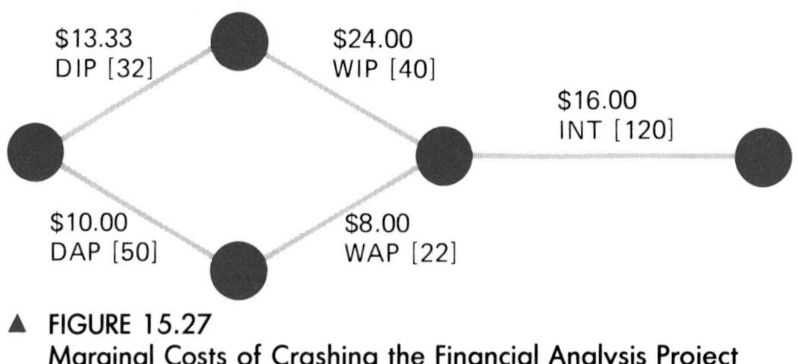

▲ FIGURE 15.27
Marginal Costs of Crashing the Financial Analysis Project

This type of analysis is very useful when your needs dictate reducing the critical path by just a few units.

crash WAP than either of the other two activities on the critical path (\$8 < \$10 and \$8 < \$16), Becky would first crash WAP by 1 hour. This decision yields a project time of 193 hours, a critical path of DAP–WAP–INT, and a total project cost of \$7216 = \$7208 + \$8. If Becky wants to achieve a time of 192 hours, exactly the same analysis would apply, and she would crash WAP by another hour and incur a marginal cost of \$8.

If Becky has crashed WAP by 2 hours to achieve a project time of 192 hours and still wants to crash the project by another hour (to achieve 191), the analysis becomes more complicated. Figure 15.27 shows the situation. The dollar figure in the diagram is the marginal cost of crashing. Note that there are now two critical paths, DIP–WIP–INT and DAP–WAP–INT, and that both require 192 hours. Crashing one of the four activities (DIP, WIP, DAP, or WAP) by 1 hour would bring one path down to 191 hours, but would still leave the project time at 192, since there would still be a critical path of 192 hours. A time of 191 could be obtained only by crashing activities on both paths. If Becky crashed DIP and WAP by 1 hour each it would reduce both paths to 191 hours, and it would cost her \$13.33 + \$8.00 = \$21.33. Alternatively, INT could be crashed by 1 hour for a cost of \$16.00. Can you see that there are other alternatives to consider?

Although it is possible to do this sort of marginal cost analysis in any CPM network, it is clear that it would be difficult and tedious to carry it out in a complicated network. This consideration leads us to an LP formulation of the problem.

A Linear Programming Model

The problem of obtaining a specific project time at minimum cost can be formulated as a linear programming problem. Figure 15.28 (on pp. 690–691) shows the formulation of the financial analysis problem with a limit of 184 hours on the project time. To understand this formulation, let

The decision variables

CWIP = hours crashed on activity WIP

ESWIP = earliest start time for activity WIP

EFINT = earliest finish time for activity INT

The other decision variables follow this same pattern. From these definitions it follows that

The objective function

1. The objective function is the total cost of crashing the network. This is the appropriate objective. The cost of completing the project on normal time is already determined. You can think of management's problem as deciding how much (and where) to crash to obtain the desired earliest finish time at minimum additional cost.

2. Rows 2 through 5 establish limits for the earliest start time for activities WIP, WAP, and INT. For example, rewriting row 2 yields

$$\text{ESWIP} \geq 32 - \text{CDIP}$$

We note that since 32 is the normal time for DIP and CDIP is the amount that DIP is crashed, the right-hand side is the time that activity DIP will take after it has been crashed. Thus, this constraint states that the earliest start time for WIP must be ≥ the modified activity time for DIP. Since DIP is *the only* predecessor for WIP, we know that the earliest start time for WIP is exactly this modified activity time of DIP. You will thus expect to see

$$\text{ESWIP} = 32 - \text{CDIP}$$

The constraints

A ≥ constraint is used rather than an = constraint because, in general, there could be several paths leading into a node, and the earliest start time of an activity leaving that node is determined by the entering path that takes the longest time. This is illustrated by rows 4 and 5. Rewriting these constraints yields

$$\text{row 4} \quad \text{ESINT} \geq 40 - \text{CWIP} + \text{ESWIP}$$

$$\text{row 5} \quad \text{ESINT} \geq 24 - \text{CWAP} + \text{ESWAP}$$

Row 4 states that INT cannot start until WIP is complete, and row 5 makes a similar statement for WAP. It will often be the case that only one of these will be active in an optimal solution.

3. Row 6 is the definition of earliest finish time for activity INT:

$$\text{EFINT} = \text{ESINT} + \underbrace{120 - \text{CINT}}_{\substack{\text{activity time for}\\ \text{INT after crashing}}}$$

4. Rows 7 through 11 limit the amount of crashing on each activity. The limit is given by column (5) in Figure 15.25 "Maximum Crash Hours."

5. Row 12 sets an upper limit on the project time we want to achieve. This constraint depends on the fact that the finish time for activity INT determines the finish time for the overall project. In general, a similar constraint would be required for each activity leading into the terminal mode. Here we have only one such activity, INT.

The solution

The solution shows that WAP should be crashed by 2 hours and INT by 8 hours to achieve a minimum cost reduction of 10 hours in the project completion time (i.e., the optimal value of EFINT is 184, and this is the project completion time). As usual with LP output, however, this is only a small part of the information available. For example, the dual price on row 12 tells us that it will cost $16 to crash the network for 1 additional hour. The right-hand-side ranges show that this rate of $16 per hour holds for another 42 hours. In this simple problem you can see that this next 42 hours of crashing (beyond the first 10) should be done on INT. In general this type of LP sensitivity information can provide useful guidance to management in the attempt to control the progress of large projects.

In concluding this section, we recall the sixth of the questions raised in Section 15.1: "How might I effectively concentrate resources on activities in order to speed up project completion?" In this section we have seen that in a context where time and costs are suitably defined, as in the CPM model, *project crashing* allows management to answer this question.

▼ FIGURE 15.28
LP Solution of the Financial Analysis Problem

```
MIN 13.33 CDIP + 24 CWIP + 10 CDAP + 8 CWAP + 16 CINT
SUBJECT TO
   2) CDIP + ESWIP > = 32
   3) CDAP + ESWAP > = 50
   4) CWIP - ESWIP + ESINT > = 40
   5) CWAP - ESWAP + ESINT > = 24
   6) CINT - ESINT + EFINT = 120
   7) CDIP < = 12
   8) CWIP < = 10
   9) CDAP < = 20
  10) CWAP < = 9
  11) CINT < = 50
  12) EFINT < = 184
```

OBJECTIVE FUNCTION VALUE

144.000000

VARIABLE	VALUE	REDUCED COST
CDIP	0.00	5.33
CWIP	0.00	16.00
CDAP	0.00	2.00
CWAP	2.00	0.00
CINT	8.00	0.00
ESWIP	32.00	0.00
ESWAP	50.00	0.00
ESINT	72.00	0.00
EFINT	184.00	0.00

ROW	SLACK	DUAL PRICES
2	0.00	−8.00
3	0.00	−8.00
4	0.00	−8.00
5	0.00	−8.00
6	0.00	−16.00
7	12.00	0.00
8	10.00	0.00
9	20.00	0.00
10	7.00	0.00
11	42.00	0.00
12	0.00	16.00

SENSITIVITY ANALYSIS
OBJ COEFFICIENT RANGES

VARIABLE	CURRENT COEF	ALLOWABLE INCREASE	ALLOWABLE DECREASE
CDIP	13.33	INFINITY	5.33
CWIP	24.00	INFINITY	16.00
CDAP	10.00	INFINITY	2.00
CWAP	8.00	2.00	5.33
CINT	16.00	5.33	8.00
ESWIP	0.00	5.33	8.00
ESWAP	0.00	2.00	8.00
ESINT	0.00	5.33	8.00
EFINT	0.00	16.00	INFINITY

RIGHTHAND SIDE RANGES

ROW	CURRENT RHS	ALLOWABLE INCREASE	ALLOWABLE DECREASE
2	32.00	2.00	7.00
3	50.00	7.00	2.00
4	40.00	2.00	7.00
5	24.00	7.00	2.00
6	120.00	42.00	8.00
7	12.00	INFINITY	12.00
8	10.00	INFINITY	10.00
9	20.00	INFINITY	20.00
10	9.00	INFINITY	7.00
11	50.00	INFINITY	42.00
12	184.00	8.00	42.00

▲ FIGURE 15.28 (Continued)

We now proceed to discuss the final question raised in Section 15.1: "What controls can be exercised on the flows of expenditures for the various activities throughout the duration of the project in order that the overall budget can be adhered to?"

15.7 Project Cost Management: PERT/Cost

The desirability of a project typically depends on its total costs and revenues. (Discounting may be necessary to express costs and/or returns in current dollars if the project is of long duration.) Once a project has been selected, effective cost management includes two important functions: planning and control.

Planning Costs for the Credit Card Project: The PERT/Cost System

This is a good example of how management science models can be hooked together. First, a PERT network model is made of the Global Oil move, then perhaps an LP model is used to crash to an acceptable time frame, and finally a simple spreadsheet financial model can be made to aid in financial planning. Thus, the output of each model becomes the input for the next, and so it is crucial to constantly check the model results for accuracy.

Large projects can strongly influence the financial situation within a firm. The need to pay for the various activities creates a demand on both the firm's overall budget and the daily cash flow. Obviously, the times at which activities are scheduled determine when budget demands occur.

It is important for a firm to be able to anticipate budget demands in order to be able to handle them economically and effectively. The **PERT/Cost** system is specifically designed to help management anticipate such demands in a clear and consistent manner. PERT/Cost is essentially an alternative approach to cost accounting. Typically, cost accounting systems are organized on a cost center basis (e.g., by departments). The PERT/Cost system is organized on a project basis, where the basic elements of control are the activities.

In order to apply the PERT/Cost system to the project of moving the credit card operation to Des Moines, Becky must now complete Figure 15.8 by filling in the final column, titled "Resources." This is an estimated or "expected" total cost of completing each activity. These expected activity costs, together with the expected activity times, the earliest start time, and the latest start time, are presented in Figure 15.29 for the redefined credit card project. The earliest start and latest start data are taken from the computer solution, Figure 15.16.

Uniform expenditure assumption

The goal of the PERT/Cost system is to construct a graph of budget demands over time. This requires knowledge of how funds will be spent throughout the life of an activity. For example, the demands on the budget are different if the $32,000 for activity E, construct the interior, is due at the beginning of the 8-week activity time or at the end of it. PERT/Cost makes the assumption that expenditures occur uniformly throughout the life of the activity; that is, for E a budget demand of $4000 occurs during each of the 8 weeks.

ACTIVITY	EXPECTED TIME	EARLIEST START	LATEST START	TOTAL RESOURCES REQUIRED ($)
A	3	0	5	2,100
B	5	0	0	5,000
C	3	5	5	1,800
D	4	8	8	4,800
E	8	12	12	32,000
F	2	8	11	1,000
G	4	10	13	2,800
H	2	10	18	7,000
I	5	5	15	4,000
J	3	14	17	30,000
K	3	10	14	1,500
Total				$92,000

▲ FIGURE 15.29
Resource Requirements for the Redesigned Project

End of week assumption

Figure 15.30 shows the budget demands by time if all activities start at their *earliest start time.* This table is constructed by assigning a row to each activity and recording the budget demands for that activity in the appropriate column (week) as determined by the earliest start time. In forming this table, "earliest start" times are interpreted as referring to the end of the appropriate week. Thus activity B starts at time 0 (the end of week 0 = beginning of week 1) and requires 5 weeks to complete. This means that activity C, as shown in Figure 15.30, cannot start until the end of week 5. It lasts 3 weeks and makes a budget demand of $600 per week. This information is summarized in the third row of Figure 15.30.

The total weekly cost is determined by adding down a column, that is, by adding the budget demands during the week from all the activities. For example, the budget demand during the thirteenth week is $5200, the sum of $4000 from E, $700 from G, and $500 from K.

The total project cost is found by cumulating the weekly costs from the beginning of the project. For example, note that the weekly cost is $1700 for each of the first 3 weeks. The total project cost after 3 weeks is therefore $5100. The total cost at the end of the project (week 20) must, of course, be the total cost for the entire project.

Figure 15.31 creates the profile of budget demands over time if each activity starts at its *latest start time.*

The information from Figures 15.30 and 15.31 is combined in Figure 15.32. The upper line is a plot of the earliest start time costs from Figure 15.30, and the lower line is a plot of the latest start time costs from Figure 15.31. The shaded area between the lines shows the area of feasible cumulative budgets for total project costs if the project is completed on time. The fact that the actual budget demands

ACTIVITY	COST PER WEEK ($)																			
	1	2	3	4	5	6	7	8	9	10	11	12	13	14	15	16	17	18	19	20
A	700	700	700																	
B	1,000	1,000	1,000	1,000	1,000															
C						600	600	600												
D									1,200	1,200	1,200	1,200								
E													4,000	4,000	4,000	4,000	4,000	4,000	4,000	4,000
F									500	500										
G											700	700	700	700						
H											3,500	3,500								
I						800	800	800	800	800										
J															10,000	10,000	10,000			
K											500	500	500							
Weekly Cost	1,700	1,700	1,700	1,000	1,000	1,400	1,400	1,400	2,500	2,500	5,900	5,900	5,200	4,700	14,000	14,000	14,000	4,000	4,000	4,000
Cumulative Project Cost	1,700	3,400	5,100	6,100	7,100	8,500	9,900	11,300	13,800	16,300	22,200	28,100	33,500	38,000	52,000	66,000	80,000	84,000	88,000	92,000

▲ FIGURE 15.30
Budget Demands: Earliest Start Time

ACTIVITY	COST PER WEEK ($)																			
	1	2	3	4	5	6	7	8	9	10	11	12	13	14	15	16	17	18	19	20
A						700	700	700												
B	1,000	1,000	1,000	1,000	1,000															
C						600	600	600												
D									1,200	1,200	1,200	1,200								
E													4,000	4,000	4,000	4,000	4,000	4,000	4,000	4,000
F												500	500							
G														700	700	700	700			
H																			3,500	3,500
I																800	800	800	800	800
J																		10,000	10,000	10,000
K															500	500	500			
Weekly Cost	1,000	1,000	1,000	1,000	1,000	1,300	1,300	1,300	1,200	1,200	1,200	1,700	4,500	4,700	5,200	6,000	6,000	14,800	18,300	18,300
Cumulative Project Cost	1,000	2,000	3,000	4,000	5,000	6,300	7,600	8,900	10,100	11,300	12,500	14,200	18,700	23,400	28,600	34,600	40,600	55,400	73,700	92,000

▲ FIGURE 15.31
Budget Demands: Latest Start Time

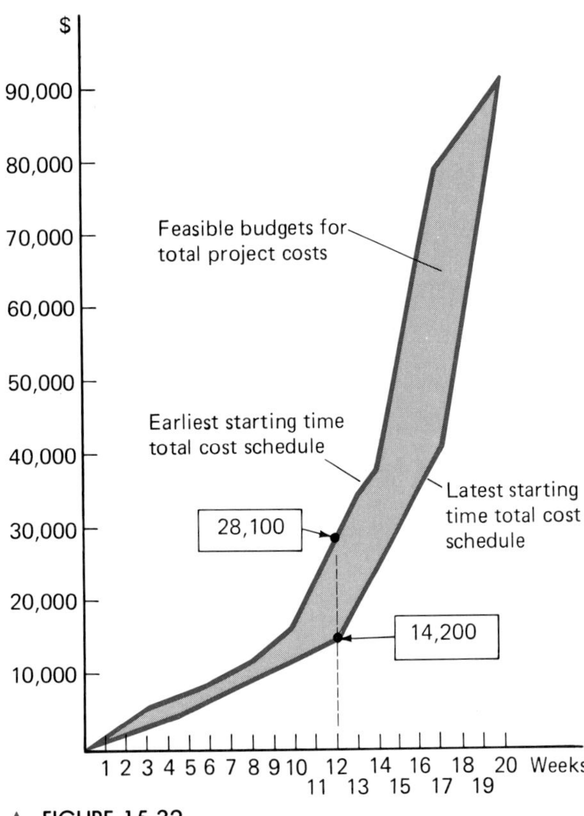

▲ FIGURE 15.32
Cumulative Budget Demands vs. Time

must fall within the envelope created by the earliest start time and the latest start time makes it easy for management to anticipate its cumulative expenditures. For example, Becky can see that by the end of week 12 Global Oil will have to have spent between $14,200 and $28,100.

We have progressed step by step through the budget calculations for the PERT/Cost planning system because this is a useful exercise from the pedagogical point of view. In practice these calculations are typically done on a computer. Figure 15.33 shows the computer output that corresponds to Figures 15.30 and 15.31.

Controlling Project Costs

The concept behind any control system is to compare the *actual performance* with *planned performance* and to take remedial action if it is necessary. The thermostat in your house is a control system that operates continuously in time by comparing the actual temperature with the desired temperature and turning the furnace (air conditioner) off or on as necessary.

The PERT/Cost system compares actual costs or budgeted project costs at regular intervals so that management has an early indication if the project is not proceeding according to plan. Management is then in a position to take appropriate action.

The PERT/Cost Control Report. Figure 15.34 is a PERT/Cost *control report* prepared 11 weeks after the start of the redefined project to move the credit card operation to Des Moines. The labels on the columns indicate how the report is prepared. Column (4), the actual cost, and column (3), the budgeted cost, provide the basic information used in the control function. The actual cost, column (4), is

RESOURCE USAGE PROFILE ACCORDING TO EARLIEST START TIME

TIME INTERVAL		RESOURCE USAGE	
FROM END OF WEEK	TO END OF WEEK	WEEKLY	CUMULATIVE
0.00→	3.00	1700.00	5100.00
3.00→	5.00	1000.00	7100.00
5.00→	8.00	1400.00	11300.00
8.00→	10.00	2500.00	16300.00
10.00→	12.00	5900.00	28100.00
12.00→	13.00	5200.00	33300.00
13.00→	14.00	4700.00	38000.00
14.00→	17.00	14000.00	80000.00
17.00→	20.00	4000.00	92000.00

RESOURCE USAGE PROFILE ACCORDING TO LATEST START TIME

TIME INTERVAL		RESOURCE USAGE	
FROM END OF WEEK	TO END OF WEEK	WEEKLY	CUMULATIVE
0.00→	5.00	1000.00	5000.00
5.00→	8.00	1300.00	8900.00
8.00→	11.00	1200.00	12500.00
11.00→	12.00	1700.00	14200.00
12.00→	13.00	4500.00	18700.00
13.00→	14.00	4700.00	23400.00
14.00→	15.00	5200.00	28600.00
15.00→	17.00	6000.00	40600.00
17.00→	18.00	14800.00	55400.00
18.00→	20.00	18300.00	92000.00

▲ FIGURE 15.33
Computer Analysis of Budget Demands

▼ FIGURE 15.34
Project Costs after 11 Weeks

ACTIVITY	(1) PERCENT COMPLETE	(2) BUDGET ($)	(3) [(1)/100] × (2) BUDGETED COST TO DATE ($)	(4) ACTUAL COST TO DATE ($)	(5) (4)-(3) COST OVERRUN TO DATE ($)
A	100	2,100	2,100	2,300	200
B	100	5,000	5,000	4,900	(100)
C	100	1,800	1,800	1,800	0
D	75	4,800	3,600	4,600	1,000
E	0	32,000	0	0	0
F	100	1,000	1,000	1,200	200
G	25	2,800	700	1,400	700
H	50	7,000	3,500	5,400	1,900
I	20	4,000	800	500	(300)
J	0	30,000	0	0	0
K	0	1,500	0	0	0
Total		92,000	18,500	22,100	3,600

self-explanatory. *The budgeted cost, column (3), is calculated on the assumption that the percentage of budget used up by an activity is the same as the percentage of that activity that is completed.* Thus, when an activity is 50% complete, its budgeted cost is 50% of the entire budget (column [2]) for that activity. Note that if an activity is completed, the entry in column (1) is 100, and this means the entry in column (3) will be the same as the entry in column (2).

Consider, for example, activity A, "select office site." We see from column (1) of Figure 15.34 that this activity, by the end of week 11, is 100% complete. Thus, its budgeted cost, column (3), is equal to its entire budget (column [2]) of $2100. Since its actual cost is $2300, there is a cost overrun of $200. This number is recorded in the last column. A similar interpretation applies to activity I, "make financial arrangements." It is 20% complete and has a budget of $4000; thus, its budgeted cost is $800 ($800 = 0.20 × $4000). Since only $500 has been spent, there is a budget surplus of $300. The parentheses in the last column indicate a budget surplus.

In this situation, since activities A and F are already completed, their cost overruns cannot be corrected. However, activities D, G, and H, none of which are yet complete, are showing significant overruns to date, and these activities should be promptly reviewed. This type of periodic managerial intervention is often required to keep the total project cost within the budget.

Potential Implementation Problems. Although PERT/Cost can provide an effective control procedure, it is well to be aware of potential implementation problems. For example, the required recording of data can involve significant clerical effort, especially when many projects with many activities are under way. Moreover, some costs, such as overhead, may be common to several activities. The allocation of such common costs can be problematic. Finally, as we mentioned at the beginning of Section 15.7, the PERT/Cost system differs in organization from typical cost accounting systems. The typical departmental cost center orientation needs to be substantially revised to handle the PERT/Cost activity-oriented system. Such redesign may be politically as well as materially expensive.

15.8 Notes on Implementation

EDS (Electronic Data Systems) has been using AutoCAD (an automatic drafting program) to draw PERT charts for clients for several years now. They find that this visual aid helps them and their clients to keep projects on track, to spot possible problems early on, and acts as a good communication device. The charts are printed across several pages, making a large "banner" that can be posted in the office.

Some 25 years after its inception, the critical path concept is an important part of current practice. Almost any time you have a large project with a number of interrelated activities, you will find a network-based planning and reporting system being used. Over time, the distinctions between PERT and CPM have become blurred. Firms have developed their own internal computer-based models incorporating those features of the original PERT and CPM systems that are important to their specific activity.

It is common to think of using critical path methods on large one-of-a-kind projects (e.g., the U.S. Space Shuttle). However, the methods can and do apply to activities that occur at quite regular intervals. A good example of such an activity is the major overhaul of the dragline in a particular coal mining operation. This maintenance must be performed on a fairly regular schedule and is of major importance because when the dragline is not operating, the mine is not operating. The firm can and does use the network for the previous overhaul in planning for an upcoming overhaul. The network plays an important role in assuring that all those involved understand the various steps and their interrelationship, as well as ensuring that all the requisite parts and materials are available when they are needed. Given the turnover in personnel, and human frailties, the network serves as a convenient way to capture past experience. The activities associated with the overhaul vary from time to time, so the chart must be reworked, but the previous version generally provides a good starting point.

For our example firm, estimating time variability is not an important part of creating their PERT-CPM network. Indeed, they rely on a single best estimate rather than the three that are part of the PERT approach. The crucial element in developing an economical plan for the overhaul is the availability of various skilled workers (electricians, pipefitters, and so on). Each time an overhaul is to be performed, the tasks vary somewhat, and thus the demand for workers varies from year to year. In addition, the supply of available workers within the firm varies from time to time depending on the level of other activities. The planning operation typically involves running the model under a variety of assumptions. Alternatives might include regular employees working regular time, regular employees doubling up (i.e., working two shifts), bringing in outside workers, and so on. Such calculations can make it clear, for example, it pays to spend $20,000 in overtime for electricians if it puts the mine back in operation a day earlier.

Impact of the computer

The computer has had a major impact on the use of CPM and PERT. Large construction projects may require 1000 or more nodes. In the 1960s it was not unusual to find the network diagram for such a project spread out over three walls of a room that was dedicated to that purpose for the duration of the project. Major changes in the plan were a major pain in their own right, and communication among the multiple contractors was cumbersome. The computer has changed all of that. The analysis is now done on a computer. Multiple runs spanning the life of the project are the order of the day. In the early phases it is important to ensure that orders for major components are placed early enough. Complicated systems (i.e., generators, furnaces, and so on) may have a delivery time of several years. Regular updating based on supplier reports enables management to see when it is necessary to expedite an order. New information is fed into the model, and the program is rerun on a weekly basis. Obviously, the information obtained from such runs influences the allocation of resources. It may even affect the design of the project. If a cost control report more or less like the one shown in Figure 15.34 indicates serious cost overruns early enough, later parts of the project may be redesigned. For example, one firm reported reworking a heating plant design based on one boiler rather than two after the cost of excavation and driving piles ran far ahead of budget. This change enabled the firm to bring the project in on time *and* within budget.

Today, there is a whole host of microcomputer software that will aid in project management, combining PERT and CPM with budget information and control. It is quite a simple matter to use the software to draw the boxes (actually combining activities and events) and then to connect them by pointing to the activities that precede each other. The program does the rest (determining the critical path, earliest and latest starting and finishing times).

15.9 Summary

This chapter dealt with the role of PERT and CPM in project management. The fundamental concept is to represent a project as a network. Section 15.2 showed how to use an activity list to construct a network diagram for a project, where the activity list identifies each activity in the project and its immediate predecessors. Section 15.3 showed how the network diagram and the expected activity times are used to determine the critical path, which is a longest path through the network. In the process, the terms *earliest start time, earliest finish time, latest start time, latest finish time,* and *slack* were defined.

Section 15.4 introduced the notion of variability in activity times. It dealt with two main topics: the PERT system of estimating times and the probability that all the activities on the critical path will be completed by a specified date. The PERT system of estimating time is based on the assumption that activity time has a beta distribution. It uses an optimistic, a most probable, and a pessimistic time estimate to derive the expected activity time and the standard deviation of the activity time.

Management would like to know the probability that the project under consideration will be completed by a specific date. If one assumes that activity times are independent and that the sum of the activity times on the critical path has a normal distribution, it is a straightforward exercise to calculate *the probability that the critical path will be completed by a specified date.* This is not the probability that the project will ultimately be completed by the specified date, for the effect of randomness could turn a supposedly noncritical path into a critical one. However, this does give an upper estimate for the probability that the overall project will be completed by a specific date.

Section 15.6 presented the CPM framework for analyzing the problem of time–cost trade-offs. The amount of time that an activity takes is determined by the level of resources devoted to that activity. The model in this section employs the notion of project crashing. The model is intended to help management select a completion time for each activity so as to achieve a specified completion date for the overall project at minimum cost. The basic input for the model is a set of functions, one for each activity. Each function portrays the activity cost as a linear function of activity time within specified limits on the time. These data are then used either in a marginal cost analysis or in a linear programming model to select the best activity times.

Section 15.7 considered project cost management via the PERT/Cost system. It dealt with both a cost planning and a cost control model. The planning model produces a graph of the feasible budget demands as a function of time. This graph is constructed from the resource usage profiles based on the earliest start time and the latest start time.

The project cost control model is a system of comparing actual costs with budgeted costs. The budgeted cost model uses the assumption that for partially completed activities, the budgeted cost is equal to the budget for the completed activity multiplied by the proportion of the activity that has been completed. The model allows management to recognize cost overruns on various activities before they are completed.

Key Terms

PERT. An acronym for Program Evaluation Review Technique, a method for scheduling and controlling projects. (*p. 664*)

CPM. An acronym for Critical Path Method, a method for scheduling and controlling projects. (*p. 664*)

Activity List. A list of jobs in a project with their immediate predecessors, expected times, and resources required. (*p. 665*)

Immediate Predecessors. Those activities that must be completed immediately prior to the start of the activity in question. (*p. 665*)

Network Diagram. A graphical method of representing a project with nodes and arcs. (*p. 667*)

Branch. A line in a PERT network indicating an activity. Also called an *arc.* (*p. 667*)

Node. A circle in a PERT network indicating the completion of certain activities and the initiation of others. (*p. 667*)

Event. The completion of all activities leading into a node in a PERT network. (*p. 667*)

Activity. A job that must be completed as part of a project, signified by a branch in a PERT network. (*p. 667*)

Dummy Activity. An imaginary activity that requires no time and is used either (1) to maintain the appropriate precedence relationships in a PERT network diagram or (2) as required by some computer programs when two activities both leave the same node and then terminate at another node together. (*p. 667*)

Path. A sequence of activities leading from the starting node to the completion node of a network. (*p. 670*)

Critical Path. A sequence of activities that determines the longest path through the network that yields the minimum time in which an entire project can be completed. (*p. 671*)

Critical Activities. The activities on the critical path. (*p. 671*)

Earliest Start Time. In a PERT network, the earliest moment at which an activity can start. (*p. 671*)

Earliest Finish Time. In a PERT network, the earliest moment at which an activity can be completed. (*p. 671*)

Forward Pass. The process of moving along a network from beginning to end, computing the earliest start time and earliest finish time for each activity. (*p. 672*)

Backward Pass. The process of moving backward along a network from end to beginning, computing the latest start time and latest finish time for each activity. (*p. 673*)

Latest Start Time. In a PERT network, the latest moment at which an activity can start without delaying completion of the overall project. (*p. 673*)

Latest Finish Time. The latest time at which an activity can be completed without delaying the completion of the overall project. (*p. 673*)

Slack. The time that an activity can be delayed beyond its earliest start time without delaying the completion of the overall project. (*p. 674*)

Optimistic Time. The time required to complete an activity if everything goes perfectly. (*p. 678*)

Most Probable Time. The time required to complete an activity under normal circumstances. (*p. 678*)

Pessimistic Time. The time required to complete an activity under the most unfavorable conditions. (*p. 678*)

Beta Distribution. A probability distribution used to model the activity times in PERT. (*p. 678*)

Normal Time. In CPM, the maximum time for completion of an activity, corresponding to minimal resource usage. (*p. 686*)

Normal Cost. The cost required to achieve the normal time. (*p. 686*)

Crash Time. In CPM, the minimum possible time for completion of an activity, corresponding to maximal resource concentration. (*p. 686*)

Crash Cost. The cost required to achieve the crash time. (*p. 686*)

Crashing. A term in the CPM method describing the process of reducing the time required to complete an activity. (*p. 687*)

PERT/Cost. A system for determining the feasible patterns of cash flow during a project. (*p. 691*)

▶ Major Concepts Quiz

True–False

1. T F In a PERT network diagram, each activity is represented by a circle called a node.

2. T F The term *event* is used to refer to nodes in a PERT network.

3. T F A dummy activity is required in a correct network representation of the following activity list.

ACTIVITY	IMMEDIATE PREDECESSORS
1	—
2	—
3	1
4	2, 3
5	2
6	5

4. T F The earliest finish time for an activity depends on the earliest finish time for the project.

5. **T F** The latest finish time for an activity depends on the earliest finish time for the project.
6. **T F** All activities on the critical path have their latest finish time equal to their earliest start time.
7. **T F** A strategic analysis of a PERT network concentrates on the allocation of resources to reduce the time on the critical path.
8. **T F** The probability of completing the project by time T is equal to the probability of completing the critical path by time T.
9. **T F** The standard deviation of an activity time is estimated as $(b - a)/6$, where b is the pessimistic and a is the optimistic time.
10. **T F** The CPM approach to time–cost trade-offs assumes that cost is a linear function of time.
11. **T F** The LP formulation of the network crashing problem minimizes the total cost of crashing subject to an upper bound on project duration.
12. **T F** In the PERT/Cost model the earliest starting time total cost schedule always is less than or equal to the latest starting time total cost schedule.
13. **T F** Time variabilities leading to a longer-than-expected total time for the critical path will always extend the project completion date.
14. **T F** If a noncritical activity is delayed more than its slack time, all other factors remaining unchanged, then the project completion date will be extended.
15. **T F** Gantt charts provide useful immediate predecessor information.

Multiple Choice

16. Of all paths through the network, the critical path
    a. has the maximum expected time
    b. has the minimum expected time
    c. has the maximum actual time
    d. has the minimum actual time

17. The earliest start time (ES) for an activity leaving node C
    a. is the Max of the earliest finish times for all activities entering node C
    b. equals the earliest finish time for the same activity minus its expected activity time
    c. depends on all paths leading from the start through node C
    d. all of the above

18. The latest finish time for an activity entering node H
    a. equals the Max of the latest start times for all activities leaving node H
    b. depends on the latest finish time for the project
    c. equals the latest start time minus the activity time for the same activity
    d. none of the above

19. The slack for activity G
    a. equals LF for G − LS for G
    b. equals EF for G − ES for G
    c. equals LS for G − ES for G
    d. none of the above

20. Estimating expected activity times in a PERT network
    a. makes use of three estimates
    b. puts the greatest weight on the most likely time estimate
    c. is motivated by the beta distribution
    d. all of the above

21. The calculation of the probability that the critical path will be completed by time T
    a. assumes that activity times are statistically independent
    b. assumes that total time of the critical path has approximately a beta distribution
    c. requires knowledge of the standard deviation for all activities in the network
    d. all of the above

22. In the CPM time–cost trade-off function
   a. the cost at normal time is 0
   b. within the range of feasible times, the activity cost increases linearly as time increases
   c. cost decreases linearly as time increases
   d. none of the above

23. The marginal cost of crashing a network could change when
   a. the activity being crashed reaches its crash time
   b. the activity being crashed reaches a point where another path is also critical
   c. both a and b

24. Fundamental ideas in the LP network crashing models are
   a. activity time equals normal time + crash time
   b. earliest start time for an activity leaving a node equals the Max of the earliest finish times for activities leaving that node
   c. earliest finish time equals latest finish time minus activity time
   d. none of the above

25. The PERT/Cost model assumes that
   a. each activity achieves its optimistic time
   b. the costs are uniformly distributed over the life of the activity
   c. activity times are statistically independent
   d. none of the above

26. The PERT/Cost control report
   a. requires a budget for each activity
   b. requires a report on the percentage of completion of each activity
   c. calculates cost overruns
   d. all of the above

Answers

1. F	**8.** F	**15.** F	**22.** c
2. T	**9.** T	**16.** a	**23.** c
3. T	**10.** T	**17.** d	**24.** d
4. F	**11.** T	**18.** b	**25.** b
5. T	**12.** F	**19.** c	**26.** d
6. F	**13.** T	**20.** d	
7. F	**14.** T	**21.** a	

Problems

2	-
1	2
3	1
4	3
6	4
5	1
8	1
7	8
10	8,5
9	6,7,10

15-1. ▲▲ The Build-Rite Construction Company has identified 10 activities that take place in building a house. They are

1. Walls and Ceiling (erect the wall frames and ceiling joists).
2. Foundation (pour the foundation slab).
3. Roof Timbers (put up the roof timbers).
4. Roof Sheathing (install roof sheathing over the timbers).
5. Electrical Wiring (install the electrical wiring).
6. Roof Shingles (shingle the roof).
7. Exterior Siding (put on the exterior siding).
8. Windows (install the window units).
9. Paint (paint the interior and exterior).
10. Inside Wall Board (hang the inside wall board).

In addition, the following customs are typically observed:

1. Wiring is done from the interior side of the wall, while the window unit is mounted after the wall frame has been erected.
2. Inside wall board and exterior siding are installed over the window unit.
3. Painting is not begun until the house is watertight.

Make a list showing each activity and its immediate predecessors.

1	-
2	-
3	-
4	1
5	1, 2
6	2, 3

15-2. ▲ Quacker Mills hires engineering undergraduates and moves them through six management experiences (activities) to prepare them to be plant managers. There are three disciplines and two positions (starting and advanced) in each discipline. These six activities are shown in Figure 15.35. Further, a person who has not been a production line engineer cannot be department head, nor can someone who has not been a foreperson be a product line scheduler. Make an activity list showing each activity and its immediate predecessors.

	DISCIPLINE		
	PLANT ENGINEERING	**LINE SUPERVISION**	**PRODUCTION PLANNING**
Starting	Production Line Engineer 1	Foreperson 2	Assistant Product Line Scheduler 3
Advanced	Plant Engineer 4	Department Head 5	Product Line Scheduler 6

▲ FIGURE 15.35

See IM

15-3. ▲ Construct the network diagram for the house construction system used by Build-Rite Construction Company in Problem 15-1.

See IM

15-4. ▲ Construct a CPM network diagram of the activities given in Figure 15.36.

Activity	Immediate Predecessors
1	—
2	—
3	2
4	1,3
5	2
6	1,5
7	1,5
8	2
9	4,6
10	6
11	7,8
12	9,10,11

▲ FIGURE 15.36

See IM; critical path: 2–1–3–4–6–9

15-5. ▲ Build-Rite has estimated the times given in Figure 15.37 as necessary to complete each of the tasks involved in building a house.
For each activity, give the

(a) Earliest start time.
(b) Earliest finish time.
(c) Latest start time.
(d) Latest finish time.
(e) Slack.

In addition, identify the critical path.

ACTIVITY NUMBER	ACTIVITY	IMMEDIATE PREDECESSORS	EXPECTED TIME (DAYS)
1	Walls and Ceiling	2	5
2	Foundation	—	3
3	Roof Timbers	1	2
4	Roof Sheathing	3	3
5	Electrical Wiring	1	4
6	Roof Shingles	4	8
7	Exterior Siding	8	5
8	Windows	1	2
9	Paint	6, 7, 10	2
10	Inside Wall Board	8, 5	3

▲ FIGURE 15.37

See IM; critical path: A–B–G–I–K–M

15-6. ▲▲ As a project manager, you are faced with the activity network and estimated activity times shown in Figure 15.38. For each activity, give the

(a) Earliest start time

(b) Earliest finish time

(c) Latest start time

(d) Latest finish time

(e) Slack

In addition, identify the critical path.

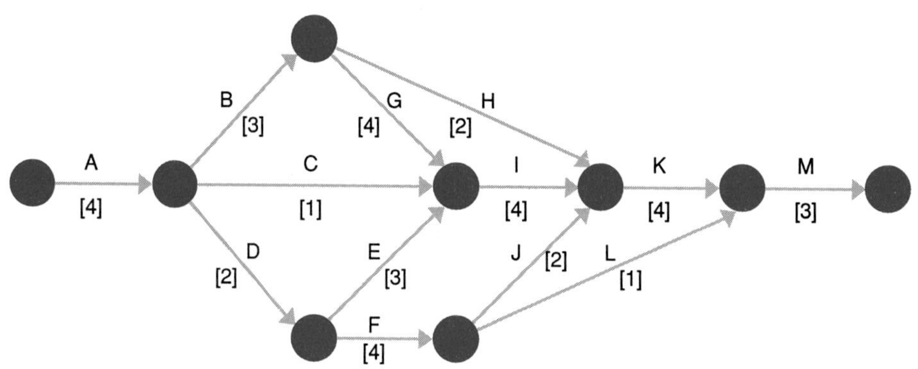

▲ FIGURE 15.38

(a) See IM; critical path: B–E–H–K–M
(b) savings = 9

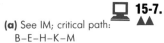

15-7. ▲▲ You are called in as a production consultant. The plant currently uses a PERT-CPM approach to a production run described by the activity network of Figure 15.39. Based on your evaluation, however, the immediate predecessors of each activity are as follows:

ACTIVITY	IMMEDIATE PREDECESSORS
A	—
B	—
C	A
D	B
E	B
F	C
G	D
H	E
I	G
J	E
K	H
L	F
M	L, I, K, J

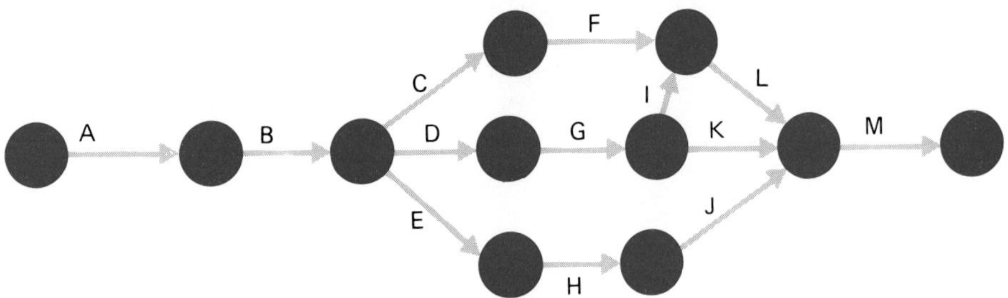

▲ FIGURE 15.39

(a) Draw the revised activity network.

(b) Compute earliest and latest start and finish times for the revised network based on the assumption that each activity takes 1 hour longer than its alphabetic predecessor (i.e., A = 1 hour, B = 2 hours, etc.). Find the slack of each activity. Identify the critical path. How much less time does the production run take under this revised activity network than it did with the original network?

(a) A–B–D–G; 14 hours
(b) 5 hours (see IM)

15-8. ▲▲▲ Consider the network and activity times shown in Figure 15.40. You would like to reduce the minimum time to complete the project. Suppose that you can reduce an activity time as much as you like as long as you increase some other activity or activities by the same amount. For example, you can reduce G by 1 hour if you increase C and D by 1/2 hour each. Assume that activity times of zero are permissible.

(a) Find the current critical path and the minimum time required to complete the project.

(b) Reallocate times to achieve the minimum possible time to complete the project. Note that in this network, the total of all activity times must equal the current total 20 hours.

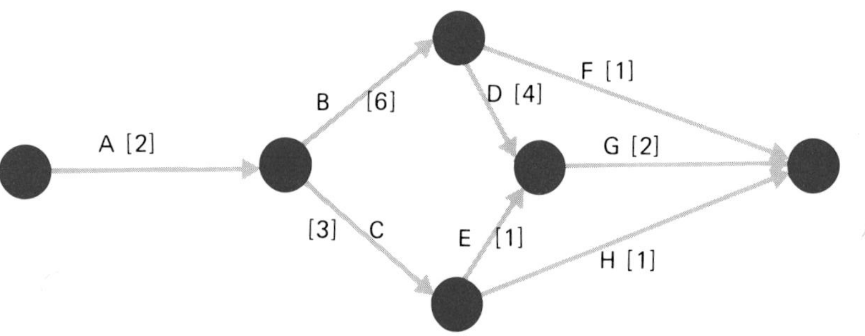

▲ FIGURE 15.40

See IM

15-9. ▲ On the basis of company history, Build-Rite's management has determined that the optimistic, most probable, and pessimistic times for each activity are as follows:

ACTIVITY NUMBER	ACTIVITY	OPTIMISTIC TIME (DAYS) a	MOST PROBABLE TIME (DAYS) m	PESSIMISTIC TIME (DAYS) b
1	Walls and Ceiling	3	5	7
2	Foundation	2	3	4
3	Roof Timbers	1	2	3
4	Roof Sheathing	1	2	9
5	Electrical Wiring	4	4	4
6	Roof Shingles	4	8	12
7	Exterior Siding	1	3	17
8	Windows	1	2	3
9	Paint	2	2	2
10	Inside Wall Board	2	3	4

Compute the expected activity time and the standard deviation for each activity.

A–B–F–H–J

15-10. On the basis of the activity network shown in Figure 15.41 and the associated activity times given below, compute the expected value and the standard deviation for each activity time. Find the earliest start times, earliest finish times, latest start times, latest finish times, and slack for each activity. Specify the critical path.

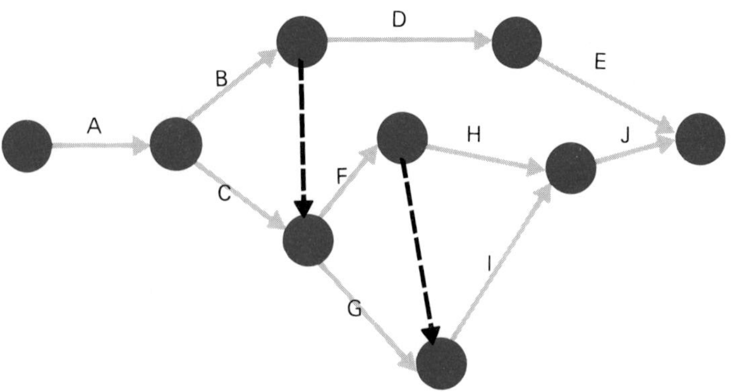

▲ FIGURE 15.41

ACTIVITY	OPTIMISTIC	MOST PROBABLE	PESSIMISTIC
A	2	3	4
B	2	4	6
C	1	2	3
D	1	3	5
E	2	3	4
F	1	4	7
G	2	2	2
H	2	5	8
I	1	3	5
J	2	3	4

P (completion time ≤ 12) = 0
P (completion time ≤ 25) = 0.84
Probability current critical path completed within 25 days ≥ probability project completed within 25 days.

15-11. Assume that activity times in Build-Rite's activity network (see Problems 15-1, 15-5, and 15-9) are independent of each other and that the sum of any combination of activity times is normally distributed. What is the probability that all the activities on the current critical path will be completed within 12 days? Within 25 days? Is this the same as the probability that a house will be completed in 25 days? Comment.

(a) 0.73
(b) 21.7 weeks

15-12. For the network in Problem 15-10, answer the following questions:

(a) Under the usual assumptions, find the probability that the activities on the critical path will be completed within 20 weeks.

(b) How many weeks should be allowed to give a 95% probability of completing the critical path on time?

(a) See IM
(b) $288
(c) $30; not possible

15-13. Build-Rite's engineers have calculated the cost of completing each activity in both normal time and crash time, where the values for normal time and crash time, respectively, correspond to the estimates of expected time and optimistic time from Problem 15-9. Their results are below.

(a) Specify the normal time, normal cost, crash time, crash cost, maximum crash days, and cost per crash day for each activity. Assume linear cost relationships.

(b) Compute the expected cost of the project (based on normal time).

(c) Suppose that the company has to reduce the completion time by 7 days. How much would this reduction cost? How much would it cost to reduce the completion time by 11 days?

NUMBER	ACTIVITY	NORMAL COST ($)	CRASH COST ($)
1	Walls and Ceiling	50	72
2	Foundation	20	30
3	Roof Timbers	15	30
4	Roof Sheathing	8	20
5	Electrical Wiring	30	30
6	Roof Shingles	13	21
7	Exterior Siding	45	65
8	Windows	45	52
9	Paint	40	40
10	Inside Wall Board	22	34

(a) See IM
(b) 19 weeks—$226; 18 weeks—$228; 17 weeks—$233
(c) See IM

15-14. ▲▲▲ Consider the activity network in Problem 15-10. The following are estimates of costs for completion in crash time and normal time, where the times correspond to the optimistic and expected time, respectively:

ACTIVITY	CRASH COST ($)	NORMAL COST ($)
A	20	12
B	50	40
C	40	30
D	20	14
E	60	45
F	35	20
G	30	30
H	25	10
I	30	15
J	12	10

(a) Prepare a table showing the normal time, normal cost, crash time, crash cost, maximum crash weeks, and cost per crash week for each activity.

(b) What would be the minimum cost of the project if it were to be completed in
(i) 19 weeks?
(ii) 18 weeks?
(iii) 17 weeks?

(c) Formulate a linear programming model that will assess the additional cost of reducing the completion time to 9 weeks.

See IM

15-15. ▲▲▲ Refer to Problems 15-3 and 15-13 and formulate a linear programming model that would allow Build-Rite to assess the cost of crashing its activity network by x hours.

(a) A–C–F–G; 16
(b) See IM

15-16. ▲▲▲ Consider the activity network and normal activity times shown in Figure 15.42, as well as the data in the table following.

▼ FIGURE 15.42

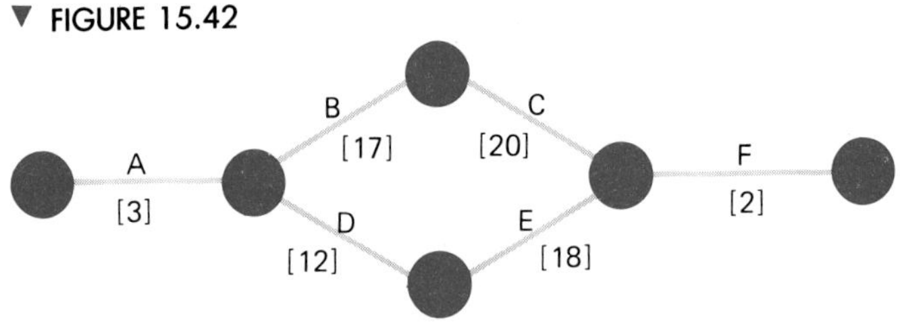

ACTIVITY	COST/CRASH UNIT	MAX. CRASH UNITS
A	10	2
B	20	8
C	5	5
D	5	5
E	15	2
F	—	0

(a) Find the critical path and the minimum time required to complete the project.

(b) Prepare a table showing which activities to crash as project length decreases.

See IM

15-17. ▲▲ Use the normal costs from Problem 15-13 and the time data from Problem 15-5 to construct early-start and late-start cost tables and the graph of cumulative expenditures versus time for Build-Rite.

See IM

15-18. ▲▲ The resources required for the activities in Problem 15-6 are given below. Construct early-start and late-start cost tables, and graph cumulative budget demands versus time, for both schedules.

ACTIVITY	TOTAL RESOURCES REQUIRED ($)
A	2,800
B	3,000
C	900
D	3,000
E	6,000
F	12,000
G	3,200
H	3,200
I	7,200
J	7,000
K	2,400
L	2,000
M	4,500

See IM

15-19. ▲▲ Build Rite's record of historical expenditures at the end of day 15 is as follows:

ACTIVITY NUMBER	ACTIVITY	COST INCURRED TO DATE ($)
2	Foundation	22
1	Walls and Ceiling	46
3	Roof Timber	15
4	Roof Sheathing	10
6	Roof Shingles	4.50
5	Electrical Wiring	20
8	Windows	22.50
10	Inside Wall Board	20
7	Exterior Siding	40
9	Paint	0

Evaluate the current project costs based on the assumptions that

(a) All activities begin on the earliest possible date and that the expected value is the time required.

(b) All activities begin on the latest possible start date and that the expected value is the time required.

In both cases, assume that budgeted cost is equal to the budget for the completed activity multiplied by the proportion of the activity that is complete.

See IM

15-20. ▲ Review the data for Problem 15-18. Prepare an analysis of the cost of the project to date if the figures below represent the status as of the end of the eighth unit of time. Assume that the budgeted cost is equal to the budget for the completed activity multiplied by the proportion of the activity that is complete.

ACTIVITY	% COMPLETE	COST TO DATE ($)
A	100	2,700
B	100	3,200
C	100	900
D	100	3,500
E	50	2,000
F	70	8,000
G	20	700
H	50	1,700
I	0	0
J	0	1,000
K	0	0
L	0	500
M	0	0

26 − 11.75 = 14.25; see IM

15-21. ▲▲▲ This is a more complex version of Problem 15-8. As the production supervisor for the Hurricane Fan Company, you have used PERT-CPM techniques to schedule your production runs. Your current activity network and activity times are shown in Figure 15.43. A production consultant has pointed out that, due to the similarity in job skills needed for each activity, resources are perfectly transferable between activities (i.e., the time required to do an activity can be reduced by any amount by increasing the time required for another job by the same amount). If the consultant is correct, how much can the time needed for each production run be reduced?

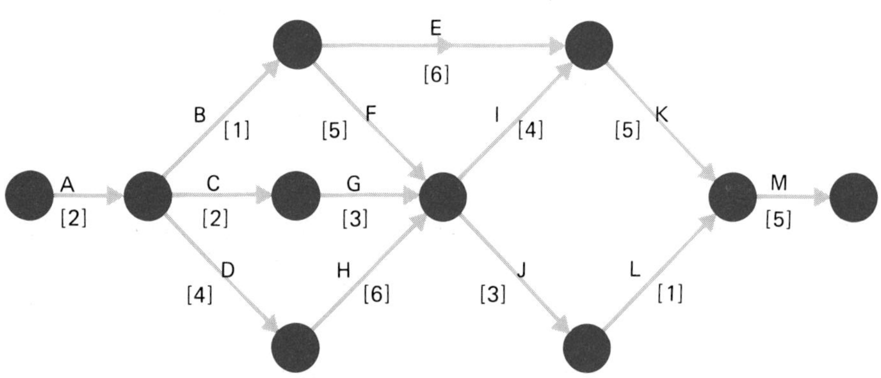

▲ FIGURE 15.43

See IM

15-22. ▲▲▲ This problem is a further examination of the PERT assumptions. Consider a project with five activities and the precedence relationships given in the table on page 710. The Range column indicates the possible range of days it might take to complete an activity.

(a) Suppose that any time within the range is equally likely. Use the standard PERT analysis and compute the expected project length. Also calculate the probability that the project will be completed in the expected project length + 5 days. Use the

Activity	Predecessors	Range
A	none	20 to 60
B	none	25 to 29
C	A	20 to 60
D	B	25 to 29
E	D	25 to 29

fact that if the range is a to b then the mean time is $\frac{(a + b)}{2}$ and the variance of the time is $\frac{(b - a)^2}{12}$.

(b) Now set up a spreadsheet to simulate the project. To generate an activity time between a and b use the formula $a + (b - a)$*@RAND or @UNIFORM(a, b) if you have @RISK. Simulate 100 trials and compute the mean project length. Is it larger or smaller than your previous answer? Why? What is the probability that the project will be completed before the expected time from part (a) + 5 days. Is it larger or smaller than your previous answer? Why?

See IM

15-23. ▲▲▲ This problem is the same as 15-22, but now assume that the activity times are normally distributed with the following means and standard deviations:

Activity	Mean	Standard Deviation
A	40	11.5
B	27	1.15
C	40	11.5
D	27	1.15
E	27	1.15

(a) Use the standard PERT analysis and compute the expected project length. Also calculate the probability that the project will be completed in the expected project length + 5 days. Is your answer the same as in part (a) of Problem 15-22? Why?

(b) Now set up a spreadsheet to simulate the project. To generate an activity time with mean μ and standard deviation σ use the formula

$$\mu + \sigma\text{*@SQRT}(-2\text{*@LN(@RAND))*@SIN(2*@PI*@RAND)}$$

or @NORMAL(μ, σ) if you have @RISK. Simulate 100 trials and compute the mean project length. Is it larger or smaller than your previous answer? Why? What is the probability that the project will be completed before the expected time from part (a) + 5 days. Is it larger or smaller than your previous answer? Why?

(c) How sensitive is the simulation analysis to the form of the activity time distribution (uniform in 15-22, normal in 15-23)?

Video Case

The Critical Path Method

In some sense, the critical path method is the quintessential illustration of good management science. It is (1) a valuable concept that is used to guide managers when no calculations or precise estimates are available, (2) an analytic approach that allows managers to control complex projects involving interrelated subprojects and various organizations, (3) a technique with an impressive record of successful applications, and (4) a source of ideas for approaching other management problems.

The notion that you cannot complete a project until the longest path through the network has been completed is obvious once you have looked at a PERT-CPM diagram. However, it is one thing to understand a concept in a textbook and quite another to make that concept part of your personal and professional life. Good managers make principles such as sunk costs and critical paths part of their personal view of the world. They are able to see the applications of the ideas and use them for everything from planning their own activities to making sure that the various projects under their control are completed on time.

PERT's ability to help manage large problems and yield pratical results was established early in the 1950s, when it was used to help control the development of the Polaris missile. It may be hard to appreciate now that the cold war has ended, but at that time there was considerable concern that the Soviet Union might be gaining nuclear superiority. The ability to have missiles based on submarines could play an important role in determining the balance of power, and so the Polaris project was a high-priority activity. It was also an extremely complicated project that involved 250 prime contractors and more than 9000 subcontractors. PERT's reputation was established in its maiden flight.

The time-estimation techniques that were introduced with PERT find potential application in a wide variety of areas. These techniques are based on two main features: (1) a three-point estimation scheme, and (2) the notion that subjective estimates by individuals who are knowledgeable about the individual processes required in a project can be used to produce useful plans and schedules. The three-point scheme of optimistic, pessimistic, and most-likely times is easy to understand and easy to relate to reality. Not only is it good for estimating the time needed to perform various tasks, but in other contexts, such fashion merchandising, it can be used to estimate the demand for specific products.

Finally, PERT is one of the early models that explicitly combines judgment and optimization. Note that in many cases, the time estimates that are the raw data in a PERT diagram include a great deal of subjective judgment. Managers of individual processes within the total project must provide estimates for activities for which, in many cases, there are no historical data. The construction company asked to dig the basement, drive the pilings, and provide the footing for a new skyscraper in downtown Chicago obviously has a lot of experience with this type of task. However, there are many uncertainties: delays can occur because of unknown and unanticipated soil contamination; it is not clear how deep the pilings must be driven in order to guarantee stable construction; excavation time depends on traffic and weather conditions; and so on. The widespread success of PERT demonstrates that management judgment and analytic techniques are not on opposite ends of some spectrum of approaches to management but can be real complements when combined in creative and innovative ways.

Questions

1. PERT and CPM assume that all precedent activities must be completed before an activity can begin. Discuss this assumption if the project is the design of a new car.
2. Discuss the potential political issues involved in obtaining estimates of completion times.
3. Discuss the impact of random completion times on the location of the critical path.

CHAPTER 16

Inventory Models with Probabilistic Demand

APPLICATION CAPSULE

Can I Get the Mickey Mouse Model with Lighted Dial in Fuchsia?

A Simple Computer Program Helps Manitoba Telephone Keep Its Inventory Costs Down*

Sometimes a very simple model provides the best means of dealing with a complicated problem. This proved to be the case for the Manitoba Telephone System(MTS), which provides phones and service to all citizens and businesses in the Canadian province of Manitoba. In Manitoba's larger cities, the company maintains phone centers (retail stores) where customers can pay bills, get information, and obtain repair services. They can also pick out a telephone.

The MTS product line includes roughly 80 telephone styles, each available in a variety of colors. MTS aims for a 95% service level—that is, to be able to satisfy customer demand from store inventory 95% of the time. To achieve this, stores had been maintaining inventory levels at 15 to 75 days of stock. Since inventory could be replenished daily, these levels were clearly excessive. Burdened by high carrying costs for floor space and high interest rates, MTS wanted to reduce its inventories to the minimum level needed to meet its service goal.

Analysis of data from the previous 13 months revealed no clear trend in customer preference or seasonal pattern of demand. Moreover, the data were not extensive enough to support the use of sophisticated forecasting techniques. The analysts therefore decided to take a simpler approach. It seemed logical that if inventories were maintained at a level sufficient to meet 95% of last year's daily demand, they should be adequate for the present year as well. A frequency table was therefore produced for each of the 62 most common style and color combinations that the store always carried in stock. The table listed the probability of a particular number of that model being ordered on any given day. From these tables it was easy to see how many of each model would be needed to satisfy customer demand 95% of the time. It was also easy to determine, for a given level of inventory, the number of demands that would not be met.

The savings realized by regulating inventories on the basis of this simple model were considerable. One phone center was able to trim its stock on hand from 267 to 147 sets—a 45% reduction. The resulting savings in capital investment amounted to nearly $5000/year and in carrying costs to nearly $1000/year. These benefits were achieved at very little expense—the simple computer program used to generate the frequency tables was very cheap and could be easily run on a PC.

*Cohen and Dunford, "Forecasting for Inventory Control: An Example When 'Simple' Means 'Better'," *Interfaces*, Vol. 16, No. 6 (Nov.–Dec. 1986).

16.1 Introduction

Dealing with uncertainty

There are many sources of uncertainty in a typical production and distribution system. There is uncertainty as to how many items customers will demand during the next week, month, or year. There is uncertainty about delivery times. If one of your suppliers says that you will receive your order before January 5, can you rely on it, or will your order arrive weeks or months later? There is uncertainty in the production processes. What happens to your production and delivery plans if a worker is sick or if a critical machine breaks down? Uncertainty exacts a toll from management in a variety of ways. A spurt in demand or a delay in production may lead to stockouts, with the potential for lost revenue and customer dissatisfaction. Alternatively, a firm might react to a current or anticipated stockout by expediting orders, placing special orders with a supplier, or working overtime—all activities that can be costly.

Many firms define the probability of being able to satisfy customer demand as "service level." Caterpillar Tractor sends all of its dealers updated tables indicating how much to order, depending on the demand per year, to achieve service levels of 90, 95, and 99%.

Firms typically hold inventory to provide protection against uncertainty. Clearly, a cushion of inventory on hand allows management to face unexpected demands or delays in delivery with a reduced chance of incurring a stockout. We have, however, already observed that holding inventory is not free. The question, then, is: "How much inventory should a firm hold to provide reasonable protection against uncertainty?"

In previous chapters we have seen that management attempts to deal with such questions about uncertainty in a variety of ways. For example, in LP models, sensitivity analysis is typically used to assure management that its decisions are not vulnerable to changes in the parameters of the model. This chapter considers uncertainty in a more formal fashion. It looks at **probabilistic demand models,** in which uncertainty is dealt with explicitly by incorporating a *probabilistic distribution of demand* into the evaluation of the various alternative inventory control schemes.

The chapter has two main divisions. The first deals with the *reorder point–reorder quantity* models that were introduced in Chapter 10. The new twist is that a distribution for lead-time demand will be introduced. Also, no backlogging will be allowed. The second division introduces *one-period inventory models.* These models are appropriate for situations in which only one ordering decision is to be made in anticipation of future demand. Such models are directly applicable to purchase decisions involving, for example, style goods or perishable products. The rationale for these models also provides the basis for more complex models involving a sequence of ordering decisions.

16.2 The Reorder Point–Reorder Quantity Model

In Chapter 10 we have seen Victor Kowalski develop a reorder point–reorder quantity model to control the inventory of appliance angles. There are three main points to review:

1. ***The rule itself:*** The operating rule in a reorder point–reorder quantity model is specified by two parameters: the *reorder point* (r) and the *reorder quantity* (Q). The operating rule states that when the inventory position[1] equals r, an order for Q items should be placed. Because this model is defined by its two parameters, it is commonly referred to as an (r, Q) model. We will adopt this notation.
2. ***Determining Q:*** The reorder quantity, Q, is determined using the EOQ (economic order quantity) model. This model must be modified to take quantity discounts and backlogging into account when such factors are appropriate.
3. ***Determining r:*** The reorder point, r, is chosen to protect the firm from running out of stock during the lead time. If demand is known with certainty, then r is set equal to the demand during the lead time.

16.3 The Appliance Angle Problem Revisited

Let us review some of the details of Victor's problem and the EOQ model that he used to solve it. The model assumed that demand occurred at a constant and known rate of 5000 items per month. The cost of placing an order and the annual holding cost per item were specified as \$25.00 and \$1.92, respectively. Steco purchased items from the mill at \$8.00 each unless orders were placed in lots of at least 5000 items, in which case the price was \$7.90 per unit. Under these conditions Victor discovered, using the EOQ formulas, that an order quantity of 5000 items minimized the annual total cost (ATC), defined as the sum of the purchase, ordering, and inventory costs during the year. (This result depends crucially on the fact that the discounted price starts at 5000 items. See Section 10.4 for a review of the relevant analysis.)

Under the assumption that demand is known and occurs at a constant rate, we saw that the reorder point r, as noted in point 3, should be set equal to the demand during the lead time. Since demand was assumed to be 5000 items per month, if the lead time was one-half month, Victor would select the reorder point of 2500 angles (i.e., $r = 2500$). With these assumptions, inventory would run out at just the instant the order arrived (see Figure 16.1).

Stockouts and Inventory Costs

We also noted in Chapter 10 that in reality demand is almost never known with certainty. We saw that in such a case the reorder point r, as described above, can result in a **stockout.** To illustrate the last point, suppose that in the angle problem the actual demand during the 2-week lead time turned out to be more than the 2500 units implied by the assumption of a constant rate of 5000 per month. Since only

[1]Inventory position is defined as inventory on hand plus that already on order.

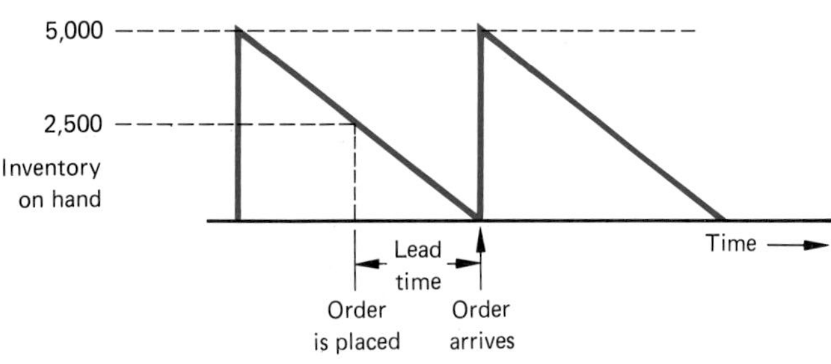

▲ FIGURE 16.1
(Q, r) Model with Known Demand

2500 units are on hand at the beginning of the 2-week lead time, and since no new units arrive until the end, if demand during that 2-week period exceeds 2500, there will be a stockout, which means, by definition, that orders arrive but inventory has been depleted.

For example, suppose that there is a demand for 2550 items rather than 2500. This is a small percentage error, but still Victor would be unable to fill 50 orders at the time they were demanded. Each unfilled order could represent a serious loss to Steco. If the customer was not willing to wait for a late delivery (i.e., demand cannot be backlogged), Steco would lose the profit from this potential sale. In addition, the customer might choose to do business in the future with a firm that could provide better service.

The cost of "opportunity loss" (being out of items) is a combination of both hard data (actual lost profit) and soft (qualitative) data. A disgruntled customer may wait a few buying turns before coming back, may never come back, or may even tell his/her friends about the experience, causing still more lost sales, etc.

One obvious way to reduce the chance of running out of stock is to increase the value of r. This was also discussed in Chapter 10. If Victor had reordered when there were 2750 items on hand, he clearly would not run out if the demand were 2550 or 2650 or even 2750. There is another side to this story, however. Increasing r increases on the average the amount of inventory that Steco will hold. If Victor increases r to 2750 and the average demand is 2500, then clearly, on the average, he will have 250 items on hand when the next order arrives. Holding inventory is not free. Indeed, one of the two cost components considered in the EOQ model is the cost of holding inventory.

How Large Should *r* Be?

Victor is thus faced with a classical management problem. If he increases r, the reorder point, he decreases the chance that he will run out of stock, but he increases his average inventory holding cost. If he decreases r, he increases the chance of running out, but decreases the average inventory holding cost. The question is: "How large should r be to achieve the proper balance between these two factors?" In the preceding chapter it was suggested that a manager might *intuitively* add an appropriate safety stock to the average lead-time demand to solve this problem. In this chapter we give a formal framework for thinking about the choice of r. It will be seen that this framework can assist management in making a more informed decision.

16.4 Victor's Choice of *r*: Uniform Lead-Time Demand

The analytic approach that is commonly used to determine the reorder point is to assume that the probability distribution of demand during the lead time is known. In other words, it is not assumed that demand is exactly known but, rather, the probabilities with which it might assume various values are assumed to be known. For example, rather than assuming that demand during the lead time is 2500 units, it might be assumed that demand would equal 2475 with probability one-half and 2525 with probability one-half. Indeed, the term *decisions under risk* is used by many authors to indicate a situation in which the probabilities of the uncertain events are known.

Victor knows something about the demand for angles from his experience in sales. It seems to him that the demand during the half-month lead time is never more than 3000 items or fewer than 2001. Between these two extremes one level of demand seems about as likely as the next. Since there are 1000 numbers in this interval, this implies that the probability that demand equals 2482 or 2535 or any other number in the interval is $1/1000$. In other words, Victor initially approaches the problem of choosing r by assuming that lead-time demand is uniformly distributed over the interval from 2001 to 3000. With this assumption, Victor can easily control the probability of a stockout. Consider the following examples:

1. If Victor sets r equal to any value larger than 3000, he will never run out during the lead time. For example, if he sets r equal to 3010, he will always have at least 10 angles on hand when the next order arrives. Since demand during the lead time is $\leq$ 3000 and he starts with 3010 on hand, he must have at least 10 on hand at the end of the lead time.
2. If an r of 2995 is selected, a stockout will occur if demand is 2996, 2997, 2998, 2999, or 3000. Since the probability of each of these quantities is $1/1000$, the probability of a stockout is $5/1000 = 0.005$.

p(s), the probability of a stockout

These examples indicate how the probability of a stockout can be controlled by the choice of r. Generalizing this discussion, we see that if the reorder point is r, with $r < 3000$, then a stockout will occur if demand is $r + 1, r + 2, \ldots, 3000$. If we let ***p(s)*** be the probability of a stockout, then if $r \geq 3000$, $p(s)$ is zero. If $r < 3000$, then

$$p(s) = \frac{3000 - r}{1000}$$

Some values of $p(s)$ and r are shown in Figure 16.2.

There is a difference between the probability of a stockout and the expected number out of stock. One can be out of 1, 2, . . . 100 units and the situation is still a "stockout." If one sets $r = 2950$, then the expected number out of stock is: 0.001(1) + 0.001(2) + 0.001(3) + . . . 0.001(50) = 1.275 units.

r	*p(s)*	*E(u)*
3010	0.00	0.000
3000	0.00	0.000
2950	0.05	1.275
2920	0.08	3.240
2870	0.13	8.515
2750	0.25	31.375
2500	0.50	125.250

r	*p(s)*
3010	0
3000	0
2950	0.05
2920	0.08
2870	0.13
2750	0.25
2500	0.50

▲ FIGURE 16.2
r, the Reorder Point, versus *p(s)*, the Probability of a Stockout, Assuming Uniform Lead-Time Demand

r vs. *p(s)*

Figure 16.2 illustrates the intuitively appealing fact that as r increases, $p(s)$ decreases. It also establishes the idea that specifying $p(s)$ dictates a value for r. To see this you must simply read Figure 16.2 from right to left. If Victor wants the probability of stocking out to equal 0.05, then he must choose $r = 2950$. Similarly, a *p(s)* of 0.13 implies an *r* of 2870.

Victor now understands that choosing *p(s)* implies a value for *r*, and vice versa. He still does not know how to choose a "good" value for *r*, or *p(s)*. One approach would be to assign a "penalty cost" per unit stockout. Victor would then choose *r* to minimize the expected holding and penalty cost during the lead time. One problem with this would be that penalty costs can be difficult to assess. In any case, an example of this type of approach is presented in the second half of this chapter in connection with the discussion of one-period inventory models.

Another way to determine *r*, or *p(s)*, is to intuitively balance several implications. This is discussed in the next three sections.

16.5 Selecting a Probability of Stocking Out

We have just illustrated the fact that choosing the reorder point *r* is equivalent to choosing *p(s)*, the probability of stocking out during the lead time to delivery. In thinking about the appropriate value for *p(s)* in the case of appliance angles, Victor considers the following facts:

1. Appliance angles are carried by all steel wholesalers.
2. The lead time for delivery from the steel mill is 2 weeks. Thus, Steco cannot quickly replenish its supply.

The result of these two facts is that if Steco is unable to fill an order when it is placed, the customer will almost always go to another supplier. Victor thus wants to make sure that Steco does not run out very often. Consequently, he wants to select a small value for *p(s)*.

Average Stockouts per Year. To get a feeling for the effects of a particular choice of *p(s)*, he might ask: "Suppose I choose $p(s) = 0.05$. How often will I stock out *during a year?*" There is no certain numerical answer to Victor's question. We can, however, make the following observations:

1. Since the order quantity Q is 5000, and since annual demand is 60,000, there are 12 orders placed per year. Thus, during each year there are 12 lead times, which means 12 opportunities to stock out. This is the maximum number of stockouts that can occur.
2. During *each* lead time Steco will stock out with a probability of *p(s)*. This is independent of whether a stockout occurred during any previous lead time.

Thus, if $p(s) = 0.05$ for *each* lead time, and we have 12 lead times a year, there will be, on the average, $(0.05)(12) = 0.6$ stockout per year, which means about 6 stockouts every 10 years. Victor may well be willing to select a value for *p(s)* on the basis, as above, of *average stockouts per year*. But he can also obtain more-specific information.

The Binomial Distribution and the Number of Stockouts. The two observations above imply that the *binomial distribution* can be used to calculate the probability of incurring any specific number of stockouts during a year. In general terms, the **binomial distribution** assumes two inputs: (1) an event that has a probability, say α, of occuring at a given trial and (2) a sequence of n independent trials. Then[2]

> The probability of having the event occur exactly x times in n trials
>
> $$= \frac{n!}{x!\,(n-x)!}\,\alpha^x(1-\alpha)^{n-x} \qquad \text{for } x = 0, 1, 2, \ldots, n$$

(16.1)

In the angles example the interpretation of a "trial" would be "lead time," and the "event" under consideration would be "a stockout during a lead time." Thus, $\alpha = p(s)$. Since there are 12 lead times per year, we would have $n = 12$. Choosing, as above, $p(s) = 0.05$, we can compute the probability of exactly x stockouts from the expression

Remember that a probability of 0.05 of stocking out means that Victor could be out 1 to 50 units *for each stockout.*

$$\frac{12!}{x!(12-x)!}\,(0.05)^x(0.95)^{n-x}$$

Victor can use this expression to calculate the probability of any specific number of stockouts in a year. For example, he computes that the probability of 0 stockouts is 0.54, and there will be exactly 1 stockout (in a year) with probability 0.34.

Although Victor now has the possibility of deriving considerable specific information, he would like a simple statistic to use in comparing the effects of alternative values of $p(s)$. Since he does not want to stock out "very often," he decides to compute the probability that he will stock out more than once during a year.

He makes use of the following relationship:

$$\text{Prob}\{\text{more than 1 stockout}\} = 1 - [\text{Prob}\{0 \text{ stockouts}\} + \text{Prob}\{1 \text{ stockout}\}] \quad \textbf{(16.2)}$$

In particular, when $p(s) = 0.05$,

$$\text{Prob}\{\text{more than 1 stockout}\} = 1 - \{0.54 + 0.34\} = 0.12$$

where, as given above, Prob{0 stockouts} = 0.54, and Prob{1 stockout} = 0.34. Similar analysis can be used to construct a table such as the one shown in Figure 16.3. This table incorporates two implications that follow from a choice of $p(s)$ or r: (1) probability of more than 1 stockout in a year and (2) average number of stockouts per year.

▼ FIGURE 16.3
Data when Demand is Uniform

$p(s)$	r	PROBABILITY OF MORE THAN ONE STOCKOUT PER YEAR	AVERAGE NUMBER OF STOCKOUTS PER YEAR
0	3000	0	0
0.02	2980	0.03	0.24
0.05	2950	0.12	0.6
0.10	2900	0.34	1.2
0.25	2750	0.84	3
0.50	2500	0.997	6

[2]The term $n! = n(n-1)(n-2)\cdots 1$. For example, $4! = 4 \cdot 3 \cdot 2 \cdot 1 = 24$. By convention, 0! is assigned the value 1.

In concluding this section, two points should be emphasized:

1. The first two columns of Figure 16.3 (i.e., the relation between r and $p(s)$) depend on the probability distribution of demand during the lead time. Recall in the discussion above that Victor assumed a probability of 1/1000 for all integer demands from 2001 to (and including) 3000.
2. The last two columns of Figure 16.3 have nothing to do with the probability distribution of lead time demand. They are based on
   a. The probability of a stockout during *each* lead time (the value of $p(s)$)
   b. The number of orders placed each year (the value of n, which is determined by Q)

Obviously, the fewer times Victor orders, the smaller the chances of stocking out during the year. Unfortunately, even though the stockout costs go down, yearly holding costs start increasing.

Effect of Order Size on Stockouts. To emphasize the last point, recall that Victor selected an order quantity Q of 5000 items. Since his model anticipates an annual demand of 60,000 items, $n = 12$ (i.e., 60,000/5000) orders are planned for each year. Suppose that, instead of 5000, an order quantity of $Q = 10{,}000$ items had been selected. In this case only six orders would be planned each year; that is, there would be six times throughout the year during which a stockout could occur. Then, with $p(s) = 0.05$ and $n = 6$, expression (16.1) produces

$$\text{probability of 0 stockouts} = \frac{6!}{0!\,6!}(0.05)^0(0.95)^6 = 0.735$$

$$\text{probability of 1 stockout} = \frac{6!}{1!\,5!}(0.05)^1(0.95)^5 = 0.232$$

Thus, the probability of more than 1 stockout during the year becomes $1 - (0.735 + 0.232) = 0.033$. This compares with 0.12 for the case of 12 orders per year. Also note that, with 6 orders per year there are, on the average, 0.3 stockouts per year, as opposed to 0.6 in the previous case. We see, then, that only Q and $p(s)$ play a role in determining the last two columns of Figure 16.3.

16.6 Victor's Choice of *r*: Normal Lead-Time Demand

Victor assumed that demand during lead time was uniformly distributed between 2001 and 3000. Many of the commercial inventory control systems find it useful to assume that the demand during the lead time has a normal probability distribution. This assumption is popular for two main reasons:

1. It is a good enough approximation to reality to yield useful results.
2. The **normal probability distribution** is completely characterized by two parameters: the mean, μ, and the standard deviation, σ. Since only two numbers are required to specify the demand for each product, it is easy to store in a computer the probability distribution for many products (in some cases, thousands). Think how much space would be required if you had to specify, for each product, a different probability distribution with 1000 possible outcomes.

Victor has just learned that ICON, the inventory control system used at Steco, assumes that demand during the lead time has a normal distribution. Since the inventory of angles will actually be controlled by this system, Victor decides to find out how this system would select r. He learns that by using past demands, the system has estimated that the demand during the lead time has a mean, μ, of 2500 and

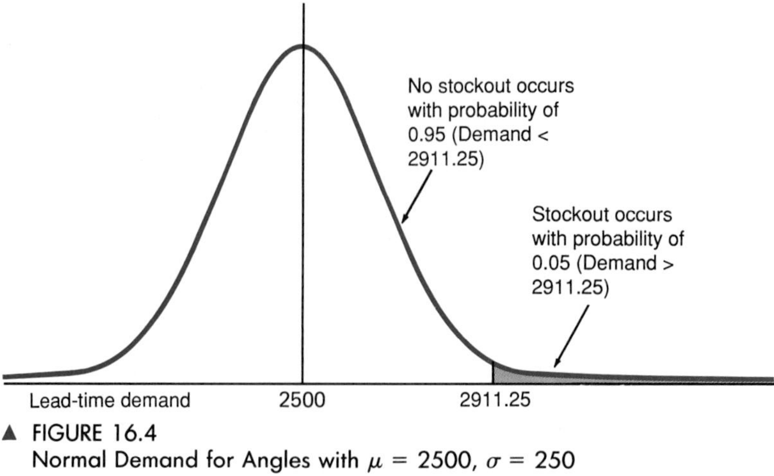

▲ FIGURE 16.4
Normal Demand for Angles with $\mu = 2500$, $\sigma = 250$

standard deviation, σ, of 250. A diagram of this distribution is shown in Figure 16.4.

Finding r given $p(s)$

The assumption that demand during the lead time has a normal distribution with $\mu = 2500$ and $\sigma = 250$ makes it possible for Victor to find the appropriate r for any value of $p(s)$, the probability of a stockout during a lead time, that he chooses. For example, suppose that he wants to have, as previously, $p(s) = 0.05$. Refer to Table A.0 in Appendix A at the end of the text, and you will see that an r value that is 1.645 standard derivations above the mean corresponds to a $p(s)$ of 0.05. It follows that for the assumed normal distribution with $\mu = 2500$ and $\sigma = 250$, as shown in Figure 16.4, the reorder point r is given by $r = 2500 + 1.645(250) = 2911.25$. Similar calculations, using different values for $p(s)$, yield the data shown in Figure 16.5.

These data should be compared with Figure 16.3. You can see that for the same values of $p(s)$ the two figures give different values for r. This shows how changing the distribution of lead-time demand changes the relation between r and $p(s)$. However, since the order quantity Q is 5000, and thus there are 12 orders per year, the last two columns of Figure 16.5 remain the same as in Figure 16.3.

p(s)	r	PROBABILITY OF MORE THAN ONE STOCKOUT PER YEAR	AVERAGE NUMBER OF STOCKOUTS PER YEAR
0.02	3013.5	0.03	0.24
0.05	2911.2	0.12	0.6
0.10	2820.2	0.34	1.2
0.25	2668.5	0.84	3
0.50	2500.0	0.997	6

▲ FIGURE 16.5
Data when Demand Is Normal with $\mu = 2500$, $\sigma = 250$

▶ 16.7 Expected Annual Cost of Safety Stock

We have discussed several implications of selecting a particular value for the reorder point, r. One is the average number of stockouts per year. Another is the probability of stocking out more than once during a year. Associated with various choices for r

will be a safety stock, and a consideration of importance is the expected annual holding cost that is associated with keeping this safety stock. Recall that the *safety stock* has been defined as the quantity that is added to the expected demand during the lead time to protect against uncertainty. Thus,

$$\text{safety stock} = r - \text{expected demand during the lead time}^3$$

Average inventory increased by safety stock

It is a fact that the average inventory on hand during a year is increased by an amount equal to the safety stock. To understand this, recall that if Victor selected a $p(s) = 0.05$, the appropriate value of r using the normal distribution for lead-time demand is 2911.2 (see Figure 16.5). Since the expected demand during the lead time is the mean of our normal distribution, namely 2500, we see that the safety stock, in this instance is 411.2 units. This situation is shown in Figure 16.6. Here we see that sometimes demand is less than and sometimes greater than the mean demand (2500). On the average, however, demand will equal 2500 units, and thus Steco will

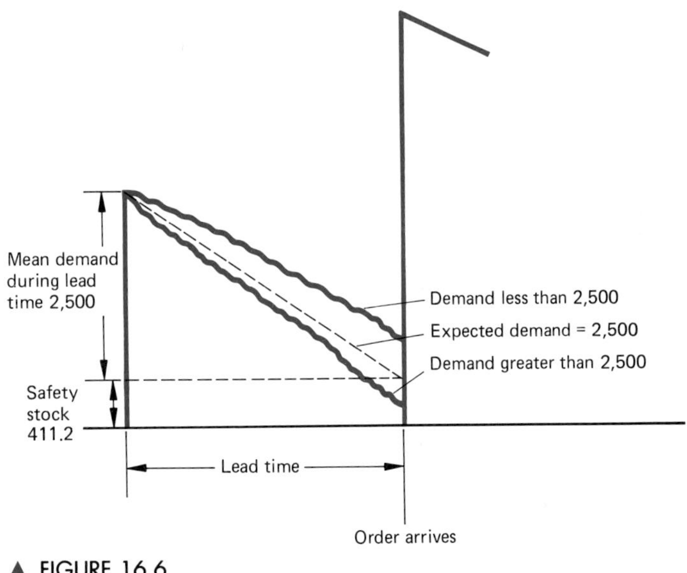

▲ FIGURE 16.6
Random Demand during the Lead Time

have increased the average amount of inventory on hand by the safety stock. Recall from Chapter 10 that C_h, Steco's cost of holding an angle in inventory for a year, is \$1.92. Then

$$\begin{aligned}\text{expected annual cost of safety stock} &= C_h(\text{safety stock})\\ &= \$1.92(411.2) = \$789.5\end{aligned}$$

Other costs could be calculated for other values of r. These calculations are combined with previous calculations in Figure 16.5 to yield Figure 16.7.

Managerial judgment needed

This table makes it easier for management to understand the trade-off between holding inventory and stocking out and provides the basis for at least a partially enlightened choice for the reorder point, r. Management can compare, for example, the case when $p(s) = 0.05$ and $r = 2911$ with the no-safety-stock situation, $p(s) = 0.5$ and $r = 2500$. Here it costs \$789.50 to decrease the probability of more than 1 stockout per year from 0.997 to 0.12 (also, to decrease the average number of stockouts per year from 6 to less than 1). Rather than asking himself, "Do I prefer a

[3]Expected demand during the lead time is the mean of the lead-time demand distribution.

$p(s)$	r	SAFETY STOCK	PROBABILITY OF MORE THAN ONE STOCKOUT PER YEAR	AVERAGE NUMBER OF STOCKOUTS PER YEAR	EXPECTED ANNUAL COST OF SAFETY STOCK ($)
0.02	3013.5	513.5	0.03	0.24	985.92
0.05	2911.2	411.2	0.12	0.6	789.50
0.10	2820.2	320.2	0.34	1.2	614.78
0.25	2668.5	168.5	0.84	3	323.52
0.50	2500	0	0.997	6	0

▲ FIGURE 16.7
Characteristics when Demand Is Normal with $\mu = 2500$, $\sigma = 250$

Management must determine the cost of being out one unit and the expected number of units out of stock for a particular value of r, to be able to determine the optimum safety stock level.

$p(s)$ of 0.50 to one of 0.05?" a manager can ask, "Is it worth about $789.50 to decrease the probability of more than 1 stockout per year from 0.997 to 0.12?" With $p(s) = 0.50$ he would expect to stock out more than once essentially every year, whereas with $p(s) = 0.05$ he would expect to stock out more than once (during the year) only about once in every 8 years ($1/8 = 0.125$). A table like Figure 16.7 provides an excellent example of how management can typically make use of formal models. The models generate data, such as those shown in the table. On the basis of these data and experience, the manager uses judgment in making the decision.

16.8 Using Simulation to Choose *r* and *Q*

The customer service division of **PROTRAC** holds inventories of literally thousands of different replacement parts. Their inventory control system is based on *monthly inspections* of the on-hand inventory (this is called **periodic review**) with a reorder point (r) and reorder quantity (Q) for each product. Although we have considered reorder point–reorder quantity (r, Q) inventory control models in Chapter 10 and this chapter, so far we have no method for finding values for r and Q that minimize the expected cost per unit of time when demand is uncertain. The selection of Q was based on the EOQ model, which assumes a constant and known rate of demand. (Thus, this model serves only as an approximation for problems such as the current one, in which demand is uncertain.) The value of r was selected independently of Q to yield a subjectively chosen probability of a stockout. Finally, we have been assuming **continuous review**—that is, we are aware of the instant the inventory position reaches r. In the situation we will now consider, the status of the system is determined only at the beginning of each month. For this reason the inventory position could be less than r when an order is placed. Simulation will provide a tool for selecting r and Q on a cost-minimizing basis.

In the context of **PROTRAC**'s customer service department, consider a particular part, the piston for the tread control unit for the D-9 crawler tractor. The inventory control system works as follows:

1. The first day of each month the inventory position for these pistons is determined, where

$$\begin{aligned}\text{inventory position} &= \text{inventory on hand} - \text{backlog} + \text{inventory on order}\\ &= \text{net inventory} + \text{inventory on order}\end{aligned}$$

2. If the inventory position is greater than r, no order is placed
3. If the inventory position is less than or equal to r, Q units are ordered.

Because demand is uncertain, it's possible that demand in a month will exceed the inventory on hand available to meet that demand. For this particular item, demand is backlogged rather than lost when this happens—that is, the customer will wait until **PROTRAC** gets the item back in stock rather than trying to obtain it elsewhere. (Backlogging in a deterministic setting was discussed in Section 10.5.)

A review of the cost, demand, and lead-time data associated with pistons yields the information shown in Figure 16.8.

cost of placing an order	= $90
cost to hold a unit for a month	= $1
cost to backlog a unit for a month	= $120
delivery leadtime	= 4 months
monthly demand: normal (μ = 20, σ = 5)	

▲ FIGURE 16.8
Cost, Demand, and Leadtime Data for Pistons

All of the numbers in Figure 16.8 are estimates. The costs are provided by the accounting group, and the assumptions about demand were developed by analyzing past data, incorporating subjective judgments, and ultimately specifying a reasonable and conveniently available probability distribution. At any rate, **PROTRAC**'s inventory control manager would be happy if he could choose inventory control parameters (values of r and Q) that yield a relatively low average cost per period (i.e., per month) when the calculations are based on the data in Figure 16.8.

Preliminary Analytical Analysis

At this point **PROTRAC** could immediately turn to a simulation study; that is, the analyst could experiment to find "good values" for r and Q. However, in many simulation projects it is useful to do some analytical analysis *before* starting the simulation. This analysis typically suggests good starting values for the decision variables (r and Q in this problem) and can significantly reduce the amount of experimentation (simulation) that must be performed to find an acceptable answer.

In this particular problem **PROTRAC** can use models from Chapter 10 to provide some guidance in choosing reasonable values of r and Q to start the simulation study. None of these models will fit this problem exactly. If they did, we would not need the simulation study—we could use the analytical result. The fundamental concept is that the models provide an idea of appropriate experimental values for r and Q in the simulation study.

The approach **PROTRAC** uses consists of two steps.

1. ***Finding a value for Q:*** In this step **PROTRAC** ignores the variability of demand in the real problem and uses the EOQ formula (see Section 10.3 for a discussion of this model) to determine Q. Thus, Q is obtained from the expression

$$Q = \sqrt{\frac{2C_oD}{C_h}} \tag{16.3}$$

where

$$\begin{aligned} C_o &= \text{fixed cost of placing an order} = \$90 \\ D &= \text{expected annual demand} \\ &= 12 \text{ months} \times 20 \text{ pistons/month} = 240 \\ C_h &= \text{cost of holding a unit in inventory for a year} \\ &= \$1/\text{month} \times 12 \text{ months} = \$12 \end{aligned}$$

The values for these parameters were taken from Figure 16.8. Making the appropriate numerical substitutions into (16.3) yields

$$Q = \sqrt{\frac{2\times 90\times 240}{12}} = \sqrt{3600} = 60$$

2. ***Finding a value for r:*** The previous discussion suggested that **PROTRAC** should select r to protect against stockouts during the leadtime. To get a rough estimate of r, we note that expected demand during the 4-month lead-time is equal to

$$4 \text{ months} \times 20 \text{ pistons/month} = 80 \text{ pistons}$$

Since demand is random, it will certainly be greater than 80 some of the time. To protect against stockouts, it seems reasonable to start the simulation study with values of r greater than or equal to 80.

Simulation Logic and Initial Conditions

In order to build a spreadsheet simulation model, we need to make some assumptions about the order in which events occur and costs are incurred. We will assume that during each month events occur in the following order:

1. At the beginning of the month, the order placed 4 months ago is received.
2. The inventory position is then checked. If it is less than or equal to r, an order is placed and the order cost is incurred.
3. Demand for the month occurs.
4. The inventory on hand and the backlog at the end of the month are calculated and the holding and backlogging costs are incurred based on the end-of-the-month values.

We also need to make an assumption about the initial conditions at the start of the simulation. We will assume that there are no outstanding orders and that the initial net inventory (on hand − backlog) is equal to the maximum net inventory, $r + Q$, when the reorder point is r and the reorder quantity is Q. The initial conditions influence how long it will take the simulation to reach *steady state* behavior. If we knew what the steady state behavior was before running the simulation, we could set the initial conditions so that the behavior of the initial months of the simulation would not be biased. Since we do not know, we will need to ignore the initial periods of the simulation when calculating our estimate of the long-run average cost per month.

The Spreadsheet Model

The spreadsheet model is shown in Figure 16.9. The values in cells A12 through A15 are zero, corresponding to the initial condition of no outstanding orders. (Think of row 16 as corresponding to the first month of the simulation). The spreadsheet currently is evaluating the policy in which $r = 80$ and $Q = 60$. Thus the ending net inventory for the month before the first month of the simulation is $60 + 80 = 140$ (the value in cell C15). Since the net inventory is positive, the ending on hand for that month is 140 and the ending backlog is 0.

The order quantity for the first month (row 16) is @IF(C15+ @SUM (D12..D15)<=$F$8,$F$7,0), because the inventory position is C15+ @SUM(D12..D15), the reorder point is $F$8, and the reorder quantity is $F$7. Demand for any month is @ROUND(@NORMAL($F$2,$F$3),0). @ROUND is used to round the decimal demand to an integer value. (Fractional demand for pistons is meaningless.) @NORMAL is the @RISK function for generating a

```
A1: [W11] 'Cost Parameters:
```

	A	B	C	D	E	F	G
1	Cost Parameters:			Demand Parameters:			
2	Ordering Cost		90	Mean Monthly Demand		20	
3	Holding Cost		1	Standard Deviation		5	
4	Backlogging Cost		120	Leadtime (months)		4	
5							
6				Inventory Control Parameters:			
7	Average Monthly Cost:			Order Quantity		60	
8	$417			Reorder Point		80	
9							
10	Order		Ending Net	Ending On	Ending		
11	Qty	Demand	Inventory	Hand	Backlog	Cost	
12	0						
13	0						
14	0						
15	0		140	140	0		
16	0	24	116	116	0	116	
17	0	22	94	94	0	94	
18	0	16	78	78	0	78	
19	60	19	59	59	0	149	
20	0	10	49	49	0	49	

▲ FIGURE 16.9
r,Q Simulation Spreadsheet

normal random demand with mean \$F\$2 and standard deviation \$F\$3. (See Section 13.5 for another method of generating normal random variables when @RISK is not available.) Ending net inventory is calculated from the formula

$$\text{Ending Net Inventory} = \text{Previous Ending Net Inventory} + \text{Quantity Ordered 4 months ago} - \text{Demand}$$

For example, the ending net inventory in cell C19 is equal to

$$59 = 78 + 0 - 19$$

When Ending Net Inventory is positive, it is equal to Ending On Hand. When Ending Net Inventory is negative, its positive numerical value (i.e., without the minus sign) is equal to Ending Backlog. For example, Ending On Hand in row 16 is 116, since the Ending Net Inventory is 116. Finally, the cost for the month is the order cost ($90 in this case) if Order Qty is positive, plus the holding cost (the holding cost per unit times Ending On Hand) plus the backlogging cost (the backlogging cost per unit times the Ending Backlog).

Running the Model. The spreadsheet model will be used to determine the average cost per month for a given *r*, *Q* policy and to find a low cost policy. To find the average cost per month for a policy, we must decide on the number of months over which to average. More months will tend to give a better estimate of the long-run average cost. But adding months increases the size of the spreadsheet and the time it takes to recalculate. As a compromise, we have chosen to simulate 8 years (96 months), discarding the first 12 months (because of the initial bias). Thus the average monthly cost of $417 shown in Figure 16.9 is an average of the last 84 values of the Cost column.

Is there a lower cost policy, and how can it be found? We will use a 2-way data table to compute the average cost for a range of *r* and *Q* values. First we need to decide on a reasonable range of *r* and *Q* values. Since the variance of monthly demand is 5^2, the variance of lead-time demand is $4 \times 5^2 = 100$. So the standard deviation of lead-time demand is 10. A reasonable first set of values for *r* is 80, 90, 100, 110, 120, and 130, i.e., the expected lead-time demand plus 0, 1, 2, 3, 4, and 5

	Q			
r	40	50	60	70
80	$539.	$413.	$417.	$286.
90	$273.	$164.	$228.	$128.
100	$134.	$86.	$127.	$86.
110	$89.	$74.	$88.	$76.
120	$88.	$84.	$84.	$86.
130	$98.	$94.	$94.	$96.

▲ FIGURE 16.10
Average Costs for Various *r*, Q Policies

standard deviations. We will also vary Q in increments of 10. The Q values will be 40, 50, 60, and 70. The results are shown in Figure 16.10.

This data suggests that among the alternatives examined, **PROTRAC** should select $r = 110$ and $Q = 50$, since this combination yields the smallest average cost per month, \$74. The Q value is fairly close to the EOQ and the reorder point is 3 standard deviations above the expected lead-time demand.

At this point we could search over an even finer grid and try to find the best r and Q to the nearest unit. But remember, we are only guaranteed of finding the best combination of r and Q values for the given set of simulated demands. (In the spreadsheet that produced Figure 16.10, only r and Q varied; the demands in each of the 96 periods were identical.) Changing the set of simulated demands could change the best combination. A complete analysis would see how sensitive the tenative solution was to a different set of demands. If the solution is very sensitive, that is an indication that the simulation needs to be run over a period longer than 8 years, or, alternatively, several 8-year periods need to be averaged when computing the average monthly cost.

Finally, we have focused on finding the policy which minimizes the expected cost, ignoring the "riskiness" of different policies. While this is possible to do in a spreadsheet program, @RISK greatly facilitates capturing the *distribution* of monthly cost for a given policy. We will leave the exploration of some of these issues to a problem at the end of the chapter.

16.9 One-Period Models with Probabilistic Demand: The Newsboy Problem

We used simulation in the previous section because there is no readily available exact analytical model for solving multi-period inventory problems. However, as we mentioned in Section 13.3, there *is* a simple analytical solution if we limit ourselves to one-period problems. We will now develop that approach, showing how it can be applied to the following typical situation.

The Wiles's Housewares Problem Revisited

As we saw in Section 13.3, Peggy McConnel is planning a promotion involving the special purchase of omelet pans from France. Peggy and her buyers must decide how many of these pans to order now, 6 long months before the sale takes place in

October. If demand were known, the decision would be easy: Order the quantity demanded. But demand is uncertain. *If they order too many, excess items will be sold at a loss. If they order too few, substitute items must be sold at a greatly reduced profit.* Unfortunately, they cannot find help by examining the (r, Q) inventory system that Wiles uses for stock items in housewares. This problem does not fit that mold. The (r, Q) model balances reorder costs and inventory holding costs. Here the ordering cost is not in question. Each item will be ordered once. Peggy needs to balance the cost of ordering too much against the cost of ordering too little. A new approach is required.

This problem occurs in many businesses. Bakeries have the same time period as the newsboy: Day-old goods must be discounted (or, if unleavened, thrown out). On the other end of the time scale, Christmas tree lots set up for business once a year and must order by August for sales in December.

The problem faced by Peggy and her staff is a classic management science problem known as the **newsboy problem.** In this problem the newsboy buys Q papers from the delivery truck driver at the beginning of the day. During the day he sells papers. How many he will sell is unknown in advance. At the end of the day the papers are worthless. If he buys more than he sells, he loses the money associated with the leftover papers. If he does not buy enough, he loses the potential profits from additional sales.

Components of the Newsboy Model

Suppose that the newsboy pays C dollars for each paper and sells them for S dollars each. Let $C = \$0.10$ and $S = \$0.25$. The model is built on three components:

1. The holding cost, h, is the cost per unit to the newsboy of each leftover paper. In this example

$$h = C = \$0.10$$

2. The penalty cost, p, is the profit that the newsboy "loses" with each paper that could have been sold but was not because he ran out. In this example,

$$\begin{aligned} p &= S - C \\ &= \$0.25 - \$0.10 \\ &= \$0.15 \end{aligned}$$

3. The probability distribution of demand.

The information about the probability that demand takes on particular values is contained in the probability distribution of demand. One would expect this distribution to be different for different products, times, and so on. Indeed, the form of the distribution can change. In some cases a normal distribution is appropriate. Other distributions may be more realistic in other cases. In this example, suppose, for simplicity, that the newsboy employs a **uniform distribution.** In particular, he believes that any demand between 1 and 100 is equally likely. Thus,

$$\begin{aligned} \text{Prob}\{\text{demand} = 1\} &= \frac{1}{100} \\ \text{Prob}\{\text{demand} = 23\} &= \frac{1}{100} \\ \text{Prob}\{\text{demand} = \text{any integer from 1 through 100}\} &= \frac{1}{100} \end{aligned}$$

Therefore,

$$\begin{aligned} \text{Prob}\{\text{demand} \le 5\} &= \frac{5}{100} = 0.05 \\ \text{Prob}\{\text{demand} \le 23\} &= \frac{23}{100} = 0.23 \end{aligned}$$

Generalizing this reasoning, we see that

$$\text{Prob}\{\text{demand} \le x\} \begin{cases} = 0 & \text{where } x \le 0 \\ = x/100 & \text{where } x = 1, 2, \ldots, 100 \\ = 1 & \text{where } x \ge 100 \end{cases}$$

The Optimal Order Quantity

This optimal quantity minimizes the "inventory" costs, balancing the holding costs with the penalty costs. This problem could also be formulated to maximize profit.

The three components (p, h, and the probability distribution of demand) come together in the following equation to determine Q^*, the optimal (i.e., *cost minimizing*) order quantity.[4]

$$Q^* \text{ is the smallest integer such that Prob}\{\text{demand} \le Q^*\} \ge \frac{p}{p+h} \quad \textbf{(16.4)}$$

In our example, $p = \$0.15$, $h = \$0.10$, and

$$\text{Prob}\{\text{demand} \le x\} = \frac{x}{100} \qquad \text{for } x = 1, 2, \ldots, 100$$

Substituting these values into (16.3) yields

$$\text{Prob}\{\text{demand} \le Q^*\} \ge \frac{p}{p+h}$$

which means

$$\frac{Q^*}{100} \ge \frac{0.15}{0.15 + 0.10} = 0.60$$
$$Q^* = 60$$

Applying the Newsboy Model to Wiles's Housewares

Problems identical to Peggy's would entail specially printed items like T-shirts for rock concerts or sporting events (World Series or Super Bowl). After the event the items generally have much less (if any) value.

If Peggy is to fit her problem into the newsboy model, she must specify each of the three components. Consider the copper omelet pan. Wiles will buy these pans for \$22 each and will sell them for \$35. Any pans left at the end of the sale will be sold to a discount chain for \$15 each. If Wiles runs out of these pans, it will substitute a pan from its regular stock, bought for \$32 each, and sell it for the sale price of \$35.

The Cost Parameters. These data provide the basis for calculating the cost parameters in the newsboy problem.

1. Let us first determine the holding cost, h. Since Wiles pays \$22 for each pan and sells each leftover pan for \$15, the store loses \$7 on each pan not sold during the sale. Thus, $h = \$7$.
2. Next, let us look at the penalty cost, p. Each time a regular pan is substituted for a sale pan to satisfy excess demand, Wiles gains \$3 (\$35 − \$32). If a sale pan had been available, Wiles would have gained \$13 (\$35 − \$22). Taking into account this "forgone gain," and treating it as an **opportunity cost,** we see that the cost per unit of running out of sale omelet pans is \$10 (\$13 − \$3).

[4]The derivation of this result would require a technical discussion that we have chosen to omit because of constraints on both space and level of treatment.

Peggy's problem of predicting the demand is compounded by the fact that there is no historical trend to look at. *Sports Illustrated* each year produces its now famous "Swimsuit Issue" and has to decide how many copies to print for the newsstands. Normally, newsstand sales account for less than 15% of its weekly sales, but for this issue they can account for up to 50%. A lot of data analysis takes place at *SI* each year to determine the number of issues to print.

3. Peggy must also specify the probability distribution of demand. This is not easy. There are no directly applicable historical data. Wiles has not tried exactly this promotion before. There is, however, information about the results of other sales. In addition, Peggy has opinions and information about the state of the economy, the desirability of this particular item, and so on.

Faced with the fact that she must specify a probability distribution, she uses the following approach:

a. Her best guess for demand during the sale is 1000 pans. She feels it is equally likely that actual demand may exceed or fall short of this best guess.
b. She feels confident that demand will not be less than 700 pans or more than 1300.
c. A demand near 1000 seems much more likely than one near 700 or 1300.

On the basis of these three observations, Peggy decides on the following model:

1. Demand is normal.
2. The mean, μ, equals her best estimate of demand, $\mu = 1000$.
3. The standard deviation, σ, is given by the calculation

$$\sigma = \frac{1300 - 700}{6} = 100$$

This calculation is based on the observation that an interval 3 standard deviations above and 3 standard deviations below the mean includes almost all possible outcomes. In other words, the distance between the largest and the smallest potential outcomes is $3 + 3 = 6$ standard deviations. This distribution is shown in Figure 16.11.

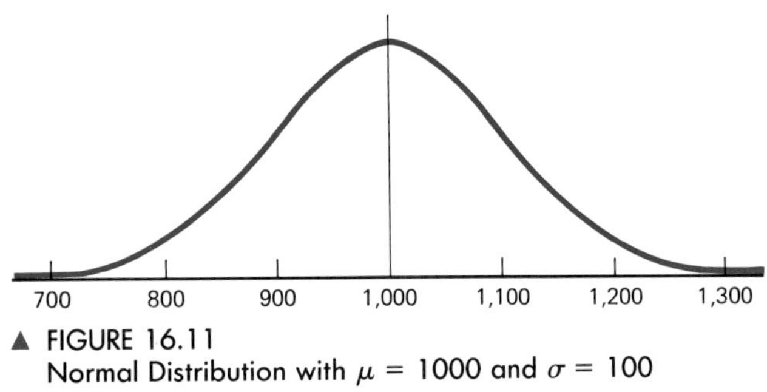

▲ FIGURE 16.11
Normal Distribution with $\mu = 1000$ and $\sigma = 100$

To help understand the calculations, let's say that Peggy finds out the pans will cost only \$20 (not \$22). Thus,
$h = (\$20 - \$15) = \$5$
$p = [\$35 - \$20] - [\$35 - \$32] = \$12$
$p/(p + h) = \$12/(\$12 + \$5) = 0.7059$.
Notice that the denominator doesn't change (still 17) but the numerator increases by 2. In this case, Peggy would order 1054 (from the normal distribution table).

Computing the Order Quantity. With the assumption that demand is normal with $\mu = 1000$ and $\sigma = 100$, and using the values determined above for h and p, the optimal order quantity Q^* is found by solving equation (16.4). Peggy must select Q^* such that

$$\text{Prob}\{\text{demand} \leq Q^*\} \geq \frac{p}{p + h} = 0.588$$

We see from Table A.0 that 0.588 of the area under the curve for a normal distribution lies to the left of a point that is about 0.22 standard deviation above the mean. Since Peggy has assumed a mean of 1000 and a standard deviation of 100,

$$Q^* = 1000 + 0.22(100) = 1022$$

In other words, given her specifications of h, p, and the probability distribution of demand, the newsboy model indicates that Peggy should order 1022 omelet pans.

Not only is the choice of distribution important, but the student needs to be reminded that the actual event will happen only once, and that the distribution covers only the range of what might happen. Even if Peggy were to choose the correct distribution, she still has to "play the odds." This type of problem could also be set up as a decision tree problem (see Chapter 14).

Importance of the Choice of Distribution. Let us now suppose that Peggy changes her distribution. Instead of using the normal, suppose that she were to assume a *uniform* distribution on the interval from 700 to 1300. In this case,

$$\text{Prob}\{\text{demand} \le x\} = \frac{x - 700}{600} \qquad \text{for } x = 701, 702, \ldots, 1300$$

and solving (16.4) for Q^* gives

$$\text{Prob}\{\text{demand} \le Q^*\} = \frac{Q^* - 700}{600} \ge 0.588$$

$$Q^* \ge 600(0.588) + 700 = 1052.8$$

and hence $Q^* = 1053$. With the normal assumption she orders 1022. Had she used the uniform distribution, she would order 1053. You can see that the assumption about the distribution of demand can be of considerable importance. It is typical of probabilistic inventory models that assumptions about the distribution of demand can greatly affect the recommended decision. That is why care must be exercised to find a distribution that best approximates reality.

You can think of the distribution itself as a model of reality—a model that we then use in another model to recommend a decision.

16.10 Notes on Implementation

The "Two-Bin" System

Inventory control is one of the oldest and most common applications of quantitative models. In manufacturing companies, the most popular implementation of inventory control models has been historically the "two-bin" inventory system. In this system a certain number of items are set aside, in bin 1, so to speak. All other items are held in another location, bin 2. Items are removed from bin 2 in order to satisfy demand. When bin 2 is empty and the stock clerk starts to use items from bin 1, this is the signal to place an order for a predetermined quantity of items. In the 1950s a computer card would be attached to bin 1. When the clerk removed the first item from bin 1 he or she also removed the computer card and sent it to inventory control. This card initiated the order for the item.

Many dry goods stores still use the "two-bin" system by inserting cards into the last few yards of a bolt of cloth to trigger the reordering. The original VW Beetle (pre-1958) had no fuel gauge but only a lever on the floor to switch to an emergency gas tank when the main one ran empty.

The two-bin system is a method of implementing the reorder point-reorder quantity model. The age of cheap computing and remote terminal entry has made this system less important. In more current versions, the process of billing a customer will often automatically adjust the inventory level. For example, the cash register in a department store, as well as itemizing your bill, will often make a record of the item you purchased. This information is fed to a computer, which adjusts the inventory level and triggers a reorder when appropriate. The data accumulated with such devices can also be used in evaluating the success of a product line and forecasting future demand.

Software Packages

A number of computer manufacturers offer an inventory control package as a standard part of their software package. Packages of some long standing include IBM's IMPACT, Honeywell's PROFIT, and RCA's WISDOM. IBM also has a more

Many companies have longed for the simplicity of a manual system after getting hooked into a computer system. The first rule of a computerized system is that it should work as well as the one it is replacing. One large computer manufacturer reportedly wouldn't use its own package at its manufacturing plant because it was too complicated! When they purchased a competitor's package, it was on the strict condition that this information be kept secret.

recent entry in the field entitled INFOREM, *In*ventory *Fo*recasting and *Re*plenishment *M*odels.

To the extent that one can generalize, these packages are based on the use of exponential smoothing (see Chapter 18) for forecasting and a reorder point-reorder quantity model as the inventory control mechanism. Each package has its own features, and we do not intend to go into detail here. It is, however, interesting to note that simulation (see Chapter 13) is an option in certain cases. This makes it possible to evaluate the operation of the system under various sets of parameters (e.g., reorder point, reorder quantity, or demand distribution) or to compare the operations of different types of systems. The very existence of these different packages indicates the importance of the inventory management function.

In some industries (or activities) inventory control has a special significance, and the assumptions underlying the standard packages (IMPACT, etc.) do not fit very well. In such cases it pays for the organization to develop its own inventory control system. One example is provided by the steel wholesaling business (like Steco). Here, for certain products, the idiosyncrasies of the supplier, the steel manufacturers, makes it difficult to use a standard approach. Certain types of steel are produced in large batches (heats) on a schedule that is known a year or so in advance. The wholesaler must determine if it wishes to buy part of a particular heat. Once a heat is sold out, prospective buyers must wait for the next heat. This uncertainty in supply must be reflected in the inventory control system for these items.

Another example, where organizations may need to develop their own self-tailored systems, is provided by the inventory of replacement parts for complicated systems. The military services have an enormous number of items of this sort. Consider an electric generator that is an important part of a nuclear submarine. The number of such items in service is small, and they fail infrequently. Since they are expensive, the inventory carrying cost is high. One thus would like to hold a minimal inventory. On the other hand, the penalty cost of running out is also high. Losing the service of a multimillion dollar submarine for several weeks while a new generator is built has high opportunity costs. In many such cases, the following type of rule is employed: "Order an item for inventory each time an item is withdrawn."

Atlanta Gas & Light in Macon, Georgia, sells 26 types of gas appliances and parts. Currently, they use a computerized system from Atlanta that must be customized to account for their seasonality, as the warehouse is fairly bursting at the seams with safety stock. The inventory decisions are based on a 95% service level, meaning that 95% of the time when a customer asks for an item, it will be in stock.

The bottom line is that inventory control is an important management function and that quantitative models have made and are making an important contribution in this area. Although the mathematics may vary from one specific model to another, the concept of balancing ordering, holding, and stockout costs remains valid across many applications. General managers should understand the assumptions and operating implications of their own system. The blind assumption that because an inventory control system is large, complex, and computerized, it therefore cannot be understood, and/or must be all right, is a large first step in the wrong direction.

16.11 Summary

This chapter considered two important inventory control models: (1) reorder point-reorder quantity (r, Q) models in which backlogging is not permitted and demand during the lead time is specified with a probability distribution; and (2) one-period problems in which demand is specified with a probability distribution.

In Chapter 10 we learned about the (r, Q) model in a deterministic setting (meaning a known constant rate of demand). We saw how Q was chosen, using the EOQ formula, to balance ordering and holding costs. The value of r was set equal to the demand that would occur during the lead time.

It can be shown that the introduction of uncertainty in demand does not greatly affect the appropriate choice for Q. Uncertainty, however, does imply that we must give more attention to the choice of r. Because of uncertain demand over the lead time, the value of r computed from the deterministic model may result in stockouts, which may be costly via the loss of future commerce. To reduce the probability of stocking out, management uses a safety stock, but this increases annual holding costs. The trade-off is as follows: Not ordering enough may lead to too many stockouts and large stockout costs; ordering too much, although reducing stockout costs, will lead to inordinately high holding costs. In this chapter some formal tools were given to help management make a decision that balances the holding and stockout costs.

A quantity of interest is $p(s)$, the probability of incurring a stockout during a lead time. This is obviously related to r, the quantity on hand when we reorder at the beginning of the lead time. The relation between $p(s)$ and r is based on the distribution of lead-time demand. Given a distribution, r determines $p(s)$, and vice versa. We used, in this chapter, two illustrative distributions, the uniform and the normal.

Several implications of a given value of $p(s)$ were given.

1. $p(s)$ and Q determine the average number of stockouts per year.
2. $p(s)$ and Q determine the probability of stocking out more than once in a year.
3. $p(s)$ and the distribution for lead-time demand determine r, and this quantity determines the safety stock level with its holding cost.

The discussion of (r, Q) models culminated in Figure 16.7. This figure provides a framework in which a manager can gauge his or her intuition about the appropriate probability of stocking out. For the case of normal lead-time demand and several values of the reorder point r, the probability of more than one stockout per year, the average number of stockouts per year, and the associated expected annual cost of safety stock are shown. This makes it possible for the manager to see how much he or she must pay to reduce the number of stockouts per year. Selecting the appropriate trade-off is left to managerial judgment.

Section 16.8 explored the use of spreadsheet simulation to identify values of r and Q that minimize expected cost when demand is uncertain.

Consideration of one-period models with probabilistic demand started with reconsideration of the Wiles housewares problem. In Section 16.9 it was established that Wiles's problem is a special case of a classic management science problem known as the newsboy problem. The solution to the newsboy problem was presented, and then Wiles's problem was solved within this context.

Key Terms

Probabilistic Demand Model. A model in which the demand for the item under consideration is specified by a probability distribution.*(p. 713)*

Stockout. Not having enough inventory on hand to satisfy demand. *(p. 714)*

***p(s)*.** The probability of a stockout during a lead time. *(p. 716)*

Binomial Distribution. A probability distribution with two parameters: the probability that an event occurs at a given trial and the number of independent trials. *(p. 714)*

Normal Distribution. A probability distribution with two parameters: μ, the mean, and σ, the standard deviation. *(p. 719)*

Expected Annual Cost of Safety Stock. The amount by which the expected annual holding cost is increased by using a safety stock. *(p. 720)*

Periodic Review. An inventory control system in which the inventory status is determined only at certain regular intervals of time. *(p. 722)*

Continuous Review. An inventory control system in which the inventory status is always known. *(p. 722)*

One-Period Model. A problem in which

there is one opportunity to order an item, and this occurs before a random demand occurs. (*p. 726*)

Newsboy Problem. A classic management science problem. A one-period inventory model with linear holding and penalty costs. (*p. 727*)

Uniform Distribution. The probability of any event in the specified range is equally likely. (*p. 727*)

Opportunity Cost. A concept of "forgone profit" used in defining the penalty cost in a newsboy model. (*p. 728*)

Major Concepts Quiz

True-False

1. **T F** In probabilistic inventory models, larger holding costs are typically used to prevent ordering too frequently.
2. **T F** The reorder point must be chosen to balance the number of stockouts versus holding cost.
3. **T F** The expected annual cost of a safety stock depends on only three quantities: r, the mean of the lead-time demand distribution, and the holding cost C_h.
4. **T F** For different lead-time demand distributions, as long as *p(s)* is the same, the safety stock level will also be the same.
5. **T F** Q plays an important role in determining the average number of stockouts per year.
6. **T F** The tools developed in this chapter serve to automate the choice of r.
7. **T F** In the newsboy model, the proper definition of penalty cost involves the concept of forgone profit, or so-called opportunity cost.
8. **T F** Suppose that known annual demand is 60,000, and each order is for 15,000 items. Then a maximum of four stockouts per year can occur.

Multiple Choice

9. Given the probability of a stockout during a lead time, the probability of incurring exactly two stockouts in a given year can be determined by using
   a. the uniform distribution
   b. the normal distribution
   c. the binomial distribution
   d. all of the above

10. The correspondence between *p(s)* and r depends on
    a. the average number of stockouts in a year
    b. the lead-time demand distribution
    c. the safety stock level

11. The choice of *p(s)*, as well as the number of orders placed per year, determine
    a. average number of stockouts per year
    b. the probability of more than one stockout in a year
    c. parameters for the binomial distribution
    d. all of the above
    e. none of the above

12. The normal distribution is convenient to work with because
    a. it is specified by only two parameters, μ and σ
    b. the same table is used no matter how one chooses μ and σ (i.e., for *any* normal distribution)
    c. it is often a good approximation of reality
    d. all of the above
    e. none of the above

13. The newsboy model
   a. balances holding and penalty costs for a one-period problem
   b. minimizes ordering, holding, and penalty costs for a one-period problem
   c. applies only to problems for which there is a uniform or normal distribution of demand
   d. all of the above

14. Consider the smallest value of Q^* that satisfies

$$\text{Prob}\{\text{demand} \le Q^*\} \ge \frac{p}{p + h}$$

   a. This value will depend on the assumed distribution of demand.
   b. This value provides the optimal order quantity for the newsboy model.
   c. This value minimizes the sum of expected holding and penalty costs in the newsboy model.
   d. All of the above.

15. The assumption about the lead-time demand distribution
   a. can affect the cost of keeping a given safety stock level
   b. will typically affect the choice of a safety stock level
   c. will affect the average number of stockouts per year
   d. both a and b

Answers

1. F	**5.** T	**9.** c	**13.** a
2. T	**6.** F	**10.** b	**14.** d
3. T	**7.** T	**11.** d	**15.** b
4. F	**8.** T	**12.** d	

Problems

QSB+ can be used to calculate an EOQ or solve a newsboy model.

$Q^* = 30$, $r = 10$

16-1. At PROTRAC's Seattle outlet the demand during a week for the overhaul kit for small marine engines is a random variable with the following distribution:

$p(0) = 0.01$	$p(7) = 0.11$
$p(1) = 0.03$	$p(8) = 0.11$
$p(2) = 0.06$	$p(9) = 0.09$
$p(3) = 0.06$	$p(10) = 0.06$
$p(4) = 0.11$	$p(11) = 0.03$
$p(5) = 0.20$	$p(12) = 0.01$
$p(6) = 0.12$	

The kits cost \$166.67 each, the cost of placing an order is \$50, the cost of holding a kit in inventory for a year is 20% of the purchase price, and delivery lead time is 1 week. Assume 50 weeks per year and derive an (r, Q) model with a probability of 0.04 of stocking out during a cycle.

16-2. ▲▲ Pierce Dears, the lead salesman for PROTRAC's Seattle outlet, has just negotiated a contract to sell 12 overhaul kits per week to Goal, the discount chain store, for the foreseeable future. Since this demand is deterministic, Pierce decides to adjust the inventory control policy as shown in Figure 16.12.

(a) No; should order more and reorder point should be increased
(b) $Q^* = 52, r^* = 22$
(c) $Q^* = 52, r^* = 21$

CHARACTERISTIC	PARAMETERS FOR THE INVENTORY POLICY IN PROBLEM 16-1	PARAMETERS FOR THE INVENTORY POLICY IN PROBLEM 16-2
Order Quantity	Q^*	$Q^* + 12T^*$
Cycle Time (Weeks)	T^*	T^*
Reorder Point	r^*	r^*

▲ FIGURE 16.12

In words, he has simply increased the order quantity to cover the demand during the cycle time. Since the additional demand is deterministic, he says there is no need to change *r*.

(a) Is this a good policy? Explain your answer.

(b) What policy would you recommend if Pierce wanted to maintain a 0.04 probability of stocking out during an inventory cycle?

(c) Management at PROTRAC's Seattle outlet decided that the 0.10 probability of a stockout per cycle would be best for them. Find Q^* and r^*.

(a) 0.052
(b) 0.058

16-3. ▲▲ Assume that PROTRAC's Seattle outlet uses the optimal policy in Problem 16-1.

(a) What is the probability of exactly two stockouts during the year?

(b) What is the probability of more than one stockout during the year?

$r \geq 9$; 0.2639

16-4. ▲▲ For Problem 16-1, for what values of *r* is the expected number of stockouts per year less than or equal to one? For the smallest value of *r*, what is the probability of more than one stockout per year?

(a) Leave it unchanged (See IM)
(b) Decrease it (See IM)

16-5. ▲ Increasing *Q*, the order quantity, will have what effect on

(a) The probability of a stockout *during an inventory cycle?*

(b) The probability of more than one stockout per year?

Explain your answers.

$r \geq 8.56$, same as before

16-6. ▲▲ If, in Problem 16-4, the lead time demand is normally distributed, with a mean of 6 and a standard deviation of 2, for what values of *r* number of is the expected stockouts per year less than or equal to one? For the smallest value of *r*, what is the probability that there is more than one stockout per year? Compare with the answers to Problem 16-4. (The number of orders per year is still 10.)

$Q^* = 500, r^* = 108$

16-7. ▲▲ At Steco the weekly demand for high-titanium rods is normally distributed with mean 100 and standard deviation 5. These rods cost \$5 each, and the cost of holding a rod in inventory for a year is equal to 20% of its cost. The cost of placing an order is \$25, independent of the quantity ordered. Delivery lead time is 1 week. Management wants a 0.06 probability of stocking out during an inventory cycle. Assume 50 weeks per year. What (*r*, *Q*) system would you recommend?

(a) $Q^* = 500, r^* = 213$
(b) None (See IM)
(c) Less rapidly (See IM)

16-8. ▲▲ Consider the data presented in Problem 16-7. Now assume that increased demand has forced Steco's supplier to increase the delivery lead time for high-titanium rods from 1 week to 2 weeks. Also, management wants a probability of 0.04 of stocking out during an inventory cycle. (HINT: Demand during the lead time is the sum of the demands during each of the 2 weeks. The demand each week has a normal distribution, and it is reasonable to assume that demands are independent from week to week.)

The following information is useful in solving Problem 16-8. Assume that X is normally distributed with mean μ_x and standard deviation σ_x, *and that* Y is also normally distributed with mean μ_Y and standard deviation σ_Y. Let $Z = X + Y$, and assume X and Y are independent. Then Z is normally distributed with mean $\mu_Z = \mu_X + \mu_Y$ and standard deviation $\sigma_Z = \sqrt{\sigma_X^2 + \sigma_Y^2}$.

(a) What (r, Q) policy would you recommend in view of this change?

(b) What effect has the change in delivery lead time had on the value for Q? Explain why.

(c) Does r increase less rapidly than, at the same rate as, or more rapidly than the lead time? Explain why.

$8

16-9. ▲ What is the expected annual cost of the safety stock associated with the (r, Q) policy you recommended in Problem 16-7?

$13

16-10. ▲ What is the expected annual cost of the safety stock associated with the (r, Q) policy you recommended in Problem 16-8?

(a) $Q^* = 575$
(b) $p(s) = 0.60$
(c) $Q^* = 729$
(d) $g = \$625$

16-11. ▲▲ The regional distribution center of Deuce Hardware sells small window air conditioners for $250 each. These units cost $200. All units not sold by September 1 are sold for one-half of the retail price in an end-of-the-season sale. Assume that demand for this air conditioner during the season is normally distributed with a mean of 600 and a standard deviation of 100.

(a) How many air conditioners should Deuce order at the beginning of the season?

(b) What is the probability that Deuce will not satisfy all demand during the season?

The management of Deuce decides to select the order quantity so that the probability of a stockout is 0.10.

(c) How many air conditioners should be ordered at the beginning of the season?

(d) What "cost of goodwill" has to be added implicitly to the financial penalty cost to justify this decision?

(a) $Q^* = 568$
(b) $Q^* = 636$
(c) $Q^* = 757$
(d) $g = 30$ cents

16-12. ▲▲ The question the concessionaire must answer is how many soft pretzels to buy for the Great Fond du Lac Boat Race. The pretzels cost $0.10 and sell for $0.25. Unsold pretzels can be returned to the supplier for a $0.05 refund. (The supplier then sells them in its Day Old Shoppe for $0.15.) Demand is normal with a mean of 500 and a standard deviation of 100.

(a) How many pretzels should be ordered?

(b) Suppose demand has a standard deviation of 200. How many pretzels should be ordered? What can you say about the relationship between the order quantity and the standard deviation?

(c) The concessionaire decides to set the probability of a stockout at 0.1. How many pretzels should be ordered? σ is now 200.

(d) What additional cost of a lost sale must implicitly be added to the financial loss to justify this decision?

See IM

16-13. ▲▲▲ In Section 16.8 we used simulation to estimate the (r, Q) combination that minimizes expected monthly costs for a particular part carried by **PROTRAC**'s customer service division. But is, in fact, the combination found ($r = 110$, $Q = 50$) the best, and how much variability is there in the average monthly costs? Use @RISK to answer the following:

(a) For a fixed set of 96 monthly demands, find the best (r, Q) values to the nearest unit. Now sample a new set of 96 demands, fix them, and find the best (r, Q) values. Are your answers the same? Explain. Suggest what you could do to get a better estimate of the optimal solution.

(b) For $r = 110$, $Q = 50$, use @RISK to calculate the average total cost for the last year of the simulation and a 90% confidence interval for the total cost of the last year of the simulation based on 100 samples of 96 monthly demands. Do the same for $r = 120$, $Q = 50$. Which policy do you prefer? Why? (HINT: To find a 90% confidence interval using @RISK, show the cumulative probability distribution and then find the values associated with target probabilities of 5% and 95%. These values will be the upper and lower limits of the confidence interval.)

See IM

16-14. ▲▲▲ Icarus Airlines is trying to decide how many customers to book on the 7 A.M. flight between Chicago and New York. There are 140 seats on the airplane. If the airline books all 140 seats, they will most likely lose revenue because of no-shows. If they book more than 140 seats and more than 140 people show up, they must compensate the passengers who miss their flight. A seat on the flight costs the customer $100. From past experience, the airline has found that there is usually someone who is willing to miss their flight if the airline pays for their ticket and gives them an additional \$200 in cash. Thus the cost of overbooking to the airline is \$300, and there is no additional cost of lost goodwill. From analysis of past data, the airline determines that, on average, 3% of the number of booked customers are no-shows. The actual number of no-shows varies according to the Poisson distribution. How many seats should the airline book so as to maximize the expected net revenue? Use a spreadsheet program or @RISK and simulation to answer this question.

Diagnostic Assignment

Inventory Turns Per Year

Introduction

Contributing to the operation of an enterprise through its various committees is an important part of the managerial function. This vignette attempts to capture some of that experience. Assume the role of Larry Luchek. You will attend the next meeting of the management committee as a replacement for Victor Kowalski. Be prepared to make a presentation to the group on the topic of inventory turns if you feel there is more to be said. Remember that the other members of the committee are not necessarily experts in current inventory control technology, so if you have a point to make you should be prepared to illustrate it with numerical examples. As you will see, such arguments are the medium of exchange in the committee under consideration.

A Management Committee Meeting

Steco's management committee is having its biweekly meeting. Frank Watson, the president; Jayne Frazier, the treasurer; and Tom Galanti, vice-president of marketing, are all assembled in the conference room. Victor Kowalski, vice-president of operations, is on a tour of West Coast facilities and cannot attend the meeting. He is represented by his assistant, Larry Luchek. The discussion proceeds as follows.

FRANK: This probably isn't the best time to raise the topic since Vic isn't here, but I want to mention it anyway so that it will be on the agenda for the next meeting. I was just reading in *Business Week* that the Japanese are beating our pants off in inventory control methods. Since inventory is our main business we have to be sure that we are doing as well as possible.

JAYNE: I read the same article, and, frankly, it wasn't very clear to me. The entire discussion was in terms of "turns." I'm quite familiar with our system, and that isn't a term we use. At any rate, the bottom line of the article is that the Japanese are doing so much better because they have many more inventory turns than the typical U.S. firm, and I inferred that more turns means you pay less inventory charges. As I recall, the typical Japanese firm averaged about 20 turns, whereas the U.S. average was about 6. The article also mentioned that European firms on the average have even a smaller number of turns; I think the average was about 2 turns. Whatever all of that proves.

LARRY: I'm sure that Vic could give you a more complete analysis of the situation than I can because I'm rather new to this assignment. However, I may be able to shed some light on the subject. Turns are defined as

$$\text{turns} = \frac{\text{annual demand}}{\text{average inventory}}$$

Jayne, your remarks are right on target. For a given annual demand, more turns means lower average inventory and, hence, lower holding costs. However, since average inventory is a function of the order quantity and our order quantities are determined by the EOQ formula, the number of turns that we have for our products must be optimal. Let's look at a specific example. We assume that demand in each month for reinforced appliance angles is a normal random variable with a mean of 50 and a standard deviation of 15. Note that this assumption yields an annual demand of 12(50) equals 600. The typical lead time is one month, and, as you know, Steco's standard practice is to have a stockout probability of 0.05. We have estimated an ordering cost of \$25.00 and a holding cost of \$1.92 per unit per year. By using the EOQ formula we can verify that Q^*, the optimal order quantity, is 125. The average inventory is one-half of the order quantity, or 62.5 angles. This yields 9.6 turns per year. Here, I'll put the calculations on the board.

$$\text{Annual demand} = D = 600 \text{ angles}$$

$$\text{Ordering cost} = C_o = \$25.00$$

$$\text{Holding cost} = C_h = \$1.92 \text{ per angle per year}$$

$$\text{Optimal order quantity} = Q^* = \sqrt{\frac{2C_oD}{C_h}} = 125$$

$$\text{Average inventory} = \frac{Q^*}{2} = 62.5$$

$$\text{Turns} = \frac{D}{(Q^*/2)} = 9.6$$

$$\text{Orders per year} = N^* = \frac{D}{Q^*}$$

therefore

$$\text{Turns} = 2N^*$$

JAYNE: Are you sure about that, Larry? I understand your calculations, but, as I recall, our inventory audit shows a larger average inventory.

LARRY: There may be some random fluctuations, but we use an (r, Q) model, and on average it will indicate how the system works. In particular, these calculations form the basis for two observations. First, we see that the number of turns (9.6) that results from our calculations is indeed smaller than the figure of 20 that you cite for Japanese firms. However, the number of turns is optimal given our current costs. In order to change the number of turns we must change the costs. Next, we see that the number of turns is simply two times the number of orders we place during a year. Thus, to increase the optimal number of orders without increasing the annual cost, we would have to lower the cost of placing an order. Since our system is already computerized, this doesn't sound very promising to me. Frankly, I don't see that there is a lot of room for improvement.

TOM: Larry, this situation reminds me of the nonreinforced appliance angle problem. I remember discussing that order with Vic because it was the case he used to learn about ICON, our inventory control system. It seems to me that because of quantity discounts we increased our order quantity from 1250 to 5000. Obviously, this large increase in the order quantity would cause a large decrease in the number of turns. If I understood your formulas correctly, increasing the order quantity by a factor of 4 would reduce the number of turns by the same factor, 4. So it is obvious that quantity discounts can play an important role in determining the number of turns. I suppose that it is possible that suppliers in the United States are more able than their Japanese competitors to demand larger order quantities in order to obtain quantity discounts, and thus the number of turns on the average is smaller here. I must say that does not sound like a reasonable hypothesis to me. There must be another explanation.

FRANK: I think that we have devoted as much time to this topic as we should in Vic's absence. We'll put it on the agenda for the next meeting. I now want to bring your attention to our current cash flow problems. The combinations of slow payment by our customers and the high interest costs are causing serious problems. . . .

Questions

1. What main point has Larry omitted from his analysis, and how (if at all) would this affect his calculation for the number of turns?
2. Larry has correctly pointed out that ordering cost will affect the number of turns. Tom has correctly pointed out that quantity discounts play a role. As a result of your analysis, what other features might management consider?

Video Case

Inventory Models with Probabilistic Demand

This is the second video devoted to JIT (just-in-time) inventory systems. In Chapter 10 we considered the importance of reduced setup costs in a JIT system and discussed the relationship between the EOQ model and JIT principles. Here we want to direct our attention to the role of delivery lead times in JIT systems and consider the relationship between JIT systems and the (r,Q) and Newsboy models discussed in this chapter.

We start by noting that there is tremendous emphasis on reducing lead times in JIT systems. This is natural; because JIT systems hold a minimum of inventory, they must be able to get quick delivery from their vendors to meet rapidly changing production plans. Companies are developing a number of approaches to aid in the drive toward reduced lead times. Here are two examples.

Electronic data interchange (EDI) plays an important role in cutting lead times. With EDI, sales information is transmitted automatically to the supplier at the time the sale occurs. This process eliminates the long delays commonly experienced in traditional hierarchical inventory systems, in which sales information is aggregated for a specified period at the retailer and then transmitted to the wholesaler, where the process is repeated.

Product design can also play a major part in reducing lead times. Companies now often use what is called a delay strategy, which involves waiting as long as possible to give a product its final form. Personal computers, for example, are designed with a number of interchangeable components. Thus any monitor may be compatible with any of several basic computers. Using the delay strategy, you need hold inventory only of each component rather than of all possible combinations of components. This approach makes it possible to have essentially every item in stock, and thus offer short delivery times.

Questions

Here are some questions that will help you relate JIT principles to the (r,Q) and Newsboy models.

1. What is the effect on the average inventory on hand of reducing lead time in the (r,Q) model?
2. What is the effect of shortening the interval between the time an order is placed and the time it arrives (the lead time) for fashion goods, i.e., items that are ordered only once?

CHAPTER 17 Queuing Models

APPLICATION CAPSULE

The BOSS Barges In: A Queuing Model Saves New York City Money by Refuting an "Obvious" Conclusion*

By 1981, many of the landfills used by the New York City Department of Sanitation (DOS) were full, or nearly so. The imminent closing of these landfills was expected to result in a doubling of the daily refuse tonnage destined for the Fresh Kills landfill on Staten Island.

To reach this landfill—the world's largest—garbage must be transported by barge. Common sense seemed to suggest that if the tonnage of refuse doubled, the size of the barge fleet would also have to double. This would require the purchase of an additional 40 barges at an estimated cost of $1 million per barge. However, DOS was dubious about this conclusion. Rather than resigning itself to such a large expense, it developed a queuing model, the Barge Operation System Simulator, or BOSS, to test the underlying logic of the "common sense" assumption.

Using the model, DOS was able to evaluate the operation of the system under different conditions, including the addition of varying numbers of barges. The simulation, in conjunction with queuing theory, showed that only 20 to 30 more barges would be needed to accommodate the increased tonnage through 1990. These results were not a surprise to the management science professionals who created the simulator. They recognized the barge operation as a "closed multi-server queuing system," and it is common for such systems to exhibit economies of scale. That is, increases in the arrival rates (garbage, in this case) of such systems can typically be accommodated with less than a proportional increase in servers (barges).

When DOS ordered the barges in 1983, they actually cost only $600,000 each. Thus the city was able to save between $6 million and $12 million. Since the BOSS study cost only $100,000, the investment in analysis yielded an impressive return.

*Richard C. Larson, "OR/MS and the Services Industries," *OR/MS Today*, April 1989, pp. 12–18.

17.1 Introduction

"Queue" is the British term for any type of line for waiting. The British always talk of "queuing up" when asking people to form a line. Students may also see the alternate spelling of "queueing" with the extra "e."

Queuing problems are everywhere. This fact is obvious even to the most casual observer. Airplanes "queue up" in holding patterns, waiting for a runway so they can land, and then they line up again to take off. People line up for tickets, to buy groceries, and, if they happen to live in England, for almost everything else. Jobs line up for machines, orders line up to be filled, and so on.

Monte Jackson might not subscribe to the notion that all of life is a queue, but as administrative director of St. Luke's Hospital in Philadelphia, he must deal with a number of situations that can be described as queuing problems. Briefly, a **queuing problem** is one in which you have a sequence of items (such as people) arriving at a facility for service, as shown in Figure 17.1. At this moment, Monte is concerned about three particular "queuing problems."

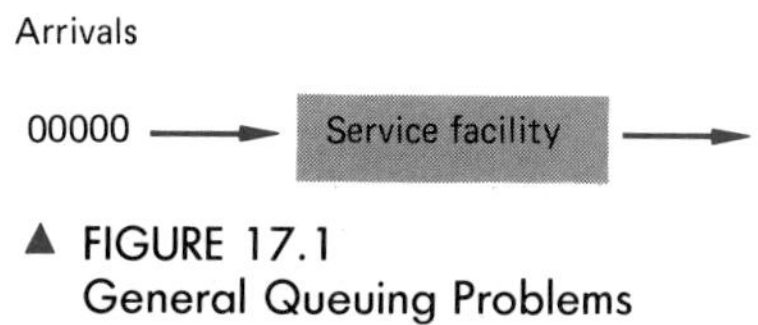

▲ FIGURE 17.1
General Queuing Problems

Problem 1: St. Luke's Hematology Lab. St. Luke's treats a large number of patients on an outpatient basis; that is, there are many patients who come to the hospital to see the staff doctors for diagnosis and treatment but who are not admitted to the hospital. Outpatients plus those admitted to the 600-bed hospital produce a large flow of new patients each day. Most new patients must visit the hematology laboratory as part of the diagnostic process. Each such patient has to be seen by a technician. The system works like this: After seeing a doctor, the patient arrives at the laboratory and checks in with a clerk. Patients are assigned on a first-come, first-served basis to test rooms as they become available. The technician assigned to that room performs the tests ordered by the doctor. When the testing is complete, the patient goes on to the next step in the process (perhaps X-ray), and the technician sees a new patient.

Monte must decide how many technicians to hire. Superficially, at least, the trade-off is obvious. More technicians means more expense for the hospital, but quicker service for the patients.

WATS (Wide Area Telephone Service) is an acronym for a special flat-rate, long-distance service offered by some phone companies. When all the phone lines allocated to WATS are in use, the person dialing out will get a busy signal, indicating that the call can't be completed (which can be confused with the destination's phone line actually being busy).

Problem 2: Buying WATS Lines. As part of its remodeling process, St. Luke's is designing a new communications system. Monte must decide how many WATS lines the hospital should buy. He knows that when people pick up the phone, they want to get through without having to try several times. How many lines he needs to achieve that result at a reasonable cost is not so clear.

Problem 3: Hiring Repairpeople. St. Luke's hires repairpeople to maintain 20 individual pieces of electronic equipment. The equipment includes measuring devices such as the electrocardiogram machine, small dedicated computers like the one used for lung analysis, and equipment such as the CAT scanner. If a piece of equipment fails and all the repairpeople are occupied, it must wait to be repaired. Monte must decide how many repairpeople to hire. He must balance their cost against the cost of having broken equipment.

As Figure 17.2 indicates, all three of these problems fit the general description of a queuing model. Monte will resolve these problems by using a combination of

The Danish engineer A. K. Erlang is credited with founding queuing theory by studying telephone switchboards in Copenhagen for the Danish Telephone Company. He developed many of the queuing results used today. One of the greatest uses of queuing theory in the United States is for analyzing automobile traffic flow—studying how many lanes to have, how to regulate the traffic lights, etc.—in order to maximize the flow of traffic.

PROBLEM	ARRIVALS	SERVICE FACILITY
1	Patients	Technicians
2	Telephone Calls	Switchboard
3	Broken Equipment	Repairpeople

▲ FIGURE 17.2
Some Queuing Problems

analytic and simulation models. However, before we reach the level of sophistication required to deal with Monte's specific problems, it is necessary for us to spend some time with the basic queuing model. In the process we will learn some terminology, and we will see the type of analytic results that are available.

17.2 The Basic Model

Consider the Xerox machine located in the fourth-floor secretarial service suite. Assume that users arrive at the machine and form a single line. Each arrival in turn uses the machine to perform a specific task. These tasks vary from obtaining a copy of a 1-page letter to producing 100 copies of a 25-page report. This system is called a single-server (or single-**channel**) queue. Questions about this or any other queuing system center on four quantities:

1. The number of people in the system: the number of people currently being served, as well as those waiting for service.
2. The number of people in the queue: the number of people waiting for service.
3. The waiting time in the system: the interval between when an individual enters the system and when he or she leaves the system. Note that this interval includes the service time.
4. The waiting time in the queue: the time between entering the system and the beginning of service.

Assumptions of the Basic Model

The exponential distribution is *not* symmetric, a fact that at first bothers many students, who think that an "average" must have as many values above the mean as below it. If customers arrive, on the average, every 5 minutes, then approximately 2/3 of them will have interarrival times less than 5 minutes, and only about 1/3 of them longer than 5 minutes (but some of those may be very long and thus "skew" the average).

1. ***Arrival Process.*** Each arrival will be called a "job." Since the time between arrivals (the **interarrival time**) is not known with certainty, we will need to specify a probability distribution for it. In the basic model a particular distribution, called the *exponential distribution* (sometimes called the *negative exponential distribution*), is used. This distribution plays a central role in many queuing models. It provides a reasonable representation of the arrival process in a number of situations, and its so-called **lack of memory** property makes it possible to obtain analytic results. The words *Poisson input* are also used to describe the arrival process when the time between arrivals has an exponential distribution. This is because of the relationship between the exponential distribution and the Poisson distribution. In particular, if the interarrival time has an exponential distribution, the number of arrivals in a specified length of time (say, three hours) has a Poisson distribution.

The exponential distribution and its relationship to the Poisson is discussed in some detail in Section 17.10. At this point, it is only necessary to understand that the exponential distribution is completely specified by one parameter. This parameter, called λ, is the *mean arrival rate,* i.e., how many jobs arrive (on the average) during a specific period of time. In a moment we will consider an example in which $\lambda = 0.05$ jobs per minute. This implies that *on the average* 5/100 of a job arrives every minute. It is probably more natural to think in terms of a longer time interval. An equivalent statement is that *on the average* one job arrives every 20 minutes. Using more technical terms, we say that *the mean interarrival time* is 20 minutes. Mean interarrival time is the average time between two arrivals. Thus, for the exponential distribution

$$\text{average time between jobs} = \text{mean interarrival time} = \frac{1}{\lambda} \qquad \textbf{(17.1)}$$

The same exponential distribution describes many services (bank tellers, postal clerks). About 2/3 of the services will be below the mean time (a lot of short, quick transactions) and 1/3 of the services will be above the mean (someone with the cash receipts from their business, or a person mailing a package overseas). Murphy's Law says that when one is in a hurry, one will always get stuck behind the person with the longest service time!

Thus, if $\lambda = 0.05$,

$$\text{mean interarrival time} = \frac{1}{\lambda} = \frac{1}{0.05} = 20$$

2. ***Service Process.*** In the basic model, the time that it takes to complete a job (the **service time**) is also treated with the exponential distribution. The parameter for this exponential distribution is called μ. It represents the *mean service rate* in jobs per minute. In other words, μT is the number of jobs that would be served (on the average) during a period of T minutes if the machine were busy during that time. In the upcoming example we will assume that $\mu = 0.10$. This implies that on the average 0.10 of a job is completed each minute. An equivalent statement is that on the average one job is completed every 10 minutes. The *mean, or average, service time* (the average time to complete a job) is $1/\mu$. When μ, the mean service rate, is 0.10, the average service time is 10 since $1/\mu = 1/0.10 = 10$.

This infinite queue assumes that when customers arrive they will enter the queue and not leave until serviced. This means that they will not **balk** (look at the long checkout line as they enter the store and decide not to shop) or **renege** (get in line with one item, get fed up with the wait, and leave the quart of milk at the counter).

3. ***Queue Size.*** There is no limit on the number of jobs that can wait in the queue. The queue is said to be infinite.
4. ***Queue Discipline.*** Jobs are served on a first-come, first-served basis; that is, in the same order as they arrive at the queue.
5. ***Time Horizon.*** The system operates as described continuously over an infinite horizon.
6. ***Source Population.*** There is an infinite population available to arrive.

Consider these assumptions in the context of the Xerox problem. Suppose that the average arrival time between jobs is 20 minutes. As we have seen, the fact that the interarrival time has an exponential distribution (see [17.1]) means that $1/\lambda = 20$, and thus $\lambda = 0.05$, or that the jobs arrive at the rate of 0.05 job per minute. Similarly, if the average time to complete a job is 10 minutes, we know that $1/\mu = 10$, $\mu = 0.10$, and that jobs are completed at the rate of 0.10 job per minute when the machine is operating.

Characteristics of the Basic Model

Formulas assume $\lambda < \mu$

The values of these two parameters (together with the assumptions) are all that is needed to calculate several important **operating characteristics** of the basic model. The necessary formulas are presented in Figure 17.3 **WARNING!** *The formulas in Figure 17.3 hold only if* $\lambda < \mu$. If this condition does not hold (i.e., if $\lambda \geq \mu$), the number of people in the queue will grow without limit. Consider, for example, a specific case where $\lambda = 0.25$ and $\mu = 0.10$. Remember that $1/\lambda$ is the average interarrival time. Thus, since $1/\lambda = 1/0.25 = 4$, on the average a job arrives every 4 minutes. Similarly, $1/\mu$ is the average time it takes to complete a job. Since $1/\mu = 1/0.10 = 10$, on the average it takes 10 minutes to complete a job. It seems clear that in this case the service operation will get further behind (the queue will grow longer) as time goes by.

Now return to the Xerox problem, in which $\lambda < \mu$ and the formulas in Figure 17.3 hold. Plugging the numerical values from the Xerox problem, $\lambda = 0.05$ and $\mu = 0.10$, into the formulas yields the results presented in Figure 17.4.

CHARACTERISTIC	SYMBOL	FORMULA
Expected number in system	L	$\frac{\lambda}{\mu - \lambda}$
Expected number in queue	L_q	$\frac{\lambda^2}{\mu(\mu - \lambda)}$
Expected waiting time (includes service time)	W	$\frac{1}{\mu - \lambda}$
Expected time in queue	W_q	$\frac{\lambda}{\mu(\mu - \lambda)}$
Probability that the system is empty	P_0	$1 - \frac{\lambda}{\mu}$

▲ FIGURE 17.3
Operating Characteristics for the Basic Model

Expected number in system	$L = \frac{\lambda}{\mu - \lambda} = \frac{0.05}{0.10 - 0.05} = 1$
Expected number in queue	$L_q = \frac{\lambda^2}{\mu(\mu - \lambda)} = \frac{0.0025}{0.10(0.10 - 0.05)} = 0.5$
Expected waiting time	$W = \frac{1}{\mu - \lambda} = \frac{1}{0.10 - 0.05)} = 20$
Expected time in queue	$W_q = \frac{\lambda}{\mu(\mu - \lambda)} = \frac{0.05}{0.10(0.10 - 0.05)} = 10$
Probability that the system is empty	$P_0 = 1 - \frac{\lambda}{\mu} = 1 - \frac{0.05}{0.10} = 0.5$

▲ FIGURE 17.4
Evaluating the Operating Characteristics of the Basic Model when $\lambda = 0.05$, $\mu = 0.10$

These values are *averages* and, as such, may have the same exponential distribution characteristics (2/3 below mean, 1/3 above). Thus, 2/3 of the customers will spend less than 10 minutes in line, while 1/3 will spend more than 10 minutes in line.

The assumption here is that enough time has passed so that the system has "settled down" and is operating normally. Mathematicians call this "steady state," as in the reaction experiments done in chemistry class. Although everything seems calm on the surface, equal and opposing chemical changes are continuously taking place, so that a dynamic balance is continued.

Steady State Results. These numbers require some interpretation. L, for example, is the expected number of people in the system (those being served plus those waiting) after the queue has reached *steady state.* In this sentence, **steady state** means that the probability that you will observe a certain number of people (say, 2) in the system does not depend on the time at which you count them. If a steady state has been achieved, the probability that there are two people using and/or waiting for the Xerox machine should be the same at 2:30 P.M. and at 4:00 P.M.

The other characteristics presented in Figures 17.3 and 17.4 have a similar interpretation. Thus, in a steady state, (1) the system is empty with a probability of one-half ($P_0 = 0.5$); (2) on the average there is 0.5 person in the queue ($L_q = 0.5$); (3) on the average an arrival must wait 10 minutes before starting to use the machine ($W_q = 10$); and (4) on the average an arrival will spend 20 minutes in the system ($W = 20$).

Using the Results. These results hold for the basic model and the particular values for the parameters ($\lambda = 0.05$ and $\mu = 0.10$). They provide information that is useful to management in analyzing this service facility. Suppose, for example, that management makes the following calculations: Since $\lambda = 0.05$, on the average 5/100 of a job arrives each minute. During each 8-hour day there are $8 \times 60 = 480$ minutes. Thus, during each day there is on the average a total of

$$(0.05)(480) = 24$$

arrivals. From the calculations in Figure 17.4 we know that on the average each person spends 20 minutes in the system ($W = 20$). Thus, a total of (24 arrivals per day) (20 minutes per arrival) = 480 minutes, or 8 hours is spent at this facility. Management might well feel that this is too long. A variety of steps might be taken:

1. A new machine might be purchased with a smaller mean service time.
2. Another machine might be purchased and both machines used to satisfy the demand. This would change the system to a two-server queue.
3. Some personnel might be sent to a different and less busy copying facility. This would change the arrival process.

Management might select one of these alternatives, or perhaps some other option. But in any case, management must balance the cost of providing service against the cost of waiting. The results in Figure 17.4 and similar results for other systems would be a central part of the analysis. These ideas will be developed in more detail in the context of Monte Jackson's problems.

17.3 A Taxonomy of Queuing Models

There are many possible queuing models. For example, if the interarrival time in the basic model had been given a different distribution (not the exponential) we would have had a different model, in the sense that the expressions for L, L_q, and so on, would no longer hold. To facilitate communication among those working on queuing models, D. G. Kendall proposed a taxonomy based on the following notation:

The notation

$$A/B/s$$

$$\text{where } A = \text{arrival distribution}$$
$$B = \text{service distribution}$$
$$s = \text{number of servers}$$

Different letters are used to designate certain distributions. Placed in the A or the B position, they indicate the arrival or the service distribution, respectively. The following conventions are in general use:

Some conventions

M = exponential distribution

D = deterministic number

G = any (a general) distribution of service times

GI = any (a general) distribution of arrival times

We can see, for example, that the Xerox problem is an $M/M/1$ model, that is, a single-server queue with exponential interarrival and service times.

APPLICATION CAPSULE

Merging Traffic: A Queuing Simulation Helps Eliminate a Costly Bottleneck*

The Westinghouse Hanford Company in Richland, Washington, is a secured work facility: All vehicles and passengers are checked at a guard station before being allowed onto the premises. This security checkpoint created enormous traffic backups during shift changes, when the volume of entering vehicles was greatest. The result was a severe hazard for the workforce and a major loss of productivity for the company as personnel were detained in long lines. An in-house engineering group was therefore asked to study the problem and make recommendations for changes.

The study group found that each workday morning an average of 7 buses and 285 cars and vans arrived at the plant. Upon approaching the entrance gate, the vehicles formed one line to pass through the checkpoint, which was normally manned by two guards during rush periods. The line extended past the available queue space (which could accommodate only 40 cars) and spilled out onto the adjacent highway, causing a major safety problem. Because of the long line, drivers of other vehicles often elected to continue down the highway to a second gate. This option meant additional time and distance for the employees, as well as an unknown wait at the other gate.

The standard analytical queuing model predicted—correctly—that because the service rate at the checkpoint was equal to the arrival rate, the queue would continue to grow without limit as long as cars kept arriving. This, however, merely confirmed what had already been observed. A simulation was therefore developed. The model was run to reproduce the current situation and then to try out alternatives.

- The first alternative scenario increased the number of guards to three while keeping the single lane of traffic. This approach reduced the maximum queue length from 45.5 to 28, but increased costs.
- The second scenario had vehicles forming two lines, with a security guard assigned to each line. When a bus arrived, it was routed around the two vehicle lines and serviced immediately by one guard while the other guard temporarily worked both lines. This solution produced a maximum queue length of 14 vehicles and a waiting time of only about 12 minutes, compared to over 30 minutes for the existing configuration.

The second scenario appeared to be a good solution involving no additional cost. When it was implemented on a trial basis, the queue length was indeed drastically reduced. The biggest surprise was that the number of vehicles using the gate rose from 285 to 345. Obviously vehicles that had been regularly bypassing the main gate had started using it. Thanks to the shorter queues, the new system easily handled the increased traffic load.

*Landauer and Becker, "Reducing Waiting Time at Security Checkpoints," *Interfaces*, Vol. 19, No. 5 (Sept.–Oct. 1989).

17.4 Little's Flow Equation and Related Results

It can be proven that in a steady-state queuing process

The flow equation

$$L = \lambda W \qquad \textbf{(17.2)}$$

This result states that L, the expected number of people in the system, equals λ, the arrival rate, times W, the expected waiting time. To perform a quick numerical check, see if the numbers derived for the Xerox problem (Figure 17.4) satisfy (17.2). The calculation is shown in (17.3).

$$L = 1.0 = 0.05 \times 20 = \lambda W \qquad \textbf{(17.3)}$$

Intuitive derivation

To understand the intuitive foundation for this result, consider the diagram in Figure 17.5. In Scene 1 our hero arrives and joins the queue. In Scene 2 he has just completed service. Assume the system is in steady state. Since in this case the average number of people in the system is independent of time, let us measure this quantity when our hero completes being served. At this time, the number of people in the system is precisely the total number who arrived after he did (i.e., the individuals who arrived during his waiting time). Therefore, if W is his waiting time and people arrive at a rate of λ, we would expect L, the average number in the system, to equal λW.

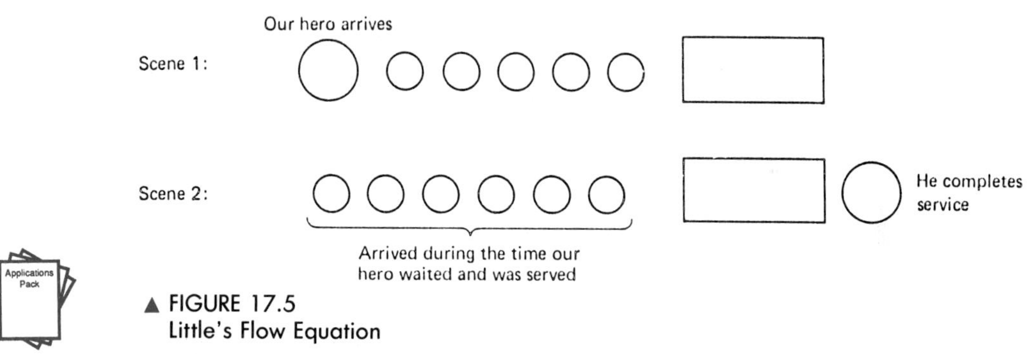

▲ FIGURE 17.5
Little's Flow Equation

Equation (17.2) is often called Little's flow equation. Note that it applies to any steady-state queuing process and is thus applicable to a wide variety of problems. The proof used to establish (17.2) also shows that

A similar equation

$$L_q = \lambda W_q \qquad \textbf{(17.4)}$$

A numerical check for the Xerox problem shows that

$$L_q = 0.5 = 0.05 \times 10 = \lambda W_q$$

which again agrees with the result in Figure 17.4.

One must take some care in applying this result in more complicated cases. It is essential that λ represents the rate at which arrivals *join* the queue. This may be different from the rate at which people "arrive." Consider, for example, a queue with an upper limit on the number of items that can wait in the queue. A modern phone system that will hold a certain number of calls (say, 10) in a queue until a

A queue with an "upper limit" is called a *finite queue*. In the phone system example, a "busy signal" causes a *balk*. A physical upper limit may be the number of phone lines, or the number of shopping carts available in a grocery store. However, the long wait on hold on the phone or in line at the checkout counter is a prime cause of *reneging* (customer spends time in the system and then decides to leave).

service representative becomes available provides a good example. In such a system a person who calls and finds the system full simply receives a busy signal—in other words, is sent away. He or she does not join the queue. This is called a **balk.** Thus, if $\lambda = 0.25$ (the arrival rate) and the mean time between calls is 4 minutes, this is *not* the rate at which people *join.* Thus, the relationship $L = 0.25W$ will not hold for this system. Similarly, a customer may tire of waiting in line and leave without being served. This is called **reneging.** Here again, $L = 0.25\,W$ will not hold for this system.

Another important general result depends on the observation that

$$\begin{aligned}\text{expected waiting time} &= \text{expected waiting time in queue}\\ &\quad + \text{expected service time}\end{aligned}$$

For the basic model we have already made use of the fact that

$$\text{expected service time} = \frac{1}{\mu}$$

Putting the general result in symbols yields

Another general result

$$W = W_q + \frac{1}{\mu} \tag{17.5}$$

For the Xerox problem we have

$$W = 20 = 10 + \frac{1}{0.10} = W_q + \frac{1}{\mu}$$

Not only does this hold for the basic model, but the general result (equation [17.5]) holds for any queuing model in which a steady state occurs.

Solving the three equations

Some students will appreciate having an alternative way of arriving at the same expected values, choosing the one that is easier for them.

Equations (17.2), (17.4), and (17.5) make it possible to compute the four operating characteristics L, L_q, W, and W_q once one of them is known. To illustrate this fact, let us start the Xerox problem over again. We begin as last time using the first formula in Figure 17.3 to calculate L:

$$L = \frac{\lambda}{\mu - \lambda} = \frac{0.05}{0.10 - 0.05} = 1$$

Now rather than using the other formulas in Figure 17.3 that are specifically for the basic model, we will use the two general results that we have just presented. First, from Little's flow equation (17.2) we know that

$$L = \lambda W$$

Thus, knowing $L = 1$ and $\lambda = 0.05$, we obtain $W = L/\lambda = 20$. Then, turning to (17.5), we see that

$$W = W_q + \frac{1}{\mu}$$

$$W_q = W - \frac{1}{\mu} = 20 - \frac{1}{0.10} = 10$$

Finally, (17.4) shows that

$$L_q = \lambda W_q = 0.05 \times 10 = 0.5$$

This alternative method of obtaining numerical results will turn out to be most useful when analyzing more complicated systems.

17.5 The $M/G/1$ Queue

While the exponential distribution accurately describes the arrival process in many situations, it may not fit the service process very well. Fortunately, there is a generalization of the basic model that permits the distribution of the service time to be arbitrary. It is not even necessary to know the service time distribution, only its mean, $1/\mu$, and its variance, σ^2. The operating characteristics for the generalized model are given in Figure 17.6.

CHARACTERISTIC	SYMBOL	FORMULA
Expected number in system	L	$L_q + \frac{\lambda}{\mu}$
Expected number in queue	L_q	$\frac{\lambda^2\sigma^2 + (\lambda/\mu)^2}{2(1 - \lambda/\mu)}$
Expected waiting time	W	$W_q + \frac{1}{\mu}$
Expected time in queue	W_q	$\frac{L_q}{\lambda}$
Probability that the system is empty	P_0	$1 - \frac{\lambda}{\mu}$

▲ FIGURE 17.6
Operating Characteristics for the Generalized Model

Note that we have made use of the results of the previous section in obtaining all the operating characteristics except for L_q. As a check on the validity of these formulas, suppose that the arbitrary service time distribution is exponential. The variance of an exponential distribution is $(1/\mu)^2$ if the mean is $1/\mu$. Therefore,

$$L_q = \frac{\lambda^2(1/\mu)^2 + (\lambda/\mu)^2}{2(1 - \lambda/\mu)} = \frac{\lambda^2}{\mu(\mu - \lambda)}$$

which is the same result as in the basic model.

As σ^2 increases, L, L_q, W, and W_q all increase. This means that the consistency of a server may be as important as the speed of the server. Suppose you must hire a secretary, and you have to select one of two candidates. Secretary 1 is very consistent, typing any document in exactly 15 minutes. Secretary 2 is somewhat faster, with an average of 14 minutes per document, but with times varying according to the exponential distribution. The workload in the office is three documents per hour, with interarrival times varying according to the exponential distribution. Which secretary will give you shorter turnaround times on documents?

Since Secretary 1 types every document in exactly 15 minutes, σ^2 is equal to 0. The values of the other parameters are $\lambda = 3$ per hour or 0.05 per minute and $\mu = 1/15$ per minute. Thus,

$$L_q = \frac{(0.05)^2(0) + [0.05/(1/15)]^2}{2[1 - 0.05/(1/15)]} = 9/8$$

$$W_q = (9/8)/0.05 = 45/2$$

$$W = 45/2 + 15 = 37.5 \text{ minutes average turnaround time}$$

If the secretary had averaged 15 minutes, with a standard deviation of 5 minutes (a fairly "fat" normal distribution), then
L_q = 1.25 documents
W_q = 25 minutes
W = 40 minutes
which dramatically illustrates the impact of the large variance of exponential distributions on waiting time.

We can use either the basic model or the generalized model to calculate the answer for Secretary 2. Using the generalized model, the parameters are $\lambda = 0.05$, $\mu = 1/14$ per minute, and $\sigma = 14$ minutes. So,

$$L_q = \frac{(0.05)^2(14)^2 + [0.05/(1/14)]^2}{2[1 - 0.05/(1/14)]} = 49/30$$

$$W_q = (49/30)/0.05 = 98/3$$

$$W = 98/3 + 14 = 46.67 \text{ minutes average turnaround time}$$

Even though Secretary 2 is "faster," the average turnaround times are longer because of the high variability of service times.

17.6 Problem 1: An *M/M/s* Queue (Hematology Lab)

Identical problems are faced by fast-food franchise managers: how many people to put on a shift to keep the average customer wait below a certain value. McDonalds reportedly figures they will lose a customer if the total wait is more than 5 minutes. Burger King has special kitchens set up to time and videotape every aspect of a model franchise. They then try different configurations of the kitchen to get the best possible work flow.

Recall that as we started this chapter, our stated goal was to attack three particular problems at St. Luke's with queuing models. In the preceding sections we have laid the groundwork for this process. We have introduced, defined, and illustrated the characteristics of the systems that we will consider (e.g., expected number in queue, expected waiting time, etc.). We have also made some general results such as Little's flow equation available for use in future analysis. We are now in a position to turn our attention to Monte Jackson's problems.

The system described in Problem 1 of Section 17.1, the blood-testing problem, is illustrated in Figure 17.7. Note that each patient joins a common queue and, on arriving at the head of the line, enters the first examining room that becomes available. This type of system must not be confused with a system in which a queue forms in front of each server, as in the typical grocery store.

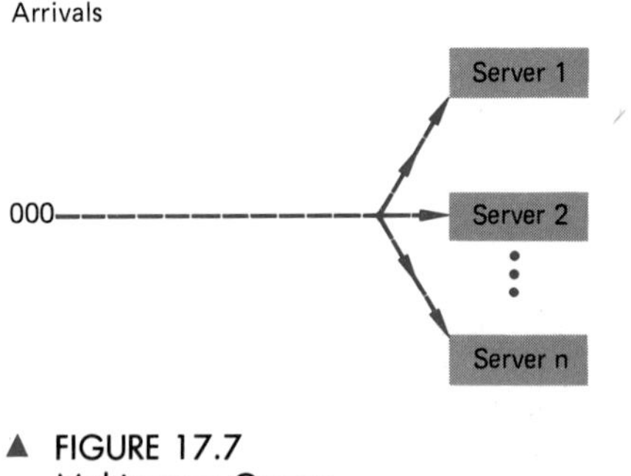

▲ FIGURE 17.7
Multiserver Queue

Assume that the interarrival time is given by an exponential distribution with parameter $\lambda = 0.20$ per minute. This implies that a new patient arrives every 5 minutes on the average, since

$$\text{mean interarrival time} = \frac{1}{\lambda} = \frac{1}{0.20} = 5$$

Also, assume that each server is identical and that each service time is given by an exponential distribution with parameter $\mu = 0.125$ per minute. This implies that the mean service time is 8 minutes, since

$$\begin{array}{l}\text{mean service time for} \\ \text{an individual server}\end{array} = \frac{1}{\mu} = \frac{1}{0.125} = 8$$

Requirement for steady state

Note that if there were only one server, the queue would grow without limit, since $\lambda > \mu$ (0.20 > 0.125). For a multiserver queue, however, a steady state will exist as long as $\lambda < s\mu$, where s is the number of servers. For example, if we have two servers, $0.20 < 2(0.125)$ or $0.20 < 0.25$.

The Key Equations. As before, we want to find values L, L_q, W, and W_q. However, since this is a multiserver queue (not a single-server queue as in the Xerox problem), we must use different formulas. To evaluate these formulas it is convenient to start with the expression for P_0, the probability that the system is empty. For this model

$$P_0 = \frac{1}{\sum_{n=0}^{s-1} \frac{(\lambda/\mu)^n}{n!} + \frac{(\lambda/\mu)^s}{s!}\left(\frac{1}{1 - (\lambda/s\mu)}\right)} \tag{17.6}$$

and L_q, the expected number of people in the queue, is expressed as

$$L_q = P_0\left[\frac{(\lambda/\mu)^{s+1}}{(s-1)!(s - \lambda/\mu)^2}\right] \tag{17.7}$$

Equations (17.6) and (17.7) and the general results in (17.2), (17.4), and (17.5) make it possible to calculate values for W_q, W, and L for any specified parameter values (μ and λ) and any number of servers (value of s).

Example Calculations. Assume, for example, that Monte decided to hire two technicians. Then, since $s = 2$, $\lambda = 0.20$, and $\mu = 0.125$, we see that $\lambda/\mu = 0.20/0.125 = 1.6$, and $\lambda/s\mu = 0.20/2(0.125) = 0.8$. Equation (17.6) becomes[1]

$$P_0 = \frac{1}{1 + 1.6 + \frac{(1.6)^2}{2}\left(\frac{1}{1 - 0.8}\right)} = 0.11$$

and the probability that the system is empty is 0.11. We can now use this result in (17.7) to find L_q.

$$L_q = 0.11\left[\frac{1.6^3}{1!(2 - 1.6)^2}\right] = 2.82$$

That is, the expected number of people in the queue is somewhat less than 3.

From (17.4), Monte knows that $L_q = \lambda W_q$. Thus,

$$W_q = \frac{L_q}{\lambda} = \frac{2.82}{0.20} = 14.10$$

or, on the average, a patient waits for 14.10 minutes before entering an examining room.

Let us now look at the general observation that

$$\begin{aligned}\text{expected waiting time} &= \text{expected waiting time in queue} \\ &\quad + \text{expected service time}\end{aligned}$$

[1]To evaluate this expression, you must use the facts that $0! = 1$ and $(1.6)^0 = 1$.

We note that the expected service time in this expression is the expected time an individual will spend being served. This does not depend on the number of servers. It depends only on the amount of time an individual server takes to do the job. In this case all servers are the same. Each has a mean service time of $1/\mu$. Since

$$W = \text{expected waiting time}$$
$$W_q = \text{expected time in queue}$$
$$\frac{1}{\mu} = \text{expected service time}$$

we have

$$\begin{aligned} W &= W_q + \frac{1}{\mu} \\ &= 14.10 + \frac{1}{0.125} \\ &= 14.10 + 8 \\ &= 22.10 \end{aligned}$$

The times for waiting in line for 2, 3, and 4 servers: $W_q(2) = 14.10$ minutes $W_q(3) = 1.57$ minutes $W_q(4) = 0.30$ minutes There is a dramatic shortening of waiting time with a third server, but at the cost of having an extra server. Another factor to take into account is how busy the servers would be. The more servers added, the higher the percentage of idle time for the technicians, which can lead to boredom and sloppy work.

On the average, then, a patient spends 22.10 minutes in the hematology area, waiting for a technician and having tests.

These calculations make the decision easy for Monte. With one technician, since $\lambda > \mu$, the system is unstable and the queue will steadily grow. This could be considered irresponsible. With two technicians, the average waiting time in the queue is less than 15 minutes. By current hospital standards, this is a small and acceptable value. If, in some cases the queue gets uncomfortably long (remember that W_q is an expected value, and the actual time in the queue will vary), the supervisors of the hematology laboratory can temporarily move one of the blood analysts to a technician's position. Monte thus feels comfortable with the idea of hiring two full-time technicians without performing a detailed cost analysis.

17.7 Economic Analysis of Queuing Systems

Monte selected the number of lab technicians to hire by looking at the operating characteristics and using his judgment. This is not an unusual approach in queuing models and is especially common in the not-for-profit sector. Monte realizes that he is balancing the cost of hiring more technicians against the costs he incurs by forcing the patients to wait. The cost of hiring additional technicians is fairly clear. The waiting cost is not.

Monte first notes that the cost to the patient is irrelevant to his decision, except as it affects the patient's willingness to use the hospital. It really does not matter who is waiting—a tax lawyer who charges \$200 per hour for his services or an unemployed person with no opportunity cost—unless the waiting time persuades the patient to use another health facility. This observation explains why certain monopolies like government bureaus and utilities can be so casual about your waiting time. There is no place else to go!

Besides the possible effect on demand, the hematology lab could cost the hospital money if it reduced the output of the hospital. Suppose, for example, that the outpatient clinics could process 50 new patients each day, but that the hematology lab could handle only 10 patients. (This is clearly an extreme example to establish a point.) In this case, the hospital would be wasting a valuable resource, the doctors and other staff in the clinics, because of a bottleneck in the hematology lab. However, having stated this, it still is not easy to assess an explicit cost of a patient waiting.

Cost Parameters. If you are willing and able to estimate certain costs, you can build expected cost models of queuing systems. Consider, for example, the hematology lab problem (in general terms any multiserver queue with exponential interarrival and service times) and suppose that management is willing to specify two costs:

C_w is a very "fuzzy" or qualitative cost, not unlike the cost of a backorder or stockout (C_b) in Section 10.5.

$$C_s = \text{cost per hour of having a server available}$$

$$C_w = \text{cost per hour of having a person wait in the system}$$

With these it is possible to calculate the total costs associated with the decision to use any particular number of servers. Let us start by calculating the total cost of hiring 2 servers for an 8-hour day. There are two components:

$$\text{server cost} = (C_s)(2)(8)$$

where C_s is the cost per hour for 1 server, 2 is the number of servers, and 8 is the number of hours each server works, and

$$\text{waiting cost} = (C_w)(L_2)(8)$$

Here we use L_2 to indicate that the average number of customers in the system is a function of the number of servers.

where L_2 is the number of people in the queue when there are 2 servers. This second calculation may not be as obvious, but the rationale is the same as for the server cost. If there are, on the average, L_2 people waiting when the system has 2 servers, then L_2 times 8 is the average number of "waiting hours" per day. Hence, $(C_w)(L_2)(8)$ is the average waiting cost for the 8-hour day.

If we wanted to calculate the total cost of using 4 servers for a 6-hour day, we would take

$$(C_s)(4)(6) + (C_w)(L_4)(6)$$

or

$$[(C_s(4) + (C_w)(L_4)]6$$

The term in square brackets, $[(C_s)(4) + (C_w)(L_4)]$, then, is the total cost per hour of using 4 servers.

The Total Cost per Hour. We now define

$$\text{TC}(s) = \text{total cost per hour of using } s \text{ servers}$$

and we see that

$$\text{TC}(s) = (C_s)(s) + (C_w)(L_s)$$

Our goal is to choose s, the number of servers, to minimize this function.

Figure 17.8 shows the general shape of the function TC(s). This function is determined by plotting the two component parts, $(C_s)(s)$ and $(C_w)(L_s)$, and adding them together.

We see that TC(s) assumes a minimum for some value s. Unfortunately it is not possible to derive a formula that gives the optimal value of s. (This is in contrast to the EOQ model, where we can find the optimal order quantity, Q*, with the equation $Q^* = \sqrt{2DC_0/C_h}$ as in Chapter 10.)

If C_s = \$50/server/hour and C_w = \$100/customer/hour, then:

S	L	TC
2	4.5	\$550
3	1.9	\$340
4	1.7	\$370

Here, it is cheaper to have 3 technicians than 2 or 4, and sensitivity analysis can be done by adjusting C_w to determine at which point it would be better to have 2 or 4 technicians. This problem might provide a nice use of spreadsheets.

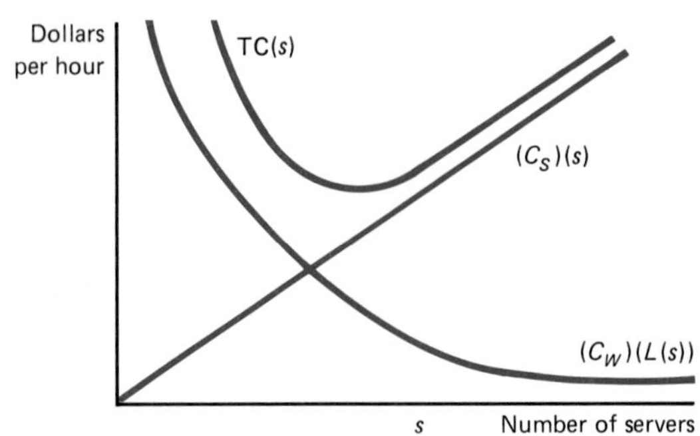

▲ FIGURE 17.8
Costs in an *M/M/s* Queue

It is, however, a relatively easy matter to attack a specific problem numerically, that is, by trying several values of s and selecting the value that yields the minimum total cost. Rather than pursuing this further, let us complete our examination of the hematology lab problem with these observations: We have seen how to find values for L, L_q, W, and W_q. These values were then used to select the appropriate number of technicians (servers). This decision might be made on intuitive grounds or on the basis of an explicit economic analysis. We now move on to Monte's second problem.

17.8 Problem 2: A Finite Queue (WATS Lines)

Do not be misled by the title of this section. It is devoted to Problem 2, Monte's attempt to select the appropriate number of WATS lines for St. Luke's. Fortunately, in this case he can expect help from the telephone company. They have a great deal of expertise in such matters, since queuing models have found extensive use in the field of telephone traffic engineering. The problem of how many lines are needed by a switchboard is typically attacked by using the *M/G/s* model, "with blocked customers cleared." You already know that this model is a multichannel queue with s servers (s lines), exponential interarrival times for the calls, and a general distribution for the service time, which in this case is the length of each call. The phrase "blocked customers cleared" is queuing jargon. It means that *when an arrival finds all of the servers occupied (all of the lines busy), he or she does not get in a queue but simply leaves.* This phrase clearly describes the behavior of the traditional telephone switchboard. More sophisticated systems now provide for queuing of a finite number of customers, in some cases even providing the lucky customer the opportunity to enjoy a Muzak version of "You Light Up My Life," or "As Time Goes By."

Here is a chance to reinforce the terms *balk* (customer receives busy signal and must hang up) and *renege* (customer gets put on hold, listens to too much Muzak, and hangs up before a service representative takes the call).

Probability of *j* Busy Servers. The problem of selecting the appropriate number of lines (servers) is attacked by computing the steady-state probability that exactly j lines will be busy. This, in turn, will be used to calculate the steady-state probability that all s lines are busy. Clearly, if you have s lines and they are all busy, the next caller will not be able to place a call.

The steady-state probability that there are exactly j busy servers given that s lines (servers) are available is given by the expression

$$P_j = \frac{(\lambda/\mu)^j/j!}{\sum_{k=0}^{s} (\lambda/\mu)^k/k!} \tag{17.8}$$

where λ = arrival rate (the rate at which calls arrive)

$\frac{1}{\mu}$ = mean service time (the average length of a conversation)

s = number of servers (lines)

The expression is called the *truncated Poisson distribution* or the *Erlang loss distribution.* It is noteworthy that although we are considering a general service-time distribution, the value P_j defined by (17.8) depends only on the mean of this distribution.

Consider a system in which $\lambda = 1$ (calls arrive at the rate of 1 per minute) and $1/\mu = 10$ (the average length of a conversation is 10 minutes). Here $\lambda/\mu = 10$. Suppose that we have five lines in the system ($s = 5$) and want to find the steady-state probability that exactly two are busy ($j = 2$). From (17.8) we see that

An alternative way of obtaining P_i:
$P_i = P_{i-1}(\lambda/\mu)/i$
$P_3 = P_2\,(10)/3$
$= (0.034)\,(10)/3$
$= 0.1133$
$P_4 = P_3\,(10)/4$
$= (0.1133)(10)/4$
$= 0.2833$
Each successive P_{i-1} is multiplied by (λ/μ) and divided by i. This alternate formulation works well on a spreadsheet.

$$P_2 = \frac{(\lambda/\mu)^2/2!}{\sum_{k=0}^{5} (\lambda/\mu)^k/k!}$$

$$= \frac{(10)^2/2 \cdot 1}{1 + 10^1/1 + 10^2/(2 \cdot 1) + 10^3/(3 \cdot 2 \cdot 1) + 10^4/(4 \cdot 3 \cdot 2 \cdot 1) + 10^5/(5 \cdot 4 \cdot 3 \cdot 2 \cdot 1)}$$

$$= \frac{50}{1 + 10 + 50 + 166.67 + 416.67 + 833.33}$$

$$= \frac{50}{1477.67} = 0.034$$

In other words, on the average, two lines would be busy 3.4% of the time.

The more interesting question is: "What is the probability that all of the lines are busy?" since in this case a potential caller would not be able to place a call. To find the answer to this question, we simply set $j = s$ in (17.8). In our example $s = 5$ and we obtain

$$P_5 = \frac{(\lambda/\mu)^5/5!}{\sum_{k=0}^{5} (\lambda/\mu)^k/k!}$$

Using values that we calculated in our evaluation of P_2, we see that

$$P_5 = \frac{833.33}{1477.67}$$

$$= 0.564$$

or on the average the system is totally occupied 56.4% of the time.

Using Graphs of $B(s, \lambda/\mu)$. The probability that the system is totally occupied (all servers are busy) is important enough that its value has been calculated for a large range of values for λ/μ and s and the results recorded in graphs. The notation $B(s, \lambda/\mu)$ is used for this probability. The B in $B(s, \lambda/\mu)$ stands for balk. This is the probability that a customer will *balk*—find the system full or busy with no waiting room. Values of B for a variety of values of s and λ/μ are presented in Figure 17.9. Let us use this figure to find $B(5, 10)$, the steady-state probability that the system is busy if there are 5 lines and $\lambda/\mu = 10$. We proceed as follows:

As technology has progressed with PCs and spreadsheets, these graphs are quickly becoming obsolete, much like tables of logarithms. Again, spreadsheets can calculate all of the expected values from a queuing situation.

1. Find the value $\lambda/\mu = 10$ on the horizontal axis.
2. Follow this line up until it intersects with the curved contour $s = 5$.
3. Finally, read on the vertical axis the value of $B(s, \lambda/\mu)$ that corresponds to this intersection.

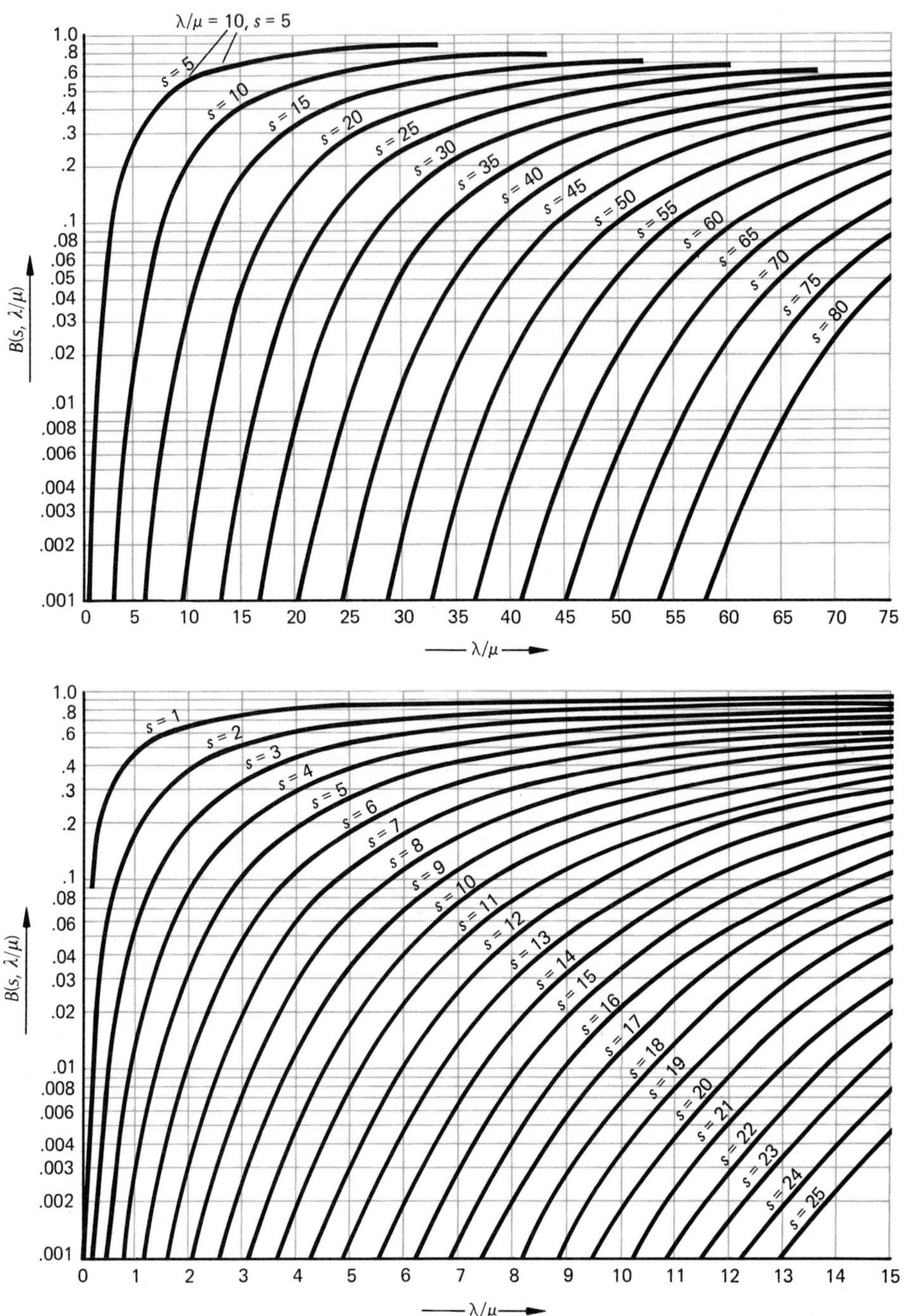

▲ FIGURE 17.9
Reprinted with permission of Macmillan Publishing Company from *Introduction to Queuing Theory* by Robert B. Cooper, Copyright © 1972 by Robert B. Cooper.

In this case (s = 5, λ/μ = 10) the value of B(5, 10) is approximately 0.56. We thus have obtained the same result with significantly less effort.

Purchasing additional lines obviously decreases the probability of finding the system busy, making $B(s, \lambda/\mu)$ smaller. Values of $B(s$, 10) with 1 to 10 servers are recorded in Figure 17.10. Here it is clear that the marginal effect of adding more servers decreases. For example, adding a second line when there was one in service decreases the probability of the system being busy by 0.089, whereas adding the tenth line when there were already nine in service decreases this probability by 0.058.

▼ FIGURE 17.10
B(s, 10) for s = 0, . . . , 10

s	B(s, 10)	DECREASE IN B(s, 10)[a]
0	1.000	
1	0.909	0.091
2	0.820	0.089
3	0.732	0.088
4	0.647	0.085
5	0.564	0.083
6	0.485	0.079
7	0.409	0.076
8	0.338	0.071
9	0.273	0.065
10	0.215	0.058

[a]The decrease in $B(s, 10)$ is defined as $B(s - 1, 10) - B(s, 10)$. It is the reduction in the probability of finding a busy system, caused by adding the sth line.

Average Number of Busy Servers. Another interesting and useful quantity in the design of phone installations is the average number of busy lines. This quantity is called the *carried load* in queuing jargon. If $\bar{N}$ is the average number of busy servers, then

$$\bar{N} = \left(\frac{\lambda}{\mu}\right)[1 - B(s, \lambda/\mu)] \tag{17.9}$$

Assume now that in Monte's problem with WATS lines for St. Luke's, $\lambda = 1$ and $1/\mu = 10$. Thus, if he purchases 10 lines, we see in Figure 17.10 that $B(10, 10) = 0.215$. It follows from (17.10) that

$$\bar{N} = 10(1 - 0.215) = 7.85$$

After $\bar{N}$ has been calculated, the server utilization can be calculated by dividing $\bar{N}$ by s (the number of servers). Thus, for the situation at St. Lukes, the server utilization is 7.85/10 = 78.5%, which means that each server (on average) is busy 78.5% of the time and idle 21.5% of the time.

In other words, the system will be busy with probability 0.215 or about one-fifth of the time and, on the average, almost 8 lines will be busy. Monte feels that this is a reasonable compromise. There does not seem to be a great deal of excess capacity, but, on the other hand, the probability of finding the system busy is in a region that he feels is appropriate for the hospital. If he is uncomfortable with this solution, based on a subjective balancing of the number of lines and the probability of finding the system busy, and is willing to specify a cost for each time a caller finds the system busy, he can select the number of lines to minimize the expected cost per hour. He would proceed in the same manner as in the $M/M/s$ system in Section 17.7.

▶ 17.9 Problem 3: The Repairperson Problem

In this problem Monte must decide how many repairpersons to hire to maintain 20 pieces of electronic equipment. Repairpersons deal with machines on a first-come (perhaps first-failed is more accurate), first-served basis.

A single repairperson treats each broken machine. You can thus think of the failed machines as forming a queue in front of multiple servers (the repairpersons).

This is another *M/M/s* problem, but it differs in a fundamental way from the *M/M/s* system (the blood-testing problem) considered in Section 17.5. In this problem there is a limited number of items (20) that can join the queue, whereas in the hematology lab problem an unlimited number could potentially join the queue.

A queuing problem, like the repairperson problem, in which only a finite number of "people" are eligible to join the queue is said to have a *finite* **calling population.** Problems with an unlimited number of possible participants are said to have an *infinite calling population.*

Consider the problem with 20 machines and 2 repairpersons. Assume that when a machine is running, the time between breakdowns has an exponential distribution with parameter $\lambda = 0.25$ per hour, that is, the average time between breakdowns is $1/\lambda = 4$ hours. Similarly, assume that the time it takes to repair a machine has an exponential distribution and that the mean repair time is 0.50 hour (i.e., $1/\mu = 0.50$). This problem is an *M/M/2* problem with a maximum of 18 items in the queue (20 including the 2 in service) and a finite calling population. In this case the general equations for the steady-state probability that there are *n* jobs in the system is a function of λ, μ, *s* (the number of repairpersons) and N (the number of machines). In particular,

Probability of *n* jobs in the system

One can see that each problem becomes a bit more complex than the previous one, and that the formulas of P_n also become more complex.

$$P_n = \frac{N!}{n!(N-n)!}(\lambda/\mu)^n P_0 \quad \text{for } 0 \le n \le s$$

$$P_n = \frac{N!}{(N-n)!\ s!\ s^{n-s}}(\lambda/\mu)^n P_0 \quad \text{for } s < n \le N \tag{17.10}$$

We also know that

$$\sum_{n=0}^{N} P_n = 1 \tag{17.11}$$

We thus have $N+1$ linear equations (N from 17.10 and 1 from 17.11) in the $N+1$ variables of interest ($P_0, P_1 \ldots P_n$). This makes it possible (if painful) to calculate values of P_n for any particular problem.

There are, however, no simple expressions (even by these standards) for the expected number of jobs (broken machines) in the system or for waiting. If the values for P_n are computed, then it is (truly) a simple task to find a numerical value for the expected number in the system. You must just calculate

$$\text{expected number in system} = L = \sum_{n=0}^{N} nP_n$$

Computers are for calculating

If God had intended humans to perform this kind of calculation by hand, He would not have let computers be invented. Figure 17.11 shows the output of a computer routine, written in FORTRAN, that can be used to compute values of P_n, the expected number in the system, and the expected number waiting, for a variety of different systems. As shown, the user enters the system parameters, and the computer does the rest. In this case, "the rest" consists of numerically evaluating the equations for P_n and using the results to find the expected number in the system. These results could equally well be obtained with any of a number of software packages. You could, for example, use Lotus 1-2-3 and its Data Matrix commands. Or you could use LINGO.

As you see in Figure 17.11, the computer stopped evaluating the number in the system at 18, since the probability was zero for any larger number. The summary data show that for this system, L_q, the average number of machines waiting for service, is 3.348 and *W,* the expected time in the system, is 1.405.

An on-line computer program such as the one used for the repairperson problem is a convenient way to obtain quick numerical results for a number of

```
HOW MANY SERVERS AND HOW MANY SPACES? (SPACES MUST AT LEAST EQUAL
SERVERS) 2, 20

INDICATE SERVICE TIME DISTRIBUTION TYPE E (EXPONENTIAL) OR C
(CONSTANT): E

POPULATION SIZE (ENTER 0 IF INFINITE) = 20

ARRIVAL RATE AND MEAN SERVICE TIME 0.25, 0.5

NO.-IN-SYS.     PROBABILITY     CUMULATIVE-PROB

     0             0.033              0.033
     1             0.083              0.116
     2             0.099              0.215
     3             0.111              0.326
     4             0.118              0.444
     5             0.118              0.563
     6             0.111              0.673
     7             0.097              0.770
     8             0.079              0.849
     9             0.059              0.908
    10             0.041              0.948
    11             0.025              0.974
    12             0.014              0.988
    13             0.007              0.995
    14             0.003              0.998
    15             0.001              1.000
    16             0.000              1.000
    17             0.000              1.000
    18             0.000              1.000

AVG.-NO.-IN-SYS. = 5.198
AVG.-NO.-WAITING = 3.348
PROBABILITY ALL SPACES FULL = 0.000
PROBABILITY FREE SERVER AVAILABLE = 0.116
AVG.-TIME-IN-SYS. FOR THOSE WHO GET SERVED = 1.405
AVG.-NO.-BUSY-SERVERS = 1.850
STOP
```

▲ FIGURE 17.11
Computer Analysis of the Repairperson Problem

queuing systems. Indeed, it could also have been used to solve Problems 1 and 2. Figure 17.12 shows the models that can be evaluated with this particular program.

▼ FIGURE 17.12
Models in the Computer-based System

QUEUING SYSTEM	QUEUE SIZE	CALLING POPULATION
M/M/s	Any specified number	Infinite
M/M/s	$N - s$	Finite, Say N
M/G/∞	0	Infinite
M/G/1	Infinite	Infinite
M/M/s	0	Finite
M/D/1	0	Finite
M/G/s	0	Infinite
M/D/s	Infinite	Infinite

17.10 Transient Versus Steady-State Results: Order Promising

This section can best be presented as either a live computer demonstration by the instructor or a laboratory exercise for the student.

It is not always the case that we are interested in steady-state results, or that an analytical model is available to predict the behavior of the queuing system of interest. In this section we will consider a situation in which we are interested in the *transient* behavior of the system and must use simulation to obtain the desired answers.

Manufacturing processes can be viewed as complex queuing systems. Probably the most frequently used management science tool in manufacturing is queuing systems simulation. Larry Lujack, a production planner at **PROTRAC** and a recent graduate, is wondering if what he learned about queuing models in his last semester of school could help him decide when to *promise* a new customer order. The order is for 20 units of an item that requires sequential processing at two work stations. The average time to process a unit at each work station is 4 hours. Each work station is available for 8 hours every working day.

By considering when the last of the 20 units will be completed, Larry initially estimates that it will take 10.5 days to process the order. The last unit must wait at Work Station 1 for the first 19 units to be completed, then it must be processed at Work Station 1 and then at Work Station 2. Assuming that it does not have to wait when it gets to Work Station 2, Larry calculates as follows:

$$(19 \text{ units} \times 4 \text{ hours/unit} + 4 \text{ hours} + 4 \text{ hours}) \div 8 \text{ hours/day} = 10.5 \text{ days}.$$

However, this analysis is somewhat simplistic. It ignores the variability of the processing times and the possibility of queuing at Work Station 2. Larry feels that the exponential distribution is an appropriate distribution for processing times because the 4-hour figure was arrived at by averaging many processing times that were less than 4 hours with a few processing times that were significantly longer than 4 hours. (See Section 17.11.) These few long processing times were due to equipment failures at a work station while processing a unit.

Next Larry checks to see whether the assumptions of the basic queuing model are met. The output from Work Station 1 are the arrivals to Work Station 2, and the time between arrivals is exponential because the processing time at Work Station 1 is exponential. The service time at Work Station 2 is exponential because it is the same as the processing time. The units are processed on a first-come, first-served basis at Work Station 2, and there is sufficient buffer capacity between the work stations so that the queue size is for all practical purposes infinite. However, the assumption of an infinite time horizon is not met. Larry is interested only in the behavior of the system until "customer" 20 ends its processing.

Larry decides to apply the basic model anyway and use it as an approximation. He approximates the time it takes to process 20 units as follows. First, he estimates that the last unit in the batch of 20 will leave Work Station 1 after $20 \times 4 = 80$ hours. Then this unit will wait in the queue in front of Work Station 2. Finally, it will complete processing at Work Station 2, at which time all 20 units will have been completed. The total time that the last unit spends at Work Station 2 is W. Thus, Larry's estimate is $20 \times 4 + W$. In the basic model, W is given by the formula $1/(\mu - \lambda)$. Larry now realizes his dilemma: μ and λ are equal (1 unit per 4 hours or 2 units per day) and the formula is valid only when μ is *greater* than λ.

Larry decides to set up a spreadsheet to simulate the flow of the 20 units through the two work stations. His spreadsheet is shown in Figure 17.13. Larry assumes that raw material is always available at Work Station 1 so that the next unit

A1: "WS 1

	A	B	C	D	E	F	G	H
1	WS 1		WS 2		Finish Time		10.5	
2	Start	Stop	Start	Stop	(days)			
3	0	4	4	8				
4	4	8	8	12				
5	8	12	12	16				
6	12	16	16	20				
7	16	20	20	24				
8	20	24	24	28				
9	24	28	28	32				
10	28	32	32	36				
11	32	36	36	40				
12	36	40	40	44				
13	40	44	44	48				
14	44	48	48	52				
15	48	52	52	56				
16	52	56	56	60				
17	56	60	60	64				
18	60	64	64	68				
19	64	68	68	72				
20	68	72	72	76				

▲ FIGURE 17.13
Order Promising Spreadsheet

at Work Station 1 can start as soon as the current unit is finished. This means that for Work Station 1 the start time of a unit is the stop time of the previous unit. For example, the formula in cell A4 of the spreadsheet is +B3. The start time of a unit at Work Station 2 is either the stop time of that unit on Work Station 1 or the stop time of the previous unit on Work Station 2, whichever is larger. So, for example, the formula in cell C4 is @MAX(B4,D3). The stop time of a unit is just the start time plus the processing time. The finish time in days is shown in cell G1 and is calculated by dividing the stop time at Work Station 2 of the last unit by 8 hours/day. The spreadsheet calculates this time to be 10.5 days *if* every unit takes exactly 4 hours at every work station.

To analyze the impact of processing time variability, Larry replaces the constant processing time of 4 in his spreadsheet with the @RISK function @EXPON(4), which samples from an exponential distribution with a mean of 4. This makes the finish time a random variable. Larry would like to know the 99th *percentile* of this random variable (the number that 99% of the time the random variable will be less than or equal to). He could then promise the order in that number of days and be 99% sure that it would actually be completed.

Using @RISK it is a simple matter to find any percentile of any random variable in the spreadsheet. Figure 17.14 shows the 99th percentile for cell G1 (the finish time in days) based on 400 iterations (400 sets of 40 random processing times—20 for Work Station 1, 20 for Work Station 2). First, note that the expected finish time ("Expected Result=" in Figure 17.14) is 12.5 days, 2 days longer than Larry's initial calculation. The extra 2 days is the average queuing delay caused by the variability of the processing times. If Larry wants to be 99% sure of having the order completed by the time he promises, he should set the due date to be 18.5 days ("Value=" in Figure 17.14) after the material becomes available at Work Station 1.

The queuing that takes place at Work Station 2 has increased the *lead-time* (time from the start of the order to its completion) 8 days (18.5 less 10.5) over what it would be if there were no variability in the processing times. Even though the basic model was not applicable in this case, it helped Larry to think about the problem and to understand this answer from his spreadsheet simulation. Problem 17-29 explores a slightly different situation in which the basic model can be used to estimate the average finish time and the 99th percentile.

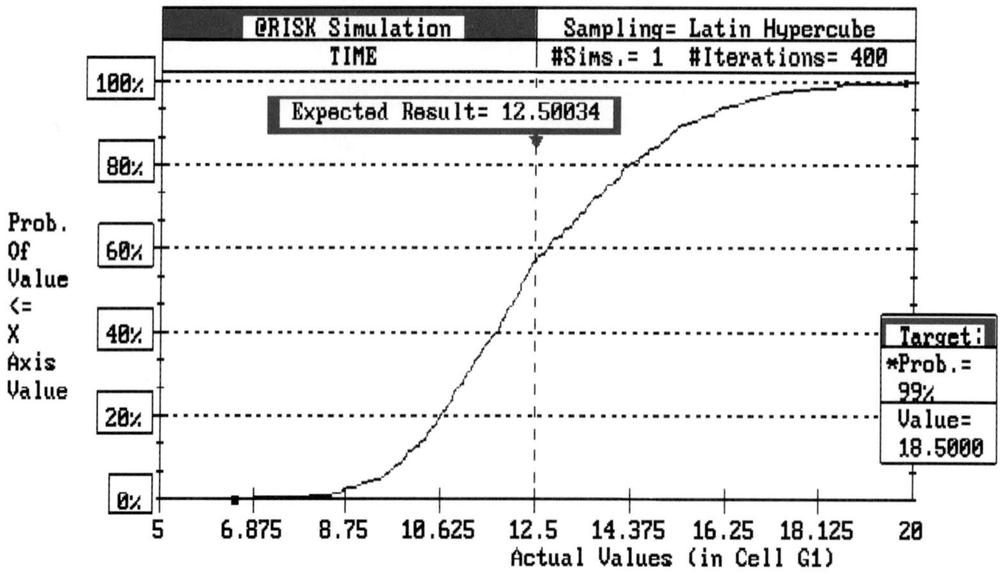

▲ FIGURE 17.14
Cumulative Distribution of Order Completion Time

17.11 The Role of the Exponential Distribution

There is an enormous body of literature concerning queuing systems, and it is virtually impossible for a manager to be aware of all the results. There are, however, some general considerations that are useful in helping a manager think about the use of queuing models. One such consideration is the role of the exponential distribution in analytic queuing models.

There are essentially no analytic results for queuing situations that do not involve the exponential distribution either as the distribution of interarrival times or service times or both. This fact makes it important for a manager to recognize the set of circumstances in which it is reasonable to assume that an exponential distribution will occur. The following three properties of the exponential distribution help to identify it:

Properties of the exponential distribution

1. ***Lack of memory:*** In an arrival process this property implies that the probability that an arrival will occur in the next few minutes is not influenced by when the last arrival occurred; that is, the system has no memory of what has just happened. This situation arises when (1) there are many individuals who could potentially arrive at the system, (2) each person decides to arrive independently of the other individuals, and (3) each individual selects his or her time of arrival completely at random. It is easy to see why the assumption of exponential arrivals fits the telephone system so well.
2. ***Small service times:*** With an exponential distribution, small values of the service time are common. This can be seen in Figure 17.15. This figure shows the graph of the probability that the service time S is less than or equal to t (Prob $\{S \leq t\}$) if the mean service time is 10, i.e., $\mu = 0.1$ and $1/\mu = 10$. Note that the graph rises rapidly and then slowly approaches the value 1.0. This indicates a high probability

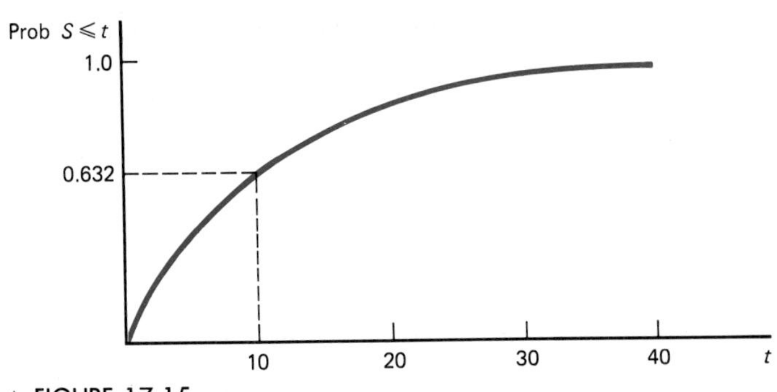

▲ FIGURE 17.15
A High Probability of Short Service Times

It is said that engineers think that the whole world is exponentially distributed, while social scientists think that the whole world is normally distributed. A quick and dirty way to check the distribution is to see if the data average is close to its standard deviation. If it is, then most likely the numbers are exponentially distributed. If it is 1/3 or less of the mean, it is probably normally distributed.

of having a short service time. For example, when $t = 10$, the probability that $S \leq t$ is 0.632. In other words, more than 63% of the service times are smaller than the average service time. This compares to a normal distribution where only 50% of the service times are smaller than the average. The practical implication of this fact is that an exponential distribution can best be used to model the distribution of service times in a system in which a large proportion of jobs take a very short time and only a few run for a long time.

3. ***Relation to the Poisson distribution:*** While introducing the basic model (Section 17.2) we noted the relationship between the exponential and Poisson distributions. In particular, if the time between arrivals has an exponential distribution with parameter λ, then in a specified period of time (say, T) the number of arrivals will have a Poisson distribution with parameter λT. Then, if X is the number of arrivals during the time T, the probability that X equals a specific number (say, n) is given by the equation

$$\text{Prob}\{X = n\} = \frac{e^{-\lambda T}(\lambda T)^n}{n!}$$

This equation holds for any nonnegative integer value of n (i.e., $n = 0, 1, 2$, and so on).

The relationship between the exponential and the Poisson distributions plays an important role in the theoretical development of queuing theory. It also has an important practical implication. By comparing the number of jobs that arrive for service during a specific period of time with the number that the Poisson distribution suggests, the analyst is able to see if his or her choices of a model and parameter values for the arrival process are reasonable.

17.12 Queue Discipline

In the previous sections we specified the arrival distribution, the service distribution, and the number of servers to define a queuing system. **Queue discipline** is still another characteristic that must be specified in order to define a queuing system. In all of the models that we have considered so far, we have assumed that arrivals were served on a first-come, first-served basis (often called FIFO, for "first-in, first-out"). This is certainly an appropriate assumption for telephone systems and for many systems where people are the arrivals. This is not necessarily the case for other systems, however. In an elevator the last person in is often the first out (LIFO). And in the repairperson model, there is really no reason to fix the machines in the same order as they break down. If a certain machine can be returned to production in 5 minutes, it seems like a good idea to do it first, rather than making it wait until a 1-hour job on a machine that broke down earlier is completed.

Adding the possibility of selecting a good queue discipline makes the queuing models more complicated. Problems of this sort are often referred to as scheduling problems, and there is an extensive literature that deals with them.

17.13 Notes on Implementation

The models discussed in this chapter are useful representatives of only a small portion of the broad expanse of queuing problems. The results presented here in general require that either the time between arrivals, the service time, or both have an exponential distribution. They are important because they yield tight analytic results and because, in many circumstances, it is reasonable to assume that the arrival process is a Poisson process. In particular, we have noted that a large (essentially infinite) calling population in which individual members of the population decide at random to arrive at service facilities generates an exponential distribution for the time between arrivals. It is not surprising, then, that the analytic models are often used on systems with this type of arrival mechanism. Communication networks (especially the telephone system) and traffic control systems are two important examples of such systems.

Digital simulation is a popular approach for studying queuing problems that do not fit the analytic mold. Indeed, current programs such as GPSS (IBM's General Purpose Systems Simulator) have been created to facilitate the simulation process.

17.14 Summary

This chapter provided an introduction to the subject of queuing. It pointed out that many interesting problems can be cast in the arrival/service mode of a queuing model.

Section 17.2 was devoted to the basic model, a single-channel queue with exponential interarrival times and service times. Four system characteristics—expected number in system, L; expected number in queue, L_q; expected waiting time, W; and expected time in queue, W_q—were defined. Formulas were presented for these characteristics as a function of the parameters of the arrival and service processes. A numerical example was presented.

Section 17.3 briefly introduced a system of notation for describing queuing systems.

Little's flow equation, $L = \lambda W$, was presented in Section 17.4. This equation plus the general fact that

$$W = W_q + \text{expected service time}$$

were offered as alternative means for computing queue characteristics.

Section 17.5 generalized the basic model to allow for an arbitrary service time distribution.

Section 17.6 considered a multiserver queue. Some new formulas were presented. These formulas were combined with results from Section 17.4 to compute numerical results for a staffing problem in a hematology lab. Section 17.7 was devoted to an economic analysis of the staffing problem in the hematology lab.

Sections 17.8 and 17.9 continued the consideration of multiserver queues. Section 17.8 was devoted to an $M/G/s$ system, in which customers who arrive and find all the servers occupied do not wait, but simply leave. This model is particularly useful in the design of telephone systems. A specific example of this type was presented.

Section 17.9 considered the repairperson problem, an *M/M/s* system with a finite calling population. It also illustrates the use of computers in obtaining numerical results for a particular problem.

Section 17.10 showed how a spreadsheet simulation can be used to explore the transient rather than the steady state behavior of a system.

Section 17.11 described the importance of the exponential distribution in the analytic analysis of queuing systems. It also presented two characteristics of the exponential distribution, the lack of memory property, and the high probability of small values.

Section 17.12 briefly considered the topic of queue discipline.

Key Terms

Queuing Problem. A problem that involves waiting in line. (*p. 741*)

Channel. A synonym for server in queuing jargon (e.g., a single-channel queue is a queue with a single server). (*p. 742*)

Arrival Process. That part of a queuing model that determines the arrival pattern. (*p. 742*)

Interarrival Time. The amount of time between two consecutive arrivals at a service facility. Typically a random quantity. (*p. 742*)

Lack of Memory. A characteristic of the exponential distribution that makes it possible to derive analytic results for many queuing models. (*p. 742*)

Service Process. That part of a queuing model that determines the service time for each item. (*p. 743*)

Service Time. The amount of time that it takes an item to pass through the service facility. Typically a random quantity. (*p. 743*)

Queue Size. The limit on the number of items that are permitted to wait in line for service. (*p. 743*)

Queue Discipline. The rule used by the service facility to determine which items to serve. First-come, first-served is a typical example. (*p. 743*)

Operating Characteristics. Quantities such as the expected number in queue that describe the operation of the queuing system. (*p. 743*)

Steady State. A condition in which the probability of viewing a certain situation (e.g., an empty queue) does not depend on the time at which you look. (*p. 744*)

Balk. A balk occurs when a customer arrives at a finite queue that is fully occupied. (*p. 748*)

Reneging. Reneging occurs when a customer leaves a system without being served. (*p. 748*)

Calling Population. The number of items that might call on the system for service; thus, a factor in determining the arrival process. (*p. 758*)

Major Concepts Quiz

True-False

1. **T F** The number of people in the system means the number waiting in line.
2. **T F** The waiting time includes the service time.
3. **T F** The exponential distribution is a two-parameter distribution that is defined by a mean and a standard deviation.
4. **T F** The mean interarrival time is the reciprocal of the mean arrival rate, and the mean service time is the reciprocal of the mean service rate.
5. **T F** The basic model is *M/M/*1.

6. **T F** As the number of servers increases, the cost of waiting generally increases.

7. **T F** The assumption that the mean service rate is less than the mean arrival rate is enough to eliminate the formation of infinitely long queues.

8. **T F** Little's flow equation states a directly proportional relationship between expected waiting time and expected number of people in the system.

9. **T F** The notation *G/M/2* means the service distribution is general, the arrival distribution is exponential, and there are two parallel servers.

Multiple Choice

10. Which of the following does not apply to the basic model?
- **a.** exponentially distributed arrivals
- **b.** exponentially distributed service times
- **c.** finite time horizon
- **d.** unlimited queue size
- **e.** the discipline is first-come, first-served

11. A major goal of queuing is to
- **a.** minimize the cost of providing service
- **b.** provide models that help the manager to trade off the cost of service
- **c.** maximize expected return
- **d.** optimize system characteristics

12. Characteristics of queues such as "expected number in the system"
- **a.** are relevant after the queue has reached a steady state
- **b.** are probabilistic statements
- **c.** depend on the specific model
- **d.** all of the above

13. In Little's flow equation, which of the following is *not* true?
- **a.** λ is the constant of proportionality between expected number in the queue and expected time in the queue.
- **b.** λ is the constant of proportionality between expected number in the system and expected time in the system.
- **c.** λ is the arrival rate, including those arrivals who choose not to join the system.

14. The most difficult aspect of performing a formal economic analysis of queuing systems is
- **a.** estimating the service cost
- **b.** estimating the waiting cost
- **c.** estimating use

15. In a multiserver system with blocked customers cleared, which one of the following does not apply?
- **a.** When all servers are busy, new arrivals leave.
- **b.** Interesting characteristics are the probability that all servers are busy and the average number of busy servers.
- **c.** One would never do an expected-cost-per-hour analysis.

16. For the exponential distribution, which of the following is *not* a characteristic?
- **a.** lack of memory
- **b.** typically yields service times greater than the mean
- **c.** a single parameter

Answers

1. F	**5.** T	**9.** F	**13.** c
2. T	**6.** F	**10.** c	**14.** b
3. F	**7.** F	**11.** b	**15.** c
4. T	**8.** T	**12.** d	**16.** b

Problems

(a) 0.5 barges/hour
(b) 2 hours
(c) 0.5 barges/hour

17-1. ▲ Barges arrive at the La Crosse lock on the Mississippi River at an average rate of one every 2 hours. If the interarrival time has an exponential distribution,

(a) What is the value of λ?

(b) What is the mean interarrival time?

(c) What is the mean arrival rate?

(a) 4 cars/hour
(b) 4 cars/hour
(c) 6 cars/hour
(d) 1/6 hour
(e) 6 cars/hour

17-2. ▲ Cars arrive at Joe's Service Station for an oil change every 15 minutes, and the interarrival time has an exponential distribution. The service station is capable of serving up to 48 cars during an 8-hour period with no idle time. Assume that the service time is also a random variable with an exponential distribution. Estimate:

(a) The value of λ.

(b) The mean arrival rate.

(c) The value of μ.

(d) The mean service time.

(e) The mean service rate.

(a) 15 people/hour
(b) 0.067 hours/person
(c) 15 people/hour

17-3. ▲ An immigration agent at Heathrow Airport in London could on the average process 120 entrants during her 8 hours on duty if she was busy all of the time. If the time to process each entrant is a random variable with an exponential distribution,

(a) What is the value of μ?

(b) What is the mean service time?

(c) What is the mean service rate?

(a) 2 cars
(b) 4/3 cars
(c) 1/2 hour
(d) 1/3 hour
(e) 1/3

17-4. ▲ For the data in Problem 17-2, determine:

(a) The expected number of cars in the system.

(b) The expected number of cars in the queue.

(c) The expected waiting time.

(d) The expected time in the queue.

(e) The probability that the system is empty.

(a) 2 persons
(b) 4/3 persons
(c) 1/5 hours/person
(d) 2/15 hours/person
(e) 1/3

17-5. ▲ Consider the immigration officer mentioned in Problem 17-3. Assume that the basic model is a reasonable approximation of her operation. Recall that if she was busy all the time she could process 120 entrants during her 8-hour shift. If on the average an entrant arrives at her station once every 6 minutes, find:

(a) The expected number in the system.

(b) The expected number in the queue.

(c) The expected waiting time.

(d) The expected time in the queue.

(e) The probability that the system is empty.

(a) 1 barge
(b) 1/2 barge
(c) 1 hour
(d) 1/2 hour
(e) 1/2
(f) $< 3/7$ hours

17-6. ▲▲ Consider the La Crosse lock mentioned in Problem 17-1. Assume that the basic model is a reasonable approximation of its operation. The new estimate of the mean interarrival time for the coming season is 60 minutes for barges, and on the average it takes 30 minutes to move a barge through the lock. Find:

(a) The expected number in the system.

(b) The expected number in the queue.

(c) The expected waiting time.

(d) The expected time in the queue.

(e) The probability that the system is empty.

(f) The longest average service time for which the expected waiting time is less than 45 minutes.

$\lambda = N/8$

17-7. ▲ Consider a single-channel queue. Assume that the basic model is a reasonable approximation of its operation. Comment on the following scheme to estimate λ:

1. Let N equal the number of arrivals between 8:00 A.M. and 4:00 P.M.
2. Set $\lambda = 8/N$.

plot $L = \frac{5}{\mu - 5}$

17-8. ▲▲ Consider the basic model. Let $\lambda = 5$, and plot the expected number in the system for $\mu = 6, 7, \cdots, 15$.

plot $P_0 = 1 - (\lambda/10)$ (see IM)

17-9. ▲▲ Consider the basic model. Let $\mu = 10$, and plot the probability that the system is empty for $\lambda = 0, 1, \cdots, 10$.

$L = \lambda W$, $1 = (1)(1)$
$L_q = \lambda W_q$, $\frac{1}{2} = (1)(\frac{1}{2})$

17-10. ▲ Use the answers to Problem 17-6 to show that Little's law holds.

See IM

17-11. ▲▲ Use Little's flow equation and the fact that $L = \lambda/(\mu - \lambda)$ in the basic model to derive the expression for W.

See IM

17-12. ▲▲ Use Little's flow equation, the expression for the mean service time, and the fact that $L = \lambda/(\mu - \lambda)$ in the basic model to derive the expression for W_q.

1.4791 people

17-13. ▲ At the Homeburg Savings and Loan, customers who wish to buy certificates of deposit form a single line and are served on a first-come, first-served basis by a specific bank officer. Service time is normally distributed with a mean of 5 minutes and a standard deviation of 1 minute. Customers arrive at the rate of one every 8 minutes. A time study shows that customers spend an average of 11.833 minutes in the system (i.e., waiting and being served). What is the average number of people in the system?

10 minutes

17-14. ▲ A doctor spends, on average, 20 minutes with her patients. If the expected waiting time is half an hour, what is the expected time in the queue?

See IM

17-15. ▲▲▲ Assume that it is stated in Problem 17-14 that patients arrive at the rate of seven per hour. Comment on this problem.

(a) 5/4 barges
(b) 3/4 barges
(c) 5/4 hours
(d) 3/4 hours
(e) 1/2

17-16. ▲ Solve (a) through (e) of Problem 17-6 using the generalized model for the case in which the variance of the service time distribution is equal to its mean.

(a) 1/9
(b) 8/9 people
(c) 2/45 hours
(d) 13/90 hours
(e) 2 8/9 people

17-17. ▲ The Homeburg Saving and Loan uses three tellers on Saturdays. The interarrival time and the service time for customers each has an exponential distribution. Customers arrive at the rate of 20 per hour, and the mean service time is 6 minutes. Customers form a single queue and are served by the first available teller. Under steady-state conditions, find:

(a) The probability that no customers are waiting or being served.
(b) The expected number of people in the queue.
(c) The expected waiting time in the queue.
(d) The expected waiting time.
(e) The expected number of people in the system.

(a) 0.043398
(b) 0.320493 faculty
(c) 0.026526 hours or 1.6 minutes
(d) 0.276526 hours
(e) 3.341084 faculty

17-18. ▲▲▲ The Business School reserves five ports on its on-line computer for faculty use. If a faculty member attempts to log on and all the ports are occupied, he receives a busy signal and must try to log on at a later time. To estimate the system characteristics, the head of the computation center wants to know the steady-state values of the characteristics assuming a finite calling population of 100 and an infinite queue. (This is an approximation because faculty receiving a busy signal must redial.) Each faculty member wants to use the computer once every 8 hours on average, and the interarrival time is exponentially distributed. Faculty spend an average of 15 minutes on the computer once logged on—again, exponentially distributed. Find:

(a) The probability that all ports are open.
(b) The expected number of people in the queue.
(c) The expected waiting time in the queue.
(d) The expected waiting time.
(e) The expected number in the system.

3-server queue with Poisson distribution of arrivals (exponential interarrival times) and deterministic service times

17-19. ▲ Describe a $M/D/3$ queuing system in words.

0.12

17-20. ▲ For Problem 17-18, estimate the probability that all ports are busy using the graphs.

(Assume an $M/G/s$ model with blocked customers cleared, an infinite calling population, and an arrival rate 100 times that for a single faculty member.)

$184.80/hour

17-21. ▲▲ Steco has 100 sales representatives in the United States. They call orders into a central office where an office worker using the central inventory control system confirms product availability, price, and delivery date. The representative calls directly from the customer's office before signing a contract. Calls are held in a queue and served by the first available office worker on a first-come, first-served basis. Calls arrive at the rate of 40 per hour, and the mean service time is 6 minutes. Management estimates that it costs $20 per hour to have a sales representative call in and order, and $12 per hour to employ an office worker. Model this situation as an $M/M/s$ queue with an infinite calling population, and calculate the expected total cost per hour if Steco hires five office workers.

$163.40

17-22. ▲▲ Find the expected total cost for the system in Problem 17-21 if Steco hires six office workers.

$C_s/C_w = 1.67$

17-23. ▲▲ Use the solutions to Problems 17-21 and 17-22 to determine the value for the ratio C_s/C_w for which Steco is indifferent between having five or six office workers.

(a) $P(0) = 0.575$; $P(1) = 0.287$; $P(2) = 0.108$; $P(3) = 0.0269$; $P(4) = 0.00310$
(b) 0.596

17-24. ▲▲▲ In a particular manufacturing cell, one repairman has to maintain four machines. For the machines, the time between breakdowns is exponentially distributed with an average of four hours. On the average, it takes half an hour to fix a machine.

(a) Find the probabilities that there are 0, 1, 2, 3 or 4 machines under repair.

(b) Find the average number of machines under repair.

(a) 0.034
(b) 0.409
(c) 5.91

17-25. ▲▲ A telephone exchange has seven lines. Calls arrive at the rate of two per minute, and the interarrival time has an exponential distribution. Conversations have a normal distribution with a mean of 5 and a standard deviation of 1. When all seven lines are occupied, the caller simply receives a busy signal.

(a) What is the probability that exactly three lines are busy?

(b) What is the probability that the system is totally occupied?

(c) What is the average number of busy servers?

(a) Since no queue forms, number in system is never > 3 regardless of arrival rate
(b) 0.182302
(c) 0.427270
(d) 2.147736

17-26. ▲▲ A market research group has three interviewers located in adjacent booths in a suburban shopping mall. A contact person meets people walking in the mall and asks them if they are willing to be interviewed. They estimate that customers willing to agree to the interview arrive at the rate of 15 per hour, and the interarrival time has an exponential distribution. On the average the interview takes 15 minutes. If all booths are occupied, a person who has agreed to be interviewed will not wait and simply goes about his or her business.

(a) Comment on the following statement: Since $\lambda > \mu s$, this system will grow without bound.

(b) Calculate the probability that exactly one interviewer is occupied.

(c) Find the probability that all three interviewers are occupied.

(d) Find the average number of busy interviewers.

(a) 0.535 barges
(b) 0.135 barges
(c) 40.1 minutes
(d) 10.1 minutes
(e) 0.60
Answers all smaller because of less variance.

17-27. ▲ Consider again the La Crosse lock mentioned in Problems 17-1 and 17-6. Suppose that the mean interarrival time is 60 minutes and that on the average it takes 30 minutes to move a barge through the lock, but that the standard deviation of this service time is 3 minutes. Reanswer (a) through (e) of Problem 17-6. How did your answers change and why?

48.75 minutes

17-28. ▲ Repair requests are handled by a handyman at an apartment complex on a first-come first-served basis. Requests arrive at the rate of 1 per hour on average. The time it takes the handyman to make a repair is normally distributed with a mean of 30 minutes and a standard deviation of 15 minutes. How long on the average is the time between when a repair request is made and the repair is completed?

See IM

17-29. ▲▲ Larry Lujack is unhappy with the long lead times he is having to quote to customers (see Section 17.10). He feels that **PROTRAC** is going to start losing business to competitors who can quote shorter lead times. Larry initially assumed that processing times were exponentially distributed. After taking a closer look at the data, he discovers that 90% of the time it takes 3 hours to process a unit on either Work Station 1 or 2 and 10% of the time it takes 13 hours on either 1 or 2. Thus the average time is $.9 \times 3 + .1 \times 13 = 4.0$ hours. After talking with the production supervisor of these stations, he learns that the high time is due to equipment failure when processing a unit. Invariably, it takes 10 hours to repair the equipment once a failure occurs. Larry has heard that preventive maintenance can reduce the chance of equipment failure and wonders what the value would be of decreasing the chance from 10% to 1%.

(a) Use a spreadsheet simulation and @RISK to find the average time to complete 20 units and the 99th percentile of the time if at each work station there is a 10% chance of equipment failure while processing a unit. How do your answers compare to those of Section 17.10, where the processing times were exponentially distributed? (HINT: Use the @RISK function @DISCRETE(3,9,13,1,2) to generate the processing times. This function will return a "3" 9 out of 9 + 1 times and a "13" 1 out of 9 + 1 times.)

(b) Now assume that at each work station there is a 1% chance of equipment failure while processing a unit. What is the value of preventive maintenance if it reduces equipment failures to this level?

See IM

17-30. ▲▲▲ Suppose Larry Lujack has another order to promise (see Section 17.10). This order is also for 20 units, but the average processing time is 6 hours per unit at Work Station 1 and 4 hours per unit at Work Station 2.

(a) Using the basic model, estimate the average time needed to complete the order.

(b) Assuming that processing times are exponentially distributed, use a spreadsheet simulation to compute the average time. How does it compare with your answer to part (a)?

(c) When both arrival and service times are exponentially distributed, then in the basic model waiting plus processing time is also exponentially distributed. Use this fact to estimate without simulation the 99th percentile of the time to complete all 20 units.

(d) Use @RISK to find the 99th percentile of the time it takes to complete all 20 units. Compare with your answer to part (c).

(e) Suppose that the times were reversed, i.e., that processing took on average 4 hours per unit at Work Station 1 and 6 hours per unit at Work Station 2. Can you use the basic model to estimate the mean and 99% fractile? Why or why not? Use simulation and compare with your answers to parts (b) and (d).

Video Case

How Many Operators?

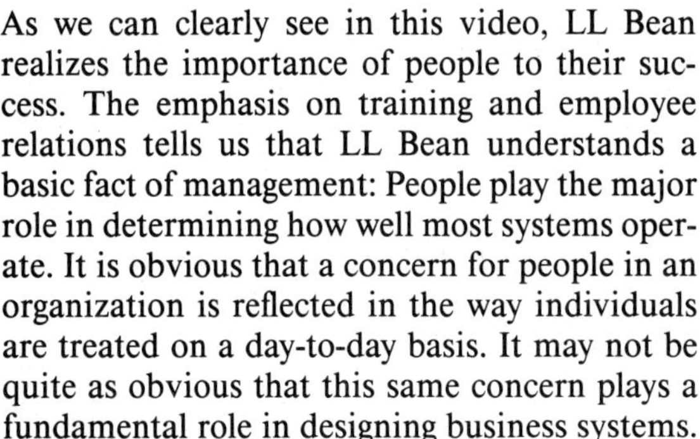

As we can clearly see in this video, LL Bean realizes the importance of people to their success. The emphasis on training and employee relations tells us that LL Bean understands a basic fact of management: People play the major role in determining how well most systems operate. It is obvious that a concern for people in an organization is reflected in the way individuals are treated on a day-to-day basis. It may not be quite as obvious that this same concern plays a fundamental role in designing business systems.

Mail order is the heart of LL Bean's business. This business is based on orders received over the phone. Bean's lines are open 24 hours a day, 365 days a year. The video indicates an average rate of 78,000 calls per day. A moment's reflection suggests that these calls do not arrive at a uniform rate. There clearly are seasonal effects, as well as variability during each day. To meet its need for phone operators, Bean offers three types of work arrangements: full time, permanent part time, and temporary. This strategy allows for great flexibility in adjusting the number of operators on duty at any moment. It also provides flexibility for employees, who can structure an arrangement that fits with other demands on their time.

However, the nagging question remains: "How many operators does Bean need, and when?" It seems clear that the company wants to balance customer service against staffing expense. Their approach is to consider each of the 8760 hours in a week as a period to be staffed. For each hour, the system is modeled as an $M/M/s$ queue—that is, a multi-server queue with exponential arrival and service times and s servers (operators). The arrival rate and service rate are estimated from historical data. Cost balancing is done in an intuitive manner: A service standard that management believes is appropriate is the basis of the design. In particular, the Bean system is designed so that no more than 15% of calls wait more than twenty seconds before reaching an operator.

We thus see that three steps are needed to determine "How many operators Bean needs, and when": (1) The estimation procedures provide parameter values for the model. (2) The model provides a distribution of waiting times for any specified number of operators on duty. (3) From the waiting times, Bean determines how many operators are needed during each hour of the week. Now, all Bean has to do is to solve a horrendous scheduling problem. (Actually, Bean did not use this model to solve the problem directly. Rather, the model was used to evaluate the proposals from four vendors for operator scheduling systems.)

Questions

1. Bean used steady state results from an $M/M/s$ queue to help determine the number of operators it needs on hand each hour. What assumptions would you be inclined to question in evaluating this model?
2. What other approach might you suggest for attacking this problem?

CHAPTER

18 Forecasting

APPLICATION CAPSULE

Yes, Virginia . . . : An Economic Forecasting Model Helps Keep an Unemployment Insurance Trust Fund in the Black*

Unemployment insurance operates on the same risk-sharing philosophy as any other insurance policy: funds are collected from a large population to help pay unexpected costs for a small percentage of that population. The obvious question is, How much must a state collect from whom in order to provide for the payments dictated by its unemployment legislation? This question can be answered only by making forecasts of future cash inflows and outflows.

The Commonwealth of Virginia has created the unemployment insurance econometric forecasting model (UIEFM) to help answer this question. The model has two main sections: a projection model and a financial forecasting model.

The projection model uses regression analysis to forecast cash *outflows* as a function of fundamental economic factors, including:

1. Rates of unemployment
2. Rates of increase in wage levels
3. Changes in the insured labor force and payrolls
4. Minimum and maximum amounts of weekly benefits.

The financial forecast program is concerned with two issues:

1. The impact of the projected cash flow on the taxing mechanism of the UI system, i.e., on the cash *inflow* to the system
2. The level of funds in the UI trust after ten years.

The financial forecast program is quite complex because the Virginia unemployment tax law includes three taxing alternatives. Virginia employers are taxed on the basis of their previous unemployment experience. The idea is that those employers who add to the ranks of the unemployed should pay a larger proportion of unemployment expenditure. In addition, each employer pays a "pool" tax to help cover expenses not covered by the experience tax. Finally, a third tax is assessed when the UI trust fund falls below the 50%

solvency level defined in the unemployment act. Indeed, a large part of the motivation for the UIEFM model came from the dramatic decline in the Unemployment Insurance Trust Fund between 1975 and 1980.

An important contribution of the forecasting model was to alert planners to the possibility of a surplus. The model predicted that under favorable economic conditions the funds in the unemployment trust could exceed the expectations of those who passed the original unemployment insurance act. As a result, several policies to deal with this situation were devised. The model was then used to evaluate their potential impact, helping legislators to choose the most effective proposals. More generally, the commissioner of the Virginia Employment Commission has stated that "the preponderance of legislation in Virginia is underpinned by simulations and analysis from the model."

*Lackman and Valz, "Risk Funding of Unemployment Insurance: An Econometric Approach," *Interfaces*, Vol. 18, No. 2 (March–April 1988).

18.1 Introduction

The date is June 15, 1941. Joachim von Ribbentrop, Hitler's special envoy, is meeting in Venice with Count Ciano, the Italian foreign minister, whereupon von Ribbentrop says: "My dear Ciano, I cannot tell you anything as yet because every decision is locked in the impenetrable bosom of the Führer. However, one thing is certain: If we attack, the Russia of Stalin will be erased from the map within eight weeks."[1] Nine days later, Nazi Germany launched operation Barbarossa and declared war on Russia. With this decision, a chain of events that led to the end of the Third Reich had been set in motion, and the course of history was dramatically changed.

There are a few "wise" sayings that illustrate the promise and frustration of forecasting:

"It is difficult to forecast, especially in regards to the future."

"It isn't difficult to forecast, just to forecast correctly."

"Numbers, if tortured enough, will confess to just about anything!"

Although few decisions are this significant, it is clearly true that many of the most important decisions made by individuals and organizations crucially depend on an assessment of the future. Predictions or forecasts with greater accuracy than that achieved by the German General Staff are thus fervidly hoped for and in some cases diligently worked for.

Economic forecasting considered by itself is an important activity. Government policies and business decisions are based on forecasts of the GNP, the level of unemployment, the demand for refrigerators, and so on. Among the major insurance companies, one is hard-pressed to find an investment department that does not have a contract with some expert or firm to obtain economic forecasts on a regular basis. Billions of dollars of investments in mortgages and bonds are influenced by these forecasts. Over 2000 people show up each year at the Annual Forecast Luncheon sponsored by the University of Chicago to hear the views of three economists on the economic outlook. The data are overwhelming. Forecasting is playing an increasingly important role in the modern firm.

Not only is forecasting increasingly important, but quantitative models are playing an increasingly important role in the forecasting function. There is clearly a steady increase in the use of quantitative forecasting models at many levels in industry and government. A conspicuous example is the widespread use of inventory control programs that include a forecasting subroutine. For economic

[1]A. L. C. Bullock, *Hitler: A Study in Tyranny* (New York: Harper & Row, 1962).

entities such as the GNP or exchange rates many firms now rely on econometric models for their forecasts. These models, which consist of a system of statistically estimated equations, have had a significant impact on the decision processes in both industry and government.

There are numerous ways to classify forecasting models and the terminology varies with the classification. For example, one can refer to "long-range," "medium-range," and "short-range" models. There are "regression" models, "extrapolation" models, and "conditional" or "precedent-based" models, as well as "nearest-neighbor" models. The major distinction we employ will be between *quantitative* and *qualitative forecasting techniques.*

18.2 Quantitative Forecasting

Advantages of quantitative forecasting models

One of the main advantages of using quantitative methods is that they are consistent, regardless of how the user "feels." They incorporate an underlying logic that is consistently applied and that does not depend on the user's mathematical knowledge or how long she has been on the job. They can be transferred to another employee and still yield the same result.

Quantitative forecasting models possess two important and attractive features:

1. They are expressed in mathematical notation. Thus, they establish an unambiguous record of how the forecast is made. This provides an excellent vehicle for clear communication about the forecast among those who are concerned. Furthermore, they provide an opportunity for systematic modification and improvement of the forecasting technique. In a quantitative model coefficients can be modified and/or terms added until the model yields good results. (This assumes that the relationship expressed in the model is basically sound.)

2. With the use of computers, quantitative models can be based on an amazing quantity of data. For example, a major oil company was considering a reorganization and expansion of its domestic marketing facilities (gasoline stations). Everyone understood that this was a pivotal decision for the firm. The size of the proposed capital investment alone, not to mention the possible influences on the revenue from gasoline sales, dictated that this decision be made by the board of directors. In order to evaluate the alternative expansion strategies, the board needed forecasts of the demand for gasoline in each of the marketing regions (more than 100 regions were involved) for each of the next 15 years. Each of these 1500 estimates was based on a combination of several factors, including the population and the level of new construction in each region. Without the use of computers and quantitative models a study involving this level of detail would generally be impossible. In a similar way, inventory control systems that require forecasts that are updated on a monthly basis for literally thousands of items could not be constructed without quantitative models and computers.

The technical literature related to quantitative forecasting models is enormous, and a high level of technical, mainly statistical, sophistication is required to understand the intricacies of the models in certain areas. In the following two sections we summarize some of the important characteristics and the applicability of such models. We shall distinguish two categories based on the underlying approach. These are *causal models* and *time-series models.*

18.3 Causal Forecasting Models

In a **causal model,** the forecast for the quantity of interest "rides piggyback" on another quantity or set of quantities. In other words, our knowledge of the value of one variable (or perhaps several variables) enables us to forecast the value of

Simply because there is a mathematical relationship does not guarantee that there is really cause and effect. Since the Super Bowl began in 1967, almost every time an old NFL team wins, the stock market Standard & Poor 500 indicator increases for that year. When an AFC team wins, the market usually goes down. In 23 years this rule has worked over 90% of the time (21 out of 23)!

another variable. In more precise terms, let y denote the true value for some variable of interest, and let $\hat{y}$ denote a predicted or forecast value for that variable. Then, in a causal model,

$$\hat{y} = f(x_1, x_2, \ldots, x_n)$$

where f is a forecasting rule, or function, and $x_1, x_2, \ldots, x_n$ is a set of variables.

In this representation the x variables are often called *independent variables,* whereas $\hat{y}$ is the *dependent* or *response variable.* The notion is that we know the independent variables and use them in the forecasting model to forecast the dependent variable.

Consider the following examples:

1. If y is the demand for baby food, then x might be the number of children between 7 and 24 months old.
2. If y is the demand for plumbing fixtures, then x_1 and x_2 might be the number of housing starts and the number of existing houses, respectively.
3. If y is the traffic volume on a proposed expressway, then x_1 and x_2 might be the traffic volume on each of two nearby existing highways.
4. If y is the yield of usable material per pound of ingredients from a proposed chemical plant, then x might be the same quantity produced by a small-scale experimental plant.

Companies often find by looking at past performance that their monthly sales are directly related to the monthly GNP, and thus figure that a good forecast could be made using next month's GNP figure. The only problem is that this is not known, or it may just be a forecast and thus not a truly independent variable.

For a causal model to be useful, the independent variables must either be known in advance or it must be possible to forecast them more easily than $\hat{y}$, the dependent variable. For example, knowing a functional relationship between the pounds of sauerkraut and the number of bratwurst sold in Milwaukee in the same year may be interesting to sociologists, but unless sauerkraut usage can be easily predicted, the relationship is of little value for anyone in the bratwurst forecasting business.

To use a causal forecasting model, then, requires two conditions:

Requirements for use

1. There must be a relationship between values of the independent and dependent variables such that the former provides information about the latter.
2. The values for the independent variables must be known and available to the forecaster at the time the forecast must be made.

One commonly used approach in creating a causal forecasting model is called **curve fitting.**

Curve Fitting: An Oil Company Expansion

The fundamental ideas of curve fitting are easily illustrated by a problem in which one independent variable is used to predict the value of the dependent variable. As a specific example, consider an oil company that is planning to expand its network of modern self-service gasoline stations. It plans to use traffic flow (measured in the average number of cars per hour) to forecast sales (measured in average dollar sales per hour).

The firm has had five stations in operation for more than a year and has used historical data to calculate the averages shown in Figure 18.1.

These data are plotted in Figure 18.2. Such a plot is often called a **scatter diagram.** We now wish to use these data to construct a function that will enable us to forecast the sales at any proposed location by measuring the traffic flow at that location and plugging its value into the function we construct. In particular, suppose that the traffic flow at a proposed location in Buffalo Grove is 183 cars per hour. How might we use the data in Figure 18.2 to forecast the sales at this location?

STATION	CARS PER HOUR	SALES PER HOUR ($)
1	150	220
2	55	75
3	220	250
4	130	145
5	95	200

▲ FIGURE 18.1
Sales and Traffic Data

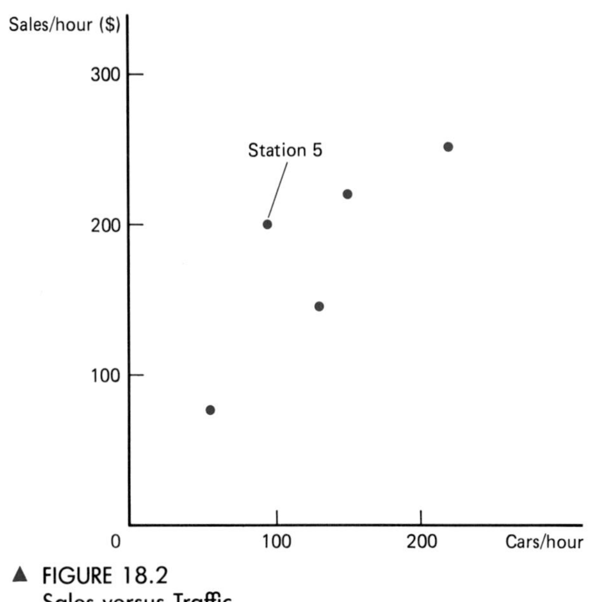

▲ FIGURE 18.2
Sales versus Traffic

A subjective method

Quick and Dirty Fits. A method that is commonly used when there is a single independent variable and a need to produce a forecast quickly is to fit a particular type of curve to the data "by eye." The goal is to find a "curve" that comes close enough to the points in the scatter diagram to satisfy the person who needs the forecast. We note that in this process it is not necessary to "touch" any data point, but the curve could pass through one or more points if it yields a good fit.

A straight line is the type of curve most commonly selected. This process is illustrated in Figure 18.3. The line shown has no special properties except that it appears (at least to the authors) to lie close to the data. Once the line is drawn, one can read from the graph a forecast of sales for any particular traffic flow. The figure shows that this particular line yields a forecast of $202.50 for a traffic flow of 183.

The better-equipped office is not limited to fitting a straight line by eye. A simple template for drawing curves of various kinds enables the decision maker to select a function that lies closer to the data. Figure 18.4 illustrates this point. Again, a forecast for a traffic flow of 183 is shown.

The straight line and the curve selected in Figures 18.3 and 18.4 yield approximately the same forecast for demand (sales/hour) when the traffic flow is 183. A larger difference, both in absolute and relative terms, would occur if these figures were used to forecast demand at a location with a traffic flow of 60. The straight line yields a forecast of 133, whereas the curve yields a forecast of 117. So which model is right?

There is no black and white answer to that question at the time the company

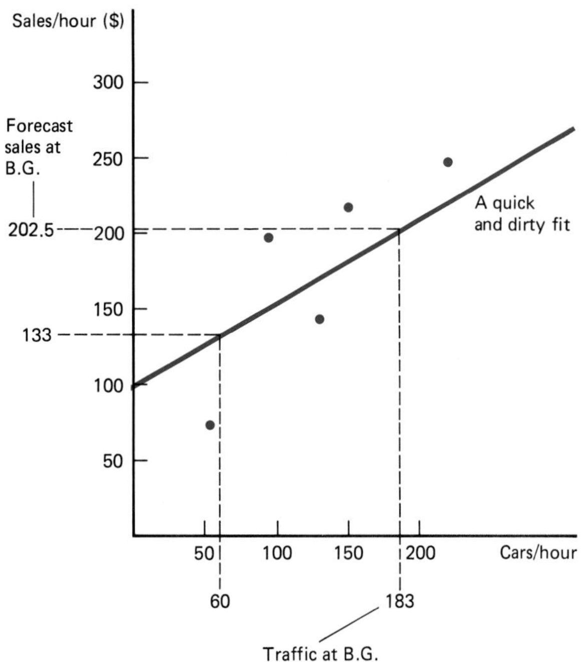

It might be pointed out that, even with the quick and dirty straight line, forecasts can have upper and lower limits. Show that if there are zero cars the station is still going to make $100! Obviously, this is a *misuse* of the quantitative model. It does not prove that the model is incorrect.

▲ FIGURE 18.3
Fitting a Line by Eye

must decide whether to build the station in Buffalo Grove. Forecasting models, like all other models, require the final step of managerial approval. *On the basis of judgment, which may be strongly influenced by direct experience with a forecasting model, the manager must decide whether to accept a particular forecast or to devote more resources to obtaining a better forecast (i.e., one in which he has more confidence).*

▼ FIGURE 18.4
Fitting a Curve by Eye

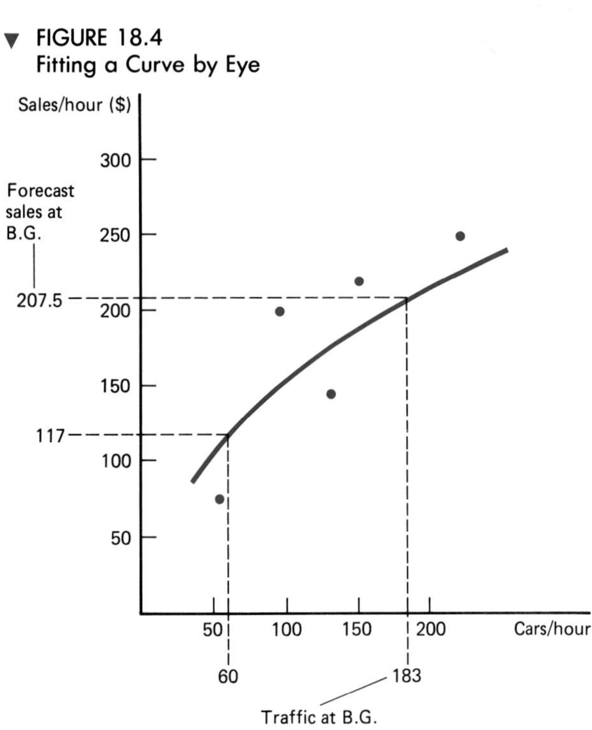

Deficiencies of the Quick and Dirty Method. The quick and dirty method just described has two major deficiencies:

1. It is impossible to extend to problems with more than one independent variable. Think of trying to use this approach if you were given historical values of sales, traffic flow, *and* the number of competing stations in a 3-mile radius. It quickly becomes clear that a ruler and/or a French curve will not provide enough help.

2. There is no measure of what a "good fit" means. Once a manager has chosen a specific functional form (say, a straight line), there is no automatic way to select one line that is better than other possible lines. Sure, the manager can look at them and pick the one he likes. However, if he can specify a measure of goodness, the process of curve fitting can be reduced to a standard and more objective technical operation.

An objective method

Least-Squares Fits. The **method of least squares** is a formal procedure for curve fitting that overcomes the two deficiencies just discussed. It is a two-step process.

Over a century ago, mathematicians could not determine the straight line that minimized the absolute error $|y - \hat{y}|$ but could use calculus to determine the line that minimized the squared error $(y - \hat{y})^2$. Thus, forecasting has been inundated with "least squares" formulas and rationalizations as to why "squared" errors should be minimized.

1. Select a specific functional form (e.g., a straight line).
2. Within the set of functions specified in step 1, choose the specific function that minimizes the sum of the squared deviations between the data points and the function values. To demonstrate this process, consider the sales-traffic flow example. In step 1, assume that we select a straight line; that is, we restrict our attention to functions of the form $y = a + bx$. Step 2 is illustrated in Figure 18.5. Here values for a and b were chosen, the appropriate line $y = a + bx$ was drawn, and the deviations between observed points and the function are indicated. For example,

$$d_1 = y_1 - [a + bx_1] = 220 - [a + 150b]$$

where y_1 = actual (observed) sales/hr at location 1 (i.e., 220)

x_1 = actual (observed) traffic flow at location 1 (i.e., 150)

a = intercept (on the vertical axis) for function in Figure 18.5

b = slope for the function in Figure 18.5

▼ FIGURE 18.5
Method of Least Squares

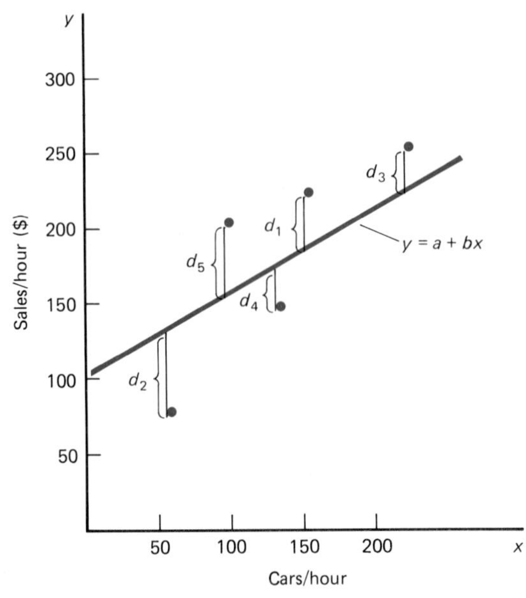

The value d_1^2 is a measure of how close the value of the function $[a + bx_1]$ is to the observed value, y_1; that is, it indicates how well the function fits at this one point.

We want the function to fit well at all points. One measure of how well it fits overall is the sum of the squared deviations, which is $\sum_{i=1}^{5} d_i^2$. Let us now consider a general problem with n as opposed to 5 observations. Then, since each $d_i = y_i - (a + bx_i)$, the sum of the squared deviations can be written as

From the formula it can be shown that:
1. All the data points are used.
2. They are all of equal importance (weighting).

$$\sum_{i=1}^{n} (y_i - [a + bx_i])^2 \tag{18.1}$$

Using the method of least squares, we select a and b so as to minimize the sum shown in expression (18.1). The rules of calculus can be used to determine the values of a and b that minimize this sum. The procedure is to take the partial derivative of the sum in expression (18.1) with respect to a and set the resulting expression equal to zero. This yields one equation. A second equation is derived by following the same procedure with b. The equations that result from this procedure are

$$\sum_{i=1}^{n} -2(y_i - [a + bx_i]) = 0 \quad \text{and} \quad \sum_{i=1}^{n} -2x_i(y_i - [a + bx_i]) = 0$$

Recall that the values for x_i and y_i are the observations, and our goal is to find the values of a and b that satisfy these two equations. The solution can be shown to be

The minimizing values of a and b

$$b = \frac{\sum_{i=1}^{n} x_i y_i - \frac{1}{n}\sum_{i=1}^{n} x_i \sum_{i=1}^{n} y_i}{\sum_{i=1}^{n} x_i^2 - \frac{1}{n}\left(\sum_{i=1}^{n} x_i\right)^2} \tag{18.2}$$

$$a = \frac{1}{n}\sum_{i=1}^{n} y_i - b\frac{1}{n}\sum_{i=1}^{n} x_i$$

Calculating a and b

The next step is to determine the values for $\sum x_i, \sum x_i^2, \sum y_i, \sum x_i y_i$. Note that these quantities depend only on the data we have observed and that we can find them with simple arithmetic operations. The table in Figure 18.6 is devoted to this purpose.

i	x_i(CARS/HR)	y_i(SALES/HR)	$x_i y_i$	x_i^2
1	150	220	33,000	22,500
2	55	75	4,125	3,025
3	220	250	55,000	48,400
4	130	145	18,850	16,900
5	95	200	19,000	9,025
Σ	650	890	129,975	99,850

▲ FIGURE 18.6
Least-Squares Calculations: The Linear Case

Since the 1970s, business and scientific calculators have provided buttons to do least squares regression for a straight line, automatically calculating these formulas.

Plugging the numerical values into the equations shown in expression (18.2), and setting $n = 5$, yields

$$b = 0.93$$

$$a = 57.1$$

The resulting least-squares line is shown in Figure 18.7 as a solid line. The quick and dirty line from Figure 18.3 is shown as a dashed line. This figure suggests that at least some individuals (e.g., the authors) are not too good at selecting by eye a line that fits the data well (by the least-squares criterion).

This forecast also "predicts" earning \$57.10 when no cars arrive. At this point it might be well to establish limits on the forecast (from 30 to 250 cars) or seek a logical explanation. Many service stations have convenience foods and also do a walk-in business. Thus "a" might represent the amount of walk-in business (which might be constant regardless of how much car traffic there is).

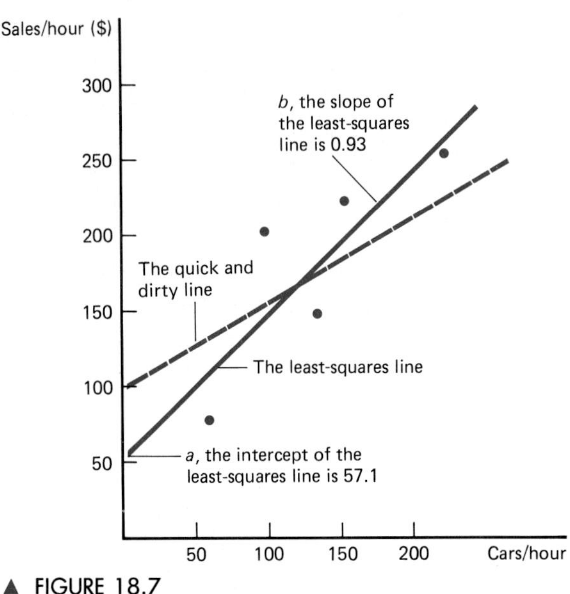

▲ FIGURE 18.7
Least-Squares Line

Fitting a Quadratic Function. The example above has shown how to make *linear fits* for the case of one independent variable. But the method of least squares can be used with any number of independent variables and with any functional form. As an illustration, suppose that we wish to fit a quadratic function of the form

$$y = a_0 + a_1x + a_2x^2$$

to our previous data with the method of least squares. Our goal, then, is to select a_0, a_1, and a_2 in order to minimize the sum of squared deviations, which is now

$$\sum_{i=1}^{5} (y_i - [a_0 + a_1x_i + a_2x_i^2])^2 \tag{18.3}$$

We proceed by setting the partial derivatives with respect to a_0, a_1, and a_2 equal to zero. This gives the equations

$$\begin{aligned} 5a_0 + (\textstyle\sum x_i)a_1 + (\sum x_i^2)a_2 &= \textstyle\sum y_i \\ (\textstyle\sum x_i)a_0 + (\sum x_i^2)a_1 + (\sum x_i^3)a_2 &= \textstyle\sum x_iy_i \\ (\textstyle\sum x_i^2)a_0 + (\sum x_i^3)a_1 + (\sum x_i^4)a_2 &= \textstyle\sum x_i^2y_i \end{aligned} \tag{18.4}$$

Point out that this is a simple set of 3 linear equations in 3 unknowns, and that if a cubic ($Y = a_0 + a_1X + a_2X^2 + a_3X^3$) were to be fitted, then 4 equations in 4 unknowns would have to be solved. Thus, the general name for this least squares curve fitting is "Linear Regression." The term "linear" comes not from a straight line being fit, but from the fact that simultaneous linear equations are being solved.

Finding the numerical values of the coefficients is a straightforward task. We proceed in the same tabular manner as in Figure 18.6. Indeed, we need all of the values calculated there. To conserve space, we use scientific notation and express numbers in powers of 10. For example, we will write 22,500 as 2.25×10^4. The calculations, to two decimals of accuracy, are shown in Figure 18.8.

The numerical values from Figure 18.8 can now be plugged into the equations presented in expression (18.4) to yield

$$5a_0 + 650a_1 + 99{,}800a_2 = 890 \tag{18.5}$$

$$6.50a_0 + 998a_1 + 172{,}600a_2 = 1300 \tag{18.6}$$

$$9.98a_0 + 1726a_1 + 322{,}500a_2 = 2153 \tag{18.7}$$

i	$x_i \times 10^2$	$y_i \times 10^2$	$x_iy_i \times 10^4$	$x_i^2 \times 10^4$	$x_i^3 \times 10^6$	$x_i^4 \times 10^8$	$x_i^2y_i \times 10^6$
1	1.50	2.20	3.30	2.25	3.38	5.06	4.95
2	0.55	0.75	0.41	0.30	0.17	0.09	0.23
3	2.20	2.50	5.50	4.84	10.65	23.43	12.10
4	1.30	1.45	1.89	1.69	2.20	2.86	2.45
5	0.95	2.00	1.90	0.90	0.86	0.81	1.80
Σ	6.50	8.90	13.00	9.98	17.26	32.25	21.53

▲ FIGURE 18.8
Least-Squares Calculations: The Quadratic Case

en making quadratic or er-order fits, because bers are being raised to fourth power or higher, erical instability may lt. There should be just unique set of values for a_1, and a_2, but another puter program computes coefficients as: $a_0 \approx$ 3.55, $a_1 \approx 2.15$, and a_2 -0.0044, which yields a ller sum of squared errors 55 versus 5398)! Different puters or programs may d different results due to erical roundoff error.

Both sides of (18.6) have been divided by 10^2, and both sides of (18.7) have been divided by 10^4 to obtain the form shown.

We are now left with the straightforward but tedious task of solving three linear equations in three unknowns. Completing this exercise yields

$$a_0 \approx -65.726$$

$$a_1 \approx 3.015$$

$$a_2 \approx -0.0074$$

To plot this function, we first evaluate it for four values of x as shown in Figure 18.9.[2]

x	$-65.726 + 3.015x - 0.0074x^2$
0	−65.726
50	66.46
100	161.52
200	240.22

▲ FIGURE 18.9
Evaluating the Quadratic Function

These points are plotted in Figure 18.10, and a curve is drawn through them. The linear least-squares fit is also shown. The quadratic function appears to fit the data better, but beware. As we have seen in the use of quick and dirty methods, the eye is not always a reliable guide to what is happening.

Comparing the Linear and Quadratic Fits. In the method of least squares, we have selected the sum of the squared deviations as our measure of "goodness of fit." We can thus compare the linear and the quadratic fit with this criterion. The calculations are shown in Figure 18.11, where columns (1) and (2) are the actual historical data from Figure 18.1, column (3) is the least-squares linear fit, and the column identified as (4) is the least-squares quadratic fit.

[2]One can use differential calculus to show that the function has a maximum value at

$$x = \frac{-a_1}{2a_2} \approx 241.3$$

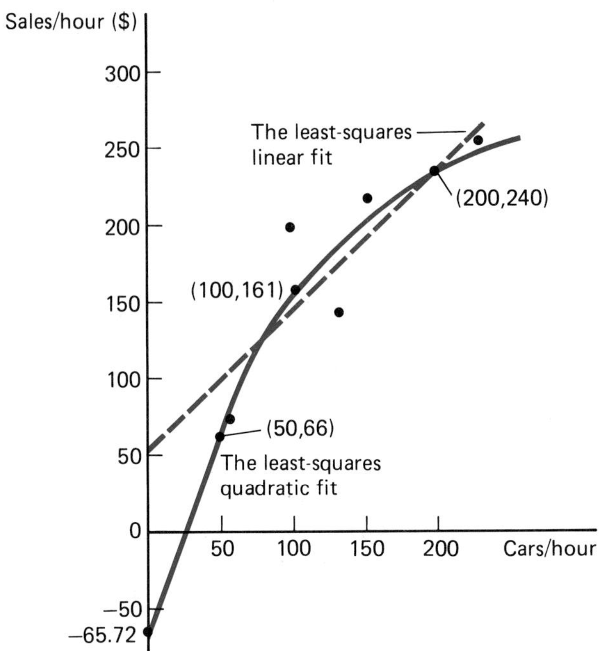

Now if there are no cars, then the service station loses \$65.72/hour. Again, this shows that there are limits to using the forecasting curve.

▲ FIGURE 18.10
Quadratic Least-Squares Function

i	(1) x_i	(2) y_i	(3) $a + bx_i$	$[(2)-(3)]^2$ d_i^2	(4) $a_0 + a_1x_i + a_2x_i^2$	$[(2)-(4)]^2$ d_i^2
1	150	220	196	576	220.57	0.32
2	55	75	108	1089	77.64	6.96
3	220	250	262	144	261.87	140.85
4	130	145	178	1089	200.71	3104
5	95	200	145	3025	246.31	2145
Σ				5923		5398

▲ FIGURE 18.11
Sum of the Squared Deviations

We see that the sum of the squared deviations for the quadratic function is indeed smaller than that for the linear function (i.e., $5398 < 5923$). Indeed, the quadratic gives us roughly a 10% decrease in the sum of squares. The general result has to hold in this direction; that is, the quadratic function must always fit better than the linear function. A linear function is, after all, a special type of a quadratic function (one in which $a_2 = 0$). It follows then that the best quadratic function must be at least as good as the best linear function.

One way of finding which fit is "better" is to compare the "mean squared error"—which is the total squared error/(number of points − number of parameters). For a linear fit, the number of parameters estimated is 2, so MSE = 5923/(5 − 2) = 1974.3, and for quadratic MSE = 5398/(5 − 3) = 2699.0. Thus, the MSE gets worse in this case, even though the total sum of squares will always be less or the same for a higher-order fit.

Which Curve to Fit?

If a quadratic function is at least as good as a linear function, why not choose an even more general form, such as a cubic or a quartic, thereby getting an even better fit? In principle the method can be applied to any specified functional form. In practice, functions of the form (again using only a single independent variable for illustrative purposes)

$$y = a_0 + a_1x + a_2x^2 + \cdots + a_nx^n$$

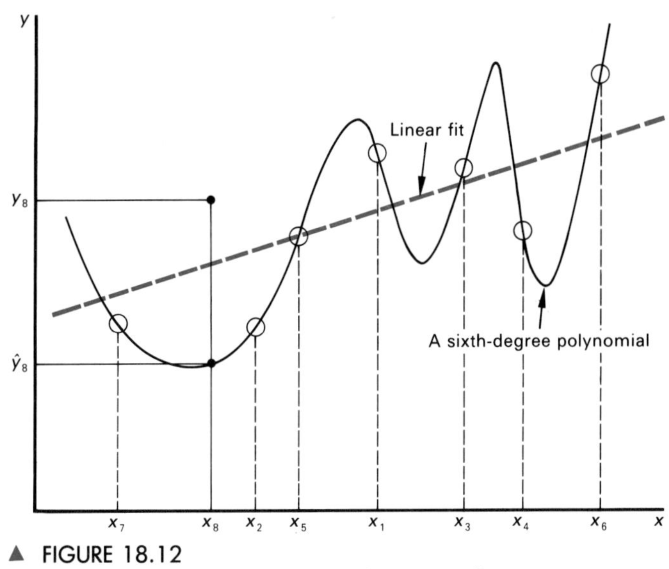

▲ FIGURE 18.12
A Sixth-Degree Polynomial Produces a Perfect Fit

Is a perfect fit the best?

are often suggested. Such a function is called a **polynomial of degree n,** and it represents a broad and flexible class of functions (for $n = 2$ we have a quadratic, $x =$ 3 a cubic, $n = 4$ a quartic, etc.). One can obtain an amazing variety of curves with polynomials, and thus they are popular among curve fitters. One must, however, proceed with caution when fitting data with a polynomial function. Under quite general conditions it is possible, for example, to find a $(k - 1)$-degree polynomial that will perfectly fit k data points. To be more specific, suppose that we have on hand seven historical observations, denoted (x_i, y_i), $i = 1, 2, \ldots, 7$. It is possible to find a sixth-degree polynomial

When there is a perfect fit, both the total sum of squares and MSE will be 0.00. Because of this, most forecasting programs will fit only up through a cubic polynomial, since higher degrees simply don't reflect the general trend of actual data.

$$y = a_0 + a_1x + a_2x^2 + \cdots + a_6x^6$$

that exactly passes through each of these seven data points (see Figure 18.12).

This perfect fit (giving zero for the sum of squared deviations), however, is deceptive, for it does not imply as much as you may think about the predictive value of the model. For example, refer again to Figure 18.12. When the independent variable (at some future time) assumes the value x_8, the true value of y might be given by y_8, whereas the predicted value is $\hat{y}_8$. Despite the previous perfect fit, the forecast is very inaccurate. In this situation a linear fit (i.e., a first-degree polynomial) such as the one indicated in Figure 18.12 might well provide more realistic forecasts, although by the criterion of least squares it does not "fit" the historical data nearly as well as the sixth-degree polynomial. Also, note that the polynomial fit has hazardous extrapolation properties. That is, the polynomial "blows up" at its extremes; x values only slightly larger than x_6 produce very large predicted y's. Looking at Figure 18.12, you can understand why high-order polynomial fits are referred to as "wild."

What Is a Good Fit? The intent of the paragraph above is to suggest that a model that has given a good fit to historical data may provide a terrible fit to future data. That is, a good historical fit may have poor predictive power. So what is a good fit?

The answer to this question involves considerations both philosophic and technical. It depends, first, on whether one has some idea about the underlying real-world process that relates the y's and the x's. To be an effective forecasting device, the forecasting function must to some extent capture important features of that process. The more one knows, the better one can do. To go very far into this topic, one must employ a level of statistics that would extend well beyond this

Statisticians assume that errors are normally distributed around the regression line, and therefore subject to analysis. Thus, when historical data are presented, each point may be shifted from where it ideally should be. Now, the regression equation is simply an approximation of an ideal curve, and the forecast is just a good guess of where the new point should appear if there were no randomness associated with the event.

Again, although the Super Bowl theory seems to work well, it is not a true model. The temptation is to keep using an irrational model (that is why fortune tellers and astrologers still make money). However, an irrational model (incorrect logic) is different from an arational model (one that works correctly but has no *distinguishable* logic).

introductory coverage. For our purposes it suffices to state that knowledge of the underlying process is typically phrased in statistical language. For example, linear curve fitting, in the statistical context, is called **linear regression.** If the statistical assumptions about the linear regression model are precisely satisfied, then in a precise and well-defined sense statisticians can prove that the linear fit is the "best possible fit."

But in a real sense, this begs the question. In the real world one can never be completely certain about the underlying process. It is never "served to us on a platter." One only has some (and often not enough) historical data to observe. The question then becomes: How much confidence can we have that the underlying process is one that satisfies a particular set of statistical assumptions? Fortunately, quantitative measures do exist. Statistical analysis, at least for simple classes of models like linear regression, can reveal how well the historical data do indeed satisfy those assumptions.

And what if they do not? One tries a different model. Let us regress (digress) for a moment to recall some of the philosophy involved with the use of optimization models. There is an underlying real-world problem. The model is a selective representation of that problem. How good is that model, or representation? One usually does not have precise measures, and many paragraphs in this text have been devoted to the role of managerial judgment and sensitivity analysis in establishing a model's credibility. Ideally, to test the goodness of a model, one would like to have considerable experience with its use. If, in repeated use, we observe that the model performs well, then our confidence is high.[3] However, what confidence can we have at the outset, without experience?

Validating Models. One benchmark, which brings us close to the current context, is to ask the question: Suppose the model had been used to make past decisions; how well would the firm have fared? This approach "creates" experience by *simulating* the past. This is often referred to as **validation** of the model. One way to use this approach, in the forecasting context, is called "divide and conquer" and is discussed in Section 18.5. Typically, one uses only a portion of the historical data to create the model—for example, to fit a polynomial of a specified degree. One can then use the remaining data to see how well the model would have performed. This procedure is specified in some detail in Section 18.5. At present, it suffices to conclude by stressing that in curve fitting the question of "goodness of fit" is both philosophic and technical, and you do not want to lose sight of either issue.

Summary Comments

A causal forecasting model uses one or more independent variables to forecast the value of a dependent or response variable. The model is often created by fitting a curve to an existing set of data and then using this curve to determine the response associated with new values of the independent variable(s). The method of least squares is a particularly useful method of fitting a curve. We illustrated the general concept of this method and considered the specific problems of fitting a straight line, a quadratic function, and higher-order polynomials to a set of data. For simplicity, all of our illustrations involved a single independent variable but the same techniques, except for quick and dirty, apply to problems with many variables.

The role of the computer

These few examples of causal forecasting models demonstrate that even in simple problems the required calculations are tedious. In most problems of an interesting size, it is impractical to perform the calculations by hand. This is

[3]No matter how much observation seems to substantiate the model, we can never conclude that the model is "true." Recall the high degree of "substantiation" of the flat earth model: "If you leave port and sail westward you will eventually fall off the earth and never be seen again."

When Lotus 1-2-3 released its version 2.0, by popular demand it included macros that do simple (linear fit) least squares regression. Couple this with the ability to graph the data and prediction curve, and one can "look" at the results and combine both quantitative and qualitative analysis.

especially true in problems where there are several independent variables. Fortunately, this is not a serious problem. The wide availability of computers and the steadily decreasing cost of computing have reduced the problem of performing the necessary calculations so that, at least in many applications, it is insignificant. The important questions are: What model, if any, can do a reliable job of forecasting, and are the data required for such a model available and reliable?

We have discussed both philosophic and technical issues that the "curve fitter" must address. Comments on the role of causal models in managerial decision making are reserved for Section 18.7. We now turn our attention to time-series analysis.

18.4 Time-Series Forecasting Models

Time-series data are historical data in chronological order, with only one value per time period. Thus, the data for the service station are *not* time-series data and cannot be analyzed using the techniques in this section.

Another class of quantitative forecasting techniques comprises the so-called **time-series models.** These models produce forecasts by *extrapolating* the *historical behavior of the values of a particular single variable of interest.* For example, one may be interested in the sales for a particular item, or a fluctuation of a particular market price with time. Time-series models use a technique to *extrapolate* the historical behavior into the future. Figuratively, the series is being lifted into the future "by its own bootstraps."

Extrapolating Historical Behavior

In order to provide several examples of bootstrap methods, let us suppose that we have on hand the daily closing prices of a January soybean futures contract for the past 12 days, including today, and that from this past stream of data we wish to predict tomorrow's closing price. Several possibilities come to mind:

Several possible approaches

1. If it is felt that all historical values are important, and that all have equal predictive power, we might take the *average* of the past 12 values as our best forecast for tomorrow.
2. If it is felt that today's value (the 12th) is far and away the most important, this value might be our best prediction for tomorrow.
3. It may be felt that in the current "fast-trending market" the first six values are too antiquated, but the most recent six are important and each has equal predictive power. We might then take the average of the most recent six values as our best estimate for tomorrow.
4. It may be felt that *all* past values contain useful information, but today's (the 12th observation) is the most important of all, and, in succession, the 11th, 10th, 9th, and so on, observations have decreasing importance. In this case we might take a *weighted average* of all 12 observations, with increasing weights assigned to each value in the order 1 through 12 and with the 12 weights summing to 1.
5. We might actually plot the 12 values as a function of time and then draw a linear "trend line" that lies close to these values. This line might then be used to predict tomorrow's value.

Let us now suppose that tomorrow's actual closing price is observed and consider our forecast for the day after tomorrow, using the 13 available historical values. Methods 1 and 2 can be applied in a straightforward manner. Now consider method 3. In this case we might take tomorrow's actual observed price, together with today's and the previous four prices, to obtain a new 6-day average. This technique is called *a simple 6-period moving average,* and it will be discussed in more detail in the following sections.

Let us now refer to method 4. In this instance, since we employ all past values, we would be using 13 rather than 12 values, with new weights assigned to these values. An important class of techniques called *exponential smoothing models* operate in this fashion. These models will also be explored in the ensuing discussion.

In this field, the error measure of M.A.D. (mean absolute deviation—what mathematicians couldn't do 100 years ago) is quite often used instead of least squares (M.S.E.).

Finally, we shall explore in more detail the technique mentioned in item 5. This provides another illustration of forecasting by a *curve-fitting method.*

We mention at this point that whenever we have values for a particular (single) variable of interest, which can be plotted against time, these values are often termed a *time series,* and any method used to analyze and extrapolate such a series into the future falls within the general category of *time-series analysis.* This is currently a very active area of research in statistics and management science. We will be able to barely scratch the surface in terms of formal development. Nevertheless, some of the important concepts, from the manager's viewpoint, will be developed.

Again, the assumption with curve fitting is that all the data are equally important (weighted). This method also produces a very *stable* forecast that is fairly insensitive to slight changes in the data.

Curve Fitting. We have already considered curve fitting in the discussion of causal models. The main difference in the time-series context is that the independent variable is time. The historical observations of the dependent variable are plotted against time, and a curve is then fitted to these data. The curve is then extended into the future to yield a forecast. In this context, extending the curve simply means evaluating the derived function for larger values of t, the time. This procedure is illustrated for a straight line in Figure 18.13.

The use of time as an independent variable has more serious implications than altering a few formulas, and a manager should understand the important difference between a causal model using curve fitting and a time-series model using curve fitting.

A different rationale

The mathematical techniques for fitting the curves are identical, but the rationale, or philosophy, behind the two models is basically quite different. To understand this difference, think of the values of y, the variable of interest, as being produced by a particular underlying process or system. The causal model assumes that as the underlying system changes to produce different values of y, it will also produce corresponding differences in the independent variables and thus, by knowing the independent variables, a good forecast of y can be deduced. The time-series model assumes that the system that produces y is essentially *stationary* (or *stable*) and will continue to act in the future as it has in the past. Future patterns in the movement of y will closely resemble past patterns. This means that time is a surrogate for many factors that may be difficult to measure but that seem to vary in a consistent and systematic manner with time. If the system that produces y significantly changes (e.g., because of changes in environment, technology, or

▼ FIGURE 18.13
Fitting a Straight Line

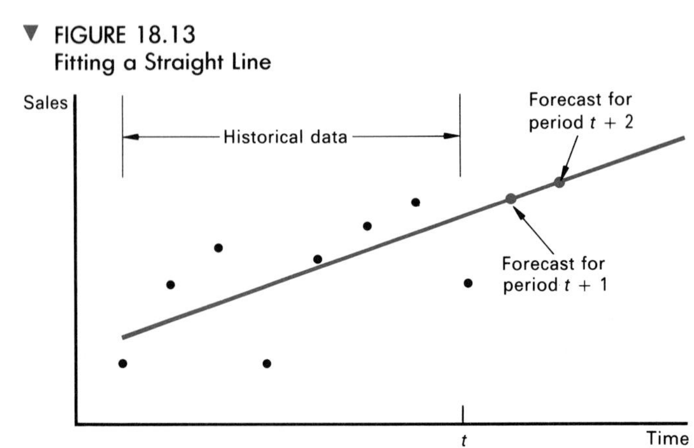

government policy) then the assumption of a *stationary process* is invalid and consequently a forecast based on time as an independent variable is apt to be badly in error.

Just as for causal models, it is, of course, possible to use other than linear functions to extrapolate a series of observations (i.e., to forecast the future). As you might imagine, one alternative that is often suggested in practice is to assume that y_t is a higher-order polynomial in t, that is,

$$y_t = b_0 + b_1t + b_2t^2 + \cdots + b_kt^k$$

As before, appropriate values for the parameters $b_0, b_1, \ldots, b_k$ must be mathematically derived from the values of previous observations. The higher-order polynomial, however, suffers from the pitfalls described earlier. That is, perfect (or at least extremely good) historical fits with little or no predictive power may be obtained.

Moving Averages: Forecasting Steco's Strut Sales. The assumption behind models of this type is that the average performance over the recent past is a good forecast of the future. It is perhaps surprising that these "naive" models are extremely important in applications. Almost all inventory control packages include a forecasting subroutine based on a particular type of moving average called exponentially weighted moving averages. On the basis of a criterion such as "frequency of use," the method of moving averages is surely an important forecasting procedure.

The fact that only the most recent data are being used to forecast the future, and perhaps the weighting of the most recent data most heavily, produces a forecast that is much more *responsive* than a curve fitting model. This type of model will be sensitive to increases or decreases in sales, or changes in the data.

One person who is deeply concerned about the use of simple forecasting models is Victor Kowalski, the new vice-president of operations of Steco. His introduction to inventory control models is discussed in Chapter 10. Since he is responsible for the inventory of thousands of items, simple (i.e., inexpensive) forecasting models are important to him. In order to become familiar with the various models, he decides to "try out" different models on some historical data. In particular he decides to use last year's monthly sales data for stainless steel struts to learn about the different models and to see how well they would have worked if Steco had been using the models last year. He is performing what is called a *validation* study.

A common notation

The forecasting models are presented, of course, in symbols. Victor feels that it would be useful to use a common notation throughout his investigation. He thus decides to let

$$y_{t-1} = \textit{observed sales} \text{ of struts in month } t-1$$
$$\hat{y}_t = \textit{forecast} \text{ of sales for struts in period } t$$

He is interested in forecasting the sales one month ahead; that is, he will take the known historical values $y_1, \ldots, y_{t-1}$ (demand in months 1 through $t-1$) and use this information to produce $\hat{y}_t$, the forecast for y_t. In other words, he will take the actual past sales, through May, for example, and use them to forecast the sales in June, then he will use the sales through June to forecast sales in July, and so on. This process produces a sequence of $\hat{y}_t$ values. By comparing these values with the observed y_t values, one obtains an indication of how the forecasting model would have worked had it actually been in use last year.

Simple n-Period Moving Average. The simplest model in the moving-average category is the **simple n-period moving average.** In this model the average of a fixed number (say, n) of the most recent observations is used as an estimate of the next value of y. For example, if n equals 4, then after we have observed the value of y in period 15, our estimate for period 16 would be

$$\hat{y}_{16} = \frac{y_{15} + y_{14} + y_{13} + y_{12}}{4}$$

MONTH	ACTUAL SALES (THOUSANDS $)	THREE-MONTH SIMPLE MOVING AVERAGE FORECAST	FOUR-MONTH SIMPLE MOVING AVERAGE FORECAST
Jan.	20		
Feb.	24		
Mar.	27		
Apr.	31	(20 + 24 + 27)/3 = 23.67	
May	37	(24 + 27 + 31)/3 = 27.33	(20 + 24 + 27 + 31)/4 = 25.50
June	47	(27 + 31 + 37)/3 = 31.67	(24 + 27 + 31 + 37)/4 = 29.75
July	53	(31 + 37 + 47)/3 = 38.33	(27 + 31 + 37 + 47)/4 = 35.50
Aug.	62	(37 + 47 + 53)/3 = 45.67	(31 + 37 + 47 + 53)/4 = 42.00
Sept.	54	(47 + 53 + 62)/3 = 54.00	(37 + 47 + 53 + 62)/4 = 49.75
Oct.	36	(53 + 62 + 54)/3 = 56.33	(47 + 53 + 62 + 54)/4 = 54.00
Nov.	32	(62 + 54 + 36)/3 = 50.67	(53 + 62 + 54 + 36)/4 = 51.25
Dec.	29	(54 + 36 + 32)/3 = 40.67	(62 + 54 + 36 + 32)/4 = 46.00

▲ FIGURE 18.14
Three- and Four-Month Simple Moving Averages

In general,

$$\hat{y}_{t+1} = \frac{1}{n}(y_t + y_{t-1} + \cdots + y_{t-n+1})$$

A simple moving average will always lag behind rising data and stay above declining data. Thus, if there are broad rises and falls, simple moving averages will not perform well. They are best suited to data with small erratic ups and downs, providing some stability in the face of the random perturbations.

The application of a three-period and a four-period moving average to Steco's strut sales data is shown in Figure 18.14.

We see that the 3-month moving average forecast for sales in April is the average of January, February, and March sales, (20 + 24 + 27)/3, or 23.67. *Ex post* (that is, after the forecast) actual sales in April were 31. Thus, in this case the sales forecast differed from the actual sales by 31 − 23.67, or 7.33.

Inspection of the data in Figure 18.14 suggests that neither forecasting method seems particularly accurate. It is, however, useful to replace this *qualitative impression* with some *quantitative measure* of how well the two methods performed. A commonly used measure of comparison is the average of the squared errors, where

A measure of forecast performance

$$\text{average squared error} = \frac{\sum_{\text{all forecasts}} (\text{forecast sales} - \text{actual sales})^2}{\text{number of forecasts}}$$

The average squared error is calculated for the 3-month (beginning with April) and 4-month (beginning with May) moving average forecast in Figure 18.15. Since the 3-month moving average yields an average squared error of 195.78, whereas the 4-month moving average yields an average squared error of 267.21, it seems (at least historically) that including more historical data harms rather than helps the forecasting accuracy.

A philosophical objection

The simple moving average has two shortcomings, one philosophical and the other operational. The *philosophical* problem centers on the fact that in calculating a forecast (say, $\hat{y}_8$), the most recent observation (y_7) receives no more weight or importance than an older observation such as y_5. This is because each of the last n observations is assigned the weight $1/n$. This procedure of assigning equal weights stands in opposition to one's intuition that in many instances the more recent data should tell us more than the older data about the future. Indeed, the analysis in Figure 18.15 suggests that better predictions for strut sales are based on the most recent data.

MONTH	ACTUAL SALES (THOUSANDS $)	THREE-MONTH SIMPLE MOVING AVERAGE FORECAST	SQUARED ERROR	FOUR-MONTH SIMPLE MOVING AVERAGE FORECAST	SQUARED ERROR
Apr.	31	23.67	53.73		
May	37	27.33	93.51	25.50	132.25
June	47	31.67	235.01	29.75	297.55
July	53	38.33	215.21	35.50	306.25
Aug.	62	45.67	266.67	42.00	400.00
Sept.	54	54.00	0	49.75	18.06
Oct.	36	56.33	413.31	54.00	324.00
Nov.	32	50.67	348.57	51.25	370.56
Dec.	29	40.67	136.19	46.00	289.00
Total			1762.20		2137.67
Average			195.78		267.21

▲ FIGURE 18.15
Average Squared Error

An operational objection

The second shortcoming, which is *operational,* is that if n observations are to be included in the moving average, then $(n - 1)$ pieces of past data must be brought forward to be combined with the current (the nth) observation. These past data must be stored in some way, in order to calculate the forecast. This is not a serious problem when a small number of forecasts is involved. The situation is quite different for the firm that needs to forecast the demand for thousands of individual products on an item-by-item basis. If, for example, Steco is using 8-period moving averages to forecast demand for 5000 small parts, then for each item 7 pieces of data must be stored for each forecast. This implies that a total of 35,000 pieces of data must be stored. In such a case storage requirements, as well as computing time, may become important factors in designing a forecasting and inventory control system.

Philosophical objection removed

Weighted n-Period Moving Average. The notion that recent data are more important than old data can be implemented with a **weighted n-period moving average.** This generalizes the notion of a simple n-period moving average, where, as we have seen, each weight is $1/n$. In this more general form, taking $n = 3$ as a specific example, we would set

$$\hat{y}_7 = \alpha_0 y_6 + \alpha_1 y_5 + \alpha_2 y_4$$

where the α's (which are called weights) are nonnegative numbers that are chosen so that smaller weights are assigned to more ancient data and all the weights sum to 1. There are, of course, innumerable ways of selecting a set of α's to satisfy these criteria. For example, if as above the weighted average is to include the last three observations (a weighted 3-period moving average), one might set

$$\hat{y}_7 = \frac{3}{6} y_6 + \frac{2}{6} y_5 + \frac{1}{6} y_4$$

Alternatively, one could define

$$\hat{y}_7 = \frac{5}{10} y_6 + \frac{3}{10} y_5 + \frac{2}{10} y_4$$

In these expressions we have decreasing weights that sum to 1. In practice, the proper choice of weights could well be a study in itself. Rather than discussing the rationale for various choices of weights, our desire is to illustrate the use of the model.

MONTH	ACTUAL SALE (THOUSANDS $)	THREE-MONTH WEIGHTED MOVING-AVERAGE FORECAST	SQUARED ERROR
Jan.	20		
Feb.	24		
Mar.	27		
Apr.	31	$[(3 \times 27) + (2 \times 24) + (1 \times 20)]/6 = 24.83$	38.07
May	37	$[(3 \times 31) + (2 \times 27) + (1 \times 24)]/6 = 28.50$	72.25
June	47	$[(3 \times 37) + (2 \times 31) + (1 \times 27)]/6 = 33.33$	186.87
July	53	$[(3 \times 47) + (2 \times 37) + (1 \times 31)]/6 = 41.00$	144.00
Aug.	62	$[(3 \times 53) + (2 \times 47) + (1 \times 37)]/6 = 48.33$	186.87
Sept.	54	$[(3 \times 62) + (2 \times 53) + (1 \times 47)]/6 = 56.50$	6.25
Oct.	36	$[(3 \times 54) + (2 \times 62) + (1 \times 53)]/6 = 56.50$	420.25
Nov.	32	$[(3 \times 36) + (2 \times 54) + (1 \times 62)]/6 = 46.33$	205.35
Dec.	29	$[(3 \times 32) + (2 \times 36) + (1 \times 54)]/6 = 37.00$	64.00
Total			1323.91
Average			147.10

▲ FIGURE 18.16
Three-Month Weighted Moving Average

To get some idea about its performance, Victor applies the 3-month weighted moving average with weights 3/6, 2/6, 1/6 to the historical stainless strut data. The forecasts and the average squared error are shown in Figure 18.16. Comparing the average squared errors of the 3-month simple moving average (195.78), the 4-month simple moving average (267.21), and the 3-month weighted moving average (147.10) confirms the suggestion, based on Figure 18.15, that recent sales results are a better indicator of future sales than are older data.

Although the weighted moving average places more weight on more recent data, it does not solve the operational problems of data storage, since $(n - 1)$ pieces of historical sales data must still be stored. We now turn to a weighting scheme that cleverly addresses this problem.

Exponential Smoothing: The Basic Model

Operational objection removed

We saw that, in using a weighted moving average, there are many different ways to assign decreasing weights that sum to 1. One way is called **exponential smoothing,** which is a shortened name for an *exponentially weighted moving average.* This is a scheme that weights recent data more heavily than past data, with weights summing to 1, but it avoids the operational problem just discussed. In this model, for any $t \geq 1$ the forecast for period t+1, denoted $\hat{y}_{t+1}$, is a weighted sum (with weights summing to 1) of the actual *observed sales in period* t (i.e., y_t) and *the forecast for period* t (which was $\hat{y}_t$). In other words,

Forecast for t+1 | Observed in t | Forecast for t

$$\hat{y}_{t+1} = \alpha y_t + (1 - \alpha)\hat{y}_t \tag{18.8}$$

Depending on the behavior of the data, it might be necessary to store a different value of α for each item, but even then much less storage would be required than if using moving averages. The thing that is nice about exponential smoothing is that by saving α and the last forecast, all the previous forecasts are being stored *implicitly.*

where α is a user-specified constant such that $0 \leq \alpha \leq 1$. The value assigned to α determines how much weight is placed on the most recent observation in calculating the forecast for the next period. Note in Equation 18.8 that if α is assigned a value close to 1, almost all the weight is placed on the demand in period t.

Exponential smoothing has important computational advantages. To compute $\hat{y}_{t+1}$, only $\hat{y}_t$ need be stored (together with the value of α). As soon as the actual y_t is observed, we compute $\hat{y}_{t+1} = \alpha y_t + (1 - \alpha)\hat{y}_t$. If Steco wanted to forecast demand for

MONTH	ACTUAL SALES (000 $)	$\alpha = 0.6$ $\hat{y}_t$	$\alpha = 0.6$ Squared Error	$\alpha = 0.4$ $\hat{y}_t$	$\alpha = 0.4$ Squared Error	$\alpha = 0.2$ $\hat{y}_t$	$\alpha = 0.2$ Squared Error
Jan.	20	40		40		40	
Feb.	24	28.00		32.00		36.00	
Mar.	27	25.60		28.80		33.60	
Apr.	31	26.44	20.79	28.08	8.53	32.28	1.64
May	37	29.18	61.21	29.25	60.09	32.02	24.76
June	47	33.87	172.39	32.35	214.66	33.02	195.46
July	53	41.75	126.60	38.21	218.77	35.82	295.31
Aug.	62	48.50	182.27	44.13	319.50	39.25	517.46
Sept.	54	56.60	6.76	51.28	7.42	43.80	104.00
Oct.	36	55.04	362.52	52.37	267.82	45.84	96.85
Nov.	32	43.62	134.93	45.82	190.97	43.87	140.97
Dec.	29	36.65	58.47	40.29	127.50	41.50	156.21
Total			1125.94		1415.25		1532.67
Average			125.10		157.25		170.30

▲ FIGURE 18.17
Exponential Smoothing (α = 0.6, 0.4, and 0.2)

5000 small parts, in each period, then 5001 items would have to be stored (the 5000 $\hat{y}_t$ values, and the value of α), as opposed to the previously computed 35,000 items needed to implement an 8-period moving average.

In order to obtain more insight into the exponential smoothing model, let us note that when $t = 1$ the expression used to define $\hat{y}_2$ is

$$\hat{y}_2 = \alpha y_1 + (1 - \alpha)\hat{y}_1$$

In this expression $\hat{y}_1$ is an "initial guess" at the value for y in period 1, and y_1 is the observed value in period 1. At this point Victor decides to use a spreadsheet to apply exponential smoothing to the stainless steel strut data. Figure 18.17 shows actual sales and three series of estimated sales for 12 months. Victor has used three different values for (0.6, 0.4, 0.2). For each series he has also calculated the total and average squared error for April through December. In this brief study we see that better forecasts are obtained by putting more weight on the most current data. Indeed, the exponential smoothing model with $\alpha = 0.6$ yields a smaller squared error than the model with smaller values of α or the moving average models (see Figures 18.15 and 18.16).

The value of y_{12} is fairly insensitive to the initial value, and by waiting until April to measure error, the effect of choosing the "wrong" value is reduced.

Victor is delighted with the results. The average squared error is smaller than what he obtained with the previous three models, and the calculations are simple. From a computational view it is reasonable to consider exponential smoothing as an affordable way to forecast the sales of the many products Steco holds in inventory.

Although the results obtained from the exponential smoothing model are impressive, it is clear that the particular numerical values in Figure 18.17 depend on the values selected for the smoothing constant α and the "initial guess" $\hat{y}_1$.

The forecast gives weight to all past observations

Because of the importance of the basic exponential smoothing model, it is worth exploring in more detail how it works and when it can be successfully applied to real problems. We will now examine some of its properties. To begin, note that if $t \geq 2$ it is possible to substitute $t-1$ for t in (18.8) to obtain

$$\hat{y}_t = \alpha y_{t-1} + (1 - \alpha)\hat{y}_{t-1}$$

Substituting this relationship back into the original expression for $\hat{y}_{t+1}$ (i.e., into [18.8]) yields for $t \geq 2$,

$$\hat{y}_{t+1} = \alpha y_t + \alpha(1-\alpha)y_{t-1} + (1-\alpha)^2\hat{y}_{t-1}$$

By successively performing similar substitutions one is led to the following general expression for $\hat{y}_{t+1}$:

$$\hat{y}_{t+1} = \alpha y_t + \alpha(1-\alpha)y_{t-1} + \alpha(1-\alpha)^2 y_{t-2} + \cdots + \alpha(1-\alpha)^{t-1}y_1 + (1-\alpha)^t\hat{y}_1 \quad \textbf{(18.9)}$$

For example,

$$\hat{y}_4 = \alpha y_3 + \alpha(1-\alpha)y_2 + \alpha(1-\alpha)^2 y_1 + (1-\alpha)^3\hat{y}_1$$

Since $0 < \alpha < 1$, it follows that $0 < 1 - \alpha < 1$. Thus,

$$\alpha > \alpha(1-\alpha) > \alpha(1-\alpha)^2$$

The weights are declining exponentially

In other words, in the previous example y_3, the most recent observation, receives more weight than y_2, which receives more weight than y_1. This illustrates the general property of an exponential smoothing model—that *the coefficients of the* y*'s decrease as the data become older.* It can also be shown that *the sum of all of the coefficients (including the coefficient of* $\hat{y}_1$*) is 1;* that is in the case of $\hat{y}_4$, for example,

$$\alpha + \alpha(1-\alpha) + \alpha(1-\alpha)^2 + (1-\alpha)^3 = 1$$

Since α is (almost) always < 1.0, raising α to a power gives it a decreasing weight for the next period. $\alpha = 1.0$ is a special case.

When $\alpha = 0.0$, this means complete trust in the last forecast and completely ignoring the last data point. This would be an extremely stable forecast. When $\alpha = 1.0$, this means throwing out the last forecast completely and using the last data point entirely. This produces an extremely responsive forecast.

We have thus seen in expression (18.9) that the general value $\hat{y}_{t+1}$ is a weighted sum of *all previous observations* (including the last observed value, y_t). Moreover, the weights sum to 1 and are decreasing as historical observations get older. The last term in the sum, namely $\hat{y}_1$, is not a historical observation. Recall that it was a "guess" at y_1. We can now observe that as t increases, the influence of $\hat{y}_1$ on $\hat{y}_{t+1}$ decreases and in time becomes negligible. To see this, note that the coefficient of $\hat{y}_1$ in (18.9) is $(1-\alpha)^t$. Thus, the weight assigned to $\hat{y}_1$ decreases exponentially with t. Even if α is small (which makes $[1-\alpha]$ nearly 1) the value of $(1-\alpha)^t$ decreases rapidly. For example, if $\alpha = 0.1$ and $t = 20$, then $(1-\alpha)^t = 0.12$. If $\alpha = 0.1$ and $t = 40$, then $(1-\alpha)^t = 0.015$. Thus, as soon as enough data have been observed, the value of $\hat{y}_{t+1}$ will be quite insensitive to the choice for $\hat{y}_1$.

Obviously, the value of α, which is a parameter input by the analyst, affects the performance of the model. As you can see explicitly in (18.8), it is the weight given to the data value (y_t) most recently observed. This implies that the larger the value of α, the more strongly the model will react to the last observation. This, as we will see, may or may not be desirable. Figure 18.18 shows values for the weights (in

▼ FIGURE 18.18
Weights for Different Values of α

VARIABLE	COEFFICIENT	α = 0.1	α = 0.3	α = 0.5
y_t	α	0.1	0.3	0.5
y_{t-1}	$\alpha(1-\alpha)$	0.09	0.21	0.25
y_{t-2}	$\alpha(1-\alpha)^2$	0.081	0.147	0.125
y_{t-3}	$\alpha(1-\alpha)^3$	0.07290	0.10290	0.0625
y_{t-4}	$\alpha(1-\alpha)^4$	0.06561	0.07203	0.03125
y_{t-5}	$\alpha(1-\alpha)^5$	0.05905	0.05042	0.01563
y_{t-6}	$\alpha(1-\alpha)^6$	0.05314	0.03530	0.00781
y_{t-7}	$\alpha(1-\alpha)^7$	0.04783	0.02471	0.00391
y_{t-8}	$\alpha(1-\alpha)^8$	0.04305	0.01729	0.00195
y_{t-9}	$\alpha(1-\alpha)^9$	0.03874	0.01211	0.00098
y_{t-10}	$\alpha(1-\alpha)^{10}$	0.03487	0.00847	0.00049
Sum of the Weights		0.68619	0.98023	0.99610

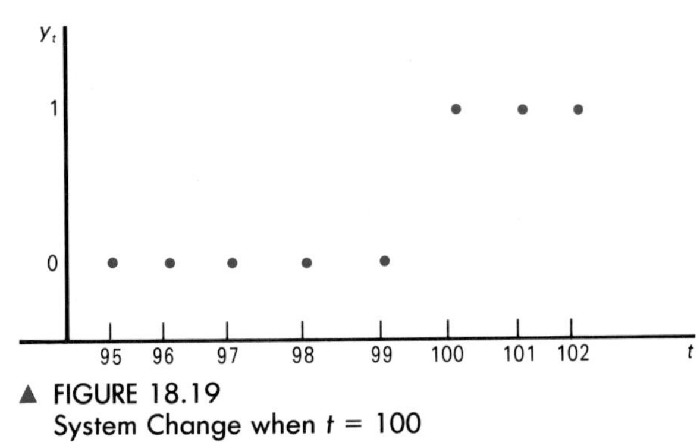

▲ FIGURE 18.19
System Change when t = 100

expression 18.9) when $\alpha = 0.1, 0.3$, and 0.5. You can see that for the larger values of α (e.g., $\alpha = 0.5$) more relative weight is assigned to the more recent observations, and the influence of older data is more rapidly diminished.

To illustrate further the effect of choosing various values for α (i.e., putting more or less weight on recent observations), we consider three specific cases.

Response to a sudden change

▶ ***Case 1:*** Suppose that at a certain point in time the underlying system experiences a rapid and radical change. How does the choice of α influence the way in which the exponential smoothing model will react? As an illustrative example consider an extreme case in which

$$y_t = 0 \quad \text{for } t = 1, 2, \ldots, 99$$
$$y_t = 1 \quad \text{for } t = 100, 101, \ldots$$

This situation is illustrated in Figure 18.19. Note that in this case if $\hat{y}_1 = 0$, then $\hat{y}_{100} = 0$ for any value of α, since we are taking the weighted sum of a series of zeros.

Thus, at time 99 our best estimate of y_{100} is 0, whereas the actual value will be 1. At time 100 we will first see that the system has changed. The question is: How quickly will the forecasting system respond as time passes and the information that the system has changed becomes available?

To answer this question, we plot $\hat{y}_{t+1}$ for $\alpha = 0.5$ and $\alpha = 0.1$ in Figure 18.20.

▼ FIGURE 18.20
Response to a Unit Change in y_t

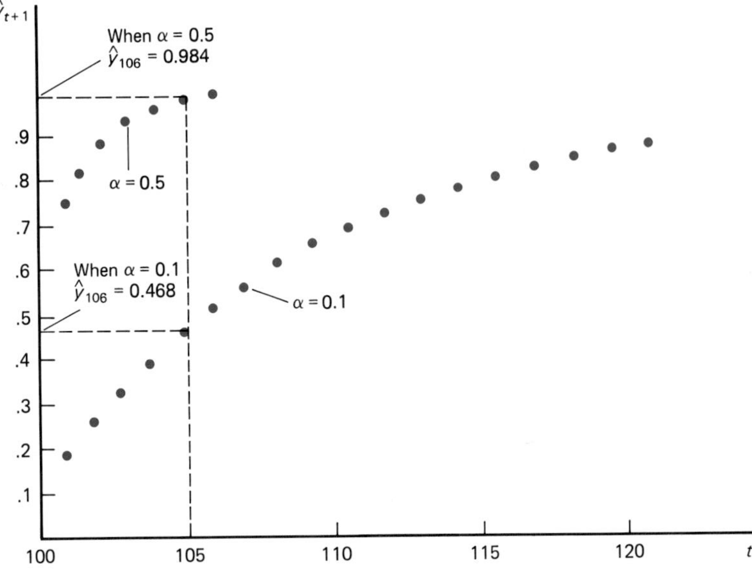

Note that when $\alpha = 0.5$, $\hat{y}_{106} = 0.984$; thus at time 105 our estimate of y_{106} would be 0.984, whereas the true value will turn out to be 1. When $\alpha = 0.1$ our estimate of y_{106} is only 0.468.

We see then that a forecasting system with $\alpha = 0.5$ responds much more quickly to changes in the data than does a forecasting system with $\alpha = 0.1$. The manager would thus prefer a relatively large α if the system is characterized by a low level of random behavior, but is subject to occasional enduring shocks. (Case 1 is an extreme example of this situation.) However, suppose that the data are characterized by large random errors but a stable mean. Then if α is large, a large random error in y_t will throw the forecast value, $\hat{y}_{t+1}$, way off. Hence, for this type of process a smaller value of α would be preferred.

Response to a steady change

▶ ***Case 2:*** As opposed to the rapid and radical change investigated in Case 1, suppose now that a system experiences a *steady* change in the value of y. An example of a steady growth pattern is illustrated in Figure 18.21. This example is called a *linear ramp.* Again the questions are: How will the exponential smoothing model respond, and how will this response be affected by the choice of α?

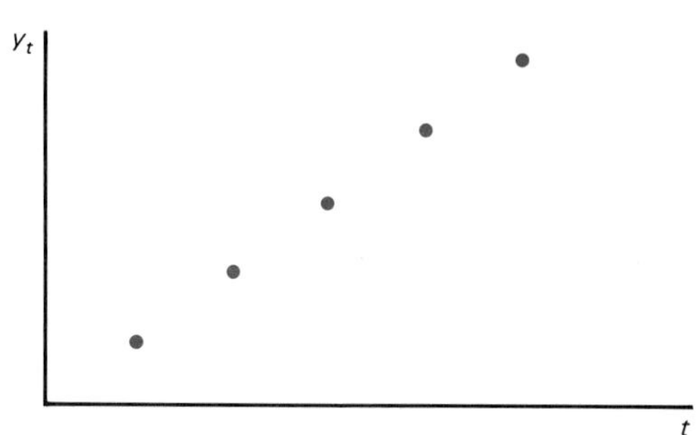

▲ FIGURE 18.21
Steadily Increasing Values of y_t (a Linear Ramp)

In this case, recall that

$$\hat{y}_{t+1} = \alpha y_t + \alpha(1 - \alpha)y_{t-1} + \cdots$$

Since all previous y's ($y_1, \ldots, y_{t-1}$) are smaller than y_t, and since the weights sum to 1, it can be shown that, for any α between 0 and 1, $\hat{y}_{t+1} < y_t$. Also, since y_{t+1} is greater than y_t, we see that $\hat{y}_{t+1} < y_t < y_{t+1}$. Thus our forecast will always be too small. Finally, since smaller values of α put more weight on older data, the smaller the value of α, the worse the forecast becomes. But even with α very close to 1 the forecast is not very good if the ramp is steep. The moral for managers is that exponential smoothing (or indeed any weighted moving average), without an appropriate modification, is not a good forecasting tool in a rapidly growing market. The model could be adjusted to include a trend, but this topic lies beyond the introductory scope of this chapter.

In this case, adjusting for trend is a much more complicated matter than adjusting with weighted moving averages.

Response to seasonal changes

▶ ***Case 3:*** Suppose that a system experiences a regular *seasonal pattern* in y (such as would be the case if y represents, for example, the demand in the city of Chicago for swimming suits). How then will the exponential smoothing model respond, and how will this response be affected by the choice of α? Consider, for example, the seasonal pattern illustrated in Figure 18.22, and suppose it is desired to extrapolate *several periods forward.* For example, suppose we wish to forecast demand in periods 8 through 11 based only on data through period 7. Then

$$\hat{y}_8 = \alpha y_7 + (1 - \alpha)\hat{y}_7$$

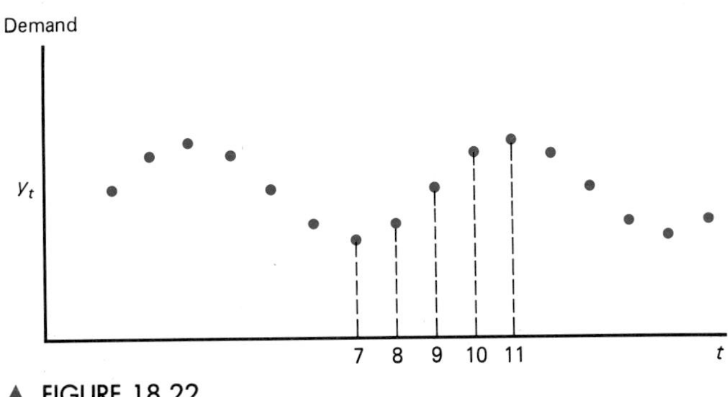

▲ FIGURE 18.22
Seasonal Pattern in y_t

When there is a discernible pattern of seasonality (which can be seen fairly easily by graphing in Lotus with each season being a different data range) there are methods, using simple moving averages, to determine a *seasonality factor*. Using this factor, the data can be "deseasonalized," exponential smoothing used, and the forecast "re-seasonalized."

Now to obtain $\hat{y}_9$, since we have data only through period 7, we assume that $y_8 = \hat{y}_8$. Then

$$\hat{y}_9 = \alpha y_8 + (1 - \alpha)\hat{y}_8 = \alpha\hat{y}_8 + (1 - \alpha)\hat{y}_8 = \hat{y}_8$$

Similarly, it can be shown that $\hat{y}_{11} = \hat{y}_{10} = \hat{y}_9 = \hat{y}_8$. In other words, $\hat{y}_8$ is the best estimate of all future demands.

Now let us see how good these predictions are. We know that

$$\hat{y}_{t+1} = \alpha y_t + \alpha(1 - \alpha)y_{t-1} + \alpha(1 - \alpha)^2 y_{t-2} + \cdots$$

Suppose that a small value of α is chosen. By referring to Figure 18.18 we see that when α is small (say, 0.1) the coefficients for the most recent terms change relatively slowly (i.e., they are nearly equal to each other). Thus, $\hat{y}_{t+1}$ will resemble a simple moving average of a number of terms. In this case the future predictions (e.g., $\hat{y}_{11}$) will all be somewhere near the average of the past observations. The forecast thus essentially ignores the seasonal pattern. If a large value of α is chosen, $\hat{y}_{11}$, which equals $\hat{y}_8$, will be close in value to y_7, which is obviously not good. In other words, the model fares poorly in this case regardless of the choice of α.

Applicability of exponential smoothing

The exponential smoothing model $\hat{y}_{t+1} = \alpha y_t + (1 - \alpha)\hat{y}_t$ is intended for situations in which the behavior of the variable of interest is essentially stable, in the sense that deviations over time have nothing to do with *time*, per se, but are caused by *random effects* that do not follow a regular pattern. This is what we have termed the *stationarity* assumption. Not surprisingly, then, the model has various shortcomings when it is used in situations (such as swimming suit demand) that do not fit this prescription. Although this statement may be true, it is not very constructive. What approach should a manager take when the exponential smoothing model as described above is not appropriate? In the case of a seasonal pattern a naive approach would be to use the exponential smoothing model on "appropriate" past data. For example, to forecast sales in June one might take a smoothed average of sales in previous Junes. This approach has two problems. First, it ignores a great deal of useful information. Certainly sales from last July through this May should provide at least a limited amount of information about the likely level of sales this June. Second, if the cycle is very long, say a year, this approach means that very old data must be used to get a reasonable sample size. The above assumption, that the system or process producing the variable of interest is essentially *stationary* over time, becomes more tenuous when the span of time covered by the data becomes quite large.

If the manager is convinced that there is either a trend (Case 2) or a seasonal effect (Case 3) in the variable being predicted, a better approach is to develop modified exponential smoothing models that incorporate these features. References to models of this sort exist in the technical literature, and the models are not exceptionally complicated. Presentation of these developments, however, carries us too far into the realm of a quite special technique and too far from our goal in this chapter of presenting mainly the basic concepts.

The Random Walk

The moving-average techniques discussed above are examples of what are called time-series models. Recently, much more sophisticated methods for time-series analysis have become available. These methods, based primarily on developments by G. E. P. Box and G. M. Jenkins[4] in the late 1960s, have already had an important impact on the practice of forecasting, and indeed the Box-Jenkins approach is incorporated in certain computer packages.

These time-series forecasting techniques are based on the assumption that the true values of the variable of interest, y_t, are generated by a stochastic (i.e., probabilistic) model. Introducing enough of the theory of probability to enable us to discuss these models in any generality seems inappropriate, but one special and very important (and very simple) process, called a **random walk,** serves as a nice illustration of a stochastic model. Here the variable y_t is assumed to be produced by the relationship

$$y_t = y_{t-1} + \varepsilon$$

where the value of ε is determined by a random event. To illustrate this process even more explicitly, let us consider a man standing at a street corner on a north-south street. He flips a fair coin. If it lands with a head showing, he walks one block north. If it lands with a tail showing, he walks one block south. When he arrives at the next corner (whichever one it turns out to be) he repeats the process. This is the classic example of a random walk. To put this example in the form of the model, label the original corner zero. We shall call this the value of the first observation, y_1. Starting at this point, label successive corners going north +1, +2, ... Also starting at the original corner label successive corners going south −1, −2, . . . (see Figure 18.23). These labels that describe the location of our random walker are the y_t's.

In the model, $y_t = y_{t-1} + \varepsilon$, where (assuming a fair coin) $\varepsilon = 1$ with probability ½ and $\varepsilon = -1$ with probability ½. If our walker observes the sequence H, H, H, T, T, H, T, T, T, he will follow the path shown in Figure 18.23.

▼ FIGURE 18.23
Classic Random Walk

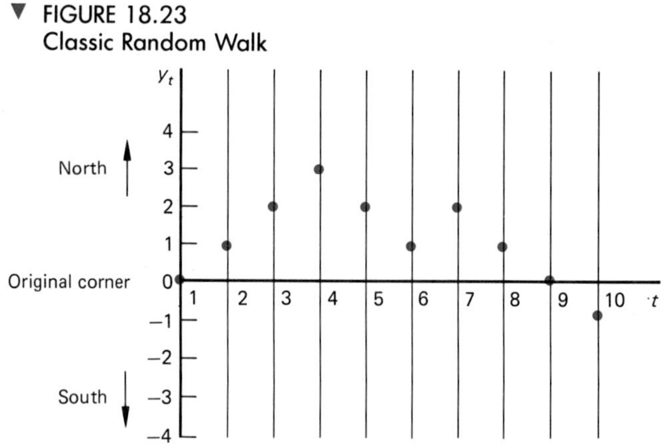

[4] G. E. P. Box and G. M. Jenkins, *Time Series Analysis, Forecasting and Control* (San Francisco: Holden-Day, Inc., 1970).

Forecasts Based on Conditional Expected Value. Suppose that after our special agent has flipped the coin nine times (i.e., he has moved nine times, and we have, starting with corner 0, 10 observations of corners) we would like to forecast where he will be after another move. This is the typical forecasting problem in the time-series context. That is, we have observed $y_1, y_2, \ldots, y_{10}$ and we need a good forecast $\hat{y}_{11}$ of the forthcoming value y_{11}. In this case, according to a reasonable criterion, the best value for $\hat{y}_{11}$ is the *conditional expected value* of the random quantity y_{11}. In other words, the best forecast is the expected value of y_{11} given that we know $y_1, y_2, \ldots, y_{10}$. From the model we know that y_{11} will equal $y_{10} + 1$ with a probability equal to ½ and y_{11} will equal $y_{10} - 1$ with a probability equal to ½. Thus, $E(y_{11}|y_1, \ldots, y_{10})$, the conditional expected value of y_{11} given $y_1, y_2, \ldots, y_{10}$, is calculated as follows:

$$E(y_{11}|y_1, \ldots, y_{10}) = (y_{10} + 1)\frac{1}{2} + (y_{10} - 1)\frac{1}{2} = y_{10}$$

Thus we see that for this model the data $y_1, \ldots, y_9$ are irrelevant, and *the best forecast of the random walker's position one move from now is his current position.* It is interesting to observe that the best forecast of y_{12} given $y_1, \ldots, y_{10}$ is also y_{10}. Indeed, the best forecast for any future value of y, given this particular model, is its current value.

There exists much heated debate (more heat than light!) about the ability to forecast the stock market. This is probably the modern equivalent of trying to find a process to turn lead into gold.

Seeing What Isn't There. This example is not as silly as it may seem at first glance. Indeed, there is a great deal of evidence that supports the idea that stock prices behave like a random walk and that the best forecast of a future stock price is its current value. Not surprisingly, this conclusion is not warmly accepted by research directors and technical chartists who make their living forecasting stock prices. One reason for the resistance to the random walk hypothesis is the almost universal human tendency when looking at a set of data to observe certain patterns or regularities, no matter how the data are produced. Consider the time-series data plotted in Figure 18.24. It does not seem unreasonable to believe that the data are following a sinusoidal pattern as suggested by the smooth curve in the figure. In spite of this impression, the data were in fact generated by the random walk model presented earlier in this section. This illustrates the tendency to see patterns where there are none. In Figure 18.24, any attempt to predict future values by extrapolating the sinusoidal pattern would have no more validity than flipping a coin.

In concluding this section we should stress that it is *not* a general conclusion of time-series analysis that the best estimate of the future is the present (i.e., that $\hat{y}_{t+1} = y_t$). This result holds for the particular random walk model presented above. The result depends crucially on the assumption that the expected or mean value of ε, the random component, is zero. If the probability that ε equals 1 had been 0.6 and the

▼ FIGURE 18.24
Time-Series Data

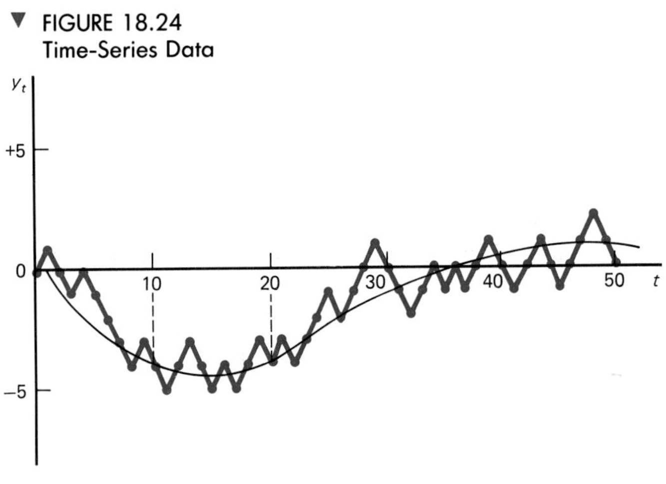

probability that ε equals −1 had been 0.4, the best forecast of y_{t+1} would not have been y_t. To find this forecast one would have had to find $E(y_{t+1}|y_1, \ldots, y_t)$. Such a model is called a *random walk with a drift.*

18.5 The Role of Historical Data: Divide and Conquer

Historical data play a critical role in the construction and testing of forecasting models. One hopes that a rationale precedes the construction of a quantitative forecasting model. There may be theoretical reasons for believing that a relationship exists between some independent variables and the dependent variable to be forecast and thus that a causal model is appropriate. Alternatively, one may take the time-series view that the "behavior of the past" is a good indication of the future. In either case, however, if a quantitative model is to be used, the parameters of the model must be selected. For example:

1. In a causal model using a linear forecasting function, $y = a + bx$, the values of a and b must be specified.
2. In a time-series model using a weighted n-period moving average, $\hat{y}_{t+1} = \alpha_0 y_t + \alpha_1 y_{t-1} + \cdots + \alpha_{n-1} y_{t-n+1}$, the number of terms, n, and the values for the weights, $\alpha_0, \alpha_1, \ldots, \alpha_{n-1}$, must be specified.
3. In a time-series model using exponential smoothing, $\hat{y}_{t+1} = \alpha y_t + (1 - \alpha)\hat{y}_t$, the value of α must be specified.

Estimating parameters and testing the model

In any of these models, in order to specify the parameter values, one typically must make use of historical data. A useful guide in seeking to use such data effectively is to "divide and conquer." More directly, this means that it is often a useful practice to use part of the data to estimate the parameters and the rest of the data to test the model.

It is also important to "clean" the data—examine it for irregularities, missing information, or special circumstances, and adjust it accordingly.

For example, suppose that a firm has weekly sales data on a particular product for the last 2 years and plans to use an exponential smoothing model to forecast sales for this product. The firm might use the following procedure:

1. Pick a particular value of α, and compare the values of $\hat{y}_{t+1}$ to y_{t+1} for $t = 25$ to 75. The first 24 values are not compared, so as to negate any initial or "startup" effect, that is, to nullify the influence of the initial guess, $\hat{y}_1$. The analyst would continue to select different values of α until the model produces a satisfactory fit during the period $t = 25$ to 75.
2. Test the model derived in step 1 on the remaining 29 pieces of data. That is, using the best value of α from step 1, compare the values of $\hat{y}_{t+1}$ and y_{t+1} for $t =$ 76 to 104.

If the model does a good job of forecasting values for the last part of the historical data, there is some reason to believe that it will also do a good job with the future. On the other hand, if by using the data from weeks 1 through 75, the model cannot perform well in predicting the demand in weeks 76 through 104, the prospects for predicting the future with the same model seem dubious. In this case, another forecasting technique might be applied.

A null test

The same type of divide-and-conquer strategy can be used with any of the forecasting techniques we have presented. This approach amounts to *simulating* the model's performance on past data. It is a popular method of testing models. It should be stressed, however, that this procedure represents what is termed a *null test.* If the model fails on historical data, the model probably is not appropriate. If the model succeeds on historical data, *one cannot be sure that it will work in the future.* Who knows, the underlying system that is producing the observations may change. It is this type of sobering experience that causes certain forecasters to be less certain.

18.6 Qualitative Forecasting

Expert Judgment

Many important forecasts are not based on formal models. This point seems obvious in the realm of world affairs—matters of war and peace, so to speak. Perhaps more surprisingly it is also often true in economic matters. For example, during the high-interest-rate period of 1980 and 1981, the most influential forecasters of interest rates were not two competing econometric models run by teams of econometricians. Rather, they were Henry Kaufman of Salomon Brothers and Albert Wojnilower of First Boston, the so-called Doctors Doom and Gloom of the interest-rate world. These gentlemen combined relevant factors such as the money supply and unemployment, as well as results from quantitative models, in their own intuitive way (their own "internal" models) and produced forecasts that had widespread credibility and impact on the financial community.

The moral for managers is that qualitative forecasts can well be an important source of information. Managers must consider a wide variety of sources of data before coming to a decision. Expert opinion should not be ignored. A sobering and useful measure of all forecasts—quantitative and qualitative—is a record of past performance. Good performance in the past is a sensible type of null test. An excellent track record does not promise good results in the future. A poor record, however, hardly creates enthusiasm for high achievement in the future. Managers should thus listen to experts cautiously and hold them to a standard of performance.

There is, however, more to qualitative forecasting than selecting "the right" expert. Techniques exist to elicit and combine forecasts from various groups of experts, and we now turn our attention to these techniques.

The Delphi Method and Consensus Panel

The **Delphi Method** confronts the problem of obtaining a combined forecast from a group of experts. One approach is to bring the experts together in a room and let them discuss the event until a consensus emerges. Not surprisingly, this group is called a **consensus panel.** This approach suffers because of the group dynamics of such an exercise. One strong individual can have an enormous effect on the forecast because of his or her personality, reputation, or debating skills. Accurate analysis may be pushed into a secondary position.

The Delphi Method was developed by the Rand Corporation to retain the strength of a joint forecast, while removing the effects of group dynamics. The method uses a coordinator and a set of experts. No expert knows who else is in the group. All communication is through the coordinator. The process is illustrated in Figure 18.25.

After three or four passes through this process, a consensus forecast typically emerges. The forecast may be near the original median, but if a forecast that is an outlier in round 1 is supported by strong analysis, the extreme forecast in round 1 may be the group forecast after three or four rounds.

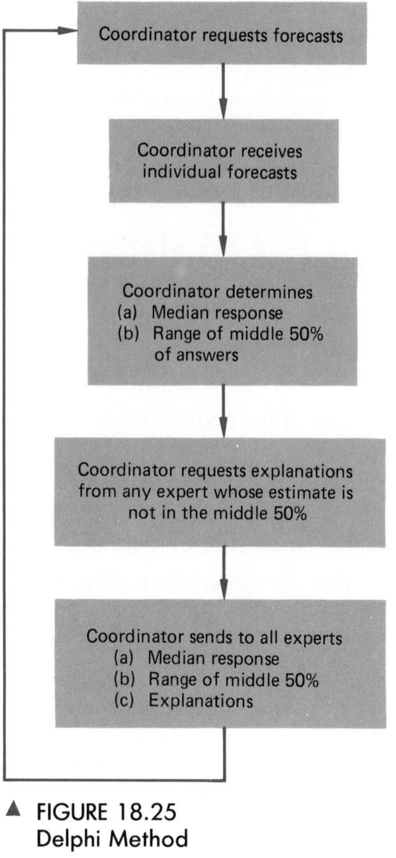

▲ FIGURE 18.25
Delphi Method

Grass Roots Forecasting and Market Research

Other qualitative techniques focus primarily on forecasting demand for a product or group of products. They are based on the concept of asking either those who are close to the eventual consumer, such as salespeople or consumers themselves, about a product or their purchasing plans.

Consulting Salesmen. In **grass roots forecasting,** salespeople are asked to forecast demand in their districts. In the simplest situations, these forecasts are added together to get a total demand forecast. In more sophisticated systems individual forecasts or the total may be adjusted on the basis of the historical correlation between the salesperson's forecasts and the actual sales. Such a procedure makes it possible to adjust for an actual occurrence of the stereotyped salesperson's optimism.

Grass roots forecasts have the advantage of bringing a great deal of detailed knowledge to bear on the forecasting problem. The individual salesperson who is keenly aware of the situation in his or her district should be able to provide better forecasts than more aggregate models. There are, however, several problems:

1. ***High cost:*** The time salespeople spend forecasting is not spent selling. Some view this opportunity cost of grass roots forecasting as its major disadvantage.
2. ***Potential conflict of interest:*** Sales forecasts may well turn into marketing goals that can affect a salesperson's compensation in an important way. Such considerations exert a downward bias in individual forecasts.
3. ***Product schizophrenia (i.e., stereotyped salesperson's optimism):*** It is important for salespeople to be enthusiastic about their product and its potential uses. It

is not clear that this enthusiasm is consistent with a cold-eyed appraisal of its market potential.

In summary, grass roots forecasting may not fit well with other organization objectives and thus may not be effective in an overall sense.

Consulting Consumers. **Market research** is a large and important topic in its own right. It includes a variety of techniques, from consumer panels through consumer surveys and on to test marketing. The goal is to make predictions about the size and structure of the market for specific goods and/or services. These predictions (forecasts) are usually based on small samples and are qualitative in the sense that the original data typically consist of subjective evaluations of consumers. A large menu of quantitative techniques exists to aid in determining how to gather the data and how to analyze them.

Market research is an important activity in most consumer product firms. It also plays an important role in the political and electoral process.

18.7 Notes on Implementation

Whether in the private or public sector, the need to deal with the future is an implicit or explicit part of every management action and decision. Because of this, managing the forecasting activity is a critical part of a manager's responsibility. A manager must decide what resources to devote to a particular forecast and what approach to use to obtain it.

What resources?

The question of "what resources" hinges on two issues:

1. The importance of the forecast, or more precisely, the importance of the decision awaiting the forecast and its sensitivity to the forecast.
2. The quality of the forecast as a function of the resources devoted to it.

In other words, how much does it matter, and how much does it cost? These are the same questions that management must ask and answer about many of the services it purchases.

What methods?

In actual applications, the selection of the appropriate forecasting method for a particular situation depends on a variety of factors. Some of the features that distinguish one situation from the next are

1. The importance of the decision.
2. The availability of relevant data.
3. The time horizon for the forecast.
4. The cost of preparing the forecast.
5. The time until the forecast is needed.
6. The number of times such a forecast will be needed.
7. The stability of the environment.

Choice of method and importance of decision

The importance of the decision probably plays the strongest role in determining what forecasting method to use. Curiously, *qualitative approaches* (as opposed to *quantitative*) dominate the stage at the extremes of important and not very important forecasts.

On the low end of the importance scale, think of the many decisions a supermarket manager makes on what are typically implicit forecasts: what specials to offer, what to display at the ends of the aisles, how many baggers to employ. In such cases, forecasts are simply business judgments. The potential return is not high enough to justify the expenditure of resources required for formal and extensive model development.

APPLICATION CAPSULE

Prescription for Profit: A Pharmaceutical Company Gets an Important Message from a Delphi Forecasting Procedure*

Syntex Laboratories, the U.S. human-pharmaceutical subsidiary of Syntex Corporation, sells seven major products, grouped into four categories: nonsteroidal antiarthritic drugs, analgesics, oral contraceptives, and topical steroids. Direct marketing is an important part of the marketing mix for a pharmaceutical company such as Syntex. In particular, Syntex salespeople visit physicians at their offices and encourage them to use Syntex products. In this environment, management faces two fundamental questions: "How many salespeople do we need?" and "How should we deploy our salespeople?"

It is clear that in order to answer these questions in a sensible manner, management must be able to estimate a sales response function: a relationship between the number of salespeople assigned to an activity and the effect this assignment will have on sales. Unfortunately, such a function cannot easily be estimated by traditional means. The relationship between a sales call and an actual sale is difficult to trace because of the way in which this industry is organized. When a doctor writes a prescription, it can be filled at any location. Moreover, the drugstore that fills the prescription may not buy directly from Syntex, but from the wholesaler. Thus there is no way of knowing whether doctors who receive sales calls are more apt to prescribe Syntex products, or if they do, whether more sales calls would produce more sales. That is, it is impossible to directly measure the efffect of sales effort.

Syntex thus turned to the use of expert judgment to estimate a sales response function. A Delphi forecasting procedure was used. A team consisting of the senior vice-president of sales and marketing, the vice-president of sales, two people from the market research department, two product managers, two regional sales managers, and two salespeople was formed. Each member of the group was asked the following question: According to the strategic plan, if the current level of sales force effort were maintained for the next four years, sales of Product A would be at the predicted level. What would happen to Product A's sale (compared with present levels) if during this same period it received

1. No sales effort?
2. One-half the current effort?
3. 50% greater sales effort?
4. A saturation level of sales effort?

These four points were used to create a smooth sales response function. Each participant formulated a set of initial estimates without discussing them with others. These responses were then summarized on a computer and discussed by the group, after which each group member had an opportunity to revise his or her estimates. Syntex found that their Delphi team converged to a consensus model on the second round.

The results of the sales response function were part of the input to two models designed to determine the best allocation of sales force effort—one among the company's various products, the other among the various medical specialists visited by the salespeople (general practitioners, orthopedists, internists, and the like). Syntex took the recommendations of these two models to heart. Because both models indicated that the sales force was below optimal size, they dramatically increased its numbers. Over a three-year period they added approximately 200 salespeople to the base of 433 that existed at the time of the study. (Historically, the sales force had grown by only 30 to 50 salespeople a year.) They also focused sales effort on Naproxyn, the largest and most profitable product in their line. As a result of these actions, Syntex laboratories enjoyed a continuing $25,000,000 increase in annual sales over those offered by the original strategic plan. The cost of developing and running the model, by contrast, was only $30,000. The experience of Syntex provides a good example of how a systematic method of soliciting business judgment within an organization can yield impressive results at little or no expense.

*Lodish, Curtis, Ness, and Simpson, "Sales Force Sizing and Deployment Using a Decision Calculus Model at Syntex Laboratories," *Interfaces*, Vol. 18, No. 1 (Jan.–Feb. 1988).

On the high end, the decisions are *too important* (and perhaps too complex) to be left entirely to formal quantitative models. The future of the company, to say nothing of the executive, may hinge on a good forecast and the ensuing decision. *Quantitative models may certainly provide important input. In fact, the higher the planning level, the more you can be sure that forecasting models will at least to some extent be employed.* But for very important decisions, the final forecast will be based on the judgment of the executive and his or her colleagues. The extent to which a quantitative model is employed as an input to this judgment will depend, in the final analysis, on management's assessment of the model's validity. A consensus panel (a management committee) is often the chosen vehicle for achieving the final forecast. For example, what forecasts do you think persuaded Henry Ford IV to reject Lee Iacocca's plan to move Ford into small, energy-efficient cars in the late 1970s? Also, what forecasts led Panasonic to introduce a tape-based system while RCA introduced a disk-based system for the TV player market? And what about the Cuban missile crisis? The Bay of Pigs? Clearly, management's personal view of the future played an important role.

Dr. Gene Woolsey, past president of The Institute of Management Sciences, has said: *"A manager would rather live with a problem that can't be solved than use a technique that can't be trusted."*

Quantitative models play a major role in producing directly usable forecasts in situations that are deemed to be of "midlevel importance." This is especially true in short-range (up to 1 month) and medium-range (1 month to 2 years) scenarios. Time-series analyses are especially popular for repetitive forecasts of midlevel importance in a relatively stable environment. The use of exponential smoothing to forecast the demand for mature products is a prototype of this type of application.

Causal models actively compete with various experts for forecasting various economic phenomena in the midlevel medium range. Situations in which a forecast will be repeated quite often, and where much relevant data are available, are prime targets for quantitative models, and in such cases many successful models have been constructed. As our earlier discussion of interest rates forecasts indicated, there is ample room in this market for the "expert" with a good record of performance. In commercial practice one finds that many management consulting groups, as well as specialized firms such as DRI, provide forecasting "packages" for use in a variety of midlevel scenarios.

The more a manager can "see" the model, work with the data, and feel comfortable with it, the more likely the model will be used, and used effectively.

As a final comment, we can make the following observations about the use of forecasting in decision making within the public sector: Just as in private industry, it is often the case that the higher the level of the planning function, the more one sees the use of forecasting models employed as inputs. In such high-level situations there is a high premium on expertise, and forecasting is, in one sense, a formal extension of expert judgment. Think of the Council of Economic Advisors, the

Chairman of the Federal Reserve Board, or the Director of the Central Intelligence Agency. You can be sure that forecasts are of importance in these contexts, and you can be sure that there is within these environments a continuing updating and, one hopes, improvement of forecasting techniques. As always, the extent to which the results of existing models are employed is a function of the executive's overall assessment of the model itself.

Key Terms

Causal Forecasting. The forecast for the quantity of interest is determined as a function of other variables. (*p. 774*)

Curve Fitting. Selecting a "curve" that passes close to the data points in a scatter diagram. (*p. 775*)

Scatter Diagram. A plot of the response variable against a single independent variable. (*p. 775*)

Method of Least Squares. A procedure for fitting a curve to a set of data. It minimizes the sum of the squared deviations of the data from the curve. (*p. 778*)

Polynomial of Degree *n*. A function of the form $y = a_0 + a_1x + a_2x^2 + \cdots + a_nx^n$. Often used as the curve in a least-squares fit. (*p. 783*)

Linear Regression. A statistical technique used to estimate the parameters of a polynomial in such a way that the polynomial "best" represents a set of data. Also sometimes used to describe the problem of fitting a linear function to a set of data (*p. 784*)

Validation. The process of using a model on past data to assess its credibility. (*p. 784*)

Time-Series Forecasting. A variable of interest is plotted against time and extrapolated into the future using one of several techniques. (*p. 785*)

Simple *n*-Period Moving Average. Average of last n periods is used as the forecast of future values; $(n - 1)$ pieces of data must be stored. (*p. 787*)

Weighted *n*-Period Moving Average. A weighted sum, with decreasing weights, of the last n observations is used as a forecast. The sum of the weights equals 1; $(n - 1)$ pieces of data must be stored. (*p. 789*)

Exponential Smoothing. A weighted sum, with decreasing weights of *all* past observations, the sum of the weights equals 1; only one piece of information need be stored. (*p. 790*)

Random Walk. A stochastic process in which the variable at time t equals the variable at time $(t-1)$ plus a random element. (*p. 796*)

Delphi Method. A method of achieving a consensus among experts while eliminating factors of group dynamics. (*p. 799*)

Consensus Panel. An assembled group of experts produces an agreed-upon forecast. (*p. 799*)

Grass Roots Forecasting. Soliciting forecasts from individuals "close to" and thus presumably knowledgeable about the entity being forecast. (*p. 800*)

Market Research. A type of grass roots forecasting that is based on getting information directly from consumers. (*p. 801*)

Major Concepts Quiz

True-False

1. **T F** Quick and dirty forecasting methods are typically based on the method of least squares.
2. **T F** Minimizing total deviations (i.e., $\sum_{i=1}^{n} d_i$) is a reasonable way to define a "good fit."
3. **T F** Least-squares fits can be used for a variety of curves in addition to straight lines.
4. **T F** Regression analysis can be used to prove that the method of least squares produces the best possible fit for any specific real problem.
5. **T F** The method of least squares is used in causal models as well as in time-series models.

6. **T F** In a weighted 3-period moving-average forecast the weights can be assigned in many different ways.
7. **T F** Exponential smoothing automatically assigns weights that decrease in value as the data get older.
8. **T F** Average squared error is one way to compare various forecasting techniques.
9. **T F** *Validation* refers to the process of determining a model's credibility by simulating its performance on past data.
10. **T F** A "random walk" is a stochastic model.
11. **T F** At higher levels of management, qualitative forecasting models become more important.

Multiple Choice

12. Quick and dirty forecasting methods
    a. consider only the last k data points
    b. primarily apply to problems with one independent variable
    c. use an intuitive measure of good fit
    d. both b and c

13. Linear regression (with one independent variable)
    a. requires the estimation of three parameters
    b. is a special case of polynomial least squares
    c. is a quick and dirty method
    d. uses total deviation as a measure of good fit

14. An operational problem with a simple k-period moving average is that
    a. it assigns equal weight to each piece of past data
    b. it assigns equal weight to each of the last k observations
    c. it requires storage of $k - 1$ pieces of data
    d. none of the above

15. A large value of α puts more weight on
    a. recent
    b. older
    data in an exponential smoothing model.

16. If the data being observed can be best thought of as being generated by random deviations about a stationary mean, a
    a. large
    b. small
    value of α is preferable in an exponential smoothing model.

17. A divide-and-conquer strategy means
    a. Divide the modeling procedure into two parts: (1) Use all the data to estimate parameter values, and (2) use the parameter values from part (1) to see how well the model works.
    b. Divide the data into two parts. Estimate the parameters of the model on the first part. See how well the model works on the second part.
    c. Compare two models on the same data base.
    d. None of the above.

18. The Delphi Method
    a. relies on the power of written arguments
    b. requires resolution of differences via face-to-face debate
    c. is mainly used as an alternative to exponential smoothing
    d. none of the above

19. Conflict of interest can be a serious problem in
    a. the Delphi Method
    b. asking salespeople
    c. market research based on consumer data
    d. none of the above

20. Quick and dirty forecasting methods are deficient in that
   a. they require the evaluation of squares and square roots
   b. they cannot be extended to more than one independent variable
   c. they have no objective measure for obtaining a good fit
   d. both b and c

Answers

1. F	**6.** T	**11.** T	**16.** b
2. F	**7.** T	**12.** d	**17.** b
3. T	**8.** T	**13.** b	**18.** a
4. F	**9.** T	**14.** c	**19.** b
5. T	**10.** T	**15.** a	**20.** d

▶ Problems

(a) See IM
(b) $\hat{y} = 21.87 + 0.361x$
(c) 65.14

18-1. ▲▲ Consider the following set of data:

x	100	70	30	40	80	60	50	20	10	90
y	57	40	35	33	56	46	45	26	26	53

(a) Plot a scatter diagram of these data.
(b) Fit a straight line to the data using the method of least squares.
(c) Use the function derived in part (b) to forecast a value for y when $x = 120$.

(a) See IM
(b) $\hat{y} = 64.667 - 1.743x$

18-2. ▲▲ Consider the following set of data where x is the independent and y the dependent variable:

x	30	25	20	15	10	5
y	15	20	30	35	45	60

(a) Plot the scatter diagram for these data.
(b) Fit a straight line to the data by the method of least squares.

(a) See IM
(b) $\hat{y} = 1.29 + 0.68x$
(c) $\hat{y} = 0.428 + 1.250x - 0.071x^2$

18-3. ▲▲ Consider the following set of data:

x	1	2	3	4	5	6	7
y	2.00	1.50	4.50	4.00	5.50	4.50	6.00

(a) Plot a scatter diagram of the data.
(b) Fit a straight line to the data by the method of least squares. Plot the line on the scatter diagram.
(c) Fit a quadratic function to the data by the method of least squares. Plot the curve on the scatter diagram.

$\hat{y} = 73.0 - 2.993x + 0.0357x^2$

18-4. ▲▲ Fit a quadratic function to the data in Problem 18-2 by the method of least squares.

Linear: sum = 4.11;
Quadratic: sum = 3.68

18-5. ▲▲ Compare the goodness of fit on the data in Problem 18-3 for the least-square linear function and the least-squares quadratic (derived in Problem 18-4) by calculating the sum of the squared deviations.

Linear: sum = 41.90;
Quadratic: sum = 12.14
sum for quadratic always ≤ sum for linear

18-6. ▲▲ Compare the goodness of fit on the data in Problem 18-2 for the least-squares linear function and the least-squares quadratic function by calculating the sum of the squared deviations. Is the answer for 18-4 always better than that for 18-2?

(a) See IM
(b) $\hat{y}_{11} = 51.50$
(c) No; doesn't take into account trend in data

18-7. Further investigation reveals that the x variable in Problem 18-1 is simply 10 times the time at which an observation was recorded, and the y variable is demand. For example, a demand of 57 occurred at time 10; a demand of 26 occurred at times 1 and 2.

(a) Plot actual demand against time.

(b) Use a simple 4-period moving average to forecast demand at time 11.

(c) By inspecting the data, would you expect this to be a good model or not? Why?

(a) See IM
(b) $\hat{y}_{13} = 55.25$
(c) 1140.69
(d) No; doesn't take into account trend in data

18-8. Consider the following data set:

TIME	1	2	3	4	5	6	7	8	9	10	11	12
DEMAND	10	14	19	26	31	35	39	44	51	55	61	54

(a) Plot this time series. Connect the points with a straight line.

(b) Use a simple 4-period moving average to forecast the demand for periods 5–13.

(c) Find the sum of squared errors.

(d) Does this seem like a reasonable forecasting device in view of the data?

(a) $\hat{y}_{11} = 53.9$
(b) Yes, weights recent observations more to capture trend in data

18-9. Consider the data in Problem 18-7.

(a) Use a 4-period weighted moving average with the weights 4/10, 3/10, 2/10, and 1/10 to forecast demand for time 11. Heavier weights should apply to more recent observations.

(b) Do you prefer this approach to the simple 4-period model suggested in Problem 18-7? Why?

(a) See IM
(b) 731.96
(c) Yes, weights recent observations more to capture trend in data

18-10. Consider the data in Problem 18-8.

(a) Use a 4-period weighted moving average with the weights 0.1, 0.2, 0.3, and 0.4 to forecast demand for time periods 5–13. Heavier weights should apply to more recent observations.

(b) Find the sum of squared errors.

(c) Do you prefer this approach to the simple 4-period model suggested in Problem 18-8? Why?

To use QSB+ to do exponential smoothing when a forecast is given for period 1, input the forecast for period 1 as the first observation, the actual for period 1 as the second observation, the actual for period 2 as the third observation, etc. The forecast QSB+ reports for period t will then actually be the forecast for period $(t - 1)$.

(a) $\hat{y}_{11} = 52.24$
(b) Larger α weights recent observations more to capture trend in data

18-11. Consider the data in Problem 18-7.

(a) Let $\hat{y}_1 = 22$ and $\alpha = 0.4$. Use an exponential smoothing model to forecast demand in period 11.

(b) If you were to use an exponential smoothing model to forecast this time series, would you prefer a larger (than 0.4) or smaller value for α? Why?

(a) $\hat{y}_{13} = 50.45$
(b) 1678.22
(c) $\hat{y}_{13} = 54.77$; 705.99
(d) Larger α weights recent observations more to capture trend in data

18-12. Consider the data in Problem 18-8.

(a) Assume that $\hat{y}_1 = 8$ and $\alpha = 0.3$. Use an exponential smoothing model to forecast demand in periods 5–13.

(b) Find the sum of squared errors.

(c) Repeat the analysis using $\alpha = 0.5$.

(d) If you were to use an exponential smoothing model to forecast this time series, would you prefer $\alpha = 0.3$, a larger (than 0.3), or smaller, value of α? Why?

Panel produces evaluation more quickly and less expensively; senior managers might unduly influence the panel.

18-13. The president of Quacker Mills wants a subjective evaluation of the market potential of a new nacho-flavored breakfast cereal from a group consisting of (1) the vice-president of marketing, (2) the marketing manager of the western region, (3) 10 district sales managers from the western region. Discuss the advantages and disadvantages of a consensus panel and the Delphi Method for obtaining this evaluation.

$\hat{y}_6 = y_5 = 1$

18-14. Given that y_t is produced by the relationship $y_t = y_{t-1} + \varepsilon$, where ε is a random number with mean zero and $y_1 = 1$, $y_2 = 2$, $y_3 = 1.5$, $y_4 = 0.8$, $y_5 = 1$, what is your best forecast of y_6?

Time series; well-established product with short time horizon

18-15. ▲▲ Given your current knowledge of the situation, would you recommend a causal or a time-series model to forecast next month's demand for Kellogg's Rice Crispies? Why?

(a) 0.2401
(b) 0.1029

18-16. ▲▲ If $\alpha = 0.3$, in calculating $\hat{y}_5$, what is the weight on

(a) $\hat{y}_1$

(b) y_1

(a) $\hat{y}_{11} = 52.2$; $\hat{w}_{11} = 55.0$
(b) Simple: avg. sq. error = 97.64
Trend-adjusted: avg. sq. error = 58.81

18-17. ▲▲▲ In some cases it is possible to obtain better forecasts by using a trend-adjusted forecast. For example, consider the following two-step procedure:

1. Calculate $\hat{y}_t$ as before.
2. Let $\hat{w}_t$ be the forecast of demand in period t based on data through period $t - 1$, given as

$$\hat{w}_t = \hat{y}_t + \alpha[\hat{y}_t - \hat{y}_{t-1}] + (1 - \alpha)[\hat{y}_{t-1} - \hat{y}_{t-2}]$$

(a) Use the above trend-adjusted model with $\alpha = 0.4$ and $\hat{y}_I = 22$ to forecast the sequence of demands in Problem 18-11.

(b) Use the average squared error measure to compare the simple exponential smoothing model (Problem 18-11) with the trend-adjusted model from part (a) on forecasting demand for periods 4 through 10, i.e., compare $\frac{1}{7}\sum_{t=4}^{10}(y_t - \hat{y}_t)^2$ with $\frac{1}{7}\sum_{t=4}^{10}(y_t - \hat{w}_t)^2$.

(a) $\hat{y}_{13} = 50.4$; $\hat{w}_{13} = 54.5$
(b) Simple: avg. sq. error = 205.7
Trend-adjusted: avg. sq. error = 110.9

18-18. ▲▲▲ **(a)** Use the trend-adjusted model with $\alpha = 0.3$ and $\hat{y}_I = 8$ to forecast the sequence of demands in Problem 18-12.

(b) As in Problem 18-17, compare the above result with the result from Problem 18-12. That is, compare $\frac{1}{9}\sum_{t=4}^{12}(y_t - \hat{y}_t)^2$ with $\frac{1}{9}\sum_{t=4}^{12}(y_t - \hat{w}_t)^2$.

See IM

18-19. ▲▲ Discuss the merit of the measure "average squared error." In comparing two methods, is the one with a smaller average squared error *always* superior?

Take the logarithm and then use the trend-adjusted model.

18-20. ▲▲ If a company experiences an exponential sales growth, how would you alter the sales forecasting model to account for this?

Appendix 18.1 Fitting Forecasting Models, the Data Table Spreadsheet Command

It probably occurred to you, as you gained experience with spreadsheet programs in earlier chapters, that Figure 18.17 can easily be generated with a spreadsheet program such as LOTUS 1–2–3. The symbolic spreadsheet for doing this is shown in Figure 18.26. Cell B1 of the spreadsheet contains the value of α used to generate the exponentially weighted moving average. Cells C3 through C14 contain the forecasts for January through December. Recall that Victor decided to use a value of 0.6 for α and a value of 40 for $\hat{y}_1$, the forecast for January. Consequently, 0.6 appears in cell B1 and 40 in cell C3. Cell D3 contains a formula for the weighted average of actual sales in January, the value of cell B3, and forecast sales, the value of cell C3. \$B\$1 is an absolute reference to the value of α in cell B1. When cell D3 is copied to cells D4 through D14, the absolute reference to cell B1 stays the same, while the other cells change. For example, in copying the formula to cell D4, cells B3 and C3 change to B4 and C4. Cells E6 through E14 contain the formulas for computing the squared difference of forecast sales in column C and actual sales in column B. The

	A	B	C	D	E
1	Alpha=	0.6			
2	Month	Actual Sales	$\hat{y}_t$	$\alpha y_t + (1 - \alpha)\hat{y}_t$	Squared Error
3	Jan.	20	40	+ \$B\$1*B3 + (1 − \$B\$1)*C3	
4	Feb.	24	+ D3	+ \$B\$1*B4 + (1 − \$B\$1)*C4	
5	Mar.	27	+ D4	+ \$B\$1*B5 + (1 − \$B\$1)*C5	
6	Apr.	31	+ D5	+ \$B\$1*B6 + (1 − \$B\$1)*C6	(C6 − B6) ^ 2
7	May	37	+ D6	+ \$B\$1*B7 + (1 − \$B\$1)*C7	(C7 − B7) ^ 2
8	June	47	+ D7	+ \$B\$1*B8 + (1 − \$B\$1)*C8	(C8 − B8) ^ 2
9	July	53	+ D8	+ \$B\$1*B9 + (1 − \$B\$1)*C9	(C9 − B9) ^ 2
10	Aug.	62	+ D9	+ \$B\$1*B10 + (1 − \$B\$1)*C10	(C10 − B10) ^ 2
11	Sept.	54	+ D10	+ \$B\$1*B11 + (1 − \$B\$1)*C11	(C11 − B11) ^ 2
12	Oct.	36	+ D11	+ \$B\$1*B12 + (1 − \$B\$1)*C12	(C12 − B12) ^ 2
13	Nov.	32	+ D12	+ \$B\$1*B13 + (1 − \$B\$1)*C13	(C13 − B13) ^ 2
14	Dec.	29	+ D13	+ \$B\$1*B14 + (1 − \$B\$1)*C14	(C14 − B14) ^ 2
15	Total				@SUM(E6. .E14)
16	Average				@AVG(E14. .E6)

▲ FIGURE 18.26
Symbolic Spreadsheet Used to Generate Figure 18.17

@SUM in cell E15 totals these squared errors and the @AVG in cell E16 computes their average.

Once the symbolic spreadsheet has been set up, it is feasible to ask "what if" questions such as "what if we change the value of α?" We would like to be able to find the value of α that gives us the lowest average squared error. This is the value of α that provides the best fit of the historical data and so would be a reasonable choice for forecasting future sales. An inefficient way to go about this is to randomly enter different values in cell B1, recalculating the spreadsheet for each new value. A more efficient way is to set up a data table.

The importance of the Data Table command is that it gives a "picture," or snapshot, of several possible values of α and gives the analyst a good idea of how it affects the forecast. Also, the data can be graphed and certain forecasts shown, to give a visual check.

Cells A21 through A31 of Figure 18.27 contain the different values of α for which we want to calculate the average squared errors. Cell B20 contains the formula used to calculate the average squared errors. The average squared errors will appear in cells B21 through B31 when the DATA TABLE command is issued. To issue this command, type /DT1. You will be prompted to enter a data table range and an input cell. The data table range is the rectangular array of cells defined by corner cells A20 and B31. The input cell is cell B1. It appears that $\alpha = 1$ will give the lowest average squared error for this set of data. Note that when $\alpha = 1$, $\hat{y}_{t+1} = y_t$; i.e., the forecast for next month's sales is simply this month's sales.

▼ FIGURE 18.27
Data Table of Average Squared Error

	A	B
20		@AVG(E6. .E14)
21	0	132.11
22	0.1	159.05
23	0.2	170.30
24	0.3	168.24
25	0.4	157.25
26	0.5	141.70
27	0.6	125.10
28	0.7	109.59
29	0.8	96.11
30	0.9	84.89
31	1	75.78 ← **Lowest Average Squared Error**

Video Case

Forecasting the Housing Market

For most individuals and families, a home is by far the most important financial asset. On the average, an investment in a home has been a good investment, at least since World War II and perhaps starting even earlier. The widely accepted view has been that real estate prices will always increase, and in general that has been true.

The video you have just seen suggests that this may be changing. A study by two Harvard economists forecasts a rather dramatic change in the real estate market. They suggest that after adjustment for inflation, housing prices will decrease by 47% over the next twenty years. As briefly described, this result is based on the "fact" that housing prices are driven by the birth rate twenty years earlier. High housing prices in the 1970s were the result of high birth rates in the 1950s. Thus, the low birth rates in the 1970s will presumably dictate low housing prices in the 1990s.

The housing industry begs to differ. Three individuals comment on this prediction. One says that the housing boom will go on as long as people want housing, and cites the increased demand for different types of housing. Another says yes, housing starts will go down; but as long as demand runs ahead of supply, prices will go up. The third speaks of California and fundamental factors such as limited land, more restrictions on development, and continuing population inflow that he suggests will keep housing prices rising.

Questions

1. What type of forecasting model is the Harvard study using?
2. What kind of implicit model is the typical potential home buyer using when he or she concludes that housing prices will go up?
3. Comment on the reaction of the first housing industry spokesperson, who talks about singles, mingles, and older people?
4. What type of forecasting is the person who talks about California using? Comment on the values of the independent variables in his model.
5. "If the Harvard team is correct, then the person who analyzes the California situation must be wrong." Comment on this assertion.
6. What does all of this mean for the potential typical home buyer?

Answers to Odd-Numbered Problems

Chapter 2

2-1. **(a)** (8) **(b)** (2) **(c)** (3) **(d)** (4) **(e)** (1) **(f)** (6) **(g)** (7) **(h)** (5)

2-3. Let A = number of product 1 produced
B = number of product 2 produced
Then the model is

$$\begin{aligned} \text{Max } & 12A + 4B \\ \text{s.t. } & A + 2B \le 800 \\ & A + 3B \le 600 \\ & 2A + 3B \le 2000 \\ & A, B \ge 0 \end{aligned}$$

2-5. Let G = number of Gofer stocks to be bought
C = number of Can Oil stocks to be bought
S = number of Sloth P. stocks to be bought
The LP model is

$$\begin{aligned} \text{Max } & 7G + 3C + 3S \\ \text{s.t. } & 60G + 25C + 20S \le 100{,}000 \\ & G \le 1{,}000 \\ & C \le 1{,}000 \\ & S \le 1{,}500 \\ & G, C, S \ge 0 \end{aligned}$$

2-7. Let A_1, A_2 = quarts of A to be used in Red Baron and Diablo, respectively. Also, let B_1, B_2 = quarts of B to be used in Red Baron and Diablo, respectively. Then the LP model is

$$\text{Max } 3.35(A_2 + B_2) + 2.85(A_1 + B_1) - 1.6(A_1 + A_2) - 2.59(B_1 + B_2)$$

$$\text{s.t.} \quad \left.\begin{array}{l} \dfrac{A_1}{A_1 + B_1} \le 0.75 \\ \\ \dfrac{A_2}{A_2 + B_2} \ge 0.25, \quad \dfrac{B_2}{A_2 + B_2} \ge 0.5 \end{array}\right\} \quad \begin{array}{l} \text{or in linear form} \\ 0.25A_1 - 0.75B_1 \le 0 \\ 0.75A_2 - 0.25B_2 \ge 0 \\ -0.5A_2 + 0.5B_2 \ge 0 \end{array}$$

$$A_1 + A_2 \le 40$$
$$B_1 + B_2 \le 30$$
$$A_1, A_2, B_1, B_2 \ge 0$$

2-9. Let A_1 = thousands of pounds of type i fertilizer to be bought. The LP model is

$$\begin{aligned} \text{Min} \quad & 10A_1 + 8A_2 + 7A_3 \\ \text{s.t.} \quad & 0.025A_1 + 0.01A_2 + 0.005A_3 \ge .010 \\ & 0.01A_1 + 0.005A_2 + 0.01A_3 \ge .007 \\ & 0.005A_1 + 0.01A_2 + 0.005A_3 \ge .005 \\ & A_1, A_2, A_3 \ge 0 \end{aligned}$$

2-11. x_1 = pounds of product 1 produced
x_2 = pounds of product 2 produced

$$\begin{aligned} \text{Max } & 4x_1 + 3x_2 \\ \text{s.t. } & 3x_1 + 2x_2 \le 10 \\ & x_1 + 4x_2 \le 16 \\ & 5x_1 + 3x_2 \le 12 \\ & x_1, x_2 \ge 0 \end{aligned}$$

2-13. Let U, D = quantities of Umidaire or Depollinator to be produced. The LP model is

$$\begin{aligned} \text{Min } & 240U + 360D \\ \text{s.t. } & U \ge 500 \\ & 450U + 700D = 240U + 360D + 390{,}000 \\ & U, D \ge 0 \end{aligned}$$

2-15. Let T, C, M, MU = dollars invested in Treasury bonds, common stock, money market, and municipal bonds, respectively. The LP model is

$$\begin{aligned} \text{Max } & 0.08T + 0.06C + 0.12M + 0.09MU \\ \text{s.t. } & T \le 5 \times 10^6 \\ & C \le 7 \times 10^6 \\ & M \le 2 \times 10^6 \\ & MU \le 4 \times 10^6 \\ & C + T \ge 3 \times 10^6 \\ & M + MU \le 4 \times 10^6 \\ & C + T + M + MU = 10^7 \\ & T, C, M, MU \ge 0 \end{aligned}$$

2-17. Let A_{ij} = number of packages sent to wholesaler j from station i, $i = 1, 2, j = 1, 2, 3, 4, 5$. The LP formulation is

$$\begin{aligned}
\text{Min. } & 5.25(A_{11} + A_{12} + A_{13} + A_{14} + A_{15}) + 5.70(A_{21} + A_{22} + A_{23} + A_{24} + A_{25}) \\
& + 0.06A_{11} + 0.04A_{12} + 0.12A_{13} + 0.09A_{14} + 0.05A_{15} \\
& + 0.15A_{21} + 0.09A_{22} + 0.05A_{23} + 0.08A_{24} + 0.08A_{25}
\end{aligned}$$

$$\begin{aligned}
\text{s.t. } A_{11} + A_{12} + A_{13} + A_{14} + A_{15} &\le 20{,}000 \\
A_{21} + A_{22} + A_{23} + A_{24} + A_{25} &\le 12{,}000 \\
A_{11} + A_{21} &= 4{,}000 \\
A_{12} + A_{22} &= 6{,}000 \\
A_{13} + A_{23} &= 2{,}000 \\
A_{14} + A_{24} &= 10{,}000 \\
A_{15} + A_{25} &= 8{,}000
\end{aligned}$$

All variables nonnegative

2-19. Let A_i = acres of A to be planted on farm i
B_i = acres of B to be planted on farm i
C_i = acres of C to be planted on farm i
$i = 1, 2, 3, 4$

The LP problem is

$$\text{Max } 500(A_1 + A_2 + A_3 + A_4) + 200(B_1 + B_2 + B_3 + B_4) + 300(C_1 + C_2 + C_3 + C_4)$$

$$\begin{aligned}
\text{s.t. } A_1 + B_1 + C_1 &\le 500 \\
A_2 + B_2 + C_2 &\le 900 \\
A_3 + B_3 + C_3 &\le 300 \\
A_4 + B_4 + C_4 &\le 700 \qquad A_1 + A_2 + A_3 + A_4 \le 700 \\
2A_1 + 4B_1 + 3C_1 &\le 1700 \qquad B_1 + B_2 + B_3 + B_4 \le 800 \\
2A_2 + 4B_2 + 3C_2 &\le 3000 \qquad C_1 + C_2 + C_3 + C_4 \le 300 \\
2A_3 + 4B_3 + 3C_3 &\le 900 \\
2A_4 + 4B_4 + 3C_4 &\le 2200
\end{aligned}$$

$$\frac{A_1 + B_1 + C_1}{500} = \frac{A_2 + B_2 + C_2}{900} = \frac{A_3 + B_3 + C_3}{300} = \frac{A_4 + B_4 + C_4}{700}$$

All variables nonnegative

2-21. Number the days 1 through 7 starting with Monday. Let w_i be the number of waiters who start their work week on day i.

$$\text{Min } \sum_{i=1}^{7} w_i$$

$$\begin{aligned}
\text{s.t. } 6(w_1 + w_4 + w_5 + w_6 + w_7) &\ge 150 \\
6(w_1 + w_2 + w_5 + w_6 + w_7) &\ge 200 \\
6(w_1 + w_2 + w_3 + w_6 + w_7) &\ge 400 \\
6(w_1 + w_2 + w_3 + w_4 + w_7) &\ge 300 \\
6(w_1 + w_2 + w_3 + w_4 + w_5) &\ge 700 \\
6(w_2 + w_3 + w_4 + w_5 + w_6) &\ge 800 \\
6(w_3 + w_4 + w_5 + w_6 + w_7) &\ge 300 \\
w_i \ge 0, \quad i &= 1, 2, \ldots, 7
\end{aligned}$$

Note that minimizing the total number of waiters is equivalent to minimizing total cost, which is $5r \sum_{i=1}^{7} w_i$, where r is the daily wage.

2-23. A_i = hours of job A handled in shop i
B_i = hours of job B handled in shop i
C_i = hours of job C handled in shop i
D_i = hours of job D handled in shop i, $i = 1, 2, 3$

$$\text{Min } 89(A_1 + B_1 + C_1 + D_1) + 81(A_2 + B_2 + C_2 + D_2) + 84(A_3 + B_3 + C_3 + D_3)$$

$$\text{s.t. } A_i + B_i + C_i + D_i \leq 160, \quad i = 1, 2, 3$$

$$\frac{A_1}{32} + \frac{A_2}{39} + \frac{A_3}{46} = 1$$

$$\frac{B_1}{151} + \frac{B_2}{147} + \frac{B_3}{155} = 1$$

$$\frac{C_1}{72} + \frac{C_2}{61} + \frac{C_3}{57} = 1$$

$$\frac{D_1}{118} + \frac{D_2}{126} + \frac{D_3}{121} = 1$$

$$A_i, B_i, C_i, D_i \geq 0, \quad \text{all } i$$

2-25. The model is

$$\text{Max } p_1x_1 + p_2x_2$$

$$\begin{aligned} \text{s.t.}\quad 3x_1 + 12x_2 &\leq 300 \quad \text{(limitation on kerosene)} \\ 9x_1 + 6x_2 &\leq 450 \quad \text{(limitation on benzene)} \\ 15x_1 + 9x_2 &\geq 600 \quad \text{(demand on starter fluid)} \\ 6x_1 + 24x_2 &\geq 225 \quad \text{(demand on lighter fluid)} \\ x_1, x_2 &\geq 0 \end{aligned}$$

2-27. Let X_j denote the pounds of food j in the "ideal daily diet." Then the model is

$$\text{Min } \sum_{j=1}^{116} c_jx_j$$

$$\text{s.t. } \sum_{j=1}^{116} a_{ij}x_j \geq N_i, \quad i = 1, \ldots, 16$$

$$x_j \geq 0, \quad \text{all } j$$

This statement of the problem ignores a technological constraint. In other words, how can we be assured that a human being will be able to process the "ideal daily diet" chosen by the model. For example, suppose that 1 pound of raw alfalfa contained exactly 1/2000 of the daily requirement of each of the 16 essential nutrients. Then 2000 pounds (1 ton) of alfalfa would satisfy the constraints. With the "right" cost coefficients this could be the optimal solution. Obviously, it is not technologically (physically) possible.

2-29.

$$\text{Min } 20P_1 + 20P_2 + \cdots + 22P_9 + .2(I_1 + I_2 + \cdots + I_9)$$

$$\text{s.t. } I_1 = P_1 - 1000$$

$$I_2 = I_1 + P_2 - 900$$

$$\vdots$$

$$I_9 = I_8 + P_9 - 500$$

$$I_t, P_t \geq 0 \qquad t = 1, \ldots, 9$$

2-31. (a)

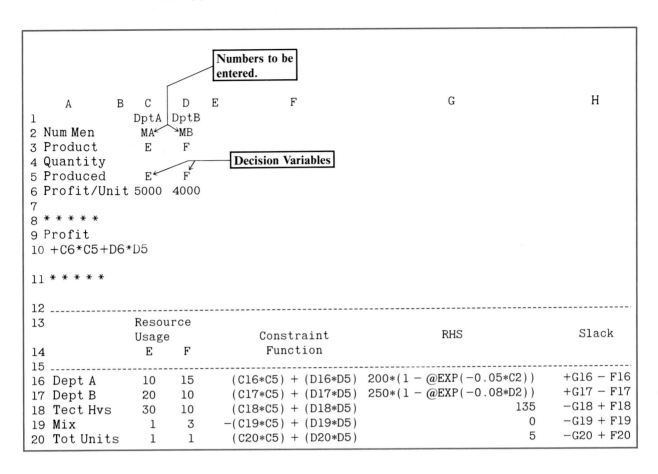

```
                                Numbers to be
                                entered.

   A         B   C      D    E          F                              G                    H
1               DptA   DptB
2 Num Men        MA     MB
3 Product        E      F
4 Quantity                          Decision Variables
5 Produced       E      F
6 Profit/Unit  5000   4000
7
8 * * * * *
9 Profit
10 +C6*C5+D6*D5

11 * * * * *

12 ------------------------------------------------------------------------------------------------------
13               Resource
                 Usage              Constraint                     RHS                          Slack
14                E      F           Function
15 ------------------------------------------------------------------------------------------------------
16 Dept A         10     15       (C16*C5) + (D16*D5)  200*(1 - @EXP(-0.05*C2))               +G16 - F16
17 Dept B         20     10       (C17*C5) + (D17*D5)  250*(1 - @EXP(-0.08*D2))               +G17 - F17
18 Tect Hvs       30     10       (C18*C5) + (D18*D5)                          135             -G18 + F18
19 Mix             1      3      -(C19*C5) + (D19*D5)                            0             -G19 + F19
20 Tot Units       1      1       (C20*C5) + (D20*D5)                            5             -G20 + F20
```

2-31. **(b)** The plan with E = 6 and F = 9 is infeasible. It requires more time in both Dep'ts. A and B than is available. **(c)** The optimal production policy is E = 5.59 and F = 7.40. **(d)** Decreasing returns to scale.

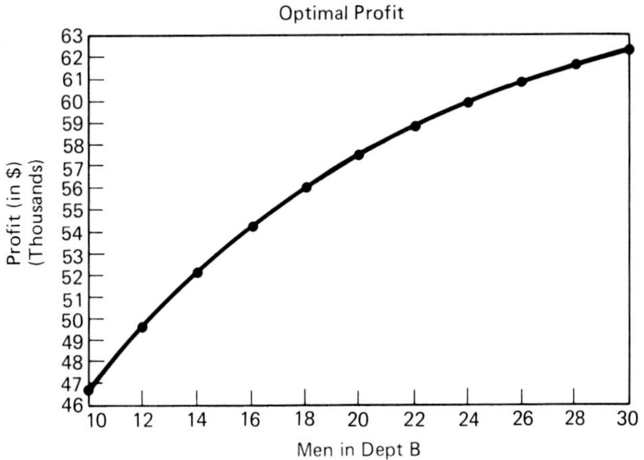

2-33. (a)

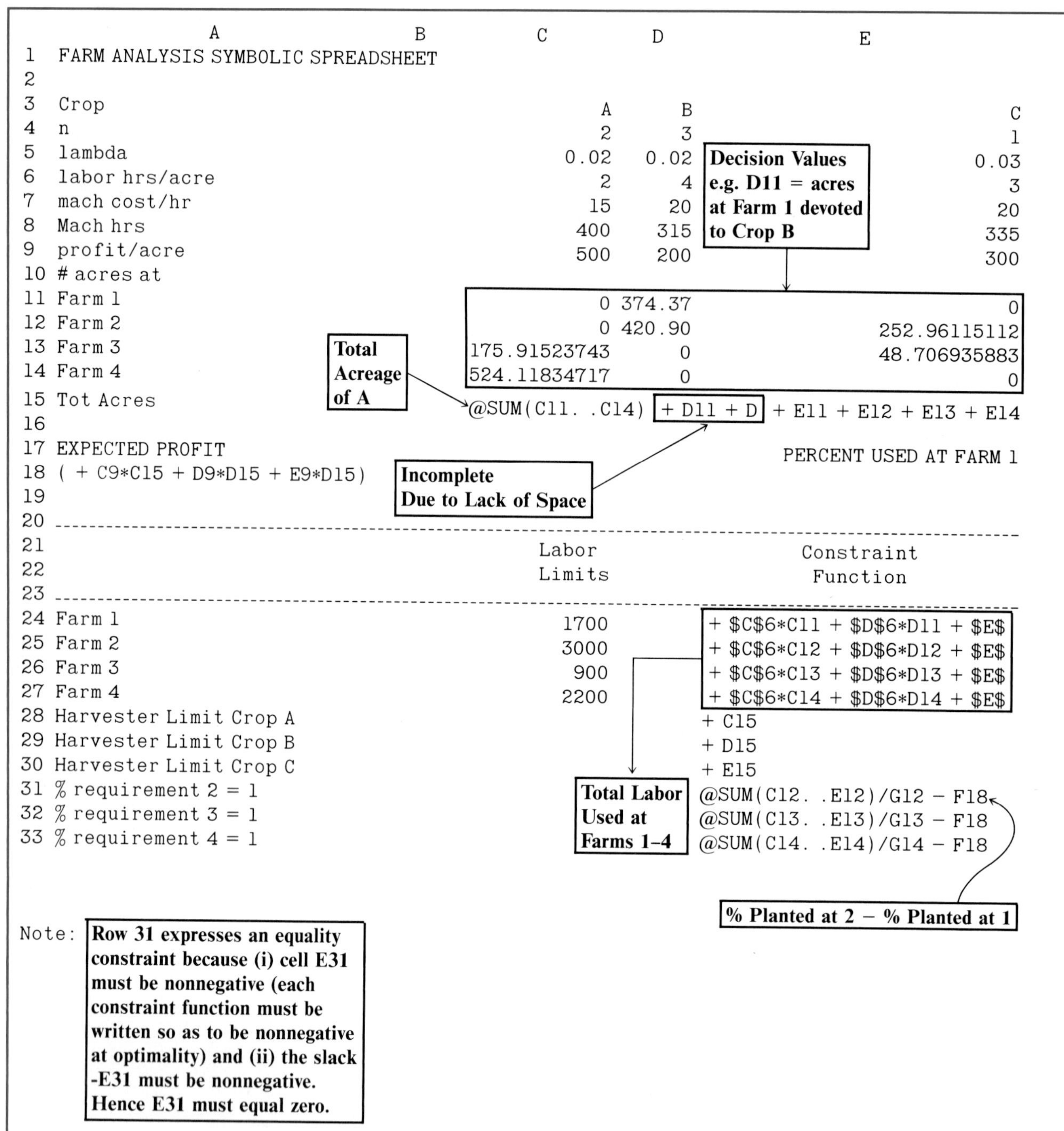

	A	B	C	D	E
1	FARM ANALYSIS SYMBOLIC SPREADSHEET				
2					
3	Crop		A	B	C
4	n		2	3	1
5	lambda		0.02	0.02	0.03
6	labor hrs/acre		2	4	3
7	mach cost/hr		15	20	20
8	Mach hrs		400	315	335
9	profit/acre		500	200	300
10	# acres at				
11	Farm 1		0	374.37	0
12	Farm 2		0	420.90	252.96115112
13	Farm 3		175.91523743	0	48.706935883
14	Farm 4		524.11834717	0	0
15	Tot Acres		@SUM(C11. .C14)	+ D11 + D	+ E11 + E12 + E13 + E14
16					
17	EXPECTED PROFIT				PERCENT USED AT FARM 1
18	(+ C9*C15 + D9*D15 + E9*D15)				
19					
20	----------				
21			Labor		Constraint
22			Limits		Function
23	----------				
24	Farm 1		1700		+ $C$6*C11 + $D$6*D11 + E
25	Farm 2		3000		+ $C$6*C12 + $D$6*D12 + E
26	Farm 3		900		+ $C$6*C13 + $D$6*D13 + E
27	Farm 4		2200		+ $C$6*C14 + $D$6*D14 + E
28	Harvester Limit Crop A				+ C15
29	Harvester Limit Crop B				+ D15
30	Harvester Limit Crop C				+ E15
31	% requirement 2 = 1				@SUM(C12. .E12)/G12 − F18
32	% requirement 3 = 1				@SUM(C13. .E13)/G13 − F18
33	% requirement 4 = 1				@SUM(C14. .E14)/G14 − F18

Note: Row 31 expresses an equality constraint because (i) cell E31 must be nonnegative (each constraint function must be written so as to be nonnegative at optimality) and (ii) the slack -E31 must be nonnegative. Hence E31 must equal zero.

F	G	H
	Fixed Co-op Investment	
	19000	
	Utilized Investment	
	+ C7*C8 + D7*D8 + E7*E8	
Acres Used	Acres Avail	Unused Acres
+ C11 + D11 + E11	500	+ G11 − F11
+ C12 + D12 + E12	900	+ G12 − F12
+ C13 + D13 + E13	300	+ G13 − F13
+ C14 + D14 + E14	700	+ G14 − F14
@SUM(C11. .E11)/G11		
RHS	Slack	Surplus
+ C24	+ F24 − E24	
+ C25 ← **Labor Hours Available**	+ F25 − E25	
+ C26	+ F26 − E26	
+ C27	+ F27 − E27	
+ $C$4*($C$8 − 1/$C$5*(1 − @EXP(− $C$5*$C$8))	+ F28 − E28	
+ $D$4*($D$8 − 1/$D$5*(1 − @EXP(− $D$5*$D$8))	+ F29 − E29	
+ $E$4*($E$8 − 1/$E$5*(1 − @EXP(− $E$5*$E$8))	+ F30 − E30	
↑ **Total Acreage of Each Crop Which Can Be Harvested**	− E31	
	− E32	
	− E33	

2-33. (b)

FARM ANALYSIS OPTIMIZED SPREADSHEET

	A	B	C	D	E	F	G	H
1	FARM ANALYSIS SPREADSHEET							
2								
3	Crop		A	B	C			
4	n		2.00	3.00	1.00			
5	lambda		0.02	0.02	0.03		Fixed Co-op Investment	
6	labor hrs/acre		2.00	4.00	3.00		19000.00	
7	mach cost/hr		15.00	20.00	20.00		Utilized Investment	
8	Mach hrs		400.00	315.00	335.00		19000.00	
9	profit/acre		500.00	200.00	300.00			
10	# acres at					Acres Used	Acres Avail	Unused Acres
11	Farm 1		0.00	374.37	0.00	374.37	500.00	125.63
12	Farm 2		0.00	420.91	252.96	673.87	900.00	226.13
13	Farm 3		175.92	0.00	48.71	224.62	300.00	75.38
14	Farm 4		524.12	0.00	0.00	524.12	700.00	175.88
15	Tot Acres		700.03	795.28	301.67			
16			Optimal Values					
17	EXPECTED PROFIT		of Decision Variables		PERCENT USED AT FARM 1			
18	599572.32					0.75		
20								
21			Labor	Constraint				
22			Limits	Function		RHS	Slack	Surplus
23								
24	Farm 1		1700.00		1497.48	1700.00	202.52	
25	Farm 2		3000.00		2442.50	3000.00	557.50	
26	Farm 3		900.00		497.95	900.00	402.05	
27	Farm 4		2200.00		1048.24	2200.00	1151.76	
28	Harvester Limit Crop A				700.03	700.03	.00	
29	Harvester Limit Crop B				795.28	795.28	.00	
30	Harvester Limit Crop C				301.67	301.67	.00	
31	% requirement 2 = 1				.00		.00	
32	% requirement 3 = 1				.00		.00	
33	% requirement 4 = 1				.00		.00	

2-33. (c) Management can select any set of hours, say T1, T2, and T3, such that $15T1 + 20T2 + 20T3 \leq 19{,}000$.

Chapter 3 **3-1.**

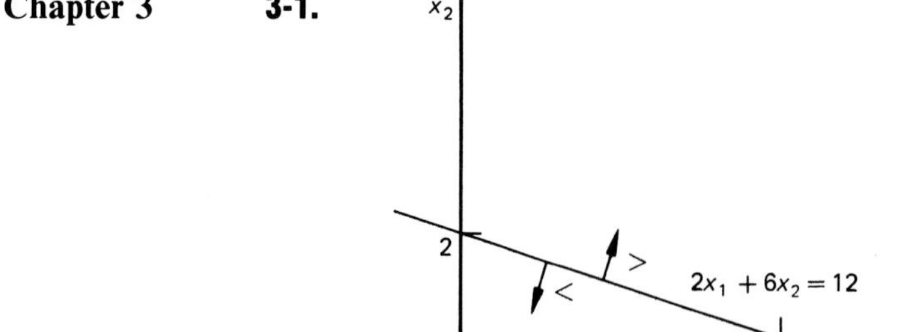

3-3. **(a)** Same as 3-1(d) **(b)** Below **(c)** Corresponds to 1(d)

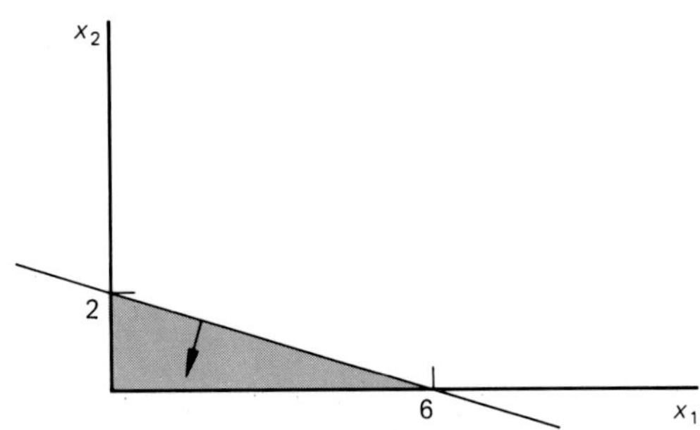

3-5. A = amps
P = preamps
Assembly: $12A + 4P \leq 60$
performance: $4A + 8P \leq 40$

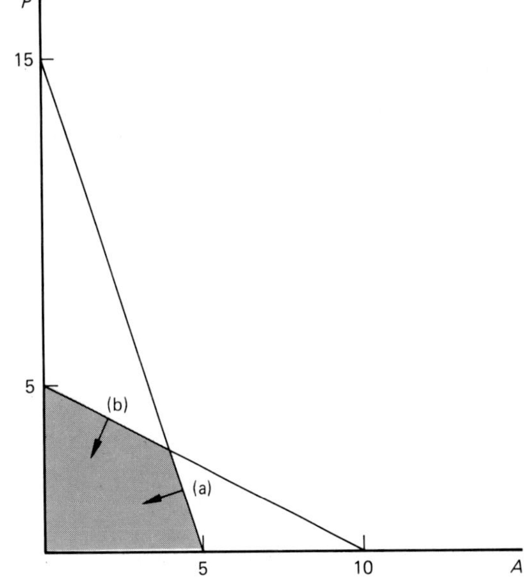

3-7.

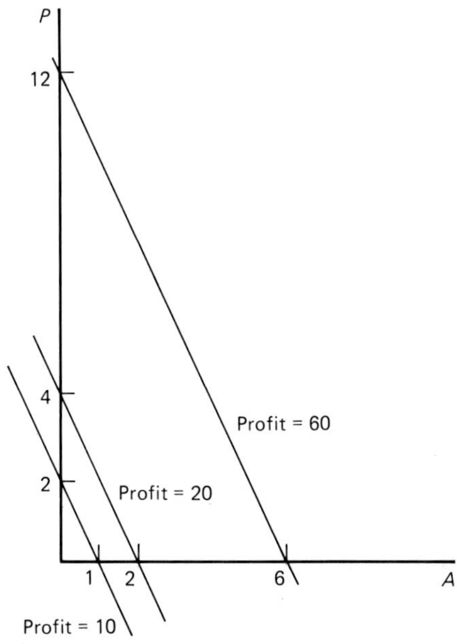

3-9. **(a)** $A^* = 4, P^* = 3$ **(b)** $\text{OV} = 10A^* + 5P^* = \$55$ **(c)** Active constraints are assembly and high-performance testing. **(d)** Inactive are

$$A \leq 6, \qquad \text{slack} = 2$$

$$P \leq 4, \qquad \text{slack} = 1$$

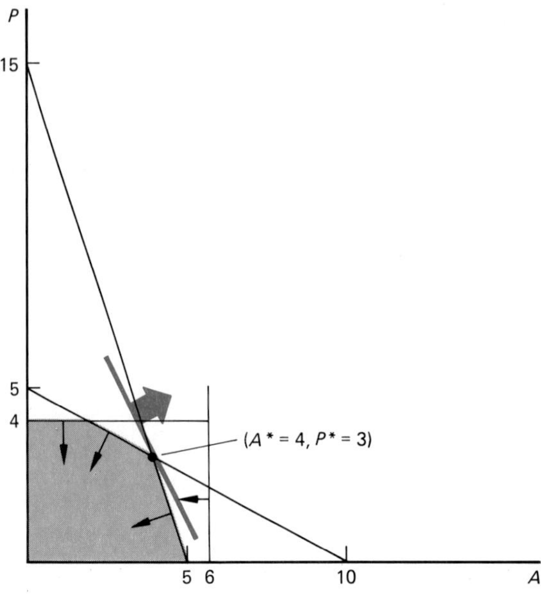

3-11. No

3-13. Makes it infeasible

3-15.

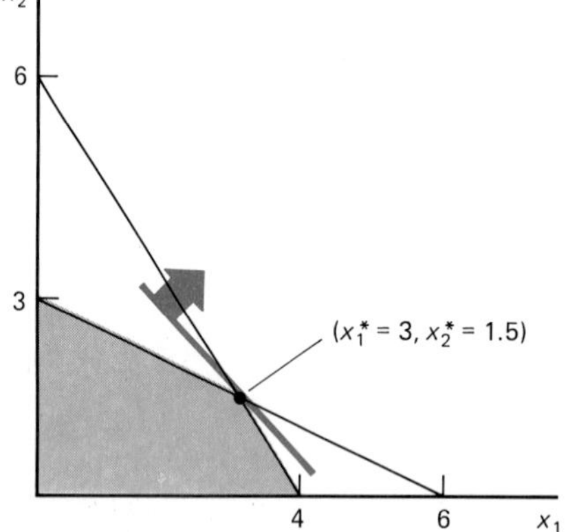

(a) $x_1^* = 3, x_2^* = 1.5$, OV = 4.5 (b) $x_1^* = 0, x_2^* = 3$ (c) Four extreme points: (0,0), (4,0), (3,1.5), (0,3)

3-17. **(a)** $x_1^* = 6\frac{2}{3}, x_2^* = 2\frac{2}{3}$, OV $= 30\frac{2}{3}$

(b) First constraint: slack $= 18\frac{2}{3}$
Second constraint: 0 slack
Third constraint: 0 surplus

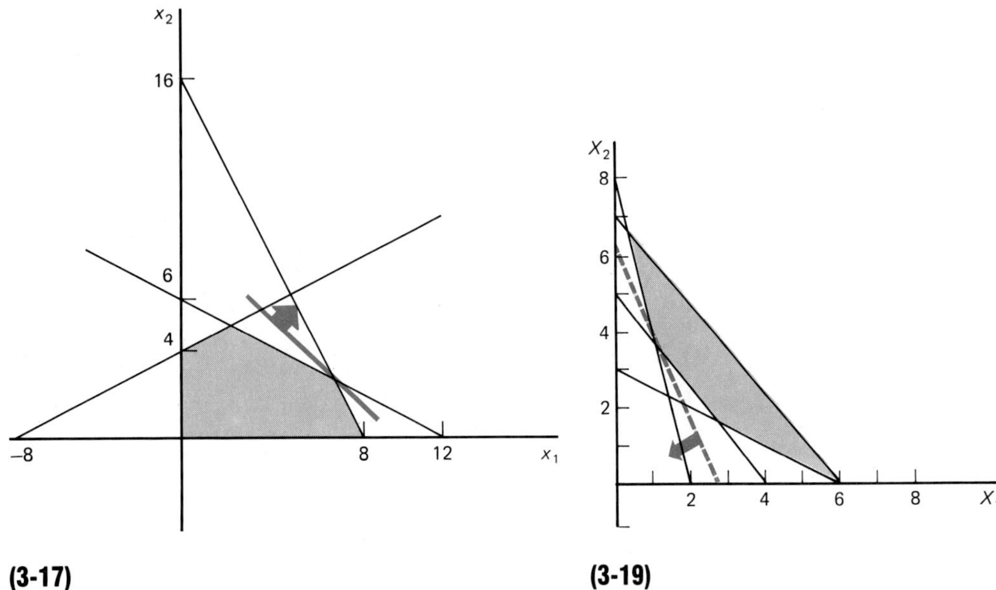

(3-17) **(3-19)**

3-19. **(a)** $x_1^* = 1\frac{1}{11}$, $x_2^* = 3\frac{7}{11}$, OV $= 12\frac{8}{11}$

(b) Active constraints are second and third; inactive constraints are first and fourth.

(c) Zero associated with second and third

First constraint: surplus is $7\frac{1}{11}$

Fourth constraint: slack is $12\frac{6}{11}$

(d) 4 (e) $(x_1^* = 1\frac{1}{11}, x_2^* = 3\frac{7}{11})$, $(x_1^* = 2\frac{2}{3}, x_2^* = 1\frac{2}{3})$

3-21. **(a)** $E^* = 118.4$, $F^* = 152.6$, OV $= 223{,}684$ **(b)** $E + F \leq 290$ **(c)** -18.496 **(d)** 0.1599 **(e)** 1667

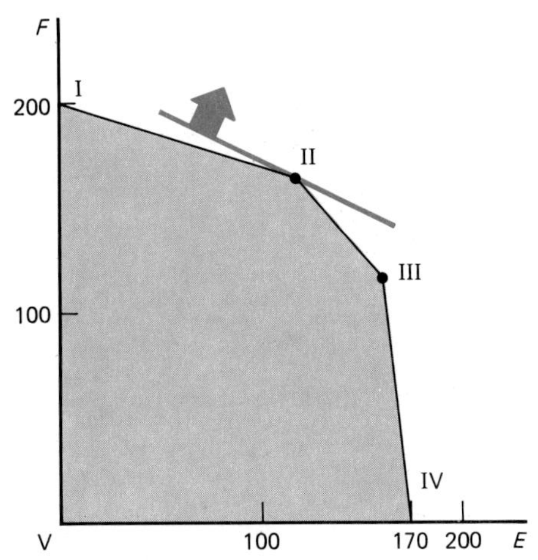

Chapter 4

4-1. **(a)** New solution is $E^* = \frac{48}{7}$, $F^* = \frac{16}{7}$. **(b)** New OV $= 38{,}857\frac{1}{7}$.

4-3. Since the relative profitability of F has increased, it is desirable to produce relatively more F. Because of the limitations on resources, this can only be done by also producing less E.

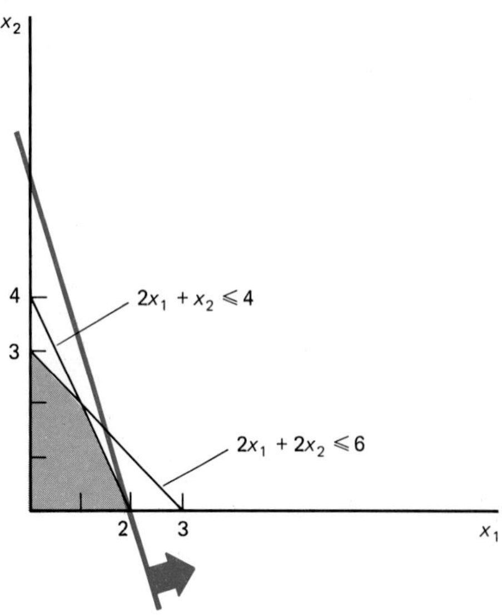

4-5. Becomes infeasible

4-7. **(a)** $x_1^* = 2, x_2^* = 0$ **(b)** Increase coefficient of x_2 to 15.
(c) 2; ($x_1^* = 2, x_2^* = 0$) and ($x_1^* = 1, x_2^* = 2$) **(d)** Can be infinitely increased. Can be decreased by 2 units.
(e) A change in either direction will change the optimal solution.
(f) The first constraint is active. The second is inactive.
(g) The optimal solution changes to ($x_1^* = \frac{1}{3}, x_2^* = 2\frac{2}{3}$) and the OV changes accordingly.
(h) No effect **(i)** Satisfies, satisfy

4-9. The first is tighter; (2, 1) satisfies both; (3, 0) satisfies the second, not the first.

4-11. The second

4-13. More, loosening

4-15. Enlarge, smaller, unchanged

4-17. The first constraint. No.

4-19. No. It may not be redundant for other values of the parameters in the model.

4-21. No.

4-23. **(a)** and (d) match with (2) and (5); (b) and (e) match with (1) and (4); (c) matches with (3).

Chapter 5

5-1.

$$\begin{aligned} &\text{Max } 3x_1 - 4x_2 \\ &\text{s.t. } 8x_1 + 12x_2 + s_1 = 49 \\ &14x_1 - 6x_2 + s_2 = 29 \\ &3x_1 + 14x_2 - s_3 = 12 \\ &x_1 + x_2 = 2 \\ &x_1, x_2, s_1, s_2, s_3 \geq 0 \end{aligned}$$

5-3. **(a)** 0 **(b)** 6 **(c)** −5

5-5. 14, counting slack and surplus variables

5-7. **(a)** OV increases by 750. **(b)** OV decreases by 3000. **(c)** Between $-\infty$ and 11.50

5-9. Zero

5-11. The current solution is degenerate.

5-13. **(a)** Same as before ($E^* = 4.5$, $F^* = 7.0$) **(b)** OV decreases by 4500.

5-15. **(a)** \$91.11 **(b)** Optimal solution unchanged, but OV decreases by 20.8. **(c)** No. Cost increases by \$25.96.

5-17. There are alternative optima.

5-19.

$$\begin{aligned} &\text{Max } 3x_1 + 17x_2 \\ &\text{s.t. } 18x_1 + 6x_2 \le 4 \\ &\qquad 12x_1 + 2x_2 \le 13 \\ x_1 \le 0,\quad &x_2 \text{ unconstrained in sign} \end{aligned}$$

5-21. **(a)** 1500 **(b)** 120 **(c)** The dual

5-23. Special structure

5-25. **(a)** Rate of improvement in the OV as the RHS increases
(b) Rate of change in the OV as the RHS increases

5-27. Let $z_1 = x_1$; $z_2 = y_1$; $z_3 = y_2$; $z_4 = x_3$ to obtain

$$\begin{aligned} &\text{Max } 4z_1 + z_2 - z_3 \\ &\text{s.t. } 3z_1 + 2z_2 - 2z_3 - z_4 + z_5 = 0 \\ &\qquad z_1 - 3z_2 + 3z_3 \qquad - z_6 = 14 \\ &\qquad z_i \ge 0, \quad i = 1, 2, 3, 4, 5, 6 \end{aligned}$$

5-29. **(a)** 128 hours on 1 and 2, 76.8 hours on 3. **(b)** Dollars per minute **(c)** 60 cents **(d)** \$1.38 per pound

5-31. **(a)** Rows 2 through 4 say that the total number of gallons of a blend produced is equal to the sum of the number of gallons of each vintage used in the blend.
(b) Rows 5 through 8 say that the number of gallons of a vintage used can not exceed the number of gallons available.
(c) Row 9 represents the restriction that Blend A must be at least 75% Vintage 1 and 2. The percentage of Vintage 1 and 2 in Blend A is given by the following expression:

$$\frac{\text{XA1+XA2}}{\text{TOTALA}} \times 100\%$$

Thus the constraint would be

$$\frac{\text{XA1+XA2}}{\text{TOTALA}} \times 100\% \ge 75\%$$

But this constraint is nonlinear, so make it linear by multiplying both sides by TOTALA. Finally, convert the percentages to fractions and bring all variable terms to the LHS.

(d) \$54,675

(e)

	VINTAGE				
BLEND	**1**	**2**	**3**	**4**	**TOTALS**
A	180	246.71		22.46	449.17
B		3.29	200	377.54	580.83
C					
Totals	180	250	200	400	1,030

(f) The current solution is degenerate because there are 12 constraints and only 9 positive variables.

(g) Since the solution is degenerate, the selling price of C would have to increase by at least the allowable increase, \$22.50, and possibly more, for the optimal solution to change to one in which it is optimal to produce blend C.

(h) \$72.50 per gallon for Vintages 1, 2, and 3 and \$22.50 per gallon for Vintage 4.

(i) The earthquake would destroy 100 gallons. The allowable decrease on row 7 is 200 gallons. Therefore the optimal solution would change, but not the basis. The optimal value would decline by $100 \times 72.5 = \$7{,}250$.

5-33. D_2 will have four more inequalities in unconstrained variables, but these four extra inequalities will give the sign conditions in D_1.

5-35. The decrease of 1500 makes the optimal objective function contour coincident to the fourth constraint line (see Figure 5.9). The decrease of 19,000 makes it coincident to the market balance line (see Figure 5.10).

Chapter 6

6-1. **(a)** (4) **(b)** (6) **(c)** (1) **(d)** (7) **(e)** (9) **(f)** (11) **(g)** (5) **(h)** (8) **(i)** (3) **(j)** (2) **(k)** (10)

6-3. **(a)**

$$\begin{aligned} 3x_1 + x_3 + s_1 - 2s_2 &= 100 \\ x_1 + x_2 \qquad + s_2 &= 200 \\ -5x_1 - 2s_1 + 4s_2 + s_3 &= 400 \\ x_i \geq 0, \quad i &= 1, 2, 3 \\ s_j \geq 0, \quad j &= 1, 2, 3 \end{aligned}$$

(b) $\{x_2, x_3, s_3\}$ **(c)** $\{x_1, s_1, s_2\}$

(d)

		20	30	25	0	0	0	
BASIC COEFFICIENT	**BASIC VARIABLE**	x_1	x_2	x_3	s_1	s_2	s_3	**VALUE**
25	x_3	3	0	1	1	−2	0	100
30	x_2	1	1	0	0	1	0	200
0	s_3	−5	0	0	−2	④	1	400
z_j		105	30	25	25	−20	0	
$c_j - z_j$		−85	0	0	−25	20	0	8500

(e) No. s_2 should enter and s_3 should exit.

(f) See below.

		20	30	25	0	0	0	
BASIC COEFFICIENT	**BASIC VARIABLE**	x_1	x_2	x_3	s_1	s_2	s_3	**VALUE**
25	x_3	$\frac{1}{2}$	0	1	0	0	$\frac{1}{2}$	300
30	x_2	$\frac{9}{4}$	1	0	$\frac{1}{2}$	0	$-\frac{1}{4}$	100
0	s_2	$-\frac{5}{4}$	0	0	$-\frac{1}{2}$	1	$\frac{1}{4}$	100
z_j		80	30	25	15	0	5	
$c_j + z_j$		−60	0	0	−15	0	−5	10,500

The optimal solution is $x_3 = 300$, $x_2 = 100$, $s_2 = 100$.

6-5. **(a)**

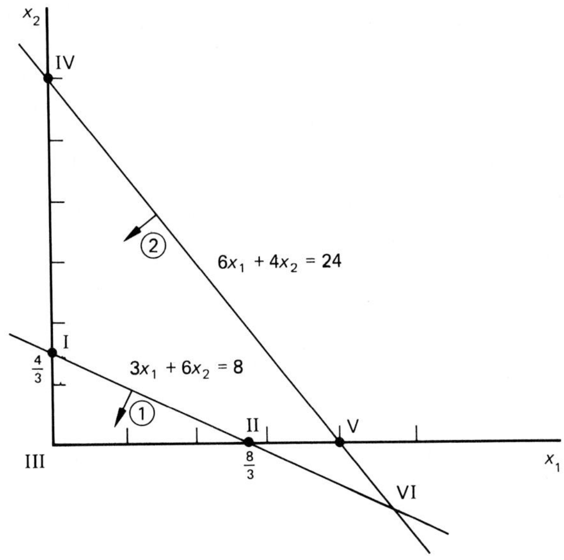

The equality form of the LP is

$$\begin{aligned} &\text{Max } 5x_1 + 6x_2 \\ &\text{s.t.} \quad 3x_1 + 6x_2 + s_1 = 8 \\ &\qquad\;\; 6x_1 + 4x_2 + s_2 = 24 \end{aligned}$$

Then we have at most $\binom{4}{2} = 6$ possible basic solutions
(b) I, II, and III in figure above are feasible.

6-7. **(a)** $\binom{4}{2} = 6$ **(b)** No **(c)** At least 1, at most 6

6-9.

		40	60	50	0	0	0	
BASIC COEFFICIENT	**BASIC VARIABLE**	x_1	x_2	x_3	s_1	s_2	s_3	**VALUE**
0	s_1	10	4	2	1	0	0	950
0	s_2	2	②	0	0	1	0	410
0	s_3	1	0	2	0	0	1	610
	z_j	0	0	0	0	0	0	
	$c_j - z_j$	40	60	50	0	0	0	0

BASIC COEFFICIENT	BASIC VARIABLE	40 x_1	60 x_2	50 x_3	0 s_1	0 s_2	0 s_3	VALUE
0	s_1	6	0	②	1	−2	0	130
60	x_2	1	1	0	0	$\frac{1}{2}$	0	205
0	s_3	1	0	2	0	0	1	610
	z_j	60	60	0	0	30	0	
	$c_j - z_j$	−20	0	50	0	−30	0	12,300

BASIC COEFFICIENT	BASIC VARIABLE	40 x_1	60 x_2	50 x_3	0 s_1	0 s_2	0 s_3	VALUE
50	x_3	3	0	1	$\frac{1}{2}$	−1	0	65
60	x_2	1	1	0	0	$\frac{1}{2}$	0	205
0	s_3	−5	0	0	−1	②	1	480
	z_j	210	60	50	25	−20	0	
	$c_j - z_j$	−170	0	0	−25	20	0	15,550

BASIC COEFFICIENT	BASIC VARIABLE	40 x_1	60 x_2	50 x_3	0 s_1	0 s_2	0 s_3	VALUE
50	x_3	$\frac{1}{2}$	0	1	0	0	$\frac{1}{2}$	305
60	x_2	$\frac{9}{4}$	1	0	$\frac{1}{4}$	0	$-\frac{1}{4}$	85
0	s_2	$-\frac{5}{2}$	0	0	$-\frac{1}{2}$	1	$\frac{1}{2}$	240
	z_j	160	60	50	15	0	10	
	$c_j - z_j$	−120	0	0	−15	0	−10	20,350

The optimal solution is $x_2 = 85$, $x_3 = 305$, $x_1 = 0$.

6-11.

BASIC COEFFICIENT	BASIC VARIABLE	25 x_1	50 x_2	0 s_1	0 s_2	0 s_3	VALUE
0	s_1	2	2	1	0	0	1000
0	s_2	3	0	0	1	0	600
0	s_3	1	③	0	0	1	600
	z_j	0	0	0	0	0	
	$c_j - z_j$	25	50	0	0	0	0

		25	50	0	0	0	
BASIC COEFFICIENT	**BASIC VARIABLE**	x_1	x_2	s_1	s_2	s_3	**VALUE**
0	s_1	$\frac{4}{3}$	0	1	0	$-\frac{2}{3}$	600
0	s_2	③	0	0	1	0	600
50	x_2	$\frac{1}{3}$	1	0	0	$\frac{1}{3}$	200
	z_j	$\frac{50}{3}$	50	0	0	$\frac{50}{3}$	
	$c_j - z_j$	$\frac{25}{3}$	0	0	0	$-\frac{50}{3}$	10,000

		25	50	0	0	0	
BASIC COEFFICIENT	**BASIC VARIABLE**	x_1	x_2	s_1	s_2	s_3	**VALUE**
0	s_1	0	0	1	$-\frac{4}{9}$	$-\frac{2}{3}$	$\frac{1000}{3}$
25	x_1	1	0	0	$\frac{1}{3}$	0	200
50	x_2	0	1	0	$-\frac{1}{9}$	$\frac{1}{3}$	$\frac{400}{3}$
	z_j	25	50	0	$\frac{25}{9}$	$\frac{50}{3}$	
	$c_j - z_j$	0	0	0	$-\frac{25}{9}$	$-\frac{50}{3}$	35,000/3

The optimal solution is: $x_1 = 200$, $x_2 = \frac{400}{3}$.

6-13.

		6	8	16	0	0	M	M	
BASIC COEFFICIENT	**BASIC VARIABLE**	x_1	x_2	x_3	s_1	s_2	a_1	a_2	**VALUE**
M	a_1	②	1	0	−1	0	1	0	5
M	a_2	0	1	2	0	−1	0	1	4
	z_j	$2M$	$2M$	$2M$	$-M$	$-M$	M	M	
	$c_j - z_j$	$6 - 2M$	$8 - 2M$	$16 - 2M$	M	M	0	0	$9M$

		6	8	16	0	0	M	M	
BASIC COEFFICIENT	**BASIC VARIABLE**	x_1	x_2	x_3	s_1	s_2	a_1	a_2	**VALUE**
6	x_1	1	$\frac{1}{2}$	0	$-\frac{1}{2}$	0	$\frac{1}{2}$	0	$\frac{5}{2}$
M	a_2	0	1	②	0	−1	0	1	4
	z_j	6	$3 + M$	$2M$	−3	$-M$	3	M	
	$c_j - z_j$	0	$5 - M$	$16 - 2M$	3	M	$M - 3$	0	$4M + 15$

BASIC COEFFICIENT	BASIC VARIABLE	6	8	16	0	0	M	M	
		x_1	x_2	x_3	s_1	s_2	a_1	a_2	VALUE
6	x_1	1	$\frac{1}{2}$	0	$-\frac{1}{2}$	0	$\frac{1}{2}$	0	$\frac{5}{2}$
16	x_3	0	($\frac{1}{2}$)	1	0	$-\frac{1}{2}$	0	$\frac{1}{2}$	2
	z_j	6	11	16	−3	−8	3	8	
	$c_j - z_j$	0	−3	0	3	8	$M - 3$	$M - 8$	47

BASIC COEFFICIENT	BASIC VARIABLE	6	8	16	0	0	
		x_1	x_2	x_3	s_1	s_2	VALUE
6	x_1	1	0	−1	$-\frac{1}{2}$	$\frac{1}{2}$	$\frac{1}{2}$
8	x_2	0	1	2	0	−1	4
	z_j	6	8	10	−3	−5	
	$c_j - z_j$	0	0	6	3	5	35

The optimal solution is: $x_1 = \frac{1}{2}$, $x_2 = 4$, $x_3 = 0$.

6-15.

BASIC COEFFICIENT	BASIC VARIABLE	6	1	3	−2	0	0	M	M	
		x_1	x_2	x_3	x_4	s_1	s_2	a_1	a_2	VALUE
0	s_1	1	1	0	0	1	0	0	0	42
M	a_1	2	3	−1	−1	0	−1	1	0	10
M	a_2	1	0	2	1	0	0	0	1	30
	z_j	$3M$	$3M$	M	0	0	$-M$	M	M	
	$c_j - z_j$	$6 - 3M$	$1 - 3M$	$3 - M$	−2	0	M	0	0	$40M$

6-17. $x_1 = 80/11$, $x_2 = 0$, $x_3 = 70/11$, $x_4 = 0$

6-19.

Variable	AI	AD
x_1	0	∞
x_2	∞	5.0
x_3	5.5	0
x_4	∞	5.0
Constraint		
1	∞	14.3
2	16.9	∞
3	70.0	40.0

Chapter 7

7-1. **(a)** (i) Northwest corner rule:

$$x_{A1} = 45,\ x_{B1} = 45,\ x_{B2} = 5,\ x_{C2} = 25,\ x_{C3} = 20,\ x_{D3} = 30$$

cost = \$1390

(ii) Vogel's approximation method:

$$x_{A3} = 45,\ x_{B1} = 15,\ x_{B2} = 30,\ x_{B3} = 5,\ x_{C1} = 45,\ x_{D1} = 30$$

cost = \$785

(b) VAM yields a better solution. This is what we expect.

7-3. **(a)** and **(b)** optimal solution:

$$x_{A3} = 45,\ x_{B1} = 15,\ x_{B2} = 30,\ x_{B3} = 5,\ x_{C1} = 45,\ x_{D1} = 30$$

cost = \$785

(c) No additional cost **(d)** 70

7-5. 85

7-7. $x_{A2} = 150$, $x_{A3} = 250$, $x_{B2} = 300$, $x_{C1} = 150$, $x_{C2} = 50$, OV = 7600

7-9. $x_{A2} = 200$, $x_{B1} = 100$, $x_{C1} = 100$, $x_{C2} = 100$, $x_{C3} = 100$, OV = 2500

7-11.

ORIGIN	DESTINATION 1	2	3	4	DUMMY	SUPPLY
A	20	19	22	24	0	800
B	26	24	28	23	0	600
C	33	25	29	28	0	700
DEMAND	300	500	400	600	300	2100

7-13. A1, B4, C3, D2, OV = 68

7-15. A4, B3, C1, D2, OV = 320

Chapter 8

8-1. **(a)**

$$\begin{aligned} \text{Max}\quad & A + 3C \\ \text{s.t.}\quad & A \le 7 \\ & 4C \le 22 \\ & 2A + 3C \le 19 \\ & A, C \ge 0 \text{ and integer} \end{aligned}$$

(b) $A = 1.25$, $C = 5.5$

(c) $A = 2$, $C = 5$ **(d)** $A = 1$, $C = 5$; Yes **(e)** \$1

8-3. Lower bound. LP relaxation is ILP problem without integer constraints.

8-5. Upper bound. LP relaxation is ILP problem without integer constraints.

8-7. x_t = \$ invested in stock i
y_t = 1 invest in stock i
0 do not invest

$$\text{Max} \sum_{t=1}^{20} r_t x_t$$

$$\begin{aligned} \text{s.t.} \sum_{i=1}^{20} x_t &\le 100{,}000 \\ x_t &\le 20{,}000 y_t \quad i = 1, \ldots, 20 \\ x_t &\ge 5{,}000 y_t \quad i = 1, \ldots, 20 \\ y_t &= 0, 1; \quad x_t \ge 0, \text{ all } i \end{aligned}$$

8-9. x_{ij} = megawatts produced by generator i in period j
y_i = 1 if generator i is started
= 0 if generator i is not started

$$\text{Min } 3000y_A + 2000y_B + 1000y_C + 5x_{A1} + 5x_{A2} + 4x_{B1} + 4x_{B2} + 7x_{C1} + 7x_{C2}$$

$$\begin{aligned} \text{s.t. } x_{A1} + x_{B1} + x_{C1} &\ge 2900 \\ x_{A2} + x_{B2} + x_{C2} &\ge 3900 \\ x_{A1} &\le 2100y_A \\ x_{A2} &\le 2100y_A \\ x_{B1} &\le 1800y_B \\ x_{B2} &\le 1800y_B \\ x_{C1} &\le 3000y_C \\ x_{C2} &\le 3000y_C \end{aligned}$$

$$x_{ij} \ge 0 \quad i = \text{A, B, C}; \quad j = 1, 2$$
$$y_i = 0 \text{ or } 1 \quad i = \text{A, B, C}$$

8-11. y_i = 1 make investment i
= 0 do not make investment i

$$\text{Max} \sum_{i=1}^{7} R_i y_i$$

$$\begin{aligned} \text{s.t. } y_2 &\le y_1 \\ y_3 &\le y_2 \\ y_2 &\le y_4 \\ y_5 &\le (1 - y_1) \\ y_5 &\le (1 - y_2) \\ y_6 &\le 2 - y_2 - y_3 \\ 2y_7 &\le y_2 + 1 - y_3 \\ \sum_{i=1}^{7} C_i y_i &\le M \end{aligned}$$

$$y_i = 0 \text{ or } 1 \quad i = 1, \ldots, 7$$

8-13. (1) Solution to LP relaxation: $A = 1.25$, $C = 5.5$, OV = 17.75.
(2) Branch on A

(a) Problem 2: add constraint $A \ge 2$
Optimal solution to LP relaxation $A = 2$, $C = 5$, OV = 17

(b) Problem 3: add constraint $A \le 1$
Optimal solution to LP relaxation $A = 1$, $C = 5.5$, OV = 17.5

(3) Branch on C in Problem 3

(a) Problem 4: add constraint $C \geq 6$
Problem infeasible

(b) Problem 5: add constraint $C \leq 5$
Optimal solution to LP relaxation $A = 1$, $C = 5$, OV = 16
Optimal solution: $A = 2$, $C = 5$, OV = 17

8-15.

RHS(b_2)	OPTIMAL VALUE
24	18
$20 \leq b_2 < 24$	17
$16 \leq b_2 < 20$	15
$12 \leq b_2 < 16$	14
$8 \leq b_2 < 12$	12
$4 \leq b_2 < 8$	10
$0 \leq b_2 < 4$	7

8-17. **(a)** $x_1 = \frac{8}{3}, x_2 = \frac{5}{3}$ **(b)** (1, 5), (1, 4), (2, 4), (2, 3), (3, 3), (3, 2), (4, 2), (4, 1), (5, 1), (6, 0) **(c)** (4, 1) **(d)** (3, 2) **(e)** No. **(f)** One more.

8-19.

$$\text{Min } 170XA1+40XA2+70XA3+160XA4+100XC1+240XC2+140XC3+60XC4$$

$$\begin{aligned}
\text{s.t.} \quad & XA1 + XC1 = 100 \\
& XA2 + XC2 = 90 \\
& XA3 + XC3 = 110 \\
& XA4 + XC4 = 60 \\
& XA1 + XA2 + XA3 + XA4 \leq 200 \\
& XC1 + XC2 + XC3 + XC4 \leq 300 \\
& X_{ij} \geq 0 \quad i = \text{A, C}; \quad j = 1, \ldots, 4
\end{aligned}$$

8-21.

$$\text{Min } 300X_1 + 670Y_1 + 950Z_1 + \cdots + 145X_5 + 322Y_5 + 458Z_5$$

$$\begin{aligned}
\text{s.t. } & C_1 = 800 + 10X_1 + 50Y_1 + 100Z_1 \\
& C_t = C_{t-1} + 10X_t + 50Y_t + 100Z_t \qquad t = 2, \ldots, 5 \\
& C_1 \geq 880, \ldots, C_5 \geq 1280 \\
& C_t \geq 0; \qquad X_1, Y_t, Z_t \geq 0 \text{ and integer } t = 1, \ldots, 5
\end{aligned}$$

8-23. Let s_i be a 0−1 variable that is 1 if the supplier makes a direct shipment to location i and is 0 otherwise, $i = 1, \ldots, 10$. Add to the objective function $Rs_1 + \ldots + Rs_{10} + Rt$. Include the constraints $x_t \leq d_i s_i$ and s_i is 0 or 1, $i = 1, \ldots, 10$.

8-25. No. There are six positive variables counting slack and surplus variables, but only five constraints.

8-27. The allowable decrease is .75 − .369 = .381.

8-29. Max $.089X + .21Y + .23Z$

s.t. $.0108075X^2 + .0583917Y^2 + .0942268Z^2 + .0248144XY + .0261502XZ + .1108528YZ \leq V$

$$X + Y + Z = 1$$

$$X \geq .75, \qquad Y \geq .75, \qquad Z \geq .75$$

$$X, Y, Z \geq 0$$

8-31. **a.** The model is

$$
\begin{aligned}
\text{Min} \quad & .01X^2 + .04Y^2 + .08Z^2 + .002XY + .002XZ - .08YZ \\
\text{s.t.} \quad & .07X + .06Y + .1Z \geq .08 \\
& X + Y + Z = 1 \\
& X, Y, Z \geq 0
\end{aligned}
$$

with solution $X = .197305$, $Y = .353476$, $Z = .449119$, and minimum variance of .009140.

b. Yes, the above solution is an example. The negative covariance between y and z allows the variance of the portfolio to be reduced.

c. The dual price on the minimum return constraint is −1.280817. Thus, we estimate that the variance would *increase* by .01(1.280817) or .01280817. The actual increase is .032525 − .009140 = .023385.

Chapter 9

9-1.

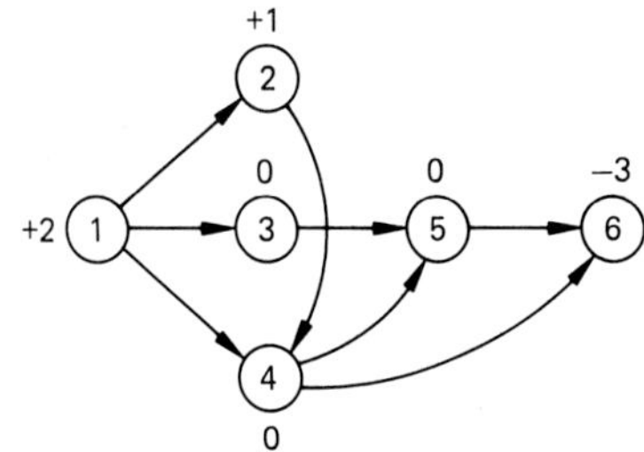

NODE	ARCS (i, j)								SUPPLIES
	(1, 2)	(1, 3)	(1, 4)	(2, 4)	(3, 5)	(4, 5)	(4, 6)	(5, 6)	
1	1	1	1						2
2	−1			1					1
3		−1			1				0
4			−1	−1		1	1		0
5					−1	−1		1	0
6							−1	−1	−3

9-3.

$$
\begin{aligned}
- x_{21} + x_{14} &= 0 \\
x_{21} + x_{24} + x_{25} &= 2 \\
x_{36} &= 8 \\
- x_{14} - x_{24} + x_{47} &= -1 \\
- x_{25} - x_{65} + x_{57} &= 0 \\
- x_{36} + x_{65} &= 0 \\
- x_{47} - x_{57} &= -9
\end{aligned}
$$

9-5.

NODE	ARCS (*i,j*)						RHS
	(1,2)	(1,3)	(2,4)	(2,5)	(3,4)	(4,5)	
1	1	1					2
2	−1		1	1			0
3		−1			1		0
4			−1		−1	1	−1
5				−1		−1	−1

9-7. The heavy lines below represent a shortest-path tree and minimum spanning tree.

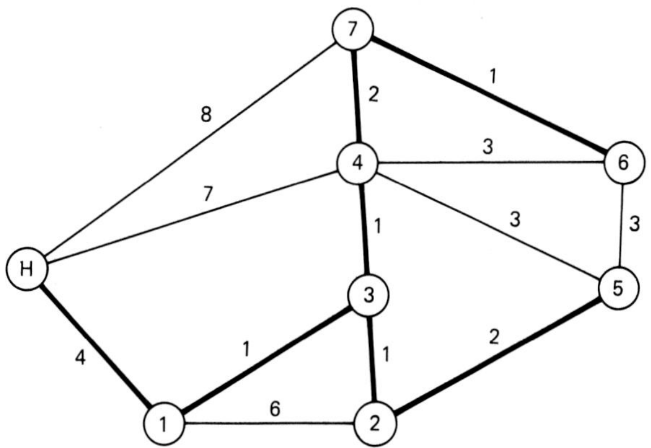

But the two algorithms do not necessarily produce the same tree. For example, consider the network

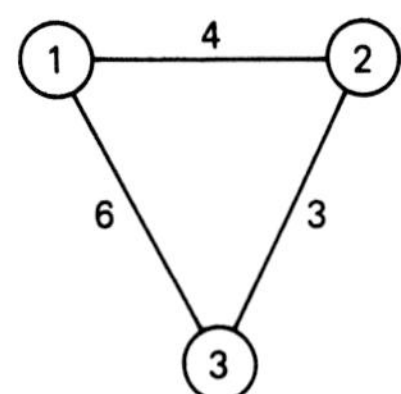

The minimum spanning tree is

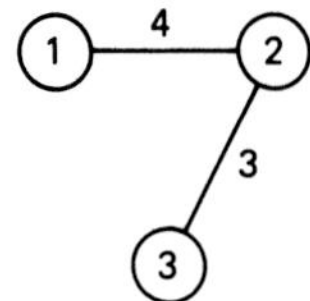

whereas the shortest-path tree (from 1) is

9-9.

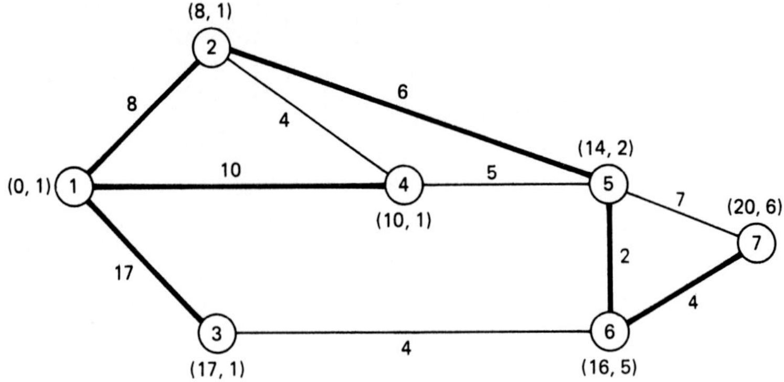

9-11.

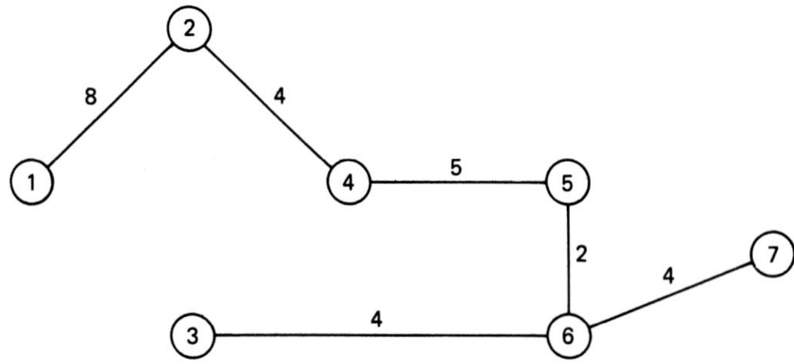

9-13.

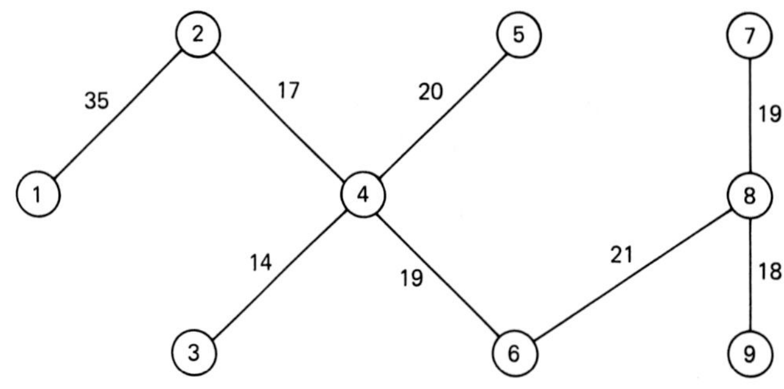

9-15.

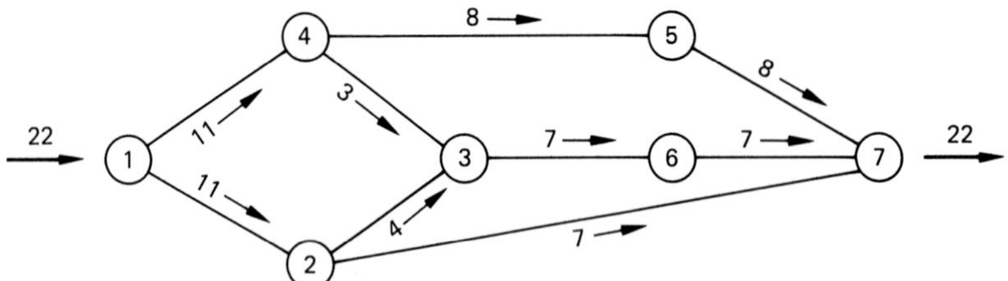

9-17.

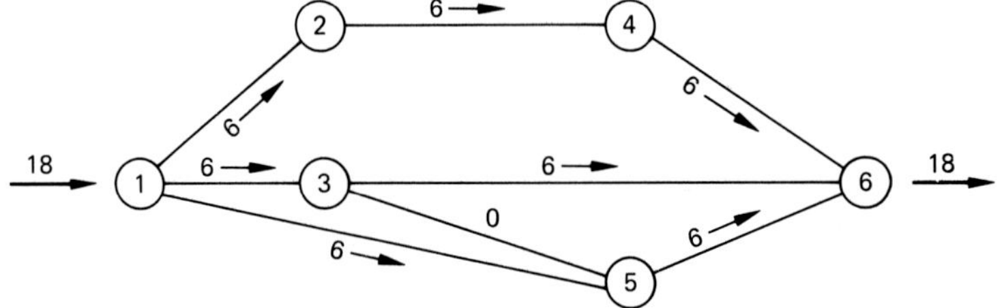

9-19. All arcs (i,j), $i = 1, \ldots, S$, $j = S+1, \ldots, S + D$ are permitted, where $i = 1, \ldots, S$ denotes origins and $j = S + 1, \ldots, S + D$ denotes destinations. There are SD arcs and $n = S + D$ nodes. For $j = 1, \ldots, S$, there are no arc (k,j), hence $\sum_k x_{kj} + 0$. Also, $L_j = S_j =$ supply at j, for $j = 1, \ldots, S$. For $j = S + 1, \ldots, S + D$, there is no arc (j, k). Hence $\sum_k x_{jk} = 0$. Also, $L_j = -D_j = -$(demand at j), for $j = S + 1, \ldots, S + D$. Thus, we get the supply and demand equations. Also, let $u_{ij} = \infty$, all (i,j).

9-21. Put a supply of 1 at the origin, a demand of 1 at the destination, and make all other nodes transshipment points.

9-23. **(a)** 17 **(b)** 9 **(c)** 5, 4, and 10 **(d)** 8, 6, and 11

(e)

From \ To	3	6	9	SUPPLY
1	5	4	10	200
5	8	6	11	150
Demands	50	250	50	

(f) 50(5) + 150(4) + 100(6) + 50(11) = 2000

Chapter 10

10-1. **(a)** 7000 **(b)** \$420 **(c)** \$1300 **(d)** \$1720 **(e)** 183,720
(f) Larger, since annual ordering cost exceeds annual holding cost

10-3. $Q^* = 3020.76$, $N^* = 3.02$

10-5. **(a)** \$48,989.80 **(b)** 48.99 **(c)** 0.020 year = 5.10 days

10-7. **(a)** \$18,974 **(b)** 12.65 **(c)** 0.079 year

10-9. **(a)** 90 dozen **(b)** 90 orders/year **(c)** .011 year = 4 days **(d)** 20 days **(e)** 450 dozen **(f)** 450 dozen

10-11. **(a)** $Q^* = 12{,}000$; $T^* = 0.1$ year = 24 days; $N^* = 10$; ATC = \$121,800
(b) 0.5% discount: \$121,432.50
0.7% discount; \$121,754.25
(c) Order 20,000

10-13. **(a)** $Q^* = 96$; $N^* = 24$; $T^* = 8.33$ days; AHO $(Q^*) = 4800$ **(b)** $C_b = \$40$
(c) $Q^* = 144$; $S^* = 80$; $N^* = 16$; $T^* = 12.5$ days; AHOB(Q^*) = \$3200 **(d)** Backlog

10-15. **(a)** $Q^* = 900$; $N^* = 20$; $T^* = 12.5$ days; $S^* = 500$; AHOB* = \$1200
(b) On hand = 4; on order = 0; position = 4 **(c)** 504 books **(d)** Yes

10-17. **(a)** $Q = 4500$ gallons; $T = 100$ days; production run = 75 days; maximum inventory level = 1125 gallons **(b)** DHS = \$23.06

10-19. 0.4%

10-21. **(a)** Engines 270, spark plug sets 145, carburetors 180, throats 30, butterfly valves 80.

(b)

DAY	11	13	16	17	22	30
ACTION	Order Throats	Order Butterfly Valves	Assemble Carburetors	Order Spark Plugs	Start Engine Assembly	Complete Order

Chapter 11

11-1. (Start III at beginning of week 1 and II at beginning of week 2) and/or (Start IX at beginning of week 5 and VII at beginning of week 7) and/or (Start IV at beginning of week 3 and III at beginning of week 4). Thus there are 7 alternative optima.

11-3. Let (i, j) mean i is assigned to j. Then the tree is

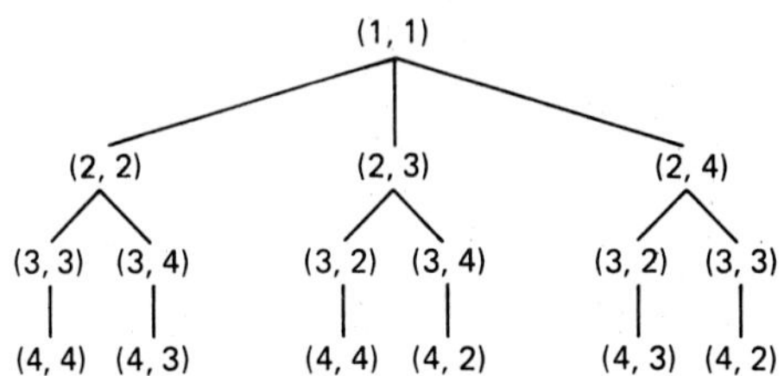

11-5. **(a)** Assign 4 to A. Delete row 4, column A. Assign 1 to C. Delete row 1, column C. Assign 5 to B. Delete row 5 and column B. Assign 3 to D, and assign 2 to E. Total Sales = 108.

(b) Transformed Data

	A	B	C	D	E
1	−5	−8	−2	0	−4
2	−10	−5	−7	−7	−8
3	−7	−7	−5	−1	0
4	0	0	0	0	0
5	−2	−4	−2	−2	−2

Assign 4 to A, 1 to D, 3 to E, 5 to C, 2 to B. Total Sales = 116.

11-7.

$$\text{Min} \sum_{i=1}^{12} u_i$$

$$\begin{aligned}
\text{s.t. } x_1 + u_1 - u_2 &= 2 \\
x_2 + u_3 - u_4 &= 10 \\
x_1 + u_5 - u_6 &= 6 \\
x_2 + u_7 - u_8 &= 6 \\
x_1 + u_9 - u_{10} &= 1 \\
x_2 + u_{11} - u_{12} &= 3 \\
u_i \geq 0, \quad i &= 1, \ldots, 12
\end{aligned}$$

11-9.

$$\begin{aligned}
\text{Min } & w_1u_1 + w_2u_2 + w_3u_3 \\
& 20x_1 + 12x_2 \leq 240 \\
& 12x_1 + 20x_2 \leq 240 \\
& x_1 + x_2 + u_1 - v_1 = 12 \\
& x_2 + u_2 - v_2 = 9 \\
& x_1 + u_3 - v_3 = 10 \\
& x_1, x_2 \geq 0, \quad u_i, v_i \geq 0, i = 1, 2, 3
\end{aligned}$$

11-11. **(a)** $x_1^* = 40, x_2^* = 40$. **(b)** Minimize underachievement, no overachievement allowed. **(c)** Minimize underachievement, overachievement allowed. **(d)** $x_1^* = 0, x_2^* = 80$

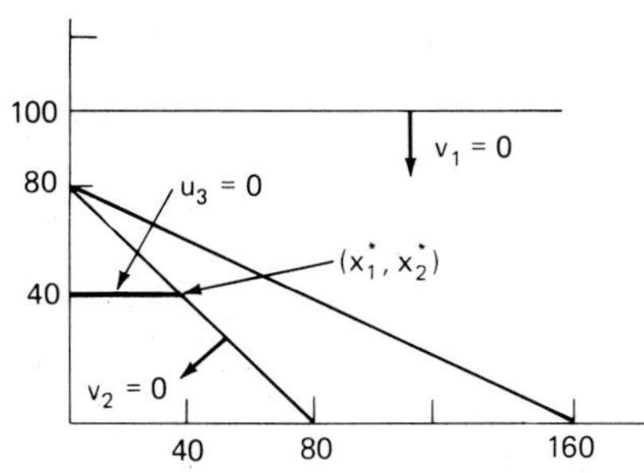

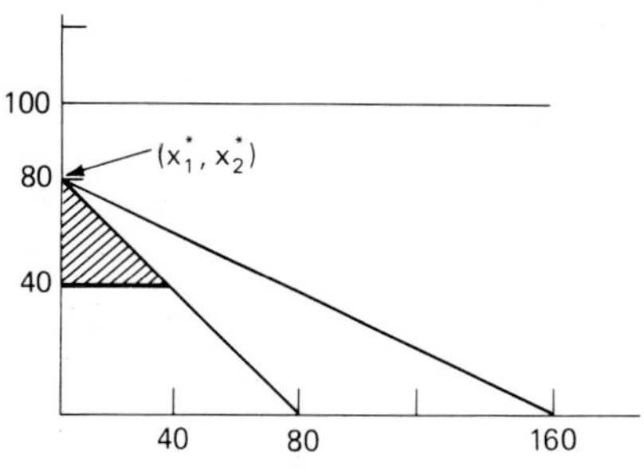

11-13. (a) $x_1^* = 100$, $x_2^* = 0$
(b) yes; $v_1^* = 20$ overachieved by 20;
$u_3^* = 45$ underachieved by 45.

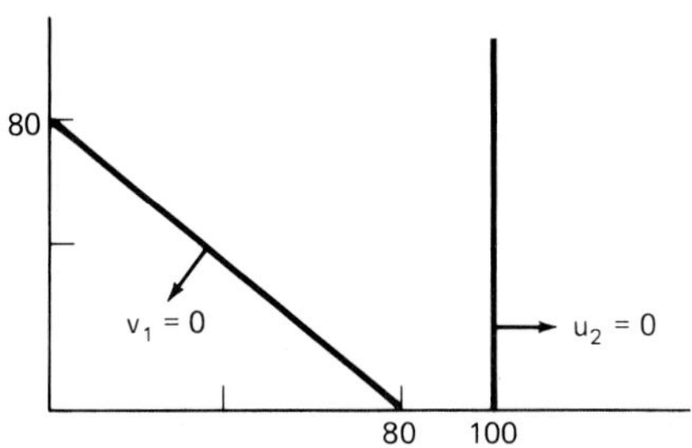

11-15. (a) $6! = 6 \times 5 \times 4 \times 3 \times 2 = 720$
(b) Sequence of jobs = D–C–A–F–E–B
Gantt Chart

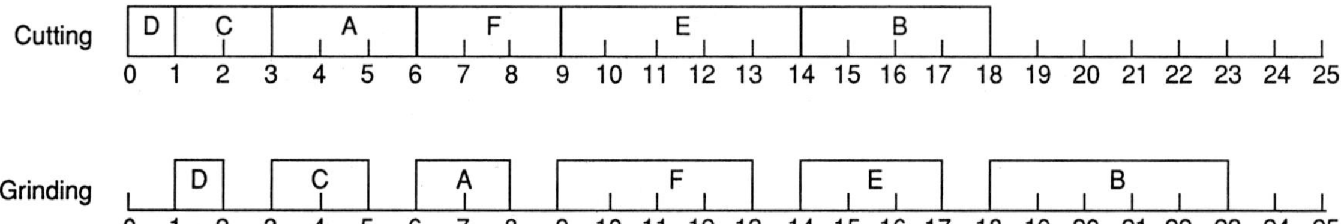

Total processing time: 23 hours

11-17. Formulation:

$$\text{Min } P_1v_1 + P_2u_2 + P_3(-200\text{A} - 200\text{B})$$
$$\text{s.t. } 400A + 600B + u_1 - v_1 = 2400$$
$$20A + 40B + u_2 - v_2 = 120$$
$$A, B, u_1, u_2, v_1, v_2 \geq 0$$

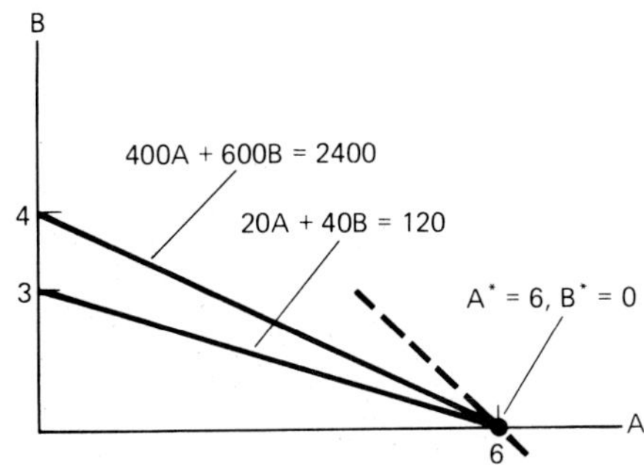

Optimal Solution: $A^* = 6$, $B^* = 0$.
The goals are exactly achieved with the optimal solution.
Net expenditure = 6(400 − 200) = 1200.
Number of jobs generated = 120.

Chapter 12

12-1. **(a)** $x^* = -\frac{7}{8}$ **(b)** Negative **(c)** $x = 1$ **(d)** Concave, because $f'' < 0$ for all x

12-3. $x^* = 25$

12-5. **(a)** saddle point **(b)** local maximizer **(c)** local maximizer

12-7. **(a)** $a^* = -5.428$, $b^* = 47.714$ **(b)** $a^* = -2$, $b^* = 45$

12-9. **(a)** $x_1^* = 3$, $x_2^* = 2$ **(b)** about 6, the value of λ^*

12-11. The stationary point is unique. Since it is a local Min it must be global.

12-13.
$$\lambda^* = \frac{1}{2}\sqrt{\frac{1}{B}\sum_{i=1}^{3}\frac{1}{p_i}}, \qquad x_i^* = \frac{B}{p_i^2 \sum_{i=1}^{3}(1/p_i)}$$

12-15.
$$x_2^* = \frac{a_1c_1 - 2b_1a_2}{4b_1b_2 - c_1^2}, \qquad x_1^* = \frac{-a_2 - 2b_2x_2^*}{c_1}$$

$b_1 > 0$ and $4b_1b_2 - c_1^2 > 0 \rightsquigarrow$ local min

$b_1 < 0$ and $4b_1b_2 - c_1^2 > 0 \rightsquigarrow$ local max

$4b_1b_2 - c_1^2 < 0 \rightsquigarrow$ saddle point

12-17. MODEL:

```
   1)  MAX = (PA - 210) * A + (PC - 230) * C;
   2)  A = 1000 - 4.7 * PA + PC
   3)  C = 1000 + 2 * PA - 6.2 * PC;
   4)  A + 2 * C < 120;
   5)  A + C < 90;

SLB     PA         .000000
SLB      A         .000000
SUB      A       70.000000
SLB     PC         .000000
SLB      C         .000000
SUB      C       50.000000

 SOLUTION STATUS: OPTIMAL TO TOLERANCES. DUAL CONDITIONS: SATISFIED.

              OBJECTIVE FUNCTION VALUE
        1)            2864.334190

VARIABLE            VALUE            REDUCED COST
      PA          248.563019            .000000
       A           70.000000         -18.894698
      PC          238.246143            .000000
       C           20.000000            .000000

   ROW         SLACK OR SURPLUS           PRICE
      2)             .000000           36.359319
      3)             .000000            6.042443
      4)           10.000000             .000000
      5)             .000000            2.203700
```

Chapter 13

13-1. Computerized war games, military exercises, training exercises.

13-3. **(a)**

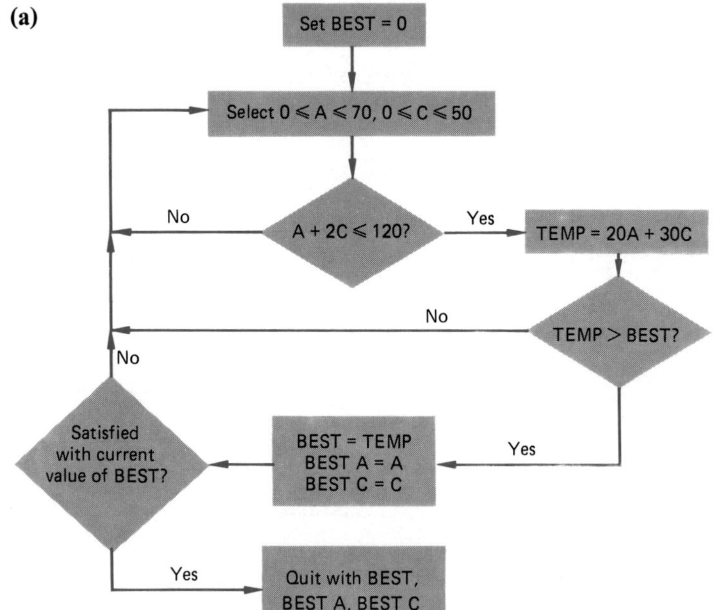

(b) A = 40, C = 30, BEST = 1700
A = 50, C = 30, BEST = 1900

13-5. False. Simplex is guaranteed to find optimum.

13-7.

EVENT	RANDOM NUMBER
Increase	00–29
Remain the Same	30–79
Decrease	80–99

13-9. 115.55

13-11. RN = 06, W = 6.0, RN = 60, W = 38.6; RN = 80, W = 44.3

13-13.

RN	90	49	06	60	92	77	38	39	84	47
Demand	13	10	8	11	13	11	10	10	12	10
Profit	139	130	90	133	139	133	130	130	136	130
Stockout	√			√	√	√			√	

(a) Average profit $= \dfrac{139 + 130 + \cdots + 130}{10} = 129$ **(b)** Number of stockouts = 5

13-15.

NUMBER OF BRAKE JOBS	RELATIVE FREQUENCY	RANDOM NUMBERS
5	3/30 = 9/90	00–08
6	8/30 = 24/90	09–32
7	9/30 = 27/90	33–59
8	6/30 = 18/90	60–77
9	4/30 = 12/90	78–89
Draw Again		90–99

	RN										
	20	82	74	08	01	69	36	35	52	99	41
Demand	6	9	8	5	5	8	7	7	7	—	7

13-17.

TIME BETWEEN ARRIVALS	RANDOM NUMBERS
5	00–24
10	25–74
15	75–99

CUSTOMER	R.N.	INTERARRIVAL TIME	ARRIVAL TIME	SERVICE STARTS	SERVICE ENDS	WAIT
1	None Needed		0	0	8	No
2	97	15	15	15	23	No
3	02	5	20	23	31	Yes
4	80	15	35	35	43	No
5	66	10	45	45	53	No
6	96	15	60	60	68	No
7	65	10	70	70	78	No
8	50	10	80	80	88	No
9	29	10	90	90	98	No
10	58	10	100	100	108	No
11	51	10	110	110	118	No
12	04	5	115	118	126	Yes
13	86	15	130	130	138	No
14	24	5	135	138	146	Yes
15	39	10	145	146	154	Yes
16	47	10	155	155	163	No

Four customers have to wait.

13-19. (a)

	A	B	C	D	E	F	G	H
1	INPUTS:							
2	Bid			$30,000.				
3	Average Annual Sales			$50,000.				
4	Operating Costs			40.%				
5	Tax Rate			33.%				
6								
7	Minimum After Tax Profit:			$14,941.				
8								
9				Year 1	Year 2	Year 3	Year 4	Year 5
10	Sales			$50,000.	$50,000.	$50,000.	$50,000.	$50,000.
11	Operating Cost			$20,000.	$20,000.	$20,000.	$20,000.	$20,000.
12	Loan Payments			$7,700.	$7,700.	$7,700.	$7,700.	$7,700.
13	Before Tax Profit			$22,300.	$22,300.	$22,300.	$22,300.	$22,300.
14	Tax			$7,359.	$7,359.	$7,359.	$7,359.	$7,359.
15	After Tax Profit			$14,941.	$14,941.	$14,941.	$14,941.	$14,941.

Average annual profit is $14,941.

(b) Answers will vary. When using @RISK with Latin Hypercube sampling and a Seed of 1, there is a 97.02% probability that over any 5 year period the minimum after-tax profit will be at least $7,000.

Chapter 14

14-1. (a) 4 (b) 3 (c) 1

(d)

	STATES OF NATURE			
	1	2	3	4
1	0	3	3	21
2	8	0	8	15
3	13	0	3	5
4	15	0	0	0

(e) 3

14-3. **(a)** 4 **(b)** 4 **(c)** Maximizing expected net dollar return and minimizing expected regret always lead to the same optimal decision.

14-5. **(a)** Accept government contract **(b)** Accept government contract

(c)

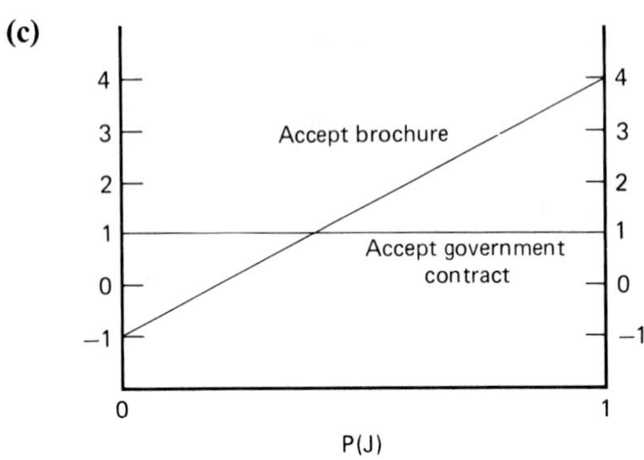

(d) 0.4 **(e)** Bid on brochure **(f)** Accept government contract **(g)** 1000 **(h)** Expected value of perfect information

14-7. **(a)** Accept government contract; 1000 **(b)** No. The risk-averse nature of the utility function will decrease the attractiveness of bidding relative to accepting the government contract. **(c)** 0.73 **(d)** $U(666.67) = 0.66 + \frac{666.67}{1000}(0.73 - 0.66) \cong 0.71$ **(e)** EU(J) = 0.66 **(f)** No. Not in general.

14-9. **(a)** $U(30) \geq 0.6$ **(b)** $U(50) \geq 0.85$ **(c)** $U(10) \leq 0.55$

14-11. $P(\text{ordering error}|\text{late}) = 0.6$
$P(\text{delivery error}|\text{late}) = 0.4$
Therefore, look for ordering error.

14-13. **(a)** $P(\frac{1}{2}) = 0.225$ **(b)** $P(A|\frac{1}{2}) = 0.44$ **(c)** ER = \$188.50

14-15. **(a)** Optimal strategy: If "sun" forecast, go ahead. If "rain" forecast, cancel.
(b) Expected value of sample information = \$6250 − \$4750 = \$1500

14-17. $P(\text{bad risk}|\text{credit}) = 0.024$

14-19. Optimal strategy: 1. Compete. 2. If order is received, use current machines.

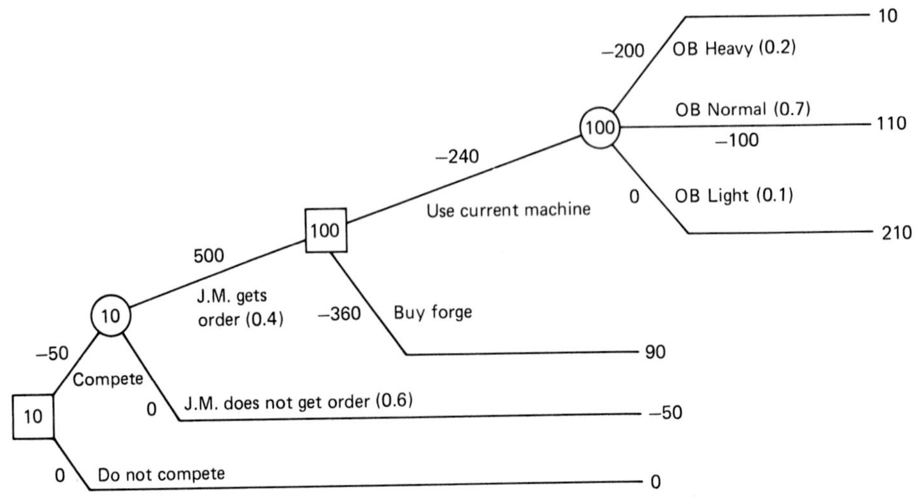

14-21. .3(200) + .6(1000) + .1(3000) = 960 > 900, sell to the movie company. .3(900) + .6(1000) + .1(3000) − 960 = 210, at most \$210,000.

14-23. Marple should make the component.

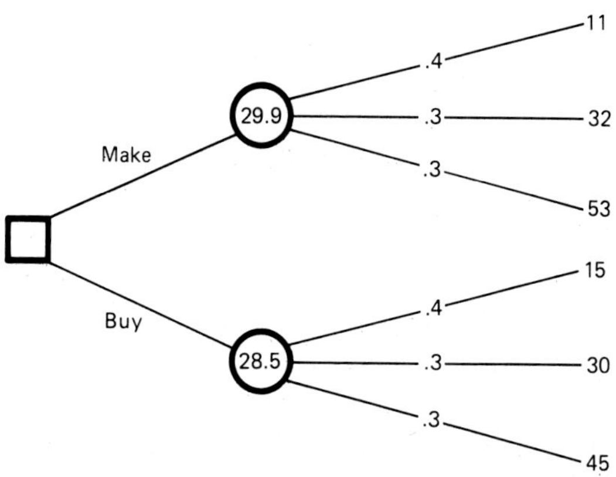

14-25. **(a)**

ORDER	DEMAND 0	1	2
0	0	100	200
1	10	10	110
2	20	20	20

(b)

ORDER	EXPECTED COST
0	$100(\frac{8}{36}) + 200(\frac{4}{36}) = \$44.44$
1	$10(\frac{24}{36}) + 10(\frac{8}{36}) + 110(\frac{4}{36}) = \$21.11$
2	\$20

Hospital should order 2 units each month.

14-27. **(a)**

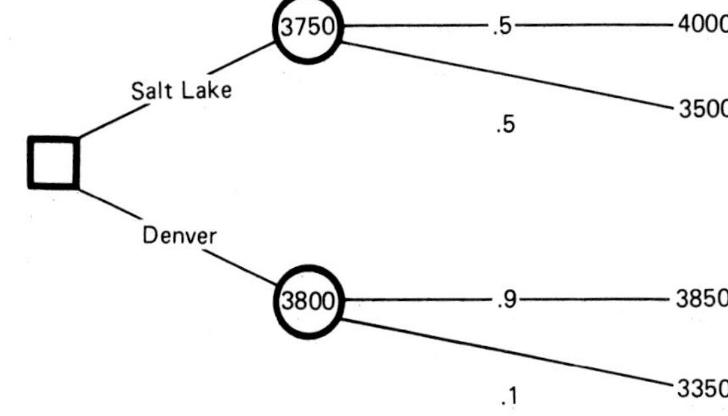

(b) Denver.

14-29. (a)

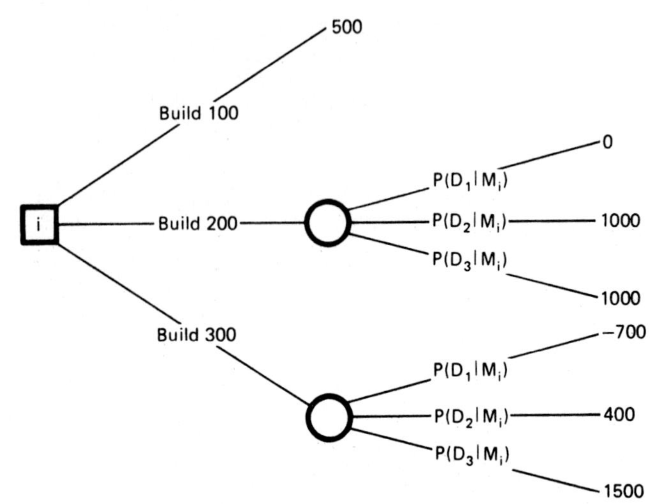

Note that there are three different trees depending on whether the measurement of demand is M_1, M_2, or M_3.

(b)

	$P(D_i \mid M_j)$			
	D_1	D_2	D_3	$P(M_j)$
M_1	.55	.39	.06	.38
M_2	.19	.62	.19	.32
M_3	.10	.50	.40	.30

	EXPECTED PAYOFF		
	M_1	M_2	M_3
Build 100	500	500	500
Build 200	450	810	900
Build 300	−139	400	730

If M_1, then Build 100, else if M_2 or M_3 Build 200.

(c) EVSI = \$719,000 − \$590,000 = \$129,000.

$$\text{EVSI/EVPI} = \frac{129{,}000}{170{,}000} = .76,$$ the survey is fairly efficient.

Chapter 15

15-1.

ACTIVITY	IMMEDIATE PREDECESSORS
2	—
1	2
3	1
4	3
6	4
5	1
8	1
7	8
10	8, 5
9	6, 7, 10

15-3.

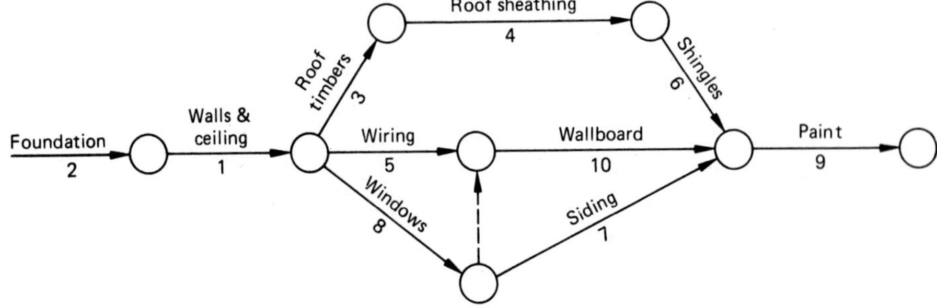

15-5.

ACTIVITY NUMBER	ACTIVITY	ES	EF	LS	LF	SLACK
2	Foundation	0	3	0	3	0
1	Walls and Ceiling	3	8	3	8	0
3	Roof Timbers	8	10	8	10	0
4	Roof Sheathing	10	13	10	13	0
6	Roof Shingles	13	21	13	21	0
5	Electrical Wiring	8	12	14	18	6
8	Windows	8	10	14	16	6
10	Inside Wall Board	12	15	18	21	6
7	Siding	10	15	16	21	6
9	Paint	21	23	21	23	0

Critical path: 2–1–3–4–6–9

15-7. **(a)**

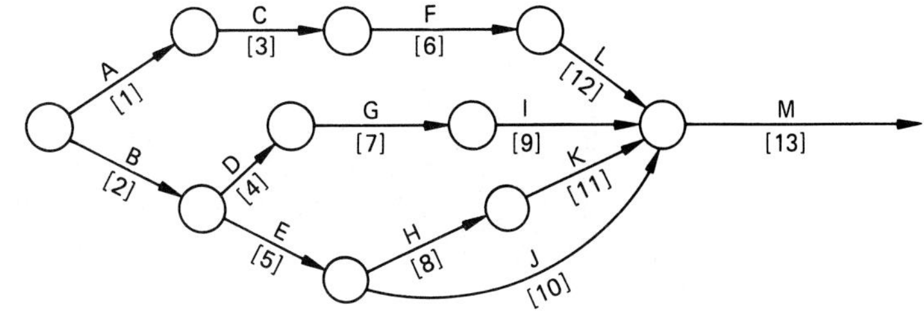

ACTIVITY	EARLIEST START	EARLIEST FINISH	LATEST START	LATEST FINISH	SLACK
A	0	1	4	5	4
B	0	2	0	2	0
C	1	4	5	8	4
D	2	6	6	10	4
E	2	7	2	7	0
F	4	10	8	14	4
G	6	13	10	17	4
H	7	15	7	15	0
I	13	22	17	26	4
J	7	17	16	26	9
K	15	26	15	26	0
L	10	22	14	26	4
M	26	39	26	39	0

Critical path: B–E–H–K–M.

(b) Savings = 9 days.

15-9.

ACTIVITY NUMBER	ACTIVITY	EXPECTED ACTIVITY TIME	STANDARD DEVIATION
2	Foundation	$\frac{2+4(3)+4}{6}=3$	$\frac{4-2}{6}=\frac{1}{3}$
1	Walls and Ceiling	$\frac{3+4(5)+7}{6}=5$	$\frac{7-3}{6}=\frac{2}{3}$
3	Roof Timbers	$\frac{1+4(2)+3}{6}=2$	$\frac{3-1}{6}=\frac{1}{3}$
4	Roof Sheathing	$\frac{1+4(2)+9}{6}=3$	$\frac{9-1}{6}=1\frac{1}{3}$
6	Roof Shingles	$\frac{4+4(8)+12}{6}=8$	$\frac{12-4}{6}=1\frac{1}{3}$
5	Electrical Wiring	$\frac{4+4(4)+4}{6}=4$	$\frac{4-4}{6}=0$
8	Windows	$\frac{1+4(2)+3}{6}=2$	$\frac{3-1}{6}=\frac{1}{3}$
7	Exterior Siding	$\frac{1+4(3)+17}{6}=5$	$\frac{17-1}{6}=2\frac{2}{3}$
10	Inside Wall Board	$\frac{2+4(3)+4}{6}=3$	$\frac{4-2}{6}=\frac{1}{3}$
9	Paint	$\frac{2+4(2)+2}{6}=2$	$\frac{2-2}{6}=0$

15-11. P (completion time $\leq$ 12) = 0; P (completion time $\leq$ 25) = 0.83
Probability critical path completed within 25 days $\geq$ probability project completed within 25 days.

15-13. **(a)**

ACTIVITY NUMBER	ACTIVITY	NORMAL TIME	NORMAL COST	CRASH TIME	CRASH COST	MAXIMUM CRASH DAYS	COST PER CRASH DAY
2	Foundation	3	\$20	2	\$30	1	$\frac{30-20}{3-2}=\$10$
1	Walls and Ceiling	5	50	3	72	2	$\frac{72-50}{5-3}=\$11$
3	Roof Timbers	2	15	1	30	1	$\frac{30-15}{2-1}=\$15$
4	Roof Sheathing	3	8	1	20	2	$\frac{20-8}{3-1}=\$6$
6	Roof Shingles	8	13	4	21	4	$\frac{21-13}{8-4}=\$2$
5	Wiring	4	30	4	30	0	n.a.
8	Windows	2	45	1	52	1	$\frac{52-45}{2-1}=\$7$
7	Siding	5	65	1	45	4	$\frac{65-45}{5-1}=\$5$
10	Inside Wall Board	3	22	2	34	1	$\frac{34-22}{3-2}=\$12$
9	Paint	2	40	2	40	0	n.a.

(b) \$288 **(c)** \$30; it is impossible

15-15.

Min 10CFOUND + 11CWALLS + 15CRTIMB + 6CRSHEA + 2CSHING + 7CWIND + 5CSIDIN + 12CWALB

s.t.

$$
\begin{aligned}
\text{ESWAL} + \text{CFOUND} &\geq 3 \\
\text{ESRTIM} + \text{CWALLS} - \text{ESWALL} &\geq 5 \\
\text{ESWIR} + \text{CWALLS} - \text{ESWALL} &\geq 5 \\
\text{ESWIN} + \text{CWALLS} - \text{ESWALL} &\geq 5 \\
\text{ESRSHE} + \text{CRTIMB} - \text{ESRTIM} &\geq 2 \\
\text{ESSHIN} + \text{CRSHEA} - \text{ESRSHE} &\geq 3 \\
\text{ESPAIN} + \text{CSHING} - \text{ESSHIN} &\geq 8 \\
\text{ESWALB} - \text{ESWIR} &\geq 4 \\
\text{ESPAIN} + \text{CWALB} - \text{ESWALB} &\geq 3 \\
\text{ESWALB} + \text{CWIND} - \text{ESWIN} &\geq 2 \\
\text{ESSID} + \text{CWIND} - \text{ESWIN} &\geq 2 \\
\text{ESPAIN} + \text{CSIDIN} - \text{ESSID} &\geq 5 \\
\text{EFPAIN} - \text{ESPAIN} &= 2
\end{aligned}
$$

$$\text{CFOUND} \leq 1, \text{CWALLS} \leq 2, \text{CRTIMB} \leq 1, \text{CRSHEA} \leq 2$$

$$\text{CSHING} \leq 4, \text{CWIND} \leq 1, \text{CSIDIN} \leq 4, \text{CWALB} \leq 1$$

$$\text{EFPAIN} + X \leq 23$$

All variables nonnegative

The last inequality represents the constraint on the total time required to complete.

23 = normal time to complete

X = desired reduction

15-17. Earliest Start

		DAY										DAY												
ACTIVITY NUMBER	ACTIVITY	1	2	3	4	5	6	7	8	9	10	11	12	13	14	15	16	17	18	19	20	21	22	23
2	Foundation	6.67	6.67	6.67																				
1	Walls and Ceiling				10	10	10	10	10															
3	Roof Timbers									7.50	7.50													
4	Roof Sheathing											2.67	2.67	2.67										
6	Roof Shingles														1.63	1.63	1.63	1.63	1.63	1.63	1.63	1.63		
5	Wiring									7.50	7.50	7.50	7.50											
8	Windows									22.50	22.50													
10	Wall Board													7.33	7.33	7.33								
7	Siding											9	9	9	9	9								
9	Paint																						20	20
Daily Project Cost		6.67	6.67	6.67	10	10	10	10	10	37.50	37.50	19.17	19.17	19	17.96	17.96	1.63	1.63	1.63	1.63	1.63	1.63	20	20
Total Project Cost		6.67	13.34	20.00	30.00	40.00	50.00	60.00	70.00	107.5	145	164.17	183.34	202.34	220.30	238.26	239.89	241.52	243.15	244.78	246.41	248	268	288

15-17. (continued) Latest Start

ACTIVITY NUMBER	ACTIVITY	DAY																						
		1	2	3	4	5	6	7	8	9	10	11	12	13	14	15	16	17	18	19	20	21	22	23
2	Foundation	6.67	6.67	6.67																				
1	Walls and Ceiling				10	10	10	10	10															
3	Roof Timbers									7.50	7.50													
4	Roof Sheathing											2.67	2.67	2.67										
6	Roof Shingles														1.63	1.63	1.63	1.63	1.63	1.63	1.63	1.63		
5	Wiring															7.50	7.50	7.50	7.50					
8	Windows															22.50	22.50							
10	Wall Board																			7.33	7.33	7.33		
7	Siding																	9	9	9	9	9		
9	Paint																						20	20
Daily Project Cost		6.67	6.67	6.67	10	10	10	10	10	7.50	7.50	2.67	2.67	2.67	1.63	31.63	31.63	18.13	18.13	17.96	17.96	17.96	20	20
Total Project Cost		6.67	13.34	20	30	40	50	60	70	77.50	85	87.67	90.34	93	94.63	126.26	157.89	176.02	194.15	212.11	230.07	248	268	288

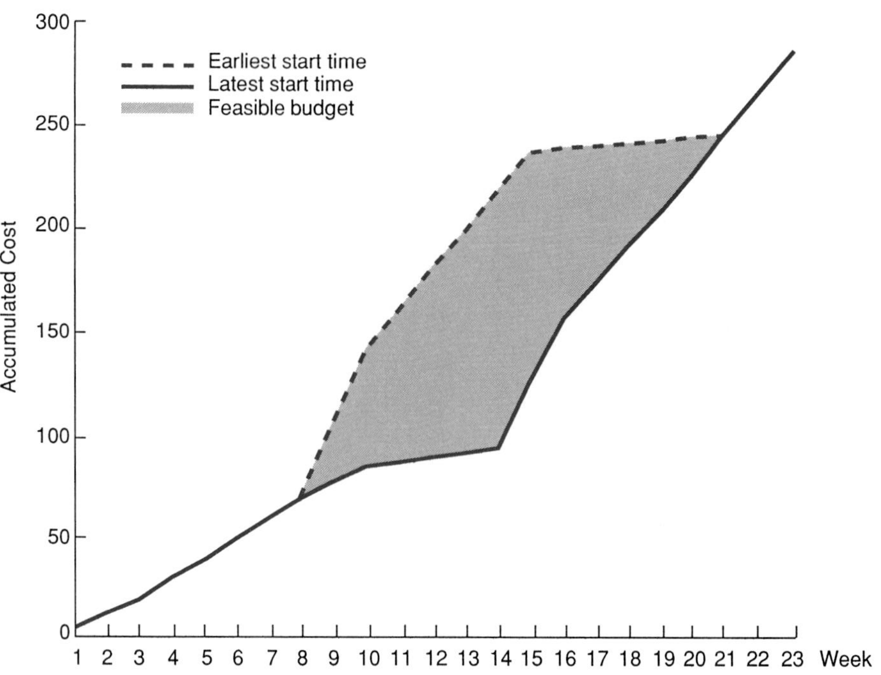

15-19.

(a)

ACTIVITY NUMBER	ACTIVITY	PERCENT COMPLETE	BUDGET	BUDGETED COST	ACTUAL COST	COST OVERRUN
2	Foundation	100	20	20	22	2
1	Walls and Ceiling	100	50	50	46	(4)
3	Roof Timbers	100	15	15	15	0
4	Roof Sheathing	100	8	8	10	2
6	Roof Shingles	25	13	3.25	4.50	1.25
5	Wiring	100	30	30	20	(10)
8	Windows	100	45	45	22.50	(22.50)
10	Inside Wall Board	100	22	22	20	(2)
7	Siding	100	45	45	40	(5)
9	Paint	0	40	0	0	0
Totals			288	238.25	200	(38.25)

(b)

ACTIVITY NUMBER	ACTIVITY	PERCENT COMPLETE	BUDGET	BUDGETED COST	ACTUAL COST	COST OVERRUN
2	Foundation	100	20	20	22	2.
1	Walls and Ceiling	100	50	50	46	(4)
3	Roof Timbers	100	15	15	15	0
4	Roof Sheathing	100	8	8	10	2
6	Roof Shingles	25	13	3.25	4.50	1.25
5	Wiring	25	30	7.50	20	12.50
8	Windows	50	45	22.50	22.50	20
10	Inside Wall Board	0	22	0	20	20
7	Siding	0	45	0	40	40
9	Paint	0	40	0	0	0
Totals			288	126.25	200	73.75

15-21. 26 − 11.75 = 14.25

15-23. **(a)** The answer is the same as for Problem 15-22 because the PERT analysis is not affected by the form of the distribution of individual activity times, but is affected by the mean and variance of those times, and these are exactly the same as in Problem 15-22.

(b) The spreadsheet is the same as before with the exception of the activity time column, which should now contain normally distributed activity times. The expected project length is longer than the answer the PERT analysis gives, 86.7 versus 81.0, while the probability of completion in 86 days is less, 0.6750 versus 0.9938. The reasons for the differences are the same as given in Problem 15-22 b.

(c) The answers from the two simulation analyses are quite close, 86.7 versus 87.0 and 0.6750 versus 0.6550. For this example, the form of the distribution of activity times (normal versus uniform) does not seem to make much difference. What does make a difference is the (erroneous) assumption made by PERT that the path with the longest expected length will always be the critical path.

Chapter 16

16-1. $r^* = 10$, $Q^* = 30$

16-3. **(a)** 0.052 **(b)** 0.058

16-5. **(a)** (iii); Q affects the number of orders per year. It has no effect on the probability of a stockout during an inventory cycle. **(b)(ii); increasing** Q decreases cycles per year and thus decreases the number of opportunities to stockout.

16-7. $r^* = 108$, $Q^* = 500$

16-9. $8

16-11. **(a)** $Q^* = 575$ **(b)** 0.60 **(c)** $Q^* = 729$ **(d)** $g = \$625.00$

16-13. **(a)** Answers will vary depending on the set of demands, because the values that are best for one set of demands will typically not be best for another set unless the number of demands sampled is very large. To get a better estimate you could either simulate more than 96 months (the best answer would vary less with different sets of demands) or simulate multiple sets of 96 monthly demands and average the cost for each policy over these multiple sets.

(b) Answers will vary depending on the set of demands. If the Seed value for the random number generator in @RISK is 1, then the results will be

Policy	Average	Lower Limit	Upper Limit
$r = 110$, $Q = 50$	$974	$792	$1644
$r = 120$, $Q = 50$	$986	$875	$1108

Some students may prefer the second policy, even though it has a higher average cost, because it is less "risky."

Chapter 17

17-1. **(a)** $\lambda = 0.5$ barges per hr **(b)** 2 hrs **(c)** 0.5 barges per hr

17-3. **(a)** $\mu = 15$ people per hr **(b)** 0.067 hrs per person **(c)** 15 people per hr

17-5. **(a)** $L = 2$ **(b)** $L_q = 4/3$ **(c)** $W = 1/5$ hr/person **(d)** $W_q = 2/15$ hr/person **(e)** $P_0 = 1/3$

17-7. (2) is wrong, for λ should be N/8.

17-9. see below

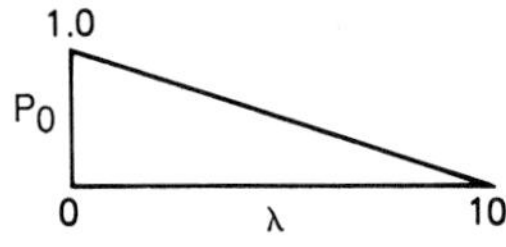

17-11. $W = L/\lambda = [\lambda/(\mu - \lambda)]/\lambda = 1/(\mu - \lambda)$

17-13. $L = 1.4791$

17-15. Since $\lambda > \mu$ the queue grows without limit unless there is balking or reneging.

17-17. **(a)** $P_0 = 1/9$ **(b)** $L = 8/9$ **(c)** $W_q = 2/45$ **(d)** $W = 13/90$ **(e)** $L = 2\ 8/9$

17-19. A three-server queue with Poisson arrivals (exponential interarrival times) and deterministic service time.

17-21. TC(5) = \$184.80 per hour.

17-23. $C_s/C_w = 1.63$

17-25. **(a)** $P_3 = 0.034$ **(b)** 0.409 **(c)** 5.91

17-27. **(a)** $L = 0.7525$ **(b)** $L_q = 0.2525$ **(c)** $W = 0.7525$ hour **(d)** $W_q = 0.2525$ hour **(e)** $P_0 = 1/2$
(a) through (d) are less because the variability of the service time is less

17-29. **(a)** The spreadsheet shown in Figure 17.12 is easily modified to answer this question: simply change the @EXPON(4) terms in columns B and D to @DISCRETE(3,9,13,1,2). Using 400 Iterations and a Seed value of 1 gives the following results: average completion time = 11.8 days, 99th percentile = 16.6 days. The assumption about the distribution of processing times is important, because when it is exponential the corresponding times are 12.5 days and 18.5 days.

(b) Now use @DISCRETE(3,99,13,1,2). The results are: average completion time = 8.3 days, 99th percentile = 10.4 days. If Larry continues to quote lead times so that he can be 99% sure of meeting them, he can reduce the lead time by 16.6 − 10.4 = 6.2 days. Thus the value of preventive maintenance is the 6.2 day reduction in lead time and the competitive advantage that brings to PROTRAC.

Chapter 18

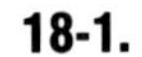

18-1. **(a)**

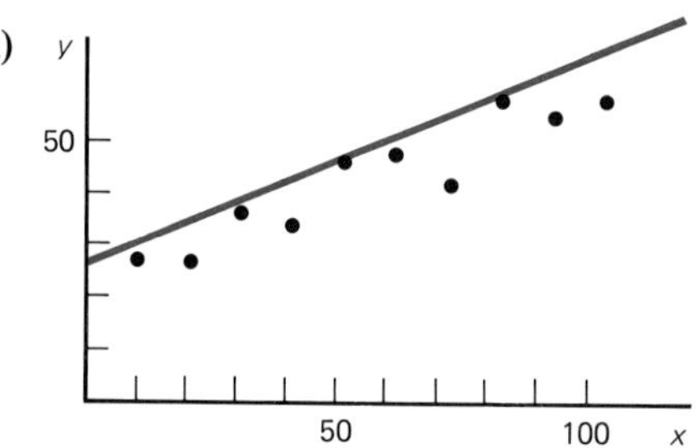

(b) Relevant data:

$$\sum x_i = 550, \quad \sum y_i = 417$$

$$\sum x_i y_i = 25{,}910, \sum x_i^2 = 38{,}500$$

$$y = 21.87 + .361x$$

(c) $y = 21.87 + 0.361(120) = 65.19$

18-3. **(a)**

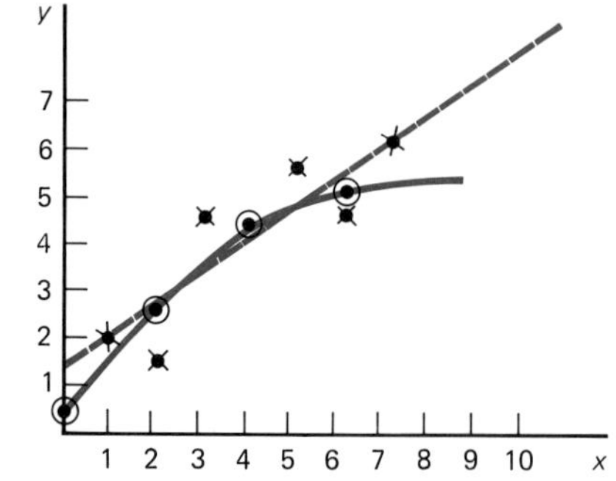

(b) Relevant data:

$$\sum x_i = 28,\quad \sum y_i = 28,\quad \sum x_i y_i = 131,\quad \sum x_i^2 = 140$$
$$\sum x_i^3 = 784,\quad \sum x_i^4 = 4676,\quad \sum x_i^2 y_i = 706$$

$y = 1.29 + 0.68x$

(c) $y = 0.428 + 1.250x - 0.071x^2$

18-5. Sum of squared deviations: linear, 4.11, quadratic, 3.68

18-7. (a)

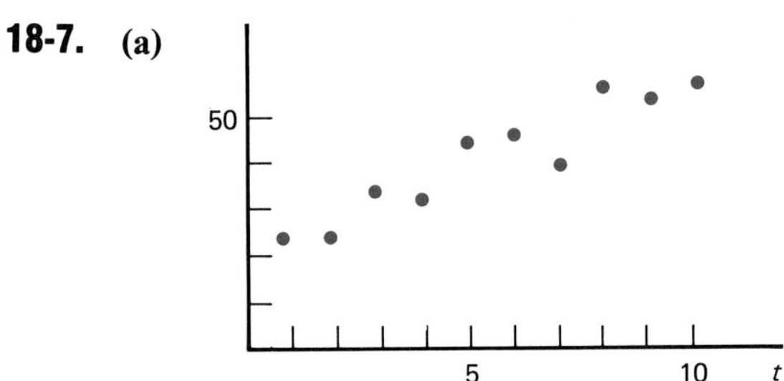

(b) $\hat{y}_{11} = 51.50$ (c) No. There seems to be a linear trend in the data and a simple moving average underestimates future demand if there is a trend.

18-9. **(a)** $\hat{y}_{11} = 53.9$ **(b)** Yes. Since there seems to be a trend, a weighted moving average with decreasing weights will underestimate demand less than a simple average. Still not as good as explicitly including the trend.

18-11. **(a)** $\hat{y}_{11} = 52.24$ **(b)** Larger. Since there seems to be a trend, we would like to put more weight on recent observations.

18-13. The anonymity of the source of each evaluation is an advantage of the Delphi Method. This is important in this case, since some of the participants are in subordinate positions. The cost and time involved are serious disadvantages of the Delphi Method as compared to the consensus panel.

18-15. Time series. The horizon is short. It is a mature product.

18-17. **(a)**

Time	4	5	6	7	8	9	10
$\hat{y}_t$	28.74	30.44	36.26	40.16	40.09	46.46	49.07
$\hat{w}_t$	30.98	33.63	39.62	45.21	42.41	48.96	53.94

(b) Simple average squared error = 97.64; trend-adjusted = 58.81.

18-19. No. Average squared error is sensitive to large but perhaps infrequent errors. Example: you might prefer errors of 0, 0, 0, 11 to +5, −5, +5, −5, but the average squared error is greater in the first case.

Appendix A: Basic Concepts in Probability

I. Introduction

Probability is the branch of mathematics that is used to model the uncertainty that occurs in nature, in science, and in business. Biologists use probability to model genetic evolution, physicists use probability to model the behavior of electrons in atoms, and economists use probability to model the behavior of stock prices. Texts such as this often use simple gambling games to motivate instruction in probability. For example, we can use probability to model the outcome of a roll of a pair of dice. The fundamental purpose of probability theory is to enable us to use what we know about simple uncertain events to calculate the probability of more complicated uncertain events. Thus, we can use our model of the probability of specific outcomes of rolling a pair of dice to calculate the probability of winning at the game of craps.

Random Variables

It is impossible to talk about probability without talking about random variables. Unfortunately, it is difficult to talk about random variables in a precise manner without getting into more abstract detail than this brief appendix allows or that is really required for this text. For our purposes, think of a random variable as an uncertain event that takes on a numerical value—for example, the face showing after the role of a die, the number of swimsuits sold by Spiegel during July, the price of General Motors stock at the end of next week, the number of snowy days in Nome, Alaska, in 1999, and so on.

Types of Probabilities

There are two basic types of probability models: discrete and continuous. The difference between them is not important in terms of the concepts used in management science. However, each type requires the use of a different branch of mathematics. Arithmetic is really all we need to handle discrete probabilities, but integral and differential calculus must be used for continuous random variables.

II. Discrete Probabilities

A. The Probability Mass Function (pmf)

Discrete probabilities are defined with the probability mass function, f(x). Specifically, f(x) is the probability that the random variable of interest takes on the value x. Consider the following examples.

Example 1: A Discrete Uniform Distribution. Suppose that we continue with the example of the roll of a die, and assume that each face of the die is equally likely to appear. Then

$$\begin{aligned} f(x) &= 1/6 \qquad (x=1, 2, 3, 4, 5, 6) \\ &= 0 \qquad (\text{otherwise}) \end{aligned}$$

The pmf for this distribution is shown in Figure A.1(a).

Example 2: An Arbitrary Discrete Distribution. Assume that an urn contains 5 balls that are identical except for the numbers written on them. Two balls have a 23 on them and the other three have 37 written on them. Assume that a ball is chosen at random, i.e., each ball is equally likely to be chosen. Then

$$\begin{aligned} f(x) &= 2/5 \qquad (x=23) \\ &= 3/5 \qquad (x=37) \\ &= 0 \qquad (\text{otherwise}) \end{aligned}$$

We note that f(x) ≥ 0 and that $\sum f(x) = 1$. These two conditions must hold for any pmf.

Example 3: The Binomial Distribution. This distribution is used to model the results of a series of independent trials when, at each trial, a specific event either occurs or does not occur. (See Section V-B, pg. A-12, for a definition of independence.) We encounter the binomial distribution in Chapter 16, where it is used to determine the probability of a specific number of stockouts in an inventory control system. This distribution has two parameters: n, the number of trials, and p, the probability that the event occurs at each trial. It follows that $(1-p)$ is the probability that the event does not occur. (The standard example is flipping a coin; the event is the occurrence of a head, and it is assumed that $p = 0.5$) The binomial distribution then is used to calculate the probability that the event occurs x times in n trials—for example, that there are 7 heads in 10 tosses of a coin. The pmf for the binomial distribution is

$$\begin{aligned} f(x) &= \binom{n}{x} p^x (1-p)^{n-x} \qquad (x=0, 1, \cdots, n) \\ &= 0 \qquad (\text{otherwise}) \end{aligned}$$

Here the symbol $\binom{n}{x}$ is the number of ways that one can select x items out of n. It is calculated as follows:

$$\binom{n}{x} = \frac{n!}{x!\,(n-x)!} = \frac{(n)\,(n-1)\cdots(1)}{[(x)\,(x-1)\cdots(1)]\,[(n-x)\,(n-x-1)\cdots(1)]}$$

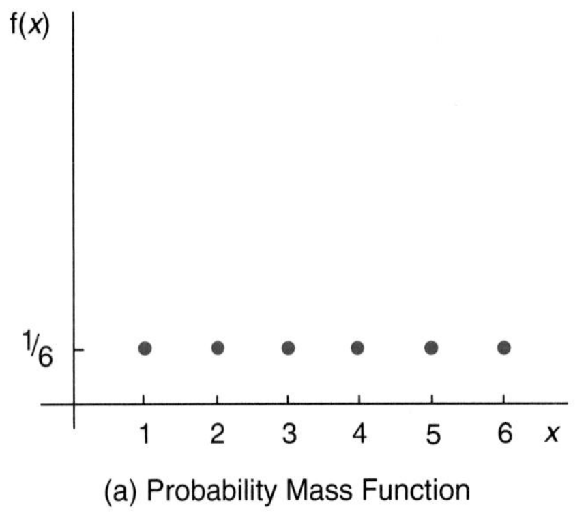

▲ Figure A.1 (a)

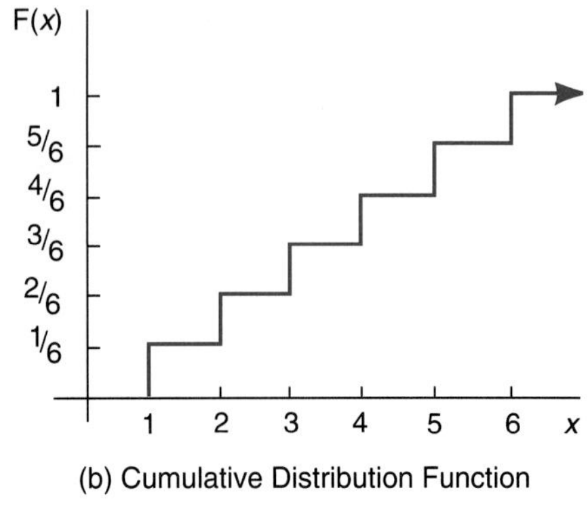

▲ Figure A.1 (b)

For example, we see that the probability of 7 heads in 10 tosses of a coin, where the probability of a head at a single toss is 0.5 (i.e., p = 0.5), is

$$f(7) = \frac{(10)\,(9)\,(8)}{(3)\,(2)\,(1)}\,(0.5^7)\,(0.5^3) = 0.117$$

Example 4: The Poisson Distribution. This distribution is often used to model the number of arrivals in a specific time interval in a queuing system (Chapter 17). The pmf is

$$\begin{aligned} f(x) &= \frac{e^{-M}M^x}{x!} && (x = 0, 1, 2, \cdots) \\ &= 0 && \text{(otherwise)} \end{aligned}$$

B. The Cumulative Distribution Function (CDF)

The cumulative distribution function F(x) is the probability that the random variable takes on a value less than or equal to x. Since the probability mass function, f(x), is the probability that the random variable takes on the value x, it follows that

$$F(x) = \sum_{j=-\infty}^{x} f(j)$$

Example 1 (continued): Discrete Uniform Distribution. If the random variable is the value showing on the throw of a fair die, then

$$\begin{aligned} F(x) &= 0 && (x < 1) \\ &= 1/6 && (1 \le x < 2) \\ &= 2/6 && (2 \le x < 3) \\ &= 3/6 && (3 \le x < 4) \\ &= 4/6 && (4 \le x < 5) \\ &= 5/6 && (5 \le x < 6) \\ &= 1 && (6 \le x) \end{aligned}$$

The CDF for this distribution is shown in Figure A.1(b)

Example 2 (continued): Arbitrary Discrete Distribution.

$$
\begin{aligned}
F(x) &= 0 && (x < 23) \\
&= 2/5 && (23 \le x < 37) \\
&= 1 && (37 \le x)
\end{aligned}
$$

III. Continuous Probabilities

A. The Probability Density Function

Continuous probabilities are defined by the probability density function (pdf). If f(x) is the pdf for a random variable, then we know that f(x) $\ge$ 0 for all x, and

$$\int_{-\infty}^{\infty} f(x)dx = 1$$

This is the continuous analog of the fact that the pmf for a discrete random variable is always greater than or equal to 0 and must sum to 1.

B. The Cumulative Distribution Function

The cumulative distribution function retains its definition for both continuous and discrete random variables—that is, F(x) is the probability that the random variable takes on a value less than or equal to x. For continuous random variables, the relationship between the probability density function (pdf) and the cumulative distribution function (CDF) is as follows

$$F(x) = \int_{-\infty}^{x} f(r)dr$$

Here we integrate the density function from $-\infty$ to x to determine the probability that the random variable is less than or equal to x. With discrete probabilities the concept is the same, but we sum the probability mass function rather than integrating the probability density function.

C. Important Examples

Here we describe three distributions that play an important role in this text and in applied business problems.

Example 5: The Continuous Uniform Distribution. The uniform distribution on the interval 0 to 1 plays a crucial role in simulation, in that it is used to generate random variables (see Chapter 13).

$$
\begin{aligned}
f(x) &= 0 && (x < 0) \\
&= 1 && (0 \le x \le 1) \\
&= 0 && (1 < x)
\end{aligned}
$$

Then by definition

$$F(x) = \int_{-\infty}^{x} f(r)\,dr$$
$$= 0 \qquad (x < 0)$$
$$= x \qquad (0 \le x \le 1)$$
$$= 1 \qquad (1 \le x)$$

Figure A.2 shows the pdf and the CDF for the continuous uniform distribution.

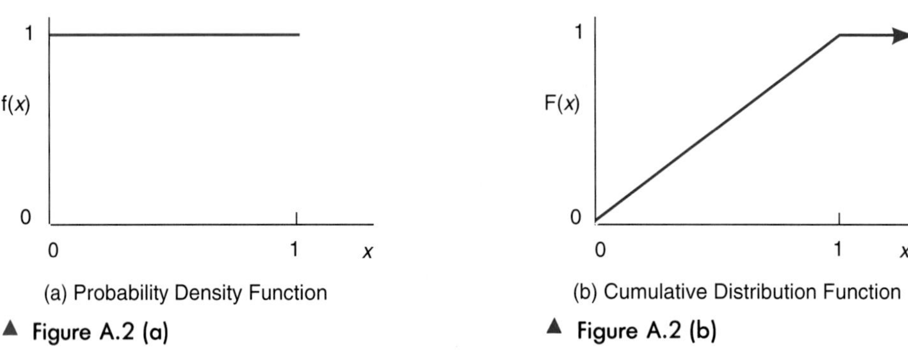

(a) Probability Density Function

▲ Figure A.2 (a)

(b) Cumulative Distribution Function

▲ Figure A.2 (b)

Example 6: The Exponential Distribution. The exponential distribution is used to describe the interarrival time between events in most queuing systems (Chapter 17). It is a one-parameter distribution. The parameter is typically denoted by λ. The pdf takes the form

$$f(x) = 0 \qquad (x < 0)$$
$$= \lambda e^{-\lambda x} \qquad (0 \le x)$$

Using the definition for the CDF we see that

$$F(x) = 0 \qquad (x < 0)$$
$$= 1 - e^{-\lambda x} \qquad (0 \le x)$$

Figure A.3 shows the pdf and the CDF for an exponential distribution with parameter $\lambda = 1$.

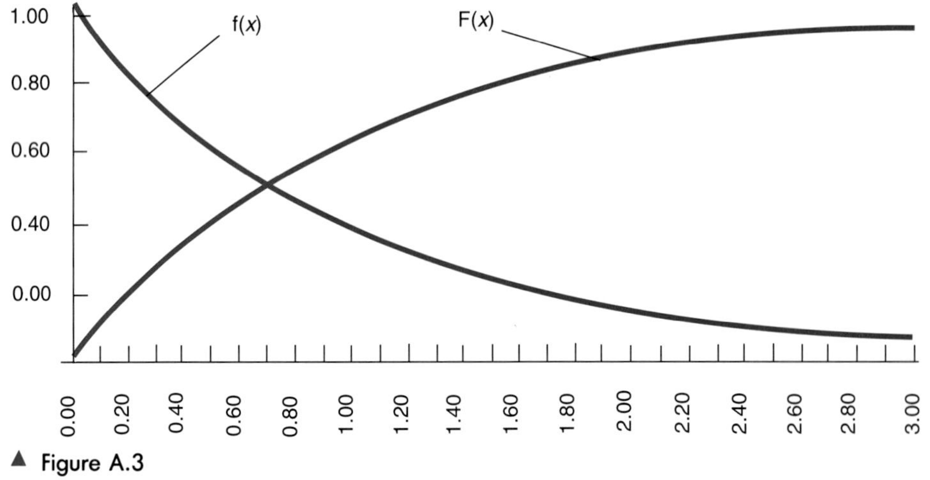

▲ Figure A.3

Example 7: The Normal Distribution. The normal distribution plays a fundamental role in probability and statistics. In this text, it occurs in a number of places—for example, it is used to represent uncertain demand in Chapters 13 and 16, as well as the probability that a project will be completed by a specific time in Chapter 15.

The normal is a two-parameter distribution. The parameters are μ, the mean, and σ, the standard deviation, which is required to be greater than 0. There is, of course, a mathematical expression for the density function of a normal pdf, but we will not show it here since we never make direct use of this expression. The pdf of the normal distribution is not integrable in closed form—that is,

$$\int_{-\infty}^{x} f(r)dr$$

cannot be written as a combination of elementary functions of x, when $f(r)$ is a normal distribution. Tables such as Table A.0 are used to evaluate $F(x)$, the CDF, for the normal distribution (represented graphically in Figure A.4). The next section is devoted to using Table A.0 to determine values for normal probabilities.

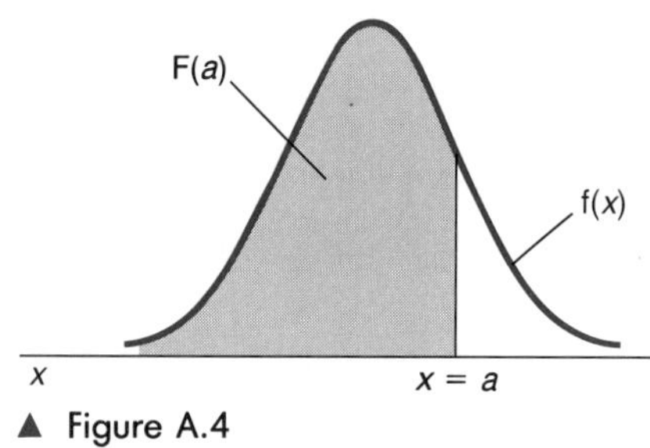

▲ Figure A.4

D. Using the Normal Table

The Standard Normal Distribution. Table A.0 can be used to find values for the CDF, $F(x)$, of a normal distribution with mean μ and standard deviation σ. (See Section IV, below, for a definition of μ and σ.) Actually, the table provides values for $F(x)$ for a normal distribution with $\mu = 0$ and $\sigma = 1$. (In a moment we will show how this table can be used to find values for the CDF of any normal distribution.) The values in the body of Table A.0 are the probability that a standard normal random variable (SNRV) takes on a value between the mean, 0, and the value of z shown in the row and column headings. Thus by looking in the row 0.4 and the column 0.05, we discover that a SNRV takes on a value between 0 and 0.45 with probability 0.1736.

Using this table and the fact that an SNRV is symmetrical about the mean allows us to find the probability that an SNRV falls into any range of numbers. Here are some examples (referring to the accompanying figure may provide some visual help in understanding the calculations).

$$\text{Prob}\{\text{SNRV} \leq 0.45\} = 0.5 + 0.1736 = 0.6736$$

$$\text{Prob}\{\text{SNRV} > 0.45\} = 1.0 - 0.6736 = 0.3264$$

$$\text{Prob}\{\text{SNRV} \leq -0.45\} = 0.5 - 0.1736 = 0.3264$$

You have probably observed that there are many different ways to calculate these results. For example, we knew that Prob{SNRV $\leq -0.45\} = 0.3264$ from the facts that Prob{SNRV $> 0.45\} = 0.3264$ and that the normal distribution is symmetrical about the mean.

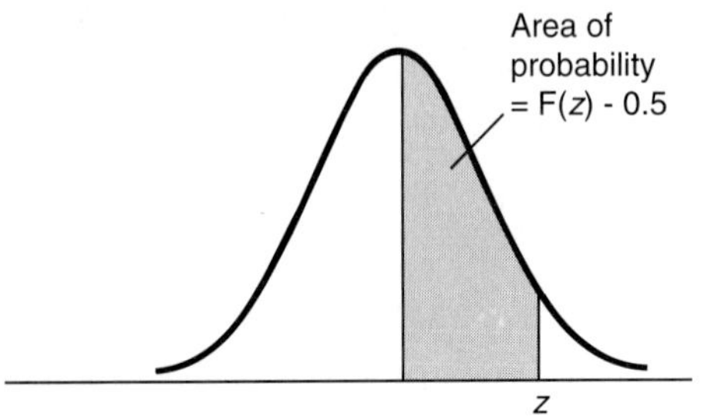

TABLE A.0
Areas for the Standard Normal Distribution

ENTRIES IN THE TABLE GIVE THE *AREA* UNDER THE CURVE BETWEEN THE MEAN AND Z STANDARD DEVIATIONS ABOVE THE MEAN. FOR EXAMPLE, FOR Z = 1.25 THE AREA UNDER THE CURVE BETWEEN THE MEAN AND Z IS 0.3944.

z	0.00	0.01	0.02	0.03	0.04	0.05	0.06	0.07	0.08	0.09
0.0	0.0000	0.0040	0.0080	0.0120	0.0160	0.0199	0.0239	0.0279	0.0319	0.0359
0.1	0.0398	0.0438	0.0478	0.0517	0.0557	0.0596	0.0636	0.0675	0.0714	0.0753
0.2	0.0793	0.0832	0.0871	0.0910	0.0948	0.0987	0.1026	0.1064	0.1103	0.1141
0.3	0.1179	0.1217	0.1255	0.1293	0.1331	0.1368	0.1406	0.1443	0.1480	0.1517
0.4	0.1554	0.1591	0.1628	0.1664	0.1700	0.1736	0.1772	0.1808	0.1844	0.1879
0.5	0.1915	0.1950	0.1985	0.2019	0.2054	0.2088	0.2123	0.2157	0.2190	0.2224
0.6	0.2257	0.2291	0.2324	0.2357	0.2389	0.2422	0.2454	0.2486	0.2518	0.2549
0.7	0.2580	0.2612	0.2642	0.2673	0.2704	0.2734	0.2764	0.2794	0.2823	0.2852
0.8	0.2881	0.2910	0.2939	0.2967	0.2995	0.3023	0.3051	0.3078	0.3106	0.3133
0.9	0.3159	0.3186	0.3212	0.3238	0.3264	0.3289	0.3315	0.3340	0.3365	0.3389
1.0	0.3413	0.3438	0.3461	0.3485	0.3508	0.3531	0.3554	0.3577	0.3599	0.3621
1.1	0.3643	0.3665	0.3686	0.3708	0.3729	0.3749	0.3770	0.3790	0.3810	0.3830
1.2	0.3849	0.3869	0.3888	0.3907	0.3925	0.3944	0.3962	0.3980	0.3997	0.4015
1.3	0.4032	0.4049	0.4066	0.4082	0.4099	0.4115	0.4131	0.4147	0.4162	0.4177
1.4	0.4192	0.4207	0.4222	0.4236	0.4251	0.4265	0.4279	0.4292	0.4306	0.4319
1.5	0.4332	0.4345	0.4357	0.4370	0.4382	0.4394	0.4406	0.4418	0.4429	0.4441
1.6	0.4452	0.4463	0.4474	0.4484	0.4495	0.4505	0.4515	0.4525	0.4535	0.4545
1.7	0.4554	0.4564	0.4573	0.4582	0.4591	0.4599	0.4608	0.4616	0.4625	0.4633
1.8	0.4641	0.4649	0.4656	0.4664	0.4671	0.4678	0.4686	0.4693	0.4699	0.4706
1.9	0.4713	0.4719	0.4726	0.4732	0.4738	0.4744	0.4750	0.4756	0.4761	0.4767
2.0	0.4772	0.4778	0.4783	0.4788	0.4793	0.4798	0.4803	0.4808	0.4812	0.4817
2.1	0.4821	0.4826	0.4830	0.4834	0.4838	0.4842	0.4846	0.4850	0.4854	0.4857
2.2	0.4861	0.4864	0.4868	0.4871	0.4875	0.4878	0.4881	0.4884	0.4887	0.4890
2.3	0.4893	0.4896	0.4898	0.4901	0.4904	0.4906	0.4909	0.4911	0.4913	0.4916
2.4	0.4918	0.4920	0.4922	0.4925	0.4927	0.4929	0.4931	0.4932	0.4934	0.4936
2.5	0.4938	0.4940	0.4941	0.4943	0.4945	0.4946	0.4948	0.4949	0.4951	0.4952
2.6	0.4953	0.4955	0.4956	0.4957	0.4959	0.4960	0.4961	0.4962	0.4963	0.4964
2.7	0.4965	0.4966	0.4967	0.4968	0.4969	0.4970	0.4971	0.4972	0.4973	0.4974
2.8	0.4974	0.4975	0.4976	0.4977	0.4977	0.4978	0.4979	0.4979	0.4980	0.4981
2.9	0.4981	0.4982	0.4982	0.4983	0.4984	0.4984	0.4985	0.4985	0.4986	0.4986
3.0	0.4986	0.4987	0.4987	0.4988	0.4988	0.4989	0.4989	0.4989	0.4990	0.4990

Reprinted with permission from Richard I. Levin and Charles A. Kirkpatrick, *Quantitative Approaches to Management, 3rd Edition*, McGraw-Hill, Inc., New York, NY, 1975.

Any Normal Random Variable. Let NRV be a normal random variable with mean μ and standard deviation σ. To find the probability that this random variable falls into a range of values, we make use of this fundamental relationship.

$$\text{Prob}\{\text{NRV} \leq x\} = \text{Prob}\{\text{SNRV} \leq (x - \mu)/\sigma\}$$

Here is an example. Suppose that NRV has $\mu = 50$ and $\sigma = 100$ and we want to find the probability that NRV ≤ 95. We proceed as follows:

$$\text{Prob}\{\text{NRV} \leq 95\} = \text{Prob}\{\text{SNRV} \leq (95-50)/100\}$$
$$= \text{Prob}\{\text{SNRV} \leq 0.45\} = 0.6736.$$

This procedure becomes second nature with a little practice.

IV. Expected Values

The expected cost or profit is often the objective in decisions under uncertainty—that is, in decision problems in which the payoff from a decision is a random variable. We first introduce the expected value of a random variable and then turn to the expected value of a function of a random variable.

A. Expected Value of a Random Variable

The expected value of a random variable—say, X—is typically written E(X). It is called the mean of the random variable, typically denoted with the Greek letter μ. We will define E(X) for both discrete and continuous random variables.

Discrete Random Variables. For a discrete random variable where f(x) is the probability mass function,

$$E(X) = \mu = \sum_{-\infty}^{\infty} x f(x)$$

Here are some examples.

Example 1 (continued): Discrete Uniform Distribution.

$$E(X) = 1\left(\frac{1}{6}\right) + 2\left(\frac{1}{6}\right) + 3\left(\frac{1}{6}\right) + 4\left(\frac{1}{6}\right) + 5\left(\frac{1}{6}\right) + 6\left(\frac{1}{6}\right) = 3.5$$

It is interesting to note that the expected value of a random variable does not have to be one of the values that the random variable can assume. For example, a die cannot take on the value 3.5. A physical interpretation is that the expected value is the center of gravity of the probability mass function. That is, if you think of the probabilities in a pmf as weights and place a fulcrum under the expected value, the pmf will balance. The expected value has a second intuitive interpretation. Think of a series of independent observations of a random variable. If you calculate the average of the values, you expect it to be close to the expected value.

Example 2 (continued): Arbitrary Discrete Distribution.

$$E(X) = 23\left(\frac{2}{5}\right) + 37\left(\frac{3}{5}\right) = 31.4$$

Example 3 (continued): Binomial Distribution. Here we state without providing a proof that for a binomial random variable, X, with parameters n and p,

$$E(X) = np$$

This result is intuitively appealing. If we flip a fair coin ten times, on the average we would expect to observe five heads.

Example 4 (continued): Poisson Distribution. The expected value of the Poisson distribution is M. The variance is M as well. These results are easily derived, but the derivations are not central to our purpose.

Continuous Random Variables. The definition of the expected value of a continuous random variable is essentially the same as for the discrete case. Here, however, we must use the pdf and integration, that is

$$E(X) = \int_{-\infty}^{\infty} x\, f(x)\, dx$$

Example 5 (continued): Continuous Uniform Distribution.

$$E(X) = \int_0^1 x \cdot 1 \cdot dx = \frac{x^2}{2}\bigg|_0^1 = \frac{1}{2}$$

It is easy to see that $\frac{1}{2}$ is the center of gravity for the density function shown in Figure A.2(a).

Example 6 (continued): Exponential Distribution.

$$E(X) = \int_0^{\infty} x\lambda e^{-\lambda x} dx = 1/\lambda$$

This integration requires a technique called integration by parts, and the details have been omitted.

B. Expected Value of a Function of a Random Variable

The General Concept. Let G(x) be any function defined on x. Then for a discrete random variable X with pmf f(x), the expected value of G(x), E[G(X)], is defined as follows:

$$E[G(X)] = \sum_{x=-\infty}^{\infty} G(x)f(x)$$

A similar definition using integrals holds for continuous random variables.

We have two main reasons for being interested in the expected value of functions of random variables. One is to define the variance of a random variable and the other is to define expected costs or profits. These topics are discussed in the following sections.

Variance and Standard Deviation of a Random Variable. The variance is a measure of dispersion of the distribution of a random variable. It is typically denoted as σ^2 and is defined as follows:

$$\mathrm{Var}(X) = \sigma^2 = E[(X-E(X))^2] = \sum_{-\infty}^{\infty}(x-E(X))^2 f(x)$$

The variance plays an important role in statistics. It is the most popular measure of dispersion of the distribution of a random variable, and it is one of the two parameters of the normal distribution (see Example 7 above). To develop a feeling for the interpretation of variance as a measure of dispersion, consider two random variables X and Y. Let $f_X(x)$ be the pmf for X and $f_Y(y)$ be the pmf for Y. Let

$$\begin{aligned} f_X(x) &= \frac{1}{2} \qquad (x = 4, 6) \\ &= 0 \qquad \text{(otherwise)} \end{aligned}$$

and

$$\begin{aligned} f_Y(y) &= \frac{1}{2} \qquad (y = 1, 9) \\ &= 0 \qquad \text{(otherwise)} \end{aligned}$$

You should be able to verify that $\text{Var}(X) = \sigma^2 = 1$ and $\text{Var}(Y) = \sigma^2 = 16$. The intuitive notion is that a random variable that has a greater probability of being further from the mean will have a larger variance. That notion is consistent with this example.

The standard deviation, typically denoted by σ, is simply the square root of the variance, that is,

$$\text{Standard Deviation of } X = (\text{Variance of } X)^{1/2}$$

or

$$\sigma = (\sigma^2)^{1/2}$$

C. Expected Return

In most business applications, management is interested in the returns (or costs) associated with the occurrence of a random event.

Discrete Random Variables. To calculate the expected return, we let $R(x)$ be the return if the random variable x occurs and use the standard definition for the expected value of a function of a random variable.

$$E[R(X)] = \sum_{x=-\infty}^{\infty} R(x)f(x)$$

Example 1 (continued): Discrete Uniform Distribution. A gambler offers to pay you $10 times the value of the face of the die that is showing if a 3, 4, 5, or 6 occurs and nothing if a 1 or 2 occurs. What is the expected value of this game?

x	R(x)	f(x)	R(x)f(x)
1	0	$\frac{1}{6}$	0
2	0	$\frac{1}{6}$	0
3	30	$\frac{1}{6}$	5
4	40	$\frac{1}{6}$	$6\frac{2}{3}$
5	50	$\frac{1}{6}$	$8\frac{1}{3}$
6	60	$\frac{1}{6}$	10
Expected value = $\sum R(x)f(x)$ = **30**			

Continuous Random Variables. The concept of finding the expected value of the function R(X) remains the same as in the discrete case. As usual, in the continuous case we must use integration and the pdf.

Example 5 (continued): Continuous Uniform Distribution. We will observe a random variable from a continuous uniform distribution on the interval 0 to 1. A gambler offers to pay 0 if the value is between 0 and 0.2 and \$10 times the value of the random variable if the value is greater than 0.2 and less than or equal to 1. It follows that

$$\begin{aligned} \mathrm{R}(x) &= 0 \qquad && (x \le 0.2) \\ &= 10x && (0.2 < x \le 1) \end{aligned}$$

Then

$$\begin{aligned} \mathrm{E}[\mathrm{R}(x)] &= \int_0^{.2} 0 \cdot 1 \cdot dx + \int_{.2}^{1} 10x \cdot 1 \cdot dx = 10\left(\frac{x^2}{2}\right)\Bigg|_{.2}^{1} \\ &= 4.8 \end{aligned}$$

V. Multivariate Distributions

This section introduces the mathematics and the concepts that are used when there is more than one random variable under consideration. Such situations are common in practice. In a PERT network (Chapter 15), the time required to complete a path in a project is equal to the sum of the times required to complete each activity on that path. Similarly, the return from a portfolio of stocks (Chapter 8) is equal to the sum of the returns of the individual stocks held in the portfolio.

Multivariate random variables are introduced in Appendix 14.2 in the discussion of Bayes's Theorem, although the term multivariate is not mentioned there. It will be useful to refer to that discussion in what follows.

A. Joint Distributions

Discrete Random Variables. It is useful to introduce some new notation in the discussion of multivariate random variables. Let

$\mathrm{f}_{X,Y}(x, y)$ = the probability that the random variable X takes on the value x *and* the random variable Y takes on the value y.

Then $\mathrm{f}_{X,Y}(x, y)$ is the *joint* probability mass function for the random variables X and Y. The word "and" is important in this definition. It indicates that both events (x, y) must happen.

The following game is introduced in Appendix 14.2.

1. A fair die is thrown.
2. The value of the die is used to determine from which of three urns we will draw a ball. Assume that each of the balls in a given urn is equally likely to be drawn.

The details are summarized in the following table.

DIE	URN	CONTENTS OF URN
1	1	28 White and 72 Black Balls
2 or 3	2	40 White and 60 Black Balls
4 or 5 or 6	3	92 White and 8 Black Balls

This game can now be used to illustrate a joint pmf. Let X be the value of the urn chosen; $Y = 1$ if a white ball is selected and $Y = 2$ if a black ball is selected. The values for $f_{X,Y}(x,y)$ are presented below.

X	Y = 1	Y = 2
1	(1/6)(28/100) = .0467	(1/6)(72/100) = .12
2	(2/6)(40/100) = .1333	(2/6)(60/100) = .10
3	(3/6)(92/100) = .4600	(3/6)(8/100) = .04

These values were derived from the definition of conditional probability:

$$f_{X,Y}(x,y) = f_X(x)f_{Y|X}(y|x)$$

A discussion of this relationship can be found in Appendix 14.2.

Continuous Random Variables. Multivariate distributions also exist for continuous random variables. Indeed, the equation that defines the relationship between joint and conditional probabilities is used to define joint probability density functions and conditional probability density functions.

B. Independent Random Variables

Two random variables, X and Y, are independent if

$$f_{X,Y}(x,y) = f_X(x)\, f_Y(y)$$

Since in general

$$f_{X,Y}(x,y) = f_{X|Y}(x|y)\, f_Y(y)$$

we see that X and Y are independent if

$$f_{X|Y}(x|y) = f_X(x)$$

The last equation says that knowing that the random variable Y takes on the value y tells us nothing about the probability that X will take on the value x. In other words, X and Y are independent.

C. Expectation and Variance of Sums

The Expected Value of $X + Y$. It is always true (whether X and Y are independent or not) that

$$E(X+Y) = E(X) + E(Y)$$

The Variance of *X*+*Y*. The variance of $(X+Y)$ is defined as follows:

$$\text{Var}(X+Y) = \text{Var}(X) + \text{Var}(Y) + 2\text{Cov}(X,Y)$$

or

$$\sigma^2_{(X+Y)} = \sigma^2_X + \sigma^2_Y + 2\sigma_{XY}$$

The Covariance of *X* and *Y*. In the previous expression, $\text{Cov}(X,Y)$ is the covariance of X and Y. It is denoted by σ_{XY} and is itself defined as follows:

$$\text{Cov}(X,Y) = \sigma_{XY} = \text{E}([X-\text{E}(X)][Y-\text{E}(Y)])$$

The covariance of X and Y is an indication of how X and Y relate to each other, but it is difficult to have an intuitive feeling for what a particular value of the covariance means. The correlation coefficient is better suited to convey this. Note, however, that when X and Y are independent random variables $\sigma_{XY} = 0$.

The Correlation Coefficient of *X* and *Y*. The correlation coefficient of X and Y is typically denoted as ρ_{XY} and is defined as follows

$$\rho_{XY} = \frac{\text{Cov}(X,Y)}{[\text{StdDev}(X)]\,[\text{StdDev}(Y)]} = \frac{\sigma_{XY}}{\sigma_X\sigma_Y}$$

The correlation coefficient can take on values from -1 to 1. A large positive value suggests that X and Y tend to move together—that is, when X is large then Y is apt to be large as well. Negative values suggest that X and Y move in opposite directions—that is, when X is large Y is apt to be small. If $\sigma_{XY} = 0$, X and Y are said to be uncorrelated.

The Expectation and Variance for the Sum of Several Random Variables. Let

$$Z = \sum_{i=1}^{N} X_i$$

That is, Z is the sum of N random variables $X_1, X_2, \ldots, X_N$. Then

$$\text{E}(Z) = \sum_{i=1}^{N} \text{E}(X_i)$$

In words, the expected value of a sum equals the sum of the expected values.

$$\text{Var}(Z) = \sum_{i=1}^{N} \text{Var}(X_i) + 2\sum_{i=1}^{N-1}\sum_{j>i}^{N} \text{Cov}(X_i,X_j)$$

In words, the variance of the sum is equal to the sum of the variances plus two times the sum of the covariances of all possible pairs of random variables.

LINDO

LOADING, RUNNING, PRINTING

Run LINDO directly from your floppy drive by placing the disk in the A: drive and typing the following commands to DOS:

A:	(make A drive the default)
LINDO	(start up the program)

To install *LINDO* on your hard disk in a subdirectory called *LINDO*, give the following commands:

C:	(make hard disk the default)
**CD **	(go to the root directory)
MD LINDO	(make LINDO subdir)
CD LINDO	(go to new LINDO subdir)
COPY A:*.*	(copy LINDO software)

You may run the program by typing:

C:
CD \LINDO
LINDO

If you're already in the proper subdirectory, just type **LINDO**.

MacLINDO

MacLINDO can be run from the floppy drive by double-clicking on the *MacLINDO* icon which appears on your screen after inserting the disk.

You should first create a *LINDO* folder by double-clicking on your hard disk icon, which appears in the upper right corner of the desktop, and choosing "**New Folder**" from the "*File*" menu. The new folder will appear under the name "**Empty Folder.**" Type "*LINDO*" to rename it.

To copy the program into the new folder on your hard disk, insert your diskette into a floppy drive, choose "**Select All**" from the file menu, and drag all selected items into the new folder on the hard disk.

Double-click the *MacLINDO* icon to start from the hard disk.

Printing

To print output from *LINDO* you should first send the output to a file. The file may then be read by a text editor and printed. For example, to create a report file called *MYREPORT* containing the formulation and solution, you would give the following commands in *LINDO*:

DIVERT MYREPORT	!OPEN OUTPUT FILE
LOOK ALL	!SEND FORMULATION TO THE FILE
GO	!SOLVE MODEL
YES	!ASK FOR RANGE ANALYSIS
RVRT	!CLOSE OUTPUT FILE

You may then start your text editor, open *MYREPORT*, and print the file with the editor's print command. While in *LINDO/PC*, you may print the current screen by holding down the shift key and pressing the PrintScreen key. **DIVERT PRN** will cause subsequent high volume output to go directly to the printer; **RVRT** stops it.

If your Mac is connected to an Imagewriter, Command-Shift-4 prints the screen; if connected to a LaserWriter, Command-Shift-3 saves the current screen to a Mac-Paint file called ScreenN, where N is a number from 0 to 10. If "Screen 0" already exists, the next created file will be called "Screen1." Once 10 such files have been created, no more may be created until earlier ones are deleted, moved, or renamed.

THE LINDO COMMAND SET

LINDO displays a " : " prompt when a command is expected. A "?" indicates that user input is appropriate. " ! " is used to begin a comment line.

Three *LINDO* commands can be used to summon help: **HELP, CATEGORIES** (or **CAT** for short), and **COMMANDS** (or COM). **HELP** followed by a given command name will yield a description of the command. **HELP** gives general information if not followed by a command name. **CAT** will list first the categories and then the commands in a specified category. To list all available commands in their categories (input, output, etc.), use **COM**.

The commands available as of 1991 as listed by **COMMAND** are:

1. *Information*

HELP	Gives help in various situations
COM	Lists commands by category
LOCAL	Gives info specific to your local installation
CAT	Lists categories of commands
TIME	Displays cumulative time of current LINDO session

2. *Input*

MAX/MIN	Start natural input
RETR	Retrieve old problem from file
RMPS	Retrieve an MPS format file
TAKE	Take terminal input from a file
LEAVE	Terminate the previous TAKE
RDBC	Retrieve old solution

3. *Display*

LOOK	Print (part of) problem in natural format
SOLUTION	Print standard solution report
RANGE	Print RANGE analysis report
PICTURE	Print logical PICTURE of matrix
SHOCOLUMN	Display a column of the problem
TABLEAU	Print current tableau
NONZEROES	Print nonzero variables solution report
BPICTURE	Print logical PICTURE of basis
CPRI	Print column information
RPRI	Print row information

4. *File output*

SAVE	Save current problem to file
DIVERT	Divert output to file
RVRT	Revert output to terminal
SDBC	Save solution in database format
SMPS	Save current problem in MPS format

5. ***Solution***

GO	Go solve the problem
PIVOT	Do the next simplex pivot

6. ***Problem editing***

ALTER	Alter some element of current problem
EXT	Extend problem by adding constraints
DEL	Delete a specified constraint
SUB	Enter a Simple Upper Bound for a variable
APPC	Append a new column to the formulation
SLB	Enter a Simple Lower Bound for a variable
FREE	Declare a variable unconstrained in sign
EDIT	Invoke *LINDO's* full-screen editor

7. ***Integer, quadratic, and parametric programs***

INT	Identify integer variables
QCP	Quadratic programming
PARA	Parametric programming
POSD	Check positive definiteness
TITAN	Tighten an IP
BIP	Set IP bound on optimal solution
GIN	Identify general integer variables
IPTOL	Set IP tolerance on optimal solution

8. ***Conversational Parameters***

WIDTH	Set terminal width
TERSE	Set conversational style to terse
VERBOSE	Set conversational style to verbose (default)
BATCH	Tell LINDO that this is a batch run
PAGE	Set page/screen size
PAUSE	Pause for keyboard action

9. ***User supplied subroutines*** (not included in Student Edition)

~~**USER**~~	~~Call user written subroutine~~

10. ***Miscellaneous***

INVERT	Invert current basis to get more accurate answers
STAT	Print matrix summary statistics
BUG	How to report a bug in the LINDO program
DEBUG	Help in debugging an infeasible model
SET	Used to set obscure solution parameters
TITLE	Assigns title to current formulation or returns current title

11. ***Quit***

QUIT	Quits *LINDO*

THE COMMANDS IN DEPTH

Many *LINDO* commands are self-explanatory; for instance, it would be difficult (although perhaps tempting after a long day) to interpret the **QUIT** command as an injunction to shut down the computer, give notice, and head for home. Commands such as **QUIT**, **GO**, and the **HELP** commands, will therefore require little exposition.

The meaning and use of many other commands, however, may not be intuitively obvious; and in many cases commands take parameters, may be typed in abbreviated form, or have other idiosyncrasies, knowledge of which will speed the modeling process. These commands are explained below, by category.

1. INFORMATION

TIME

Returns the cumulative time of the cuurent *LINDO* session. Useful in determining the time needed to solve or display a solution. For instance, in **TERSE** mode (to avoid output intervening between TIME readouts), enter **TIME**, then **GO**, then **TIME** again. The difference between the two TIME returns gives solution time.

2. INPUT

MAX/MIN

Begins input of a problem formulation, indicates that the objective function is to be Maximized or Minimized, and removes any previous formulation and solution report from memory, once a return is entered at the end of the line. Also entered as a value to the parameter DIR under ALTER, q.v. END is entered to indicate the end of problem input.

RETRIEVE Syntax: RETRIEVE <path:fileName>

May be abbreviated **RETR**. Retrieves a problem saved in *LINDO's* compressed format with the **SAVE** command, q.v. **RETRIEVE** typed alone will yield the standard file dialog (see **TAKE**); in DOS only, wildcards may be entered to limit the display. In the Macintosh environment, only compressed format files will be visible. Entering the entire path as argument will bypass the file dialog.

RMPS Syntax: RMPS <path:fileName>

Opens a file saved in the industry standard MPS format. See **SMPS**.

TAKE Syntax: TAKE <path:fileName>

Allows you to take commands from a standard ASCII file created in a text editor.

For DOS: Implements a standard DOS file search.The simple command **TAKE** will display a screen showing all files in the default directory and allowing you to select one and input it. **TAKE C:mydir*.*** will display all files in the directory mydir on the C drive.

For MAC: **TAKE** alone displays the standard Macintosh file dialog; only text files will be displayed. **TAKE** followed by a filename will attempt to **TAKE** that file if it is in the current directory. If it is not in the current directory, the message **UNSUCCESSFUL OPEN** is displayed. **TAKE** followed by a complete pathname and the filename will attempt to take the file specified. A colon must separate path elements; wildcard characters are not allowed in the Mac file search.

In either environment: if an invalid command is encountered in the **TAKE** file, the **TAKE** operation is stopped where the invalid command was encountered and the message **INVALID COMMAND: <command>** is displayed. If the first command is invalid, no **TAKE** is performed. To see the **TAKE** file as it is input, see **BATCH**.

LEAVE

Used to terminate a **TAKE** file.

RDBC Syntax: RDBC <path:fileName>

RDBC reads the contents of an SDBC created file. LINDO attempts to "install" the solution found in the SDBC file into the current formulation. This may provide a good starting point for solving the current model if the SDBC file was saved from a very similar one. Note, however, that even if the two formulations are identical, several pivots may be required when GO is typed after the RDBC is read in; this is because the SDBC file does not contain information about dual prices. RDBC typed alone will yield the standard file dialog, prompting the entry of the filename.

3. DISPLAY

LOOK Syntax: LOOK <rowNumber-rowNumber | all>

Look at an area of the problem. If **LOOK** is typed alone, *LINDO* asks for a row specification. Some responses might be 3, or 1-2, or ALL, causing, respectively, row 3, or rows 1 through 2 or all the rows to be printed to the screen.

SOLUTION

May be abbreviated **SOLU**. Displays the solution to a model.

RANGE

Causes the Range Analysis report to be displayed.

PICTURE

Displays logical **PICTURE** of the matrix. May be abbreviated PIC.

SHOCOLUMN Syntax: SHOCOLUMN <variableName>

May be abbreviated **SHOC**. Displays all information about a given column (i.e., a given variable).

TABLEAU

May be abbreviated **TABL**. Displays the Simplex Tableau of the current formulation.

NONZEROES

Displays all nonzero variables (and their values) in the solution report of the present formulation.

BPICTURE

Displays logical **PICTURE** of the basis. May be abbreviated BPIC.

CPRI/RPRI Syntax: CPRI | RPRI<printList> : <conditions>

Allows you to display columns/rows which satisfy specified conditions and print various attributes of the columns/rows. Symbols for column and row attributes are:

N	Name
P	Primal value (slack for rows)
D	Dual value (reduced cost for columns)
R	Rim (objective coefficient for columns; RHS for rows)
U	simple Upper bound
L	simple Lower bound
T	type ("C", "I", or "F"; "<", "=", or ">")
Z	number of nonzeroes in a column or row
%	wild card character in names

Other symbols are:

Arithmetic	*Logical*	*Relational*	*Order*
+ - / ^	**AND.**	< > = #	( )
LOG( ) EXP( )	**OR.**		
ABS( )	**NOT.**		

Example: **CPRI N P : P > 0** prints names and values of variables greater than zero.

4. FILE OUTPUT

SAVE Syntax: SAVE <path:fileName>

Saves problem in *LINDO's* own compressed file format. **SAVE** typed alone yields file dialog, prompting entry of a filename. Entering the entire path as argument bypasses file dialog.

DIVERT Syntax: DIVERT <path:fileName>

Diverts all high volume output to a text file. Objective function value is still displayed on screen. **DIVERT** typed alone yields the standard file dialog, prompting entry of the file name. Entering the entire path as argument bypasses the file dialog. May be abbreviated **DIVE**.

RVRT

Undo preceding **DIVERT**, restoring subsequent output to screen.

SDBC Syntax: SDBC <path:fileName>

A file saved with **SDBC** is best used by **RDBC** to get a "running start" when solving a slight modification of the same problem in a later session. SDBC saves a file describing the columns part of the solution, containing one line for each column (i.e., variable) and one for the objective. Each line contains the variable name, current value, reduced cost, type (C, I, or F for continuous, integer or free), and simple upper (not lower) bound. **SDBC** typed alone will yield the standard file dialog, prompting the entry of the filename. Entering the entire path as argument will bypass the file dialog.

SMPS Syntax: SMPS <path:fileName>

Save the current problem as an **MPS** file: the machine independent industry standard format for transferring LP problems between *LINDO* and other LP programs. **SMPS** typed alone will yield the standard file dialog, prompting the entry of the filename. Entering the entire path as argument will bypass the file dialog.

5. SOLUTION

GO

GO solve the problem.

PIVOT

Causes *LINDO* to perform the next step in the solution process; solves LP's step-by-step.

6. PROBLEM EDITING

ALTER Syntax : ALTER<row> <variableName | dir |rhs>

Alter an element of the current problem. If **ALTER** is typed alone, *LINDO* will ask for a row, then a variable in that row, then a new coefficient for that variable. If **ALTER 2** is typed, *LINDO* will ask for the name of the variable to alter, then the new coefficient for the variable. If **ALTER 2 X** is typed, *LINDO* will ask for the new coefficient for the variable named X in row 2. If **ALTER 2 DIR** is typed, LINDO will ask **NEW DIRECTION?** "<", ">", and "=" are acceptable answers. If **ALTER 2 RHS** is typed, *LINDO* will ask **NEW COEFFICIENT?** At this point you may enter the new coefficient for the right-hand-side of the row.

In **ALTER**ing row 1, the objective function, using the argument **DIR** will cause *LINDO* to ask **NEW DIRECTION**? **MAX** and **MIN** are acceptable answers. **ALT** is acceptable as an abbreviation.

EXT

Add a constraint to the formulation. **END** is entered to indicate the end of new input.

DEL Syntax: DEL <row>

Deletes the given row. In the absence of a specification, the program asks for one. Only one row may be deleted at a time.

SUB Syntax: SUB <variableName> <Upper Bound>

Allows you to enter a Simple Upper Bound on a variable. If only SUB is typed, LINDO asks for the variable and the bound. The variable and its bound are noted at the end of the formulation.

APPC Syntax: APPC <variableName>

Add a variable (APPend a Column) to the formulation. If **APPC FRED** is typed, *LINDO* will display a "?" prompt and await a row specification; once the row specification is entered, the program will prompt with **COEF**, at which point FRED's coefficient for that row should be entered. If **APPC** alone is typed, *LINDO* will ask **NAME** before proceeding as above. (Variables may also be added through use of the **ALTER** command.)

SLB Syntax: SLB <variableName> <Lower Bound>

Allows you to enter a Simple Lower Bound on a variable. If only **SLB** is typed, *LINDO* asks for the variable and the bound. The variable and its bound are noted at the end of the formulation.

FREE Syntax: FREE <variableName>

Renders the specified variable unconstrained in sign.

EDIT

Invokes *LINDO's* full-screen editor. Line numbers, supplied by the editor.for help in navigating,are for reference only. They are not part of the model. When you press the Esc key in edit mode, *LINDO* will try to compile (make sense of) your model. For most keys other than the arrow keys, pressing a key when in edit mode will cause the character associated with that key to be inserted at the cursor position. The effects of other special keys are summarized in the following table.

KEY	*EFFECT*
→	Moves cursor right one character
←	Moves cursor left one character
↑	Moves cursor up one line
↓	Moves cursor down one line
Home	Moves cursor to beginning
End	Moves cursor to end
PageUp	Moves cursor up one screen
PageDown	Moves cursor down one screen
Ctrl S	Moves cursor to start of current line
Ctrl E	Moves cursor to end of current line
Ctrl Æ	Moves cursor to end of current word
Ctrl ¨	Moves cursor to beginning of current word
Delete	Deletes character at current cursor position
Enter	Inserts a carriage return at current cursor position
Insert	Inserts a carriage return at current cursor position
Backspace	Deletes character to the left of cursor
Esc	Exit the editor and try to interpret edited model
Ctrl Break	Exit the editor without interpreting edited model

7. INTEGER, QUADRATIC, AND PARAMETRIC PROGRAMS

INTEGER Syntax:INTEGER<variableName | numberOfVariables>

Declares a variable or series of variables to be 0/1.The first form identifies the named variable only. The second form identifies the first *numberOf Variables* variables in the current formulation as being 0/1. The order of the variables is determined by their order in the input and is as listed in the solution report. If the user knows the exact order of the variables the second form requires less typing.

QCP Syntax: QCP <row>

Used after entering a Quadratic program to specify the row which contains the first real constraint.

PARARHS Syntax: PARARHS <row> <value>

PARARHS, abbreviated **PARA**, allows the value of the right-hand-side of a given row to be changed; thereupon the new objective value, dual price, and **RHS** are displayed along with their original values. Variables whose values have increased from zero as a result of the RHS change are listed under **VAR IN**; variables whose values have been driven to zero as a result of the RHS change are listed under **VAR OUT.** The number of the row whose constraint forced the variable into or out of the solution is listed under **PIVOT ROW**.

POSD

In Quadratic programs POSD ascertains the definiteness of the submatrix corresponding to the quadratic part of the objective. If the matrix is found by **POSD** not to be symmetric, **POSD** identifies the elements in violation; it is useful in debugging a quadratic programming model. **POSD** will ascertain whether the submatrix is a) indefinite (neither convex or concave), b) positive definite (convex), c) negative definite (concave), d) positive semidefinite (loosely convex), or e) negative semidefinite (loosely concave). **POSD** should be applied to any quadratic program on first developing the model.

TITAN

It is important that IP formulations be "tight": when the model is solved as an LP, the solution should be similar to the IP solution. Many of the IP variables should be naturally integer and the LP objective value should be approximately equal to the IP objective value. **TITAN** will do some of this tightening. It finds tighter upper bounds for continuous variables and then, using this information, lowers the coefficients of integer variables where justified. The nonzero IP variables will be closer to 1 than they otherwise would have been, when the modified problem is solved as an LP.

BIP Syntax: BIP <boundOnSolution>

Knowing a good, but not necessarily optimal solution to an IP, allows the reduction of search time by avoiding examination of solutions which are clearly not optimal in light of this prior information. The **BIP** command allows you to do so by entering the bound as its argument. For a **MAX** problem, *LINDO* will then not examine solutions with objective less than or equal to the argument; for a **MIN** problem, greater than or equal to the argument. **BIP** is cancelled once the current problem is altered in any way.

GIN Syntax: GIN<variableName | numberOfVariables>

Declares a variable or series of variables to be general integer (0,1 2,3...).The first form identifies the named variable only. The second form identifies the first *numberOf Variables* variables in the current formulation as being general integer. The order of the variables is determined by their order in the input and is as listed in the solution report. If the user knows the exact order of the variables the second form requires less typing.

IPTOL Syntax: IPTOL<fraction>

Truncating an IP search with the IPTOL command may be of value in cases in which a percentage of variance from the true optimum is acceptable. The allowed variance is expressed as a nonnegative fraction. Once a feasible IP solution is found, a branch in the tree will be pursued only if it can improve on the current best solution by at least the fraction specified. IPTOL often reduces IP solution times dramatically.

TERSE /VERBOSE

Toggles dispay mode. *LINDO's* default mode is called **VERBOSE**. In **VERBOSE** mode *LINDO* displays the entire solution and asks whether the **RANGE** report is desired. If the **TERSE** command is typed, *LINDO* will not display the solution report nor offer to display the **RANGE** report. **TERSE** mode is appropriate for very large problems in which it would be impractical to display the entire solution report. (You could, of course, view selected sections of the solution with the **CPRI** and **RPRI** commands discussed below.) **TERSE** or **VERBOSE** mode remains in force until the user next types its opposite.

WIDTH

Specifies a display width to *LINDO* in characters.

PAGE Syntax: PAGE <lines per page>

Sets the number of lines in a page or screen. **PAGE 24** is appropriate for most crt terminals. 12 is the lowest acceptable value for this parameter, with the exception of 0. **PAGE 0** will disable paging until some other parameter is entered; with paging set at 0 the display will not automa-tically pause. You may, of course, pause and resume with the DOS command ctrl-S on PC's.

BATCH

Toggles input echo on and off. If the first command of a **TAKE** file is **BATCH** (or **BAT**), every line of input is echoed to the output. This will cause every line of the model to be displayed without the **LOOK** command. The next **BAT** will turn external input display off.

PAUSE

PAUSE command is useful when taking input via a **TAKE** file. A **PAUSE** command before the formulation in the file will cause the program to wait for a carriage return to be typed. Text after the word **PAUSE** in the same line is displayed and the program awaits a carriage before resuming. For example, if the line: **PAUSE HIT CARRIAGE RETURN WHEN READY TO PROCEED** is encountered in a **TAKE** file, then the message **HIT CARRIAGE RETURN WHEN READY TO PROCEED** will be displayed. No further commands will be read from the TAKE file until a carriage return is typed.

MISCELLANEOUS

INVERT

INVERT resolves the set of simultaneous linear equations implied by the current basis. The inverse is represented by a product of elementary matrices(i.e., identity matrix except for one column). Inversion tries to permute the rows and columns of the basis so that the matrix is as close to triangular as possible. The rows which cannot be triangularized constitute the "bump." The columns in the bump which protrude above the diagonal are called "spikes." **INVERT** prints a short summary describing the basis, the new inverse, and the bump and spike structure. **INVERT** followed by **BPIC** (p. 5) is useful in revealing the structure of the solution.

BUG

Displays information on how to report a bug in *LINDO*.

DEBUG

Identifies parts of a model which may be in error.

STAT

STAT yields some simple summary statistics of the current model. Most statistics in the **STAT** report are straightforward, such as the **ROWS, VARS** (columns) and **NO. INTEGER VARS**. counts. A misspelled variable name should result in a **VARS** count which is greater than expected, because the typical variable appears several places in the model but is misspelled only once. The number of **NONZEROES** gives another measure of problem size. The **CONSTRAINT NONZeroes** is the count when the objective function is not included. If the **CONSTRAINT NONZeroes** are +1 or -1 the problem tends to be easier, so this count is given. The DENSITY is the fraction (not the percent) of the elements in the problem which are nonzero. If a decimal point in a coefficient is grievously misplaced it will manifest itself as either an extremely small number or an extremely large number. Thus, the SMALLEST AND LARGEST ELEMENTS IN ABSOLUTE VALUE are given. If either of these is "out of line," a bug is likely in the vicinity. The fourth line of the **STAT** report gives the count of the number of rows of each type, the direction (**MAX** or MIN) of the objective, and the **GUBS**,or General Upper Bounds statistic. This is a measure of problem simplicity. It is an upper bound on the number of nonintersecting constraints in the model. If all the constraints were nonintersecting, the problem could be solved by inspection by considering each constraint as a separate problem. A problem for which the **GUBS** statistic is high relative to the row count tends to be easier to solve. The **SINGLE COLS** statistic is a count of the number of variables which appear in only one row. Such a variable is effectively a slack. If you did not explicitly add slack variables to your model, and the **SINGLE COLS** count is greater than zero, it suggests a misspelled variable name. For more detailed analysis see **CPRI/RPRI**.

SET Syntax: SET<parameterID> <newValue>

SET is used to reset some of LINDO's internal solution parameters. This will seldom be necessary; if done without proper understanding may yield inaccurate results; and in most cases is not recommended.

The following parameters are accessible through SET:

ID	*Purpose*
1	Final Constraint Tolerance
2	Initial Constraint Tolerance
3	Entering Variable Reduced Cost Tolerance
4	Fixing Threshold for IP Variables

TITLE Syntax: TITLE<title>

TITLE returns the title of the present formulation if one has been entered; changes the present title or assigns one if text follows the **TITLE** command. The assigned text string is saved with the formulation when **SAVEd**, **SMPS** saved, or **DIVErted** to an ASCII file.

Acknowledgements

The LINDO software was written by Linus Schrage and Kevin Cunningham. Macintosh version adapted by Jorge Herrada.

WRITE:

LINDO Systems, Inc.
P.O.B. 148231
Chicago, IL 60614

LINDO LICENSE AGREEMENT

Subject to the following terms and conditions, LINDO Systems Inc. grants to you, and you hereby accept, a personal nonexclusive license to use the LINDO software program (the "SOFTWARE") contained on the enclosed disks and related documentation.

LICENSE

LINDO grants to you the right to use the SOFTWARE on a single computer. You may make one copy of the SOFTWARE solely for backup or archival purposes. You may move the software from one computer to another, so long as you can ensure that there is no possibility that the SOFTWARE is used on more than one computer at one time.

TRANSFER

The software may be transferred to another party only if the other party accepts the terms and conditions of this License Agreement. At the time of transfer of the SOFTWARE, you must at the same time transfer all disks and documentation including any updated disks and documentation.

COPYRIGHT

The SOFTWARE and its related documentation are copyrighted and protected by United States copyright laws and international treaty provisions. You may not use, copy, modify, or transfer the software or related documentation or any copy except as expressly provided in this license agreement or with written permission of LINDO Systems Inc.

RESTRICTIONS AGAINST DISTRIBUTION

You may not distribute, lease, sublease, rent, sublicense or disclose the SOFTWARE or related documentation without written permission of LINDO Systems Inc.

LIMITED WARRANTY

LINDO Systems Inc. warrants that the enclosed disks and the copy of the related documentation to be free of defects in materials and workmanship for a period of one year from receipt of your payment. Due to the inherent complexity of computer programs and mathematical models, the SOFTWARE and your mathematical models may not be completely free of errors. You are advised to verify your answers before basing decisions on them. NEITHER LINDO SYSTEMS INC. NOR ANYONE ASSOCIATED WITH THE CREATION, PRODUCTION, OR DISTRIBUTION OF THE SOFTWARE MAKES ANY OTHER EXPRESSED WARRANTIES REGARDING THE DISKS OR DOCUMENTATION AND MAKES NO WARRANTIES AT ALL, EITHER EXPRESSED OR IMPLIED, REGARDING THE SOFTWARE, INCLUDING BUT NOT LIMITED TO IMPLIED WARRANTIES OF MERCHANTABILITY, FITNESS FOR A PARTICULAR PURPOSE OR OTHERWISE.

REMEDY

LINDO's entire liability and your exclusive remedy for breach of this Limited Warrant shall be, at LINDO's Option, either return of the price paid or replacement of defective disks or documentation. In no event shall LINDO Systems Inc. be liable for any damages including but not limited to loss of profit, data, or direct, indirect, incidental, special or consequential damages, even if LINDO has been specifically advised of the possibility of such damages.

GENERAL

This agreement gives you specific rights, and you may also have other rights that vary from state to state. Some states do not allow limitations on duration of an implied warranty, or the exclusion or limitation of liability of incidental or consequential damages, so some of the above may not apply to you. If any provision of this License Agreement is determined by a court to be invalid under any applicable statute or rule of law, it shall be deemed omitted and the remaining provisions shall continue in full force and effect. This License Agreement is governed by, and shall be construed in accordance with, the laws of the State of Illinois. Should you have any questions concerning this agreement, please contact in writing: LINDO Systems Inc., Customer Sales and Service, P.O.B. 148231, Chicago, IL 60614.

▶ The Traveling Salesman Problem and LINDO

In this section we use LINDO to solve a classic management science problem, known as the traveling salesman problem. It is discussed here both to serve as an introduction to the problem and to provide an example of a LINDO application.

I. Problem Statement and Formulation

Consider a salesman who starts at home, visits (n-1) other cities, and returns home. He must visit each city once and only once. There is a specific, known cost associated with traveling between each pair of cities, and the salesman naturally wants to minimize the total cost of his round trip.

At first blush, the traveling salesman problem sounds like the shortest-route problem in Section 9.4 in that it involves finding a shortest route on a network. There is an important difference, however. In the shortest-route problem, the goal is to find the shortest route from a base to all other cities, and the solution is thus *a set of routes* leading from the base to each of the other cities. In the traveling salesman problem, by contrast, *a single round-trip route* is sought.

We wish to model this problem as an integer programming problem. We therefore let c_{ij} be the segment cost of going from city i to city j. (Values of c_{ij} for a six-city problem are shown in Figure L.1.) We then let $x_{ij} = 1$ if the salesman goes from city i to city j and $x_{ij} = 0$ if he doesn't.

▼ FIGURE L.1
Costs for a Six-City Traveling Salesman Problem

CITY	1	2	3	4	5	6
1	—	25	22	20	28	30
2	23	—	30	25	21	27
3	28	20	—	30	25	23
4	28	30	22	—	20	18
5	30	25	20	27	—	23
6	15	17	20	18	28	—

The problem can be formulated as follows. (We show the model as it would appear in LINDO.)

```
MIN 25 X12 + 22 X13 + 20 X14 + 28 X15 + 30 X16 + 23 X21 + 30 X23
    + 25 X24 + 21 X25 + 27 X26 + 28 X31 + 20 X32 + 30 X34 + 25 X35
    + 23 X36 + 28 X41 + 30 X42 + 22 X43 + 20 X45 + 18 X46 + 30 X51
    + 25 X52 + 20 X53 + 27 X54 + 23 X56 + 15 X61 + 17 X62 + 20 X63
    + 18 X64 + 28 X65

SUBJECT TO
    2) X12 + X13 + X14 + X15 + X16 = 1
    3) X21 + X23 + X24 + X25 + X26 = 1
    4) X31 + X32 + X34 + X35 + X36 = 1
    5) X41 + X42 + X43 + X45 + X46 = 1
    6) X51 + X52 + X53 + X54 + X56 = 1
    7) X61 + X62 + X63 + X64 + X65 = 1
    8) X21 + X31 + X41 + X51 + X61 = 1
```

```
 9)  X12 + X32 + X42 + X52 + X62 = 1
10) X13 + X23 + X43 + X53 + X63 = 1
11) X14 + X24 + X34 + X54 + X64 = 1
12) X15 + X25 + X35 + X45 + X65 = 1
13) X16 + X26 + X36 + X46 + X56 = 1

END
INTE 30
```

The objective function consists of 30 terms. Each term is the cost of a particular segment (e.g., $c_{23} = 30$) multiplied by the decision variable for that segment, in this case x_{23}. The first six constraints, rows 2 through 7, are departure constraints. For example, row 2 says that the salesman must leave city 1 and go to one of the other cities. Rows 3 through 7 say the same thing for each of the other cities. Rows 8 through 13 are arrival constraints. For example, row 8 says that the salesman must leave some city and arrive in city 1. Rows 9 through 13 say the same thing for each of the other cities. The INTE 30 command after the END command means that all 30 of the x_{ij} variables must take on the value 0 or 1.

You may recognize the problem shown above as the assignment problem (Section 7.5). Thus the values of the decision variables will all be 0 or 1 if we solve this problem as a linear programming problem. Adding the integer constraint, however, does no harm, since as we saw in Chapter 8, the first step in solving an integer programming problem with the branch-and-bound algorithm is to solve the LP relaxation.

II. Creating the Formulation in LINDO

The formulation shown above is printed from LINDO. It is worth noting that the formulation was originally created in WordPerfect. (Other word processors would work equally well.) While LINDO has a full screen editor, it does not have the copying or search-and-replace commands of a full-featured word processor. The WordPerfect version was then saved as an ASCII file under the name *travsals.dos* using the TEXT IN/OUT command in WordPerfect. We then exited WordPerfect and called up LINDO. We wanted to get the formulation into LINDO and to review it. LINDO uses a colon as a prompt. We used the TAKE command to bring the formulation into LINDO as follows. We will boldface commands within LINDO.

: **TAKE *travsals.dos***

LINDO responds with a colon to let us know that it has the formulation. To review the formulation we used the LOOK command.

: **LOOK all**

This tells LINDO that we want to look at all the rows.

: **GO**

This tells LINDO to solve the problem. LINDO solves this problem quickly, and the solution appears on the screen. It is evident that most of the decision variables take on the value 0. We are interested only in those that take on the value 1. We thus use the NONZERO command to simplify the output.

:**NONZERO**

The output from LINDO follows.

OBJECTIVE FUNCTION VALUE

1) 114.000000

VARIABLE	VALUE	REDUCED COST
X14	1.000000	.000000
X25	1.000000	.000000
X32	1.000000	.000000
X46	1.000000	.000000
X53	1.000000	.000000
X61	1.000000	.000000

This is actually just part of the solution report—we have omitted the section that presents information on the dual prices.

III. Do We Have a Solution?

LINDO has solved the problem that we formulated, but is it a solution to the real problem? Let's check the answer. We see that the salesman should take the following route: $1 \rightarrow 4 \rightarrow 6 \rightarrow 1$ and $2 \rightarrow 5 \rightarrow 3 \rightarrow 2$. So we do not have a solution to the real problem. Our formulation allows the salesman to make what are called subtours—that is, this formulation does not necessarily produce a single route that takes the salesman through every city. It is perhaps surprising that this complete tour requirement is what makes the traveling salesman problem so hard to solve. Without it, we have the assignment problem, one of the easiest integer programming problems to solve. With it, the traveling salesman problem becomes one of a large set of integer programming problems that are very hard to solve.

IV. Using LINDO to Introduce Tour Breakers

A practical method for solving small traveling salesman problems is to append constraints that eliminate the subtours. (Doing this also presents an opportunity to show how easy it is to work with LINDO in an interactive mode.) In this particular problem we know that one of the variables x_{14}, x_{46}, x_{61}, x_{25}, x_{53}, x_{32} will have to assume the value 0 if a complete tour is to be realized. We thus add a constraint that forces the sum of these six variables to be less than or equal to 5 to the model. This eliminates the current solution, as the sum of these variables is six in the current solution. The EXTEND command makes this a simple procedure.

: EXTEND

LINDO responds by telling us to begin in row 14 and prompts with a question mark. After we enter the constraint and strike the return key, LINDO replies with another question mark prompt. To end this process, type END. The new formulation is the same as the previous solution through line 13. The new constraint (line 14) and part of the nonzero solution report follow:

14) X14 + X25 + X32 + X46 + X53 + X61 ≤ 5

END
INTE 30

OBJECTIVE FUNCTION VALUE
1) 121.000000

VARIABLE	VALUE	REDUCED COST
X14	1.000000	20.000000
X25	1.000000	21.000000
X32	1.000000	20.000000
X43	1.000000	22.000000
X56	1.000000	23.000000
X61	1.000000	15.000000

We see that the new route, $1 \rightarrow 4 \rightarrow 3 \rightarrow 2 \rightarrow 5 \rightarrow 6 \rightarrow 1$, is a complete tour and that the real problem has been solved. It is not guaranteed that an optimal solution will be reached by inserting a single tour breaker. That is, the solution to the new problem might have consisted of a different set of subtours. If so, more tour breakers would have to be appended, and the process would continue until the solution was a complete tour.

We note that the new solution has an objective value of 121, whereas the objective value for the first solution was 114. This illustrates again the concept from Chapter 4 that adding a constraint eliminates some solutions that were previously feasible. Clearly, eliminating possible solutions cannot help and might hurt the value of the objective function. Here we see that adding an additional constraint increased the minimum value by 7.

V. Obtaining Hard Copy of LINDO Output

It is easy to obtain output from LINDO in a form that can be taken directly into a word processor. The DIVERT command diverts all output from the screen into a file of our choice. The RVRT command returns all output to the screen. Once we have stored the LINDO output in a file, it can be retrieved by a word processor and become an integral part of a management report. Exactly that approach was used in preparing the manuscript for this section.

Index

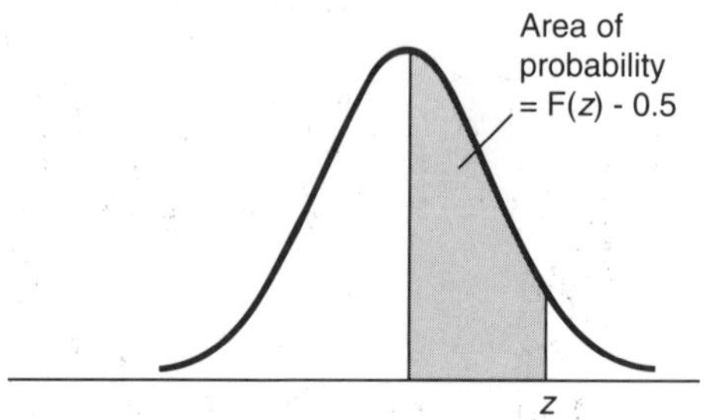

▼ TABLE A.0
Areas for the Standard Normal Distribution

Entries in the the table give the *Area* under the curve between the mean and z standard deviations above the mean. For example, for $z = 1.25$ the area under the curve between the mean and z is 0.3944.

z	0.00	0.01	0.02	0.03	0.04	0.05	0.06	0.07	0.08	0.09
0.0	0.0000	0.0040	0.0080	0.0120	0.0160	0.0199	0.0239	0.0279	0.0319	0.0359
0.1	0.0398	0.0438	0.0478	0.0517	0.0557	0.0596	0.0636	0.0675	0.0714	0.0753
0.2	0.0793	0.0832	0.0871	0.0910	0.0948	0.0987	0.1026	0.1064	0.1103	0.1141
0.3	0.1179	0.1217	0.1255	0.1293	0.1331	0.1368	0.1406	0.1443	0.1480	0.1517
0.4	0.1554	0.1591	0.1628	0.1664	0.1700	0.1736	0.1772	0.1808	0.1844	0.1879
0.5	0.1915	0.1950	0.1985	0.2019	0.2054	0.2088	0.2123	0.2157	0.2190	0.2224
0.6	0.2257	0.2291	0.2324	0.2357	0.2389	0.2422	0.2454	0.2486	0.2518	0.2549
0.7	0.2580	0.2612	0.2642	0.2673	0.2704	0.2734	0.2764	0.2794	0.2823	0.2852
0.8	0.2881	0.2910	0.2939	0.2967	0.2995	0.3023	0.3051	0.3078	0.3106	0.3133
0.9	0.3159	0.3186	0.3212	0.3238	0.3264	0.3289	0.3315	0.3340	0.3365	0.3389
1.0	0.3413	0.3438	0.3461	0.3485	0.3508	0.3531	0.3554	0.3577	0.3599	0.3621
1.1	0.3643	0.3665	0.3686	0.3708	0.3729	0.3749	0.3770	0.3790	0.3810	0.3830
1.2	0.3849	0.3869	0.3888	0.3907	0.3925	0.3944	0.3962	0.3980	0.3997	0.4015
1.3	0.4032	0.4049	0.4066	0.4082	0.4099	0.4115	0.4131	0.4147	0.4162	0.4177
1.4	0.4192	0.4207	0.4222	0.4236	0.4251	0.4265	0.4279	0.4292	0.4306	0.4319
1.5	0.4332	0.4345	0.4357	0.4370	0.4382	0.4394	0.4406	0.4418	0.4429	0.4441
1.6	0.4452	0.4463	0.4474	0.4484	0.4495	0.4505	0.4515	0.4525	0.4535	0.4545
1.7	0.4554	0.4564	0.4573	0.4582	0.4591	0.4599	0.4608	0.4616	0.4625	0.4633
1.8	0.4641	0.4649	0.4656	0.4664	0.4671	0.4678	0.4686	0.4693	0.4699	0.4706
1.9	0.4713	0.4719	0.4726	0.4732	0.4738	0.4744	0.4750	0.4756	0.4761	0.4767
2.0	0.4772	0.4778	0.4783	0.4788	0.4793	0.4798	0.4803	0.4808	0.4812	0.4817
2.1	0.4821	0.4826	0.4830	0.4834	0.4838	0.4842	0.4846	0.4850	0.4854	0.4857
2.2	0.4861	0.4864	0.4868	0.4871	0.4875	0.4878	0.4881	0.4884	0.4887	0.4890
2.3	0.4893	0.4896	0.4898	0.4901	0.4904	0.4906	0.4909	0.4911	0.4913	0.4916
2.4	0.4918	0.4920	0.4922	0.4925	0.4927	0.4929	0.4931	0.4932	0.4934	0.4936
2.5	0.4938	0.4940	0.4941	0.4943	0.4945	0.4946	0.4948	0.4949	0.4951	0.4952
2.6	0.4953	0.4955	0.4956	0.4957	0.4959	0.4960	0.4961	0.4962	0.4963	0.4964
2.7	0.4965	0.4966	0.4967	0.4968	0.4969	0.4970	0.4971	0.4972	0.4973	0.4974
2.8	0.4974	0.4975	0.4976	0.4977	0.4977	0.4978	0.4979	0.4979	0.4980	0.4981
2.9	0.4981	0.4982	0.4982	0.4983	0.4984	0.4984	0.4985	0.4985	0.4986	0.4986
3.0	0.4986	0.4987	0.4987	0.4988	0.4988	0.4989	0.4989	0.4989	0.4990	0.4990